Interest and Prices

Interest and Prices

Foundations of a Theory of Monetary Policy

MICHAEL WOODFORD

Princeton University Press

Princeton and Oxford

ISBN 0-691-01049-8

Library of Congress Control Number 2003106560

British Library Cataloging-in-Publication Data is available

This book has been composed in New Baskerville and Officina Serif
by Princeton Editorial Associates, Inc., Scottsdale, Arizona

www.pupress.princeton.edu

10 9 8 7 6 5 4 3 2 1

For Argia

CONTENTS

APPENDIXES

PREFACE

This book is a progress report on my struggles with two problems that have
engaged me since graduate school. The first is the problem of reconciling
macroeconomics with microeconomic theory without simply ignoring the
main concerns of the tradition of macroeconomic thought that stretches
back long before Keynes—above all, the question of how to understand and
mitigate the temporary departures from an efficient utilization of existing
productive capacity that result from slow adjustment of wages or prices.
My advisor, Bob Solow, always insisted on the unity of microeconomics and
macroeconomics, and wore both hats with equal flair. He challenged me,
while I was still writing my dissertation, to try to integrate sticky prices
into the kind of intertemporal general-equilibrium models that were then
becoming the dominant paradigm for macroeconomic analysis. Another
of my teachers, Peter Diamond, insisted upon the importance of a public
economics that would allow an integrated treatment of inefficient allocation
of resources across sectors and macroeconomic stabilization. It has taken me
twenty years to come up with a response to these challenges that I am not
embarrassed to submit. I hope that tardiness will not be judged sufficient
grounds in itself for a failing grade.

The second is the problem of reconciling central bankers' understanding
of what they do with the way that monetary policy is conceived in theoretical monetary economics. It has long been the understanding of bankers
that the crucial monetary policy question is that of the appropriate level
for short-term nominal interest rates. Yet the theoretical literature has, until recently, always modeled monetary policy in terms of a central bank's
control of the supply of base money or the implications of its actions for
the evolution of some broader monetary aggregate. In the literature that I
studied in school, interest rates were not only not central to the way in which
candidate policies for analysis were described; much of the time, theoretical

frameworks were used in which interest rates were not even determined or (if an interest rate was defined) in which the nominal interest rate would necessarily be zero at all times, regardless of the monetary policy chosen. The Wicksellian tradition of monetary analysis, which I first learned about from Axel Leijonhufvud, has been an important source of inspiration for my efforts to show that one can indeed conceive of monetary policy in terms of rules for the adjustment of an operating target for an overnight interest rate, while at the same time insisting upon clear foundations for monetary analysis within the broader framework of intertemporal general equilibrium theory.

The idea of attempting a systematic exposition of this material first originated when I was asked to give a one-week course in macroeconomic theory as part of the Netherlands Network of Economics (NAKE) summer school in Wageningen, in June 1998. I repeated a version of the same lecture series in August of that year at the Federal Reserve Bank of Kansas City and presented a somewhat longer version as a three-week course for doctoral students at the London School of Economics in February 1999. After this, I felt that I had a fairly clear view of what I wanted to say, and began work on this book. Completing the task has taken somewhat longer than I had expected when starting out, partly because research in the area has developed so rapidly since then. Probably the drafts of this manuscript that have circulated since the spring of 1999 have helped to accelerate this, but I have at times wondered if the present moment is really as ripe for a systematic exposition of theory of monetary policy as I had imagined. The present volume is surely not the last word on the subject, but it may perhaps help others to join the conversation.

Most of the research described here has been joint work with a series of co-authors, namely Julio Rotemberg, Ben Bernanke, Lars Svensson, Marc Giannoni, and Pierpaolo Benigno (in roughly chronological sequence). Many of the ideas in this work have really been theirs, though I must take responsibility for any inadequacy of the formulation offered here. I hope that they will forgive me for not mentioning them more frequently in the pages that follow. The general program of research discussed here has also been greatly advanced by the work of a number of my students. In addition to those listed above as co-authors, these include Robert Kollman, Chris Erceg, Stephanie Schmitt-Grohé, Martin Uribe, Peter Ireland, Tim Fuerst, Tack Yun, Thomas Laubach, Eduardo Loyo, Rochelle Edge, Kosuke Aoki, Jon Steinsson, Gauti Eggertsson, Bruce Preston, and Hong Li. I would not have gotten as far in my own understanding of these topics without their help.

Given the subject addressed, it should be no surprise that many of my most valuable interlocutors have been in central banks. My research agenda has been particularly shaped by the two years that I served as a consultant to the Federal Reserve Bank of New York, in 1995–1997, and by the period I was able to spend as a Professorial Fellow at the Reserve Bank of New Zealand in the summer of 2000. I have also benefited greatly from shorter visits to the Federal Reserve Board, the Bank of Canada, the Bank of England, the European Central Bank, the Bank of Sweden, the Bank of Italy, the Bank of Japan, and the Hong Kong Monetary Authority while preparing this study. I am especially grateful to David Archer, Andy Brookes, Kevin Clinton, Chuck Freedman, Spence Hilton, Chris Ryan, and William Whitesell for their patient efforts to educate me about the implementation of monetary policy at their respective central banks.

I owe a considerable debt to Ed Nelson and Argia Sbordone for carefully reading much of this manuscript (and sometimes multiple drafts). I also thank Pierpaolo Benigno, Pelin Berkmen, Olivier Blanchard, Jean Boivin, Michael Dotsey, Peter Dougherty, Gauti Eggertsson, Pedro Garcia Duarte, Tim Fuerst, Jeff Fuhrer, Marvin Goodfriend, Bob Hall, Michael Kiley, Jinill Kim, Hong Li, Eduardo Loyo, Bennett McCallum, Rick Mishkin, Athanasios Orphanides, David Romer, Julio Rotemberg, Juha Seppala, Jon Steinsson, Brad Strum, Lars Svensson, and Marco Vega for comments on various parts of the manuscript, and Gauti Eggertsson, Marc Giannoni, Hong Li, Eduardo Loyo, and Brad Strum for their assistance with the research reported here. Among my Harvard students, Yves Nosbuch deserves special mention for finding the largest number of typos.

I am grateful to the National Science Foundation for supporting the research described here, through a series of grants to the National Bureau of Economic Research, and to the John Simon Guggenheim Memorial Foundation and the Center for Economic Policy Studies, Princeton University, for their support of the sabbatical year during which I was able to plan and begin work on this book. Finally, I thank Peter Dougherty for his continuing enthusiasm for a project that must at some points have seemed unlikely to reach a conclusion.

And most of all, my thanks to Argia, brave and loyal as Hyginus would have it, for her faith.

Interest and Prices

CHAPTER 1

The Return of Monetary Rules

If it were in our power to regulate completely the price system of the future, the ideal position . . . would undoubtedly be one in which, without interfering with the inevitable variations in the relative prices of commodities, the general average level of money prices . . . would be perfectly invariable and stable.

And why should not such regulation lie within the scope of practical politics? . . . Attempts by means of tariffs, state subsidies, export bounties, and the like, to effect a partial modification of the natural order of [relative prices] almost inevitably involve some loss of utility to the community. Such attempts must so far be regarded as opposed to all reason. Absolute prices on the other hand—money prices—are a matter in the last analysis of pure convention, depending on the *choice of a standard of price* which it lies within our own power to make.

—Knut Wicksell
Interest and Prices, 1898, p. 4

The past century has been one of remarkable innovation in the world's monetary systems. At the turn of the twentieth century, it was taken for granted by practical men that the meaning of a monetary unit should be guaranteed by its convertibility into a specific quantity of some precious metal. Debates about monetary policy usually concerned the relative advantages of gold and silver standards or the possibility of a bimetallic standard. But through fits and starts, the world's currencies have come progressively to be more completely subject to "management" by individual central banks. Since the collapse of the Bretton Woods system of fixed exchange rates in the early 1970s, the last pretense of a connection of the world's currencies to any real commodity has been abandoned. We now live instead in a world of pure "fiat" units of account, where the value of each depends solely upon the policies of the particular central bank with responsibility for it.

This has brought both opportunities and challenges. On the one hand, vagaries of the market for gold or some other precious metal no longer cause variations in the purchasing power of money, with their disruptions of the pattern of economic activity. The recognition that the purchasing

1

power of money need not be dictated by any "natural" market forces and is instead a proper subject of government regulation, as proposed by the monetary reformer Knut Wicksell a century ago, should in principle make possible greater stability of the standard of value, facilitating contracting and market exchange. At the same time, the responsibilities of the world's central banks are more complex under a fiat system than they were when the banks' tasks were simply to maintain convertibility of their respective national currencies into gold, and it was not immediately apparent how the banks' new freedom should best be used. Indeed, during the first decade of the new regime, the policies of many industrial nations suffered from a tendency toward chronic inflation, leading to calls from some quarters in the 1980s for a return to a commodity standard.

This has not proven to be necessary. Instead, since the 1980s the central banks of the major industrial nations have been largely successful at bringing inflation down to low and fairly stable levels. Nor does this seem to have involved any permanent sacrifice of other objectives. For example, real GDP growth has been if anything higher on average, and certainly more stable, since inflation was stabilized in the United States. Somewhat paradoxically, this period of improved macroeconomic stability has coincided with a *reduction,* in certain senses, in the ambition of central banks' efforts at macroeconomic stabilization. Banks around the world have committed themselves more explicitly to relatively straightforward objectives with regard to the control of inflation, and have found when they do so that not only is it easier to control inflation than previous experience might have suggested, but that price stability creates a sound basis for real economic performance as well.

What appears to be developing, then, at the turn of another century, is a new consensus in favor of a monetary policy that is disciplined by clear rules intended to ensure a stable standard of value, rather than one that is determined on a purely discretionary basis to serve whatever ends may seem most pressing at any given time. Yet the new monetary rules are not so blindly mechanical as the rules of the gold standard, which defined monetary orthodoxy a century ago. They are instead principles of systematic conduct for institutions that are aware of the consequences of their actions and take responsibility for them, choosing their policies with careful attention to what they accomplish. Indeed, under the current approaches to rule-based policymaking, more emphasis is given to explicit commitments regarding desired economic outcomes, such as a target rate of inflation, than to particular technical indicators that the central bank may find it useful to monitor in achieving that outcome.

The present study seeks to provide theoretical foundations for a rule-based approach to monetary policy of this kind. The development of such a theory is an urgent task, for rule-based monetary policy in the spirit that I have described is possible only when central banks can develop a conscious and articulate account of what they are doing. It is necessary in order for them to know how to act systematically in a way that can serve their objectives, which are now defined in terms of variables that are much further removed from their direct control. It is also necessary in order for them to be able to communicate the nature of their systematic commitments to the public, despite the absence of such mechanical constraints as a commitment to exchange currency for some real commodity. As I explain below, the advantages of a sound monetary policy are largely dependent upon the policy's being *understood* and relied upon by the private sector in arranging its affairs.

There can be little doubt that the past decade has seen a marked increase in the self-consciousness of central banks about the way in which they conduct monetary policy and in the explicitness of their communication with the public about their actions and the considerations upon which they are based. A particularly important development in this regard has been the adoption of "inflation targeting" as an approach to the conduct of monetary policy by many of the world's central banks in the 1990s.[1] As I subsequently discuss in more detail, this approach (best exemplified by the practices of such innovators as the Bank of England, the Bank of Canada, the Reserve Bank of New Zealand, and the Swedish Riksbank) is characterized not only by public commitment to an explicit target, but also by a commitment to explain the central bank's policy actions in terms of a systematic decisionmaking framework that is aimed at achieving this target. This has led to greatly improved communication with the public about the central bank's interpretation of current conditions and the outlook for the future, notably through the publication of detailed *Inflation Reports*. It has also involved fairly explicit discussion of the approach that they follow in deliberating about policy actions and, in some cases, even publication of the model or models used in producing the forecasts that play a central role in these deliberations. As a consequence, these banks in particular have found themselves in need of a clear theory of how they can best achieve their objectives and have played an important role in stimulating reflection on this problem.

It is true that the conceptual frameworks proposed by central banks to deal with their perceived need for a more systematic approach to policy were, until quite recently, largely developed without much guidance from the academic literature on monetary economics. Indeed, the central questions of practical interest for the conduct of policy—how should central banks decide about the appropriate level of overnight interest rates? how should monetary policy respond to the various types of unexpected disturbances that occur?—had in recent decades ceased to be considered

---

1. See, e.g., Bernanke et al. (1999) for a thorough discussion of this development.

suitable topics for academic study. Reasons for this included the trenchant critique of traditional methods of econometric-policy evaluation by Lucas (1976); the critique of the use of conventional methods of optimal control in the conduct of economic policy by Kydland and Prescott (1977); and the development of a new generation of quantitative models of business fluctuations ("real-business-cycle theory") with more rigorous microeconomic foundations, but which implied no relevance of monetary policy for economic welfare.

Nonetheless, recent developments, to be discussed in detail in this volume, have considerably changed this picture. The present study seeks to show that it is possible to use the tools of modern macroeconomic theory—intertemporal equilibrium modeling, taking full account of the endogeneity of private-sector expectations—to analyze optimal interest-rate setting in a way that takes the concerns of central bankers seriously, while simultaneously taking account of the "New Classical" critique of traditional policy-evaluation exercises. In this way, the basic elements are presented of a theory that can provide the groundwork for the kind of systematic approach to the conduct of monetary policy that many central banks are currently seeking to develop. In the present chapter, I review some of the key features of this theory, as preparation for the more systematic development that begins in Chapter 2.

1 The Importance of Price Stability

A notable feature of the new rule-based approaches to monetary policy is the increased emphasis given to a particular policy objective: maintaining a low and stable rate of inflation. This is most obvious in the case of countries with explicit inflation targets. But it also seems to characterize recent policy in the United States as well, where the past decade has seen unusual stability of the inflation rate and many econometric studies have found evidence of a stronger Fed reaction to inflation variations. (See further discussion of recent U.S. policy in Section 4.1.)

Yet the justification of such an emphasis from the standpoint of economic theory may not be obvious. Standard general-equilibrium models—and the earliest generation of quantitative equilibrium models of business fluctuations, the real-business-cycle models of the 1980s—indicate that the absolute level of prices should be irrelevant for the allocation of resources, which depends only on *relative* prices. Traditional Keynesian macroeconometric models, of course, imply otherwise: Variations in the growth rate of wages and prices are found to be associated with substantial variations in economic activity and employment. Yet the existence of such "Phillips-curve" relations has typically been held to imply that monetary policy should be used to achieve output or employment goals, rather than giving priority to price stability.

The present study argues instead for a different view of the proper goals of monetary policy. Its use to stabilize an appropriately defined price index is in fact an important end toward which efforts should be directed—at least to a first approximation, it should be the primary aim of monetary policy. But this is *not*, as proponents of inflation targeting sometimes argue, because variations in the rate of inflation have no real effects. Rather, it is exactly because instability of the general level of prices causes substantial real distortions—leading to inefficient variation both in aggregate employment and output and in the sectoral composition of economic activity—that price stability is important.

Moreover, the existence of predictable real effects of shifts in monetary policy need not imply that policy should be based primarily on a calculation of its effects on output or employment. For the efficient aggregate level and sectoral composition of real activity is likely to vary over time, as a result of real disturbances of a variety of types. The market mechanism performs a difficult computational task—much of the time, fairly accurately—in bringing about a time-varying allocation of resources that responds to these changes in production and consumption opportunities. Because of this, variation over time in employment and output relative to some smooth trend cannot in itself be taken to indicate a failure of proper market functioning. Instead, instability of the general level of prices *is* a good indicator of inefficiency in the real allocation of resources—at least when an appropriate price index is used—because a general tendency of prices to move in the same direction (either all rising relative to their past values or all falling) is both a cause and a symptom of systematic imbalances in resource allocation.

This general vision is in many respects an attempt to resurrect a view that was influential among monetary economists prior to the Keynesian revolution. It was perhaps best articulated by the noted Swedish economic theorist Knut Wicksell at the turn of the previous century, along with his followers in the "Stockholm school" of the interwar period (such as Erik Lindahl and Gunnar Myrdal) and others influenced by Wicksell's work, such as Friedrich Hayek. However, these authors developed their insights without the benefit of either modern general-equilibrium theory[2] or macroeconometric modeling techniques, so that it may be doubted whether Wicksellian theory can

2. Of course, Wicksell and his followers were quite familiar with Walrasian general-equilibrium theory and used it as a starting point for their own thought. But at the time, general-equilibrium theory meant a *static* model of resource allocation, not obviously applicable to the problems of intertemporal resource allocation with which they were primarily concerned. See, e.g., Myrdal (1931, chap. 2, sec. 4, and chap. 3, sec. 5).

provide a basis for the kind of quantitative policy analysis in which a modern central bank must engage—and which has become only more essential given current demands for public justification of policy decisions. This book seeks to provide theoretical foundations for the view just sketched that meet modern standards of conceptual rigor and are capable of elaboration in a form that can be fit to economic time series.

1.1   Toward a New "Neoclassical Synthesis"

The approach to monetary policy proposed here builds upon advances in the analysis of economic fluctuations and, in particular, of the monetary transmission mechanism over the past few years.[3] The models analyzed in this volume differ in crucial respects from the first two generations of equilibrium business-cycle models, namely, the New Classical models that Lucas (1972) took as a starting point and the real-business-cycle (RBC) models pioneered by Kydland and Prescott (1982) and Long and Plosser (1983). Neither of these early illustrations of the possibility of rigorous intertemporal general-equilibrium analysis of short-run fluctuations contained elements that would make them suitable for the analysis of monetary policy. While the Lucas model allows for real effects of unexpected variations in monetary policy (modeled as stochastic variation in the growth rate of the money supply), it implies that any real effects of monetary policy must be purely transitory and that monetary disturbances should have *no* real effects to the extent that their influence on aggregate nominal expenditure can be forecast in advance. Yet, as shown Chapter 3, VAR evidence on the effects of identified monetary policy shocks is quite inconsistent with these predictions. Rather, these effects on aggregate nominal expenditure are forecastable at least 6 months in advance on the basis of federal funds rate movements, whereas the (similarly delayed) effects on real activity are substantial and persist for many quarters. Nor is this empirical failure of the model one of minor import for the analysis of monetary policy. The conclusion that only unanticipated monetary policy can have real effects leads fairly directly to the skeptical conclusions of Sargent and Wallace (1975) about the necessary ineffectiveness of any attempt to use monetary policy to stabilize real activity.

The RBC models of the 1980s offered a very different view of the typical nature of short-run fluctuations in economic activity. But the classic models in this vein similarly imply no scope at all for monetary stabilization policy because real variables are modeled as evolving in complete independence of any nominal variables. Monetary policy is thus (at least implicitly) assumed

---

3. Useful surveys of recent developments include Goodfriend and King (1997) and Gali (2001).

to be of no relevance as far as fluctuations in real activity are concerned. Since neither the empirical evidence from VAR studies nor the practical experience of central bankers supports this view, I am reluctant to discuss the nature of desirable monetary policy rules using models of this kind.

Chapters 3 through 5 review a more recent literature that has shown, instead, how one can develop models with equally rigorous foundations in intertemporal optimizing behavior that allow a more realistic account of the real effects of monetary disturbances. These models also imply that systematic monetary policy can make a substantial difference for the way that an economy responds to real disturbances of all sorts, and this is actually the prediction that is of greatest importance for the concerns here. VAR models typically do *not* imply that a large part of the variance of fluctuations in real activity should be attributed to monetary policy shocks—that is, to the purely random component of central-bank interest-rate policy. Moreover, in any event, one does not really need to understand exactly what the effects of such shocks are, since under almost any view it is desirable to eliminate such shocks (i.e., to render monetary policy predictable) to the greatest extent possible. (Here, I discuss the ability of the models being proposed to account for evidence with regard to the effects of such shocks only because this is the aspect of the effects of monetary policy that can be *empirically identified* under relatively weak, and hence more convincing, identifying assumptions.) On the other hand, I am very interested in what a model implies about the way in which alternative systematic monetary policies determine the effects of real disturbances. The question of practical importance in central banking is never "should we create some random noise this month?," but rather "does this month's news justify a change in the level of interest rates?" To think about this, one needs to understand the consequences of different types of possible monetary responses to exogenous disturbances.

The key to obtaining less trivial consequences of systematic monetary policy in the models proposed here is the assumption that prices and/or wages are not continually adjusted, but remain fixed for at least short periods (a few months, or even a year) at a level that was judged desirable at an earlier time. However, this postulate does not mean accepting the need for mechanical models of wage and price adjustment of the kind that were at the heart of the Keynesian macroeconometric models of the 1960s. Rather than postulating that prices or wages respond mechanically to some measure of market disequilibrium, they are set optimally, that is, so as to best serve the interests of the parties assumed to set them, according to the information available at the time they are set. The delays involved before the next time that prices are reconsidered (or perhaps, before a newly chosen price takes effect) are taken here to be an institutional fact, just like the available production technology. However, the resulting constraints are taken account of by the decisionmakers who set them. Thus the assumed "stickiness" of prices implies that when they are reconsidered, they are set in a *forward-looking* manner, on the basis of expectations regarding future demand and cost conditions, and not simply in response to current conditions. As a result, expectations turn out to be a crucial factor in the equilibrium relation between inflation and real activity (as argued by Phelps and Friedman in the 1960s). Under certain special assumptions, described in Chapter 3, the relation is of exactly the form assumed in the New Classical literature: Deviations of output from its "natural rate" are proportional to the unexpected component of inflation. However, this is not true more generally. Other models, which I would judge to be more realistic, also lead to "expectations-augmented Phillips-curve" relations of a sort, but not of the precise sort that implies that anticipated monetary policy cannot have real effects.

It is also important to note that the emphasis here upon nominal rigidities does not in any way mean ignoring the real factors in business fluctuations stressed by RBC theory. One important achievement of the RBC literature has been to show that the equilibrium level of output can easily be disturbed by real disturbances of many sorts—variations in the rate of technical progress, variations in government purchases, changes in tax rates, or different kinds of shifts in tastes. I do not want to abstract from the existence of such disturbances in the proposed models. After all, it is only the existence of real disturbances (i.e., disturbances other than those originating from randomness in monetary policy itself) that gives rise to nontrivial questions about monetary policy, and I strive to obtain results that remain valid for as broad a class of possible disturbances as possible. Of course, the predicted effects of real disturbances are not necessarily the same in the models presented here as in RBC theory, which, in its classic form, assumes complete flexibility of both wages and prices. Rather, in these models, the predicted effects of real disturbances depend on the nature of monetary policy.

Nonetheless, the predicted evolution of real variables under complete wage and price flexibility—the topic studied in RBC theory—represents an important benchmark in the theory developed here. The level of output that *would* occur in an equilibrium with flexible wages and prices, given current real factors (tastes, technology, government purchases)—what is called the "natural rate" of output, following Friedman (1968)—turns out to be a highly useful concept, even if the present theory does not imply that this is the *actual* level of output, regardless of monetary policy. It is the gap between actual output and this natural rate, rather than the level of output as such (or output relative to trend) that is related to inflation dynamics in a properly specified Phillips-curve relation, as I show in Chapter 3. It is also this concept of the output gap to which interest rates should respond if a "Taylor rule" is to be a successful approach to inflation stabilization, as I discuss in Chapter 4; it is this concept of the output gap that monetary policy should aim to stabilize in order to maximize household welfare, as shown in Chapter 6; and it is this concept of the output gap to which optimal interest-rate rules and/or optimal inflation targets should respond, as shown in Chapter 8. From the point of view of any of these applications, the fact that the natural rate of output may vary at business-cycle frequencies, as argued in the RBC literature, is of tremendous practical importance. I am also quite interested in the consequences of time variation in what Wicksell (1898) called the "natural rate of interest"—the equilibrium real rate of interest in the case of flexible wages and prices, given current real factors.[4] Once again, RBC theory has a great deal to tell us about the kind of factors that should cause the natural rate of interest to vary. Hence RBC theory, when correctly interpreted, constitutes an important building block of the theory to be developed here.

It is for this reason that Goodfriend and King (1997) speak of models of this kind as representing a "new neoclassical synthesis," in the spirit of the synthesis between Keynesian short-run analysis and neoclassical long-run analysis proposed by Hicks and Samuelson. In the modern, more explicitly dynamic version of such a synthesis, the neoclassical theory (i.e., RBC theory) defines not a static "long-run equilibrium" but rather a dynamic path that represents a sort of *virtual* equilibrium for the economy at each point in time—the equilibrium that one *would* have if wages and prices were not in fact sticky. The evolution of the virtual equilibrium matters because the gaps between actual quantities and their virtual equilibrium values are important measures of the incentives for wage and price adjustment and hence determinants of wage and price dynamics.

At the same time, the stickiness of prices and/or wages implies that short-run output determination can be understood in a manner reminiscent of Keynesian theory. Indeed, the basic analytical framework in this study has the structure of a simple model consisting of an "IS equation," a monetary policy rule, and an "AS equation." (The monetary policy rule—which I often suppose is something similar to a Taylor rule—replaces the "LM equation" of Hicksian pedagogy, since for the most part I am not interested

---

4. This is of course the origin of the natural rate terminology—Friedman's (1968) concept of a "natural rate of unemployment" appealed to an analogy with Wicksell's "natural rate of interest," a concept with which his readers were presumed to be familiar. Nowadays, many readers are more familiar with Friedman's concept and find the natural rate of interest most easy to understand as an analogy with Friedman's natural rate. In fact, Wicksell was also an early proponent of the "natural rate hypothesis" enunciated in Friedman's address. "Those people who prefer a continually upward moving to a stationary price level forcibly remind one of those who purposely keep their watches a little fast so as to be more certain of catching their trains. But to achieve their purpose they must not be conscious . . . of the fact that their watches are fast; otherwise they become accustomed to take the extra few minutes into account and so after all, in spite of their artfulness, arrive too late" (Wicksell, 1898, pp. 3–4).

here in the consequences of monetary targeting.) Nonetheless, even for purposes of "short-run" analysis, the proposed model is less static than an old-fashioned Keynesian model; in particular, *expectations* will be crucial elements in its structural relations (e.g., its "intertemporal IS relation"), so that anything that causes a change in expectations should shift them.

The inclusion of significant forward-looking terms in the key structural relations has substantial consequences for the analysis of the character of optimal policy, just as Lucas (1976) argued, even if the consequences are not necessarily the ones suggested in the New Classical literature. For example, estimated IS equations in traditional macroeconometric models often indicate an effect of *lagged* rather than current interest rates on aggregate demand, since the coefficients on lagged rates are found to be more significant than those on a current interest rate in the case of a regression seeking to explain aggregate real expenditure in terms of observable variables. On the other hand, in the optimization-based model estimated by Rotemberg and Woodford (1997), the observed delay in the effects of an interest-rate innovation on real GDP is explained by an assumption that the interest-sensitive component of private spending is predetermined, though chosen in a forward-looking way. Thus current aggregate demand is assumed to depend on *past expectations* of *current and future* interest rates, rather than on past interest rates.

Econometrically, the two hypotheses are not easily distinguished, given the substantial serial correlation of observed interest rates. Yet the second hypothesis, I would argue, has a much simpler logic in terms of the optimal timing of expenditure, once one grants the hypothesis of predetermination of spending decisions (just as with pricing decisions). Moreover, the specification assumed matters greatly for one's conclusions about the conduct of policy. If expenditure is really affected solely by lagged interest rates, it becomes important for the central bank to adjust interest rates in response to its *forecast* of how it would like to affect aggregate demand at a later date; "preemptive" actions are essential. If instead only past expectations of current and future interest rates matter, then *unforecastable* interest-rate movements will not affect demand, so that immediate responses to news will serve no purpose. It will then be important for interest rates to continue to respond to the outlook that *had* been perceived in the past, even if more recent news has substantially modified the bank's forecasts. This *inertial* character of optimal interest-rate policy is discussed further in Chapters 7 and 8.

1.2 Microeconomic Foundations and Policy Analysis

I consider the development of a model of the monetary transmission mechanism with clear foundations in individual optimization to be important for two reasons: It allows us to evaluate alternative monetary policies in a way

that avoids the flaw in policy evaluation exercises using traditional Keynesian macroeconometric models stressed by Lucas (1976); and the outcomes
resulting from alternative policies can be evaluated in terms of the preferences of private individuals that are reflected in the structural relations of
one's model.

Lucas (1976) argued that traditional policy evaluation exercises using
macroeconometric models were flawed by a failure to recognize that the relations typically estimated—a "consumption equation," a "price equation,"
and so on—were actually (at least under the hypothesis of optimizing behavior by households and firms) reduced-form rather than truly structural
relations. In particular, in the estimated equations, expectations regarding
future conditions (future income in the case of consumers and future costs
and future demand in the case of pricesetters) were proxied for by current and lagged observable state variables. But the correlation of expectations with those observables ought to be expected to change in the case of
a change in the government's policy rule, as contemplated in the policy-
evaluation exercise.

This problem can be addressed by making use of structural relations
that explicitly represent the dependence of economic decisions upon expectations regarding future endogenous variables. The present study illustrates how this can be done, deriving the structural relations that are to be
used in the calculation of optimal policy rules from the first-order conditions (Euler equations) that characterize optimal private-sector behavior.
These conditions explicitly involve private-sector expectations about the future evolution of endogenous variables, and often they only *implicitly* define
private-sector behavior, rather than giving a consumption equation or price
equation in closed form. My preference for this form of structural relations
is precisely that they are ones that should remain invariant (insofar as the
proposed theory is correct) under changes in policy that alter the stochastic
laws of motion of the endogenous variables.

Of course, the mere fact that the structural relations derived here follow
from explicit optimization problems for households and firms is no guarantee that they are correctly specified; the (fairly simple) optimization problems that I consider here may or may not be empirically realistic. (Indeed,
insofar as I illustrate the principles of my approach in the context of very
simple examples, one can be certain that they are not very precise representations of reality.) But this is not an objection to the method that I advocate here. It simply means that there is no substitute for careful empirical
research to flesh out the details of a quantitatively realistic account of the
monetary transmission mechanism. While the present study does include
some discussion of the extent to which the simple models presented here
are consistent with empirical evidence, in order to motivate the introduction of certain model elements, no attempt is made to set out a model that

is sufficiently realistic to be used for actual policy analysis in a central bank. Nonetheless, the basic elements of an optimizing model of the monetary transmission mechanism, developed in Chapters 3 through 5, are ones that I believe are representative of crucial elements of a realistic model; and indeed, the illustrative models discussed here have many elements in common with rational-expectations models of the monetary transmission mechanism that are already being used for quantitative policy evaluation at a number of central banks.

A second advantage of proceeding from explicit microeconomic foundations is that in this case, the welfare of private agents—as indicated by the utility functions that underlie the structural relations of one's model of the transmission mechanism—provides a natural objective in terms of which alternative policies should be evaluated. In taking this approach, the present study seeks to treat questions of monetary policy in a way that is already standard in other branches of public economics, such as the analysis of optimal tax policy. Nonetheless, the approach is not common in the literature on monetary policy evaluation, which instead typically evaluates alternative policies in terms of ad hoc stabilization objectives for various macroeconomic indicators.

Until recently, welfare-theoretic analyses of monetary policy have been associated exclusively with the problem of reducing the transactions frictions (sometimes called "shoe-leather costs") that account for the use of money in purchases.[5] This is because this was for a long time the only sort of inefficiency present in general-equilibrium monetary models, which typically assumed perfectly flexible wages and prices and perfect competition. Here I show how welfare analysis of monetary policy is also possible in settings that incorporate nominal rigidities. Allowing for these additional frictions— crucial to understanding the real effects of alternative monetary policies— provides a welfare-theoretic justification for additional policy goals.

As shown in Chapter 6, taking account of delays in the adjustment of wages and prices provides a clear justification for an approach to monetary policy that aims at price stability. It might seem more obvious that allowing for real effects of monetary policy provides a justification for concern with output stabilization. The stickiness of prices explains why actual output may differ from the natural rate, and so justifies a concern for the stabilization of the "output gap," that is, the discrepancy between the actual and natural levels of output. But price stickiness also justifies a concern with price stability. For when prices are not constantly adjusted, instability of the general level of prices creates discrepancies between relative prices owing to the absence of perfect synchronization in the adjustment of the prices of different

---

5. For reviews of that traditional literature, see Woodford (1990) and Chari and Kehoe (1999).

goods. These relative-price distortions lead in turn to an inefficient sectoral allocation of resources, even when the *aggregate* level of output is correct.

Moreover, the present theory implies not only that price stability should matter *in addition* to stability of the output gap, but also that, at least under certain circumstances, inflation stabilization eliminates any need for further concern with the level of real activity. This is because, at least under the conditions described more precisely in Chapter 6, the time-varying efficient level of output is the *same* (up to a constant, which does not affect the basic point) as the level of output that eliminates any incentive for firms on average to either raise or lower their prices. It then follows that there is no conflict between the goal of inflation stabilization and output-gap stabilization, once the welfare-relevant concept of the output gap is properly understood. Furthermore, because of the difficulty involved in measuring the efficient level of economic activity in real time—depending as this does on variations in production costs, consumption needs, and investment opportunities—it may well be more convenient for a central bank to concern itself simply with monitoring the stability of prices.

The development of an explicit welfare analysis of the distortions resulting from inflation variations has advantages beyond the mere provision of a justification for central bankers' current concern with inflation stabilization. For the theory presented here also provides guidance as to *which* price index it is most desirable to stabilize. This is a question of no small practical interest. For example, the stock-market booms and crashes in many industrial nations in the late 1990s led to discussion of whether central banks ought not target an inflation measure that took account of "asset-price inflation" as well as goods prices.[6]

The answer provided by the theory developed here is *no.* The prices that monetary policy should aim to stabilize are the ones that are infrequently adjusted and that consequently can be expected to become misaligned in an environment that requires these prices to move in either direction. Large movements in frequently adjusted prices—and stock prices are among the most flexible—can instead be allowed without raising such concerns, and if allowing them to move makes possible greater stability of the sticky prices, such instability of the flexible prices is desirable.[7] In Chapter 6, I show how such a conclusion can be justified from the point of view of welfare

6. For examples of scholarly attention to the question, see Goodhart (1999) and Bryan et al. (2002).

7. The basic point was already evident to authors of the Stockholm school: "If one desires the greatest possible diminution of the business cycle . . . then one must try to stabilize an index of those prices which are sticky in themselves. . . . Stability of the level of the sticky prices permits a certain freedom for all other price levels, including capital values. . . . It is evident that [the price of capital goods] is the last price that one should try to stabilize in a capitalist society. . . . The same is naturally true for all indices of flexible commodity prices" (Myrdal,

economics. I further show how to develop a quantitative measure of the
deadweight loss resulting from stabilization of alternative price indices, so
that more subtle distinctions between the relative stickiness of different
prices can be dealt with.

In addition to implying that an appropriate inflation target ought not
involve asset prices, the present theory suggests that not all goods prices are
equally relevant. Rather, central banks should target a measure of "core"
inflation that places greater weight on those prices that are stickier. Furthermore, insofar as wages are also sticky, a desirable inflation target should
take account of wage inflation as well as goods prices. The empirical results
discussed in Chapter 3 suggest that wages and prices are sticky to a similar
extent, suggesting (as I show in Chapter 8) that a desirable inflation target
should put roughly equal weight on wage and price inflation.

2   The Importance of Policy Commitment

Thus far, I have summarized a theoretical justification for the concern of
the inflation-targeting central banks with price stability. But why should
it follow that there is a need for public commitment to a target inflation
rate, let alone for commitment to a systematic procedure for determining
appropriate instrument settings? Why is it not enough to appoint central
bankers with a sound understanding of the way the economy works and
then grant them complete discretion to pursue the public interest in the way
that they judge best? Should it not follow from my analysis that this would
result in price stability, to the extent that it is possible given the instruments
available to the central bank and the information available at the time that
policy decisions must be made?

I argue instead that there is good reason for a central bank to commit
itself to a systematic approach to policy that not only provides an explicit
framework for decisionmaking within the bank, but that is also used to explain the bank's decisions to the public. There are two important advantages
of commitment to an appropriately chosen *policy rule* of this kind. One is
that the effectiveness of monetary policy depends as much on the public's
expectations about future policy as upon the bank's actual actions. Hence
it is important not only that a bank manage to make the right decision as
often as possible, but that its actions be *predictable*.

The second, and subtler, reason is that even if the public has no difficulty
in correctly perceiving the pattern in the central bank's actions—as assumed

---

1931, pp. 192–193). Simons (1948) and Meade (1951) advocated targeting a domestic-goods
price index rather than a consumer price index on similar grounds; the CPI would include the
prices of imported goods, that could vary freely through exchange-rate movements. Clarida
et al. (2001) also obtain the latter conclusion, in the context of a fully articulated open-
economy sticky-price model.

under the hypothesis of rational expectations—if a bank acts at each date under the assumption that it cannot commit itself to any future behavior (and is not bound by any past commitments), it will choose a systematic pattern of behavior that is suboptimal. I take up each of these arguments in turn.

2.1   Central Banking as Management of Expectations

The first advantage of commitment to a policy rule is that it facilitates public understanding of policy. It is important for the public to understand the central bank's actions, to the greatest extent possible, not only for reasons of democratic legitimacy—though this is an excellent reason itself, given that central bankers are granted substantial autonomy in the execution of their task—but also in order for monetary policy to be most effective.

For successful monetary policy is not so much a matter of effective control of overnight interest rates as it is of shaping market *expectations* of the way in which interest rates, inflation, and income are likely to evolve over the coming year and later. On the one hand, optimizing models imply that private sector behavior should be forward looking; hence expectations about future market conditions should be important determinants of current behavior. It follows that, insofar as it is possible for the central bank to affect expectations, this should be an important tool of stabilization policy. Moreover, given the increasing sophistication of market participants about central banking over the past two decades, it is plausible to suppose that a central bank's commitment to a systematic policy will be factored into private-sector forecasts—at least insofar as the bank's actions are observed to match its professed commitments.

Not only do expectations about policy matter, but, at least under current conditions, very little *else* matters. Few central banks of major industrial nations still make much use of credit controls or other attempts to directly regulate the flow of funds through financial markets and institutions. Increases in the sophistication of the financial system have made it more difficult for such controls to be effective, and in any event the goal of improvement of the efficiency of the sectoral allocation of resources stressed previously would hardly be served by such controls, which (if successful) inevitably create inefficient distortions in the relative cost of funds to different parts of the economy.

Instead, banks restrict themselves to interventions that seek to control the overnight interest rate in an interbank market for central-bank balances (e.g., the federal funds rate in the United States). But the current level of overnight interest rates *as such* is of negligible importance for economic decisionmaking. If a change in the overnight rate were thought to imply only a change in the cost of overnight borrowing for that one night, then even a large change (say, a full percentage point increase) would make little difference to anyone's spending decisions. The effectiveness of changes in central-bank targets for overnight rates in affecting spending decisions (and hence ultimately pricing and employment decisions) is wholly dependent upon the impact of such actions upon other financial-market prices, such as longer-term interest rates, equity prices, and exchange rates. These are plausibly linked, through arbitrage relations, to the short-term interest rates most directly affected by central-bank actions. But it is the expected future path of short-term rates over coming months and even years that should matter for the determination of these other asset prices, rather than the current level of short-term rates by itself.[8]

Thus the ability of central banks to influence expenditure, and hence pricing, decisions is critically dependent upon their ability to influence market expectations regarding the *future path* of overnight interest rates, and not merely their current level. Better information on the part of market participants about central-bank actions and intentions should increase the degree to which central-bank policy decisions can actually affect these expectations and so increase the effectiveness of monetary stabilization policy. Insofar as the significance of current developments for future policy is clear to the private sector, markets can to a large extent "do the central bank's work for it," in that the actual changes in overnight rates required to achieve the desired changes in incentives can be much more modest when expected future rates move as well.[9]

An obvious consequence of the importance of managing expectations is that a transparent central-bank decisionmaking process is highly desirable. This has come to be widely accepted by central bankers over the past decade. (See Blinder et al., 2001, for a detailed and authoritative discussion.) But it is sometimes supposed that the most crucial issues are ones such as the frequency of press releases or the promptness and detail with which the

8. An effect of the same kind is obtained in the basic "neo-Wicksellian" model developed in Chapter 4, insofar as the short-run real rate of interest determines not the absolute level of desired private-sector expenditure, but rather the current level relative to the expected future level of expenditure, as a result of an Euler equation for the optimal timing of expenditure. Expected future expenditure, relative to expected expenditure even farther in the future, similarly depends upon expected future short rates, and so on for expectations regarding the still farther future.

9. There is evidence that this is already happening, as a result both of greater sophistication on the part of financial markets and greater transparency on the part of central banks, the two developing in a sort of symbiosis with one another. Blinder et al. (2001, p. 8) argue that in the period from early 1996 through the middle of 1999, one could observe the U.S. bond market moving in response to macroeconomic developments that helped to stabilize the economy, despite relatively little change in the level of the federal funds rate, and suggest that this reflected an improvement in the bond market's ability to forecast Fed actions before they occur. Statistical evidence of increased forecastability of Fed policy by the markets is provided by Lange et al. (2001), who show that the ability of Treasury bill yields to predict changes in the federal funds rate some months in advance has increased since the late 1980s.

minutes of policy deliberations are published. Instead, from the perspective suggested here, what is important is not so much that the central bank's deliberations themselves be public, as that the bank give clear signals about what the public should expect it to do in the future. The public needs to have as clear as possible an understanding of the *rule* that the central bank follows in deciding what it does. Inevitably, the best way to communicate about this is by offering the public an explanation of the decisions that have already been made; the bank itself would probably not be able to describe how it might act in all conceivable circumstances, most of which will never arise.

Some good practical examples of communication with the public about the central bank's policy commitments are provided by the *Inflation Reports* of the leading inflation-targeting banks. These reports do not pretend to give a blow-by-blow account of the deliberations by which the central bank reached the position that it has determined to announce, but they do explain the *analysis* that justifies the position that has been reached. This analysis provides information about the bank's systematic approach to policy by illustrating its application to the concrete circumstances that have arisen since the last report; and it provides information about how conditions are likely to develop in the future through explicit discussion of the bank's own projections. Because the analysis is made public, it can be expected to shape future deliberations, with the bank knowing that it should be expected to explain why views expressed in the past are not being followed later. Thus a commitment to transparency of this sort helps to make policy more fully rule based and also increases the public's understanding of the rule.

It is perhaps worth clarifying further what I intend by "rule-based" policy. I do not mean that a bank should commit itself to an explicit state-contingent plan for the entire foreseeable future, specifying what it would do under every circumstance that might possibly arise. That would obviously be impractical, even under complete unanimity about the correct model of the economy and the objectives of policy, simply because of the vast number of possible futures. But it is also not necessary. To obtain the benefits of commitment to a systematic policy, it suffices that a central bank commit itself to a systematic way of determining an appropriate response to future developments, without having to list all of the implications of the rule for possible future developments.[10]

Nor is it necessary to imagine that commitment to a systematic rule means that once a rule is adopted it must be followed forever, regard-

---

10. I show in Chapter 8 how policy rules can be designed that can be specified without any reference to particular economic disturbances, but that nonetheless imply an optimal equilibrium response to additive disturbances of an arbitrary type. The targeting rules advocated by Svensson (1999, 2003b) are examples of rules of this kind.

less of subsequent improvements in understanding the effects of monetary policy on the economy, including experience with the consequences of implementing the rule. If the private sector is forward looking, and it is possible for the central bank to make the private sector aware of its policy commitments, then there *are* important advantages of commitment to a policy other than discretionary optimization—that is, simply doing what seems best at each point in time, with no commitment regarding what may be done later. This is because there are advantages to having the private sector able to anticipate *delayed* responses to a disturbance that may not be optimal ex post if one reoptimizes taking the private sector's past reaction as given. But one can create the desired anticipations of subsequent behavior—and justify them—without committing to following a fixed rule in the future no matter what may happen in the meantime.

It is enough that the private sector have no grounds to forecast that the bank's behavior will be *systematically* different from the rule that it pretends to follow. This will be the case if the bank is committed to choosing a rule of conduct that is justifiable on certain *principles*, given its model of the economy. (An example of the sort of principles that I have in mind is given in Chapter 8.) The bank can then properly be expected to continue to follow its current rule, as long as its understanding of the economy does not change. Furthermore, as long as there is no *predictable* direction in which its future model of the economy should be different from its current one, private-sector expectations should not be different from those in the case of an indefinite commitment to the current rule. Yet changing to a better rule remains possible in the case of improved knowledge (which is inevitable); and insofar as the change is justified in terms of both established principles and a change in the bank's model of the economy that can itself be defended, this need not impair the credibility of the bank's professed commitments.

It follows that rule-based policymaking necessarily means a decision process in which an explicit *model* of the economy (albeit one augmented by judgmental elements) plays a central role, both in the deliberations of the policy committee and in explanation of those deliberations to the public. This too has been a prominent feature of recent innovations in the conduct of monetary policy by the inflation-targeting central banks. While there is undoubtedly much room for improvement in both current models and current approaches to the use of models in policy deliberations, one can only expect the importance of models to policy deliberations to increase in a world of increasingly sophisticated financial markets.

2.2 Pitfalls of Conventional Optimal Control

It is not enough that a central bank have sound objectives (reflecting a correct analysis of social welfare), that it make policy in a systematic way, using a correct model of the economy and a staff that is well trained in numerical optimization, and that all this be explained thoroughly to the public. A bank that approaches its problem as one of optimization under *discretion*—deciding afresh on the best action in each decision cycle, with no commitment regarding future actions except that they will be the ones that seem best in whatever circumstances may arise—may obtain a substantially worse outcome, from the point of view of its own objectives, than one that commits itself to follow a properly chosen policy *rule*. As Kydland and Prescott (1977) first showed, this can occur even when the central bank has a correct quantitative model of the policy trade-offs that it faces at each point in time and the private sector has correct expectations about the way that policy will be conducted.

At first thought, discretionary optimization might seem exactly what one would want an enlightened central bank to do. All sorts of unexpected events constantly occur that affect the determination of inflation and real activity, and it is not hard to see that, in general, the optimal level of interest rates at any point in time should depend on precisely what has occurred. It is plainly easiest, as a practical matter, to arrange for such complex state dependence of policy by having the instrument setting at a given point in time be determined only after the unexpected shocks have already been observed. Furthermore, it might seem that the dynamic programming approach to the solution of intertemporal optimization problems provides justification for an approach in which a planning problem is reduced to a series of independent choices at each of a succession of decision dates.

But standard dynamic programming methods are valid only for the optimal control of a system that evolves mechanically in response to the current action of the controller, as in the kind of industrial problems of typical interest in engineering control theory. The problem of monetary stabilization policy is of a different sort, in that the consequences of the central bank's actions depend not only upon the sequence of instrument settings up until the present time, but also upon private-sector expectations regarding future policy. In such a case, sequential (discretionary) optimization leads to a suboptimal outcome because at each decision point, prior expectations are taken as *given*, rather than as something that can be affected by policy. Nonetheless, the predictable character of the central bank's decisions, taken from this point of view, does determine the (endogenous) expectations of the private sector at earlier dates, under the hypothesis of rational expectations. A commitment to behave differently that is made credible to the private sector could shape those expectations in a different way, and because expectations matter for the determination of the variables that the central bank cares about, in general outcomes can be improved through shrewd use of this opportunity.

The best-known example of a distortion created by discretionary optimization is the "inflation bias" analyzed by Kydland and Prescott (1977) and Barro and Gordon (1983). In the presence of a short-run Phillips-curve trade-off between inflation and real activity (given inflation expectations) and a target level of real activity higher than the one associated with an optimal inflation rate (in the case of inflation expectations also consistent with that optimal rate), these authors showed that discretionary optimization leads to a rate of inflation that is inefficiently high on average, owing to neglect of the way that pursuit of such a policy raises inflation expectations (causing an adverse shift of the short-run Phillips curve). A variety of solutions to the problem of inflation bias have been proposed. One influential idea is that this bias can be eliminated by assigning the central bank targets for inflation and output that differ from those reflected in the true social welfare function (i.e., the central-bank objective assumed by Kydland and Prescott or Barro and Gordon), without otherwise constraining the central bank's discretion in the selection of policies to achieve its objective. This is one of the primary reasons for the popularity of inflation targeting, which involves commitment of a central bank to the pursuit of an assigned target rather than being left to simply act as seems best for society at any point in time, while leaving the bank a great deal of flexibility as to the way in which the assigned goal is to be pursued.

However, the distortions resulting from discretionary optimization go beyond simple bias in the *average* levels of inflation or other endogenous variables; this approach to the conduct of policy generally results in suboptimal responses to shocks as well, as shown in Chapter 7. For example, various types of real disturbances can create temporary fluctuations in what Wicksell called the "natural rate of interest," meaning (as shown in Chapter 4) that the level of nominal interest rates required to stabilize both inflation and the output gap varies over time. However, the amplitude of the adjustment of short-term interest rates can be more moderate—and still have the desired size of effect on spending and hence on both output and inflation— if it is made more *persistent*, so that when interest rates are increased, they will not be expected to quickly return to their normal level, even if the real disturbance that originally justified the adjustment has dissipated. Because aggregate demand depends upon expected future short rates as well as on current short rates, a more persistent increase of smaller amplitude can have an equal affect on spending. If one also cares about reducing the volatility of short-term interest rates, a more inertial interest-rate policy of this kind is preferable; that is, the anticipation that the central bank will follow such a policy leads to a preferable rational-expectations equilibrium. But a central bank that optimizes under discretion has no incentive to continue to maintain interest rates high once the initial shock has dissipated. At that point, prior demand has already responded to whatever interest-rate expectations were held then, and the bank has no reason to take into account any effect upon demand at an earlier date in setting its current interest-rate target.

This distortion in the dynamic response of interest-rate policy to disturbances cannot be cured by any adjustment of the targets that the bank is directed to aim for regardless of what disturbances may occur. Rather, policy must be made *history dependent,* that is, dependent upon past conditions even when they are no longer relevant to the determination of the current and future evolution of the variables that the bank cares about. Indeed, in general no *purely forward-looking* decision procedure—one that makes the bank's action at each decision point a function solely of the set of possible paths for its target variables from that time onward—can bring about optimal equilibrium responses to disturbances. Discretionary optimization is an example of such a procedure, and it continues to be when the bank's objective is modified, if the modification does not introduce any history dependence. But other popular proposals are often purely forward looking as well. Thus the classic "Taylor rule" (Taylor, 1993) prescribes setting an interest-rate operating target at each decision point as a function of current estimates of inflation and the output gap only (see below), and Taylor (1999b) expresses skepticism about the desirability of partial-adjustment dynamics of the kind that characterize most estimated central-bank reaction functions. Popular descriptions of inflation-forecast targeting are typically purely forward looking as well. The interest-rate setting at each decision point is to be determined purely as a function of the forecast from that date forward for inflation (and possibly other target variables). Thus the intuition that optimal policy *should* be purely forward looking seems to be fairly commonplace; but when the private sector is forward looking, any purely forward-looking criterion for policy is almost invariably suboptimal.

Obtaining a more desirable pattern of responses to random disturbances therefore requires commitment to a systematic policy rule, and not just a (one-time) adjustment of the bank's targets. The primary task of this study is to provide principles that can be used in the design of such rules. By saying that a *policy rule* is necessary, I mean to draw a distinction with two other conceptions of optimal policy. One is discretionary optimization, as just discussed; specifying a rule means a more detailed description of the way in which a decision is to be reached than is involved in a simple commitment to a particular objective. But I also mean to distinguish the approach advocated here from the usual understanding of what an *optimal commitment* involves.

In the literature that contrasts policy commitment with discretionary policymaking, following Kydland and Prescott, "commitment" is generally taken to mean a specification, once and for all, of the state-contingent action to be taken at each subsequent date. An optimal commitment is then a choice of such a state-contingent plan so as to maximize the ex ante expected value of the policymaker's objective, as evaluated at the initial date t_0 at which the commitment is chosen. This leads to a description of optimal policy in terms of a specification of the instrument setting as a function of the history of exogenous shocks since date t_0.

But the solution to such an optimization problem is not an appealing policy recommendation in practice. For it is generally not *time consistent*: Solving the same optimization problem at a later date t_1 to determine the optimal commitment from *that* date onward does not result in a state-contingent plan from date t_1 onward that continues the plan judged to be optimal at date t_0. This is because the commitment chosen at date t_0 takes account of the consequences of the commitments made for dates t_1 and later for expectations between dates t_0 and t_1, while at date t_1 these expectations are taken as historical facts that cannot be changed by the policy chosen from then on. (This is just the reason why discretionary optimization does not lead to the same policy as an optimal commitment.) Hence this policy proposal cannot be regarded as proposing a decision procedure that can be used at each date to determine the best action at that date. Rather, a state-contingent plan must be determined once and for all, for the rest of time, and thereafter simply implemented, whether it continues to appear desirable or not.

Such a proposal is not a practical one for two reasons. First, enumeration in advance of all of the possible subsequent histories of shocks is not feasible—the kinds of situations that the central bank may face at a given date are too various to possibly be listed in advance. Second, the arbitrariness of continuing to stick to a particular specified policy simply because it looked good at a particular past date—the date t_0 at which one happened to make the commitment—is sufficiently unappealing that one cannot imagine a central bank binding itself to behave in that way or the private sector believing that it had. Here my argument is not that central bankers are *incapable* of commitment to a systematic rule of conduct, so that they are inevitably discretionary optimizers; it is rather that their commitment must be based upon an understanding of the rational justification of the rule, and not on the mere fact that it happens to have been chosen (even by themselves) on a past occasion.

Both problems can be avoided by commitment to a systematic rule for determining their policy action at each decision point that does not reduce to a once-and-for-all specification of the instrument setting as a function of the history of shocks. In Chapter 8, it is shown that one can design rules for setting the central bank's interest-rate operating target that lead to optimal dynamic responses to shocks, without the rule specification having to refer to the various disturbances that may have occurred. The disturbances affect the instrument setting, of course. But they affect it either as a result of having influenced endogenous variables, such as inflation and output, to which the instrument setting responds or as a result of being factored into the central bank's projections of the future evolution of the economy under alternative possible instrument settings. Such a rule can result in optimal equilibrium responses to disturbances of any of a vast number of possible types, so that the potential disturbances need not even be listed in advance in order to describe the rule and evaluate its desirability.

The optimal rules derived in accordance with the principles set out in Chapter 8 are also time invariant in form. This means that the optimal rule that would be derived at date t_0, on the basis of a particular structural model of the monetary transmission mechanism and a particular understanding of the central bank's stabilization objectives, is also derived at date t_1, assuming that the bank's model and objectives remain the same. A commitment to conduct policy in accordance with a rule that is judged optimal by this criterion is thus *time consistent*, in the sense that reconsideration of the matter at a later date on the basis of the same principle leads to a decision to continue the same course of action as had been intended earlier.[11]

Because of this, adherence to a policy rule need not be taken to mean adoption of a rule at some initial date, after which the rule is followed blindly, without ever again considering its desirability. Instead, *rule-based policymaking* as the term is intended here means that at each decision point an action is taken that conforms to a policy rule, which rule is itself one that is judged to be optimal (from a "timeless perspective" that is explained in Chapter 7) given the central bank's understanding of the monetary transmission mechanism *at the time that the decision is made.* The desire to follow a rule (and so to avoid the trap of discretionary optimization) does not mean that the bank must refrain from asking itself whether adherence to the rule is consistent with its stabilization objectives. It simply means that whenever this question is taken up, the bank should consider what an optimal *rule* of conduct would be, rather than asking what an optimal *action* is on the individual occasion, and that it should consider the desirability of alternative rules from an impartial perspective that does not amount to simply finding a rationalization for the action it would like to take on this particular occasion.[12] A central bank might reconsider this question as often as it likes,

11. Note that "time consistency" in the sense that I use the term here does *not* mean that the policymaker does not believe at any time that it is possible to achieve a higher expected value for its objective by deviating from its intended rule. Time consistency does not require this, because this is not the criterion according to which the central bank's action is judged to be optimal at *any* time, including the initial date t_0.

12. The distinction between these two perspectives is similar to the distinction that is made in ethical theory between "rule utilitarianism" and "act utilitarianism" (Brandt, 1959; Harsanyi, 1982). Act utilitarianism is the view that the right act on any occasion is the one that will maximize social utility in the situation that the actor is in at that time. Rule utilitarianism instead maintains that a right act is one that conforms to the correct rule for this sort of situation, where a correct rule is one that would maximize social utility if *always* followed in all situations of this type.

without being led into the kind of suboptimal behavior that results from discretionary optimization. Moreover, when considering the desirability of a policy rule, it is correct for the bank to consider the effects of its being expected to follow the rule indefinitely, even though it does not contemplate *binding* itself to do so; for as long as its view of the policy problem does not change (which it has no reason to expect), a commitment to rule-based policymaking should guarantee that it will continue to act according to the rule judged to be optimal.

Rule-based policymaking in this sense avoids the sorts of rigidity that are often associated with commitment to a "rule" and that probably account for much of the resistance that central bankers often display toward the concept of a policy rule. A commitment to rule-based policymaking does not preclude taking account of all of the information, from whatever sources, that the central bank may have about current economic conditions, including the recognition that disturbances may have occurred that would not have been thought possible a few months earlier. For a policy rule need not specify the instrument setting as a function of a specified list of exogenous states, and indeed it is argued in Chapter 7 that an optimal rule should in general *not* take this form. Nor does it preclude changing the form of the policy rule when the bank's view of the monetary transmission changes, as it surely will, owing both to institutional change in economies themselves and to the progress of knowledge in economics. Hence it allows the sort of flexibility that is often associated with the term "discretion," while at the same time eliminating the systematic biases that follow from policy analysis that naively applies dynamic-programming principles.

3   Monetary Policy without Control of a Monetary Aggregate

Thus far I have discussed the desirability of a monetary policy rule without saying much about the precise form of rule that is intended. To be more concrete, the present study considers the design of a rule to be used in determining a central bank's operating target for a short-term nominal interest rate. This target will ordinarily be revised at intervals of perhaps once a month (as at the ECB) or eight times a year (as in the United States).[13]

My focus on the choice of an *interest-rate rule* should not surprise readers familiar with the current practice of central banks. Monetary policy decisionmaking almost everywhere means a decision about the operating target for an overnight interest rate, and the increased transparency about policy in recent years has almost always meant greater explicitness about

13. The question of the optimal frequency of reconsideration of the interest-rate target is one of obvious practical interest. But I shall not take it up in this study, as I consider optimal policy in the context of a discrete-time model of the transmission mechanism with "periods" corresponding to the length of the central bank's decision cycle.

the central bank's interest-rate target and the way in which its interest-rate decisions are made. In such a context, it is natural that adoption of a policy rule should mean commitment to a specific procedure for deciding what interest-rate target is appropriate.

Nonetheless, theoretical analyses of monetary policy have until recently almost invariably characterized policy in terms of a path for the money supply, and discussions of policy rules in the theoretical literature have mainly considered money-growth rules of one type or another. This curious disjunction between theory and practice predates the enthusiasm of the 1970s for monetary targets. Goodhart (1989) complains of "an unhelpful dichotomy, between the theory and the reality of Central Bank operations," which equally characterized the work of John Maynard Keynes and Milton Friedman:

> When either of these two great economists would discuss practical pol-
> icy matters concerning the level of short-term interest rates, they had no
> doubts that these were normally determined by the authorities, and could
> be changed by them, and were not freely determined in the market. . . . But
> when they came to their more theoretical papers, they often reverted to the
> assumption that the Central Bank sets the nominal money stock, or alterna-
> tively fixes the level of the monetary base, [with] the demand and supply of
> money . . . equilibrated in the short run . . . by market-led developments in
> nominal interest rates. (pp. 330–331)

The present study seeks to revive the earlier approach of Knut Wicksell and considers the advantages of systematic monetary policies that are de-scribed in terms of rules for setting a nominal interest rate. While the im-plied evolution of the money supply is sometimes discussed, the question is often ignored. Some of the time, I do not bother to specify policy (or an economic model) in sufficient detail to determine the associated path of the money supply, or even to tell if one can be uniquely determined in principle. Some readers may fear as a result that I consider an ill-posed question—that the "policy rules" studied here may not represent sufficiently complete de-scriptions of a policy to allow its consequences to be determined or may not represent states of affairs that the central bank is able to bring about. Hence some general remarks may be appropriate about why it is possible to conceive of the problem of monetary policy as a problem of interest-rate policy before turning to examples of the specific types of interest-rate rules that I wish to consider.

3.1 Implementing Interest-Rate Policy

An argument that is sometimes advanced for specifying monetary policy in terms of a rule for base-money growth rather than an interest-rate rule is that central banks do not actually fix overnight interest rates. Even when banks have an operating target for the overnight rate, they typically seek to implement it through open-market operations in Treasury securities or their equivalent—that is, by adjusting the supply of central-bank liabilities to a level that is expected to cause the market for overnight cash to clear near the target rate. Thus it may be argued that the action that the central bank actually takes each day is an adjustment of the nominal magnitude of the monetary base, so that a complete specification of policy should describe the size of this daily adjustment.

But even when banks implement their interest-rate targets entirely through quantity adjustments, as is largely correct as a description of current U.S. arrangements, this conclusion hardly follows. Central banks like the U.S. Federal Reserve determine their quantity adjustments through a two-step procedure: first the interest-rate target is determined by a monetary policy committee (the Federal Open Market Committee in the United States) without consideration of the size of the implied open-market operations, and then the appropriate daily open-market operations required to maintain the funds rate near the target are determined by people closer to the financial markets (mainly the Trading Desk at the New York Fed). The higher-level policy decision about the interest-rate target is the more complicated one, made much less frequently because of the complexity of the deliberations involved,[14] and it is accordingly this decision with which the present study is concerned.

Nor is it the case that a central bank's interest-rate target *must* be implemented through choice of an appropriate supply of central-bank liabilities. A central bank can also influence the interest rate at which banks lend overnight cash to one another through adjustment of the interest rate paid on overnight balances held at the central bank and/or the interest rate at which the central bank is willing to lend overnight cash to banks that run overdrafts on their clearing accounts at the central bank. These are important policy tools outside the United States, and in some countries are the primary means through which the central bank implements its interest-rate targets.

As is discussed in more detail in Woodford (2001c), countries like Canada, Australia, and New Zealand now implement monetary policy through a "channel system." In a system of this kind, the overnight interest rate is kept near the central bank's target rate through the provision of standing

---

14. The comparative simplicity of the decision about each day's open-market operation is not so much because each day's demand for Fed balances is highly predictable as because the Fed learns immediately how much it has misjudged market demand each day and can act the following day in response to the previous day's gap between the actual funds rate and the target rate. Owing to intertemporal substitution in the demand for reserves under U.S. regulations, a credible commitment by the Fed to respond the following day is enough to keep the funds rate from deviating too much from the target most of the time. See Taylor (2001) for further discussion of the Trading Desk's reaction function.

facilities by the central bank, with interest rates determined by the central bank's current target interest rate $\bar{\imath}_t$. In addition to supplying a certain aggregate quantity of clearing balances (adjusted through open-market operations), the central bank offers a lending facility through which it stands ready to supply an arbitrary amount of additional overnight balances at an interest rate determined by a fixed spread over the target rate (i.e., $i_t^l = \bar{\imath}_t + \delta$). In the countries just mentioned, the spread δ is generally equal to 25 basis points, regardless of the level of the target rate. Finally, depository institutions that settle payments through the central bank also have the right to maintain excess clearing balances overnight with the central bank at a deposit rate $i_t^d = \bar{\imath}_t - \delta$, where δ is the same fixed spread.

The lending rate, on the one hand, and the deposit rate, on the other, then define a channel within which overnight interest rates should be contained.[15] Because these are both standing facilities (unlike the Fed's discount window in the United States), no bank has any reason to pay another bank a higher rate for overnight cash than the rate at which it could borrow from the central bank. Similarly, no bank has any reason to lend overnight cash at a rate lower than the rate at which it can deposit with the central bank. The result is that the central bank can control overnight interest rates within a fairly tight range regardless of what the aggregate supply of clearing balances might be; frequent quantity adjustments accordingly become less important.

Woodford (2001c) describes a simple model of overnight interest-rate determination under such a system. In this model, the daily demand for clearing balances by depository institutions depends only on the location of the interbank market rate relative to the channel established by the two standing facilities, rather than on the absolute level of this interest rate. The interbank market then clears at an interest rate

$$i_t = i_t^d + F(-S_t/\sigma_t)\left(i_t^l - i_t^d\right), \tag{3.1}$$

where S_t is the aggregate supply of clearing balances (determined by the central bank's open-market operations), σ_t is a factor measuring the degree of uncertainty about payment flows on a given day, and F is a cumulative distribution function that increases monotonically from 0 (when its argument is $-\infty$) to 1 (as the argument approaches $+\infty$).

---

15. It is arguable that the actual lower bound is somewhat above the deposit rate because of the convenience and lack of credit risk associated with the deposit facility, and similarly that the actual upper bound is slightly above the lending rate because of the collateral requirements and possible stigma associated with the lending facility. Nonetheless, market rates are observed to stay within the channel established by these rates (except for occasional slight breaches of the upper bound during the early months of operation of Canada's system—see Figure 1.1), and typically near its center.

As noted, the market overnight rate is necessarily within the channel: $i_t^d \leq i_t \leq i_t^l$. Its exact position within the channel should be a decreasing function of the supply of central-bank balances. The model predicts an equilibrium overnight rate at exactly the target rate (the midpoint of the channel) when the supply of clearing balances is equal to

$$S_t = -F^{-1}(1/2)\, \sigma_t. \qquad (3.2)$$

If the probability distribution of unexpected payment flows faced by each institution is roughly symmetric, so that $F(0)$ is near one-half, then the aggregate supply of clearing balances required to maintain the overnight rate near the target rate should not vary much with changes in σ_t. Even if this is not quite true, the adjustments of the supply of clearing balances required by (3.2) are unrelated to changes in the target level of interest rates.

Thus achievement of the central bank's operating target does not require any quantity adjustments through open-market operations in response to deviations of the market rate from the target rate; nor are any changes in the supply of central-bank balances required when the bank wishes to change the level of overnight interest rates. The target level of clearing balances in the system (3.2) has to be adjusted only in response to "technical" factors (e.g., changes in the volume of payments on certain days that can be expected to affect the σ_i), but *not* on occasions when it is desired to "tighten" or "loosen" monetary policy. Instead, changes in the level of overnight rates, when desired, are brought about through the shifts in the deposit rate and lending rate that automatically follow from a change in the target rate (and constitute the operational meaning of such a change), without any need for quantity adjustments.

This type of system has proven highly effective in Canada, Australia, and New Zealand in controlling the level of overnight interest rates. For example, Figure 1.1 plots the overnight rate in Canada since the adoption of the Large-Value Transfer System for payments in February 1999, at which time the standing facilities described previously were adopted.[16] One observes that the channel system has been quite effective, at least since early in 2000, in keeping the overnight interest rate not only within the Bank's 50-basis-point operating band or channel, but usually within about 1 basis point of the target rate. Australia and New Zealand similarly now achieve considerably tighter control of overnight interest rates than is realized under the current operating procedures employed in the United States.[17] For purposes of comparison, Figure 1.2 plots the federal funds rate together

16. A system of the kind described here has been used in Australia since June 1998, and in New Zealand since March 1999.

17. See Woodford (2001c) for corresponding plots for the other two countries, and for discussion of the differences in the four countries' ability to respond to the Y2K panic without loss of control of short-term interest rates.

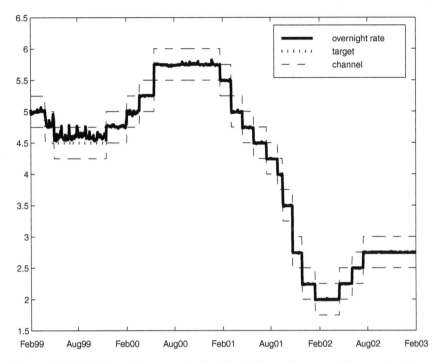

Figure 1.1   *The channel or operating band and the market overnight rate since intro-duction of the LVTS system in Canada. Source: Bank of Canada.*

with the Fed's operating target over the same time period. Note that the standard deviation of the gap between the target and actual federal funds rate is much larger in the United States than in the countries using channel systems (about 1 basis point for Canada, but over 10 basis points for the United States), even under normal circumstances. At times of particular uncertainty about money demand (the Y2K panic, the 9/11/01 attacks on the United States), the deviations from the target funds rate in the United States have been much larger, whereas the same events had little effect on overnight rates in countries like Canada.

Thus the quantity adjustments of the supply of central-bank balances[18] that are involved in implementation of interest-rate policy are quite different

18. I refer here to adjustments of the supply of central-bank balances rather than adjust-ments of the monetary base because in all of the countries under discussion, changes in the public's demand for currency are automatically accommodated by open-market operations that change the monetary base while seeking to insulate the supply of central-bank balances from the effects of such developments. Thus despite the emphasis of the academic literature on monetary-base rules, in practice a quantity-targeting rule that is intended to directly specify the central bank's daily open-market operation would have to specify a target supply of central-bank balances rather than a target value for the monetary base.

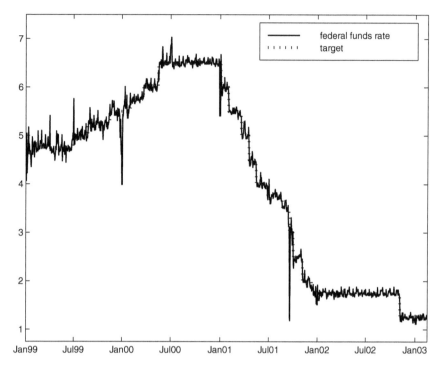

Figure 1.2   *The U.S. federal-funds rate and the Fed's operating target. Source: Federal Reserve Board.*

under a channel system as opposed to the system used in the United States. In the latter, policy can be tightened *only* by restricting the supply of Fed balances, so that the equilibrium spread between the return available on interbank lending and that available on Fed balances increases; in Canada, on the other hand, there need be no change in supply, as there is no desire to change the spreads $i_t^l - i_t$ or $i_t - i_t^d$. Yet there is no reason to believe that these institutional details have any important consequences for the effects of interest-rate policy on these economies, and hence for the way in which it makes sense for these different central banks to determine their interest-rate operating targets. It follows that these conclusions would be of less universal validity if I were to formulate them in terms of a rule for determining the appropriate size of open-market operations, assuming American institutional arrangements.

Furthermore, for a country with a channel system, it would *not be possible* to formulate this advice in terms of a quantity-targeting rule. On the occasions upon which it is appropriate for the central bank to tighten or loosen policy, this does not imply any change in the appropriate target for the supply of central-bank balances; yet this does not at all mean that the central bank should not act! Because the crucial policy instruments in these countries are in fact the interest rates associated with the two standing facilities, which are in turn directly based on the time-varying interest-rate target, a policy rule for such countries must necessarily be formulated as an interest-rate rule. In fact, this way of specifying monetary policy is equally convenient for a country like the United States, and is the one that I use in this study.

3.2 Monetary Policy in a Cashless Economy

Another case in which a monetary policy prescription would *have* to be specified in terms of an interest-rate rule would be if the foregoing advice were to be applicable to a "cashless" economy, by which I mean an economy in which there are *no monetary frictions* whatsoever. In a hypothetical economy of this kind, central-bank liabilities have no special role to play in the payments system that results in a willingness to hold them despite the fact that they yield a lower return than other, equally riskless short-term claims. Consideration of this extreme case is of interest for two reasons.

First, it is possible to imagine that in the coming century the development of electronic payments systems could not only substitute for the use of currency in transactions, but also eliminate any advantage of clearing payments through accounts held at the central bank, as discussed by King (1999). This prospect is highly speculative at present; most current proposals for variants of "electronic money" still depend upon the final settlement of transactions through the central bank, even if payments are made using electronic signals rather than old-fashioned instruments such as paper checks.[19] Yet it is possible that in the future central banks will face the problem of what their role should be in such a world. Moreover, the question of how the development of electronic money should be regulated will face them much sooner. If one takes the view that monetary policy can be implemented only by rationing the supply of something that fulfills an essential function in the payments system, it is likely to be judged important to *prevent* the development of alternatives to payments using central-bank money in order to head off a future in which the central bank is unable to do anything at all on behalf of macroeconomic stabilization—in which it becomes "an army with only a signal corps," in the evocative phrase of Benjamin Friedman (1999).

19. Charles Freedman (2000), for one, argues that the special role of central banks in providing for final settlement is unlikely ever to be replaced, owing to the unimpeachable solvency of these institutions, as government entities that can create money at will. Some, such as Goodhart (2000), equally doubt that electronic media can ever fully substitute for the use of currency.

A second reason why it is useful to consider policy implementation in this hypothetical case is that if I can show that effective interest-rate control is possible even in the complete absence of monetary frictions, it may well simplify the analysis basic issues in the theory of monetary policy to start from the frictionless case, just as a physicist does when analyzing the motion of a pendulum or the trajectory of a cannonball. The appeal of this analytical approach was clear already to Wicksell (1898), who famously began his analysis (though writing at the end of the nineteenth century!) by considering the case of a "pure credit economy," defined as

> A state of affairs in which money does not actually circulate at all, neither in the form of coin (except perhaps as small change) nor in the form of notes, but where all domestic payments are effected by means of . . . bookkeeping transfers. (p. 70)

This is the approach that is taken in the chapters to follow. The basic model (developed beginning in Chapter 2) is one that abstracts from monetary frictions, in order to focus attention on more essential aspects of the monetary transmission mechanism, such as the way that spending decisions depend on expected future interest rates as well as current ones or the way in which fluctuations in nominal expenditure affect real activity. I then pause at various points to consider the modifications of the analysis that are required in order to take account of the monetary frictions that evidently exist, given the observation that non-interest-earning currency continues to be held. It is shown that, as a quantitative matter, these modifications are of relatively minor importance.

In the discussion of interest-rate determination under a present-day channel system, I have supposed that there is a demand for at least a small quantity of central-bank balances for clearing purposes, and these are held despite the existence of a small opportunity cost (25 basis points on average). But once the idea has been accepted that the central bank can vary the overnight interest rate without ever having to vary the size of this return spread, the functioning of the system no longer depends on the existence of a clearing demand. Consider instead the supposition that balances held with the central bank cease to be any more useful to commercial banks than any other equally riskless overnight investment. In this case, the demand for central-bank balances is zero for all interest rates higher than the deposit rate i_t^d. But banks should still be willing to hold arbitrary balances at the central bank as long as the market overnight rate is no higher than the rate paid by the central bank. In this case, it would no longer be possible to induce the overnight cash market to clear at a target rate higher than the rate paid on overnight balances at the central bank; for equation (3.1) reduces to $i_t = i_t^d$ in the case of any positive supply of central-bank balances.

But the central bank could still control the equilibrium overnight rate, by using the deposit rate as its policy instrument.[20] Such a system would differ from current channel systems in that an overnight lending facility would no longer be necessary, so that there would no longer be a "channel."[21] Furthermore, the rate paid on central-bank balances would no longer be set at a fixed spread δ below the target overnight rate, but rather at exactly the target rate.

Perfect control of overnight rates should still be possible through adjustments of the rate paid on overnight central-bank balances, and changes in the target overnight rate would not have to involve any change in the target supply of central-bank balances, just as is true under current channel systems. Indeed, in this extreme case, any variations that did occur in the supply of central-bank balances would cease to have any effect at all upon the equilibrium overnight rate.

But how can interest-rate variation be achieved without any adjustment at all of the supply of central-bank balances? Informal discussions often treat interest-rate control by the central bank like a species of price control. Certainly, if a government decides to peg the price of some commodity, it may be able to do so, but only by holding stocks of the commodity that are sufficiently large relative to its world market, and by standing ready to vary those holdings by large amounts as necessary. If the market in question is a large one (more to the point, if either supply or demand in the market is relatively price elastic) relative to the size of the balance sheet of the government entity seeking to control the price, one doubts that such efforts will be effective. What is different about controlling short-term nominal interest rates?

The difference is that there is no inherent "equilibrium" level of interest rates to which the market would tend in the absence of central-bank intervention and against which the central bank must therefore exert a significant countervailing force in order to achieve a given operating

---

20. Grimes (1992) makes a related point, showing that variation of the interest rate paid on central-bank balances would be effective in an environment in which central-bank reserves are no more useful for carrying out transactions than other liquid government securities, so that open-market purchases or sales of such securities are completely ineffective. Hall (1983, 2002) has also proposed this as a method of price-level control in the complete absence of monetary frictions. Hall speaks of control of the interest yield on a government "security," without any need for a central bank at all. But because of the special features that this instrument would need to possess, which are not possessed by privately issued securities—it is a claim only to future delivery of more units of the same instrument, and society's unit of account is defined in terms of this instrument—it seems best to think of it as still taking the same institutional form that it does today, namely, balances in an account with the central bank.

21. This presumes a world in which no payments are cleared using central-bank balances. Of course, there would be no harm in continuing to offer such a facility as long as the central-bank clearing system were still used for at least some payments.

target.[22] This is because there is no inherent value (in terms of real goods and services) for a fiat unit of account such as the "dollar," except insofar as a particular exchange value results from the monetary policy commitments of the central bank. The basic point was clear to Wicksell (1898, pp. 100–101), who compares relative prices to a pendulum that always returns to the same equilibrium position when perturbed, while the money prices of goods in general are compared to a cylinder resting on a horizontal plane, which can remain equally well in any location on the plane to which it may happen to be moved.[23] Alternative price-level paths are thus equally consistent with market equilibrium in the absence of any intervention that would vary the supply of any real goods or services to the private sector; and associated with these alternative paths for the general level of prices are alternative paths for short-term nominal interest rates.

Of course, this analysis might suggest that while central banks can bring about an arbitrary level of *nominal* interest rates (by creating expectations of the appropriate rate of inflation), they should not be able to significantly affect *real* interest rates, except through trades that are large relative to the economy that they seek to affect. It may also suggest that they should be able to move nominal rates only by altering inflation expectations; yet banks generally do not feel that they can easily alter expectations of inflation over the near term, so that one might doubt that they should be able to affect *short-term* nominal rates through such a mechanism.

However, once one recognizes that many prices (and wages) are fairly sticky over short time intervals, the arbitrariness of the path of nominal prices (in the sense of their underdetermination by real factors alone) implies that the path of real activity and the associated path of equilibrium real interest rates are equally arbitrary. It is equally possible, from a logical standpoint, to imagine allowing the central bank to determine, by arbitrary fiat, the path of aggregate real activity, or the path of real interest rates, or the path of nominal interest rates as it is to imagine allowing it to determine the path of nominal interest rates.[24] In practice, it is easiest for central

22. This does not mean that Wicksell's notion of a natural rate of interest determined by real factors is of no relevance to the consideration of the policy options facing a central bank. It is indeed, as argued in Chapter 4. But the natural rate of interest is the rate of interest required for *an equilibrium with stable prices;* the central bank nonetheless can arbitrarily choose the level of interest rates (within limits), because it can choose the degree to which prices will increase or decrease.

23. This is the grounds for his argument—in the quotation from the introduction to his book that begins this chapter—that control of the general level of prices involves no interference with the market mechanism of the kind that is required if some relative price is to be controlled.

24. This does not mean, of course, that absolutely any paths for these variables can be achieved through monetary policy; the chosen paths must be consistent with certain constraints

banks to exert relatively direct control over overnight nominal interest rates, and so they generally formulate their short-run objectives (their operating target) in terms of the effect that they seek to bring about in this variable rather than in one of the others.

Even recognizing the existence of a very large set of rational-expectations equilibria—equally consistent with optimizing private-sector behavior and with market clearing, in the absence of any specification of monetary policy —one might nonetheless suppose, as Fischer Black (1970) once did, that in a fully deregulated system the central bank should have no way of using monetary policy to select among these alternative equilibria. The path of money prices (and similarly nominal interest rates, nominal exchange rates, and so on) would then be determined solely by the self-fulfilling expectations of market participants. Why should the central bank play any special role in determining which of these outcomes should actually occur if it does not possess any monopoly power as the unique supplier of some crucial service?

The answer is that the unit of account in a purely fiat system is *defined* in terms of the liabilities of the central bank.[25] A financial contract that promises to deliver a certain number of U.S. dollars at a specified future date is promising payment in terms of Federal Reserve notes or clearing balances at the Fed (which are treated as freely convertible into one another by the Fed). Even in the technological utopia imagined by the enthusiasts of electronic money—where financial-market participants are willing to accept as final settlement transfers made over electronic networks in which the central bank is not involved—if debts are contracted in units of a national currency, then clearing balances at the central bank still define the thing to which these other claims are accepted as equivalent.

This explains why the nominal interest yield on clearing balances at the central bank can determine overnight rates in the market as a whole. The central bank can obviously define the nominal yield on overnight deposits in its clearing accounts as it chooses; it is simply promising to increase the nominal amount credited to a given account, after all. It can also determine

---

implied by the conditions for a rational-expectations equilibrium, e.g., those presented in Chapter 4. But this is true even in the case of the central bank's choice of a path for the price level. Even in a world with fully flexible wages and prices, for instance, it would not be possible to bring about a rate of deflation so fast as to imply a negative nominal interest rate.

25. See Hall (2002) and White (2001) for expressions of similar views. White emphasizes the role of legal-tender statutes in defining the meaning of a national currency unit. But such statutes do not represent a restriction upon the means of payment that can be used within a given geographical region—or at any rate, there need be no such restrictions upon private agreements for the point to be valid. What matters is simply what contracts written in terms of a particular unit of account are taken to mean, and the role of law in stabilizing such meanings is essentially no different than, say, in the case of trademarks.

this independently of its determination of the quantity of such balances that it supplies. Commercial banks may exchange claims to such deposits among themselves on whatever terms they like. But the market value of a dollar deposit in such an account cannot be anything other than a dollar—*because this defines the meaning of a "dollar"!*

This places the Fed in a different situation than any other issuer of dollar-denominated liabilities.[26] Citibank can determine the number of dollars that one of its jumbo CDs will be worth at maturity, but must then allow the market to determine the current dollar value of such a claim; it cannot determine *both* the quantity that it wishes to issue of such claims and the interest yield on them. Yet the Fed can, and does so daily—though at present it chooses to fix the interest yield on Fed balances at zero and only to vary the supply. The Fed's current position as monopoly supplier of an instrument that serves a special function is necessary in order for variations in the quantity supplied to affect the equilibrium spread between this interest rate and other market rates, but *not* in order to allow separate determination of the interest rate on central-bank balances and the quantity of them in existence.

Yes, some may respond, a central bank would still be able to determine the interest rate on overnight deposits at the central bank, and thus the interest rate in the interbank market for such claims, even in a world of completely frictionless financial markets. But would control of *this* interest rate necessarily have consequences for other market rates, the ones that matter for critical intertemporal decisions such as investment spending? The answer is that it must—and all the more so in a world in which financial markets have become highly efficient, so that arbitrage opportunities created by discrepancies among the yields on different market instruments are immediately eliminated. Equally riskless short-term claims issued by the private sector (say, shares in a money-market mutual fund holding very short-term Treasury bills) would not be able to promise a different interest rate than the one available on deposits at the central bank; otherwise, there would

---

26. Costa and De Grauwe (2001) instead argue that "in a cashless society . . . the central bank cannot 'force the banks to swallow' the reserves it creates" (p. 11), and speak of the central bank being forced to "liquidate . . . assets" in order the redeem the central-bank liabilities that commercial banks are "unwilling to hold" in their portfolios. This neglects the fact that the definition of the U.S. dollar allows the Fed to honor a commitment to pay a certain number of dollars to account holders the next day by simply crediting them with an account of that size at the Fed—there is no possibility of demanding payment in terms of some other asset valued more highly by the market. Similarly, Costa and De Grauwe argue that "the problem of the central bank in a cashless society is comparable to [that of a] central bank pegging a fixed exchange rate" (footnote 15). But the problem of a bank seeking to maintain an exchange-rate peg is that it promises to deliver a foreign currency in exchange for its liabilities, not liabilities of its own that it freely creates. Costa and De Grauwe say that they imagine a world in which "the unit of account remains a national affair . . . and is provided by the state" (p. 1), but seem not to realize that this means defining that unit of account in terms of central-bank liabilities.

be an excess supply or demand for the private-sector instruments. Moreover, determination of the overnight interest rate would also have to imply determination of the equilibrium overnight holding return on longer-lived securities, up to a correction for risk; and so determination of the expected future path of overnight interest rates would essentially determine longer-term interest rates.

The special feature of central banks, then, is simply that they are entities whose liabilities happen to be used to define the unit of account in a wide range of contracts that other people exchange with one another. There is perhaps no deep, universal reason why this need be so; it is certainly not essential that there be one such entity per national political unit. Nonetheless, the provision of a well-managed unit of account—one in terms of which the equilibrium prices of many goods and services are relatively stable—clearly facilitates economic life. Furthermore, given the evident convenience of having a single unit of account used by most of the parties with whom one wishes to trade, one may well suppose that this function should properly continue to be taken on by the government, even in a world of highly efficient information processing. I assume here a world in which central banks (whether national or supranational, as in the case of the ECB) continue to fulfill this function, and in which they are interested in managing their fiat currency in the public interest. The present study aims to supply a theory that can help them to do so.

4 Interest-Rate Rules

I have argued that the central problem of the theory of monetary policy is to provide principles that can be used in selecting a desirable rule for setting a central bank's interest-rate operating target. It is perhaps worth saying a bit more at this point about exactly what form of rules I have in mind and what sort of questions I would like to answer about them. This will provide a more concrete background for the analysis to be developed in the chapters to come.

Probably the earliest example of a prescription for monetary policy in terms of an interest-rate rule is due to Wicksell (1898, 1907). Although writing at a time when the leading industrial nations remained committed to the gold standard, with even most scholars assuming the necessity of a commodity standard of one sort or another, Wicksell foresaw the possibility of a pure fiat standard and indeed argued that it was essential for the development of "a rational monetary system." The soundness of his advocacy of price-level targeting in the context of a pure fiat monetary standard was shown during the 1930s, when Sweden abandoned the gold standard that had become an engine of worldwide deflation. The Swedish Riksbank adopted a price-level target as a substitute and used its interest-rate policy to achieve this target as recommended by Wicksell. The policy was quite successful, especially in comparison with the price-level fluctuations suffered by many other countries during this period (Jonung, 1979). Nonetheless, the experiment was radical for its time and was not to be repeated for another 50 years.[27]

Wicksell advocated not only price-level targeting, but a specific form of interest-rate rule for the management of such a system. His original (1898) statement of the proposed rule was as follows:

> So long as prices remain unaltered the [central] banks' rate of interest[28] is to remain unaltered. If prices rise, the rate of interest is to be raised; and if prices fall, the rate of interest is to be lowered; and the rate of interest is henceforth to be maintained at its new level until a further movement of prices calls for a further change in one direction or the other. (p. 189, italicized in original)

Wicksell's proposal can be represented mathematically as a commitment to set the central bank's interest-rate operating target i_t according to a relation of the form[29]

$$i_t = \bar{i} + \phi p_t, \tag{4.1}$$

where p_t is the log of some general price index (the one that the policy aims to stabilize) and ϕ is a positive response coefficient, or alternatively by a rule of the form

$$\Delta i_t = \phi \pi_t \tag{4.2}$$

where $\pi_t \equiv \Delta p_t$ is the inflation rate.[30] I discuss price-level determination under policy rules of this kind in Chapter 2 and argue that such a rule

27. For an example of favorable academic comment on the Swedish experiment at the time, see Fisher (1934, pp. 399–410).

28. In the passage quoted here, Wicksell proposes a coordinated policy by the world's central banks in order to establish a stable world unit of account. Elsewhere he offers similar advice for the stabilization of the value of a single national unit of account.

29. Wicksell proposes nothing so specific as a log-linear relation of this kind, of course; he only describes a monotonic relationship. The log-linear specification is useful for the simple calculations of the next section. In Chapter 2, I discuss the usefulness of this sort of log-linear approximation of what is necessarily not a globally log-linear rule. The specification (4.1) cannot be maintained for all possible price levels, owing to the requirement that the nominal interest rate be nonnegative.

30. Note that a commitment to set the interest rate according to (4.2) from some date t_0 forward is equivalent to a commitment to set it according to a rule of the form (4.1), where the intercept $\bar{i}$ corresponds to $i_{t_0-1} - \phi p_{t_0-1}$. Fuhrer and Moore (1995c) propose a more complicated interpretation of Wicksell's proposal, in which the interest change is instead a

should indeed succeed in stabilizing the price index around a constant level. The principles that determine the equilibrium price level under such a regime are briefly sketched in Section 4.3 of this introduction.

A simple Wicksellian rule such as this has certain advantages as well, at least in comparison to other equally simple rules, as discussed by Giannoni (2000). Nonetheless, I do not confine my attention to rules of this kind. My primary interest in this study is in the analysis of proposals that are closer in form to the policies currently followed by many central banks. These rules involve an (explicit or implicit) target for the *inflation rate*, rather than for the *price level;* nor are they expressible solely in terms of interest-rate *changes,* so that they are equivalent to a rule that responds to the price level, as in the case of (4.2). The rules typically allow for "base drift" in the price level as a result—even if the inflation rate is kept within a narrow interval at all times, there is no long-run mean reversion in the price level, or even in the price level deflated by some deterministic target path. Moreover, as I eventually conclude in Chapter 8, optimal interest-rate rules are likely to have this property.

4.1   Contemporary Proposals

The best-known example of a proposed rule for setting interest rates is prob-ably the one proposed by John Taylor (1993), both as a rough description of the way that policy had actually been made by the U.S. Federal Reserve under Alan Greenspan's chairmanship and as a normative prescription (on the basis of stochastic simulations using a number of econometric models). According to the Taylor rule, as it has come to be known, the Fed's funds-rate operating target i_t is set as a linear function of measures of the current inflation rate and the current gap between real output and potential:

$$i_t = 0.04 + 1.5(\bar{\pi}_t - 0.02) + 0.5\left(y_t - y_t^p\right), \tag{4.3}$$

where $\bar{\pi}_t$ is the rate of inflation (the change in the log GDP deflator over the previous four quarters in Taylor's illustration of the rule's empirical fit), y_t is log output (log real GDP in Taylor's plot), and y_t^p is log "potential" output (log real GDP minus a linear trend in Taylor's plot). The constants in Taylor's numerical specification indicate an implicit inflation target of 2 percent per annum, and an estimate of the long-run real federal funds rate of 2 percent per annum as well, so that a long-run average inflation rate at the target requires a long-run average funds rate of 4 percent. A slightly

---

function of the price *level.* While their rule is slightly more difficult to analyze, it does not lead to substantially different conclusions about the consequences of commitment to a Wicksellian rule.

simpler rule in the same vein was proposed for the United Kingdom by Charles Goodhart (1992), according to which "there should be a presumption" that the nominal interest rate would satisfy an equation of the form

$$i_t = 0.03 + 1.5\,\bar{\pi}_t,$$

and "the Governor should be asked, say twice a year, to account for any divergence from that 'rule' " (p. 324).

The coefficients 1.5 and 0.5 in the Taylor rule are round figures argued to approximately characterize U.S. policy between 1987 and 1992 and that were found to result in desirable outcomes (in terms of inflation and output stability) in simulations.[31] In Taylor's discussions of the rule, he places particular stress upon the importance of responding to inflation above the target rate by raising the nominal interest-rate operating target by *more than the amount* by which inflation exceeds the target; the importance of this "Taylor principle" is considered in detail in Chapters 2 and 4. Taylor (1999c) argues that the Fed did not adhere to this principle before 1979 (at which time Fed chairman Paul Volcker instituted a radical shift in policy), and this failure may well have been responsible for the greater U.S. macroeconomic instability during the 1960s and 1970s. Taylor illustrates the change in policy by estimating simple Fed reaction functions of the form

$$i_t = \bar{i} + \phi_\pi(\bar{\pi}_t - \bar{\pi}) + \phi_x x_t \tag{4.4}$$

for two different sample periods, using ordinary least squares; his coefficient estimates are shown in Table 1.1. (Here I introduce the notation x_t for the *output gap,* again equated with deviations of log real GDP from trend in Taylor's empirical work.) Nelson (2001) finds that estimates of Taylor-type rules for the United Kingdom tell a similar story. Prior to the adoption of inflation targeting in 1992, U.K. interest rates rose less than one-for-one with increases in inflation (and in the mid-1970s responded little or not at all), but since 1992, the long-run inflation response coefficient is estimated to have been nearly 1.3.

Estimates of empirical central-bank reaction functions typically find that a dynamic specification fits the data better, whatever the validity may be of Taylor's (1999b) preference for a purely contemporaneous specification on normative grounds.[32] For example, Judd and Rudebusch (1998) estimate

---

31. A similar form of policy rule was advocated, also on the basis of simulation studies, at around the same time by Henderson and McKibbin (1993).

32. This is also true of the estimates for the United Kingdom reported in Nelson (2001). This is why I refer to Nelson's "long-run inflation response coefficient" in the previous paragraph, rather than to a contemporaneous response coefficient of the kind estimated by Taylor (1999c).

TABLE 1.1   Alternative estimates of Fed reaction functions[a]

	ϕ_π	(s.e.)	ϕ_x	(s.e.)	γ	ρ_1	(s.e.)	ρ_2	(s.e.)
Taylor (1999c)									
1960–1979	0.81	(.06)	0.25	(.05)					
1987–1997	1.53	(.16)	0.77	(.09)					
Judd-Rudebusch (1998)									
1979–1987	1.46	(.26)	1.53	(.80)	1	0.56	(.12)		
1987–1997	1.54	(.18)	0.99	(.13)	0	0.72	(.05)	0.43	(.10)
Clarida et al. (2000)									
1960–1979	0.83	(.07)	0.27	(.08)		0.68	(.05)	*	
1979–1996	2.15	(.40)	0.93	(.42)		0.79	(.04)	*	
Orphanides (2003)									
1966–1979	1.49	(.38)	0.46	(.13)		0.68	(.07)	0.26	(.14)
1979–1995	1.89	(.64)	0.18	(.20)		0.77	(.10)	0.08	(.19)

[a] Asterisks indicate values not constrained to be zero in the estimation, but not reported in the published account of regression results.

Fed reaction functions according to which the funds-rate operating target adjusts in response to changes in an implicit desired level of the funds rate $\bar{\imath}_t$ according to partial-adjustment dynamics of the form[33]

$$i_t = (1 - \rho_1)\bar{\imath}_t + \rho_1 i_{t-1} + \rho_2(i_{t-1} - i_{t-2}). \tag{4.5}$$

The desired level of the funds rate in turn depends upon inflation and the output gap in a manner similar to that postulated by Taylor,

$$\bar{\imath}_t = \bar{\imath} + \phi_\pi(\bar{\pi}_t - \bar{\pi}) + \phi_x(x_t - \gamma x_{t-1}), \tag{4.6}$$

except that the allowance for nonzero γ means that the desired funds rate may respond to the rate of change of the output gap as well as (or instead of) its level. The Judd-Rudebusch estimated coefficients for two different sample periods, corresponding to the Fed chairmanships of Paul Volcker and Alan Greenspan, respectively, are also reported in Table 1.1.[34] Taylor's view of the nature of policy in the Greenspan period is largely confirmed, with the exception that Judd and Rudebusch estimate partial-adjustment

33. Here as in all other regressions reported in this section, periods are assumed to be quarters, and quarterly data are used in the estimation.
34. In their preferred estimates, the value of γ is imposed rather than estimated. The extreme values assumed for the separate periods, however, are suggested by preliminary regressions in which the value of γ is unconstrained.

dynamics implying substantial persistence. They give a similar characterization of policy in the Volcker period, except that the desired funds rate is
found to depend on the rate of change of the output gap, rather than its
level.[35]

Many recent discussions of central-bank behavior, both positive and normative, argue instead for specifications in which a bank's operating target
depends on forecasts. For example, Clarida et al. (2000) estimate Fed reaction functions of the form[36]

$$\bar{\imath}_t = \bar{\imath} + \phi_\pi E[\pi_{t+1} - \bar{\pi}|\Omega_t] + \phi_x E[x_t|\Omega_t], \tag{4.7}$$

where Ω_t is the information set assumed to be available to the Fed when setting i_t, and the actual operating target is again related to the desired funds
rate $\bar{\imath}_t$ through partial-adjustment dynamics. Like Taylor, these authors find
an important increase in the degree to which the Fed's desired level for
the funds rate responds to inflation variations since 1979, though in their
specification the Fed responds to an inflation *forecast* rather than inflation
that has already occurred.[37]

Finally, it should be noted that the view that the Fed has responded more
vigorously to inflation variations since 1979 has not gone unchallenged. Orphanides (2003) argues that the findings of Taylor and the other authors
just cited are distorted by the use of inflation and output-gap data (especially
the output-gap estimates), which were not available to the Fed at the time
that its interest-rate decisions were made. When he estimates Fed reaction
functions of the kind assumed by Clarida et al. using the forecasts actually
produced by Fed staff at the time rather than econometric projections using the data available now, he obtains much more similar estimates for the
pre-Volcker and post-Volcker periods, as shown in Table 1.1. The inflation-
response coefficient ϕ_π is well above one in both periods, according to Orphanides's estimates; he instead emphasizes the reduction in the size of ϕ_x
as the crucial policy change after 1979, and the key to U.S. macroeconomic

35. Judd and Rudebusch also estimate a reaction function for the period (1970–1978)
corresponding to the chairmanship of Arthur Burns. Like Taylor, in this period they estimate
an inflation-response coefficient ϕ_π less than one, though not significantly so in their case.

36. Clarida et al. also estimate variants of the rule in which the forecast horizon is assumed
to be more than one quarter in the future. The policies of inflation-targeting central banks
have often been represented by rules in which the interest-rate operating target responds to a
forecast of inflation as many as 8 quarters in the future. See, e.g., Black et al. (1997b), Batini
and Haldane (1999).

37. Like Taylor, they also suggest that this change has led to greater macroeconomic stability in the later period. They provide a theoretical analysis of why this could have been so,
in terms of the vulnerability of an economy to instability due to self-fulfilling expectations in
the case of a policy rule of the kind that they estimate for the period 1960–1979. Reasons for
this are discussed in Chapter 4.

stability since the mid-1980s. I do not seek to resolve this debate about historical Fed policy here, but simply note that much current debate about both the explanation of recent U.S. policy successes and the reason for past policy failures turns upon claims concerning the desirability of particular coefficients in Taylor-type rules.

These alternative characterizations suggest a number of questions about the form of a desirable interest-rate rule. One obvious question is whether the variables to which the Fed is described as responding in the Taylor rule and the estimated reaction functions just discussed—some measures of inflation and the output gap—are ones that make sense. Is it desirable for interest rates to be adjusted in response to variations in these variables, and with the signs proposed by Taylor? Are there any grounds for thinking it more important to respond to variations in these variables than in others? Is responding to variations in these variables an adequate substitute for attempting to respond to the underlying disturbances that are perceived to be currently affecting the economy?

If it does make sense to respond to these variables, how exactly should they be defined? Which sort of price index is most appropriately used in the inflation measure? Relative to what concept of potential output should the output gap measure be defined? And how strongly is it desirable to respond to variations in these variables? Is a value of ϕ_π greater than one essential, as argued by Taylor? Is a large value of ϕ_x dangerous, as argued by Orphanides?

I am also interested in the most desirable dynamic specification of such an interest-rate rule. Are purely contemporaneous responses, as prescribed by Taylor, preferable? Is there any justification for the more inertial interest-rate dynamics indicated by the estimated reaction functions? If so, how inertial is it desirable for interest-rate policy to be? Is it preferable to respond to forecasts rather than to current or past values of inflation and the output gap? If so, how far in the future should the forecasts look?

Another type of policy rule that has figured prominently both in recent descriptions of actual central-bank behavior and in normative prescriptions is an *inflation-forecast targeting* rule. A classic example is the sort of rule that is often used to explain the current procedures of the Bank of England (e.g., Vickers, 1998). According to the formula, the Bank should be willing to adopt a given operating target i_t for the overnight interest rate at date t if and only if the Bank's forecast of the evolution of inflation over the next 2 years, conditional upon the interest rate remaining at the level i_t, implies an inflation rate of 2.5 percent per annum (the Bank's current inflation target) 2 years after date t. This is an example of what Svensson (1999, 2003b) calls a "targeting rule" as opposed to an instrument rule. No formula is specified for the central bank's interest-rate operating target. Rather, it is to be set at whatever level may turn out to be required in order for the bank's projections to satisfy a certain target criterion. That criterion need not involve only future inflation; for example, Svensson (1999) advocates a flexible inflation-targeting rule in which the interest rate is adjusted at date t so as to ensure that

$$E_t \pi_{t+j} + \lambda E_t x_{t+k} = \bar{\pi}, \tag{4.8}$$

where $\bar{\pi}$ is the average inflation target, the coefficient $\lambda > 0$ depends on the relative importance of output-gap stabilization, and the horizons j and k are not necessarily the same distance in the future.

I also wish to consider the desirable specification of a target criterion in the case of a policy rule of this sort. Again, a basic question is whether it makes sense to define the target criterion in terms of projections for these particular variables, inflation and the output gap, rather than others, such as monetary aggregates. If so, what should determine the relative weight, if any, to be placed on the output-gap forecast? How far into the future should the forecasts in the target criterion look? And is a desirable criterion *purely* forward looking, as in the case of the two examples just mentioned, or should the inflation target be history dependent, in addition to (possibly) depending on projected future output gaps?

This study will seek to elaborate a methodology that can be used to give quantitative answers to questions of this sort about optimal policy rules. Of course, the answers obtained depend on the details of what one assumes about the nature of the monetary transmission mechanism, and I do not propose to argue for a specific quantitative rule. The aim of the present study is more to suggest a way of approaching the problem than to announce the details of its solution. However, certain model elements recur in many of the models currently used in studies of the effects of monetary policy, both in the academic literature and in central banks; and given the likelihood that a reasonable model is judged to include these features, I may obtain some tentative conclusions as to the likely form of reasonable policy rules.

4.2   General Criticisms of Interest-Rate Rules

Before taking up specific questions of these kinds about the form of de- sirable interest-rate rules, it is first necessary to address some more basic issues. Would *any* form of interest-rate rule represent a sensible approach to monetary policy? Proponents of monetary targeting have often argued against interest-rate control *as such*—asserting not that skill is required in the choice of an interest-rate operating target, but that it is a serious mistake to have one at all.

One famous argument, mentioned previously, is that of Sargent and Wal- lace (1975). These authors consider a general class of money-supply rules on the one hand, and a general class of interest-rate rules on the other, and argue that while *any* of the money-supply rules leads to a determinate rational-expectations equilibrium (in the context of a particular rational-expectations IS-LM model), *none* of the interest-rate rules do. By *determinacy* of the equilibrium I mean that there is a unique equilibrium satisfying certain bounds, made precise in Chapter 2. Sargent and Wallace argue that interest-rate rules lead to *indeterminacy*, meaning that even if one restricts one's attention to bounded solutions to the equilibrium relations (as I largely do in this study), there is an extremely large set of equally possible equilibria. These include equilibria in which endogenous variables such as inflation and output respond to random events that are completely unrelated to economic "fundamentals" (i.e., to the exogenous disturbances that affect the structural relations that determine inflation and output) and also equilibria in which "fundamental" disturbances cause fluctuations in equilibrium inflation and output that are arbitrarily large relative to the degree to which the structural relations are perturbed. Thus in such a case, macroeconomic instability can occur owing purely to self-fulfilling expectations. This is plainly undesirable, if one's objective is to stabilize inflation and/or output.[38] Hence Sargent and Wallace argue that interest-rate rules can be excluded from consideration as a class; the problem of optimal monetary policy is then properly framed as a question of what the best money-supply rule would be.

However, as McCallum (1981) notes, the Sargent-Wallace indeterminacy result applies, even in the context of their own model, only in the case of interest-rate rules that specify an *exogenous* evolution for the nominal interest rate. This includes the possibility of rules that specify the nominal interest rate as a function of the history of exogenous disturbances, but not rules that make the nominal interest rate a function of *endogenous* variables, such as inflation or output. Yet the Taylor rule, and the other interest-rate rules discussed previously, are all rules of the latter sort, so that the Sargent-Wallace result need not apply. The same is shown to be true, in Chapters 2 and 4, in the case of the optimizing models of inflation and output determination considered here. Indeed, I find that, at least in the case of the simple model of the monetary transmission mechanism that is most extensively analyzed here, *either* the type of feedback from the general price level to the interest rate (or from changes in the price level to changes in the interest rate) advocated by Wicksell *or* the type of feedback from inflation and output to the central bank's interest-rate operating target prescribed by Taylor would suffice to imply a determinate rational-expectations equilibrium. In

---

38. The point remains valid if one's objective is, as I argue that it should be, to stabilize output relative to its natural rate, rather than output stabilization as such. For the fluctuations in output owing purely to self-fulfilling expectations will imply fluctuations in the output gap as well.

the case of a level-to-level (or change-to-change) Wicksellian specification, it is only necessary that the sign of the response be the one advocated by Wicksell. In the case of a change-to-level specification such as that proposed by Taylor, the Taylor principle mentioned earlier—the requirement that a sustained increase in inflation eventually result in an increase in nominal interest rates that is even larger in percentage points—turns out to be the critical condition that determines whether equilibrium should be determinate or not.[39]

A related criticism of interest-rate targeting also maintains that such a policy is dangerous because it allows instability to be generated by self-fulfilling expectations, but is not based on the possibility of multiple rational-expectations equilibria. Friedman (1968) argues that attempting to control nominal interest rates is dangerous on the basis of Wicksell's (1898, 1907) famous analysis of the "cumulative process." With a nominal interest rate that is fixed at a level below the natural rate, inflation is generated that increases inflation expectations, which then stimulates demand even further owing to the reduction in the real rate, generating even faster inflation, further increasing inflation expectations, and so on without bound.[40] The same process should occur with the opposite sign if the interest rate happens to be set above the natural rate; thus any attempt to fix the nominal interest rate would seem almost inevitably to generate severe instability of the inflation rate. (In Friedman's analysis, there is no indeterminacy of the path of inflation, as inflation expectations are assumed to be a specific function of previously observed inflation.)

As is discussed in Chapter 4, this analysis can be formalized in the context of an optimizing model in which inflation and income forecasts are based on extrapolation from past data (e.g., using empirical time-series models). But once again, the classic analysis applies only in the case of a policy that exogenously specifies the path of nominal interest rates. If instead a surge in inflation and output leads to increases in nominal interest rates large enough to raise real rates, then demand should be damped, tending to lower inflation as well—so that there should be no explosive instability of either inflation or output dynamics under adaptive learning. Indeed, the analyses of Bullard and Mitra (2002) and Preston (2002a) find that conformity

39. Clarida et al. (2000) argue on this basis that the macroeconomic instability of the 1970s in the United States may have been increased by self-fulfilling expectations, given that their estimates (see Table 1.1) imply that the Taylor principle has been satisfied by post-1979 policy but not by previous policy.

40. This summarizes Friedman's account, rather than Wicksell's original discussion. Wicksell does not discuss endogenous inflation expectations and so concludes that the price level rather than the inflation rate should rise without bound. Lindahl (1939) was the first to introduce endogenous inflation expectations into the analysis and so to conclude that the inflation rate could rise without bound.

to the Taylor principle is both a necessary and sufficient condition (at least within certain simple classes of policy rules) for adaptive learning dynamics to converge to a stationary rational-expectations equilibrium, in which inflation and output fluctuate only in response to "fundamentals."

Thus it is important to realize that these well-known criticisms of interest-rate targeting assume that under such a policy the interest-rate target would remain *fixed,* regardless of the path of inflation. The analyses are quite inapplicable in the case of policy rules such as Wicksell's rule, the Taylor rule, or typical inflation-forecast targeting rules, which require that interest rates be raised sharply if inflation is either observed or forecasted to exceed the target rate consistently for a substantial period of time. In fact, in these conventional arguments for monetary targeting, the reason for control of money growth is precisely that this is a policy commitment that ensures that an excessive rate of inflation will lead to interest-rate increases sufficient to curb the growth of nominal expenditure. A fixed target path for the money supply (or more generally, a path that is contingent only upon exogenous state variables, not upon the path of the price level) implies that if the price level grows more rapidly, the private sector will be forced to operate with a lower level of real money balances. This will require interest-rate increases and/or a reduction in real activity sufficient to reduce desired real money balances to the level of the real money supply.

But the same kind of automatic increase in interest rates, curbing expenditure, can be arranged through a simple commitment of the central bank to raise interest rates in response to deviations of the general level of prices from its desired path, as first proposed by Wicksell. Moreover, once one recognizes that quantity control is not necessary for such a system to work, it is hard to see why one should wish to be encumbered by it. Over the course of the twentieth century, it came to be accepted that no convertibility of national currencies into a real commodity such as gold was necessary in order for central banks to act in a way that controlled the value of their currencies. Moreover, once this was accepted, it quickly became evident that nations were better off *not* relying upon such a crude mechanism as a gold standard, which left the value of the national unit of account vulnerable to fluctuations in the market for gold. Similarly, once one accepts that the adjustment of interest rates to head off undesired price-level variation can be managed by central banks without any need for so mechanical a discipline as is provided by a money-growth target, it should be clear that a properly chosen interest-rate rule can be more efficient than monetary targeting, which has the unwanted side effect of making interest rates (and hence the pace of aggregate expenditure) vulnerable to variations in the relation between desired money balances and the volume of transactions.

A more subtle criticism of interest-rate rules as an approach to systematic monetary policy would argue that even if such rules lead to well-defined, well-behaved equilibria, the description of policy in this way may still not be useful to a central bank that wishes to understand, and thus to accurately calibrate, the consequences of its actions. It is often supposed that the key to understanding the effects of monetary policy on inflation must always be the quantity theory of money, according to which the price level is determined by the relation between the nominal money supply, on the one hand, and the demand for real money balances, on the other. It may then be concluded that what matters about *any* monetary policy is the implied path of the money supply, whether this is determined through straightforward monetary targeting or in some more indirect manner.[41] From such a perspective, it might seem that a clearer understanding of the consequences of a central bank's actions would be facilitated by an explicit focus on what evolution of the money supply the bank intends to bring about—that is, by monetary targeting—rather than by talk about interest-rate policy that, even if it does imply a specific path for the money supply, does not make the intended path entirely transparent.

   The present study aims to show that the basic premise of such a criticism is incorrect. One of the primary goals of Part I of this book is the development of a theoretical framework in which the consequences of alternative interest-rate rules can be analyzed, which does not require that they first be translated into equivalent rules for the evolution of the money supply. Indeed, much of the time I analyze the consequences of interest-rate rules without having to solve for the implied path of the money supply, or even having to specify the coefficients of a "money-demand" relation. In the case of an economy without monetary frictions—a case that I argue is an analytically convenient approximation for many purposes, and that may well represent the future, as discussed earlier—there will not even be any meaningful money supply or demand to be defined. If instead one takes account of the sort of frictions that evidently still exist in an economy like that of the United States at present, then the models imply an equilibrium path for the money supply along with other endogenous variables. But the factors determining the equilibrium paths of both inflation and output continue to be nearly the same as in the frictionless economy, so that it does not seem at all natural or useful to try to *explain* the predicted paths of inflation and output as *consequences* of the implied path of the money supply. Instead, it proves to be possible to discuss the determinants of inflation and output in a fairly straightforward way in terms of the coefficients of an interest-rate rule. Thus the characterizations of central-bank policy offered previously are found to be quite convenient for analysis of the consequences of one quantitative specification or another. I further show, in Chapter 8, that optimal policy

---

41. This is, e.g., the perspective taken in the *Monetary History* of Friedman and Schwartz (1963).

can be conveniently represented in terms of specifications of exactly this sort, leading to answers to the very specific questions about interest-rate policy posed in the previous section.

4.3   Neo-Wicksellian Monetary Theory

The non-quantity-theoretic analytical framework developed here develops several important themes from the monetary writings of Knut Wicksell (1898, 1906, 1907, 1915). Wicksell argued that even the variations in the price level observed in his own time, under the international gold standard, were not primarily due to variations in the world gold supply, but rather to two other factors—the policies followed by central banks, adjusting the "bank rate" at which they were willing to discount short-term bills, on the one hand, and real disturbances, affecting the natural rate of interest, on the other. In Wicksell's view, price stability depended on keeping the interest rate controlled by the central bank in line with the natural rate determined by real factors (such as the marginal product of capital). Inflation occurred whenever the central banks lowered interest rates without any decline in the natural rate having occurred to justify it or whenever the natural rate of interest increased (due, e.g., to an increase in the productivity of investment opportunities) without any adjustment of the interest rates controlled by central banks in response. Deflation occurred whenever a disparity was created of the opposite sign.

Whatever the validity of such a non-quantity-theoretic approach for the analysis of price-level determination under the gold standard, Wicksell's approach is a particularly congenial one for thinking about our present circumstances—a world of purely fiat currencies in which central banks adjust their operating targets for nominal interest rates in response to perceived risks of inflation, but pay little if any attention to the evolution of monetary aggregates—to say nothing of the one toward which we may be headed, in which monetary frictions become negligible.[42] In such a world, where the concepts of money supply and demand become inapplicable, what is there to determine an equilibrium value for the general level of money prices? One possible answer is the role of *past* prices in determining

---

42. As noted earlier, Wicksell's basic exposition of his theory is for the case of a "pure credit economy." On the non-quantity-theoretic character of Wicksell's explanation of price-level determination, see in particular Haavelmo (1978), Leijonhufvud (1981), and Niehans (1990). Others have insisted on the compatibility of Wicksell's analysis with a quantity-theoretic framework; see, e.g., Humphrey (2002). I do not deny the *consistency* of a neo-Wicksellian account of a price-level determination under an interest-rate rule with a standard quantity-theoretic model; see, e.g., Section 3 of Chapter 4. But I show that the existence of a well-defined demand for money is not *essential* to the logic of such an account, which is consequently equally applicable to a world in which money-demand relations are undefined or unstable.

current equilibrium prices, due either to wage or price stickiness or to the effect of past prices on expectations regarding future prices (the critical factor in Wicksell's own analysis). Thus once prices have been at a certain level (for whatever arbitrary reason), this historical initial condition ties down their subsequent evolution, though they may subsequently drift arbitrarily far from that level. But probably the most important factor, in general, is *the interest-rate policy of the central bank,* insofar as this responds to the evolution of some price index. A state of affairs in which all wages and prices were 10 percent higher than they presently are would not be equally possible as an equilibrium, if the observation of such a jump in the price level would trigger an increase in interest rates, as called for under either a Wicksellian rule or the Taylor rule.

The way in which the equilibrium price level can be determined by the central bank's interest-rate response to price-level variations, without any reference to the associated fluctuations in any monetary aggregate, can be illustrated very simply. Suppose that the equilibrium real rate of interest is determined by real factors (such as time preference and the productivity of capital), in complete independence of how nominal quantities may evolve,[43] and let $\{r_t\}$ be an exogenous stochastic process for this real rate. It then follows that the short-term nominal interest rate i_t and the log price level p_t must at all times satisfy the Fisherian relation

$$p_t = E_t p_{t+1} + r_t - i_t, \tag{4.9}$$

assuming rational expectations on the part of the private sector. Because r_t is a certain function of exogenous real factors, rather than the measured real rate of return, this is an *equilibrium* relation—the condition required for equality between aggregate saving and investment—rather than an identity. This "flexible-price IS equation" indicates how the price level that clears the goods market—or equivalently, that equates saving and investment—depends on the expected future price level, real factors affecting saving and investment, and the nominal interest rate controlled by the central bank.

Now suppose that the central bank sets the short-term nominal interest rate according to the Wicksellian rule

$$i_t = \bar{\imath}_t + \phi p_t, \tag{4.10}$$

which generalizes (4.1) in allowing for a time-varying intercept, indicating possible shifts over time in monetary policy. Suppose further that $\{\bar{\imath}_t\}$ is another exogenous stochastic process (i.e., determined independently of the

---

43. In Chapter 2, I present assumptions under which this is true in an explicit intertemporal equilibrium model with flexible prices.

evolution of prices), which may or may not be correlated with the exogenous fluctuations in the equilibrium real rate of interest. Then substituting (4.10) into (4.9) to eliminate i_t, one obtains a relation of the form

$$p_t = \alpha E_t p_{t+1} + \alpha (r_t - \bar{i}_t) \qquad (4.11)$$

to determine the equilibrium evolution of the price level, given the exogenous processes $\{r_t, \bar{i}_t\}$, where $\alpha \equiv 1/(1 + \phi)$ is a coefficient satisfying $0 < \alpha < 1$.

In the case that $\{r_t, \bar{i}_t\}$ are bounded processes, equation (4.11) has a unique bounded solution, obtained by "solving forward," namely,

$$p_t = \sum_{j=0}^{\infty} \alpha^{j+1} E_t \left(r_{t+j} - \bar{i}_{t+j} \right). \qquad (4.12)$$

Thus the equilibrium price level fluctuates in a bounded interval around the long-run average value

$$\bar{p} \equiv \phi^{-1} (\bar{r} - \bar{i}),$$

where $\bar{r}, \bar{i}$ are the long-run average values of r_t and $\bar{i}_t$, respectively. This analysis shows how a policy rule that involves no targets for any monetary aggregate can nonetheless control the long-run price level. It also shows how the determinants of equilibrium inflation can be understood without any reference to the determinants of either the money supply or money demand—indeed, it does not matter for the analysis just presented whether there is any well-defined demand function for the monetary base.

The account of price-level determination implied by this theory has a strongly Wicksellian flavor. One observes from (4.12) that the equilibrium price level at any date t is increased by either a loosening of monetary policy—represented by a reduction of the intercept term $\bar{i}_t$—not justified by any decline in the equilibrium real rate or by an increase in the equilibrium real rate r_t that is not matched by a tightening of policy. The proposed forward-looking model also implies that any news that allows the private sector to forecast the future occurrence of either of these things should stimulate inflation immediately.

In the simple model sketched here, there is no distinction of the sort that Wicksell makes between the actual real rate of return and the natural rate that would occur in an intertemporal equilibrium with flexible prices. In Chapter 4, however, I show how one can usefully introduce such a distinction, in the context of a model with sticky prices. When prices are temporarily sticky, the real rate of return at which borrowing and lending occurs can differ from the natural rate of interest, just as the level of output can differ from its natural rate; and the degree to which both occur depends on the degree of instability of the overall price level, as it is only when the general level of prices is changing that price rigidity creates distortions. Equilibrium condition (4.9) must then be replaced by a more general one, of the form

$$i_t - E_t \pi_{t+1} = r_t^n + \delta(\pi_t, \ldots), \tag{4.13}$$

where r_t^n is the natural rate of interest (still assumed to depend only on exogenous real factors) and the discrepancy $\delta(\cdot)$ is a function of both current and expected future inflation.[44] The system consisting of conditions (4.10) and (4.13) can again be solved for a unique bounded process for the price level, and the solution is of the form

$$p_t = \sum_{j=0}^{\infty} \psi_j E_t \left(r_{t+j}^n - \bar{\imath}_{t+j} \right)$$

for certain coefficients $\{\psi_j\}$. Thus in the more general case, it is variation in the *natural rate* of interest due to real disturbances of various sorts, to the extent that such variation is not matched by corresponding adjustment of the central bank's reaction function, that causes inflation variation. Just as in Wicksell's theory, real disturbances affecting desired saving and investment are predicted to be important sources of price-level variations; and as in that theory, the implied variation in the natural rate of interest is a useful summary statistic for the way in which a variety of real disturbances should affect the rate of inflation.

In Chapters 2 and 4, I show how a similar analysis of equilibrium inflation determination is possible in the case of a rule like the Taylor rule. In this case a positive response of the interest rate to fluctuations in the inflation rate is not sufficient to guarantee a determinate equilibrium (a unique nonexplosive equilibrium path for the inflation rate, rather than the price level). It is instead necessary that the response coefficient be greater than one, in accordance with the Taylor principle mentioned earlier. But in that case similar results are obtained; equilibrium inflation is a function of current and expected future gaps between the natural rate of interest and the intercept term in the Taylor rule.

One finds, then, that it is possible to determine the consequences for inflation dynamics of a given monetary policy rule when it is expressed in terms of an interest-rate rule, without any need to first translate the rule into an implied state-contingent path for the money supply. Hence the

---

44. In the case of the basic neo-Wicksellian model developed in Chapter 4, δ is a function of π_t, $E_t \pi_{t+1}$, and $E_t \pi_{t+2}$.

terms used to describe both actual central-bank policies and simple policy prescriptions in the literature summarized previously are not inappropriate ones. The consequences of systematic policies of these types can conveniently be analyzed as functions of exactly the coefficients appearing in Table 1.1.

While the usefulness of the neo-Wicksellian framework sketched here is perhaps most evident in the case of an economy without monetary frictions, so that the familiar quantity-theoretic apparatus is plainly inapplicable, it is also equally useful in the case of an economy in which monetary frictions still exist, at least of the modest sort that are indicated by the observed willingness to hold non-interest-earning currency in an advanced economy like that of the United States today. In what I have written previously, I have not actually relied upon any assumed absence of monetary frictions, except in assuming that the equilibrium real rate of interest (or more generally, the natural rate of interest) is independent of the evolution of nominal variables. But even in the presence of transactions frictions resulting in a demand for base money despite its below-market rate of return, it is unlikely that the natural rate of interest is much affected, as a quantitative matter, by variations in the rate of inflation. (The accuracy of the approximation involved in neglecting such effects is considered numerically in Chapters 2 and 4.) Hence the approach proposed here is also appropriate for analysis of the effects of a Taylor rule in an economy like that of the United States, where changes in the Fed's interest-rate operating target are implemented through adjustments in the supply of (non-interest-earning) Fed balances. The monetary frictions that create a demand for such balances are important for the size of quantity adjustment required to achieve a given change in the funds rate, but are of little significance for the effects upon output and inflation of any given change in the path of the funds rate.

Nor are the predictions of the neo-Wicksellian theory really any different from those of a standard quantity-theoretic analysis, despite the apparent dissimilarity of approach. In a quantity-theoretic analysis of inflation determination, central importance is given to the money-demand relation that describes desired real money balances as a function of interest rates and other variables. However, in the case of an interest-rate rule like any of those described earlier, the money supply varies passively so as to satisfy this relation; hence the relation places no restrictions upon the equilibrium evolution of interest rates and goods prices. Thus in such a system, the equilibrium paths of interest and prices are determined by solving equations (4.9) and (4.10), or equations (4.10) and (4.13) in the case of sticky prices, just as previously. Once one knows the equilibrium paths of interest and prices, the money-demand relation can then be used to determine the implied evolution of the money supply as well. But this last relation does not play an important role in determining equilibrium inflation under such an analysis. Moreover, insisting upon first solving for the state-contingent path of the money supply implied by the policy rule and then deriving the equilibrium path of inflation from this along quantity-theoretic lines would be an unnecessarily roundabout procedure, given that one must first solve for the path of prices and interest rates in order to determine the path of the money supply.

The neo-Wicksellian approach is thus clearly preferable, even granting the existence of a well-defined, econometrically stable money-demand relation, if one wishes to analyze the consequences of interest-rate rules such as the Taylor rule. But, it might be asked, is it clear that *desirable* policy rules should belong to this class, regardless of the current popularity of such prescriptions? Might not a money-growth rule be preferable, in which case a more traditional quantity-theoretic approach would also be necessary in order to explain its effects?

The results of this study suggest that the answer is no. As is shown in Chapter 8, it is possible to derive optimal policy rules that indicate how a short-term nominal interest-rate operating target should be set, as a function of the projected evolution of inflation and the output gap, without any reference to the paths of monetary aggregates. It is further argued that this form of prescription has the advantage, relative to other possible characterizations of optimal policy, of being invariant under a larger class of possible exogenous disturbances. For example, in the case of an economy with a well-defined demand for base money, it is possible to compute both the state-contingent evolution of overnight interest rates and the state-contingent evolution of the monetary base in an optimal equilibrium. However, the desired evolution of the monetary base, even when well defined, depends upon factors that are of little or no relevance to the desired evolution of interest rates, and this makes it simpler to characterize optimal policy in terms of an interest-rate operating target.

One such factor is the dependence of the optimal path of the monetary base on changes in the transactions technology—for example, available opportunities for substitution among alternative means of payment. Such changes may have significant effects on money demand in the presence of a given interest differential between base money and other riskless assets, but have little effect on the relations between interest rates and the incentives for intertemporal substitution of expenditure that determine the desired evolution of interest rates. (In an economy where the financial system is already highly efficient, one expects further innovations to represent movements from one highly efficient system to another, so that the relations between interest rates and the real allocation of resources remain near those predicted by a model with no financial frictions; but money demand may be greatly affected in percentage terms, as it ceases to be defined in the frictionless limit.) Another factor is the dependence of the optimal evolution of the monetary base on the details of monetary policy implementation.

The desired path of money-market interest rates is largely independent of the rate of interest paid on the monetary base. This depends instead on the intertemporal marginal rates of substitution, the marginal products of real investment implied by the desired allocation of resources, and the desired path for inflation. But the desired path of the monetary base depends greatly on whether it is assumed for institutional reasons that zero interest is paid on base money or whether instead the interest paid on money varies when other short-term interest rates vary; for the demand for base money depends not on the absolute level of nominal interest rates, but on the *spread* between the interest rate paid on base money and that available on other assets.

Thus even when the desired evolution of the monetary base is well defined, it is more dependent on special "technical" factors than is the desired evolution of short-term nominal interest rates. This makes a description of optimal monetary policy in terms of a state-contingent money growth rate less convenient. Moreover, if, as some forecast, monetary frictions are largely eliminated in the coming century owing to the development of electronic payments media, a description of optimal policy in terms of the desired evolution of a monetary aggregate is likely to become awkward if not altogether impossible. Yet a description of optimal policy in terms of the principles that should regulate the adjustment of an interest-rate operating target should still be possible. Indeed, increasing efficiency of the financial system should only simplify the description of optimal policy in these terms, insofar as the arbitrage relations that connect the overnight interest rate directly targeted by the central bank to other interest rates and asset prices become simpler and more reliable. Hence the neo-Wicksellian framework proposed here directs attention to precisely those elements of the monetary transmission mechanism that are likely to remain of fundamental importance for the design of effective monetary policies in a world of increasingly efficient financial markets and institutions.

5 Plan of the Book

Part I develops a theoretical framework that can be used to analyze the consequences of alternative monetary policy rules in a way that takes full account of the implications of forward-looking private sector behavior. Chapter 2 begins by considering price-level determination when monetary policy is specified by an interest-rate rule in the case of a model where, for simplicity, prices are completely flexible and the supply of goods is given by an exogenous endowment. This chapter demonstrates the possibility of a coherent theory of price-level determination even in the complete absence of monetary frictions—a special case that is considered repeatedly in what follows, in order to direct attention more closely to the economic relations that are considered to be of more fundamental importance for the characterization of optimal policy. But it also considers price-level determination under an interest-rate rule in a standard optimization-based monetarist framework, allowing a comparison between the consequences of monetary targeting and those of commitment to an interest-rate rule, and an analysis of the extent to which the presence of monetary frictions changes one's conclusions about the effects of such a rule.

Chapter 3 then introduces endogenous goods supply and nominal price and wage rigidities, so that monetary policy can affect the level of real activity as well as the inflation rate. Considerable attention is given to the microeconomic foundations of the aggregate-supply relations that result from delays in the adjustment of prices or wages, in order to select specifications (from among those that might appear similarly consistent with econometric evidence) with clear behavioral interpretations that thereby allow one to take account of the "Lucas critique." At the same time, attention is also paid to the need to find a specification of the dynamic relations between real activity and inflation that is consistent with econometric evidence regarding the effects of identified monetary disturbances. A series of modifications of a basic sticky-price model are introduced that can improve the model's fit with estimated responses on various dimensions.

Chapter 4 then integrates the analysis in Chapters 2 and 3, considering the effects of interest-rate rules in a framework where monetary policy can affect real activity and where feedback from measures of real activity to the central bank's interest-rate operating target matter for the predicted effects of such rules. In the neo-Wicksellian framework developed here, inflation dynamics results from the interaction between real disturbances on the one hand and the central bank's interest-rate rule on the other. Wicksell's natural rate of interest is shown to play a central role, summarizing the effects of a variety of real disturbances that are relevant for inflation and output-gap determination in the case of a class of policy rules that may be thought of as generalized Taylor rules. The chapter also includes a first analysis of the consequences of such a framework for the design of desirable policy rules by considering the conditions under which a Taylor-like rule should be able to stabilize inflation and the output gap.

Chapter 5 discusses further elaborations of the basic neo-Wicksellian model, mainly with regard to aggregate-demand determination, that allow the model to better match econometric evidence regarding the effects of monetary policy. Various reasons are discussed for delayed effects of interest-rate changes on aggregate demand to differ from the immediate effect, and then some simple examples are presented of small optimizing models of the U.S. monetary transmission mechanism that have been fit to U.S. time series. This discussion of empirical models is intended to motivate the kinds of model specifications that are considered in the remainder of this study.

Part II then considers the optimal conduct of monetary policy in the light of the theoretical framework introduced in the earlier chapters. Chapter 6 begins by considering appropriate stabilization goals for monetary policy. An advantage of the derivation of the proposed model's structural relations from explicit microeconomic foundations in Part I is that it is possible to ask what sort of monetary policy would best serve economic welfare, given the objectives and constraints of the agents whose decisions account for the observed effects of monetary policy. Chapter 6 considers the connection between the obvious measure of economic welfare in such a model—the expected utility of the representative household—and the stabilization of macroeconomic aggregates such as inflation and the output gap.

It is shown that a quadratic approximation to expected utility, which suffices (under certain conditions) for the derivation of a linear approximation to an optimal policy rule, can be expressed in terms of the expected value of squared deviations of certain aggregate variables from target values for those variables. The variables that are relevant and the details of the quadratic loss function that can be justified on welfare-theoretic grounds depend on the microeconomic foundations of one's model of the monetary transmission mechanism. In particular, it is shown that different assumptions regarding price and/or wage stickiness imply that price and/or wage inflation should enter the central bank's loss function in different ways. Nonetheless, it is argued that price stability, suitably interpreted—for example, quite possibly in terms of an index that includes wages as well as the prices of final goods and services—should be an important consideration, though not necessarily the only one, in the selection of a monetary policy rule. Grounds for inclusion of output-gap stabilization and interest-rate stabilization objectives in the loss function as well are considered; but it is argued that in practice, these additional concerns are not likely to justify either an average rate of inflation much greater than zero or substantial variability in the rate of inflation in response to shocks.

Chapter 7 then considers the optimal state-contingent evolution of inflation, output, and interest rates in response to real disturbances of various sorts, from the point of view of the sort of loss function argued for in Chapter 6 and in the context of a forward-looking model of the monetary transmission mechanism of the kind developed in Part I. An important general issue treated in this chapter is the way in which optimal control techniques must be adapted in the case of control of a forward-looking system. The responses to shocks under an optimal commitment are distinguished from the equilibrium responses under discretionary optimization by the central bank. Particular attention is given to the fact that in general, optimal responses will be *history dependent* in a way that is inconsistent with any purely forward-looking decision procedure for monetary policy. Alternative approaches to introducing the desired sort of history dependence into the conduct of policy are surveyed. The one that is emphasized in this study is the possibility of commitment to a *policy rule* that is history dependent in the desired way. Commitment to a *targeting rule*, such as a flexible inflation target, is shown to be an especially desirable way of formulating such a policy commitment.

Finally, Chapter 8 considers the problem of choice of a policy rule to implement the desired state-contingent evolution of inflation, output, and interest rates, as derived in Chapter 7. From the standpoint taken here, this problem of *implementation* of the desired equilibrium is a nontrivial part of the characterization of optimal policy. The mapping from the history of exogenous disturbances to the desired overnight interest rate at any point in time is not a suitable description of an optimal policy rule, for reasons taken up in this chapter. Instead, it is argued that a more suitable policy prescription should relate the instrument setting to the evolution (observed or projected) of endogenous variables such as inflation and the output gap, as in the proposals mentioned earlier. A general method is described for constructing optimal policy rules of this form in the case of a fairly general class of log-linear structural models and quadratic loss functions. The method is then applied to several of the simple optimizing models of the monetary transmission mechanism developed in previous chapters.

It is shown that optimal rules can easily take the form of generalized Taylor rules or of target criteria for a forecast-targeting procedure like that used at the Bank of England. However, even in the case of fairly simple models of the transmission mechanism, the optimal rules are somewhat different from the proposals described earlier. While there is a fairly clear logic for rules that respond to (and perhaps only to) variations in inflation and in the output gap, the theoretically appropriate measures of inflation and of the output gap may not be the ones used in the characterizations above of current central-bank behavior. Moreover, the optimal rules that I obtain are also typically different in their dynamic specifications. Optimal rules are history dependent in ways other than those of the classic Taylor rule or familiar descriptions of inflation-forecast targeting; and while they may well be more forward looking than the classic Taylor rule, in all of the calibrated examples they are considerably less forward looking than the procedures currently used at the inflation-targeting central banks.

Conclusions about the precise content of an optimal policy rule depend, of course, on the details of one's model of the transmission mechanism, and I do not attempt here to reach final conclusions in that regard. The answer is likely to be somewhat different for different countries in any event. My more important goal is to provide a method that individual central banks can use in order to choose sensible systematic policies on the basis of their own research on the nature of the transmission mechanism in their respective economies. It is hoped that the present volume can provide useful guidelines for such an inquiry.

PART I

Analytical Framework

CHAPTER 2

Price-Level Determination under Interest-Rate Rules

While virtually all central banks use a short-term nominal interest rate (typically an overnight rate, such as the federal funds rate in the United States) as their instrument, and an extensive empirical literature characterizes actual monetary policy in terms of estimated central-bank "reaction functions" for setting such interest rates, the theoretical literature in monetary economics has concerned itself almost entirely with the analysis of policies that are described by alternative (possibly state-contingent) paths for the money supply. The aim of this chapter is to remedy this oversight by presenting a theory of price-level determination under interest-rate rules of the sort that are often taken to describe actual central-bank policies.

I argue that it is not necessary, in order to understand the consequences of such rules, to first determine their consequences for the evolution of the money supply and then analyze the equivalent money-supply rule. Rather, it is possible to analyze price-level determination under such rules in terms of an explanatory framework that assigns no importance to either the evolution of the money supply or the determinants of money demand. In this neo-Wicksellian framework, the fundamental determinants of the equilibrium price level are instead the real factors that determine the equilibrium real rate of interest, on the one hand, and the systematic relation between interest rates and prices established by the central bank's policy rule, on the other.

I first expound this approach in the context of a purely cashless economy—one in which there are assumed to be no transactions frictions that can be reduced through the use of money balances, and that accordingly provide a reason for holding such balances even when they earn a rate of return that is dominated by that available on other assets. Such a setting—one that is commonly assumed in financial economics and in purely real models of economic fluctuations alike—allows one to display the relations that are of central importance in the neo-Wicksellian theory in their simplest form.

At the same time, neither the usefulness nor the validity of the approach proposed here depends on a claim that monetary frictions do not exist in actual present-day economies. After expounding the theory for the cashless case, I show how the framework can easily be generalized to allow for monetary frictions, modeled in one or another of the ways that are common in monetarist models of inflation determination (by including real balances in the utility function or assuming a cash-in-advance constraint). I show in this case that equilibrium relations continue to be obtained that are direct generalizations of those for the cashless economy and that need not even imply results that are too different as a quantitative matter, if the monetary frictions are parameterized in an empirically plausible way. Hence the cashless analysis can be viewed as a useful approximation even in the case of an economy where money balances do facilitate transactions to some extent.

In the case of an economy with transactions frictions, one can *also* analyze price-level determination along traditional monetarist lines: One may view the equilibrium price level as being determined by the expected path of the money supply, although the latter quantity is endogenous, in the case of an interest-rate rule such as the Taylor rule, so that money, prices, and interest rates must be simultaneously determined. In the models considered here, this approach would not yield different ultimate conclusions than the neo-Wicksellian analysis, for the system of equilibrium conditions to be solved is actually the same despite the differing direction of approach. Nonetheless, I argue that the neo-Wicksellian interpretation of these equilibrium conditions is a particularly fruitful one, not least because it continues to be possible in the limiting case of a cashless economy.

In this chapter, I expound the basic outlines of the neo-Wicksellian theory in the context of a model with flexible prices and an exogenous supply of goods. This allows me to address a number of basic issues in a particularly simple context; it also allows direct comparison of this theory with the standard quantity-theoretic approach, which, when derived from optimizing models, is also most often expounded in a model with flexible prices. A more complete development of the theory is possible only after the introduction of nominal price rigidities in the following chapter.

1 Price-Level Determination in a Cashless Economy

I begin by considering price-level determination in an economy in which both goods markets and financial markets are completely frictionless: Markets are perfectly competitive, prices adjust continuously to clear markets, and there exist markets in which state-contingent securities of any kind may be traded. Under the assumption of frictionless financial markets, it is natural to suppose that no "monetary" assets are needed to facilitate transactions.

However, I assume that there exists a monetary *unit of account* in terms of which prices (of both goods and financial assets) are quoted. This unit of account is defined in terms of a claim to a certain quantity of a liability of the central bank, which may or may not have any physical existence.[1] This liability is not a claim to future payment of anything except future units of the central-bank liability. As argued in Section 3.2 of Chapter 1, the special situation of the central bank, as issuer of liabilities that promise to pay only additional units of its own liabilities, allows the central bank to fix both the nominal interest yield on its liabilities and the quantity of them in existence.

While I assume that there is no reason why private parties need to hold this particular asset, or receive any benefit from doing so that would not be obtained by holding any other similarly riskless financial claim denominated in terms of the same unit of account, I also assume that they choose to hold financial claims on the government along with privately issued financial claims. The conditions under which the private sector is willing to hold the liabilities of the central bank, along with other government liabilities, are described by arbitrage relations of the kind that are familiar from financial economics. In an equilibrium, where these relations are satisfied, there then exists a well-defined exchange ratio between money and real goods and services.

In a frictionless world of this kind, base money—the monetary liabilities of the central bank—is a perfect substitute for other riskless nominal assets of similarly short maturity, whether these are private obligations or other (nonmonetary) government obligations. As a result, variations in the nominal size of the monetary base, due, for example, to open-market purchases of other sorts of government obligations by the central bank, need have no effect on the prices or interest rates that represent a market equilibrium. Yet this does not mean that in such a world, the central bank has no control over the equilibrium prices of goods in terms of money. As we shall see, the central bank's policy rule is one of the key determinants of the equilibrium price level even in a cashless economy; and it is possible, at least in principle, for the central bank to stabilize the price level around a desired level

---

1. Under current U.S. arrangements, which are fairly typical, Federal Reserve notes (U.S. currency) and Federal Reserve balances (credits in an account at the Fed, which can be used for clearing purposes and to satisfy reserve requirements) are freely convertible into one another, and a promise to pay "a dollar" may be discharged by transfer to the creditor (or its bank) of either of these types of financial claim, in the amount of one dollar. In a cashless economy of the kind that some envision for the future, currency need no longer exist; in such a world, the "dollar" would be defined by a claim to a one-dollar balance at the Fed. The fact that in such a world there would be no physical dollars (i.e., dollar bills) would not prevent the use of dollar accounts in making payments; after all, even now, the dollar is not a claim to anything *else* and is accepted in payment only because of the expectation that it can be transferred to someone else in a subsequent transaction.

(or deterministic trend path) through skillful use of the tools at its disposal.
But in such a world, the crucial tool available to the central bank will not
be open-market operations, but the possibility of adjusting the interest rate
paid on central-bank balances.

1.1 An Asset-Pricing Model with Nominal Assets

Consider an economy made up of a large number of identical households.
The representative household seeks to maximize the expected value of a
discounted sum of period contributions to utility of the form

$$E_0 \left\{ \sum_{t=0}^{\infty} \beta^t u(C_t; \xi_t) \right\}. \tag{1.1}$$

Here $0 < \beta < 1$ is a discount factor, and the period contribution to utility u depends upon the level of consumption C_t of the economy's single
good. I also allow for exogenous stochastic disturbances ξ_t to the period
utility function, which one may think of as representing variation in households' impatience to consume. The presence of this term represents a first
simple example of something of considerable importance for the general
conception of the problem facing central banks, namely, the existence of
real disturbances that should be expected to change the equilibrium real
rate of return and hence the level of nominal interest rates required for
price stability. For any given realization of ξ_t, I assume that the period utility
function $u(C; \xi_t)$ is concave and strictly increasing in C.

   As noted in the introduction, I assume *complete financial markets*, that is,
that available financial assets completely span the relevant uncertainty faced
by households about future income, prices, taste shocks, and so on, so that
each household faces a single intertemporal budget constraint. Under the
assumption of complete markets, a household's *flow* budget constraint each
period can be written in the form

$$M_t + B_t \leq W_t + P_t Y_t - T_t - P_t C_t. \tag{1.2}$$

Here M_t denotes the household's nominal end-of-period balances in the
distinguished financial asset (the monetary base) that represents the economy's unit of account, B_t represents the nominal value (in terms of this unit
of account) of the household's end-of-period portfolio of all *other* financial
assets (whether privately issued or claims on the government), W_t represents *beginning*-of-period financial wealth (now counting the monetary base
along with other assets), Y_t is an exogenous (possibly stochastic) endowment of the single good, P_t is the price of the good in terms of the monetary
unit, and T_t represents net (nominal) tax collections by the government.

The constraint says that total end-of-period financial assets (money plus bonds) can be worth no more than the value of financial wealth brought into the period plus nonfinancial income during the period net of taxes and the value of consumption spending. Interest income is not written explicitly in (1.2) because it is assumed to accrue *between* the discrete dates at which decisions are made; thus W_t already includes the interest earned on bonds held at the end of period $t - 1$.[2]

It is important to note that in (2.2), B_t does not refer to the quantity held of some *single* type of bond. As I assume complete markets, households must be able, at least in principle, to hold any of a wide selection of instruments with different state-contingent returns. However, I need not introduce any notation for the particular types of financial instruments that are traded. (This is one of the conveniences of the assumption of complete markets.) Since any pattern of future state-contingent payoffs that a household may desire can be arranged (for the appropriate price), I can write the household's consumption planning and wealth-accumulation problems without any explicit reference to the quantities that it holds of particular assets; and if there are redundant assets, there will not actually be determinate demands for individual assets (the assumption in the case of the monetary base). I distinguish the household's holdings of the monetary base from the rest of its end-of-period portfolio, however, in order to allow me to discuss explicitly the central bank's supply of this asset and the interest paid on it.

In the proposed notation, I may simply represent the household's portfolio choice as a choice of the state-contingent value A_{t+1} of its nonmonetary portfolio at the beginning of the next period. Total beginning-of-period wealth in the following period is then given by

$$W_{t+1} = \left(1 + i_t^m\right)M_t + A_{t+1},\tag{1.3}$$

where i_t^m is the nominal interest rate paid on money balances held at the end of period t. Note that this implies that W_{t+1}, as a function of the state of the world realized in period $t + 1$, is determined by decisions made in period t; thus W_t is a predetermined state variable in (2.2).

At the time of the portfolio decision, A_{t+1} is a random variable, whose value will depend upon the state of the world in period $t + 1$. But the household chooses the complete specification of this random variable: its value in every possible state. The absence of arbitrage opportunities (a

---

2. See equation (1.6). Though I often refer to a succession of "periods," as is common in the macroeconomic literature, the present models are formally ones in which trading occurs at a sequence of discrete points in time. References to "beginning-of-period" and "end-of-period" portfolios are simply notation to keep track of the effects of trades, not references to different points in time between which interest may accrue.

necessary requirement for equilibrium) then requires that there exist a (unique) *stochastic discount factor* (or asset-pricing kernel) $Q_{t,t+1}$ with the property that the price in period t of any bond portfolio with random value A_{t+1} in the following period is given by

$$B_t = E_t \left[Q_{t,t+1} A_{t+1} \right]. \tag{1.4}$$

(As of date t, $Q_{t,t+1}$ remains a random variable; and E_t refers to the expectation conditional upon the state of the world at date t.) In terms of this discount factor, the riskless *short-term* (one-period) *nominal interest rate* i_t corresponds to the solution to the equation

$$\frac{1}{1+i_t} = E_t \left[Q_{t,t+1} \right]. \tag{1.5}$$

Note that if it happens that the representative household chooses to hold a purely riskless portfolio (in nominal terms), so that A_{t+1} is perfectly forecastable at date t, equation (1.4) states simply that $A_{t+1} = (1 + i_t)B_t$. Substituting this into (1.3), and the resulting expression for W_t into (2.2), which holds with equality in equilibrium, yields the familiar difference equation

$$M_t + B_t = \left(1 + i^m_{t-1}\right) M_{t-1} + (1 + i_{t-1}) B_{t-1} + P_t Y_t - T_t - P_t C_t \tag{1.6}$$

for the evolution of B_t. This will actually be an equilibrium condition in the case that the government issues only riskless one-period debt; but it is still important, even in that case, to recognize that an individual household's budget constraint allows it the possibility of shifting wealth across states of the world in other ways.[3]

More generally, then, equations (2.2), (1.3) and (1.4) together give a complete description of the household's flow budget constraint. With the use of (1.3) and (1.4) to eliminate B_t from (1.2), the constraint can alternatively be written

$$\left(1 - E_t Q_{t,t+1}(1 + i^m_t)\right) M_t + E_t \left[Q_{t,t+1} W_{t+1} \right] \le W_t + [P_t Y_t - T_t - P_t C_t].$$

---

3. Condition (1.6) actually represents the correct flow budget constraint if we assume such radically incomplete markets that households can neither borrow nor lend except in terms of the single instrument assumed to be issued by the government. This case of a single traded asset is often considered in the literature on consumption theory (see, e.g., Obstfeld and Rogoff, 1996, sec. 2.3). In the present context, with identical households, it makes no real difference what one assumes about the number of financial markets that are open. However, the characterization of optimal household plans is simplest in the case of complete markets, and the introduction of market valuations for arbitrary random income streams proves useful in the next chapter, when I need to consider the optimal pricing decisions of firms.

Using (1.5) gives

$$P_t C_t + \Delta_t M_t + E_t \left[Q_{t,t+1} W_{t+1} \right] \leq W_t + [P_t Y_t - T_t]. \tag{1.7}$$

where

$$\Delta_t \equiv \frac{i_t - i_t^m}{1 + i_t}. \tag{1.8}$$

It is clear from this version that the interest-rate differential Δ_t between non-monetary and monetary assets represents the opportunity cost of holding wealth in monetary form. Given its planned state-contingent wealth W_{t+1} at the beginning of the following period, the household can choose any values C_t, $M_t \geq 0$ that satisfy (1.7).[4]

A complete description of the household's budget constraints requires that I also specify a limit on borrowing to prevent "Ponzi schemes" of the kind that would otherwise be consistent with the infinite sequence of flow budget constraints in an infinite-horizon model. In the spirit of the assumption of perfectly frictionless financial markets, it is natural to suppose that there is no obstacle to borrowing against after-tax endowment income that may be anticipated (even if in only some states of the world) at any future date. The implied constraint is then that the household must hold a net portfolio at the end of period t (possibly including *issuance* of some securities, in order to borrow against future income) such that the wealth W_{t+1} transferred into the next period satisfies the bound

$$W_{t+1} \geq - \sum_{T=t+1}^{\infty} E_{t+1} \left[Q_{t+1,T}(P_T Y_T - T_T) \right] \tag{1.9}$$

with certainty, that is, in *each* state of the world that may be reached in period $t+1$. Here the general stochastic discount factor $Q_{t,T}$ for discounting (nominal) income in period T back to an earlier period t is defined by

$$Q_{t,T} \equiv \prod_{s=t+1}^{T} Q_{s-1,s}.$$

4. I assume that money balances must be nonnegative because this asset is *defined* as a liability of the central bank, which accordingly cannot be issued by any other parties, even though (under the assumption of complete markets) private securities are issued that are equivalent in terms of their state-contingent payouts. This nonnegativity constraint is another reason to single out this asset from the others in writing the household's budget constraints; for I assume no short-sale constraints in the case of any other securities in my model with frictionless financial markets.

(I also use the notation $Q_{t,t} \equiv 1$.) Condition (1.9) then says that a household cannot plan to be indebted in any state in an amount greater than the present value of all subsequent after-tax nonfinancial income.

The entire infinite sequence of flow budget constraints (1.7) and borrowing limits (1.9) is equivalent to a single *intertemporal* (or lifetime) budget constraint for the household. I note first of all that unless the present value on the right-hand side of (1.9) is well defined (i.e., the infinite sum converges), the household has no budget constraint: Ponzi schemes are possible; hence unlimited consumption is affordable. Furthermore, if the present value is infinite looking forward from any state of the world, at any date, unbounded consumption is possible not only at that date and in all other states (including along histories under which the state in question never occurs). For with complete markets, it is possible to borrow against that state to finance unbounded consumption in any other state.

One may thus restrict attention to the case in which Ponzi schemes are not possible because

$$\sum_{T=t}^{\infty} E_t \left[Q_{t,T}(P_T y_T - T_T) \right] < \infty \qquad (1.10)$$

at all times.[5] The budget constraint is also undefined unless interest rates satisfy the lower bound

$$i_t \geq i_t^m \qquad (1.11)$$

at all times. For otherwise, an arbitrage opportunity exists; a household can finance unlimited consumption by shorting riskless one-period bonds (i.e., borrowing at the short riskless rate, assumed to be negative) and using the proceeds partly to hold cash sufficient to repurchase the bonds (repay its debt) a period later and partly to finance additional consumption. Because utility is assumed to be strictly increasing in consumption, such an operation continues to increase utility no matter how much it may be engaged in. Hence one may also restrict attention to the case in which (1.11) holds at all times.

One is then able to establish that the infinite sequence of flow budget constraints (1.7) is equivalent to a single intertemporal budget constraint.

PROPOSITION 2.1. Consider positive-valued stochastic processes $\{P_t, Q_{t,T}\}$ satisfying (1.10) and (1.11) at all dates, and let $\{C_t, M_t\}$ be non-negative-

5. Throughout, it should be understood that when I say that such a relation holds "at all times," this also means in all possible states of the world at each date.

valued processes representing a possible consumption and money-accumulation plan for the household. Then there exists a specification of the household's portfolio plan at each date satisfying both the flow budget constraint (1.7) and the borrowing limit (1.9) at each date, if and only if the plans $\{C_t, M_t\}$ satisfy the constraint

$$\sum_{t=0}^{\infty} E_0 Q_{0,t} [P_t C_t + \Delta_t M_t] \leq W_0 + \sum_{t=0}^{\infty} E_0 Q_{0,t} [P_t Y_t - T_t]. \qquad (1.12)$$

The proof is given in Appendix A. Note that the intertemporal budget constraint states simply that the present value of the household's planned consumption over the entire indefinite future plus the cost to it of its planned money holdings must not exceed its initial financial wealth plus the present value of its expected after-tax income from sources other than financial assets. One can also show (see the proof in Appendix A) that the household's continuation plan, looking forward from any date t (i.e., its plan for dates $T \geq t$ in all of the states that remain possible given the state of the world at date t), must satisfy the corresponding intertemporal budget constraint

$$\sum_{s=t}^{\infty} E_t Q_{t,s} [P_s C_s + \Delta_s M_s] \leq W_t + \sum_{s=t}^{\infty} E_t Q_{t,s} [P_s Y_s - T_s]. \qquad (1.13)$$

The household's optimization problem is then to choose processes C_t, $M_t \geq 0$ for all dates $t \geq 0$, satisfying (1.12) given its initial wealth W_0 and the goods prices and asset prices (indicated by the stochastic discount factors $Q_{t,t+1}$) that it expects to face, so as to maximize (1.1). Given an optimal choice of these processes, an optimal path for W_t may be constructed as in the proof of Proposition 2.1. Given a stochastic process for W_{t+1}, the implied processes for A_{t+1} and for B_t are given by (1.3) and (1.4).

Because this is essentially a standard concave optimization problem subject to a single budget constraint, necessary and sufficient conditions for household optimization are easily given. First of all, (1.10) and (1.11) must hold at all times, since otherwise no optimal plan exists (as more consumption is always possible). Second, since in the cashless economy there is no nonpecuniary benefit to holding money balances, household optimization requires that either

$$M_t = 0 \qquad (1.14)$$

or

$$i_t = i_t^m \qquad (1.15)$$

at each date and in each possible state (though which condition obtains may
differ across dates and across states).

Third, by equating marginal rates of substitution to relative prices, I
obtain the first-order conditions

$$\frac{u_c(C_t; \xi_t)}{u_c(C_{t+1}; \xi_{t+1})} = \frac{\beta}{Q_{t,t+1}} \frac{P_t}{P_{t+1}}. \tag{1.16}$$

Here U_c is the partial derivative of U with respect to the level of consumption. This condition must hold for each possible state at each date $t \geq 0$
and for each possible state that may occur at date $t + 1$, given the state that
has occurred at date t. ($Q_{t,t+1}$ indicates the value of the discount factor in a
particular state at date $t + 1$.) With (1.5), condition (1.16) implies that the
short-term nominal interest rate must satisfy

$$1 + i_t = \beta^{-1} \left\{ E_t \left[\frac{u_c(C_{t+1}; \xi_{t+1})}{u_c(C_t, ; \xi_t)} \frac{P_t}{P_{t+1}} \right] \right\}^{-1} \tag{1.17}$$

at each date.

Finally, optimization requires that the household exhaust its intertemporal budget constraint; that is, (1.13) must hold as an equality at each date.
Equivalently, the flow budget constraint (2.2) must hold as an equality at
each date, and in addition, the household's wealth accumulation must satisfy the *transversality condition*

$$\lim_{T \to \infty} E_t \left[Q_{t,T} W_T \right] = 0. \tag{1.18}$$

(Condition (1.13), stated as a strict equality, implies both that (2.2) must
hold as a strict equality at each date $T \geq t$ and that (1.18) must hold.
Conversely, the latter set of conditions implies that (1.13) holds with strict
equality, looking forward from date t.) Finally, given that (1.13) must hold
with strict equality, condition (1.10) may equivalently be written as

$$E_t \left\{ \sum_{T=t}^{\infty} Q_{t,T} \left[P_T C_T + \Delta_T M_T \right] \right\} < \infty. \tag{1.19}$$

One thus obtains a set of conditions—(1.2) as a strict equality; the requirement that either (1.14) or (1.15) hold with equality, in addition to the inequality conditions (1.11) and $M_t \geq 0$; (1.16); (1.18); and (1.19)—that must
hold at all times in order for the representative household's actions to be
optimal. At the same time, one can show that these conditions suffice for
optimality as well.

I may now state the complete set of conditions for a rational-expectations (or intertemporal) equilibrium in this model. In addition to the conditions just stated for household optimization, markets must clear at all dates. This means that household demands must satisfy

$$C_t = Y_t, \qquad M_t = M_t^s, \qquad A_{t+1} = A_{t+1}^s$$

at all dates. Here M_t^s refers to the supply of base money by the central bank, which I assume to be positive at all dates. A_{t+1}^s refers to the aggregate value at the beginning of period $t+1$ of government bonds in the hands of the public at the end of period t. (In general, it would not suffice for bond-market clearing to require that $B_t = B_t^s$, where B_t^s denotes the market value of government bonds outstanding at the end of period t, as this could allow households to demand a portfolio with different state-contingent payoffs than the aggregate supply of government bonds.) If I specify the supply of government bonds in more primitive terms by specifying the variables $\{B_{t,t+j}^s\}$, where for each date t and each $j \geq 1$, $B_{t,t+j}^s$ denotes the total (nominal) coupons that the government promises to pay at date $t+j$ on bonds that are outstanding at the end of period t, then

$$A_{t+1}^s \equiv \sum_{j=1}^{\infty} E_{t+1}\left[Q_{t+1,t+j} B_{t,t+j}^s\right]$$

in each possible state that may be reached at date $t+1$. Finally, note that I abstract here from government purchases of real goods and services (though the model is subsequently extended to allow for them).

Given that $M_t^s > 0$, market clearing implies that (1.14) cannot hold, and hence that (1.15) must hold at all times. Substituting the market-clearing conditions into conditions (1.16) and (1.17) for household optimization yields equilibrium conditions

$$\frac{u_c(Y_t; \xi_t)}{u_c(Y_{t+1}; \xi_{t+1})} = \frac{\beta}{Q_{t,t+1}} \frac{P_t}{P_{t+1}}, \tag{1.20}$$

$$1 + i_t = \beta^{-1} \left\{ E_t \left[\frac{u_c(Y_{t+1}; \xi_{t+1})}{u_c(Y_t; \xi_t)} \frac{P_t}{P_{t+1}} \right] \right\}^{-1} \tag{1.21}$$

for each date. Note that the latter relation takes the form of a "Fisher equation" for the nominal interest rate, where the intertemporal marginal rate of substitution of the representative household plays the role of the real-interest factor.

Finally, with substitution of solution (1.20) for the stochastic discount factor into (1.18) and (1.19), the latter conditions take the form

$$\lim_{T\to\infty} \beta^T E_t\big[u_c(Y_T; \xi_T) W_T^s/P_T\big] = 0, \qquad (1.22)$$

$$\sum_{T=t}^{\infty} \beta^T E_t\,[u_c(Y_T; \xi_T)Y_T] < \infty. \qquad (1.23)$$

(Here I have also used the market-clearing conditions to equate W_T with $W_T^s \equiv (1 + i_{T-1}^m)M_{T-1}^s + A_T^s$, the total supply of nominal claims on the government at the beginning of period T, and (1.15) to substitute for the factor Δ_T in (1.19).) A rational-expectations equilibrium is then a collection of processes that satisfy (1.15) and (1.21)–(1.23) at all dates $t \geq 0$.

The transversality condition (1.22) can equivalently be written in a possibly more familiar form in terms of the end-of-period value of total government liabilities, $D_t \equiv M_t^s + B_t^s$.

PROPOSITION 2.2. Let assets be priced by a system of stochastic discount factors that satisfy (1.20), and consider processes $\{P_t, i_t, i_t^m, M_t^s, W_t^s\}$ that satisfy (1.15), (1.21), and (1.23) at all dates, given the exogenous processes $\{Y_t, \xi_t\}$. Then these processes satisfy (1.22) as well if and only if they satisfy

$$\lim_{T\to\infty} \beta^T E_t\,[u_c(Y_T; \xi_T)D_T/P_T] = 0. \qquad (1.24)$$

The proof is given in Appendix A. It follows that one can equivalently define equilibrium as follows.

DEFINITION. A *rational-expectations equilibrium* of the cashless economy is a pair of processes $\{P_t, i_t\}$ that satisfy (1.15) and (1.21)–(1.24) at all dates $t \geq 0$, given the exogenous processes $\{Y_t, \xi_t\}$ and evolution of the variables $\{i_t^m, M_t^s, D_t\}$ consistent with the monetary-fiscal policy regime.

This latter formulation is especially useful in that it allows one to specify fiscal policy in terms of restrictions on the evolution of the total government liabilities, or alternatively, restrictions on the path of the conventional government budget deficit.

Note that if one is interested only in the determination of equilibrium prices and interest rates, the additional equilibrium condition (1.20) in the definition of rational-expectations equilibrium need not be included. (The additional condition must be appended to the system if one is interested in other equilibrium asset prices.) Nor is there any additional equilibrium condition corresponding to the requirement that (2.2) hold with equality. This condition is necessarily satisfied (when one substitutes the market-clearing conditions) as long as the supplies of government liabilities evolve in accordance with the flow *government budget constraint*

$$E_t \left[Q_{t,t+1} W_{t+1}^s \right] = W_t^s - T_t - \Delta_t M_t^s. \tag{1.25}$$

I assume that the monetary-fiscal policy regime satisfies this constraint at all times. I then have a system of two equalities at each date, (1.15) and (1.21), to determine the two endogenous variables P_t and i_t, together with the bounds (1.23) and (1.24) that the solution must satisfy.

The notation thus far allows only for fiscal policies consisting of taxes or transfers. But the previous framework is easily extended to allow for government purchases of goods and services as well, without any material change being required in the equilibrium conditions. Let government purchases of the single good in period t be denoted G_t, and suppose that $\{G_t\}$ is an exogenous process, such that $G_t < Y_t$ at all dates.[6] Market clearing then requires that $C_t + G_t = Y_t$ at all dates. Substitution of this relation into the conditions for optimization by the representative household then leads to equilibrium conditions such as

$$1 + i_t = \beta^{-1} \left\{ E_t \left[\frac{u_c(Y_{t+1} - G_{t+1}; \xi_{t+1})}{u_c(Y_t - G_t; \xi_t)} \frac{P_t}{P_{t+1}} \right] \right\}^{-1}, \tag{1.26}$$

generalizing (1.21).

I note that (1.26) is obtained from equation (1.21) by replacing $u_c(Y_t; \xi_t)$ by $u_c(Y_t - G_t; \xi_t)$ each time it occurs. The same is true for the other equilibrium conditions (1.20), (1.23) and (1.24) as well. Alternatively, I obtain the equilibrium conditions for the general case by replacing the "direct" utility function $u(C_t; \xi_t)$ throughout the calculations by the "indirect" utility

$$\tilde{u}(Y_t; \tilde{\xi}_t) \equiv u(Y_t - G_t; \xi_t), \tag{1.27}$$

indicating the utility flow to the representative household as a function of its "total demand" for resources Y_t, where total demand adds the resources consumed by the government on the household's behalf (its per capita share of government purchases) to the household's private consumption.[7] In this indirect utility function, $\tilde{\xi}_t$ indicates a vector of disturbances that includes both G_t and the taste shock ξ_t.

---

6. One might, of course, also consider fiscal policies under which G_t is endogenously determined, e.g., as the solution to some welfare-maximization problem of the government's. In the present study, however, I assume that government purchases are given exogenously. I allow for endogeneity of the level of net tax collections, as, e.g., in the next section, and this is of some importance for the present theory of price-level determination. See Section 4 of Chapter 4 for further discussion.

7. Here I use the same notation Y_t for a choice variable of the household as was used previously for the exogenous supply of goods. In fact, in the model with endogenous output presented in Chapter 4, equilibrium conditions such as (1.27) continue to apply, but with Y_t referring to aggregate demand, and *not* to any exogenously given supply of goods.

The household's problem can then be written as one of choosing the state-contingent evolution of total demand to maximize its expected discounted flow of indirect utility subject to an intertemporal budget constraint of the form (1.12), if C_t in this constraint is taken to refer to total demand, and T_t to the primary government budget surplus (tax collections in excess of government spending).[8] In this case, I can derive exactly the same equilibrium conditions as were obtained earlier, except that the function u is everywhere replaced by $\tilde{u}$. Hence variations in the level of government purchases G_t have exactly the same effect as the taste shock ξ_t; they are simply another source of exogenous variations in the relation $\tilde{u}_c(Y_t; \tilde{\xi}_t)$ between the marginal utility of income to the representative household and aggregate output, and hence of variations in the equilibrium real rate of interest.

1.2 A Wicksellian Policy Regime

I now offer a simple example of a complete specification of monetary and fiscal policy rules for a cashless economy and consider the determinants of the equilibrium path of the money price of goods under such a regime. Note that as a consequence of the forward-looking character of households' asset accumulation problems, the determination of equilibrium at any point in time requires that one specify how policy is expected to be conducted into the indefinite future, and in all possible future states. This is one reason for the present specification of government policy in terms of systematic *rules* for the determination of both the central bank's actions and the government's budget.

This specification of monetary policy is in the spirit of Wicksell's (1898, 1907) proposed rule. As discussed in the previous chapter, this rule can be expressed in terms of a formula for the central bank's interest-rate operating target. I also explicitly specify the way in which the central bank adjusts the two instruments at its disposal—the nominal value of the monetary base M_t^s, on the one hand, and the interest rate i_t^m paid on base money on the other—in order to achieve its operating target. In a world with monetary frictions (discussed in Section 3), it is possible to use *either* of these instruments to affect the level of short-term nominal interest rates, and as discussed in Chapter 1, actual central banks differ in the extent to which

---

8. The definition of equilibrium that results from this formulation of the household's problem is equivalent to the standard one, subject to the proviso that the processes $\{G_t, Y_t, \xi_t\}$ are such that the present value of government purchases is finite. Technically, one can imagine an equilibrium in which the present value of per capita output is not finite, though the present value of the resources left for the private sector to consume is finite. But this special case is of little interest and is ignored here.

they use these two means to implement policy (though almost all central banks formulate policy in terms of an interest-rate operating target). In the cashless economy described previously, however, changes in the quantity of base money (e.g., through open-market purchases of government securities) have no consequences for the equilibrium determination of interest rates or other variables. (Note that M_t^s does not appear in any of the equilibrium conditions obtained at the end of the previous section.) Hence policy targets must be implemented exclusively through adjustment of the interest paid on base money.

Specifically, I assume a regime under which the interest paid on base money is equal at all times to the central bank's current interest-rate target, determined in response to the bank's assessment of current aggregate conditions. Such a system would resemble the channel systems described in Chapter 1, under which the interest paid on central-bank balances is equal to the target rate minus a fixed spread. Here the spread is assumed to be zero, since in equilibrium, the market interest rate i_t is actually equal to i_t^m, and not i_t^m plus any positive spread. It is true that current channel systems pay interest only on central-bank clearing balances, and not on currency. But one can interpret the regime analyzed here to have this property as well. In a cashless world, this would simply mean that currency would not be held in equilibrium (any initially existing currency would be promptly deposited with the central bank in an interest-earning account), so that base money M_t^s would correspond to the supply of clearing balances.

Under a Wicksellian rule for the interest-rate target, the interest rate paid on central-bank balances equals

$$i_t^m = \phi(P_t/P_t^*; v_t), \tag{1.28}$$

where $P_t^* > 0$ defines a target path for the price level, v_t is an additional possible exogenous random disturbance to the policy rule (or to its implementation), and $\phi(\cdot; v)$ is a non-negative-valued, nondecreasing function for each possible value of the disturbance v.[9]

Here the function ϕ indicates the rule used by the central bank to set its operating target, while equation (1.28) indicates the way in which the

9. The function is assumed to be nonnegative on the grounds that it is not possible for the central bank to drive nominal interest rates to negative levels. I assume that, as under typical current arrangements, the holders of central-bank balances have the right to ask for currency in exchange for such balances at any time, and that it is infeasible to pay negative interest on currency. Hence an attempt to pay negative interest on central-bank balances would lead to zero demand for such balances, and a market overnight interest rate of zero (the rate available on currency), rather than a negative overnight interest rate. The assumed nonnegativity of the function requires that $\phi(P/P^*; v)$ not be an exactly linear function of $\log(P/P^*)$, though I make use of a local log-linear approximation to the function below.

rule is implemented. The inclusion of a time-varying price-level target P_t^* allows one to treat the case of a rule that seeks to stabilize the price level around a modestly growing trend path—say, a rule that provides for 1 or 2 percent inflation per year, perhaps to compensate for bias in the price index that is targeted—rather than necessarily assuming a constant price-level target, as Wicksell did. The inclusion of the random disturbance v_t allows one to consider the effects of random variations in policy, or in its implementation, that I may not wish to model as changes in the target price level itself. This includes the possibility that the central bank may respond to output variations as well as the path of prices, as called for by the Taylor (1993) rule, or that the central bank may respond to perceived variation in the equilibrium real rate of return. (In the present model, both output and the equilibrium real interest rate are purely exogenous; hence systematic responses to these variables can be modeled by the inclusion of an exogenous disturbance term in the policy rule.)

I also need to specify the rule by which the evolution of the monetary base is determined. Here the assumption is simply that $\{M_t^s\}$ is an exogenous, positive-valued sequence. The logic of the Wicksellian regime requires no variation over time in the supply of base money at all; however, I allow for possible variation over time in the monetary base, in order to analyze the equilibrium consequences of this kind of policy action.

Finally, fiscal policy is specified by a rule for the evolution of the total supply of government liabilities $\{D_t\}$ and by a specification of the composition of government liabilities (debt-management policy) at each point in time. For simplicity, let $\{D_t\}$ be an exogenous process. One simple example of such a fiscal rule would be a *balanced-budget rule* of the kind analyzed by Schmitt-Grohé and Uribe (2000), where $\Delta D_t = 0$ each period; another would be a policy under which no government bonds are ever issued, so that $D_t = M_t^s$ each period. I also simplify by assuming that all government debt consists entirely of riskless one-period nominal bonds. The variable B_t^s then indicates the supply of such bonds at the end of period t, in terms of their nominal value at the time of issuance (rather than maturity). The implied rule for net tax collections T_t is then given by

$$T_t = (1 + i_{t-1})(D_{t-1} - \Delta_{t-1}M_{t-1}^s) - D_t, \tag{1.29}$$

using the fact that $A_t^s = (1 + i_{t-1})B_{t-1}^s = (1 + i_{t-1})(D_{t-1} - M_{t-1}^s)$.

A rational-expectations equilibrium is then a set of processes $\{P_t, i_t, i_t^m\}$ that satisfy (1.15), (1.21), (1.23), (1.24), and (1.28) at all dates $t \geq 0$, given the exogenous processes $\{Y_t, \xi_t, M_t^s, D_t\}$.[10] Using (1.15) to eliminate i_t^m in (1.28) yields

---

10. In the case in which one allows for government purchases, one should replace u by $\tilde{u}$ in each equation, and ξ_t by $\tilde{\xi}_t$.

$$i_t = \phi(P_t/P_t^*; v_t), \tag{1.30}$$

as an equilibrium condition linking the paths of interest rates and prices. (Note that this equation directly expresses the interest-rate rule that the central bank implements through its adjustment of the interest rate paid on base money.) Note further that condition (1.23) does not involve any endogenous variables and thus plays no role in equilibrium determination. I assume processes $\{Y_t, \xi_t\}$ that satisfy this condition, and, having done so, can drop (1.23) from the list of requirements for equilibrium. I can thus identify rational-expectations equilibrium with a set of processes $\{P_t, i_t\}$ that satisfy (1.21), (1.24), and (1.30) each period.

I am interested not only in whether a solution to this system of equilibrium conditions *exists*, but in whether these relations suffice to uniquely determine the equilibrium paths of interest rates and prices. The question of the *determinacy* of equilibrium is a preliminary, more basic issue, before one can hope to address the question of what factors affect the equilibrium price level and how they affect it. Moreover, there are obvious reasons to worry about determinacy under the kind of regime just described. In the celebrated analysis of Sargent and Wallace (1975), interest-rate rules as such are to be avoided, on the grounds that they result in indeterminacy of the equilibrium price level (and hence, in their model, of the equilibrium paths of real variables as well). It is also often a concern that in a cashless economy, there might be nothing to pin down the equilibrium price level, given that there is in such an environment no determinate demand for the monetary base. This is sometimes argued to be an important reason to head off financial innovations that could lead to this kind of world (e.g., Friedman, 1999).

A general analysis of the existence and uniqueness of solutions to the system of equations for arbitrary monetary and fiscal policy rules is beyond the scope of this study. Rather, I address here, and in most of this study, a more limited question: namely, the *local* determinacy of equilibrium in the case of policies that involve only small fluctuations over time in the monetary policy rule, assuming as well that other exogenous disturbances are similarly small. By local determinacy I mean the question of whether there is a unique equilibrium within a sufficiently small neighborhood of certain paths for the endogenous variables. If so, this equilibrium is at least *locally* unique, and such local uniqueness makes possible a well-defined "comparative-statics" analysis of the effects of small disturbances or parameter changes.[11] In fact, I analyze the effects of small fluctuations in the price-level target and other small disturbances through exactly such a consideration of how the steady-state equilibrium associated with steady trend growth of the price-level target and zero disturbances is perturbed by small stochastic variations in the exogenous variables.

11. See Section A.3 of Appendix A for further discussion.

An advantage of restricting attention to this question is that it can be addressed using purely linear methods. I analyze a log-linear approximation to the structural equations derived earlier and characterize the (bounded) log-linear solutions to these equations. This way of characterizing both the important structural relations implied by the present model and the predicted equilibrium evolution of economic time series under alternative policies is useful not only because of its tractability, but because of the ubiquity of linear time-series models in empirical studies. My approach will thus allow a direct mapping between the predictions of optimizing models of economic behavior and the kinds of structural models and data characterizations already used in quantitative monetary policy analysis. This will facilitate both evaluation of the empirical adequacy of the optimizing models and productive dialogue between optimization-based and more traditional approaches to policy evaluation.

Furthermore, such an analysis corresponds reasonably closely to the way that the determinacy of rational-expectations equilibrium is considered by Sargent and Wallace (1975). That paper assumes a log-linear model and considers the uniqueness of nonexplosive solutions to the log-linear structural equations. The method herein is essentially the same, except that the log-linear structural equations can be justified as a log-linear approximation to exact relations derived from an explicit intertemporal general equilibrium model, and I am more explicit about the class of solutions to be considered. Thus the analysis here suffices to address the particular issue relating to determinacy of equilibrium under interest-rate rules raised by Sargent and Wallace.[12]

I begin by characterizing the steady state near which I look for other solutions. Consider an environment in which $Y_t = \bar{Y} > 0$ and $\xi_t = 0$ at all times. Assume a policy regime under which the price-level target grows at the constant rate

$$P^*_{t+1}/P^*_t = \bar{\Pi} > \beta$$

at all dates (with some initial $P^*_0 > 0$), $v_t = 0$ at all dates, and suppose that the function ϕ satisfies

$$1 + \phi(1; 0) = \bar{\pi}/\beta,$$

so that the policy rule is consistent with the assumed target path for prices. Also assume a fiscal rule under which

---

12. In Chapter 4, I consider an extension of the model in this chapter that is essentially a rational-expectations IS-LM model, though not identical in structure to the one analyzed by Sargent and Wallace (1975). The determinacy of equilibrium under alternative policy rules is taken up again in that chapter.

$$D_{t+1}/D_t = \gamma_D < \bar{\pi}/\beta$$

at all dates (given initial government liabilities $D_0 > 0$), and an open-market policy under which $\{M_t^s\}$ is an arbitrary sequence, satisfying

$$0 < M_t^s < D_t \tag{1.31}$$

at all times. Under such a policy regime, we easily observe that the paths

$$P_t = P_t^*, \qquad i_t = \bar{i} \equiv (\bar{\pi} - \beta)/\beta > 0$$

for all t represent a rational-expectations equilibrium.

Next, consider an environment in which there are only small fluctuations in the exogenous variables Y_t, P_{t+1}^*/P_t^*, v_t, and D_{t+1}/D_t around the constant values specified in the previous paragraph. (Specifically, suppose that each of these variables remains forever within a bounded interval containing a neighborhood of the steady-state value.) I also continue to assume that the process $\{M_t^s\}$ satisfies the bounds (1.31). I wish to look for rational-expectations equilibria in which the endogenous variables i_t and P_t/P_t^* similarly remain forever within certain neighborhoods of their steady-state values. In this case, condition (1.24) is necessarily satisfied (for any tight enough bounds on the allowable variation in the variables listed above); thus I need only consider the (local) existence and uniqueness of solutions to the system of equations consisting of (1.21) and (1.30).

In the case of tight enough bounds on the variations that are considered in these variables, it suffices to take into account only the *bounded* solutions to a system consisting of *log-linear approximations* to conditions (1.21) and (1.30).[13] For the sake of simplicity (and continuity with the assumptions made in more complex examples in the next two chapters), I specify that the steady state around the log-linearization is one in which $\bar{\Pi} = 1$, so that there is zero inflation. (This does not require that the analysis consider only policies under which there is no trend growth in the price-level target: it only requires that the target inflation rate is *never very large*.)

A log-linear approximation to (1.21) is then given by[14]

$$\hat{i}_t = \hat{r}_t + E_t \pi_{t+1}, \tag{1.32}$$

---

13. As is further explained in Section A.3 of Appendix A, this amounts to using the inverse function theorem to demonstrate local uniqueness of the solution to this system of equilibrium conditions, and using the implicit function theorem to give a log-linear local approximation to the solution.

14. Note that the appearance in (1.32) of the inflation rate rather than of the inflation rate relative to steady-state inflation depends on the assumption that the steady-state inflation rate is zero.

where

$$\hat{\imath}_t \equiv \log\left(\frac{1+i_t}{1+\bar{\imath}}\right), \qquad \pi_t \equiv \log\left(\frac{P_t}{P_{t-1}}\right).$$

Here the (percentage deviation in the) ex ante short-term *equilibrium real rate of return* $\hat{r}_t$ is an exogenous process given by

$$\hat{r}_t = \sigma^{-1}\left[E_t(\hat{Y}_{t+1} - g_{t+1}) - (\hat{Y}_t - g_t)\right], \qquad (1.33)$$

where the constant coefficient

$$\sigma \equiv -\frac{u_c}{u_{cc}\bar{Y}} > 0$$

measures the intertemporal elasticity of substitution of aggregate expenditure and the disturbance term

$$g_t \equiv -\frac{u_{c\xi}}{\bar{Y}\,u_{cc}}\xi_t$$

indicates the percentage increase in output required to keep the marginal utility of income constant, given the change that has occurred in the impatience to consume.

In the case of the model extended to allow for government purchases, equations (1.32) and (1.33) still apply, under the alternative definitions $\sigma \equiv s_C\sigma_C$, where $s_C \equiv \bar{C}/\bar{Y}$ is the steady-state share of private expenditure in total demand and

$$\sigma_C \equiv -\frac{\tilde{u}_c}{\tilde{u}_{cc}\bar{C}} > 0$$

is the intertemporal elasticity of substitution of private spending; and $g_t = \hat{G}_t + s_C\bar{c}_t$, where $\hat{G}_t \equiv (G_t - \bar{G})/\bar{Y}$ indicates fluctuations in government purchases, measured in units of steady-state output, and

$$\bar{c}_t \equiv -\frac{\tilde{u}_{c\xi}}{\bar{C}\tilde{u}_{cc}}\xi_t$$

indicates the percentage change in private expenditure required to keep marginal utility constant. (In fact, the notation g_t is used for the disturbance in (1.33) because variations in government purchases are among the most obvious reasons for the existence of shifts in this factor.)

A corresponding log-linear approximation to the Wicksellian policy rule (1.30) is given by

$$\hat{\imath}_t = \phi_p \hat{P}_t + v_t, \tag{1.34}$$

where $\hat{P}_t \equiv \log(P_t/P_t^*)$, and $\phi_p \geq 0$ represents the elasticity of ϕ with respect to P/P^*, evaluated at the steady-state values of its arguments.[15] To the system of log-linear equations (1.32) and (1.34) I must also adjoin the identity

$$\pi_t = \hat{P}_t - \hat{P}_{t-1} + \pi_t^*, \tag{1.35}$$

where $\pi_t^* \equiv \log(P_t^*/P_{t-1}^*)$ indicates the exogenous fluctuations, if any, in the target inflation rate. I then wish to examine the bounded solutions to the system of log-linear equations (1.32), (1.34), and (1.35).

Using (1.34) and (1.35) to substitute for $\hat{\imath}_t$ and π_{t+1} in the Fisher equation (1.32) results in an expectational difference equation in the variable $\hat{P}_t$ alone, given by

$$(1 + \phi_p)\hat{P}_t = E_t \hat{P}_{t+1} + (\hat{r}_t + E_t \pi_{t+1}^* - v_t). \tag{1.36}$$

Given a policy rule for which $\phi_p > 0$, as called for by Wicksell, so that $0 < (1 + \phi_p)^{-1} < 1$, this equation can be solved forward (as discussed further in Appendix A) to obtain a unique bounded solution

$$\hat{P}_t = \sum_{j=0}^{\infty} (1 + \phi_p)^{-(j+1)} E_t \left[\hat{r}_{t+j} + \pi_{t+j+1}^* - v_{t+j} \right], \tag{1.37}$$

in the case of any bounded exogenous processes $\{\hat{r}_t, \pi_t^*, v_t\}$. Substitution of this solution into (1.34) then yields an associated unique bounded solution for the nominal interest-rate dynamics as well, namely,

$$\hat{\imath}_t = \sum_{j=0}^{\infty} \phi_p (1 + \phi_p)^{-(j+1)} E_t \left[\hat{r}_{t+j} + \pi_{t+j+1}^* - v_{t+j} \right] + v_t, \tag{1.38}$$

while substitution into (1.35) yields a corresponding solution for the equilibrium rate of inflation.

I thus obtain the main result of this section.[16]

---

15. In writing the disturbance term simply as v_t, we adopt the normalization under which $\partial \phi / \partial v = 1 + \bar{\imath} = \beta^{-1}$, when also evaluated at the steady-state values of the arguments.

16. Kerr and King (1996) provide an early discussion of the determinacy of equilibrium under a rule of this kind, in a log-linear framework similar to the one derived here as an approximation to the exact equilibrium conditions. Woodford (1998) demonstrates determinacy of equilibrium under a Wicksellian regime in the context of a complete intertemporal equilibrium model, along lines similar to those followed here, although the means by which the central bank is assumed to implement its interest-rate operating target is different there.

PROPOSITION 2.3. Under a Wicksellian policy rule (1.30) with $\phi_p > 0$, the rational-expectations equilibrium paths of prices and interest rates are (locally) determinate; that is, there exist open sets $\mathcal{P}$ and $\mathcal{I}$ such that in the case of any tight enough bounds on the fluctuations in the exogenous processes $\{\hat{r}_t, \pi_t^*, \nu_t\}$, there exists a unique rational-expectations equilibrium in which $P_t/P_t^* \in \mathcal{P}$ and $i_t \in \mathcal{I}$ at all times. Furthermore, equations (1.37) and (1.38) give a log-linear (first-order Taylor series) approximation to that solution, accurate up to a residual of order $\mathcal{O}(\|\xi\|^2)$, where $\|\xi\|$ indexes the bounds on the disturbance processes.

See further discussion in Appendix A.

Thus there may be a well-defined rational-expectations equilibrium path for the price level, even in a purely cashless economy, and even under a policy rule that is formulated in terms of an interest-rate rule—that is, a rule for setting a short-term nominal interest rate that is independent of the evolution of any monetary aggregate. It is true that the regime described above assumes an exogenously given path for the monetary base M_t^s. But it should not therefore be taken for granted that it is the existence of a "money-growth target" that is responsible for the existence of a determinate price level; for the equilibrium price level (1.37) is independent of the assumed path of the monetary base.

Indeed, in a cashless economy, a money-growth target will *not* succeed in determining an equilibrium price level—at least if such a policy is understood to involve a constant (typically zero) rate of interest on the monetary base. In the case that no interest is paid on money, the following result implies that no equilibrium price level is possible at all.

PROPOSITION 2.4. Consider a monetary policy under which the monetary base is bounded below by a positive quantity: $M_t^s \geq \underline{M} > 0$ at all times. (For example, perhaps the monetary base is nondecreasing over time, starting from an initial level $M_0^s > 0$.) Suppose further that government debt is nonnegative at all times, so that $D_t \geq M_t^s$. Finally, suppose that $i_t^m = 0$ at all times. Then in the cashless economy previously described, there exists no rational-expectations equilibrium path for the price level $\{P_t\}$.

The proof is in Appendix A. Results of this kind are often taken (see, e.g., Sargent, 1987, sec. 4.1) to imply that it is not possible to model the determinants of the exchange value of money without introducing some kinds of frictions that create a demand for money despite its low rate of return. Hence monetary frictions are thought to be an essential element of any theory of the effects of monetary policy. But we have seen instead that an equilibrium in which money exchanges for goods is possible even in a cashless economy, as long as the rate of interest paid on money is high enough relative to the growth rate of the money supply.

Of course, in actual economies like that of the United States, interest is *not* paid on the monetary base, so that the policy regime in place would seem to be one to which Proposition 2.4 would apply, were the economy cashless. One might then conclude that monetary frictions are essential to understanding inflation determination in such an economy. But in fact, monetary frictions are essential only to understand one aspect of current U.S. policy—the fact that it is possible for the Fed to implement its operating target for the federal funds rate without paying interest on Fed balances. As we shall see, the details of how the Fed is able to implement its interest-rate target are of relatively little importance for the effects of its interest-rate policy on price-level determination; and a cashless model may give a good account of the latter issue.

Even when interest is paid on the monetary base at a sufficient rate to allow a monetary equilibrium to exist, if the interest rate on money is *constant*, the equilibrium price level is indeterminate, as a consequence of Proposition 2.5 in the next section, whether or not the monetary base is kept on a precise deterministic growth path. Determinacy of equilibrium requires a regime under which interest rates respond systematically—in the right way, of course—to variations in the price level. In standard models with monetary frictions, money-growth targeting (with a constant rate of interest on money) is an example of a policy with this property: price-level increases automatically result in increases in short-term nominal interest rates. But in a cashless economy, money-growth targeting has no such consequence for interest rates, and so fails to determine an equilibrium price level. It is actually the presence of a systematic relation between prices and interest rates, of the kind called for by Wicksell, that is essential for determinacy of equilibrium, and not control of the money supply as such.

Proposition 2.3 does not simply establish conditions under which a monetary equilibrium is possible: It gives a precise account of the factors that determine the equilibrium price level under such a regime. Equation (1.37) may equivalently be written

$$\log P_t = \sum_{j=0}^{\infty} \varphi_j E_t \big[\log P_{t+j}^* + \phi_p^{-1}(\hat{r}_{t+j} - v_{t+j}) \big], \tag{1.39}$$

where the weights $\varphi_j \equiv \phi_p (1 + \phi_p)^{-(j+1)}$ are all positive and sum to one. Thus the equilibrium log price level is equal (up to terms of order $\mathcal{O}(\|\xi\|^2)$) to a weighted average of the current and expected future log price level targets, plus a deviation term that is itself a weighted average of current and expected future disturbances to the equilibrium real rate of interest and disturbances to the monetary policy rule other than those represented by variations in the target price level.[17] The determinants of variations in the equilibrium real interest rate are in turn given by (1.33); these depend solely upon exogenous real factors, independent of monetary policy. Note that the associated evolution of the monetary base $\{M_t^s\}$ is *not* among the relevant factors.

The theory of price-level determination obtained under such a regime has, in fact, a distinctly Wicksellian flavor. Equation (1.39) indicates that increases in the equilibrium price level result either from exogenous increases in the equilibrium real rate of return (Wicksell's natural rate of interest)[18] that are not sufficiently offset by an adjustment of the central bank's operating target or from a loosening of monetary policy (corresponding either to an increase in P_t^* or a decrease in v_t) that is not justified by any real disturbance. This emphasis upon the interplay between variations in the equilibrium real rate and the stance of monetary policy (and specifically upon the gap between the current level of the natural rate of interest and the interest rate controlled by the central bank) as the source of inflationary or deflationary pressures recalls Wicksell's (1898, 1915) theory.

Of course, the present rational-expectations equilibrium version of Wicksellian theory differs in important ways from the original. For example, solution (1.39) for the equilibrium price level is *forward looking*, in much the same way as the rational-expectations monetarist analysis presented in Section 3.3. It is not simply the current equilibrium real rate of return that matters, but a weighted average of current and expected future rates, and it is not simply the current stance of monetary policy that matters, but a weighted average of the current and expected future shifts in the central bank's feedback rule. Perhaps more crucially, this theory does not determine an equilibrium price level as a function of the path (even including expectations about the future path) of the central bank's interest-rate instrument. Rather, the price level depends upon the current and expected future *feedback rules* for determination of the interest rate as a function of the

---

17. Note that insofar as the target price level is regarded as being implicit in the central bank's reaction function, rather than an explicit target, the distinction between variations in the target price level and variations in v_t is an arbitrary one; and as should be expected, (1.39) indicates that only the difference $\log P_t^* - (\phi_p^{-1} + 1)v_t$ actually matters in the log-linear approximation, for determination of the equilibrium price level. But for some purposes, it remains useful to distinguish the two components; e.g., one allows $\log P_t^*$ to possess a trend, but assumes that v_t is stationary.

18. In the simple analysis here, there is no distinction between the actual and "natural" *real* rates of interest. This is introduced in Chapter 4, where one finds that it continues to be possible to understand price-level determination along similar lines.

evolution of the price level. (For, as shown earlier, an exogenously specified interest-rate process leaves the price level indeterminate.)

Nonetheless, the implications of this theory for the conduct of monetary policy with a view to price stability are reminiscent of Wicksell's prescriptions. First of all, suppose that the target price level P_t^* is constant,[19] and let $\phi_p > 0$ be fixed; then monetary policy achieves the constant price level $P_t = P^*$ if and only if $v_t = \hat{r}_t$ at all times. Failure of policy to track such variations in the natural rate with sufficient accuracy was, in Wicksell's account, the primary explanation for price-level instability.[20]

Second, the present study implies that for any given degree that the shift factor v_t fails to track the exogenous variation in $\hat{r}_t$, the price-level instability that results can be reduced by a sharper automatic positive response of the central bank's operating target to price-level increases. The effects upon $\log P_t$ of variations in the gap $\hat{r}_t - v_t$ vary inversely with ϕ_p, and in fact they can be made arbitrarily small, in principle, by choosing a large enough ϕ_p.[21] Thus, a positive automatic response to price-level deviations from target is desirable, not only because it is necessary for determinacy (this would be achieved by even a very small $\phi_p > 0$), but because it reduces the degree to which accurate direct observation of the current equilibrium real rate is necessary in order for price-level variability to be kept at a given level. This too is a theme in Wicksell's discussions of desirable policy.

2 Alternative Interest-Rate Rules

While most central banks organize their monetary-policy deliberations around the choice of an operating target for a short-term nominal interest rate and pay a great deal of attention to inflation measures in those deliberations, it would be hard to argue that the Wicksellian rule (1.30)

19. Similar conclusions are reached in the case of a target price level that grows at a constant rate; one must simply add a constant to the value of v_t required each period to achieve the target.

20. See, e.g., Wicksell (1915, sec. IV.9). He found evidence for this in the often-remarked tendency of the price level to covary positively with the level of nominal interest rates during the period of the classical gold standard (the so-called "Gibson paradox"). Note that if $v_t = 0$, (1.39) implies that $\log P_t$ should vary with exogenous variations in the real rate, while (1.34) then implies that the endogenous variations in the short nominal rate should perfectly coincide with these fluctuations in the price level. A similar conclusion is obtained if v_t covaries positively, but less than one-for-one, with the variations in r_t, so that the inflationary and deflationary impulses are not completely eliminated.

21. It is unlikely to be desirable, however, to seek to completely eliminate price-level variation without any need to directly respond to variations in the equilibrium real rate by choosing a rule with an extremely large elasticity ϕ_p. For in this case, errors in the measurement of the price level by the central bank would have very large effects upon policy, and hence upon the economy, as discussed in Bernanke and Woodford (1997).

represents even a rough description of the current behavior of any central banks. (In particular, central banks clearly accept "base drift" in the price level, rather than seeking to stabilize a price index around an exogenously given target path.) Nor do I argue that this is actually an optimal rule, though such a rule can be shown to have desirable properties, relative to other rules of equal simplicity (Giannoni, 2000). It is therefore useful to extend the present analysis to other types of interest-rate rules. While a complete treatment of the topic is beyond the scope of this study, I take up a few additional cases here suggested by the discussion of empirical central-bank reaction functions in Chapter 1.

2.1   Exogenous Interest-Rate Targets

The simplest sort of interest-rate rule, of course, would be one that involves *no* feedback from any endogenous variables. One might instead suppose that the central bank's interest-rate operating target is given by some exogenous stochastic process $\{\bar{\imath}_t\}$. This need not imply that the sole objective of policy is interest-rate stabilization (or maintenance of "easy money"). A central bank concerned with price stability, and believing in the theoretical model of Section 1, might reason that a rational-expectations equilibrium with constant prices is possible only if

$$1 + i_t = 1 + r_t \equiv \beta^{-1} \left\{ E_t \left[\frac{u_c(Y_{t+1}; \xi_{t+1})}{u_c(Y_t; \xi_t)} \right] \right\}^{-1}, \qquad (2.1)$$

as a consequence of (1.21). If it is supposed that it is possible for the central bank to measure the exogenous variation in the right-hand side of this equation in time to use this information in the conduct of policy, would the bank achieve its objective by committing itself to a policy of always adopting the current value of r_t as its operating target? (Such a proposal might appear to be suggested by a Wicksellian analysis of the determinants of inflation, although, as noted in Chapter 1 and in the previous section, this is the not the kind of rule actually proposed by Wicksell.)

While such a policy would be *consistent* with the desired rational-expectations equilibrium, it would also be equally consistent with an extremely large class of alternative rational-expectations equilibria, in most of which prices vary randomly. This is true even if, as before, attention is restricted to alternative equilibria that remain forever *near* the reference equilibrium, that is, the steady state with zero inflation. In fact, this is a consequence of *any* policy commitment that makes the interest-rate operating target purely a function of the economy's exogenous state (i.e., the history of disturbances alone), regardless of how sensibly the exogenous sequence of interest-rate targets may have been chosen.

PROPOSITION 2.5. Let monetary policy be specified by an exogenous sequence of interest-rate targets, assumed to remain forever within a neighborhood of the interest rate $\bar{\imath} > 0$ associated with the zero-inflation steady state; and let these be implemented by setting i_t^m equal to the interest-rate target each period. Let $\{M_t^s, D_t\}$ be exogenous sequences of the kind assumed in Proposition 2.3. Finally, let $\mathcal{P}$ be any neighborhood of the real number zero. Then for any tight enough bounds on the exogenous processes $\{Y_t, \xi_t \, D_t/D_{t-1}\}$ and on the interest-rate target process, there exists an uncountably infinite set of rational-expectations equilibrium paths for the price level, in each of which the inflation rate satisfies $\pi_t \in \mathcal{P}$ for all t. These include equilibria in which the inflation rate is affected to an arbitrary extent by "fundamental" disturbances (unexpected changes in Y_t or ξ_t), by pure "sunspot" states (exogenous randomness unrelated to the "fundamental" variables), or both.

In this case, any process $\{P_t\}$ that satisfies both (1.21) and (1.24), given the exogenous processes $\{Y_t, \xi_t, i_t^m, M_t^s, D_t\}$ and with the exogenous target i_t^m substituted for i_t in (1.21), represents a rational-expectations equilibrium. For any tight enough bounds on the exogenous processes and on the neighborhood $\mathcal{P}$, (1.24) is necessarily satisfied, so the question reduces to an analysis of the local uniqueness of solutions to (1.21) for a given interest-rate process. As in the previous section, this can be addressed through a consideration of the uniqueness of bounded solutions to the log-linearized equilibrium condition (1.32). This now takes the form

$$\bar{\imath}_t = \hat{r}_t + E_t \pi_{t+1}, \tag{2.2}$$

where $\bar{\imath}_t$ indicates the exogenous fluctuations in the interest-rate target and $\hat{r}_t$ the exogenous fluctuations in r_t owing to random fundamentals, again given by (1.33). This equation obviously has a unique solution for $E_t \pi_{t+1}$, and if the exogenous terms are bounded, the implied fluctuations in the expected inflation rate is bounded as well. But this equation does *not* have a unique bounded solution for the stochastic process $\{\pi_t\}$, for absolutely any pattern of bounded fluctuations in the unexpected component of the inflation rate is consistent with it.

Writing this explicitly, one observes that

$$\pi_t = \bar{\imath}_{t-1} - \hat{r}_{t-1} + \nu_t \tag{2.3}$$

is a bounded solution to (2.2), where $\{\nu_t\}$ represents any mean-zero bounded process that is completely unforecastable a period in advance, that is, that satisfies

$$E_t \nu_{t+1} = 0$$

at all dates. It then follows that one similarly has an uncountably infinite set of bounded solutions to the exact equilibrium condition (1.21).[22]

It is important to note that the conclusion obtained here depends on a particular assumption about the character of fiscal policy. If fiscal policy were not assumed to be "locally Ricardian," then there might be a locally, or even globally, unique equilibrium in the case of an exogenous path for the interest-rate operating target. This occurs, for example, in the analysis of price-level determination under a bond-price support regime in Woodford (2001b). See further discussion in Section 4 of Chapter 4.

Here the random variable v_t may be correlated in an arbitrary way with unforecastable variations in "fundamental" variables such as $\bar{\imath}_t$, $\hat{Y}_t$, and ξ_t; but it may also be completely unrelated to economic fundamentals. Thus even when attention is restricted to nearby solutions, the rational-expectations equilibrium price level is quite indeterminate under such a regime. Note further that even though one considers only alternative solutions in which inflation is always within a certain neighborhood of zero, this set of solutions includes alternative paths for the *price level* that wander arbitrarily far from one another, once sufficient time has passed. This is the basis for the conclusion of Sargent and Wallace (1975) that interest-rate rules are flawed as a general approach to monetary policy and that policy should instead be formulated in terms of monetary targets.[23]

One might ask, is this sort of price-level indeterminacy really a *problem?* It will be observed in the discussion here that *real* quantities are unaffected by the indeterminacy of the price level, and the same conclusion is true even in the case of the model with monetary frictions considered in Section 3, and even in a more elaborate model in which output is endogenous and may depend upon the level of real money balances. Thus no variables that actually influence household utility are affected. However, the indeterminacy is plainly undesirable if price stability is a concern, as Sargent and Wallace assume in their analysis of optimal monetary policy. Indeed, since the class of bounded solutions includes solutions in which the unexpected fluctuations in inflation are arbitrarily large, at least *some* of the equilibria consistent with the interest-rate targeting policy are worse (assuming a loss function that penalizes squared deviations of inflation from target, say) than

---

22. This can actually be shown directly in the present case, without any need for linearization of the model, as shown in section A.6 of Appendix A. More generally, however, the existence of an infinite multiplicity of bounded solutions to the linearized equations implies the similar existence of an infinite number of solutions to the exact equilibrium conditions, arbitrarily close to the steady state, in the case of any small enough fluctuations in the disturbance processes, as shown in Woodford (1986).

23. See Walsh (1998, sec. 10.2.1) for an exposition of their analysis in the context of an IS-LM model with rational expectations that is closer to the structure of the model actually used in the original paper.

the equilibrium associated with *any* policy that makes equilibrium determinate. Furthermore, similar conclusions are subsequently shown (in Chapter 4) to hold in the case of a model with nominal price rigidity, in which case the self-fulfilling expectations also affect real variables, which matter for household utility. Thus, if one evaluates policy rules according to how bad is the *worst* outcome that they might allow, it would be appropriate to assign an absolute priority to the selection of a rule that would guarantee determinacy of equilibrium.

This argument might seem inconsistent with my earlier use of a purely *local* analysis of determinacy. One response to such a concern would be to present an exact analysis of the solutions to the equilibrium conditions and show that there are indeed solutions involving arbitrarily large unexpected changes in the log price level, as would be possible in this simple case. But in fact the local analysis also allows one to address this issue, when correctly interpreted. I fix neighborhoods of the steady-state values of π_t, i_t, and so on, that are small enough that the approximation error in the log-linearized relation (1.32) is of an acceptable size for all paths remaining within these neighborhoods and restrict attention to solutions of this kind. The analysis of the log-linearized equations shows that in the case of the exogenous interest-rate target, there exist solutions in which the inflation rate fluctuates over the *entire* admissible neighborhood, *no matter how small* the fluctuations in the exogenous disturbances may be. Now compare such a policy to one that results in a determinate equilibrium (and hence a solution in which π_t and the other endogenous variables are linear functions of the exogenous disturbances, with coefficients that are independent of the assumed shock variances). One then observes that by making the exogenous disturbances small enough, one obtains a case in which the inflation variability in at least certain equilibria associated with interest-rate targeting is much greater than in the locally unique equilibrium associated with the other policy. Thus, at least in the case of small enough exogenous disturbances, the conclusion reached from the analysis of the log-linearized equations is correct.

Whether one should only care about the worst possible equilibrium might be doubted, if a particular policy also allows very desirable equilibria that are better than those associated with any other policies. But in fact, this is unlikely to be a serious problem, once the class of considered policies is sufficiently broad; for it is often possible to achieve any desired equilibrium through a policy rule that makes equilibrium determinate, in addition to its being consistent with rules that would make equilibrium indeterminate. There are typically many policy rules consistent with the desired equilibrium. These coincide in what they prescribe should occur in the desired equilibrium, but differ in how policy is specified "off the equilibrium path," and thus may differ as to whether they exclude other nearby equilibria. In such a case, it seems reasonable to accept as a principle of policy design that one should choose one of the rules that makes the desired equilibrium at least locally determinate, if not globally unique. I take this perspective in the current study; see Chapter 8.

Fortunately, interest-rate rules as such need not imply indeterminacy of equilibrium, as McCallum (1981) first noted in the context of the model of Sargent and Wallace. A rule that involves a commitment to feedback from endogenous state variables such as the price level to the level of nominal interest rates can result in a determinate equilibrium, as the analysis of Wicksellian rules in Section 1 has shown. I now turn to additional examples that are better descriptions of current policies.

2.2   The Taylor Principle and Determinacy

As discussed in Chapter 1, the well-known Taylor rule (Taylor, 1993) differs from Wicksell's classic proposal in that it directs the central bank to respond to deviations of the *inflation rate* from a target level, without any reference to the absolute level that prices may have reached. Such concern with the inflation rate rather than the level of prices would seem to characterize policy in all advanced nations, at least since the breakdown of the Bretton Woods system in the early 1970s. Thus there is greater relevance for contemporary policy discussions in considering a Taylor rule of the form

$$i_t = \phi\big(\Pi_t / \Pi_t^*;\ \nu_t\big) \tag{2.4}$$

for central bank policy, where $\Pi_t \equiv P_t/P_{t-1}$ is the gross inflation rate, Π_t^* is a (possibly time-varying) target rate, ν_t again represents exogenous shifts in this relation, and $\phi(\cdot;\nu)$ is an increasing function for each value of ν. Once again, I suppose that in a cashless economy, the central bank's interest-rate operating target is implemented by setting i_t^m each period equal to the right-hand side of (2.4), so that (2.4) holds in equilibrium as a consequence of (1.15). Once again, $\{M_t^s\}$ is allowed to be an arbitrary process, and fiscal policy is specified by an exogenous process $\{D_t\}$.

Again I consider equilibria near a zero-inflation steady state. With the assumption that $\phi(1; 0) = \beta^{-1} - 1$, such a steady state is an equilibrium in the case that $\Pi_t^* = 1$, $Y_t = \bar{Y} > 0$, and $\nu_t = \xi_t = 0$ at all times. One looks for equilibria in which Π_t and i_t fluctuate within neighborhoods of their steady-state values, assuming that the exogenous variables $\{Y_t, \xi_t, \Pi_t^*, \nu_t\}$ all remain forever within neighborhoods of their steady-state values.

A log-linear approximation to (2.4) is given by

$$\hat{\imath}_t = \phi_\pi \big(\pi_t - \pi_t^*\big) + \nu_t,$$

or equivalently by

$$\hat{\imath}_t = \bar{\imath}_t + \phi_\pi \pi_t, \tag{2.5}$$

where now $\pi_t^* \equiv \log \Pi_t^*$, $\phi_\pi > 0$ is the elasticity of ϕ with respect to its first argument, evaluated at the steady state, and $\bar{\imath}_t \equiv v_t - \phi_\pi \pi_t^*$ measures the total exogenous shift in the central bank's reaction function. Substitution of this into (1.32) yields an expectational difference equation for the inflation rate,

$$\phi_\pi \pi_t = E_t \pi_{t+1} + (\hat{r}_t - \bar{\imath}_t). \tag{2.6}$$

In the case of a rule that conforms to what may be called the Taylor principle —that the central bank should raise its interest-rate instrument *more than one-for-one* with increases in inflation,[24] so that $\phi_\pi > 1$—(2.6) can again be solved forward, yielding a unique bounded solution of the form

$$\pi_t = \sum_{j=0}^{\infty} \phi_\pi^{-(j+1)} E_t \left[\hat{r}_{t+j} - \bar{\imath}_{t+j} \right], \tag{2.7}$$

which leads to the following result.

PROPOSITION 2.6. If monetary policy is characterized by an interest-rate feedback rule of the form (2.4), with $\phi_\pi > 1$, then the rational-expectations equilibrium paths of inflation and the nominal interest rate are (locally) determinate; that is, there exist open sets $\mathcal{P}$ and $\mathcal{I}$ such that in the case of any tight enough bounds on the fluctuations in the exogenous processes $\{\hat{r}_t, \pi_t^*, v_t\}$, there exists a unique rational-expectations equilibrium in which $\pi_t \in \mathcal{P}$ and $i_t \in \mathcal{I}$ at all times. Furthermore, equation (2.7) gives a log-linear (first-order Taylor series) approximation to the evolution of inflation in that equilibrium. If instead $0 \leq \phi_\pi < 1$, rational-expectations equilibrium is indeterminate, as in Proposition 2.5.

Here the proof follows exactly the same lines as our proofs of Propositions 2.3 and 2.5 above.

When the Taylor principle is satisfied, one finds once again that an interest-rate feedback rule can be compatible with a determinate equilibrium price level.[25] One also observes that equilibrium inflation is again

24. The rule described in Taylor (1993) obviously conforms to this principle, as it specifies that $\phi_\pi = 1.5$. Discussions of the general desirability of such a principle include Taylor (1995, 1999c).

25. It should be observed that the price *level*, and not just the inflation rate, is determined in the solution represented by (2.7). This is because the previous period's price level P_{t-1} is given at any date t as a predetermined state variable; unique determination of Π_t then implies a unique equilibrium price level P_t. The "nominal anchor" that allows determination of the absolute price level is thus the dependence of (2.4) on P_{t-1} through its dependence upon Π_t.

determined by interaction between the real determinants of the equilibrium real rate of return, on the one hand, and the nature of the central-bank feedback rule for setting the nominal interest rate, on the other, quite independently of the associated evolution of any monetary aggregate. Moreover, the present theory of inflation determination once again has a Wicksellian flavor: Increases in the equilibrium real rate that are not offset by sufficient tightening of monetary policy result in inflation, as do loosenings of policy (decreases in $\bar{\imath}_t$) that are not warranted by an exogenous decline in the equilibrium real rate. Moreover, once again, it is only current and expected future values of the "gap" variable $\hat{r}_t - \bar{\imath}_t$ that matter for the generation of inflationary or deflationary impulses. Finally, given any stochastic process for the gap variable, the resulting equilibrium inflation variability varies inversely with the response elasticity ϕ_π.

The main qualitative difference between this family of rules and the Wicksellian regimes considered earlier is that transitory fluctuations in the gap variable $\hat{r}_t - \bar{\imath}_t$ now give rise to transitory fluctuations in inflation, which *permanently* shift the absolute level of prices. Thus such a regime almost inevitably results in *price-level drift* (a unit root in the log price level) of the kind that has in fact been observed in all advanced countries in recent decades. This contrasts with the stationarity of the fluctuations in $\hat{P}_t$ under the Wicksellian regime; there, a deterministic trend for P_t^* would suffice to imply trend stationarity of the equilibrium price level.

Note that this last result holds even in the case of very small positive values of ϕ_p, which correspond to policies that stabilize nominal interest rates to an arbitrarily great extent. Thus price-level drift is not a necessary consequence of policies that achieve a great deal of nominal interest-rate smoothing. The result of Goodfriend (1987), according to which a policy that aims to reduce interest-rate variability, among other objectives, results in price-level drift, actually depends upon his specification of the central bank's objectives *other* than interest-rate smoothing. Because the central bank is assumed to care only about the variability of inflation over a short horizon, and not about the size of cumulative changes in the price level, almost any obstacle to complete inflation stabilization (whether due to infeasibility of perfect control or to the presence of a conflicting objective such as Goodfriend's assumed concern with interest-rate variability) results in its choosing a path that sacrifices price-level stability for a less variable inflation.[26]

Another important difference between this family of rules and the Wicksellian rules is that here a positive response of the interest-rate operating target to deviations of inflation from its target level does not suffice for determinacy. If one assumes instead that $\phi_\pi < 1$, (2.6) has an infinity of

26. See, e.g., Van Hoose (1989).

bounded solutions, so that equilibrium inflation in this case is indeterminate, just as in the case of pure interest-rate control.[27]

Interestingly, Taylor (1999c) finds that U.S. monetary policy during the 1960s and 1970s did not conform to the Taylor principle, as discussed in Chapter 1. At least in the case of a flexible-price model of the kind considered in this chapter, a systematic policy of the kind that Taylor estimates for the period 1960–1979 would imply indeterminacy of the equilibrium price level. Clarida et al. (2000) reach a similar conclusion, on the basis of an estimated forward-looking rule, and propose that the indeterminacy of equilibrium explains the instability of U.S. inflation and real activity during the 1970s.[28]

Of course, such an interpretation depends on an assumption that the interest-rate regressions of these authors correctly identify the character of systematic monetary policy during the period. In fact, an estimated reaction function of this kind could easily be misspecified. For example, consider the equilibrium described by (1.39) in the case of a Wicksellian regime and suppose that P_t^* grows deterministically at a constant rate. Since in equilibrium $\hat{\imath}_t$ is equal to ϕ_p times $\hat{P}_t$, $\hat{P}_t$ is a stationary series, and π_t is equal to its first-difference (up to a constant), one can show that the (asymptotic) coefficient of a regression of $\hat{\imath}_t$ on π_t (rather than upon the correct variable, $\hat{P}_t$) equals $\phi_p/2$. This coefficient could easily be much less than one—suggesting violation of the Taylor principle and that the price level should be indeterminate—even though in fact, as $\phi_p > 0$, the price level is determinate. Thus Taylor's interpretation of his finding of positive coefficients much less than one on inflation in estimated Taylor rules for the classical gold standard period (e.g., a coefficient of only 0.02 for the period 1879–1891), as indicating an even more extreme version of

27. This result was first obtained by Leeper (1991) using similar linearization methods to those employed here. Leeper distinguishes between "active" monetary policies (rules of the form (2.5) with $\phi_\pi > 1$) and "passive" policies (rules with $\phi_\pi < 1$). The present results correspond to Leeper's case in which fiscal policy is "passive," though the specification here of fiscal policy in terms of an exogenous path for $\{D_t\}$ does not correspond exactly to any member of his parametric family of fiscal rules. See further discussion in Chapter 4, Section 4. Kerr and King (1996) also contains an early discussion of the connection between the Taylor principle and determinacy of equilibrium.

28. Indeterminacy of the equilibrium inflation rate also implies indeterminacy of equilibrium real activity in the context of a model with sticky prices of the kind discussed in Chapter 4. Lubik and Schorfheide (2002) estimate an equilibrium process for the pre-Volcker period in the United States in which sunspot variables account for part of the volatility of U.S. inflation, consistent with the hypothesis of Clarida et al. Chari et al. (1998) also argue that the instability of the 1970s can be attributed to self-fulfilling expectations; but in their analysis, the multiplicity of equilibria results from an absence of commitment on the part of the Fed, rather than from a commitment to systematic policy of an unfortunate sort.

the kind of unduly passive interest-rate responses seen in the 1960s and 1970s, may well be incorrect.

A less dramatic case of the same problem may bias downward Taylor's estimate of the inflation response coefficient in the period 1960–1979 as well, as Orphanides (2003) argues.[29] Yet the suggestion that the policy mistakes of the period may have been related to a failure to understand the restrictions upon monetary policy required for price-level determinacy is an intriguing one, which suggests that an improved theoretical understanding of this issue could be of considerable practical importance.[30]

2.3   Inertial Responses to Inflation Variation

The simple class of Taylor rules (2.4) allows only the crudest sort of approximation to actual central-bank policies for a number of reasons. One of the more obvious is the allowance for feedback only from the current period's rate of inflation. In practice, monetary policy will never involve feedback from an *instantaneous* rate of inflation (as is sometimes assumed in continuous-time treatments of the problem), because available inflation measures are always time-averaged over a period of at least a month. In fact, Taylor's (1993) account of recent U.S. policy assumes that the operating target for the funds rate is a function of inflation over the previous *year*. It is thus desirable to consider rules involving feedback from the rate of inflation averaged over a time longer than one "period." A case in which the analysis remains quite simple (even if it is not realistic as a literal representation of central-bank procedures) is that in which the central bank responds to an exponential moving average of past inflation rates of the form

$$\bar{\pi}_t \equiv (1 - \delta) \sum_{j=0}^{\infty} \delta^j \pi_{t-j}, \qquad (2.8)$$

---

29. In Orphanides's analysis, systematic overestimation of potential output during the 1970s gave policy an inflationary bias, even though the Fed followed a rule similar to the Taylor rule that describes its later behavior. Regressions using revised estimates of the output gap, rather than the real-time estimates on which policy was actually based, then lead to a downward-biased estimate of the inflation-response coefficient, since the period in which policy was looser due to the omitted variable was a period of higher-than-average inflation.

30. For example, Kiley (2003) shows, in the context of a particular model of staggered price setting, that equilibrium can be indeterminate even in the case of response coefficients of the magnitude estimated by Orphanides in the case of a forward-looking Taylor rule. On the consequences for determinacy of equilibrium of this particular kind of rule, see Section 2.2 of Chapter 4.

for some decay factor $0 < \delta < 1$. This case is simple to analyze because the relevant inflation measure evolves according to a simple partial-adjustment formula

$$\bar{\pi}_t = (1 - \delta)\pi_t + \delta\bar{\pi}_{t-1}.$$

Let the central bank's log-linear feedback rule be given by

$$\hat{\imath}_t = \bar{\imath}_t + \Phi_\pi \bar{\pi}_t, \tag{2.9}$$

instead of (2.5), where $\bar{\pi}_t$ is defined by (2.8). One then obtains the following result.

PROPOSITION 2.7. Let monetary policy be described by a feedback rule of the form (2.9), at least near the zero-inflation steady state, with $\Phi_\pi \geq 0$. Then equilibrium is determinate if and only if $\Phi_\pi > 1$. When this condition is satisfied, a log-linear approximation to the equilibrium evolution of the smoothed inflation process is given by

$$\bar{\pi}_t = (1 - \delta)\sum_{j=0}^{\infty}(\delta + (1 - \delta)\Phi_\pi)^{-(j+1)}E_t[\hat{r}_{t+j} - \bar{\imath}_{t+j}]. \tag{2.10}$$

A corresponding approximation to the equilibrium evolution of the single-period inflation rate π_t is then obtained by substituting (2.10) into

$$\pi_t = \frac{\bar{\pi}_t - \delta\bar{\pi}_{t-1}}{1 - \delta}. \tag{2.11}$$

The proof is given in Appendix A. Note that determinacy is once again obtained if and only if $\Phi_\pi > 1$, as required by the Taylor principle. Furthermore, in the determinate case, the smoothed inflation rate $\bar{\pi}_t$ bears the same qualitative relation as above to expectations regarding the equilibrium real rate and future monetary policy shifts: It rises when the natural rate rises without an offsetting tightening of policy, either currently or anticipated to occur in the future.

Estimated central-bank reaction functions also typically differ from the simple rule (1.30) in that they incorporate some degree of partial-adjustment dynamics for the interest rate itself; that is, the current setting of the operating target for the interest rate inevitably depends positively upon one or more lags of itself, in addition to measures of current economic conditions such as some measure of inflation. As a simple example, one may consider a rule of the form

$$\hat{\imath}_t = \bar{\imath}_t + \rho(\hat{\imath}_{t-1} - \bar{\imath}_{t-1}) + \phi_\pi \pi_t, \qquad (2.12)$$

where again $\phi_\pi \geq 0$, and the coefficient $\rho \geq 0$ measures the degree of intrinsic inertia in the central bank's adjustment of its operating target. Note that when $\rho < 1$, this rule can be represented as a partial-adjustment rule, like those discussed in Chapter 1. However, it is also of interest to consider rules with $\rho = 1$ (i.e., rules in which it is the *change* in the operating target that is a function of current inflation, as assumed in some estimated central-bank reaction functions, e.g., that of Fuhrer and Moore, 1995b), or even "superinertial" rules with $\rho > 1$, like those considered by Rotemberg and Woodford (1999a).

In the case that $\rho < 1$, the feedback rule (2.12) can actually be equivalently expressed in the form (2.9), simply by solving backward to eliminate the dependence upon the lagged interest rate. In this alternative representation, the response coefficient Φ_π in (2.9) corresponds to $\phi_\pi/(1 - \rho)$ in the new notation, and the decay factor δ in (2.8) corresponds to ρ in the new notation. Thus Proposition 2.7 applies, and equilibrium is determinate if and only if $\Phi_\pi > 1$, again in accordance with the Taylor principle. (In a case of this kind, the principle must be understood to require that the *eventual* increase in the nominal interest rate as a result of a *sustained* increase in the inflation rate is more than one-for-one.) Furthermore, once again, an appropriate moving average of inflation is positively related to an average of current and expected future values of the gap between the natural rate of interest and the policy stance measure $\bar{\imath}_t$.

But well-behaved rational-expectations equilibria can also exist in the case of rules with $\rho \geq 1$. In fact, one can show the following.

PROPOSITION 2.8. Let monetary policy be described by a feedback rule of the form (2.12), at least near the zero-inflation steady state, with $\phi_\pi, \rho \geq 0$. Then equilibrium is determinate if and only if $\phi_\pi > 0$ and

$$\phi_\pi + \rho > 1. \qquad (2.13)$$

When these conditions are satisfied, a log-linear approximation to the equilibrium evolution of inflation is given by

$$\pi_t = -\frac{\rho}{\phi_\pi}(\hat{\imath}_{t-1} - \bar{\imath}_{t-1}) + \sum_{j=0}^{\infty}(\phi_\pi + \rho)^{-(j+1)}E_t\big[\hat{r}_{t+j} - \bar{\imath}_{t+j}\big], \qquad (2.14)$$

where the interest rate evolves according to

$$\hat{\imath}_t = \bar{\imath}_t + \sum_{j=0}^{\infty}\phi_\pi(\phi_\pi + \rho)^{-(j+1)}E_t\big[\hat{r}_{t+j} - \bar{\imath}_{t+j}\big]. \qquad (2.15)$$

The proof is again in Appendix A. When $\rho < 1$, this condition is equivalent to the requirement that $\Phi_\pi > 1$, just discussed. But (2.13) applies more generally. In fact, it shows that if $\rho \geq 1$, *any* positive value for ϕ_π suffices for determinacy. Indeed, if $\rho > 1$, the equilibrium inflation rate is determinate even in the case of moderate negative values of ϕ_π, as is discussed further in Appendix A. Determinacy, however, requires that $\phi_\pi \neq 0$, since in the absence of any feedback from inflation, Proposition 2.5 applies.

Equation (2.14) also provides a direct generalization of the earlier solution (2.7) for the equilibrium path of the inflation rate. Again it can be seen that a weighted average of current and expected future gap terms determines the current inflation rate, given the lagged interest rate (which affects current inflation in the same way as an exogenous shift in the current stance of monetary policy). The pair of equations (2.14) and (2.15) can be solved iteratively for the entire paths of inflation and the nominal interest rate, given an initial lagged interest rate and the paths of the exogenous disturbances.

For example, suppose that the equilibrium real rate follows an AR(1) process with autoregressive coefficient $0 < \rho_r < 1$ and consider policies of the form (2.12) with $\bar{\imath}_t = 0$ at all times (the central bank reacts only to inflation, with no target changes and no control errors). Then in the solution described by (2.15), the nominal interest rate is perfectly correlated (positively) with fluctuations in the real rate. But inflation fluctuations are less persistent than the real-rate fluctuations, because the effect of an innovation in the real rate at date t upon $E_t\pi_{t+1}$ is $(\rho_r - \rho)$ times its effect upon π_t, whereas the effect upon $E_t\hat{r}_{t+1}$ is ρ_r times its effect upon $\hat{r}_t$. If $\rho = \rho_r$, the inflation fluctuations become purely transitory, and for larger values of ρ, they actually become antipersistent, that is, the effect a period after the shock is actually of the *opposite* sign to the initial effect. Figure 2.1 plots impulse responses to a 1 percent increase in the equilibrium real rate, assuming $\phi_\pi = 0.7$, $\rho_r = 0.8$, and a variety of values for ρ consistent with (2.13). Panel (a) shows the impulse response of the nominal interest rate for each value of ρ, and panel (b) shows the impulse response of the inflation rate.

This simple example illustrates two desirable features of a more inertial response to inflation variations, relative to the purely contemporaneous specification (2.4). First of all, inertia allows a given degree of reduction of the variance of inflation to be achieved with *less interest-rate variability*. This is an implication of the following result.

PROPOSITION 2.9. Suppose that the equilibrium real rate $\{\hat{r}_t\}$ follows an exogenously given stationary AR(1) process, and let the monetary policy rule be of the form (2.12), with $\rho \geq 0, \phi_\pi > 0$, and a constant intercept consistent with the zero-inflation steady state (i.e., $\bar{\imath}_t = 0$). Consider the choice of a policy rule (ρ, ϕ_π) within this class so as to bring about a certain

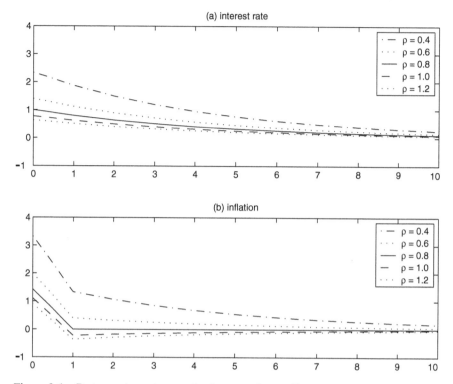

Figure 2.1 *Responses to an increase in the natural rate of interest.*

desired unconditional variance of inflation var(π) > 0 around the mean inflation rate of zero. For any large enough value of ρ, there exists a ϕ_π satisfying (2.13) such that the unconditional variance of inflation in the stationary rational-expectations equilibrium associated with this rule is of the desired magnitude. Furthermore, the larger ρ, the *smaller* the unconditional variance of interest-rate fluctuations var($\hat{\imath}$) in this equilibrium.

The proof is in Appendix A. I argue in Chapter 6 that the reduction of both interest-rate variability and inflation variability are appropriate goals of monetary policy. It follows that inertial rules, even *superinertial* rules (with $\rho > 1$), have an advantage over other members of the class (2.12).

Second, an inertial rule allows a greater degree of stabilization of the *long-run price level*, by making inflation fluctuations less persistent (or even antipersistent, so that increases in the price level are subsequently offset). I argue in Chapter 6 that the variability of the rate of inflation over a short horizon is more directly related to welfare losses that monetary policy should seek to minimize than is instability of the long-run price level. Nonetheless, some have argued that stabilization of the long-run price level is also an appropriate goal of policy, for example, in order to facilitate long-term contracting (see, e.g., Hall and Mankiw, 1994).

One possible measure of long-run price-level instability (proposed in Rotemberg and Woodford, 1999a) is the variance of innovations in the Beveridge-Nelson (1981) price-level trend. Define the long-run price level as

$$\log P_t^\infty \equiv \lim_{j \to \infty} E_t \left[\log P_{t+j} - jE(\pi) \right], \tag{2.16}$$

where $E(\pi)$ is the unconditional expectation of the rate of inflation.[31] The innovation in this variable at date t is then defined as

$$\log P_t^\infty - E_{t-1} \left[\log P_t^\infty \right] = \sum_{j=0}^{\infty} \left[E_t \pi_{t+j} - E_{t-1} \pi_{t+j} \right].$$

In the equilibrium just described, this innovation is equal to $(1 - \rho)(1 - \rho_r)^{-1}(\phi_\pi + \rho - \rho_r)^{-1}$ times the innovation in the equilibrium real rate of return. Thus the variability of such innovations is minimized, and in fact reduced to zero, when $\rho = 1$. In this case, the log price level is actually *trend-stationary*, so that the long-run price level defined in (2.16) is deterministic. For values of ρ near one, the price level still possesses a unit root, but the long-run price level still evolves relatively smoothly.

The fact that a rule with $\rho = 1$ exactly stabilizes the price *level* is less mysterious once one recalls the equivalence between rules of the form (2.12) and rules of the form (2.9). For $0 < \rho < 1$, the rule (2.12) is equivalent to making the interest rate a function of a weighted average of past rates of inflation. As ρ approaches one, the effective weights on past rates of inflation cease to be discounted relative to more recent rates, so that the rule effectively responds to cumulative inflation over the entire past, which is to say, the price level. In the limit, a rule of this kind thus becomes equivalent to a Wicksellian rule of the form (1.30),[32] which as shown earlier stabilizes the price level.

It may be wondered why rules with $\rho \geq 1$ do not lead to *instrument instability*, that is, a nonstationary process for the central bank's operating target. In fact, if an arbitrary stationary stochastic process for inflation is fed into (2.12), a nonstationary interest-rate process is almost inevitably implied. However, in a rational-expectations equilibrium, the only kind of inflation processes that occur are exactly the kind that *do not* cause the interest rate

---

31. This definition assumes that inflation is a stationary variable, i.e., that $\log P_t$ is difference-stationary. Note that all of the equilibria discussed here have this property.

32. Note that when $\rho = 1$, (2.12) is just a first-differenced version of (1.34).

to be nonstationary. Think again about the Wicksellian regime. For most stationary inflation processes, the price *level* has a unit root, so a policy that responds to deviations of the price level from a deterministic path should result in a unit root in the interest rate as well, under the reasoning just suggested. The reason this does not happen is that, in equilibrium, a policy of responding to price level deviations makes the price *level* stationary, and not just the rate of inflation. This explains why $\rho = 1$ does not create a problem, but the logic is exactly the same in the case that $\rho > 1$.

Rules with $\rho > 1$ might seem implausible, because commitment to such a rule implies a commitment to continue raising interest rates to higher and higher levels, at an explosive rate, if inflation is ever even temporarily above its target level, as long as it never subsequently falls *below* the target rate. Of course, in equilibrium, these extreme actions need never be taken, as any temporary increase in inflation is followed by subsequent *undershooting* of the target rate, as shown in Figure 2.1(b). But it might be suspected that they fail to be triggered only because of the anticipation that they would be a "threat" that might properly be considered incredible.[33] In fact, this is not so. Note that in the equilibrium calculated previously, equilibrium inflation fluctuates over a bounded interval, as does the nominal interest rate. Hence only the definition of the policy rule (2.12) for inflation rates and lagged interest rates within those intervals matters for the conclusion that (2.14) describes a locally unique equilibrium. I could change the specification of the rule in the case of more extreme values of the endogenous variables—in particular, change it to specify that interest rates would never be raised above some finite level, as seems more credible—and still obtain exactly the same conclusions as before. Such a change would at most affect the conclusions about the existence of *other* rational-expectations equilibria, which do not remain forever near the steady state, a topic not yet addressed.

A commitment to indefinitely follow a superinertial instrument rule implies a certain restriction upon the expected evolution of inflation that must hold in any bounded rational-expectations equilibrium. In the case of a rule of the form (2.12), the restriction takes the following form.

PROPOSITION 2.10. Consider a policy rule of the form (2.12), where $\rho > 1$ and $\{\bar{\imath}_t\}$ is a bounded process, to be adopted beginning at some date t_0. Then any bounded processes $\{\pi_t, \hat{\imath}_t\}$ that satisfy (2.12) for all $t \geq t_0$ must be such that the predicted path of inflation, looking forward from any date $t \geq t_0$, satisfies

---

33. At a conference, Bob Hall compared policies with $\rho > 1$ to the "Doomsday Machine" in *Doctor Strangelove*.

$$\sum_{j=0}^{\infty} \rho^{-(j+1)} \phi_\pi \, E_t \pi_{t+j} = -(\hat{\imath}_{t-1} - \bar{\imath}_{t-1}). \tag{2.17}$$

Conversely, any bounded processes satisfying (2.17) for all $t \geq t_0$ also satisfy (2.12) for all $t \geq t_0$.

The proof is in Appendix A. Condition (2.17) is a restriction upon the expected future path of inflation that must be satisfied (in any nonexplosive rational-expectations equilibrium) given the commitment to the rule (2.12), which is quite independent of any other assumptions about the conditions required for an equilibrium.

In fact, the policy can alternatively be stated as a commitment to adjust interest rates as necessary in order to ensure that the projected future path of inflation always satisfies the target criterion (2.17). This way of stating the rule is an example of an inflation-forecast *targeting rule* of the kind discussed by Svensson (1997a, 1999a, 2003b), though it differs from the simpler examples he referred to in that the target for the weighted average of future inflation forecasts is time-varying, both in response to variation in the lagged level of the nominal interest rate and owing to the exogenous policy shifts represented by the $E_t \bar{\imath}_{t+j}$ terms. I have just shown that a commitment to the instrument rule (2.12) implies that one must expect the target criterion (2.17) to be satisfied at each date; and conversely, a policy that ensures that the target criterion is satisfied at each date must involve an interest-rate path that satisfies (2.12) at each date.

Thus these two superficially different forms of policy commitment are actually *equivalent*, at least as far as the set of bounded rational-expectations equilibria associated with either of them is concerned; and this equivalence is independent of the details of the structural model of the monetary transmission mechanism that is used to predict the consequences of following either rule. Which way of describing the policy commitment should be preferred depends on which is judged more effective as a way of communicating the policy commitment to the public. In Chapter 8, I show that in the context of at least some plausible models of the monetary transmission mechanism, an optimal policy rule can be represented as a more complicated version of a rule of this kind. There I discuss the representation of optimal policy in terms of both a superinertial instrument rule and a forecast-targeting rule.

3 Price-Level Determination with Monetary Frictions

I now take up the question of how the equilibrium prices of goods in terms of money are determined in an economy where the monetary liabilities of the central bank *do* facilitate transactions, contrary to the simplifying assumption in the previous two sections. In all actually existing economies, one observes that positive quantities of base money are held by private parties despite the fact that this asset yields a lower return than other very short-term riskless assets. This indicates that there must be advantages to holding money not allowed for in the previous model. My earlier analysis is only useful in understanding actual economies; then, if I can show that even when such transactions services of money are allowed for, the conclusions about price-level determination are fairly similar to those obtained when abstracting from this complication. Introducing transactions frictions also allows comparison of this neo-Wicksellian theory of inflation determination with the implications of a traditional quantity-theoretic analysis.

3.1 A Model with Transactions Frictions

I now extend the above analysis to allow for transactions frictions that can be ameliorated through the use of central-bank monetary liabilities. For simplicity, I employ a model that has been used extensively in rational-expectations monetarist analyses: the representative-household model of Sidrauski (1967) and Brock (1974, 1975).[34] In this approach, the transactions frictions are not explicitly modeled; instead, the *transactions services* supplied by real money balances are directly represented as an argument of household utility functions.[35]

I again assume a representative-household economy, but now with a household objective of the form

$$E_0 \left\{ \sum_{t=0}^{\infty} \beta^t u(C_t, M_t/P_t; \xi_t) \right\}, \tag{3.1}$$

where M_t again measures the household's end-of-period money balances, and P_t is the price of the single good in terms of money in period t. The function u is now an indirect utility function, incorporating the costs of transacting with a given level of money balances; hence the vector of exogenous disturbances ξ_t may now include random variation in the transactions technology, as well as actual preference shocks.[36] For any given realization

---

34. For other recent expositions of the model, see, e.g., Obstfeld and Rogoff (1996, sec. 8.3) and Walsh (1998, sec. 2.3).

35. In the alternative analysis presented in section A.16 of Appendix A, the transactions frictions are more represented by a cash-in-advance constraint. On the similarity between models with transactions frictions of that sort and models with money in the utility function, see also Feenstra (1986), Lucas and Stokey (1987), and Woodford (1994b, 1998).

36. It is important to note that I do not assume that ξ_t is a scalar process; e.g., ξ_t might contain two components, one of which represents variation in impatience and the other

of ξ_t, I assume that the period utility function $u(c, m; \xi_t)$ satisfies standard neoclassical assumptions: It is concave and strictly increasing in each of the arguments (c, m).[37] I also suppose that u implies that both consumption and real balances are (strict) *normal goods;* that is, I assume that income-expansion paths are upward sloping in the case of any finite positive relative price for the two "goods."

The household's budget constraints remain of the form assumed in Section 1. Note that I allowed there for a possible return differential between money and other riskless nominal claims, even though it turned out that no such differential exists in equilibrium (in the cashless economy). Hence the household's problem is to choose processes $\{C_t, M_t\}$ satisfying (1.12) given its initial wealth W_0, so as to maximize (3.1). Necessary and sufficient conditions for this problem are derived along the same lines as before.

Once again, (1.10) and (1.11) must hold at all times, since otherwise no optimal plan exists. The first-order conditions for optimal choice of the household's money balances now require that $M_t \geq 0$ and

$$\frac{u_m(C_t, M_t/P_t; \xi_t)}{u_c(C_t, M_t/P_t; \xi_t)} \leq \Delta_t$$

at each date, with at least one condition holding with equality at each date; thus at any date at which $M_t > 0$, one must have

$$\frac{u_m(C_t, M_t/P_t; \xi_t)}{u_c(C_t, M_t/P_t; \xi_t)} = \Delta_t. \tag{3.2}$$

(Note that this condition generalizes (1.15) to the case in which utility is increasing in real balances.) Conditions (1.16) and (1.17) as well as the exhaustion of the intertemporal budget constraint are again necessary as before, with only the change that now the marginal utility of consumption must be written $u_c(C_t, m_t; \xi_t)$. Moreover, once again this set of conditions can be shown to be both necessary and sufficient for optimality of the household's plan.

---

variation in the liquidity services provided by money balances. The use of the single symbol ξ_t to represent both shocks does not imply anything about their assumed correlation; the two components of the vector might, e.g., be distributed independently of one another.

37. The existence of a finite level of money balances at which there is satiation in money, which level is typically increasing in the level of consumption, creates only minor technical complications. And indeed, many explicit models of transactions frictions, such as cash-in-advance models, imply that such a satiation level should exist. But whether there is satiation does not matter, for present purposes, except for the question of whether it is possible to reduce nominal interest rates all the way to zero. I suppose in general that there is no wish to do so, though the reason for this (distortions associated with deflation) will only be introduced after I extend the model to include nominal rigidities.

Substituting the relations implied by market clearing into the conditions for household optimization and assuming a policy regime under which $M_t^s > 0$ at all times, I again obtain equilibrium conditions (1.20), (1.21), and (1.22) for each date, together with the conditions

$$\frac{u_m(Y_t, M_t^s/P_t; \xi_t)}{u_c(Y_t, M_t^s/P_t; \xi_t)} = \Delta_t \qquad (3.3)$$

and

$$\sum_{T=t}^{\infty} \beta^T E_t \left[u_c(Y_T, M_T^s/P_T; \xi_T) Y_T + u_m(Y_T, M_T^s/P_T; \xi_T) M_T^s/P_T \right] < \infty, \qquad (3.4)$$

generalizing (1.15) and (1.23), respectively. These relations, together with a specification of the policy regime, provide a complete description of a rational-expectations equilibrium.

Note that under the assumption that both consumption and real balances are normal goods, u_m/u_c is increasing in consumption and decreasing in real balances. It follows that I can solve (3.3) for equilibrium real balances,[38] obtaining a relation of the form

$$M_t^s/P_t = L(Y_t, \Delta_t; \xi_t). \qquad (3.5)$$

Here the *liquidity preference* function L is increasing in Y_t and decreasing in Δ_t for any value of the disturbance vector ξ_t. Note that equation (3.5) corresponds to the LM equation of the Keynesian system, or to the money-market equilibrium condition of a monetarist model. (In the case that $i_t^m = 0$, as in standard treatments, one can alternatively write the liquidity preference function in terms of Y_t and i_t.) From a quantity-theoretic point of view, it is this equilibrium condition that is regarded as determining the price level at each point in time, given the money supply M_t^s at that date.

Finally, I can show once again that condition (1.22) may equivalently be written in the form (1.24),[39] and thus obtain the following generalization of my previous definition.

---

38. Technically, monotonicity of u_m/u_c is not quite enough: It implies that there is a well-defined level of equilibrium real money balances for Δ_t in some interval (that may depend on Y_t and ξ_t), but it does not exclude the possibility that no solution exists for interest rates that are either too high or too low. I simplify the analysis, when necessary, by assuming boundary conditions on preferences that imply a solution for any $\Delta_t > 0$; specifically, I suppose that u_m becomes unboundedly large as real balances are made small, and arbitrarily small as real balances are made large enough, which may or may not involve satiation at a finite level of real balances. Note that the primary concern here is with stationary fluctuations around an equilibrium steady state, and for these purposes such boundary conditions are irrelevant.

39. In the presence of monetary frictions, Proposition 2.2 must be restated as Proposition 2.2′, which is stated and proved in section A.2 of Appendix A.

DEFINITION. A *rational-expectations equilibrium* of the Sidrauski-Brock model is a pair of processes $\{P_t, i_t\}$ that satisfy (1.21), (1.24),[40] (3.4), and (3.5) at all dates $t \geq 0$, given the exogenous processes $\{Y_t, \xi_t\}$ and evolution of the variables $\{i_t^m, M_t^s, D_t\}$ consistent with the monetary-fiscal policy regime.

3.2 Interest-Rate Rules Reconsidered

I now turn to the specification of the monetary-fiscal policy regime. In an economy with monetary frictions, it is no longer necessary for equilibrium that either $i_t = i_t^m$ or $M_t^s = 0$; this increases the range of possible ways in which monetary policy may be specified. The central bank may freely choose (within certain bounds) any two of the variables i_t, i_t^m, and M_t^s, leaving the third to be endogenously determined by the LM relation (3.5). In particular, it might choose a target for the monetary base M_t^s while maintaining a fixed rate (zero) for i_t^m and let market nominal interest rates be endogenously determined, as in many textbook analyses; but it might also choose a short-run operating target for i_t while maintaining a fixed rate (zero) for i_t^m, and let the monetary base be endogenously determined, as under current Fed procedures. The central bank's choice of an interest rate to pay on central-bank balances no longer implies a particular operating target for short-term market interest rates, and it is now important to distinguish between these two aspects of the monetary policy regime.

In one case, however, the details of the way in which the central bank chooses to implement its interest-rate operating targets is irrelevant for price-level determination. This is the case, often assumed for pedagogical purposes, in which $u(C, m; \xi)$ is additively separable between the arguments C and m for each possible vector of disturbances ξ.[41] In this familiar case, the marginal utility of consumption is independent of real money balances, just as in the cashless economy, even though now $u_m > 0$ in the case of a low enough level of real balances.

Let monetary policy be specified by an interest-rate rule, such as the Wicksellian rule (1.30), together with an additional equation that specifies either the supply of base money M_t^s or the interest paid on base money i_t^m. If the additional equation specifies the supply of base money, then the interest-rate target is implemented by adjusting i_t^m as necessary in order for the target interest rate i_t to satisfy (3.5), given the supply of base money. (This generalizes the method of policy implementation assumed above for the cashless economy, where (1.15) played the role of equilibrium

---

40. In writing (1.21) and (1.24) for this model, one must express the marginal utility of consumption as $u_c(Y_t, M_t^s/P_t; \xi_t)$.

41. See, e.g., the presentation of the model by Obstfeld and Rogoff (1996, sec. 8.3) or Walsh (1998, sec. 2.3).

condition (3.5).) If instead the additional equation specifies the interest paid on money (perhaps specifying $i_t^m = 0$ at all times), then the interest-rate target is implemented by adjusting M_t^s so as to satisfy (3.5). (This is a stylized representation of the current method of policy implementation in countries like the United States.) I suppose once again that fiscal policy is specified by an exogenous process $\{D_t\}$.

I have already shown that in the cashless case, conditions (1.21) and (1.30) alone suffice to determine locally unique rational-expectations equilibrium paths for the variables $\{P_t, i_t\}$, as long as $\phi_p > 0$. The same argument continues to apply here, given that the marginal utility of consumption in (1.21) is once again a function only of the exogenous states (Y_t, ξ_t). Corresponding to these paths are locally unique paths for $\{M_t^s, i_t^m\}$, obtained by solving (3.5) together with the additional equation that specifies one or the other of these variables each period. Thus the conditions under which the interest-rate rule implies a determinate rational-expectations equilibrium are exactly the same as in a cashless economy, and (1.37) and (1.38) continue to provide a log-linear approximation to the equilibrium evolution of prices and interest rates in response to small enough exogenous disturbances.

The same is true if the interest-rate rule is of a form such as (2.4), (2.9), or (2.12) rather than (1.30). The neo-Wicksellian account of price-level determination developed above continues to apply even in the presence of transactions frictions that allow for a nonnegligible interest differential Δ_t in equilibrium. In the present model with transactions frictions, the money-demand or LM relation (3.5) is a requirement for equilibrium, yet it plays no role in determining the equilibrium evolution of prices under a given interest-rate rule. This relation is relevant only to the question of how the central bank must adjust the instruments under its direct control (M_t^s and i_t^m) so as to *implement* its interest-rate operating targets.

3.3   A Comparison with Money-Growth Targeting

The money-demand relation is, of course, a crucial element in the theory of price-level determination in the case of a money-growth rule, that is, a monetary policy specified in terms of exogenous paths for the monetary base $\{M_t^s\}$ and the interest rate paid on money $\{i_t^m\}$, with the interest rate $\{i_t\}$ left to be determined by the market. I consider the case in which M_t^s/M_{t-1}^s and i_t^m remain forever within bounded intervals containing the steady-state values 1 and $0 \leq \bar{\imath}^m < \beta^{-1} - 1$, respectively, and look for rational-expectations equilibria in which $m_t \equiv M_t^s/P_t$ and i_t remain forever near the constant values

$$\bar{m} \equiv L(\bar{Y}, \bar{\Delta}; 0),$$

$$\bar{\imath} = \beta^{-1} - 1 > 0$$

associated with a zero-inflation steady state. (Here $\bar{\Delta} \equiv 1 - \beta(1 + \bar{\imath}^m) > 0$ is the steady-state interest differential.)

Log-linearizing (3.5) around this steady state yields a relation of the form

$$\hat{m}_t = \eta_y \hat{Y}_t - \eta_i \left(\hat{\imath}_t - \hat{\imath}_t^m \right) + \epsilon_t^m, \tag{3.6}$$

where

$$\hat{m}_t \equiv \log \left(\frac{m_t}{\bar{m}} \right), \qquad \hat{\imath}_t^m \equiv \log \left(\frac{1 + i_t^m}{1 + \bar{\imath}^m} \right).$$

Here the constant coefficients are

$$\eta_y \equiv \frac{\bar{Y}}{\bar{m}} \frac{\partial L}{\partial y} > 0, \qquad \eta_i \equiv -\frac{1 - \bar{\Delta}}{\bar{m}} \frac{\partial L}{\partial \Delta} > 0,$$

with the partial derivatives evaluated at the steady-state values of the arguments of L, and the exogenous disturbance term is

$$\epsilon_t^m \equiv \frac{1}{\bar{m}} \frac{\partial L}{\partial \xi} \xi_t.$$

(The signs asserted above for these coefficients follow from the assumptions regarding preferences stated earlier.) Note that η_y and η_i measure the income elasticity and interest semielasticity of money demand, respectively; numerical values for these coefficients and for the statistical properties of the disturbance term can thus be obtained from standard econometric studies of money demand.

One can then study the local determinacy of equilibrium under such a policy by considering the bounded processes $\{\hat{m}_t, \hat{\imath}_t\}$ that satisfy the log-linear equilibrium relations (1.32) and (3.6) at all times. I obtain the following result.

PROPOSITION 2.11. In the context of a Sidrauski-Brock model with additively separable preferences, consider the consequences of a monetary policy specified in terms of exogenous paths $\{M_t^s, i_t^m\}$, together with a fiscal policy specified by an exogenous path $\{D_t\}$. Under such a regime, the rational-expectations equilibrium paths of prices and interest rates are (locally) determinate; that is, there exist open sets $\mathcal{P}$ and $\mathcal{I}$ such that in the case of any tight enough bounds on the fluctuations in the exogenous processes $\{Y_t, \xi_t, M_t^s/M_{t-1}^s, i_t^m, D_t/D_{t-1}\}$, there exists a unique rational-expectations equilibrium in which $P_t/M_t^s \in \mathcal{P}$ and $i_t \in \mathcal{I}$ at all times. Furthermore, a log-linear approximation to the equilibrium path of the price level, accurate up to a residual of order $\mathcal{O}(\|\xi\|^2)$, takes the form

$$\log P_t = \sum_{j=0}^{\infty} \varphi_j E_t\big[\log M_{t+j}^s - \eta_i \log\left(1 + i_t^m\right) - u_{t+j}\big] - \log \bar{m}, \quad (3.7)$$

where the weights

$$\varphi_j \equiv \frac{\eta_i^j}{(1 + \eta_i)^{j+1}} > 0$$

sum to one, and u_t is a composite exogenous disturbance

$$u_t \equiv \eta_y \hat{Y}_t - \eta_i \hat{r}_t + \epsilon_t^m - \eta_i \log(1 + \bar{i}^m).$$

The proof is given in Appendix A.

I thus obtain a well-defined rational-expectations equilibrium price level under such a policy for arbitrary bounded fluctuations in the rate of money growth. This is the determinacy result that Sargent and Wallace (1975) stress in their argument for the money supply as the "optimal instrument of monetary policy." However, we have seen that policy rules need not take this form in order to imply a determinate equilibrium path for the price level; interest-rate rules such as those advocated by Wicksell and Taylor also have this property.

Equation (3.7) also provides a simple theory of price-level determination. In the case that one abstracts from disturbances other than the fluctuations in the rate of money growth, it states that the log price level at any point in time is (up to a constant) just a weighted average of current and expected future logs of the money supply.[42] This appealingly simple result may suggest that even in the analysis of other types of possible policy regimes, what matters about any regime is the path of the money supply that it implies.[43]

42. This result is most often presented as the implications of a rational-expectations version of the Cagan model of inflation determination. (See McCallum, 1989, chap. 8, or Obstfeld and Rogoff, 1996, sec. 8.2.1, for standard expositions.) In Cagan's (1956) model, desired log real money balances are a decreasing linear function of the expected rate of growth of the log price level. A (discrete-time) relation of exactly this kind is obtained by substituting (1.32) into (3.6) to eliminate i_t, except that in the present case there is also a time-varying intercept for this relation, equal to $\log \bar{m} + u_t + \eta_i \log(1 + i_t^m)$.

43. The determinacy result in Proposition 2.11 applies only to policies that make the money supply an exogenously specified process, and not to general feedback rules for determination of the money supply. The derivation of equation (3.7) as an implication of the requirements for rational-expectations equilibrium also goes through more generally, assuming that the infinite sum on the right-hand side is well defined. But in the case of feedback from endogenous variables (such as the price level) to the money supply, the expressions on the right-hand sides of equations such as (3.7) need not be uniquely defined. That is, there may be a large number of equilibria, in each of which (3.7) is valid, but in each of which the expression on

It might then seem natural that alternative strategies for policy should be considered in terms of how one wishes to have the money supply evolve. But as we have seen, a straightforward analysis of the consequences for inflation of alternative policy rules is equally possible without any reference to either the evolution of the money supply or the determinants of money demand.

In fact, the previous conclusions about the consequences of alternative interest-rate rules can be viewed as more basic, for Proposition 2.11 is actually a *consequence* of my earlier analysis of Wicksellian rules.[44] For solving the money-demand relation (3.5) for the equilibrium nominal interest rate, we obtain an equation of the form

$$i_t = \iota\left(P_t/M_t^s;\ i_t^m,\ Y_t,\ \xi_t\right), \tag{3.8}$$

where ι is an increasing function of its first argument, for any values of i_t^m, Y_t, ξ_t. This is just Keynes's (1936) "liquidity preference theory" of the interest rate. If i_t is graphed as a function of Y_t, suppressing the other arguments, this is the Hicksian LM curve. When Y_t is exogenous and prices are flexible, as here, it is more useful to think of this as an equilibrium relation between i_t and P_t, as in some presentations of a "flexible-price IS-LM" model.

This equilibrium relation between interest rates and prices, established through the central bank's control of its instruments M_t^s and i_t^m, is just an example of an interest-rate feedback rule of the form (1.30), in which $P_t^* = M_t^s/\bar{m}$, $v_t = (i_t^m, Y_t, \xi_t)$,[45] and

$$\phi(p;\ v) = \iota(p/\bar{m};\ v).$$

It then follows that in the log-linear approximation (1.34), $\phi_p = \eta_i^{-1} > 0$ and

$$v_t = \hat{\imath}_t^m + \eta_i^{-1}\left(\eta_y \hat{Y}_t + \epsilon_t^m\right).$$

---

the right-hand side takes a different value, as a result of different evolution of the endogenous determinants of the money supply.

44. See Taylor (1999c) for motivation of the Taylor rule in terms similar to these. Taylor's discussion, however, elides the distinction between rules such as (1.30), which respond to deviations of the price *level* from a target path, and rules such as (2.4), which respond to deviations of the *inflation rate* from its target.

45. Here I extend the previous notation in (1.30) by allowing a vector v_t of exogenous variables to affect the function ϕ.

As this is a policy rule under which $\phi_p > 0$, Proposition 2.3 applies, and making the above substitutions for ϕ_p, P_t^*, and ν_t, one finds that (3.7) is just the price-level path predicted by the previous result (1.39) for a general rule of the Wicksellian type.

The prior formulation is the more general one, since it applies to Wicksellian rules in which the elasticity of interest-rate response to price-level deviations need not equal exactly η_i^{-1}. Furthermore, it is clear even from (3.7)—which follows from a traditional quantity-theoretic analysis, as shown in Appendix A—that the path of the money supply *as such* is not important for price-level determination. What matters is the way in which the central bank chooses to adjust the composite variable $\log M_t^s - \eta_i \log(1 + i_t^m)$. It does not matter to what extent this is achieved by varying the money supply as opposed to the interest rate paid on base money (except, of course, that if there is to be trend growth in this variable it must occur through trend growth in the money supply, owing to the impossibility of reducing i_t^m below zero). The reason for this is simple: It is the shift in this composite variable that indicates the extent to which the central bank's actions shift the equilibrium relation (3.8) between interest rates and prices.

Of course, one could also develop a theory of price-level determination under money-supply feedback rules in which the path of the monetary base is not specified exogenously, but is instead a specified function of the price level. Wicksellian rules (1.30) could then be equivalently described as rules of the form

$$M_t^s = M^s(P_t; P_t^*, i_t^m, Y_t, \xi_t, \nu_t), \tag{3.9}$$

where the function M^s is obtained by substituting (1.30) for i_t in (3.5), and solving for M_t^s as a function of the other variables. But subsuming the present theory of price-level determination under interest-rate rules under such a theory of endogenous-money rules is not obviously desirable. First of all, the theory of price-level determination under interest-rate rules expounded above continues to apply in a cashless economy (the form in which I first expounded it), whereas a theory of endogenous-money rules of the form (3.9) would not be possible in that case.

Even when a well-defined money-demand relation (3.5) exists, it is not obvious that (1.30) and (3.9) are equally useful ways of specifying monetary policy in order to achieve the equilibrium described by (1.39). For (1.30) suffices to specify the aspects of policy that matter for the central bank's stabilization objective (here assumed to be control of the price level), whereas (3.9) does not—the latter rule must be supplemented by a policy rule for the control of i_t^m in order for the price level to be determined. (Of course, in traditional accounts, it is taken for granted that $i_t^m = 0$.) Moreover, even granting a specific, known policy with regard to interest payments on money,

(1.30) may be a more useful policy prescription. This is because implementation of (3.9) requires that the central bank take account of the current value of the disturbance ϵ_t^m to the money-demand equation in setting its money-supply instrument, whereas knowledge of this state is irrelevant for purposes of implementation of the interest-rate rule (1.30).

Since, in practice, the central bank is not able to estimate this random disturbance with perfect precision, adoption of a monetary-base target necessarily results in interest-rate variations in response to money-demand disturbances that could be avoided through the use of an interest-rate instrument. Interest-rate variations in response to these shocks are not desirable, from the point of view of price-level stabilization, unless they are positively correlated with exogenous variations in the equilibrium real rate of interest. As the primary source of money-demand variation is probably developments in the payments system that have important effects upon money demand without being of particular consequence for equilibrium real rates of return, this seems an implausible line of argument.

The point that money-demand disturbances make an interest-rate operating target more desirable than a money-supply target is of course a central argument in the celebrated analysis of Poole (1970). Poole also argues that if, instead, IS shocks are a more important source of instability than LM shocks, monetary control is superior to interest-rate control. This might make it seem uncertain which concern, in practice, ought to dominate. But let us recall the nature of the argument for a monetary instrument in the case of IS shocks. It is desirable on stabilization grounds that interest rates rise in response to demand stimulus (in Wicksellian terms, because these disturbances raise the natural rate of interest), but it is assumed that with interest-rate control, interest rates will not rise. Instead, with control of the money supply, such disturbances raise output (or in the present flexible-price model, the price level), and as a result increase money demand, leading to an automatic interest-rate increase, which aids stabilization. But this argument requires not only that the central bank is unable to respond directly to the disturbance, but that it *cannot condition its interest-rate instrument upon output or the price level* except indirectly by letting interest rates be affected by an increase in money demand. If one assumes instead that the central bank *can* make its instrument a function of current prices and output directly, even though it cannot make it a direct function of exogenous disturbances, then the interest-rate instrument is unambiguously superior.

3.4 Consequences of Nonseparable Utility

The strong irrelevance result obtained in Section 3.2—according to which an interest-rate rule such as (1.30) or (2.4) suffices to determine the equilibrium path of prices quite independently of how the central bank implements its interest-rate operating targets through adjustment of the monetary base and/or the interest rate paid on money—depends, of course, on the special assumption of an additively separable (indirect) utility function $u(C, m; \xi)$. This assumption is not very realistic, despite its frequent appearance in textbook treatments. If real balances supply a nonpecuniary yield owing to their usefulness in conducting transactions, it makes sense that the marginal benefit of additional real balances should depend on the volume of purchases that the household makes.[46] (The most plausible assumption, on intuitive grounds, would probably be that $u_{cm} > 0$, so that consumption expenditure and real balances are complements.)

Yet one can justify the neglect of real-balance effects on the marginal utility of income in equations such as (1.21) without assuming either additive separability or a genuinely cashless economy (with the counterfactual implication that money must earn the same rate of return as other riskless assets). In what Woodford (1998) calls a "cashless limiting economy," the marginal utility of additional real balances becomes quite large as household real balances fall to zero (assuming real purchases of a magnitude near $\bar{Y}$), so that it is possible in equilibrium to have a nontrivial interest-rate differential Δ_t. Yet, at the same time, the transactions that use money are sufficiently unimportant that variations in the level of real balances sufficient to require a substantial change in the interest-rate differential have only a negligible effect on the marginal utility of real income (or of consumption).

The idea is that in such an economy money is used for transactions of only a very few kinds, though it is essential for those. As a result, positive real balances are demanded even in the case of a substantial interest-rate differential (and hence, a substantial opportunity cost of holding money); but equilibrium real balances are very small relative to national income. Equation (3.3) requires that in such an equilibrium, an increase in real balances *equal in value to a substantial share of aggregate expenditure* would have to increase utility by as much as a substantial percentage increase in consumption; but if equilibrium real balances are tiny in value relative to national income, a substantial *percentage increase* in real balances may still have a negligible effect on utility. As this effect may continue to be negligible for different levels of consumption, the effect on the marginal utility of consumption of a substantial percentage change in real balances may also be negligible. This then justifies neglecting real-balance effects in equations such as (1.21).

---

46. As discussed in Section A.16 of Appendix A, one also has $\chi \neq 0$ even in the case of additively separable preferences, in the case that one uses an alternative timing convention that often appears in the literature. However, it is shown there that even under the alternative timing convention, the "separable" case analyzed previously remains a theoretical possibility; it is simply that the kind of separability required in order for χ to equal zero is of a different sort.

Formally, the elasticity of u_m, the marginal utility of additional real money balances, with respect to changes in the level of real expenditure is equal to

$$v \equiv \bar{Y} u_{mc} / u_m,$$

a quantity that I have argued should plausibly have a nontrivial positive value. But what matters for the extent to which variations in the level of real balances affect the Fisher relation (1.21) is the elasticity of u_c, the marginal utility of additional expenditure, with respect to changes in the level of real balances, or

$$\chi \equiv \bar{m} u_{cm} / u_c. \tag{3.10}$$

Note that $\chi = s_m v$, where

$$s_m \equiv \bar{m} u_m / \bar{Y} u_c = \bar{\Delta}(\bar{m}/\bar{Y})$$

is the flow rate of effective expenditure by households on liquidity services (measured by the interest foregone on the money balances that they hold) expressed as a proportion of national income. It follows that χ and v must have the same sign. But in a "cashless limiting economy," s_m is infinitesimally small (even though $\bar{\Delta}$ is not), as a result of which χ is infinitesimally small (even though v is not).[47] Because χ is negligible, a log-linear approximation to (1.21) again takes the simple form (1.32); yet this is not equivalent to assuming additive separability, for one need not assume that v is negligible. (The latter quantity matters for the predictions of one's analysis regarding the percentage fluctuations in the money supply that should occur in equilibrium under a particular approach to implementation of the interest-rate rule.)[48]

Thus the case of a cashless limiting economy is another in which one may legitimately abstract from any effects of variations in real balances on

47. Woodford (1998) displays a parametric family of transactions technologies in which this limiting case is approached as a certain parameter α, measuring the fraction of goods that are purchased using cash, is made arbitrarily small. The paper shows that the equilibrium solution for the state-contingent evolution of prices is continuous in the parameter α, so that the conclusions reached under the assumption that $\chi = 0$, as in a cashless model, provide an accurate approximation to the equilibrium dynamics in the case of any economy with a small enough value of α. At the same time, the interest-rate differential remains bounded away from zero as α is made small; hence the equilibrium of the cashless limiting economy is in this respect different from that of a genuinely cashless economy of the kind presented in Section 1.

48. The assumption of a cashless limiting economy leaves one free to assume elasticities η_y, η_i in the money-demand relation (3.6) in accordance with empirical estimates, whereas the assumption of additive separability would imply a restriction upon these elasticities that is not in accordance with typical estimates, as discussed later.

the equilibrium conditions that determine the evolution of prices under an interest-rate rule. How accurately this limiting case approximates the situation of an actual economy in which central-bank money still provides some valuable services remains, of course, a question for quantitative analysis. I turn, then, to the question of the extent to which the previous results must be modified if I allow for a nonnegligible value of the elasticity χ defined in (3.10).

In the general case of the Sidrauski-Brock model, a log-linear approximation to (1.21) takes the form

$$\hat{\imath}_t = \hat{r}_t + E_t \pi_{t+1} - \chi E_t(\hat{m}_{t+1} - \hat{m}_t), \tag{3.11}$$

where $\hat{r}_t$ continues to be defined by (1.33). (Note, however, that $\hat{r}_t$ no longer has the interpretation of being the equilibrium real rate of return; the latter quantity is no longer completely exogenous.) Substituting (3.6) for the equilibrium level of real balances in this equation, one obtains a relation of the form

$$(1 + \eta_i \chi)\hat{\imath}_t = \tilde{r}_t + E_t \pi_{t+1} + \eta_i \chi E_t \hat{\imath}_{t+1} - \eta_i \chi E_t \left(\hat{\imath}^m_{t+1} - \hat{\imath}^m_t\right), \tag{3.12}$$

where the composite exogenous disturbance in this relation is given by

$$\tilde{r}_t \equiv \hat{r}_t - \eta_y \chi E_t\left(\hat{Y}_{t+1} - \hat{Y}_t\right) - \chi E_t\left(\epsilon^m_{t+1} - \epsilon^m_t\right).$$

Then if one specifies the policy rule in a way that allows both i_t and i^m_t to be determined as functions of the path of prices, equation (3.12) alone, together with the policy rule, suffices to determine the equilibrium paths of interest rates and prices, just as in the analyses in Sections 1 and 2.

For example, consider a policy regime under which the central bank seeks to maintain a constant interest-rate differential $\bar{\Delta}$ between overnight market rates and the interest paid on the monetary base (as is true of the channel systems described in Chapter 1, at least in the case of the interest paid on central-bank balances). In such a case, monetary policy may be specified by an interest-rate rule, such as the Wicksellian rule (1.30), together with the equation

$$\Delta_t = \bar{\Delta} > 0, \tag{3.13}$$

indicating the way in which the interest paid on money varies with the changes in the interest-rate target required by the Wicksellian rule. (I assume that $\bar{\Delta} > 0$ because of the observed preference of central banks with channel systems for maintaining a small positive spread.) Fiscal policy can again be specified by an exogenous sequence $\{D_t\}$.

In order to analyze local equilibrium determination under such a regime, it suffices that one consider the log-linear relations (1.34) and (3.12), together with the equation

$$\hat{\imath}_t = \hat{\imath}_t^m, \tag{3.14}$$

representing the log-linearization of (3.13). Using (3.14) to eliminate $\hat{\imath}_t^m$ from (3.12), one obtains a relation of the form

$$\hat{\imath}_t = \tilde{r}_t + E_t \pi_{t+1}.$$

This is of exactly the same form as (1.32), except that the term $\hat{r}_t$ is replaced by $\tilde{r}_t$, a different function of the exogenous disturbances. One observes from (3.15) that $\tilde{r}_t$ can be interpreted as the equilibrium real rate of return in the case that a constant interest-rate differential is maintained. (It is only under the latter stipulation that one can define an equilibrium real rate that is purely exogenous, in the case of nonseparable utility.)

I now look for bounded solutions $\{\hat{P}_t, \hat{\imath}_t\}$ to the system of equations (1.34) and (3.15). As (3.15) is identical to (1.32), except for the replacement of $\hat{r}_t$ by $\tilde{r}_t$, the previous results are directly applicable. Proposition 2.3 then implies that equilibrium is determinate in the case of any rule with $\phi_p > 0$, and a log-linear approximation to the equilibrium price process is given by (1.39), with $\tilde{r}_{t+j}$ replacing $\hat{r}_{t+j}$ in each term.[49] Hence the same theory of price-level determination as derived above continues to apply, with a small modification of the interpretation of the exogenous disturbance term. The same is true for other families of interest-rate rules, such as (2.4) or (2.12).

Suppose instead that policy is implemented in a way that involves a fixed rate of interest on the monetary base (e.g., a zero interest rate, as in the United States at present). In this case, (3.13) is replaced by the condition $i_t^m = \bar{\imath}$. I can again eliminate $\hat{\imath}_t^m$ from (3.12), and obtain a system of two equations to solve for the equilibrium evolution of prices and interest rates. Similar methods as have been used before can then be employed to derive generalizations of the previous results.

PROPOSITION 2.12. In a Sidrauski-Brock model, where utility is not necessarily separable, let monetary policy be specified by a Wicksellian rule (1.30) for the central bank's interest-rate operating target. Suppose that $i_t^m = \bar{\imath}$ at all times, for some $0 \leq \bar{\imath} < \beta^{-1} - 1$; and let fiscal policy again be specified by an exogenous process $\{D_t\}$. Finally, suppose that

---

49. In fact, the previous results for the Wicksellian regime in a cashless economy can be recognized as a special case of the more general result obtained here. For that regime was also one in which (3.13) held at all times, with the value $\bar{\Delta} = 0$; and the composite disturbance $\hat{r}_t$ is just the value of $\tilde{r}_t$ in the case of a cashless economy, since $\chi = 0$ in that case.

$$\chi > -1/2\eta_i. \tag{3.16}$$

Then equilibrium is determinate in the case of any policy rule with $\phi_p > 0$. A log-linear approximation to the locally unique equilibrium price process is given by

$$\log P_t = \phi_p^{-1} \sum_{j=0}^{\infty} \varphi_j E_t \tilde{r}_{t+j} + \sum_{j=0}^{\infty} \tilde{\varphi}_j E_t \left[\log P^*_{t+j} - \phi_p^{-1} v_{t+j} \right], \tag{3.17}$$

where the weights are given by

$$\varphi_j \equiv \frac{(1 + \eta_i \chi \phi_p)^j \phi_p}{[1 + (1 + \eta_i \chi)\phi_p]^{j+1}}, \tag{3.18}$$

$$\tilde{\varphi}_0 \equiv \frac{(1 + \eta_i \chi)\phi_p}{1 + (1 + \eta_i \chi)\phi_p}, \qquad \tilde{\varphi}_j \equiv \frac{(1 + \eta_i \chi \phi_p)^{j-1} \phi_p}{[1 + (1 + \eta_i \chi)\phi_p]^{j+1}} \qquad \text{for } j \geq 1. \tag{3.19}$$

The proof is given in Appendix A. Here the solution (3.17) generalizes the previous result (1.39), to which it reduces in the case that $\chi = 0$. As long as χ also satisfies $\chi > -(\phi_p \eta_i)^{-1}$, the weights $\{\varphi_j, \tilde{\varphi}_j\}$ are all positive, and again both series of weights sum to one, though for $\chi \neq 0$, the weight $\tilde{\varphi}_j$ no longer exactly equals φ_j.

Thus as long as $\chi \geq 0$ (the case of greatest empirical plausibility), and even for sufficiently small negative values of χ, the same condition as before suffices for determinacy. One also obtains a qualitatively similar theory of price-level determination: Again, the log price level is equal to a weighted average of current and future price-level targets plus a discrepancy that involves current and expected future fluctuations in the (suitably qualified) equilibrium real rate of return $\tilde{r}_t$ and in the reaction-function shift factor v_t in a manner similar to the previous equation (1.39). The solution (3.17) is also observed to be continuous in χ, so that for any economy in which χ is small enough, the equations derived for the cashless economy provide a close approximation to the equilibrium evolution of prices.

I can similarly extend the results derived earlier for the case of a generalized Taylor rule (2.12).

PROPOSITION 2.13. Let monetary policy instead be specified by an interest-rate rule of the form (2.12), with coefficients $\phi_\pi, \rho \geq 0$, and again suppose that $i_t^m = \bar{i}_t^m$ at all times. Finally, suppose again that χ satisfies (3.16). Then equilibrium is determinate if and only if $\phi_\pi > 0$ and (2.13) holds. When these conditions are satisfied, a log-linear approximation to the equilibrium evolution of inflation is given by

$$\pi_t = -\frac{\rho}{\phi_\pi}(\hat{\imath}_{t-1} - \bar{\imath}_{t-1}) + \sum_{j=0}^{\infty} \varphi_j E_t \tilde{r}_{t+j} - \sum_{j=0}^{\infty} \tilde{\varphi}_j E_t \bar{\imath}_{t+j}, \qquad (3.20)$$

where the weights are given by

$$\varphi_j \equiv \frac{(1 + \eta_i \chi \phi_\pi)^j}{[(1 + \eta_i \chi)\phi_\pi + \rho]^{j+1}}, \qquad (3.21)$$

$$\tilde{\varphi}_0 \equiv \frac{(1 + \eta_i \chi)}{(1 + \eta_i \chi)\phi_\pi + \rho},$$

$$\tilde{\varphi}_j \equiv \frac{[1 + (1 - \rho)\eta_i \chi](1 + \eta_i \chi \phi_\pi)^{j-1}}{[(1 + \eta_i \chi)\phi_\pi + \rho]^{j+1}} \quad \text{for } j \geq 1. \qquad (3.22)$$

The proof is in Appendix A. Thus the Taylor principle is again necessary and sufficient for determinacy, as long as χ does not take a large negative value. The solution (3.20) generalizes (2.14), to which it reduces when $\chi = 0$. Again the weights $\tilde{\varphi}_j$ are no longer exactly equal to the φ_j weights when $\chi \neq 0$. However, the weights all continue to be positive, if $\rho \leq 1$ and χ is not too negative.

I have found that the qualitative results are largely unaffected by taking account of real-balance effects on the equilibrium real rate of interest. How much are such effects likely to matter quantitatively? The size of the required correction can be numerically calibrated from estimates of money demand. The present simple model implies that the money-demand elasticities should be the same at both high and low frequencies, and if one expects the disturbances ϵ_t^m to be unimportant at low frequencies, low-frequency relations among the variables m_t, Y_t, and i_t will be most revealing about these elasticities. As a typical example, Lucas (2000) finds that low-frequency variations in real M1 for the United States over the twentieth century are fairly well fit (up to a constant) by the variations in log $Y_t - .5$ log i_t.[50] Linearization of (3.3) in the logs of Y_t, m_t, and i_t indicates that according to the present model, $\hat{m}_t$ should be proportional to

$$[\sigma^{-1} + \upsilon]\hat{Y}_t - \beta \log(i_t/\bar{\imath}).$$

50. The present model should really be interpreted as one of demand for the monetary base, but empirical studies more often model the demand for a broader aggregate such as M1. At the low frequencies with which we are here concerned, M1 and the base move roughly in proportion to one another, so I use Lucas's estimated elasticities as estimates of the corresponding elasticities of demand for the monetary base.

(Here it should be recalled that one log-linearizes around a steady state with zero inflation, and assumes zero interest on the monetary base, as is true for the United States.) Thus $\beta^{-1}[\sigma^{-1} + \upsilon]$ should be the ratio of the income elasticity to the interest elasticity of money demand. According to Lucas's estimates, this ratio is approximately 2.[51]

From this one can infer that

$$\chi = s_m \upsilon = s_m(2\beta - \sigma^{-1}). \tag{3.23}$$

If σ is greater than 0.5, as I assume,[52] it follows that $\chi > 0$, as previously argued on intuitive grounds. At the same time, no matter how large σ is assumed to be, the factor in parentheses in (3.23) cannot exceed 2, so that χ cannot realistically be assigned a value larger than twice the size of s_m. For the United States, the value of the monetary base is about 25 percent of a quarter's GDP, so that (using the value $\beta = .99$ for a quarterly model) s_m is approximately 0.0025. This suggests a value of χ no larger than 0.005. Alternatively, if one uses Lucas's estimated coefficients for a semilogarithmic specification of money demand, namely, $\eta_y = 1$ and $\eta_i = 7$ years (or 28 quarters), then the implied ratio of elasticities would be $\eta_y/(1 - \beta)\eta_i = 1/0.28 = 3.6$. This would allow χ to be a larger multiple of s_m, but only by a factor of less than 2, so that χ should be no larger than 0.01. Since the monetary base is equally small for most industrial economies, a similar conclusion as to the plausible size of real-balance effects would be reached for many economies.

As an illustration of how much allowing for $\chi > 0$ would affect the calculations, consider the solution (3.20) for the case of an inertial Taylor rule. Take a policy rule with $\rho = 0.8$, a fairly typical degree of interest-rate inertia in estimated Fed reaction functions for the United States using quarterly data (see Table 1.1), and $\phi_\pi = 0.3$, implying a long-run inflation response coefficient of $\Phi_\pi = 1.5$, Taylor's (1993) value for the Greenspan period. Then the weights φ_j and $\tilde{\varphi}_j$ appearing in the solution (3.20) for various future horizons j are plotted in Figure 2.2. The figure shows the weights both under the assumption that $\chi = 0$ (as in the first approach here), and for the positive value $\chi = 0.02$. The latter is likely to be an over-estimate of the actual size of real-balance effects on the marginal utility of income, but is considered to show that even under the most generous

---

51. Here one may observe the way in which the assumption of an additively separable utility function, implying $\upsilon = 0$, would restrict the model's implications regarding money demand in an undesirable way. One would obtain a necessary relation between the degree of interest sensitivity of private expenditure, on the one hand, and the income elasticity and interest elasticity of money demand on the other. A negligible value of χ is instead consistent with arbitrary values of these other elasticities, as long as one assumes a small enough value for s_m.

52. See Chapter 4 for further discussion of the calibration of this parameter.

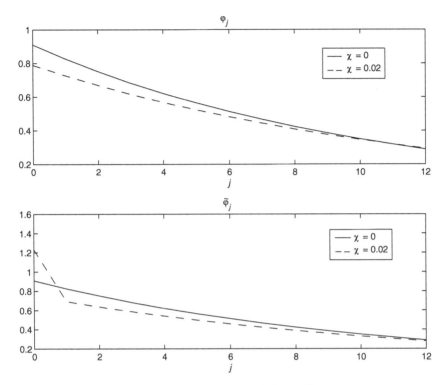

Figure 2.2   *The weights φ_j with and without real-balance effects.*

assumptions real-balance effects should not matter greatly. (The value $\eta_i = 28$ quarters is assumed in both cases.)

While the real-balance effect matters for such a calculation, neglecting it would not lead to extremely misleading conclusions, either. Perhaps the most important qualitative difference is that setting $\chi = 0.02$ results in a slightly larger relative weight on the current period's intercept $\bar{\imath}_t$ as opposed to expected future intercepts. Especially in the (realistic) case that both the equilibrium real rate $\tilde{r}_t$ and the monetary policy disturbance $\bar{\imath}_t$ exhibit substantial positive serial correlation, so that it is only smoothed versions of the coefficients φ_j and $\tilde{\varphi}_j$ that matter in practice, the predictions for inflation under the two assumptions are quite similar. For example, suppose that $\tilde{r}_t$ follows a stationary AR(1) process with serial correlation coefficient $0 < \rho_r < 1$. Then the predicted initial-period jump in the price level in response to a unit positive innovation in the natural rate of interest[53] is given by

---

53. I understand this to mean a jump of 1 percentage point *per annum* in the natural rate, meaning that $\tilde{r}_t$ jumps by Δ, where Δ is the length of a period in years.

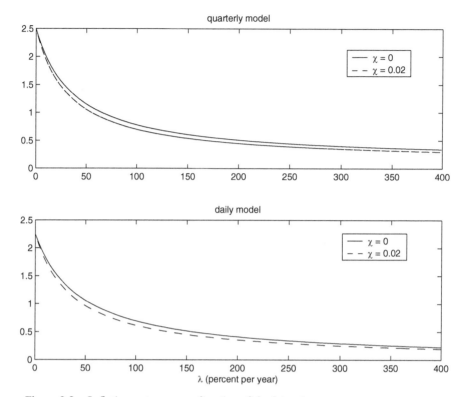

Figure 2.3 *Inflation response as a function of shock persistence.*

$$\Delta \sum_{j=0}^{\infty} \varphi_j \rho_r^j.$$

This quantity is plotted as a function of the degree of persistence of the shocks in the top panel of Figure 2.3. Here the measure of persistence on the horizontal axis is the rate of decay of the disturbances per unit of calendar time, $\lambda \equiv -(\log \rho_r)/\Delta$, where Δ is the length of a period in years.[54] The results are plotted both under the assumption that $\chi = 0$ and for the upper-bound case $\chi = 0.02$. Observe that the error involved in neglecting the real-balance effects is quite small.

One case in which real-balance effects would matter a great deal, however, is that of a rule (2.4) in which the interest rate depends only upon

---

54. This measure is used, instead of ρ_r itself, in order to allow comparability across models with different period lengths. In the first panel, $\Delta = 0.25$ years.

contemporaneous inflation, in the case that the periods are very short. Consider the behavior of the solution to the equations as the length of a period ($\Delta > 0$ units of calendar time) is made progressively shorter. I fix numerical values for the rate of time preference $\delta \equiv (-\log \beta)/\Delta > 0$, the intertemporal elasticity of substitution $\sigma > 0$, the steady-state share of expenditure on liquidity services s_m, the interest-rate semielasticity of money demand in units of calendar time $\tilde{\eta}_i \equiv \Delta \eta_i > 0$, and the income elasticity of money demand η_y, which are independent of the assumed size of Δ. Then the same reasoning used to derive (3.23) implies that as Δ is made small, the value of χ approaches a well-defined limiting value

$$\bar{\chi} = s_m \left(\frac{\eta_y}{\delta \tilde{\eta}_i} - \sigma^{-1} \right). \tag{3.24}$$

I then obtain the following result.

PROPOSITION 2.14. Consider a sequence of economies with progressively smaller period lengths Δ, calibrated so that $\bar{\chi} \neq 0$. Assume in each case that monetary policy is specified by a contemporaneous Taylor rule (2.4), with a positive inflation-response coefficient $\phi_\pi \neq 1$ that is independent of Δ. Assume also that zero interest is paid on money. Then equilibrium is determinate for all small enough values of Δ if $\phi_\pi > 1$ and $\bar{\chi} > 0$, or if $0 < \phi_\pi < 1$ and $\bar{\chi} < 0$, but not otherwise.

The proof is in Appendix A.[55] This result clearly implies that the solution for equilibrium inflation in the short-period limit cannot be a continuous function of χ for values of χ near zero. Thus the value of χ matters in this case, even if it is very small.

However, this failure of continuity in χ in the short-period limit occurs only in the case of a policy rule that makes the interest-rate operating target a purely contemporaneous function of the current period's inflation. As periods are made shorter, the central bank is assumed to respond to a higher-frequency measure of inflation, and in the limit policy is assumed to respond solely to an instantaneous rate of inflation. This is plainly a case of no practical interest. If I assume instead that policy responds to a smoothed

55. My result agrees with the continuous-time analysis of Benhabib et al. (2001a), who find that the range of values of ϕ_π that result in determinacy depends on the sign of u_{cm}. Note that the result does not contradict Proposition 2.13. That proposition asserts that even in the case of a rule with $\rho = 0$, one has determinacy in the case of $\phi_\pi > 1$ for all values of χ greater than the negative lower bound (3.16). However, in the sequence of economies with progressively shorter period lengths considered in Proposition 2.14, the value of η_i increases as Δ^{-1}. Hence for any sequence of economies in Proposition 2.14 for which $\bar{\chi} < 0$, (3.16) is violated for all small enough values of Δ, and Proposition 2.13 ceases to apply.

inflation measure (2.8), and let the rate of decay (in calendar time) of the exponential weights on past inflation be fixed as I make the periods shorter, no such problem arises. The same is true in the equivalent case of a policy rule (2.12) with partial adjustment of the interest rate toward a desired level that depends on the current instantaneous rate of inflation, if the rate of adjustment $\psi \equiv -\log \rho/\Delta > 0$ is held fixed as Δ is made smaller. (One must also assume that ϕ_π is reduced along with Δ, so as to hold fixed the long-run response coefficient $\Phi_\pi \equiv (1-\rho)^{-1}\phi_\pi$.) In this case I obtain the following.

PROPOSITION 2.15. Again consider a sequence of economies with progressively smaller period lengths Δ, and suppose that

$$\bar{\chi} > -1/\psi \, \Phi_\pi \bar{\eta}_i. \tag{3.25}$$

Let monetary policy instead be specified by an inertial Taylor rule (2.12), with a long-run inflation-response coefficient $\Phi_\pi \equiv \phi_\pi/(1-\rho)$ and a rate of adjustment $\psi \equiv -\log \rho/\Delta > 0$ that are independent of Δ. Assume again that zero interest is paid on money. Then rational-expectations equilibrium is determinate if and only if $\Phi_\pi > 1$, that is, if and only if the Taylor principle is satisfied.

The unique bounded solution for the path of nominal interest rates in the determinate case is of the form

$$\hat{\imath}_t = \Lambda \bar{\imath}_t + \Gamma(1-\gamma) \sum_{j=0}^{\infty} \gamma^j E_t \tilde{r}_{t+j} - \tilde{\Gamma}(1-\gamma) \sum_{j=0}^{\infty} \gamma^j E_t \bar{\imath}_{t+j}, \tag{3.26}$$

with the solution for $\{\pi_t\}$ then obtained by inverting (2.12). In this solution, the coefficients $\Lambda, \Gamma, \tilde{\Gamma}$ approach well-defined limiting values as Δ is made arbitrarily small, while the rate of decay of the weights on expected disturbances farther in the future,

$$\xi \equiv -\log \gamma/\Delta > 0,$$

also approaches a well-defined limiting value. Furthermore, these limiting values are all continuous functions of $\bar{\chi}$ for values of $\bar{\chi}$ in the range satisfying (3.25), including values near zero.

Again the proof is in Appendix A. Proposition 2.15 implies that in the case of this kind of rule, small nonzero values of χ (of either sign) make no important difference for the conclusions regarding price-level determination, even in the limiting case of arbitrarily short periods.[56] For example,

---

56. Wicksellian policy rules of the form (1.30) can similarly be shown to be well behaved in the continuous-time limit.

the previous conclusions about the small consequences of allowing for a realistic positive value for χ continue to hold in the case of periods shorter than a quarter. As an illustration, the lower panel of Figure 2.3 shows the same calculations as in the top one, but for a model in which the period is only a day. Thus as long as one assumes either a modest degree of time averaging in the inflation measure to which the central bank responds or of inertia in the central bank's adjustment of its interest-rate operating target in response to inflation variations—both of which are always characteristic of actual central-bank policies—one continues to find that the cashless analysis gives a good approximation to the results obtained under a realistic nonzero value of χ, regardless of the assumed period length.

4 Self-Fulfilling Inflations and Deflations

Thus far I have considered only the problem of *local* determinacy of equilibrium. But it is appropriate also to consider, at least briefly, the question whether rational-expectations equilibrium is *globally* unique under one policy rule or another. Certainly one may have greater confidence that a particular policy regime is desirable if a desirable outcome represents not merely a locally unique equilibrium, but the unique rational-expectations equilibrium, period. Moreover, insofar as regimes may differ in the matter of global uniqueness, even when they are equally consistent with the same desired equilibrium, and equally serve to make it locally determinate, considerations of global uniqueness provide a reasonable further criterion for refining one's policy prescription.

The question of global uniqueness requires that I return to a consideration of the exact, nonlinear equilibrium conditions, as the log-linear approximations can be relied upon to be accurate only in the case of equilibria in which the variables remain within a sufficiently small neighborhood of the values at which the log-linearization is done. This makes a complete treatment of the issue rather complex and beyond the scope of the present study. However, a simple example serves to illustrate how global multiplicity of equilibrium is possible, despite local determinacy. I also give examples of policy regimes that would resolve this problem.

4.1 Global Multiplicity Despite Local Determinacy

My example illustrates the potential problem of multiplicity of equilibria under a Taylor rule as discussed by Schmitt-Grohé and Uribe (2000) and by Benhabib et al. (2001b). Consider a deterministic interest-rate feedback rule of the form

$$i_t = \phi(\Pi_t), \tag{4.1}$$

where $\Pi_t \equiv P_t/P_{t-1}$ is again the gross inflation rate and ϕ is an increasing continuous function satisfying $\phi(\Pi) \geq 0$ for all $\Pi > 0$. I suppose once again that this rule incorporates an implicit target inflation rate $\Pi^* > \beta$ satisfying $\phi(\Pi^*) = \beta^{-1}\Pi^* - 1$. The stipulated lower bound—which is of some importance for the present discussion—is necessary because it is impossible for the central bank to force nominal interest rates to be negative, no matter how much it may increase the monetary base.

Following Benhabib et al. (2001b), let fiscal policy now be specified by a rule of the form

$$T_t = \alpha W_t - \frac{i_t}{1 + i_t} M_t \tag{4.2}$$

for determination of net tax collections at each date, for some constant $0 < \alpha \leq 1$. Using the flow government budget constraint (1.7), we see that this rule implies that

$$E_t\left[Q_{t,t+1} W_{t+1}\right] = (1 - \alpha) W_t.$$

Thus this fiscal policy has the "Ricardian" property that the transversality condition (1.18) necessarily holds, regardless of the evolution of the endogenous variables.[57] This means that one may omit the transversality condition from the list of requirements for an equilibrium. Note also that under such a fiscal policy, debt management policy is irrelevant for equilibrium determination.

Under such a regime, a rational-expectations equilibrium is a pair of processes $\{P_t, i_t\}$ satisfying (4.1) and

$$1 + i_t = \beta^{-1} E_t \left[\frac{\lambda(y_{t+1}, i_{t+1}; \xi_{t+1})}{\lambda(y_t, i_t; \xi_t)} \frac{P_t}{P_{t+1}} \right]^{-1} \tag{4.3}$$

at all dates, together with the bound

$$\sum_{T=t}^{\infty} \beta^T E_t \lambda(y_T, i_T; \xi_T) \left[y_T + \frac{i_T}{1 + i_T} L(y_T, i_T; \xi_T) \right] < \infty. \tag{4.4}$$

Here (4.3) rewrites (1.21) using the function $\lambda(y, i; \xi)$ that gives the value of U_c as a function of those arguments (by substituting equilibrium real balances for the second argument of U_c), and (4.4) similarly rewrites (1.23), also using (3.2) to substitute for U_m.

---

57. Here the terminology follows Benhabib et al. (2001b). See Woodford (2001b) and Section 4 of Chapter 4 for further discussion.

The general existence of multiple solutions can be shown by considering the set of perfect-foresight equilibria (i.e., deterministic solutions) in the absence of shocks ($y_t = \bar{y}, \xi_t = 0$ for all t). Then, substituting (4.1) into (4.3), I obtain a nonlinear difference equation for the inflation rate,

$$\Pi_{t+1}\lambda(\phi(\Pi_{t+1}))^{-1} = \beta(1 + \phi(\Pi_t))\lambda(\phi(\Pi_t))^{-1}, \tag{4.5}$$

where for $\lambda(\bar{y}, i; 0)$ I now write simply $\lambda(i)$. In the cashless limit (or the case of additive separability), this reduces to

$$\Pi_{t+1} = \beta(1 + \phi(\Pi_t)). \tag{4.6}$$

It is clear in this last case that there exists a solution for $\Pi_{t+1} > 0$ in the case of any given $\Pi_t > 0$. Hence starting from any arbitrarily chosen initial inflation rate $\Pi_0 > 0$, I can construct a sequence $\{\Pi_t\}$ that satisfies (4.6) at all dates. Associated with this is a sequence of nonnegative interest rates, given by (4.1). As long as these sequences satisfy the bound (4.4), they represent a perfect-foresight equilibrium. In the case that desired real money balances $L(\bar{y}, i; 0)$ are bounded above as i approaches zero,[58] because there is satiation at a finite level of real money balances, this holds for any sequence $\{i_t\}$. In such a case, it is clear that there exists a continuum of perfect-foresight equilibria, one corresponding to each possible initial inflation rate Π_0.

This result obtains even if the rule (4.1) satisfies $\phi_\pi > 1$ near the target inflation rate Π^*, so that the Taylor principle is satisfied, at least locally. In such a case, one has a large multiplicity of equilibria *globally*, despite local determinacy. This is illustrated in Figure 2.4, where the solid curve plots the locus of pairs (Π_t, Π_{t+1}) that satisfy (4.6). Note that this locus crosses the diagonal at the target inflation rate Π^*, indicating that $\Pi_t = \Pi^*$ forever is one solution. The Taylor principle implies that the curve cuts the diagonal from below at this point. In such a case, the fact that $\phi(\Pi) \geq 0$ for all Π implies that there also must be another steady state (constant inflation rate satisfying (4.6)), at some lower rate of inflation. At this lower steady state, the curve must cut the diagonal from above; thus, as Benhabib et al. stress, the Taylor principle *cannot* be globally valid. In the case shown in the figure, the Taylor principle is adhered to as far as possible, which means that the lower steady state corresponds to a zero nominal interest rate. In this case, the lower steady-state inflation rate is

---

58. In fact, it suffices that $iL(\bar{y}, i; 0)$ be bounded. Thus even in the case of the log-log money demand function preferred by Lucas (2000), in which desired real balances decline as $i^{-1/2}$, condition (4.4) is satisfied by all interest-rate sequences.

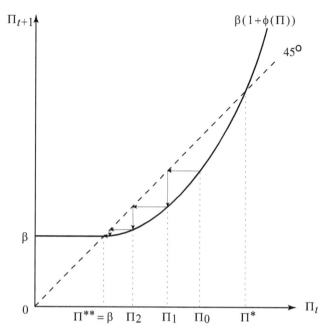

Figure 2.4 *A self-fulfilling deflation under a Taylor rule.*

$\Pi^{**} = \beta$, corresponding to deflation at the Friedman rate, the rate of time preference of the representative household.

The sequence of inflation rates corresponding to any given initial inflation rate Π_0 may be constructed geometrically as indicated in Figure 2.4. For each value of Π_t, one finds the associated value of Π_{t+1} using the curve, then reflects this value down to the horizontal axis using the diagonal, and repeats the construction. In the figure, a value $\Pi_0 < \Pi^*$ is considered. This is consistent with perfect-foresight equilibrium only if $\Pi_1 < \Pi_0$, which in turn requires $\Pi_2 < \Pi_1$, and so on. One is able to continue the construction forever, and in the case shown in Figure 2.4 (where $\phi(\Pi) < \beta^{-1}\Pi - 1$ for all $\Pi > \beta$, while $\phi(\Pi) = 0$ for all $\Pi \le \beta$), one finds that the inflation rate must decline monotonically over time, approaching the value $\Pi^{**} = \beta$ asymptotically. This indicates the possibility of a *self-fulfilling deflation* under such a regime—inflation that is perpetually lower than the target rate and, eventually, actual deflation, which represents an equilibrium only because even lower inflation is expected in the future. Along such a path, interest rates are constantly being lowered in response to the decline in inflation, but because *expected* future inflation falls at the same time, *real* interest rates are not reduced, and continue to be high enough to restrain demand despite the falling prices.

Such an equilibrium exists for each possible choice of Π_0 in the interval $\beta < \Pi_0 < \Pi^*$. At the same time, for any inflation rate *higher* than the target rate, there exists an equilibrium in which the equilibrium inflation rate *rises* over time, eventually growing unboundedly large. Thus *self-fulfilling inflation* is equally possible under such a regime. Furthermore, because (4.3) need only hold *in expectation* for an inflation process $\{\Pi_t\}$ to constitute a rational-expectations equilibrium, there is also an even larger set of equilibria in which the rate of inflation or deflation depends upon sunspot variables.[59]

Note that this global multiplicity of solutions does not contradict the previous results with regard to local determinacy. One observes from Figure 2.4 that any deterministic equilibrium other than the one with $\Pi_t = \Pi^*$ forever involves an inflation rate that diverges further and further from the target inflation rate as time passes. Thus every other equilibrium eventually leaves a neighborhood of Π^*, even if the initial inflation rate is very close to it. The same can be shown to be true of all of the stochastic equilibria as well,[60] so that the desired equilibrium is indeed locally unique in the sense discussed above. Note also that equilibrium is indeterminate even locally, near the deflationary steady state; for any neighborhood of Π^{**}, there exists a continuum of distinct equilibria in which inflation remains forever within this range. But this too is consistent with the previous results, since the Taylor principle is violated near this steady state.

These conclusions are largely unchanged when one takes account of real-balance effects. As long as $\Pi/\lambda(\phi(\Pi))$ is still a monotonically increasing function of Π, (4.5) can be solved in the same manner as (4.6). In the case that real balances are complementary with private expenditure ($u_{cm} > 0$), as was previously suggested to be reasonable, $\lambda(i)$ is a decreasing function, and this condition is necessarily satisfied. Moreover, even if $u_{cm} < 0$, the monotonicity condition may still hold—it suffices that λ not be too strongly increasing in i.[61] In particular, as long as $\lambda(i)$ has a finite limiting value for $i = 0$—which makes sense, as there should be a limit to the value of expenditure, even when it is completely unimpeded by transactions frictions—then the previous assumptions about the form of $\phi(\Pi)$ suffice to imply that the curve in Figure 2.4 cuts the diagonal from above at the Friedman rate of deflation. This suffices to imply the existence of a continuum of solutions to (4.5) involving self-fulfilling deflation. These solutions also satisfy (4.4),

59. The analysis of this possibility may be conducted along lines followed in Woodford (1994b) in the analysis of multiple equilibria under a money growth rule.

60. Again, see the related analysis in Woodford (1994b).

61. As discussed in Sections A.16 and A.17 in Appendix A, it is common for cash-in-advance models to imply that λ should be an increasing function of i, as in the case of a Sidrauski-Brock model with $u_{cm} < 0$. Even so, it is probably not plausible for such an effect to be quantitatively large in the case of moderate levels of the nominal interest rate.

and hence represent perfect-foresight equilibria, as long as desired real balances are bounded, or, indeed, as long as $iL(\bar{y}, i; 0)$ has a finite bound for i near zero.

These results may make it seem that a Taylor rule is not a very reliable way of ensuring a determinate equilibrium price level after all, even if the Taylor principle is adhered to except when interest rates become very low (in which case it cannot be). Several responses may be made to this criticism. One is to note that the equilibrium in which inflation is stabilized at the target level is nonetheless *locally* unique, which may be enough to allow expectations to coordinate upon that equilibrium rather than on one of the others. Here it might seem that the existence of other equilibria with initial inflation rates arbitrarily close to the target rate should make it easy for the economy to "slip" into one of those other equilibria. Indeed, it is often said that in the case of perfect-foresight dynamics like those shown in Figure 2.4, the steady state with inflation rate Π^* is "unstable," implying that an economy should be expected almost inevitably to experience either a self-fulfilling inflation or a self-fulfilling deflation under such a regime.

Such reasoning involves a serious misunderstanding of the causal logic of difference equation (4.5). The equation does not indicate how the equilibrium inflation rate in period $t+1$ is determined by the inflation that happens to have occurred in the previous period. If it did, it would be correct to call Π^* an unstable fixed point of the dynamics—even if that point were fortuitously reached, any small perturbation would result in divergence from it. But instead, the equation indicates how the equilibrium inflation rate in period t is determined by *expectations* regarding inflation in the following period. These expectations determine the real interest rate, and hence the incentive for spending, associated with the nominal rate that the central bank sets in response to any given current inflation rate. The equilibria that involve initial inflation rates near (but not equal to) Π^* can only occur as a result of expectations of *future* inflation rates (at least in some states) that are even *further* from the target inflation rate. Thus the economy can only move to one of these alternative paths if expectations about the future change significantly, something that one may suppose would not easily occur.

Indeed, many analyses of convergence to rational-expectations equilibrium as a result of adaptive learning dynamics find that equilibria are stable under the learning dynamics in the same case that they are "stable under the backward perfect-foresight dynamics," which is exactly the case of the steady state Π^* in Figure 2.4.[62] The key to such results is that any deviation in

---

62. For examples of results of this kind, see Grandmont (1985), Grandmont and Laroque (1986), Marcet and Sargent (1989), and Lettau and Van Zandt (2000). Lucas (1986) uses a result of this kind to argue that self-fulfilling inflations should not be expected to occur in the case of a monetary targeting regime. See also the discussion of least-squares learning

expected future inflation from the target rate results in an actual inflation rate that is closer to the target rate than is the expected rate. If expectations evolve relatively slowly (as an average of experience over a period of time), then one will persistently observe inflation closer to the target rate than one is expecting, as a result of which expectations eventually adjust toward a value closer to the target rate themselves. But this makes actual inflation even closer to the target rate, and so on, until the process eventually converges to an equilibrium in which both expected and actual inflation equal the target rate forever.

Nonetheless, other types of learning processes, which allow extrapolation of paths diverging from the target steady state, can result in convergence to one of the other equilibria.[63] Furthermore, even if one regards the target steady state as locally stable, one must worry that a large shock could nonetheless perturb the economy enough that expectations settle upon another equilibrium; thus the problem of self-fulfilling inflations and deflations should probably not be dismissed out of hand. But it is also important to note that this problem is in no way special to the formulation of monetary policy in terms of an interest-rate feedback rule. In particular, exactly the same sort of problems may arise in the case of monetary targeting.

Let us recall the equations that defined equilibrium real balances in the case of a monetary targeting regime, and once again focus on the case in which there are no exogenous shocks ($\mu_t = \bar{\mu} > \beta, y_t = \bar{y}, \xi_t = 0$ for all t). Solving (3.3) for i_t and substituting this into the Fisher equation (1.21) yields a stochastic difference equation for real balances of the form

$$F(m_t) = \beta/\bar{\mu}E_t G(m_{t+1}), \qquad (4.7)$$

where

$$F(m) \equiv [U_c(\bar{y}, m; 0) - U_m(\bar{y}, m; 0)]m, \qquad G(m) \equiv U_c(\bar{y}, m; 0)m.$$

This is exactly the equation for which (A.29) represents a log-linear approximation, except that I have here suppressed the dependence upon exogenous disturbances.

If one again considers perfect-foresight solutions, one looks for sequences $\{m_t\}$ that satisfy

$$G(m_{t+1}) = \bar{\mu}/\beta F(m_t). \qquad (4.8)$$

---

dynamics in a sticky-price model in Section 2.3 of Chapter 4, where one finds that the rational-expectations equilibrium is stable under learning dynamics in the same cases in which it is locally determinate, meaning stable in a *backward* rational-expectations recursion.

63. See Grandmont and Laroque (1986) and Lettau and Van Zandt (2000).

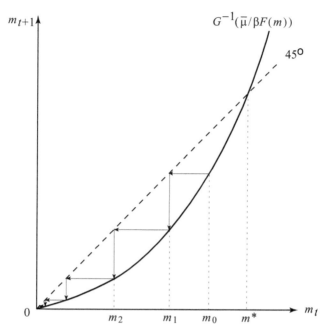

Figure 2.5   *A self-fulfilling inflation under monetary targeting.*

In the additively separable case, $G(m)$ is linearly increasing in m, and so can be inverted, whereas the function $F(m)$ equals m times an increasing function of m. If this latter function $(U_c - U_m)$ is positive for all $m > 0$—which is to say, if desired real balances can be made arbitrarily small by making the interest rate high enough—then $F(m)$ is positive, increasing, and convex, and takes the limiting value $F(0) = 0$. In such a case, (4.8) can be uniquely solved for $m_{t+1} > 0$ given any value $m_t > 0$, and the graph of the solution is of the form shown in Figure 2.5. Once again, the steady-state level of real money balances $m^* = L[\bar{y}, (\bar{\mu} - \beta)/\beta; 0]$ is the point at which this graph intersects the diagonal. Note that at this point the curve necessarily cuts the diagonal from below; and once again there is a second steady state, this time at zero real balances.

Just as in the case of the Taylor rule, it is observed that there is a distinct perfect-foresight equilibrium corresponding to each possible value of m_0. If $m_0 < m^*$, real balances must be expected to decrease over time (as in the equilibrium illustrated in Figure 2.4), converging to zero asymptotically. This corresponds to a self-fulfilling inflation. For the progressively lower levels of real balances are associated with progressively higher nominal interest rates, which in turn require progressively higher rates of inflation.

Asymptotically, inflation approaches the rate (that may or may not be finite) that causes complete demonetization of the economy. If instead $m_0 > m^*$, real balances must increase over time, eventually increasing without bound. If desired real balances are finite at all positive interest rates, then such equilibria involve interest rates falling to zero, at least asymptotically, and so eventually involve deflation at a rate approaching the Friedman rate. They thus correspond to the self-fulfilling deflations discovered to be possible in the case of a Taylor rule. Thus, as a general rule, monetary targeting as such does not avoid either of these types of potential problem.

In fact, as we shall see, it is possible to choose a policy regime under which equilibrium is globally unique. But here again, there is little difference between the degree to which this is possible when monetary policy takes the form of an interest-rate feedback rule, such as a Taylor rule, and when it takes instead the form of monetary targeting.

4.2   Policies to Prevent a Deflationary Trap

The result that self-fulfilling deflations are possible in the case of monetary targeting may seem surprising, as many papers that consider equilibrium in the case of a constant money supply find that such equilibria are impossible.[64] But the reason for this is that standard analyses do not specify a Ricardian fiscal policy, as I did earlier. As noted in Section 1.2, analyses of monetary targeting typically assume a fiscal policy under which there is zero government debt at all times. Under this specification, the transversality condition (1.24) is no longer redundant; it holds only if the path of real balances satisfies

$$\lim_{T \to \infty} \beta^T E_t [u_c(Y_T, m_T; \xi_T) m_T] = 0. \tag{4.9}$$

As a result, self-fulfilling deflations generally cannot occur in a rational-expectations equilibrium if the money growth rate satisfies $\bar{\mu} \geq 1$, that is, the money supply is nondecreasing. This is most easily shown in the case that there is satiation in real balances at some finite level. Then for all values of m above this level, $F(m) = G(m)$, and (4.8) requires that

$$m_{t+1} = \bar{\mu}/\beta \, m_t$$

each period, after real balances exceed the satiation level. At the same time, $U_c(\bar{y}, m_t; 0)$ remains constant, even if preferences are not additively separable. It follows that in the case of any deflationary solution to (4.8),

---

64. See, e.g., Brock (1975), Obstfeld and Rogoff (1986), and Woodford (1994b).

$$\beta^T U_c(\bar{y}, m_T; 0) m_T = \beta^t \bar{\mu}^{T-t} U_c(\bar{y}, m_t; 0) m_t \geq \beta^t U_c(\bar{y}, m_t; 0) m_t > 0$$

at all dates $T \geq t$, where t is some date at which real balances have already reached the satiation level. Thus the transversality condition is violated in the case of any such path, and it does not represent a perfect-foresight equilibrium. A generalization of this argument can be used to exclude stochastic equilibria in which real balances eventually exceed the satiation level as well. As a result one can show that one must have $m_t \leq m^*$ at all times in any rational-expectations equilibrium.[65]

However, this result has nothing to do with the fact that monetary policy is specified in terms of a target path for the money supply. Rather, it depends upon the fact that *fiscal* policy under such a regime is assumed not to be Ricardian. Government policy implies that not just the money supply, but also the nominal value of government liabilities D_t, grows at the rate $\bar{\mu}$, and it is the latter fact that rules out self-fulfilling deflations. But one could equally well combine this kind of fiscal policy with an interest-rate rule by specifying the former in terms of a target path for D_t, as in Section 2.1. One would then obtain exactly the same result.

Let total nominal government liabilities D_t be specified to grow at a constant rate $\bar{\mu} \geq 1$, starting from an initial size $D_0 > 0$, while monetary policy is described by the Taylor rule (4.1). (Note that a balanced-budget policy, in the sense of Schmitt-Grohé and Uribe (2000), is one example of such a fiscal policy.) Let us also suppose, to simplify the analysis, that there exists an inflation rate $\underline{\Pi} > \beta$ such that $\phi(\Pi) = 0$ for all $\Pi \leq \underline{\Pi}$.[66]

Then any deflationary solution to (4.5) involves a zero nominal interest rate in each period after some finite date t, which in turn implies that $\Pi_T = \beta$ for all $T \geq t + 1$. It follows that

$$\beta^T \lambda(i_T) D_T / P_T = \beta^t \bar{\mu}^{T-t} \lambda(0) D_t / P_t \geq \beta^t \lambda(0) D_t / P_t > 0$$

at all dates $T > t$, so that the transversality condition (1.24) is violated in the case of any such path.[67] In essence, the specified fiscal policy is too stimulative, in the case of a deflationary path, to be consistent with market clearing. If the private sector consumes only as much as the economy produces, it finds that its real wealth grows explosively, as a result of which it wishes to consume more.[68]

---

65. See Woodford (1994b) for details.

66. One interpretation of this assumption is that the policy rule conforms to the Taylor principle except when the zero bound prevents any further decreases in the nominal interest rate.

67. This is how self-fulfilling deflations are excluded under a Taylor rule in Schmitt-Grohé and Uribe (2000), in the context of a related model, discussed further in Section A.17 of Appendix A.

68. The effects of fiscal policy upon aggregate demand under a non-Ricardian regime are discussed further in Chapter 5.

The result just mentioned depends upon interest rates being driven to zero sufficiently quickly in the event that inflation falls. However, even if $\phi(\Pi) > 0$ for all $\Pi > \beta$, as long as $\phi(\Pi) < (\Pi - \beta)/\beta$ for all $\beta < \Pi < \Pi^*$, one can still exclude self-fulfilling deflations in the case of any fiscal policy that ensures a growth rate $\bar{\mu} > 1$ for government liabilities. For this ensures that every deflationary solution involves an inflation rate converging to $\Pi^{**} = \beta$, as shown in Figure 2.4. Hence there must exist a date t such that $1 + \phi(\Pi_T) \geq \bar{\mu}$ for all $T \geq t$. It follows that

$$\beta^T \lambda(i_T) D_T / P_T = \beta^t \lambda(i_t) \prod_{s=t}^{T-1} (1 + i_s)^{-1} \bar{\mu}^{T-t} D_t / P_t \geq \beta^t \lambda(i_t) D_t / P_t > 0,$$

so that again the transversality condition is violated. Finally, even if interest rates level off sooner, so that there exists a lower steady-state inflation rate $\Pi^{**} > \beta$, the same argument works as long as $\bar{\mu} > \beta^{-1} \Pi^{**}$.

Thus, in the case of an appropriate fiscal policy rule, a deflationary trap is not a possible rational-expectations equilibrium, even under an interest-rate rule. Furthermore, the type of fiscal commitment that is required to exclude such a possibility is essentially the same in the case of an interest-rate rule as in the case of monetary targeting: Fiscal policy must ensure that the nominal value of total government liabilities D_t will not decline, even in the case of sustained deflation.[69]

Indeed, an interest-rate rule has an advantage over the classic formulation of a monetary targeting regime in at least one regard. Self-fulfilling deflations may be excluded in the case of an interest-rate rule, even when the target inflation rate Π^* associated with the Taylor rule (or with a Wicksellian regime with a nonconstant target path for the price level) implies *deflation* at a rate less than the rate of time preference ($\beta < \Pi^* < 1$). However, under the monetary targeting regime (with fiscal policy maintaining zero government debt at all times) the previous argument to exclude self-fulfilling deflations fails when $\bar{\mu} < 1$. In this case, the transversality condition *is* satisfied by all of the solutions to (4.8) that involve inflation rates eventually falling to the level $\Pi_t = \beta$, and so a continuum of perfect-foresight equilibria (and similarly a large set of sunspot equilibria) exists.[70] Of course, this result could be avoided if one assumes a different fiscal policy; it is simply necessary that the nominal value of total liabilities be nondecreasing, even as the money supply contracts. Thus Dupor (1999) shows that self-fulfilling deflations can be avoided if the money supply is contracted through open-market operations (that replace the money with corresponding increases in government debt), rather than through the lump-sum tax collections

---

69. For further discussion, see Benhabib et al. (2002).
70. See Woodford (1994b) for demonstration of this for a closely related model.

envisioned by Friedman (1969). But this emphasizes that monetary targeting as such is not the key to excluding the possibility of a deflationary trap.

It is sometimes supposed that the conduct of monetary policy through interest-rate control leaves monetary policy impotent in the case of a deflationary trap, because the nominal interest-rate instrument cannot be lowered below zero, whereas it is actually still possible to stimulate aggregate demand by increasing the money supply. But monetary control has no such advantage. It is important to remember that *there is no real-balance effect* once the short nominal interest rate falls to zero, even if it is still possible to increase the size of the excess real money balances (i.e., balances in excess of the satiation level) held by the public. This is because higher real balances increase desired spending, for any given expected path of real interest rates, only insofar as they are able to increase the marginal utility of additional expenditure associated with a given level of real expenditure. Once the satiation level of real balances is reached, additional money balances no longer lead to any further relaxation of constraints upon transactional flexibility, so they cannot stimulate aggregate demand.

Recall that in Section 3.3, I was able to replace the function $U_c(y_t, m_t; \xi_t)$ describing the marginal utility of additional expenditure by $\lambda(y_t, i_t; \xi_t)$. Thus additional real balances affect the marginal utility of expenditure only insofar as they can reduce the short-term nominal interest rate i_t, which indicates the value of further relaxation of transaction constraints. Once the nominal interest rate cannot be further lowered, an increase in real money balances as such can have no effect upon aggregate demand, through *either* a real-interest-rate effect or a direct real-balance effect. Thus monetary policy is impotent under such circumstances, but this is not a limitation of the use of an interest-rate instrument.

Alternatively, it is sometimes argued that even when increases in the current money supply are ineffective, due to the economy's being in a "liquidity trap" (i.e., money balances already in excess of the satiation level), a commitment to *future* money supply increases can nonetheless stimulate aggregate demand. The idea is that increasing the expected future price level can lower real interest rates even when nominal rates cannot be further reduced (Krugman, 1998). This is right, but there is no special efficacy in a commitment to monetary targets in this regard. Commitment to a high rate of money growth does nothing to exclude a deflationary trap when coupled with a Ricardian fiscal policy; the deflationary equilibrium simply involves a higher level of excess money balances in that case. Only an antideflationary fiscal commitment can solve this problem, and it can do so whether or not there are monetary targets.[71]

---

71. A commitment to a positive floor for the monetary base can, however, be relevant in conjunction with a fiscal commitment which ensures that the present value of *government*

On the other hand, the problem of a country like Japan at present may not be so much that it has fallen into a self-fulfilling deflationary trap, despite the existence of an equilibrium with stable prices if only expectations were to coordinate upon it, as that a temporary reduction in the equilibrium real rate of return has made stable prices incompatible with the zero bound on nominal interest rates, as suggested by Krugman. In such a case, the only way to avoid a period of sharp deflation when the disturbance occurs may be a regime that creates expectations of subsequent *inflation*. Let us suppose that the problem of self-fulfilling deflations may be put aside (perhaps because of an appropriate fiscal commitment) and that the economy is expected to converge to a near-steady-state equilibrium after the real disturbance subsides (and the equilibrium real rate returns to its normal positive level). Then whether the path of this sort that is followed involves a sharp initial deflation or not depends upon expected monetary policy after the shock subsides, although, for some expectations regarding future policy, there may be nothing current monetary policy can do to prevent deflation. In such a case, as Krugman argues, the future monetary policy commitment and its credibility are crucial. But the kind of policy commitment that can imply expectations of a suitably high future price level may well be a Wicksellian regime or a Taylor rule, which would determine the expected future price level in the way explained in Section 2.[72]

4.3 Policies to Prevent an Inflationary Panic

I next consider the opposite sort of instability due to self-fulfilling expectations, the possibility of spontaneous flight from a country's currency, with its loss in value over each time period resulting from expectations of even further declines in value, at an even faster rate, in the near future. In the literature on monetary targeting regimes, such *self-fulfilling inflations* have generally been considered a more troubling possibility than *self-fulfilling deflations*. However, conditions have been identified under which such equilibria would not exist in the case of a constant money-growth rate.

In particular, Obstfeld and Rogoff (1983) show that in the model considered here, if preferences are of the additively separable form considered in Section 3.3 and if

---

debt far in the future is necessarily zero—i.e., that government liabilities classified as "debt" will eventually be "repaid"—rather than a commitment to a Ricardian policy in the sense of Benhabib et al. (2001b), which ensures that the present value of *government liabilities including the monetary base* far in the future must be zero. For further discussion, see Eggertsson and Woodford (2003).

72. See Eggertsson and Woodford (2003) for characterization of the optimal commitment with regard to the eventual path of the price level, in the context of a sticky-price model of the kind introduced in Chapter 4, which allows a utility-based analysis of appropriate stabilization goals.

$$\lim_{m \to 0} mu_m(m; 0) > 0, \qquad (4.10)$$

then no such perfect-foresight equilibria exist under monetary targeting. For in this case, the function $F(m)$ is negative for all levels of real balances below a critical level $\underline{m} > 0$, as a result of which the graph of (4.8) cuts the horizontal axis at the point $m_t = \underline{m} > 0$, rather than passing through the origin as shown in Figure 2.5. Thus no equilibrium can ever have $m_t \leq \underline{m}$. But then it follows from (4.8) that no perfect-foresight equilibrium can ever have

$$m_t \leq \underline{m}_1 \equiv F^{-1}(\beta/\bar{\mu} G(\underline{m})),$$

as a result of which no perfect-foresight equilibrium can ever have

$$m_t \leq \underline{m}_2 \equiv F^{-1}\big(\beta/\bar{\mu} G(\underline{m}_1)\big),$$

and so on. One shows in this way that no equilibrium is possible with $m_t < m^*$ at any time.

Condition (4.10) was excluded in my previous analysis by the assumption that desired real balances can be made arbitrarily small by sufficiently increasing the interest rate; for it implies that $L(\bar{y}, i; 0)$ is bounded below by $\underline{m}$ for all i. (The existence of such a bound is the key to the earlier construction, for which additive separability is actually not important.) Obstfeld and Rogoff point out that the conditions required for this to be true are somewhat implausible, though theoretically possible. Observed hyperinflations in several countries have also shown that real balances do indeed fall to a small fraction of their normal level when inflation becomes sufficiently severe, and the money demand functions estimated from such data (as in the classic study by Cagan, 1956) imply that real balances should approach zero in the case of high enough expected inflation. Hence it is not clear that one can rely upon this mechanism to prevent self-fulfilling inflations in an actual economy.

What if monetary policy is specified instead by a Taylor rule of the form (4.1)? A similar argument excluding self-fulfilling inflations would be possible only if the graph of (4.5) becomes vertical at some finite inflation rate $\bar{\pi}$, so that (4.5) has no solution for Π_{t+1} in the case of $\Pi_t > \bar{\pi}$. In the additively separable case, this might seem to be impossible, as there could fail to be a solution for Π_{t+1} in (4.6) only if $\phi(\Pi_t)$ is itself not defined. However, it is not clear that a function ϕ that becomes unboundedly large at a finite inflation rate $\bar{\pi}$ must be excluded as a possible policy. After all, in the case of monetary targeting when (4.10) holds, the policy that excludes self-fulfilling inflations is one of commitment never to supply more than a certain quantity of money, no matter how high this may require interest rates to be driven. This is equivalent to a Wicksellian rule (1.30) in which the function ϕ becomes unboundedly large at a finite level of P_t/P_t^*. If such a policy is considered to be feasible, despite the fact that it commits the central bank to something that is simply impossible in the case of too high a price level, then it is not clear why a Taylor rule that makes ϕ undefined for $\Pi_t \geq \bar{\pi}$ is not an equally feasible policy. However, if one considers that a Taylor rule of this kind represents a credible commitment, then such a strategy to exclude self-fulfilling inflations should actually be superior to monetary targeting. For its applicability would not depend upon the implausible assumption that desired real balances are bounded away from zero.

Furthermore, under some circumstances it is possible to exclude self-fulfilling inflations through commitment to increase interest rates sufficiently sharply at high rates of inflation, even when $\phi(\Pi)$ is well defined for any finite inflation rate. If $u_{cm} < 0$ at low levels of real balances, the function $\lambda(i)$ is increasing in i at high levels of i.[73] Suppose that in fact the elasticity of $\lambda(i)$ with respect to $1 + i$ is positive, but bounded below one for all high enough i. Then the right-hand side of (4.5) increases with Π_t, for high inflation rates, eventually growing without bound. However, if $\phi(\Pi)$ increases sufficiently rapidly for high values of Π, the function $\Pi/\lambda[\phi(\Pi)]$ may be bounded above. In this case, (4.5) has no solution for Π_{t+1} in the case of values of Π_t above some finite bound $\bar{\pi}$.[74]

But this then allows one to exclude self-fulfilling inflations altogether among the set of perfect-foresight equilibria, using an iterative argument like that advanced earlier in the case of the lower bound on real balances. Then, assuming a fiscal policy of the kind previously discussed, which excludes self-fulfilling deflations, one can show that the equilibrium with inflation forever at the target inflation rate Π^* is the unique perfect-foresight equilibrium. In fact, using similar arguments, one can show that it is the unique rational-expectations equilibrium, even allowing for stochastic equilibria of arbitrary form. Furthermore, at least in the case of sufficiently small random variations in the exogenous variables $\{y_t, \xi_t, \nu_t, \Pi_t^*\}$, the locally

---

73. Cash/credit goods models of the transactions technology, discussed in Section A.16 of Appendix A, provide an alternative and especially natural reason for $\lambda(i)$ to be increasing in i. In these models, $\lambda(i)$ corresponds to the marginal utility of additional cash goods purchases, and it is then plausible that a higher interest rate, and accordingly lower real money balances, should be associated with lower cash goods purchases and so a higher marginal utility of additional purchases of this kind. While such effects on the marginal utility of income are probably not very large in the case of fluctuations in interest rates around a low value, they might plausibly become substantial under circumstances of hyperinflation, which is all that matters for the argument here.

74. This is the way in which self-fulfilling inflations are excluded under a Taylor rule in the analysis of Schmitt-Grohé and Uribe (2000). See Section A.17 of Appendix A for the functional forms used in their example.

unique equilibrium that was approximately characterized in Section 2.3 can similarly be shown to be globally unique.

Even if solutions of these kinds are unavailable, self-fulfilling inflations may be excluded through the addition of policy provisos that apply only in the case of hyperinflation. For example, Obstfeld and Rogoff (1986) propose that the central bank commit itself to peg the value of the monetary unit in terms of some real commodity by standing ready to exchange the commodity for money in the event that the real value of the total money supply ever shrinks to a certain very low level. If it is assumed that this level of real balances is one that would never be reached except in the case of a self-fulfilling inflation, the commitment has no effect except to exclude such paths as possible equilibria. Obstfeld and Rogoff propose this as a solution to the problem of self-fulfilling inflations under a regime that otherwise targets the money supply; but it has no intrinsic connection to monetary targeting and could equally well be added as a hyperinflation proviso in a regime that otherwise follows a Taylor rule.

CHAPTER 3

Optimizing Models with Nominal Rigidities

I turn now to the analysis of models in which monetary policy affects the level of real economic activity, and not just the level of money prices of goods and services. This requires going beyond the analysis of endowment economies, as in the previous chapter, and allowing instead for endogenous supply decisions. But as is well-known, even when one allows for endogenous supply, monetary policy can have only small effects on the equilibrium allocation of resources in an environment with perfect wage and price flexibility (and identical information on the part of all decisionmakers). Hence I also extend the analytical framework to allow for delays in the adjustment of prices and/or wages to changing aggregate conditions. In this way, I allow for nontrivial real effects of monetary policy.

This extension of the framework is also important for a more realistic discussion of central-bank interest-rate policy. In the basic model of Chapter 2, the equilibrium real rate of return is completely independent of monetary policy. This means that a central bank can have no effect on nominal interest rates except insofar as it can shift inflation expectations. In the earlier analysis I assumed that it is able to do so as long as the change in expectations that is called for involves no violation of the postulate of rational expectations on the part of the private sector; but that analysis may give the appearance of assuming precise central-bank control of something upon which banks have little direct influence in reality. The introduction of price stickiness makes the assumption that the central bank can set a short-term nominal interest rate less paradoxical. If private-sector inflation expectations do not change when the central bank seeks to adjust the nominal interest rate, it does not prevent the bank from achieving its operating target. It simply means that the private sector perceives the *real* interest rate to have changed, which affects desired expenditure and hence the degree of utilization of existing productive capacity. (I reexamine the topic of inflation determination under an interest-rate rule in the context of models with nominal rigidities in Chapter 4.)

I focus primarily on models with sticky prices, though I discuss the consequences of wage stickiness as well. In this I follow most of the literature of the past 20 years, but the choice perhaps deserves brief comment. One reason for emphasizing price stickiness, at least for pedagogical purposes, is simply that models with only sticky prices provide a *simpler* framework for the consideration of basic issues regarding the nature of inflation determination. If I am to talk about the determinants of inflation (which in the context of current policy debate almost invariably means the rate of increase in goods prices rather than wages), I must model the goods market. Moreover, if I am to consider such central issues as the relation between interest rates and expenditure decisions, I have to adjust the nominal interest rate for the expected rate of price inflation as well. On the other hand, it is not equally essential to consider wage determination explicitly. It is possible to model endogenous supply decisions without any reference to a labor market at all, as in the familiar "yeoman farmer" models; and so the simplest models developed here are of this form or are equivalent in their implications to such a model, even if a (completely frictionless) labor market is represented.

It is also often argued that there is more reason to believe that the stickiness of prices matters for the allocation of resources. A well-known criticism of the models of nominal wage rigidity popular in the 1970s was that the mere observation of infrequent changes in individual nominal wages did not in itself prove the existence of a nominal rigidity with any allocative consequences (Barro, 1977; Hall, 1980). Because employment is an ongoing relationship rather than a spot-market transaction, the effective cost to a firm of increased employment of labor inputs at a point in time need not equal the wage paid per hour of work at that time; and under an efficient implicit contract, wages might well be smoother than the effective cost of labor, owing to a preference of workers for a smoother income stream. On the other hand, it is less plausible that the observed rigidity of consumer-goods prices should not have allocative consequences, given the absence of a similar kind of ongoing relationship between the suppliers of consumer goods and their customers (Rotemberg, 1987). However, no convincing evidence has ever been offered that the stickiness of nominal wages does *not* result in stickiness of the effective nominal cost of labor inputs. Furthermore, evidence described later—indicating that the evolution of U.S. inflation can be well explained by the evolution of unit labor costs—suggests that a model of supply costs that treats the reported wage as the true marginal cost of additional hours of labor is not too inaccurate. Thus a more empirically realistic model is likely to involve both wage and price stickiness. I treat models of that kind in Section 4.

I devote particular attention to the derivation of models with sticky prices and/or wages in which prices and wages are nonetheless set *optimally* on the occasions when they are adjusted. Allowing for optimal price- and wage-setting is important for several reasons. One is that it allows one to high-light the importance of *expectations* for wage and price dynamics. As we see in later chapters, forward-looking private-sector behavior, in this and other respects, has profound consequences for the optimal conduct of monetary policy. It would thus be a serious mistake to simply assume mechanical wage- and price-adjustment equations (perhaps drawn from the econometric lit-erature) and treat these as structural for purposes of an analysis of optimal monetary policy, as Lucas (1976) so forcefully argued.

Another reason for modeling optimal price- and wagesetting is that I am interested in the welfare evaluation of alternative monetary policies. An es-pecially appealing basis for such evaluation is to ask how alternative possible equilibria compare from the point of view of the private-sector objectives that underlie the behavior assumed in one's model of the effects of alter-native policies; but this is only possible insofar as the structural equations of the present model of the monetary transmission mechanism are derived from optimizing foundations. As is seen in Chapter 6, alternative assump-tions about the nature of price and wage stickiness imply that alternative stabilization objectives for monetary policy are appropriate.

While I give detailed attention to the consequences of assumed delays in the adjustment of prices and/or wages, I do not attempt to say anything new here about the underlying *reasons* for these delays. My assumptions about the frequency with which firms adjust their prices or the time lag that may be involved between the decision about a price and the time that the new price takes effect are treated as structural features of the environment in which firms sell their products, with the same status as their production functions. How reasonable this is depends on the question that one intends to ask of one's model. The "endogenous growth" literature has emphasized that, when thinking about the determinants of economies' long-run growth prospects, it is probably a mistake to ignore the endogeneity of production functions—for changes in economic conditions can change the incentives of private parties to devote resources to research and development, to intro-duce new products, and so on. On the other hand, for purposes of a compar-ison of alternative monetary policy rules, it may not be a bad approximation to assume given production functions. The real effects of alternative mone-tary policies are relatively shortlived, and over this short horizon production possibilities are unlikely to be much affected by the temporary alteration of incentives to innovate that may have occurred.

Similarly, if one wished to analyze the consequences of highly inflation-ary policies, one would surely *not* want to treat as given the frequency of price adjustment, the degree of indexation of wage contracts, or even the currency in terms of which prices are quoted; it is known that practices ad-just in all of these respects (and for reasons that are easy to understand) in economies that suffer from sustained high inflation. But my interest in the present study is in the identification of better monetary policies within the class of policies under which inflation is never very great. In fact, I make extensive use of approximations that are expected to be accurate only for the analysis of policies of that kind. (It is perhaps not giving away too much to divulge at this point that, according to my analysis, optimal policy will indeed involve low and stable inflation!) For this purpose, treating the delays involved in price and wage adjustment as structural may not be a bad approximation. The sizes of wage and price increases do clearly vary from year to year, in response to changes in perceived market conditions; practices with regard to the times at which prices or wages are reconsidered, or the units in which they are announced, occur much less often and only in response to more drastic changes in the economic environment.

Finally, I freely grant that the simple models presented here should be viewed only as crude approximations to the actual monetary transmission mechanism. A realistic quantitative model would need to incorporate a large number of complications from which I abstract here, in order to clarify basic concepts. One may wish to add endogenization of the timing of price and wage adjustments to the list of refinements that one would like to incorporate into an eventual, truly accurate model. It is not clear, however, that this particular one should be placed too high on the list of refinements when ranked in terms of their likely quantitative importance for the analysis of monetary policy.

Nor is it even clear that any of the models with endogenous timing of price changes that currently exist should be regarded as more realistic than the models presented here, quite apart from the question of complexity. Some feel that models of "state-dependent pricing," such as those of Caplin and Leahy (1991) or Dotsey et al. (1999), have *better microfoundations* than do the sorts of models presented here, which assume a given timing for price and wage changes. But this is not obvious. These models assume that firms are constantly reevaluating the price that they *would* adopt if they were to change their price and the expected benefits from the change, and then weighing these benefits against the current "menu cost" of a price change to decide whether to actually change their price or not. Yet in reality, the main benefit of infrequent price changes is not lower menu costs, but reduction of the costs associated with information collection and decisionmaking (Zbaracki et al., 1999). Obtaining this benefit necessarily means that the timing of the occasions upon which prices are reconsidered is largely independent of current market conditions; for example, firms often reconsider pricing policy at a particular time of year.

I begin in Section 1 with a basic model of monopolistic competition, in which the prices of some goods must be determined a period in advance. This very simple example of price stickiness is useful for introducing a number of basic concepts. It also provides optimizing foundations for a familiar aggregate-supply specification, the New Classical Phillips curve, used in many well-known analyses of optimal monetary policy, such as those of Kydland and Prescott (1977) and Barro and Gordon (1983). While the literature using this specification has produced a number of insights of more general importance, this relation is quite inadequate as a realistic account of the co-movement of real and nominal variables. For example, it does not allow any persistent effects of monetary policy on real activity or any effects of anticipated policy. These strong conclusions are not general consequences of optimal pricesetting, as I show in Section 2 through the analysis of the Calvo (1983) model of staggered pricesetting. While still very simple, the Calvo model implies an aggregate-supply relation, sometimes called the "New Keynesian Phillips curve," that has proven capable of explaining at least some of the more gross features of inflation dynamics in the United States and elsewhere. Section 3 discusses still more complex specifications with increased empirical realism that introduce delays in the effects of monetary policy changes on inflation. Finally, Section 4 discusses models in which nominal wages as well as prices are sticky.

1 A Basic Sticky-Price Model

I begin by displaying the structure of a very basic model in which monetary policy has real effects as a result of some goods prices being fixed in advance. A number of issues that are easy to analyze in this simple context turn out to be relevant to the more realistic models to be developed in later sections.

3.1 Pricesetting and Endogenous Output

In order to be able to model pricesetting, one must first extend the representative-household model introduced in the previous chapter in certain respects that are quite distinct from the issue of whether prices are assumed to be *sticky*. In particular, one must allow for endogenous goods supply, rather than simply assuming a given endowment of goods. This requires the introduction of a production technology and at least one variable factor of production (which is labor in this basic model). I am concerned with understanding the determinants of the costs of supplying goods, as supply costs are a prime determinant of optimal pricing. I also introduce differentiated goods and monopolistic competition among the suppliers of these goods, as in the New Keynesian literature originated by Rotemberg (1982), Mankiw (1985), Svensson (1986), and Blanchard and Kiyotaki (1987), rather than assuming a single good in competitive supply. This last device, which is now quite commonplace, allows individual suppliers a degree of market power and hence a decision about how to set their prices. It also implies that a supplier that fails to immediately adjust its price in response to a change in demand conditions does not suffer an unboundedly large (percentage) change in its sales, so that it becomes more plausible that prices should not be constantly adjusted.[1]

Thus I now assume that the representative household seeks to maximize a discounted sum of utilities of the form

$$E_0 \left\{ \sum_{t=0}^{\infty} \beta^t \left[u(C_t, M_t/P_t; \xi_t) - \int_0^1 v(h_t(i); \xi_t) di \right] \right\}. \tag{1.1}$$

Here C_t is now an *index* of the household's consumption of each of the individual goods that are supplied, and P_t is a corresponding index of the prices of these goods, while $h_t(i)$ is the quantity of labor of type i supplied. I assume that each of the differentiated goods (indexed by i over the unit interval) uses a specialized labor input in its production (and in this chapter, this will be the *only* variable input); labor of type i is used to produce differentiated good i.

Introducing differentiated labor inputs is not necessary for an analysis of a monopolistically competitive goods supply, but as we shall see, it is convenient to do so. One reason is that I am able, in this case, to derive a model with factor markets that is equivalent to the frequently used yeoman farmer model, in which households are assumed to supply goods directly. A more important reason is that it turns out that the strategic complementarity among different suppliers' pricing decisions is greater when it is assumed that they do not hire labor from a single homogeneous (competitive) labor market. Because I regard the conclusion obtained in the case of differentiated labor inputs as the more realistic one, I choose this specification as the baseline model. (The case of a single homogeneous labor market is discussed in Section 1.4.)

The term $v(h_t(i); \xi_t)$ represents the disutility of supplying labor of type i. I assume that for each possible value of ξ, $v(\cdot; \xi)$ is an increasing, convex function,[2] and have written (1.1) as if the representative household simultaneously supplies *all* of the types of labor. However, I might equally well

---

1. The size of the menu costs required to rationalize the failure of suppliers to adjust their prices immediately has been the subject of an extensive literature. I do not pursue this issue here, though I note that the same sorts of "strategic complementarities" in pricesetting that increase the degree of stickiness of the general price level (as discussed below) when price adjustment is asynchronous also tend to reduce the size of the costs of price changes to individual suppliers that are required to rationalize a failure to adjust prices in response to an aggregate-demand disturbance. On this latter point, see in particular Ball and Romer (1990).

2. Once again, ξ_t is a vector, so that the use of the same notation for exogenous disturbances to the functions u and v involves no assumption about statistical dependence between the shifts in these two functions.

assume that each household specializes in the supply of only *one* type of labor, but that there are an equal number of households supplying each type. In this case, a household that supplies labor of type i seeks to maximize

$$E_0 \left\{ \sum_{t=0}^{\infty} \beta^t \left[u(C_t, M_t/P_t; \xi_t) - v(h_t(i); \xi_t) \right] \right\}.$$

When not all goods prices are set at the same time, households' wage incomes will be different, depending upon the type of labor they supply. But it may be assumed that there exist competitive financial markets in which these risks are efficiently shared.

In this case, and if all households start with initial financial assets that give them the same initial intertemporal budget constraints,[3] since households value consumption streams (and money balances) identically and face the same prices, all households choose identical consumption and real balances in all states. (Note that while I have allowed for preference shocks ξ_t in (1.1), I assume that these are the same for all households—here I contemplate only *aggregate* shocks.) They also choose portfolios of financial assets that ensure that they continue to have identical intertemporal budget constraints at all subsequent dates.[4] The common intertemporal budget constraint in each state is in turn exactly that of a household that supplies *all* of the types of labor, and pools the wage income received.

Because each household chooses exactly the same state-contingent consumption plan, the first-order conditions for optimal supply of each type of labor are exactly the same as when a single household type supplies all types of labor so as to maximize (1.1). Thus the conditions that determine equilibrium prices and quantities are the same in the two models. Furthermore, if the welfare criterion in the specialized-labor model is the average level of utility of all households, the level of social welfare associated with a given equilibrium is measured by the value of (1.1). Thus it makes no difference to my conclusions which version of the model is assumed. The fiction that each household supplies all types of labor directly, and so receives its pro rata share of the aggregate wage bill of the entire economy, simplifies the

3. This means that if any households face different present values of their expected wage incomes as of date zero, they hold initial financial claims W_0 that differ in exactly the way necessary to offset the difference in their expected wages. Note that if this condition has *ever* held, then optimization in the presence of complete financial markets implies that it will hold *forever after*, regardless of which values may be realized for the exogenous disturbances.

4. Here my argument relies upon the assumption in (1.1) that the disutility of labor supply is additively separable from the other terms. This implies that even if households expect to work different amounts in particular states, they equalize their marginal utility of income in each state by holding assets that allow them to afford to consume exactly the same amount and hold exactly the same money balances as one another.

exposition in that it allows one to dispense with explicit discussion of the risk-sharing arrangements just referred to.

Following Dixit and Stiglitz (1977), I assume that the index C_t is a constant-elasticity-of-substitution aggregator

$$C_t \equiv \left[\int_0^1 c_t(i)^{(\theta-1)/\theta} \, di \right]^{\theta/(\theta-1)} \tag{1.2}$$

with $\theta > 1$, and that P_t is the corresponding price index

$$P_t \equiv \left[\int_0^1 p_t(i)^{1-\theta} \, di \right]^{1/(1-\theta)}. \tag{1.3}$$

Note that (1.3) defines the minimum cost of a unit of the aggregate defined by (1.2), given the individual goods prices $\{p_t(i)\}$. Since a household cares only about the number of units of this aggregate that it can purchase, deflation by P_t is an appropriate measure of the purchasing power of nominal money balances M_t.

The household's budget constraints are then the same as in Chapter 2, except that the term $p_t c_t$ for nominal consumption expenditure must now be replaced by $\int_0^1 p_t(i) c_t(i) \, di$, and the term $p_t y_t$ for income from the sale of goods must now be replaced by

$$\int_0^1 w_t(i) h_t(i) \, di + \int_0^1 \Pi_t(i) \, di, \tag{1.4}$$

where $w_t(i)$ is the nominal wage of labor of type i in period t, and $\Pi_t(i)$ represents the nominal profits from sales of good i. In writing this last expression, I assume that each household owns an equal share of all of the firms that produce the various goods. Again, given the assumption of complete financial markets, this assumption of distributed ownership is irrelevant. I could also introduce trading in the shares of the firms without any change in the conditions for a rational-expectations equilibrium, except that then equilibrium share prices would also be determined. As these extensions of the framework have no consequences for the equilibrium evolution of goods prices or the quantities of goods supplied, I omit further discussion of them.

As in Chapter 2, each household then faces a single intertemporal budget constraint. Optimal (pricetaking) household behavior is then described by the conjunction of three sets of requirements. First, the household's consumption spending must be optimally allocated *across differentiated goods* at each point in time, taking as given the overall level of expenditure. Thus the relative expenditures on different goods must be such as to maximize the index (1.2) given the level of total expenditure. As in other applications of the Dixit-Stiglitz model, this requires that purchases of each good i satisfy

$$c_t(i) = C_t \left(\frac{p_t(i)}{P_t} \right)^{-\theta}. \tag{1.5}$$

This rule for distributing expenditure is easily seen to imply that total expenditure is equal to $P_t C_t$. Using this substitution, I can write *both* the household's utility and its budget constraints solely in terms of P_t and C_t, without any reference to quantities or prices of the individual goods that are purchased.

Second, taking as given the optimal allocation of consumption expenditure at each date (just described) and the amount of labor supplied (considered below), the household must choose optimal levels of total consumption expenditure at each date, an optimal level of money balances to hold at each date, an optimal amount of financial wealth to accumulate, and an optimal portfolio allocation across the various types of state-contingent bonds that are available. Necessary and sufficient conditions for optimization in this respect are given by *exactly the same* conditions as in Chapter 2—namely, conditions (1.2), (1.12), (1.13), (1.15), and (1.16) of that chapter must again hold at all times, except that now P_t now refers to the price index (1.3); c_t is replaced by the index C_t defined in (1.2); and y_t is replaced by Y_t, a similarly defined aggregate of the quantities supplied of the various differentiated goods.[5] This is because both preferences over alternative streams of the consumption aggregate and budget constraints written in terms of affordable paths for the consumption aggregate are exactly the same as in Chapter 2.[6]

Finally, the household must choose an optimal quantity of each kind of labor to supply, given the wages that it faces and the value to it of additional income (determined by the consumption-allocation problem just described). The first-order condition for optimal supply of labor of type i at date t is given by

$$\frac{v_h(h_t(i); \xi_t)}{u_c(C_t, m_t; \xi_t)} = \frac{w_t(i)}{P_t}. \tag{1.6}$$

---

5. The relative quantities supplied of the various goods must be distributed in the same way as the relative demands implied by (1.5). (When I later allow for government purchases, I assume that the government seeks to maximize a similar aggregate of its purchases and so distributes them in the same manner.) It then follows that total nonfinancial income (1.4), which must equal total sales revenues of all of the firms, can be written as $P_t Y_t$.

6. Here the additive separability of the disutility-of-labor terms in (1.1) is again crucial, allowing me to obtain preferences over paths for the consumption aggregate and real balances that are the same as in the earlier model with no labor-supply decision.

These conditions, together with those listed earlier, constitute a complete set of necessary and sufficient conditions for household optimization.

I turn next to the specification of production possibilities. I assume that each good i has a production function

$$y_t(i) = A_t f(h_t(i)),\tag{1.7}$$

where $A_t > 0$ is a time-varying exogenous technology factor, and f is an increasing, concave function. Here labor is represented as the only factor of production (with one specific type of labor being used in the production of each good). One may think of capital as being allocated to each firm in a fixed amount, with capital goods never depreciating, never being produced, and (because they are specific to the firm that uses them) never being reallocated among firms; in this case, the additional argument of the production function may be suppressed. (An extension of the model to allow for endogenous capital accumulation is presented in the next chapter.)

It follows that the variable cost of supplying a quantity $y_t(i)$ of good i is given by

$$w_t(i)f^{-1}(y_t(i)/A_t).$$

Differentiating this, we find that the (nominal) marginal cost of supplying good i is equal to

$$S_t(i) = \frac{w_t(i)}{A_t} \Psi(y_t(i)/A_t),\tag{1.8}$$

where

$$\Psi(y) \equiv \frac{1}{f'(f^{-1}(y))}\tag{1.9}$$

is an increasing positive function.

Here I assume that the producer is a wagetaker, even though I have supposed that the supplier of each differentiated good uses a different type of labor with its own market. But an assumption of differentiated labor inputs need not imply that each producer is a monopsonist in its labor market. The only assumption that is important for the subsequent results is that producers that change their prices at different times also hire labor inputs from distinct markets. I might, for example, assume a double continuum of differentiated goods, indexed by (I, j), with an elasticity of substitution of θ between any two goods, as previously. It might then be assumed that all goods with the same index I (goods in the same "industry") change their prices at the same time (and so always charge the same price), and are also all produced using the same type of labor (type I labor).[7] The degree of market power of each producer in its product market would then be as assumed here, but the fact that a continuum of producers all bid for type I labor would eliminate any market power in their labor market. In this model, the marginal cost for each firm $i = (I, j)$ would equal $w_t(I)f^{-1}(y_t(i)/A_t)$, and the industry wage would satisfy (1.6) with $h_t(I) \equiv \int_j h_t(I, j) dj$, the total labor demand in industry I, replacing $h_t(i)$. However, in equilibrium, the firms in a given industry would produce the same amount each period, so that $h_t(i) = h_t(I)$ for each $i = (I, j)$, and the expressions given here for the wage and for marginal cost would be correct.

Substituting the labor-supply function (1.6) for the wage in (1.8) yields a relation between the real marginal supply cost and the quantity supplied:

$$s_t(i) \equiv S_t(i)/P_t = s(y_t(i), Y_t; \tilde{\xi}_t),$$

where the *real marginal cost function* is defined by

$$s(y, Y; \tilde{\xi}) = \frac{v_h(f^{-1}(y/A); \xi)}{u_c(Y; \xi)A} \Psi(y/A). \tag{1.10}$$

In this last expression, $\tilde{\xi}_t$ represents the complete vector of exogenous disturbances, in which the preference shocks ξ_t have been augmented by the technology factor A_t, we have substituted into the labor supply function the sectoral labor requirement as a function of sectoral output, and we have used the fact that in equilibrium, the index of aggregate consumption C_t must at all times equal the index of output Y_t.[8]

Note also that I have suppressed real balances as an argument of u_c (and hence as an argument of the real marginal cost function) in the denominator. Abstracting from such real-balance effects can be justified along any

---

7. It might be wondered why one should assume that the producers who happen to share factor markets should also change their prices at the same time. The analysis of Lau (2001) of a strategic model with endogenous timing of price changes—which finds that synchronization of price changes arises as an equilibrium phenomenon in the case of producers whose pricing decisions are "strategic substitutes," while staggering of price changes arises in the case of producers whose pricing decisions are "strategic complements"—makes this a plausible assumption. For as shown later, the pricing decisions of firms that share the same factor markets are more likely to be strategic substitutes.

8. When I allow for exogenous variation in government purchases, I can still apply this equation, if I understand $u(Y_t; \xi_t)$ to mean the function $\tilde{u}(Y_t; \tilde{\xi}_t)$ introduced in Section 1.1 of Chapter 2, measuring household utility flow as a function of *aggregate demand* rather than consumption expenditure. Under this interpretation, the level of government purchases is just one element of the vector of exogenous disturbances $\tilde{\xi}$ that shifts this relation. When I allow for endogenous variations in investment spending, matters are more complex; in such a case, it is important to remember that it is really $u_c(C; \xi)$ rather than $u_c(Y; \xi)$ that belongs in the denominator of (1.10).

of several grounds discussed in Chapter 2. It is simplest to suppose that the economy considered in this chapter is a cashless one, in which monetary policy is implemented in the way considered in Section 1 of Chapter 2.[9] As in Chapter 2, I assume here a cashless economy as the baseline model; the consequences of real-balance effects are considered in Section 3.2 of Chapter 4.

This model of production costs might alternatively be derived from a yeoman farmer model, in which households supply goods directly, seeking to maximize

$$E_0 \left\{ \sum_{t=0}^{\infty} \beta^t \left[u(C_t, M_t/P_t; \xi_t) - \int_0^1 \tilde{v}(y_t(i); \tilde{\xi}_t) di \right] \right\}. \tag{1.11}$$

If I convert the marginal disutility of supply of good i into units of an equivalent quantity of the consumption aggregate, I obtain a *real marginal cost* of good i equal to

$$\frac{\tilde{v}_y(y_t(i); \tilde{\xi}_t)}{u_c(Y_t; \xi_t)}.$$

This is in fact identical to (1.10) if the disutility of output supply is given by

$$\tilde{v}(y; \tilde{\xi}) \equiv v(f^{-1}(y/A); \xi).$$

This concept of real marginal cost plays exactly the same role in optimal pricing in the yeoman farmer model as does the more conventional concept in the case of supply by firms that purchase inputs, and the results that are obtained here are identical to those that one would obtain from a yeoman farmer model. As noted earlier, this is one reason for interest in the model with differentiated labor inputs assumed here. However, explicitly modeling the labor market has the advantage of allowing me to derive additional implications of the model. It also makes the subsequent extension to a model with sticky wages as well as sticky prices more straightforward.

---

9. Alternatively, the results apply to a Sidrauski-Brock model in which utility is separable, as discussed in Section 3.2 of Chapter 2; to a cash-in-advance model of the special type discussed in Section A.16 of Appendix A; or to a cashless limiting economy of the sort discussed in Section 3.4 of Chapter 2. They also apply to a much broader class of models with transactions frictions, in the case that monetary policy is implemented through a procedure under which the interest-rate differential Δ_t is held constant, under a suitable reinterpretation of the parameter σ and the disturbance g_t, so that $-\sigma^{-1}(\hat{Y}_t - g_t)$ is the deviation of the log marginal utility of real income from its steady-state level in the case of a constant interest-rate differential (rather than a constant level of real balances). For discussion of this last case, see Section 3.2 of Chapter 4, especially footnote 59.

With a theory of marginal supply costs in place, I now turn to the question of optimal pricing, and examine first the case of *perfectly flexible* prices; that is, I assume that the supplier of each good chooses a price for it each period, not constrained in any way by the price that has been charged for the good in the past and with full information about current demand and cost conditions. As usual in a model of monopolistic competition, it is assumed that each supplier understands that its sales depend upon the price charged for its good, according to the demand function

$$y_t(i) = Y_t \left(\frac{p_t(i)}{P_t} \right)^{-\theta}. \tag{1.12}$$

(The form of the demand curve assumed here follows from (1.5); when all purchases are for private consumption, the index of aggregate demand Y_t corresponds simply to the representative household's choice of the index C_t.) Because good i accounts for only an infinitesimal contribution to households' budgets and their utility from consumption, the supplier of an individual good does not believe that his pricing decision can affect the evolution of either the index of aggregate demand Y_t or the price index P_t; thus $p_t(i)$ is chosen taking the latter two quantities as given. Optimization by the supplier of good i then involves setting a price $p_t(i) = \mu S_t(i)$, where $\mu \equiv \theta/(\theta - 1) > 1$ is the seller's *desired markup*, determined by the usual Lerner formula.

It follows that each supplier wishes to charge a relative price satisfying

$$\frac{p_t(i)}{P_t} = \mu s(y_t(i), Y_t; \tilde{\xi}_t). \tag{1.13}$$

Then from (1.12), the relative supply of good i must satisfy

$$\left(\frac{y_t(i)}{Y_t} \right)^{-1/\theta} = \mu s(y_t(i), Y_t; \tilde{\xi}_t).$$

Because s is increasing in its first argument, this equation must have a unique solution for $y_t(i)$ given Y_t. It follows that in equilibrium, the same quantity must be supplied of each good, and that common quantity must equal Y_t. Equilibrium output must then be given by $Y_t = Y^n(\tilde{\xi}_t)$, where the latter function indicates the solution to the equation

$$s \left(Y_t^n, Y_t^n; \tilde{\xi}_t \right) = \mu^{-1}. \tag{1.14}$$

Because s is also increasing in its second argument, this equation as well must have a unique solution for each specification of the exogenous shocks $\tilde{\xi}_t$.

One thus finds that in the case of fully flexible prices, equilibrium output is completely *independent of monetary policy*. Given this solution for aggregate output as a function of the exogenous shocks, this model of price-level determination then reduces to exactly the model analyzed in Chapter 2 (where an exogenous supply of goods was simply assumed). Thus neither the introduction of endogenous supply nor the assumption of monopolistic competition has any necessary consequences for the effects of monetary policy. But they now make it possible to consider other assumptions about pricing behavior, and we shall see that in the case of sticky prices the conclusions *are* different.

The solution to equation (1.14)—which I call the *natural rate of output* following Friedman (1968)—continues to be a useful construct even in the case of sticky prices (though it no longer need equal the *equilibrium* level of output at all times).[10] This is because a log-linear approximation to the real marginal cost function (1.10) is given by

$$\hat{s}_t(i) = \omega \hat{y}_t(i) + \sigma^{-1} \hat{Y}_t - \left(\omega + \sigma^{-1}\right) \hat{Y}_t^n, \tag{1.15}$$

where $\omega > 0$ represents the elasticity of s with respect to its first argument, and $\sigma > 0$ is the intertemporal elasticity of substitution of private expenditure, as in Chapter 2. Here I log-linearize around the steady-state equilibrium in the case of flexible prices and $\tilde{\xi}_t = 0$ at all times.[11] Letting $\bar{Y}$ be the constant level of output in this steady state, I define $\hat{Y}_t$ as in Chapter 2 and correspondingly define $\hat{y}_t(i) \equiv \log\left(y_t(i)/\bar{Y}\right)$, $\hat{Y}_t^n \equiv \log(Y_t^n/\bar{Y})$, and $\hat{s}_t(i) \equiv \log\left(\mu s_t(i)\right)$. Thus the natural rate of output provides a useful summary of the way in which disturbances shift the real marginal cost function, whether prices are constantly adjusted or not.

For later purposes it is useful to note that in (1.15), the elasticity ω can be decomposed as

$$\omega = \omega_w + \omega_p, \tag{1.16}$$

where $\omega_w > 0$ is the elasticity of the marginal disutility of work with respect to output increases, and $\omega_p > 0$ is the elasticity of the function Ψ defined in (1.9). Thus ω_w indicates the elasticity of real wage demands with respect to the level of output, holding fixed the marginal utility of income, while ω_p

---

10. Some authors would say that it *is* the equilibrium level of output, but that the level of output actually observed as a result of sticky prices is instead a disequilibrium level of output. I avoid this terminology in this study; here, equilibrium always refers to the prediction of the model, whether it involves fully flexible prices or not.

11. The element of $\tilde{\xi}_t$ that measures aggregate technology is here taken to be $a_t \equiv \log A_t$ rather than A_t itself. Thus the steady-state value of the technology factor A_t is normalized as one.

indicates the negative of the elasticity of the marginal product of labor with respect to the level of output.[12]

It is also worth noting that both the neutrality result just obtained, and the usefulness of the concept of the natural rate of output, apply to a broader range of specifications of the structure of costs and of demand than those described previously. In any of a range of models (further examples of which are discussed in Section 1.4), the nominal profits in period t of the supplier of good i are given by a function of the form

$$\Pi_t(i) = \Pi\big(p_t(i), p_t^I, P_t; Y_t, \tilde{\xi}_t\big), \tag{1.17}$$

where $p_t(i)$ is the price charged for good i, p_t^I is an index of the prices charged in industry I (to which good i belongs), and P_t is an economy-wide price index. The industry is assumed to be a collection of suppliers that always change their prices at the same time (this matters only when I introduce sticky prices), and also hire inputs in common factor markets as well (see text at footnote 7 above). As an example, in the baseline model introduced above, the profit function is given by

$$\Pi(p, p^I, P; Y, \tilde{\xi}) \equiv pY(p/P)^{-\theta}$$
$$- \frac{v_h(f^{-1}(Y(p^I/P)^{-\theta}/A); \xi)}{u_c(Y - G; \xi)} P f^{-1}(Y(p/P)^{-\theta}/A), \tag{1.18}$$

where it is assumed that the wage faced by each supplier depends on total labor demand in its industry.[13] However, one might vary the specification in any of several respects and still obtain a profit function of the general form (1.17).

I wish to make the following general assumption regarding the profit function.

ASSUMPTION 3.1. The function Π is homogeneous degree one in its first three arguments and a single-peaked function of its first argument, with a maximum at some positive price for any values of its other arguments.

---

12. In a model with wage- and pricesetting, ω_w indicates the degree to which higher economic activity increases workers' desired wages given prices, while ω_p indicates the degree to which higher economic activity increases producers' desired prices given wages.

13. Because in equilibrium each supplier in the same industry always chooses the same price, it suffices to evaluate the profit function under the assumption that all suppliers in industry I other than firm i choose a common price p^I, though the consequences for i of deviating from this must be considered. In (1.18) it is also assumed that i's own labor demand will have a negligible impact on industry labor demand, so that the individual supplier is a wagetaker, as discussed previously.

The elements of Assumption 3.1 are easily seen to be satisfied in the previous example. The single-peakedness follows from the fact that revenues are a concave (increasing) function of the quantity sold of good i, while the labor requirement $f^{-1}(y_t(i)/A_t)$ is a convex (increasing) function of the same variable. Hence profits are a concave function of $y_t(i)$; and since marginal revenue becomes unboundedly large as sales approach zero and approaches zero as sales are made sufficiently large, there is necessarily an interior maximum for this function. Then, since sales of good i are a monotonically decreasing function of $p_t(i)$, it follows that profit as a function of $p_t(i)$ is also single-peaked.

In this general formalism, the first-order condition for optimal pricing by the supplier of good i takes the form

$$\Pi_1\left(p_t(i), p_t^I, P_t; Y_t, \tilde{\xi}_t\right) = 0, \tag{1.19}$$

and under Assumption 3.1, this equation must have a unique solution that corresponds to the interior profit maximum. In a flexible-price equilibrium, then, the common price chosen by all suppliers must satisfy

$$\Pi_1\left(P_t, P_t, P_t; Y_t, \tilde{\xi}_t\right) = 0. \tag{1.20}$$

But under Assumption 3.1, the homogeneity of the function Π implies that Π_1 must be a function that is homogeneous of degree zero in its first three arguments. Hence the left-hand side of (1.20) is independent of the value of P_t, and this equilibrium condition can be solved for Y_t, independently of monetary policy. I thus obtain the following generalization of the earlier result.

PROPOSITION 3.1. Let the profit function of the supplier of an individual good be of the form (1.17) and satisfy Assumption 3.1, and suppose that all prices are flexible. Then the equilibrium level of output of each good is independent of monetary policy, and given by $y_t(i) = Y_t^n$, where the *natural rate of output* is implicitly defined by the equation

$$\Pi_1\left(1, 1, 1; Y_t^n, \tilde{\xi}_t\right) = 0. \tag{1.21}$$

Of course, the result here that monetary policy is *completely* irrelevant to the determination of real activity is rather special. If, for example, one allows for real-balance effects, one finds that monetary policy can affect equilibrium output even under flexible prices, owing to the effects of expected inflation upon equilibrium real balances. Moreover, if one allows for endogenous capital accumulation, one finds that the natural rate of output depends upon the capital stock, and insofar as real-balance effects are able to affect equilibrium capital accumulation, they may have a further effect upon equilibrium output under flexible prices through this channel as well. However, these effects are not plausibly very large in quantitative terms, as studies such as that of Cooley and Hansen (1989) have shown. Thus the conclusion from the present simple model remains essentially correct.

1.2 Consequences of Prices Fixed in Advance

I now contrast these results to those obtained under a simple form of price stickiness. Suppose that all prices $p_t(i)$ must be fixed *a period in advance;* that is, when $p_t(i)$ is chosen, the exogenous disturbances (including possible random variation in monetary policy) realized in periods $t - 1$ or earlier are known, but not any of the disturbances that are to be realized only in period t. (Whether the stickiness of prices results because the price that applies in period t has to be announced at an earlier time or simply because pricesetters make their decision on the basis of old information does not matter for my conclusions.) I assume that the supplier of good i is committed to supply whatever quantity buyers may wish to purchase at the predetermined price $p_t(i)$, and hence to purchase whatever quantity of inputs may turn out to be necessary to fill orders.

When the price $p_t(i)$ is chosen, in period $t-1$, the consequences for sales and profits in period t are not yet known with certainty. Hence I assume that the firm seeks to maximize the *present value* of period t profits, given by

$$E_{t-1}\left[Q_{t-1,t}\Pi\left(p_t(i), p_t^I, P_t; Y_t, \tilde{\xi}_t\right)\right], \tag{1.22}$$

where $Q_{t-1,t}$ is the stochastic discount factor introduced in Chapter 2, and the profit function Π is the one introduced in the previous section. The supplier of good i chooses $p_t(i)$ on the basis of information available at date $t - 1$ so as to maximize this expression, given the expected state-contingent values of the random variables $Q_{t-1,t}$, Y_t, p_t^I, P_t, and the exogenous disturbances $\tilde{\xi}_t$.

The first-order condition for this problem is given by

$$E_{t-1}\left[Q_{t-1,t}\Pi_1\left(p_t(i), p_t^I, P_t; Y_t, \tilde{\xi}_t\right)\right] = 0. \tag{1.23}$$

In an equilibrium in which all prices are set at date $t - 1$ by firms solving this same pricing problem, and hence all take a common value, it must be the case that

$$E_{t-1}\left[Q_{t-1,t}\Pi_1\left(P_t, P_t, P_t; Y_t, \tilde{\xi}_t\right)\right] = 0.$$

Again, because Π_1 is a homogeneous degree-zero function of its first three arguments, this condition is independent of the value of P_t, and may equivalently be written

$$E_{t-1}\left[Q_{t-1,t}\Pi_1\left(1,1,1;Y_t,\tilde{\xi}_t\right)\right]=0. \tag{1.24}$$

In the case of the profit function (1.18) associated with the model introduced in the previous section, this condition takes the form

$$E_{t-1}\left\{u_c(Y_t;\xi_t)Y_t\left[\mu^{-1}-s(Y_t,Y_t;\tilde{\xi}_t)\right]\right\}=0, \tag{1.25}$$

where I have also substituted the form for the stochastic discount factor obtained in Chapter 2 in the case of preferences of the kind assumed in this model.

Here (1.24), or (1.25) in the case of the baseline model, represents a restriction that must be satisfied by the joint distribution of Y_t and the exogenous disturbances $\tilde{\xi}_t$, conditional upon information at date $t-1$; note that it involves no nominal variables. It is a weaker version of the result in the case of flexible prices, where $Y_t = Y_t^n$ at all times. Output equal to the natural rate is equivalent to requiring that $s(Y_t, Y_t; \tilde{\xi}_t) = \mu^{-1}$ at all times; instead, (1.24) requires only that this hold "on average" (where the average in question does not involve weights exactly equal to the probability of each state's occurrence).

Together with the stipulation that P_t is predetermined, (1.24) represents an *aggregate supply* relation for this model. One can examine its implications, without needing to specify the rest of the model, if one supposes that monetary policy is used to achieve an exogenous target path for nominal GDP: $\mathcal{Y}_t = P_t Y_t$. This sort of aggregate demand specification is very commonly assumed in the literature on sticky-price models, usually by stipulating that nominal GDP is proportional to the money supply, and then that monetary policy is specified by an exogenous target path for the money supply. It is not attractive, for present purposes, to assume either a constant velocity of money or monetary targeting. But I may nonetheless examine an equivalent aggregate demand specification by assuming that policy is specified in terms of a target path for nominal GDP, which is then achieved by adjusting the interest-rate instrument as necessary. In addition to allowing comparisons with familiar literature, this assumption allows me to examine the consequences of alternative aggregate supply specifications without needing to specify the way in which monetary policy affects aggregate spending. Accordingly, aggregate demand is specified in terms of an exogenous process $\{\mathcal{Y}_t\}$ throughout the present chapter. (The interest-rate adjustments required in order to control aggregate spending are then taken up in Chapter 4.)

Substituting $Y_t = \mathcal{Y}_t/P_t$ into (1.25), one observes that the equilibrium price level is given by the solution to the equation

$$E_{t-1}\left\{u_c(\mathcal{Y}_t/P_t;\xi_t)\mathcal{Y}_t\left[\mu^{-1}-s(\mathcal{Y}_t/P_t,\mathcal{Y}_t/P_t;\tilde{\xi}_t)\right]\right\}=0. \tag{1.26}$$

This implies that P_t is a function solely of the joint distribution of $\{\mathcal{Y}_t, \tilde{\xi}_t\}$, conditional upon information at date $t-1$, and that this function is homogeneous of degree one in the distribution of values anticipated for $\mathcal{Y}_t$. Given the value of P_t determined by this ex ante distribution, the level of output Y_t is then determined by the ex post realization of $\mathcal{Y}_t$. The homogeneity property just referred to implies that Y_t depends only upon the level of $\mathcal{Y}_t$ *relative* to the distribution of levels of nominal spending that were regarded as possible at date $t-1$.

This result can be stated more simply if one makes use of a log-linear approximation to the aggregate-supply relation (1.24). I log-linearize around the steady-state equilibrium in which $\tilde{\xi}_t = 0$ and $\mathcal{Y}_t/\mathcal{Y}_{t-1} = 1$ at all times and obtain an expression that approximates the exact solution as long as $\tilde{\xi}_t$ and $\mathcal{Y}_t/\mathcal{Y}_{t-1}$ are always sufficiently *close* to these values. If $\bar{Y} > 0$ again denotes the natural rate of output implicitly defined by (1.21) when $\tilde{\xi}_t = 0$, log-linearization of (1.21) implies that

$$\Pi_1\left(P_t, P_t, P_t; Y_t, \tilde{\xi}_t\right) = \psi_y\left(\hat{Y}_t - \hat{Y}_t^n\right) \tag{1.27}$$

to a first-order approximation, for arbitrary P_t and any values of Y_t close enough to $\bar{Y}$ and $\tilde{\xi}_t$ small enough, where ψ_y is a positive coefficient. Then log-linearization of (1.24) and substitution of (1.27) yields

$$E_{t-1}\left[\hat{Y}_t - \hat{Y}_t^n\right] = 0.$$

Thus the result described intuitively in the previous paragraph can in fact be justified as a log-linear approximation, independently of the specific assumptions made in (1.25). With the substitution $Y_t = \mathcal{Y}_t/P_t$, this in turn implies that the equilibrium price level is approximately given by

$$\log P_t = E_{t-1}\log \mathcal{Y}_t - E_{t-1}\log Y_t^n,$$

from which it follows that

$$\log Y_t = E_{t-1}\log Y_t^n + [\log \mathcal{Y}_t - E_{t-1}\log \mathcal{Y}_t].$$

One then observes that the component of output that can be forecasted a period in advance is always equal to the forecast of the natural rate,

$$E_{t-1}\log Y_t = E_{t-1}\log Y_t^n,$$

and hence is independent of monetary policy. The unexpected component of output fluctuations, by contrast, is equal to the unexpected component of nominal GDP (or of nominal GDP growth):

$$\log Y_t - E_{t-1} \log Y_t = \log \mathcal{Y}_t - E_{t-1} \log \mathcal{Y}_t.$$

Thus monetary policy affects real activity in this model only insofar as it causes unexpected variation in nominal spending, and the resulting variations in output must themselves be purely unexpected.

1.3   A New Classical Phillips Curve

The previous model can be generalized by allowing some prices to be flexible, though others are fixed in advance. This enables consideration of the robustness of the previous conclusions to allowing some prices to be flexible, even in the very short run (as is in fact observed). It also permits one to derive a Phillips-curve relation between price movements and output movements of a kind familiar from the New Classical literature of the 1970s.

Suppose now that a fraction $0 < \iota < 1$ of the goods prices are fully flexible—which is to say, set each period on the basis of full information about current demand and cost conditions—while the remaining $1 - \iota$ are set a period in advance, as in the previous subsection. The supplier of each flexible-price good then sets its price each period according to (1.19), whereas the supplier of each sticky-price good sets its price in advance according to (1.23). Under the assumption that the goods in a given industry are either all flexible-price goods or all fixed-price goods, it follows that all flexible-price goods have a common price p_{1t}, and all sticky-price goods similarly have a common price p_{2t}. These two prices satisfy

$$\Pi_1\left(p_{1t}, p_{1t}, P_t; Y_t, \tilde{\xi}_t\right) = 0, \tag{1.28}$$

$$E_{t-1}\left[Q_{t-1,t}\Pi_1\left(p_{2t}, p_{2t}, P_t; Y_t, \tilde{\xi}_t\right)\right] = 0, \tag{1.29}$$

where P_t is an aggregate of the two prices, with the additional stipulation that p_{2t} must depend only on information available at date $t - 1$.

In order to characterize the real effects of variations in aggregate nominal expenditure, it is again useful to compute a log-linear approximation to these pricing relations. Note that Assumption 3.1 implies that for any values of the arguments, $\Pi_1(p, p, P; Y, \tilde{\xi})$ depends only on the values of p/P, Y, and $\tilde{\xi}$. Taking a log-linear approximation to Π_1 in terms of the latter three arguments, near the values $(1, \bar{Y}, 0)$, and then substituting (1.27), yields

$$\Pi_1\left(p_t, p_t, P_t; Y_t, \tilde{\xi}_t\right) = \psi_p \log(p_t/P_t) + \psi_y\left(\hat{Y}_t - \hat{Y}_t^n\right),$$

where $\psi_p < 0$ as a consequence of Assumption 3.1. This can alternatively be written

$$\Pi_1\left(p_t, p_t, P_t; Y_t, \tilde{\xi}_t\right) = \psi_p\left[\log(p_t/P_t) - \zeta\left(\hat{Y}_t - \hat{Y}_t^n\right)\right], \tag{1.30}$$

where $\zeta \equiv -\psi_y/\psi_p > 0$. (The significance of the numerical value of ζ and its determinants are discussed in the next section.)

Taking a log-linear approximation to the two pricing equations (1.28) and (1.29) gives

$$\log p_{1t} = \log P_t + \zeta\left(\hat{Y}_t - \hat{Y}_t^n\right), \tag{1.31}$$

$$\log p_{2t} = E_{t-1}\left[\log P_t + \zeta\left(\hat{Y}_t - \hat{Y}_t^n\right)\right].$$

These approximations apply as long as the fluctuations in p_{it}/P_t, Y_t, and Y_t^n around the values near which I log-linearize are small enough. These relations imply that up to the log-linear approximation,

$$\log p_{2t} = E_{t-1}\log p_{1t}.$$

A corresponding log-linear approximation to the aggregate price index (1.3) yields

$$\log P_t = \iota \log p_{1t} + (1 - \iota) \log p_{2t}.$$

It follows that

$$\pi_t - E_{t-1}\pi_t = \log P_t - E_{t-1}\log P_t = \frac{\iota}{1-\iota}(\log p_{1t} - \log P_t).$$

Then using (1.31) yields the following New Classical aggregate-supply relation.

PROPOSITION 3.2. Let the profit function of the supplier of an individual good again be of the form (1.17) and satisfy Assumption 3.1, but suppose now that fraction $0 < \iota < 1$ of goods prices are flexible, while the other fraction $1 - \iota$ are fixed one period in advance. Then the aggregate inflation rate and aggregate output in any period t must satisfy an aggregate-supply relation of the form

$$\pi_t = \kappa\left(\hat{Y}_t - \hat{Y}_t^n\right) + E_{t-1}\pi_t, \tag{1.32}$$

where

$$\kappa \equiv \frac{\iota}{1-\iota}\zeta > 0.$$

Note that this relation has the form of an expectations-augmented Phillips curve of the kind hypothesized by Phelps (1967) and Friedman (1968), in which the specific inflation expectation that is relevant is the expectation at the time at which current predetermined prices were fixed regarding inflation over the interval until the present. This particular form of dependence of aggregate supply upon inflation expectations was stressed in the New Classical literature of the 1970s (e.g., Sargent and Wallace, 1975).

This aggregate-supply relation implies once again that

$$E_{t-1} \log Y_t = E_{t-1} \log Y_t^n,$$

so that the component of output that can be forecasted a period in advance is still independent of monetary policy. However, unexpected variations in aggregate demand now give rise to inflation variation as well, rather than affecting only output. Again taking the stochastic process for aggregate nominal spending $\mathcal{Y}_t$ as given, (1.32) implies that aggregate output equals

$$\log Y_t = \log Y_t^n + (1+\kappa)^{-1} \left(\log \mathcal{Y}_t - E_{t-1} \log \mathcal{Y}_t \right), \qquad (1.33)$$

so that the aggregate price level equals

$$\log P_t = \left(E_{t-1} \log \mathcal{Y}_t - \log Y_t^n \right) + \frac{\kappa}{1+\kappa} (\log \mathcal{Y}_t - E_{t-1} \log \mathcal{Y}_t).$$

How does the degree of price flexibility affect the impact of fluctuations in nominal spending upon real activity? Not surprisingly, a larger number of flexible prices (larger ι) implies a higher value of κ (steeper short-run Phillips curve), and hence a smaller value of the elasticity of output with respect to unexpected variations in nominal spending in (1.33). In the limit as ι approaches one (all prices flexible), κ becomes unboundedly large, and the output effects of variations in nominal spending approach zero, as found earlier. More interesting is the question of whether intermediate values of ι result in effects more like those of the fully flexible limit or the fully sticky limit. This turns out to depend upon the size of ζ.

Figure 3.1 plots the elasticity $1/(1+\kappa)$ occurring in (1.33) as a function of ι, for each of several values of ζ. In each case, the function is monotonically decreasing, as one would expect, and takes the same values in the two limiting cases of $\iota = 0$ and $\iota = 1$. However, when $\zeta > 1$, the function is convex (and more so the larger is ζ), whereas when $\zeta < 1$, the function is concave (and more so the smaller is ζ). Thus if ζ is large, even *some* goods having flexible prices is enough to prevent variations in nominal spending from having much effect on aggregate output. In such a case, the flexible-price model provides a reasonable approximation to the evolution of aggregate prices and quantities. But if ζ is small, even *some* prices being sticky is enough to result in a substantial effect of variations in nominal spending upon output. Indeed, in such a case, the overall price index responds very little to unexpected variations in nominal spending, and the simple model

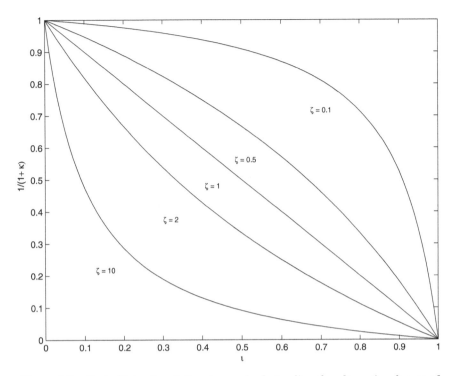

Figure 3.1 *Real effects of variation in nominal spending for alternative degrees of strategic complementarity in pricesetting.*

in which all prices were assumed to be predetermined is a reasonably good guide to aggregate outcomes.

There is a simple intuition for the significance of the parameter ζ: It describes the degree of *strategic complementarity* between the pricesetting decisions of the suppliers of different goods. Consider the following simple game among pricesetters. Aggregate nominal spending $\mathcal{Y}_t$ is given, and the suppliers of individual goods i are to simultaneously choose the prices $p_t(i)$ for their goods. In what way does a given supplier's optimal price depend upon the level of the prices chosen by the other suppliers? One says that the pricing decisions are *strategic complements* if an increase in the prices charged for other goods *increases* the price that it is optimal to charge for one's own good. Correspondingly, one may speak of *strategic substitutes* if an increase in the other prices makes it optimal for one to *reduce* the price of one's own good.[14]

14. See Bulow et al. (1985) for the general notion of strategic complementarity and Halti-wanger and Waldman (1989) for discussion of it in the context of adjustment to aggregate shocks more generally.

To determine the answer to this question, one must first consider what may be called the *notional* short-run aggregate-supply (SRAS) curve, which indicates how each industry's relative price would vary with the level of aggregate activity, *if* prices in that industry could be freely set on the basis of demand and cost conditions at date t, independent of any prices charged or announced in the past, and with no consequences for the prices that could be charged at any later dates as well. This is a purely notional supply curve in that it need not indicate how the prices of any goods are *actually* set in an economy where prices are sticky. Nonetheless, we shall see that the concept is a useful one, even when no prices are perfectly flexible. This notional SRAS curve is implicitly defined by the relation

$$\Pi_1\left(p_t^I, p_t^I, P_t; Y_t, \tilde{\xi}_t\right) = 0.$$

Using the approximation (1.30), it can be seen that a log-linear approximation to this relation is of the form

$$\log\left(p_t^I / P_t\right) = \zeta\left(\hat{Y}_t - \hat{Y}_t^n\right). \tag{1.34}$$

Hence the coefficient ζ, shown to be of importance for the slope of the inflation-output trade-off in the New Classical model, is just the elasticity of the notional SRAS curve. Ball and Romer (1990) refer to an economy in which this elasticity is small as being characterized by *real rigidities*.[15]

Best-response curves for individual pricesetters can then be derived by substituting the identity $Y_t = y_t/P_t$ into the notional SRAS curve to obtain p_t^I as a function of P_t, y_t, and the exogenous disturbances. The degree of strategic complementarity is then indicated by the partial derivative of this solution for p_t^I with respect to P_t. Using the approximation (1.34) to the notional SRAS curve, one finds that strategic complementarity exists (a positive partial derivative) if and only if $\zeta < 1$,[16] whereas the pricing decisions of the separate firms are strategic substitutes if $\zeta > 1$.

---

15. The analogy is with "nominal rigidity," a situation in which the nominal price charged by a given supplier (rather than its relative price) is insensitive to the quantity that it must supply. Because the nominal SRAS as defined here is independent of any specification of the speed at which prices may be adjusted, the degree to which an economy is characterized by "real rigidities" depends solely upon real factors: the structure of production costs and of demand. The term, though widely used, is somewhat unfortunate, as it suggests that there are costs of adjusting real quantities, whereas in fact it means a situation in which (notional) supply is very *elastic*. I thus mainly speak here of "elastic supply" or "strategic complementarity in pricesetting" instead.

16. Note that the question of whether different firms' pricing decisions are strategic complements is only defined relative to a particular pricing game in which aggregate nominal spending is taken as given, independent of the prices chosen by any of the firms. This is a

Thus it is the existence (or not) of strategic complementarity that determines whether the fraction of the suppliers with sticky prices exert a disproportionate effect upon the degree of adjustment of the aggregate price index. The intuition for this is simple: If prices are strategic complements, then the fraction of prices that do not adjust in response to a disturbance to nominal spending lead even the flexible-price suppliers to adjust their prices by less than they would otherwise. If the strategic complementarity is strong enough, there is little aggregate-price adjustment (and so a large output effect) even if the fraction of flexible-price suppliers is large (though less than one). On the other hand, if prices are strategic substitutes, then the aggregate price level may adjust nearly in proportion to the unexpected change in nominal spending, even when many prices are sticky. For in this case, the fact that some prices do not adjust causes the flexible-price suppliers to compensate by adjusting their prices even *more* than they would in a flexible-price equilibrium. In the case of a high degree of strategic substitutability (large ζ), this can result in the aggregate price index adjusting nearly in proportion to the change in nominal spending; but it does not adjust by quite that amount, else there would be no change in real aggregate demand, and so no desire on the part of flexible-price suppliers to change their relative prices.

The possibility of strategic substitutability explains why some authors, such as Ohanian et al. (1995) and Christiano et al. (1997), find in models with sticky prices for only some goods that the partial price stickiness has little effect upon the aggregate effects of monetary shocks. These papers assume parameter values that imply an elasticity ζ greater than one, the case of strategic substitutes. At the same time, the New Keynesian literature of the 1980s routinely assumed an elasticity $\zeta < 1$, and hence found that pricing decisions should be strategic complements. This result favored the conclusion that it was plausible to suppose that nominal rigidities mattered a great deal for the character of short-run responses to shocks. It is thus worth considering in further detail possible determinants of the degree of strategic complementarity in pricing and the plausible size of the elasticity ζ.

1.4 Sources of Strategic Complementarity

I begin by considering the determinants of the elasticity ζ in the baseline model described in Section 1.1. It follows from (1.18) that in that model,

---

useful question to consider, however, when analyzing the dynamics of prices and output under an arbitrarily specified stochastic process for nominal spending, as is done repeatedly in this chapter.

$$\Pi_1\left(p, p, P; Y, \tilde{\xi}\right) = -(\theta - 1)Y(p/P)^{-\theta-1}\left[p/P - \mu s\left(Y(p/P)^{-\theta}, Y; \tilde{\xi}\right)\right],$$

so that the notional SRAS curve is implicitly defined by

$$p^I/P = \mu s\left(Y\left(p^I/P\right)^{-\theta}, Y; \tilde{\xi}\right),$$

where the real marginal cost function is defined in (1.10). Using the log-linear approximation (1.15) to the latter function yields a log-linear notional SRAS relation of the form (1.34), in which

$$\zeta = \frac{\omega + \sigma^{-1}}{1 + \omega\theta} > 0. \tag{1.35}$$

Most early New Keynesian literature[17] assumes linear utility of consumption. This corresponds in my notation to the limiting case $\sigma^{-1} = 0$, in which case (1.35) reduces to

$$\zeta = \frac{\omega}{1 + \omega\theta}.$$

Given that one must have $\theta > 1$, this expression implies that $\zeta < 1$, so that the pricing decisions of different suppliers are necessarily strategic complements—the conclusion relied upon in that literature. However, this conclusion is less obviously true if, more realistically, one assumes a finite value for the intertemporal elasticity of substitution σ.[18]

Indeed, many of the authors in the early 1990s seeking to incorporate sticky prices into otherwise standard RBC models adopted numerical calibrations (derived from the RBC literature) that implied strategic substitutability. One reason for this was the widespread assumption, unlike what I have supposed above, of common economy-wide factor markets, so that the marginal cost of supply would be equal for all goods i at any point in time.[19] The marginal cost of supplying any good is given by

---

17. See, e.g., the presentation in Blanchard and Fischer (1989, sec. 8.1).

18. Razin and Yuen (2002) point out that the effective value of σ should be higher in an open economy with capital mobility, insofar as variations in domestic output in that case imply less variation in domestic consumption, and hence in the marginal utility of income in the domestic economy. (The significance of σ^{-1} in expression (1.35) is as a measure of the extent to which increases in domestic economic activity are associated with reductions in the marginal utility of income, and hence increased wage demands.) Razin and Yuen suggest that this may explain the fact that empirical Phillips curves are found to be steeper in countries with greater restrictions on capital mobility (Loungani et al., 2001).

19. The consequences of this issue for the degree of strategic complementarity in pricing are stressed by Kimball (1995).

$$S_t = \frac{w_t}{A_t f'(h_t)},$$

where w_t is the wage paid by all producers for the homogeneous labor input and h_t is the common labor-capital ratio chosen by all producers. Capital is reallocated among firms so as to allow all firms to use the same efficient labor-capital ratio, even if they produce different quantities of their respective goods; this common labor-capital ratio is given by $h_t = f^{-1}(X_t/A_t)$, where the common output-capital ratio X_t satisfies

$$X_t = \int_0^1 y_t(i)\, di. \tag{1.36}$$

Finally, the economy-wide wage w_t satisfies (1.6), where the representative household's labor supply must equal h_t. Marginal supply cost is therefore given by

$$S_t(i) = P_t s\left(X_t, Y_t; \tilde{\xi}_t\right),$$

independent of the quantity produced of the individual good i, where s is again the function defined in (1.10).

In this case the profit function is given by

$$\Pi\left(p, P; X, Y, \tilde{\xi}\right) \equiv pY(p/P)^{-\theta} - \frac{v_h\left(f^{-1}(X/A); \xi\right)}{u_c(Y - G; \xi)} P\psi(X/A)Y(p/P)^{-\theta},$$

rather than (1.17). Here the ratio X/Y depends on the structure of industry prices; but on the assumption that a single industry has only a negligible effect on economy-wide factor demands, it may be taken as independent of the industry's relative price in deriving the notional SRAS curve. The notional SRAS curve is then given simply by

$$p/P = \mu s\left(X, Y; \tilde{\xi}\right).$$

Log-linearizing once again around an equilibrium in which all relative prices equal one, using (1.15) and noting that to first order, $\hat{X}_t = \hat{Y}_t$, one again obtains a log-linear SRAS relation (1.34), but now with

$$\zeta \equiv \omega + \sigma^{-1} > 0.$$

In the RBC literature, it is standard to assume that $\sigma = 1$. (See, e.g., Cooley and Prescott, 1995.) Under this assumption, $\zeta > 1$, and pricing decisions are *strategic substitutes*, regardless of the (necessarily positive) value assigned to ω.

For example, the baseline calibration of Chari et al. (2000) implies that $\omega = 1.25$, while $\sigma = 1$. As they assume common factor markets, their parameterization implies a value of $\zeta = 2.25$, and thus a considerable degree of strategic substitutability. Moreover, even if they were to assume linear utility of consumption ($\sigma^{-1} = 0$), despite the implausibility of such an extreme value, the assumed degree of diminishing returns to labor in the production function and the assumed degree of increasing marginal disutility of work (which together imply their value of ω) would still imply $\zeta = 1.25$, so that there would still be strategic substitutability. On the other hand, even with their assumed values for ω and σ, if these authors were to assume specific factor markets (as in the analysis above), then (given that they also assign the value $\theta = 10$) they would have found that $\zeta = 0.17$, using (1.35). This would imply a great degree of strategic complementarity. Thus it is the assumption of common factor markets that makes the most crucial difference for the finding of these and other authors that pricing decisions are strategic substitutes.

It can be seen that the assumption of common factor markets is far from innocuous. It is also far from realistic. Of course, it makes sense that high wages in one part of the economy eventually raise wages in the rest, as workers migrate from low-wage to high-wage labor markets. Similarly, it makes sense that high returns to capital in one part of the economy eventually raise the rental rate for capital services throughout the economy, as capital is shifted to higher-return uses (if only through the allocation of new investment). A failure to allow for these factor-price equalization mechanisms makes the present model of specific factor markets unrealistic as a model of the long-run effects upon sectoral marginal costs of a *permanent* failure of prices in one sector to adjust.

Nonetheless, the opposite extreme assumption—that all factor prices are *instantaneously* equalized across the suppliers of different goods—is also unrealistic. In the short run, it is not easy for workers to migrate to regions, specialties, or even firms that happen to have temporarily higher labor demand; and it is even less easy to reassign capital goods, once installed, to firms with a temporarily high rate of utilization of their capital stock. This "quasi-fixed" character of factor inputs allows equilibrium factor prices to vary across suppliers for some period following a shock that affects them asymmetrically; and it is mainly these short-run dynamics of factor prices that matter for determining the short-run dynamics of price adjustment in response to shocks, which are what matter for comparing the real allocation of resources under alternative monetary policies.[20]

---

20. In Chapter 4, I show how endogenous reallocation of capital across sectors can be added to the model, so that the rental price of capital must be equalized across sectors in

Factor specificity need not be an all-or-nothing assumption. For example, one might assume (as in Sbordone, 1998) that all suppliers hire the same kind of labor inputs in a single economy-wide labor market, but that each firm has a production function of the form $y_t(i) = A_t f(h_t(i))$, where f is strictly concave. This amounts to assuming that each firm's allocation of capital goods remains fixed, rather than letting capital be reallocated to equalize its rental rate. In this case, real marginal costs are given by

$$\hat{s}_t(i) = \omega_p \hat{y}_t(i) + \left(\omega_w + \sigma^{-1}\right)\hat{Y}_t - \left(\omega + \sigma^{-1}\right)\hat{Y}_t^n,$$

where $\omega_p, \omega_w > 0$ are the two components of ω introduced in (1.16). It then follows that

$$\zeta = \frac{\omega + \sigma^{-1}}{1 + \omega_p \theta} > 0. \tag{1.37}$$

This value of ζ is higher than that implied by (1.35), so that there is less strategic complementarity than in the case of specific labor markets as well (given a finite Frisch elasticity of labor supply, so that $\omega_w > 0$). But it remains a lower value than is obtained under the assumption of common factor markets, that is, instantaneous equalization of the rental price of capital services. For example, Chari et al. (2000) assume a Cobb-Douglas production function with a labor share of .67, which implies $\omega_p = 0.5$. Thus under their baseline calibration, if they were to assume a common labor market but specific capital inputs, they would have obtained $\zeta = 0.38$, and so a substantial degree of strategic complementarity in pricesetting.

There are other reasons as well to believe that the simple model with common factor markets set out above underestimates the likely degree of strategic complementarity in pricesetting. One that has received some attention in the literature is the possibility that preferences over differentiated goods need not be of the constant-elasticity (Dixit-Stiglitz) form (1.2). The result is that the elasticity of demand, and hence the desired markup of price over marginal cost, need not be independent of the relative quantities produced of different goods. In particular, Kimball (1995) shows that if the elasticity of demand is lower for the products of suppliers who sell more (because they have relatively low prices), this increases strategic complementarity, and hence the real effects of variations in nominal spending. For in the event of a decline in nominal spending, price cuts by flexible-price suppliers lead to an increase in their relative sales (though a reduction in the absolute

---

the long run. I nonetheless find that in the presence of adjustment costs for investment, the short-run dynamics of marginal supply costs are not too different from those predicted by the simple model with a fixed allocation of capital to firms.

quantity sold), because the sticky-price suppliers fail to cut their prices. If this increase in relative sales leads to less-elastic demand for their products, their desired markups will rise, mitigating the effect upon their desired relative price of the decline in their sales (and hence reduction in their marginal supply cost). This causes them to cut their prices less, so that the decline in their output is greater.

Following Kimball, one may generalize (1.2) by assuming that the consumption aggregate C_t is implicitly defined by a relation of the form

$$\int_0^1 \psi(c_t(i)/C_t)\, di = 1, \tag{1.38}$$

where $\psi(x)$ is an increasing, strictly concave function satisfying $\psi(1) = 1$. (Note that this reduces to (1.2) if $\psi(x) = x^{\theta-1/\theta}$.) As shown in Section B.1 of Appendix B, the desired relative price of a flexible-price supplier is in this case given by

$$p_t(i)/P_t = \mu\left(y_t(i)/Y_t\right) s(y_t(i), Y_t; \tilde{\xi}_t), \tag{1.39}$$

generalizing (1.13). Here the constant (desired) markup in our baseline model has been replaced by an endogenously varying markup that depends on the relative sales of good i.

Log-linearization of this relation in turn yields

$$\log p_t(i) = \log P_t + \epsilon_\mu\left(\hat{y}_t(i) - \hat{Y}_t\right) + s_y\left(\hat{y}_t(i) - \hat{Y}_t^n\right) + s_Y\left(\hat{Y}_t - \hat{Y}_t^n\right), \tag{1.40}$$

where ϵ_μ is the elasticity of $\mu(x)$ at the value $x = 1$, and s_y and s_Y are the elasticities of the real marginal cost function with respect to its first two arguments, respectively. (I now introduce general notation for these elasticities in order to be able to treat both the case of specific factor markets, as in the baseline model, and the case of homogeneous factor markets, discussed earlier in this section.) While the demand function is no longer exactly log-linear in the case of non-CES preferences, one can still derive a log-linear approximation to the demand function

$$\hat{y}_t(i) = \hat{Y}_t - \theta(\log p_t(i) - \log P_t),$$

where here θ refers to the elasticity of demand in the case of a small deviation from a situation in which all relative prices equal one (i.e., $\theta(1)$, where the function $\theta(\cdot)$ is defined in Appendix B). Using this relation to eliminate $\hat{y}_t(i)$ in (1.40) and then solving for $\log p_t(i)$, one obtains a log-linear notional SRAS curve and observes that now

$$\zeta = \frac{s_y + s_Y}{1 + \theta(\epsilon_\mu + s_y)}. \tag{1.41}$$

For given values of the other parameters, it is observed that a positive ϵ_μ—which means $\theta(x)$ decreasing in x, as discussed above—lowers the value of ζ, thus increasing the degree of strategic complementarity.

In principle, as Kimball shows, ϵ_μ could be an arbitrarily large quantity, and so this factor could result in ζ being arbitrarily small, regardless of the size of the coefficients s_y, s_Y, and θ. (Note that $\zeta \to 0$ as $\epsilon_\mu \to \infty$.) Bergin and Feenstra (2000), however, argue that a plausible calibration would assign a value of approximately $\theta\epsilon_\mu = 1$, so that ϵ_μ is positive but not extremely high. If the desired markup depends upon relative demand for different goods as before, one can show that the desired price of supplier i satisfies

$$\log p_t(i) = \frac{1}{1 + \theta\epsilon_\mu} \log S_t(i) + \frac{\theta\epsilon_\mu}{1 + \theta\epsilon_\mu} \log P_t,$$

regardless of the determinants of nominal marginal cost $S_t(i)$. Bergin and Feenstra note that the literature on exchange-rate pass-through typically finds that a devaluation raises the domestic-currency price of imported goods by only about 0.5 of the percentage of the devaluation. If one interprets this as measuring the elasticity of $p_t(i)$ with respect to changes in $S_t(i)$ (on the assumption that the devaluation does not affect the foreign-currency marginal cost of supplying the imported goods or the domestic-currency prices of most goods in the domestic price index), then one may conclude that $\theta\epsilon_\mu$ equals approximately 1.[21]

In the case of homogeneous factor markets ($s_y = 0$, $s_Y = \omega + \sigma^{-1}$), assumed by Bergin and Feenstra, (1.41) reduces to

$$\zeta = \frac{\omega + \sigma^{-1}}{1 + \theta\epsilon_\mu}.$$

In this case, their suggested value of ϵ_μ reduces ζ by a factor of two relative to what one would obtain under the assumption of Dixit-Stiglitz preferences. This is not enough to radically change one's views about the real effects of monetary policy (as they conclude), but it is nonetheless a nontrivial correction. However, in the case of specific factor markets ($s_y = \omega$, $s_Y = \sigma^{-1}$), the correction matters much less. In this case, (1.41) reduces to

---

21. Bergin and Feenstra also note that this size of markup elasticity would be implied by the translog specification of preferences that has been popular in econometric studies of demand.

$$\zeta = \frac{\omega + \sigma^{-1}}{1 + \theta(\epsilon_\mu + \omega)}.$$

Here setting $\theta\epsilon_\mu$ equal to one instead of zero does not make such a great difference, since the term $\theta\omega$ in the denominator is now likely to be much greater than one. For example, in the case of the Chari et al. values for ω, σ, and θ discussed above, allowing for the variation in desired markups only reduces the predicted ζ from 0.17 to 0.16.

Another reason for greater strategic complementarity than is indicated by the previous baseline analysis is the economy's input-output structure, stressed by Basu (1995). My earlier analysis of marginal supply costs assumes that labor is the only variable factor of production and ignores the role of intermediate inputs. While this is a familiar assumption in equilibrium business-cycle models (it is, e.g., routine in the RBC literature), it is far from being literally correct. The production function for output as a function of capital and labor inputs that one typically encounters in such models must be interpreted as a functional relation between the *value added* in production (GDP) and *primary* factor inputs, rather than a relation between gross output and all factors of production (including those that are themselves produced). Under certain conditions, and for some purposes, it suffices to model the economy as if this value-added production function were the actual production function of individual producers—for example, for purposes of predicting the evolution of real GDP in the context of a flexible-price, perfectly competitive model, as in RBC theory. But as Rotemberg and Woodford (1995) note, it is important not to conflate gross-output and value-added production functions in the case of a model with imperfect competition and prices that do not co-move perfectly with marginal cost.

Rotemberg and Woodford (1995) propose a simple gross-output production function of the form[22]

$$y_t(i) = \min\left[\frac{A_t f(h_t(i))}{1 - s_m}, \frac{m_t(i)}{s_m}\right], \tag{1.42}$$

where $A_t f(h_t(i))$ is the value-added production function (as before), $m_t(i)$ is the quantity of materials inputs used by firm i, and $0 \le s_m < 1$ is a parameter of the production technology (that can be identified, for purposes of

---

22. Basu (1995) and Bergin and Feenstra (2000) instead assume that gross output is a Cobb-Douglas function of labor and materials inputs. The simple analysis here, however, which has the advantage of nesting my previous specification as a limiting case, allows me to reach quite similar conclusions about the consequences of the input-output structure for the degree of strategic complementarity in pricing in a highly transparent way. There seems in any event to be no argument other than tractability offered for the Cobb-Douglas specification used in these other papers.

calibration, with the share of materials costs in the value of gross output). The argument $m_t(i)$ refers to the number of units of the aggregate defined in (1.2)—or more generally in (1.38)—that are purchased for use in producing good i. It is thus a composite of all of the goods produced in the economy, which are all assumed to be equally both final goods and intermediate inputs. In this case I obtain the following generalization of (1.41).

PROPOSITION 3.3. Suppose that preferences over differentiated goods are defined by (1.38) and the production technology by (1.42). Then one again obtains a log-linear approximation to the notional SRAS curve of the form (1.34), with elasticity

$$\zeta = \frac{(1 - \mu s_m)(s_y + s_Y)}{1 + \theta[\epsilon_\mu + (1 - \mu s_m)s_y]}. \tag{1.43}$$

Here s_y denotes the elasticity of the real marginal cost of supplying value added by firm i with respect to the value added by that firm, and s_Y is the elasticity with respect to aggregate value added. Once again, in the case of specific factor markets (as in Section 1.1), this expression holds with $s_y = \omega$, $s_Y = \sigma^{-1}$; instead, in the case of homogeneous factor markets (discussed earlier in this section), $s_y = 0$, $s_Y = \omega + \sigma^{-1}$.

Details of the derivation are given in Appendix B.

One observes that allowing for a positive materials share lowers ζ for given values of the other parameters; and once again, this effect could in principle result in an arbitrarily small value for ζ, regardless of the values of the other parameters. (Note that $\zeta \to 0$ as $s_m \to \mu^{-1} < 1$.) However, the share of materials costs in total costs for U.S. manufacturing sectors is typically on the order of 50 or 60 percent, which suggests that a reasonable calibration would be on the order of $\mu s_m = 0.6$.[23] In the case of homogeneous factor markets ($s_y = 0$), this implies that ζ is reduced by a factor of 2.5 (i.e., it is multiplied by 0.4). This is again a significant reduction, and if this effect is combined with the degree of variation in the

23. This would correspond to a materials share of 54 percent, if one assumes $\theta = 10$ as do Chari et al. (2000). Note that Basu (1995) suggests that a share parameter as high as $s_m = 0.9$ could be reasonable, on the grounds that the share of intermediate inputs in marginal cost could be substantially higher than their share in average cost. Under such an assumption this correction would be much more important than under the calibration suggested here; e.g., the assumption $s_m = 0.9$ combined with an assumption $\theta = 10$ would imply that $\zeta = 0$. But such a calibration is not easy to interpret. If, e.g., one proposes that a large fraction of primary input purchases represent fixed or overhead costs, this would imply substantial increasing returns (average cost much higher than marginal cost), which would in turn not be consistent with equilibrium in the absence of an implausibly high degree of market power.

desired markup argued for above, the value of ζ is only one-fifth the size indicated by the baseline calculation of Chari et al.—0.45 instead of 2.25, which is to say well below 1 (implying strategic complementarity) rather than being well above 1 (implying strategic substitutability). On the other hand, in the case of specific factor markets, this correction matters much less, unless s_m is assumed to be much closer than μ^{-1} than seems realistic. Using the calibration discussed above, assuming $\mu s_m = 0.6$ rather than zero reduces ζ from 0.17 to 0.15 (in the constant-markup case), or from 0.16 to 0.13 (in the variable-markup case). These reductions make no dramatic difference in one's conclusions about the degree of strategic complementarity.

Our conclusions about the effects of these several corrections, in the case of the calibrations just discussed, are summarized in Table 3.1. The left side of the table gives the value of ζ under the assumption that $\omega = 1.25$, $\sigma = 1$, and $\theta = 10$, as assumed by Chari et al., under eight different cases, representing three binary choices. These are the assumption of homogeneous factor markets ($s_y = 0$, $s_Y = \omega + \sigma^{-1}$) versus specific factor markets ($s_y = \omega$, $s_Y = \sigma^{-1}$); the assumption of a constant desired markup ($\epsilon_\mu = 0$) versus a realistic degree of markup variation ($\theta\epsilon_m u = 1$); and the assumption of no intermediate inputs ($s_m = 0$) versus a realistic intermediate input share in costs ($\mu s_m = .6$). In each case, the simple assumption made in the baseline case of Chari et al. is the one least favorable to strategic complementarity. Changing any of these assumptions individually reduces ζ substantially relative to their baseline case. However, it is the allowance for factor specificity that matters most, if one accepts that this is the more realistic assumption. For whereas each of the other two corrections makes a significant difference in the case of homogeneous factor markets, and together they make an even larger difference (as stressed by Bergin and Feenstra), in the case of specific factor markets even their combined effect is not at all dramatic. Furthermore, factor specificity alone reduces the value of ζ much more than the other two factors combined do, if the importance of these latter factors is calibrated in what seems a reasonable way.

TABLE 3.1   The value of ζ under alternative assumptions

		$\sigma^{-1} = 1$, $\omega = 1.25$		$\sigma^{-1} = 0.16$, $\omega = 0.47$	
$\theta\epsilon_\mu$	μs_m	Homogeneous factor	Specific factor	Homogeneous factor	Specific factor
0	0	2.25	0.17	0.63	0.11
1	0	1.13	0.16	0.32	0.09
0	.6	0.90	0.15	0.25	0.09
1	.6	0.45	0.13	0.13	0.06

The right side of Table 3.1 offers a similar comparison when lower values are assumed for both σ^{-1} and ω. The values suggested here are those obtained by Rotemberg and Woodford (1997) when a slightly more complicated version of this pricing model is fit to U.S. time series, as discussed further in Chapter 4. The higher value of σ (implying much greater interest sensitivity of private expenditure) is needed in order to account for the observed size of the effects of an identified monetary policy shock on real aggregate demand; the lower value of ω (implying much more elastic labor supply) is needed in order to account for the observed modest declines in real wages that accompany such a large decline in output. Under these alternative assumptions regarding preferences, $\zeta < 1$, implying a modest degree of strategic complementarity, even in the case of homogeneous factor markets, Dixit-Stiglitz preferences, and no intermediate inputs. But once again the degree of real rigidity is increased by modifying any of these last three assumptions. It is interesting to observe in this case that even under the assumption of homogenous-factor markets, one obtains a value of $\zeta = 0.13$, if we make realistic assumptions about the other two sources of real rigidity. Thus a value of ζ in the range between 0.10 and 0.15 does not require implausible assumptions. This is a value that implies substantial strategic complementarity, and as we shall see, enough to explain roughly the observed degree of sluggishness of aggregate-price adjustment in response to variations in nominal expenditure, given the observed frequency of price adjustment in economies like that of the United States.

2 Inflation Dynamics with Staggered Pricesetting

One unsatisfactory feature of the "New Classical" aggregate-supply relation derived earlier is its implication that *only* unanticipated fluctuations in nominal spending have any effect upon real activity, and that equilibrium fluctuations in the output gap must be completely *unforecastable*. These strong predictions were the occasion of a great deal of discussion and criticism during the 1970s and early 1980s (see, e.g., Sheffrin, 1996, chap. 2). They imply that only the *immediate* effects of a monetary policy shock upon nominal expenditure should have any consequences for real activity; delayed effects (effects on nominal spending after the "period" in which the shock occurs) should not affect output at all, but only the price level. Moreover, such real effects of a monetary policy shock as occur must be purely transitory, that is, must last no longer than the period for which the sticky prices are fixed in advance.

These predictions are quite inconsistent with the effects identified in the "structural VAR" literature. As an example, Figure 3.2 plots the impulse response of nominal GDP to an identified monetary policy shock, according

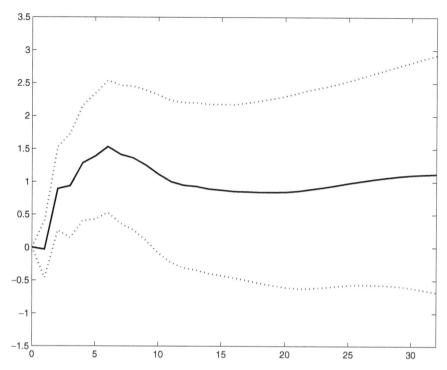

Figure 3.2 *Impulse response of nominal GDP to an unanticipated interest-rate reduction in quarter zero. Periods on horizontal axis represent quarters and the vertical axis measures the effect on log nominal GDP in percentage points. Source: Christiano et al. (2001).*

to the structural VAR model of Christiano et al. (2001).[24] There is practically no measurable effect of an unexpected interest-rate reduction in quarter zero upon nominal GDP until the second quarter following the monetary policy shock, though there is a strong increase in nominal GDP at that time.[25] But this means that according to the New Classical aggregate-supply

24. This particular impulse response is not reported in their paper, though the point estimates here are implied by the inflation and real GDP responses that are reported there. I thank Charlie Evans for supplying the data plotted in this and subsequent figures. The impulse responses indicated by this particular VAR study are representative of those found in many others; see Christiano et al. (1999) for a review.

25. The fact that there is zero effect upon nominal GDP in quarter zero is an artifact of the authors' identification scheme, which assumes that any contemporaneous correlation between interest-rate innovations and innovations in either real GDP or inflation is due to feedback from the latter variables to the current interest-rate operating target, as under a Taylor rule. However, the estimated effect in quarter one is in no way constrained by the identification

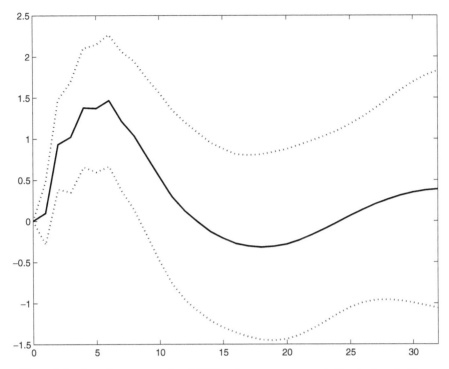

Figure 3.3 *Impulse response of real GDP to the same monetary policy shock as in Figure 3.2. The vertical axis measures the effect on log real GDP in percentage points. Source: Christiano et al. (2001).*

relation, monetary shocks should have *no* effect upon real activity at all, unless the period for which sticky prices are fixed in advance is longer than 6 months.

Figure 3.3 next shows the estimated impulse response of real GDP to the same shock in quarter zero. Contrary to the suggestion just mentioned, there is a substantial real effect of the shock. (Note that in both figures, the monetary policy shock is normalized so that the long-run effect on nominal GDP is an increase of 1 percentage point.) Furthermore, the effect occurs with a substantial delay; there is essentially no effect on output until the second quarter following the policy shock,[26] and the peak output effect

---

scheme; the fact that neither output nor inflation is estimated to be significantly affected in quarter one provides some support for the assumption relied upon in the identification scheme.

26. It may be wondered why I assert that the shock actually occurs in quarter zero, given that there is no effect on nominal expenditure until quarter two. The occurrence of the policy

occurs only in the sixth quarter following the shock. The estimated effect is still more than two standard errors greater than zero a full 2 years after the shock, and (at least according to the point estimate) the effect is still at more than a third of its maximum level ten quarters after the shock. Such long-lasting effects are inconsistent with the New Classical aggregate-supply relation, unless the period for which prices are fixed in advance is longer than 2 years. But survey evidence on price changes (e.g., Blinder et al., 1998) finds that the majority of firms change their prices more frequently than once a year, so that more than half of all prices should have been adjusted at least once within the first two quarters following a shock.

However, this undesirable feature of the model can be avoided—without abandoning the assumption that prices are set optimally (under rational expectations) when they are adjusted and without assuming counterfactually long intervals between price changes—by supposing that the intervals over which the prices of different goods remain fixed overlap, rather than being perfectly synchronized. As Phelps (1978) and Taylor (1979a, 1980) first pointed out,[27] such staggering of price changes can lead to a sluggish process of adjustment of the overall price level, even when individual prices are adjusted relatively frequently.

This is because, if individual suppliers' pricing decisions are strategic complements, then the fact that some prices are not yet being adjusted restrains the degree to which prices are changed by those suppliers that do adjust their prices. At a later date, the adjustment of the prices that earlier were sticky are in turn restrained by the fact that the prices that earlier were adjusted were not changed very much. As a result of this process, the level of prices prior to a shock can continue to have a significant effect on the general level of prices even after most prices have been adjusted at least once since the shock. If the strategic complementarity between pricing decisions is great enough, the adjustment of the general level of prices can be quite slow, even though individual price adjustments are frequent. The consequence will be prolonged effects on real activity of a sustained change in the level of nominal spending.

As we shall see, this theory of pricing can again justify an aggregate-supply relation that takes the form of an expectations-augmented Phillips-curve relation. However, in this variant case, the kind of inflation expectations that determine the location of the short-run Phillips curve are current

---

shock is indicated by the substantial decline in the federal funds rate in quarter zero; see Christiano et al. (2001) for a plot of this response.

27. These first applications of the idea assumed that wages, rather than prices, were fixed for a period of time (owing to wage contracts), and thus concerned the effects of staggered wage negotiations rather than staggered pricesetting. But as Blanchard (1983) pointed out, the same principle can be applied to pricesetting.

expectations regarding future inflation, rather than past expectations regarding current inflation. This might seem a small difference (given the degree of serial correlation in inflation expectations, at least in recent decades), but it is a crucial one because the aggregate-supply relation together with rational expectations no longer exclude the possibility of forecastable variations in the output gap. With this modification, the model becomes consistent with the occurrence of prolonged fluctuations in real activity following a monetary policy shock of at least roughly the kind estimated in the VAR literature.

2.1 The Calvo Model of Pricesetting

Here I present a particular example of a model with staggered pricesetting, a discrete-time variant of a model proposed by Guillermo Calvo (1983).[28] In this model, a fraction $0 < \alpha < 1$ of goods prices remain unchanged each period, whereas new prices are chosen for the other $1 - \alpha$ of the goods. For simplicity, the probability that any given price will be adjusted in any given period is assumed to be $1 - \alpha$, independent of the length of time since the price was set and of what the particular good's current price may be.

These last assumptions are plainly unrealistic, but they are very convenient in simplifying the analysis of equilibrium inflation dynamics, as they greatly reduce the size of the state space required to characterize those dynamics.[29]

---

28. See also Rotemberg (1987) for discussion of this model, and the similarity of its implications for aggregate dynamics to those of a model with convex costs of price adjustment. The first use of a discrete-time version of Calvo's model of pricesetting, in the context of a complete intertemporal equilibrium model of aggregate fluctuations, was in the work of Yun (1996). Other early applications of the same device include Woodford (1996), King and Watson (1996), King and Wolman (1996), and Goodfriend and King (1997). Kimball (1995) also assumes Calvo pricing, albeit in continuous time, in another important early study of an intertemporal equilibrium model with sticky prices.

29. Generalization of the theory presented here to deal with other, possibly more realistic, distributions of intervals between price changes, is an important topic for future research. Some qualitative similarities between the dynamics implied by the Calvo model and other variants clearly exist; e.g., the measure of real rigidities ζ is quite generally a critical determinant of the degree of persistence of the real effects of a monetary disturbance. Nonetheless, alternative specifications can make substantial differences in the quantitative conclusions that one obtains. For example, Kiley (2002) finds that models in which price commitments last for a fixed number of periods imply substantially smaller welfare costs of monetary instability; Erceg and Levin (2002) find that models of that kind imply a larger relative weight on output-gap stabilization in the welfare-theoretic stabilization objective implied by the nominal rigidities; and Mash (2002) finds such that models, or other generalizations of the Calvo model, can more easily explain the persistence of equilibrium fluctuations in inflation. There has thus far been little empirical work that seeks to evaluate the relative fit of alternative specifications, but this too is clearly needed. (See Jadresic, 2000, for an early effort in this vein.)

As each supplier that chooses a new price for its good in period t faces exactly the same decision problem, the optimal price p_t^* is the same for all of them, and so in equilibrium, all prices that are chosen in period t have the common value p_t^*. The remaining fraction α of prices charged in period t are simply a subset of the prices charged in period $t-1$, with each price appearing in the period t distribution of unchanged prices with the same relative frequency as in the period $t-1$ price distribution. (For this last argument it is crucial that each price has an equal probability of being adjusted in a given period.) Then the Dixit-Stiglitz price index (1.3) in period t satisfies

$$P_t^{1-\theta} \equiv \int_0^1 p_t(i)^{1-\theta}\,di = (1-\alpha)p_t^{*\,1-\theta} + \alpha \int_0^1 p_{t-1}(i)^{1-\theta}\,di,$$

so that

$$P_t = \left[(1-\alpha)p_t^{*\,1-\theta} + \alpha P_{t-1}^{1-\theta}\right]^{1/(1-\theta)}. \tag{2.1}$$

It follows that in order to determine the evolution of this price index, one need only know its initial value and the single new price p_t^* that is chosen each period. The determination of p_t^*, in turn, depends upon current- and expected-future-demand conditions for the individual good, but (1.12) implies that other prices affect the demand curve for good i only through the value of the price index P_t. Thus one can determine the equilibrium value of the index P_t as a function of its previous period's value, the expected-future path of this same index, and current and expected future values of aggregate real variables. There is no need for reference to additional information about past prices.[30]

A supplier that changes its price in period t chooses its new price $p_t(i)$ to maximize

$$E_t\left\{\sum_{T=t}^{\infty}\alpha^{T-t}Q_{t,T}\Pi\left(p_t(i), p_T^I, P_T; Y_T, \tilde{\xi}_T\right)\right\}, \tag{2.2}$$

---

30. This is only precisely true in the case of the baseline model with specific factor markets, since in this case the real marginal cost of supplying a given good depends only upon the quantity supplied of that good $y_t(i)$, aggregate output Y_t, and the vector of aggregate shocks $\tilde{\xi}_t$. If I instead assume common-factor markets, as in Yun (1996), real marginal cost depends upon the alternative output aggregate X_t defined in (1.36), and not solely upon the Dixit-Stiglitz aggregate Y_t. This means that the equilibrium conditions for the evolution of P_t also involve a second price index, as shown by Yun. However, even in that case, up to a log-linear approximation the equilibrium conditions can be written solely in terms of the index P_t because the two price aggregates that are required for the exact dynamics are equal to one another up to a log-linear approximation.

where the profit function is defined in the same way as in any of the various models discussed in Section 1. Here the factor α^{T-t} multiplying the stochastic discount factor indicates the probability that price $p_t(i)$ will still be charged in period T.[31] The price $p_t(i)$ is chosen on the basis of information available at date t so as to maximize this expression, given the expected state-contingent values of the random variables $Q_{t,T}$, Y_T, P_T, and p_T^I and the exogenous disturbances.

Corresponding to (1.23) one obtains in this case the first-order condition

$$E_t \left\{ \sum_{T=t}^{\infty} \alpha^{T-t} Q_{t,T} \Pi_1 \left(p_t(i), p_T^I, P_T; Y_T, \tilde{\xi}_T \right) \right\} = 0. \tag{2.3}$$

Under the assumption that all firms in a given industry change their prices at the same time (so that the Calvo lottery is actually over industries rather than individual suppliers), the common new price p_t^* chosen by all firms that revise their prices at date t is implicitly defined by the relation

$$E_t \left\{ \sum_{T=t}^{\infty} \alpha^{T-t} Q_{t,T} \Pi_1 \left(p_t^*, p_t^*, P_T; Y_T, \tilde{\xi}_T \right) \right\} = 0. \tag{2.4}$$

This condition together with (2.1) then determines the evolution of the aggregate price index given the evolution of aggregate output and the real disturbances. These equations together constitute the aggregate-supply block of the model with staggered pricing.

Once again, one may usefully approximate the equilibrium dynamics of inflation in the case of small enough disturbances by considering a log-linear approximation to these equations. If $\tilde{\xi}_t = 0$ and $Y_t = \bar{Y}$ at all times, equations (2.1) and (2.4) have a solution with zero inflation, in which $P_t = p_t^* = P_{t-1}$ each period. In the case of small enough fluctuations in $\tilde{\xi}_t$ and Y_t around these values, one accordingly looks for a solution in which P_t/P_{t-1} and p_t^*/P_t remain always close to 1, though the (log) price level may contain a unit root.[32] As log-linear approximations to (2.1), and (2.4), respectively, I obtain

31. Note that (2.2) reduces to (1.22) if the factor α^{T-t} is replaced by one that takes the value one if $T = t + 1$ and the value zero for all other T.

32. The algebra at this point is simplified by log-linearizing around a steady state with a zero inflation rate, rather than some other constant inflation rate. The resulting log-linear structural equations thus apply only to the determination of equilibrium in the case of a policy rule that does in fact generate inflation near zero at all times. This does not mean, however, that one can consider only policy rules that make the average inflation rate exactly zero or that involve a target inflation rate of zero. It is only necessary that the average inflation rate be sufficiently small (of order φ, where φ is an expansion parameter characterizing monetary policy, such that the average inflation rate is zero for policies with $\varphi = 0$), if I want the

$$\log P_t = \alpha \log P_{t-1} + (1 - \alpha) \log p_t^*, \tag{2.5}$$

and

$$\sum_{T=t}^{\infty} (\alpha\beta)^{T-t} E_t \left[\log p_t^* - \log P_T - \zeta \left(\hat{Y}_T - \hat{Y}_T^n \right) \right] = 0. \tag{2.6}$$

This model of pricing behavior is appealing in that it implies that aggregate price indices should be smoothed, relative to the degree of high-frequency variation in the factors that should affect desired prices in a flexible-price model. To analyze the empirical fit of equations (2.5) and (2.6), of course, one needs an empirical proxy for the output gap $\hat{Y}_t - \hat{Y}_t^n$. Simply using a detrended output measure of one type or another is not obviously justifiable. For according to our theoretical definition of the natural rate of output, $\hat{Y}_t^n$ should vary in response to real disturbances of any of several types (productivity shocks, taste shocks of various sorts, and variations in government purchases have already been discussed), and there is no a priori reason to suppose that these disturbances should be either small or properly described by smooth time series.

In fact, Sbordone (1998, 2002) and Gali and Gertler (1999) have argued that the most direct measure of time variation in the output gap that is relevant to equation (2.6) would not be one based on output data at all, but rather on variation in production costs.[33] One may recall that in the case of the baseline model in Section 1.1, I showed that the real-marginal-cost function could be approximated by (1.15). Averaging this relation over goods i yields

$$\hat{s}_t = \left(\omega + \sigma^{-1} \right) \left(\hat{Y}_t - \hat{Y}_t^n \right), \tag{2.7}$$

where now $\hat{s}_t$ refers to the deviation of the log economy-wide *average* level of real marginal cost from its steady-state value ($\log \bar{s} = -\log \mu$). Thus

---

error in my characterization of the evolution of inflation and other variables to be of order $\mathcal{O}(\|\varphi, \tilde{\xi}\|^2)$, where $\|\tilde{\xi}\|$ is a bound on the size of the disturbances. As I argue (see Chapters 6 and 7) that desirable policies do imply a low average inflation rate, this does not seem an inconvenient restriction, from the standpoint of my goal of characterizing optimal policy. Characterization of the effects of policy in a high-inflation economy might require a more accurate approximation. But the Calvo pricing model itself is implausible as a model of pricing under such circumstances, as many individual prices are likely to be indexed to some broader price index (or to an exchange rate). The model with backward-looking price indexation, discussed in Section 3.2, would perhaps be more realistic for such purposes.

33. Other proposals for theory-based proxies for the output gap include the measure based on hours worked used by McCallum and Nelson (1999b) and the real-interest-rate gap series used by Nelson and Nikolov (2001).

the output that is relevant as a measure of inflationary pressure should be monotonically related to variations in the level of real marginal cost.

Nor is this conclusion special to the particular structure of production costs and demand assumed in Section 1.1. In the case of any of the models discussed in Section 1.4, the price that would be chosen by a flexible-price supplier can be expressed in the form

$$
\begin{aligned}
\log p_t(i) - \log P_t &= \log \mu_t(i) + \log s_t(i)\\
&= \epsilon_\mu(\hat{y}_t(i) - \hat{Y}_t) + s_y(\hat{y}_t(i) - \hat{Y}_t) + \hat{s}_t\\
&= -\theta(\epsilon_\mu + s_y)(\log p_t(i) - \log P_t) + \hat{s}_t,
\end{aligned}
$$

where s_y is used to denote the elasticity of relative real marginal cost with respect to the relative output of good i.[34] This implies that

$$
\log p_t(i) - \log P_t = \left[1 + \theta(\epsilon_\mu + s_y)\right]^{-1} \hat{s}_t.
$$

Comparison with (1.30) indicates that one must have[35]

$$
\hat{s}_t = \left[1 + \theta(\epsilon_\mu + s_y)\right] \zeta\left(\hat{Y}_t - \hat{Y}_t^n\right).
$$

The appearance of the expected log real marginal cost (i.e., the expected gap between log marginal cost and the log price index) in the first-order condition (2.6) also makes sense insofar as it is this gap, rather than the level of real activity as such, that is directly related to the incentives that suppliers have to adjust their prices.

If I replace each term of the form $\zeta(\hat{Y}_T - \hat{Y}_T^n)$ by $(1 + \tilde{\omega}\theta)^{-1}\hat{s}_T$, where $\tilde{\omega} \equiv \epsilon_m u + s_y$,[36] then (2.6) can be written

$$
\log p_t^* = \frac{1 - \alpha\beta}{1 + \tilde{\omega}\theta} \sum_{T=t}^{\infty} (\alpha\beta)^{T-t} E_t[\log \mu + \log S_T + \tilde{\omega}\theta \log P_T], \quad (2.8)
$$

where now $\log S_t$ represents the average log *nominal* marginal cost across sectors. This form, however, still expresses p_t^* (and hence P_t) as a function of the expected evolution of the aggregate price index. Sbordone (1998, 2002) shows that under the assumption that the aggregate price index in

---

34. This corresponds to the quantity denoted $(1 - \mu s_m)s_y$ in (1.43), where s_y is used to denote the elasticity of the real marginal cost of supplying *value added*, rather than gross output.

35. Note that this result provides another derivation of (1.43), given the fact that for the model discussed in Proposition 3.3, $\hat{s}_t = (1 - \mu s_m)(s_y + s_Y)(\hat{Y}_t - \hat{Y}_t^n)$, in terms of the notation used there.

36. Note that this quantity corresponds to ω in the case of the baseline model introduced in Section 1.1.

all future periods will evolve according to this same relation, one can solve
for the rational-expectations equilibrium path of the price index as follows.

PROPOSITION 3.4. Suppose that $\{\log S_t\}$ is a difference-stationary process.
Then there is a unique solution to equations (2.5) and (2.8) for the price-
index process such that $\{\log P_t\}$ is also difference-stationary (i.e., inflation
is a stationary process), given by

$$\log P_t = \lambda_1 \log P_{t-1} + (1 - \lambda_1)\left(1 - \lambda_2^{-1}\right) \sum_{j=0}^{\infty} \lambda_2^{-j} [\log \mu + E_t \log S_{t+j}], \quad (2.9)$$

where $0 < \lambda_1 < 1 < \beta^1 < \lambda_2$ are the two roots of the characteristic polynomial

$$\beta\lambda^2 - (1 + \beta + \xi)\lambda + 1 = 0, \tag{2.10}$$

in which

$$\xi \equiv \frac{1 - \alpha}{\alpha} \frac{1 - \alpha\beta}{1 + \tilde{\omega}\theta} > 0. \tag{2.11}$$

The proof is given in Appendix B. Note that (2.9) implies that the price
index evolves through partial-adjustment dynamics (with weight λ_1 on the
lagged price index in the partial-adjustment dynamics) toward a time-
varying target price that is a weighted average of current and expected-
future values of $\log \mu + \log S_{t+j}$ (with weights on future marginal costs that
decline as λ_2^{-j}). Thus the price index is predicted to be smoothed relative
to the fluctuations in average marginal cost.

This prediction of the Calvo pricing model is in fact independent of any
specification of the determinants of average marginal costs. Tests of the empirical adequacy of this theory of pricing are therefore more appropriately
focused upon this prediction, rather than upon the accuracy of the New Keynesian aggregate-supply relation derived later (which depends as well upon
the details of one's theory of supply costs). This is the approach taken by
Sbordone (1998, 2002), who uses data on the average level of unit labor cost
in the U.S. economy as a measure of nominal marginal cost.[37] She estimates
a small atheoretical VAR model with which to forecast the future path of
unit labor costs, using quarterly U.S. data over the period 1960–1997. This
then allows one to construct an implied series for the forward-looking terms

---

37. Note that according to the model developed in Section 1.1, average marginal supply
cost should be proportional to average unit labor cost under the assumption of a production
technology with a constant elasticity of output with respect to the labor input (e.g., the familiar
Cobb-Douglas specification). See Rotemberg and Woodford (1999b) for further discussion of
this common measure of marginal cost and alternatives.

on the right-hand side of (2.9), for any assumed values of β and ξ (which then imply values for λ_1 and λ_2). Starting from an initial condition for the price level (given by its historical value in the initial quarter), one can then simulate (2.9) to obtain a predicted time path for the price level, given the observed path of unit labor costs (and of forecasted future labor costs). One can then compare this prediction to the actual path of the aggregate price level over the same period.

Note that in the case of flexible prices (the $\xi \to \infty$ limit of the above model), the predicted price series would simply be given by $\log P_t = \log \mu + \log S_t$, so that predicted inflation would be given by the percentage growth in nominal unit labor costs from one quarter to the next. As shown in Figure 3.4, this would be quite a poor explanation of actual U.S. inflation; in particular, one observes that inflation has been much less volatile than the growth rate of unit labor costs. Alternatively, as shown in Figure 3.5, there has been substantial variation in the ratio of price to unit labor cost

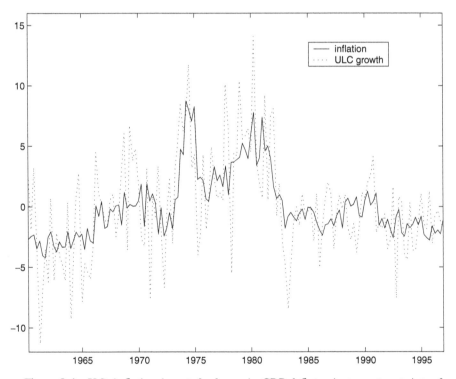

Figure 3.4 *U.S. inflation (quarterly change in GDP deflator, in percentage points of equivalent annual rate) compared to growth rate of unit labor cost. Source: Sbordone (2002).*

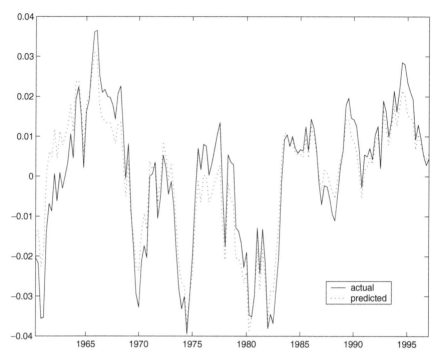

Figure 3.5   *Actual path of price/ULC ratio (quarterly U.S. data, reported as log deviation from mean) compared to prediction of the Calvo pricing model. Source: Sbordone (2002).*

from year to year, whereas the model implies that this should be constant. In the case of sticky prices (ξ finite), the model implies less volatile inflation, and, in fact, for a certain value of ξ, it predicts a path for the price level quite similar to its actual path. Figure 3.5 compares the actual path of the (demeaned, log) price/ULC ratio to the model's prediction in the case that $\xi = .055$.[38] The fit is quite good; the mean-squared error of the predicted price/ULC series is only 12 percent as large as the variance of the actual price/ULC series. Furthermore, even this statistic fails to emphasize the extent to which the model succeeds in explaining the timing of quarterly changes in the ratio; the discrepancy between the predicted and actual series is mainly at quite low frequencies. Figure 3.6 similarly compares the actual path of U.S. inflation (measured by growth in the GDP deflator)

38. Sbordone selects this value as her estimate, on the grounds that it minimizes the mean-squared error of the model's predicted path for $\log P_t$, when β is assigned a value of 1. Note that she actually reports the value of $\xi^{-1} = 18.3$.

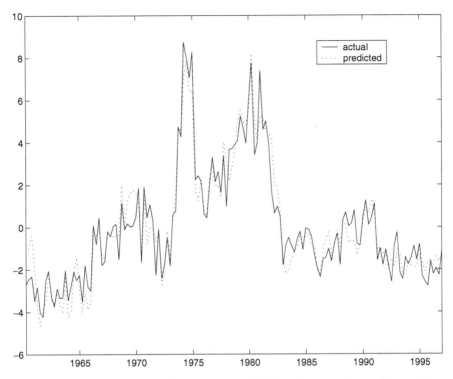

Figure 3.6 *Actual path of inflation (quarterly U.S. data) compared to prediction of the Calvo pricing model. Source: Sbordone (2002).*

with the path predicted by the model. The fit is again quite good (which is another way of seeing that the discrepancy in Figure 3.5 is almost entirely at low frequencies).[39]

These results provide persuasive evidence for price stickiness of at least roughly the sort implied by the Calvo pricing model. The degree to which

---

39. Gali and Gertler (1999) obtain similar results for U.S. inflation, using an instrumental-variables strategy for estimating the inflation equation (2.14) derived later. Gali and Gertler find that they can statistically reject this baseline pricing model in favor of a generalization in which some pricesetters use a backward-looking rule of thumb, resulting in a specification closely related to (3.6) below. However, they find that the baseline model already explains historical inflation dynamics quite well, as Figure 3.6 shows; and the validity of the standard errors used to determine that the rejection of the baseline model is statistically significant might also be questioned. Batini et al. (2000) similarly find that the Calvo pricing model can explain U.K. inflation dynamics, while Gali et al. (2001) obtain similar results for several European countries. For further discussion of the degree of empirical support for this pricing theory, see Gali et al. (2003), Guerrieri (2001), Jondeau and LeBihan (2001), Kurmann (2002), Linde (2002), and Sbordone (2003).

the model fits U.S. inflation dynamics is perhaps surprising, given that the assumption of a fixed probability of price change for all suppliers has been chosen for analytical convenience rather than out of any belief that it ought to be realistic. Probably this reflects the fact that, given the small value of ξ implied by Sbordone's estimates (and hence the high degree of smoothing of marginal cost in the price dynamics), the details of the distribution of intervals between price changes does not matter much for the evolution of the aggregate price index, but only the average rate at which prices are revised. But the fit of the model *does* clearly depend upon the existence of staggered price changes of the kind assumed by Calvo. The New Classical pricing model considered above, for example, would imply that fluctuations in the ratio of price to marginal cost should be unforecastable, so that the predicted P/ULC series would necessarily exhibit no serial correlation. The significant serial correlation of the P/ULC series shown in Figure 3.5 and the closely similar degree of serial correlation of the series predicted by the Calvo model[40] suffice to show that the kind of price stickiness allowed in that model cannot similarly explain the U.S. data. Perhaps more surprisingly, Sbordone shows that the U.S. price index cannot be fit nearly as well by any purely backward-looking moving average of unit labor costs either. The kind of smoothing reflected in the figures depends importantly upon the presence of the forward-looking terms on the right-hand side of (2.9), and not simply upon the partial-adjustment term.[41]

One might, of course, doubt the accuracy of the simple unit-labor-cost measure of marginal cost, for various reasons that are reviewed by Rotemberg and Woodford (1999b). But it seems fortuitous that such a simple model of pricesetting can explain actual inflation dynamics so well, if unit labor cost is not in fact a fairly accurate measure of variations in marginal cost, at least at moderate frequencies.[42] In fact, Sbordone experiments with a number of possible corrections to her simple measure of marginal cost and finds that none of them improves the fit of the pricing model. One might also wonder whether forecasts based on a VAR model with constant coefficients fit to the entire period 1960–1997 should correspond very closely to

40. The autocorrelation functions of both series, with standard errors for the data series, are presented in Sbordone (1998, 2002).

41. Sbordone shows this formally by separately estimating the weights λ_1 and λ_2^{-1} in (2.9), without imposing the restriction that they correspond to the two roots of (2.10). She finds not only that both coefficients are significantly positive, but that the values that yield the best fit are nearly equal in size, as the Calvo pricing model would imply. (Note that the two roots of (2.10) necessarily satisfy $\lambda_1 \lambda_2 = \beta^{-1}$.)

42. Because of the degree of smoothing involved in (2.9), high-frequency error in the measure of marginal cost has relatively little effect upon the predicted path for prices; Figure 3.5 itself indicates at least a small amount of low-frequency specification error, which might be due to low-frequency error in the measure of marginal cost.

people's expectations, even assuming that their expectations were rational, on the ground that the dynamics of unit labor costs need not have been constant over this period. (One might think, e.g., that inflation dynamics have been substantially different since the disinflation of the early 1980s; but this would imply that unit labor cost dynamics should have been different as well.) But, once again, the close fit of the model and the fact that it fits equally well both before and after the 1979–1982 period suggest that the hypothesis of a common (and at least roughly unbiased) forecasting rule over the entire period is not too inaccurate.

2.2 A New Keynesian Phillips Curve

I can use the model of optimal pricesetting just derived to obtain an aggregate supply relation—that is, a structural relation between inflation dynamics and the level of real activity—by again considering the implications of the first-order condition (2.4), expressed in terms of the output gap.

PROPOSITION 3.5. *Let the profit function of the supplier of an individual good again be of the form* (1.17) *and satisfy Assumption 3.1, but suppose now that a fraction* $0 < \alpha < 1$ *of goods prices remain fixed each period, with each price having an equal probability of being revised in any given period, as in the model of Calvo (1983). Suppose also that profits are discounted using a stochastic discount factor that is equal on average to* β, *where* $0 < \beta < 1$.[43] *Then the aggregate inflation rate and aggregate output in any period* t *must satisfy an aggregate-supply relation of the form*

$$\pi_t = \kappa \left(\hat{Y}_t - \hat{Y}_t^n \right) + \beta E_t \pi_{t+1}, \tag{2.12}$$

where

$$\kappa = \frac{(1-\alpha)(1-\alpha\beta)}{\alpha} \zeta > 0. \tag{2.13}$$

The derivation is given in Appendix B. The determinants of (1.35) in (2.13) are again those discussed in Section 1.4. For example, in the case of the baseline model,

$$\kappa \equiv \left(\omega + \sigma^{-1} \right) \xi = \frac{(1-\alpha)(1-\alpha\beta)}{\alpha} \frac{\omega + \sigma^{-1}}{1 + \omega\theta}.$$

A more general expression can be obtained using Proposition 3.3.

---

43. It is not necessary for this result that the factor β coincide with the utility discount factor of the representative household.

Equation (2.12) is what Roberts (1995) calls the New Keynesian Phillips curve, as this specification, or one similar to it, is implied by a variety of simple models of optimal pricesetting.[44] From (2.13) it can be observed once again that the short-run Phillips curve is flatter (for any given inflation expectations) the smaller the value of ζ, and thus the greater the degree of strategic complementarity in pricesetting. It is also flatter as α is larger, which is to say, the longer the average time interval between price changes.

The aggregate-supply relation again has the form of an expectations-augmented Phillips curve, but now the inflation expectations that shift the curve are current expectations of future inflation, rather than past expectations of the current inflation rate as in (1.32). The difference turns out to be crucial for the model's ability to allow for forecastable fluctuations in the output gap. It is now possible for nonzero values of $\hat{Y}_t - \hat{Y}_t^n$ to be forecasted at some earlier date $t - j$; this simply requires that $E_{t-j}\pi_t$ not equal $\beta E_{t-j}\pi_{t+1}$.

It is worth noting that (2.12) can alternatively be expressed in the form

$$\pi_t = \xi \hat{s}_t + \beta E_t \pi_{t+1}, \tag{2.14}$$

where $\xi > 0$ is defined as in (2.11), by again replacing the term $\zeta(\hat{Y}_t - \hat{Y}_t^n)$ with $(1 + \tilde{\omega}\theta)^{-1}\hat{s}_t$. In fact, this version of the relation is in a number of respects more useful than the more familiar relation (2.12). In particular, it holds under weaker assumptions; for example, it does not depend on the particular theory of wagesetting used in deriving (2.12). This makes it especially appropriate to test the empirical validity of (2.14) when seeking to determine the degree of accuracy of the Calvo model of pricing, as Gali and Gertler (1999) emphasize. It is also the form of the relation that more directly generalizes to models such as the multisector model considered in Section 2.5.

2.3 Persistent Real Effects of Nominal Disturbances

I return now to the question of the persistence of the real effects of disturbances to nominal spending. Once again, I assume a given stochastic process for aggregate nominal spending y_t and consider what processes for P_t and Y_t are then implied by the aggregate-supply relation (2.12). As a simple

---

44. Notably, the same form of aggregate supply relation, up to the log-linear approximation, is implied by a model with convex costs of price adjustment, as shown by Rotemberg (1987). Note that in Roberts's presentation of the New Keynesian Phillips curve, the discount factor β is set equal to one. This simplification may seem appealing, in that it implies a vertical "long-run" inflation-output trade-off. But correctly accounting for the presence of the discount factor in (2.12) has important consequences for the analysis of optimal policy, as is shown in Chapters 6 and 7.

example, suppose that an unexpected disturbance permanently increases $\log \mathcal{Y}$ by a unit amount at date zero, which is then expected to maintain the higher value. One may suppose that aggregate nominal spending evolves according to a stochastic process of the form

$$\log \mathcal{Y}_t = \log \mathcal{Y}_{t-1} + \epsilon_t + q_t, \qquad (2.15)$$

where $\{\epsilon_t\}$ is an i.i.d. mean-zero random variable, and $\{q_t\}$ is some stochastic process that is independent of the process $\{\epsilon_t\}$. Because of this assumed independence, (2.15) implies that a unit increase in the realization of ϵ_t raises $E_t \log \mathcal{Y}_{t+k}$ by one for all $j \geq 0$, regardless of the statistical properties of the process $\{q_t\}$. I suppose that ϵ_t represents a purely *monetary* disturbance at date t, that is, one due to a change in monetary policy (possibly one that is due to error on the part of the central bank, but an error that is assumed to be independent of the real disturbances to the economy), and hence that the exogenous process $\{\hat{Y}_t^n\}$ is independent of $\{\epsilon_t\}$. Note that it need not be assumed that the other (independent) determinants of aggregate expenditure, represented by the process $\{q_t\}$, are *unrelated* to monetary policy. I am simply supposing that *one kind* of monetary disturbance is the shock $\{\epsilon_t\}$ and wish to determine the consequences of this kind of disturbance, when it occurs.

The consequences of this kind of disturbance may be calculated as follows. It follows from (2.12) that

$$E_t \pi_{t+k} = \kappa E_t \left(\hat{Y}_{t+k} - \hat{Y}_{t+k}^n \right) + \beta E_t \pi_{t+k+1}$$

for each $k \geq 0$. Using the identities $\pi_t \equiv \log P_t - \log P_{t-1}$ and $\hat{Y}_t - \hat{Y}_t^n = \log \mathcal{Y}_t - \log P_t - \log Y_t^n$, this can alternatively be written

$$E_t(\log P_{t+k} - \log P_{t+k-1}) = \kappa E_t \left(\log \mathcal{Y}_{t+k} - \log P_{t+k} - \log Y_{t+k}^n \right)$$
$$+ \beta E_t \left(\log P_{t+k+1} - \log P_{t+k} \right).$$

Then, differentiating with respect to the realization of ϵ_t yields

$$\tilde{p}_k - \tilde{p}_{k-1} = \kappa(1 - \tilde{p}_k) + \beta(\tilde{p}_{k+1} - \tilde{p}_k), \qquad (2.16)$$

where

$$\tilde{p}_k \equiv \frac{\partial}{\partial \epsilon_t} E_t \log P_{t+k}.$$

(Here I have used the derivatives of $E_t \log \mathcal{Y}_{t+k}$ and $\log Y_{t+k}^n$ discussed in the previous paragraph.) Equation (2.16) is a difference equation to solve for the sequence $\{\tilde{p}_k\}$, which describes the *impulse-response function* of the log price level in response to this kind of shock.

Similarly, introducing the notation

$$\tilde{y}_k \equiv \frac{\partial}{\partial \epsilon_t} E_t \log Y_{t+k},$$

I note that if the rational-expectations equilibrium is one in which deviations of output from trend are stationary, I must have

$$\lim_{k \to \infty} \tilde{y}_k = 0.$$

Given my conclusion about the effect of the shock on $E_t \log \mathcal{Y}_{t+k}$, this requires that

$$\lim_{k \to \infty} \tilde{p}_k = 1. \tag{2.17}$$

I also have as an initial condition

$$\tilde{p}_{-1} = 0, \tag{2.18}$$

since obviously an unexpected shock at date t cannot affect the price level in the previous period.

I accordingly try to find a sequence $\{\tilde{p}_k\}$ that satisfies (2.16) for each $k \geq 0$ and is consistent with terminal condition (2.17) and initial condition (2.18). The solution is given in the following proposition.

PROPOSITION 3.6. Suppose that aggregate nominal expenditure evolves according to (2.15), where ϵ_t is an unforecastable monetary policy shock at date t, and the process $\{q_t\}$ is independent of the process $\{\epsilon_t\}$. Then in an economy with an aggregate-supply relation of the New Keynesian form (2.12), the impulse-response functions of the log price index and log real GDP to a unit positive innovation in ϵ_t (i.e., an unexpected permanent increase of one unit in the log of aggregate nominal expenditure) are given by

$$\tilde{p}_k = 1 - \lambda^{k+1},$$
$$\tilde{y}_k = \lambda^{k+1},$$

for $k \geq 0$, where $0 < \lambda < 1$ is the smaller of the two real roots of the characteristic polynomial

$$\beta \lambda^2 - (1 + \beta + \kappa)\lambda + 1 = 0. \tag{2.19}$$

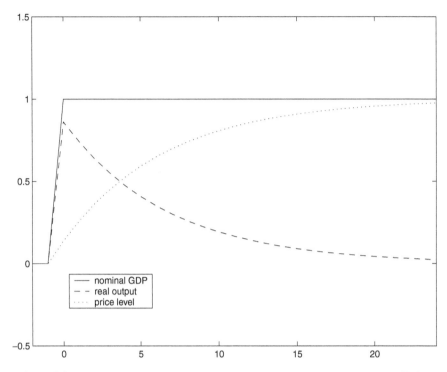

Figure 3.7 *Impulse responses to an immediate permanent increase in nominal GDP.*

Further details of the proof are given in Appendix B. Observe that the log price level is expected to rise monotonically, asymptotically reaching a level proportional to the increase in nominal spending. Output increases in the period of the disturbance, by an amount less than (though possibly close to) proportional to the increase in nominal spending, then decays monotonically back to its original level. (These impulse responses of the price level and of output are plotted in Figure 3.7, for the illustrative parameter values $\beta = .99$ and $\kappa = 0.024$.[45])

The degree of persistence of the effect upon real activity is thus dependent upon the size of the root λ; the closer λ is to one (its theoretical upper bound), the longer the time it takes for real activity to return to its "potential" level following a nominal disturbance. (Note that λ also determines the size of the initial effect upon real activity in period zero, as well. Thus the same factors that increase the *amplitude* of the effect upon real activity— by making aggregate price adjustment more sluggish—also make the effect

---

45. These values are taken from the estimates of Rotemberg and Woodford (1997), discussed further in Chapter 5.

more *persistent*.) It is easily seen, in turn, that the smaller root of $P(\lambda)$ varies inversely with the size of κ, with a value that approaches zero in the case of very large κ and a value that approaches one for κ near zero. Thus a small value of κ (a flat short-run Phillips curve) is required for significant persistence. This in turn could occur either as a result of α being near one (infrequent price changes) or ζ being small (strong strategic complementarity).

It is perhaps most interesting to observe that the degree of strategic complementarity can have a considerable effect upon the degree of persistence, holding fixed the frequency of price changes. Note that for any value of α, the value of κ can be made arbitrarily small, or arbitrarily large, through assignment of an appropriate value to ζ. The effects of α and ζ upon the degree of persistence are shown quantitatively in Figure 3.8, where the implied value of λ is plotted as a function of these two parameters, assuming the value $\beta = .99$.

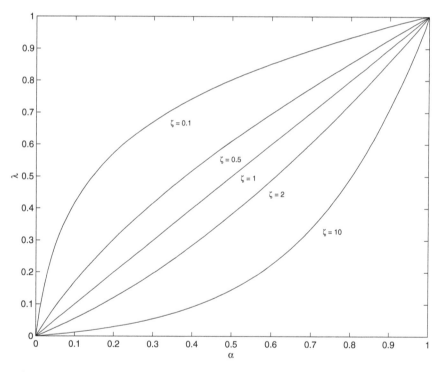

Figure 3.8   *Persistence of real effects of an increase in nominal spending as a function of the frequency of price adjustment for alternative degrees of strategic complementarity in pricesetting.*

One observes that $\lambda > \alpha$ if and only if $\zeta < 1$, that is, if and only if pricing decisions are strategic complements in the sense discussed above. This can be shown analytically by observing that

$$\mathcal{P}(\alpha) = (1 - \alpha)(1 - \alpha\beta)(1 - \zeta),$$

where $\mathcal{P}(\lambda)$ is the characteristic polynomial on the left-hand side of (B.20), and I have used (2.13) to substitute for κ. Thus $\mathcal{P}(\alpha) > 0$, so that $\alpha < \lambda < 1$, if and only if $\zeta < 1$. In this case the rate of adjustment of the aggregate price index is slower than would be expected mechanically as a result of the fact that not all prices have yet had an opportunity to be updated since the occurrence of the shock. (The fraction of prices in period t that have not yet been adjusted even once since the shock is given by α^{t}.) In such a case, Taylor (1980) speaks of the existence of a "contract multiplier" as a result of the staggering of price adjustments.[46] Such a multiplier depends upon the existence of strategic complementarity among different suppliers' pricing decisions, so that the fact that other prices have not fully adjusted makes an individual supplier adjust its own price less. In the case of strategic substitutes ($\zeta > 1$), there is actually even *less* persistence than one would expect for purely mechanical reasons ($\lambda < \alpha$), because the first prices that are adjusted actually overadjust in reaction to the failure of other prices to adjust in proportion to the increase in nominal spending.

Can staggering of price changes give rise to an empirically realistic degree of persistence, assuming an empirically realistic average interval between price changes? Chari et al. (2000) argue that it cannot. However, their conclusion depends both upon an exaggeration of the size of the contract multiplier that would be needed and an underestimate of the empirically plausible degree of strategic complementarity. They define the contract multiplier as "the ratio of the half-life of output deviations after a monetary shock with staggered pricesetting to the corresponding half-life with synchronized pricesetting" (p. 1152). In the analysis above of the response of output under Calvo pricesetting to a monetary shock that permanently increases the level of nominal GDP,[47] I have shown that the level of output

46. In Taylor's original formulation, it is actually the staggered negotiation of *wage* contracts that gives rise to the multiplier.

47. This is not exactly the form of monetary shock considered by Chari et al., who instead assume an exogenous process for the money supply, and consider its implications within a complete general-equilibrium model of the monetary transmission mechanism. However, in their analysis of a stripped-down version of their baseline model, they assume a static money demand function according to which nominal GDP is at all times proportional to the money supply, and also assume a random walk for the (log) money supply; this is thus an experiment of exactly the kind I consider here.

returns to its steady-state level following a shock as λ^t, where λ is the smaller root of (2.19). Thus the half-life with staggered pricesetting would equal $\log 2/\log \lambda^{-1}$ periods.

By the corresponding half-life with synchronized pricesetting, Chari et al. mean the case in which each price that is revised after the shock occurs is immediately adjusted all the way to the new expected long-run price level, so that the fraction of the eventual aggregate price adjustment that has occurred at any time is equal to the fraction of prices that have been revised at least once since the occurrence of the monetary shock. In the case of the Calvo pricing model, the fraction of prices that have not yet been adjusted k periods following a shock is α^{k+1}, so that the half-life with synchronized pricesetting would equal $\log 2/\log \alpha^{-1}$.[48] The contract multiplier implied by the Calvo pricing model is then equal to $\log \alpha^{-1}/\log \lambda^{-1}$. It follows from the previous results that the multiplier is greater than one if and only if $\zeta < 1$, which is to say if and only if there is strategic complementarity in the pricing decisions of different suppliers.[49] In fact, in the continuous-time limit of the Calvo model, one can show that the contract multiplier is equal to

$$\frac{2a^*}{[4a^*(a^*+1)\zeta+1]^{1/2}-1},\qquad (2.20)$$

where a^* is the ratio of the (continuous) rate of price adjustment to the (continuous) rate of time preference, independent of the values of the other parameters.[50] In the case that $a^* \gg 1$, this is approximately $\zeta^{-1/2}$, regardless of the size of a^*; this provides an analytical explanation for the finding of Chari et al. that the predicted contract multiplier in a model with staggered pricesetting depends little upon the assumed length of time between price changes.

Chari et al. argue that a very large multiplier would be needed in order for staggered pricesetting to account for observed persistence. They fit a

48. Chari et al. instead assume fixed-length price commitments, as a result of which this half-life is equal to $N/2$ periods, where N is the number of periods that each price remains fixed.

49. As noted in the previous two footnotes, Chari et al. consider a different model of staggered pricing, but obtain the same conclusion; their finding that the multiplier is necessarily less than one in their stripped-down model follows from the fact that ζ is necessarily greater than one, for the reasons that I discussed above. (They call this parameter γ; their equation (34) shows that it must exceed one.) In their analysis, as here, the question of whether a contract multiplier much greater than one is possible amounts largely to a consideration of whether ζ can plausibly be much less than one.

50. Here I fix ζ and let α and β decrease with Δ, the period length, so that as $\Delta \to 0$, $\log \beta^{-1}/\Delta$ and $\log \alpha^{-1}/\Delta$ both approach positive constants ρ and a, respectively. Then, expanding the characteristic polynomial (2.19) in powers of Δ, one can show that $\log \lambda^{-1}/\Delta$ approaches a positive constant n as well, which depends upon ζ and the ratio $a^* \equiv a/\rho$. The multiplier (2.20) is then equal to a/n.

univariate ARMA model to detrended real GDP for the postwar United States, and conclude that the half-life of output fluctuations around trend is approximately ten quarters. At the same time, they argue that a reasonable length of time to assume that prices are fixed would be only one quarter, implying a half-life with synchronized pricesetting of only half a quarter. Thus they argue that a contract multiplier of twenty would be needed; this would be possible only if ζ were quite small (0.004 in the case of the continuous-time limit).[51] Instead, they find that their baseline parameter values imply a value of ζ well above one, and so a contract multiplier less than one; and while alternative parameter values can raise the multiplier somewhat, they argue that it cannot plausibly be greater than two. They conclude that one must believe that prices remain fixed for many years in order to account for observed persistence.

However, this way of identifying the persistence of the output effects of monetary shocks assumes that *all* fluctuations of output around a deterministic trend path are due to monetary shocks. There is no reason to assume this; indeed, a central contention of this study is that the task of monetary policy is to respond appropriately to a large variety of types of *real* disturbances to which economies are subject. One may attribute great importance to monetary policy without holding that any large fraction of the overall variability of output is due (in the sense of ultimate causation) to the random component of monetary policy, for systematic monetary policy can greatly change the effects of real disturbances. For example, the estimated model of Rotemberg and Woodford (1997), discussed in Chapter 5, attributes only a few percent of the overall variance of real GDP around trend over the sample period to monetary policy shocks; yet the counterfactual simulations reported in that paper show that alternative systematic monetary policies would have implied greatly different paths of real as well as nominal variables.

One needs, then, to identify the real effects of monetary policy shocks *alone* in order to determine the relevant half-life. This may be much shorter than the one estimated by Chari et al., without any implication that monetary policy is unimportant for business fluctuations. For example, the impulse response reported in Figure 3.3 shows that only 3 quarters after the peak output response, the level of (log) output has already returned halfway to the level that would have been expected prior to the shock; and two quarters after that, the response has fallen to only 20 percent of its peak level. This suggest a half-life of only 2.5 to 3 quarters. The structural VAR of Rotemberg and Woodford (1997), discussed in Chapter 5, yields an output

---

51. This value follows from (2.20) under the assumption that $a^* = 33$, a value suggested by survey evidence on the frequency of price change in the U.S. economy, as discussed later. Note, however, that a similarly small value of ζ is required in the case of any large value for a^*.

response that involves more nearly exponential decay after the quarter in which output is first substantially affected; this response, shown later in Figure 5.2, exhibits a half-life of only about 3 quarters.[52]

Furthermore, survey evidence indicates that many prices remain unchanged for longer than a quarter on average. For example, the survey of Blinder et al. (1998) indicates an average time between price changes (for a representative sample of U.S. firms) of 9 months.[53] This suggests that the continuous rate of price change should be parameterized as approximately 0.33/quarter, implying a half-life of 2.08 quarters. Thus the required contract multiplier is only 1.44, within the range that Chari et al. find to be possible. In the continuous-time limit of the Calvo pricing model previously derived,[54] this requires only that $\zeta = 0.49$, and (as shown in Table 3.1) a value this low or even lower is easily consistent with the assumptions about preferences and technology made by Chari et al., once I allow for non-CES preferences and intermediate inputs or, alternatively, for at least some degree of factor specificity.[55] A larger value of σ makes this even easier, and as I argue in Chapter 4, it is most reasonable to calibrate this model with a value of σ much larger than one.

In fact, the present discussion has indicated that a variety of plausible assumptions can justify a value of ζ in the range of 0.10–0.15. This would imply a contract multiplier (in the continuous-time limit of our model) in the range of 2.6 to 3.3, or a half-life for the output response (assuming the rate of price adjustment indicated by the survey evidence) between 5.5 and 6.8 quarters. This is a degree of persistence of the effects on real activity of an increase in nominal expenditure considerably greater than the one indicated by the VAR evidence cited by Rotemberg and Woodford, but is

52. As shown in Figure 5.2, the peak (and first significant) output contraction occurs two quarters following a contractionary policy shock; log output has returned about halfway to its trend level by the fifth quarter following the shock. Nonetheless, the model of Rotemberg and Woodford is fully consistent with the observed degree of persistence of the deviations of output from trend; compare the predicted and estimated autocorrelation functions reproduced in Figure 5.3 below.

53. See Rotemberg and Woodford (1997) for discussion of other survey evidence from studies of smaller sectors of the economy.

54. Here I use (2.20), assuming that $a = 0.33$/quarter and $\rho = 0.01$/quarter, so that $a^* = 33$.

55. In fact, the model of Rotemberg and Woodford is not able to reproduce their estimated impulse-response function for real GDP in response to a monetary policy shock without a considerably smaller value of ζ, approximately 0.13. The difference is obtained because their model is a discrete-time model with periods of 3 months (which results in a degree of persistence somewhat different than that in the continuous-time limit), because they set $\alpha = 2/3$ (so that exactly one-third of all prices are changed each quarter, rather than the fraction $1 - e^{-a} = 0.28$ implied by integration of the continuous-time model), and because their identified monetary policy shock does not result in an immediate, permanent increase in nominal GDP as assumed above.

comparable to the degree of persistence indicated by some other studies of the effects of identified monetary shocks.[56]

2.4 Consequences of Persistence in the Growth of Nominal Spending

I have thus far considered only the response of real activity to an unexpected, permanent increase in nominal spending. While this particular thought experiment allows for a clear definition of the degree of persistence, such a perturbation of the expected path of nominal spending has little similarity to the estimated responses of nominal spending to the monetary policy shocks identified in the VAR literature. Thus the model's predictions for this case cannot be directly compared to any empirical estimates. Identified monetary policy shocks tend to affect nominal spending only slightly (if at all) in the first few months, with an effect that increases cumulatively over a period of several quarters, eventually bringing expected future nominal spending to a new permanent level.

As a simple case that allows for shocks of this kind, I assume that the growth rate of nominal spending follows a process of the form

$$\Delta \log \mathcal{Y}_t = \rho \Delta \log \mathcal{Y}_{t-1} + \epsilon_t + q_t \qquad (2.21)$$

with $0 < \rho < 1$, where ϵ_t is again an i.i.d. mean-zero random variable and $\{q_t\}$ is again a process independent of $\{\epsilon_t\}$. This specification implies that an innovation ϵ_t increases the conditional expectation $E_t \log \mathcal{Y}_{t+k}$ by an amount $(1 - \rho)^{-1}(1 - \rho^{k+1})\epsilon_t$, which increases monotonically with k, asymptotically approaching a permanent effect that is $(1 - \rho)^{-1} > 1$ times as large as the initial effect.[57] Consider the impulse response to a positive innovation $\epsilon_0 = 1 - \rho$, which results in a unit increase in the expected long-run level of nominal spending, adopting the notation

$$\tilde{p}_k \equiv (1 - \rho) \frac{\partial}{\partial \epsilon_t} E_t \log P_{t+k},$$

---

56. The real effects of the identified monetary policy shocks obtained by Rotemberg and Woodford (1997) are less persistent than those obtained in some other VAR studies, mainly using longer sample periods. For example, in the baseline results of Christiano et al. (1999), using quarterly data and identifying monetary policy shocks with innovations in the federal funds rate (first column of their fig. 2), the peak contraction in real GDP following an unexpected monetary tightening occurs only 5 to 6 quarters after the shock, while output has returned halfway to its original trend path by the 11th quarter following the shock; this would indicate a half-life of 5 to 6 quarters. The later results of Christiano et al. (2001) indicate a half-life of less than 3 quarters, however, as previously noted.

57. This form of stochastic process is used as a rough approximation of actual U.S. time series in Rotemberg (1996).

$$\tilde{y}_k \equiv (1 - \rho)\frac{\partial}{\partial \epsilon_t} E_t \log Y_{t+k}$$

for these responses. I obtain in this case the following generalization of Proposition 3.6.

PROPOSITION 3.7. Suppose that aggregate nominal expenditure evolves according to (2.21), where $0 < \rho < 1$, with $\rho \neq \lambda$, where $0 < \lambda < 1$ is again defined as in Proposition 3.6; ϵ_t is an unforecastable monetary policy shock at date t; and the process $\{q_t\}$ is independent of the process $\{\epsilon_t\}$. Then in an economy with an aggregate-supply relation of the New Keynesian form (2.12), the impulse-response function of log real GDP to a positive innovation of size $1 - \rho$ in ϵ_t (implying an eventual permanent increase of one unit in the log of aggregate nominal expenditure) is given by

$$\tilde{y}_k = \frac{(1 - \rho)(1 - \beta\rho)}{(\lambda - \rho)(\lambda^{-1} - \beta\rho)} \left(\lambda^{k+1} - \rho^{k+1}\right)$$

for each $k \geq 0$. The corresponding impulse response function for the log price level is given by

$$\tilde{p}_k = 1 - \rho^{k+1} - \tilde{y}_k.$$

(Note that in the limiting case $\rho = 0$, these solutions reduce to those given in Proposition 3.6.)

The proof is given in Appendix B. Note that the sequence $\{\tilde{y}_k\}$ is the difference of two exponentially decaying series, where the component that enters with a positive sign is the slower-decaying series and has the larger value for all k, so that $\tilde{y}_k > 0$ for all k. A difference of two exponentials of this kind either decays monotonically back to zero after a peak in the period of the shock, or it first increases to a peak, and then decays monotonically back to zero (a hump-shaped response). Since $\tilde{y}_2 = (\lambda + \rho)\tilde{y}_1$, the response function for output is hump-shaped if and only if $\lambda + \rho > 1$, that is, if and only if $\rho > 1 - \lambda$. As an example of how this kind of response is possible, the impulse responses of the log price level and log output are plotted in Figure 3.9, for the illustrative parameter values $\beta = .99$, $\kappa = 0.024$, and $\rho = .4$, along with the impulse response of nominal spending itself.[58]

The reason for such an equilibrium response is simple. Even though prices do not change much immediately following the shock, the increase in

58. The figure also shows the impulse response of the inflation rate, here measured in annual percentage points, so that the inflation rate plotted is defined as $4\Delta \log P_t$. The dynamics of the inflation rate are discussed further in Section 3.

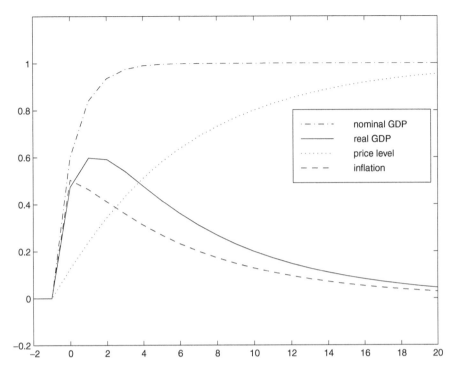

Figure 3.9   *Impulse responses to an innovation in nominal GDP in the case of persistence in nominal GDP growth.*

output is not initially large because nominal spending has not yet increased much. As nominal spending increases further, real output increases as well. Eventually, prices adjust, and real activity falls back to its original level (or, in a model with trend output growth, back to its original trend).

The hump-shaped output response shown in Figure 3.9 is at least roughly of the kind typically estimated using structural VAR methodology (see, e.g., Figure 3.3). Indeed, Cochrane (1998) finds that a slightly modified version of the New Keynesian aggregate-supply relation (2.12) can more closely match the estimated response of output to a monetary policy shock than any of the other simple aggregate-supply relations that he considers.[59] A particular advantage of this specification is that it can allow significant output effects of a nominal disturbance even when there is little immediate effect upon nominal spending. This can be seen by considering the previous calculation in the case in which ρ is close to 1. In such a case, there is little increase in nominal spending in period zero ($\log y_0$ increases only

59. The form used by Cochrane is actually equation (3.2), with a delay $d = 1$ quarter.

by $1 - \rho$), yet the peak output effect may be an arbitrarily large fraction of 1. (For small enough κ, the value of λ may be made arbitrarily close to 1, so that the adjustment of prices is slow compared to the rate at which expected nominal spending approaches its long-run value.) This contrasts sharply with the prediction of the New Classical aggregate-supply relation (1.32), which implies that the peak output effect (which must occur in period zero) is bounded above by $1 - \rho$, no matter how flat the short-run Phillips curve may be.

2.5 Consequences of Sectoral Asymmetries

Thus far I have considered only a completely symmetric model, in the sense that all preferences and production relations would remain the same if the labels of different goods were interchanged. In particular, I have assumed that all real disturbances affect supply and demand conditions for all goods in exactly the same way: Technical progress lowers the cost of producing each good in exactly the same proportion, and so on. In reality, of course, there are many kinds of disturbances that differentially affect various sectors of the economy. Here I briefly consider an extension of the basic model with staggered pricing that allows for several kinds of asymmetries. One reason for interest in this extension is that in the presence of such asymmetries, it is no longer generally the case that stabilization of an aggregate price index and stabilization of an aggregate output gap are equivalent policies (an important but obviously special implication of the New Keynesian Phillips curve (2.12)). Allowing for sectoral asymmetries is also especially important in analyzing monetary policy for an open economy (where, e.g., one wants to consider the consequences of shocks that affect the terms of trade), though I do not develop that extension here.[60]

Instead of assuming that the consumption index C_t that enters the utility function of the representative household is defined by the CES index (1.2), let us suppose that it is a CES aggregate of two subindices,

$$C_t \equiv \left[(n_1 \varphi_{1t})^{1/\eta} C_{1t}^{(\eta-1)/\eta} + (n_2 \varphi_{2t})^{1/\eta} C_{2t}^{(\eta-1)/\eta} \right]^{\eta/(\eta-1)}, \qquad (2.22)$$

for some elasticity of substitution $\eta > 0$. The subindices are in turn CES aggregates of the quantities purchased of the continuum of differentiated goods in each of the two sectors,

$$C_{jt} \equiv \left[n_j^{-1/\theta} \int_{N_j} c_t(i)^{(\theta-1)/\theta} \, di \right]^{\theta/(\theta-1)},$$

---

60. In fact, the two-sector model presented here closely resembles the treatment of a two-country monetary union in Benigno (2003).

for $j = 1, 2$, where the intervals of goods belonging to the two sectors are, respectively, $N_1 \equiv [0, n_1]$ and $N_2 \equiv (n_1, 1]$, and once again $\theta > 1.$[61] In the aggregator (2.22), n_j is the number of goods of each type ($n_2 \equiv 1 - n_1$), and the random coefficients φ_{jt} are at all times positive and satisfy the identity $n_1 \varphi_{1t} + n_2 \varphi_{2t} = 1$. (The variation in the φ_{jt} thus represents a single disturbance each period, a shift in the relative demand for the two sectors' products.)

It follows from this specification of preferences that the minimum cost of obtaining a unit of the sectoral composite good C_{jt} is given by the sectoral price index

$$P_{jt} \equiv \left[n_j^{-1} \int_{N_j} p_t(i)^{1-\theta} \, di \right]^{1/(1-\theta)} \tag{2.23}$$

for $j = 1, 2$, and that the minimum cost of obtaining a unit of C_t is correspondingly given by the overall price index

$$P_t \equiv \left[n_1 \varphi_{1t} p_{1t}^{1-\eta} + n_2 \varphi_{2t} p_{2t}^{1-\eta} \right]^{1/(1-\eta)}.$$

The optimal allocation of demand across the various differentiated goods by pricetaking consumers satisfies

$$c_t(i) = \frac{1}{n_j} C_{jt} \, (p_t(i)/P_{jt})^{-\theta}$$

for each good i in sector j, and the index of sectoral demand satisfies

$$C_{jt} = n_j \varphi_{jt} \, C_t \, (P_{jt}/P_t)^{-\eta}$$

for each sector, regardless of total consumption expenditure in a given period. Note that the random factors φ_{jt} appear as multiplicative disturbances in the sectoral-demand functions. The aggregators have been normalized so that in the event of a common price p for all goods, the price indices are each equal to that common price, and the demands are equal to $c_t(i) = \varphi_{jt} C_t$ for each good i in sector j.

I also assume a disutility of supplying labor of type i equal to $v(h_t(i); \xi_{jt})$ in the case of each good i in sector j; thus I allow for a sector-specific (though not good-specific) disturbance to preferences regarding labor supply. The production function for this good is assumed to be of the form

---

61. I need not assume that $\eta > 1$ in order for there to be a well-behaved equilibrium of the two-sector model under monopolistic competition. In fact, the limiting case in which $\eta \to 1$ and the aggregator (2.22) becomes Cobb-Douglas is frequently assumed; see, e.g., Benigno (2003).

$$y_t(i) = A_{jt} f(h_t(i)),$$

where the function $f(\cdot)$ is common to all goods as before, but I now allow for a sector-specific technology disturbance as well. With the assumption that each firm is a wagetaker in a firm-specific labor market as in Section 1.1, nominal profits for firm i in sector j are given by

$$\Pi_t^{ij} = Y_{jt} P_{jt}^{\theta} p_t(i)^{1-\theta} - w_t(i) f^{-1}\big(Y_{jt} P_{jt}^{\theta} p_t(i)^{-\theta}/A_{jt}\big),$$

generalizing (1.18).

Suppose further that there is Calvo-style staggered pricing in each of the two sectors, with α_j the fraction of goods prices that remain unchanged each period in sector j. A supplier in sector j that changes its price in period t chooses its new price $p_t(i)$ to maximize

$$E_t \left\{ \sum_{T=t}^{\infty} \alpha_j^{T-t} Q_{t,T} \big[\Pi_T^{ij}\big] \right\}, \tag{2.24}$$

generalizing (2.2). This implies a first-order condition that when log-linearized as before is of the form

$$\log p_{jt}^* = \frac{1-\alpha\beta}{1+\omega\theta} \sum_{T=t}^{\infty} (\alpha_j\beta)^{T-t} E_t \big[\log \mu + \log S_{jT} + \omega\theta \log P_{jT}\big], \tag{2.25}$$

generalizing (2.8), where $\log S_{jt}$ is log nominal marginal cost in period t, averaged across the firms of sector j.[62] Log-linearization of (2.23) further implies that

$$\log P_{jt} = \alpha_j \log P_{j,t-1} + (1-\alpha_j) \log p_{jt}^*, \tag{2.26}$$

generalizing (2.5).

Equations (2.25) and (2.26) then determine the evolution of the sectoral price level as a function of expected future inflation in that sector and expectations regarding nominal marginal costs in the sector at all future

---

62. It is this form of the optimal pricesetting condition, rather than (2.6), that most directly generalizes to the multisector case. For the relation used previously between the partial derivative of the profit function and the gap between price and marginal cost continues to hold, even when only averaged over a particular sector of the economy. The average sectoral gap between price and marginal cost cannot, however, be made a monotonic function of a sectoral output gap, as the gap between actual sectoral output and equilibrium sectoral output under flexible prices is not in general independent of the sectoral output gaps (or sectoral average markups) in other parts of the economy. See Section B.7 of Appendix B for details.

dates T. It is no longer possible, however, to express the gap between price and marginal cost in a given sector j as a function solely of economic activity in that sector, together with exogenous disturbances, as was possible in the single-sector model. In the two-sector model, the aggregate-supply relation between sectoral inflation and sectoral activity also depends on activity in the other sector, or alternatively on the aggregate output gap as well as the sectoral gap. Instead of writing the sectoral aggregate-supply relations in terms of both aggregate and relative output gaps, one can write them in terms of the aggregate output gap, and a *relative-price gap* $\hat{p}_{Rt} - \hat{p}_{Rt}^n$, where $\hat{p}_{Rt} \equiv \log(p_{2t}/p_{1t})$, and $\hat{p}_{Rt}^n$ is the value of this relative price in the flexible-price equilibrium (a function solely of the exogenous real disturbances, like the natural rate of output).

PROPOSITION 3.8. Consider a two-sector model of the kind previously described, with Calvo pricing in each sector (and the fraction of prices that remain unchanged each period in sector j equal to $0 < \alpha_j < 1$), and sector-specific disturbances to tastes and technology. For each sector $j = 1, 2$, let $\pi_{jt} \equiv \log(P_{jt}/P_{j,t-1})$ be the rate of inflation in that sector. Then for each sector, the sectoral inflation rate is related to the aggregate output gap through a relation of the form

$$\pi_{jt} = \kappa_j(\hat{Y}_t - \hat{Y}_t^n) + \gamma_j(\hat{p}_{Rt} - \hat{p}_{Rt}^n) + \beta E_t \pi_{j,t+1}, \qquad (2.27)$$

generalizing (2.12), where

$$\kappa_j \equiv \frac{(1 - \alpha_j)(1 - \alpha_j \beta)}{\alpha_j} \frac{\omega + \sigma^{-1}}{1 + \omega\theta} > 0$$

for $j = 1, 2$, and

$$\gamma_1 \equiv n_2 \frac{(1 - \alpha_1)(1 - \alpha_1 \beta)}{\alpha_1} \frac{1 + \omega\eta}{1 + \omega\theta} > 0,$$

$$\gamma_2 \equiv -n_1 \frac{(1 - \alpha_2)(1 - \alpha_2 \beta)}{\alpha_2} \frac{1 + \omega\eta}{1 + \omega\theta} < 0,$$

where $0 < n_j < 1$ is the number of goods in sector j.

Details of this derivation are given in Appendix B.

Inflationary pressure in each sector can thus be expressed as a function of the aggregate level of real activity (relative to its natural level) *and* of the sector's relative price index (relative to the natural value of this relative price). High aggregate output increases inflationary pressure in both sectors, whereas a high relative price in one sector reduces inflationary pressure in that sector. Combining equations (2.27) for $j = 1, 2$ with the identity

$$\hat{p}_{Rt} = \hat{p}_{R,t-1} + \pi_{2t} - \pi_{1t}, \qquad (2.28)$$

one has a complete system of equations for the evolution of the price indices for both sectors given the evolution of aggregate real activity and the two composite real disturbances $\hat{Y}_t^n$ and $\hat{p}_t^R$. The latter term reflects the various ways in which the real disturbances differentially affect the two sectors, and is given by

$$\hat{p}_{Rt}^n \equiv (1/\eta)\big[(\hat{\varphi}_{2t} - \hat{\varphi}_{1t}) - \big(\hat{Y}_{2t}^n - \hat{Y}_{1t}^n\big)\big].$$

In general, this model implies that inflation in both sectors, and hence aggregate inflation as well, depends on a lagged endogenous variable, $\hat{p}_{R,t-1}$; thus inflation is not so purely forward looking in this theory as in the fully symmetric (one-sector) case. However, in the case that prices are equally sticky in both sectors ($\alpha_1 = \alpha_2$), $\xi_1 = \xi_2$, and hence

$$n_1\xi_1 + n_2\xi_2 = 0.$$

It follows that if the relation (2.27) is averaged over the two sectors, weighting each relation by the size of the corresponding sector, once again equation (2.12) is obtained for the evolution of aggregate inflation. Thus one finds that the existence of an equilibrium relation of the form (2.12)—implying that there is no incompatibility between stabilization of the overall price index and stabilization of the output gap $\hat{Y}_t - \hat{Y}_t^n$—does not require that all real disturbances affect the demand for and cost of production of each good identically, as assumed earlier. In the case of a model that is otherwise symmetrical (the same degree of price stickiness for all goods, the same form of production function for all goods up to a multiplicative technology factor, and so on), a relation of this kind is obtained even in the presence of several types of asymmetric disturbances: disturbances to the relative disutility of supplying different types of labor, disturbances to the relative productivity of labor in different sectors, and shifts in the relative preferences of households for different goods.

On the other hand, if prices are not equally sticky for different types of goods, it ceases to be true that the same policy can simultaneously stabilize the aggregate output gap and the overall inflation rate. The consequences of the resulting trade-off for optimal stabilization policy are considered in Section 4.3 of Chapter 6.

3 Delayed Effects of Nominal Disturbances on Inflation

We have seen that the assumption of staggered pricesetting (as interpreted by Calvo in particular) gives rise to an aggregate-supply relation that fits much better with basic facts about the effects of monetary disturbances than the simple New Classical Phillips curve. For this reason, the New Keynesian Phillips curve has been employed in many recent discussions of monetary policy that seek to take account of forward-looking private-sector behavior. Nonetheless, even this model has been subject to a good bit of criticism as not fitting too well with econometric evidence regarding the co-movements of real and nominal variables.

A central criticism has been that the model implies that inflation should be a more *purely forward-looking* process than it seems to be in reality. Note that (2.12) can be solved forward to yield

$$\pi_t = \kappa \sum_{j=0}^{\infty} \beta^j E_t \big[\hat{Y}_{t+j} - \hat{Y}_{t+j}^n \big]. \tag{3.1}$$

Thus the predicted rate of inflation at any time should depend solely upon the predicted output gaps at that time and later, in a way that is completely independent of either output gaps or inflation in the past. This does not square well with many economists' intuitive view of the inflation process or with the inflation dynamics implied by the models currently used in most central banks. These models instead assume a substantial degree of *inertia* in the inflation process, so that recent past inflation figures as an important determinant of current inflation.

Clear evidence that the New Keynesian Phillips curve cannot account for the co-movement that is observed between real activity and inflation, or for the persistence of inflation dynamics themselves, is not as easy to obtain as often seems to be assumed. Claims that the equation is grossly at odds with the facts are often based upon the use of one or another conventional output-gap series as a proxy for $\hat{Y}_t - \hat{Y}_t^n$. For example, (2.12) implies that the series $\pi_{t+1} - \beta^{-1}\pi_t$, which is essentially the rate of acceleration of inflation, should be negatively correlated with $\hat{Y}_t - \hat{Y}_t^n$.[63] Instead, conventional series for the U.S. output gap (which subtract one relatively smooth trend or another from a log real GDP series) are generally found to be *positively* correlated with the subsequent acceleration of inflation. But the present model gives good reason to suppose that $\hat{Y}_t^n$ may not be a smooth trend. It should be affected immediately by changes in government purchases or other "autonomous" components of expenditure and by variations in household impatience to consume or in attitudes toward work, in addition to such slower-moving factors as capital accumulation, technical progress,

---

63. To be precise, it implies that this quasi-acceleration statistic should equal $-\beta^{-1}\kappa \, (\hat{Y}_t - \hat{Y}_t^n)$ plus a forecast error that should be uncorrelated with all period t information, including $\hat{Y}_t - \hat{Y}_t^n$.

and growth in the labor force. If there are relatively high-frequency variations in $\hat{Y}_t^n$, traditional gap measures could easily be *negatively* correlated
with $\hat{Y}_t - \hat{Y}_t^n$, owing to policies tending to stabilize output around a smooth
trend rather than around the time-varying natural rate (Gali, 2002). The
fact that average real unit labor costs—which should correspond to variations in $\hat{Y}_t - \hat{Y}_t^n$ under fairly general assumptions about the nature of the
disturbances, as discussed above—are negatively correlated with detrended
real GDP suggests that this may well be the case. In fact, real unit labor costs
are *negatively* correlated with inflation acceleration in U.S. data, and the
New Keynesian Phillips curve accounts quite well for U.S. inflation dynamics
when real unit labor costs are used to measure $\hat{Y}_t - \hat{Y}_t^n$, as discussed above.

However, evidence that the simple New Keynesian Phillips curve may indeed be too forward looking can be found by considering the dynamics of
output and inflation in response to identified monetary policy shocks. If the
identification of monetary shocks in the VAR studies mentioned earlier is
correct, then the estimated impulse responses for real GDP should also correspond to the impulse response for the theoretically correct gap measure,
$\hat{Y}_t - \hat{Y}_t^n$, since the path of $\hat{Y}_t^n$ should be unaffected.[64] Hence the estimated
impulse responses for real GDP and inflation should satisfy (2.12), or equiv-
alently (3.1).

Typically, they do not. In particular, one generally observes that the main
effect of a monetary policy shock on inflation occurs in the quarters *following* those in which the output response is strongest. (For example, Figure
3.10 shows the responses obtained in the study of Christiano et al., 2001, discussed earlier.) But this is inconsistent with (3.1), regardless of the assumed
parameter values, because this equation states that the inflation response
each quarter should be an increasing function of the output responses that
are expected in that quarter and *later.* Thus the effect on inflation should *pre-
cede* the effect on output, insofar as the latter effect is predictable in advance
(as the output impulse response indicates to be the case); and it should
peak earlier than the effect on output, since once the peak output effect is
reached, the output gaps that can be anticipated from then on are smaller
than those that could still be expected a short while earlier. This is not what
the VAR studies indicate. Rather, the effects of monetary disturbances on

---

64. This is no longer exactly true once one allows for endogenous capital accumulation,
as I do in Chapter 4. But even so, the effect upon $\hat{Y}_t^n$ owing to endogenous variation in the
capital stock should not be large during the first few quarters. Furthermore, taking account of
this effect will only exacerbate the problem sketched here: The true output gap really returns
to its previously expected level even *faster* than real GDP because increased investment during
the early quarters following an interest-rate reduction should raise the natural rate of output.
This would only make the tendency of inflation to peak *after* the main effect on the output gap
even more dramatic than it appears to be in Figure 3.10.

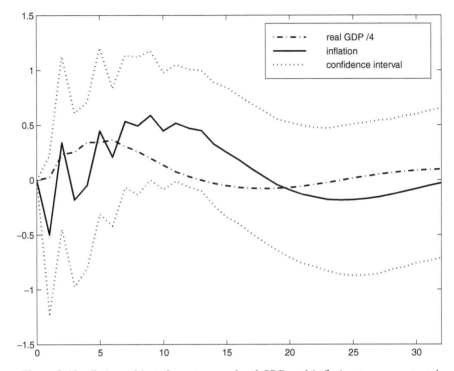

Figure 3.10 *Estimated impulse responses of real GDP and inflation to an unexpected interest-rate reduction. Source: Christiano et al. (2001).*

inflation are delayed and more persistent than would be predicted by the simple model of staggered pricing.

However, the present model of staggered pricing can be extended in a number of ways that make it more realistic in this respect, while continuing to derive inflation dynamics from optimal pricing decisions, subject to certain assumed constraints. Here I focus particular attention to two approaches that have been useful in reconciling optimizing models with VAR evidence.

3.1 Staggered Pricing with Delayed Price Changes

One simple way of avoiding the counterfactual prediction that—because of the forward-looking character of inflation in the Calvo model—the rate of inflation should respond *immediately* to a monetary disturbance that is expected to affect nominal expenditure eventually is to modify the assumption that newly chosen prices take effect immediately. I have assumed in the previous derivation that the fraction $1 - \alpha$ of prices that change in a given period are chosen optimally, given aggregate conditions in the period in which the new price takes effect. One reason for this assumption was that it allowed me to nest the case of fully flexible prices within my specification (as the limiting case in which $\alpha = 0$). However, the literature on staggered wage- and pricesetting has often assumed that new wage contracts and/or price commitments are chosen at a date *before* they first take effect—and as a result are optimal only conditional upon the information that was available at that earlier date. Allowing for a delay before newly chosen prices take effect obviously has the consequence that a monetary policy shock will not affect prices until after this delay. It could then also affect output sooner than it affects inflation.

I can easily modify my earlier presentation of the discrete-time Calvo model to allow for such delays in the introduction of new prices. Suppose that each of the new prices chosen in period t takes effect only in period $t + d$, for some integer $d \geq 0$. Conditional upon a new price being chosen for a given good in period t, that price applies in periods prior to period $t + d$ with probability zero, in period $t + d$ with probability 1, in period $t + d + 1$ with probability α, and more generally in period $t + d + k$ with probability α^k, for any $k \geq 0$. A supplier i that chooses a new price in period t chooses that new price $p_{t+d}(i)$ to maximize

$$E_t \left\{ \sum_{T=t+d}^{\infty} \alpha^{T-t-d} Q_{t,T} \Pi\big(p_{t+d}(i), p_T^I, P_T; Y_T, \tilde{\xi}_T\big) \right\},$$

generalizing (2.2), where nominal profits each period are again given by (1.18). I obtain in this case the first-order condition

$$E_t \left\{ \sum_{T=t+d}^{\infty} (\alpha\beta)^{T-t-d} u_c(Y_T; \xi_T) Y_T P_T^\theta \left[p_{t+d}^* - \mu P_T s\big(Y_T P_T^\theta p_{t+d}^{*-\theta}, Y_T; \tilde{\xi}_T\big) \right] \right\} = 0$$

to implicitly define the optimal price p_{t+d}^*, which is the same for all suppliers choosing a new price at date t. The value of p_t^* then determines the evolution of the price index P_t through (2.1), just as before.

Through a series of manipulations similar to those used in the proof of Proposition 3.5, log-linearization of the above first-order condition yields a log-linear aggregate supply relation of the form

$$\pi_t = \kappa E_{t-d}\big(\hat{Y}_t - \hat{Y}_t^n\big) + \beta E_{t-d}\pi_{t+1}, \tag{3.2}$$

generalizing (2.12). (All variables and coefficients in this equation have the same definitions as before.) In the case that $d = 1$, this is the form of aggregate-supply relation used by Cochrane (1998) and by Bernanke and

Woodford (1997). Note that the right-hand side of (3.2) consists entirely of terms that are a function of period $t - d$ information. Thus this model implies that inflation π_t is a predetermined variable, depending only upon disturbances in period $t - d$ or earlier. In this case, only fluctuations in $E_{t-d}\hat{Y}_t^n$, the *forecastable component* of the natural rate of output, matter for inflation and output determination.

An alternative interpretation of this model would be not that price changes must actually be determined in advance (say, because advance notice to customers is expected), but rather that when an opportunity to change price arises at date t, the new price (that applies beginning in period t) is chosen on the basis of *old information,* namely, the state of the world as of period $t - d$. This assumption would result in exactly the same optimality criterion for new prices as above, and hence exactly the same aggregate-supply relation (3.2). Thus the hypothesis may alternatively be described as one involving *information delays,* as, for example, in the work of Mankiw and Reis (2001a,b).[65]

Under either interpretation, the model implies that a monetary policy shock in period t has no effect on inflation before period $t + d$. This eliminates an embarrassing feature of the basic New Keynesian specification that is especially evident when one recognizes that, according to the VAR studies, monetary disturbances affect aggregate nominal expenditure only with a delay (as in Figure 3.2). Suppose that nominal GDP evolves according to a stochastic process of the form

$$\Delta \log \mathcal{Y}_t = \rho \Delta \log \mathcal{Y}_{t-1} + \epsilon_{t-s} + q_t, \tag{3.3}$$

where the integer $s \geq 0$ indicates the lag between the time at which the monetary policy shock occurs and the first time at which it affects nominal GDP. (As before, ϵ_t is assumed to be a mean-zero disturbance realized at date t, completely unforecastable before that date, and the process $\{q_t\}$ is assumed to be independent of the process $\{\epsilon_t\}$.) One can once again solve for the equilibrium paths of inflation and output given the aggregate supply relation (3.2). I now wish to consider the consequences of alternative assumed delays d in the latter relation.

Figure 3.11 shows the implied impulse responses of inflation and output to a monetary disturbance at date zero according to the standard New

---

65. One advantage of the hypothesis of information delays is that one need not assume the same delay in the case of all types of news. In order to obtain the result that monetary policy shocks do not affect inflation within the first year, e.g., it would be necessary to assume a delay of a year in the receipt of information about changes in interest rates; but one might simultaneously assume that other kinds of disturbances are observed by suppliers much more quickly, so that one would not have to assert that *all* price changes are determined entirely by conditions in the previous year and earlier. I do not pursue this extension here, however.

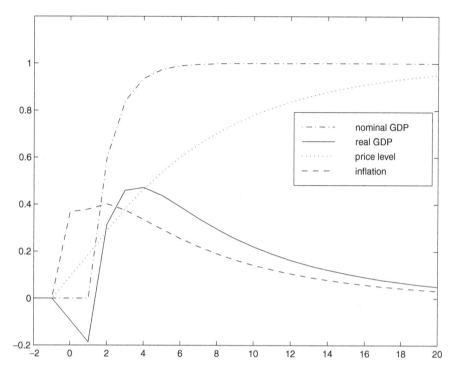

Figure 3.11 *Impulse responses to a monetary disturbance with a delayed effect on nominal expenditure (s = 2), according to the basic Calvo model.*

Keynesian Phillips curve in the case that the effect of the disturbance on nominal GDP is delayed. The shock is once again an unexpected loosening of policy that implies an eventual increase in nominal GDP of 1 percentage point, and the assumed value of ρ is equal to 0.4, as in Figure 3.9; but I now assume that $s = 2$, to match the delay in the effect of an interest-rate reduction on nominal GDP shown in Figure 3.2. (The values assumed for β and κ are the same as in the case of Figure 3.9.)

In the case of the basic New Keynesian specification, I obtain the embarrassing prediction that a monetary disturbance that is expected to increase nominal expenditure beginning two periods later should *contract* real activity in the short run. This is because an expectation of higher real activity and/or inflation two periods from now implies that those suppliers who change prices sooner than that (but after learning of the shock) should already raise their prices at a higher than normal rate, in anticipation of high demand and high competitors' prices in the future. Inflation should thus increase immediately in response to the expectation of higher nominal

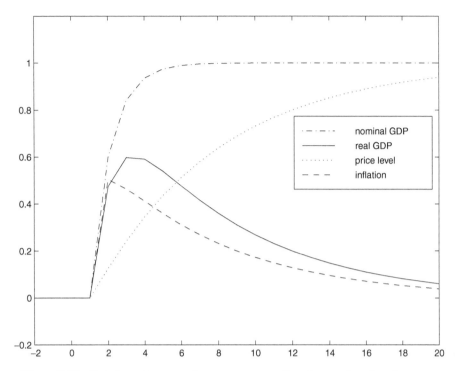

Figure 3.12 *Impulse responses to the same monetary disturbance when $d = 2$ quarters in AS relation (3.2).*

expenditure in the near future; but since nominal expenditure does *not* increase immediately (by hypothesis), this implies a temporary *contraction* of real activity. This is not, of course, at all what estimated output response is like (recall Figure 3.3).

The problem can be solved by assuming a delay $d = 2$ quarters before newly chosen prices take effect (replacing (2.12) by (3.2)). The corresponding impulse responses in this case are shown in Figure 3.12. The predicted responses of all variables are exactly the same as in Figure 3.9, except that all the impulse-response functions are shifted to the right by two quarters. Note that the hypothesis of delayed price changes also implies no effect of the monetary shock on output until two quarters later, given the assumption of a delay in the effect of the shock on nominal GDP.[66] The implied response of output in this case is qualitatively fairly similar to what the VAR

66. Of course, the question remains why an interest-rate reduction should have no effect on nominal GDP until two quarters later. This is a question about the aggregate-demand block of the model, to be deferred until the next chapter.

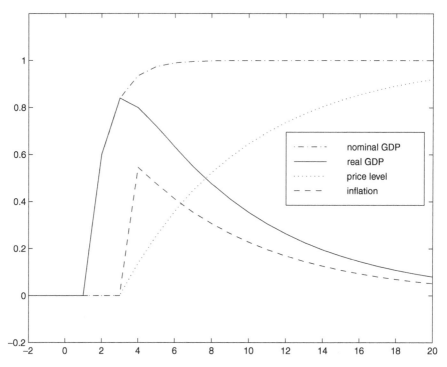

Figure 3.13 *Impulse responses to the same monetary disturbance when d = 4 quarters.*

studies estimate—an effect that is delayed for two quarters, hump-shaped thereafter, persistent, and never significantly negative.

This figure still differs from the responses shown in Figure 3.10, though, in that the inflation effect peaks earlier than the output effect. This problem can be ameliorated by assuming an even longer delay d before price changes take effect. (Note that the response shown in Figure 3.10 implies that the price level is no higher than it would have been in the absence of the shock, until six quarters following the shock; so these estimated responses are consistent with d being as long as six quarters.) Figure 3.13 shows the corresponding impulse responses in the case that $d = 4$ quarters. It can now be observed that the effect of the shock on real output peaks before there is any effect on inflation at all (i.e., in the third quarter following the shock).

Even so, the effects on inflation, once the delay d is past, are predicted to appear abruptly; the peak effect on inflation is very clearly in the first quarter in which any effect on prices can occur, with a sharp decline in the inflation effect thereafter. Thus the predicted inflation response still does not exhibit the kind of persistence seen (at least according to the point estimates) in Figure 3.10. A further modification of the Calvo model can help with this.

3.2 Consequences of Indexation to Past Inflation

In the classic Calvo model, it is assumed that prices remain fixed in money terms between those occasions upon which they are reoptimized. While this is a simple way of resolving the question of what to do about prices between revisions, and the assumption conforms with apparent practice at many firms, I have certainly not shown that there is anything optimal about this aspect of the Calvo pricing model. I have instead analyzed optimal pricing policy taking this feature of it as a constraint. One might instead assume that prices are automatically raised in accordance with some mechanical rule between the occasions on which they are reconsidered. If the rule is simple enough, the fact that firms refrain from reconsidering the optimality of their prices for intervals of months at a time still results in substantial savings on managerial costs, and so it may be plausible that such an interim rule of thumb would be used.

One obvious type of a more sophisticated interim rule than simply fixing prices in terms of money is one that seeks to correct, in at least a simple way, for increases in the general price index. As an example, Yun (1996) assumes that prices are automatically increased at some rate $\bar{\pi}$ between occasions on which they are reconsidered, where $\bar{\pi}$ is the actual long-run average rate of inflation in the economy. This results in an aggregate-supply relation of the form

$$\pi_t = (1 - \beta)\bar{\pi} + \kappa(\hat{Y}_t - \hat{Y}_t^n) + \beta E_t \pi_{t+1},$$

generalizing (2.12). In comparing the expected consequences of monetary policy rules that imply different long-run average rates of inflation, Yun assumes that the parameter $\bar{\pi}$ of firms' pricing policies should change accordingly; this results in a vertical long-run Phillips-curve relation, unlike the classic Calvo model.

In practice, in economies where inflation has been enough of a problem for indexation of long-term monetary commitments to be worth undertaking, indexation schemes are generally based on a measure of inflation over some relatively short recent time interval, as there is no presumption that inflation can always be expected to remain near some nonzero steady-state value. (Of course, this is related to the fact that there was little experience of stable commitment to a fixed inflation target in any country prior to the past decade!) This suggests that it may be more plausible to assume automatic indexation of price commitments (or wages, as discussed in the next section) to the change in the overall price index over some recent past period.

Note, however, that it is not realistic to assume that it should be possible to index individual prices to the *current* price index. Apart from the simultaneity problem that this would create, the assumption that this is possible would not be in the spirit of my assumption that continual monitoring of current conditions in order to maintain a constantly optimal price is too costly to be worthwhile. It is far more plausible, then, to imagine a policy of automatic indexation of one's price (between the occasions on which a full review of the optimality of the price is undertaken) to the change in an overall price index over some *past* time interval.

Christiano et al. (2001), Smets and Wouters (2002), and Giannoni and Woodford (2003b) assume partial or full indexation of this kind for both wages and prices and argue that this extension of the Calvo pricing model improves the empirical fit of their models. Here I examine the consequences of backward-looking indexation for inflation dynamics, continuing for now to assume efficient labor-market contracting. Let us suppose once again that each period a randomly chosen fraction $1 - \alpha$ of all prices are reconsidered, and that these are set optimally; but the price of each good i that is *not* reconsidered is adjusted according to the indexation rule

$$\log p_t(i) = \log p_{t-1}(i) + \gamma \, \pi_{t-1}, \tag{3.4}$$

where $0 \leq \gamma \leq 1$ measures the degree of indexation to the most recently available inflation measure. (Note that even when $\gamma = 1$, as assumed by Christiano et al., nominal rigidities still matter for the effects of aggregate disturbances because of the one-quarter lag in the indexation.)

This assumption about how prices are adjusted in the interim between reoptimizations affects the way in which prices should be set when they are reconsidered. If one assumes, as in the basic Calvo model, that newly optimized prices take effect immediately, then a new price $p_t(i)$ chosen in period t should be selected to maximize

$$E_t \left\{ \sum_{T=t}^{\infty} \alpha^{T-t} Q_{t,T} \left[\Pi_T^i (p_t(i) \, (P_{T-1}/P_{t-1})^{\gamma}) \right] \right\}.$$

This results in a first-order condition

$$E_t \left\{ \sum_{T=t}^{\infty} (\alpha\beta)^{T-t} u_c(Y_T; \xi_T) \, Y_T P_T^{\theta} \left(\frac{P_{T-1}}{P_{t-1}} \right)^{\gamma(1-\theta)} \right.$$

$$\left. \times \, \left[p_t^* - \mu P_T s \big(Y_T (p_t^*/P_T)^{-\theta} (P_{T-1}/P_{t-1})^{-\gamma\theta}, \, Y_T; \tilde{\xi}_T \big) \right] \right\} = 0$$

to implicitly define the optimal price p_t^*, once again the same for all suppliers choosing a new price at date t. Given the choice of p_t^* each period, the overall price index then evolves according to

$$P_t = \left[(1 - \alpha)p_t^{*1-\theta} + \alpha \left(P_{t-1} \left(\frac{P_{t-1}}{P_{t-2}} \right)^{\gamma} \right)^{1-\theta} \right]^{1/(1-\theta)}, \qquad (3.5)$$

generalizing (2.1).

Log-linearization of the first-order condition and of the law of motion (3.5) for the Dixit-Stiglitz price index, together with a series of manipulations analogous to those used in the proof of Proposition 3.5, then yields a log-linear aggregate-supply relation of the form

$$\pi_t - \gamma \pi_{t-1} = \kappa \left(\hat{Y}_t - \hat{Y}_t^n \right) + \beta E_t(\pi_{t+1} - \gamma \pi_t), \qquad (3.6)$$

where β, κ, and $\hat{Y}_t^n$ all have the same definitions as in (2.12). The allowance for backward-looking indexation generalizes the New Keynesian Phillips curve in a fairly straightforward way: It is now the quasi-differenced inflation rate, $\pi_t - \gamma \pi_{t-1}$, rather than the inflation rate itself, that is related to the output gap in the way indicated by the previous relation.

In particular, it is still possible to solve (3.6) forward to obtain

$$\pi_t = \gamma \pi_{t-1} + \kappa \sum_{j=0}^{\infty} \beta^j E_t \left[\hat{Y}_{t+j} - \hat{Y}_{t+j}^n \right],$$

generalizing (3.1). The quasi-differenced inflation rate is still a purely forward-looking function of the expected path of the output gap. However, now the inflation rate predicted for periods t and later depends not only upon the predicted path of the output gap in those periods, but also upon the initial inflation rate π_{t-1}. Thus the extended theory implies *inflation inertia*, to an extent that is greater as the indexation parameter γ is larger.

The difference made by a substantial degree of indexation can be illustrated by again considering the predicted impulse responses of inflation and output to a monetary policy shock that results in a persistent increase in the growth rate of nominal GDP. Figure 3.14 shows the predicted impulse responses in the case of aggregate-supply relation (3.6), in the case $\gamma = 1$, when (as in Figure 3.9) there is no delay in the effect of the shock on nominal expenditure. It can now be seen that even without the hypothesis of delay before new prices can take effect, it is possible to explain the observed delay in the effect of a monetary disturbance on inflation, relative to its effect on output. It can also be observed that in this model, the inflation response is hump shaped, rather than immediately declining sharply after the quarter of the disturbance, as is predicted by the basic Calvo model (see Figure 3.9).

A number of authors have argued that this kind of modification of the basic Calvo model results in a more realistic specification. Christiano et al. (2001) argue that a model with $\gamma = 1$ better fits their estimated impulse

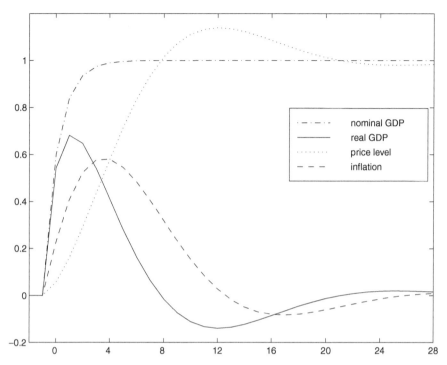

Figure 3.14 *Impulse responses to the same monetary disturbance as in Figure 3.9 (s =
0) in the case of backward-looking indexation of prices (γ = 1).*

responses than the standard model with $\gamma = 0$. Smets and Wouters (2002)
treat γ as a free parameter (in addition to using a different estimation
strategy) and conclude that the best-fitting value of γ is an intermediate
value, approximately 0.64. Giannoni and Woodford (2003b) also treat γ as
a free parameter, but (using an estimation strategy closer to that of Christiano et al., discussed in Chapter 5) find that $\gamma = 1$ is the best-fitting
value.

It should also be noted that when $\gamma = 1$, relation (3.6) is essentially
identical to the aggregate-supply relation of Fuhrer and Moore (1995a,b),
which has been popular in econometric work.[67] Relation (3.6) is also of essentially the same form as the generalization of the Calvo model proposed
by Gali and Gertler (1999). These authors assume that prices remain fixed
in monetary terms for stochastic intervals of time, as in the Calvo model; but
when prices are adjusted, some prices are chosen optimally (as in the Calvo

---

67. In the limiting case $\beta = 1$, the relation is identical to that of Fuhrer and Moore,
although the derivation that they offer for their relation is different from the one given here.

model), whereas others are adjusted according to a backward-looking rule of thumb that introduces dependence upon lagged inflation. The fraction of suppliers who are backward looking is treated as a free parameter, and variation in this parameter has essentially the same effect as variation in γ in the indexation model. In the limiting case $\beta = 1$, the two models have identical implications. Relation (3.6) for any given value of γ can be obtained from the Gali-Gertler model through an appropriate choice of the fraction of backward-looking pricesetters. While Gali and Gertler find that the basic Calvo model fits U.S. inflation dynamics fairly well (once real unit labor cost is used as a proxy for the output gap, rather than a traditional output-based measure), their instrumental variables estimates indicate significant rejection of the hypothesis of no backward-looking pricesetters. Their point estimates for U.S. data since 1980 indicate a fraction of backward-looking pricesetters that would imply (in terms of my notation) a value of γ on the order of 0.6. Gali et al. (2001) obtain similar results using European data. Thus there exists a fair amount of consensus—using a variety of empirical proxies for the output gap and a variety of estimation strategies—that the relation (3.6) better characterizes U.S. inflation dynamics when an indexation parameter between 0.5 and 1.0 is included.

The backward-looking indexation model retains one unfortunate feature of the basic Calvo model, however, even when γ is large: that if a monetary disturbance increases nominal GDP only with a lag, as indicated in Figure 3.2, the model predicts that output should initially *contract* in response to such a shock. The reason is that the expectation of a future output increase implies a desire to increase $\pi_t - \gamma\pi_{t-1}$ immediately; so there should be an increase in inflation even before nominal GDP begins to increase.

This problem can be solved, once again, by assuming a delay of d quarters before a newly chosen price takes effect. (In the meantime, a firm's price continues to be adjusted using (3.4).) In this case, the aggregate-supply relation becomes instead

$$\pi_t - \gamma\pi_{t-1} = \kappa E_{t-d}\left(\hat{Y}_t - \hat{Y}_t^n\right) + \beta E_{t-d}(\pi_{t+1} - \gamma\pi_t). \tag{3.7}$$

Figure 3.15 shows the dynamic responses of output and inflation to an innovation in the process (3.3) for nominal GDP assuming $s = 2$ quarters for conformity with Figure 3.2 and an aggregate-supply relation (3.7) with $\gamma = 1$ and $d = 2$. In this case there is no effect on output until two quarters following the shock, and then a hump-shaped response, as in Figure 3.3. In addition, inflation exhibits a hump-shaped response of its own, which peaks later than the output response. In this respect, note that Figure 3.15 is much more similar to Figure 3.10 than was Figure 3.12 (the case $\gamma = 0$). Figure 3.16 shows the responses to the same disturbance in the case that $d = 4$. This results in a stronger output response and a further delay in the

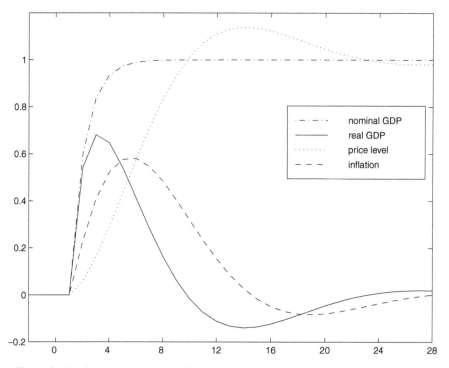

Figure 3.15   *Impulse responses to the same monetary disturbance as in Figures 3.11–3.13 (s = 2), in the case of backward-looking indexation (γ = 1) and a delay of d = 2 quarters in price changes.*

inflation response. Figure 3.16 results in predicted responses that are most similar to those implied by the VAR estimates shown in Figure 3.10.[68]

4   Consequences of Nominal Wage Stickiness

Thus far the only form of nominal rigidity considered is a delay of one sort or another in the adjustment of the money prices at which goods are offered for sale. In particular, I have not assumed any corresponding stickiness of nominal wages, though this is another familiar explanation for the real effects of monetary policy, emphasized, for example, in Keynes (1936). I

---

68. I could do better at quantitatively matching the responses shown in Figure 3.10 if I were to treat κ as a free parameter. In the experiments reported here, I have fixed the value of κ at the value estimated by Rotemberg and Woodford (1997). However, their estimates are for a model without backward-looking indexation, in addition to being based on a VAR and a sample period different from those of Christiano et al.

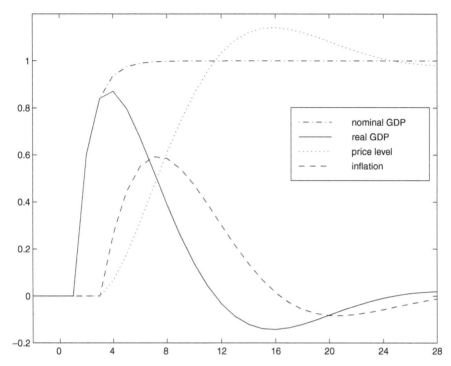

Figure 3.16 *Impulse responses to the same monetary disturbance as in Figure 3.15 in the case that $\gamma = 1$ and $d = 4$ quarters.*

have instead assumed that wages are fully flexible, or equivalently (as far as the derivation of the aggregate-supply relations is concerned) that there is efficient contracting between firms and their workers.[69]

My exclusive emphasis upon price stickiness has allowed the present models to take an especially simple form. In particular, it has been possible, for many purposes, to analyze inflation and output dynamics without any reference to the labor market. Furthermore, as between the two simple hypotheses (*only* sticky prices or *only* sticky wages), the hypothesis of sticky prices is often regarded as more compelling on both theoretical and empirical grounds. I mentioned in the introduction to this chapter the objection

---

69. As far as the relation between price changes and output is concerned, it is enough that goods suppliers face a cost of marginal labor input at each point in time that is equal to the marginal disutility of labor supply expressed in the monetary unit of account. It does not matter whether this occurs because this is the wage that clears a competitive spot market for labor (as assumed explicitly in the previous discussion of the relation between unit labor costs and prices), or because an efficient labor contract leads firms to internalize the cost to their workers of requiring additional hours of work.

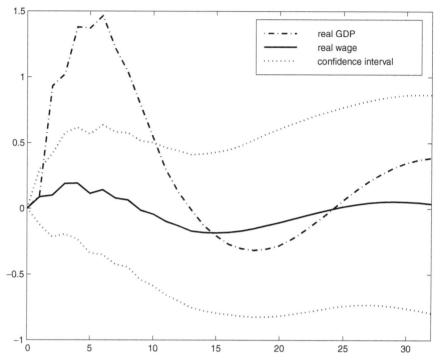

Figure 3.17 *Estimated impulse response of the real wage to an unexpected interest-rate reduction. Source: Christiano et al. (2001).*

that nominal wages might be constant in the face of disturbances even when the effective cost of marginal hours of labor to firms changes, owing to the existence of implicit contracts between firms and workers. The hypothesis of pure wage stickiness has also often been criticized on account of its implication that real wages should move countercyclically (a criticism of Keynes's model first raised by Dunlop, 1938, and Tarshis, 1939). More relevant than overall business-cycle correlations is the finding, in VAR studies such as that of Christiano et al. (1999, 2001), of mildly pro-cyclical real-wage movements in response to identified monetary policy disturbances. (See, e.g., Figure 3.17, which shows the estimated impulse response of the average real wage from the latter study. Here the impulse response of real GDP to the same type of disturbance is also shown for purposes of comparison.) Since these responses ought to be uncorrelated with changes in technology, the failure of the real wage to decline sharply at the time of the increase in real activity is difficult to reconcile with a sticky-wage/flexible-price model.

But even if a model with *only* sticky wages is unappealing, it may be desirable to allow for stickiness of wages as well as prices. Indeed, the study by Christiano et al. (1999) criticizes sticky-price (but flexible-wage) models of the monetary transmission mechanism on the grounds that they imply *too sharp* a real-wage decline in response to a tightening of monetary policy— one so strong that producers' profits ought actually to increase, despite their reduced sales (and contrary to fact). This problem can be ameliorated by assuming preference parameters that imply a more elastic labor supply, as in the model of Rotemberg and Woodford (1997). But slow adjustment of wages to changes in labor demand may be a more plausible explanation for the relatively modest response of real wages seen in Figure 3.17, and, as I discuss in Chapter 6, the choice between these two explanations matters for welfare analysis. Hence I develop here an extension of the baseline model that incorporates wage as well as price stickiness.

4.1 A Model of Staggered Wagesetting

Here I follow Erceg et al. (2000) and model wagesetting in a way that is directly analogous to the model of staggered pricing introduced by Calvo (1983). I introduce wagesetting agents by assuming monopolistic competition among the suppliers of differentiated types of labor, analogous to the earlier treatment of the goods market.[70] The exposition is simplest if I follow Erceg et al. in assuming a single economy-wide labor market, with the producers of all goods hiring the same kinds of labor and facing the same wages.[71] However, I assume that the labor used to produce each good is a CES aggregate of the continuum of individual types of labor supplied by the representative household, defined by

$$H_t \equiv \left[\int_0^1 h_t(j)^{(\theta_w - 1)/\theta_w} \, dj \right]^{\theta_w/(\theta_w - 1)} \tag{4.1}$$

for some elasticity of substitution $\theta_w > 1$. Here $h_t(j)$ is the labor of type j that is hired. Note that the continuum of differentiated types of labor is no longer identified with the continuum of differentiated goods indexed by i, as labor of all types is used in producing each good. It follows that the demand for labor of type j on the part of wagetaking firms is given by

$$h_t(j) = H_t \left(\frac{w_t(j)}{W_t} \right)^{-\theta_w}, \tag{4.2}$$

---

70. For a detailed discussion of optimizing models with sticky nominal wages, see Bénassy (2002).

71. The model presented here differs from that of Erceg et al. in that I do not assume that capital can be instantaneously reallocated among firms so as to equalize the return to capital services across firms that change their prices at different times. Instead, as in the baseline model of the previous section, capital is assumed to be completely immobile. I also adopt fewer parametric specifications of preferences and technology than in the paper of Erceg et al.

where $w_t(j)$ is the (nominal) wage demanded for labor of type j and W_t is a wage index defined analogously with (1.3).

I assume that the wage for each type of labor is set by the monopoly supplier of that type, who then stands ready to supply as many hours of work as turn out to be demanded at that wage. As in the present model of monopolistic competition in the goods market, I assume an independent wage-setting decision for each type j, made under the assumption that the choice of that individual wage has no nonnegligible effect upon the the wage index W_t or upon the demand H_t for the labor aggregate.[72] I furthermore assume, as in the Calvo model of staggered pricing, that each of the wages is adjusted with only a probability $1 - \alpha_w$ each period, for some $0 < \alpha_w < 1$, which probability is independent of the time since a given wage was last adjusted or the current level of that wage.

It follows that a wage $w_t(j)$ that is adjusted in period t should be chosen to maximize

$$E_t \left\{ \sum_{T=t}^{\infty} (\alpha_w \beta)^{T-t} \left[\Lambda_T w_t(j) h_T(w_t(j)) - v(h_T(w_t(j)); \xi_T) \right] \right\}, \quad (4.3)$$

where Λ_T is the representative household's marginal utility of nominal income in period T and the dependence of labor demand $h_T(j)$ upon the wage is given by (4.2).[73] (I have omitted a j in the notation for this last function because the function $h_T(w)$ is the same for all j.) The solution to this problem satisfies the first-order condition

$$E_t \left\{ \sum_{T=t}^{\infty} \alpha_w^{T-t} Q_{t,T} H_T W_T^{\theta_w} \left[w_t(j) - \mu_w V(h_T(j), C_T; \xi_T) P_T \right] \right\} = 0, \quad (4.4)$$

which has a form analogous to the previous first-order condition for optimal pricesetting. Here

72. Both the assumption of a monopoly supplier of each type of labor and that the supplier of an individual type of labor has no power to affect the wage index W_t indicate that I can no longer assume a continuum of identical households, each supplying the same continuum of types of differentiated labor. Instead, I must assume that households specialize in supplying a particular type of labor, the disutility of which is additively separable from the utility of consumption as before. Risk-sharing among the households that supply types of labor that set their wages at different dates can then result in a common budget constraint for each of the households, which is the same as if each household were to receive its pro rata share of the economy's total wage bill, as earlier.

73. Note that although there is technically not a representative household in the present model, in the sense of a household whose trades are equal to its per capita share of all trades in the economy (owing to labor specialization), it remains true that all households have the same consumption budget and choose the same consumption. Hence they have the same marginal utility of income Λ_t at all times, equal to $u_c(C_t; \xi_t)/P_t$.

$$\mathcal{V}(h, C; \xi) \equiv \frac{v_h(h; \xi)}{u_c(C; \xi)} \tag{4.5}$$

is the marginal rate of substitution between work and consumption for the supplier of a given type of labor, and $\mu_w \equiv \theta_w/(\theta_w - 1) > 1$ is the desired markup of a household's real-wage demand over its marginal rate of substitution owing to its monopoly power. If I substitute (4.2) for $h_T(j)$ in (4.4), I obtain a relation that implicitly defines the optimal wage choice w_t^*, which is the same for all wages j that are adjusted at date t. The choice of w_t^* then determines the evolution of the wage index W_t through a law of motion analogous to (2.1).

Again it is useful to approximate equilibrium wage dynamics in the case of small disturbances using a log-linear approximation, computed under the assumption that W_t/P_t, P_t/P_{t-1}, and w_t^*/W_t all remain close to their steady-state values ($\bar{w}$, 1, and 1, respectively) at all times. For the law of motion of the wage index I obtain

$$\log W_t = \alpha_w \log W_{t-1} + (1 - \alpha_w) \log w_t^*, \tag{4.6}$$

which is directly analogous to the earlier law of motion (2.5) for the price index in the Calvo model.

The log marginal rate of substitution (MRS) for the supplier of a given type of labor j in period t can be written in the form

$$\log v_t + v \log(h_t(j)/H_t),$$

where v_t is the geometric average of the MRS across different types of labor, and

$$v \equiv \frac{v_h h(\bar{h}; 0)}{\bar{h} v_h(\bar{h}; 0)} > 0.$$

The average desired nominal wage (under flexible wages) can then be approximated by $\log \mu_w + \log V_t$, where $\mu_w \equiv \theta_w/(\theta_w - 1) > 1$ is the desired wage markup and $V_t \equiv v_t P_t$ is the average MRS expressed in monetary units. Using this notation, one can write a log-linear approximation to (4.4) as

$$\log w_t^* = \frac{1 - \alpha_w \beta}{1 + v\theta_w} \sum_{T=t}^{\infty} (\alpha_w \beta)^{T-t} E_t[\log \mu_w + \log V_T + v\theta_w \log W_T], \tag{4.7}$$

an expression that is directly analogous to (2.8) in the case of the Calvo model of pricing. Equations (4.6) and (4.7) then describe the equilibrium dynamics of the wage index given the expected evolution of the nominal

MRS, which plays a role analogous to marginal cost in the present model of pricesetting.

Manipulations directly analogous to those used in the derivation of (2.14) then allow me to obtain a relation of the form

$$\Delta \log W_t = \xi_w[\hat{v}_t + \log \bar{w} + \log P_t - \log W_t] + \beta E_t[\Delta \log W_{t+1}] \quad (4.8)$$

for the dynamics of the wage index, where

$$\xi_w \equiv \frac{(1 - \alpha_w)(1 - \alpha_w \beta)}{\alpha_w(1 + v\theta_w)} > 0.$$

If I continue to assume a production function of the form (1.7) for each good (i.e., a fixed allocation of capital across firms, even though there is a single economy-wide labor market), the corresponding equation for the price dynamics is

$$\Delta \log P_t = \xi_p[\hat{\psi}_t - \log \bar{w} + \log W_t - \log P_t] + \beta E_t[\Delta \log P_{t+1}], \quad (4.9)$$

where $\hat{\psi}_t$ denotes minus the average deviation of the log marginal product of labor from its steady-state value. Here

$$\xi_p \equiv \frac{(1 - \alpha_p)(1 - \alpha_p \beta)}{\alpha_p(1 + \omega_p \theta_p)} > 0,$$

where the parameters previously denoted α and θ are now denoted α_p and θ_p, and ω_p is defined as in (1.16). Note that equation (4.9) is just an alternative way of writing (2.14), given that

$$\hat{s}_t = \log W_t - \log P_t + \hat{\psi}_t.$$

(The only difference is that the expression for ξ_p is different now owing to the assumption of an economy-wide labor market.)

Finally, log-linearizing (4.5), I obtain

$$\hat{v}_t = v[\phi(\hat{Y}_t - a_t) - \bar{H}_t] + \sigma^{-1}(\hat{Y}_t - g_t) \quad (4.10)$$

as an expression for log deviations of the MRS from its steady-state value as a function of fluctuations in aggregate output, where

$$\phi_h \equiv \frac{f(\bar{h})}{\bar{h}f'(\bar{h})} > 1$$

is the elasticity of a firm's labor demand with respect to the demand for its product, $\bar{H}_t$ is the log deviation in the level of labor supply associated with a constant marginal disutility of working, g_t is the log deviation in the level of output required for a constant marginal utility of consumption, and $a_t \equiv \log A_t$ is the log deviation in the technology factor (assumed to equal 1 in the steady state). Equation (4.10) can equivalently be written

$$\hat{v}_t = (\omega_w + \sigma^{-1})\hat{Y}_t - (\omega + \sigma^{-1})\hat{Y}_t^n + (1 + \omega_p)a_t,$$

where $\omega_w \equiv v\phi_h > 0$, as in (1.16). The assumed form of production function implies that

$$\hat{\psi}_t = \omega_p \hat{Y}_t - (1 + \omega_p)a_t,$$

where $\omega_p > 0$ is also defined as in (1.16). Note that these expressions indicate that the log deviation of average real marginal cost in a model with flexible wages would equal

$$\hat{v}_t + \hat{\psi}_t = (\omega + \sigma^{-1})(\hat{Y}_t - \hat{Y}_t^n),$$

in accordance with (1.15).

Combining these equations for $\hat{v}_t$ and $\hat{\psi}_t$ with the wage- and price-inflation equations (4.8) and (4.9), I finally obtain a pair of equations for the evolution of wages and prices given variations in real activity.

PROPOSITION 3.9. *If wages and prices are both staggered, as in the model of Erceg et al. (2000), then the joint evolution of the wage index, the price index, and aggregate real output must satisfy the relations*

$$\Delta \log W_t = \kappa_w(\hat{Y}_t - \hat{Y}_t^n) + \xi_w(\log w_t^n + \log P_t - \log W_t) + \beta E_t[\Delta \log W_{t+1}], \tag{4.11}$$

$$\Delta \log P_t = \kappa_p(\hat{Y}_t - \hat{Y}_t^n) + \xi_p(\log W_t - \log P_t - \log w_t^n) + \beta E_t[\Delta \log P_{t+1}] \tag{4.12}$$

each period, where

$$\kappa_w \equiv \xi_w(\omega_w + \sigma^{-1}) > 0, \qquad \kappa_p \equiv \xi_p \omega_p > 0,$$

and

$$\log w_t^n \equiv \log \bar{w} + (1 + \omega_p)a_t - \omega_p \hat{Y}_t^n$$

represents the natural real wage, that is, the equilibrium real wage when both wages and prices are fully flexible.

These equations generalize the aggregate-supply relation (2.12) derived earlier for the flexible-wage model in an obvious respect. Note that if one defines a particular weighted average of wage and price inflation,

$$\bar{\pi}_t \equiv \frac{\xi_p^{-1}\pi_t + \xi_w^{-1}\pi_{wt}}{\xi_p^{-1} + \xi_w^{-1}}, \tag{4.13}$$

then the corresponding weighted average of (4.11) and (4.12) reduces to

$$\bar{\pi}_t = \kappa(\hat{Y}_t - \hat{Y}_t^n) + \beta E_t \bar{\pi}_{t+1}, \tag{4.14}$$

where

$$\kappa \equiv \frac{\sigma^{-1} + \omega}{\xi_p^{-1} + \xi_w^{-1}} > 0 \tag{4.15}$$

is a coefficient that is smaller the greater the degree of rigidity of *either* wages or prices. In the limit as $\alpha_w \to 0$, $\xi_w \to \infty$, $\bar{\pi}_t$ simply measures price inflation, and (4.14) is again the aggregate-supply relation (2.12) obtained earlier, in which (4.15) corresponds once more to (2.13) using the value (1.37) for ζ. More generally, it is found that an alternative inflation index is the same kind of purely forward-looking function of the output gap, but this index involves wage inflation with a weight that is greater the greater the relative stickiness of wages. In the limiting case that *only* wages are sticky, (4.14) becomes a Phillips curve for wages.

4.2 Sticky Wages and the Real Effects of Nominal Disturbances

I turn now to the implications of wage stickiness for the real effects of fluctuations in nominal expenditure due to a purely monetary disturbance. As is well-known, nominal wage stickiness implies that such disturbances should have temporary effects on real activity, during the time that it takes for wages to adjust, even in the case of fully flexible goods prices. A more subtle question is whether this mechanism should result in real effects that are more or less persistent than those that would result from sticky prices. Some authors (e.g., Andersen, 1998; Huang and Liu, 1998) have argued that sticky wages result in more persistent effects than sticky prices and that the assumption of sticky prices (as in the treatment in the earlier part of this chapter) therefore underestimates the likely importance of the real effects of monetary policy.

In order to compare the degree of persistence resulting from wage stickiness with that resulting from price stickiness, it is useful to consider once again the effects of an unexpected permanent increase in nominal GDP, unrelated to any real disturbance (that could affect $\hat{Y}_t^n$ or w_t^n). I again assume a shock that results in (2.15) holding for all $t \geq 0$ and consider the expected paths $E_0 \log P_t$, $E_0 \log W_t$, and $E_0 \log Y_t$ that are consistent with the system (4.11) and (4.12), given initial conditions $\log W_{-1} = \log P_{-1} = 0$.

In the case of sticky wages but purely flexible prices, (4.12) reduces to an equilibrium relation between the real wage and the output gap, which can be written in the form

$$\log W_t - \log P_t = \log w_t^n - \frac{\omega_p}{1 + \omega_p} \left(\log \mathcal{Y}_t - \log W_t + \log w_t^n - \log Y_t^n \right). \quad (4.16)$$

Substituting this into (4.11) yields

$$\Delta \log W_t = \hat{\kappa} \left[\log \mathcal{Y}_t - \log W_t + \log w_t^n - \log Y_t^n \right] + \beta E_t \left[\Delta \log W_{t+1} \right]$$

for nominal wage dynamics given the evolution of nominal GDP and the real disturbances, where

$$\hat{\kappa} \equiv \frac{\kappa}{1 + \omega_p} > 0.$$

This equation has the same form as the equation for *price* dynamics in the model with flexible wages and sticky prices, and so my reasoning in the proof of Proposition 3.6 directly applies. It follows that if I let $\tilde{w}_k$ denote the change in $E_t \log W_{t+k}$ made by a unit increase in ϵ_t, the unique bounded solution is of the form

$$\tilde{w}_k = 1 - \lambda^{k+1},$$

by analogy with the solution for $\tilde{p}_k$ in Proposition 3.6. Here $0 < \lambda < 1$ is the smaller root of (2.19) when $\hat{\kappa}$ is substituted for κ. Then noting that (4.16) also implies that

$$\log Y_t = \log Y_t^n + \frac{1}{1 + \omega_p} \left(\log \mathcal{Y}_t - \log W_t + \log w_t^n - \log Y_t^n \right),$$

one sees that (4.2) indicates an output response of the form

$$E_0 \log Y_t = -(1 + \omega_p)^{-1} \tilde{w}_t = (1 + \omega_p)^{-1} \lambda^{t+1}.$$

The degree of persistence of the output response thus depends upon the root λ, and hence upon the size of $\hat{\kappa}$, in the same way as in the sticky-price model. The only possibility of a difference between the two models as to the likely degree of persistence would be if it is judged more plausible that

$\hat{\kappa}$ should be small in the case of the sticky-wage model than that κ should be small in the case of the sticky-price model. One possible reason for this, of course, would be if it were observed that wages are in fact adjusted less frequently than prices. But it is not obvious that this is true to any dramatic extent; in an economy like that of the United States, most wages, like most prices, are adjusted annually if not more often. (In any event this is not the basis of Andersen's argument, which assumes two-period commitments in each case.)

I consider instead the likelihood of the existence of a contract multiplier in the sense discussed earlier. We have seen that in the case of the sticky-price model, $\lambda > \alpha_p$, so that output effects decay more slowly than the rate at which prices are revised following the shock if and only if $\zeta < 1$ (the case of strategic complementarity among pricing decisions), where ζ is again given (for the present setup) by (1.37). One can similarly show that for the sticky-wage model, $\lambda > \alpha_w$ if and only if $\tilde{\zeta} < 1$, where

$$\tilde{\zeta} = \frac{\omega + \sigma^{-1}}{(1 + \nu\theta_w)(1 + \omega_p)}. \tag{4.17}$$

(Once again, the size of $\tilde{\zeta}$ can be interpreted as a measure of the degree of strategic complementarity among the wagesetting decisions of suppliers of different types of labor.) The question then reduces to asking whether it is more plausible that $\tilde{\zeta}$ should be less than one in the sticky-wage model than it is that ζ should be less than one in the sticky-price model.

This turns out to be true in the analysis of Andersen (1998), but his simple model omits a number of important considerations. His analysis of the sticky-wage model effectively assumes (in terms of the present notation) that $\nu = \sigma^{-1} = 0$ (which also implies that $\omega_w = 0$), and hence concludes that

$$\tilde{\zeta} = \frac{\omega_p}{1 + \omega_p} < 1,$$

indicating the existence of a contract multiplier regardless of the size of $\omega_p > 0$. However, this result is not as general as it would appear. A contract multiplier less than one is still theoretically possible in the sticky-wage model (if, e.g., one assumes $\nu = 0$ but $\sigma < 1$).

Andersen's analysis of the sticky-price model similarly effectively assumes that $\omega_p = \sigma^{-1} = 0$ (which also implies that $\omega_w = \nu$), and hence concludes that $\zeta = \nu$, which may or may not be less than one.[74] But this comparison of

---

74. Andersen suggests that the most plausible assumption about preferences would involve $\nu > 1$; smaller values are popular in calibrated quantitative business-cycle models in order to account for the relative acyclicality of real wages, but he proposes that this reflects wage stickiness rather than the nature of preferences regarding labor supply.

the two models is misleading. In fact, as we have seen, the numerators of the expressions for ζ and $\tilde{\zeta}$ are identical, both being equal to $\omega + \sigma^{-1}$; Andersen obtains the value ω_p for the sticky-wage model (which should be small even if ν is large) only because he has assumed $\nu = 0$ in that model. The most important difference between the two cases is rather the presence of the factor $(1 + \nu\theta_w)$ in the denominator of (4.17), whereas the corresponding factor in the denominator of (1.37) is $(1 + \omega_p\theta_p)$—neither of which factors appears in Andersen's analysis. If one regards ν as being substantially larger than ω_p[75] and supposes that there is at least as much substitutability among types of labor as among different goods (so that $\omega_w \geq \omega_p$), then it would indeed follow that $\tilde{\zeta}$ should be significantly smaller than ζ, and wage stickiness would lead to more output persistence than would price stickiness.

This is in fact the basis for the conclusions of Huang and Liu (1998), who also present a comparison of the consequences of wage and price stickiness, but with explicit micro-foundations for the assumed wage- and pricesetting equations (and hence consistent assumptions about preferences and technologies in the two cases). Their basic model (abstracting from capital accumulation and endogenous velocity of money) is a special case of the one just presented, in which the production function $f(\cdot)$ is assumed to be linear, so that $\omega_p = 0$ and $\omega_w = \nu$, and in which $u(C) = \log C$, so that $\sigma = 1$. They accordingly find that

$$\tilde{\zeta} = \frac{1 + \nu}{1 + \nu\theta_w} < 1, \qquad \zeta = 1 + \nu > 1,$$

so that there is necessarily strategic complementarity in the sticky-wage model and necessarily none in the sticky-price model.

Yet this conclusion depends upon ignoring a number of reasons discussed earlier for a low value of ζ to be plausible in the model with only sticky prices. In particular, I have already shown that if one assumes that the producers of different goods hire labor from distinct labor markets, the value of ζ is then given by (1.35). In this case, the factor in the denominator is $(1 + \omega\theta_p)$. This is larger than the factor that appears in (1.37), and especially noteworthy is the fact that a large value for ν increases the size of this factor in much the same way as in the case of (4.17). Indeed, under the special parametric assumptions of Huang and Liu, one would find

---

75. It is not obvious that this must be true. For example, Hansen (1985) argues for preferences with $\nu = 0$, as a result of the indivisibility of labor; in his model, variation in hours worked is entirely associated with variation in the number of workers who work a shift of fixed length, rather than variation in the number of hours worked by each member of the labor force, as assumed in the representative-household model used here.

$$\zeta = \frac{1+\nu}{1+\nu\theta_p},$$

which is just as small as the value that they obtain for $\tilde{\zeta}$ as long as $\theta_p \geq \theta_w$, that is, as long as pricesetters have no more market power than wagesetters. Thus there is little reason to expect that persistence should be greater in the case of a sticky-wage model than in that of a sticky-price model, once one allows for specific labor markets in the former.[76]

It is nonetheless true that wage stickiness generally increases the size and persistence of the real effects of nominal disturbances, holding fixed the degree of price stickiness. Note that subtracting (4.12) from (4.11) yields

$$\Delta \log w_t = -(\xi_w + \xi_p)\big(\log w_t - \log w_t^n\big)$$
$$+ (\kappa_w - \kappa_p)\big(\log Y_t - \log Y_t^n\big) + \beta E_t[\Delta \log w_{t+1}], \tag{4.18}$$

where $w_t \equiv W_t/P_t$ is an aggregate real wage. In the special case that $\kappa_w = \kappa_p$ (so that wages are sticky to roughly the same extent as prices), the output term drops out, and the only endogenous variable in (4.19) is the real wage. One easily verifies that this equation has a unique bounded solution for the path of the real wage, given a bounded process for the exogenous disturbance w_t^n. Hence in this case, the equilibrium real wage is determined by this equation alone, independent of monetary policy or any other factors that affect only the demand side of the model. Let the solution for w_t be denoted $\bar{w}_t$. Then substitution of this solution into (4.12) gives us an equation for price inflation of the form

$$\pi_t = \kappa\big(\hat{Y}_t - \hat{Y}_t^n\big) + E_t\pi_{t+1} + u_t, \tag{4.19}$$

where κ is the common value of κ_w and κ_p, and u_t is an exogenous term defined as

$$u_t \equiv \xi_p\big(\log \bar{w}_t - \log w_t^n\big). \tag{4.20}$$

This is again an aggregate-supply relation of the same form as (2.12), except that the exogenous intercept is no longer equal to $\hat{Y}_t^n$. It follows that the effect upon output of a monetary disturbance is exactly the same as in my previous analysis and depends upon the value of κ in the way discussed earlier. (The nature of the exogenous intercept term does not matter for this question, since in any event it is unaffected by a purely

76. Edge (2002) demonstrates this quantitatively in the case of a complete general-equilibrium model of the monetary transmission mechanism with endogenous capital accumulation. See also Ascari (2001) for further discussion of this point.

monetary disturbance.) Note that in the present case (with both wages and prices sticky), the slope coefficient κ is equal to $\xi_p \omega_p$, whereas in the case of flexible wages analyzed earlier, it was equal to $\xi_p(\omega + \sigma^{-1})$. Thus κ is a smaller positive quantity in the present case (assuming that all parameters take the same values, except the parameter α_w determining the degree of wage stickiness), implying both larger and more persistent output effects of a monetary disturbance.

Allowing for wage stickiness can also be important in improving the ability of the model to account for the observed behavior of wages as well as prices. The model with fully flexible wages implies that a monetary contraction should lower wages by more than the decline in prices, for in this limiting case, (4.11) reduces to the equilibrium relation

$$\log W_t - \log P_t = \log w_t^n + \left(\omega_w + \sigma^{-1}\right)\left(\hat{Y}_t - \hat{Y}_t^n\right). \tag{4.21}$$

Thus the predicted decline in real wages must be substantial relative to the decline in output, unless both ω and $\sigma - 1$ are quite small in value; in particular, this requires that ν be quite small (as it is necessary that $\omega > \nu$). But if wages are sticky as well as prices, it is possible for the decline in real wages to be small, or even nonexistent, even if ν is of substantial magnitude. Indeed, we have just seen that if $\kappa_w = \kappa_p$, there is no effect of a monetary disturbance upon the real wage at all, and this condition can hold regardless of the value of ν. (For any values of the other parameters, it is possible to arrange that $\kappa_w = \kappa_p$ simply by assigning an appropriate value to α_w.) [77]

The model with both wage and price stickiness also allows for more complicated wage dynamics than can be achieved in the flexible-wage model through any choice of the parameters ω and σ, for it ceases to be necessary that the effects of monetary policy on the real wage be any constant multiple of the effects upon real GDP. For arbitrary coefficients $\xi_w, \xi_p > 0$ and bounded processes $\{Y_t, Y_t^n, w_t^n\}$, equation (4.19) has a unique bounded solution for the real wage. This is given by

$$\log w_t = \lambda_1 \log w_{t-1} + \beta^{-1} \sum_{j=0}^{\infty} \lambda_2^{-j-1} E_t z_{t+j}, \tag{4.22}$$

where $0 < \lambda_1 < 1 < \lambda_2$ are the two roots of the characteristic polynomial

$$P(\lambda) \equiv \beta\lambda^2 - (1 + \beta + \xi_w + \xi_p)\lambda + 1 = 0,$$

---

77. If wages are made sufficiently sticky, the model would predict an actual increase in the real wage following a monetary contraction (the prediction of the classic Keynesian model), though evidence such as that presented by Christiano et al. (1997) does not indicate that this actually occurs.

and the forcing process $\{z_t\}$ is defined by

$$z_t \equiv (\xi_w + \xi_p) \log w_t^n + (\kappa_w - \kappa_p)(\log Y_t - \log Y_t^n).$$

A monetary disturbance affects the path of z_t solely through its effect on Y_t, as the other terms are exogenous. In the case that either wages or prices are perfectly flexible (so that either ξ_w or ξ_p is unboundedly large), both λ_1 and λ_2^{-1} equal zero, and (4.22) implies that $\log w_t$ is a multiple of z_t; but when both are sticky, so that $\xi_w + \xi_p$ is finite, $\log w_t$ is instead proportional to a smoothed version of the forcing process.

The effects of wage stickiness are illustrated in Figure 3.18. Here a given impulse-response function for output in response to a monetary disturbance is assumed, and the implied response of the real wage to the same disturbance is then inferred from (4.22). The implied real-wage responses are plotted along with the output response for each of several alternative assumed degrees of nominal wage stickiness, corresponding to different values of ξ_w. Here the assumed response of output is the same as in Figure 3.9, and the values assumed for the parameters ξ_p, ω_w, ω_p, and σ are again

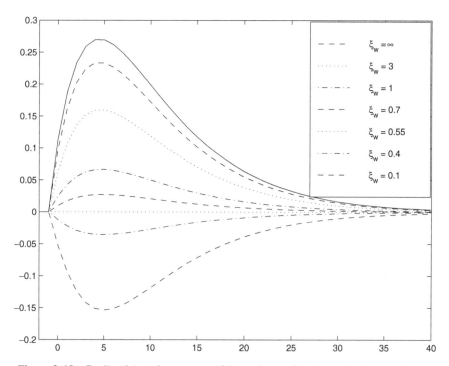

Figure 3.18 *Predicted impulse response of the real wage for alternative degrees of wage stickiness. The solid line indicates the response of real GDP.*

those of Rotemberg and Woodford (1997) (see Table 4.1). The limiting case $\xi_w = \infty$ (complete wage flexibility) corresponds to the assumptions of Rotemberg and Woodford; the other cases shown each involve some degree of wage stickiness.

As the degree of wage stickiness increases, the size of the real-wage increase associated with a given size of effect on output declines. When $\xi_w = 0.55$, κ_w falls to a value equal to that of κ_p, and wages and prices are in a sense "equally sticky"; in this case, there is no longer any real-wage response at all to a monetary disturbance that increases output. For even lower values of ξ_w, wages are stickier than prices, and the real wage is predicted to move countercyclically.

The estimated real-wage response shown in Figure 3.17 suggests that the empirically relevant case is one in which κ_w is slightly larger than κ_p, but not much. Amato and Laubach (2003a) reach a similar conclusion when they estimate a model that allows for wage as well as price stickiness, as discussed in Section 2.2 of Chapter 5. Christiano et al. (2001), Altig et al. (2002), and Smets and Wouters (2002) similarly find that the impulse responses to identified monetary policy shocks are best fit by a model that incorporates both wage and price stickiness.

Furthermore, allowing for wage as well as price stickiness leads to additional ways in which real disturbances may shift the aggregate-supply curve, that is, the short-run relation between inflation and output for given inflation expectations. In the aggregate-supply relation (2.12) derived under the assumption of sticky prices but flexible wages, any of a variety of real disturbances can cause a shift—variation in the rate of technical progress, government purchases, and various types of shifts in preferences—but in each case, the relation is shifted exactly to the extent that the disturbance in question changes the natural rate of output (i.e., the equilibrium output level with flexible wages and prices). However, in (4.19), this is no longer true, unless the term u_t is zero.

In general this term is not identically zero (i.e., $\bar{w}_t \neq w_t^n$), even when the degree of wage stickiness is exactly that required to make $\kappa_w = \kappa_p$. One notes that $w_t = w_t^n$ is a solution to (4.19) in the case that $\kappa_w = \kappa_p$ only if $\Delta \log w_t^n = \beta E_t \Delta \log w_{t+1}^n$, which in turn is possible, if w_t^n is a stationary process, only if w_t^n is a constant—that is, if the real disturbances present in the model would never affect the equilibrium real wage in the case of flexible wages and prices. This is true only for extremely special parameter values and/or assumptions about the kinds of real disturbances that can occur. Under any other assumptions, solving (4.19) allows one to determine how various types of real disturbances shift the aggregate-supply relation in a way that differs from their effect upon the natural rate of output.[78] Here

---

78. For general parameter values, of course, one is not able to solve for the equilibrium real wage independent of the evolution of real activity, as indicated by (4.22). In the general case

I do not pursue the topic further, except to note that the existence of a nonzero u_t term implies a tension between the goals of stabilizing inflation and stabilizing the output gap $\hat{Y}_t - \hat{Y}_t^n$ that does not appear in the baseline sticky-price model. The consequences of this for optimal stabilization policy are taken up in Section 4.4 of Chapter 6.

Finally, I note that infrequent reoptimization of wage demands need not mean that wages remain fixed in money terms between the occasions on which they are reoptimized; instead, wages might be indexed to an aggregate price index in the interim, just as in the discussion of goods-price indexation in Section 3.2. Indeed, indexation schemes of this kind for wages are sometimes a part of multiyear union contracts, so that there is more direct evidence for the idea of indexation in the case of wages than prices; and in practice, such indexation is always to a lagged price index. Suppose I let $0 \leq \gamma_w \leq 1$ be the indexation rate for wages that are not reoptimized; that is, if the wage demanded for labor of type j is not reoptimized in period t, it is adjusted according to the indexation rule

$$\log w_t(j) = \log w_{t-1}(j) + \gamma_w \pi_{t-1}.$$

This modifies the relations for optimal wagesetting in a way that is directly analogous to our discussion of optimal pricesetting with backward-looking indexation in Section 3.2.

The result is that the system (4.11) and (4.12) becomes instead

$$\pi_t^w - \gamma_w \pi_{t-1} = \kappa_w \left(\hat{Y}_t - \hat{Y}_t^n \right) + \xi_w \left(\log w_t^n - \log w_t \right)$$
$$+ \beta E_t \left[\pi_{t+1}^w - \gamma_w \pi_t \right], \tag{4.23}$$

$$\pi_t - \gamma_p \pi_{t-1} = \kappa_p \left(\hat{Y}_t - \hat{Y}_t^n \right) + \xi_p \left(\log w_t - \log w_t^n \right)$$
$$+ \beta E_t \left[\pi_{t+1} - \gamma_p \pi_t \right], \tag{4.24}$$

where $\pi_t^w \equiv \Delta \log W_t$ is the rate of wage inflation, $w_t \equiv W_t/P_t$ is the aggregate real wage, γ_p is the rate of indexation of price commitments (called simply γ in Section 3.2), and the coefficients $\kappa_w, \kappa_p, \xi_w, \xi_p$ are again defined exactly as in (4.11) and (4.12). These equations once again provide a coupled pair for the evolution of the aggregate wage and price indices, given the path of aggregate output and the real disturbances. Note that in the case that $\gamma_w = \gamma_p = 1$, this represents a simplified version of the aggregate-supply block of the model of Christiano et al. (2001), in which

---

there is no exogenous term u_t for which an aggregate supply relation of the simple form (4.19) holds. But our more general point, that when both wages and prices are sticky it is no longer true that inflation stabilization and output-gap stabilization imply one another, continues to hold.

I abstract from complications such as endogenous capital accumulation. Smets and Wouters (2002) also estimate a model with an aggregate-supply block of this kind, but treat γ_w and γ_p as free parameters to be estimated. (Their best-fitting values are $\gamma_p = .64$, $\gamma_w = .42$.) Both sets of authors find that a model of this type—incorporating staggered wagesetting as well as staggered pricesetting and automatic indexation of both wages and prices to recent past inflation—can account fairly well for the joint dynamics of wages, prices, and real activity.

The existence of the additional terms due to indexation results in inflation inertia much as has already been discussed in the context of the flexible-wage model of Section 3.2. For example, the inflation dynamics associated with the Fuhrer-Moore aggregate-supply relation (3.6) can occur as a result of wage rather than price indexation. In the case of fully flexible (and hence nonindexed) prices and the special case of a linear production function (so that $\omega_p = 0$), (4.16) reduces to $w_t = w_t^n$, in which case (4.11) implies that

$$\pi_t - \gamma \pi_{t-1} = \kappa\left(\hat{Y}_t - \hat{Y}_t^n\right) + \beta E_t[\pi_{t+1} - \gamma \pi_t] + u_t, \qquad (4.25)$$

where $\gamma = \gamma_w$, $\kappa = \kappa_w$, and

$$u_t \equiv \beta E_t \Delta \log w_{t+1}^n - \Delta \log w_t^n.$$

Alternatively, similar inflation dynamics can result from a similar degree of indexation of wages and prices. For example, in the special case that $\gamma_w = \gamma_p = \gamma$ and $\kappa_w = \kappa_p = \kappa$, subtracting (4.24) from (4.23) again yields an equation that can be solved for the real-wage dynamics independent of monetary policy. Substituting this solution $w_t = \bar{w}_t$ into (4.24) again yields an aggregate supply relation of the form (4.25), but where u_t is now defined as in (4.20).

Thus I find that allowing for wage stickiness does not matter all that much, if the goal is simply to construct a positive model of the co-movement of inflation and output, and the way that both can be affected by monetary policy. (Stickiness of wages reduces the slope of the short-run Phillips curve, but a similar degree of flatness could alternatively be obtained by choosing different values for other parameters in a flexible-wage model, without any counterfactual consequences for the dynamics of output and inflation; stickiness of wages creates a new way in which real disturbances can shift the short-run Phillips curve, but similar consequences for the evolution of inflation and the output gap would be obtained by simply postulating an exogenous "cost-push shock" as many authors do.) To this extent, the relative neglect of wagesetting in the early literature on the optimizing models with nominal rigidities can be given a justification.

On the other hand, we shall see that there is an important respect in which it does matter whether one thinks that wages, prices, or both are sticky. This has to do with the proper goals of monetary stabilization policy from a welfare-theoretic point of view. If one takes as given an ad hoc stabilization goal, defined in terms of the stability of a certain price index and a certain measure of the output gap, then an adequate model for determining how policy can best achieve this goal may well be formulated without having to take a stand on the question of wage stickiness. But if one asks whether it is really appropriate, from the point of view of economic welfare, to define the goal of policy in that way, it turns out to matter after all whether one believes that wages are sticky. Even in the cases discussed above in which monetary policy is unable to affect the evolution of the real wage (so that the effects of purely monetary disturbances on wage and price inflation must be identical), it does not follow that wage and price inflation should be indistinguishable: They are differentially affected by *real* disturbances. But it then follows that seeking to stabilize wage inflation and seeking to stabilize price inflation are not equivalent policies. Which is the more appropriate goal? The answer depends on the degree to which wages as opposed to prices are sticky, as I show in Chapter 6.

CHAPTER 4

A Neo-Wicksellian Framework for the Analysis of Monetary Policy

I am now ready to consider the effects of alternative interest-rate rules for monetary policy in a setting in which such policy has real effects owing to the nominal rigidities discussed in the previous chapter. As in Chapter 2, a crucial first issue in the choice of an interest-rate feedback rule is to select one that results in a determinate equilibrium. I reconsider this issue (previously treated under the case of full price flexibility) and show that the Taylor principle—the requirement that interest rates be increased more than one-for-one in response to sustained increases in the inflation rate—continues to be essential for determinacy.

I then consider the nature of inflation and output determination in the case where a determinate equilibrium exists. Once again, I show that the equilibrium evolution of these variables can be understood without reference to either the implied path of the money supply or the determinants of money demand. When monetary policy is specified in terms of an interest-rate feedback rule—a specification that more directly matches the terms in which monetary policy is discussed within actual central banks—it is possible to understand the effects of such policies by directly modeling the effects of interest rates upon spending and pricing decisions, without attaching any central importance to the question of how various monetary aggregates may also happen to evolve. This is in fact the approach already taken in many of the econometric models used for policy simulations within central banks or international institutions.[1] A primary goal of the present exposition is to show how models with this basic structure—roughly speaking, models that

---

1. See, e.g., Black et al. (1997a), Brayton et al. (1997), and Coletti et al. (1996) for discussions of the models currently used at the U.S. Federal Reserve Board, the Bank of Canada, and the Reserve Bank of New Zealand, or Laxton and Pesenti (2002) for a description of the IMFs Global Economic Model. A similar approach is also already common in small macroeconometric models used for policy evaluation in the academic literature as well (e.g., Fuhrer and Moore, 1995b), but such models are typically not derived from explicit optimizing foundations.

consist of an IS block, an aggregate-supply (AS) block, and an interest-rate feedback rule—can be derived from explicit optimizing foundations. In this way it is established that a nonmonetarist analysis of the effects of monetary policy does not involve any theoretical inconsistency or departure from neo-classical orthodoxy.

Rather, I argue that inflation and output determination can be usefully explained in Wicksellian terms—as depending upon the relation between a natural rate of interest determined primarily by real factors and the central bank's rule for adjusting the short-term nominal interest rate that serves as its operating target. Increases in output gaps and in inflation result from increases in the natural rate of interest that are not offset by a corresponding tightening of monetary policy (positive shift in the intercept term of the interest-rate feedback rule), or alternatively from loosenings of monetary policy that are not justified by declines in the natural rate of interest.[2]

While this basic approach to inflation determination has already been discussed in Chapter 2, it is only in an environment with sticky prices that one is able to introduce the crucial Wicksellian distinction between the actual and the natural rate of interest, as the discrepancy between the two arises only as a consequence of a failure of prices to adjust sufficiently rapidly. Here I also discuss the underlying real determinants of variation in the natural rate of interest and the way in which a central bank would respond to such variations in order to maintain stable prices or a stable rate of inflation.

I first expound my neo-Wicksellian analysis in the context of a very simple intertemporal equilibrium model, in which I abstract from endogenous variation in the economy's capital stock. I then extend the model in Chapter 5 to consider the consequences for the monetary transmission mechanism of endogenous capital accumulation, in addition to various other extensions of the basic framework to allow for more realistic dynamics. I also first expound the model for the case of a purely cashless economy and then discuss its extension to a model that allows a role for money in the determination of aggregate demand in Section 3.

1 A Basic Model of the Effects of Monetary Policy

I first present a complete general-equilibrium model of the monetary transmission mechanism, which I use frequently in the remainder of this book. (References later to "the basic model" refer to the model presented in this section.) This model combines the relation between interest-rate targeting by the central bank and intertemporal resource allocation developed in

---

2. See Chapter 1 for an introduction to Wicksell's views. Recent discussions include Humphrey (1992, 2002), Fuhrer and Moore (1995c), and Woodford (1998).

Section 1 of Chapter 2 with the relation between real activity and inflation developed in Section 2 of Chapter 3. One should note that the assumptions made in separately deriving these equilibrium relations are in fact mutually consistent, so that my separate partial results can be combined to yield a complete, though highly stylized, model. The resulting framework indicates how interest rates, inflation, and real output are jointly determined in a model that abstracts from endogenous variations in the capital stock and assumes perfectly flexible wages (or some other mechanism for efficient labor contracting), but monopolistic competition in goods markets and sticky prices that are adjusted at random intervals in the way assumed by Calvo (1983).[3]

1.1 Nonlinear Equilibrium Conditions

The requirements for rational-expectations equilibrium that represent the aggregate-demand block of the basic model are the same as those in the (cashless) flexible-price model of Chapter 2. Recall from Section 1.1 of Chapter 2 that the equilibrium paths of aggregate real expenditure Y_t and the price index P_t must satisfy the Euler equation

$$1 + i_t = \beta^{-1} \left\{ E_t \left[\frac{u_c(Y_{t+1} - G_{t+1}; \xi_{t+1})}{u_c(Y_t - G_t; \xi_t)} \frac{P_t}{P_{t+1}} \right] \right\}^{-1} \tag{1.1}$$

at all times as a result of household optimization of the timing of expenditure, where i_t is the riskless one-period nominal interest rate controlled by the central bank.[4] Household optimization similarly requires that the paths of aggregate real expenditure and the price index satisfy the bounds

$$\sum_{T=t}^{\infty} \beta^T E_t \left[u_c(Y_T - G_T; \xi_T)(Y_T - G_T) \right] < \infty, \tag{1.2}$$

3. The model expounded here was first presented as a simple example of an optimizing framework for the analysis of alternative monetary policies in Woodford (1994a, 1996). Similar models have been extensively used in the recent literature; see, e.g., Kerr and King (1996), Bernanke and Woodford (1997), Rotemberg and Woodford (1997, 1999a), McCallum and Nelson (1999a), and Clarida et al. (1999).

4. As discussed in Chapter 2, in a cashless economy the central bank achieves its operating target for i_t by adjusting the interest rate i_t^m paid on the monetary base; an arbitrage relation then requires that $i_t = i_t^m$ in any equilibrium, given a positive supply of base money at all times. Here I simplify by supposing that the central bank can directly control the short-term market rate i_t and by writing the monetary policy directly in terms of a feedback equation for i_t rather than for i_t^m. This simplifies the translation of the results to the case of an economy with monetary frictions in Section 3, in which case i_t and i_t^m are no longer equal, but monetary policy is still specified in terms of a rule that determines the central bank's operating target for i_t.

$$\lim_{T \to \infty} \beta^T E_t[u_c(Y_T - G_T; \xi_T)D_T/P_T] = 0, \qquad (1.3)$$

given the evolution of real government purchases G_t and the nominal value of government liabilities D_t under the monetary-fiscal policy regime.

In the flexible-price model of Chapter 2, Y_t is an exogenous variable. Equations (1.1)–(1.3), together with an interest-rate rule linking the paths of i_t and P_t and a fiscal rule specifying the path of D_t then suffice to determine the equilibrium paths of P_t and i_t. In a model with an endogenous goods supply of the kind developed in Chapter 3, this is no longer the case, but equations (1.1)–(1.3) are still all requirements for equilibrium. Because households are pricetakers in this model, the first-order conditions for an optimal spending plan are the same, regardless of whether prices are flexible; and household consumption demand C_t plus government purchases G_t must add up to aggregate output Y_t regardless of whether the latter quantity is exogenously given.

Instead of an exogenous endowment process $\{Y_t\}$, I now assume a production technology and pricing behavior of the kind introduced in Chapter 3. Specifically, in the basic model I assume Calvo-style staggered pricing as in Section 2 of Chapter 3, and a production technology in which labor is the only variable factor of production.[5] In this model, the aggregate price index P_t evolves according to a law of motion

$$P_t = \mathcal{P}(p_t^*, P_{t-1}), \qquad (1.4)$$

where p_t^* is the new price chosen in period t by those firms that adjust their prices in that period, and $\mathcal{P}(p, P)$ is a homogeneous function of degree one.[6]

The optimal pricing decision p_t^* each period satisfies a first-order condition of the form

$$E_t \left\{ \sum_{T=t}^{\infty} (\alpha\beta)^{T-t} u_c(Y_T - G_T; \xi_T) P_T^{-1} \Pi_1 \left(p_t^*, p_t^*, P_T; Y_T, \tilde{\xi}_T \right) \right\} = 0, \qquad (1.5)$$

---

5. As discussed in Chapter 3, one may assume that capital is used along with labor in production, but that the capital stock is fixed (either at the level of the individual firm or in aggregate). One may also assume that produced goods are used as intermediate inputs in the production of other goods, as long as the intermediate input in the production of each good is the same composite good as is demanded by consumers and by the government. These alternative assumptions correspond simply to alternative functional forms for the profit function $\Pi(p^i, p^I, P; Y; \tilde{\xi})$ referred to in equation (1.5).

6. In the case of the Dixit-Stiglitz preferences assumed in the baseline model of Chapter 3, the aggregator function is $\mathcal{P}(p, P) = [(1-\alpha)p^{1-\theta} + \alpha P^{1-\theta}]^{1/(1-\theta)}$, where $\theta > 1$ is the elasticity of substitution across alternative goods. But as discussed in Section 1.4 of Chapter 3, one may also allow for non-CES preferences, which are arguably more realistic.

where $0 < \alpha < 1$ is the fraction of goods prices that remain unchanged each period, and $\Pi(p^i, p^I, P; Y; \tilde{\xi})$ is the function that indicates the nominal profits obtained in any period by the supplier of a good that charges a price p^i. Here the index of prices in that supplier's industry in the same period is p^I, the economy-wide general price index is P, the index of real aggregate demand is Y, and $\tilde{\xi}$ is the current value of a vector of exogenous disturbances to preferences, technology, and the level of government purchases.[7] The form of the first-order condition (1.5) indicates that the supplier of good i (any such supplier that adjusts prices in period t) chooses a new price to maximize its own expected present value of profits, taking as given the prices of all other goods, including those in its industry; but all other firms in its industry choose their own new prices at the same time and solve an identical optimization problem. Equations (1.4) and (1.5) jointly determine the evolution of both p_t^* and the price index P_t given the evolution of aggregate demand Y_t and the real disturbances $\tilde{\xi}_t$; this pair of equations constitutes the aggregate-supply block of the basic model.

The system of equations (1.1)–(1.5) represents the complete system of requirements for rational-expectations equilibrium, apart from those imposed by the rules describing monetary and fiscal policy, assuming that the latter rules do not depend on endogenous variables other than P_t, Y_t, and i_t.[8] For example, monetary policy might be specified by a Taylor rule of the form

$$i_t = \phi\left(\Pi_t/\Pi_t^*; \ Y_t, v_t\right) \tag{1.6}$$

where $\Pi_t \equiv P_t/P_{t-1}$ is the gross inflation rate, Π_t^* is an exogenously varying target rate, and v_t is an additional exogenous disturbance term (representing, e.g., control errors or mismeasurement by the central bank). Fiscal policy might be specified by an exogenous target path $\{D_t\}$ for the value of government liabilities, an exogenous path $\{d_t\}$ for real government liabilities $(d_t \equiv D_t/P_t)$, or perhaps an exogenous path for real government liabilities as a proportion of GDP. The complete system of equilibrium conditions is then the following.

DEFINITION. A *rational-expectations equilibrium* of the basic neo-Wicksellian model is a triple of processes $\{P_t, Y_t, i_t\}$ that satisfy (1.1)–(1.6) at all

---

7. A profit function of this form is shown to exist in the case of any model within a class of alternatives discussed in Chapter 3. In each case, Π is homogeneous of degree one in the arguments (p^i, p^I, P).

8. If, e.g., the monetary policy rule were to involve feedback from nominal wage inflation or from a long bond rate, one would need to adjoin to the above system an additional equilibrium wage relation or an equilibrium pricing relation for the long bond. The equations needed can be found in Chapters 2 and 3.

dates $t \geq 0$, given the exogenous disturbance processes and evolution of $\{D_t\}$ consistent with the fiscal rule.

Note that while the form of equilibrium condition (1.1) is exactly the same as in the flexible-price model of Chapter 2, its interpretation is now somewhat different. When we first encountered this relation (as equation (1.21) in Chapter 2), its natural interpretation was as a relation that determined the equilibrium real rate of return, given the economy's exogenous supply of goods. In the present context it is instead most usefully viewed as the analog, in an intertemporal equilibrium model, of the Hicksian IS curve.[9] That is, it determines the level of real aggregate demand associated with a given real interest rate, and then since output is demand determined in the present model, it determines the equilibrium level of output associated with a given real interest rate.

An obvious difference between this equilibrium relation and that of Hicks, of course, is that in the present model there is no mention of investment spending (the I in IS). But one need not understand the model to assume that investment demand is zero. (This point matters when it comes time to calibrate the model for use in quantitative analysis.) A more generous view of the basic model would be that it abstracts from the effects of variations in private spending (including those classified as investment expenditure in the national income accounts) upon the economy's productive capacity. The theory of marginal supply cost that underlies the model of optimal pricing behavior assumes that the capital stock in each sector of the economy evolves exogenously, so that any variations can be subsumed under variation in the exogenous technology factor A_t. In addition, it assumes that the marginal utility of additional real private expenditure at any point in time is a function solely of the aggregate level of such expenditure, together with exogenous factors—*as if* all forms of private expenditure (including those classified as investment expenditure) were like nondurable consumer purchases. This is not a preposterous theory of "investment" spending, since the existence of convex adjustment costs of the sort assumed in standard neoclassical investment theory *does* imply that the marginal utility of additional investment spending at a given point in time is decreasing in the real quantity of investment spending at that time. However, neoclassical investment theory does imply in general that the marginal utility of additional investment spending *also* depends upon other endogenous factors, such as variations in expected future returns to capital, and the present model must

---

9. The analogy between this equilibrium relation and the IS curve is stressed in particular in Woodford (1994a, 1996), Kerr and King (1996), Bernanke and Woodford (1997), and McCallum and Nelson (1999a). An early derivation of an IS relation from intertemporal optimization in the same spirit was provided by Koenig (1987, 1993).

be understood to abstract from variations in these factors. (The implications of a fully developed neoclassical model of investment demand are presented in Chapter 5 and compared to those of the present model.)

This simple model of the effects of real interest rates on aggregate demand is obviously extremely stylized, and it might be wondered why I even bother to derive it from optimizing foundations if I intend to abstract from so many features of a more realistic equilibrium model. The answer is that the model's simplicity makes it useful as a source of insight into basic issues; yet the consideration of intertemporal optimization introduces some subtleties, even in this simple specification, that I believe are of considerable general significance. The most important advantage of (1.1) over many simple IS specifications (including those often assumed in linear rational-expectations models with an IS-LM structure) is that it implies that *expected future* real interest rates, and not just a current short real rate, matter for the determination of aggregate demand. This point can be made most clearly by log-linearizing the equilibrium relations.

1.2 A Log-Linear Approximate Model

For most purposes in this study, I am interested solely in characterizing equilibria involving small fluctuations around a deterministic steady state. In this case it suffices to use a log-linear approximation of the equilibrium conditions, as in Chapters 2 and 3. As in Chapter 2, a log-linear approximation to (1.1) this takes the form

$$\hat{Y}_t = g_t + E_t(\hat{Y}_{t+1} - g_{t+1}) - \sigma(\hat{\imath}_t - E_t \pi_{t+1}), \tag{1.7}$$

where once again the parameter $\sigma > 0$ measures the intertemporal elasticity of substitution of aggregate expenditure,[10] and g_t is a composite exogenous disturbance that indicates the shift in the relation between real income Y_t and the marginal utility of real income, due either to preference shocks or to variation in government purchases.[11] Furthermore, in the case of any solutions in which Y_t and g_t are both stationary variables, it follows from (1.7) that

---

10. To be precise, $\sigma \equiv s_C \tilde{\sigma}$, where $s_C \equiv \bar{C}/\bar{Y}$ is the share of private expenditure in total aggregate demand, and $\tilde{\sigma} \equiv -u_C/\bar{C}u_{CC}$ is the usual intertemporal elasticity of substitution in private expenditure.

11. See equations (1.32) and (1.33) of Chapter 2. Here I have written the equilibrium relation somewhat differently. I no longer subsume all sources of variation in the equilibrium real rate of return under a single term $\hat{r}_t$ because output is no longer an exogenous factor, and I put $\hat{Y}_t$ on the left-hand side, to stress that the equation may now be viewed as determining aggregate demand.

$$\hat{Y}_t = \hat{Y}_\infty + g_t - \sigma \sum_{j=0}^{\infty} E_t\big(\hat{\imath}_{t+j} - \pi_{t+j+1}\big), \tag{1.8}$$

using the fact that

$$\lim_{T\to\infty} E_t\big(\hat{Y}_T - g_T\big) = \hat{Y}_\infty, \tag{1.9}$$

where $\hat{Y}_\infty$ is the long-run average value of $\hat{Y}_t$ under the policy regime in question.[12]

Thus aggregate demand in this model depends upon *all* expected future short real rates, and not simply upon a current ex ante short real rate of return; and unless fluctuations in short rates are both highly unforecastable and highly transitory, expectations of *future* short rates are more significant than the current short rate.[13] The exact way in which expectations of future short rates matter in (1.8) is undoubtedly special and unlikely to be precisely correct in reality. (I reconsider the question later in the context of a more sophisticated model of investment dynamics.) Nonetheless, the conclusion that expected future short rates matter a great deal is likely to be robust, and, as we shall see, this general insight is of considerable importance for the theory of monetary policy. It implies that a central bank's primary impact on the economy comes about not through the level at which it sets current overnight interest rates, but rather through the way it affects private-sector expectations about the likely *future* path of overnight rates.

---

12. The long-run average value of g_t is assumed to be zero, by definition. The long-run average value of $\log Y_t$ is not necessarily equal to $\log \bar{Y}$, the zero-inflation steady-state level around which I log-linearize. In the case of the New Keynesian aggregate-supply relation (1.10), a policy that results in a long-run average rate of inflation π_∞ different from zero also implies a nonzero value for $\hat{Y}_\infty$, namely, $(1 - \beta)/\kappa$ times π_∞; and while my approximations assume that the inflation rate is always near zero, they do not require that inflation be exactly zero on average. If instead I assume either the New Classical AS relation discussed in Chapter 3 or complete indexation of prices to a lagged price index (AS relation (2.36), with $\gamma = 1$), then any policy that makes the inflation rate a stationary variable results in $\hat{Y}_\infty = 0$.

13. One way of interpreting (1.8) is by saying that it is a *long-term* real rate of interest, rather than a short rate, that determines aggregate demand in this model. In fact, the part of the term structure that matters according to (1.8) is the yield on a bond of infinite duration, i.e., the sort of "very long discount" (VLD) bond discussed by Kazemi (1992) and Fisher and Gilles (2000). These authors show that in an environment of the kind assumed here, the yield on the VLD bond defines the stochastic discount factor that can be used to price all financial assets; as it happens, it also suffices to determine the optimal level of private expenditure, given the value of the preference shock g_t. The reason is that additive separability of preferences over time allows one to define a "Frisch demand function" for consumption, in which desired consumption at any point in time is a function of the marginal utility of income at that time. The marginal utility of income that enters that function is in turn just the stochastic discount factor that is shown in the asset-pricing literature to equal the yield on a VLD bond.

This in turn implies that the credibility of policy commitments must be a paramount concern, that discretionary optimization will almost surely lead to a suboptimal outcome, and that interest-rate smoothing is desirable, among other consequences, as I discuss in Chapters 7 and 8.

Log-linearization of (1.4) and (1.5) and elimination of the variable p_t^* yields a log-linear aggregate-supply relation. This is the so-called New Keynesian Phillips curve,

$$\pi_t = \kappa\left(\hat{Y}_t - \hat{Y}_t^n\right) + \beta E_t \pi_{t+1}, \tag{1.10}$$

derived in Section 2 of Chapter 3, where $\kappa > 0$ is a coefficient that de-pends upon both the frequency of price adjustment and the elasticity of real marginal cost with respect to the level of real activity, and $\hat{Y}_t^n$ represents exogenous variation in the natural rate of output as a result of any of several types of real disturbances. Finally, log-linearization of the Taylor rule (1.6) yields

$$\hat{i}_t = \bar{i}_t + \phi_\pi (\pi_t - \bar{\pi}) + \phi_y \hat{Y}_t / 4, \tag{1.11}$$

where $\bar{i}_t$ is an exogenous (possibly time-varying) intercept reflecting pos-sible variation in both the Π_t^* and v_t terms, and ϕ_π, ϕ_y and the (implicit, long-run) inflation target $\bar{\pi}$ are constant policy coefficients.[14] I then obtain a complete system of equations for determination of the three endogenous processes $\{\hat{i}_t, \pi_t, \hat{Y}_t\}$, given the evolution of the exogenous disturbances $\{g_t, \hat{Y}_t^n, \bar{i}_t\}$. As long as the only endogenous variables to which the central bank's reaction function responds are inflation and output (as in the spec-ification (1.11)), these three equations suffice for equilibrium determina-tion under such a policy rule.[15] (Dependence upon additional lags of the interest rate instrument, inflation, or output, considered later, does not change this conclusion, nor does arbitrary dependence upon exogenous state variables.)

It is often useful to write my system of equilibrium conditions in terms of the *output gap* $x_t \equiv \hat{Y}_t - \hat{Y}_t^n$. This allows me (at least under the baseline assumptions) to write the AS relation without any residual term; and it is shown in Chapter 6 that (under those same assumptions) it is fluctuations in x_t rather than in $\hat{Y}_t$ that are relevant for welfare. Taylor rules are also often

---

14. Here I write the coefficient on the output term as $\phi_y/4$ so that ϕ_y corresponds to the output coefficient in a standard Taylor rule written in terms of annualized interest and inflation rates. In terms of the notation here, these annualized rates are $4\hat{i}_t$ and $4\pi_t$, respectively.

15. The other equilibrium conditions listed in the previous section place no restrictions on possible paths $\{\hat{i}_t, \pi_t, \hat{Y}_t\}$ that remain forever close enough to the steady-state values of these variables, as discussed in Chapter 2. This depends on a particular assumption about the character of fiscal policy, discussed further in Section 4.

specified in terms of a response to variations in the output gap, though a question must raised as to whether the output-gap measure that would be used in practice corresponds to the theoretical definition here. (I can in any event write the interest-rate rule in terms of the gap, as a purely notational matter, by allowing the intercept to be a function of the natural rate of output.) The basic model then consists of the equations

$$x_t = E_t x_{t+1} - \sigma \left(\hat{i}_t - E_t \pi_{t+1} - \hat{r}_t^n \right), \tag{1.12}$$

$$\pi_t = \kappa x_t + \beta E_t \pi_{t+1}, \tag{1.13}$$

together with an interest-rate rule such as

$$\hat{i}_t = \bar{i}_t + \phi_\pi (\pi_t - \bar{\pi}) + \phi_x (x_t - \bar{x})/4. \tag{1.14}$$

Note that this equation describes the same family of policy rules as (1.11), but that the exogenous term $\bar{i}_t$ is not the same under the two representations of any given rule. Here I have also written the gap term in the rule as $x_t - \bar{x}$, where $\bar{x} \equiv (1 - \beta)\bar{\pi}/\kappa$ is the steady-state value of the output gap consistent with the inflation target $\bar{\pi}$, so that in an equilibrium in which the inflation target is achieved on average, the nominal interest rate $\hat{i}_t$ is on average equal to $\bar{i}_t$.

The intertemporal IS relation (1.12) now involves a composite exogenous disturbance term[16]

$$\hat{r}_t^n \equiv \sigma^{-1} \left[\left(g_t - \hat{Y}_t^n \right) - E_t \left(g_{t+1} - \hat{Y}_{t+1}^n \right) \right]. \tag{1.15}$$

This represents deviations of the Wicksellian natural rate of interest from the value consistent with a zero-inflation steady state,[17] a concept about which I have more to say in the next section. Here it suffices to note that the *only* exogenous disturbance terms in the system consisting of (1.12)–(1.15) are the terms $\hat{r}_t^n$ and $\bar{i}_t$. Hence insofar as my policy rule implies

---

16. Note that the framework used by Clarida et al. (1999) includes an IS relation of exactly this form, but with a disturbance term g_t, which is described as a demand shock. This interpretation is somewhat misleading, since it is apparent from (1.15) that any source of transitory variation in the natural rate of output also affects the natural rate of interest. As a result, the conclusions of Clarida et al. about the optimal policy response to supply shocks as opposed to demand shocks must be interpreted with care. Real disturbances that have a transitory effect upon the natural rate of output are not supply shocks in the sense of Clarida et al. because they do not result in any disturbance term in equation (1.10), whereas they are demand shocks in the sense of those authors because they affect the disturbance term in equation (1.12).

17. The steady-state value of the natural rate is equal to the value of the nominal interest rate consistent with that same zero-inflation steady state, so (1.15) takes the same form if one interprets $\hat{i}_t$ as the (continuously compounded) nominal interest rate itself and $\hat{r}_t^n$ as the (continuously compounded) natural rate of interest.

a determinate rational-expectations equilibrium, it must be one in which fluctuations in both inflation and the output gap are due *solely* to variations in these two factors—variations in the natural rate of interest due to real disturbances, on the one hand, and variations in monetary policy (whether deliberate or accidental), on the other. The exact way in which these factors affect inflation and the output gap is explored further in the next section.

2 Interest-Rate Rules and Price Stability

I turn now to a brief consideration of implications of the baseline framework for the explanation of economic fluctuations and the choice of a monetary policy rule. As in Chapter 2, a first question to be addressed concerns the conditions under which an interest-rate rule such as (1.15) implies a determinate rational-expectations equilibrium. In the case that equilibrium is determinate, I then inquire as to how equilibrium inflation and real activity are affected by both real disturbances and shifts in monetary policy. Finally, I use this analysis to consider the design of a monetary policy rule that should maintain stable prices. The question of the extent to which price stability should be the goal of monetary policy is deferred to Chapter 6.

2.1 The Natural Rate of Interest

I first consider the relatively simple question of how interest rates must be adjusted in order for monetary policy to be consistent with stable prices. To answer this question, I simply solve the AS and IS relations for the equilibrium paths of output and interest rates, under the assumption of zero inflation at all times. I first observe from the AS relation that $\pi_t = 0$ at all times requires that $x_t = 0$ at all times, that is, that output equal the natural rate of output at all times. From the derivation of the AS relation in Chapter 3, one observes that this conclusion is exact, and not merely a property of the log-linear approximation. For the natural rate of output is exactly the level of output in all sectors for which real marginal cost of supplying each good will equal μ^{-1}, the reciprocal of the desired gross markup. This latter quantity is equal to marginal revenue for a firm that adjusts its price, in the case that all firms charge identical prices. Thus $Y_t = Y_t^n$ is exactly the condition needed for no firm to wish to charge a price different from the common price charged by all other firms, which is in turn the condition under which firms that adjust their prices continue to charge the same price as firms that do not, so that there is no inflation.

Substituting these paths for inflation and output into the intertemporal IS relation, one obtains the required path of nominal interest rates. Substituting $\Pi_t = 1$ and $Y_t = Y_t^n$ into (1.1), one sees that interest rates must satisfy $i_t = r_t^n$ at all times, where

$$1 + r_t^n \equiv \beta^{-1} \left\{ E_t \left[\frac{u_c(Y_{t+1}^n; \xi_{t+1})}{u_c(Y_t^n; \xi_t)} \right]^{-1} \right\}. \tag{2.1}$$

That is, the interest rate must at all times equal the Wicksellian *natural rate of interest*, which may be defined as the equilibrium real rate of return in the case of fully flexible prices. Under this definition, one observes a direct correspondence with the previously introduced concept of the natural rate of output.[18] Indeed, the natural rate of interest is just the real rate of interest required to keep aggregate demand equal at all times to the natural rate of output.[19] Log-linearizing (2.1), one observes that the exogenous term $\hat{r}_t^n$ in (1.15) corresponds to the percentage deviation of the natural rate of interest from its steady-state value,

$$\hat{r}_t^n \equiv \log \left(\frac{1 + r_t^n}{1 + \bar{r}^n} \right) = \log(1 + r_t^n) + \log \beta.$$

I have thus far referred only to the conditions under which one could obtain complete price stability in the sense of a constant price level (and hence zero inflation). As we shall see, there is a certain normative interest in this case, as, at least under the assumptions of the baseline model, it would eliminate the distortions resulting from price stickiness. Yet most inflation-targeting countries instead seek to maintain inflation at a low positive level, and so policies that stabilize inflation at some constant target level $\bar{\pi}$ are also of obvious interest. In fact, in the log-linear approximation, my conclusions are exactly the same in that case, up to certain constant terms. The required path for the output gap is still a constant (though not zero unless $\bar{\pi} = 0$), and the required path for the nominal interest rate is now

$$\hat{\imath}_t = \hat{r}_t^n + \bar{\pi}.$$

Though the average values of output and of the nominal interest rate depend upon the target inflation rate, the way in which they should respond to shocks does not (up to a log-linear approximation).

Equation (2.1) (or equally usefully for most purposes, the log-linear version (1.15)) provides a theory of how various types of real disturbances affect the natural rate of interest and hence a theory of how the interest rate controlled by the central bank should respond to those disturbances in an equilibrium characterized by price stability. To consider the effects

18. Of course, Friedman (1968) originally proposed the concept of a natural rate of output (or of unemployment) by analogy with Wicksell's concept of a natural rate of interest, a notion that was at that time more familiar!

19. The concept is thus closely related to Blinder's (1998, chap. 2, sec. 3) notion of the "neutral" rate of interest.

of individual disturbances, one needs first to recall how various real disturbances affect the natural rate of output. Log-linearization of equation (1.13)
from Chapter 3 implies that

$$\hat{Y}_t^n \equiv \frac{\sigma^{-1}g_t + \omega q_t}{\sigma^{-1} + \omega}, \tag{2.2}$$

where g_t denotes the variation in log output required to maintain a constant
marginal utility of real income as in (1.7), q_t correspondingly denotes the
variation in log output required to maintain a constant marginal disutility
of output supply as in Chapter 3, $\sigma > 0$ is the intertemporal elasticity of
substitution of private expenditure as in (1.7), and $\omega > 0$ is the elasticity of
real marginal cost with respect to a firm's own output, as in Chapter 3.

Furthermore, these composite disturbance terms can be expressed in
terms of more fundamental disturbances as

$$g_t = \hat{G}_t + s_C \bar{c}_t,$$
$$q_t = \left(1 + \omega^{-1}\right)a_t + \omega^{-1}v\bar{h}_t. \tag{2.3}$$

Here, as in Chapter 2, $\hat{G}_t$ denotes the deviation of government purchases
from their steady-state level, measured as a percentage of steady-state output
$\bar{Y}$, which shifts the level of private expenditure implied by any given level
of aggregate demand $\hat{Y}_t$, and $\bar{c}_t$ denotes the percentage shift in the Frisch
(constant marginal utility of income) consumption demand due to a shift
in the utility-of-consumption function; and as in Chapter 3, a_t represents
variation in the log of the multiplicative technology factor that is common
to all sectors, and $\bar{h}_t$ is the percentage shift in the Frisch labor supply due
to a shift in the disutility-of-labor function v. (The exogenous shifts in the
Frisch demand schedules are measured at the steady-state values of their
arguments.) Finally, $v > 0$ is the inverse of the Frisch (or intertemporal)
elasticity of labor supply.

It then follows from (2.2) that

$$\hat{Y}_t^n = \frac{\sigma^{-1}}{\sigma^{-1} + \omega}\left(\hat{G}_t + s_C\bar{c}_t\right) + \frac{1}{\sigma^{-1} + \omega}\left((1 + \omega)a_t + v\bar{h}_t\right).$$

One observes that *each* of the exogenous disturbances $\hat{G}_t$, $\bar{c}_t$, a_t, and $\bar{h}_t$
increases the natural rate of output. It follows that under a policy aimed
at price stability, each of them must be allowed to perturb the equilibrium
level of economic activity $\hat{Y}_t$.

Substituting this solution into (1.15), one can determine the effects of
each of the various types of real disturbances on the evolution of the natural

rate of interest. The following provides a simple example of the kind of results that may be obtained.

PROPOSITION 4.1. Suppose that each of the exogenous disturbances $\{\hat{G}_t,$ $\bar{c}_t, a_t, \bar{h}_t\}$ follows an independent first-order autoregressive process, and let $\rho_G, \rho_c, \rho_a,$ and ρ_h be the respective autocorrelation coefficients of these processes. Then in a rational-expectations equilibrium with stable prices, (real and nominal) interest rates must track the exogenously varying *natural rate of interest* given by

$$\hat{r}_t^n = (\sigma + \omega^{-1})^{-1}\big[(1 - \rho_G)\hat{G}_t + s_C(1 - \rho_c)\bar{c}_t$$
$$- (1 + \omega^{-1})(1 - \rho_a)a_t - \omega^{-1}v(1 - \rho_h)\bar{h}_t\big]. \tag{2.4}$$

Since stationarity requires that $\rho_i < 1$ in each case, one observes that un-der this assumption, interest rates must increase in response to temporary increases in government purchases or in the impatience of households to consume and decrease in response to temporary increases in productivity or in the willingness of households to supply labor. In each case, the effects upon the natural rate of interest are larger the more temporary the distur-bance (i.e., the less positive the serial correlation).

This prescription may appear quite different from that of Clarida et al. (1999), who state (in their Result 4) that optimal policy involves "adjusting the interest rate to perfectly offset demand shocks," while "perfectly accom-modat[ing] shocks to potential output by keeping the nominal interest rate constant." In fact, the variable (their g_t) here referred to as a demand shock corresponds to my natural rate of interest r_t^n.[20] What these authors mean by "perfectly offsetting" movements in this variable is that the central bank's interest-rate instrument should move one-for-one with variations in the nat-ural rate of interest. (Thus perfectly offsetting the shocks does not mean that output is insulated from them, but that the *output gap* is so insulated.) Moreover, what they mean by "perfectly accommodating shocks to potential output" is that, *given* the value of the natural rate of interest, the interest rate should be independent of the natural rate of output. That is, disturbances to the natural rate of output *that do not shift the natural rate of interest* should not affect nominal interest rates. Stated this way, there is no difference between their recommendation and mine.[21] However, it is *not* true, in general, that

20. The variable is evidently thought of as a demand shock because it is the disturbance term in the Euler equation (1.12). But because this condition has been written in terms of the *output gap* x_t rather than the level of output $\hat{Y}_t$, the composite disturbance $\hat{r}_t^n$, unlike my variable g_t, cannot properly be regarded as a pure demand shock, if one supposes the occurrence of transitory disturbances to the natural rate of output.

21. Actually, the results referred to in Clarida et al. are characterizations of optimizing central-bank policy under discretion, which is *not* in general optimal policy, in the sense of the

optimal policy involves no interest-rate response to shocks that affect the natural rate of output, because as shown by (2.4) such shocks almost always do affect the natural rate of interest to some extent.

It is worth noting that the required interest-rate variations (2.4) in response to the various types of shocks cannot be achieved, in general, through a simple Taylor rule under which the nominal interest rate is a function solely of inflation and the deviation of output from trend. In an equilibrium with completely stable prices, inflation does not vary in response to the shocks at all, and so conveys no information about them. Output does vary in response to each of the shocks, but the desired interest-rate response is not proportional to the desired output response across the various types of shocks; indeed, one wants interest rates to vary procyclically in the case of government-purchase or consumption-demand shocks, but countercyclically in response to technology or labor-supply shocks. Thus if its aim is complete price stability, the central bank needs additional information in order to implement its policy.

Analysis of the sources of variation in the natural rate of interest is also important in determining whether complete price stability is necessarily *feasible*. The previous analysis suggests that it should be, insofar as I have been able to solve for paths of output and interest rates that would imply that the IS and AS relations would be satisfied at all times by a zero inflation rate. However, even supposing that the central bank possesses the information required to adjust its interest-rate instrument as required by that analysis, there is another potential problem: The natural rate of interest may sometimes be *negative*.[22] If this occurs, it is not possible for the nominal interest rate to perfectly track the natural rate, owing to the zero lower bound on nominal interest rates. How likely the natural rate of interest is to ever be negative is a topic of some debate, though Summers (1991) has suggested that it fluctuates sufficiently in the United States for an inflation target several percentage points above zero to be desirable in order to allow more successful stabilization, and Krugman (1998) has argued that it has recently been far below zero in Japan. Here I note simply that the present theory allows for variation over time in the natural rate for a variety of reasons, and there is no reason why it should not sometimes be negative. (The model does imply a positive *average* level of the natural rate, determined by the rate of time preference of the representative household.) Policy options

---

policy that best achieves the central bank's assumed objectives, as I explain in Chapter 7. However, in the case that complete stabilization of both inflation and the output gap are possible, doing so corresponds *both* to optimal policy and to the result of discretionary optimization, as we shall see.

22. Another possible problem is the existence of a non-Ricardian fiscal policy of a sort that makes a constant price level inconsistent with the condition that households exhaust their intertemporal budget constraints. This potential problem and its implications are taken up in Section 4.

when the natural rate of interest is temporarily negative are discussed in Eggertsson and Woodford (2003), using the framework set out here.

2.2 Conditions for Determinacy of Equilibrium

I have thus far only considered how interest rates would have to vary in order for there to be an equilibrium with stable prices. My answer to this question does not yet, in itself, explain what sort of interest-rate rule would be suitable to *bring about* an equilibrium of this kind. In particular, it should *not* be inferred from the previous discussion that a suitable policy rule would be simply to set the central bank's interest-rate instrument to equal its estimate of the current natural rate of interest. A policy rule of the form $\hat{\imath}_t = \hat{r}_t^n$ would be *consistent* with the desired equilibrium, but might allow many other, less desirable equilibria as well. Such a rule makes the nominal interest rate a function of purely exogenous state variables, and just as in the flexible-price analysis of Chapter 2, *all* such rules imply *indeterminacy* of rational-expectations equilibrium. I thus must again take up the question of the determinacy of equilibrium under alternative interest-rate rules, but now in the context of the model with sticky prices and endogenous output variation.

I begin with a formal consideration of interest-rate rules, such as the one just proposed, under which $\{\hat{\imath}_t\}$ is an exogenous process. In this case I wish to solve the system (1.12) and (1.13) for the endogenous variables $\{\pi_t, x_t\}$, given exogenous stationary processes $\{\hat{r}_t^n, \hat{\imath}_t\}$. One observes that this system can be written in the form

$$E_t z_{t+1} = A z_t + a \left(\hat{r}_t^n - \hat{\imath}_t \right), \tag{2.5}$$

where the vector of endogenous variables is

$$z_t \equiv \begin{bmatrix} \pi_t \\ x_t \end{bmatrix}, \tag{2.6}$$

and the matrices of coefficients are

$$A \equiv \begin{bmatrix} \beta^{-1} & -\beta^{-1}\kappa \\ -\beta^{-1}\sigma & 1 + \beta^{-1}\kappa\sigma \end{bmatrix}, \qquad a \equiv \begin{bmatrix} 0 \\ -\sigma \end{bmatrix}.$$

The matrix A has characteristic equation

$$\mathcal{P}(\mu) = \mu^2 - [1 + \beta^{-1}(1 + \kappa\sigma)]\mu + \beta^{-1} = 0.$$

As the parameters satisfy $\kappa, \sigma > 0$ and $0 < \beta < 1$, it can be seen that $\mathcal{P}(0) > 0, \mathcal{P}(1) < 0$, and $\mathcal{P}(\mu) > 0$ again for large enough $\mu > 1$. Hence A has two real eigenvalues, satisfying

$$0 < \mu_1 < 1 < \mu_2.$$

Since neither endogenous state variable is predetermined, the existence of an eigenvalue $|\mu_1| < 1$ implies that rational-expectations equilibrium is indeterminate, just as in the flexible-price model of Chapter 2 (and in the rational-expectations IS-LM-AS model of Sargent and Wallace, 1975). I thus obtain the following important result.

PROPOSITION 4.2. In the context of the basic neo-Wicksellian model set out in Section 1, suppose that monetary policy is conducted so as to ensure that the short-term nominal interest rate follows an exogenously specified (bounded) target process $\{\bar{\imath}_t\}$. Then rational-expectations equilibrium is *indeterminate*, regardless of the nature of the target process (e.g., the correlation that may or may not exist between target changes and other exogenous disturbances).

As in Chapter 2, this means that there are an infinite number of different possible equilibrium responses of the endogenous variables to real disturbances, including some in which the fluctuations in inflation and output are disproportionately large relative to the size of the change in "fundamentals" that has occurred and some in which inflation and output vary in response to random events with no fundamental significance whatsoever. Here the situation differs from that in Chapter 2 in that the alternative stationary solutions include a large number of alternative stochastic processes for output (as well as for the expected component of inflation), rather than it being only the *unexpected* component of inflation that fails to be uniquely determined. In the present context it is also clearer that this indeterminacy is undesirable, since in the presence of staggered pricesetting, variations in inflation due to self-fulfilling expectations create real distortions (of a kind further characterized in Chapter 6).

This result implies that even if the central bank has perfect information about the exogenous fluctuations in the natural rate of interest, a desirable interest-rate rule also has to involve feedback from endogenous variables such as inflation and/or real activity, if only to ensure determinacy of equilibrium. In fact, if one is seeking to find a rule that implements the equilibrium with completely stable prices (or more generally, a completely stable inflation rate), then neither the variable π_t nor x_t is useful as a source of *information* about the real disturbances to the economy, for in the desired equilibrium neither variable responds at all to any of the real disturbances.[23]

---

23. This is a common problem for an approach to stabilization policy based upon a commitment to respond solely to deviations of one's target variables from their (constant) target values, discussed in Bernanke and Woodford (1997). It should be noted, however, that if complete stabilization of inflation and the output gap is not desirable—owing, say, to a desire to

Nonetheless, it may be desirable for the central bank to commit itself to respond to fluctuations in these variables, *in addition* to its response to other sources of information about the real disturbances, in order to render equilibrium determinate.

I illustrate this possibility by considering the determinacy of equilibrium under a Taylor rule of the form (1.14). (Note that it is now necessary to write explicitly the dependence of the interest-rate operating target upon the output gap, since output here is an endogenous variable.) In this case, I obtain the following generalization of Proposition 4.2.

PROPOSITION 4.3. *Suppose instead that monetary policy is conducted so as to ensure that the nominal interest rate satisfies a rule of the form (1.14), where* $\phi_\pi, \phi_x \geq 0$. *Then equilibrium is determinate if and only if*[24] *the response coefficients satisfy*

$$\phi_\pi + \frac{1-\beta}{4\kappa}\phi_x > 1. \tag{2.7}$$

The proof is in Appendix C.

Condition (2.7) for determinacy can be given a simple interpretation. Note that the New Keynesian Phillips curve implies that each percentage point of permanently higher inflation (i.e., quarterly inflation π_t permanently higher by $1/4$ of a percent) implies a permanently higher output gap of $(1-\beta)/4\kappa$ percentage points.[25] Hence the left-hand side of (2.7) represents the long-run increase in the nominal interest rate prescribed by (1.14) for each unit permanent increase in the inflation rate. The condition then corresponds once more to the Taylor principle: At least in the long run, nominal interest rates should rise by more than the increase in the inflation rate.

Contrary to the result in Chapter 2, determinacy now depends upon the output response coefficient ϕ_x, and not solely upon the inflation response coefficient ϕ_π; and indeed, a large enough positive value of *either*

---

reduce the degree of interest-rate volatility—then it may be possible to implement an optimal equilibrium through commitment to a rule that responds directly to no variables other than inflation and the output gap, as shown in Chapter 8.

24. Here and in the subsequent results regarding the conditions for determinacy of equilibrium, my "necessary and sufficient" are only *generically* necessary. I omit discussion of various knife-edge cases in which an eigenvalue lies exactly on the unit circle; in such cases one cannot generally reach a conclusion regarding determinacy simply on the basis of a log-linear approximation to the equilibrium conditions.

25. Thus the long-run Phillips curve is not perfectly vertical in this model. I show, however, in Chapters 6 and 7 that this does not imply that the optimal long-run inflation rate is positive, even if the optimal output level exceeds the natural rate.

coefficient suffices to guarantee determinacy. This complicates slightly our interpretation of the Taylor (1999) contrast between pre-Volcker and post-Volcker U.S. monetary policy. Taylor's estimates (discussed above in Section 2.3 of Chapter 2) imply that $\phi_\pi < 1$ in his pre-Volcker sample; but as they also imply that $\phi_x > 0$ in that period, this does not in itself suffice to indicate that equilibrium should have been indeterminate under the earlier policy. Still, plausible numerical values for the parameters of the NKPC imply this, at least if Taylor's point estimates for the policy-rule coefficients are taken to be correct. For example, if one assumes the parameter values given in Table 5.1 (based upon the estimates of Rotemberg and Woodford (1997)), then determinacy would require that the inflation coefficient plus 0.1 times the output coefficient be greater than one. Taylor's estimates for the period 1960–1979 would then imply an interest-rate increase of only $0.81 + 0.1(0.25) = 0.84$ percentage points per percentage point long-run increase in inflation. Thus just as I concluded in Chapter 2, these estimates suggest that equilibrium should have been indeterminate under the pre-Volcker regime, though clearly determinate under the post-Volcker regime.

As discussed in Chapter 1, most empirical estimates of Taylor rules incorporate some form of partial adjustment of the short-term interest-rate instrument toward an implicit target that depends upon the current inflation rate and output gap. (I also argue in Chapter 8 that rules of that kind are desirable on normative grounds.) It is therefore of some interest to consider the effects of interest-rate inertia upon the question of determinacy. For the sake of simplicity I restrict the present analysis to the family of generalized Taylor rules

$$\hat{\imath}_t = \bar{\imath}_t + \rho(\hat{\imath}_{t-1} - \bar{\imath}_{t-1}) + \phi_\pi(\pi_t - \bar{\pi}) + \phi_x(x_t - \bar{x})/4, \qquad (2.8)$$

where it is assumed that $\rho, \phi_\pi, \phi_x \geq 0$. I can now further generalize Proposition 4.3 as follows.

PROPOSITION 4.4. Suppose that monetary policy is conducted so as to ensure that the nominal interest rate satisfies a rule of the form (2.8), where $\rho, \phi_\pi, \phi_x \geq 0$. Then equilibrium is determinate if and only if the response coefficients satisfy

$$\phi_\pi + \frac{1-\beta}{4\kappa}\phi_x > 1 - \rho. \qquad (2.9)$$

Again the proof is in Appendix C.

Condition (2.9) will be recognized as a generalization of (2.7), and once again it can be interpreted as requiring adherence to the Taylor principle. In the case that $\rho < 1$, the rule (2.8) implies that a sustained increase in inflation of a certain size results in an eventual cumulative increase in the nominal interest rate of $\Phi_\pi \equiv (1 - \rho)^{-1}\phi$ times as much; similarly, a sustained increase in the output gap results in an eventual cumulative increase in the interest rate of $(1/4$ of$)$ $\Phi_x \equiv (1 - \rho)^{-1}\phi_x$ times as much.[26] In this case, (2.9) can equivalently be written as

$$\Phi_\pi + \frac{1 - \beta}{4\kappa}\Phi_x > 1,$$

which clearly has the same interpretation as (2.7) in the noninertial case. Furthermore, if $\rho \geq 1$, the eventual cumulative increase in the nominal interest rate is infinite if at least one of ϕ_π or ϕ_x is positive, so that the Taylor principle is necessarily satisfied; but (2.9) is necessarily satisfied in this case as well. Thus (2.9) is equivalent to requiring conformity with the Taylor principle.[27] This result—that the Taylor principle continues to be a crucial condition for determinacy, once understood to refer to *cumulative* responses to a *permanent* inflation increase, even in the case of an inertial interest-rate rule—recalls the finding in Chapter 2 in the case of a flexible-price model. The finding that a determinate rational-expectations equilibrium necessarily exists for rules with $\rho \geq 1$ (superinertial rules) also recalls an earlier result.

Some empirical papers (e.g., Clarida et al., 2000; Bernanke and Boivin, 2000) estimate forward-looking variants of the Taylor rule, in which interest rates respond to deviations of expected *future* inflation from its target level, instead of responding to the amount that prices have already risen. As a simple example, consider the family of rules

26. It may be recalled that the estimated Fed reaction functions described in Chapter 1 are described in terms of the values of these long-run response coefficients Φ_π and Φ_x rather than the immediate responses ϕ_π and ϕ_x.

27. In fact, one finds for a wide variety of types of simple interest-rate rules that the Taylor principle is one of the conditions required for determinacy, even if it is not a sufficient condition in itself, as is true here. This should not be too surprising. One observes quite generally—in the case of *any* family of policy rules that involve feedback only from inflation and output, regardless of how many lags of these might be involved—that the boundary between sets of coefficients that satisfy the Taylor principle and those that do not will consist of coefficients for which there is an eigenvalue exactly equal to 1. The eigenvalue of 1 exists for any policy rule with the property that the long-run increase in the nominal interest rate is exactly equal to the long-run increase in the inflation rate, for the associated right eigen-vector is one with an element 1 for each current or lagged value of inflation or the interest rate, and an element $(1 - \beta)/4\kappa$ for each current or lagged value of the output gap. This is because under the hypothesis about the policy rule, the IS relation, the AS relation, and the policy rule all share the property that the equation continues to be satisfied if inflation, output, and interest rates are increased at all dates by the constant factors just mentioned. It follows that a real eigenvalue crosses the unit circle as the sign of the inequality corresponding to the Taylor principle changes. This boundary is therefore one at which the number of unstable eigenvalues increases by one. Often this results in moving from a situation of indeterminacy to determinacy, though I do not seek to establish general conditions for this.

$$\hat{\imath}_t = \bar{\imath}_t + \phi_\pi (E_t \pi_{t+1} - \bar{\pi}) + \phi_x (x_t - \bar{x})/4, \qquad (2.10)$$

where I again assume that $\phi_\pi, \phi_x > 0$. In this case, the result obtained in Proposition 4.3 must be slightly modified.

PROPOSITION 4.5. Suppose that monetary policy is conducted so as to ensure that the nominal interest rate satisfies a rule of the form (2.10), where $\phi_\pi, \phi_x \geq 0$. Then equilibrium is determinate if and only if the response coefficients satisfy both (2.7) and

$$\phi_\pi < 1 + \frac{1+\beta}{4\kappa} \left(\phi_x + 8\sigma^{-1} \right). \qquad (2.11)$$

Again the proof is in Appendix C.

Note that condition (2.7) again corresponds to the Taylor principle, so that also in this case conformity to that principle is a necessary condition for determinacy. But in the present case, one finds that it is not sufficient. In particular, condition (2.11) fails to hold for large enough values of ϕ_π, even though the Taylor principle is satisfied. Thus adjusting interest rates in response to deviations of expected future inflation from target can give rise to equilibrium fluctuations due purely to self-fulfilling expectations, as shown by Bernanke and Woodford (1997) for a closely related model. This problem does not arise in the case of a strong response to the inflation that has already occurred no matter how large ϕ_π is made. The region in which equilibrium is determinate for rules of this family is illustrated in Figure 4.1, assuming values for the structural parameters β, σ, κ taken from Table 5.1. As Clarida et al. (2000) also conclude, indeterminacy results from too high a value of ϕ_π only in the case of quite high values relative to empirical estimates for any central banks. However, this could be a problem if a central bank were to attempt to demonstrate the seriousness with which it takes its inflation target by responding extremely vigorously to any deviations in an inflation forecast.[28]

The interest-rate rule estimated by Clarida et al. (2000) for the Fed is more complicated than rules of the family (2.10), most notably because it allows for interest-rate inertia. Thus in order to interpret their results I have to consider forward-looking rules of the more general family[29]

28. See also Proposition 7.13 in Chapter 7, for a further illustration of the way that excessive responsiveness of an interest-rate rule to an inflation forecast can make possible self-fulfilling expectations. Kiley (2003) proposes an alternative model, under which a forward-looking Taylor rule of the form (2.10) may result in indeterminacy regardless of the strength of the response to inflation.

29. Note that even this family is still too restricted to include any of the rules actually estimated by Clarida et al., as they also replace the output gap term by a forecast of the future

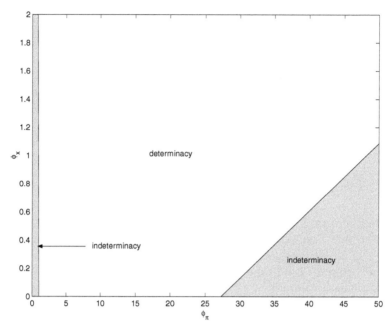

Figure 4.1 *Regions of determinacy and indeterminacy for forward-looking Taylor rules.*

$$\hat{\imath}_t = \bar{\imath}_t + \rho\left(\hat{\imath}_{t-1} - \bar{\imath}_{t-1}\right) + \phi_\pi\left(E_t\pi_{t+1} - \bar{\pi}\right) + \phi_x\left(x_t - \bar{x}\right)/4. \quad (2.12)$$

PROPOSITION 4.6. Suppose that monetary policy is conducted so as to ensure that the nominal interest rate satisfies a rule of the form (2.12), where $\rho, \phi_\pi, \phi_x \geq 0$. Then it is necessary for determinacy of equilibrium that the response coefficients satisfy both (2.9), generalizing (2.7), and

$$\phi_\pi < 1 + \rho + \frac{1+\beta}{4\kappa}\left(\phi_x + 8\sigma^{-1}(1+\rho)\right), \quad (2.13)$$

generalizing (2.11).

---

output gap. However, analysis of the family of rules (2.12) does allow insight into how the three key parameters estimated by these authors should be expected to affect the determinacy of equilibrium, and indeed their own numerical examination of the conditions under which equilibrium is determinate considers this family of rules, rather than anything more general. Furthermore, for the reason explained in footnote 27, the Taylor principle has the same importance for the eigenvalues of the equation system if the current output gap is replaced by an expected future output gap; so the most important of the conditions for determinacy is likely to continue to apply.

Again the proof is in Appendix C. Note that in this case, I have not established whether conditions (2.9) and (2.11) are also sufficient for determinacy in the absence of further restrictions on parameter values. However, I have obtained a direct generalization of the necessary conditions given in Proposition 4.5 for the case $\rho = 0$ (in which case these conditions are also sufficient). It is worth noting that for this class of rules, (2.9) corresponds to the Taylor principle, which thus is again necessary, though not sufficient, for determinacy of equilibrium.

As in the $\rho = 0$ case already treated in Proposition 4.4, one finds that in addition to requiring that ϕ_π be large enough to satisfy the Taylor principle, it is at the same time necessary that ϕ_π satisfy an upper bound, expressed in (2.13). Observe that higher values of ρ relax this constraint, but do not eliminate it. Thus it continues to be true that too great a degree of sensitivity of the interest rate to the inflation forecast results in indeterminacy. This is illustrated in Figure 4.2, where the values of ϕ_π and ρ consistent with a determinate equilibrium are indicated, in the case of rules of the form (2.12) with $\phi_x = 0$, assuming the same model parameters as in Figure 4.1.[30]

In the case of rules with coefficients in the range that is likely to be of practical interest, however, the other requirements for determinacy do not seem likely to be a problem. The requirement for determinacy that is of most practical interest thus remains the Taylor principle.[31] Like Taylor, Clarida et al. find that an estimated policy rule for the period 1960–1979 involves an insufficient response to inflation to be consistent with determinacy, whereas their estimated rule for the period 1982–1996 satisfies the Taylor principle and would imply a determinate equilibrium. For example, their baseline estimates for the earlier period are $\rho = 0.68$, $\phi_\pi = 0.27$, $\phi_x = 0.09$. In the absence of any increase in the output gap, these values

30. In graphing the regions in which determinacy obtains, one checks as well the sufficient conditions discussed in Appendix C, Section C.5. It turns out that these are satisfied, at least in this example, whenever the necessary conditions stated in Proposition 4.6 are met. Thus the two boundaries shown in the figure correspond to the two restrictions stated in the proposition.

31. Kiley (2003), however, finds that in the case of an alternative model of staggered pricing (with price commitments that always last for two periods), equilibrium is indeterminate under a forward-looking Taylor rule, *regardless* of the size of the response coefficients, if the rule implies a target inflation rate that is sufficiently large. In the case considered by Kiley, satisfaction of the Taylor principle is not at all a sufficient condition for determinacy. An interesting feature of Kiley's result is that it makes possible an explanation of U.S. macroeconomic instability in the 1970s as due to a monetary policy rule that caused equilibrium to be indeterminate, even under Orphanides's (2003) characterization of U.S. monetary policy. According to Orphanides, as discussed in Chapter 1, U.S. monetary policy in the 1970s conformed to a forward-looking Taylor rule with coefficients that satisfied the Taylor principle. However, the shift in the 1970s to a policy consistent with a fairly high average inflation rate—owing to systematic overestimation of potential output, rather than a conscious decision to increase the inflation target—would by itself have resulted in indeterminacy of equilibrium in the model proposed by Kiley.

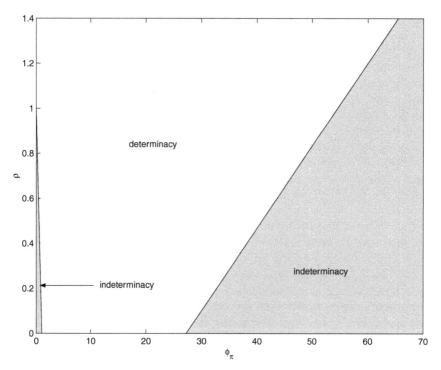

Figure 4.2 *Regions of determinacy and indeterminacy for forward-looking Taylor rules with interest-rate inertia.*

imply that a sustained increase in inflation of 1 percentage point would eventually raise nominal interest rates by only 83 basis points. Thus the Taylor principle is violated unless the associated increase in the output gap is quite large. Condition (2.9) is satisfied only if $\kappa < 0.4(1 - \beta)$, which is to say, if $\kappa < 0.004$; this is an extremely small value, from the point of view of either the underlying microfoundations of price adjustment or of estimated Phillips curves.[32] On the other hand, their baseline estimates for the later period are $\rho = 0.79$, $\phi_\pi = 0.45$, and $\phi_x = 0.20$. Since in this case $\phi_\pi > 1 - \rho$, the Taylor principle is satisfied regardless of the assumed slope of the long-run Phillips curve. On the other hand, because $\phi_\pi < 1$, condition (2.13) is necessarily satisfied as well, and such a policy rule implies a determinate equilibrium.

Another class of possible policy rules that is of at least theoretical interest is that of rules that incorporate a *price-level* target—the Wicksellian rules

32. See Chapter 5 for examples of estimated parameter values.

considered in Chapter 2. In the case of a model with endogenous output, one must also consider the consequences of possible feedback from the level of output, and so the class of rules considered in Chapter 2 may be generalized to include all rules of the form

$$\hat{\imath}_t = \bar{\imath}_t + \phi_p(p_t - \bar{p}_t) + \phi_x(x_t - \bar{x}), \tag{2.14}$$

where now p_t is the log price level, and $\{\bar{p}_t\}$ is a target path for the log price level, growing deterministically at some rate $\bar{\pi}$ (to which $\bar{x}$ again corresponds). Giannoni (2000) establishes the following result.

PROPOSITION 4.7. Suppose that monetary policy is conducted so as to ensure that the nominal interest rate satisfies a rule of the form (2.14), where $\phi_p > 0$, $\phi_x \geq 0$. Then equilibrium is necessarily determinate.

Again the proof is in Appendix C.

Note that in the case that $\phi_p = 0$, a rule of this kind corresponds to a rule of the form (1.14) with $\phi_\pi = 0$, and so one knows from Proposition 4.3 that determinacy obtains in that case only if

$$\phi_x > \frac{\kappa}{1 - \beta}. \tag{2.15}$$

(This is the case in which such a rule would satisfy the Taylor principle.) If $\phi_p > 0$, however—that is, if the rule responds at all to deviations from the price-level target—equilibrium is determinate regardless of the size of the output response coefficient. This, however, is also in conformity with the Taylor principle. For a sustained inflation rate in excess of the target rate (the rate at which the price-level target path grows deterministically) eventually results in an arbitrarily large deviation $p_t - \bar{p}_t$. Hence no matter how small $\phi_p > 0$ may be, the rule requires that the nominal interest rate would eventually be (permanently) raised by more than the amount of the excess inflation. Thus the Taylor principle is satisfied by any such rule with $\phi_p > 0$, regardless of the size of ϕ_x. The fact that the condition required for determinacy is necessarily satisfied, rather than depending on the strength of the response coefficients as in the case of the present results for Taylor-type rules, is one of the appealing features of rules of this kind, as discussed by Giannoni.

2.3 Stability under Learning Dynamics

I have shown in the previous section that a commitment to an interest-rate rule need not be vulnerable to the critique of Sargent and Wallace (1975), according to which interest-rate rules result in indeterminacy of the rational-expectations equilibrium. Interest-rate targeting as an approach to the conduct of monetary policy has also been criticized, however, on an independent, though related ground by Milton Friedman (1968). Friedman also warns that interest-rate targeting can leave the economy vulnerable to instability as a result of self-fulfilling expectations. But his argument is not one that depends upon the existence of a multiplicity of alternative rational-expectations equilibria; rather, it is based on concern for whether expectations can actually be relied upon to converge to the (desirable) rational-expectations equilibrium.

Friedman argues that an attempt to peg the level of nominal interest rates through monetary policy is an unsound policy, even if the level of nominal rates that is chosen is a sensible one—one equal to the Wicksellian natural rate of interest, and hence consistent with a rational-expectations equilibrium (r.e.e.) with stable prices—because that equilibrium is unlikely to be realized.[33] For even in that case, any small discrepancy between the inflation expectations of the public and the ones required for realization of the rational-expectations equilibrium will set in motion a dynamic process in which their expectations are driven *ever farther* from consistency with the r.e.e. If people expect even a small amount of inflation, they will perceive the available real rate of return to be less than the natural rate of interest and hence demand more current goods than are consistent with production at the natural rate of output. This will cause inflation, observation of which will lead to even greater anticipation of inflation by the private sector. More expected inflation will imply an even lower perceived real rate of return, stimulating even more demand, creating even more inflation, justifying still greater expectations of inflation, and so on, in an explosive spiral that can only end in disaster if the interest-rate peg is not abandoned.

Friedman's analysis parallels (and indeed, explicitly recalls) Wicksell's (1898) celebrated analysis of the "cumulative process" of inflation set in motion by a discrepancy between the natural rate of interest and the interest rate maintained through central-bank policy. Wicksell's point, however, was not the importance of a money-growth rule; rather, it was to argue for a *particular type* of interest-rate rule. As was discussed in Chapter 1, Wicksell argued for the importance of increasing the nominal interest rate controlled by the central bank in response to any observed increase in the general level of prices, in order to head off instability of this sort. As we shall see, explicit analyses of adaptive learning dynamics confirm the reasonableness of this as an alternative solution to the problem that Friedman

---

33. Because Friedman's address was given prior to the rational-expectations revolution of the 1970s, he does not describe matters in precisely these terms. But the analysis that he gives of expectational instability can easily be cast in these terms. Howitt (1992) explicitly reformulates Friedman's critique as a failure of convergence of learning dynamics to rational-expectations equilibrium.

warns against. These analyses indicate that there is indeed a danger of instability due to self-fulfilling expectations in the case of a policy that fixes the
nominal interest-rate target *independently of what may happen to the level of prices*
even when the interest-rate target is based on a sophisticated awareness of
the correct current value of the natural rate of interest. However, they also
show that a suitably chosen commitment to an interest-rate *feedback rule* can
ensure convergence to the rational-expectations equilibrium when expectations are based on extrapolation from experience. Moreover, one type of
feedback rule that suffices for stability of the r.e.e. under learning dynamics,
at least in the simple frameworks discussed here, is a rule of exactly the kind
proposed by Taylor (1993).

Bullard and Mitra (2002) provide an explicit analysis of learning dynamics under Taylor-type interest-rate rules.[34] They assume a log-linear model
of the transmission mechanism in which inflation and the output gap are
determined by a system of equations of the form

$$\pi_t = \kappa x_t + \beta \hat{E}_t \pi_{t+1}, \tag{2.16}$$

$$x_t = \hat{E}_t x_{t+1} - \sigma\left(\hat{\imath}_t - \hat{E}_t \pi_{t+1} - \hat{r}_t^n\right), \tag{2.17}$$

where $\hat{E}_t z_{t+1}$ indicates the *subjective* expectation of private agents in period t
regarding the variable z in period $t+1$. (Note that under the hypothesis of
rational expectations—that subjective expectations coincide with the true
conditional expectations according to the probability distribution implied
by the model, so that $\hat{E}_t z_{t+1} = E_t z_{t+1}$—the predictions of this model are identical to those of the basic neo-Wicksellian model, characterized by equations
(1.12) and (1.13).) If these are supplemented by an interest-rate feedback
rule of the form (1.14), one has a system of three equations that determine
the equilibrium values of π_t, x_t, and $\hat{\imath}_t$ each period as linear functions of
the exogenous disturbances $\hat{r}_t^n$, $\bar{\imath}_t$ and current subjective expectations. The
solution for inflation and output can be written in the form

$$z_t = \bar{z} + B\left[\hat{E}_t z_{t+1} - \bar{z}\right] + b\left(\hat{r}_t^n - \bar{\imath}_t\right), \tag{2.18}$$

where z_t is the same vector as in (2.6), $\bar{z}$ is the average r.e.e. value of this
vector, and B and b are matrices of coefficients. (The matrix B is just the
inverse of the matrix A in (2.5).)

Completion of the model of learning dynamics requires a specification
of how the subjective expectations $\hat{E}_t z_{t+1}$ evolve. Bullard and Mitra assume
least-squares learning dynamics, which means that expectations are formed
by linear regression of the observed (past) values of the variables to be

---

34. See Evans and Honkapohja (2002c) for a review of recent literature on learning dynamics under alternative monetary policy rules.

forecasted on the corresponding (past) values of some vector of variables that can be used as the basis for a forecast a period in advance. The stability concept that they employ is the criterion of "expectational stability," or "E-stability," advocated by Evans and Honkapohja (2001). This criterion is defined in terms of a mapping from the class of forecasting models contemplated by private agents into itself, which maps a given subjective model to the one that actually best describes the data that are generated when agents believe in the first model.

This concept can be illustrated with a simple example. Suppose that agents believe, in the case of both inflation and the output gap, that the best forecast is an unknown constant value; that is, they do not believe that any variables that are observed a period in advance can improve their forecasts. (This corresponds to the trivial case of regression on a constant, and no other regressors.) The forecasting model in period t can then simply be represented by two numbers, the elements of z_t^e, indicating current beliefs about the correct value of $\hat{E}_t z_{t+1}$. Belief in a given forecasting model z^e results in a data-generating process (d.g.p.)

$$z_t = \bar{z} + B[z^e - \bar{z}] + b(\hat{r}_t^n - \bar{\imath}_t),$$

as a consequence of (2.18). If the forecasting model is estimated on the basis of data generated by this d.g.p.—that is, if the mean of the vector z_t is estimated when z_t is generated in this way—then the correct model (to which a consistent estimator should converge with sufficient data) is given by

$$E[z] = \bar{z} + B[z^e - \bar{z}] \equiv T(z^e). \tag{2.19}$$

The mapping $T(\cdot)$ defined in (2.19) is the mapping from subjective to correct beliefs mentioned above. A fixed point of this mapping defines a *self-consistent equilibrium* (s.c.e.): Beliefs that generate data that should confirm those beliefs (abstracting from sampling error). An s.c.e. will correspond to a r.e.e. if the class of forecasting models is flexible enough so that the optimal forecasting rule, given a d.g.p. resulting from subjective beliefs in this class, belongs to the class. In the present example, the unique s.c.e. is the belief $z^e = \bar{z}$, in the (generic) case that B has no eigenvalue equal exactly to one.[35] This is also an r.e.e. in the case that $\hat{r}_t^n$ and $\bar{\imath}_t$ are i.i.d. (and hence unforecastable) random variables.

An s.c.e. is said to be *E-stable* if it is a locally stable rest point of the dynamics defined by the ordinary differential equation

---

35. This is true as long as (2.7) does not hold as an equality. Even in the special case where it does, $z^e = \bar{z}$ is a fixed point and so an s.c.e.; but the s.c.e. is not unique in this special case. This results in a particular kind of learning dynamics, as discussed below.

$$\dot{z}^e = T(z^e) - z^e. \tag{2.20}$$

Here the idea is that agents' beliefs about the correct forecasting model should evolve over time in the direction of the current discrepancy between their current beliefs (z^e) and the correct model of the data that are generated as a result of their current beliefs ($T(z^e)$). This clearly is the direction in which beliefs should evolve on average in this simple example. If beliefs about the correct forecast are obtained from the sample mean of data observed before the current period,

$$z_t^e = t^{-1} \sum_{k=0}^{t-1} z_k,$$

then the expected change in beliefs from one period to the next equals

$$z_{t+1}^e - z_t^e = (t+1)^{-1}\left(z_t - z_t^e\right), \tag{2.21}$$

so that the mean dynamics are given by

$$E_{t-1}\left[z_{t+1}^e - z_t^e\right] = (t+1)^{-1}\left(T(z_t^e) - z_t^e\right),$$

using (2.19). This can be written

$$E_{t-1}\left[\frac{\Delta z_{t+1}^e}{\Delta \tau_{t+1}}\right] = T(z_t^e) - z_t^e, \tag{2.22}$$

where τ_t is a rescaled time variable defined by

$$\tau_t \equiv \sum_{k=1}^{t} \frac{1}{k}.$$

For dates t far enough in the future, the discrete increments in the variable τ_t become arbitrarily small, and the mean dynamics described by (2.22) come to approximate the continuous-time dynamics implied by the system (2.20) arbitrarily closely.[36]

One can also show (as discussed by Evans and Honkapohja) that asymptotically, the probability of large deviations of the actual dynamics of beliefs from the mean dynamics becomes smaller and smaller. Intuitively, the fact that the change in beliefs each period under (2.21) resulting from a given discrepancy between the forecast and what occurs becomes smaller and

36. As shown by Evans and Honkapohja (2001), a similar relation between the ordinary differential equation system (2.20) and the mean dynamics resulting from least-squares learning continues to exist in the case of forecasting by regression on a vector of several regressors.

smaller means that eventually beliefs change only in response to the average discrepancy over a large number of independent realizations of the exogenous disturbances, during which time the mean discrepancy $T(z^e) - z^e$ remains nearly the same; the law of large numbers then implies that eventually the direction of change in beliefs is almost certainly nearly equal to that implied by the mean dynamics. Hence local stability of a s.c.e. under the dynamics (2.20) implies that there exists a compact set, containing a neighborhood of the s.c.e., with the property that if beliefs are restricted to never leave this region (perhaps as a result of a priori restrictions upon the range of possibly correct forecasting models), they must eventually converge with probability 1 to the s.c.e. Under certain circumstances, global stability of the s.c.e. under the dynamics (2.20) also suffices to establish convergence of beliefs with probability 1 to the s.c.e. under least-squares learning, even in the absence of any proviso that beliefs be restricted to a compact set.

The local stability of an s.c.e. $\bar{z}$ under the dynamics (2.20) depends on the eigenvalues of the Jacobian matrix $DT(\bar{z}) - I$; the s.c.e. is E-stable if and only if all of these eigenvalues have negative real part.[37] In the present application, the mapping T is linear, and its derivative DT is simply the matrix B. Furthermore, because $B = A^{-1}$, where A is the matrix in (2.5), the eigenvalues of B are simply the inverses of the eigenvalues of A, and they can be determined through study of the same characteristic polynomial as is considered in the proof of Proposition 4.3. I thus obtain the following result.

PROPOSITION 4.8. Suppose that the mapping from beliefs to outcomes is the one proposed by Bullard and Mitra (equations (2.16) and (2.17)): Policy is conducted according to an interest-rate rule in the class (1.14), with coefficients $\phi_\pi, \phi_x \geq 0$; and agents forecast inflation and the output gap using the sample means of past observations of these variables, without taking into account any other information. Then the s.c.e. in which expected inflation and the expected output gap are equal to $\bar{\pi}$ and $\bar{x}$, respectively, is *E-stable* if and only if the response coefficients of the policy rule satisfy (2.7), that is, if and only if policy conforms to the Taylor principle.

One thus finds that learning dynamics of this kind do not necessarily converge to beliefs consistent with rational expectations, or indeed converge at all. In the case that the response coefficients are too weak to satisfy (2.7), the matrix B has an eigenvalue with a positive real part, and the dynamics of expectations described by (2.20) are explosive and diverge from the neighborhood of the s.c.e. even starting from almost all points near it. (The dynamics implied by (2.20) in this case are graphed in the $x^e - \pi^e$ plane in

37. As with the discussion of the determinacy of equilibrium in the previous section, I ignore nongeneric cases in which eigenvalues have a real part equal exactly to zero.

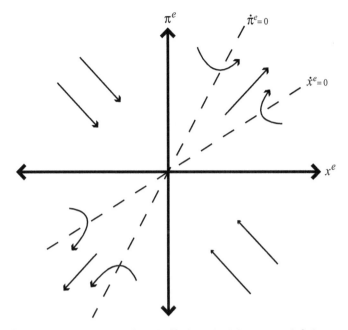

Figure 4.3 *Learning dynamics when the Taylor principle is not satisfied.*

Figure 4.3.[38]) One case in which this occurs is if the interest-rate target does not respond at all to variations in inflation or real activity, as assumed in Friedman's discussion ($\phi_\pi = \phi_x = 0$). In that case, inflation expectations in excess of $\bar{\pi}$ and output-gap expectations in excess of $\bar{x}$ are self-reinforcing in an inflationary spiral of the kind described by Friedman.

On the other hand, in the case of an interest-rate rule that satisfies the Taylor principle, this does not occur. (The dynamics in this case are graphed in Figure 4.4.[39]) Inflation expectations in excess of $\bar{\pi}$ would tend to stimulate demand and hence create inflation, but insofar as they do so, they result in an increase in the central bank's interest-rate target that offsets the incentive for higher spending. Demand is sufficiently restrained that the inflation

38. In the figure, the origin corresponds to the point $(\bar{x}, \bar{\pi})$. The figure is drawn for the case in which the left-hand side of (2.7) is greater than $1 - ((1 - \beta)/\kappa\sigma)$, though less than 1. When the response coefficients are smaller than this, the $\dot{\pi}^e = 0$ locus rotates through the vertical axis, so that inflation expectations are monotonically increasing everywhere in the positive orthant; but the phase diagram remains otherwise similar to the one shown.

39. The figure is drawn for the case in which ϕ_π is less than β^{-1}. When the inflation-response coefficient is larger than this, the $\dot{x}^e = 0$ locus rotates through the vertical axis, so that output-gap expectations are monotonically decreasing everywhere in the positive orthant; but the phase diagram remains otherwise similar to the one shown.

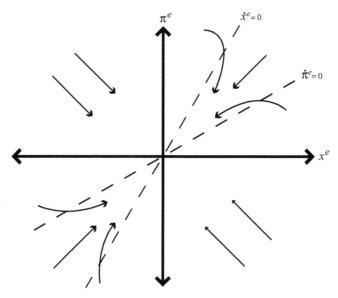

Figure 4.4   *Learning dynamics when the Taylor principle is satisfied.*

generated is less than what people expect, pulling their expectations back to conformity with the s.c.e.

It can be observed from Figures 4.3 and 4.4 that the E-stability of the s.c.e. depends on the relative slopes of the loci where $\dot{\pi}^e = 0$ and $\dot{x}^e = 0$. Increasing either of the response coefficients in the Taylor rule rotates the $\dot{\pi}^e = 0$ locus in the clockwise direction, and at the same time rotates the $\dot{x}^e = 0$ locus in the counterclockwise direction. The point at which (2.7) holds with equality is the point at which the two loci coincide and represents the point at which one passes from the configuration shown in Figure 4.3 to the one shown in Figure 4.4. (In this nongeneric case, there is a continuum of stationary equilibrium levels of inflation that are consistent with both the structural equations and the policy rule; thus there is a line in the $x^e - \pi^e$ plane at any point along which expectations are self-confirming.)

It may seem surprising that exactly the same inequality (2.7) determines both whether or not rational-expectations equilibrium is locally unique and whether or not this equilibrium is stable under learning dynamics. But this is not accidental. A rational-expectations equilibrium of this model is a solution to the system of log-linear equations

$$z_t = \bar{z} + B[E_t z_{t+1} - \bar{z}] + b(\hat{r}_t^n - \bar{\imath}_t).$$

A r.e.e. is determinate if and only if B has both eigenvalues inside the unit circle, so that $B^j \to 0$ as j is made large; this is the case in which the difference equation can be solved forward to yield a unique bounded solution. But this same property of the matrix B is closely related to the one that is necessary for E-stability.

The connection is especially close in the case of what Evans and Honkapohja call "iterative E-stability." The s.c.e. is said to be iteratively E-stable if the discrete-time dynamics

$$z_{\tau+1}^e = T\left(z_\tau^e\right) \equiv \bar{z} + B\left[z_\tau^e - \bar{z}\right] \tag{2.23}$$

converge to the s.c.e. for large τ, in the case of any initial beliefs in a neighborhood of the s.c.e. This can be interpreted as a learning process as follows. Suppose that for some "epoch" τ (an interval of time over which many successive observations of inflation and output are made) beliefs remain fixed at the value z_τ^e, and data are generated by the d.g.p. corresponding to these beliefs. At the end of the epoch, the forecasting model is reestimated, using only the data from epoch τ, and the new estimates form the beliefs $z_{\tau+1}^e$, on the basis of which agents make decisions during all of the following epoch. The mean dynamics are given in this case by (2.23), and in the case that epochs are long enough, the actual learning dynamics (despite sampling error) should evolve close to those indicated by (2.23) with high probability.

It can be observed that the condition required for iterative E-stability of the s.c.e. $\bar{z}$ is the same as the one required for determinacy of r.e.e.; and indeed, one iterates the same linear operator to convergence in establishing both results, though in one case the operator maps $E[z_{\tau+1}]$ into $E[z_\tau]$, while in the other case it maps z_τ^e into $z_{\tau+1}^e$. The condition required for E-stability under the continuous dynamics (2.20), corresponding to continuous adjustment of the estimates as new data are received, is slightly different, but still closely related. Determinacy (like iterative E-stability) obtains if and only if both eigenvalues of B have moduli less than 1; continuous E-stability obtains if and only if both eigenvalues of B have a real part less than 1 (so that the eigenvalues of $B - I$ have a negative real part). When the Taylor principle is not satisfied, one eigenvalue is real and greater than 1, meaning both a modulus greater than 1 and a real part greater than 1; however, when the Taylor principle is satisfied, both eigenvalues have moduli less than 1 and, consequently, real parts less than 1 as well.

Essentially, both types of vulnerability to self-fulfilling expectations—indeterminacy of rational-expectations equilibrium and the possibility of learning dynamics that diverge from the r.e.e. (or s.c.e.)—require that changes in expectations result in changes in actual inflation and output that are *even larger,* so that changes in expectations are justified or reinforced by the actual dynamics. Adherence to the Taylor principle makes actual inflation and output less sensitive to current expectations (i.e., makes the norm of the matrix B smaller in (2.18)). As a consequence, it reduces the economy's vulnerability to both potential threats.

Proposition 4.8 shows only that it is possible for agents to learn to correctly forecast the unconditional means of inflation and the output gap, if these are inferred from the sample means of past observations. This suffices for learning the r.e.e. only in the case of i.i.d. disturbances. However, one can similarly show that when the Taylor principle is satisfied, agents can learn r.e.e. beliefs through least-squares estimation, even in the case of arbitrary linear processes for the exogenous disturbances. Let the dynamics of the disturbances be specified in state-space form,

$$s_t = Cs_{t-1} + e_t,$$
$$u_t = f's_t. \tag{2.24}$$

Here s_t is a vector of exogenous states that include all information at date t about current and future disturbances to the structural equations, C is a matrix with all eigenvalues inside the unit circle (so that the vector process $\{s_t\}$ is stationary), e_t is a vector of i.i.d. innovations, $u_t \equiv [\hat{r}_t^n \ \bar{\imath}_t]'$ is the vector of disturbances to the period t temporary-equilibrium relations (2.18), and f is a vector of coefficients that identifies the current disturbances from the complete state vector s_t. Then suppose that agents forecast inflation and the output gap using a linear model of the form

$$z_{t+1} = \Gamma \bar{s}_t + \epsilon_{t+1}, \tag{2.25}$$

where the vector of forecasting variables $\bar{s}_t$ consists of a constant plus the elements of s_t (assumed to be fully observable), and the vector of residuals ϵ_{t+1} is assumed to be unforecastable in period t. Thus subjective expectations in period t are given by

$$\hat{E}_t z_{t+1} = \Gamma_t \bar{s}_t \equiv \Gamma_{0t} + \Gamma_{st} s_t,$$

where Γ_t represents the matrix of current estimates of coefficients of the linear model, based on past observations $\{z_{\tau+1}, \bar{s}_\tau\}$.

In this case, belief in any forecasting model of the form (2.25), parameterized by coefficients $\hat{\Gamma}$, results in actual inflation and output given by

$$z_t = \bar{z} + B[\hat{\Gamma}\bar{s}_t - \bar{z}] + b[1-1]f's_t,$$

as a result of (2.18). This (together with the law of motion (2.24) for the exogenous state vector) implies that the fluctuations in inflation and output are correctly described by a linear model of the form (2.25), but one in which the correct coefficients Γ are given by

$$\Gamma_0 = \bar{z} + B[\hat{\Gamma}_0 - \bar{z}], \tag{2.26}$$

$$\Gamma_s = \left(B\hat{\Gamma}_s + b[1 - 1]f' \right)C, \qquad (2.27)$$

and the residuals by

$$\epsilon_{t+1} = \left(B\hat{\Gamma}_s + b[1 - 1]f' \right)e_{t+1}.$$

Thus if beliefs remain fixed upon any member of this family of forecasting models, it is *correct* to forecast using a model in this family (albeit not necessarily the one that people actually use). From this it follows that a self-confirming equilibrium is actually a rational-expectations equilibrium.

Equations (2.26) and (2.27) define a mapping $\Gamma = T(\hat{\Gamma})$, identifying correct beliefs as a function of those actually held.[40] Once again the fixed point $\bar{\Gamma}$ of this mapping is generically unique, and now it corresponds to an r.e.e. In the case that (2.7) is satisfied, so that the r.e.e. is determinate, the fixed point of $T(\cdot)$ is just the unique bounded r.e.e.

E-stability may once more be defined as local stability of the fixed point under the dynamics

$$\dot{\Gamma} = T(\Gamma) - \Gamma.$$

I then obtain the following generalization of Proposition 4.8.[41]

PROPOSITION 4.9. Again suppose that the mapping from beliefs to outcomes is the one proposed by Bullard and Mitra (equations (2.16) and (2.17)), and that policy is conducted according to an interest-rate rule in the class (1.14), with coefficients $\phi_\pi, \phi_x \geq 0$, but suppose now that agents forecast inflation and the output gap through linear regression of z_τ on $\bar{s}_{\tau-1}$, with the coefficient estimates $\hat{\Gamma}_t$ used to forecast in period t based on inflation and output data from periods $\tau < t$. Then the r.e.e. $\bar{\Gamma}$ is *E-stable* if and only if the response coefficients of the policy rule satisfy (2.7), that is, if and only if policy conforms to the Taylor principle.

The proof is in Appendix C. It is in fact the possible instability of the dynamics of estimates of the constant terms Γ_0 in the forecasting model that is the relevant threat; and whether this occurs or not is determined by whether

---

40. Evans and Honkapohja (2001) refer to this as a mapping from a "perceived law of motion" to an "actual law of motion," though it seems most relevant to speak of a mapping from one forecasting rule to another, in which the specification of the forecasting rule need not involve a complete specification of a d.g.p. that justifies it.

41. Bullard and Mitra (2002) establish this result for the special case in which $\{\hat{r}_t^n\}$ is a stationary AR(1) process and $\{\bar{\imath}_t\}$ is a constant, and the sole forecasting variable s_t is the current value of $\hat{r}_t^n$. Note that in Proposition 4.9, the state vector s_t may include redundant state variables, such as sunspot variables.

or not the Taylor principle is adhered to, as in Proposition 4.8. Thus in the case that the r.e.e. is found to be determinate, this equilibrium is also one to which least-squares learning dynamics converge. And contrariwise, in the case in which the Taylor principle is *not* satisfied, one finds that policy is doubly problematic. Not only is the r.e.e. determinate, so that one may fear instability due to self-fulfilling expectations even if one is confident that the economy should settle upon some nonexplosive r.e.e., but plausible learning dynamics may also fail to converge to any r.e.e. at all, and may instead result in an explosive inflationary (or deflationary) spiral.

While the model of learning dynamics proposed by Bullard and Mitra has identical rational-expectations equilibria to those of the basic neo-Wicksellian model, expounded in Section 1, it does not really correspond to a model with the same microeconomic foundations as that model, simply substituting an alternative model of expectations formation. As Preston (2002a) notes: In the model of Bullard and Mitra, inflation and output depend only on private-sector forecasts of inflation and output a period in the future, whereas in the model developed in Section 1, pricing and spending decisions depend on forecasts of future income and prices indefinitely far into the future.

Preston shows that a log-linear approximation to the spending rule of a typical household in the basic neo-Wicksellian model (written as a function of arbitrary expectations about future real income, real rates of return on saving, and preference shocks) takes the form

$$
\hat{C}_t^i = \bar{C}_t + (1 - \beta)s_C^{-1}\hat{W}_t^i + \hat{E}_t^i \sum_{T=t}^{\infty} \beta^{T-t}\big[(1 - \beta)s_C^{-1}(\hat{Y}_T - G_T) \tag{2.28}
$$
$$
- (1 - \beta)\bar{C}_T - \beta\tilde{\sigma}(\hat{i}_T - \pi_{T+1})\big],
$$

where $\hat{W}_t^i$ denotes net real wealth of the household at the beginning of period t, relative to the steady-state income level $\bar{Y}$, and $\hat{E}_t^i[\hat{Y}_T - \hat{G}_T]$ denotes expected after-tax real income in period T, on the assumption that government purchases are financed through immediate taxation, so as to maintain zero government debt at all times.[42] (Note that this corresponds to a log-linear version of the familiar permanent-income hypothesis, in which the expected real rate of return on savings is not assumed to equal the rate of time preference at all times, and preference shocks are allowed for.)

---

42. This last assumption is one of many ways in which one might specify a Ricardian fiscal policy, in the sense defined in Section 4, and beliefs on the part of agents that policy is Ricardian, so that they expect a present value of future tax liabilities that coincides with their forecast of the present value of government spending (inclusive of debt service). It is only the hypothesis of Ricardian fiscal expectations that matters for the learning analysis presented by Preston.

Using the identity

$$\hat{Y}_t = s_C \int_i \hat{C}_t^i \, di + \hat{G}_t$$

to define aggregate demand, together with the fact that $\int_i \hat{W}_t^i \, di = 0$ at all times given that there is zero government debt, Preston obtains from (2.28) an aggregate-demand relation

$$\hat{Y}_t = g_t + \hat{E}_t \sum_{T=t}^{\infty} \beta^{T-t} \left[(1 - \beta)(\hat{Y}_T - g_T) - \beta \sigma (\hat{\imath}_T - \pi_{T+1}) \right],$$

where $\hat{E}_t[\cdot] \equiv \int_i \hat{E}_t^i[\cdot]$ denotes the average private-sector forecast of the variables in question. This can be written in terms of output-gap forecasts as

$$x_t = \hat{E}_t \sum_{T=t}^{\infty} \beta^{T-t} \left[(1 - \beta) x_{T+1} - \sigma (\hat{\imath}_T - \pi_{T+1} - \hat{r}_T^n) \right]. \tag{2.29}$$

Note that under the assumption of rational expectations ($\hat{E}_t[\cdot] = E_t[\cdot]$), the expectation that (2.29) will hold each period from t onward implies that (2.17) should be expected to hold from period t onward, and vice versa. However, the relations do not imply one another under more general forecasting rules—in particular, when private agents' forecasting rules do not have to be consistent with an economic model that incorporates either of these structural relations.

Preston similarly obtains a temporary-equilibrium relation for inflation determination under arbitrary expectations that involves long-horizon forecasts. Log-linearizing (1.5) in the case of arbitrary expectations, he obtains a log-linear decision rule,

$$\hat{p}_t^j = \hat{E}_t^j \sum_{T=t}^{\infty} (\alpha \beta)^{T-t} \left[(1 - \alpha \beta) \zeta x_T + \alpha \beta \pi_{T+1} \right],$$

for the log relative price chosen by the supplier of good j, if that supplier is one that revises its price in period t. Then given that a log-linear approximation to the definition of the aggregate price index implies that

$$\pi_t = \frac{1 - \alpha}{\alpha} \int \hat{p}_t^j \, dj,$$

he obtains an inflation equation

$$\pi_t = \hat{E}_t \sum_{T=t}^{\infty} (\alpha \beta)^{T-t} \left[\kappa x_T + (1 - \alpha) \beta \pi_{T+1} \right] \tag{2.30}$$

that is valid under arbitrary subjective expectations. Once again, under the assumption of rational expectations, (2.30) implies (2.16) and vice versa. Preston thus obtains a pair of equations (2.29) and (2.30) to determine inflation and the output gap each period as a function of the current interest rate, the current natural rate of interest, and current private-sector expectations.

In this framework, it is necessary to specify a forecasting model for the private sector that allows forecasts to be generated for inflation, the output gap, the nominal interest rate, and the natural rate of interest arbitrarily far in the future. One may assume once again that agents estimate a linear model of the form (2.25), where now the vector z_{t+1} includes $\hat{\imath}_{t+1}$ in addition to the inflation rate and output; but this must now be supplemented by an estimated law of motion for the exogenous states, which I assume to be of the form (2.24). The estimated matrices of coefficients $\hat{\Gamma}$ and $\hat{C}$ then determine the subjective forecasts $\hat{E}_t z_T$ for any horizon $T > t$ as linear functions of the current state vector $\bar{s}_t$.

Given any beliefs of this kind and a monetary policy rule of the form (1.14), the elements of z_t are determined as linear functions of $\bar{s}_t$ and hence of $\bar{s}_{t-1}$ plus a residual not forecastable at date $t - 1$. The temporary-equilibrium relations (2.29) and (2.30) plus the monetary policy rule thus define a mapping

$$(\Gamma, C) = T(\hat{\Gamma}, \hat{C})$$

that defines the correct forecasting model in the case of a d.g.p. that results from the use of a given forecasting model by private agents. (Here C is given by a constant function, as the true law of motion for the exogenous states is independent of private beliefs.) Once again, the (generically unique) fixed point $(\bar{\Gamma}, C)$ of this mapping is an r.e.e., which is E-stable if and only if all eigenvalues of $DT(\bar{\Gamma}, C) - I$ have a negative real part. Preston establishes the following.

PROPOSITION 4.10. Let the exogenous states evolve according to a law of motion of the form (2.24), where all of the eigenvalues of the matrix C are real, and suppose that the mapping from beliefs to outcomes is the one proposed by Preston equations (2.29) and (2.30). Suppose again that policy is conducted according to an interest-rate rule in the class (1.14), with coefficients ϕ_π, $\phi_x \geq 0$, and that agents forecast inflation and the output gap through linear regression of z_τ and $\bar{s}_\tau$ on $\bar{s}_{\tau-1}$, with the coefficient estimates $\hat{\Gamma}_t$, $\hat{C}_t$ used to forecast in period t based on inflation and output data from periods $\tau < t$. Then the r.e.e. $(\bar{\Gamma}, C)$ is *E-stable* if and only if the response coefficients of the policy rule satisfy (2.7), that is, if and only if policy conforms to the Taylor principle.

Details of the proof may be found in Preston (2002a).

Somewhat surprisingly, the conditions required for stability of r.e.e. under least-squares learning turn out to be the same in this case as those found by Bullard and Mitra. Some intuition for this may be given as follows. Because the part of the T mapping that determines C is a constant function, the eigenvalues of DT consist of a set of zeros (which thus have a real part less than one) plus the eigenvalues of $DT_\Gamma(\bar{\Gamma})$, where T_Γ is the mapping

$$\Gamma = T_\Gamma(\hat{\Gamma}),$$

which identifies the correct forecasting model Γ as a function of $\hat{\Gamma}$ in the case that $\hat{C} = C$. E-stability then depends purely on the eigenvalues of $DT_\Gamma - I$. As in the proof of Proposition 4.9, a subset of these eigenvalues is the set of eigenvalues of $DT_0(\bar{\Gamma}_0) - I$, where T_0 is the part of the mapping T_Γ that defines Γ_0 (the correct intercept terms in the forecasting equations) as a function of the beliefs $\hat{\Gamma}_0$. Moreover, as in the proof of Proposition 4.9, all the eigenvalues of $DT_\Gamma - I$ have a negative real part if the eigenvalues of $DT_0 - I$ do. Hence it is once again the character of the mapping from beliefs about the mean values of the endogenous variables to their actual mean values that is critical for E-stability of the r.e.e.

Finally, two of the three eigenvalues of DT_0 are the eigenvalues of $D\hat{T}_0$, where $\hat{T}_0$ is the restriction of the mapping T_0 to the two-dimensional subspace of mean beliefs that are consistent with the Taylor rule (1.14). (Note that if private agents have mean beliefs in this subspace, the actual means $E[z]$ will also lie in this subspace.) Preston shows that only the dynamics on this subspace are potentially unstable. Hence the question of E-stability reduces once again, as in the proofs of both Propositions 4.8 and 4.9, to the study of a mapping from beliefs z^e about the mean values of inflation and the output gap to the actual means $E[z]$ of these two variables. Furthermore, the mapping in question is once again of the form (2.19), except that the matrix B must be replaced by a matrix $\tilde{B} \neq A^{-1}$ in the case of Preston's model of learning dynamics.

E-stability depends on the properties of the matrix $\tilde{B}$ in exactly the same way as was discussed in connection with Proposition 4.8; the unstable and stable cases again correspond to dynamics of the sort shown in Figures 4.3 and 4.4, respectively. The boundary between E-instability and E-stability is again the case in which the $\dot{\pi}^e = 0$ and $\dot{x}^e = 0$ loci coincide; but this once again corresponds to the case in which there exists a continuum of steady-state equilibrium inflation rates. Moreover, the conditions under which there exists a continuum of steady states are the same for Preston's model as for that of Bullard and Mitra, given that *the rational-expectations equilibria* of the models coincide, even if the implied learning dynamics are generally different. Thus the critical parameter values in both cases are exactly those for which (2.7) holds with equality.

The present conclusions in the case of the simple family of policy rules (1.14) should not be taken to imply that the conditions for E-stability and those for determinacy of r.e.e. are always the same; in many cases they are not, as Bullard and Mitra (2002) and Evans and Honkapohja (2002b) emphasize. (Nor is it generally the case that the conditions for E-stability implied by the approach of Bullard and Mitra always coincide with those implied by an analysis like that of Preston, as illustrated in Preston (2002b).) Hence the question whether given policy rules result in an equilibrium that is stable under learning dynamics deserves separate study.[43] The important conclusion from this section should be rather that it is possible to design interest-rate feedback rules so that they imply that plausible learning dynamics should converge to a rational-expectations equilibrium associated with the rule. If r.e.e. is determinate in the case of such a rule, the equilibrium to which the learning dynamics converge is typically the unique stationary equilibrium.

2.4 Determinants of Inflation

Having established that interest-rate rules can result in a determinate equilibrium, and even that plausible learning dynamics may be expected to converge to the beliefs required for this equilibrium, I turn now to the further characterization of the dynamics of endogenous variables in such an equilibrium. I am particularly interested in the determinants of equilibrium inflation under the kinds of policies just considered and the conditions under which fluctuations in the price level can be minimized.

I have discussed several classes of simple interest-rate rules with the property that the equilibrium conditions can be written entirely in terms of $\pi_t - \bar{\pi}$, $x_t - \bar{x}$, $\hat{\imath}_t - \bar{\imath}_t$, and $r_t^n - \bar{\imath}_t + \bar{\pi}$. This implies that when equilibrium is determinate, it is possible to solve for the endogenous variables in this list (the first three) as a function of initial conditions and the current and expected future values of the exogenous variable (the last one). In the case of policy rules (1.14) or (2.10), the equation system involves *no* predetermined endogenous variables, so that there are no relevant initial conditions (other than those relating to the path of the exogenous variables). One therefore obtains in these cases a solution of the form

$$\pi_t = \bar{\pi} + \sum_{j=0}^{\infty} \psi_j^{\pi} E_t\left(\hat{r}_{t+j}^n - \bar{\imath}_{t+j} + \bar{\pi}\right), \tag{2.31}$$

$$x_t = \bar{x} + \sum_{j=0}^{\infty} \psi_j^{x} E_t\left(\hat{r}_{t+j}^n - \bar{\imath}_{t+j} + \bar{\pi}\right), \tag{2.32}$$

43. I consider this question again in the context of rules that seek to implement optimal policy in Section 5 of Chapter 7.

$$\hat{\imath}_t = \bar{\imath}_t + \sum_{j=0}^{\infty} \psi_j^i E_t\big(\hat{r}_{t+j}^n - \bar{\imath}_{t+j} + \bar{\pi}\big). \tag{2.33}$$

In particular, if both eigenvalues of A are outside the unit circle (the condition for determinacy), then A^{-1} is a stable matrix, and one can obtain a unique bounded solution to (C.19) by solving forward, namely,

$$z_t = \sum_{j=0}^{\infty} A^{-j-1} a E_t\big(\hat{r}_{t+j}^n - \bar{\imath}_{t+j} + \bar{\pi}\big). \tag{2.34}$$

This allows one to identify the coefficients in equations (2.31) and (2.32). Substitution of the solutions for these variables into the policy rule then permits identification of the coefficients in (2.33) as well.

However, in the case of a rule such as (2.8) or (2.12), the lagged nominal interest rate is a predetermined endogenous variable that is relevant for equilibrium determination because of the way that it enters the policy rule. In cases of this sort, one obtains instead solutions of the form

$$\pi_t = \bar{\pi} + \omega^{\pi}\,(\hat{\imath}_{t-1} - \bar{\imath}_{t-1}) + \sum_{j=0}^{\infty} \psi_j^{\pi} E_t\big(\hat{r}_{t+j}^n - \bar{\imath}_{t+j} + \bar{\pi}\big),$$

and similarly for the other endogenous variables.

Thus the model implies that for policy rules of these types, equilibrium inflation depends solely upon the path of the *gap* between the natural rate of interest $\hat{r}_t^n$ and the intercept term $\bar{\imath}_t$ indicating the tightness of central-bank policy. In the case of the inertial interest-rate rules, equilibrium inflation also depends upon a lagged interest rate (specifically, upon $\hat{\imath}_{t-1} - \bar{\imath}_{t-1}$), but in equilibrium this variable is itself a function of the history of the gaps $\hat{r}_{t-j}^n - \bar{\imath}_{t-j}$. As has already been noted in Chapter 2, the present theory of inflation determination thus has a distinctively Wicksellian flavor: Variations in the rate of inflation depend upon the interaction between the real factors that determine the natural rate of interest, on the one hand, and the way in which the central bank adjusts short-term nominal interest rates, on the other. Inflation will be stable insofar as the stance of monetary policy is varied to keep up with the exogenous variations in the natural rate of interest that occur as a result of real disturbances and not varied otherwise; it will be variable insofar as either factor varies other than in perfect tandem with the other. The analysis here has a more fully Wicksellian character than that presented in Chapter 2, because I am now able to distinguish between the natural rate of interest (which *would* be the equilibrium real rate of return in the absence of nominal rigidities and depends purely upon real factors) and the actual real rate of return (which can differ from the natural rate as a result of short-run disequilibrium and is affected by monetary

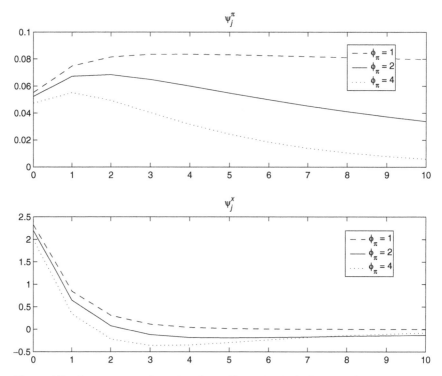

Figure 4.5 *Consequences of varying the coefficient ϕ_π in the Taylor rule.*

policy among other factors). Thus I am now able to explain economic fluctuations in terms of the development of a gap between the natural and the actual real rate of return and discuss the role of monetary policy in helping to minimize such gaps.

Examples of numerical solutions for the coefficients $\{\psi_j^\pi\}$ and $\{\psi_j^x\}$ in the case of the Taylor rules of the form (1.14) are presented in Figures 4.5 and 4.6. The numerical values assigned to the structural parameters β, σ, κ are again taken from Table 5.1. Here I take as the baseline policy rule a Taylor rule with coefficients $\phi_\pi = 2$, $\phi_x = 1$. Figure 4.5 then illustrates the consequences of varying ϕ_π around this baseline value, while Figure 4.6 illustrates the consequences of varying ϕ_x. Observe that for a range of parameter values representing reaction functions similar to actual central-bank policies, the coefficients ψ_j^π and ψ_j^x are positive for all small enough j, which are the coefficients of primary importance in determining the equilibrium responses to typical shocks.[44] Thus one finds that higher output gaps

44. The coefficients for large j would dominate in computing the effects of news about the natural rate or monetary policy only if the news were to affect expectations *only* about conditions many quarters in the future.

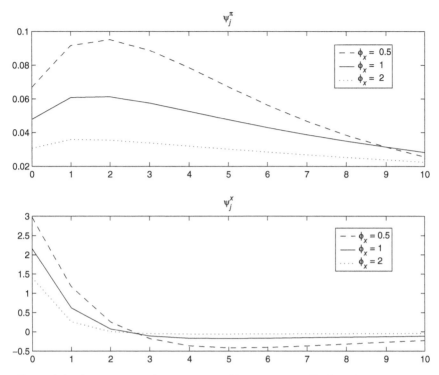

Figure 4.6   *Consequences of varying the coefficient ϕ_x in the Taylor rule.*

and inflation result from increases in the current or expected future natural rate of interest, not offset by a sufficient tightening of monetary policy, or by current or expected future loosening of monetary policy, not justified by a decline in the natural rate of interest. This is essentially a forward-looking variant of the traditional Wicksellian analysis. Also observe that a higher response coefficient on inflation in the Taylor rule results in weaker equilibrium responses of inflation to exogenous disturbances, especially to disturbances expected several quarters in the future; the response of output is also reduced, though less dramatically. A higher response coefficient on the output gap in the Taylor rule significantly attenuates the equilibrium response of the output gap to news about the natural rate or monetary policy in the current quarter or the next one, and this also weakens the equilibrium response of inflation.

  The consequences of interest-rate inertia in the Taylor rule are shown in Figure 4.7. Here one assumes a rule of the form (2.8), with values for ϕ_π and ϕ_x as in the baseline case of Figures 4.5 and 4.6, but with various positive values for ρ. Observe that for given ϕ_π and ϕ_x, a higher value of ρ reduces the equilibrium response of both inflation and output, though

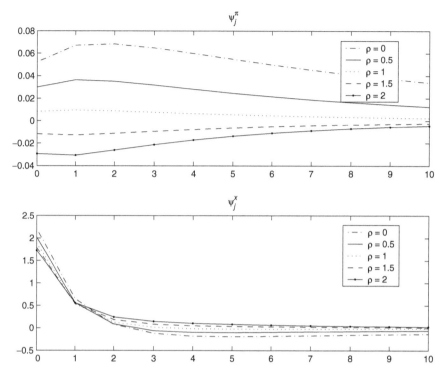

Figure 4.7 *Consequences of varying the coefficient ρ in the Taylor rule with interest-rate inertia.*

the effect is much more dramatic in the case of the inflation response. This should be intuitive, since for given ϕ_π and ϕ_x, a higher ρ implies a larger *eventual* interest-rate response to a sustained increase in inflation or the output gap. When one considers superinertial rules (i.e., rules with $\rho > 1$), the response of inflation to an increase in the natural rate (not offset by a corresponding tightening of monetary policy) actually becomes *negative*. This is because the output gap still increases, as a result of which interest rates increase; the strong interest-rate inertia then implies an expectation of much higher *future* interest rates as well, even if the output gap no longer exists. The expectation of future tightening leads to an expectation of *lower* future output gaps, which in turn motivates an immediate reduction in inflation, despite the initially higher output gap. (The reduction in inflation is insufficient to prevent interest rates from rising under the policy rule, as there would otherwise be no increase in expected future interest rates to generate the incentive to disinflation.)

These figures indicate the immediate response of inflation and output to a disturbance that shifts the current and/or expected future values of $\hat{r}_t^n$

or $\bar{\imath}_t$. The figures do not, however, indicate the dynamic response to such disturbances. In the case that $\rho = 0$, inflation and the output gap are both purely forward-looking functions of the current and expected future disturbances, as indicated in (2.31) and (2.32). In this case, the dynamics of the response of inflation and output to a shock are a straightforward consequence of the dynamics of the disturbance itself. (A transitory disturbance must have a purely transitory effect; a more persistent disturbance has a correspondingly more persistent effect, though the effect is also larger, owing to the effects of the anticipation of the continued disturbance in the future.) But when the policy rule incorporates feedback from lagged endogenous variables, it is also possible to obtain persistent effects on inflation and output from even a purely transitory disturbance. Since estimated central-bank reaction functions generally incorporate lagged endogenous variables of several sorts, both lagged interest rates and lags of variables such as inflation and the output gap as well (as discussed in Chapter 1), it is not implausible to assume such lags in seeking to account for the degree of persistence of the responses of output and inflation to identified monetary policy shocks in historical data. Alternatively, of course, one could simply assume that the monetary policy disturbance $\{\bar{\imath}_t\}$ is serially correlated. This would suffice to allow the model to predict persistent responses to a monetary policy shock, and indeed the two explanations are not even conceptually distinguishable. For example, a policy rule of the form (1.14) where

$$\bar{\imath}_t - \bar{\pi} = \rho(\bar{\imath}_{t-1} - \bar{\pi}) + \epsilon_t$$

and $\{\epsilon_t\}$ is an i.i.d. mean-zero shock is equivalent to a policy rule of the form

$$(\tilde{\imath}_t = \rho\tilde{\imath}_{t-1}) + \phi_\pi(\tilde{\pi}_t - \rho\tilde{\pi}_{t-1}) + (\phi_x/4)(\tilde{x}_t - \rho\tilde{x}_{t-1}) + \epsilon_t, \qquad (2.35)$$

where

$$\tilde{\imath}_t \equiv i_t - \bar{r} - \bar{\pi}, \qquad \tilde{\pi}_t \equiv \pi_t - \bar{\pi}, \qquad \tilde{x}_t \equiv x_t - \bar{x}.$$

This representation of the policy rule now has a serially uncorrelated disturbance term, but feedback from lagged endogenous variables.

As an example of the kind of persistent response to a transitory shock that can result in the case of feedback from lagged endogenous variables, Figure 4.8 presents impulse responses to a monetary policy shock in the case of a policy rule of the form (2.35), where again $\{\epsilon_t\}$ is an i.i.d. mean-zero shock. In the figure, the inertia coefficients are set equal to $\rho = 0.6, 0.7$, or 0.8, while ϕ_π and ϕ_x are chosen to imply the same long-run responses $\Phi_\pi \equiv (1-\rho)^{-1}\phi_\pi = 2$ and $\Phi_x \equiv (1-\rho)^{-1}\phi_x = 1$ in each case. Because these coefficients satisfy (2.7) in each case, equilibrium is determinate. The figure shows the dynamic response to an unexpected monetary tightening (an unexpected increase in ϵ_t that raises the short-term interest rate by 1 percentage point for given values of the other arguments of the central-bank reaction function).[45] The baseline case is chosen to be $\rho = 0.7$ because this is approximately the sum of the coefficients on lags of the federal funds rate in the rule estimated by Rotemberg and Woodford (1997), as discussed below, and I wish to provide insight into the theoretical responses obtained in their more complicated model.

One observes that the responses of both output and inflation to such a shock last for many quarters; in the case of the present completely forward-looking model of inflation and output determination, the degree of persistence of all four responses is determined directly by the assumed value of ρ in the policy rule. The amplitude of the equilibrium responses for any given long-run responses to inflation and output in the policy rule also depends on the value of ρ. The initial effect on output is essentially the same regardless of ρ, but the effect is more persistent as ρ is larger; and a more persistent output contraction reduces inflation more (and more persistently). Hence the reduction in inflation is greater, and the effects on both variables are more persistent for larger values of ρ.

In the case of sufficiently modest values of ρ, a contractionary monetary policy shock is associated with a temporary increase in nominal interest rates; but for $\rho = 0.7$ or larger, the predicted inflation reduction is strong enough that nominal interest rates are actually predicted to *decrease* temporarily. Thus the prediction is for no "liquidity effect" in the latter cases, a feature that has often been considered an embarrassment for calibrated optimization-based models of the monetary transmission mechanism (see, e.g., Kimball, 1995, or Edge, 2000). Figure 4.8 shows that a liquidity effect is possible for some parameter values. However, a more satisfactory resolution of the problem requires that additional delays in the effects of monetary policy be introduced, as discussed in Chapter 5. There I argue that the response shown in Figure 4.8 for the case $\rho = 0.7$ is not too different from the empirically estimated responses for the second quarter following the shock and later. (By that time, nominal interest rates are predicted to return nearly to the level that would have been expected in the absence of the shock, as shown in Figure 5.2.) It is the estimated responses in the first two quarters that cannot be explained by this simple model; and here the real puzzle is not that nominal interest rates temporarily increase, but rather that output and inflation do not *immediately fall*, as indicated in Figure 4.8. Once that problem is solved, the problem of obtaining a liquidity effect is easily solved as well.

---

45. The responses plotted for the nominal and real interest rate and for inflation are all expressed in percentage points of the equivalent annualized rate, so that "inflation" actually means the variable $4\pi_t$, and so on. The shock increases $4\hat{\imath}_0$ by 1 percentage point.

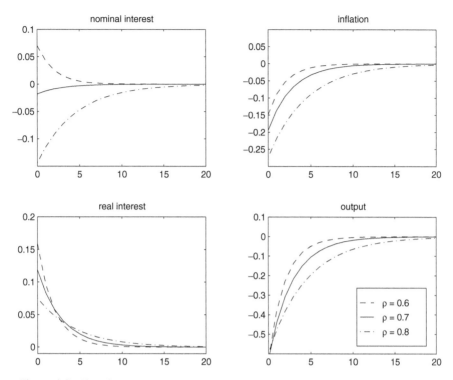

Figure 4.8 *Impulse responses to a contractionary monetary policy shock for alternative degrees of policy inertia.*

The present model can also be used to predict the response of the economy to real disturbances of various sorts, under one or another monetary policy rule. This is important for the explanation of business fluctuations, since it is widely agreed that the greater part of cyclical variation in real activity is ultimately caused by real disturbances rather than by random monetary policy.[46] But it is also important for the choice of a monetary policy rule, for the crucial question for the theory of monetary policy has to do with the choice of the *systematic* component of monetary policy (and not the exogenous random component, which one plainly wishes to eliminate to the extent possible), in the light of the implications of alternative systematic policies for the way that the economy responds to disturbances that, in their origin, have nothing to do with monetary policy.

46. This is the implication, e.g., of the variance decompositions implied by typical VAR studies. Again see, e.g., Christiano et al. (1999).

I do not attempt a detailed treatment of this issue here. However, two general lessons from the baseline model are worth pointing out. The first is that, insofar as I am concerned solely with the responses of inflation, the output gap, and nominal interest rates to the real disturbances (and in Chapter 6 I explain why these are exactly the variables that should matter from the point of view of social welfare under the assumptions that underlie the present model), and insofar as I restrict attention to policy rules of the general type considered here (and in Chapter 8 I show that optimal policy can be represented in this way), then the only feature of the real disturbances that matters is *their effect upon the path of the natural rate of interest.* The second is that the responses of inflation and the output gap to a disturbance to the natural rate of interest *are exactly the same* as their responses to a monetary policy shock (disturbance to the $\bar{\imath}_t$ term in the policy rule) that has the same serial correlation properties and the opposite sign. Both conclusions follow from the fact that in the case of the classes of policy rules considered above, equilibrium inflation and the output gap are functions solely of the path of the gap $\hat{r}_t^n - \bar{\imath}_t$. Thus Figure 4.8, for example, also indicates the response of inflation and the output gap to an unexpected reduction in the natural rate of interest, if the natural rate follows a first-order autoregressive process with a coefficient of ρ and the monetary policy rule is of the form (1.14).

Thus far I have considered inflation and output-gap determination only in the case of a purely forward-looking model of inflation determination, namely, the basic Calvo pricing model introduced in Chapter 3. But as discussed in Section 3.2 of that chapter, there is a fair amount of evidence suggesting that a model that allows for some degree of inflation inertia can better explain observed inflation dynamics. To what extent does allowance for inflation inertia require a modification of the neo-Wicksellian account just developed?

In fact, inflation inertia of the kind assumed by Christiano et al. (2001) makes only a small difference for the present qualitative results, though, of course, the exact specification matters for quantitative purposes. Let the aggregate-supply relation (1.13) be replaced by

$$\pi_t - \gamma \pi_{t-1} = \kappa x_t + \beta E_t [\pi_{t+1} - \gamma \pi_t], \tag{2.36}$$

where $0 \leq \gamma \leq 1$ indicates the degree of indexation of individual prices to a lagged price index, as in Section 3.2 of Chapter 3. For simplicity again consider a policy rule of the form (1.14). The complete system of equations for the determination of the equilibrium paths of inflation, output, and the nominal interest rate then consists of equations (1.12), (1.14), and (2.36). It is then easily seen that in the case of a policy rule that implies a determinate equilibrium, this equilibrium is described by laws of motion of the form

$$\pi_t = \bar{\pi} + \omega_\pi (\pi_{t-1} - \bar{\pi}) + \sum_{j=0}^{\infty} \psi_j^\pi E_t (\hat{r}_{t+j}^n + \bar{\pi} - \bar{\iota}_{t+j}), \qquad (2.37)$$

$$x_t = \bar{x} + \omega_x (\pi_{t-1} - \bar{\pi}) + \sum_{j=0}^{\infty} \psi_j^x E_t (\hat{r}_{t+j}^n + \bar{\pi} - \bar{\iota}_{t+j}), \qquad (2.38)$$

$$\hat{\iota}_t = \bar{\iota}_t + \omega_i (\pi_{t-1} - \bar{\pi}) + \sum_{j=0}^{\infty} \psi_j^i E_t (\hat{r}_{t+j}^n + \bar{\pi} - \bar{\iota}_{t+j}). \qquad (2.39)$$

Figure 4.9 plots the numerical values of the coefficients ψ_j^π and ψ_j^x as a function of the horizon j for three alternative values of γ. Here the assumed values of β, σ, and κ are again taken from Table 5.1, while the coefficients assumed in the policy rule are $\phi_\pi = 2$, $\phi_x = 1$. (Thus the case $\gamma = 0$ in this

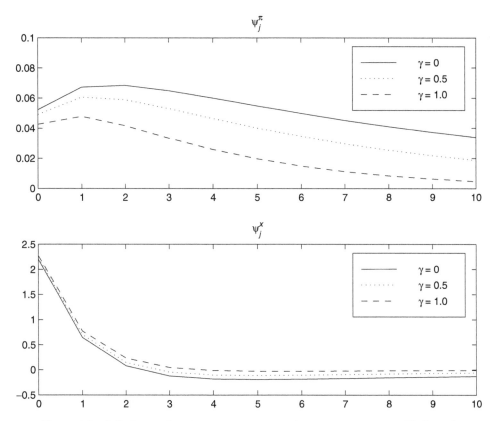

Figure 4.9 *Inflation and output-gap responses under a contemporaneous Taylor rule for alternative degrees of inflation inertia.*

figure corresponds once again to the baseline cases of Figures 4.5 and 4.6, and to the $\rho = 0$ case of Figure 4.7.) Observe once again that the qualitative impact on inflation and the output gap of news at date t is the same as discussed earlier: An increase in the expected natural rate of interest (now or in the near future) increases both inflation and the output gap, whereas a tightening of monetary policy lowers both. The main difference made by a positive value of γ in this regard is that the inflation rate is more sensitive to expectations regarding the natural rate and the policy-rule intercept many quarters in the future.

The other difference in the response of inflation and the output gap to these two types of disturbances results from the presence of the $\pi_{t-1} - \bar{\pi}$ terms in the equations (2.37) and (2.38). When $\gamma = 0$, these terms are zero, but as γ increases, ω_π takes an increasingly larger positive value, whereas ω_x takes an increasingly larger negative value.[47] In this model, for any given expectations regarding current and future natural rates of interest and monetary policy, the fact of a higher rate of inflation in the past acts as an adverse "supply shock," increasing current inflation while lowering the current output gap. This results in an additional mechanism for the propagation of the effects of fluctuations in the natural rate and/or in the monetary policy rule applied by the central bank. Nonetheless, it continues to be true that the natural rate of interest is a sufficient statistic for the effects of all real disturbances on the evolution of inflation and the output gap; that it is only the gap between the natural rate and the Taylor-rule intercept at each date that matters in this regard; and that at least the immediate effects of disturbances have the same sign as in the earlier analysis.

2.5   Inflation Stabilization through Commitment to a Taylor Rule

I now briefly consider the implications of the model of inflation determination just developed for the design of a monetary policy that would succeed in stabilizing the general level of prices, or more generally in stabilizing the rate of inflation around some target rate.[48] The theory of inflation implied by solutions such as (2.31) yields a simple prescription for a policy under which (if the private sector regards the central bank's policy commitment as perfectly credible) inflation should never deviate from the target rate $\bar{\pi}$. The central bank can commit itself to a policy rule belonging to

---

47. For the parameter values used in Figure 4.9, one obtains $\omega_\pi = 0.42$, $\omega_x = -1.95$ in the case $\gamma = 0.5$, and $\omega_\pi = 0.73$, $\omega_x = -3.17$ in the case $\gamma = 1$.

48. Here I assume without further discussion a locally Ricardian fiscal regime, in the sense discussed in Section 4; the role of fiscal policy in the design of a regime conducive to price stability is taken up further there. I also take it for granted that price stability is the goal of monetary policy, without seeking to justify such an objective; the welfare-theoretic justification for such a goal is treated in Chapter 6.

one of the families discussed in the previous section (or a generalization of these), with the further stipulations that (i) the time-varying intercept term $\bar{\imath}_t$ should track the exogenous variation in the natural rate of interest, so that $\bar{\imath}_t = \hat{r}_t^n + \bar{\pi}$ at all times, and (ii) response coefficients such as ϕ_π, ϕ_x, and ρ should be chosen so as to imply a determinate rational-expectations equilibrium. The latter proviso implies that the rule should respect the Taylor principle (at least in the case of each of the simple families considered above), but it may also place further restrictions on the response coefficients as well.

As shown in the previous section, as long as the policy rule involves feedback only from current, lagged, or expected future values of the variables $\pi_t - \bar{\pi}$, $x_t - \bar{x}$, and $\hat{\imath}_t - \bar{\imath}_t$, then *if* equilibrium is determinate, the solution makes each of the variables just listed a function solely of current and expected future values of the gap terms $\hat{r}_t^n - \bar{\imath}_t + \bar{\pi}$ plus lagged values of the endogenous variables that enter the central bank's feedback rule and/or the aggregate supply relation.[49] This means that if $\bar{\imath}_t = \hat{r}_t^n + \bar{\pi}$ at all times, there are no equilibrium fluctuations in the endogenous variables, except those due to nonzero initial values of those variables; the latter variation is purely deterministic, and approaches zero as time passes, assuming a credible permanent commitment to the policy. Thus such a policy should succeed in principle in complete stabilization of both inflation and the output gap (as here defined).[50] Note that this conclusion holds equally in the case that one assumes an aggregate-supply relation of the form (2.36) incorporating inflation inertia.

Such an approach to policy would make the natural rate of interest a key concept in monetary policymaking. Furthermore, unlike some discussions (see, e.g., Monetary Policy Committee, 1999) of the "neutral rate of interest," which imply that this should not vary over time, the present theoretical analysis implies that the natural rate of interest should vary in response to any of a wide range of types of real disturbances, and keeping track of its current value would be an important (and far from trivial) task of central-bank staff under such a regime. Of course, insofar as the policy rule involves feedback from the output gap, as allowed for in the previous discussion, implementation of such a rule would also require a central bank to track variations in the current natural rate of output (a topic already much discussed in most central banks). However, the previous analysis implies that

49. A similar conclusion holds if I allow for lagged endogenous terms in the IS relation as well, as discussed in Section 1.2 of Chapter 5.

50. That it is possible to completely stabilize both inflation and the output gap depends, of course, upon the absence in the baseline model of inefficient supply disturbances of the kind discussed in Section 4.5 of Chapter 6. The nature of the trade-off between inflation stabilization and output-gap stabilization goals that arises in the presence of such disturbances is considered in detail in Chapters 6 through 8.

this concept is less essential to the central bank's task. For given an ability to adjust $\bar{\iota}_t$ perfectly in response to variations in the natural rate of interest, it would not matter what the responses to endogenous variables are, as long as the response coefficients are large enough to imply determinacy. As we have seen, the latter concern does not require any nonzero response to the output gap. Thus it would be possible, in principle, to commit to a rule such as (1.14) with $\bar{\iota}_t = r_t^n + \bar{\pi}$, $\phi_\pi > 1$, and $\phi_x = 0$, and completely stabilize inflation and the output gap; but the implementation of such a rule would not require the central bank to be aware of the current natural rate of output.

On the other hand, simply producing an accurate estimate of the current natural rate of interest and adjusting the bank's operating target for an overnight interest rate accordingly is not quite sufficient for inflation stabilization; a commitment to the right sort of response to variations in endogenous variables such as inflation is also necessary in order to ensure determinacy. It is true that if the central bank's adjustment of $\bar{\iota}_t$ so as to track variations in the natural rate of interest is exact, the precise *degree* of response to endogenous state variables is irrelevant as long as it suffices to put one in the range required for determinacy. This is because, in equilibrium, variations in those variables never occur; the commitment to a response to them matters not in order to change the nature of the desired equilibrium, but simply in order to exclude *other* possible equilibria. However, one must recognize that in practice, perfect tracking of the current natural rate of interest is impossible, as real-time information about the natural rate is inevitably imprecise.[51] In this case, for any given degree of irreducible variation in the gap process $\hat{r}_t^n - \bar{\iota}_t$ due to limits on the central bank's ability to track variations in the natural rate, the equilibrium fluctuations in inflation implied by a solution such as (2.31) also depend upon the policy rule's response coefficients.

If one's goal is simply to stabilize inflation (and the output gap, as these goals are equivalent in the present model) to the greatest extent possible, then one would want to choose response coefficients that make the coefficients $\{\psi_j^\pi\}$ and $\{\psi_j^x\}$ as small as possible. In the case of the backward-looking Taylor rules, (1.14) or (2.8), one can make all of these coefficients simultaneously as close to zero as one likes simply by making the response coefficients ϕ_π and ϕ_x large enough. (In fact, it suffices to make *either* of these coefficients sufficiently large; for an equilibrium with small fluctuations in the output gap must also have small fluctuations in inflation, and vice versa.) Through this approach one can, in principle, make the equilibrium fluctuations in inflation arbitrarily small, even without attempting to track variations in the natural rate of interest at all. This represents an

---

51. The way in which optimal policy is affected by imperfect observability of the current state of the economy is considered formally in Chapter 8.

advantage of backward-looking Taylor rules over the forward-looking variants; for in the latter case, making the response coefficient on the inflation forecast too large results in indeterminacy (see Figure 4.1), as is also found by Bernanke and Woodford (1997) in a related model. There is thus a limit on the extent to which inflation fluctuations in response to real disturbances can be reduced using a forward-looking rule, if one restricts attention to rules that result in a determinate equilibrium.[52]

However, complete reliance upon the threat of extreme responses to inflation and/or output-gap variations should they occur, as a means of preventing such variations from ever occurring, is not obviously the most desirable approach. For under such a regime, there is clearly a danger that random noise in the particular measure to which the central bank responds might require violent adjustments of interest rates, which in turn create havoc in the economy. If one supposes that the inflation measure to which the central bank responds represents the average of the prices set by optimizing suppliers, plus an exogenous measurement error term, then a policy rule with a very large coefficient ϕ_π would cause no great trouble *if* pricesetters were able to observe the quarter t measurement-error disturbance *before* choosing new prices for quarter t. In that case, the equilibrium rate of actual inflation would adjust to (nearly perfectly) offset the measurement error, so that the inflation measure used by the central bank would be nearly perfectly stabilized. This would result in some variation in actual inflation, but this would be limited by the size of the measurement error, and fluctuations in interest rates would be minimal. However, in the more realistic case that quarter t prices are chosen *prior* to private-sector observation of the measurement error in the government statistics, it would not be possible for private-sector pricing decisions to offset the measurement error, and large interest-rate variations would occur in equilibrium. This could make too extreme a version of such a strategy highly undesirable. Thus if one wishes to stabilize inflation to the greatest extent possible, it is fairly certain that attempting to vary policy in response to estimates of the natural rate of interest improves policy.

On the other hand, as I show in Chapters 6 and 7, there are good reasons why a central bank may not wish to fully stabilize inflation—for example, because the amount of interest-rate variation required would be undesirable. In this case, a constrained-optimal equilibrium still involves nontrivial fluctuations in inflation and the output gap in response to real disturbances,

---

52. In the case of rules in the family (2.10), it is still possible to reduce inflation fluctuations to an arbitrary extent without loss of determinacy by making the output-gap coefficient ϕ_x large. But this term in the rule is the same as in a backward-looking (standard) Taylor rule, and a rule with the main weight on that term is essentially equivalent to a backward-looking rule.

and as a result, feedback from these endogenous variables may substitute for response to more direct measures of the real disturbances. It then may be possible, as I show in Chapter 8, to find an optimal policy rule that may be expressed as an interest-rate feedback rule in which there is no time-varying term $\bar{\imath}_t$ at all.

2.6 Inflation Targeting Rules

In an alternative possible approach to ensuring price stability, the policy rule to which the central bank is committed need involve no explicit reference to the natural rate of interest: The central bank commits itself to a *targeting rule,* according to which it is committed to adjust its interest-rate instrument to whatever extent appears to be necessary in order to ensure that a certain *target criterion* is continuously fulfilled.[53] Under such a specification of the policy rule, the central bank's explicit commitment is to the achievement of the target criterion, which need not involve any explicit reference to the desired path of the nominal interest rate, even though this is the central bank's policy instrument.

For example, the central bank might be committed to ensure the target criterion

$$\pi_t = \bar{\pi}, \tag{2.40}$$

where $\bar{\pi}$ is a desired rate of inflation. (This is sometimes called "strict inflation targeting," to distinguish such a commitment from a target criterion that takes into account both the projected inflation rate and other variables such as the output gap.) In order for this to represent a coherent policy commitment, there must *exist* an equilibrium in which the target criterion is continuously satisfied under some possible evolution of the nominal interest rate. Furthermore, this equilibrium must be *determinate,* so that a commitment to achievement of the target criterion suffices to determine the required evolution of the interest rate. (This is an additional reason to be concerned with determinacy in the case of a targeting rule, apart from the concern raised in Section 2.2, which is that a policy that results in indeterminacy may allow undesirable fluctuations to occur.)

One is thus led to study the set of solutions to a system of equations consisting of the structural equations plus a target criterion such as (2.40),

---

53. This is what Svensson (1999a) and Svensson and Woodford (2003) call a "specific targeting rule," to distinguish this kind of policy commitment from a conception of inflation targeting in which the central bank is committed to a loss function by means of which it evaluates alternative possible outcomes, but not to bring about an outcome with any specific property, such as a particular inflation rate. In this study, "targeting rules" always refer to specific targeting rules.

intended to specify a monetary policy commitment. This question can be studied using similar methods as in the case that the policy commitment is specified by an interest-rate feedback rule. In the context of the basic neo-Wicksellian model, a commitment of the form (2.40) does imply a determinate equilibrium. Using (1.13), one sees that if (2.40) holds for each period $t \geq 0$, one must have $x_t = \bar{x}$ at all times, where $\bar{x}$ is again the steady-state output gap consistent with the inflation target $\bar{\pi}$. Substituting these solutions for inflation and output into (1.12), one finds that it is necessary that $\hat{i}_t = \hat{r}_t^n + \bar{\pi}$ at all times. If this implied interest-rate path is consistent with the zero lower bound (a question that depends both on how negative the natural rate of interest sometimes becomes and on how high the target rate of inflation $\bar{\pi}$ has been chosen), then such an equilibrium exists, and it is furthermore uniquely determined.

However, the question of determinacy is not so trivial as this example may suggest. Suppose instead that the target criterion is of the form

$$E_t \pi_{t+k} = \bar{\pi}, \qquad (2.41)$$

for some horizon $k \geq 1$. This means that the central bank's instrument decision for period t is chosen with a view toward the effect of a given interest-rate decision on its forecast of inflation in a future period $t + k$. This is a type of target criterion that is often discussed in the literature on inflation targeting, and it corresponds to the criterion that is the official basis for policy decisions by the Bank of England, namely, a commitment to ensure that RPIX inflation is predicted to equal 2.5 percent at a horizon eight quarters in the future (Vickers, 1998).

A policy that ensures that the criterion (2.41) is satisfied in all periods $t \geq 0$ similarly implies that in any rational-expectations equilibrium, $E_t x_{t+k} = \bar{x}$ and $E_t \hat{i}_{t+k} = E_t \hat{r}_{t+k}^n + \bar{\pi}$ for all $t \geq 0$, through an argument like the one just made. But the components of these variables that are *not* forecastable k periods in advance are *not* determined. This can easily be seen. Consider any stochastic process for inflation of the form

$$\pi_t = \bar{\pi}_t + u_t, \qquad (2.42)$$

where u_t is a random variable with the property that $E_t u_{t+k} = 0$. Now suppose that (2.42) were itself to represent the policy commitment, for some particular (exogenously specified) process $\{u_t\}$. By the same reasoning as before, an equilibrium exists in which this inflation process can be achieved, as long as it implies a path for the nominal interest rate that is always non-negative. (In the generic case, if $\bar{\pi}$ is chosen high enough for there to be *any* equilibria consistent with (2.41) holding in all periods, then it is possible to choose an infinite number of processes $\{u_t\}$ in which the fluctuations are modest enough for this property to be satisfied.) Hence to *each* choice of the process $\{u_t\}$ for which the implied nominal interest-rate process is always nonnegative there corresponds a distinct equilibrium inflation process consistent with criterion (2.41). This is thus an example of an inflation-targeting rule that leads to indeterminacy.

This conclusion does not depend on the assumption of a purely forward-looking model of inflation determination. If the aggregate-supply specification (1.13) is replaced with (2.36), the conclusion still obtains. Once again, one can solve the AS relation for the implied process for the output gap and then the IS relation for the implied process for the nominal interest rate, starting from any inflation process of the form (2.42), as long as the process $\{u_t\}$ satisfies certain bounds that ensure a nonnegative implied nominal interest rate.

The argument that is typically made for the desirability of a target criterion such as (2.41), with a horizon k some years in the future, is that it would be undesirable not to allow temporary fluctuations in inflation in response to real disturbances, while the central bank should nonetheless provide clear assurances that inflation will eventually be returned to its long-run target level. But while a pattern of response of this general type to certain kinds of disturbances may well be desirable, as we shall see in Chapter 7, it does not follow that a commitment *solely* to keep medium-term inflation expectations anchored suffices to define a desirable policy rule. If (2.41) is taken to be *the* target criterion that should determine the central bank's instrument choice in period t (rather than merely one among several criteria that an optimal equilibrium should jointly satisfy), then it is inadequate to the task, as it fails to define an action that is required for consistency with the target criterion, in addition to failing to specify what sort of transitory variation in inflation in response to real disturbances is actually to be desired.

But target criteria can be defined that suffice to determine an equilibrium; (2.40) is a simple example. Moreover, I argue in Chapter 7 that targeting rules have important advantages as a way of specifying a monetary policy commitment. A characteristic feature of the optimal targeting rules that I discuss in Chapters 7 and 8 is that they are defined entirely in terms of the projected paths of "target variables" such as inflation and the output gap, variables in terms of which it is possible to measure the deadweight losses associated with incomplete macroeconomic stabilization.

The natural rate of interest then plays no role in the expression of an optimal target criterion, as neither it nor the gap between market interest rates and the natural rate plays the role of a target variable in the present characterization (see Chapter 6) of welfare-theoretic stabilization objectives. Nonetheless, the natural rate of interest plays an important role under such a policy as a critical piece of information for the central bank in seeking to *implement* the targeting rule. In order to implement a targeting rule, the central bank must determine what interest-rate setting is consistent with projected paths for the target variables of the right sort. According to the model developed in this chapter, the natural rate of interest is a key summary statistic, describing the way in which real disturbances of many sorts may change the instrument setting that is necessary to achieve given paths for inflation and the output gap—the two variables that are most commonly considered appropriate target variables for monetary stabilization (and with considerable reason, as we shall see).

As an example, one may consider the problem of implementing the strict inflation target (2.40). Because the central bank must choose an interest-rate operating target for period t before the inflation rate π_t is observed (and indeed, in the present model, π_t is partially *determined* by the central bank's decision), the interest-rate decision must be based on a *projection* of what current-period inflation is expected to be as a function of the central bank's interest-rate decision. One way that one might imagine this occurring is the following. Suppose that in each period t, the period t exogenous disturbances are first realized and observed by the private sector; period t private-sector expectations are then formed; the central bank observes both the current disturbances and the current state of private-sector expectations and decides upon its target for i_t; and finally, private spending and pricing decisions for period t are made, in response to the current disturbances, private expectations, and the level of interest rates.

The output gap determined in this last step is given by (1.12), while the inflation rate is given by (1.13), with (1.12) used to substitute for x_t in this equation. The solution thus obtained for inflation is

$$\pi_t = (\beta + \kappa\sigma)E_t\pi_{t+1} + \kappa E_t x_{t+1} - \kappa\sigma\left(\hat{\imath}_t - \hat{r}_t^n\right). \tag{2.43}$$

Suppose that the central bank uses this (correct) model[54] to project period t inflation as a function of its interest-rate decision. Then the interest-rate target that would lead it to project an inflation rate consistent with the target criterion (2.40) is obtained by equating the right-hand side of (2.43) to $\bar{\pi}$ and solving for $\hat{\imath}_t$. One obtains

$$\hat{\imath}_t = \hat{r}_t^n + \bar{\pi} + (1 + \beta/\kappa\sigma)[E_t\pi_{t+1} - \bar{\pi}] + \sigma^{-1}[E_t x_{t+1} - \bar{x}], \tag{2.44}$$

using the substitution $\bar{x} \equiv ((1 - \beta)/\kappa)\bar{\pi}$.

---

54. In solving in this way, the central bank assumes the existence of a rational-expectations equilibrium, so that (1.12) and (1.13) should be satisfied, though it does not assume the particular equilibrium processes that it wishes to implement. In the event that private-sector expectations may not be rational, longer-horizon private-sector expectations should also matter for a correct projection of inflation, as discussed in Section 2.3. See also Section 5.2 of Chapter 7.

Equation (2.44) describes the *reaction function* of the central bank that implements the targeting rule (2.40). Given the specification of the structural model used by the central bank in implementing the targeting rule, the policy rules specified by (2.40) and (2.44) are equivalent; supplementing the structural equations of the model with *either* of these equations as a specification of monetary policy yields an equivalent system of equations (with a unique stationary solution, the r.e.e. in which inflation equals $\bar{\pi}$ at all times). One description of policy (in terms of the target criterion) is more useful as a way of communicating with the public about the nature of the central bank's policy commitment; but the other (in terms of the reaction function) is of great practical importance to the central bank in seeking to fulfill this commitment.[55]

At the level of its implied reaction function, the inflation-targeting rule is seen to be equivalent to a type of Taylor rule. Once more, it is found that a policy that succeeds in completely stabilizing inflation corresponds to a Taylor rule with an intercept term that varies one-for-one with shifts in the natural rate of interest. Moreover, because the coefficients of the rule satisfy $\phi_\pi > 1, \phi_x > 0$, the Taylor rule that corresponds to inflation targeting is consistent with the Taylor principle.

The inflation-targeting rule, however, corresponds to a quite specific interest-rate rule from among the many possible Taylor rules with these general features. It is interesting to note that it is also a *forward-looking* Taylor rule, similar to the kind estimated by Clarida et al. (2000), discussed in Chapter 1. The rule is forward looking, however, not because the *target criterion* involves future inflation rather than nearer-term inflation—as we have seen, that proposal would instead lead to an ill-defined rule and indeterminacy of equilibrium—but because it is necessary for the central bank to *respond* to fluctuations in private-sector expectations to prevent them from causing inflation to deviate from the target, in the same way as it must respond to exogenous fluctuations in the natural rate of interest. As in the previous section, a commitment to respond to these fluctuations in expectations strongly enough to satisfy the Taylor principle is necessary in order for the desired equilibrium to be the *only* stationary equilibrium consistent with the central-bank reaction function, even though in that equilibrium no such responses are ever called for. Furthermore, feedback of this very specific kind from forecasts does not give rise to the potential instability discussed in Section 2.2 as a problem with some other forecast-based feedback rules; for in this case, the feedback is calculated to *offset* the effects of the changes in private expectations on the evolution of the target variable, and hence to *weaken* the sensitivity of aggregate outcomes to the current state of

---

55. See Svensson and Woodford (2003) for further comparison between these alternative levels of specification of a monetary policy rule.

expectations, rather than increasing the sensitivity of the economy to fluctuations in expectations by making monetary policy dependent upon them.

3 Money and Aggregate Demand

Thus far, my analysis of the effects of monetary policy has made no reference
to the evolution of the money supply, which may seem to some a surprising
omission. Here I discuss the way in which the analysis can be extended to
include the evolution of the money supply under alternative policy rules,
should that be desired, in the case that there exist monetary frictions sufficient for a well-defined money-demand function to exist. This extension
of the model also makes it possible to consider monetary targeting rules or
rules that respond to variations in money growth among the candidate policy proposals. I also consider the extent to which allowance for real-balance
effects would modify the conclusions reached earlier about inflation determination under interest-rate rules.

3.1 An Optimizing IS-LM Model

I now again assume the existence of transactions frictions of the kind considered in Chapter 2, which can be represented by the inclusion of liquidity
services from real money balances in the household utility function. Once
again, this results in a first-order condition for the representative household's optimal demand for money balances of the form

$$\frac{U_m(C_t, m_t; \xi_t)}{U_c(C_t, m_t; \xi_t)} = \frac{i_t - i_t^m}{1 + i_t}, \tag{3.1}$$

where m_t denotes the household's end-of-period real money balances, and
i_t^m is the interest (if any) paid on such balances. As with the earlier discussion
of the intertemporal IS relation, I note that the first-order conditions describing the optimal behavior of a pricetaking household are the same in the
case of the sticky-price model considered in this chapter as in the flexible-
price model of Chapter 2. (The only difference here is that C_t now refers to
an index of consumption of a large number of differentiated goods, rather
than the single consumer good of Chapter 2.) Imposing the requirements
that the demands of the representative household equal the economy's aggregate supply of both goods and financial assets, I obtain the equilibrium
condition

$$M_t^s/P_t = L(Y_t, \Delta_t; \xi_t), \tag{3.2}$$

where $\Delta_t \equiv (i_t - i_t^m)/(1+i_t)$ is the interest differential between nonmonetary
and monetary assets and the money demand function $L(y, \Delta; \xi)$ has the

same properties as in Chapter 2. When (3.2) is log-linearized around the steady-state equilibrium with zero inflation, I again obtain a relation of the form

$$\hat{m}_t = \eta_y \hat{Y}_t - \eta_i \left(\hat{\imath}_t - \hat{\imath}_t^m \right) + \epsilon_t^m, \tag{3.3}$$

where $\eta_y, \eta_i > 0$ and ϵ_t^m is an exogenous disturbance process.

The other equilibrium conditions used in the analysis thus far continue to apply in the presence of monetary frictions. As discussed in Chapter 2, the only difference between a cashless economy and one in which central-bank money facilitates transactions is that in the latter case, the marginal utility of additional real expenditure by the representative household is given by $u_c(C_t, M_t/P_t; \xi_t)$, the value of which depends in general on the level of real money balances in addition to the level of real expenditure. However, in either the case of preferences additively separable between consumption and real balances or the cashless limit discussed in Section 3.4 of Chapter 2, one may neglect the effect of variations in real money balances on the value of u_c, and the intertemporal IS relation and aggregate-supply relation take exactly the forms assumed above.[56] The complete system of equilibrium conditions for determination of the nominal interest rate, the price level, and output (in the case of a money-growth rule) or the price level, output, and the money supply (in the case of an interest-rate rule) is then given by the IS and AS relations considered previously, together with (3.2) or (3.3). This system of equations has essentially the structure of an IS-LM-AS system of the kind familiar from undergraduate textbooks, though here the IS and AS relations are not purely static ones. Note also that the LM relation (3.2), considered as an equilibrium relation between i_t and Y_t, is shifted by variations in either M_t^s or i_t^m, which appear as two separate instruments through which monetary policy may be implemented, in addition to potentially being shifted by the exogenous disturbances ξ_t.

In the case of an interest-rate rule of one of the forms considered above, the equilibrium paths of inflation and output are determined by the IS and AS relations as before, but the LM relation now allows one to solve for the implied path of the money supply as well, under an assumption about the path of the interest rate on money (such as the conventional specification $\hat{\imath}_t^m = 0$).[57] In the case of a cashless limiting economy—perhaps the most attractive justification for my neglect of real-balance effects in the

<hr/>

56. The same is true in the case of a cash-in-advance model under which the disutility associated with making purchases without using cash is additive separable from the direct utility obtained from consumption of purchased goods (whether purchased using money or not), as discussed in Section A.16 of Appendix A.

57. It is worth noting, however, that in the absence of a constraint on the evolution of i_t^m, the required path of the money supply is not uniquely determined; for a given interest-rate

analysis thus far—the absolute size of equilibrium real money balances is assumed to be negligible. However, this does not mean that there may not be nonnegligible (and well-defined) fluctuations in equilibrium real balances *relative* to their (extremely small) steady-state level, indicated by the variable $\hat{m}_t$ in (3.2). Similarly, there may be nonnegligible, well-defined fluctuations in the rate of growth of the nominal money supply, even in the absence of a well-defined absolute level of the equilibrium money supply.

For example, one may consider how money growth must respond to various kinds of real disturbances under a policy that succeeds in stabilizing inflation and the output gap. To answer this question, I simply substitute the required interest-rate variations, discussed in Section 2.1, into equation (3.3) to determine the implied path of the money supply. One finds that, in general, the money supply should be allowed to vary in response to all four of the types of exogenous disturbances considered in Section 2.1, so that a constant money growth rate is certainly not the best way to stabilize inflation.

Nor does the path of the money supply required for price stability necessarily involve "leaning against the wind." For example, *procyclical* variations in the money supply are required in response to temporary fluctuations in productivity, as argued by Ireland (1996)[58]; for an increase in a_t raises $\hat{Y}_t^n$ while lowering $\hat{r}_t^n$, thus warranting an increase in $\log M_t^s$ at the same time as an increase in $\hat{Y}_t$. The same is true of temporary labor-supply shocks, and while the result depends upon parameter values, it is also true of government-purchase shocks and consumption-demand shocks, at least if these are sufficiently persistent. Furthermore, in the case of technology or labor-supply shocks, it is actually desirable for the money supply to be *more* procyclical than would be the case if interest rates were held unchanged; for one actually wants nominal interest rates to *decline* in response to a positive shock. In the case of the other two shocks, this is not true, but it is still possible that holding the nominal interest rate fixed is closer to the optimal response than holding the money supply fixed; in particular, this is necessarily true if the shocks are sufficiently persistent, as in that case the natural rate of interest is affected very little.

Thus variations in the rate of money growth should not, in general, be a very accurate indicator of whether interest rates have been allowed to

---

policy may be implemented using *either* quantity variations or variations in the interest paid on money, or using some combination of the two.

58. Aiyagari and Braun (1998) reach a similar conclusion, in the case of their model with sticky prices, though they assume convex costs of price changes, following Rotemberg (1996), rather than predetermined prices as in the models considered here. These authors also reach a similar conclusion with regard to government-purchase shocks, in the case of their numerical calibration of their model.

adjust to the extent that they ought to in response to disturbances. Monetary targeting amounts to an automatic mechanism for bringing about procyclical interest-rate variation (and interest-rate increases in response to price-level increases as well); but the required change in the level of interest rates for stabilization—which depends upon the change in the natural rate of interest—might not even have the same *sign*. Monetary targeting also causes interest rates to vary in response to money-demand disturbances, even though these should have negligible effects upon the natural rate of interest, so that it is not desirable for interest rates to respond to them. One should therefore expect to be able to do better by adopting an interest-rate rule that: (i) achieves a desired degree of response of interest rates to price-level and/or output-gap increases through explicit feedback from measures of these variables, as called for in the Taylor rule; and (ii) incorporates a direct response to changes in the central bank's estimate of the current natural rate of interest.

The foregoing conclusions with regard to the usefulness of monetary targeting contrast with the classic analysis of Poole (1970), according to which monetary targeting should be desirable as long as money-demand disturbances are of less importance than real disturbances to aggregate demand (IS shocks). What I call government-purchase or consumption-demand shocks presumably correspond to what Poole intends by IS shocks; yet even in the case of these shocks, I have argued that some degree of accommodation (allowing the money supply to vary in order to reduce the interest-rate response) is often desirable. Moreover, if the shocks are sufficiently persistent, the optimal degree of accommodation of the IS shift may be nearly 100 percent. The difference, of course, is that Poole assumes that output stabilization should be the goal of policy, whereas here I assume a goal of stabilizing the output *gap* instead,[59] by which I mean output relative to a natural rate that is affected by IS shocks among other real disturbances. If I consider the possibility of technology or labor-supply shocks, neglected by Poole altogether, the results are even more different, and even more strongly support a presumption in favor of accommodation.

But the most important limitation of Poole's analysis is that it assumes that monetary targeting is the only alternative to a complete interest-rate peg. Yet the kind of policy that has been proposed here (or that has been advocated by Wicksell or by Taylor) is not one that fixes nominal interest rates in the face of changing macroeconomic conditions. Once one recognizes that an interest-rate rule may specify interest-rate adjustments in response to changes in the price level and/or in output, then Poole's IS-LM analysis provides no grounds whatsoever for belief that it is desirable to respond to changes in monetary aggregates *as well*.

---

59. This objective is justified in terms of social welfare in Chapter 6.

One might, of course, make a case for responding to changes in the growth rate of monetary aggregates if such statistics provide more up-to-date information about prices and/or output than is otherwise available. This seems unlikely; at best, one might on these grounds justify paying attention to monetary aggregates along with a large number of other indicators.[60] But even in this case, it would be most useful to understand the central bank's policy commitment in terms of its response to its estimates of inflation and the output gap, rather than in terms of a commitment to respond to—let alone to stabilize—particular indicators.

3.2 Real-Balance Effects

Thus far I have considered only models in which monetary policy affects aggregate demand through the effects of real interest rates on the desired timing of private expenditure. While this is surely the most important single channel through which monetary policy matters, it is sometimes argued that this channel is not the only one way in which monetary policy matters, and that under at least some circumstances the neglect of other mechanisms may lead to significantly misleading conclusions. One proposal of this kind with an especially venerable history is the argument that the level of real money balances held by the private sector should directly influence aggregate demand, for reasons that are independent of the reduction in equilibrium interest rates that ordinarily accompany a higher real money supply in order to induce the private sector to choose to hold the higher money balances. Pigou (1943) argued for the existence of such a real-balance effect, and proposed that its existence was especially important in guaranteeing the effectiveness of monetary policy even under the circumstances of a liquidity trap of the kind posited by Keynes (1936).

It is first important to note that I have *not* omitted any effect of real money balances upon aggregate demand that results from a simple (Hicksian) wealth effect, as Pigou supposed. The Euler equation for the optimal timing of private expenditure from which I have derived the crucial equilibrium condition (1.1) does not in any way contradict the contribution of financial wealth to the intertemporal budget constraint of the representative household (discussed in detail in Chapter 2). Furthermore, solving the log-linearized Euler equation forward to obtain a relation of the form (1.8) between the level of aggregate expenditure at a given date and a very-long-term real rate (or equivalently, a distributed lead of expected future short real rates) involves no neglect of any wealth effects. It is true that, for an individual household, optimal consumption demand is a function

---

60. The optimal use of indicator variables given that inflation and the output gap are not perfectly observed in real time is treated in Chapter 8.

of the household's current financial wealth in addition to its future (after-tax) income expectations and its expectations regarding the available rate of return on its savings. (See (2.28) for a log-linear approximation to this decision rule.) But still, optimal current expenditure *relative* to expected future expenditure depends only on the expected rates of return on assets between now and the future date; for greater financial wealth should imply greater expected future spending in the same proportion as it increases desired current spending. Moreover, for households in aggregate, expected spending in the long-run future must be tied down by the exogenous evolution (in the kind of model considered here) of the natural rate of output. Given this anchor for the representative household's expected long-run level of expenditure, the sequence of expected future real interest rates does suffice to determine what optimal expenditure must be in the present.

Nonetheless, there is a type of real-balance effect from which this analysis has abstracted. Thus far, I have assumed that the marginal utility of real income to the representative household depends only upon the quantity of real resources produced and consumed (and upon exogenous disturbances, including the level of government purchases), and not on the household's money balances. This can be justified, in the context of the Sidrauski-Brock model, under the assumption of preferences that are additively separable between consumption and real money balances, as in Section 3.1 of Chapter 2.[61] This familiar assumption makes the algebra simpler in many places, but it can hardly be defended as realistic. If utility is obtained from holding money, this must be because money balances facilitate transactions, and it is hardly sensible that the benefits of such balances should be independent of the real volume of transactions that a household actually undertakes. But if u_m is increasing in C_t, u_c must also be increasing in m_t, the household's real balances.

Accordingly I consider here how the foregoing results extend to the case of a more general preference specification. I argue that the simple case treated earlier remains a good guide to intuition and, indeed, that it may be justified as an approximation without any appeal to the plausibility of additive separability. But it is also useful to be able to see how real-balance effects require the previous calculations to be modified, if one wishes to be more precise.

Recall from Chapter 2 that in the general case, the equilibrium condition derived from the Euler equation for the optimal timing of private expenditure takes the form

---

61. An alternative justification is proposed in Section A.16 of Appendix A, but this too depends on a special functional form.

$$1 + i_t = \beta^{-1} \left\{ E_t \left[\frac{U_c\left(Y_{t+1}, M^s_{t+1}/P_{t+1}; \xi_{t+1}\right)}{U_c\left(Y_t, M^s_t/P_t; \xi_t\right)} \Pi_{t+1}^{-1} \right] \right\}^{-1}. \tag{3.4}$$

This reduces to equation (1.1) only under the assumption of additively separable preferences (or the absence of nonnegligible transactions frictions). In the general case, a log-linear approximation to this relation takes the form

$$\hat{\imath}_t = \sigma^{-1} \left[E_t \left(\hat{Y}_{t+1} - g_{t+1} \right) - \left(\hat{Y}_t - g_t \right) \right] - \chi (E_t \hat{m}_{t+1} - \hat{m}_t) + E_t \pi_{t+1}, \tag{3.5}$$

generalizing (1.7), where

$$\chi \equiv \bar{m} U_{cm}/U_c$$

with partial derivatives evaluated at the steady state. Here g_t is again the exogenous factor defined in (2.3), where the shift in the marginal utility of consumption $\bar{C}_t$ is now evaluated at the steady-state values of both C_t and m_t. Note that (3.5) is the same as equation (3.11) of Chapter 2, except that now the dependence on real output is explicit, as output is no longer exogenous.

Solving (3.5) forward again yields an IS equation of the form

$$\hat{Y}_t = \hat{Y}_\infty + g_t + \chi \sigma \hat{m}_t - \sigma \sum_{j=0}^{\infty} E_t [\hat{\imath}_{t+j} - \pi_{t+j+1}]. \tag{3.6}$$

If $\chi > 0$, then there is indeed a real-balance effect upon aggregate demand. This results not from a wealth effect, but from the fact that even controlling for the path of real interest rates, times when real balances are high are particularly convenient times to spend, due to the way in which money balances facilitate transactions. One can also show that, contrary to Pigou's suggestion, this effect does not imply that increases in the money supply can increase demand even in a liquidity trap; see Eggertsson and Woodford (2003).

I first consider instead the consequences of the existence of a real-balance effect for inflation determination under an interest-rate rule in the case of only small fluctuations around the zero-inflation steady state (so that the zero lower bound on nominal interest rates is never approached). As in Section 3.4 of Chapter 2, it is convenient to use (3.3) to eliminate real balances from the intertemporal IS equation (3.5), yielding

$$(1 + \eta_i \chi)\hat{\imath}_t = \left(\sigma^{-1} - \eta_y \chi\right)\left(E_t \hat{Y}_{t+1} - Y_t\right) + E_t \pi_{t+1}$$
$$+ \eta_i \chi E_t \hat{\imath}_{t+1} - \eta_i \chi \left(E_t \hat{\imath}^m_{t+1} - \hat{\imath}^m_t\right) + v_t, \tag{3.7}$$

where

$$v_t \equiv -\sigma^{-1}(E_t g_{t+1} - g_t) - \chi(E_t \epsilon^m_{t+1} - \epsilon^m_t) \qquad (3.8)$$

collects the exogenous disturbance terms unrelated to policy. This gives an equilibrium relation written solely in terms of the evolution of interest rates, inflation, and output, like (1.7).[62]

I then define the natural rate of output Y_t^n as the equilibrium level of output at each point in time that would obtain under flexible prices, given a monetary policy that maintains a constant interest-rate spread Δ_t between nonmonetary and monetary riskless short-term assets. This last stipulation in the definition is now necessary, as when utility is nonseparable, equilibrium output under flexible prices is no longer independent of monetary policy.[63] Similarly define the natural rate of interest r_t^n as the equilibrium real rate of interest under the same hypothetical circumstances. As (3.7) must hold equally whether prices are flexible or sticky, one must have

$$\hat{r}_t^n = \left(\sigma^{-1} - \eta_y \chi\right)\left(E_t \hat{Y}_{t+1}^n - Y_t^n\right) - \sigma^{-1}\left(E_t g_{t+1} - g_t\right) - \chi\left(E_t \epsilon_{m,t+1} - \epsilon_{mt}\right). \qquad (3.9)$$

Note that this reduces to the previous definition (1.15) in the case that $\chi = 0$. Using this to substitute for terms on the right-hand side of (3.7) and rearranging terms yields

$$\left(1 - \sigma \eta_y \chi\right)x_t = \left(1 - \sigma \eta_y \chi\right)E_t x_{t+1} - \sigma\left(\hat{\imath}_t - E_t \pi_{t+1} - \hat{r}_t^n\right)$$
$$+ \sigma \eta_i \chi\left[E_t\left(\hat{\imath}_{t+1} - \hat{\imath}_{t+1}^m\right) - \left(\hat{\imath}_t - \hat{\imath}_t^m\right)\right], \qquad (3.10)$$

generalizing (1.12), where again $x_t \equiv \hat{Y}_t - \hat{Y}_t^n$. Thus I once more obtain an intertemporal IS relation in terms of the output gap x_t in which the

62. It is worth noting that in the case of a monetary policy that is implemented in a way that preserves a constant interest-rate differential Δ_t at all times, so that (in the log-linear approximation) $\hat{\imath}_t = \hat{\imath}_t^m$ at all times, equation (3.7) is equivalent in form to relation (1.1) under a reinterpretation of the coefficient σ and the disturbance term g_t in the previous relation. (Specifically, one must replace σ^{-1} by $\sigma^{-1} - \eta_y \chi$ and g_t by $g_t + \sigma \chi \epsilon_t^m$.) One might plausibly consider these alternative expressions to be the appropriate *definitions* of σ and g_t in the case of a model with nonseparable utility; that is, one might define these quantities so that $-\sigma^{-1}(\hat{Y}_t - g_t)$ is the deviation of the log marginal utility of real income from its steady-state level in the case of a constant interest-rate differential (rather than a constant level of real balances). In that case, (1.1) would apply in the case of a constant-interest-differential policy, regardless of additive separability. In the text, however, I continue to define σ and g_t in terms of partial derivatives of the utility function, holding real balances fixed, so as to avoid confusion.

63. One might, of course, choose other definitions of the natural rate, such as the flexible-price level of output in the case of a monetary policy that results in a stable price level. The choice made here turns out to be convenient in simplifying the welfare analysis of Chapter 6.

only exogenous disturbance term is the shift in the natural rate of interest $\hat{r}_t^n$.[64]

Allowing for nontrivial transactions frictions and nonseparable utility between consumption and real balances also requires modification of the derivation of the aggregate-supply relation (1.10). (Throughout Chapter 3, I assumed either negligible transactions frictions or separable utility.) In the case of nonseparable utility, the marginal utility of income depends upon real money balances as well as real expenditure, so that the household labor-supply equation becomes

$$w_t(i) = \frac{v_h(h_t(i); \xi_t)}{u_c(C_t, m_t; \xi_t)}.$$

It follows that the real marginal cost of supplying good i, when log-linearized, is given by

$$\hat{s}_t(i) = \omega(\hat{y}_t(i) - q_t) + \sigma^{-1}(\hat{Y}_t - g_t) - \chi \hat{m}_t,$$

where the exogenous disturbances q_t and g_t continue to be defined as before. Substituting (3.3) for real money balances $\hat{m}_t$, and recalling the definition just proposed for the natural rate of output, one can write average real marginal cost in the form

$$\hat{s}_t = \epsilon_{mc}(\hat{Y}_t - \hat{Y}_t^n) + \eta_i \chi(\hat{\imath}_t - \hat{\imath}_t^m), \tag{3.11}$$

where the elasticity of average marginal cost with respect to aggregate output is now equal to

$$\epsilon_{mc} = \omega + \sigma^{-1} - \eta_i \chi, \tag{3.12}$$

and the natural rate of output is now given by

$$\hat{Y}_t^n = \frac{\omega q_t + \sigma^{-1} g_t + \chi \epsilon_t^m}{\epsilon_{mc}}, \tag{3.13}$$

generalizing (2.2).

Expression (3.11) can alternatively be written in the form

$$\hat{s}_t = \epsilon_{mc}\left[x_t + \varphi\left(\hat{\imath}_t - \hat{\imath}_t^m\right)\right],$$

64. Note that in the case of flexible prices and an exogenous goods supply, so that necessarily $x_t = 0$ at all times, equation (3.10) reduces to equation (3.12) of Chapter 2, with $\hat{r}_t^n$ corresponding to the composite exogenous disturbance $\hat{r}_t$ of that model.

where

$$\varphi \equiv \eta_i \chi / \epsilon_{mc}.$$

The case that would seem to be of greatest empirical relevance is that in which χ satisfies the bounds

$$0 \le \chi < \eta_y^{-1} \left(\omega + \sigma^{-1} \right),$$

in which case both ϵ_{mc} and φ are positive coefficients.[65] A calculation exactly parallel to that given in Chapter 3 then allows one to derive an aggregate-supply relation of the form

$$\pi_t = \kappa \left[x_t + \varphi \left(\hat{\imath}_t - \hat{\imath}_t^m \right) \right] + \beta E_t \pi_{t+1}, \qquad (3.14)$$

generalizing (1.10). Here

$$\kappa \equiv \frac{(1-\alpha)(1-\alpha\beta)}{\alpha} \frac{\epsilon_{mc}}{1+\omega\theta}$$

as before, but ϵ_{mc} is now given by (3.12). It is found that in the nonseparable case, inflationary pressure depends not only on the output gap, but also on the interest differential between nonmonetary and monetary assets. The greater this return differential is, the greater the cost of holding the money balances needed to facilitate transactions; hence the greater is the marginal cost of supplying a given level of output and, ultimately, the incentive to raise prices.

How much of a difference is made by the inclusion of the additional terms in (3.10) and (3.14)? If I assume an interest-rate rule of one of the kinds considered in Section 2, and add the additional stipulation that the interest rate i_t^m paid on the monetary base is adjusted along with all changes in the central bank's interest-rate operating target, so as to maintain a constant spread Δ_t, then the previous conclusions are *entirely unchanged* under an appropriate calibration of the numerical coefficients. The reason is that in the case that $\hat{\imath}_t^m = \hat{\imath}_t$ at all times, equations (3.10) and (3.14) reduce to *precisely* the previous equations (1.12) and (1.10), respectively, given the new definition (3.9) of the natural rate of interest, with one exception: in the IS

---

65. As discussed in Section 2.1 of Chapter 5, Rotemberg and Woodford (1997) argue that a reasonable value for ϵ_{mc} is about 0.63 for the U.S. economy. I argued in Chapter 2 that a realistic value for $\chi \eta_y$ for the United States would be about 0.01, so this would imply a value for $\sigma^{-1} + \omega$ of about 0.64. Even if these values are inaccurate, $\sigma^{-1} + \omega$ is likely to be much larger than $\chi \eta_y$.

relation (3.4), the coefficient indicating the interest sensitivity of real expenditure is no longer σ, as in (1.12), but rather $(\sigma^{-1} - \eta_y\chi)^{-1}$.[66] As long as $\chi < (\eta_y\sigma)^{-1}$—the empirically realistic case, under the calibration proposed below[67]—then there is no qualitative change in the previous conclusions; I would obtain identical numerical results to those presented in the earlier figures under a suitably different calibration of the value of σ.

Inflation and the output *gap* (the latter, rather than detrended output, being the welfare-relevant quantity, as I argue in Chapter 6) thus evolve according to exactly the formulas derived earlier, once I take into account the modification of the effects of real disturbances on the natural rate of interest. (Computation of the implied path of detrended output requires that one also take into account the modified expression for the effects of real disturbances on the natural rate of output.) Thus the previous results apply not only to fully (or nearly) cashless economies and to economies in which preferences are additively separable between consumption and real balances, but also to economies in which central-bank interest-rate targets are implemented through adjustments of the interest paid on the monetary base, rather than through adjustments of the supply of base money.[68]

If, however, interest-rate adjustments are implemented through variation in the supply of base money, holding fixed the rate of interest paid on the monetary base—as under current U.S. monetary arrangements, for example—then the additional terms in both the IS relation and the AS relation matter, assuming nontrivial monetary frictions and nonseparable preferences. Nonetheless, for many purposes the additional terms do not

66. In the analysis of price-level determination under this kind of policy in Chapter 2, where I assumed flexible prices, this difference did not matter, as no fluctuations in the output gap x_t could occur in equilibrium. In the case of price stickiness, the additional qualification is needed.

67. In a more realistic extension of the present model, where I distinguish among different categories of private expenditure with differing degrees of interest sensitivity, this would be even more clearly true. For one might well calibrate a lower degree of interest elasticity (larger σ^{-1}) for those expenditures that are complementary with real money balances (the ones for which $\chi > 0$).

68. Another case in which the previous results apply would be a hybrid of two of those just mentioned. Suppose that utility each period is given by $u(C_t, m_t^{cb}; \xi_t) + v(m_t^{cu}; \xi_t)$, where m_t^{cb} indicates the real value of the clearing balances held at the central bank to facilitate payments and m_t^{cu} indicates the real value of currency in circulation. (Here the liquidity services provided by clearing balances are assumed to depend on the volume of aggregate transactions in the economy, while the usefulness of currency is assumed to be largely unaffected by variations in aggregate real expenditure.) Then it suffices for the validity of the previous results that the interest rate i_t^{cb} paid on clearing balances be adjusted so as to maintain a constant spread between this and the central bank's interest-rate operating target, as is true under the channel systems mentioned in Chapter 1; it does not matter whether there is any interest paid on currency as well.

seem likely to have too large an effect on the quantitative conclusions. I can illustrate this by considering a numerical calibration of the model based on U.S. data.

As argued in Section 3.4 of Chapter 2, evidence on long-run U.S. money demand suggests money-demand elasticities on the order of $\eta_y = 1$, $\eta_i = 28$ quarters, and a value of at most $\chi = 0.02$ for the elasticity of the marginal utility of expenditure with respect to additional real money balances. Suppose that the other coefficients of the structural equations are based on the parameter values used by Rotemberg and Woodford (1997), shown in Table 5.1 in the next chapter, and discussed further there. Since Rotemberg and Woodford infer the value of ω from their estimate of ϵ_{mc}, rather than the reverse, allowing for $\chi \neq 0$ does not imply any change in the calibrated value of ϵ_{mc}. Thus the value that I assume for φ is $(0.02)(28)/(0.63) = 0.89$ quarters.[69] The values assumed for the parameters β, σ, and κ are those reported in Table 5.1.

Using similar methods, one can show that in the case that a determinate equilibrium exists,[70] an interest-rate rule of the form (1.14)[71] together with the stipulation that $\hat{\imath}_t^m = 0$ implies equilibrium paths for the endogenous variables of the form

$$\pi_t = \bar{\pi} + \sum_{j=0}^{\infty} \tilde{\psi}_j^{\pi} \left(E_t \hat{r}_{t+j}^n + \bar{\pi} \right) - \sum_{j=0}^{\infty} \tilde{\psi}_j^{\pi} E_t \bar{\imath}_{t+j}, \tag{3.15}$$

$$x_t = \bar{x} + \sum_{j=0}^{\infty} \tilde{\psi}_j^{x} \left(E_t \hat{r}_{t+j}^n + \bar{\pi} \right) - \sum_{j=0}^{\infty} \tilde{\psi}_j^{x} E_t \bar{\imath}_{t+j}, \tag{3.16}$$

$$\hat{\imath}_t = \bar{\imath}_t + \sum_{j=0}^{\infty} \tilde{\psi}_j^{i} \left(E_t \hat{r}_{t+j}^n + \bar{\pi} \right) - \sum_{j=0}^{\infty} \tilde{\psi}_j^{i} E_t \bar{\imath}_{t+j}. \tag{3.17}$$

In the case that $\chi \neq 0$, the coefficients $\tilde{\psi}_j^{\pi}$ and so on are no longer exactly equal to the coefficients ψ_j^{π} and so on. The extent to which allowance for real-balance effects influences the quantitative size of these coefficients is shown in Figures 4.10 and 4.11, for the calibrated parameter values stated in the previous paragraph.

---

69. This value multiplies a quarterly interest rate; if instead the interest rate is expressed as an annualized rate, φ should equal 0.22 years.

70. The conditions for determinacy of equilibrium can also be generalized using the same methods as above. One again obtains a set of inequalities that the coefficients of the interest-rate rule must satisfy, and these expressions are continuous functions of χ, so that the set of interest-rate rules that imply a determinate equilibrium remain nearly the same when one assumes a small positive value for χ.

71. Once again, I assume an output-gap target $\bar{x}$ consistent with the inflation target $\bar{\pi}$. In the case that $\chi \neq 0$, this requires that $\bar{x} = (1 - \beta)\bar{\pi}/\kappa + \varphi\bar{\pi}$.

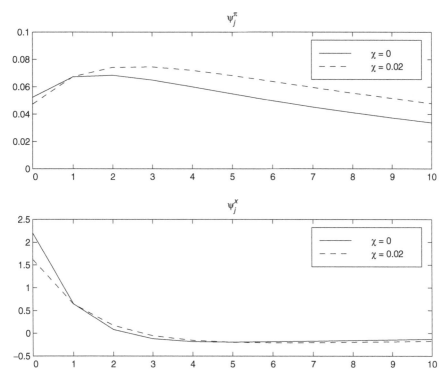

Figure 4.10 *Effects of anticipated natural-rate fluctuations under a simple Taylor rule allowing for real-balance effects.*

The figures show the results in the case of a rule with $\phi_\pi = 2, \phi_x = 1$, corresponding to the baseline case in Figures 4.5 and 4.6. Figure 4.10 shows the coefficients ψ_j^π and ψ_j^x, while Figure 4.11 shows the coefficients $\tilde{\psi}_j^\pi$ and $\tilde{\psi}_j^x$, for various future horizons j. In each panel, the coefficients are computed both for the parameter values given previously (the dashed lines) and for the same values of β, σ, and κ, but under the assumption that χ and φ are equal to zero (as in the earlier figures). Observe that the predicted effects of both types of disturbances on inflation and the output gap are not much modified by allowing for real-balance effects. The main difference is a greater inflationary impact of increases in the natural rate of interest that are foreseen several quarters in advance, as a result of the contribution of the resulting increase in the interest differential to the marginal cost of supply. But even this matters for predicted inflation dynamics only to the extent that fluctuations in the natural rate of interest are predictable several quarters in advance.

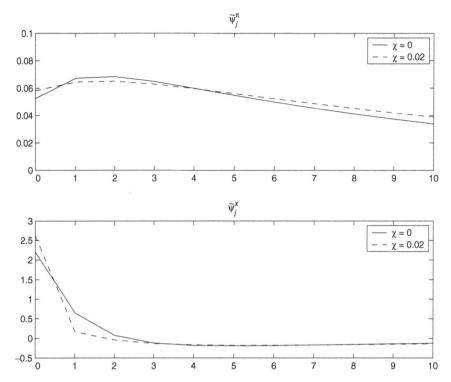

Figure 4.11 *Effects of anticipated policy shifts under a simple Taylor rule allowing for real-balance effects.*

In the case of an interest-rate rule of the form (2.8), again combined with the stipulation that $\hat{\imath}_t^m = 0$, one correspondingly obtains solutions of the form

$$\pi_t = \bar{\pi} + \omega^{\pi}(\hat{\imath}_{t-1} - \bar{\imath}_{t-1}) + \sum_{j=0}^{\infty} \psi_j^{\pi} E_t(\hat{r}_{t+j}^n + \bar{\pi}) - \sum_{j=0}^{\infty} \tilde{\psi}_j^{\pi} E_t \bar{\imath}_{t+j},$$

and similarly for the other endogenous variables. Once again, the coefficients $\tilde{\psi}_j^{\pi}$ and so on are no longer exactly equal to the coefficients ψ_j^{π} when $\chi \neq 0$. The quantitative significance of the allowance for real-balance effects is shown in Figures 4.12 and 4.13, using the same format as in Figures 4.10 and 4.11. Here the assumed coefficients of the policy rule are $\phi_{\pi} = 0.6$, $\phi_x = 0.3$, and $\rho = 0.7$, as in the baseline case of Figure 4.8. The conclusions in this case are essentially the same.

Another way of considering the consequences of real-balance effects for the previous conclusions is to compute the predicted impulse responses of inflation, the output gap, and the nominal interest rate to a monetary policy

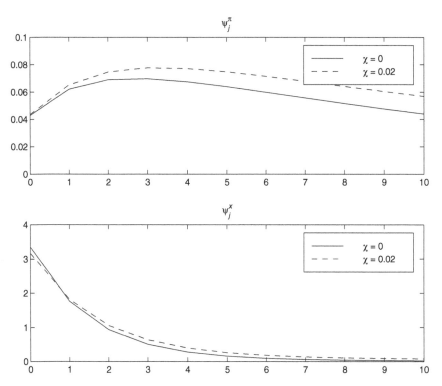

Figure 4.12 *Effects of anticipated natural-rate fluctuations under an inertial Taylor rule allowing for real-balance effects.*

shock using the modified structural equations. Again consider a policy rule of the form (2.35), with coefficients $\phi_\pi = 0.6, \phi_x = 0.3$, and $\rho = 0.7$, as in the baseline case of Figure 4.8. The impulse responses to an unexpected monetary tightening, both in the case that $\chi = 0$ (as in Figure 4.8) and in the case that $\chi = 0.02$, are shown in Figure 5.1. (The responses shown in that figure are actually for a variant model in which there is no effect on inflation or output during the quarter of the policy shock; but the responses shown for quarter one and later are identical to those implied by the model with structural equations (3.10) and (3.14). Note that the responses indicated by the solid lines in Figure 5.1 are identical for periods one and later to those shown by the solid lines in Figure 4.8.) Observe that the responses of all of the variables are not very different when real-balance effects are considered, relative to the overall scale of variation in the variables in question.[72]

---

72. In the case of the nominal interest rate, allowance for real-balance effects would predict a substantially greater decline, *relative* to the size of the decline predicted in the baseline case

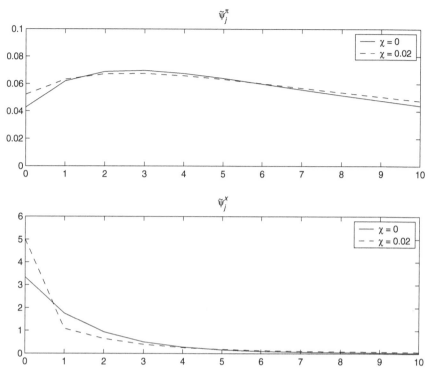

Figure 4.13 *Effects of anticipated policy shifts under an inertial Taylor rule allowing for real-balance effects.*

Thus far I have only considered how large real-balance effects might be expected to be, according to the present theory, when the model parameters are calibrated on the basis of the observed demand for money in the United States. One might also wonder whether there is much evidence for real-balance effects in IS or AS relations from econometric estimates of those relations. To answer this question, Ireland (2001) presents maximum-likelihood estimates of a structural model consisting of equations (3.3),

---

(which is very small), if one did not assume a one-quarter delay in the effects of monetary policy shocks on spending and pricing decisions. However, this is of little importance, since empirical estimates (see Figures 5.2, 5.4, or 5.5 in the next chapter) indicate that most of the variation in nominal interest rates due to identified monetary policy shocks represents responses that occur prior to any effect on real expenditure. A substantial proportionate effect on the response predicted in those later periods still makes very little difference to the overall predicted variation in nominal interest rates.

(3.10), and (3.14), together with a monetary policy rule, estimated using quarterly U.S. data on inflation, output, nominal interest rates, and money growth. His estimated value for $\chi\sigma$, the coefficient indicating the size of the effect of variations in real money balances on aggregate demand, is -0.02, with a standard error of nearly 0.04; it is thus not significantly different from zero. Nor is this result obtained only because the effect is not precisely estimated; the 95 percent confidence interval implied by Ireland's results would allow the coefficient to have as large a positive value as 0.05 or as negative a value as -0.09, but it would not allow values as large as the coefficient of 0.13 assumed in the case shown in Figures 4.10–4.13. Thus Ireland's estimates would imply real-balance effects even more modest than the ones exhibited in these figures.

4 Fiscal Requirements for Price Stability

In my account of aggregate-demand determination thus far, I have made little mention of fiscal policy. I have been able to avoid it thanks to my (tacit) assumption again in this chapter of the kind of fiscal policy assumed in Chapter 2, namely, an exogenous target path for total nominal government liabilities of a kind consistent with price stability. In this section, I discuss more generally the kind of assumption about fiscal policy that is necessary for the results of the previous sections to obtain and also the way in which the conclusions would change in the event of other specifications.

I wish to consider the topic, neglected thus far in the present chapter, of the evolution of the government debt under alternative monetary-fiscal regimes. A complete specification of policy must specify the composition of the government debt at each point in time; here, to simplify, suppose that all government debt consists of riskless, one-period nominal debt. The analysis is also simplified by again treating the case of a cashless economy, as in Sections 1 and 2. Then D_t, the nominal value of government liabilities at the end of period t, represents the value of the public debt,[73] and also the quantity outstanding of one-period government bonds (measured by their value at issuance rather than at maturity). This quantity evolves over time according the law of motion

$$D_t = (1 + i_{t-1})D_{t-1} + (P_t G_t - T_t), \tag{4.1}$$

---

73. It should actually include the monetary base since, in the exposition in Chapter 2 of the implementation of monetary policy in a cashless economy, there remains a positive monetary base in such an economy, though the private sector suffers no opportunity cost of holding such assets and the government earns no seignorage. But since the same interest rate i_t is paid on the monetary base as on government debt, there is no need to distinguish the monetary base from the rest of the government debt in the present model.

where T_t represents nominal tax collections in period t. Note that monetary policy (the choice of i_t) affects the evolution of the public debt, even in the absence of seignorage revenues, through its consequences for debt service on existing government debt. In most advanced economies, this is actually the most important fiscal consequence of monetary policy, and I consider it here exclusively.

I continue to regard the path of real government purchases $\{G_t\}$ as exogenously given, but now wish to consider alternative rules for the determination of the level of net tax collections T_t. As with the analysis thus far, I restrict attention to local equilibrium determination. Hence I consider only fiscal rules that are nearly consistent with a steady state in which both real tax collections $\tau_t \equiv T_t/P_t$ and the maturity value of real public debt $b_t \equiv (1 + i_t)D_t/P_t$ are equal to certain constant values $\bar{\tau}, \bar{B} > 0$ in each period[74] in the case of zero inflation and no real disturbances (meaning $Y_t = \bar{Y} > 0$, $G_t = \bar{G} \geq 0$, and $i_t = \bar{i} \equiv \beta^{-1} - 1 > 0$ each period). In order to be consistent with (4.1), these steady-state fiscal values must satisfy $\bar{\tau} = \bar{G} + (1 - \beta)\bar{B}$.

For purposes of analyzing the existence of equilibria near this steady state, it suffices to linearize (4.1) around the steady-state values, obtaining

$$\hat{b}_t = \beta^{-1}\left[\hat{b}_{t-1} - \bar{b}\pi_t + \hat{G}_t - \hat{\tau}_t\right] + \bar{b}\hat{i}_t, \tag{4.2}$$

where $\hat{b}_t \equiv (b_t - \bar{B})/\bar{Y}$ and $\hat{\tau}_t \equiv (\tau_t - \bar{\tau})/\bar{Y}$ are defined by analogy with the previous definition of $\hat{G}_t$, and the coefficient $\bar{b} \equiv \bar{B}/\bar{Y}$. I define a fiscal rule (tax rule) as *locally Ricardian* if when substituted into the flow budget constraint (4.1) (or its local version (4.2)) it implies that $\{b_t\}$ remains forever within a bounded neighborhood of $\bar{B}$, for all paths of the endogenous variables $\{\pi_t, Y_t, i_t\}$ that remain forever within some sufficiently small neighborhoods of the steady-state values $(0, \bar{Y}, \bar{i})$, and all small enough values of the exogenous disturbances (including $\{\hat{G}_t\}$).[75]

---

74. I assume that $\bar{\tau}, \bar{B} > 0$, as government liabilities include at least the monetary base used to define the unit of account and as taxes have to be collected to pay interest on this base, even if there is no other government spending.

75. This is the definition that is appropriate in the case of a monetary policy rule that involves no reference to an absolute price level, in which case determinacy of equilibrium is taken to mean existence of a unique bounded equilibrium process for the inflation rate, but not necessarily an equilibrium with a stationary process for the price level. In the case of a Wicksellian policy rule such as (2.14), however, the appropriate definition requires only that $\{b_t\}$ remain forever within a bounded neighborhood in the case of all sufficiently tightly bounded fluctuations in $\{P_t/P_t^*\}$, where $\{P_t^*\}$ is the target path for the price level, rather than for all bounded fluctuations in the inflation rate. In this case, an example of a locally Ricardian fiscal rule would be one that specifies a target path for $\{D_t\}$, as considered in Chapter 2, where D_t/P_t^* remains forever within a bounded interval. As discussed in Chapter 2, Section 4, this

In the event that fiscal policy is locally Ricardian, one can be sure that $\{b_t\}$ remains forever bounded, and hence that the transversality condition (1.3) is satisfied in the case of any processes $\{\pi_t, Y_t, i_t\}$ close enough to the steady-state values of these variables. Thus the equilibrium condition (1.3) may be neglected in the analysis of rational-expectations equilibria near the steady state, as was done in the previous sections of this chapter. If in addition the monetary policy rule does not depend on the paths of either of the purely fiscal variables $\{D_t, \tau_t\}$, as has been true of the examples considered in this chapter, then the details of the fiscal policy rule (apart from the stipulation that it is locally Ricardian) are irrelevant to the determination of equilibrium inflation, output, and interest rates.

However, the previous results need not hold in the case of a locally non-Ricardian policy. Suppose that the tax rule is of the form

$$\tau_t = \tau(b_{t-1}, G_t, \pi_t, Y_t, i_t; v_t), \tag{4.3}$$

where τ is a time-invariant function and v_t is an exogenous disturbance (fiscal policy shock), and suppose, for simplicity, that the rule is consistent (in the absence of disturbances) with the steady state around which (4.2) has been linearized, that is, that

$$\tau(\bar{b}, \bar{G}, 0, \bar{Y}, \bar{i}; 0) = \bar{\tau}.$$

For purposes of the local analysis of equilibrium determination, it suffices that I consider a linear approximation to (4.3) given by

$$\hat{\tau}_t = \tau_b \hat{b}_{t-1} + \tau_g \hat{G}_t + \tau_\pi \pi_t + \tau_y \hat{Y}_t + \tau_i \hat{i}_t + v_t. \tag{4.4}$$

Substitution of this into (4.2) yields

$$\hat{b}_t = \beta^{-1}\left[(1 - \tau_b)\hat{b}_{t-1} - (\bar{b} + \tau_\pi)\pi_t + (1 - \tau_g)\hat{G}_t - \tau_y \hat{Y}_t\right] \\ + (\bar{b} - \beta^{-1}\tau_i)\hat{i}_t - \beta^{-1}v_t \tag{4.5}$$

as an implied law of motion for real government debt. It follows from (4.5) that this sort of tax rule is locally Ricardian if and only if

$$\left|\beta^{-1}(1 - \tau_b)\right| < 1,$$

so that the implied dynamics of real government debt are bounded when arbitrary bounded processes for the other endogenous variables and for the

---

kind of fiscal commitment has the advantage of ruling out self-fulfilling deflations, in addition to being a locally Ricardian policy.

exogenous disturbances are substituted into (4.5). If I restrict attention to rules in which $\tau_b \leq 1$, so that end-of-period public debt is at least a weakly increasing function of beginning-of-period debt, then fiscal policy is locally Ricardian if and only if $\tau_b > 1 - \beta$.

Following Leeper (1991) and Woodford (1996),[76] define equilibrium to be (locally) *determinate* if and only if there are unique bounded equilibrium processes for all of the endogenous variables $\{b_t, \pi_t, Y_t, i_t\}$ in the case of any sufficiently tightly bounded processes for the exogenous disturbances. I then obtain the following result regarding determinacy of equilibrium under a Taylor rule.

PROPOSITION 4.11. Consider again the basic neo-Wicksellian model of a cashless economy, and suppose that monetary policy is conducted in accordance with a rule of the form (1.14), where $\phi_\pi, \phi_x \geq 0$, while fiscal policy is determined by a rule of the form (4.3), with $\tau_b \leq 1$. Then if fiscal policy is *locally Ricardian* (i.e., if $\tau_b > 1 - \beta > 0$), the results reported in Proposition 4.3 apply: Equilibrium is determinate if and only if the monetary policy rule conforms to the Taylor principle, that is, the response coefficients satisfy (2.7). If the inequality in (2.7) is reversed, equilibrium is *indeterminate* as discussed in Section 2.

If, instead, fiscal policy is *locally non-Ricardian* (i.e., if $\tau_b < 1 - \beta$), equilibrium is determinate if and only if the monetary policy rule *violates* the Taylor principle, that is, the inequality in (2.7) is reversed. If monetary policy conforms to the Taylor principle, there is (for almost all possible initial conditions and realizations of the exogenous disturbances) no equilibrium in which the paths of the endogenous variables $\{b_t, \pi_t, Y_t, i_t\}$ remain forever within small intervals around their steady-state values, no matter how small the open sets of values from which the initial conditions and disturbances may be selected.

The proof is given in Appendix C. This result, first obtained by Woodford (1996) for a version of the basic neo-Wicksellian model that allowed for monetary frictions, directly parallels the results of Leeper (1991) in the context of a flexible-price model.[77]

---

76. One might arguably prefer a weaker condition than boundedness of the real public debt process, given that this is not required for satisfaction of the transversality condition. The definition proposed here has the advantage that it can be analyzed using solely the linear approximations to both the tax rule and the law of motion for government debt. The results of Evans and Honkapohja (2002b), finding E-stability of the r.e.e. that are locally determinate in this sense in Leeper's (1991) model, provide a further ground for thinking that this conception of determinacy of equilibrium is of interest.

77. Leeper classifies fiscal rules as passive when policy is locally Ricardian and active otherwise, and classifies monetary policy as active when it conforms to the Taylor principle (in the

I have already indicated why Proposition 4.3 applies in the case of a locally Ricardian fiscal policy. In this case, equilibrium inflation, output, and nominal interest rates are determined in the way discussed in Section 2.4, and are completely independent of fiscal developments. If instead policy is locally non-Ricardian, it is no longer the case that $\{b_t\}$ remains bounded for all possible bounded paths for the other endogenous variables. The requirement that $\{b_t\}$ remain bounded under the dynamics implied by (4.5) places a linear restriction on the possible evolution of inflation, output, and interest rates. In the generic case, this additional linear restriction suffices to determine the equilibrium evolution of those variables in the case that the other log-linear structural relations fail to uniquely determine an equilibrium. In that case, equilibrium is determinate, and the evolution of inflation depends on fiscal variables (both the level of real public debt carried into the period and news about current and future fiscal shocks), in accordance with what is sometimes called "the fiscal theory of the price level."

In the case in which the equilibrium relations studied in previous sections *do* already suffice to uniquely determine equilibrium paths $\{\pi_t, Y_t, i_t\}$ without reference to fiscal policy, these paths will not generically also be consistent with the restriction required for bounded evolution of the government debt. In the latter case, equilibrium is *over*determined. Leeper's (1991) conclusion is that the monetary and fiscal policy specifications are therefore inconsistent and that one will have to change. An alternative possibility is that a rational-expectations equilibrium exists, but involves explosive paths for some or all of these variables. In the flexible-price model considered by Loyo (1999), there is a unique rational-expectations equilibrium, but it involves explosive inflation dynamics, despite adherence to a monetary policy that conforms to the Taylor principle. Under some assumptions about what happens to fiscal policy when extreme levels of public debt are reached, there may also be an equilibrium in which inflation remains bounded, but the real public debt grows explosively until a crisis is triggered that leads to fiscal reform. Under any of these conclusions about what happens in the case of local overdetermination, it is undesirable (if even feasible) to adhere to the Taylor principle in conjunction with a locally non-Ricardian fiscal policy.

The conclusions about the consequences of alternative forms of interest-rate rules are therefore quite different depending whether fiscal policy is assumed to be locally Ricardian. One possible response would be to deny that fiscal policies are ever non-Ricardian, and hence to ignore the possibility of the second case treated in Proposition 4.11. Some have suggested that

---

form appropriate to his flexible-price model) and passive otherwise. His central result is then that equilibrium is determinate if and only if either monetary or fiscal policy is active, while the other is passive.

a model in which fiscal policy is not specified in such a way that the transversality condition (1.3) is necessarily satisfied is incoherent, as the government is not required to respect its "intertemporal budget constraint."[78]

This does not seem to be correct; for example, Bassetto (2000) gives a careful strategic analysis of a model of a bond price-support regime with a non-Ricardian fiscal policy in which the out-of-equilibrium strategies of all players (including the government) are fully specified. Furthermore, the reason why the government need not be subject to an intertemporal budget constraint of the kind that constrains other borrowers is fairly straightforward, at least in the case of a bond price-support regime; unlike the debt of private borrowers, government debt is only a promise to deliver *additional financial liabilities of its own* at maturity.[79]

A full discussion of this question would be tangential to the concerns of the present study, and it suffices here to note that whatever one thinks of the possibility of a commitment to a *globally* non-Ricardian policy, which would imply debt dynamics that fail to satisfy (1.3) even asymptotically, it is surely possible for fiscal policy to be *locally* non-Ricardian. For example, one may suppose, as proposed by McCallum (2001), that explosive dynamics of the real public debt would eventually trigger a crisis that would require a change in fiscal policy so that the transversality condition is satisfied after all, and that one can therefore be confident that (1.3) will be satisfied regardless of the expected paths of inflation, output, or interest rates. Even so, there is no reason why fiscal policy might not conform to a non-Ricardian rule (say, one in which tax collections are not affected by the size of the existing public debt, so that $\tau_b = 0$) *until* extreme regions of the state space are reached. In this case, fiscal policy would be locally non-Ricardian in the sense defined above.

This would mean that it would still be possible for a determinate equilibrium to result under a monetary rule that fails to conform to the Taylor principle, as in Woodford's (1995, 2001b) analysis of inflation determination under a bond price-support regime. Under the assumption that fiscal policy is *globally* non-Ricardian (i.e., that real tax collections would continue to evolve exogenously, regardless of the size of the real public debt), the equilibrium described in those papers is also *globally* unique; but even if a change in fiscal policy were to be forced under extreme conditions in order to satisfy the transversality condition asymptotically, this would result at most in additional possible rational-expectations equilibria (the ones involving eventual fiscal crises) that are far from the fiscalist one, which remains *locally* unique. Moreover, the fact that Evans and Honkapohja (2002b) find

---

78. See, e.g., Buiter (2002).
79. See Cochrane (2000), Sims (1999), and Woodford (2001b) for further discussion of this point.

that the fiscalist equilibrium is (at least locally) E-stable under least-squares learning suggests that it is not implausible to suppose that the economy could settle upon such an equilibrium, despite the existence in principle of others.

Similarly, the conclusion that no equilibrium exists in which small disturbances give rise to correspondingly small fluctuations in all endogenous variables when monetary policy conforms to the Taylor principle would remain disturbing even if one supposes that the locally non-Ricardian fiscal policy should nonetheless be globally Ricardian. For even if it is assumed that the equilibrium that is most likely to be reached in such a case is the one in which inflation, output, and interest rates are bounded (rather than an equilibrium with explosive inflation as in Loyo's (1999) analysis),[80] the fact that fiscal policy must change as the result of a debt crisis hardly recommends this policy configuration as one likely to promote macroeconomic stability.

Thus the possibility of locally non-Ricardian fiscal policy cannot be simply declared to be impossible or to be of no import for the effects of monetary policy. Nonetheless, the policy design problem with which I am concerned in this study is one of choosing a desirable interest-rate rule to accompany a commitment to locally Ricardian fiscal policy (e.g., a commitment to balanced budgets), and I analyze the consequences of alternative monetary policy rules, as in the previous sections of this chapter, under the assumption of a fiscal commitment of this kind. Thus while it would not be true, independently of the character of fiscal policy, that conduct of monetary policy in accordance with a Taylor rule or an inflation-targeting rule should lead to a stable macroeconomic environment (as Loyo's analysis of Brazil in the 1980s illustrates), I nonetheless argue for the desirability of commitment to policy rules of this kind. I simply emphasize that a suitable *fiscal policy commitment* is an essential part of a policy framework to achieve macroeconomic stability, in addition to a suitable monetary policy commitment.

This means, obviously, that a fiscal policy consistent with a reasonable degree of price stability must be chosen. But one can go farther and argue that it is not enough to choose a fiscal policy rule that would be consistent with certain *particular* paths for the price level that do not involve extreme inflation, or even one that is consistent with perfect constancy of the general price index, but that is *not* also consistent with most other *nearby* paths for

---

80. This is not obviously the outcome that one should expect, however, even if policy is globally Ricardian. Woodford (2001b) presents an analysis according to which Loyo's equilibrium, rather than any of those with explosive debt dynamics, is the one that is stable under learning dynamics. Evans and Honkapohja (2002b) also find that when an interest-rate rule conforming to the Taylor principle is combined with a locally non-Ricardian fiscal rule, then (for some parameter values) the uniquely E-stable equilibrium is a fiscalist equilibrium characterized by explosive inflation dynamics.

inflation. For in such a case (which would include many types of locally non-Ricardian fiscal rules), the nonexplosive paths that happen to be consistent with the fiscal rule could easily fail to coincide with any of those that are consistent with the monetary policy rule. Hence a commitment to a locally Ricardian fiscal policy—for example, to limits on deficits or on the ratio of public debt to GDP, as under the Stability and Growth Pact of the EMU—is desirable as a way of ensuring that a suitably chosen monetary policy rule can lead to price stability.[81]

Of course, one might ask why one could not equally well solve the problem of ensuring the existence of a determinate equilibrium with bounded fluctuations in inflation, output, and interest rates by committing oneself to the other possibility revealed by Proposition 4.11—a commitment *not* to adjust tax collections too much in response to fluctuations in the value of the public debt, together with a commitment *not* to adjust interest rates too much in response to variations in inflation or output. Such a regime is consistent in principle with a fairly stable macroeconomic environment, and indeed Woodford (2001b) proposes that the stable prices of the late 1940s in the United States illustrate this possibility. Nonetheless, such a regime, while rendering equilibrium determinate (and so ensuring that large fluctuations should not occur in the absence of any large change in fundamentals), leaves macroeconomic stability relatively precarious, in the sense that *fiscal expectations* come to rank among the kinds of fundamentals that may require inflation and output to vary substantially, whereas they have no effect under a regime that combines a locally Ricardian fiscal commitment with a monetary policy rule that satisfies the Taylor principle. Because long-run fiscal expectations are highly uncertain (the dramatic swings in budget projections in the U.S. policy debate over the past 5 years alone should make this clear to contemporary observers!), this seems likely to be a substantial disadvantage of non-Ricardian/passive money regimes. Indeed, the bond-price support regime of the 1940s in the United States was abandoned (with the Fed-Treasury "Accord" of 1951) precisely because a change in the fiscal outlook with the outbreak of war in Korea had abruptly turned a regime that had previously been generating mild deflation into an "engine of inflation."

Another reason can be given for not further exploring the possibilities of non-Ricardian–passive-money regimes in this study. In Chapter 8, I show

81. Our discussion here assumes an economy not subject to such severe fiscal difficulties as to make such a fiscal commitment unduly costly from other points of view. The framework for policy analysis proposed here is therefore not necessarily applicable to all countries and all times; it might, e.g., not be applicable without qualification to the situations of some developing economies or to transition economies, for reasons discussed by Jonas and Mishkin (2003) and Sims (2003). The special problems of monetary policy in countries subject to severe fiscal instability are beyond the scope of the present study.

how it is possible to design an optimal monetary policy rule. There I proceed, not by optimizing over the equilibria associated with a particular predefined class of policy regimes, but by finding the optimal state-contingent evolutions of inflation and output from among all those that could be consistent with rational-expectations equilibrium, regardless of the character of policy, and then finding a policy rule that can implement the desired equilibrium. This means that I do not simply compute the optimal equilibrium from among those consistent with a locally Ricardian fiscal policy, while the possibilities that might be made possible by non-Ricardian fiscal policy remain unexplored. Instead, I find the best possible equilibrium responses to real disturbances from among those that could be achieved by *any* policy, and then show that a regime that combines a locally Ricardian fiscal commitment with a monetary policy commitment of the kind that results in determinacy of equilibrium under this kind of fiscal policy is a possible approach to implementing the optimal equilibrium. Hence the outcome achieved by this kind of policy is as good as one can possibly hope to attain by any policy.

The result that I achieve in Chapter 8 is actually even stronger. I do not ask simply for *some* policy commitment consistent with the desired equilibrium; I seek a policy rule that is *robustly optimal*, so that the same rule continues to be optimal despite changes in the assumed character of the stochastic disturbances affecting the economy. This additional requirement proves to place tight restrictions on the form of the optimal monetary policy rule. Nonetheless, I find, for a broad class of possible economic models, that it is possible to find an optimal monetary rule in the desired sense. Moreover, in the cases treated in Chapter 8, the optimal monetary policy rule turns out to be one that implies determinacy of equilibrium in the *case of a locally Ricardian fiscal policy*, but that would imply nonexistence of a nonexplosive equilibrium in the case of a locally non-Ricardian fiscal policy. Hence the pursuit of a policy rule that is not merely consistent with optimal equilibrium responses to disturbances in the case of a particular specification of the disturbance processes, but that would *continue* to be optimal in the case of (unexpected) additional types of disturbances as well, requires that the optimal equilibrium be implemented through a commitment to active monetary policy, combined with a commitment to locally Ricardian fiscal policy.

CHAPTER 5

Dynamics of the Response to Monetary Policy

In the previous chapter I analyzed the effects of various types of policy rules in a simple but complete intertemporal general-equilibrium framework with nominal rigidities. I now consider various extensions of the simple framework that are necessary in order for a model of the monetary transmission mechanism to make some claim to quantitative realism. In particular, I discuss elaborations of the aggregate demand block of the model that allow for more complex dynamics of the response of inflation and output to changes in monetary policy.

I emphasize extensions of the proposed framework in two main directions here. First, I discuss ways in which the specification of aggregate demand must be modified to incorporate delays in the effects of monetary policy shocks on wages, prices, and economic activity of the kinds that are found in the empirical responses estimated using VAR methods. In Chapter 3, I discussed modifications of the supply side of the present model to account for delayed responses, taking as given a delayed response of aggregate nominal expenditure to the monetary policy shock, but did not seek to explain why aggregate nominal expenditure should not respond immediately to a change in interest rates. I take up that question in Section 1 of this chapter.

Second, I discuss the consequences of separately modeling consumption and investment spending, rather than supposing that all interest-sensitive private expenditure can be modeled as if it were nondurable consumer spending. In addition to being a necessary step in accounting for more detailed aspects of the observed responses to monetary policy, taking account of the effects of endogenous private investment expenditure on the evolution of productive capacity (treated as exogenous in Chapter 4) introduces an additional channel through which monetary disturbances may have longer-lasting effects. I consider the effects of endogenous capital accumulation in Section 3 of this chapter and offer a preliminary assessment of the likely quantitative significance of such effects.

I do not attempt here to offer a fully realistic quantitative model of the monetary transmission mechanism. The development of realistic models with optimizing foundations that can be used for quantitative policy evaluation is currently an active area of research, but one that is sure to develop further in the next few years, so any announcement of the correct quantitative specification is likely to be outdated by the time this book is published. I do, however, review several modeling techniques that are used in a number of recent examples of estimated models with optimizing foundations. The discussion is intended to provide insight into the effects of policy in those models, which are often more complicated than the simpler specifications presented here. This discussion will also set the stage for a consideration, in Part II, of the consequences for the character of optimal policy of assuming aggregate demand specifications of these more complex sorts.

1 Delayed Effects of Monetary Policy

The simple optimizing model of the effects of interest-rate changes on aggregate demand presented previously differs in a number of respects from the kind of specification that is common in the macroeconometric models used in central banks. One is the degree to which the model is *forward looking*. The aggregate-demand specification of the basic neo-Wicksellian model of Chapter 4,

$$\hat{Y}_t = \hat{Y}_\infty + g_t - \sigma \sum_{j=0}^{\infty} E_t(\hat{\imath}_{t+j} - \pi_{t+j+1}), \tag{1.1}$$

implies that changes in expected future interest rates should affect current aggregate expenditure as much as do changes in current (short-term) interest rates. However, in practice, expected future interest rates (at least, insofar as these expectations are based on atheoretical time-series models) co-move very closely with current short-term interest rates, as shown by Fuhrer and Moore (1995b). Thus the coefficients multiplying current short rates in the expenditure equations of econometric models might simply be proxies for a long distributed lead of expected future short rates. While the two specifications may allow a similar fit to historical data, the forward-looking model has a much clearer rationale in terms of optimizing behavior (for any of a variety of reasons, as noted in Chapter 1). Moreover, taking account of the forward-looking character of aggregate demand has important consequences for my analysis of optimal policy in Part II.

Another difference between the optimizing model and common econometric specifications, however, gives one more reason to doubt the empirical realism of the theoretical model. This is the fact that the model implies that aggregate expenditure responds to current as opposed to *lagged* interest rates. Hence the model predicts that a monetary policy disturbance should immediately affect real expenditure, as shown, for example, in Figure 4.8 (where, in fact, the maximum effect on real activity occurs in the quarter of the shock). Instead, the conventional wisdom in central banks is that monetary policy can have little immediate effect on either real activity or inflation, and VAR studies typically confirm this view. For instance, the estimated impulse response of real GDP shown in Figure 3.3 shows no non-negligible effect until two quarters following the quarter of the monetary policy shock.[1] This would be consistent with an equation for aggregate expenditure involving only interest rates two or more quarters in the past, but not with the theory that I have derived from consideration of the optimal timing of expenditure.

In this section, I briefly discuss ways in which the basic model can be extended to allow for a more realistic delay in the predicted effects of a change in monetary policy. As we shall see, optimization-based theories incorporating such delays continue to imply that interest-rate *expectations* should matter as much as actual interest rates. Moreover, they continue to imply that the key to inflation stabilization should be a policy under which the interest rate controlled by the central bank tracks variations in the natural rate of interest as accurately as possible. Thus central insights derived from the previous analysis continue to apply in more realistic settings.

1.1 Consequences of Predetermined Expenditure

One simple way in which one can explain the observed delay in the effect of monetary policy shocks on aggregate expenditure is to assume that expenditure decisions are, to some significant extent, made in advance, just as some or all prices are determined in advance in the pricing models introduced in Chapter 3. Alternatively, one might assume that many expenditure decisions are based on old information. I first present a model in which expenditure decisions are predetermined, that is, in which aggregate real expenditure in period t must be decided upon in period $t - d$. Later I discuss a closely related model in which expenditure decisions are not based on completely up-to-date information about financial-market conditions. In either case, the level of expenditure in period t must be a function solely of period $t - d$ information about interest rates, and so can depend on monetary policy shocks in period $t - d$ and earlier, but not on any more recent shocks.

How plausible are such assumptions? In the strict forms in which they have just been stated, both assumptions are obviously too extreme to be

---

1. The same is true of Figures 5.2, 5.4, and 5.5, showing the impulse response functions obtained from other identified VAR studies.

entirely realistic. Nonetheless, they capture in a simple way a feature of many actual expenditure decisions. Many of the most interest-sensitive components of expenditure, such as investment spending, are in fact predetermined to a significant extent, owing both to the existence of planning lags and to the fact that individual projects require expenditure over a period of time ("time to build," in the terminology of Kydland and Prescott, 1982), which expenditure will in most cases be worth continuing once the project has been started. (See, e.g., Edge, 2000, for discussion of both types of delay and their likely quantitative magnitudes.) Once again, whereas here I model all interest-sensitive expenditure as if it were household consumption (abstracting from any effects of this expenditure on productive capacity), the model should really be interpreted as one of the timing of private expenditure more generally, and the relevant delays are those that apply to the most interest-sensitive components of such expenditure. Furthermore, even in the case of household consumption, Gabaix and Laibson (2002) have argued that it makes sense to model households as changing their planned consumption levels only intermittently; they show that this hypothesis can help to reconcile the behavior of aggregate consumption with the behavior of asset prices. The simple model of predetermined expenditure decisions proposed here is in the spirit of such a model, though it involves a cruder hypothesis.[2]

As a simple example, suppose that the state-contingent consumption plan from date t onward is chosen to maximize

$$E_{t-d}\left\{\sum_{s=t}^{\infty}\beta^{s-t}u(C_s;\xi_s)\right\},$$

subject to an intertemporal budget constraint of the form

$$\sum_{s=t}^{\infty}E_{t-d}Q_{t-d,s}P_sC_s \leq E_{t-d}Q_{t-d,t}W_t + \sum_{s=t}^{\infty}E_{t-d}Q_{t-d,s}[P_sY_s - T_s], \quad (1.2)$$

where $\{Q_{t,s}\}$ is the same system of stochastic discount factors as in Chapter 2. Here d is the assumed length of the delay (in periods) between expenditure decisions and the time that the expenditure actually occurs (or alternatively, the delay in the receipt of new information about aggregate conditions). The intertemporal budget constraint (1.2) has to hold only in present value discounting back to the state of the economy at date $t - d$, because as before I assume (sequentially) complete financial markets, allowing a household

---

2. Intermittent adjustment of consumption as proposed by Gabaix and Laibson also leads to expenditure dynamics similar to those implied by the hypothesis of habit persistence, discussed in Section 1.2.

to insure itself at date $t - d$ against the realization of state at date t in which the present value of its subsequent after-tax income is unusually low. The present value $E_{t-d}Q_{t-d,t}W_t$ of period t initial wealth is given as an initial condition, as it follows from period $t - d$ wealth, the consumption path already chosen for periods $t-d$ through $t-1$, after-tax income expectations for those same periods, and financial-market prices.

A necessary condition for an interior solution to this optimization problem is that

$$\beta^d E_{t-d} u_c(C_t; \xi_t) = \Lambda_{t-d} \, E_{t-d}[Q_{t-d,t}P_t] \tag{1.3}$$

at each date $t - d \geq 0$ and each possible state at that date, where $\Lambda_{t-d} > 0$ is the Lagrange multiplier on the household's budget constraint (1.2) looking forward from that date, indicating the shadow value (in terms of period $t - d$ utility) of additional nominal income at date $t - d$. Another necessary condition, given the existence of complete financial markets, is that

$$\Lambda_t Q_{t,s} = \beta^{s-t} \Lambda_s \tag{1.4}$$

for any two dates $0 \leq t < s$ and any possible state at date s. Note further that using (1.4), one can equivalently write (1.3) as

$$E_{t-d} u_c(C_t; \xi_t) = E_{t-d}[\Lambda_t P_t]. \tag{1.5}$$

An optional plan is then characterized by a system of Lagrange multipliers $\{\Lambda_t\}$ and a consumption plan $\{C_t\}$ such that (i) for each date, C_t depends only on the state of the world at $t - d$; (ii) conditions (1.4) and (1.5) are satisfied in each possible state at each date; and (iii) the intertemporal budget constraint (1.2) holds with equality, looking forward from the initial date.[3]

As in Section 1, it is useful to give an approximate characterization of the optimal timing of private expenditure in the case of small disturbances by log-linearizing these equilibrium conditions around the deterministic steady-state consumption plan that is optimal in the case of no real disturbances and a monetary policy consistent with zero inflation and a nominal interest rate equal to the rate of time preference. Substituting $Y_t - G_t$ for C_t in (1.5) and log-linearizing yields

---

3. Here it is assumed that the household faces prices such that the right-hand side of (1.2) is well defined and finite; otherwise, no optimal plan is possible, as before. Thus this condition is also a requirement for equilibrium, as in Chapter 2. Similarly, if one assumes that households can choose to hold a nonnegative quantity of non-interest-bearing currency if they wish, then it is also a requirement for the existence of an optimal plan that the household face a nonnegative nominal interest at all times.

$$\hat{Y}_t = g_t - \sigma E_{t-d}\hat{\lambda}_t, \tag{1.6}$$

where $\hat{\lambda}_t \equiv \log(\Lambda_t P_t / u_c(\bar{C}; 0))$. Here the composite disturbance term is defined as

$$g_t = \hat{G}_t + s_C E_{t-d}\bar{c}_t,$$

generalizing equation (2.3) of Chapter 4. Note that this need not be pre-determined at date $t - d$, if government purchases are not determined as far in advance as interest-sensitive private expenditure.[4] The disturbances $\hat{G}_t$, $\bar{C}_t$ and the coefficient $\sigma > 0$ are defined as before.

Equation (1.4) implies that

$$1 + i_t = \beta^{-1}\Lambda_t[E_t\Lambda_{t+1}]^{-1},$$

which when log-linearized becomes

$$i_t = \hat{\lambda}_t + E_t[\pi_{t+1} - \hat{\lambda}_{t+1}].$$

This can be solved forward to yield

$$\hat{\lambda}_t = \hat{\lambda}_\infty + \sum_{j=0}^{\infty} E_t(i_{t+j} - \pi_{t+j+1}),$$

which, when substituted into (1.6), yields

$$\hat{Y}_t = \hat{Y}_\infty + g_t - \sigma \sum_{j=0}^{\infty} E_{t-d}(\hat{i}_{t+j} - \pi_{t+j+1}), \tag{1.7}$$

generalizing (1.1). Alternatively, the intertemporal "IS relation" can be written in differenced form as

$$\hat{Y}_t = g_t + E_{t-d}(\hat{Y}_{t+1} - g_{t+1}) - \sigma E_{t-d}(i_t - \pi_{t+1}). \tag{1.8}$$

This is essentially the same form of IS relation as in the basic model, except that now it is *past expectations* of current and future real interest rates that matter, rather than current interest rates or current expectations. Such a specification implies that an unexpected change in monetary policy in period t can have no effect on aggregate real expenditure before period

---

4. The assumption that g_t is not public knowledge at $t - d$ does not require that the government has better information about macroeconomic conditions or a shorter planning horizon than the private sector. It simply indicates exogenous random variation in government purchases that cannot be forecast d periods in advance on the basis of public information.

$t + d$. Yet the delayed effect of a monetary policy shock does not occur because it is actual past interest rates, rather than current or expected future rates, that matter for current expenditure. Only past expectations regarding real rates of return *from now on* are relevant to the desired substitution between current and future expenditure, even when the decision itself was made at a past date.

The difference between this specification and an IS relation according to which current real expenditure depends on lagged (but not current) interest rates has quite important implications for the conduct of monetary policy. If expenditure depended on actual lagged interest rates, it would follow that interest rates should be adjusted now to offset disturbances that are expected to affect the output gap in the future, even if these disturbances have no immediate effect; for once the disturbances have their effect, it may be too late for an interest-rate change to have any countervailing influence on expenditure. Thus policy should be forward looking and respond immediately to news that affects the economic outlook some quarters in the future. If, instead, as in this optimizing model, expenditure depends on *past expectations* of current and future rates, it follows that interest-rate policy affects expenditure only to the extent that it is *forecastable* in advance. There would therefore be no advantage (from the point of view of output-gap stabilization) in responding at all to news except after it has been known to the public for d periods. Instead, it would be important to base current interest rates on past conditions (possibly including past perceptions of the outlook for the future), in order to bring about forecastable interest-rate variations that could be used to offset the effects of predictable disturbances.

Under this alternative specification of our forward-looking model of the determinants of real expenditure, the effects of an (anticipated future) monetary disturbance are similar to those analyzed earlier, only delayed in time. Suppose, for example, that there is a lag of the same length before new price decisions take effect, so that the aggregate-supply relation is of the form

$$\pi_t = \kappa E_{t-d} x_t + \beta E_{t-d} \pi_{t+1},\tag{1.9}$$

where once again $x_t \equiv \hat{Y}_t - \hat{Y}_t^n$, and $\hat{Y}_t^n$ is defined as in Chapter 3. Furthermore, the component of the output gap that is forecastable d periods in advance satisfies

$$E_{t-d} x_t = E_{t-d} x_{t+1} - \sigma E_{t-d}(\hat{\imath}_t - \pi_{t+1} - \hat{r}_t^n),\tag{1.10}$$

as a consequence of (1.8). This relation together with

$$x_t = E_{t-d} x_t + (g_t - \hat{Y}_t^n) - E_{t-d}(g_t - \hat{Y}_t^n)\tag{1.11}$$

is in fact equivalent to (1.8).

Finally, let monetary policy be specified by a rule of the form

$$\tilde{\imath}_t = \rho \tilde{\imath}_{t-1} + \phi_\pi (\tilde{\pi}_t - \rho \tilde{\pi}_{t-1}) + (\phi_x/4)(\tilde{x}_t - \rho \tilde{x}_{t-1}) + \epsilon_t, \qquad (1.12)$$

as in Figure 4.8, where again tildes are used to denote deviations of each variable from its target value. Then for the same parameter values as are assumed in the baseline case ($\rho = 0.7$) of that figure, but with a delay of $d = 1$ quarter, the predicted impulse responses to a contractionary monetary policy shock are those shown by the solid lines in Figure 5.1. Note that for quarters 1 and later following the shock, the responses are identical to those shown earlier in Figure 4.8. The only difference is that there are no effects on output or inflation in the quarter of the shock itself; as a consequence, the initial increase in the nominal interest rate is much larger, as the increase in $\tilde{\imath}_t$ is not offset by the reaction to any immediate declines in output or inflation (as was the case in Figure 4.8). This modification of the model greatly increases its realism, not only because the effects on output and inflation are delayed, but because of the prediction of a transitory

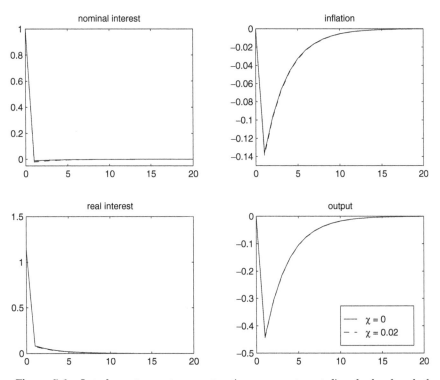

Figure 5.1 *Impulse responses to a contractionary monetary policy shock when both expenditure and prices are predetermined for one quarter.*

"liquidity effect" of a monetary tightening. Note that the predicted initial increase in nominal interest rates is weaker (or even absent, as in the cases $\rho = 0.7$ or 0.8) in Figure 4.8. The responses shown in Figure 5.1 are much more similar to empirical estimates, discussed further in the next section.[5]

Under this extension of the basic model, the key to inflation and output-gap stabilization continues to be the adjustment of interest rates so as to track the variations in the natural rate of interest owing to exogenous real disturbances. For example, suppose that monetary policy is described by a Taylor rule of the form

$$\hat{\imath}_t = \bar{\imath}_t + E_{t-d}[\phi_\pi (\pi_t - \bar{\pi}) + \phi_x(x_t - \bar{x})], \qquad (1.13)$$

where $\bar{x}$ is consistent with $\bar{\pi}$, as assumed earlier, and $\bar{\imath}_t$ is again an exogenous intercept term.[6] The evolution of the forecastable components of inflation, the output gap, and the nominal interest rate is then determined by the system of equations consisting of (1.9), (1.10), and the equation obtained by taking the conditional expectation of both sides of (1.13) at date $t - d$. This system of equations has a structure that is precisely analogous to the system consisting of equations (1.12)–(1.14) of Chapter 4 in the case of the basic neo-Wicksellian model. It implies a determinate rational-expectations equilibrium in exactly the same case as with the previous system, that is, if and only if the coefficients satisfy the Taylor principle,

$$\phi_\pi + \frac{1-\beta}{4\kappa}\phi_x > 1. \qquad (1.14)$$

In this case, the unique bounded solution is given by

$$\pi_t = \bar{\pi} + \sum_{j=0}^{\infty} \psi_j^\pi E_{t-d}\left(\hat{r}_{t+j}^n - \bar{\imath}_{t+j} + \bar{\pi}\right), \qquad (1.15)$$

$$x_t = \bar{x} + \sum_{j=0}^{\infty} \psi_j^x E_{t-d}\left(\hat{r}_{t+j}^n - \bar{\imath}_{t+j} + \bar{\pi}\right) + \left(g_t - \hat{Y}_t^n\right) - E_{t-d}\left(g_t - \hat{Y}_t^n\right), \qquad (1.16)$$

$$\hat{\imath}_t = \bar{\imath}_t + \sum_{j=0}^{\infty} \psi_j^i E_{t-d}\left(\hat{r}_{t+j}^n - \bar{\imath}_{t+j} + \bar{\pi}\right), \qquad (1.17)$$

5. The figure also shows the predicted impulse responses in the case that I allow for real-balance effects, parameterizing monetary frictions in the way discussed in Section 3.2 of Chapter 4. These are not substantially different from those predicted in the cashless case. Hence we continue to abstract from real-balance effects in the remainder of this chapter.

6. The assumption that the endogenous terms involve only the components of inflation and the output gap that are forecastable at $t - d$ is purely notational. For it follows from (1.9) that π_t is entirely forecastable at $t - d$, while it follows from (1.11) that the unforecastable component of x_t is purely exogenous.

where the coefficients $\{\psi_j^y\}$ for $y = \pi, x, i$ are exactly the same as before. Here the solutions for the forecastable components of all three variables are given by the forecasts d periods in advance of the solutions previously presented in equations (2.31)–(2.33) of Chapter 4. The variables π_t and $\hat{\imath}_t - \bar{\imath}_t$ have no unforecastable components, while the unforecastable component of x_t is given by (1.11).

This solution implies, once again, that inflation and the output gap are both stabilized, to the greatest extent possible, by commitment to a Taylor rule in which the intercept term tracks variation in the natural rate of interest. The only difference is that now it is only necessary to track the fluctuations in the natural rate that can be forecast d periods in advance. A rule of the form (1.13) with $\bar{\imath}_t = E_{t-d}\hat{r}_t^n$ and coefficients ϕ_π, ϕ_x satisfying (1.14) implies a determinate equilibrium in which

$$\pi_t = \bar{\pi}, \qquad E_{t-d}x_t = \bar{x}$$

at all times. This obviously stabilizes inflation to the greatest extent possible. Since the forecastable and unforecastable components of the output gap are necessarily uncorrelated,

$$\text{var}\{x_t\} = \text{var}\{E_{t-d}x_t\} + \text{var}\{x_t - E_{t-d}x_t\}$$
$$= \text{var}\{E_{t-d}x_t\} + \text{var}\{(g_t - \hat{Y}_t^n) - E_{t-d}(g_t - \hat{Y}_t^n)\},$$

as a consequence of (1.11). Given that the second term is independent of monetary policy, the most that can be done to stabilize the output gap is to reduce the variance of the forecastable component to zero; the proposed policy achieves this.

Certain complications arise when one seeks to combine this alternative model of the effects of interest rates on aggregate demand with aggregate-supply relations of the sort derived in Chapter 3. The derivations in Chapter 3 assume that period t expenditure is chosen optimally on the basis of period t information, so that (1.6) holds with $d = 0$. The place at which this assumption was used in Chapter 3 was in replacing the marginal utility of income by a function of current consumption in the account there of optimizing labor supply (and hence of the marginal cost of supplying goods). More generally, the (log-linearized) real-marginal-cost function for the model with flexible wages is given by

$$\hat{s}_t(i) = \omega(\hat{y}_t(i) - \hat{Y}_t^n) + \sigma^{-1}(\hat{Y}_t - \hat{Y}_t^n) - \mu_t, \tag{1.18}$$

where

$$\mu_t \equiv \hat{\lambda}_t - \sigma^{-1}(g_t - \hat{Y}_t) \tag{1.19}$$

is the discrepancy between the (log) marginal utility of real income and the (log) marginal utility of consumption. When period t expenditure is chosen optimally at date t, $\mu_t = 0$ and the aggregate-supply relations derived in Chapter 3 are correct. But when interest-sensitive private expenditure must be chosen in advance, (1.6) implies only that $E_{t-d}\mu_t = 0$, whereas μ_t need not equal zero.

Now suppose that even though the aggregate index of demand (i.e., the demand for the composite good) is determined d periods in advance, the way that this demand is allocated across the various differentiated goods is *not* committed in advance. It follows that a supplier who considers a price change that will take effect in less than d periods will still calculate the optimal price taking into account the effect on demand for its good from the first period in which the price change takes effect. Then in the case of random intervals between price changes of the kind assumed by Calvo (1983) and a delay of s periods before a newly chosen price takes effect, the aggregate-supply relation should be of the form

$$\pi_t = \kappa E_{t-s} x_t - (\kappa/\epsilon_{mc}) E_{t-s}\mu_t + \beta E_{t-s}\pi_{t+1}, \tag{1.20}$$

where $\epsilon_{mc} > 0$ is the elasticity of average real marginal cost with respect to the level of aggregate output.

Only in the case that $s \geq d$ could the $E_{t-s}\mu_t$ term be neglected (as in (1.9) above). If $s < d$, one would instead need to use the form (1.20), together with the relation

$$\mu_t = \sum_{j=0}^{d-1} E_t\left[\hat{\imath}_{t+j} - \pi_{t+j+1}\right] + \sigma^{-1}\left[\left(\hat{Y}_t - g_t\right) - E_t\left(\hat{Y}_{t+d} - g_{t+d}\right)\right] \tag{1.21}$$

relating μ_t to observables using (1.6).[7] The presence of the $E_{t-s}\mu_t$ term indicates a moderating effect on expected supply costs in period t, and hence on inflationary pressure, of an expectation at $t - s$ of real rates of return between periods t and $t + d - s$ that are higher than those that were anticipated at the time that expenditure was planned for periods t through $t + d - s - 1$. Unexpectedly high real rates of return increase the value of income in period t, and so lower average wage demands, even if they occur as a result of shocks that (because unanticipated) do not affect aggregate demand.

There appears, however, to be little evidence of an effect of interest rates on supply costs of the kind implied by the $E_{t-s}\mu_t$ term in (1.20). If anything, unexpected interest-rate increases probably *increase* supply costs in the short run, as found by Barth and Ramey (2000) and Christiano et al. (2001). It

---

7. See the empirical model of Rotemberg and Woodford (1997) for an illustration.

is thus important to note that this effect appears in (1.20), even under the assumption that $s < d$, only in the case that the delay in the effect of interest rates on expenditure is derived from a planning delay rather than a delay in obtaining up-to-date information about financial conditions.

Under an alternative interpretation of (1.7), period t spending decisions are made at date t, but on the basis of an estimate of the household's marginal utility of real income that reflects information available at date $t-d$ rather than the complete information available to financial-market participants at date t. Suppose that each household has an agent that optimally manages its investments. This agent, with full information about financial market conditions (as well as about the household's tastes and labor-income prospects), produces an estimate of the marginal utility of additional wealth. Individual household members who go into the goods markets then purchase individual goods to the point at which the marginal utility from an additional dollar of spending on a given good equals the current estimate of the marginal utility of wealth. But suppose there is a time delay in the transmission of the financial advisor's estimate, so that in period t the household's spending decisions are based on the financial advisor's period $t - d$ estimate of what the household's marginal utility of real wealth in period t would be.

Suppose further that the household members simply use this estimate, rather than updating it on the basis of what they should be able to infer about unexpected changes in financial conditions from the prices that they observe.[8] The level of expenditure C_t is then determined at date t to satisfy the first-order condition

$$u_c(C_t; \xi_t) = E_{t-d}[\Lambda_t P_t], \tag{1.22}$$

where the right-hand side is the signal transmitted by the financial advisor at date $t - d$. This has implications that are identical to those of (1.5), except that taste shocks ξ_t that are not forecastable at date $t - d$ can still affect private expenditure in this version.[9] Equating C_t with $Y_t - G_t$ and log-linearizing, we again obtain (1.6), except that in this case g_t is again defined as

$$g_t = \hat{G}_t + s_C \bar{c}_t,$$

as in Chapter 4. We then again obtain an IS relation of the form (1.7).

---

8. There is admittedly an element of bounded rationality in this assumption, which is not required if one assumes that the household has committed itself in advance to a particular level of real expenditure.

9. An appealing feature of this alternative derivation is that it makes it clear why expenditure at date t on individual goods should still depend on the prices of the individual goods, as I have assumed, rather than only on the forecast of their prices at date $t - d$.

Under this alternative interpretation, however, each household's labor-supply decisions should *also* be affected by its imperfect information about current financial-market conditions. Thus real wages, and hence real marginal costs, should depend on $E_{t-d}\hat{\lambda}_t$ rather than on the true value of $\hat{\lambda}_t$, as this would be evaluated by the household's financial advisor. But (1.6) implies that $E_{t-d}\hat{\lambda}_t$ can be written as $-\sigma^{-1}(\hat{Y}_t - g_t)$, even if $\hat{\lambda}_t$ cannot. Thus one obtains (1.18) without the μ_t term, and correspondingly (1.20) without the $E_{t-s}\mu_t$ term. That is, one gets exactly the form of AS relation derived in Chapter 3 for the case $d = 0$.

1.2 Habit Persistence in Private Expenditure

An alternative reason for delays in the effect of interest-rate changes on aggregate expenditure—or at any rate for the initial effect to be smaller than the eventual effect in the case of a change in interest rates that is relatively persistent—is the hypothesis that the current level of aggregate real expenditure depends positively on the recent past level of expenditure, so that aggregate demand should change only gradually even in the case of an abrupt change in the path of interest rates. This is often a feature of ad hoc macroeconometric "IS relations" (e.g., Fuhrer and Moore, 1995b). A simple theoretical interpretation of such a specification in terms of optimizing behavior is to assume that private expenditure exhibits "habit persistence" of the sort assumed in the case of consumption expenditure by authors such as Fuhrer (2000), Edge (2000), Christiano et al. (2001), Altig et al. (2002), and Smets and Wouters (2002).

Here, as in Chapter 4 and in the previous section, I model all interest-sensitive private expenditure as if it were nondurable consumption; that is, I abstract from the effects of variations in private expenditure on the evolution of productive capacity. Hence I assume habit persistence in the level of aggregate private expenditure and not solely in consumption, as in the models of Amato and Laubach (2000) and Boivin and Giannoni (2003). This might seem odd, given that I do not really interpret the "C_t" in my model as referring mainly to consumption expenditure. But quantitative models that treat consumption and investment spending separately often indicate that the dynamics of investment spending are also best captured by specifications of adjustment costs that imply inertia in the rate of investment spending (e.g., Edge, 2000; Christiano et al., 2001; Altig et al., 2002; Basu and Kimball, 2002). The "habit persistence" assumed here should be understood as a proxy for adjustment costs in investment expenditure of that sort and not solely (or even primarily) as a description of household preferences with regard to personal consumption.

Following Boivin and Giannoni (2003), suppose that the utility flow of any household h in period t depends not only on its real expenditure C_t^h in that period, but also on that household's level of expenditure in the previous period.[10] Specifically, I assume that the utility flow from expenditure is given by a function of the form

$$u\big(C_t^h - \eta C_{t-1}^h; \xi_t\big),$$

where ξ_t is a vector of exogenous taste shocks, $u(\cdot; \xi)$ is an increasing, concave function for each value of the exogenous disturbances, and $0 \leq \eta \leq 1$ measures the degree of habit persistence.[11] (The model of Chapter 4 corresponds to the limiting case $\eta = 0$ of this one.) The household's budget constraint remains as before.

In this extension of the present model, the marginal utility for the representative household of additional real income in period t is no longer equal to the marginal utility of consumption in that period, but rather to

$$\lambda_t = u_c(C_t - \eta C_{t-1}; \xi_t) - \beta \eta E_t [u_c(C_{t+1} - \eta C_t; \xi_{t+1})]. \qquad (1.23)$$

The marginal utility of income in different periods continues to be linked to the expected return on financial assets in the usual way, so that equilibrium requires that

$$\lambda_t = \beta E_t [\lambda_{t+1}(1 + i_t)P_t/P_{t+1}]. \qquad (1.24)$$

Using (1.23) to substitute for the λ's in (1.24), I obtain a generalization of the previous Euler equation for the intertemporal allocation of aggregate expenditure given expected rates of return.

Log-linearization of this Euler equation yields a generalization of the previous IS relation of the form

$$\tilde{x}_t = E_t \tilde{x}_{t+1} - \varphi^{-1} \big[\hat{\imath}_t - E_t \pi_{t+1} - \hat{r}_t^n\big], \qquad (1.25)$$

where

$$\tilde{x}_t \equiv (x_t - \eta x_{t-1}) - \beta \eta E_t(x_{t+1} - \eta x_t),$$

$$\varphi^{-1} \equiv (1 - \beta \eta)\sigma > 0,$$

and $\sigma \equiv -u_c/(\bar{Y} u_{cc})$ as before. Here x_t is again the log gap between actual output and the flexible-price equilibrium level of output, and r_t^n is again

---

10. Note that the consumption "habit" is assumed here to depend on the household's own past level of expenditure, and not on that of other households.

11. In the case that C_t^h is actually interpreted as investment expenditure, one can make sense of this specification by supposing that investment adjustment costs are of the specific kind postulated by Basu and Kimball (2002). See Section D.1 of Appendix D.

the flexible-price equilibrium real interest rate, that is, the real interest rate associated with an equilibrium in which $x_t = 0$ at all times. Note that when $\eta = 0$, φ reduces to σ^{-1}, $\tilde{x}_t$ reduces to x_t, and (1.25) reduces to the IS relation of the basic neo-Wicksellian model. In the general case, the log marginal utility of real income is negatively related to $\tilde{x}_t$, rather than to x_t, which is why $\tilde{x}_t$ appears in the generalized IS relation (1.25).

This can be solved forward to yield

$$x_t - \eta x_{t-1} = \sum_{j=0}^{\infty} (\beta \eta)^j E_t \tilde{x}_{t+j}$$

$$= (1 - \eta) x_{\infty} - \sum_{k=0}^{\infty} \xi_k E_t \left[\hat{\imath}_{t+k} - \pi_{t+k+1} - \hat{r}_{t+k}^n \right],$$

where

$$\xi_k = \varphi^{-1} \frac{1 - (\beta \eta)^{k+1}}{1 - \beta \eta} > 0$$

for each $k \geq 0$. Hence in this extension of the basic model, the output gap at a given point in time is a decreasing function of expected real interest-rate gaps as before, but also now an increasing function of the previous period's output gap. There is thus intrinsic persistence in the dynamics of the output gap. Purely transitory fluctuations in the real interest-rate gap will result in the output gap following an AR(1) process, with the coefficient of autocorrelation given by η; instead, AR(1) fluctuations in the interest-rate gap, with a substantial degree of persistence, will result in the output gap following an AR(2) process, with innovations in the interest-rate gap giving rise to hump-shaped dynamics of the output gap. Hence a model of this kind provides a further reason for the effects of changes in monetary policy on aggregate expenditure to be delayed—at least, a reason why the maximum effect on expenditure may occur several quarters later than the maximum effect on real interest rates.

This modification of preferences changes the form of the aggregate-supply relation appropriate to the present model as well. For simplicity, I consider here only the case of a model with flexible wages and Calvo pricing, as in the basic neo-Wicksellian model of Chapter 4. In the derivation of my previous aggregate-supply relation (in Chapter 3), I assumed that the log marginal utility of real income (which affects real supply costs owing to its effect on real wage demands) can be replaced by a linear function of x_t. But just as in the case of the IS relation, this must now be written as a linear function of $\tilde{x}_t$ instead. One then obtains an aggregate-supply relation of the form

$$\pi_t = \xi_p [\omega x_t + \varphi \tilde{x}_t] + \beta E_t \pi_{t+1}, \tag{1.26}$$

where $\xi_p > 0$ is the same coefficient as in equation (4.9) of Chapter 3. (This reduces to the aggregate-supply relation used in Chapter 4 in the limiting case that $\eta = 0$, recalling that $\kappa \equiv \xi_p(\omega + \sigma^{-1})$ in the notation used earlier.)

This relation can be rewritten equivalently in the form

$$\pi_t = \kappa[(x_t - \delta x_{t-1}) - \beta\delta E_t(x_{t+1} - \delta x_t)] + \beta E_t \pi_{t+1}, \tag{1.27}$$

where $0 \le \delta \le \eta$ is the smaller root of the quadratic equation

$$\eta\varphi(1 + \beta\delta^2) = [\omega + \varphi(1 + \beta\eta^2)]\delta, \tag{1.28}$$

and

$$\kappa \equiv \xi_p \eta\varphi/\delta > 0. \tag{1.29}$$

[Note that in the limiting case in which $\eta = 0$, $\delta = 0$, while δ/η approaches the well-defined limit $\varphi/(\omega + \varphi)$, so that $\kappa = \xi_p(\omega + \varphi) = \xi_p(\omega + \sigma^{-1})$. Thus in this limit, the definition of κ given in (1.29) coincides with the one given in Chapter 3.] This alternative form will be especially useful when I consider optimal stabilization policy in Part II.

Suppose now that monetary policy is specified by a Taylor rule of the form

$$\hat{\imath}_t = \bar{\imath}_t + \phi_\pi(\pi_t - \bar{\pi}) + \phi_x(x_t - \bar{x}), \tag{1.30}$$

where again $\bar{x}$ is consistent with $\bar{\pi}$ and $\bar{\imath}_t$ is an exogenous intercept term. The equilibrium evolution of inflation, the output gap, and the nominal interest rate is then determined by the system consisting of equations (1.25), (1.26) or (1.27), and (1.30). Once again, I can use (1.30) to substitute for $\hat{\imath}_t$ in (1.25), and obtain a system of two equations to solve for the paths of π_t and x_t, in which the only exogenous disturbance is the composite term $\hat{r}_t^n - \bar{\imath}_t$.

It follows that whenever the response coefficients of the monetary policy rule are in the range that implies determinacy of equilibrium, the unique bounded solution to these equations are of the form

$$\pi_t = \bar{\pi} + \omega_\pi(x_{t-1} - \bar{x}) + \sum_{j=0}^{\infty} \psi_j^\pi E_t(\hat{r}_{t+j}^n - \bar{\imath}_{t+j} + \bar{\pi}), \tag{1.31}$$

$$x_t = \bar{x} + \omega_x(x_{t-1} - \bar{x}) + \sum_{j=0}^{\infty} \psi_j^x E_t(\hat{r}_{t+j}^n - \bar{\imath}_{t+j} + \bar{\pi}), \tag{1.32}$$

$$\hat{\imath}_t = \bar{\imath}_t + \omega_i(x_{t-1} - \bar{x}) + \sum_{j=0}^{\infty} \psi_j^i E_t(\hat{r}_{t+j}^n - \bar{\imath}_{t+j} + \bar{\pi}), \tag{1.33}$$

for some coefficients ω_y and $\{\psi_j^y\}$. I thus obtain, once again, the same general result as in Chapter 4: Inflation and the output gap are both stabilized, to the greatest extent possible, by commitment to a Taylor rule in which the intercept term tracks variation in the natural rate of interest.

2 Some Small Quantitative Models

I now review some examples of fairly small estimated models of the U.S. monetary transmission mechanism with complete optimizing foundations. These models remain simpler than the ones that would probably best be offered as examples of the current state of the art, but they incorporate many key elements of the most sophisticated optimizing models currently being used for the quantitative analysis of monetary policy,[12] and their structure can be discussed relatively briefly. A presentation of the numerical parameter values obtained for these models offers some sense of what reasonable quantitative magnitudes might be for critical parameters of the theoretical models on which I base my analysis of optimal policy in Part II.

2.1 The Rotemberg-Woodford Model

A model only slightly more complex than those described in Section 1.1 is used by Rotemberg and Woodford (1997, 1999a) as a basis for quantitative analysis of alternative interest-rate rules for the U.S. economy. Rotemberg and Woodford assume an intertemporal IS equation of the form (1.8) with a delay of $d = 2$ quarters and interpret the delay as being due to predeterminedness of interest-sensitive private expenditure. Their AS equation is instead a more complex version of (1.9), in which the delay required before revised prices take effect is not the same for all goods. Instead, it is assumed that for a fraction φ of all goods, a new price that is chosen in period t (or at any rate, on the basis of public information in period t) applies to purchases beginning in period $t + 1$, whereas for the remaining goods, a new price chosen in period t takes effect only beginning in period $t + 2$. In the case of both types of goods, it is assumed (as in the Calvo model) that a fraction $1 - \alpha$ of all goods prices are revised each period, with the price of each good having the same probability of being revised in any given period.

   In this case, the aggregate supply relation (1.20) generalizes to

$$\pi_t = \frac{1}{1+\psi}\left\{\kappa E_{t-1}x_t - \frac{\kappa}{\epsilon_{mc}}E_{t-1}\mu_t + \beta E_{t-1}\pi_{t+1}\right\}$$

12. As examples of current best practice, one might mention the work of Christiano et al. (2001), Altig et al. (2002), Smets and Wouters (2002), and the new Global Economic Model under development at the IMF (see, e.g., Laxton and Pesenti, 2002).

$$+ \frac{\psi}{1+\psi} \{\kappa E_{t-2}x_t + \beta E_{t-2}\pi_{t+1}\}, \tag{2.1}$$

where $\psi \equiv (1 - \varphi)/\varphi\alpha > 0$, while (1.21) implies that

$$E_{t-1}\mu_t = E_{t-1}\left[\hat{\imath}_t - \pi_{t+1}\right] + \sigma^{-1}\left[\left(\hat{Y}_t - g_t\right) - \left(\hat{Y}_{t+1} - g_{t+1}\right)\right]. \tag{2.2}$$

(Note that when $d = 2$, (1.8) implies that the value of the second term in square brackets here is known at date $t - 1$, so that we may omit the conditional expectation operator for that term.) The log-linearized structural equations of the Rotemberg-Woodford model then consist of the intertemporal IS relation (1.8) with $d = 2$; the aggregate-supply relation obtained by substituting (2.2) into (2.1); a specification of the exogenous disturbance processes $\{g_t, \hat{Y}_t^n\}$; and a monetary policy rule specifying $\hat{\imath}_t$ as function of its own history, current and lagged values of inflation and output, and a serially uncorrelated exogenous monetary policy shock.[13] Once the processes $\{g_t, \hat{Y}_t^n\}$ have been specified, the evolution of the natural rate of interest $\hat{r}_t^n$ that appears in (1.8) is given by

$$\hat{r}_t^n \equiv \sigma^{-1}\left[\left(g_t - \hat{Y}_t^n\right) - E_t\left(g_{t+1} - \hat{Y}_{t+1}^n\right)\right]. \tag{2.3}$$

The monetary policy rule, the laws of motion for the exogenous disturbances, and certain parameters of the structural equations are also specified so as to allow the model to fit as well as possible the joint evolution of short-term nominal interest rates, inflation, and output in the U.S. economy. Rotemberg and Woodford characterize the co-movements of these latter three variables by estimating an unrestricted VAR model for the federal funds rate, the rate of growth of the GDP deflator, and the linearly detrended log of real GDP, using quarterly data for the sample period 1980:1–1995:2. These particular measures of the interest rate, inflation, and output are used following Taylor (1993), as one equation of the VAR should represent an estimate of the Fed's reaction function. The sample period begins at the beginning of 1980 because of the general recognition that an important change in the way that monetary policy was conducted in the United States occurred around this time. (Recall the discussion in Chapter 1 of the alternative interest-rate rules estimated for different sample periods. An even shorter sample period might be preferred on the same grounds— say, a post-1987 sample as in Taylor, 1993, 1999c—but this would allow even less precise estimates of the impulse responses to a monetary policy shock.)

---

13. Note that if a sufficient number of lags of the endogenous variables are included, this specification is equivalent to one in which the monetary policy disturbance is allowed to be an arbitrary autoregressive process.

In the VAR model, $\hat{\imath}_t$, π_{t+1}, and $\hat{Y}_{t+1}$ are regressed on three lags of each of these variables, with the coefficients otherwise unrestricted. (Additional lags are not included as they were found not to be significant.) The particular lags that are included in the case of each variable are chosen in this way because the model implies that $\hat{\imath}_t$, π_{t+1}, and $\hat{Y}_{t+1}$ are all part of the same information sets: These variables are known by period t (in particular, before the period $t+1$ interest-rate decision is made), because both inflation and output are predetermined,[14] but not yet known in period $t-1$ (i.e., before the period t interest-rate decision is made). Because the model implies that the period t interest-rate decision cannot affect the determination of either period t output or period t inflation, an OLS regression of $\hat{\imath}_t$ on the lags of all three variables (which include π_t and $\hat{Y}_t$) should identify the coefficients of the monetary policy rule, and the residual of this equation should identify the sequence of monetary policy shocks.[15] The two VAR residuals orthogonal to this one are interpreted instead as the two innovations in the joint exogenous process for the disturbances $\{g_t, \hat{Y}_t^n\}$.

With this identification of the historical monetary policy shocks, the just identified VAR model can be used to estimate the impulse responses of all three variables to a monetary policy shock. Figure 5.2 plots the estimated responses, together with the associated (± 2 s.e.) confidence intervals, in the case of a one-standard-error innovation in the federal funds rate, that is, an unexpected monetary tightening. By construction, the funds rate increases, whereas there is no effect on either output or inflation in the quarter of the shock. However, the results also indicate (as in Figure 3.3) that there is no noticeable effect on output in the following quarter either, though output sharply declines in the second quarter following the shock; this is the reason for the inclusion of a delay $d = 2$ quarters in the determination of private expenditure in the Rotemberg-Woodford model. The contraction of output relative to trend persists for several quarters, though Rotemberg and Woodford find a peak output effect in the second quarter following the monetary shock, which is sooner than what is indicated by most studies using a longer sample.[16] (Compare Figure 3.3.) The effects of

14. Note that it is assumed that the composite exogenous disturbance g_t is known at date $t-1$, i.e., prior to the determination of the period t interest rate. Since government purchases are in fact typically budgeted in advance, this is not implausible.

15. The assumptions used to identify the monetary policy shock here are common in the structural VAR literature on this question; see, e.g., Christiano et al. (1999).

16. Boivin and Giannoni (2003) compare the results that would be obtained using a similar method to analyze the response to monetary policy shocks in a pre-1980 sample. They argue that much of the difference can be accounted for by the change in their estimated monetary policy rule between the pre-1980 and post-1980 samples, though they also find that a better fit to the pre-1980 responses is possible in the case of a model that incorporates additional grounds for persistence in the effects of interest-rate changes on private-sector expenditure, as discussed below.

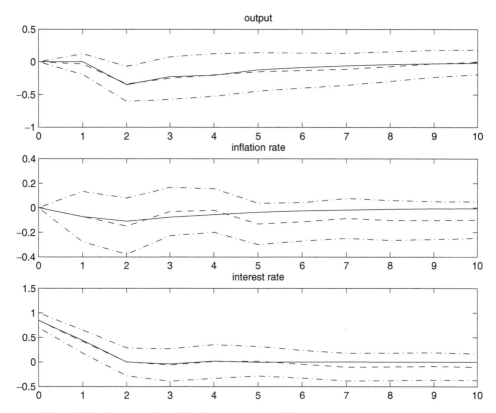

Figure 5.2 *Predicted [solid line] and estimated [dashed line] impulse responses to a monetary policy shock. Dash-dotted lines indicate bounds of the confidence intervals for the estimated responses. Source: Rotemberg and Woodford (1997).*

a monetary policy shock on inflation are less well estimated, but the point estimates indicate lower inflation for many subsequent quarters as a result of the policy tightening.

One equation of the VAR can also be interpreted as indicating the Fed's reaction function over this period. The estimated coefficients on the three lags of the funds rate itself are all positive, and they sum to 0.69. This implies substantial inertia in the Fed's interest-rate policy, as in the estimated rules discussed in Chapter 1. The sums of the coefficients on current and lagged values of inflation and detrended output are also both positive and imply long-run interest-rate responses to sustained increases in these two variables of $\Phi_\pi = 2.13$ and $\Phi_y = 0.47$, respectively. Thus except for the additional dynamics implied by the inclusion of lags of all three variables, the estimated reaction function is similar to Taylor's (1993) characterization of Fed policy under Greenspan's chairmanship.

Rotemberg and Woodford then estimate certain parameters of their model so as to fit the estimated responses to a monetary policy shock as closely as possible, given that monetary policy is described by the estimated interest-rate rule. It can be shown that the model's predicted responses depend only on the parameters β, σ, κ, and a certain function of ω and ψ, in addition to the coefficients of the monetary policy rule.[17] There are thus at most four free parameters that can be chosen (within certain a priori bounds) so as to improve the model's fit. Furthermore, because the model implies that $\beta^{-1} - 1$ should equal the long-run average real rate of interest, Rotemberg and Woodford calibrate the discount factor $\beta = .99$ on these grounds, rather than using information about the responses to shocks to estimate this parameter. They then estimate the values of the other three parameters that minimize the distance between the predicted impulse responses and those implied by the unrestricted VAR estimates. The predicted impulse responses in the case of these parameter values are shown by the solid lines in Figure 5.2.

Note that the model can account quite well for both the size and the persistence of the estimated response of real GDP. The predicted output response is in fact essentially the same as the one shown in Figure 4.7 for the inertial policy rule with $\rho = 0.7$, with the magnitude of the policy shock appropriately rescaled and the response delayed for two quarters.[18] For the IS and AS relations of the Rotemberg-Woodford model are identical to those of the basic neo-Wicksellian model if one takes expectations conditional upon information two quarters earlier. It follows that the predicted responses of all variables two or more quarters following the shock are the same as in the analysis in Chapter 4, if the initial conditions that apply two quarters later are appropriately adjusted; the result follows for the same reason as in the case of the one-quarter delay shown in Figure 5.1. Thus the predicted output response would be exactly the same as in Figure 4.7 or 5.1, but with a two-quarter delay, if the policy rule were of the simpler form assumed in those figures.

The model also accounts well for the estimated response of the funds rate itself to a monetary policy shock: The theoretical model predicts, as the VAR indicates, that the funds rate returns essentially to the level that would have been predicted in the absence of any shock within two quarters following the shock. (This occurs for the same reason that in Figure 4.7 there is very little response of the nominal interest rate to the policy shock, and that in Figure 5.1 the interest rate returns to its normal level after one quarter.) Note

17. Parameter identification, along with other aspects of the estimation strategy, are discussed in detail in the appendix to Rotemberg and Woodford (1998).

18. The size of the effective shift in the intercept term of the policy rule in the second period following the shock is found by substituting the predicted responses in the previous two periods for the lagged interest-rate and inflation terms in the rule.

TABLE 5.1   Parameter values in the quarterly model of Rotemberg and Woodford (1997)

α	0.66	ν	0.11	ϵ_{mc}	0.63
β	0.99	ϕ_h^{-1}	0.75	$(\theta - 1)^{-1}$	0.15
φ	0.63	ω_w	0.14	ζ	0.14
ψ	0.88	ω_p	0.33	κ	0.024
σ^{-1}	0.16	ω	0.47		

that this fact does *not* mean, as is sometimes supposed, that an "interest-rate channel" cannot account for the timing of the observed real effects of monetary policy disturbances, which instead only *begin* two quarters after the shock. The reason is that it is the real rate of interest, and not the nominal rate, that matters primarily for aggregate demand. Moreover, if a monetary tightening is expected to lower inflation for several quarters (as predicted both by the theoretical responses and the VAR), this implies a higher real rate of interest that persists for several quarters, even if the nominal rate has returned to its normal level. The predicted and estimated inflation responses do not match as well as in the case of the other two variables, but it should be noted that the estimated responses are highly imprecise.

The parameter values required for this degree of fit are consistent with the a priori restrictions implied by the model's microeconomic foundations. The values estimated by Rotemberg and Woodford are shown in Table 5.1, which also includes their "calibrated" values for several model parameters that cannot be identified from the impulse responses. These are included so as to provide further insight into the economic significance (and plausibility) of the estimated parameters and also because some of the additional parameters matter for the welfare evaluation of alternative policies.

As in most of the equilibrium business-cycle literature, they assume a Cobb-Douglas aggregate production function, $f(h) = h^\lambda$, and calibrate the elasticity λ to be .75 on the basis of the observed labor share in national income.[19] This implies that the component of the elasticity of real marginal cost with respect to output that is due to the diminishing marginal product of labor should equal $\omega_p = 0.33$. They further propose, on the basis of other structural VAR studies that estimate real-wage responses, that the elasticity of the real wage with respect to output changes not associated with any change in production possibilities is approximately of the magnitude 0.3. This would imply an overall elasticity of average real marginal cost with respect to aggregate output of $\epsilon_{mc} = 0.63$.

---

19. Because the assumed value of θ implies a ratio of price to marginal cost of 1.15, a labor elasticity of .75 implies that one should observe a labor share of .75/1.15 = .65, which is about what is observed on average for the United States.

Since in their cashless model, $\epsilon_{mc} = \omega + \sigma^{-1}$, the estimated value of σ^{-1} implies that $\omega = \omega_w + \omega_p = 0.47$, and hence that $\omega_w = 0.14$. Since $\omega_w = \nu\phi$, where ν measures the curvature of the disutility of labor function and ϕ_h is the inverse of the labor elasticity, the implied value of ν is $.75(0.14) = 0.11$. This is a very low degree of curvature, but still a positive one, so the implied preferences for the representative household satisfy the standard concavity restrictions. While the implication of highly elastic responses of voluntary labor supply to real-wage variations may be judged implausible, the problem is a familiar one for equilibrium business-cycle models (such as standard RBC models) that incorporate a wage-taking representative-household model of labor supply.[20]

Given this value for ω, it is then possible to estimate a value for ψ, namely 0.88. This value is also positive, as required by the model. A variety of values of α and φ would be consistent with this value for ψ. Rotemberg and Woodford calibrate $\alpha = .66$ on the basis of survey evidence on the typical frequency of price changes in the U.S. economy, such as that of Blinder et al. (1998, table 4.1). (This value of α implies a mean time between price changes of three quarters.) The estimate of ψ then implies the value $\varphi = .63$, which is between zero and one as required by the theory.

Finally, given these values for α and β, the estimated value of κ is consistent with the theoretical prediction that[21]

$$\kappa \equiv \frac{(1-\alpha)(1-\alpha\beta)}{\alpha}\,\zeta$$

in the case that ζ (the measure of "real rigidity" from a variety of sources, discussed in Chapter 3) is equal to 0.14. Under the Rotemberg-Woodford assumptions regarding the structure of production costs and demand, the degree of real rigidity should be given by

$$\zeta = \frac{\epsilon_{mc}}{1+\omega\theta},$$

as shown in Chapter 3. Hence the required value of ζ is consistent with the values obtained for ϵ_{mc} and ω in the case that the elasticity of substitution among alternative differentiated goods is equal to $\theta = 7.88$. This value is greater than one, as required by the theoretical model, and is also a fairly plausible magnitude; it is neither so small as to imply an implausible degree of market power for the typical producer in the U.S. economy (it implies an

---

20. Rotemberg and Woodford point out that the assumption of extremely elastic labor supply is not necessary to make their estimated low value of κ consistent with the theoretical restrictions of the model, but only to make the model consistent with the observation of an only modestly procyclical real-wage response to monetary policy shocks.

21. See equation (2.12) of Chapter 3.

average markup of prices over marginal cost of less than 15%), nor so large as to make it implausible that suppliers leave their prices unchanged for a period of 9 months on average.

It is thus possible to account for the estimated impulse responses to an identified monetary policy shock fairly accurately, assuming parameter values that are not only theoretically possible, but are also consistent with a variety of other observations about the U.S. economy. Once the parameters of the structural equations have been assigned numerical values in this way, it is then possible to specify the joint stochastic process for the two composite real disturbances $\{g_t, \hat{Y}_t^n\}$ so as to match other features of the estimated joint distribution of the three time series characterized by the Rotemberg-Woodford VAR. Figure 5.3 shows the extent to which this is possible. The figure plots the estimated autocovariance and cross-covariance functions for the three variables (the ones implied by the estimated VAR model) and

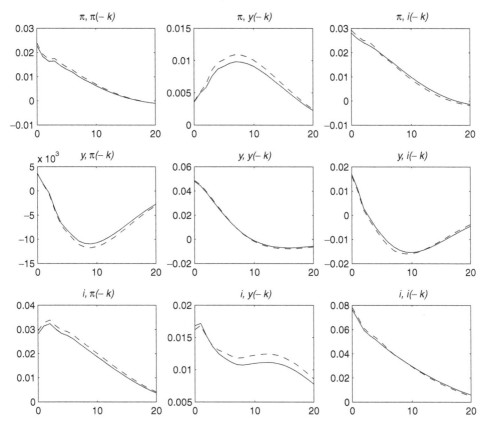

Figure 5.3 *Predicted [solid line] and estimated [dashed line] second moments of quarterly U.S. data, 1980:1–1995:4. Source: Rotemberg and Woodford (1997).*

the predictions of the theoretical model given the Rotemberg-Woodford specification of the exogenous disturbance processes. These match quite closely. For example, it is worth noting that the model has no difficulty accounting for the observed degree of persistence of both the fluctuations in inflation and the deviations of output from trend over this sample period. Nor does it have difficulty accounting for such often-remarked features of the data as the negative correlation between output and lagged interest rates and the positive correlation between output and interest-rate leads.

Of course, these last successes of the theoretical model are mainly a result of assuming real disturbances with the proper statistical properties. Rotemberg and Woodford impose no a priori restrictions on the joint law of motion for the two composite disturbances, apart from insisting that they be stationary processes that evolve independently of the monetary policy shocks. As the structural VAR model indicates that only a small amount of the variability of any of the three variables is ultimately caused by the identified monetary policy disturbances, the restriction that the assumed real disturbances be independent of the identified monetary policy shocks constrains only slightly their ability to choose disturbance processes that imply the desired second moments for the data series. If one were to start instead with tightly parameterized a priori assumptions about the laws of motion of the disturbance processes, as is common in the literature on both maximum-likelihood estimation of structural macroeconometric models and calibrated equilibrium business-cycle models, one might find that the model would fit the properties of the time series less well.[22] Yet the theory developed here gives one no reason to assume particular kinds of "simple" laws of motion for the real disturbances. Indeed, it implies that each of the real disturbances is actually a composite of many different sorts of underlying real disturbances and that many kinds of real disturbances should affect both g_t and $\hat{Y}_t^n$, albeit with different dynamics. Thus there is no reason to expect the two processes to have simple serial correlation properties or to be uncorrelated with one another.

As the approach to the design of optimal monetary policy rules emphasized later in Chapter 8 makes the form of an optimal policy rule independent of the statistical properties of the real disturbances, I do not discuss the details of the disturbance processes estimated by Rotemberg and Woodford any further here. However, it is perhaps of some interest to note the implications of their estimates for the question of the variability of the natural rate

---

22. For criticism of the model on these grounds, see Fuhrer (1997), who assumes that the real disturbances should be serially uncorrelated. McGrattan (1999) also finds considerably worse performance when the real disturbance processes are assumed to consist solely of a production-function residual and variation in real government purchases. But the theoretical model allows for preference disturbances as well, which may play an important role in accounting for the historical time series.

of interest. In their IS relation (1.8), it is only the forecastable component $E_t \hat{r}_{t+2}^n$ that matters, owing to the assumption that interest-sensitive private expenditure is predetermined two quarters in advance. Thus it seems most appropriate to ask about the variability of this exogenous term that is implied by the residuals of the estimated IS relation. As reported in Woodford (1999a), this (annualized) series has a standard deviation of 3.72 percentage points. Since the estimated long-run average funds rate and inflation rate imply a mean natural rate of interest of only 2.99 percentage points, this implies that even a one-standard deviation decline in the natural rate involves a natural rate well below zero.[23]

Thus these estimates imply that the natural rate of interest should be negative fairly often. This means that a policy under which the funds rate would always equal $E_{t-2} \hat{r}_t^n + \bar{\pi}$—as would be necessary, according to the Rotemberg-Woodford model, in order to completely stabilize both $E_{t-2} \pi_t$ and $E_{t-2} x_t$—would be consistent with the zero lower bound for the funds rate only if the inflation target $\bar{\pi}$ is well above zero. Thus the zero bound creates a tension between inflation stabilization and the pursuit of a low average rate of inflation, as is discussed further in Section 4.2 of Chapter 6.[24]

2.2 More Complex Variants

Amato and Laubach (2003a) extend the analysis of Rotemberg and Woodford by adding a real-wage series to the VAR and estimating the impulse response of wages as well as prices to a monetary policy shock. Their estimated impulse responses to an identified monetary policy shock are shown in Figure 5.4. They find that the real-wage response is never significantly different from zero, just as in the estimates of Christiano et al. (2001) reported in Figure 3.17. As a result, the estimated responses (taking account of the real-wage response along with the others, which are changed very little by the inclusion of the additional series in the VAR) are no longer consistent with the simple Rotemberg-Woodford model with wage-taking households

---

23. Using a quite different approach, Laubach and Williams (2001) estimate a natural-rate series for the United States that exhibits substantial variability, though not quite so much. When they assume that the component of the natural rate of interest owing to factors other than variation in the economy's long-run growth rate is a stationary AR(2) process, they estimate the standard deviation of the natural rate to be 1.98 percentage points. Their estimate of low-frequency variation implies that the natural rate was as low as only 10 basis points in late 1994. Since their method seeks only to isolate a low-frequency component of natural-rate variations, while theory indicates that higher-frequency variations are likely as well, it is quite plausible that the overall variability of the natural rate should be greater than that estimated by Laubach and Williams, even assuming that they correctly identify low-frequency variations.

24. The trade-off between these two objectives is demonstrated quantitatively in the context of the estimated model in Rotemberg and Woodford (1997, fig. 5).

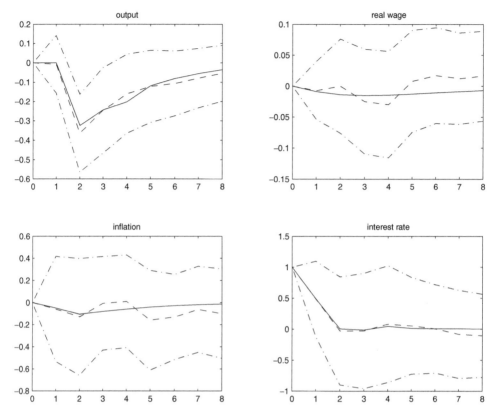

Figure 5.4 *Predicted [solid line] and estimated [dashed line] impulse responses to a monetary policy shock. Source: Amato and Laubach (2003a).*

for any assumed preference parameters. Amato and Laubach extend the model to allow wages as well as prices to be sticky, along the lines of the models discussed in Section 4 of Chapter 3. The aggregate-supply block of their model consists of a pair of wage and price inflation equations that generalize equations (4.11) and (4.12) of Chapter 3 to incorporate predetermined wage and price changes like those in the Rotemberg-Woodford model.

The numerical parameter values in the Amato-Laubach model are given for comparison purposes in Table 5.2. Here the meaning of the parameters is the same as in the model of Erceg et al. (2000) discussed in Chapter 3, except for the introduction of the parameters φ_w, φ_p (assumed for simplicity to take a common value) that indicate the fraction of newly revised wages and prices, respectively, that take effect after only one quarter. The values of α_p, β, and ω_p are calibrated as in Rotemberg and Woodford, and $\alpha_w = \alpha_p$

TABLE 5.2 Parameter values in the quarterly model of Amato and Laubach (2003a)

α_w, α_p	0.66	ω_w	0.27	ξ_w	0.066
β	0.99	ω_p	0.33	ξ_p	0.058
φ_w, φ_p	0.56	$(\theta_w - 1)^{-1}$	0.13	κ_w	0.035
σ^{-1}	0.26	$(\theta_p - 1)^{-1}$	0.19	κ_p	0.019

and $\gamma_w = \gamma_p$ are assumed to reduce the number of free parameters. Given the calibrated value for ω_p, the ratio κ_p/ξ_p is also fixed. The free parameters σ, ξ_w, κ_w, κ_p, and the common value of ψ in both inflation equations are then estimated to minimize a measure of the distance between the theoretical and estimated impulse responses. These estimates then imply the remaining parameter values listed in the table.

The Amato-Laubach parameter values imply predicted responses of output, inflation, and the nominal interest rate quite similar to those of the Rotemberg-Woodford model, but in addition these values imply a smaller real-wage response, which is also more gradual and more persistent than the output response. (The responses predicted by their model, given the estimated parameter values, are shown in Figure 5.4.) The model yields these predictions as a result of substantial wage as well as price stickiness, indicated by the small estimated value for κ_w. Whereas κ_w is estimated to be larger than κ_p, so that the real wage is predicted to move slightly procyclically (see Figure 3.18), the two coefficients are similar in magnitude, and the predicted real-wage response is quite small. Note that despite the fact that wages are estimated to be relatively sticky, the estimated model still implies very low curvature of the disutility of labor supply. Even though ω_w can no longer be inferred directly from the relative magnitudes of the output and real-wage responses, it can be inferred from the relative magnitudes of κ_w and ξ_w. The fact that Amato and Laubach estimate that ξ_w is large relative to the size of κ_w can be reconciled with the underlying microeconomic foundations of the model only if the marginal disutility of working does not rise much with increases in employment.

Another weakness of the simple Rotemberg-Woodford model is its failure to predict an inflation response as persistent as the one indicated by the VAR. This response is estimated quite imprecisely by their VAR; but as discussed in Chapter 3, a large number of other studies also conclude that inflation responses are both more delayed and more persistent than predicted by their model. A simple way to increase the realism of this aspect of their model is to assume that prices are indexed to a lagged price index between the occasions on which they are reoptimized, as discussed in Section 3.2 of Chapter 3. Boivin and Giannoni (2003) estimate a variant of the Rotemberg-Woodford model that is extended to allow this kind of indexation of prices, as well as habit persistence of the kind discussed above in Section 1.2. Giannoni and Woodford (2003b) in turn extend this model to allow for sticky wages as well as prices and indexation of wages as well as prices to the lagged price index, as in the model of Christiano et al. (2001).

As in the Rotemberg-Woodford model, Giannoni and Woodford assume that aggregate private expenditure is predetermined two quarters in advance, but also assume habit persistence in these expenditures. As a result of the predetermination of private expenditure, the IS relation (1.25) now takes the form

$$E_{t-2}\tilde{x}_t = E_{t-2}\tilde{x}_{t+1} - \varphi^{-1}E_{t-2}\left[\hat{\imath}_t - \pi_{t+1} - \hat{r}_t^n\right] \tag{2.4}$$

for determination of the predictable component of the output gap, where both the coefficient φ and the variable $\tilde{x}_t$ are defined as in Section 1.2. The actual output gap is then given by the predictable component plus a purely exogenous term,

$$\tilde{x}_t = E_{t-2}\tilde{x}_t + \left(\breve{g}_t - \tilde{Y}_t^n\right) - E_{t-2}\left(\breve{g}_t - \tilde{Y}_t^n\right)$$
$$- \beta\eta\left[E_t\left(x_{t+1} + \hat{Y}_{t+1}^n\right) - E_{t-2}\left(x_{t+1} + \hat{Y}_{t+1}^n\right)\right]. \tag{2.5}$$

Owing to the inflation inertia introduced through the assumption of indexation, Giannoni and Woodford need assume only that all price revisions are predetermined for only one quarter (following Boivin and Giannoni (2003) in this regard). The aggregate-supply block of the model then consists of a pair of equations for price and wage inflation of the form

$$\pi_t - \gamma_p\pi_{t-1} = \xi_p\omega_p E_{t-1}x_t + \xi_p E_{t-1}\left(w_t - w_t^n\right) + \beta E_{t-1}\left(\pi_{t+1} - \gamma_p\pi_t\right), \tag{2.6}$$

$$\pi_t^w - \gamma_w\pi_{t-1} = \xi_w E_{t-1}\left(\omega_w x_t + \varphi\tilde{x}_t\right) - \xi_w E_{t-1}\mu_t + \xi_w E_{t-1}\left(w_t^n - w_t\right)$$
$$+ \beta E_{t-1}\left(\pi_{t+1}^w - \gamma_w\pi_t\right), \tag{2.7}$$

together with an identity that links the change in the log real wage w_t to wage and price inflation. Here γ_p and γ_w indicate the degree of indexation of prices and wages, respectively, to the lagged price index. The other coefficients all have the same meaning as in the case of the Amato-Laubach model, and the term μ_t is defined as in (1.19) when the latter relation is appropriately generalized to take account of the habit persistence.

Giannoni and Woodford estimate the coefficients of their model so as to fit the estimated impulse responses of the same four variables as in the case of Amato and Laubach, but their responses are derived from a VAR model estimated on quarterly U.S. data for the sample period 1980:1–2002:2. (Their estimated responses are consequently somewhat different

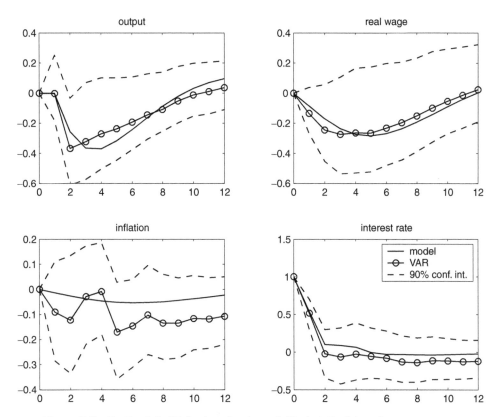

Figure 5.5 *Predicted [solid line] and estimated [dashed line] impulse responses to a monetary policy shock. Source: Giannoni and Woodford (2003b).*

from those of Amato and Laubach; in particular, they find a larger decline in the real wage in response to a contractionary monetary policy shock.) The estimated responses implied by their VAR and the predictions of the theoretical model in the case of the best-fitting parameter values are shown in Figure 5.5.

As with the other studies discussed above, Giannoni and Woodford calibrate certain parameter values, and then estimate the others so as to minimize the distance between predicted and estimated impulse responses. In their case, the calibrated parameter values are α_p, α_w, β, ω_p, and ϕ_h. These are each calibrated in the same way as in Table 5.1. The estimated parameter values are φ and η in the IS relation (2.4), ξ_p and γ_p in the inflation equation (2.6), and ξ_w, ω_w, and γ_w in the wage-inflation equation (2.7). These values are required to be positive, and a theoretical upper bound of 1 is imposed in the case of the parameters η, γ_w, and γ_p. (The latter three bounds all

TABLE 5.3   Parameter values in the quarterly model of Giannoni and
Woodford (2003b)

α_w, α_p	0.66	γ_w	1.00	$(\theta_w - 1)^{-1}$	0.54
β	0.99	γ_p	1.00	$(\theta_p - 1)^{-1}$	0.004
φ	0.75	ν	14.7	ξ_w	0.0042
η	1.00	ω_w	19.6	ξ_p	0.0020
ϕ_h^{-1}	0.75	ω_p	0.33	κ_p	0.0007

bind, though the nonnegativity constraints do not.) The estimated parameter values (together with the calibrated parameters and some others implied
by these) are shown in Table 5.3.[25]

While some of the model parameters are not estimated too precisely, the
estimation results are consistent with the theory insofar as positive values are
estimated for the response coefficients φ, ξ_p, ξ_w, and ω_w. Overall, the model
is able to replicate the impulse responses estimated by the VAR (the dashed
lines) fairly well, and the predicted responses remain consistently within
the 90 percent confidence intervals. In particular, the model replicates the
estimated hump-shaped output and real-wage responses. While it still does
not match the estimated dynamics of inflation too well (which are in any
event again estimated quite imprecisely), the model does deliver a more
persistent decline in inflation following a monetary contraction than either
of the previous two models.

Giannoni and Woodford also test the restrictions associated with three
restricted versions of their model: one with zero habit persistence, as in
the models of Rotemberg and Woodford (1997) and Amato and Laubach
(2003a); one with no indexation of either wages or prices to the lagged
price index, also like the two models just mentioned; and one with flexible
wages, as in the models of Rotemberg and Woodford (1997) and Boivin and
Giannoni (2003).[26] The values of the objective function for the best-fitting
versions of each of these restricted models (weighted squared distances
between the predicted and estimated impulse responses, with weights given
by the inverse of the squared standard error of the estimated response) are
reported in Table 5.4, which also shows the *p*-values for the Wald test in each
case of the null hypothesis that the restricted model is correct. Giannoni and
Woodford find that each of these restrictions, assumed in earlier studies, can
be individually rejected, though the assumption of flexible wages is the one
that would reduce the model's ability to fit the estimated impulse-response
functions to the greatest extent.

25. Note that φ has a different meaning here than in Table 5.1.
26. The restricted model with flexible wages is exactly the model of Boivin and Giannoni,
though Boivin and Giannoni use a somewhat different method to estimate its parameters.

TABLE 5.4   Tests of various restricted cases of the model of Giannoni and Woodford (2003b)

	Baseline	No habit, $\eta = 0$	No indexation, $\gamma_p = \gamma_w = 0$	Flexible wages, $\xi_w^{-1} = 0$
Objective function value	13.110	15.886	16.580	18.837
Wald test (p-value)	—	0.000	0.000	0.000

It is striking to note that the model fits the impulse responses best when the degree of inflation indexing (γ_p) and wage indexing to inflation (γ_w) reach their upper bound at 1. This corresponds to the assumption of full wage and price indexing made by Christiano et al. (2001). A value of $\gamma_p = 1$ is also roughly consistent with the weight on lagged inflation in the "hybrid" aggregate-supply relation estimated by Gali and Gertler (1999), and results in an aggregate-supply relation quite similar to the one proposed by Fuhrer and Moore (1995a,b).

The relatively small values of ξ_p, and ξ_w suggest that changes in the output gap and the real wage gap have a relatively small impact on price and wage inflation. (It is worth noting that ξ_p is nonetheless estimated to be significantly positive.) However, the estimated value of ω_w suggests that a 1 percent increase in economic activity increases workers' desired wages by nearly 20 percent for given prices. Thus labor supply is estimated to be quite inelastic (as far as household preferences are concerned: The Frisch elasticity of labor supply ν^{-1} is only 0.07), though the assumed contracting mechanism requires households to elastically supply whatever amount of labor happens to be demanded at the current wage. The estimate of φ corresponds to an elasticity of intertemporal substitution (adjusted by the degree of habit formation) of $\varphi^{-1} = 1.3$. Authors such as Fuhrer (2000) and Christiano et al. (2001), among others, have estimated substantial degrees of habit formation, but the estimate lies at the upper bound of 1.

It is also worth noting that the estimated parameter values, together with the calibrated values mentioned previously, can be used once again to derive implied elasticities of substitution among alternative goods θ_p as well as among alternative types of labor θ_w. The values of these elasticities implied by our estimates indicate a gross markup of prices over marginal costs of only $\mu_p = \theta_p / (\theta_p - 1) = 1.004$ in the goods market, but a considerably higher gross markup of $\mu_w = \theta_w / (\theta_w - 1) = 1.54$ in the labor market. The fact that these implied markups are greater than 1 (i.e., that the implied elasticities of substitution are greater than 1) again indicates consistency of our estimates with our theoretical model. (The difference between the implied elasticities of substitution in goods as opposed to labor markets is of some importance for welfare analysis and hence for the conclusions as to optimal policy in this model discussed in Chapter 8.)

The complications found to improve the fit of the relatively simple models discussed here—predetermined wages, prices, and real expenditure; sticky (and staggered) wages as well as prices; wages and prices both indexed to a lagged price index; and habit persistence—all figure as well in the more complex models that Christiano et al. (2001), Altig et al. (2002), and Smets and Wouters (2002) estimate using considerable larger sets of U.S. time series. In order to fit additional series, these models introduce a number of further complications, including separate modeling of consumption and investment dynamics (taken up in the next section), adjustment costs for investment, variable utilization of capital, and financial frictions. Discussion of all of these elements is beyond the scope of the present book. However, the fact that the more ambitious empirical studies just mentioned also emphasize the importance of the model elements listed previously suggests that it will be of some interest to understand the consequences of the incorporation of such elements into one's model of the monetary transmission mechanism for the optimal conduct of monetary policy. I accordingly focus substantial attention on the consequences of each of these factors in my analysis of optimal policy in Part II.

3 Monetary Policy and Investment Dynamics

One of the more obvious omissions in the basic neo-Wicksellian model developed in Chapter 4 is the absence of any effect of variations in private spending upon the economy's productive capacity and hence upon supply costs in subsequent periods. This means that I have treated all private expenditure as if it were nondurable consumption expenditure. While this has kept the analysis of the effects of interest rates on aggregate demand quite simple, one may doubt the accuracy of the conclusions obtained, given the obvious importance of variations in investment spending both in business fluctuations generally and in the transmission mechanism for monetary policy in particular. I have suggested that the basic neo-Wicksellian model ought not be interpreted as one in which investment spending is literally constant. In particular, I have argued that the parameter σ in that model ought not be "calibrated" on the basis of studies of intertemporal substitution of consumer expenditure, but should be taken instead to refer to the degree of intertemporal substitutability of overall private expenditure, largely as a result of intertemporal substitution in investment spending. In this section I develop an extended version of the model in which investment spending is modeled explicitly to see to what extent it has properties different than those of the basic model when the latter is calibrated to reflect an elasticity of intertemporal substitution of overall spending that is several times as large as the elasticity of nondurable consumption.

3.1 Investment Demand with Sticky Prices

A first task is to develop a model of optimizing investment demand by suppliers with sticky prices that are demand-constrained as a result. I begin by modifying the production function to include an explicit representation of the effects of variation in the capital stock. The production function for good i is assumed to be of the form

$$y_t(i) = k_t(i)f(A_t h_t(i)/k_t(i)), \tag{3.1}$$

where f is an increasing, concave function as before, with $f(0) = 0$. Note that when $k_t(i)$ is a constant, this reduces to the form of production function assumed in Chapter 3, except that the technology factor A_t is now assumed to multiply the labor input rather than the entire production function ("labor-augmenting" technical progress). I now change the specification of the technology factor so that a 1 percent increase in A_t will still result in a 1 percent long-run increase in equilibrium output, now that the eventual increase in the capital stock is taken into account. (In the model with endogenous capital accumulation, the capital used per unit of labor will eventually increase in proportion to the increase in A_t, in order to maintain a constant long-run relation between the marginal product of capital and the rate of time preference of households.)

I assume that each monopolistic supplier makes an independent investment decision each period. There is a separate capital stock $k_t(i)$ for each good, which can be used only in the production of good i, rather than a single capital stock that can be "rented" for use in any sector at a single economy-wide "rental rate" for capital services. The latter assumption is remarkably common in the literature on intertemporal general-equilibrium models with sticky prices. Important early examples of models of that kind include Hairault and Portier (1993), Kimball (1995), Yun (1996), King and Watson (1996), King and Wolman (1996), and Chari et al. (2000), among others. Simplicity probably accounts for this (together with the bad example set by early intertemporal general-equilibrium models with imperfect competition, such as Rotemberg and Woodford, 1992). However, the assumption of a single economy-wide rental market for capital is plainly unrealistic, and its consequences are far from trivial in the present context: It would imply that differences in the demand for goods that have their prices set at different times should result in instantaneous reallocation of the economy's capital stock from lower-demand to higher-demand sectors, and this in turn has an important effect upon the degree to which marginal cost of supply should vary with the demand for a given good. I showed in Chapter 3 that the assumption of economy-wide factor markets greatly reduces the predicted degree of strategic complementarity of the pricing decisions of different suppliers and thus increases the speed of adjustment of the

overall level of prices to varying demand conditions. Here I assume instead
that while all sectors purchase investment goods from the same suppliers
(i.e., that the investment goods used by the different sectors are perfect
substitutes for their *producers*), these goods cease to be substitutable once
they have been purchased for use in production in a particular sector. Capital can be reallocated from low-demand to high-demand sectors only over
time, through reduced new investment in the former sectors and increased
new investment in the latter, and the speed with which this occurs is limited
by the assumption of adjustment costs. The resulting model is more realistic and also represents a more direct generalization of the constant-capital
model developed in Chapter 3. (That model implicitly assumed a constant
quantity of capital $k_t(i)$ available for the production of each individual good,
rather than a constant aggregate capital stock that would be efficiently reallocated among sectors in each period. I show later that the constant-capital
model can be recovered as a limiting case of the present one, in the limit of
very high adjustment costs for investment.)

I assume convex adjustment costs, of the usual kind assumed in neoclassical investment theory for investment by each firm. Increasing the capital
stock to the level $k_{t+1}(i)$ in period $t+1$ requires investment spending in
the amount $I_t(i) = I(k_{t+1}(i)/k_t(i))k_t(i)$ in period t. Here $I_t(i)$ represents
purchases by firm i of the composite good, defined as the usual Dixit-Stiglitz
aggregate over purchases of each of the continuum of goods (with the same
constant elasticity of substitution $\theta > 1$ as for consumption purchases). In
this way, the allocation of investment expenditure across the various goods
is in exactly the same proportion as consumption expenditure, resulting in
a demand curve for each producer that is again of the form

$$y_t(i) = Y_t\left(\frac{p_t(i)}{P_t}\right)^{-\theta}, \tag{3.2}$$

but where now aggregate demand is given by $Y_t = C_t + I_t + G_t$, in which
expression I_t denotes the integral of $I_t(i)$ over the various firms i. I assume as
usual that the function $I(\cdot)$ is increasing and convex, the convexity implying
the existence of costs of adjustment. I further assume that near a zero growth
rate of the capital stock, this function satisfies $I(1) = \delta$, $I'(1) = 1$, and
$I''(1) = \epsilon_\psi$, where $0 < \delta < 1$ and $\epsilon_\psi > 0$ are parameters. This indicates
that in the steady state to which the economy converges in the absence of
shocks (which involves a constant capital stock as we abstract from trend
growth), the steady rate of investment spending required to maintain the
capital stock is equal to δ times the steady-state capital stock (so that δ can be
interpreted as the rate of depreciation). It also implies that near the steady
state, a marginal unit of investment spending increases the capital stock by
an equal amount (as there are locally no adjustment costs). Finally, in our

log-linear approximation to the equilibrium dynamics, ϵ_ψ is the parameter that indexes the degree of adjustment costs.

Profit-maximization by firm i then implies that the capital stock for period $t + 1$ is chosen in period t to satisfy the first-order condition

$$I'(k_{t+1}(i)/k_t(i)) = E_t Q_{t,t+1} \Pi_{t+1}\{\rho_{t+1}(i)$$
$$+ (k_{t+2}(i)/k_{t+1}(i))I'(k_{t+2}(i)/k_{t+1}(i)) - I(k_{t+2}(i)/k_{t+1}(i))\},$$

where $\rho_{t+1}(i)$ is the (real) shadow value of a marginal unit of additional capital for use by firm i in period $t + 1$ production, and $Q_{t,t+1}\Pi_{t+1}$ is the stochastic discount factor for evaluating real-income streams received in period $t + 1$. Expressing the real stochastic discount factor as $\beta\lambda_{t+1}/\lambda_t$ (where λ_t is the representative household's marginal utility of real income in period t) and then log-linearizing this condition around the steady-state values of all state variables yields

$$\hat{\lambda}_t + \epsilon_\psi(\hat{k}_{t+1}(i) - \hat{k}_t(i)) = E_t\hat{\lambda}_{t+1} + [1 - \beta(1-\delta)]E_t\hat{\rho}_{t+1}(i)$$
$$+ \beta\epsilon_\psi E_t(\hat{k}_{t+2}(i) - \hat{k}_{t+1}(i)), \qquad (3.3)$$

where $\hat{\lambda}_t \equiv \log(\lambda_t/\bar{\lambda})$, $\hat{k}_t(i) \equiv \log(k_t(i)/\bar{K})$, $\hat{\rho}_t(i) \equiv \log(\rho_t(i)/\bar{\rho})$, and variables with bars denote steady-state values.

Note that $\rho_{t+1}(i)$ would correspond to the real "rental price" for capital services if a market existed for such services, though we do not assume one. It is *not* possible in the present model to equate this quantity with the marginal product or even with the marginal revenue product of capital (using the demand curve (3.2) to compute marginal revenue). For suppliers are demand-constrained in their sales, given the prices that they have posted; it is not possible to increase sales by moving down the demand curve. Thus the shadow value of additional capital be computed instead as the reduction in labor costs through substitution of capital inputs for labor, while still supplying the quantity of output that happens to be demanded. I thus obtain

$$\rho_t(i) = w_t(i)\left(\frac{f\left(\tilde{h}_t(i)\right) - \tilde{h}_t(i)f'\left(\tilde{h}_t(i)\right)}{A_t f'\left(\tilde{h}_t(i)\right)}\right),$$

where $w_t(i)$ is the real wage for labor of the kind hired by firm i and $\tilde{h}_t(i) \equiv A_t h_t(i)/k_t(i)$ is firm i's effective labor-capital input ratio.[27] I can alternatively

---

27. Note that in the case of a flexible-price model, the ratio of $w_t(i)$ to the denominator would always equal marginal revenue, so this expression would equal the marginal revenue product of capital, though it would be a relatively cumbersome way of writing it.

express this in terms of the output-capital ratio for firm i (in order to derive an "accelerator" model of investment demand), by substituting (3.1) to obtain

$$\rho_t(i) = \frac{w_t(i)}{A_t} f^{-1}(y_t(i)/k_t(i))[\phi(y_t(i)/k_t(i)) - 1], \tag{3.4}$$

where $\phi(y/k)$ is the reciprocal of the elasticity of the function f, evaluated at the argument $f^{-1}(y/k)$.

Recall from Chapter 3 the first-order condition for optimizing labor supply, which may be written in the form

$$w_t(i) = \frac{v_h\left(f^{-1}(y_t(i)/k_t(i))k_t(i)/A_t; \xi_t\right)}{\lambda_t}, \tag{3.5}$$

again writing labor demand in terms of the demand for good i. Substituting this into (3.4) and log-linearizing yields

$$\hat{\rho}_t(i) = \left(v\phi_h + \frac{\phi}{\phi - 1}\omega_p\right)(\hat{y}_t(i) - \hat{k}_t(i)) + v\hat{k}_t(i) - \hat{\lambda}_t - \omega q_t, \tag{3.6}$$

where $\phi_h > 1$ is the steady-state value of $\phi(y/k)$, that is, the reciprocal of the elasticity of the production function with respect to the labor input, $\omega_p > 0$ is the negative of the elasticity of $f'(f^{-1}(y/k))$ with respect to y/k, and $v > 0$ is once again the elasticity of the marginal disutility of labor with respect to labor supply. The composite exogenous disturbance q_t is again defined as

$$q_t \equiv (1 + \omega^{-1})a_t + \omega^{-1} v \bar{h}_t.$$

Substituting (3.4) into (3.3), I then have an equation to solve for the dynamics of firm i's capital stock, given the evolution of demand $\hat{y}_t(i)$ for its product, the marginal utility of income $\hat{\lambda}_t$, and the exogenous disturbance q_t.

As the coefficients of these equations are the same for each firm, an equation of the same form holds for the dynamics of the aggregate capital stock (in the log-linear approximation). The equilibrium condition for the dynamics of the capital stock is thus of the form

$$\hat{\lambda}_t + \epsilon_\psi(\hat{K}_{t+1} - \hat{K}_t) = \beta(1 - \delta)E_t\hat{\lambda}_{t+1} + \left[1 - \beta(1 - \delta)\right][\rho_y E_t \hat{Y}_{t+1}$$

$$- \rho_k \hat{K}_{t+1} - \omega q_t] + \beta\epsilon_\psi E_t(\hat{K}_{t+2} - \hat{K}_{t+1}), \tag{3.7}$$

where the elasticities of the marginal valuation of capital are given by

$$\rho_y \equiv v\phi_h + \frac{\phi_h}{\phi_h - 1}\omega_p > \rho_k \equiv \rho_y - v > 0.$$

The implied dynamics of investment spending are then given by

$$\hat{I}_t = k\left[\hat{K}_{t+1} - (1 - \delta)\hat{K}_t\right], \tag{3.8}$$

where $\hat{I}_t$ is defined as the percentage deviation of investment from its steady-state level, as a share of steady-state output, and $k \equiv \bar{K}/\bar{Y}$ is the steady-state capital-output ratio.

I have derived here investment dynamics as a function of the evolution of the marginal utility of real income of the representative household. This is in turn related to aggregate spending through the relation $\lambda_t = u_c(Y_t - I_t - G_t; \xi_t)$, which may be log-linearized as

$$\hat{\lambda}_t = -\sigma^{-1}\left(\hat{Y}_t - \hat{I}_t - g_t\right), \tag{3.9}$$

where the composite disturbance g_t once again reflects the effects both of government purchases and shifts in private impatience to consume.[28] Finally, if one recalls the relation between the marginal utility of income process and the stochastic discount factor that prices bonds, the nominal interest rate must satisfy

$$1 + i_t = \left\{\beta E_t\left[\lambda_{t+1}/(\lambda_t \Pi_{t+1})\right]\right\}^{-1},$$

which may be log-linearized as

$$\hat{\imath}_t = E_t \pi_{t+1} + \hat{\lambda}_t - E_t \hat{\lambda}_{t+1}. \tag{3.10}$$

The system of equations (3.7)–(3.10) then comprise the "IS block" of the extended model. Jointly these suffice to determine the paths of the variables $\{\hat{Y}_t, \hat{I}_t, \hat{K}_t, \lambda_t\}$, given an initial capital stock and the evolution of short-term real interest rates $\{\hat{\imath}_t - E_t \pi_{t+1}\}$. The nature of the effects of real interest-rate expectations on these variables is discussed further in Section 3.3.

3.2 Optimal Pricesetting with Endogenous Capital

I turn next to the implications of an endogenous capital stock for the price-setting decisions of firms. The capital stock affects a firm's marginal cost, of course; but more subtly, a firm considering how its future profits will be affected by the price it sets must also consider how its capital stock will evolve over the time that its price remains fixed.

---

28. Note that the parameter σ in this equation is no longer the intertemporal elasticity of substitution in consumption, but rather $\bar{C}/\bar{Y}$ times that elasticity. In a model with investment, these quantities are not exactly the same, even in the absence of government purchases.

I begin with the consequences for the relation between marginal cost and output. Real marginal cost can be expressed as the ratio of the real wage to the marginal product of labor. Again writing the factor input ratio as a function of the capital/output ratio, and using (3.5) for the real wage, I obtain

$$s_t(i) = \frac{v_h\left(f^{-1}(y_t(i)/k_t(i))k_t(i)/A_t; \xi_t\right)}{\lambda_t A_t f'\left(f^{-1}(y_t(i)/k_t(i))\right)}$$

for the real marginal cost of supplying good i. This can be log-linearized to yield

$$\hat{s}_t(i) = \omega\left(\hat{y}_t(i) - \hat{k}_t(i)\right) + v\hat{k}_t(i) - \hat{\lambda}_t - \left[v\bar{h}_t + (1+v)a_t\right], \qquad (3.11)$$

where once again $\omega \equiv \omega_w + \omega_p \equiv v\phi_h + \omega_p > 0$ is the elasticity of marginal cost with respect to a firm's own output, and

$$q_t \equiv \omega^{-1}\left[v\bar{h}_t + (1+v)a_t\right]$$

is the percentage change in output required to maintain a constant marginal disutility of output supply when the firm's capital remains at its steady-state level.[29]

Letting $\hat{s}_t$ without the index i denote the average level of real marginal cost in the economy as a whole, one notes that (3.11) implies that

$$\hat{s}_t(i) = \hat{s}_t + \omega\left(\hat{y}_t(i) - \hat{Y}_t\right) - (\omega - v)\left(\hat{k}_t(i) - \hat{K}_t\right).$$

Then using (3.2) to substitute for the relative output of firm i, one obtains

$$\hat{s}_t(i) = \hat{s}_t - (\omega - v)\tilde{k}_t(i) - \omega\theta\hat{p}_t(i), \qquad (3.12)$$

where $\hat{p}_t(i) \equiv \log(p_t(i)/P_t)$ is the firm's relative price, and $\tilde{k}_t(i) \equiv \hat{k}_t(i) - \hat{K}_t$ is its relative capital stock.

As in Chapter 3, the Calvo pricesetting framework implies that if firm i resets its price in period t, it chooses a price to satisfy the (log-linear approximate) first-order condition

---

29. That is, q_t measures the output change that would be required to maintain a fixed marginal disutility of supply given possible fluctuations in preferences and technology, but not taking account of the effect of possible fluctuations in the firm's capital stock; thus q_t is again an exogenous disturbance term. Note that the expression given here for q_t in terms of the underlying disturbances differs from that in Section 2.1 above, because of our differing specification here of how the technology factor A_t shifts the production function. Nonetheless, this definition of q_t is directly analogous to that used in the case of the constant-capital model; it is actually my use of the notation a_t that is different here.

$$\sum_{k=0}^{\infty}(\alpha\beta)^k E_t\left[\hat{p}_{t+k}(i) - \hat{s}_{t+k}(i)\right] = 0.$$

Substituting (3.12) for $s_{t+k}(i)$ in this expression gives

$$\sum_{k=0}^{\infty}(\alpha\beta)^k E_t\left[(1+\omega\theta)\hat{p}_{t+k}(i) - \hat{s}_{t+k} + (\omega - v)\tilde{k}_{t+k}(i)\right] = 0. \quad (3.13)$$

I can as before express the entire sequence of values $\{\hat{p}_{t+k}(i)\}$ as a linear function of the relative price $\hat{p}_t^*$ chosen at date t and aggregate variables (namely, the overall rate of price inflation over various future horizons). However, I cannot yet solve for the optimal choice of $\hat{p}_t^*$ because (3.13) also involves the relative capital stock of firm i at a sequence of future dates, and this depends upon the investment policy of the firm.

I must therefore use the investment theory of the previous section to model the evolution of firm i's relative capital stock, as a result of which I obtain a result of the following form.

PROPOSITION 5.1. In the model with endogenous capital accumulation the optimal relative price of a firm that revises its price in period t is given by

$$(a - b)\hat{p}_t^* = \sum_{k=0}^{\infty}(\alpha\beta)^k E_t \hat{s}_{t+k} + a\sum_{k=1}^{\infty}(\alpha\beta)^k E_t\pi_{t+k} - b\sum_{k=1}^{\infty}\mu_2^{-k}E_t\pi_{t+k}, \quad (3.14)$$

where

$$a \equiv \frac{1+\omega\theta}{1-\alpha\beta} + (\omega - v)\frac{\alpha}{1-\alpha\beta}\frac{\Xi}{(1-\alpha\beta\mu_1)(1-\alpha\beta\mu_2)} > 0,$$

$$b \equiv (\omega - v)\frac{\alpha}{1-\mu_2^{-1}}\frac{\Xi}{(1-\alpha\beta\mu_1)(1-\alpha\beta\mu_2)} > 0,$$

$$\Xi \equiv (1 - \beta(1-\delta))\rho_y\theta\epsilon_\psi^{-1} > 0,$$

and μ_2 is the root greater than β^{-1} of the equation

$$\mathcal{P}(\mu) \equiv \beta\mu^2 - \left[1+\beta+(1-\beta(1-\delta))\rho_k\epsilon_\psi^{-1}\right]\mu + 1 = 0. \quad (3.15)$$

The derivation of this result is given in Appendix D. Proposition 5.1 allows us to solve for the average relative price chosen at date t by optimizing price-setters as a function of information at that date about the future evolution of average real marginal costs and the overall rate of price inflation.

As in Chapter 3, it is useful to quasi-difference this pricing relation in order to obtain an aggregate-supply relation. Equation (3.14) implies that

$$(a - b)E_t[(1 - \alpha\beta L^{-1})(1 - \mu_2^{-1}L^{-1})\hat{p}_t^*] = E_t[(1 - \mu_2^{-1}L^{-1})\hat{s}_t]$$

$$+ a\alpha\beta E_t[(1 - \mu_2^{-1}L^{-1})\pi_{t+1}] - b\mu_2^{-1}E_t[(1 - \alpha\beta L^{-1})\pi_{t+1}].$$

(3.16)

Recall that in the Calvo pricing model the overall rate of price inflation is given by

$$\pi_t = \frac{1 - \alpha}{\alpha}\hat{p}_t^*.$$

Using this to substitute for $\hat{p}_t^*$ in (3.16), I obtain an inflation equation of the form

$$\pi_t = \xi_0\hat{s}_t - \xi_1 E_t\hat{s}_{t+1} + \psi_1 E_t\pi_{t+1} - \psi_2 E_t\pi_{t+2},$$

(3.17)

where

$$\xi_0 \equiv \frac{1 - \alpha}{\alpha}\frac{1}{a - b}, \qquad \xi_1 \equiv \mu_2^{-1}\xi_0$$

and

$$\psi_1 \equiv \frac{a(\beta + \mu_2^{-1}) - b(\alpha\beta + \alpha^{-1}\mu_2^{-1})}{a - b}, \qquad \psi_2 \equiv \beta\mu_2^{-1}.$$

Once again, this allows us to solve for equilibrium inflation as a function of the current and expected future average level of real marginal costs across sectors. (The sign of this relationship is investigated numerically below.)

It remains to connect the expected evolution of real marginal costs, in turn, with expectations regarding real activity. Averaging (3.11) over firms i and substituting (3.9) to eliminate $\hat{\lambda}_t$ yields

$$\hat{s}_t = (\omega + \sigma^{-1})\hat{Y}_t - \sigma^{-1}\hat{I}_t - (\omega - \nu)\hat{K}_t - [\sigma^{-1}g_t + \omega q_t].$$

(3.18)

Once again, real marginal costs are increasing in the current level of real activity. However, now this relation is affected not merely by exogenous disturbances to tastes and technology, but also by fluctuations in the aggregate capital stock and by the share of current aggregate demand that is investment as opposed to consumption demand. Equations (3.17) and (3.18) constitute the "aggregate-supply block" of the extended model. Jointly they replace the aggregate-supply relation of the basic model and serve to determine equilibrium inflation dynamics as a function of the expected evolution of aggregate real expenditure, the aggregate capital stock, and aggregate investment spending.

3.3   Comparison with the Basic Neo-Wicksellian Model

The complete extended model then consists of the system of equations (3.7) and (3.10) and (3.17)–(3.18), together with an interest-rate feedback rule specifying monetary policy. This is a system of seven expectational difference equations per period to determine the equilibrium paths of seven endogenous variables, namely, $\{\pi_t, \hat{\imath}_t, \hat{Y}_t, \hat{K}_t, \hat{I}_t, \hat{s}_t, \hat{\lambda}_t\}$, given the paths of three composite exogenous disturbances $\{g_t, q_t, \bar{\imath}_t\}$. It is useful to comment upon the extent to which the structure of the extended (variable-capital) model remains similar, though not identical, to that of the basic (constant-capital) model.

I have already noted that the equations of the extended model consist of an IS block(which allows us to solve for the paths of real output and of the capital stock, given the expected path of real interest rates and the initial capital stock), an AS block (which allows us to solve for the path of inflation given the paths of real output and of the capital stock), and a monetary policy rule (which implies a path for nominal interest rates given the paths of inflation and output). In this overall structure it is similar to the basic neo-Wicksellian model, except that the present model involves an additional endogenous variable, the capital stock, which is determined by the IS block and taken as input to the AS block, along with the level of real activity.[30] It also continues to be the case that real disturbances affect the determination of inflation and output only through their effects upon the two composite disturbances g_t and q_t. Previously, I emphasized the disturbances g_t and $\hat{Y}_t^n$, but these contained the same information as a specification of g_t and q_t. (The appropriate definition of the natural rate of output in the context of the extended model is deferred to the next subsection.) In the case of inflation determination alone (and determination of the output *gap*) I was previously able to further reduce these to a single composite disturbance $\hat{r}_t^n$. In the case of the extended model this is no longer possible, although, as I discuss in the next subsection, one can still explain inflation determination in terms of the gap between an actual and a "natural" real rate of interest. The problem is that with endogenous variation in the capital stock, the natural rate of interest is no longer a purely exogenous state variable.

Note also that the extended model's AS block continues to be nearly as forward looking as that of the basic model. The inflation equation (3.17) can once again be "solved forward" to yield a solution of the form[31]

---

30. The structure of the model is thus similar to rational-expectations IS-LM models such as that of Sargent and Wallace (1975), which allows for an endogenous capital stock.

31. The existence of a unique bounded solution of this form depends as usual upon the roots of a characteristic equation satisfying certain conditions, which I do not examine further here. Note, however, that in the numerical work presented here, the relevant condition is satisfied in the case of what are judged to be empirically realistic parameter values.

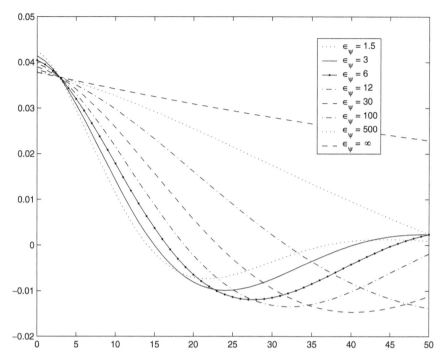

Figure 5.6 *The coefficients Ψ_j in inflation equation (3.19), for alternative sizes of investment adjustment costs.*

$$\pi_t = \sum_{j=0}^{\infty} \Psi_j E_t \hat{s}_{t+j}, \qquad (3.19)$$

where the $\{\Psi_j\}$ are constant coefficients. In the case of the basic model, the coefficients of this solution are necessarily all positive and decay exponentially: $\Psi_j = \xi \beta^j$, for some $\xi > 0.$[32] In the extended model, the coefficients are not necessarily all positive. Nonetheless, numerical analysis suggests that for empirically realistic parameter values, one has $\Psi_j > 0$ for all small enough values of j.

This point is illustrated in Figure 5.6 in the case of parameter values chosen in the following way. The values used for parameters α, β, ϕ_h, ν, ω_p, ω, and θ are those given in Table 5.1, drawn from the work of Rotemberg and Woodford (1997). The value used for σ is not the same as in that study.

---

32. This follows from "solving forward" the corresponding inflation equation (2.13) of Chapter 3.

Rather, as discussed earlier, as the parameter σ of the basic neo-Wicksellian model (and similarly of the Rotemberg-Woodford model) should not be interpreted as the intertemporal elasticity of substitution of nondurable consumption expenditure, it indicates instead the substitutability of private expenditure as a whole. In the extended model, then, σ refers solely to the substitutability of consumption, so this parameter is now calibrated to equal 1, which is roughly the degree of substitutability typically assumed in the RBC literature (see, e.g., Kydland and Prescott, 1982, or King et al., 1988).[33]

One must also assign values to two new parameters, δ and ϵ_ψ, which relate to the dynamics of the capital stock. Note that the present model implies that the steady-state capital-output ratio $k \equiv \bar{K}/\bar{Y}$ must satisfy

$$\beta^{-1} = \frac{\theta - 1}{\theta} \frac{\phi_h - 1}{\phi_h} \frac{1}{k} + (1 - \delta).$$

Given the values just assumed for β, θ, and ϕ_h in this quarterly model, it follows that the model will predict an average capital-output ratio of ten quarters (roughly correct for the United States) if and only if I assume a quarterly depreciation rate of $\delta = .012$ (about 5% per year). Finally, the figure compares the consequences of a range of different possible positive values for ϵ_ψ. Here the value $\epsilon_\psi = 3$ (indicated by the solid line in the figure) is the one that I regard as most empirically plausible. As we shall see, this results in a degree of responsiveness of overall private expenditure to monetary policy shocks that is similar to that estimated by Rotemberg and Woodford. But I also consider the consequences of smaller and larger values for this crucial new parameter.

In the limit of an extremely large value for ϵ_ψ, the coefficients reduce to those implied by the constant-capital model. One observes from the form given for the polynomial $Q(L)$ in (D.3) that as ϵ_ψ is made large, the two roots approach limiting values $\mu_1 \to 1$, $\mu_2 \to \beta^{-1}$. It then follows that the coefficients in (3.14) approach limiting values $a \to (1 + \omega\theta)/(1 - \alpha\beta)$, $b \to 0$, and hence that the coefficients in (3.17) approach limiting values

$$\xi_0 \to \xi \equiv \frac{1-\alpha}{\alpha} \frac{1-\alpha\beta}{1+\omega\theta} > 0, \qquad \xi_1 \to \beta\xi > 0,$$

$$\psi_1 \to 2\beta, \qquad \psi_2 \to \beta^2.$$

Thus in the limit, (3.17) takes the form

---

33. Strictly speaking, my calibration here is not identical to the standard RBC choice. For as noted above, my σ is actually the consumption share in output times the intertemporal elasticity of substitution of consumption, rather than the elasticity itself; thus a value of 0.7 would be closer to the standard RBC assumption. But I have no grounds for choosing a precise value and so choose 1 as a round number.

$$E_t\left[\left(1 - \beta L^{-1}\right)\pi_t\right] = \xi E_t\left[\left(1 - \beta L^{-1}\right)\hat{s}_t\right] + \beta E_t\left[\left(1 - \beta L^{-1}\right)\pi_{t+1}\right].$$

This relation has the same bounded solutions as the simpler relation

$$\pi_t = \xi\hat{s}_t + \beta E_t\pi_{t+1}$$

derived for the baseline model in Chapter 3, and in particular it implies that (3.19) holds with coefficients $\Psi_j = \xi\beta^j$. (These are the coefficients indicated by the upper dashed curve in Figure 5.6.)

If ϵ_ψ is finite but still quite large, the coefficients $\{\psi_j\}$ again decay only relatively gradually as j increases, though more rapidly than would be predicted by the basic neo-Wicksellian model. If, instead, ϵ_ψ takes a more moderate value (anything in the range that one could consider empirically plausible), the coefficients decline more sharply with j, and indeed become negative if horizons as long as 5 or 6 years in the future are considered. Intuitively, the expectation of a high average level of real marginal cost several years in the future is no longer a motive for increasing prices now, if firms can plan to build up their capital stocks in the meantime. Nonetheless, higher expected future real marginal costs continue to increase inflation as long as the expectations relate to horizons 3 years in the future or less. Moreover, if the expectations relate to the coming year (i.e., the next four quarters), then the coefficients are not just positive but of roughly the same magnitude as in the basic model; and it is these coefficients for low j that mainly matter, given that shocks will typically have a relatively transient effect on average real marginal costs. (With flexible prices, average real marginal costs would never vary at all; even with a realistic degree of price stickiness, price adjustment is rapid enough to make mean reversion in the level of real marginal costs relatively rapid.)

The remaining relation in the AS block of the extended model is the real marginal cost relation (3.18), which reduces to the same one as in the basic model if the $\hat{I}_t$ and $\hat{K}_t$ terms are omitted. The relation between real marginal costs and output is not as simple in the extended model, owing to the presence of those additional terms. However, insofar as cyclical variation in investment is highly correlated with cyclical variation in output and cyclical variation in the capital stock is not too great, the implied cyclical variation in real marginal costs in the extended model is not too different. (In this case, the cyclical variation in $\hat{Y}_t - \hat{I}_t$ is highly correlated with, but smaller in amplitude than, the cyclical variation in $\hat{Y}_t$ itself. One corrects for the difference in amplitude by using a substantially larger value for σ^{-1} when calibrating the constant-capital model.) I illustrate this further on when I report the impulse response of real marginal costs to a monetary policy shock in Figure 5.8. Of course, in the limiting case of large ϵ_ψ, the equilibrium fluctuations in both $\hat{I}_t$ and $\hat{K}_t$ are negligible, and the entire AS block reduces to an AS relation like that of the basic model.

The IS block of the extended model also retains broad similarities to that of the basic model. It is first useful to consider the implied long-run average values for capital, output, and investment as a function of the long-run average rate of inflation π_∞ resulting from a given monetary policy. Equations (3.8) and (3.9) indicate that the long-run average values of the various state variables must satisfy

$$\hat{\lambda}_\infty = \rho_y \hat{Y}_\infty - \rho_k \hat{K}_\infty,$$

$$\hat{I}_\infty = \delta k \hat{K}_\infty,$$

$$\hat{\lambda}_\infty = -\sigma^{-1}(\hat{Y}_\infty - \hat{I}_\infty).$$

These relations can be solved for $\hat{Y}_\infty$, $\hat{I}_\infty$, and $\hat{K}_\infty$ as multiples of $\hat{\lambda}_\infty$, which generalizes the relation between $\hat{Y}_\infty$ and $\hat{\lambda}_\infty$ obtained for the basic model. Equation (3.11) similarly implies that the long-run average level of real marginal cost must satisfy

$$\hat{s}_\infty = \omega \hat{Y}_\infty - (\omega - \nu) \hat{K}_\infty - \hat{\lambda}_\infty.$$

Substituting the above solutions, one obtains $\hat{s}_\infty$ as a multiple of $\hat{\lambda}_\infty$ as well. Finally, (3.17) indicates that

$$\pi_\infty = \frac{\xi_0 - \xi_1}{1 - \psi_1 + \psi_2} \hat{s}_\infty.$$

Using this together with the previous solution allows one to solve for $\hat{\lambda}_\infty$, and hence for $\hat{Y}_\infty$, $\hat{I}_\infty$, and $\hat{K}_\infty$ as well, as multiples of π_∞.

I turn next to the characterization of transitory fluctuations around these long-run average values. Using (3.8) and (3.9) to eliminate $\hat{Y}_{t+1}$ from (3.7) yields a relation of the form

$$E_t\left[A(L)\hat{K}_{t+2}\right] = E_t\left[B(L)\hat{\lambda}_{t+1}\right] + z_t, \tag{3.20}$$

where $A(L)$ is a quadratic lag polynomial, $B(L)$ is linear, and z_t is a linear combination of the disturbances g_t and q_t. For empirically realistic parameter values, the polynomial $A(L)$ can be factored as $(1 - \tilde{\mu}_1 L)(1 - \tilde{\mu}_2 L)$, where the two real roots satisfy $0 < \tilde{\mu}_1 < 1 < \tilde{\mu}_2$. It follows that there is a unique bounded solution for $\hat{K}_{t+1}$ as a linear function of $\hat{K}_t$, the expectations $E_t\hat{\lambda}_{t+j}$ for $j \geq 0$, and the expectations $E_t z_{t+j}$ for $j \geq 0$. Then solving (3.10) forward to obtain

$$\hat{\lambda}_t = \hat{\lambda}_\infty + \sum_{j=0}^{\infty} E_t\left(\hat{\imath}_{t+j} - \pi_{t+j+1}\right), \tag{3.21}$$

and using this to eliminate the expectations $E_t\hat{\lambda}_{t+j}$, I finally reach a solution of the form

$$\hat{K}_{t+1} = (1 - \tilde{\mu}_1)\hat{K}_\infty + \tilde{\mu}_1\hat{K}_t - \sum_{j=0}^{\infty} \tilde{\chi}_j E_t\left(\hat{i}_{t+j} - \pi_{t+j+1}\right) + e_t^k, \qquad (3.22)$$

where the $\{\tilde{\chi}_j\}$ are constant coefficients and e_t^k is an exogenous disturbance term (a linear combination of the $\{E_t z_{t+j}\}$). This can be solved iteratively for the dynamics of the capital stock, starting from an initial capital stock and given the evolution of the exogenous disturbances and of real interest-rate expectations.

Equation (3.21) can also be substituted into (3.9) to yield

$$\hat{Y}_t = \left(\hat{Y}_\infty - \hat{I}_\infty\right) + \hat{I}_t + g_t - \sigma \sum_{j=0}^{\infty} E_t\left(\hat{i}_{t+j} - \pi_{t+j+1}\right),$$

a direct generalization of (1.1), which now, however, takes account of investment spending. Using (3.8) and (3.22) to substitute for $\hat{I}_t$, it is found that this expression takes the form

$$\hat{Y}_t = \left(\hat{Y}_\infty - \Sigma\hat{K}_\infty\right) + \Sigma\hat{K}_t - \sum_{j=0}^{\infty} \chi_j E_t\left(\hat{i}_{t+j} - \pi_{t+j+1}\right) + e_t^y, \qquad (3.23)$$

where $\Sigma \equiv k[\tilde{\mu}_1 - (1 - \delta)]$, $\{\chi_j\}$ is another set of constant coefficients, and e_t^y is another exogenous disturbance term (a linear combination of g_t and of the $\{E_t z_{t+j}\}$). The joint evolution of output and the capital stock is then determined by the pair of equations (3.22) and (3.23), starting from an initial capital stock and given the evolution of the exogenous disturbances and of real interest-rate expectations.

Except for the need to jointly model the evolution of output and the capital stock, this system of equations has implications rather similar to those of the IS relation (1.1) of the basic neo-Wicksellian model. In particular, for typical parameter values, the coefficients $\{\chi_j\}$ in (3.23) are all positive and even of roughly similar magnitude for all j. For example, these coefficients are plotted in Figure 5.7 for a model that is calibrated in the same way as in Figure 5.6, again allowing for a range of different possible values of ϵ_ψ. In the limit of very large ϵ_ψ, the coefficients all approach the constant value σ (here assigned the value 1), as in (1.1). For most lower values of ϵ_ψ, the coefficients are not exactly equal in magnitude, and each coefficient becomes larger as the adjustment costs associated with investment spending are made smaller. However, the coefficients all remain positive and quite similar in magnitude to one another, especially for values of ϵ_ψ near the baseline value of 3.

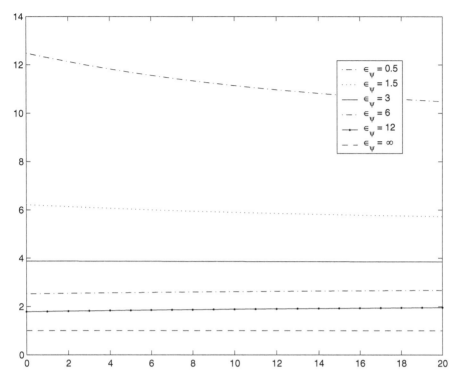

Figure 5.7 *The coefficients χ_j in aggregate demand relation (3.23) for alternative sizes of investment adjustment costs.*

I can show analytically that χ_j takes the same value for all j (though a value greater than σ) if it happens that $B(L)$ in (3.20) is of the form $-h(1 - \mu_2 L)$, where $h > 0$ and μ_2 is the root greater than 1 in the factorization of $A(L)$. In this case (3.20) is equivalent to

$$(1 - \mu_1 L)\hat{K}_{t+1} = -h\hat{\lambda}_t,$$

and substitution of (3.21) yields a solution for aggregate demand of the form (3.23) with $\chi_j = \sigma + h$ for all $j \geq 0$. For the calibrated parameter values, the root of $B(L)$ coincides with a root of $A(L)$ in this way if and only if ϵ_ψ happens to take a specific value, equal approximately to 3.23. This is in fact not an unrealistic value. Perhaps more interesting, however, is the fact that the coefficients $\{\chi_j\}$ are all reasonably similar in magnitude even when ϵ_ψ is larger or smaller than the critical value.

Thus it continues to be true, as in the basic model, that changes in interest-rate expectations (due, e.g., to a shift in monetary policy) affect aggregate demand through their effect on a *very long* real rate. The existence of endogenous variation in investment spending simply makes the degree of sensitivity of aggregate demand to the level of the very long real rate greater. For example, one sees from Figure 5.7 that when $\epsilon_\psi = 3$, the degree of interest sensitivity of aggregate demand is about four times as great as if ϵ_ψ is extremely large; the response to interest-rate changes is thus roughly the same as in a constant-capital model with a value of σ near 4, rather than equal to 1 as assumed here. This justifies my use of a value of σ much larger than 1 when calibrating the basic model.

However, even if I adjust the value assumed for σ in this way, the predictions of the constant-capital model as to the effects of real interest-rate changes are not exactly the same as those of the model with variable capital. This is because lower investment spending as a result of high long real rates of interest soon results in a lower capital stock, and once this occurs aggregate demand is affected through the change in the size of the $\Sigma \hat{K}_t$ term in (3.23). In the case of sufficiently moderate adjustment costs (the empirically realistic case), the value of Σ is negative; for given real interest-rate expectations, a higher existing capital stock depresses investment demand (because returns to existing capital are low).[34] Thus a sustained increase in long real rates of interest will initially depress aggregate demand in the variable-capital model by more than it does later on. Once the capital stock has fallen this fact helps investment demand to recover, despite the continued high real rates.

The degree to which endogenous variation in the capital stock is likely to matter in practice can be illustrated by considering the predicted effects of a monetary policy shock in the case of a systematic monetary policy rule again given by (1.12) with coefficients $\phi_\pi = 0.6$, $\phi_x = 0.3$, and $\rho = 0.7$.[35] Impulse responses to an unexpected monetary tightening (again increasing nominal interest rates by 1% per year) are plotted in Figure 5.8, which also reproduces the predictions of the basic model corresponding to the case $\rho = 0.7$ in Figure 4.7. Observe that when one assumes $\epsilon_\psi = 3$ (and all other parameter values as in Figures 5.6 and 5.7), the predicted output response in the extended model is essentially the same as in the basic model. (It is for this reason that I choose $\epsilon_\psi = 3$ as my baseline calibration of the extended model.)

However, this does not mean that the extended model with $\epsilon_\psi = 3$ and $\sigma = 1$ makes predictions that are identical in all respects to those

---

34. For the particular parameter values discussed in the text, the baseline value $\epsilon_\psi = 3$ implies that $\Sigma = -1.246$ in the quarterly model. Note that the model does not require Σ to be negative. One can show that $\Sigma > 0$ (because $\mu_1 > 1 - \delta$) if and only if ϵ_ψ exceeds the critical value $\rho_k(1 - \delta)/\delta > 0$. For the calibrated parameter values, this critical value is approximately equal to 114.5, and thus would imply a level of adjustment costs in investment that would be inconsistent with the observed degree of volatility of investment spending.

35. These values imply that $\Phi_\pi = 2$, $\Phi_x = 1$ and correspond to the baseline case from Figure 4.7, and to the case considered again in Figure 5.1.

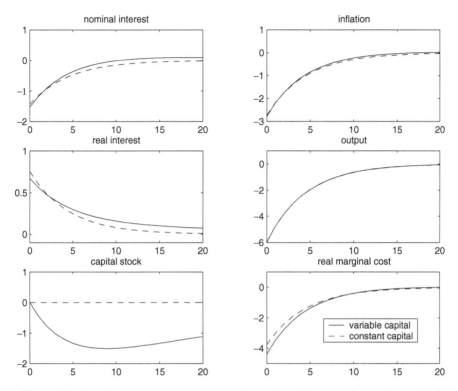

Figure 5.8 *Impulse responses to an unexpected monetary tightening: the constant-capital and variable-capital models compared.*

of a constant-capital model with $\sigma = 6.37$. For example, one sees from Figure 5.7 that when $\epsilon_\psi = 3$, the coefficients $\{\chi_j\}$ of the IS relation are approximately constant, but the constant value is a bit less than 4, rather than being greater than 6 as in the basic model. One could arrange for the extended model to predict the same degree of interest sensitivity of aggregate demand as the basic model if one were to assume a value near $\epsilon_\psi = 1.5$. But this would lead to *overprediction* of the output contraction that should result from a monetary policy tightening. The reason has to do with the effects of endogenous variation in the capital stock, which have been abstracted from in the basic model. The $\Sigma \hat{K}_t$ term in (3.23) contributes a positive stimulus to output (i.e., reduces the size of the output decline) several quarters after the shock, as the low capital stock induces greater investment spending than would otherwise be chosen given the higher-than-average real interest rates.[36] This means that an output response that

36. The effect is quite significant. For example, in the simulation shown in Figure 5.8, by the eighth quarter following the shock the positive effect of the $\Sigma \hat{K}_t$ term is 65% of the size of

decays at the same rate as in the constant-capital model (and as in the estimates of Rotemberg and Woodford, 1997, discussed above) requires a *more persistent* increase in real interest rates in the case of the variable-capital model. (One can see from Figure 5.8 that the simulation does indeed have this property.) On the other hand, because of the very forward-looking character of the model—real-interest-rate expectations several years in the future affect aggregate demand to essentially the same extent as the current short-term real rate—a more persistent increase in the short-term real rate will cause a larger immmediate contraction of aggregate demand, unless the size of the coefficients $\{\chi_j\}$ is reduced. This is achieved in the simulation shown in Figure 5.8 by assuming a large enough value of ϵ_ψ to reduce the interest-rate sensitivity of aggregate demand by a factor of about 40 percent relative to the basic model.

Whether or not one allows for endogenous capital accumulation, the impulse responses resemble the results of VAR studies more closely if one introduces delays of the sort discussed in Section 1.1 above. If one assumes that both consumption and investment spending are determined a period in advance, then the IS block of the endogenous-capital model takes the form

$$\hat{K}_{t+1} = (1 - \tilde{\mu}_1)\hat{K}_\infty + \tilde{\mu}_1\hat{K}_t - \sum_{j=0}^{\infty} \tilde{\chi}_j E_{t-1}(\hat{\imath}_{t+j} - \pi_{t+j+1}) + e_{t-1}^k, \qquad (3.24)$$

$$\hat{Y}_t = \left(\hat{Y}_\infty - \Sigma\hat{K}_\infty\right) + \Sigma\hat{K}_t - \sum_{j=0}^{\infty} \chi_j E_{t-1}(\hat{\imath}_{t+j} - \pi_{t+j+1}) + e_{t-1}^y, \qquad (3.25)$$

where all coefficients remain the same functions of underlying parameters as in (3.22) and (3.23). Similarly, if all new prices must be determined a period in advance, the AS block takes the form

$$\pi_t = \xi_0 E_{t-1}\hat{s}_t - \xi_1 E_{t-1}\hat{s}_{t+1} + \psi_1 E_{t-1}\pi_{t+1} - \psi_2 E_{t-1}\pi_{t+2}, \qquad (3.26)$$

together with (3.18), where the coefficients in (3.26) are the same as those in (3.17).

The impulse responses to a monetary disturbance in the case of the variable-capital model with one-period delays and a monetary policy rule of the same kind as in Figure 5.8 are shown by the solid lines in Figure 5.9. (Here all parameters except the length of the delays are calibrated as in Figure 5.8.) The dashed lines in the figure also reproduce the impulse responses to the same kind of monetary policy disturbance in the case of

---

the cumulative negative effect of all of the real-interest-rate terms, so that the contraction in aggregate demand is only a bit more than a third of the size it would have been otherwise.

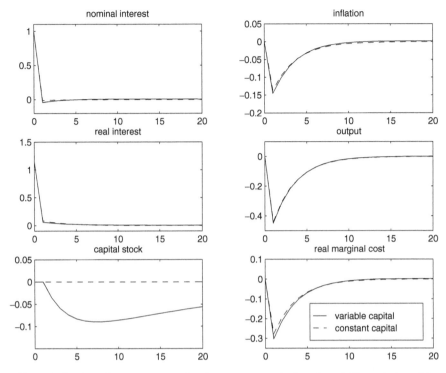

Figure 5.9 *Impulse responses under the constant-capital and variable-capital models compared in the case of predetermined spending and pricing decisions (d = 1).*

the constant-capital model considered in Figure 5.1. (The responses plotted here are those of the case shown in Figure 5.1 in which there are no real-balance effects.) Again, one observes that the variable-capital model with $\sigma = 1$ and $\epsilon_\psi = 3$ predicts output and inflation responses quite similar to those predicted by the constant-capital model in the case of a value of σ greater than 6. In this case, the predicted responses under both models are reasonably similar to the VAR responses shown in Figure 5.2. While I do not explore here the ability of a more complex variable-capital model to fit estimated impulse-response functions, it seems likely that a variable-capital model would fit the estimated responses as well as the constant-capital Rotemberg-Woodford model discussed in Section 2.1, but without requiring a large value of σ to do so.

The fact that constant-capital and variable-capital models can be calibrated so as to predict very similar output and inflation dynamics in response to the same kind of monetary policy shock indicates that the predictions of the models need not be too different; indeed, their respective abilities to fit empirical evidence as to the response to a particular kind of (historically typical) disturbance might well be quite similar. On the other hand, the mechanisms within the models that produce these predictions are not too closely parallel, owing to the significant effects of endogenous capital accumulation in the extended model. This means that even if the models are calibrated so as to predict similar responses to a particular kind of policy (as in Figures 5.8 and 5.9), it will not follow that the models calibrated in this way would also predict similar responses to all other policies that might be contemplated. Thus while a number of general lessons that may be drawn from the basic model (e.g., the degree to which aggregate demand should depend upon expected real rates years in the future) are found to be robust to an explicit consideration of endogenous capital accumulation, accurate quantitative conclusions about the nature of optimal monetary policy are likely to require explicit allowance for the dynamics of the capital stock.

3.4   Capital and the Natural Rate of Interest

I now consider the extent to which the concept of the "natural rate of interest," introduced in Chapter 4, Section 2, in connection with the basic neo-Wicksellian model, can be extended to a model that allows for endogenous variation in the capital stock. The most important difference in the case of the extended model is that the equilibrium real rate of return under flexible prices is no longer a function solely of current and expected future exogenous disturbances, but depends as well upon the capital stock, which is now an endogenous state variable (and so a function of past monetary policy, among other things, when prices are sticky). Hence if I continue to define the natural rate of interest in this way, it ceases to refer to an exogenous process.

An alternative possibility (pursued in Neiss and Nelson, 2003) would be to define the "natural rate of interest" as what the equilibrium real rate of return would be if prices were not only currently flexible and expected always to be flexible in the future, but also *had always been flexible in the past*—so that what matters for the computation is not the capital stock that actually exists, but the one that *would* exist if prices had been flexible, given the actual history of exogenous real disturbances. Under that definition the natural rate of interest would be exogenous, but at the cost of less connection with equilibrium determination in the actual (sticky-price) economy. It seems odd to define the economy's "natural" level of activity, and correspondingly the associated "natural" level of interest rates, in a way that makes the capital stock that actually exists and the effects of this upon the economy's productive capacity irrelevant. Moreover, a clear cost of the alternative definition would be less connection between this concept of "natural" output and the efficient level of output, which clearly depends on the actual capital stock.

For this reason, I continue to define the "natural rates" of output and interest as those that would result from price flexibility now and in the future, *given* all exogenous and predetermined state variables, including the economy's capital stock.

Since the equilibrium with flexible prices at any date t depends only on the capital stock at that date and on current and expected future exogenous real disturbances,[37] I can write a log-linear approximation to the solution in the form

$$\hat{Y}_t^n = \hat{Y}_t^{ncc} + \eta_y \hat{K}_t,$$

$$\hat{r}_t^n = \hat{r}_t^{ncc} + \eta_r \hat{K}_t,$$

and so on, where the terms $\hat{Y}_t^{ncc}$ and $\hat{r}_t^{ncc}$ refer to exogenous processes (functions solely of the exogenous real disturbances). These "intercept" terms in each expression indicate what the level of real output (or the real interest rate, and so on) *would* be, given current and expected future real disturbances, if prices were flexible *and* the capital stock did not vary from its steady-state level. I call this the *constant-capital natural rate* of output (or of interest, and so on). I also find it useful to define a "natural rate" of investment $\hat{I}_t^n$ and of the marginal utility of income $\hat{\lambda}_t^n$ in a similar way. One can even define a "natural" capital stock $\hat{K}_{t+1}^n$, as what the capital stock in period $t + 1$ would be if it had been chosen in a flexible-price equilibrium in period t as a function of the actually existing capital stock $\hat{K}_t$ and the exogenous disturbances at that time. Thus I similarly write

$$\hat{K}_{t+1}^n = \hat{K}_{t=1}^{ncc} + \eta_k \hat{K}_t.$$

Finally, I use tildes to indicate the "gaps" between the actual and "natural" values of these several variables: $\tilde{Y}_t \equiv \hat{Y}_t - \hat{Y}_t^n$, $\tilde{r}_t \equiv \hat{r}_t - \hat{r}_t^n$, and so on.

Once again, in a flexible-price equilibrium, real marginal cost must at all times be equal to a constant $(\theta - 1)/\theta$. It then follows from (3.18) that fluctuations in the natural rate of output satisfy

$$\hat{Y}_t^n = \frac{\omega - \nu}{\omega + \sigma^{-1}} \hat{K}_t + \frac{\sigma^{-1}}{\omega + \sigma^{-1}} \hat{I}_t + \frac{\sigma^{-1}}{\omega + \sigma^{-1}} g_t + \frac{\omega}{\omega + \sigma^{-1}} q_t.$$

This relation generalizes equation (2.2) of Chapter 4 for the basic neo-Wicksellian model. Note that this does not allow me to solve for the natural rate of output as a function of the capital stock and the real disturbances

---

37. This is true up to the log-linear approximation that I use here to characterize equilibrium. More precisely, it would depend on the capital stock in place in each of the firms producing differentiated goods.

without simultaneously solving for the natural rate of investment. However, comparison with (3.18) allows me to derive an expression for real marginal cost in terms of the gaps,

$$\hat{s}_t = \left(\omega + \sigma^{-1}\right)\tilde{Y}_t - \sigma^{-1}\tilde{I}_t, \tag{3.27}$$

generalizing equation (2.7) of Chapter 3.

One can also write condition (3.7) in terms of the gap variables, obtaining the following.

PROPOSITION 5.2. Let $\tilde{Y}_t \equiv \hat{Y}_t - \hat{Y}_t^n$, where the natural rate of output $\hat{Y}_t^n$ represents the flexible-price equilibrium level of output given $\hat{K}_t$, and similarly let $\tilde{K}_{t+1} \equiv \hat{K}_{t+1} - \hat{K}_{t+1}^n$, where $\hat{K}_{t+1}^n$ represents the flexible-price equilibrium capital stock given $\hat{K}_t$ (the *actual* capital stock in period t, rather than what it *would* have been if prices had been flexible in earlier periods). Then optimizing investment demand implies that the joint dynamics of the output and capital gaps $\{\tilde{Y}_t, \tilde{K}_{t+1}\}$ satisfy

$$\begin{aligned}
[1 - \beta(1 - \delta)] &\left[\rho_y \left(E_t \tilde{Y}_{t+1} + \eta_y \tilde{K}_{t+1}\right) - \rho_k \tilde{K}_{t+1}\right] \\
&+ \beta \epsilon_\psi \left[\left(E_t \tilde{K}_{t+2} + \eta_k \tilde{K}_{t+1}\right) - \tilde{K}_{t+1}\right],
\end{aligned} \tag{3.28}$$

where the coefficients ρ_y, ρ_k, η_y, η_k are again defined as in (3.7).

The calculation is explained in the appendix. Note that equation (3.28) is similar in form to (3.7), *except* that it is purely forward looking; it determines the equilibrium size of the gap $\tilde{K}_{t+1}$ without any reference to predetermined state variables such as $\tilde{K}_t$.

Equations (3.8)–(3.10) must hold similarly in a flexible-price equilibrium, which implies that the gaps must also satisfy the following equations:

$$\tilde{I}_t = k\tilde{K}_{t+1}, \tag{3.29}$$

$$\tilde{\lambda}_t = -\sigma^{-1}\left(\tilde{Y}_t - \tilde{I}_t\right), \tag{3.30}$$

$$\tilde{r}_t = \tilde{\lambda}_t - \left(E_t \tilde{\lambda}_{t+1} + \eta_\lambda \tilde{K}_{t+1}\right). \tag{3.31}$$

Using equations (3.29) and (3.30) to eliminate $\tilde{\lambda}_t$ and $\tilde{K}_{t+1}$ from (3.28) and (3.31), I am left with a system of two equations that can be written in the form

$$E_t z_{t+1} = A z_t + a \tilde{r}_t, \tag{3.32}$$

for a certain matrix A and vector a of coefficients, where now

$$z_t \equiv \begin{bmatrix} \tilde{Y}_t \\ \tilde{I}_t \end{bmatrix}.$$

This pair of coupled difference equations generalizes the "gap" version (equation (1.12) of Chapter 4) of the IS relation of the basic neo-Wicksellian model.

One can now close the system by specifying monetary policy in terms of an interest-rate feedback rule of the form

$$\hat{\imath}_t = \bar{\imath}_t + \phi_\pi(\pi_t - \bar{\pi}) + \phi_x(x_t - \bar{x})/4, \tag{3.33}$$

where I reintroduce the notation $x_t \equiv \tilde{Y}_t$ for the output gap. (Once again, $\bar{x}$ is the steady-state output gap corresponding to the steady-state inflation rate $\bar{\pi}$.) With policy specified by a "Taylor rule" of this kind, the interest-rate gap is given by

$$\tilde{r}_t = \left(\bar{\imath}_t - \hat{r}_t^n - \bar{\pi}\right) - E_t(\pi_{t+1} - \bar{\pi}) + \phi_\pi(\pi_t - \bar{\pi}) + \phi_x(x_t - \bar{x})/4. \tag{3.34}$$

Note that in this last relation, the only endogenous variables are gap variables *if* one makes the further assumption that

$$\bar{\imath}_t = \bar{\imath}_t^{cc} + \eta_r \hat{K}_t, \tag{3.35}$$

where $\{\bar{\imath}_t^{cc}\}$ is an exogenous process. This implies that in addition to systematic responses to endogenous variation in inflation and in the output gap, the policy rule (3.33) also involves a systematic response of a specific sort to endogenous variation in the capital stock: The central bank's interest-rate operating target is adjusted to exactly the same extent as the natural rate of interest is changed by the variation in the capital stock. This is obviously a special case, but not an entirely implausible one if we posit a desire to stabilize inflation and hence to arrange for interest rates to vary one-for-one with variation in the natural rate of interest. Of all the possible sources of variation in the natural rate of interest, variations owing to changes in the economy's aggregate capital ought to be the easiest for a central bank to track with some accuracy (owing to the slowness of movements in the capital stock).

A complete system of equilibrium conditions for the determination of the variables $\{\tilde{Y}_t, \tilde{I}_t, \tilde{r}_t, \hat{s}_t, \pi_t\}$ is then given by (3.17), (3.27), (3.32), and (3.34). The system of equations may then be written in the form

$$E_t \hat{z}_{t+1} = \hat{A} \hat{z}_t + \hat{a}\left(\hat{r}_t^n - \bar{\imath}_t + \bar{\pi}\right), \tag{3.36}$$

where now

$$\hat{z}_t \equiv \begin{bmatrix} \tilde{Y}_t - \bar{x} \\ \tilde{I}_t - \bar{I} \\ E_t \pi_{t+1} - \bar{\pi} \\ \pi_t - \bar{\pi} \end{bmatrix},$$

with $\bar{I}$ the steady-state value of $\tilde{I}_t$ corresponding to steady inflation at the rate $\bar{\pi}$, and $\hat{A}$ and $\hat{a}$ again a matrix and vector of coefficients. One gets this system as follows. The first two rows are obtained by substituting for $\tilde{r}_t$ in (3.32) using (3.34),[38] and the third row by solving (3.17) for $E_t \pi_{t+2}$ and then substituting for $\hat{s}_t$ and $E_t \hat{s}_{t+1}$ using (3.27). We finally substitute for $E_t \tilde{Y}_{t+1}$ and $E_t \tilde{I}_{t+1}$ using the first two rows of (3.36) just derived. The fourth row is simply an identity.

Because the system (3.36) is purely forward looking (i.e., there are no predetermined endogenous state variables), a policy rule of the kind defined by (3.33) and (3.35) results in determinate equilibrium dynamics for inflation and the output gap (among other variables) if and only if the matrix $\hat{A}$ has all four eigenvalues outside the unit circle. When this is true, the system can be solved forward in the usual way to obtain a unique bounded solution. The solutions for inflation and the output gap and the implied solution for the nominal interest rate are once again of the form

$$\pi_t = \bar{\pi} + \sum_{j=0}^{\infty} \psi_j^{\pi} E_t \left(\hat{r}_{t+j}^n - \bar{\iota}_{t+j} + \bar{\pi} \right), \tag{3.37}$$

$$x_t = \bar{x} + \sum_{j=0}^{\infty} \psi_j^x E_t \left(\hat{r}_{t+j}^n - \bar{\iota}_{t+j} + \bar{\pi} \right), \tag{3.38}$$

$$\hat{\iota}_t = \bar{\iota}_t + \sum_{j=0}^{\infty} \psi_j^i E_t \left(\hat{r}_{t+j}^n - \bar{\iota}_{t+j} + \bar{\pi} \right), \tag{3.39}$$

as in the case of the basic neo-Wicksellian model (Section 2.4 of Chapter 4). However, the numerical values of the coefficients $\{\psi_j^{\pi}, \psi_j^x, \psi_j^i\}$ in these expressions are different. Figure 5.10 plots coefficients $\{\psi_j^{\pi}, \psi_j^x\}$ for $j = 0$ through 10, in the case of model parameters chosen as in the earlier figures, and a policy rule of the form defined by (3.33) and (3.35), with feedback coefficients $\phi_{\pi} = 2$, $\phi_x = 1$. Here the solid line indicates the coefficients in the case of the variable-capital model, and the dashed line the coefficients

---

38. Note that all of these equations continue to be valid when we replace variables by the difference of those variables from their steady-state values. I choose to express the equations in this form in (3.36) because the policy rule (3.33) has already been expressed in this form.

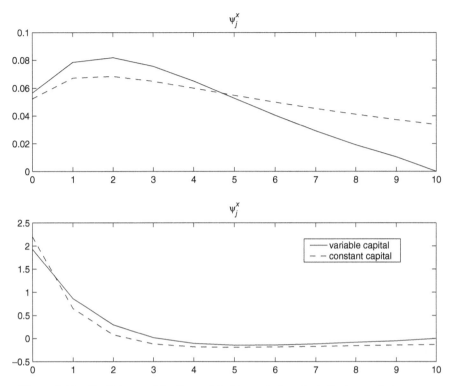

Figure 5.10 *Coefficients of the forward-looking solution for inflation and the output gap.*

in the case of the basic model. (The dashed line here corresponds to the baseline case shown in Figures 4.4 and 4.5.)

Once again one finds that, at least in the case of changes in the expected gap $E_t(\hat{r}^n_{t+j} - \bar{\imath}_{t+j})$ only a few quarters in the future, increases in the expected gap increase both inflation and the output gap. Once again, this is true even many quarters in the future in the case of inflation, whereas expected gaps $E_t(\hat{r}^n_{t+j} - \bar{\imath}_{t+j})$ more than a few quarters in the future have little effect upon the output gap. Thus fluctuations in inflation and the output gap can still be explained in essentially the same way as in the constant-capital model. Once again, inflation and positive output gaps result from increases in the natural rate of output that are not fully matched by a tightening of monetary policy or by loosenings of monetary policy not justified by any decline in the natural rate of interest.

An immediate consequence is that once again a possible approach to the goal of inflation stabilization is to commit to a policy rule of the form (3.33) such that (i) the coefficients ϕ_π, ϕ_x are chosen so as to imply a determinate equilibrium, and (ii) the intercept adjustments track variations in the natural rate of interest as well as possible, that is, the central bank seeks to set $\bar{\imath}_t = \hat{r}_t^n + \bar{\pi}$ at all times. (Note that this is an example of a rule of the form (3.35), with $\bar{\imath}_t^{cc} = \hat{r}_t^{ncc}$.) If it is possible to satisfy this condition with sufficient accuracy, then inflation can in principle be completely stabilized with finite response coefficients. Thus the requirement of tracking variations in the natural rate of interest continues to be as important to the pursuit of price stability as in our analysis of the basic neo-Wicksellian model.

PART II

Optimal Policy

CHAPTER 6

Inflation Stabilization and Welfare

I turn now to the evaluation of alternative monetary policy rules, using the analytical framework developed in the previous chapters. A first question, of course, is what the goals of monetary policy should be. Most discussions give primary, if not exclusive, attention to two goals in terms of which alternative policies should be evaluated. The first, which has attained particular prominence in recent discussion, is maintaining a low and stable rate of inflation. It is sometimes argued that this should be the exclusive goal of monetary policy, and various recent developments—the explicit responsibility given to several central banks in the 1990s for achievement of inflation targets or the exclusive concern with price stability that is specified in the Maastricht treaty as the goal of the European Central Bank—indicate that this view has become influential among policymakers.[1] At the same time, most discussions of actual monetary policy, even now and even in countries with inflation-targeting central banks, assume at least some degree of concern with the stabilization of economic activity as well; in the early literature (e.g., Poole, 1970), this was often treated as the primary goal of monetary stabilization policy.

There is thus a fair amount of consensus in the academic literature that a desirable monetary policy is one that achieves a low expected value of a discounted-loss function, where the losses each period are a weighted average of terms quadratic in the deviation of inflation from a target rate and in some measure of output relative to potential. But even agreement upon this general form of the objective still allows considerable scope for disagreement about details that may well matter a great deal for the design of an optimal policy. First of all, obviously, there is the question of the relative weight to be placed upon inflation stabilization and output stabilization. But this is hardly the only ambiguity in the conventional prescription. For

---

1. It may, however, be questioned whether the inflation-targeting central banks should be understood to care solely about inflation stabilization. See, e.g., Svensson (1999a).

instance, which kind of output measure should be stabilized? In particular, should one seek to stabilize output relative to a concept of "potential output" that varies in response to real disturbances that shift the short-run aggregate-supply curve, or should one seek to stabilize output relative to a smooth trend?[2]

Similarly, in which sense should price stability be pursued? Should one seek to stabilize deviations of the *price level* from a deterministic target path (as proposed, e.g., by Hall and Mankiw, 1994), so that unexpected inflation in excess of one's target rate should subsequently be deliberately counteracted, in order to bring the price level back to its target path? Or should one seek to stabilize deviations of the *inflation rate* from its target level (as assumed, e.g., by Svensson, 1997a), so that—assuming that the variance of the unforecastable component of inflation cannot be reduced by policy—one should *not* seek to counteract past inflation fluctuations in order to minimize variation in the forecastable component of inflation? Should greater priority perhaps be given to reducing the variability of *unforecastable* inflation, on the grounds that this is what causes unexpected modifications of the real consequences of preexisting nominal contracts, whereas forecastable variations in inflation can simply be incorporated into contracts? Or should greater priority be given to stabilization of *forecastable* inflation, on the grounds that expected inflation distorts incentives (like an anticipated tax), whereas unforecastable inflation has no incentive effects (like an unanticipated wealth levy)?

The aim of the present chapter is to show how economic analysis can be brought to bear upon these questions. An important advantage of using a model founded upon private-sector optimization to analyze the consequences of alternative policy rules is that there is a natural welfare criterion in the context of such a model, provided by the preferences of private agents, which are displayed in the structural relations that determine the effects of alternative policies. Such a utility-based approach to welfare analysis has long been standard in the theory of public finance. It is not yet too common in analyses of monetary policy, perhaps because it is believed that the main concerns of monetary stabilization policy are assumed away in models with explicit micro-foundations. But we have seen that models founded on individual optimization can be constructed that, thanks to the presence of nominal rigidities, allow for realistic effects of monetary policy upon real variables. Here we shall see those same nominal rigidities provide welfare-economic justification for central bankers' traditional concern for price stability.

---

2. Different answers to this question lead Bean (1983) and West (1986) to reach diametrically opposite conclusions about the case in which nominal GDP targeting would be preferable to money-supply targeting.

It is not assumed, of course, that individuals care directly about prices; their economic welfare depends directly only upon the goods they consume and the amount of effort they expend upon production. But just as taxes can cause deadweight losses because of their effects on the equilibrium allocation of resources, so can inflation. In a model with nominal rigidities—more specifically, in one in which it is recognized that prices are not adjusted in perfect synchronization with one another (which requires, but is stronger than, the observation that they are not all adjusted continually)—instability of the general price level leads to unnecessary and undesired variation in the relative prices of goods whose prices are adjusted at different times. These relative price distortions result in deadweight losses, just as in the case of distorting taxes. We shall see that this effect can justify not only a loss function that penalizes inflation variations, but indeed—if one assumes parameter values implied by the apparent degree of nominal rigidity in actual economies—a much larger relative weight on inflation variation than upon output variation than is assumed in the loss functions used in many monetary policy evaluation exercises.

Deriving a utility-based welfare criterion in this way can not only allow one to justify a general concern with price stability, but can furthermore provide exact answers to the questions raised previously about the precise formulation of the appropriate loss function. These answers depend, of course, upon the assumptions one makes about the structure of the economy; for example, they depend crucially upon the nature of the nominal rigidities that are present. Insofar as the correct structural relations of the present model of the economy remain controversial, the proper welfare criterion to use in evaluating policy remains controversial as well; and my goal here is more to illustrate a method than to reach final conclusions. But insofar as particular parameter values are found to be empirically justified in that they are required in order for my structural equations to fit historical data, they contain important information about the proper welfare criterion as well.

1   Approximation of Loss Functions and Optimal Policies

The method that I employ in the following analysis derives a quadratic loss function that represents a quadratic (second-order Taylor series) approximation to the level of expected utility of the representative household in the rational-expectations equilibrium associated with a given policy. There are several reasons for resorting to this approximation. One is simply mathematical convenience; with a quadratic approximation to the objective function and linear approximations to the structural equations, I can address the nature of optimal policy within a linear-quadratic optimal control framework that has been studied extensively, and in which the characterization of optimal policy is relatively simple. This convenience is especially great when turning to questions such as the optimal use of indicator variables under circumstances of partial information.[3]

But there are other advantages as well. One is comparability of the results with those of the traditional literature on monetary policy evaluation, which almost always assumes a quadratic loss function of one sort or another. Casting my own results in this familiar form allows me to discuss similarities and differences between my utility-based welfare criterion and those assumed in other studies without letting matters be obscured by superficial differences in functional form that may have relatively little consequence for the results obtained.

Finally, it does not make sense to be concerned with a higher-order approximation to the welfare criterion if I do not plan to characterize the effects of alternative policies with a degree of precision sufficient to allow computation of those higher-order terms. In the first part of this study, I have shown how to derive a log-linear approximation to the equilibrium fluctuations in inflation and output under alternative policies, using a log-linear approximation to the exact structural equations of the model. Using this method, I compute the equilibrium fluctuations in these variables only up to a residual of order $\mathcal{O}(\|\xi\|^2)$, where $\|\xi\|$ is a bound on the amplitude of the exogenous disturbances. Given that I do not compute the terms of second order in $\|\xi\|$ in characterizing equilibrium fluctuations, I cannot expect to compute the terms of third or higher order in $\|\xi\|$ in evaluating the expected utility of the representative household.[4] Of course, one might also wish to undertake a more accurate approximation of the predicted evolution of the endogenous variables under alternative regimes. However, such a study would introduce a large number of additional free parameters to which numerical values would have to be assigned for purposes of computation; and there is often little empirical basis for the assignment of such values, given the degree to which the empirical study of macroeconomic time series makes use of linear models.[5]

---

3. See Chapter 8, Section 3.4.

4. There is thus no obvious advantage to the approach sometimes adopted in utility-based welfare analyses, such as Ireland (1997) or Collard et al. (1998), of evaluating an exact utility function but using a log-linear approximation to the model's structural equations in order to compute the equilibrium.

5. A common approach in the quantitative equilibrium business-cycle literature, of course, is to assume special functional forms for preferences and technology that allow the higher derivatives of these functions to be inferred from the same small number of parameters as determine the lower-order derivatives, which may then be inferred from first and second moments of the time series alone. This approach often obscures the relation between the properties of the time series and the model parameters that are identified by them, and allows "identifications" that are in fact quite sensitive to the arbitrary functional form assumption. I prefer instead to assume functional forms that are as general as possible and then to emphasize that only a finite number of derivatives of these functions matter for the calculations.

However, even a second-order approximation to utility can be computed on the basis of a merely linear approximation to the model structural equation only under certain circumstances. I assume that these hold in the calculations here, but it is important to be clear about the scope of validity of the results. Let x represent a vector of endogenous variables, and suppose that one wishes to evaluate $E[U(x; \xi)]$ under alternative policies, where ξ is a vector of random exogenous disturbances, and $U(\cdot; \xi)$ is a concave function for each possible realization of ξ and at least twice differentiable. Now suppose that one is able to compute a linear (or log-linear) approximation to the equilibrium responses of the endogenous variables for any policy rule in a given class of the form

$$x = x^0 + A\xi + \mathcal{O}\big(\|\varphi, \xi\|^2\big), \qquad (1.1)$$

where the coefficients x^0 and A depend on policy, and φ indexes an aspect of policy discussed later. For any given policy rule, this represents a first-order Taylor-series approximation to the exact equilibrium responses $x(\xi)$, assumed to be nonlinear but differentiable, taken around the mean values $\xi = 0$. I arrive at this approximate solution by solving a system of approximate structural equations (including an approximate policy rule), obtained by linearizing the exact equations around some value $\bar{x}$ of the vector of state variables and the value $\xi = 0$ for the disturbances.[6] The value $\bar{x}$ around which I linearize need not correspond exactly to x^0, the equilibrium values in the absence of disturbances, for I wish to consider alternative policy rules (which need not all imply identical values of x^0) using a single approximate model. Nonetheless, given a choice of $\bar{x}$ around which to expand the equations of the model, my approximation methods are only accurate in the case of policies that imply values of x^0 close enough to $\bar{x}$. To be precise, in order for the residual in (1.1) to be only of order $\mathcal{O}(\|\varphi, \xi\|^2)$, regardless of the policy rule, when the linear approximate solution is obtained by solving the structural equations linearized around $\bar{x}$, I must assume that $\tilde{x}^0 \equiv x^0 - \bar{x} = \mathcal{O}(\|\varphi\|)$. Thus the parameter vector φ indexes aspects of the policy rule that affect the equilibrium outcome in the absence of disturbances, where $\varphi = 0$ implies that $x^0 = \bar{x}$, and the results apply to policies for which $\|\varphi\|$ is small.

I can take a similar Taylor-series expansion of the utility function, obtaining

$$U(x; \xi) = \bar{U} + U_x \tilde{x} + U_\xi \xi + \tfrac{1}{2} \tilde{x}' U_{xx} \tilde{x} + \tilde{x}' U_{x\xi} \xi$$

$$+ \tfrac{1}{2} \xi' U_{\xi\xi} \xi + \mathcal{O}\left(\|\varphi, \xi\|^3\right), \qquad (1.2)$$

---

6. The conditions under which the solution to the linearized structural equations yields a valid approximation of this kind to the solution to the exact structural equations are discussed in Appendix A.

where $\bar{U} \equiv U(\bar{x}; 0)$, $\tilde{x} \equiv x - \bar{x}$, and all partial derivatives of U are evaluated at $(\bar{x}; 0)$. In bounding the residual, I have used the fact that (1.1) implies that $\tilde{x} = \mathcal{O}(\|\varphi, \xi\|)$. Taking the expected value of (1.2) and using the fact that ξ is normalized so that $E(\xi) = 0$ yields the approximate welfare criterion

$$E[U] = \bar{U} + U_x E[\tilde{x}] + \tfrac{1}{2}\mathrm{tr}\{U_{xx}\mathrm{var}[x]\} + \mathrm{tr}\{U_{x\xi}\mathrm{cov}(\xi, \tilde{x})\}$$
$$+ \tfrac{1}{2}\mathrm{tr}\{U_{\xi\xi}\mathrm{var}[\xi]\} + \mathcal{O}(\|\varphi, \xi\|^3). \tag{1.3}$$

Here I use the notation $E[z]$ for the expectation of a random vector z, $\mathrm{var}[z]$ denotes its variance-covariance matrix, and $\mathrm{cov}(z_1, z_2)$ the matrix of covariances between two random vectors z_1, z_2.

I now wish to consider whether the linear approximation

$$x^{(1)} \equiv x^0 + A'\xi \tag{1.4}$$

to the equilibrium fluctuations in x under a given policy rule can be validly used to compute a second-order approximation to expected utility. Substituting $\tilde{x}^{(1)} \equiv x^{(1)} - \bar{x}$ for $\tilde{x}$ in (1.3) yields the estimate

$$U^{(1)} \equiv \bar{U} + U_x\tilde{x}^0 + \tfrac{1}{2}\mathrm{tr}\{U_{xx}A\Omega A'\} + \mathrm{tr}\{U_{x\xi}\Omega A'\} + \tfrac{1}{2}\mathrm{tr}\{U_{\xi\xi}\Omega\},$$

where $\Omega \equiv \mathrm{var}[\xi]$. But note that

$$E[U] = U^{(1)} + U_x E[\tilde{x} - \tilde{x}^0] + \mathcal{O}(\|\varphi, \xi\|^3).$$

This means that the criterion $U^{(1)}$ cannot be expected to correctly rank alternative policies among those implying the same average outcome x^0,[7] even in the case of an arbitrarily small bound on the amplitude of the disturbances, unless one is sure that

$$U_x E[\tilde{x} - \tilde{x}^0] = \mathcal{O}(\|\varphi, \xi\|^3). \tag{1.5}$$

Condition (1.5) need not hold simply as a result of the standard regularity assumptions needed to justify the use of the Taylor-series approximations. For there may be *second-order* terms in a correct approximation to $E[x]$ that

---

7. Of course, in the case of policies that imply different values for $U_x\tilde{x}^0$, a correct welfare ranking is possible in the case of small enough disturbances using the zeroth-order approximation $U^{(0)} \equiv \bar{U} + U_x\tilde{x}^0$, since (1.3) implies that $E[U] = U^{(0)} + \mathcal{O}(\|\varphi, \xi\|^3)$. But since x^0 is independent of the way in which policy responds to disturbances, this criterion can tell us nothing about optimal *stabilization* policy—only about issues such as the optimal target value for long-run average inflation.

are left as part of the residual in (1.1) but that make a nonzero second-order contribution to the left-hand side of (1.5).[8] Moreover, the question whether such terms are nonzero or not cannot generally be determined without considering the second-order terms in an approximate solution for the equilibrium of the model, which in turn requires the use of a second-order approximation of the model structural equations.

One case in which it is nonetheless possible to legitimately use the solutions to linearized structural equations to obtain valid welfare rankings of alternative policy rules in the case of small enough shocks is when

$$U_x(\bar{x}; 0) = 0, \tag{1.6}$$

so that (1.5) necessarily holds. In this case $U^{(1)}$ provides a valid second-order approximation to $E[U]$, and comparisons of the value of $U^{(1)}$ provide a correct welfare ranking of alternative policies in the case of small enough disturbances and policies that imply values of x^0 close enough to $\bar{x}$. As is shown in the next section, it is possible to define models for which this condition holds, and hence for which the second-order expansion (1.2) contains no linear terms.

Equation (1.6) is observed to be just the condition for the optimality of $\bar{x}$ as an outcome in the absence of disturbances. It might be thought that the condition in question is simply an instruction about the point around which the model equations should be log-linearized: One should expand around the values of the state variables that would maximize welfare in the absence of disturbances. But $\bar{x}$ must also be a point such that x^0 is near it under the policies that one is interested in evaluating, and this may contradict the other requirement. For example, in a model of monopolistically competitive pricing of the kind presented in Chapter 3, the equilibrium level of output (in the absence of an output subsidy) under flexible prices, or more generally under a policy that leads to stable prices, is inefficiently low. One might propose to expand around an allocation of resources in which $y_t(i) = Y^*$ for each good in each period, where Y^* is the welfare-maximizing level of production in the absence of disturbances. But then a policy that leads to stable or nearly stable prices need not be one that leads to an equilibrium outcome in the absence of shocks that is near the point around which one has linearized the model equilibrium conditions. Consequently, the approximate welfare measure $U^{(0)}$ may be inaccurate in the case of such policies, owing to the inaccuracy of the log-linearized equations for the purpose of analyzing policies of this kind. Yet these are the policies

---

8. See, for example, Kim and Kim (2003) for an example of the kind of mistake in welfare analysis that can be made by neglecting this issue.

that I am interested in, and indeed, I establish (here and in Chapter 7) conditions under which they are optimal. So one must expand around the allocation of resources corresponding to an equilibrium with stable prices in the absence of disturbances. Condition (1.6) is then a condition that may or may not be satisfied, depending on whether distortions remain even in an environment with no stochastic disturbances and stable prices.

Condition (1.6) is not just a property of the economy for which one analyzes alternative policy rules; in the case of a given economic model, it may or may not be satisfied depending on the choice of variables in terms of which the quadratic welfare criterion is expressed. Suppose, for example, that in the model of monopolistic competition there is a production subsidy, as considered in Section 2, of a size that causes the flexible-price equilibrium level of output to be efficient. Even so, if one writes utility as a function of the consumption and labor supply of the representative household and expands utility as a quadratic function of consumption and hours around the flexible-price equilibrium levels of these variables when there are no disturbances, condition (1.6) is not satisfied, despite the optimality of this allocation. This is because neither the marginal utility of consumption nor the marginal disutility of work is equal to zero (or need even be small) at the allocation around which one expands. The allocation $\bar{x}$ is optimal, but only when one takes into account the relation between consumption and work that characterizes feasible outcomes as a result of the production function. Moreover, to obtain a valid welfare ranking of alternative policies, one needs to substitute the production function into the utility function, as I do in Section 2, and express utility as a function of the level of production, a state variable in terms of which the utility gradient is zero. This change of variables matters for the second-order approximation to expected utility because one substitutes the production function into the utility function before computing the quadratic approximation. In doing so one makes use of a second-order approximation to the production function, whereas with the other choice of variables, the relation between consumption and work would be one of the structural relations of the model and merely log-linearized. Thus the choice of variables needs to be made with care.[9]

9. The example of Kim and Kim (2003) can be understood in this light. These authors consider a welfare comparison between two policies, autarchy versus international risk pooling in the case of a two-country endowment economy. When the vector x consists of the log consumption levels in the two countries (and the linearized structural relations are log-linear solutions for each country's consumption as a function of the two random endowments), the invalid conclusion is obtained that risk pooling may lower average expected utility. Condition (1.6) fails to hold because the marginal utility of consumption is positive in both countries. If, however, one let the state variable x be a measure of the transfer from one country to the other, and wrote average utility as a function of the two endowments and the size of the transfer, then for an appropriate choice of $\bar{x}$ condition (1.6) would be satisfied. In this case, a linear

One can weaken condition (1.6) somewhat, requiring only that

$$U_x(\bar{x}; 0) = \mathcal{O}(\|\Phi\|), \tag{1.7}$$

where Φ is a vector of parameters of the structural model that determines the degree of inefficiency of the allocation $\bar{x}$ around which the Taylor-series expansions are taken. Under this assumption, one has

$$U_x E\left[\tilde{x} - \tilde{x}^0\right] = \mathcal{O}\left(\|\Phi, \varphi, \xi\|^3\right), \tag{1.8}$$

as a result of which

$$E[U] = U^{(1)} + \mathcal{O}\left(\|\Phi, \varphi, \xi\|^3\right).$$

Hence the quadratic approximation to expected utility (1.3) provides a valid second-order approximation to expected utility when evaluated using the solution to linear approximate structural relations, as long as: (i) the disturbances are small enough, (ii) the policies considered imply outcomes in the absence of shocks that are close enough to the allocation around which the expansions are taken, and (iii) certain distortions are small enough. In the sticky-price model with monopolistic competition considered in the next section, condition (ii) obtains in the case of policies that imply a long-run average inflation rate that is small enough. Condition (iii) obtains in the case that the inefficiency of the flexible-price equilibrium level of output is small enough, owing to weak market power and/or the existence of a subsidy that sufficiently offsets the market power of the monopolistic suppliers of differentiated goods.

Considering Taylor-series expansions of the equations in Φ along with the other parameters allows consideration of the consequences of distortions that are not eliminated by a policy of price stability and an absence of stochastic disturbances, but only in limited respects. In the linear approximation (1.1) to equilibrium outcomes under alternative policies, the proposed approximation takes account of the effects of small distortions $\Phi \neq 0$ on the constant term x^0, but does not consider the effects of such distortions on the responses to disturbances given by the matrix A, as such effects would be of second order if the distortions are only of first order. Similarly, in the quadratic approximation (1.3) to expected utility, this method takes account of the interaction between the distortions and the average values

---

approximation to the structural relation—i.e., the linear equation that specifies the transfer as a function of the random endowments, under either policy—when substituted into a quadratic approximation to expected average utility yields the correct welfare ranking for all values of the model parameters.

of the endogenous variables, but not of any effects of the distortions on the welfare consequences of the way in which the endogenous variables are affected by disturbances. Hence, to this order of approximation, the linear characterizations of the optimal responses to disturbances are independent of Φ, and hence the same as in an economy with $\Phi = 0$.[10] Nonetheless, taking account of the consequences of $\Phi \neq 0$ in even this limited sense is of considerable interest. In particular, it allows us to determine the consequences for the optimal long-run average inflation rate of a situation in which the optimal level of output is higher on average than the one consistent with stable prices, a situation (in conjunction with the existence of a short-run Phillips-curve trade-off) that is often argued to provide a motive for inflationary policy.

Dealing with the case in which the distortions that are not eliminated by price stability are more substantial, so that a small-Φ expansion is inadequate, requires additional information. One approach would simply be to compute an approximate solution to the equilibrium conditions for any given policy rule that is accurate to second order and substitute this into (1.3). Perturbation methods (and numerical algorithms) that can be used for this purpose are discussed by Collard and Juillard (2001), Anderson and Levin (2002), Jin and Judd (2002), Kim et al. (2003), and Schmitt-Grohé and Uribe (2002). As shown by Sutherland (2002), in some cases the required calculations can be simplified given that for purposes of welfare analysis one needs only to compute a second-order approximation to the mean values of the state variables, $E[x]$.

Benigno and Woodford (2003) show rather that even when (1.6) does not hold, and a small-Φ approximation does not suffice, it may well be possible to find a quadratic approximation to expected utility that possesses no linear terms. That is, one may be able to find a quadratic form V such that

$$E[U] = \bar{U} + E[\tilde{z}' V \tilde{z}] + \mathcal{O}\big(\|\varphi, \xi\|^3\big) \tag{1.9}$$

regardless of the policy rule that is considered, where $\tilde{z} \equiv [\tilde{x}' \; \xi']'$, even though (1.6) does not hold and $V \neq U_{zz}$. If a representation of the form (1.9) is possible, then

$$E[U] = V^{(1)} + \mathcal{O}\big(\|\varphi, \xi\|^3\big),$$

---

10. It is not intended here to claim that the optimal responses to disturbances are not affected by the value of Φ; this is not always true, as discussed in Section 5. The point is simply that any effects of $\Phi \neq 0$ on the optimal response of x to disturbances represent a contribution to x that is at least of order $\mathcal{O}(\|\Phi, \varphi, \xi\|^2)$, and that accordingly can be neglected in a first-order characterization of optimal policy in the sense proposed here.

where

$$V^{(1)} \equiv \bar{U} + \text{tr}\{V_{xx} A\Omega A'\} + 2\text{tr}\{V_{x\xi}\Omega A'\} + \text{tr}\{V_{\xi\xi}\Omega\}$$

is the estimate arrived at by substituting the first-order approximate solution (1.4) for x into the terms on the right-hand side of (1.9). This means that a valid second-order approximation to welfare can be obtained using only a linear approximation to the equilibrium outcomes under alternative policies; hence it suffices to use the linearized equilibrium conditions to predict the consequences of alternative policies.

The method of Benigno and Woodford amounts to using a second-order approximation to the structural relations (*not* including any specification of the monetary policy rule) to obtain an expression for the term in (1.3) that involves the mean levels of the endogenous variables of the form

$$U_x E[\tilde{x}] = E[\tilde{z}' W \tilde{z}] + \mathcal{O}(\|\varphi, \xi\|^3), \qquad (1.10)$$

which must hold regardless of the policy rule; (1.3) then implies (1.9) under the definition

$$V = \tfrac{1}{2} U_{zz} + W.$$

The possibility of a representation (1.10) being possible depends, in general, on the expansion point $\bar{x}$ being *constrained*-optimal, even if not an unconstrained optimum of the function U; the gradient must be zero in the particular directions in which it is possible for policy to move x^0. But it may well be possible to arrange this through a suitable choice of $\bar{x}$; and such a constrained-optimal choice of $\bar{x}$ would then represent an outcome of the sort that x remains near under desirable policies, making $\bar{x}$ a suitable choice for the point around which to expand. I show in Section 5, for example, that this method can be applied to the present baseline model with staggered pricing, even in the case of nonnegligible distortions resulting from market power and/or taxation.

The use of this method requires the computation of a second-order approximation to the structural relations, or at least some of them, in order to obtain the representation (1.10). However, this calculation need only be done once, and not separately for each type of policy that one may wish to analyze, as in the case of the second-order solution methods mentioned earlier. Hence one can use this method to characterize fully optimal policy, and not merely to find the optimal rule within some parametric class of simple policy rules for which the second-order expansion of the complete set of equilibrium conditions has been computed (as in the analysis of Sutherland, 2002, e.g.). Furthermore, because the optimal-policy problem can be cast in a familiar linear-quadratic form, a variety of powerful results for problems of that kind can be brought to bear. These include the methods used to characterize the optimal state-contingent responses to exogenous disturbances in Chapter 7 and to derive optimal linear policy rules in Chapter 8.

2 A Utility-Based Welfare Criterion

I turn now to the computation of a utility-based approximate welfare criterion, of the kind discussed in the previous section, for the case of the baseline model. In this section, I restrict attention to the simple case of the small-Φ expansion discussed in the previous section.[11] The natural welfare criterion in the model is the level of expected utility

$$E\left\{\sum_{t=0}^{\infty}\beta^t U_t\right\} \tag{2.1}$$

associated with a given equilibrium, where the period contribution to utility U_t is given by

$$U_t = u(C_t; \xi_t) - \int_0^1 v(h_t(i); \xi_t)\,di, \tag{2.2}$$

in which C_t denotes the Dixit-Stiglitz consumption aggregate, and $h_t(i)$ is the supply of labor of the type used in sector i.[12] In this section, I abstract from the welfare consequences of monetary frictions.[13]

Then, using the equilibrium condition $C_t + G_t = Y_t$ and the production function $y_t(i) = A_t f(h_t(i))$ to substitute for consumption and hours, I can express the period utility of the representative household as a function solely of the level of production of each of the goods in period t,

$$U_t = \tilde{u}\left(Y_t; \tilde{\xi}_t\right) - \int_0^1 \tilde{v}\left(y_t(i); \tilde{\xi}_t\right)di, \tag{2.3}$$

where the indirect utility functions are defined as[14]

---

11. The derivation follows essentially the lines of that presented in Rotemberg and Woodford (1997, 1999a) in the context of a variant model with additional decision lags.

12. Here I derive the welfare criterion under the assumption of specific factor markets, discussed in Chapter 3. The general method expounded here applies equally, however, under alternative assumptions about factor market structure.

13. The welfare criterion derived in this section thus applies to a cashless economy, or to a cashless limiting economy, of the kind introduced in Chapter 2. The additional terms that must be added in the case of nonnegligible monetary frictions are considered in Section 4.1.

14. Note that one may alternatively assume a yeoman farmer model, as in Rotemberg and Woodford (1997, 1999a), in which case $\tilde{v}(y_t(i); \tilde{\xi}_t)$ can be interpreted as directly specifying the household's disutility of supplying good i.

$$\tilde{u}(Y; \tilde{\xi}) \equiv u(Y - G; \xi), \tag{2.4}$$

$$\tilde{v}(y; \tilde{\xi}) \equiv v(f^{-1}(y/A); \xi), \tag{2.5}$$

as in Chapters 2 and 3, and $\tilde{\xi}_t$ denotes the complete vector of exogenous disturbances $(\xi_t, G_t, \text{ and } A_t)$. The index Y_t (like C_t and G_t) is a Dixit-Stiglitz aggregate,

$$Y_t \equiv \left[\int_0^1 y_t(i)^{(\theta-1)/\theta} \, di \right]^{\theta/(\theta-1)}, \tag{2.6}$$

where $y_t(i)$ measures the production (and consumption) in period t of differentiated good i.[15]

2.1 Output-Gap Stability and Welfare

Under my previous assumptions, $\tilde{u}$ is an increasing, concave function of Y, and $\tilde{v}$ is an increasing, convex function of y, for each possible value of $\tilde{\xi}$. Thus (2.3) implies that U_t is a concave function of the entire vector of levels of production of the various goods. Note also that in terms of this notation, the real marginal cost function introduced in Chapter 3 is given by

$$s(y, Y; \tilde{\xi}) = \tilde{v}_y(y; \tilde{\xi})/u_c(Y; \xi). \tag{2.7}$$

It follows that the elasticity of $\tilde{v}_y$ with respect to y is given by $\omega > 0$, the elasticity of real marginal cost with respect to own output, introduced in Chapter 3. One may also observe that the elasticity of real marginal cost with respect to aggregate output is given by σ^{-1}, where once again

$$\sigma \equiv -u_c/\bar{Y}u_{cc} > 0$$

measures the intertemporal elasticity of substitution of aggregate expenditure.

The steady-state level of output associated with zero inflation in the absence of real disturbances (i.e., when $\tilde{\xi}_t = 0$ at all times[16]) is the quantity $\bar{Y}$ that satisfies

$$s(\bar{Y}, \bar{Y}; 0) = (1 - \tau)/\mu \equiv 1 - \Phi_y. \tag{2.8}$$

---

15. If there is trend growth in productivity and output, the variables Y_t, $y_t(i)$, and A_t should all be interpreted as having been deflated by a common exponential trend factor to render them stationary.

16. Here I assume for notational convenience that the elements of $\tilde{\xi}$ that measure variations in government purchases and in technology are $\hat{G}_t$ and a_t, which are monotonic transformations of G_t and A_t, rather than G_t and A_t themselves.

Here τ is the constant proportional tax rate on sales proceeds, and $\mu \equiv \theta/(\theta - 1)$ is the desired markup as a result of suppliers' market power. The parameter Φ_y then summarizes the overall distortion in the steady-state output level as a result of both taxes and market power. Since the efficient output level Y^* for all goods in the absence of shocks satisfies $s(Y^*, Y^*; 0) = 1$, it is observed that $\bar{Y}/Y^*$ is a decreasing function of Φ_y, equal to one when $\Phi_y = 0$. When Φ_y is small, one may make use of the log-linear approximation

$$\log\left(\bar{Y}/Y^*\right) = -\left(\omega + \sigma^{-1}\right)^{-1} \Phi_y + \mathcal{O}\left(\|\Phi_y\|^2\right). \tag{2.9}$$

The empirically realistic case is clearly that in which $\Phi_y > 0$. However, I assume in this section that Φ_y is small and treat it as one of the expansion parameters in the Taylor-series approximations, as discussed in the previous section.[17] Note that the introduction of the distorting tax rate τ allows one to contemplate a series of economies in which Φ_y is made progressively smaller, without this having to involve any change in the size of θ, and so without any implication for the coefficients of the log-linearized structural relations that determine the consequences of alternative policies.[18]

I now proceed to compute a quadratic Taylor-series approximation to (2.3).

PROPOSITION 6.1. In the case of small enough fluctuations in the production of each good $\hat{y}_t(i)$ around the level $\bar{Y}$, small enough disturbances, and a small enough value of Φ_y, the utility flow to the representative household each period can be approximated by

$$U_t = -\frac{\bar{Y} u_c}{2} \left\{ \left(\sigma^{-1} + \omega\right)\left(x_t - x^*\right)^2 + \left(\theta^{-1} + \omega\right) \mathrm{var}_i \hat{y}_t(i) \right\}$$

$$+ \mathrm{t.i.p.} + \mathcal{O}\left(\|\Phi_y, \hat{y}, \tilde{\xi}\|^3\right). \tag{2.10}$$

Here $\hat{y}_t(i) \equiv \log(y_t(i)/\bar{Y})$; $x_t \equiv \hat{Y}_t - \hat{Y}_t^n$, where $\hat{Y}_t \equiv \log(Y_t/\bar{Y})$ and $\hat{Y}_t^n$ denotes the (log of the) *natural rate* of output, the equilibrium level of out-

---

17. For the extension of the results of this section to the case of larger Φ, see Section 5.

18. Rotemberg and Woodford (1997, 1999a) instead assume that τ is of exactly the (negative) size required to offset the distortion due to market power, so that $\Phi_y = 0$. They propose to consider optimal monetary stabilization policy as part of a broader analysis of optimal policy, in which another instrument (tax policy) is assigned responsibility for achieving the optimal average level of economic activity, while monetary policy is used to ameliorate the economy's response to shocks. However, it is clear that monetary policy must in practice be chosen in an environment in which such an output subsidy does not exist. Furthermore, the fact that the natural rate of output is inefficiently low is of importance for certain issues, notably the inflationary bias associated with discretionary policymaking, treated in Chapter 7. Hence here I allow for $\Phi_y > 0$, while still assuming that Φ_y is small.

put under complete price flexibility (as defined in Chapter 3), and $x^* \equiv \log(Y^*/\bar{Y})$ is the efficient level of the output gap, given by (2.9). The term "t.i.p." collects terms that are independent of monetary policy, either constants or functions purely of exogenous disturbances and so irrelevant to the welfare ranking of alternative equilibria.

Details of this calculation are given in Appendix E.

One can alternatively bound the residual in terms of a bound on certain parameters of the policy rule, φ, that determine the long-run equilibrium values of the endogenous state variables in the absence of disturbances. I normalize these parameters so that $\varphi = 0$ implies a long-run output level $Y^\infty = \bar{Y}$ and for any small enough φ, $\log(Y^\infty/\bar{Y}) = \mathcal{O}(\|\varphi\|)$. Furthermore I restrict attention to equilibria in which the endogenous variables, such as $y_t(i)$, fluctuate around their long-run equilibrium values to an extent that is bounded by $\|\tilde{\xi}\|$.[19] I am thus able to write $\|\hat{y}\| = \mathcal{O}(\|\varphi, \tilde{\xi}\|)$, so that (2.10) may alternatively be written

$$U_t = -\frac{\bar{Y} u_c}{2} \left\{ \left(\sigma^{-1} + \omega\right)\left(x_t - x^*\right)^2 + \left(\theta^{-1} + \omega\right) \mathrm{var}_i \hat{y}_t(i) \right\}$$

$$+ \text{t.i.p.} + \mathcal{O}\left(\|\Phi_y, \varphi, \tilde{\xi}\|^3\right). \tag{2.11}$$

Expressing the bounds in the approximation errors in terms of the coefficients φ reminds one that the approximate welfare measure is only valid in the case of policies that are close enough to consistency with a long-run average output level of $\bar{Y}$.

Note that the exogenous shocks $\tilde{\xi}_t$ to preferences, technology, and government purchases matter, in this approximation, only through their effects on a single (composite) exogenous state variable, the natural rate of output $\hat{Y}_t^n$. Furthermore, output variability as such does not matter for the utility-based welfare criterion; rather, it is the variability of the *output gap* that is significant, and the measure of potential output with respect to which the gap should be measured for purposes of the welfare criterion is the *same natural rate* of output that (as shown in Chapter 3) determines the short-run relation between output and inflation. Thus I can already offer an answer to one question posed in the introduction to this chapter. It is the output gap x_t, rather than output relative to trend, that one should seek to stabilize, and— if the only distortions in the economy are those associated with monopolistic

---

19. I now include in $\tilde{\xi}$ a parameterization of initial conditions, so that $\tilde{\xi} = 0$ implies initial conditions consistent with an equilibrium in which $y_t(i) = \bar{Y}$ for all t in the case of a policy with $\varphi = 0$, and the extent to which output must differ from $\bar{Y}$, even initially, under such a policy but alternative initial conditions, is bounded by $\|\tilde{\xi}\|$. I also include in $\tilde{\xi}$ any random disturbance terms in the monetary policy rule itself; the approximation applies only to the case in which both nonmonetary disturbances and monetary policy shocks are sufficiently small.

competition, a constant level of distorting taxes, sticky prices, and the cumulative effect of the first two distortions is small—the welfare-relevant output
gap is the same one that appears in the short-run aggregate-supply curve.

However, (2.10) implies that stabilization of the output gap should not
be the sole concern of policy, since the dispersion of output levels across
sectors matters as well.[20] In fact, in the baseline framework, there is no
reason for equilibrium output to be different for different goods, except
as a result of relative price distortions that result from sticky prices in an
environment where the overall price level is unstable. It is through this
channel that price stability turns out to be relevant for welfare, in a way
that goes beyond the mere association between inflation and the level of
the aggregate output gap.

Specifically, the assumed CES (Dixit-Stiglitz) preferences over differentiated goods imply that each supplier faces a constant-elasticity demand curve
of the form

$$\log y_t(i) = \log Y_t - \theta(\log p_t(i) - \log P_t). \tag{2.12}$$

It follows from this that

$$\operatorname{var}_i \log y_t(i) = \theta^2 \operatorname{var}_i \log p_t(i),$$

so that (2.11) may equivalently be written

$$U_t = -\frac{\bar{Y} u_c}{2} \left\{ (\sigma^{-1} + \omega)(x_t - x^*)^2 + \theta(1 + \omega\theta) \operatorname{var}_i \log p_t(i) \right\}$$

$$+ \text{t.i.p.} + \mathcal{O}\big(\|\Phi_y, \varphi, \tilde{\xi}\|^3\big). \tag{2.13}$$

Thus one finds that, in addition to stabilization of the output gap, it is also
appropriate for policy to aim to reduce price dispersion. In the present
framework, this is achieved by stabilizing the general price level; but the
exact way in which fluctuations in the general price level affect price dispersion, and hence welfare, depend upon the details of pricesetting.

2.2   Inflation and Relative-Price Distortions

The approximation (2.13) to the utility of the representative household applies to any model with no frictions other than those due to monopolistic

---

20. More generally, it is the dispersion of output *gaps* across sectors that matters, along
with the *aggregate* output gap. Here I consider only disturbances $\tilde{\xi}_t$ that affect the natural rate
of output in an identical way in all sectors, so that the dispersion of output gaps across sectors
is identical to the dispersion of output levels. In Section 4.3, I consider the consequences of
allowing for shocks with asymmetric effects on different sectors.

competition and sticky prices, regardless of the nature of the delays involved in pricesetting. The relation between the price dispersion term and the stability of the general price level depends instead upon the details of pricesetting. Here I do not attempt a general treatment, but illustrate the form of the relation in three simple examples, including the baseline model of staggered pricesetting from Chapter 3.

As a first example, consider again the case, discussed in Section 1.3 of Chapter 3, of an economy in which a fraction $0 < \iota < 1$ of goods prices are fully flexible, while the remaining $1 - \iota$ must be fixed a period in advance. In such an economy, as shown above, the aggregate-supply relation takes the familiar New Classical form

$$\pi_t = \kappa x_t + E_{t-1} \pi_t, \tag{2.14}$$

where the slope coefficient is given by

$$\kappa \equiv \frac{\iota}{1 - \iota} \frac{\sigma^{-1} + \omega}{1 + \omega \theta} > 0.$$

(Equation (2.14), like the other log-linear structural relations recalled below, is accurate only up to a residual of order $\mathcal{O}(\|\varphi, \tilde{\xi}\|^2)$.)

In this model, in any period all flexible-price goods have the same price, p_t^1, and all sticky-price goods have the same price, p_t^2, and

$$\log p_t^2 = E_{t-1} \log p_t^1 + \mathcal{O}(\|\tilde{\xi}\|^2). \tag{2.15}$$

Furthermore, the overall price index (defined by equation (1.3) of Chapter 3) satisfies

$$\log P_t = \iota \log p_t^1 + (1 - \iota) \log p_t^2 + \mathcal{O}(\|\tilde{\xi}\|^2),$$

so that

$$\pi_t - E_{t-1} \pi_t = \iota \left[\log p_t^1 - E_{t-1} \log p_t^1 \right] + \mathcal{O}(\|\tilde{\xi}\|^2)$$

$$= \iota \left[\log p_t^1 - \log p_t^2 \right] + \mathcal{O}(\|\tilde{\xi}\|^2),$$

using (2.15). It follows that under this assumption about pricing,

$$\text{var}_i \log p_t(i) = \iota (1 - \iota) \left(\log p_t^1 - \log p_t^2 \right)^2$$

$$= \frac{1 - \iota}{\iota} (\pi_t - E_{t-1} \pi_t)^2 + \mathcal{O}(\|\tilde{\xi}\|^3).$$

As asserted earlier, equilibrium price dispersion is closely connected with the stability of the general price level; but in this special case, it is only the volatility of the *unexpected component* of inflation that matters.

Substituting this expression into (2.13), I obtain the following welfare-theoretic objective for monetary policy.[21]

PROPOSITION 6.2. In the case of the New Classical model of Chapter 3, the utility flow to the representative household each period can be approximated by

$$U_t = -\Omega L_t + \text{t.i.p.} + \mathcal{O}\big(\|\Phi_y, \tilde{\xi}\|^3\big),$$

where Ω is a positive constant and L_t is a quadratic loss function of the form

$$L_t = (\pi_t - E_{t-1}\pi_t)^2 + \lambda\big(x_t - x^*\big)^2, \tag{2.16}$$

with a relative weight on output gap variability of $\lambda = \kappa/\theta$, and an optimal output gap of

$$x^* = \big(\omega + \sigma^{-1}\big)^{-1} \Phi_y. \tag{2.17}$$

I thus obtain precise conclusions regarding both the sense in which aggregate output and inflation variations matter for welfare (it is the output *gap* that is significant, and the *unexpected* component of inflation), and the relative weight that should be placed upon the two concerns (the relative weight on output-gap variations is proportional to the slope κ of the short-run Phillips curve).

In fact, in the context of this model, there is no tension between the goals represented by the two terms of (2.16). For (2.14) implies that the output gap is itself proportional to the surprise component of inflation. Thus one can simplify (2.16) further and say that the sole goal of policy should be to minimize the variability of unexpected inflation or, alternatively, that the sole goal should be to stabilize the output gap (when properly measured).[22]

---

21. Here I am able to omit any bound on policy parameters φ in the bound on the residual, since in the case of this particular model of pricing, equilibrium output levels fluctuate around $\bar{Y}$ regardless of the nature of the policy rule.

22. However, if one allows for disturbances to the short-run aggregate-supply relation (2.14) that—unlike the preference, technology, or government-purchase shocks considered in Chapter 3—do not shift the efficient level of output to the same extent, then the loss function (2.16) would still be correct, whereas the output gap that appears in this formula would no longer coincide perfectly with unexpected inflation. In that extension of the model,

While I obtain a simple result in this case, the model is not a very realistic one, since, as discussed earlier, it is unable to account for the persistence of the observed output effects of monetary disturbances. Consider instead, then, the consequences of the kind of staggered pricing assumed in the baseline model, a discrete-time version of the Calvo (1983) pricing model. In this model, a fraction $0 < \alpha < 1$ of all prices remain unchanged each period, with the probability of a price change assumed to be independent of both the length of time since the price was last changed and of the degree to which that good's price is out of line with others. As shown in Chapter 3, the aggregate-supply relation in this case takes the New Keynesian form

$$\pi_t = \kappa x_t + \beta E_t \pi_{t+1}, \tag{2.18}$$

where now the slope coefficient is given by

$$\kappa \equiv \frac{(1-\alpha)(1-\alpha\beta)}{\alpha} \frac{(\sigma^{-1} + \omega)}{1 + \omega\theta} > 0. \tag{2.19}$$

Under this assumption about the timing of price revisions, one can establish the following connection between price dispersion at a point in time and the overall rate of inflation.

PROPOSITION 6.3. Suppose that price changes are staggered as in the discrete-time Calvo model expounded in Chapter 3, with fraction α of prices remaining unchanged each period, and let price dispersion at any point in time be measured by

$$\Delta_t \equiv \mathrm{var}_i \log p_t(i).$$

Then this dispersion measure evolves over time according to

$$\Delta_t = \alpha \Delta_{t-1} + \frac{\alpha}{1-\alpha}\pi_t^2 + \mathcal{O}\big(\|\Delta_{t-1}^{1/2}, \varphi, \tilde{\xi}\|^3\big) \tag{2.20}$$

in the case of a small enough initial price dispersion, small enough disturbances, and a policy rule (corresponding to a small value of φ) that ensures a long-run average inflation rate near zero.

---

it would be quite important to know the correct relative weight λ to place on output-gap variations. See Section 4.5. Moreover, even for the kind of disturbances considered thus far, the welfare-relevant output gap no longer co-moves perfectly with unexpected inflation when Φ_y is nonnegligible, though a quadratic loss function of the form (2.16) continues to represent a correct approximation to expected utility. See Benigno and Woodford (2003).

The proof is in Appendix E. Note that the evolution of the measure of price dispersion again depends (to second order) solely upon the behavior of the aggregate price index, but the relationship is now a dynamic one. Note also that in this calculation, I assume an initial degree of price dispersion Δ_{t-1} that is only of second order; it then follows that this measure of price dispersion continues to be of only second order in the case of first-order deviations of inflation from zero.

Integrating forward (2.20), starting from any (small) initial degree of price dispersion Δ_{-1} in the period before the first period for which a new policy is contemplated, one finds that the degree of price dispersion in any period $t \geq 0$ under the new policy is given by

$$\Delta_t = \alpha^{t+1}\Delta_{-1} + \sum_{s=0}^{t} \alpha^{t-s}\left(\frac{\alpha}{1-\alpha}\right)\pi_s^2 + \mathcal{O}\big(\|\Delta_{-1}^{1/2}, \varphi, \tilde{\xi}\|^3\big).$$

Note that the first term is independent of the policy that one chooses to apply in periods $t \geq 0$. Thus if one takes the discounted value of these terms over all periods $t \geq 0$, one obtains

$$\sum_{t=0}^{\infty}\beta^t\Delta_t = \frac{\alpha}{(1-\alpha)(1-\alpha\beta)}\sum_{t=0}^{\infty}\beta^t\pi_t^2 + \text{t.i.p.} + \mathcal{O}\big(\|\Delta_{-1}^{1/2}, \varphi, \tilde{\xi}\|^3\big).$$

Substituting this in turn into (2.13), I obtain the following.

PROPOSITION 6.4. In the case of the New Keynesian model of Chapter 3 (i.e., the basic model with Calvo pricing), the discounted sum of utility of the representative household can be approximated by

$$\sum_{t=0}^{\infty}\beta^t U_t = -\Omega\sum_{t=0}^{\infty}\beta^t L_t + \text{t.i.p.} + \mathcal{O}\big(\|\Phi_y, \Delta_{-1}^{1/2}, \varphi, \tilde{\xi}\|^3\big), \qquad (2.21)$$

where $\Omega > 0$ and the normalized quadratic loss function is given by

$$L_t = \pi_t^2 + \lambda(x_t - x^*)^2. \qquad (2.22)$$

Here the relative weight on output-gap variability is again given by $\lambda = \kappa/\theta$, but now the value of κ referred to is that given in (2.19).[23] The optimal output gap x^* is again given by (2.17).

23. Note that the values of Ω and λ obtained here are slightly different from those that follow from the derivation presented in Rotemberg and Woodford (1999a). The reason is that here I am interested in approximating the expected value of the discounted sum of utilities, conditioning upon the preexisting degree of price dispersion at date -1, whereas they

The loss function (2.22) is in fact of a form widely assumed in the literature on monetary policy evaluation (and also in positive models of central bank behavior).[24] Here, however, I am able to present a theoretical justification for the attention to variations in inflation (rather than, say, variations in the price level), as well as for the common assumption that inflation variations are equally costly whether forecastable or not, in terms of the relative-price distortions resulting from price-level instability in the Calvo model of staggered pricesetting. I am also able to derive an optimal rate of inflation with respect to which deviations should be measured (namely, zero, as it is in this case that no relative-price distortions result from imperfect synchronization of price changes). Finally, I am again able to derive an optimal relative weight upon output-gap variation as opposed to inflation variation. This depends upon model parameters, but in a way that makes an estimate of the slope of the short-run aggregate-supply curve directly informative about the proper size of this weight.[25]

As is discussed further in Section 4.2, Rotemberg and Woodford's (1997) estimate of the slope of the short-run aggregate-supply curve for the United States implies a value for λ_x on the order of .05, if the output gap is measured in percentage points and inflation is measured as an annualized percentage rate.[26] This value is much lower than the value $\lambda_x = 1$ often assumed in the literature on evaluation of monetary policy rules, on a ground such as "giving equal weight to inflation and output" as stabilization objectives.[27] Our utility-based analysis implies instead that if one assumes the degree of price stickiness that is needed to account for the persistence of the real effects of monetary policy shocks, the distortions associated with inflation

---

compute an unconditional expectation. Note that the loss measure that is computed here for a given policy does not depend upon the initial price dispersion Δ_{-1}. Nonetheless, it matters whether one conditions upon the value of Δ_{-1} in computing the expected utility. Computing the unconditional expectation, rather than conditioning upon the value of Δ_{-1}, also penalizes policies that lead to higher average price dispersion for the higher average value that is assumed for Δ_{-1} if one integrates over the unconditional distribution of values for Δ_t associated with a given stationary equilibrium.

24. See, e.g., Walsh (1998, chap. 8), Clarida et al. (1999), or Svensson (1999a).

25. The size of this weight is of greater interest in the case of this model, since aggregate-supply relation (2.18) does not imply that inflation and the output gap should perfectly covary under most circumstances. It is true that complete stabilization of one implies complete stabilization of the other, as I discuss further in the next section, and in this sense there is no tension between the two goals if (2.18) holds. But it may not be possible to achieve complete stabilization, e.g., because of the zero lower bound on nominal interest rates, informational restrictions on feasible policies, or "cost-push shocks" of the kind discussed in Section 4.5; and in such cases optimal policy generally depends upon the relative weight placed upon the two goals.

26. This is actually the numerical value of $16\kappa/\theta$, the appropriate weight on $(x_t - x^*)^2$ relative to $(4\pi_t)^2$, since $4\pi_t$ is the annualized inflation rate in the quarterly model of Rotemberg and Woodford (1997).

27. See, e.g., Rudebusch and Svensson (1999) and Williams (1999).

are more important than those associated with variation in the aggregate output gap.

As yet another alternative, suppose that prices are indexed to a lagged price index between the occasions on which they are reoptimized, as in the model with inflation inertia set out in Section 3.2 of Chapter 3. In this case, the aggregate-supply relation takes the form

$$\pi_t - \gamma \pi_{t-1} = \kappa x_t + \beta E_t[\pi_{t+1} - \gamma \pi_t], \tag{2.23}$$

generalizing (2.18), where γ measures the degree of indexation to the lagged price index and κ is again defined as in (2.19). Recall that in the periods in which a given price is not reoptimized, it is automatically increased by an amount

$$\log p_t(i) = \log p_{t-1}(i) + \gamma \pi_{t-1}$$

owing to the change in the lagged price index. It follows that (2.20) generalizes to

$$\Delta_t = \alpha \Delta_{t-1} + \frac{\alpha}{1-\alpha}(\pi_t - \gamma \pi_{t-1})^2 + \mathcal{O}\big(\|\Delta_{t-1}^{1/2}, \varphi, \tilde{\xi}\|^3\big). \tag{2.24}$$

(The proof follows lines exactly parallel to the proof of Proposition 6.3 given in Appendix E.) Price dispersion is increased only when the prices that are reoptimized are increased by an amount different than $\gamma \pi_{t-1}$, the amount by which the prices that are not reoptimized increase. This occurs if and only if the overall rate of inflation π_t differs from $\gamma \pi_{t-1}$. It is then straightforward to obtain the following generalization of Proposition 6.4.

PROPOSITION 6.5. *In the case of the model of inflation inertia due to backward-looking indexation (derived in Section 3.2 of Chapter 3), the discounted sum of utility of the representative household can be approximated by an expression of the form (2.21), where the normalized quadratic loss function is now given by*

$$L_t = (\pi_t - \gamma \pi_{t-1})^2 + \lambda(x_t - x^*)^2, \tag{2.25}$$

in which $0 \le \gamma \le 1$ *measures the degree of indexation. Once again, the relative weight on output-gap variability is given by* $\lambda = \kappa/\theta$, *where* κ *is defined in (2.19), and* x^* *is given by (2.17).*

In the case of full indexation of individual prices to the lagged price index ($\gamma = 1$),[28] Proposition 6.5 implies that it is the rate of inflation acceleration,

---

28. Note that in this case, the aggregate-supply relation is essentially identical to the popular empirical specification proposed by Fuhrer and Moore (1995a, 1995b).

$\Delta\pi_t$, rather than the rate of inflation itself, that should be stabilized around zero in order to reduce the distortions associated with price dispersion.[29] Owing to the existence of complete indexation to past inflation, there are no distortions resulting from *constant* inflation, only from *changes* in the rate of inflation. In its implication that steady inflation at any rate causes no harm, this model is like the New Classical model (with which it shares the prediction of a vertical long-run Phillips curve). But in the model with full indexation, inflation *changes* distort the allocation of resources, whether they are predictable in advance or not.

Another way in which the basic neo-Wicksellian model is often argued to be excessively forward looking is in its specification of aggregate-demand determination, as discussed in Chapter 5. Suppose instead that there is habit persistence in private expenditure, modeled as in Section 1.2 of that chapter. The representative household's utility flow from expenditure each period is then of the form

$$u\big((Y_t - G_t) - \eta(Y_{t-1} - G_{t-1}); \xi_t\big), \tag{2.26}$$

generalizing (2.4). I then obtain the following generalization of Proposition 6.1 (following Amato and Laubach, 2001, and Giannoni and Woodford, 2003b).

PROPOSITION 6.6. Suppose that the preferences of the representative household exhibit habit persistence of the form (2.26), for some $0 \le \eta \le 1$. Then under the same assumptions (otherwise) as in Proposition 6.1, the utility flow to the representative household each period can be approximated by

$$U_t = -\frac{\bar{Y}u_c}{2}\left\{\mu_x\left(x_t - \delta x_{t-1} - \hat{x}^*\right)^2 + \left(\theta^{-1} + \omega\right)\mathrm{var}_i\hat{y}_t(i)\right\} \tag{2.27}$$
$$+ \text{t.i.p.} + \mathcal{O}(\|\Phi_y, \hat{y}, \tilde{\xi}\|^3),$$

where the coefficient $0 \le \delta \le \eta$ is again the smaller root of equation (1.28) in Chapter 5,

29. Steinsson (2002) and Amato and Laubach (2003b) similarly find, in the case of an AS relation with inflation inertia owing to the presence of backward-looking rule-of-thumb pricesetters of the kind proposed by Gali and Gertler (1999), that the utility-based loss function should penalize variations in $\Delta\pi_t$ as well as variations in π_t. However, the result (2.25) is simpler than the one obtained by these authors, and leads to simpler conclusions regarding the character of optimal policy in the presence of inflation inertia. This is one reason that I emphasize indexation to a lagged price index as a possible source of inflation inertia in this study.

$$\mu_x \equiv \frac{1 - \beta\eta}{1 + \beta\delta^2} \left[\omega + \varphi \left(1 + \beta\eta^2 \right) \right] > 0,$$

and

$$\hat{x}^* \equiv \frac{1 + \beta\delta^2}{1 - \beta\delta} \frac{\Phi_y}{\omega + \varphi \left(1 + \beta\eta^2 \right)} \geq 0,$$

in which expressions $\varphi > 0$ is again defined as in equation (1.25) of Chapter 5.

Details of this calculation are given in Appendix E.

The fact that the utility flow in period t depends on expenditure relative to the previous period's expenditure, rather than the current level of real expenditure alone, results in a stabilization objective for the output gap relative to the previous period's output gap, rather than the current output gap alone. The weight δ on the lagged output gap depends on (and is an increasing function of) the size of η, as discussed in Chapter 5. However, it is generally smaller than η, and can be much smaller, as is true in the case of the estimates of Giannoni and Woodford (2003b). If the rate at which the marginal disutility of output supply increases with additional current output is substantially greater than the rate at which the marginal utility of expenditure declines with additional current expenditure, then δ is small (distortions depend mainly on the distance of current output from the current natural rate, and not on the relation of current output to the previous period's output) even if η is large.

Note that I use the notation $\hat{x}^*$ for the target value because it is now a target for the quasi-differenced output gap, rather than for the level of the gap. As long as $\delta < 1$, the gap term in (2.27) can alternatively be written as

$$\mu_x \left[\left(x_t - x^* \right) - \delta \left(x_{t-1} - x^* \right) \right]^2,$$

where x^* is a target level for the output gap. However, expression (2.27) is also correct in the limiting case that $\delta = 1$ (however implausible these preferences may be), and it is worth noting that $\hat{x}^*$ need not equal zero in that case.

Proposition 6.6 can then be used, in conjunction with one or another hypothesis about the timing of price changes, to derive a welfare-theoretic loss function in terms of inflation and the output gap. For example, in the case of Calvo pricing, one can show that (2.21) holds for an appropriate definition of Ω and a normalized quadratic loss function of the form

$$L_t = \pi_t^2 + \lambda \left(x_t - \delta x_{t-1} - \hat{x}^* \right)^2, \qquad (2.28)$$

where once again $\lambda = \kappa/\theta > 0$, and κ is now defined as in equation (1.29) of Chapter 5. In the case of indexation of prices to a lagged price index, this generalizes to

$$L_t = (\pi_t - \gamma\pi_{t-1})^2 + \lambda(x_t - \delta x_{t-1} - \hat{x}^*)^2, \tag{2.29}$$

where the definition of λ remains the same.

Recall from Section 1.2 of Chapter 5 that in the case of habit persistence and Calvo pricing, the aggregate-supply relation takes the form

$$\pi_t = \kappa\left[(x_t - \delta x_{t-1}) - \beta\delta E_t(x_{t+1} - \delta x_t)\right] + \beta E_t\pi_{t+1}, \tag{2.30}$$

where κ and δ are the same coefficients as in (2.28). Similarly, one can show that if in addition prices are indexed to a lagged price index, the aggregate-supply relation takes the form

$$\pi_t - \gamma\pi_{t-1} = \kappa\left[(x_t - \delta x_{t-1}) - \beta\delta E_t(x_{t+1} - \delta x_t)\right] + \beta E_t(\pi_{t+1} - \gamma\pi_t). \tag{2.31}$$

Thus once again there is a close relation between the way in which a change in assumptions affects the aggregate-supply relation and the way in which the welfare-theoretic loss function should change.

3 The Case for Price Stability

While each of the loss measures derived earlier under the various assumptions about the timing of pricing decisions is different in certain respects, they all share an important common property: The deadweight losses due to relative price distortions can in each case be completely eliminated, in principle, by stabilizing the aggregate price level. The intuition for this result is simple. The aggregate price level is stabilized by creating an environment in which suppliers who choose a new price have no desire at any time to set a price different from the average of existing prices. But if this is so, the average of existing prices never changes, and so the new prices that are chosen at all times are always the same, and eventually all goods prices are equal to that same, constant value. Thus aggregate price stability is a sufficient condition for the absence of price dispersion in the present simple framework.

At the same time, in most cases, it is also a necessary condition. This is not true in the pure New Classical case, as in that case it is only necessary that there be no *unexpected* changes in the aggregate price level in order for there to be no price dispersion. But this is clearly a highly special case; even if some prices are fully flexible, if the sticky goods prices are set as in the Calvo model, complete price stability will again be necessary to eliminate distortions. Similarly, even in the model of Mankiw and Reis (2001a), which is like the New Classical model in assuming that each goods price at any date is set optimally, conditional on information available at some prior date (though the dates are different for different goods), complete price stability is necessary to eliminate distortions. This is because in the Mankiw-Reis model, for any horizon k, there are a positive fraction of goods prices that are set more than k periods in advance (or on the basis of information that is more than k periods out of date). This means that relative-price distortions are created in the case of any disturbance that affects the price level, even if it has no effect upon the price level until k periods later. Since this is true for arbitrary k, distortions are completely eliminated only if exogenous disturbances *never* imply any change in the price level.

Similarly, in the model with staggered pricing and full indexation to a lagged price index, price stability is not necessary for the absence of price dispersion; it is simply necessary that the inflation rate be constant over time. But again this is a highly special case. If the indexation parameter γ takes any value other than one, only zero inflation is consistent with an absence of price dispersion.[30] The same conclusion would be reached if only *some* prices are indexed to the lagged price index.

The argument for the necessity of stability of the general price index for the elimination of price dispersion is also independent of the specific details of the way that the timing of price changes is modeled by Calvo (1983). One need not assume that the probability of revision of any given price in a given period is the same for all prices; one might instead assume that prices are revised at fixed time intervals, as in the models of Taylor (1980), Blanchard and Fischer (1989, sec. 8.2), King and Wolman (1999), or Chari et al. (2000), among others, or one might endogenize the timing of price revisions as in the model of Dotsey et al. (1999). In any of these cases, price dispersion is eliminated only by a policy that completely stabilizes the general price index.

Moreover, price stability is desirable not only because the distortions associated with an inefficient output *composition* are eliminated. As we shall see, it is also the route to minimization of the distortions associated with an inefficient *level* of output; and so, in the context of the kind of simple model considered thus far, it is an unambiguously desirable goal for monetary policy. The argument for this is simplest in the case that the equilibrium level of output under flexible prices is optimal, so I take up this case first.

---

30. To be precise, an absence of price dispersion requires that prices change at a common rate π_t satisfying the difference equation $\pi_t = \gamma \pi_{t-1}$, given some arbitrary initial rate of inflation. But when $\gamma < 1$, this implies zero inflation every period, at least asymptotically. A *stationary* policy regime that fully eliminates distortions resulting from price dispersion would have to be one with zero inflation at all times.

But as we shall see, the conclusions require only minor modification even when I allow for the possibility that the natural rate of output is inefficiently low, as long as the distortions are not too large.

3.1 The Case of an Efficient Natural Rate of Output

Here I assume not merely that the inefficiency wedge Φ_y defined in (2.8) is small (so that a small-Φ_y Taylor-series expansion is appropriate), but that it is equal to zero. This implies that $\bar{Y} = \bar{Y}^*$, so that the steady-state level of output under flexible prices is efficient. Since I have verified that per-centage *fluctuations* in the natural rate are equal (to second order) to the percentage fluctuations in the efficient level of output, this actually implies that (to second order) the natural rate of output coincides with the efficient level of output at all times.

In this case, I easily reach a very simple conclusion about the nature of optimal monetary policy. For *each* of the individual terms in the quadratic loss function can be shown to achieve its minimum possible value, zero, if inflation is zero at all times. I have just discussed the fact that this is true of the terms that measure the deadweight loss due to an inefficient composition of output. But in the present case, $x^* = 0$, so that the term in the loss function that involves the aggregate output gap is also minimized (and equal to zero) if and only if $x_t = 0$ at all times. Each of the aggregate-supply relations (2.14), (2.18), and (2.23) implies that this is true in the case of zero inflation at all times.[31]

In the informal argument just given, I have ignored the role of initial conditions that may not be consistent with an equilibrium with zero infla-tion and zero output gap at all times. If one wishes to consider optimal policy from some initial date, however, the initial conditions that happen to exist— not necessarily ones that result from an anticipation of the policy that will be followed from now on—may constrain possible outcomes from now on. Thus it may not be possible to completely stabilize both inflation and the output gap at zero each period from the initial period onward.

In the case of the New Keynesian aggregate-supply relation (2.18), there is no problem; because this AS relation is purely forward looking, the set of paths for inflation and the output gap that are feasible from date zero onward are independent of anything that has happened previously. In this case, $\pi_t = 0$ and $x_t = 0$ for all $t \geq 0$ is a possible equilibrium outcome regardless of initial conditions, and so this is plainly the optimal outcome

---

31. Here I assume the baseline preference specification, in which there is no habit per-sistence. However, the same claim is true in the case of habit persistence, if I replace x_t by $x_t - \delta x_{t-1}$ and x^* by $\hat{x}^*$.

given a loss function (2.22).[32] On the other hand, in the case of the New Classical AS relation (2.14), such an outcome represents a possible equilibrium only in the case of initial conditions under which $E_{-1}\pi_0 = 0$. In the case of other initial conditions, it is obvious that an optimal policy involves $\pi_0 = E_{-1}\pi_0 \neq 0$ and $x_0 = 0$, which reduces the period zero loss (2.16) to its minimum possible value, zero. A loss of zero is also possible in all later periods, through commitment to any path for inflation that is completely predictable a period or longer in advance; in particular, a commitment to $\pi_t = 0$ in all periods $t > 0$ is one way of achieving the minimum possible discounted stream of losses.

Thus a commitment to price stability would again represent an optimal policy, except possibly during a brief transition period. Moreover, I argue in Chapters 7 and 8[33] that one should choose a time-invariant policy rule that achieves the pattern of behavior that it would be optimal to commit *eventually* to follow. In the present context, a commitment to price stability would be an example of such a policy. One reason why it might be sensible to commit to follow such a rule from the beginning, even when $E_{-1}\pi_0 \neq 0$, is that a willingness to deliver whatever rate of inflation may have been anticipated "just this once" may allow the private sector to expect that the same principle would be followed in the future as well, if it ever turned out that $E_{t-1}\pi_t$ differed from zero. But in this case there would be no determinate equilibrium level of inflation for the private sector to expect.

In the case of indexation to a lagged price index, resulting in an AS relation (2.23) that implies inflation inertia, matters are still more complex. An equilibrium with $\pi_t = 0$ and $x_t = 0$ for all $t \geq 0$ is possible only in the case of initial conditions under which $\pi_{-1} = 0$. However, it is evident from the form of the AS relation that the set of possible paths for the variables $\pi_t^d \equiv \pi_t - \gamma\pi_{t-1}$ and x_t from period zero onward is independent of the initial conditions, and one also notes that the utility-based loss function (2.25) depends only on the paths of these two variables. It is thus obvious that the optimal policy, from the point of view of minimizing the discounted sum of losses from period zero onward given the economy's prior state, is one under which $\pi_t = \gamma\pi_{t-1}$ and $x_t = 0$ for all $t \geq 0$. Thus the resulting path of inflation depends on the economy's initial rate of inflation prior to adoption of the optimal policy; specifically it satisfies $\pi_t = \gamma^{t+1}\pi_{-1}$.

---

32. This is only precisely true in the exact model, as opposed to the log-linear approximation, in the case that one starts from an initial condition in which all goods prices are the same, i.e., there is zero price dispersion. More generally, optimal policy will involve a rate of inflation and an output gap that depend on the degree of dispersion of existing prices. But on the assumption (made earlier) that the initial dispersion measure Δ_{-1} is of only second order, the optimal deviation from the zero-inflation steady state is only of second order, and the statement in the text is correct as a first-order approximation to the optimal paths of inflation and the output gap.

33. See the discussion in those chapters of policymaking "from a timeless perspective."

As long as $\gamma < 1$, optimal policy in this case is again one under which the inflation is *asymptotically* equal to zero—and not just on average, but in all possible states of the world. Thus optimal policy involves a commitment to eventual stabilization of the price level. Furthermore, even in the transition period, the optimal path of inflation is deterministic, which implies that it is unaffected by any random disturbances that may occur from period zero onward. Thus optimal policy has the immediate consequence that the price level should no longer be affected at all by any random disturbances that may occur, be they disturbances to technology, to preferences, or to the level of government purchases. The existence of inflation inertia only affects the rate at which it is optimal for the central bank to commit to lowering the rate of inflation (assuming an initial positive level) to its long-run target of zero.

It is only in the special case that $\gamma = 1$ (full indexation to the lagged price index) that this result is not obtained. In that case, the optimal commitment given initial conditions is to a constant inflation rate $\pi_t = \pi_{-1}$ for all $t \geq 0$; it is therefore optimal *never* to disinflate once inflation has been allowed to begin. But such a result plainly depends on the absence, in this simple model, of any distortions associated with steady inflation. If the prices of even a few goods are *not* fully indexed to the lagged price index, zero inflation is required to eliminate relative-price distortions. Similarly, if the adjustment of prices as a result of indexation is not continuous, but occurs only occasionally (though more frequently than reoptimizations of pricing policy), relative-price distortions are again completely eliminated only in the case of zero inflation. In either case, optimal policy will steadily reduce inflation over time to a long-run rate of zero, as there is always a motive for some reduction in the inflation rate (as long as the current rate remains positive) but never a motive for increasing it (as opposed to keeping it near its recent level). Thus one finds quite generally that optimal policy involves a commitment to price stability, at least eventually. And this means that eventually inflation will not only equal zero on average, but zero regardless of the real disturbances that may affect the economy.

Matters are only slightly more complex in the case of habit persistence in private expenditure (abstracted from in my remarks thus far). In this case, the welfare-theoretic stabilization objective consists of a discounted sum of terms of the form $(\pi_t - \gamma \pi_{t-1})^2$ and $(x_t - \delta x_{t-1})^2$, as a consequence of (2.29). But given an aggregate-supply relation of the form (2.31), it is possible to simultaneously achieve a zero value for each of these terms by following a monetary policy under which $\pi_t = \gamma \pi_{t-1}$ each period, implying that $x_t = \delta x_{t-1}$ each period as well. Thus under optimal policy, the path of inflation is never affected by any real disturbances, and as long as $\gamma < 1$, inflation should eventually be reduced to zero.

This strong conclusion regarding the optimality of complete price stability depends upon various details of the present model, as discussed further in Section 3.3. Nonetheless, it is interesting to note that it holds despite my having allowed for several different kinds of stochastic disturbances. In particular, the framework allows for exogenous disturbances to technology, to government purchases, to households' impatience to consume, to their willingness to supply labor, or to the transactions technology that determines their demand for money balances. In the face of each of these types of disturbance, it remains optimal, under the circumstances assumed here, for the general level of prices to be held fixed.

The generality of the conclusion results from a simple intuition, stressed by Goodfriend and King (1997). Under the circumstances assumed here, the failure of prices to be continually adjusted is the *only* distortion that prevents rational-expectations equilibrium from achieving an optimal allocation of resources. Thus an optimal monetary policy is one that achieves *the same allocation of resources as would occur with flexible prices*, if this is possible. Flexible-price equilibrium models of aggregate fluctuations (i.e., RBC models[34]) are then of practical interest, not as descriptions of what aggregate fluctuations should be like *regardless* of the monetary policy regime, but as descriptions of what they would be like under an *optimal* policy regime. Finally, these models of optimal pricesetting imply that price stickiness has no effect upon equilibrium outcomes in the case that monetary policy keeps the general price level completely unchanged over time, since in this case suppliers of goods would not wish to change their prices more frequently even if it were costless for them to do so. Thus complete price stability achieves the optimal allocation of resources.

Verifying that it is in fact possible, in principle, to achieve this first-best allocation through suitable monetary policy requires that I verify that I can solve the equations of the present model for the evolution of all variables (including the interest-rate instrument of the central bank) under the assumption that $\pi_t = 0$ at all times. As discussed in Chapter 4, this is possible as long as the natural rate of interest r_t^n is always nonnegative. In this case, what

---

34. Standard RBC models (King and Rebelo, 1999) differ from the flexible-price limit of the model assumed here in that product markets are competitive, rather than monopolistically competitive; in that all output is produced using inputs purchased from the same factor markets, so that there is a common level of marginal cost for all firms at any time; and in that the endogenous dynamics of the capital stock in response to shocks is modeled, and indeed emphasized (as the only endogenous propagation mechanism in simple RBC models). However, in the flexible-price limit of the baseline model, all goods prices move together, and similarly the levels of production of each good, so that marginal cost is in fact the same for all firms. If one assumes, as in this section, that an output or employment subsidy offsets the distortion due to firms' market power, the flexible-price equilibrium is equivalent to that of a competitive model with a single good. Finally, if one extends the baseline model to take account of capital-accumulation dynamics (which, as I have argued in Chapter 4, are not so important for my concerns), then the flexible-price dynamics of the present model are fully equivalent to those of a standard RBC model. Note that these models, like the cashless model, abstract from real-balance effects upon consumption demand, labor supply, and so on.

is required is that output equal the natural rate of output at all times and that the nominal interest rate equal the natural rate of interest at all times. Hence such an equilibrium is possible (under the qualification stated), and thus such an outcome is the one that an optimal policy would aim at.

Further discussion of exactly what kinds of output and interest-rate variations in response to real disturbances this should imply can be found in Section 2.1 of Chapter 4. Here I recall simply that in the case of none of the types of real disturbances discussed there would it be desirable to use monetary policy to suppress all effects of the real disturbance on aggregate output. Nor can I support, in general, so simple a conclusion as that reached by Ireland (1996), who argues that one should use monetary policy to "insulate aggregate output" against "shocks to demand," while accommodating "shocks to supply." Many readers might assume that shocks to demand would include disturbances such as government-purchase or consumption-demand shocks, but the result just derived here (together with the discussion in Chapter 4 of variation in the natural rate of output) implies that it is not optimal to stabilize output in response to these shocks. In fact, in Ireland's theoretical analysis, the term shocks to demand refers solely to money-demand shocks, as this is the only type of exogenous disturbance other than technology shocks that he considers.

3.2 Consequences of a Mildly Inefficient Natural Rate of Output

I now consider the extent to which the conclusions just reached must be modified in the case that (quite realistically) one assumes that $\Phi_y > 0$, so that the equilibrium rate of output under flexible prices would be inefficiently low. I continue, however, to assume that Φ_y is small, so that a Taylor-series expansion in Φ_y is appropriate. (This means that Φ_y must be made sufficiently small in order for the characterization of optimal policy to achieve a certain degree of accuracy.) The case in which Φ_y is allowed to be larger (and is not treated as an expansion parameter) is deferred to Section 5.

The distortions represented by the coefficient Φ_y, that is, the market power resulting from monopolistic competition and the constant rate of distorting taxation τ, introduce a wedge between this natural rate of output and the efficient output level. However, this wedge is assumed to be constant over time, so that *percentage changes* in the natural rate still correspond precisely (in the log-linear approximation) to percentage changes in the efficient level of output.[35] Thus, as shown above, the distortions associated with a suboptimal aggregate level of economic activity are still measured by

---

35. The consequences of time variation in the size of this wedge are considered in Section 4.5.

a quadratic function of the output gap, $\lambda(x_t - x^*)^2$, even if now the constant x^* is assumed to be positive.

While this difference matters for the optimal *average* levels of inflation and output—that is, for the deterministic part of the earlier description of the optimal policy commitment—it has *no* effect (in the log-linear approximation to optimal policy) on the optimal responses to shocks.[36] I first demonstrate this in the simple context of the New Classical model of price-setting. In this case, the normalized quadratic loss function (2.16) can be written

$$L_t = (\pi_t - E_{t-1}\pi_t)^2 - 2\lambda x^* x_t + \lambda x_t^2, \qquad (3.1)$$

dropping the term λx^{*2} that is independent of policy. The second term on the right-hand side now indicates a welfare gain from an increase in the expected output gap in any period. However, because x^* is of order $\mathcal{O}(\|\Phi_y\|)$, a *first-order* approximation to the solution for x_t suffices to give a *second-order* approximation to this term; and the (first-order approximate) aggregate-supply relation (2.14) implies that, to first order, $E_0 x_t = 0$ for all $t > 0$ regardless of policy. Hence all of the linear terms in x_t except the x_0 term may be eliminated from the evaluation of the expected value of the discounted-loss criterion (2.21).

Thus if I take the expected discounted value of (3.1), also using (2.14) to substitute for the x_0 term (and dropping the term $E_{-1}\pi_0$ that is independent of policy), I obtain the utility-based welfare criterion

$$E_0\left\{\sum_{t=0}^{\infty}\beta^t L_t\right\} = -2\theta^{-1}x^*\pi_0 + E_0\left\{\sum_{t=0}^{\infty}\beta^t\left[(\pi_t - E_{t-1}\pi_t)^2 + \lambda x_t^2\right]\right\}. \quad (3.2)$$

Note that there remain no terms proportional to x^*, except the one indicating a welfare gain from surprise inflation at date zero, the time at which a new policy commitment is adopted. Because it is not possible to commit in advance to an inflation *surprise* at any later date, the corresponding terms for dates $t \geq 1$ do not matter. But this means that allowing for $x^* > 0$ has no effect upon the nature of the optimal policy commitment, except in the initial (transitional) period, when it is possible to take advantage of the fact that private sector expectations of period-zero inflation are already

36. Of course, the content of this claim is simply that well-behaved small-Φ_y limiting values of the response coefficients describing the economy's optimal state-contingent evolution exist. Allowing for the dependence of the response coefficients on Φ_y would require a second-order approximation to optimal policy, when Φ_y is an expansion parameter. I show how the dependence of the response coefficients on Φ_y can be determined in Section 5 below, where I no longer treat Φ_y as an expansion parameter.

given, before the policy is adopted.[37] It is arguable (as discussed in the next chapter) that it does not make sense to behave differently in this initial period than one commits to behave later, if one wants the commitment to be credible. But regardless of how one manages the transition to the optimal regime, it is optimal to commit to an eventual zero rate of inflation and to a path for inflation that is unaffected by any stochastic disturbances.[38]

It might be thought that this result depends upon the fact that in the special case in which all prices are changed every period (though some are committed a period in advance), only *unexpected* inflation has an effect upon output. Yet a similar conclusion is obtained in the baseline model, with Calvo pricesetting. In this case, the period loss function can be written as

$$L_t = \pi_t^2 - 2\lambda x^* x_t + \lambda x_t^2, \tag{3.3}$$

again showing the existence of a term linear in x_t when $x^* > 0$. The New Keynesian AS relation (2.18) no longer implies that $E_{t-1} x_t = 0$ regardless of policy. Nonetheless, one can forward integrate (2.18) to yield the implication

$$\pi_0 = \kappa E_0 \left\{ \sum_{t=0}^{\infty} \beta^t x_t \right\}, \tag{3.4}$$

which must hold (to first order) regardless of policy. One can use this relation to eliminate the discounted sum of $E_0 x_t$ terms from the evaluation of the expected discounted value of (3.3), obtaining

$$E_0 \left\{ \sum_{t=0}^{\infty} \beta^t L_t \right\} = -2\theta^{-1} x^* \pi_0 + E_0 \left\{ \sum_{t=0}^{\infty} \beta^t \left[\pi_t^2 + \lambda x_t^2 \right] \right\}. \tag{3.5}$$

Once again all of the terms proportional to x^* have been eliminated, except the one indicating welfare gains from a surprise inflation in period zero. Committing in advance to nonzero inflation in any later period does *not* produce any such effect. For the value of the increase in output in any period $t \geq 1$ resulting from higher inflation in period t must be offset by the cost of the *reduction* in output in period $t-1$ as a result of *expectation*

---

37. Of course, this different prescription in the case of the initial period shows that optimal policy is not *time consistent* in this case. This issue is taken up in the next chapter.

38. Of course, in this model, there is no advantage of complete price stability over any other policy that makes inflation completely forecastable a period in advance. But in order to stress the similarity of the results obtained under the alternative aggregate-supply specifications, it is worth noting that also in this case there is no *advantage* to any variation in inflation in response to shocks.

of that higher inflation in period t. From the standpoint of the discounted-loss criterion (3.2), the costs resulting from the anticipation of the inflation are weighted more strongly (by a factor of $\beta^{-1} > 1$), as they occur earlier in time. On the other hand, the output effect of anticipated inflation, by shifting the short-run aggregate-supply curve, is also smaller than the effect of current inflation by exactly the factor $\beta < 1$, with the result that the two effects exactly cancel to first order (which is to say, to second order when multiplied by x^*). Thus once again there is no welfare gain, up to the order of approximation, from a commitment to inflation that can be anticipated in advance. In particular, one finds once again that except for transition effects, resulting from the different term in (3.5) for the initial period, it is again optimal to commit to zero inflation, independent of the shocks to the economy.

Nonetheless, the term in (3.5) that is linear in π_0 now affects the optimal commitment for periods later than π_0 as well. That is because of the intertemporal linkage implied by aggregate-supply relation (2.18). The welfare gain from inflation at date zero can be obtained with less increase in the period-zero output gap (and hence less increase in the λx_0^2 term) if it is accompanied by an increase in expected inflation at date one; and since the welfare loss from such inflation is merely quadratic, it is optimal to commit to some amount of such inflation. Thus the inflation associated with the transition to the optimal regime lasts for more than a single period in this case.

The optimal transition path is characterized in Section 1 of Chapter 7. Here I am content with a few observations about the form of the solution to this problem. First, because the only reason to plan a nonzero inflation rate in period one is for the sake of the effect of expected period-one inflation on the location of the period-zero output-inflation trade-off, there is no gain from planning on a period-one inflation rate that is not deterministic. The same is true of planned inflation in all later periods. Thus the optimal commitment from date zero onward involves a deterministic path for inflation; it continues not to be optimal for the inflation rate to respond at all to real disturbances of the various types considered thus far. In addition, as shown in the next chapter, the deterministic path for planned inflation should converge asymptotically to zero, the rate that would be optimal but for the opportunity to achieve an output gain from unexpected inflation in the initial period.

Thus it is optimal (from the point of minimizing discounted losses from date zero onward) to arrange an initial inflation, given that the decision to do so can have no effect upon expectations prior to date zero (if one is not bothered by the non-time-consistency of such a principle of action). The optimal policy involves positive inflation in subsequent periods as well, but there should be a commitment to reduce inflation to its optimal long-run

value of zero asymptotically. Moreover, the rate at which inflation is committed to decline to zero should be completely unaffected by random disturbances to the economy in the meantime.[39] Thus the allowance for $\Phi_y > 0$
makes no difference for the conclusions of the previous section with regard
to the optimal response to shocks. Furthermore, if one takes the view (as I
argue in the next chapter) that one should actually conduct policy as one
would have optimally committed to do far in the past, thus foregoing the temptation to exploit the private sector's failure to anticipate the new policy, then
it is optimal simply to choose $\pi_t = 0$ at all times—that is, to completely
stabilize the price level—just as in the previous section.

It is interesting to note that this result—that the optimal commitment
involves a long-run inflation rate of zero, even when the natural rate of
output is inefficiently low—does *not* depend upon the existence of a vertical
long-run Phillips-curve trade-off. For the aggregate-supply relation (2.18) in
our baseline model implies an upward-sloping relation

$$x^{ss} = (1 - \beta)\kappa^{-1}\pi^{ss}$$

between steady-state inflation π^{ss} and the steady-state output gap x^{ss}. (This
is because the expected-inflation term has a coefficient $\beta < 1$, unlike
that of the New Classical relation (2.14).) It is sometimes supposed that
the existence of a long-run Phillips-curve trade-off, together with an inefficient natural rate, should imply that the Phillips curve should be ex-
ploited to some extent, resulting in positive inflation forever, even under
commitment. But here that is not true because the smaller coefficient on the
expected-inflation term relative to that on current inflation—which results
in the long-run trade-off—is exactly the size of the shift term in the short-
run aggregate-supply relation that is needed *to precisely eliminate any long-run
incentive for nonzero inflation* under an optimal commitment. If one were instead to "simplify" the New Keynesian aggregate-supply relation, putting a
coefficient of one on expected inflation (as is done in some presentations,[40]
presumably in order to conform to the conventional wisdom regarding the
long-run Phillips curve), one would then fail to obtain such a simple result.
The optimal long-run inflation rate would actually be found to be *negative,*
as the stimulative effects of lower expected inflation would be judged to be
worth more than the output cost of lower current inflation—even though
there would actually be no long-run output increase as a result of the policy!

Moreover, once again, the character of optimal policy in the presence of
inflation inertia due to partial indexation to a lagged price index can be

39. These results agree with those of King and Wolman (1999) in the context of a model
with two-period overlapping price commitments in the style of Taylor (1980).
40. See, e.g., Roberts (1995).

determined directly from the results for the Calvo pricing model with no indexation; the optimal time path for π_t in the case of the model without indexation becomes the optimal time path for $\pi_t^d \equiv \pi_t - \gamma\pi_{t-1}$ in the case with indexation. It then follows that once again the optimal path of inflation is completely deterministic. Furthermore, whereas there will be initial inflation (even starting from an initial condition with $\pi_{-1} = 0$) if the central bank allows itself to exploit initial expectations by choosing $\pi_0^d > 0$, optimal policy involves a commitment to reduce π_t^d asymptotically to zero. In the case of any $\gamma < 1$, this once again means a commitment to eventual price stability; and optimal policy has this character despite the fact that the level of output associated with stable prices is inefficiently low and despite the existence of a positively sloped long-run Phillips-curve trade-off, as this is ordinarily defined.

3.3 Caveats

We have seen that, within the class of sticky-price models that has been discussed here, the optimality of a monetary policy that aims at complete price stability is surprisingly robust. Not only does this conclusion not depend upon the fine details of how many prices are set a particular time in advance or left unchanged for a particular length of time, but it remains valid in the case of a considerable range of types of stochastic disturbances and in the case of an inefficient natural rate of output. Nonetheless, it is likely that some degree of deviation from full price stability is warranted in practice. Some of the more obvious reasons for this are sketched here.

First of all, complete price stability may not be *feasible*. I have just argued, in Section 3.2, that in the baseline model, it is feasible, because one is able to solve for the required path of the central bank's nominal interest-rate instrument. This is correct as long as the random disturbances are small enough in amplitude. But if they are larger, such a policy might not be possible because it might require the nominal interest rate to be *negative* at some times, which, as explained in Chapter 2, is not possible under any policy. Specifically, this occurs if it is ever the case that the natural rate of interest is negative. On average, it does not seem that it should be, and thus zero inflation *on average* would seem to be feasible; but it may be temporarily negative as a result of certain kinds of disturbances, and this is enough to make complete price stability infeasible. As a result, a policy has to be pursued that involves less volatility of the short nominal interest rate in response to shocks, and some amount of price stability thus has to be sacrificed.[41] The way in which optimal monetary policy is different in the presence of such a concern is an important issue in Chapter 7.

---

41. In general, it is optimal to back off from complete price stability both by allowing inflation to vary somewhat in response to disturbances *and* by choosing an average rate of

Varying nominal interest rates as much as the natural rate of interest varies may also be desirable as a result of the "shoe-leather costs" involved in economizing on money balances. As argued by Friedman (1969), the size of these distortions is measured by the level of nominal interest rates, and they are eliminated only if nominal interest rates are zero at all times.[42] Taking account of these distortions—from which I have abstracted thus far in my welfare analysis—provides another reason for the equilibrium with complete price stability, even if feasible, not to be fully efficient; for as Friedman argues, a zero nominal interest rate typically requires expected *deflation* at a rate of at least a few percent per year.

One might think that this should make no more difference to the analysis of optimal policy than the existence of an inefficient natural rate of output due to market power—that it may similarly affect the *deterministic* part of the optimal path for inflation without creating any reason for inflation to vary in response to random shocks. But monetary frictions do not have implications only for the optimal *average* level of nominal interest rates. As with distorting taxes, it is plausible that the deadweight loss is a convex function of the relative-price distortion, so that temporary increases in nominal interest rates are more costly than temporary decreases of the same size are beneficial. In short, monetary frictions provide a further reason for it to be desirable to reduce the *variability* of nominal interest rates, even if one cannot reduce their average level. (At the same time, reducing their average level requires less variable rates, because of the zero floor.) Insofar as these costs are important, they too justify a departure from complete price stability, in the case of any kinds of real disturbances that cause fluctuations in the natural rate of interest, in order to allow greater stability of nominal interest rates. This trade-off is treated more explicitly in Section 4.1.

Even apart from these grounds for concern with interest-rate volatility, it should be recognized that the class of sticky-price models analyzed previously is still quite special in certain respects. One of the most obvious is that it is assumed that there are no shocks as a result of which the relative prices of any of the goods with sticky prices would vary over time in an *efficient* equilibrium (i.e., the shadow prices that would decentralize the optimal allocation of resources involve no variation in the relative prices of such goods). This is because I have assumed that only goods prices are sticky, that all goods enter the model in a perfectly symmetrical way, and that

---

inflation that is somewhat greater than zero, as suggested by Summers (1991), in order to allow more room for interest-rate fluctuations consistent with the zero lower bound. However, the quantitative analysis undertaken below finds that the effect of the interest-rate lower bound on the optimal response of inflation to shocks is more significant than the effect upon the optimal average rate of inflation.

42. See Woodford (1990) for justification of this relation in a variety of alternative models of the demand for money.

all random disturbances have perfectly symmetrical effects upon all sectors of the economy. These assumptions are convenient, but plainly an idealization. Yet it should be clear that they are relied upon in the conclusion that stability of the general price level suffices to eliminate the distortions that are due to price stickiness.

If an efficient allocation of resources requires relative price changes, owing to asymmetries in the way that different sticky-price commodities are affected by shocks, this will not be true. However, I show in Section 4.3 that even in the presence of asymmetric shocks, it is possible to define a symmetric case in which it is still optimal to completely stabilize the general price level, even though this does not eliminate all of the distortions resulting from price stickiness. But this holds exactly only in a special case in which different goods are similar, among other respects, in the *degree* of stickiness of their prices. If sectors of the economy differ in their degree of price stickiness (as is surely realistic), then complete stabilization of an aggregate price index is not optimal. Stabilization of an appropriately defined *asymmetric* price index (that puts more weight on the stickier prices) is a better policy, as argued by Aoki (2001) and Benigno (2003), though even the best policy of this kind need not be fully optimal.

An especially important reason for disturbances to require relative-price changes between sticky commodities with sticky prices is that *wages* are probably as sticky as prices. Real disturbances almost inevitably require real-wage adjustments in order for an efficient allocation of resources to be decentralized, and if *both* wages and prices are sticky, it is then not possible to achieve all of the relative prices associated with efficiency simply by stabilizing the price level—specifically, the real wage is frequently misaligned, as are the relative wages of different types of labor if these are not set in perfect synchronization. In such circumstances, complete price stability may not at all be a good approximation to the optimal policy, as Erceg et al. (2000) show. As I demonstrate in Section 4.4, stabilization of an appropriately weighted average of prices and wages may still be a good approximation to optimal policy, and fully optimal in some cases. Thus concerns of this kind are not so much reasons not to pursue price stability as they are reasons why care in the choice of the index of prices (including wages) that one seeks to stabilize may be important.

Yet another qualification to the results in this section is that I have assumed a framework in which the flexible-price equilibrium rate of output is efficient, or at most differs from the efficient level by only a small constant factor. As we have seen, this assumption is compatible with the existence of a variety of types of economic disturbances, including technology shocks, preference shocks, and variations in government purchases. But it would not hold in the case of other sorts of disturbances that cause *time variation in the degree of inefficiency* of the flexible-price equilibrium. These could include variation in the level of distorting taxes, variation in the degree of market power of firms or workers, or variation in the size of the wage premium that must be paid on efficiency-wage grounds.

The empirical importance of disturbances of any of these kinds remains a matter of considerable controversy. However, in the case that the gap between the flexible-price equilibrium level of output and the efficient level of output is large on average (owing to the existence of substantial distortions due to taxes or market power), it is no longer the case, in general, that disturbances shift the efficient level of output and the flexible-price equilibrium level of output to the same extent (even to a first-order approximation). This is true even if the disturbances are of the sorts—preference shocks, technology shocks, variations in government purchases—assumed thus far in this chapter, as discussed in Section 5. This is a reason of even clearer empirical relevance to allow for a time-varying gap between the efficient level of output and the flexible-price equilibrium level (i.e., for what are sometimes called "cost-push shocks").

In the case of a time-varying gap between the flexible-price equilibrium level of output and the efficient level, complete stabilization of inflation is no longer sufficient for complete stabilization of the welfare-relevant output gap. For while inflation stabilization may imply a level of output at all times equal to the flexible-price equilibrium level, as previously discussed, this no longer minimizes the variability of the gap between actual output and the efficient level of output. As a result, complete stabilization of inflation is not generally optimal. It is also not obvious that stabilization of any alternative price index makes sense as a solution to the problem in this case, whereas some degree of concern for stabilization of the (appropriately measured) output gap is clearly appropriate, even if it should not wholly displace a concern for inflation stabilization. This is an especially serious challenge to the view that price stability should be the sole goal of monetary policy, and I give considerable attention in Chapters 7 and 8 to the characterization of optimal monetary policy in this case. However, even if the fluctuations in the gap between the flexible-price equilibrium output level and the efficient level are of substantial magnitude, the degree of departure from price stability that can be justified on welfare-theoretic grounds may well be less than is often supposed, as I show in Section 4.5.

4 Extensions of the Basic Analysis

Here I sketch extensions of the utility-based welfare criterion to incorporate several complications from which I have abstracted in the basic analysis presented in Section 2. I focus particularly on complications that illustrate some of the reasons just sketched for complete stabilization of the price level not to be optimal.

4.1   Transactions Frictions

In Section 2, I abstracted from the welfare consequences of the transactions frictions that account for the demand for the monetary base. The results therefore apply to a cashless economy of the kind discussed in Chapter 2. Here I consider the way in which they must be modified in order to allow for nonnegligible welfare effects of transactions frictions.

As in Chapter 2, one may represent the welfare consequences of variations in the degree to which these frictions distort transactions by including real money balances as an additional argument of the utility function of the representative household. This generalization makes real marginal cost, and hence the equilibrium level of output under flexible prices, a function of the (endogenous) level of real balances in addition to the exogenous state of preferences and technology, in the case that the indirect utility function $u(c, m)$ is not additively separable. Substituting the equilibrium level of real balances

$$\hat{m}_t = \eta_y \hat{Y}_t - \eta_i \left(\hat{\imath}_t - \hat{\imath}_t^m \right) + \epsilon_t^m \qquad (4.1)$$

into the household labor-supply relation, I have shown in Chapter 4 that average real marginal cost is given by

$$\hat{s}_t = \epsilon_{mc} \left[x_t + \varphi \left(\hat{\imath}_t - \hat{\imath}_t^m \right) \right], \qquad (4.2)$$

where

$$\epsilon_{mc} \equiv \sigma^{-1} + \omega - \chi \eta_y, \qquad (4.3)$$

$$\varphi \equiv \eta_i \chi / \epsilon_{mc}, \qquad (4.4)$$

and $x_t \equiv \hat{Y}_t - Y_t^n$, where now

$$\hat{Y}_t^n \equiv \frac{\sigma^{-1} g_t + \omega q_t + \chi \epsilon_t^m}{\epsilon_{mc}}. \qquad (4.5)$$

In these expressions, I once again use the coefficient $\chi \equiv \bar{m} u_{cm} / u_c$ to measure the degree of complementarity between private expenditure and real balances.

Here the natural rate of output $\hat{Y}_t^n$ is defined as the flexible-price equilibrium level of output when the interest-rate differential Δ_t is fixed at its steady-state level $\bar{\Delta}$, so that $\hat{Y}_t^n$ is again an exogenous process. This definition also has the advantage that, up to a log-linear approximation, the amount by which the (log) efficient level of output exceeds the (log) natural rate is a constant, to first order,[43] in the case that both the steady-state inefficiency wedge Φ and the steady-state interest-rate differential $\bar{\Delta} \equiv (\bar{\imath} - \bar{\imath}^m)/(1 + \bar{\imath})$ are small (and treated as expansion parameters). This constant gap (up to a residual of order $\mathcal{O}(\|\Phi, \bar{\xi}\|^2)$, where Φ is now the vector of steady-state distortions, with elements Φ_y and $\bar{\Delta}$) is given by

$$x^* \equiv \frac{\Phi_y + s_m \eta_y}{\epsilon_{mc}}, \tag{4.6}$$

where $s_m \equiv \bar{m} u_m / \bar{c} u_c \geq 0$ measures the interest cost of real balances as a fraction of the value of private expenditure. I assume as in Chapter 4 that $\epsilon_{mc} > 0$, so that if $\Phi_y \geq 0$, $x^* > 0$. It can then be seen that the signs of the effects upon the natural rate of output of the various real disturbances discussed in Section 3.2 remain the same. Now, however (if $\chi \neq 0$), disturbances to the money-demand function, possibly due to shifts in the transactions technology, also affect the natural rate of output.

It follows from (4.2) that in this more general case, the New Classical aggregate-supply relation takes the form

$$\pi_t = \kappa \left[x_t + \varphi \left(\hat{\imath}_t - \hat{\imath}_t^m \right) \right] + E_{t-1} \pi_t \tag{4.7}$$

instead of (2.14), where again $x_t \equiv \hat{Y}_t - \hat{Y}_t^n$, and

$$\kappa \equiv \frac{\iota}{1 - \iota} \frac{\epsilon_{mc}}{1 + \omega\theta} > 0.$$

On the other hand, in the case of Calvo pricing, the aggregate-supply relation now takes the form

$$\pi_t = \kappa \left[x_t + \varphi \left(\hat{\imath}_t - \hat{\imath}_t^m \right) \right] + \beta E_t \pi_{t+1}, \tag{4.8}$$

where again

$$\kappa \equiv \frac{(1 - \alpha)(1 - \alpha\beta)}{\alpha} \frac{\epsilon_{mc}}{1 + \omega\theta} > 0.$$

Note that in either case the interest-rate differential appears as a shift factor in the aggregate-supply relation because of its (small) effect on the real marginal cost of supply.

---

43. In the present case, the efficient level of output at any point in time is the solution to two equations, stating that real marginal cost is equal to one and that there is satiation in real money balances. Because the second condition implies a zero interest-rate differential regardless of the real disturbances, both the natural rate of output and the efficient level can be defined as output variations in response to real disturbances that maintain real marginal cost constant in the case of a constant interest differential.

In computing the quadratic approximation to expected utility, I rely upon the following assumption about preferences.

ASSUMPTION 6.1. The transactions technology implies that there is satiation in real money balances at a finite level; in the case of the level of output $\bar{Y} > 0$ associated with a flexible-price equilibrium steady state with interest-rate differential $\bar{\Delta} = 0$, the associated satiation level of real money balances is the finite quantity $\bar{m} > 0$. Furthermore, all first and second partial derivatives of utility with respect to c and m have well-defined, finite limiting values as (c, m) approach $(\bar{Y}, \bar{m})$, with m approaching $\bar{m}$ from below, and the limiting value of u_{mm} from below is negative.

The assumption that u_{mm} is bounded away from zero as m approaches $\bar{m}$ from below implies that u_{mm} must be discontinuous at the satiation point, since $u_m = 0$ for all m greater than or equal to the satiation level. However, this assumption corresponds to the existence of a well-defined (finite) interest-rate semielasticity of money demand (the coefficient η_i in (4.1)) as one approaches satiation, given by

$$\eta_i = -\frac{u_c}{\bar{m}u_{mm}} > 0.$$

(The discontinuity of u_{mm} corresponds to a discontinuity in the interest-elasticity of money demand when the satiation point is reached, and money demand necessarily becomes infinitely elastic.) While not uncontroversial, this is a feature of many econometrically estimated money-demand functions. It is also a feature of many theoretical models of transactions technologies, such as the cash/credit goods models of Appendix A, Section A.16.

I can then again approximate the utility from private expenditure using a second-order Taylor series expansion, obtaining the following generalization of Proposition 6.1.

PROPOSITION 6.7. Assume a transactions technology satisfying Assumption 6.1. Then in the case of small enough fluctuations in the production of each good $\hat{y}_t(i)$ around the level $\bar{Y}$, small enough fluctuations in the interest-rate differential Δ_t around the level $\bar{\Delta}$, small enough disturbances, and small enough values of the steady-state distortions Φ, the utility flow to the representative household each period can be approximated by

$$U_t = -\frac{\bar{Y}u_c}{2}\left\{\epsilon_{mc}(x_t - x^*)^2 + \bar{v}^{-1}\eta_i\left(\hat{\imath}_t - \hat{\imath}_t^m + \bar{\Delta}\right)^2 + \left(\theta^{-1} + \omega\right)\operatorname{var}_i\hat{y}_t(i)\right\}$$

$$+ \text{t.i.p.} + \mathcal{O}\left(\|\Phi, \hat{y}, \hat{\Delta}, \tilde{\xi}\|^3\right). \tag{4.9}$$

Here ϵ_{mc} is defined by (4.3), x_t is the output gap relative to the natural rate of output defined by (4.5), x^* is defined by (4.6), $\bar{v} \equiv \bar{Y}/\bar{m} > 0$ is the steady-state "velocity of money," and $\eta_i > 0$ is the limiting value of the interest-rate semielasticity of money demand.

Details of the calculation are given in Appendix E. Note that it follows from (4.6) that $x^* = \mathcal{O}(\|\Phi\|)$, and it similarly follows from the relation $s_m = \bar{\Delta}/(s_C\bar{v})$ that $s_m = \mathcal{O}(\|\Phi\|)$. Hence the quadratic approximation to welfare in (4.9) involves coefficients on the linear terms that are of order $\mathcal{O}(\|\Phi\|)$, as required for characterization of optimal policy up to a log-linear approximation using only a log-linear approximation to the structural equations of the model. Also note that (4.9) implies that the optimal level for the interest-rate differential is zero, since the condition $i_t = i_t^m$, the Friedman (1969) condition for satiation in real money balances, corresponds to $\hat{i}_t = \hat{i}_t^m - \bar{\Delta} + \mathcal{O}(\bar{\Delta}^2)$.

Given (4.9), I can again substitute for output dispersion as a function of inflation as before, in order to obtain a quadratic loss function expressed in terms of the paths of output and inflation. In the case of the baseline (Calvo) model of pricesetting, I obtain the following.

PROPOSITION 6.8. In the case of the model set out in Chapter 4, Section 3, with Calvo pricing and a transactions technology satisfying Assumption 6.1, the discounted sum of utility of the representative household can again be approximated by an expression of the form (2.21), with a residual of order $\mathcal{O}(\|\Phi, \Delta_{-1}^{1/2}, \varphi, \tilde{\xi}\|^3)$. In this expression, I once again have $\Omega > 0$, but the normalized quadratic loss function is now given by

$$L_t = \pi_t^2 + \lambda_x(x_t - x^*)^2 + \lambda_i(\hat{i}_t - \hat{i}_t^m + \bar{\Delta})^2, \qquad (4.10)$$

with weights

$$\lambda_x = \frac{\kappa}{\theta} > 0, \qquad \lambda_i = \frac{\eta_i}{\bar{v}\epsilon_{mc}}\lambda_x > 0, \qquad (4.11)$$

and an optimal value x^* given by (4.6).

The proof follows exactly the same lines as that of Proposition 6.4, given Proposition 6.7. It is also worth noting that an alternative expression for the weight on the interest-rate term, equivalent under the small-$\bar{\Delta}$ approximation, though applicable only in the case that $\chi \neq 0$,[44] is

---

44. As shown in the proof of Proposition 6.8 in Appendix E, the limiting value of η_y as $\bar{\Delta} \to 0$ is zero in the case that $\chi = 0$.

$$\lambda_i = \frac{\eta_i}{\eta_y}\varphi\lambda_x. \tag{4.12}$$

Thus taking account of transactions frictions adds an additional term to the loss function, with a positive weight on squared deviations of the interest-rate differential from its optimal size, which is zero. Note that in the cashless limit discussed in Chapter 2, $\bar{v}^{-1} \to 0$, so that $\lambda_i \to 0$, and I recover the foregoing results for the cashless model. However, it is important to note that the interest-rate variability term does *not* vanish under the assumption that utility is additively separable between consumption and real balances, so that $u_{cm} = 0$. While this last assumption (which implies that $\chi = 0$) results in the disappearance of real-balance effects from both the aggregate-supply and IS relations of the model of the transmission mechanism, and similarly implies that money-demand disturbances have no effect on the natural rates of output or of interest, it does not imply that $\lambda_i = 0$. Thus it makes a difference whether one assumes that χ is negligible in size because of approximate additive separability, or rather because equilibrium real balances are small (velocity is large).

One case in which the previous conclusions are largely unaffected is that in which the central bank's interest-rate operating target is implemented through adjustments of the interest paid on the monetary base, so that Δ_t is equal to a fixed spread at all times, regardless of how i_t varies.[45] In this case, the $(\hat{i}_t - \hat{i}_t^m + \bar{\Delta})^2$ term in (4.10) is a constant, independent of how inflation, output, and interest rates vary over time. Optimal policy then is again one that minimizes a loss function of the form (2.22); the only difference that monetary frictions make would be to the definitions of ϵ_{mc} (and hence of κ and λ_x) and of $\hat{Y}_t^n$. In particular, it is found once again that optimal policy involves complete stabilization of the price level, just as in the earlier analysis of the cashless model.

If, instead, the interest paid on the monetary base is equal to a constant $\bar{i}^m$ at all times (perhaps zero, as in the United States at present), then the final term in (4.10) is not irrelevant. In this case, the welfare-theoretic loss function reduces to

$$L_t = \pi_t^2 + \lambda_x(x_t - x^*)^2 + \lambda_i(\hat{i}_t - i^*)^2, \tag{4.13}$$

where now the optimal nominal interest rate is given by

$$i^* \equiv \log \frac{1+\bar{\imath}^m}{1+\bar{\imath}} = -\bar{\Delta} + \mathcal{O}(\bar{\Delta}^2),$$

that is, it is equal to the constant interest rate paid on the monetary base. Note that the final term results in a loss function of the kind assumed by Williams (1999), though Williams motivates the additional term by reference to "aversion to interest-rate variability."

The additional term means that complete stabilization of the price level is no longer optimal, for two reasons. The first is that as long as $i^m < \bar{\imath} \equiv \beta^{-1} - 1$, the steady-state nominal interest rate that minimizes the last term in (4.10) requires expected deflation, as argued by Friedman (1969). There is thus now a conflict between the steady-state rate of inflation needed to minimize the first term and that needed to minimize the third. In fact, the long-run inflation rate under an optimal policy commitment, in the absence of stochastic disturbances, is generally intermediate between the two—higher than the Friedman rate (i.e., minus the rate of time preference), but still negative, as shown in Chapter 7.

Second, there is now a conflict between the pattern of responses to shocks that minimizes the first term (i.e., no inflation variation at all) and the pattern required to minimize the third term (no interest-rate variation). Insofar as shocks affect the natural rate of interest (and I have shown that many different types of real disturbances all should), nominal interest-rate variations are required to keep inflation stable, and vice versa. In addition, it need not even be true any longer that complete inflation stabilization minimizes the second term—for if $\kappa_i > 0$, the interest-rate variations required to stabilize inflation result in at least a small amount of output-gap variation as well.

A special case is possible in which no such conflict arises. Suppose that one assumes instead the New Classical model of pricing, in which all prices are adjusted each period, though some new prices are chosen a period in advance. Again suppose that $i_t^m = \bar{\imath}^m$ at all times. In this case, it follows from Proposition 6.7 that the corresponding normalized loss function is given by

$$L_t = (\pi_t - E_{t-1}\pi_t)^2 + \lambda_x(x_t - x^*)^2 + \lambda_i(\hat{\imath}_t - i^*)^2, \tag{4.14}$$

where the weights are again given by (4.11), but using the definition of κ in (4.7). If it is also assumed that $\Phi_y = 0$, (4.6) implies that $x^* = -\varphi i^* > 0$, up to a residual of order $\mathcal{O}(\bar{\Delta}^2)$. This means that the aggregate-supply relation (4.7) can alternatively be written

$$\pi_t = \kappa \left[(x_t - x^*) + \varphi (\hat{\imath}_t - i^*) \right] + E_{t-1}\pi_t. \tag{4.15}$$

There is then no problem with simultaneously minimizing all three terms in (4.14). This simply requires that one set $\hat{\imath}_t = i^*$ each period and make inflation equal whatever value was forecasted in the previous period, in which case (4.7) implies that $x_t = x^*$ as well. Minimization of the interest-rate variation term has implications only for *expected* inflation, whereas minimization of the term representing the costs of price dispersion has implications only for *unexpected* inflation; thus, in this special case, there is no conflict between fully achieving both goals at all times.

Even if $\Phi_y > 0$, (4.6) implies that

$$x^* + \varphi i^* = \Phi_y / \epsilon_{mc} > 0. \tag{4.16}$$

Using this to substitute for x^*, one can write the discounted-loss measure as

$$E_0 \left\{ \sum_{t=0}^{\infty} \beta^t L_t \right\} = -2 \frac{\Phi_y}{\theta \epsilon_{mc}} \left[\pi_0 - \kappa_i \hat{\imath}_0 \right] + E_0 \left\{ \sum_{t=0}^{\infty} \beta^t \left[(\pi_t - E_{t-1}\pi_t)^2 \right. \right.$$
$$\left. \left. + \lambda_x (x_t + \varphi i^*)^2 + 2 \frac{\lambda_x \varphi \Phi_y}{\epsilon_{mc}} (\hat{\imath}_t - i^*) + \lambda_i (\hat{\imath}_t - i^*)^2 \right] \right\}, \tag{4.17}$$

generalizing (3.2). All terms on the right-hand side except the first are again minimized by setting $\hat{\imath}_t = i^*$ and $\pi_t = E_{t-1}\pi_t$ each period. (The third term inside the large square brackets is necessarily nonnegative each period because of the equilibrium requirement that $i_t \geq \bar{\imath}^m$, or $\hat{\imath}_t \geq i^*$.) The first term indicates that there is an additional welfare gain from unexpected inflation in period zero, because what is decided for this period cannot affect inflation expectations in the previous period; and if one allows oneself to take advantage of that opportunity, the inflation rate in period zero should be chosen to be somewhat higher than had been expected. But thereafter, one makes unexpected inflation equal zero every period, as this is not inconsistent with setting $\hat{\imath}_t = i^*$ in every period. Furthermore, under a policy that is optimal from a timeless perspective, one simply arranges for zero unexpected inflation and $\hat{\imath}_t = i^*$ each period.

But this case, in which the distortions resulting from price stickiness can be completely eliminated without putting any restriction upon the process that expected inflation may follow, is clearly a very special one. In general, variations in expected inflation as a result of fluctuations in the natural rate of interest (as is required in order to maintain $\hat{\imath}_t = i^*$ at all times) results in relative-price distortions. Hence the goal of minimizing the distortions associated with transactions frictions conflict with that of minimizing the distortions resulting from price stickiness. Before discussing further the nature of this tension between alternative stabilization objectives, I argue that a similar concern with nominal interest-rate stabilization can be justified on alternative grounds.

4.2   The Zero Interest-Rate Lower Bound

Even in the case of a cashless economy, incomplete inflation stabilization may be optimal, in order to reduce the variability of nominal interest rates in response to shocks, the reason being the equilibrium requirement that $i_t \geq 0$ at all times.[46] If shocks are sufficiently small, this poses no obstacle to complete inflation stabilization, but if the natural rate of interest is sometimes negative (and by this I mean the natural *short* rate, which is more volatile than the associated natural longer rates), complete stabilization of inflation is infeasible.

In that case, which seems reasonably likely, it is of some interest to consider the nature of optimal policy subject to the constraint of respecting the zero lower bound. It is reasonably clear that such policy involves less variation in nominal interest rates than occurs in the natural rate of interest; in particular, market rates do not fall as much as the natural rate in those states in which it becomes negative. Characterizing the optimal behavior of market rates is a problem beyond the scope of the linear-quadratic optimization methods used here; however, I can consider a related problem that gives some insight into the way in which such a constraint should affect optimal policy: To replace the constraint that the nominal interest must be nonnegative in every period with a constraint upon its *variability*.[47]

Specifically, Rotemberg and Woodford (1997, 1999a) propose to approximate the effects of the lower bound by imposing a requirement that the mean federal funds rate be at least k standard deviations above the theoretical lower bound, where the coefficient k is large enough to imply that violations of the lower bound should be infrequent. The alternative constraint, while inexact, has the advantage that checking it requires only computation of first and second moments under alternative policy regimes, whereas checking whether the funds rate is predicted to be negative in *any* state would depend upon fine details of the distribution of shocks. In addition, a constraint of this form has the advantage that, assuming linear structural

---

46. More generally, the requirement is that $i_t \geq i_t^m$, but here I suppose that zero interest is paid on the monetary base, in order to make this constraint as weak as possible. I assume that the payment of negative interest on the monetary base, as proposed by Gesell and by Keynes (1936), is technically infeasible.

47. Eggertsson and Woodford (2003) consider the optimal nonlinear policy when the exact, nonlinear zero-bound constraint is imposed, rather than the approximation discussed here. The optimal nonlinear policy is in some respects similar to the linear policy that solves the approximate problem discussed here: In particular, it ceases to be optimal to completely stabilize inflation and the output gap, and the optimal policy involves a higher average inflation rate than would be optimal if the zero bound were never to bind. The interest-rate response to variations in the natural rate of interest is also *history-dependent* under the optimal nonlinear policy, just as it is in the linear policy that solves the approximate problem discussed here, as shown in Chapter 7, Section 2.2.

equations and a quadratic loss function, the constrained-optimal policy is a linear rule, just like the unconstrained optimum. Hence my linear methods can still be used to characterize optimal policy.

Note that the proposed constraint can equivalently be expressed as a requirement that the average value of i_t^2 be not more than $K \equiv 1 + k^{-2}$ times the square of the average value of i_t,[48] which latter average must also be nonnegative. If one uses discounted averages, for conformity with the other terms in the welfare measure, one obtains constraints of the form

$$E_0 \left\{ (1 - \beta) \sum_{t=0}^{\infty} \beta^t i_t \right\} \geq 0, \tag{4.18}$$

$$E_0 \left\{ (1 - \beta) \sum_{t=0}^{\infty} \beta^t i_t^2 \right\} \leq K \left[E_0 \left\{ (1 - \beta) \sum_{t=0}^{\infty} \beta^t i_t \right\} \right]^2. \tag{4.19}$$

Optimal policy subject to these additional constraints can in turn be described as the policy that minimizes a modified objective function.

PROPOSITION 6.9. Consider the problem of minimizing an expected discounted sum of quadratic losses

$$E_0 \left\{ (1 - \beta) \sum_{t=0}^{\infty} \beta^t L_t \right\} \tag{4.20}$$

subject to (4.18) and (4.19), and let m_1, m_2 be the discounted average values of i_t and i_t^2 associated with the optimal policy. Then the optimal policy also minimizes a modified discounted-loss criterion of the form (4.20), but with L_t replaced by

$$\tilde{L}_t \equiv L_t + \tilde{\lambda}_i \left(\hat{\imath}_t - i^{**} \right)^2, \tag{4.21}$$

under no constraints other than the structural equations. Here $\tilde{\lambda}_i \geq 0$, with a strictly positive value if and only if the constraint (4.19) binds. Moreover, in the event that the constraint binds, $i^{**} > 0$; that is, the target interest rate is higher than the nominal interest rate $\bar{\imath}$ associated with the zero-inflation steady state.

Thus the optimal policy minimizes the expected discounted value of a quadratic loss function (4.21), subject to the constraints imposed by the structural equations of the model. If the latter are linear, the optimal policy

---

48. By the expression i_t here, I actually mean $\log(1 + i_t)$, or $\hat{\imath}_t + \bar{\imath}$.

is itself linear. Note that the effective loss function (4.21) contains a quadratic penalty for interest-rate variations (in the case that constraint (4.19) binds), even if the "direct" social loss function L_t is independent of the path of the interest rate. For example, consider again the basic model of Calvo pricing, in the cashless limit. The direct loss function is then given by (2.22), which involves only inflation and the output gap. But if the fluctuations in the natural rate of interest are large enough for (4.19) to bind—that is, if (4.19) is violated by the solution $\hat{\imath}_t = \hat{r}^n_t$—then optimal policy actually minimizes a loss function of the form (4.10), exactly as I previously concluded by taking account of transactions frictions. The particular *type* of departure from price stability that is motivated by the need to respect the interest-rate lower bound is exactly the same as the kind that results from taking account of transactions frictions.

The primary qualitative difference between the loss functions motivated in the two ways is that transactions frictions lead to a loss function (4.10) with a target interest rate $i^* < 0$ (i.e., lower than the steady-state interest rate $\bar{\imath}$ consistent with zero inflation), whereas the interest-rate lower bound alone would suggest a target interest rate $i^{**} > 0$. For I have already shown that when (4.19) does not bind, optimal policy in the cashless limit involves a deterministic component of inflation that is nonnegative (and converging asymptotically to zero); hence average inflation is nonzero. If instead (4.19) does bind, the only reason to choose a different deterministic component for inflation would be in order to relax the constraint, which would involve making average inflation higher (so that the average funds rate can be higher).

If transactions frictions are nonnegligible *and* the interest-rate lower bound binds as well, the quadratic interest-rate term in (4.21) is added to the quadratic interest-rate term already present in (4.10). The result is a loss function that again has the same form:

$$\hat{L}_t = \pi_t^2 + \lambda_x \left(x_t - x^* \right)^2 + \hat{\lambda}_i (\hat{\imath}_t - \hat{\imath})^2, \qquad (4.22)$$

where now $\hat{\lambda}_i = \lambda_i + \mu_2$ is an even larger positive coefficient, whereas $\hat{\imath}$ is intermediate between i^* and i^{**} (and thus may have either sign). In fact, the value of $\hat{\imath}$, like the value of x^*, matters only for the deterministic component of optimal policy; the optimal responses to shocks depend only upon the weights λ_x, $\hat{\lambda}_i$ of the loss function. Thus in this regard both considerations point in the same direction, toward the likely importance of including a quadratic interest-rate term in the loss function. Hence I give considerable attention in Chapter 7 to the consequences for optimal policy of including such a term.[49]

___

49. Note, however, that both considerations justify a concern to reduce the variability of the *level* of interest rates, and *not* a concern with the variability of interest-rate *changes*. The

How much are such considerations likely to matter? I investigate this numerically in a calibrated example. The values of the parameters α, β, σ, κ, and ϵ_{mc} are as in Table 5.1, based upon the estimates of Rotemberg and Woodford (1997) discussed in Chapter 5.[50] The values for η_y, η_i, and χ given in the table are those implied by estimates of long-run money demand for the United States, as discussed in Chapter 2.[51]

For present purposes, the only aspect of the exogenous disturbances that matters is the implied evolution of the natural rate of interest $\hat{r}_t^n$; for simplicity, I assume that this variable follows a stationary first-order autoregressive process, with a mean of zero, and a standard deviation and serial correlation coefficient as specified in Table 5.1. As I explain further in Chapter 7, these numerical values are motivated by aspects of the estimated model of Rotemberg and Woodford (1997), though that model involves a more complex specification of the shock processes.

Finally, the structural parameters given in Table 5.1 imply a value for θ equal to 7.88. Using this, I am able to obtain a theoretical value for λ_x in the utility-based loss function (2.22), which value is also given in the table.[52] I simplify my calculations by assuming that $\Phi_y = 0$, so that $x^* = 0$.

Using these parameter values, I can explore the trade-off between minimization of the deadweight losses measured by (2.22) and stabilization of the short-term nominal interest rate. Letting L_t^0 be this loss function (i.e., the loss function abstracting from any costs of interest-rate variability), one can compute its expected discounted value,

$$\hat{E}[L^0] \equiv (1 - \beta) \sum_{t=0}^{\infty} \beta^t E\left[L_t^0\right], \tag{4.23}$$

in the case of any stochastic processes for inflation and the output gap. Here I use the notation $\hat{E}$ to denote a discounted expectation rather than simply

---

latter sort of "interest-rate-smoothing" goal is often assumed to characterize the behavior of actual central banks. As I show in Chapter 7, it is possible to justify the assignment of such a goal to the central bank as part of an optimal *delegation* problem, even if it is not part of the *social* loss function which is the concern here.

50. Note that the value of ω reported in Table 5.1 is not exactly the one implied by the values given here, since in Rotemberg and Woodford the value of ω is inferred from the value of ϵ_{mc} assuming that $\chi = 0$.

51. The value for χ used here is actually slightly higher than that derived in Chapter 2, as the value of χ implied by the long-run money-demand estimates depends upon the assumed value of σ. However, the values used in both chapters agree to the first three decimal places.

52. Note that the value given here is equal to $16\kappa/\theta$, rather than κ/θ. This is because I report the loss-function weights λ_x, λ_i that are appropriate when inflation and interest rates are measured as annualized percentage rates, despite the fact that the model is quarterly. The square of the annualized percentage inflation rate is thus not π_t^2 but $16\pi_t^2$, in terms of the notation used in the earlier theoretical derivations.

TABLE 6.1   Calibrated parameter values for the quarterly model used for Figure 6.1

Structural parameters		Shock process		Loss function		Interest-rate bound	
α	0.66	ρ_r	0.35	x^*	0	k	2.26
β	0.99	$sd(\hat{r}^n)$	3.72	λ_x	0.048	$\bar{r}$	2.99
σ^{-1}	0.16			λ_i	0.077		
κ	0.024						
ϵ_{mc}	0.63						
η_y	1						
η_i	28						
χ	0.02						

the unconditional expectation (or long-run average value) of the random variable L_t^0. The operator E on the right-hand side should be understood to mean an unconditional expectation over possible initial states of the exogenous disturbance $\hat{r}_0^n$, while assuming initial lagged values for any endogenous variables that may matter under the policy rule being considered that are consistent with the zero-inflation steady state.[53] I measure the degree of interest-rate variability associated with any possible equilibrium in terms of the statistic

$$V[i] \equiv (1 - \beta) \sum_{t=0}^{\infty} \beta^t \text{var}(\hat{\imath}_t),$$

where the unconditional variance $\text{var}(\hat{\imath}_t)$ again involves an integral over the possible initial values r_0^n. I then consider the policies that minimize $\hat{E}[L^0]$ subject to a constraint that $V[i]$ not exceed some finite value.

The efficient frontier for these two statistics is shown in Figure 6.1. (The nature of the constrained-efficient policies is discussed in the next chapter.) Observe that it is possible to achieve the theoretical lower bound of zero for $\hat{E}[L^0]$ by completely stabilizing inflation and the output gap, as discussed

53. The reason that this matters is that I wish to compare alternative policies in terms of the discounted losses that they imply, looking forward from date zero, at which time the policy is adopted; and for a fair comparison I wish to assume the same distribution of initial conditions, regardless of the degree of variability of endogenous variables that may occur under the different policies. For example, under a policy that creates substantial persistence in the (mean-zero) equilibrium fluctuations in inflation, the unconditional expectation (or long-run average value) of π_t^2 is greater than $\hat{E}[\pi^2]$ because in computing the latter statistic, $\pi_{-1} = 0$ is assumed, which implies that π_t is near zero with high probability for early periods $t \geq 0$ as well, even though inflation eventually fluctuates over a wider range of values. Such a policy would be unduly penalized if one were to look at the long-run average value of π_t^2, when one really cares about the discounted sum of deadweight losses that can be expected from adopting the policy at date zero.

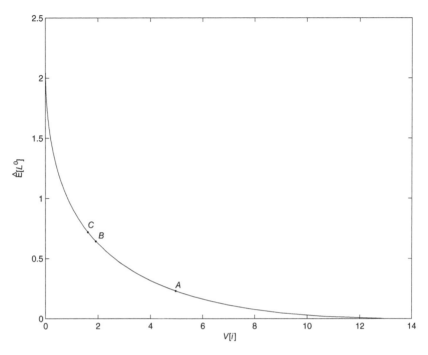

Figure 6.1 *The trade-off between inflation/output-gap stabilization and interest-rate stabilization.*

in Section 3, only if one is willing to tolerate an interest-rate variability of $V[i] = 13.83$, corresponding to a (discounted) standard deviation of 3.72 percentage points for the federal funds rate. (This is, of course, just the assumed standard deviation of fluctuations in the natural rate of interest.) Lower interest-rate variability requires that one accept less complete stabilization of inflation and the output gap, indicated by a positive value for $\hat{E}[L^0]$. Complete interest-rate stabilization would require that $\hat{E}[L^0]$ take a value of 2.10, a level of deadweight loss more than twice that associated with steady inflation of 1 percent per year.[54] Statistics relating to the variability of inflation, the output gap, and the federal funds rate in these two extreme cases are given by the first and last lines of Table 6.2, using measures analogous to $V[i]$ in the case of the other two variables as well. Note that in terms of these measures,

$$\hat{E}[L^0] = V[\pi] + \lambda_x V[x],$$

54. A similar efficient frontier in the case of the more complicated model estimated by Rotemberg and Woodford (1997) is shown in Figure 5 of that paper.

TABLE 6.2   Examples of policies on the efficient frontier

$\hat{\lambda}_i$	$V[\pi]$	$V[x]$	$V[i]$	$\hat{E}[L^0]$
0	0	0	13.83	0
0.077	0.037	4.015	4.961	0.231
0.236	0.130	10.60	1.921	0.643
0.277	0.151	11.75	1.623	0.719
∞	0.677	29.35	0	2.096

given that both inflation and the output gap have mean zero in all of the policies considered in this table.

This frontier indicates how a concern with interest-rate variability, for whatever reason, would affect the degree to which it would be optimal to stabilize inflation and the output gap. I am particularly interested, however, in the degree of attention to this goal that would be justified by either of the two considerations treated earlier. Taking account of transactions frictions, I would wish to minimize $\hat{E}[L]$, where now L_t is the loss function (4.10) including an interest-rate variability term. The fact that $i^* \neq 0$ in (4.10) affects only the deterministic part of the optimal paths of the endogenous variables, as with the discussion of the case $x^* \neq 0$ in Section 3; it has no effect upon the optimal responses to shocks. Thus the optimal responses to shocks can be determined by minimizing $\hat{E}[L]$ with i^* set equal to zero, which amounts to minimizing $\hat{E}[L^0] + \lambda_i V[i]$. This policy corresponds to a point on the frontier in Figure 6.1, namely, the point at which the slope is equal to $-\lambda_i$, where λ_i is given by (4.12).

Assuming the structural parameters given in Table 6.1, one sees that equation (4.4) implies that for the United States, φ should equal approximately 0.22 years. Then (4.12) implies that $\lambda_i = 0.077$, the value also given in the table.[55] This corresponds to point A on the frontier in Figure 6.1.[56]

55. This value, based on an assumption that $\chi = 0.02$, is probably too large by a factor of two or more, for reasons discussed in Chapter 2. Williams (1999), e.g., assumes a value (if the weight on the squared inflation term is normalized as one) equal to 0.02.

56. In order to show the optimal equilibria under differing assumptions on a single diagram, I use the same structural model in each case—namely, the baseline model, abstracting from real-balance effects, which is also used in the numerical analysis of Chapter 7—simply varying the assumed welfare criterion in each case. This means that in the case of point A, I am actually assuming parameter values in the structural equations ($\chi = 0$) that are not completely consistent with those used to derive the loss function ($\chi = 0.02$). However, this makes only a small difference to the characterization of optimal policy when transactions frictions are allowed for; the most important effect is upon the loss function, rather than upon the structural equations. Were I to assume additively separable preferences $u(c, m)$, there would be no effect upon the structural equations at all, but the loss function would nonetheless be modified as indicated in (4.10).

Line 2 of Table 6.2 reports the variability of each of the endogenous variables in this equilibrium.

Now suppose instead that I abstract from transactions frictions, but take account of the lower bound on nominal interest rates, or more precisely, that I impose the constraints (4.18) and (4.19). Following Rotemberg and Woodford (1997), let k equal the ratio of the standard deviation of the funds rate to its mean in the long-run stationary distribution implied by their estimated VAR model of U.S. data, and assume a value for $\bar{\imath}$, the steady-state real funds rate, equal to the mean real funds rate implied by this same long-run stationary distribution. These values are indicated in Table 6.1.

As shown before, the optimal policy subject to these constraints minimizes $\hat{\mathrm{E}}[\tilde{L}]$, where $\tilde{L}_t$ is defined by (4.21) with L_t equal to L_t^0. Once again, the fact that $i^{**} \neq 0$ does not affect the optimal responses to shocks, and so these are as in one of the equilibria on the frontier shown in Figure 6.1. Under the assumed parameter values, the implied value of $\tilde{\lambda}_i$ in (4.21), given by the Lagrange multiplier on constraint (4.19), is equal to 0.236. The corresponding optimal responses to shocks are those associated with point B on the frontier, which is the point at which the frontier has this steeper slope. The third line of Table 6.2 reports the variability of each of the endogenous variables in this equilibrium. (In the computations reported in the table, the deterministic component of each variable is equal to zero in all periods, so that these statistics refer only to the variations in the variables due to fluctuations in the natural rate of interest.) The higher effective penalty upon interest-rate variability results in less equilibrium variation in nominal interest rates, at the cost of more variation in both inflation and the output gap.

Finally, suppose that in the welfare analysis one takes account both of transactions frictions and of the lower bound on nominal interest rates. One then finds the policy that minimizes $\hat{\mathrm{E}}[\tilde{L}]$ when L_t is given by (4.10) rather than by L_t^0. As noted earlier, this policy minimizes a criterion of the form $\hat{\mathrm{E}}[\hat{L}]$, where $\hat{L}_t$ is given by (4.22). In the case of the assumed parameter values, $\hat{\lambda}_i$ is equal to 0.277, a larger value than would be obtained taking account of either of these considerations individually. Once again, the optimal responses to shocks correspond to a point on the frontier shown in Figure 6.1, the point labeled C. The variability of the endogenous variables in this equilibrium is indicated on the fourth line of Table 6.2.

It is interesting to note that the value $\hat{\lambda}_i$ is not greatly larger than $\tilde{\lambda}_i$, so that point C is not too much higher than point B on the efficient frontier. This indicates that taking account of transactions frictions does not matter as much for the welfare analysis, once one has taken account of the interest-rate lower bound, though the reverse is not true. There is a simple intuition for this result. Whether or not one allows for transactions frictions, imposition of constraint (4.19) makes it optimal to choose a policy under which interest-rate variability is roughly of the size that makes (4.19) consistent with an average inflation rate of zero.[57] The level of interest-rate variability that this would involve, the point on the frontier corresponding to it, and the associated weight on interest-rate variations in the effective loss function (which is given by the negative of the slope of the efficient frontier at that point) are all independent of whether the loss function directly penalizes interest-rate variations (because of transactions frictions) or not.

For this reason, increasing the weight λ_i on interest-rate variations in the direct loss function L_t has relatively little effect on the weight $\hat{\lambda}_i$ in the effective loss function. The increase in λ_i results in a smaller Lagrange multiplier on constraint (4.19), as there is less desire to vary interest rates even in the absence of the constraint; and so the sum of the two weights increases much less than the increase in λ_i. Thus there is not a great loss in accuracy involved in neglecting the welfare consequences of transactions frictions, if the interest-rate lower bound has already been taken into account (as in Rotemberg and Woodford, 1997, 1999a, or Woodford, 1999a). Furthermore, the conclusions reached in those analyses are the same as would have been obtained if transactions frictions were allowed for but with the lower bound treated as slightly less of a constraint—as, for example, if one assumed slightly less variability or a slightly higher average value of the natural rate of interest.

4.3 Asymmetric Disturbances

Next I consider the consequences of real disturbances that, unlike those considered in Section 2, do not have identical effects upon demand and supply conditions for all goods. Instead, I wish to allow for the kinds of disturbances that would affect equilibrium relative prices even in the case that all prices were fully flexible. In the presence of such disturbances, it is generally not possible to arrange for the equilibrium of an economy with sticky prices to reproduce the state-contingent resource allocation of a flexible-price economy simply by choosing a monetary policy that stabilizes an aggregate price index. I also allow for asymmetries between sectors in that I no longer assume that the frequency of price adjustments must be the same for all goods. (This introduces another reason for different sectors of the economy to be differentially affected by shocks.) What are appropriate stabilization goals in such a case?

---

57. When one takes account of only the interest-rate lower bound, it is already optimal to reduce interest-rate variability to a degree consistent with a long-run average inflation rate of only 14 basis points per year. When one takes account of the welfare consequences of transactions frictions as well, it becomes instead optimal to reduce interest-rate variability to an extent consistent with a long-run average inflation rate of negative 11 basis points per year. This does not require a great deal of further reduction in the variability of the short-term interest rate.

The analysis here generalizes the work of Aoki (2001) and is essentially a closed-economy interpretation of the analysis of Benigno (2003).[58] I again return to the model with asymmetric disturbances described in Section 2.5 of Chapter 3. The welfare measure is again given by the utility of the representative household, which is once again of the form (2.3), except that now Y_t is a (time-varying) CES aggregate of the sectoral indices of aggregate demand Y_{1t} and Y_{2t}, and the disturbances affecting the disutility of output supply (2.5) are now allowed to be different in the case of goods i in different sectors.

In this case, I obtain the following generalization of Proposition 6.1.

PROPOSITION 6.10. Consider the two-sector model with asymmetric disturbances described in Section 2.5 of Chapter 3. Let n_1, n_2 be the (steady-state) shares of the two sectors in national income, and let $\eta > 0$ be the elasticity of substitution in household preferences between the consumption aggregates of the two sectors. Then in the case of small enough fluctuations in aggregate output Y_t around the level $\bar{Y}$, small enough fluctuations in relative prices $\hat{p}_t(i) \equiv \log(p_t(i)/P_t)$ (and hence small variations in the relative quantities produced and consumed of different goods), small enough disturbances, and a small enough value of Φ_y, the utility flow to the representative household each period can be approximated by

$$U_t = -\frac{\bar{Y}u_c}{2}\left\{ \left(\sigma^{-1}+\omega\right)\left(x_t - x^*\right)^2 + n_1 n_2 \eta(1+\omega\eta)\left(\hat{p}_{Rt} - \hat{p}_{Rt}^n\right)^2 \right.$$

$$(4.24)$$

$$\left. + \theta(1+\omega\theta)\sum_{j=1}^{2} n_j \mathrm{var}_i^j \log p_t(i) \right\} + \mathrm{t.i.p.} + \mathcal{O}\left(\|\Phi_y, \hat{Y}, \hat{p}, \xi\|^3\right).$$

Here x_t once again denotes the output gap $\hat{Y}_t - \hat{Y}_t^n$, where $\hat{Y}_t^n$ is the (log of the) equilibrium level of aggregate output under complete price flexibility (defined in Chapter 3), and the efficient level of the output gap x^* is again given by (2.17). I also use the notation $\hat{p}_{Rt} \equiv \log(P_{2t}/P_{1t})$ for the (log) sectoral relative price and $\hat{p}_{Rt}^n$ for its natural value, that is, the equilibrium relative price under full price flexibility (a function solely of the asymmetric exogenous disturbances).

---

58. In the model of Benigno, there are two countries that specialize in the production of different sets of goods, and real disturbances may have differential effects upon the markets for goods produced in a given country. Here the two sets of goods are instead interpreted as simply two sectors of a single national economy. However, my conclusions with regard to appropriate stabilization objectives follow directly from his analysis of stabilization objectives for a two-country monetary union.

This quadratic approximation to the utility flow each period is valid regardless of my assumptions about pricing. If I assume Calvo-style staggered pricesetting in each sector, I obtain the following welfare-theoretic loss function, expressed in terms of stabilization objectives for aggregate output and sectoral price indices.

PROPOSITION 6.11. Consider a two-sector model with staggered (Calvo) pricing in each sector, but possibly with different frequencies of price adjustment in the two sectors. Then the discounted sum of utility of the representative household can again be approximated by an expression of the form (2.21), where now the period loss function is of the form

$$L_t = \sum_{j=1}^{2} w_j \, \pi_{jt}^2 + \lambda_x \big(x_t - x^* \big)^2 + \lambda_R \big(\hat{p}_{Rt} - \hat{p}_{Rt}^n \big)^2, \tag{4.25}$$

generalizing (2.22). Here π_{jt} is the rate of price inflation in sector j, and the weights (normalized so that $w_1 + w_2 = 1$) are given by

$$w_j \equiv \frac{n_j \kappa}{\kappa_j} > 0, \qquad \lambda_x \equiv \frac{\kappa}{\theta} > 0, \qquad \lambda_R \equiv \frac{n_1 n_2 \eta (1 + \omega \eta)}{\sigma^{-1} + \omega} \, \lambda_x > 0,$$

where the coefficients κ_j are defined as in Proposition 3.8, and

$$\kappa \equiv \big(n_1 \kappa_1^{-1} + n_2 \kappa_2^{-1} \big)^{-1} > 0$$

is a geometric average of the two.

The proof is in Appendix E. One now finds that deadweight loss depends not only upon the economy-wide average rate of inflation, but on the rate of inflation in each of the sectors individually; the relative weight on inflation variations in sector j is greater the larger the relative size of this sector, and also the smaller the relative value of κ_j, which measures the degree of price stickiness in sector j. (A smaller value of κ_j indicates slower price adjustment in sector j; κ_j is unboundedly large in the limit of perfectly flexible prices in sector j.) The relative weight on aggregate output-gap variations depends as before on the measure κ of the overall degree of price stickiness in the economy. Finally, misalignments of the relative price between the two sectors (relative to what it would be under fully flexible prices) also distort the allocation of resources.[59] The relative weight on this

---

59. In Benigno's open-economy application, this corresponds to the real exchange rate, and one obtains a welfare-theoretic justification for a real exchange-rate stabilization objective.

stabilization objective is greater the larger the elasticity of substitution η between the products of the two sectors.

In general, it is not possible to satisfy all of these stabilization objectives simultaneously. In particular, if the natural relative price $\hat{p}_{Rt}^n$ varies over time, it is not possible to stabilize inflation in both sectors *and* to eliminate gaps between the relative price and its natural value at the same time. Accordingly, in this case one must consider second-best optimal policies; and in general, complete stabilization of the aggregate inflation rate

$$\pi_t \equiv n_1\pi_{1t} + n_2\pi_{2t}$$

is *not* the best available policy. This is most easily seen in the case considered by Aoki (2001), in which prices are fully flexible in one sector, but sticky in the other. If prices are fully flexible in sector j, $\kappa_j^{-1} = 0$, so that $w_j = 0$. In this limiting case, one can also show that the relative-price gap $\hat{p}_{Rt} - \hat{p}_{Rt}^n$ is a constant multiple of the output gap x_t, regardless of policy, so that the same policy completely stabilizes both gap variables, and that complete stabilization of both gaps implies zero inflation in the sticky-price sector.

Hence all three terms in (4.25) with nonzero weights are minimized by the same policy, one that completely stabilizes the price index for the sticky-price sector, and this is clearly the optimal policy in this case. (Aoki interprets this policy as stabilization of an index of core inflation.) Again the intuition is a simple one: Such a policy achieves the same allocation of resources as would occur under complete price flexibility, since no suppliers in the sticky-price sector have any desire to change their prices more frequently than they already do. But in general, such a policy does not completely stabilize the broader price index, despite the fact that an alternative policy exists that would do so. For if $\hat{p}_{Rt}$ is to track $\hat{p}_{Rt}^n$ while the sticky-price index remains constant, there must be a variable inflation rate in the flexible-price sector.

There is one case in which complete stabilization of the broad inflation measure π_t continues to be optimal even in the presence of relative-price disturbances: the case in which prices are equally sticky in the two sectors (in addition to the sectors being symmetrical in the other ways assumed in Chapter 3). When $\alpha_1 = \alpha_2$, so that $\kappa_1 = \kappa_2$, $w_1 = w_2 = 0.5$, and the loss function can alternatively be written

$$L_t = \pi_t^2 + \tfrac{1}{4}\left(\hat{p}_{Rt} - \hat{p}_{R,t-1}\right)^2 + \lambda_x\left(x_t - x^*\right)^2 + \lambda_R\left(\hat{p}_{Rt} - \hat{p}_{Rt}^n\right)^2.$$

However, it should be noted that it is the gap between the real exchange rate and its natural level that should be stabilized, rather than the real exchange rate itself.

As shown in Chapter 3, in this symmetric case, stabilization of the aggregate inflation rate π_t is equivalent to stabilization of the aggregate output gap x_t, whereas the relative price $\hat{p}_{Rt}$ evolves in the same way regardless of monetary policy. Thus while it is not possible for any policy to reduce all terms in L_t to zero each period (since $\hat{p}_{Rt} \neq \hat{p}_{Rt}^n$ in general), a policy that completely stabilizes π_t reduces the value of each term to the greatest extent possible, and so is optimal.

More generally, Benigno finds that a policy that completely stabilizes an appropriately weighted average of the sectoral inflation rates,

$$\pi_t^{targ} \equiv \phi\pi_{1t} + (1 - \phi)\pi_{2t}, \tag{4.26}$$

typically provides a reasonably good approximation to optimal policy, if the weight $0 \leq \phi \leq 1$ is properly chosen. (I have just described cases in which each of the values $\phi = 0, 1/2$, or 1 is optimal, suggesting the interest of this general family of rules.) This can be illustrated in a calibrated example.

Suppose that $n_1 = n_2 = 1/2$, $\eta = 1$, and let $\beta, \sigma, \kappa, \omega$, and θ take the values reported in Table 4.1, derived from the study of Rotemberg and Woodford (1997).[60] The implied values of α_1 and α_2 are then derived from these coefficient values for an arbitrary choice of the relative weight $0 \leq w_2 \leq 1$. (In the case that $w_2 = 0.5$ is chosen, $\alpha_1 = \alpha_2$, and the common value of α is the one reported in Table 4.1.) This allows us to vary the assumed relative stickiness of prices in the two sectors between the two extremes of complete flexibility in sector two ($w_2 = 0$) and complete flexibility in sector one ($w_2 = 1$), while assuming the same overall degree of price stickiness (as measured by κ). Note that the assumed coefficients λ_x and λ_R in the loss function (4.25) remain the same as w_2 is varied; the values implied by the above calibration are indicated in Table 6.3.[61] The tensions between alternative stabilization objectives just discussed exist only insofar as the natural relative price $\hat{p}_{Rt}^n$ is not constant; for purposes of illustration, I assume that this follows an AR(1) process with an autoregressive coefficient of .8. The assumed variance of the innovations in this process do not matter for the results (all of the expected losses are proportional to this assumed variance), so it is set equal to one without loss of generality.[62]

---

60. Note that the model of Rotemberg and Woodford can be interpreted as a two-sector model in which $\alpha_1 = \alpha_2$. Because no data on relative prices are used in that study, it provides no estimate of η.

61. As in Table 6.1, the reported weights λ_x and λ_R are sixteen times as large as those implied by the formulas given above, so that they correspond to the relative weights on these terms in the loss function when the inflation rate is measured as an annual rather than a quarterly rate.

62. Note that an innovation variance of 1 implies a variance of $1/1 - (.8)^2$ for the disturbance process, or a standard deviation of 1.67.

TABLE 6.3   Calibrated parameter values for the quarterly model used for Figure 6.2

Additional structural parameters		Shock process		Loss function	
n_1, n_2	0.5	$\rho(\hat{p}_R^n)$	0.8	x^*	0
η	1	$sd(\hat{p}_R^n)$	1.67	λ_x	0.048
				λ_R	0.028

The solid line in Figure 6.2 plots the minimum attainable value for the expected discounted period loss $\hat{E}[L]$, again defined as in (4.23), for each possible choice of the coefficient w_2 measuring the relative stickiness of sector two.[63] Only in the case that w_2 takes one of the extreme values (i.e., prices are completely flexible in one sector or the other) is the minimum attainable value zero, for only in this case is it is possible for monetary policy to achieve the allocation of resources associated with complete price flexibility. The expected loss under a policy that strictly targets (completely stabilizes) aggregate inflation is shown by the dashed line. The two lines coincide only when $w_2 = .5$, the only case in which aggregate-inflation targeting is optimal. Whenever the degrees of price stickiness in the two sectors differ, aggregate-inflation targeting results in greater losses, and the losses associated with this policy are greater the greater the degree of asymmetry, whereas the unavoidable losses are smaller the greater the asymmetry. The expected losses resulting from strict targeting of the weighted index (4.26), where the weight ϕ is optimally chosen for each value of w_2, is instead shown by the dotted line. This coincides with the solid line when $w_2 = 0, .5,$ or 1 (the three special cases already discussed), but not otherwise; thus these are the only cases in which optimal policy is exactly described by a simple targeting rule of this kind. But even in other cases, the dotted line is only slightly above the solid line; thus a rule of this kind is a reasonable approximation to optimal policy, if ϕ is properly chosen.

The optimal value of ϕ for each value of w_2 is shown in Figure 6.3. The optimal values are $\phi = 1$ when $w_2 = 0$, $\phi = .5$ when $w_2 = .5$, and $\phi = 0$ when $w_2 = 1$, for reasons already discussed. More generally, the optimal ϕ is a decreasing function of w_2, as the special cases had already suggested: The near-optimal policy stabilizes an inflation measure that puts more weight on prices in the sector where they are stickier. As Aoki suggests, this provides theoretical justification for a policy that targets core inflation rather than the growth of a broader price index, and offers a theoretical criterion for the construction of such an index. It also explains why it is not appropriate to target an inflation measure that includes "asset-price inflation" along

---

63. The precise definition of constrained-optimal policy that I assume in cases like this and the Lagrangian method that I use to characterize it are explained in Chapter 7.

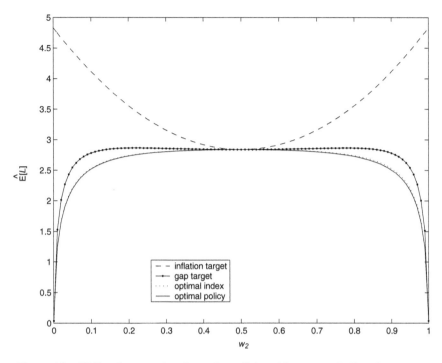

Figure 6.2 *Welfare losses under alternative policies with asymmetric disturbances.*

with goods-price increases, as is sometimes proposed; even if asset prices are also prices and can also be affected by monetary policy, they are among the prices that are most frequently adjusted in response to new market conditions, and so their movements do not indicate the kind of distortions that one seeks to minimize.

The choice of the right rule of the form (4.26) depends, however, on an accurate estimate of the relative stickiness of prices in the two sectors. A simple rule that performs relatively well regardless of the value of w_2 is strict targeting of the *output gap*, using monetary policy to ensure that $x_t = 0$ at all times. The expected loss resulting from this rule is shown in Figure 6.3 by the dotted solid line. This policy is only fully optimal in three cases ($w_2 = 0, .5,$ or 1), and otherwise it is somewhat worse than the best weighted-inflation targeting rule; but it is relatively good over the entire range of possible values of w_2 (unlike the equal-weighted inflation targeting rule, e.g.), despite involving no coefficients that must be assigned values that vary with the changing value of w_2.

In fact, the output-gap targeting rule is reasonably successful regardless of the value of w_2 because it incorporates the principle of stabilizing to the

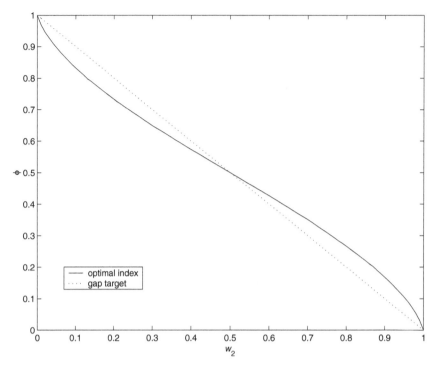

Figure 6.3   *The optimal price index to stabilize as a function of the relative stickiness of prices in the two sectors. The dotted line shows the price index that is equivalent to output-gap targeting.*

greatest extent the prices that are most sticky. If one multiplies the inflation equation for sector j (equation (2.27) of Chapter 3) by w_j and sums over j, one obtains

$$\bar{\pi}_t = \kappa x_t + \beta E_t \bar{\pi}_{t+1},$$

where

$$\bar{\pi}_t \equiv w_1 \pi_{1t} + w_2 \pi_{2t}.$$

From this it follows that output-gap stabilization is equivalent to stabilization of $\bar{\pi}_t$. This is thus a policy of the form (4.26), with $\phi = w_1$. Hence the weights are automatically adjusted to place less weight on the prices in the sector with more flexible prices. This is not done in precisely the optimal way (see the comparison of this function of w_2 with the optimal one in Figure 6.3), but this simple rule is not too different from the optimal member of the family (4.26) for any value of w_2.

Thus I conclude that even in the case of asymmetric disturbances, stabilization of a price index provides a fairly good recipe for monetary policy, as long as the right price index is chosen. On the other hand, this does not mean that seeking to stabilize the output gap cannot be a sound approach as well, as long as the output gap is properly measured; in fact, in the absence of information about which sector's prices are more sticky, an output-gap target is a more robustly desirable simple policy rule. The choice between the two approaches, then, must turn on which sorts of information the central bank is able to rely upon with more confidence. In practice, banks are likely to be more confident that they can estimate the relative stickiness of different prices with some confidence than that they can accurately track the natural rate of output in real time; for the former question can be studied using past data, whereas the latter depends upon correctly judging the economy's current state despite the possible occurrence of a vast number of different types of disturbances. For this reason, one may still conclude that an appropriately chosen inflation target represents a sensible approach to policy.

4.4 Sticky Wages and Prices

Similar issues arise if one assumes that wages as well as prices are sticky. Once again, some types of real disturbances modify the natural relative price, that is, the equilibrium real wage under flexible wages and prices, so that no monetary policy can eliminate all of the distortions resulting from wage and price stickiness. Here I analyze welfare-theoretic stabilization goals for the model with sticky wages and prices set out in Section 4 of Chapter 3; my results essentially recapitulate those of Erceg et al. (2000).

In this model, all firms hire the same composite labor input; nonetheless, there exist differential demands for the labor supplied by different households j, owing to wage dispersion (as a result of staggered wage adjustment). The demand for each differentiated type of labor is given by

$$h_t(j) = H_t\left(\frac{w_t(j)}{W_t}\right)^{-\theta_w},\qquad (4.27)$$

where $\theta_w > 1$ is the elasticity of substitution among different types of labor on the part of firms. I allow the elasticity of substitution between different types of labor θ_w to differ from the elasticity of substitution between differentiated goods, now denoted θ_p.

When wages as well as prices are sticky, it is useful to decompose the elasticity ω of average real marginal cost with respect to aggregate output (holding fixed the marginal utility of income) under flexible wages into two components,

$$\omega = \omega_w + \omega_p.$$

Here $\omega_w \geq 0$ is the elasticity of the real wage that a flexible-wage supplier of labor would demand (again, holding fixed the marginal utility of income) with respect to aggregate output, and $\omega_p \geq 0$ is the negative of the elasticity of the marginal product of labor with respect to aggregate output. It is also useful to factor the elasticity ω_w as

$$\omega_w = \nu\phi_h,$$

where $\nu \geq 0$ is the elasticity of the desired real wage with respect to the quantity of labor demanded (inverse of the Frisch elasticity of labor supply), and $\phi_h > 0$ is the inverse of the elasticity of output with respect to additional labor input in the production technology.

I then obtain the following generalization of Proposition 6.1.

PROPOSITION 6.12. Consider a model with sticky wages as well as prices, as described in Chapter 3, Section 4. Then in the case of small enough fluctuations in aggregate output Y_t around the level $\bar{Y}$, small enough fluctuations in relative prices $\hat{p}_t(i) \equiv \log(p_t(i)/P_t)$ and relative wages $\hat{w}_t(j) \equiv \log(w_t(j)/W_t)$, small enough disturbances, and a small enough value of Φ_y, the utility flow to the representative household each period can be approximated by

$$U_t = -\frac{\bar{Y}u_c}{2}\left\{(\sigma^{-1} + \omega)\left(x_t - x^*\right)^2 + \theta_p(1 + \omega_p\theta_p)\mathrm{var}_i \log p_t(i)\right.$$

$$\left. +\theta_w\phi_h^{-1}(1 + \nu\theta_w)\mathrm{var}_j \log w_t(j)\right\} + \text{t.i.p.} + \mathcal{O}\big(\|\Phi_y, \hat{Y}, \hat{p}, \hat{w}, \tilde{\xi}\|^3\big),$$

$$(4.28)$$

where the output gap x_t is defined as in the flexible-wage model, and the optimal output gap x^* is again given by (2.17).

The proof is in Appendix E. When both wages and prices are sticky, wage dispersion across different types of labor results in deadweight losses, for essentially the same reason as does price dispersion when prices are sticky.

This quadratic approximation to the utility flow each period is valid regardless of my assumptions about the nature of wage- and pricesetting. If I assume Calvo-style staggering of both wages and prices, following Erceg et al., I obtain the following generalization of Proposition 6.4.

PROPOSITION 6.13. Consider a model with Calvo-style staggering of both wages and prices, as described in Chapter 3, Section 4, but allowing for different frequencies of adjustment of wages as opposed to prices. Then the discounted sum of utility of the representative household can again be approximated by an expression of the form (2.21), where now the period loss function is of the form

$$L_t = \lambda_p \pi_t^2 + \lambda_w \pi_{wt}^2 + \lambda_x (x_t - x^*)^2.$$

(4.29)

Here the weights (normalized so that $\lambda_p + \lambda_w = 1$) are given by

$$\lambda_p = \frac{\theta_p \xi_p^{-1}}{\theta_p \xi_p^{-1} + \theta_w \phi_h^{-1} \xi_w^{-1}} > 0, \qquad \lambda_w = \frac{\theta_w \phi^{-1} \xi_w^{-1}}{\theta_p \xi_p^{-1} + \theta_w \phi_h^{-1} \xi_w^{-1}} > 0,$$

$$\lambda_x = \frac{\sigma^{-1} + \omega}{\theta_p \xi_p^{-1} + \theta_w \phi_h^{-1} \xi_w^{-1}} > 0,$$

where $\xi_w, \xi_p > 0$ are again the elasticities appearing in equations (4.8) and (4.9) of Chapter 3, measuring the effects of a real wage gap on wage inflation and price inflation, respectively.

I omit details of the derivation, which follows exactly the same lines as the proofs of Propositions 6.3 and 6.4.

One should note that the relative weight on output-gap stabilization is again related to the slope of the aggregate supply relation in a similar way as in the basic (flexible-wage) model. In particular, in the case that $\theta_w \phi_h^{-1} = \theta_p$, the expression for λ_x reduces to κ/θ, where $\kappa > 0$ is the slope of the short-run Phillips-curve relation between a weighted average of price and wage inflation and the output gap (equation (4.14) of Chapter 3) and $\theta > 1$ is the common value of θ_p and $\theta_w \phi_h^{-1}$. However, the weight on inflation stabilization is now divided between a price-inflation-stabilization goal and a wage-inflation-stabilization goal; the relative weights on each depend on the relative stickiness of wages and prices (as indicated by the relative sizes of ξ_w^{-1} and ξ_p^{-1}). If only prices are sticky ($\xi_w \to +\infty$), only price inflation matters ($\lambda_w = 0$), and optimal policy involves complete stabilization of prices (as this also completely stabilizes the output gap). If only wages are sticky ($\xi_p \to +\infty$), only wage inflation matters ($\lambda_p = 0$), and optimal policy involves complete stabilization of wages (which also completely stabilizes the output gap). In the intermediate case, both goals matter, and complete stabilization is impossible in the presence of fluctuations in the natural real wage w_t^n.

An intermediate case in which optimal policy is nonetheless simple to characterize is the special case in which $\theta_w \phi_h^{-1} = \theta_p$ and $\kappa_w = \kappa_p$, where κ_w, κ_p are the coefficients indicating the effects of output-gap variations on wage and price inflation, respectively (see equations (4.11) and (4.12) of Chapter 3). Note that (4.29) can alternatively be written

$$L_t = \bar{\pi}_t^2 + \lambda_p \lambda_w \left(\log w_t - \log w_{t-1}\right)^2 + \lambda_x \left(x_t - x^*\right)^2, \qquad (4.30)$$

where

$$\bar{\pi}_t \equiv \lambda_p \pi_t + \lambda_w \pi_{wt}$$

and w_t is the real wage. In the case that $\kappa_w = \kappa_p$, the evolution of the real wage is independent of monetary policy, as shown in Chapter 3; hence the middle term in (4.30) is irrelevant. In the case that $\theta_w \phi_h^{-1} = \theta_p$, the weights λ_p, λ_w define a weighted average of price and wage inflation that is stabilized if and only if the output gap is stabilized. (This follows from equation (4.14) of Chapter 3.) Hence the two terms in (4.30) that can be affected by monetary policy are both minimized by the same policy, one that completely stabilizes $\bar{\pi}_t$.[64]

This last result suggests that even when both wages and prices are sticky, and L_t cannot be reduced to zero by *any* policy, a policy that stabilizes a weighted inflation measure of the form

$$\pi_t^{targ} \equiv \phi \pi_{1t} + (1 - \phi)\pi_{2t} \qquad (4.31)$$

may be desirable. In fact, except in the special case just described, fully optimal policy cannot be represented by such a simple rule, but numerical experimentation suggests that a targeting rule of this kind can nonetheless be nearly optimal, if the weight ϕ is appropriately chosen.

This can be illustrated by a calibrated example. Again let the parameters $\beta, \sigma, \omega_w, \omega_p$, and θ_p take the values estimated by Rotemberg and Woodford (1997) and reported in Table 5.1,[65] and in the absence of any direct evidence I assume the same value for $\theta_w \phi^{-1}$ as for θ_p. I wish to let the assumed relative degree of wage as opposed to price stickiness vary between the two extremes of full wage flexibility and full price flexibility, but I assume a given degree of overall nominal rigidity by fixing the value of the slope coefficient κ in the generalized Phillips-curve relation described by equation (4.14) of Chapter 3. The value assumed for κ is again the one shown in Table 5.1. (Note that in the case of wage flexibility as assumed by Rotemberg and Woodford, the estimated coefficient κ corresponds to the κ of this model, rather than to κ_p.) This implies a fixed value for the sum $\xi_w^{-1} + \xi_p^{-1}$, shown in Table 6.4,[66] though I wish to vary the relative contributions of the two terms to this sum

---

64. Even when $x^* > 0$, one can show that this is the optimal policy from the "timeless perspective," which is explained further in Chapter 7.

65. Note that the parameter θ_p is referred to simply as θ in Table 5.1.

66. Note that the estimates of Amato and Laubach (2002), reported in Table 5.2, would instead imply a value of 32.4, or a slightly greater overall degree of nominal rigidity than is assumed here.

TABLE 6.4   Calibrated parameter values for the quarterly model used for Figure 6.4

Additional structural parameters		Shock process		Loss function	
θ_p	7.88	$\rho(\hat{w}^n)$	0.8	x^*	0
$\theta_w \phi_h^{-1}$	7.88	$sd(\hat{w}^n)$	1.67	λ_x	0.048
$\xi_w^{-1} + \xi_p^{-1}$	26.7				
κ	0.024				

(between $\xi_w^{-1} = 0$ and $\xi_p^{-1} = 0$ when wages and prices, respectively, are fully flexible). I parameterize my assumption about the relative degree of wage and price stickiness by the value of $\lambda_w = \xi_w^{-1}/(\xi_w^{-1} + \xi_p^{-1})$, which I allow to vary over the interval from zero to one. The assumed value of $\xi_w^{-1} + \xi_p^{-1}$ implies a value for λ_x that is independent of the choice of λ_w; once again this is the same as in Table 6.1.

The only exogenous disturbance that matters for the optimal state-contingent evolution of wages and prices is the natural-real-wage process $\hat{w}_t^n$. For the sake of illustration, I assume an AR(1) process with the properties listed in Table 6.4. (Note that once again the assumed variance of the disturbance has no effect on the results, other than to scale up the expected value of each term of the loss function equally.)

The solid line in Figure 6.4 then shows the minimum attainable value of $\hat{E}[L]$ associated with these parameter values for each possible value of λ_w. As in Figure 6.3, distortions can be reduced to zero only in the two extreme cases (here corresponding to full wage flexibility when $\lambda_w = 0$ and full price flexibility when $\lambda_w = 1$). The dashed line shows the expected discounted loss associated with a policy of complete stabilization of the rate of price inflation π_t; this policy is optimal only if $\lambda_w = 0$ (completely flexible wages) and grows worse the greater the relative stickiness of wages. The expected loss achievable by targeting a weighted average of wage and price inflation, when the weight ϕ is optimally chosen, is indicated by a dotted line. This coincides exactly with the solid line (indicating that the optimal policy belongs to this simple family) only at three points, when $\lambda_w = 0$, .48, or 1. (The intermediate special case is that in which $\lambda_w = (\sigma^{-1} + \omega_w)/(\sigma^{-1} + \omega)$, so that $\kappa_w = \kappa_p$.) However, the dotted line can barely be distinguished from the solid line over the entire interval; hence a well-chosen policy of this form offers a good approximation to optimal policy in all cases. The optimal choice of the weight ϕ is plotted as a function of λ_w in Figure 6.5. Note that it is monotonically decreasing: The optimal weight to put on price as opposed to wage inflation is lower the greater the relative stickiness of wages.

Once again, it is also found that output-gap targeting is a fairly robust policy that does not require knowledge of the exact degrees of wage and price stickiness. The expected losses associated with this policy are shown by

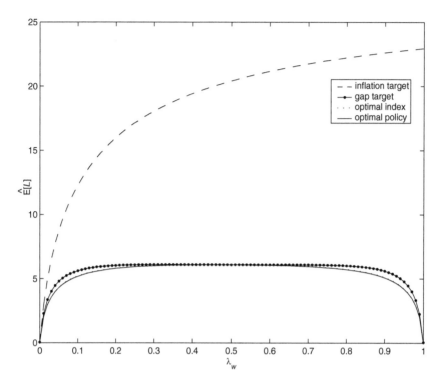

Figure 6.4   *Welfare losses under alternative policies with sticky wages and prices.*

the dotted solid line in Figure 6.4. Output-gap targeting is only fully optimal in the three special cases just mentioned, and otherwise it is also not as good as the best policy within the generalized inflation-targeting family. In fact, output-gap targeting is equivalent to a generalized inflation-targeting policy, corresponding to an index with $\phi = \lambda_p = 1 - \lambda_w$. But as shown in Figure 6.5, this choice of ϕ is not too different from the optimal one, regardless of the relative stickiness of wages and prices; this is exactly why output-gap targeting is a relatively robust policy prescription. Yet once again, this observation is only of practical importance if direct measures of the output gap in real time are fairly accurate. In practice, the best way to stabilize the output gap may well be to seek to stabilize an appropriate weighted average of wage and price inflation.

4.5   Time-Varying Tax Wedges or Markups

Finally, as discussed above, complete stabilization of inflation ceases to be optimal, even when this implies that aggregate output should perfectly track the equilibrium level of output under flexible wages and prices, if the gap

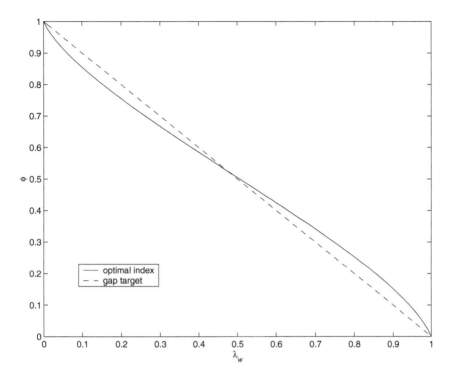

Figure 6.5 *The optimal index to stabilize as a function of the relative stickiness of wages and prices. The dotted line shows the generalized inflation-targeting rule that is equivalent to output-gap targeting.*

between this latter quantity and the *efficient* level of output is not a constant. In such a case, unlike those considered in the previous two subsections, there are time-varying distortions that do not result from delays in the adjustment of any kind of prices; thus there is no way of defining the price index to be stabilized that can make price stability an adequate proxy for welfare-maximizing policy. Hence the challenge to price stability as a goal of policy is strongest in this case.

For simplicity, assume again a model in which wages are flexible, all prices are equally sticky, and all real disturbances affect the demand for and production costs of all goods symmetrically, as in the models considered in Section 2. However, suppose as well that the relative price $p_t(i)/P_t$ at which the supplier of a differentiated good i would be willing to supply a quantity $y_t(i)$ of that good, under conditions of full price flexibility, is given by

$$\tilde{p}(y_t(i), Y_t; \tilde{\xi}_t, \mu_t) \equiv \mu_t \frac{\tilde{v}_y(y_t(i); \tilde{\xi}_t)}{\tilde{u}_c(Y_t; \tilde{\xi}_t)}, \tag{4.32}$$

where $\mu_t > 1$ is an exogenous time-varying markup factor. The term μ_t includes the distortions resulting from the market power of the supplier of each differentiated good and from the existence of distorting taxes on output, consumption, employment, or wage income. I allowed for these distortions earlier, but assumed them to be constant over time (and represented their composite effect by a *constant* factor $1/(1 - \Phi_y)$); I now allow them to vary over time, but assume that their variation is exogenous. The composite distortion μ_t can also include the effects of a wedge between the representative household's marginal rate of substitution between leisure (less supply of the labor used in producing good i) and consumption and the real wage demanded from producers of good i as a result of (possibly time-varying) market power in labor supply.

The flexible-price equilibrium level (or natural rate) of output for each good Y_t^n is then implicitly defined at each time by the relation

$$\tilde{p}\left(Y_t^n, Y_t^n; \tilde{\xi}_t, \mu_t\right) = 1, \tag{4.33}$$

and the time-varying efficient level of output Y_t^e is implicitly defined by the relation

$$\frac{\tilde{v}_y\left(Y_t^e; \tilde{\xi}_t\right)}{\tilde{u}_c\left(Y_t^e; \tilde{\xi}_t\right)} = 1. \tag{4.34}$$

Note that Y_t^e is a function solely of the exogenous disturbances to tastes, technology, and government purchases at date t, reflected by the vector $\tilde{\xi}_t$. The natural rate Y_t^n is also a function solely of exogenous disturbances at date t; but the exogenous disturbances that affect it include all of the various disturbances that affect the value of μ_t. These latter disturbances result in inefficient variations in the flexible-price equilibrium. In particular, log-linearizing both (4.33) and (4.34) and comparing terms, one finds that

$$\log Y_t^n = \log Y_t^e - \left(\omega + \sigma^{-1}\right)^{-1} \log \mu_t + \mathcal{O}\left(\|\Phi_y, \tilde{\xi}\|^2\right),$$

under the usual small-Φ_y approximation.

Repeating the derivation in Chapter 3 of the New Keynesian aggregate-supply relation, one finds that even with the above modification of assumed pricing behavior, a log-linear approximate aggregate-supply relation takes the form

$$\pi_t = \kappa\left(\hat{Y}_t - \hat{Y}_t^n\right) + \beta E_t \pi_{t+1}, \tag{4.35}$$

where $\hat{Y}_t^n$ refers to deviations from trend of the natural-rate concept defined in (4.33). On the other hand, repeating the derivations given in the proof of Proposition 6.4, one finds that, once again, discounted utility can be approximated by an expression of the form (2.21), where now the normalized quadratic loss function is given by

$$L_t = \pi_t^2 + \lambda\big(\log Y_t - \log Y_t^e\big)^2, \tag{4.36}$$

where Y_t^e is the efficient level of output defined by (4.34). Note that the derivation given in the proof of Proposition 6.4 applies without change to the model with time-varying tax wedges or markups, except for the fact that the definition of $\hat{Y}_t^n$ in terms of underlying disturbances has changed. (The correct welfare measure, expressed as a function of inflation, output, and exogenous disturbances, is unchanged.) The quantity x_t in (2.22) therefore corresponds not to $\log Y_t - \log Y_t^n$ in the current notation, but to $\log Y_t - (\log Y_t^n + (\omega + \sigma^{-1})^{-1}\hat{\mu}_t)$, or equivalently (to first order), to[67]

$$\log Y_t - \log Y_t^e + x^*. \tag{4.37}$$

Thus (4.36) is just expression (2.22) in terms of the new notation.

I find that the aggregate-supply relation and the welfare-theoretic loss function both take the same form as before, except that they now involve *different* output-gap concepts: It is $\log Y_t - \log Y_t^n$ that is relevant for measuring inflationary pressure in the AS relation, whereas it is $\log Y_t - \log Y_t^e$ that is relevant for the welfare evaluation of alternative equilibria. Here I follow a common practice in the literature on monetary policy evaluation and represent the existence of a time-varying gap between these two concepts by the addition of a stochastic residual term to the aggregate-supply relation, rather than a stochastic target term in the loss function. (See, e.g., Clarida et al., 1999.) Thus in the presence of inefficient shifts in the natural rate of output, I define the output gap x_t to refer to the welfare-relevant output gap, the target value of which is constant, that is, to expression (4.37). It then follows that (2.22) is once again the correct welfare-theoretic stabilization objective.

In terms of this new definition of the output gap, the aggregate supply relation (4.35) can alternatively be written

$$\pi_t = \kappa x_t + \beta E_t \pi_{t+1} + u_t, \tag{4.38}$$

where the residual term

$$u_t \equiv \frac{\kappa}{\omega + \sigma^{-1}}\hat{\mu}_t \tag{4.39}$$

---

67. Here I define $\hat{\mu}_t \equiv \log \mu_t - \log \bar{\mu}$, where $\log \bar{\mu} = \Phi_y + \mathcal{O}(\|\Phi_y\|^2)$.

is a composite exogenous disturbance that Clarida et al. (1999) refer to as a cost-push shock.[68] The appearance of the random term u_t in the relation (4.38) implies that it is no longer possible to simultaneously stabilize both inflation and the welfare-relevant output gap.

The trade-off that exists between these two stabilization goals in the presence of inefficient supply shocks can be illustrated, for a calibrated numerical example, using a figure of a kind popularized by Taylor (1979b). The coefficients β and κ of the AS relation are again calibrated as in Table 6.1; the exogenous disturbance u_t is assumed to be an AR(1) process with serial correlation $\rho_u = 0.8$ and an innovation variance of one.[69] (Once again, the assumed variance of the single disturbance is irrelevant for my conclusions, though it determines the scale of the axes in Figure 6.6.) I then compute the *efficient frontier* in $V[\pi] - V[x]$ space by computing the policy commitment that minimizes $\hat{E}[L]$ for arbitrary values of $\lambda > 0$ in the loss function (2.22). The values of $V[\pi]$ and $V[x]$ associated with each possible value of λ are then plotted as the lower of the two convex curves (i.e., the one closer to the origin) in Figure 6.6.[70] Point A (optimal policy when $\lambda = 0$) indicates how much variability of the output gap must be accepted in order to completely stabilize inflation, while point E (optimal policy when λ is unboundedly large) indicates how much variability of inflation must be accepted in order to completely stabilize the output gap. Points B, C, and D represent optimal policies for various finite, positive values of λ.

Since $\lambda > 0$ in the utility-based loss function, complete stabilization of inflation is seen not to be optimal. However, this does not mean that the optimal degree of variability in inflation need be very great. First of all, one observes from the figure that the efficient frontier is quite flat in the lower right region; thus it is possible to substantially reduce the variability of the output gap without too much variability of inflation being required. On the other hand, on the upper part of the frontier, where efficient policies

68. The terminology is not entirely satisfactory, however, as there is no necessary connection between shocks that affect inflation by increasing costs of production and time variation in the degree of inefficiency of the natural rate of output. Technology shocks, energy price shocks, or variations in labor supply may all shift the aggregate-supply curve in terms of the output relative to trend, without (to first order) changing the relation between inflation and the output gap as I have defined it.

69. To be more precise, it is assumed that a one-standard-deviation innovation in the cost-push shock raises the annualized inflation rate $4\pi_t$ by 1 percentage point. In Figure 6.6, $V[\pi]$ refers to the variability of the *annualized* inflation rate, and the units on both axes are percentage points squared.

70. The other curve shows the best possible combinations of $V[\pi]$ and $V[x]$ that are attainable using policies that are purely forward-looking in a sense defined in Chapter 7. The equilibria corresponding to points on this inner frontier represent the "optimal noninertial plan," also discussed in Chapter 7, for alternative assumed relative weights on inflation and output-gap stabilization.

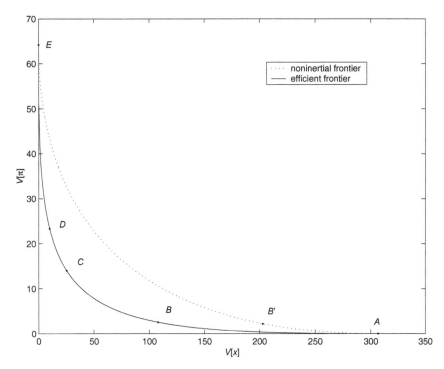

Figure 6.6 *The trade-off between inflation and output-gap stabilization in a model with inefficient supply shocks. The solid line shows the efficient frontier, while the dotted line corresponds to a class of rules that are efficient among purely forward-looking policies (see Chapter 7).*

involve substantial inflation variability, the frontier is quite steep. Thus policies on that part of the frontier would be optimal only if the relative weight λ on output-gap stabilization were quite large. Second, the value of λ that can be justified on welfare-theoretic grounds is likely to be quite small. As shown in Table 4.1, my calibrated parameter values imply a value of $\lambda = 0.05$. In Figure 6.6, the point on the efficient frontier that minimizes this weighted average of the two criteria (and hence that represents optimal policy) is point B. This policy involves quite a modest degree of inflation variability, relative, for example, to the inflation variability that would be required to fully stabilize the output gap.

The value of λ in the utility-based loss function is much smaller than the relative weight on output-gap stabilization that is often assumed in ad hoc policy objectives in the literature on monetary policy evaluation. A commonly assumed value would be $\lambda = 1$, which would correspond to point D in Figure 6.6. It can be seen that optimal policy involves much more stable inflation than would be chosen under an ad hoc criterion of that kind. As another example of a familiar policy recommendation, it has sometimes been proposed that given the existence of supply shocks, and hence a necessary tension between output stabilization and inflation stabilization, nominal GDP targeting would represent a reasonable balance between the two goals. In the present model, in the case that there are no fluctuations in Y_t^e (so that *all* variations in the output level consistent with price stability are inefficient, as arguments for nominal GDP targeting typically assume), nominal GDP targeting is a policy on the efficient frontier, as shown in Chapter 7.[71] However, for my calibrated parameter values, nominal GDP targeting would correspond to point C on the frontier, which still involves considerably more variation in inflation than an optimal policy under the utility-based criterion. Thus according to the utility-based analysis, the degree of departure from complete inflation stabilization that can be justified even in the case of inefficient supply shocks of significant magnitude is quite modest.

It should also be noted that the quantitative importance of shocks of this kind is far from clear. The literature on monetary policy evaluation has given considerable emphasis to the tension between the goals of inflation stabilization and output stabilization created by the existence of supply shocks. It is taken as well established that such shocks are an important factor in practical monetary policy. But the mere existence of supply shocks, in the sense of real disturbances that shift the short-run Phillips curve, does not imply the existence of *inefficient* supply shocks, the kind of shifts resulting from variation in Φ_t as opposed to the elements of $\tilde{\xi}_t$. As we have seen, the vector ξ_t includes a variety of types of real disturbances that are of clear importance in actual economies, and that can easily cause substantial fluctuations in the flexible-price equilibrium level of output; but in our model, these fluctuations are (to a first-order approximation) also shifts in the *efficient* level of output. While one can also think of possible sources of variation in the flexible-price equilibrium level of output that would clearly not be efficient, such as variations in tax distortions or in market power, such factors have not been clearly established as important sources of short-run fluctuations in economic activity. Thus while it is certainly possible that substantial disturbances of this kind occur, the matter is far from established.

I nonetheless give considerable attention in the next two chapters to the design of optimal policies in the case that inefficient supply shocks occur.

---

71. The policies on the efficient frontier correspond to complete stabilization of $\log P_t + \phi x_t$ for alternative values of $\phi > 0$. The value of λ required to make one of these policies optimal is $16\kappa\phi$. In the case that Y_t^e (and hence Y_t^n) is a constant, so that $x_t = \hat{Y}_t$, nominal GDP targeting represents the efficient policy corresponding to a weight $\lambda = 16\kappa$. In my calibrated example, this corresponds to $\lambda = 0.38$.

One reason for this is that, as explained in Chapter 8, I wish to choose policy rules that are robust to alternative beliefs about the nature of the real disturbances to the economy—for example, to alternative beliefs about how frequently particular types of shocks occur. Thus I wish to consider the *possibility* of inefficient supply shocks and to choose policy rules that would be optimal *whether or not* disturbances of this kind are a significant source of macroeconomic instability in a given economy. In order to undertake this challenge, I must consider what optimal policy would seek to achieve in the case that such shocks occur.

5   The Case of Larger Distortions

I turn now to a brief discussion of the extent to which the previous analysis must be modified if one is not willing to assume that the degree of inefficiency of the flexible-wage and -price equilibrium in the absence of shocks is minimal, and hence is not content with a small-Φ_y approximation. Benigno and Woodford (2003) show that it is possible even in this case to derive a quadratic approximation to expected utility with the property that a correct log-linear approximation to optimal policy can be derived by minimizing the quadratic loss function subject to the constraints implied by a log-linear approximation to the model structural equations. However, the derivation of the quadratic loss function in this case requires an additional step.

Consider again the basic one-sector cashless-economy model, with flexible wages and Calvo pricing, as in Section 2. As before, one may compute a Taylor-series expansion for the utility flow U_t in a given period, expanding around the allocation associated with the zero-inflation steady state, that is, the allocation in which $y_t(i) = \bar{Y}$ for each good i. Even though this level of output is no longer assumed to be near the efficient level, it is desirable to compute the local approximations to both the structural equations and the welfare measure around this equilibrium, as optimal policy is found to require an equilibrium near it.

Following the same steps as in the proof of Proposition 6.1 yields

$$U_t = -\frac{\bar{Y}u_c}{2}\left\{\left[\sigma^{-1}+\omega-\Phi_y(1+\omega)\right]\hat{Y}_t^2 + 2\left[\Phi_y+\sigma^{-1}g_t+(1-\Phi_y)\omega q_t\right]\hat{Y}_t\right.$$

$$\left.+(1-\Phi_y)(\theta^{-1}+\omega)\operatorname{var}_i\hat{y}_t(i)\right\} + \text{t.i.p.} + \mathcal{O}\left(\|\hat{y},\tilde{\xi}\|^3\right), \tag{5.1}$$

where Φ_y is no longer an expansion parameter. In the small-Φ_y case, I was able to make the substitutions

$$\left[\sigma^{-1}+\omega-\Phi_y(1+\omega)\right] = \left(\sigma^{-1}+\omega\right) + \mathcal{O}(\Phi_y),$$

$$\left[\Phi_y+\sigma^{-1}g_t+(1-\Phi_y)\omega q_t\right] = \left(\sigma^{-1}+\omega\right)\left(x^*+\hat{Y}_t^n\right) + \mathcal{O}\left(\|\Phi_y,\tilde{\xi})\|^2\right),$$

and reduce (5.1) to (2.10). I now wish to avoid this simplification, in order to consider the consequences of a larger value of $\Phi_y > 0$. (Note, however, that necessarily $\Phi_y < 1$, no matter how large market power and tax distortions may be.) Instead, Proposition 6.3 can be used together with (5.1) to establish the following generalization of Proposition 6.4.

PROPOSITION 6.14. In the case of the New Keynesian model of Chapter 3 (in which I no longer assume that Φ_y is necessarily small), the discounted sum of utility of the representative household can be approximated by

$$\sum_{t=0}^{\infty} \beta^t U_t = -\Omega \sum_{t=0}^{\infty} \beta^t L_t + \text{t.i.p.} + \mathcal{O}\left(\|\Delta_{-1}^{1/2}, \varphi, \tilde{\xi}\|^3\right), \qquad (5.2)$$

where again $\Omega > 0$, and the normalized quadratic loss function is given by

$$L_t = \pi_t^2 + \lambda_{yy} \hat{Y}_t^2 - 2\gamma_t \hat{Y}_t, \qquad (5.3)$$

where

$$\lambda_{yy} = \frac{\kappa}{\theta} \frac{\omega + \sigma^{-1} - \Phi_y(1+\omega)}{(1-\Phi_y)(\omega + \sigma^{-1})},$$

$$\gamma_t = \frac{\kappa}{\theta} \frac{\Phi_y + \sigma^{-1} g_t + (1-\Phi_y)\omega q_t}{(1-\Phi_y)(\omega + \sigma^{-1})}.$$

Except in the case of very large Φ_y, I again find that $\lambda_{yy} > 0$, and in this case the loss function can again be written (neglecting a term independent of policy) in the form

$$L_t = \pi_t^2 + \lambda_{yy} \left(\hat{Y}_t - \tilde{Y}_t - g^*\right)^2,$$

where $\tilde{Y}_t$ is a mean-zero exogenous term and g^* a positive constant (increasing in Φ_y). I thus obtain once again a quadratic stabilization objective in terms of the inflation rate and an output gap $\hat{Y}_t - \tilde{Y}_t$. However, this approximate welfare measure does not have the properties that are required, following the discussion in Section 1, to allow me to compute an accurate log-linear characterization of optimal policy using only a log-linear approximation to the structural equations of the model. For the fact that $g^* > 0$ means that second-order terms in the solution for $\hat{Y}_t$ under a given policy make a second-order contribution to the evaluation of this loss function.

It is nonetheless possible to obtain a quadratic loss function of the desired form by using a quadratic approximation to the structural equations to substitute a quadratic expression with zero linear terms for the term linear in $\hat{Y}_t$ in (5.3). While this requires computing quadratic (rather than merely log-linear) approximations to at least some of the structural equations, the quadratic approximation is required only at the stage of the derivation of a welfare-theoretic objective for stabilization policy. One does *not* need to use the quadratic approximation to the structural equations to compute a second-order approximation to equilibrium under each of the policies that one may wish to compare in order to obtain a welfare ranking of policies that is accurate to second order. The reason that it is possible to eliminate these linear terms was pointed out in Section 3.2, when I forward integrated the (log-linearized) AS relation to obtain (3.4), and used this to eliminate the linear terms in output from the discounted-loss criterion. In that section, because I was content with a small-Φ_y approximation and $g^* = \mathcal{O}(\Phi_y)$, a log-linear approximation to the AS relation sufficed to substitute for the linear terms in output. However, when Φ_y is not assumed to be small, one must take account of quadratic terms in the AS relation as well. But the additional terms add additional quadratic terms to the approximate welfare measure, not any additional linear terms. Hence, as shown earlier, one is able to eliminate all linear terms except a term linear in the initial inflation rate, which has no effect on the characterization of optimal policy in the long run (or optimal policy from the timeless perspective discussed in Chapter 7).

To simplify the discussion of the second-order terms in the aggregate-supply relation, here I restrict attention to the "isoelastic" case of preferences and technology of the following special forms.

ASSUMPTION 6.2. Preferences and technology are given by

$$u(C_t; \xi_t) = (1 - \tilde{\sigma})^{-1} \bar{C}_t^{\tilde{\sigma}} C_t^{1-\tilde{\sigma}}, \qquad v(h_t(j); \xi_t) = \lambda \bar{h}_t^{-\nu} h_t(j)^{1+\nu},$$

$$f(h_t(j)) = h_t(j)^{1/\phi_h},$$

for some constants $\lambda, \tilde{\sigma}, \nu > 0$, $\phi_h > 1$, and stationary exogenous disturbance processes $\{\bar{C}_t, \bar{h}_t\}$.

Benigno and Woodford (2003) show that in this case,[72] a quadratic approximation to the aggregate supply relation of the basic New Keynesian model can be forward integrated to yield

---

72. Benigno and Woodford derive a more general version of this result, applicable to general twice-differentiable functions satisfying only the standard neoclassical restrictions.

$$\pi_0 + Q_0 = \kappa E_0 \left\{ \sum_{t=0}^{\infty} \beta^t \left(\hat{Y}_t - \hat{Y}_t^n \right) \right\} + \frac{\mu_y}{2} E_0 \left\{ \sum_{t=0}^{\infty} \beta^t \hat{Y}_t^2 \right\} - E_0 \left\{ \sum_{t=0}^{\infty} \beta^t \delta_t \hat{Y}_t \right\}$$

$$+ \frac{\mu_\pi}{2} E_0 \left\{ \sum_{t=0}^{\infty} \beta^t \pi_t^2 \right\} + \text{t.i.p.} + \mathcal{O}\big(\|\Delta_{-1}^{1/2}, \varphi, \tilde{\xi}\|^3\big), \tag{5.4}$$

generalizing (3.4). Here Q_0 is a quadratic function (equal to zero to first order) of period-zero state variables, and of period-zero conditional expectations of the future paths of the state variables; δ_t is a composite exogenous disturbance term with mean zero. The coefficients μ_y, μ_π are certain functions of the model parameters. Note that only the first terms on the left- and right-hand sides, respectively, are of first order, and that the t.i.p. contains only second-order terms, so that one easily verifies that to first order, (5.4) reduces to (3.4).

Using this relation to eliminate the discounted sum of $E_0 \hat{Y}_t$ terms from the evaluation of (5.2), I can obtain an alternative quadratic approximation to expected utility.

PROPOSITION 6.15. Suppose that in the New Keynesian model of Chapter 3, preferences and technology satisfy Assumption 6.2. Then regardless of the size of Φ_y, one can approximate the expected value of the discounted utility of the representative household by

$$\sum_{t=0}^{\infty} \beta^t U_t = W_0 - \tilde{\Omega} \sum_{t=0}^{\infty} \beta^t \tilde{L}_t + \text{t.i.p.} + \mathcal{O}\big(\|\Delta_{-1}^{1/2}, \varphi, \tilde{\xi}\|^3\big), \tag{5.5}$$

where the term W_0 depends only on a transitory, deterministic component of policy, the coefficient $\tilde{\Omega} > 0$, and the normalized quadratic loss function is given by

$$L_t = \pi_t^2 + \tilde{\lambda} \big(\hat{Y}_t - \hat{Y}_t^* \big)^2, \tag{5.6}$$

where

$$\tilde{\lambda} = \frac{\kappa}{\theta} \left(1 - \frac{\Phi_y \left(s_C^{-1} - 1 \right)}{\omega + \sigma^{-1} + \Phi_y \left(1 - \sigma^{-1} \right)} \frac{\sigma^{-1}}{\omega + \sigma^{-1}} \right) \tag{5.7}$$

and

$$\hat{Y}_t^* = \omega_1 \hat{Y}_t^n - \omega_2 \hat{G}_t + \omega_3 \hat{\mu}_t, \tag{5.8}$$

with

$$\omega_1 = \frac{\kappa}{\tilde{\lambda}\theta},$$

$$\omega_2 = \frac{\Phi_y s_C^{-1} \sigma^{-1}}{\left(\omega + \sigma^{-1}\right)^2 + \Phi_y \left[\left(1 - \sigma^{-1}\right)\left(\omega + \sigma^{-1}\right) - \left(s_C^{-1} - 1\right)\sigma^{-1}\right]},$$

$$\omega_3 = \frac{1 - \Phi_y}{\left(\omega + \sigma^{-1}\right) + \Phi_y \left[\left(1 - \sigma^{-1}\right) - \left(s_C^{-1} - 1\right)\sigma^{-1}\left(\omega + \sigma^{-1}\right)^{-1}\right]}.$$

Here $\hat{Y}_t^n$ refers to variation in the flexible-price equilibrium level of output, and $\hat{\mu}_t$ to variation in a markup factor due either to a time-varying wage markup owing to the market power of wagesetters, a time-varying tax on wage income, or a time-varying sales tax.[73]

Details of the derivation are given in Benigno and Woodford (2003).

This alternative quadratic approximation to expected utility is more complex, owing to the presence of the term W_0, which is equal to a quadratic function of π_0 plus a term proportional to $\pi_0 Z_0$, where the variable Z_0 is defined as

$$Z_0 = E_0 \left\{ \sum_{t=0}^{\infty} (\alpha\beta)^t \hat{Y}_t + \psi \pi_{t+1} \right\}$$

for a certain coefficient ψ, and a term proportional to $\pi_0 e_0$, where e_0 is a composite exogenous disturbance term. The term W_0 is not independent of policy, as it depends on the values of both π_0 and Z_0, which are endogenous. However, both π_0 and Z_0 depend only on the *deterministic component* of policy, that is, on the conditional expectations of the inflation and output as of date zero, and not on the planned responses to unexpected shocks. Furthermore, W_0 depends on the conditional expectations of inflation and output at future dates t only with weights that die out at a rate *faster* than β^t; hence the contribution of the W_0 term to the loss function becomes negligible, even in judging the optimality of the deterministic component, when policy sufficiently far in the future is considered. This is what is meant by saying that W_0 "depends only on a transitory, deterministic component of policy."

In Chapter 7, I argue that it is appropriate to judge proposed policy rules according to the optimality of (i) the long-run average values of inflation

---

73. The type of sales tax referred to here is one that, like American sales taxes, is paid in addition to the (sticky) posted price of goods. The results are slightly different in the case of a European-style value-added tax, which rate is included in the posted price of goods, if it is the price inclusive of tax that is sticky. See Benigno and Woodford (2003) for treatment of the other case as well.

and output that they imply, and (ii) the equilibrium responses to shocks that they imply. (I refer to this criterion as judging the optimality of policy "from a timeless perspective.") In evaluating policies from this point of view, it does not matter whether the objective function contains a transitory, deterministic term such as W_0 or not. Hence Proposition 6.15 once again justifies judging alternative policy rules using a discounted quadratic criterion of the form

$$E_0 \left\{ \sum_{t=0}^{\infty} \beta^t \left[\pi_t^2 + \tilde{\lambda} x_t^2 \right] \right\}, \tag{5.9}$$

if the welfare-relevant output gap is now defined as $x_t \equiv \hat{Y}_t - \hat{Y}_t^*$, where $\hat{Y}_t^*$ is given by (5.8). The output gap is once again the discrepancy between actual log real GDP and an ideal value that depends on the exogenous disturbances; but the ideal value no longer corresponds, in general, to the flexible-price equilibrium level of output $\hat{Y}_t^n$.

One important implication of this can already be noted (though I discuss it further in the next chapter): Even when the distortions measured by Φ_y are substantial in magnitude, the *optimal long-run inflation rate is zero*. For even when Φ_y is not assumed to be small, I can express the quadratic welfare measure (up to a transitory term) in the form (5.9). Moreover, the two objectives indicated by this loss function (keeping the inflation rate near zero and keeping the output gap near zero) are *both* consistent with an inflation rate that is zero on average, since $\hat{Y}_t^*$ is not different *on average* from $\hat{Y}_t^n$, the equilibrium level of output under a policy of price stability. Hence the conclusion obtained earlier under the assumption that $\Phi_y = 0$, and then again under the assumption that Φ_y was small enough to be treated as an expansion parameter, is in fact true regardless of the size of Φ_y.

Allowing for nontrivial steady-state distortions does, however, complicate my previous conclusions as to the optimality of complete stability in the face of exogenous disturbances. To address this question, I must consider the trade-off between the inflation-stabilization and output-gap-stabilization objectives represented by the two terms of (5.6). The relative weight on the output-gap-stabilization objective, $\tilde{\lambda}$, is positive as long as

$$\frac{\Phi_y \left(s_C^{-1} - 1 \right) \sigma^{-1}}{\omega + \sigma^{-1}} < \omega + \left(1 - \Phi_y \right) \sigma^{-1} + \Phi_y. \tag{5.10}$$

Note that this condition necessarily holds for all Φ_y small enough, and also for all values of s_C close enough to one (i.e., for all values of $\bar{G}/\bar{Y}$ small enough). I restrict attention to this case. Given (5.10), one can also conclude that $\omega_1 \geq 1$, and that $\omega_j > 0$ for $j = 2, 3$, for any $0 < \Phi_y < 1$.

It is possible to rewrite the aggregate-supply relation (4.35) in terms of the welfare-relevant output gap. In this case I again obtain a relation of the form (4.38), where the residual term (the cost-push shock) is given by

$$u_t = \kappa(\omega_1 - 1)\hat{Y}_t^n - \kappa\omega_2\hat{G}_t + \kappa\omega_3\hat{\mu}_t. \qquad (5.11)$$

When $\Phi_y = 0$, $\omega_1 = 1$, and $\omega_2 = 0$, while

$$\omega_3 = \left(\omega + \sigma^{-1}\right)^{-1},$$

so that the cost-push term is again given by (4.39). However, when $\Phi_y > 0$, one can have a nonzero cost-push term even in the absence of variations in tax wedges or markups.

Another case in which one obtains a relatively simple conclusion is that in which $\bar{G} = 0$, so that in steady state, there are no government purchases (though one may consider transitory fluctuations in the value of government purchases around this value). In this case, $\omega_1 = 1$, and so (5.11) reduces to

$$u_t = -\kappa\omega_2\,\hat{G}_t + \kappa\omega_3\hat{\mu}_t.$$

In this case, none of the real disturbances that have been considered thus far give rise to a cost-push term (other than the tax wedges or markups), *except* variations in government purchases. An increase in government purchases causes a negative cost-push shock, meaning that inflation must fall if there is not to be an increase in the welfare-relevant output gap.[74]

This is the case considered by Khan et al. (2002), who compute a log-linear approximation to optimal policy (using a method different from this one, and for a slightly different model[75]). They find, numerically, that the optimal response to a technology shock involves complete stabilization of the price level, while output responds exactly as it would in an equilibrium with flexible prices (i.e., according to the prediction of a RBC model). This

---

74. Note that the effects of variations in government purchases are not equivalent to those of variations in the preference parameter $\bar{C}_t$. The reason is that in the case of the isoelastic preference specification described in Assumption 6.2, one disturbance represents an additive shift in the relationship between aggregate demand Y_t and the marginal utility of income, whereas the other represents a multiplicative shift. The difference does not matter for a log-linear approximation to this relationship, which is all that one needs to derive the log-linear aggregate-supply relation. But the difference does matter for the quadratic approximation that is required for the evaluation of welfare when Φ_y is of nonnegligible magnitude.

75. Their model assumes staggered prices, but with a distribution of random intervals between price changes that differs from the exponential distribution of the Calvo model. I refer to their results for the version of their model that abstracts from monetary frictions, as I do here.

is the conclusion that I would also obtain as a result of Proposition 6.15. Such
a disturbance creates no cost-push term, so that it is possible to fully stabilize
all terms in the quadratic objective function (5.9) by completely stabilizing
inflation and the welfare-relevant output gap. They also find that the optimal response to an increase in government purchases involves a temporary
reduction in inflation below its steady-state level, together with a greater
contraction of private consumption (and a smaller increase in output) than
would occur in the flexible-price equilibrium or would result from a monetary policy that completely stabilized inflation. This also corresponds with
my analytical results here. A negative cost-push shock means that it is not
possible to maintain $\hat{Y}_t$ equal to $\hat{Y}_t^*$ without deflation (as $\hat{Y}_t^*$ rises less than
does the natural rate $\hat{Y}_t^n$). The optimal trade-off involves accepting some
deflation, though not as much as would be required to maintain $\hat{Y}_t$ equal
to $\hat{Y}_t^*$; this involves output temporarily lower than the natural rate, though
higher than $\hat{Y}_t^*$.[76] We thus obtain yet another case in which complete price
stability is not optimal.

In the case that $\bar{G} > 0$, moreover, $\omega_1 > 1$, and the expression for u_t is
no longer so simple. *Any* of the real disturbances that affect the natural rate
of output—variations in impatience to consume, variations in preferences
affecting labor supply, technology shocks, or government purchases—in
general have a nonzero effect on the u_t term, as these disturbances do
not shift $\hat{Y}_t^*$ and $\hat{Y}_t^n$ by identical amounts. The same is usually true, as
Benigno and Woodford show, once one leaves the special isoelastic case
defined in Assumption 6.2.[77] Hence it is quite likely that nontrivial variations
in the cost-push disturbance term must be included in a realistic model.
Accordingly, I give considerable attention in the remainder of this volume to
the problem of conducting monetary policy so as to minimize a discounted-
loss criterion of the form (5.9) subject to a constraint of the form (4.38).

Here it is worth mentioning one important conclusion from that analysis:
The optimal long-run inflation target is zero in this model, *no matter how large*
the steady-state distortions may be. In Section 3.2, I argued that the optimal
long-run inflation target continued to be zero even when $\Phi_y > 0$, despite
the existence of an upward-sloping long-run Phillips-curve trade-off, in the
case that Φ_y was not too large (so that a small-Φ_y expansion represented an
acceptable approximation). The argument there turned on the fact that it

---

76. The algebraic characterization of the optimal dynamic responses to such a disturbance
is given in Chapter 7, Section 2.1.

77. In fact, the reason that it matters whether $\bar{G} > 0$ in the case considered here is that
when $\bar{G} > 0$, the relation between aggregate demand and the marginal utility of income ceases
to be of the isoelastic form, $\lambda_t = (Y_t/\bar{C}_t)^{1-\tilde{\sigma}}$. Similar results are obtained with regard, say, to
the effects of a technology shock on the cost-push term if the relation is nonisoelastic for some
other reason.

was possible to use the aggregate-supply relation to substitute for the linear output-gap terms in the discounted-loss function, leaving a quadratic approximation to welfare with no linear terms other than transitory ones (a term linear in π_0). This relied upon an approximation to the aggregate-supply relation that was accurate only to first order, so that it sufficed to evaluate welfare to second order only in the small-Φ_y approximation. But now we see that a second-order approximation to the aggregate-supply relation can be used to derive a quadratic approximation to welfare with no linear terms other than transitory ones, even when Φ_y is large. Hence one continues to find that the optimal long-run inflation target is zero, regardless of the size of Φ_y.[78]

---

78. In Section 1 of Chapter 7, I show how to explicitly analyze the optimal path of inflation in the presence of a transitory motive for nonzero inflation, and verify that the optimal path converges to zero asymptotically in models of the kind discussed informally here. I also argue that in such cases it is reasonable to judge a policy rule to be optimal that involves a zero average inflation rate.

Gains from Commitment to a Policy Rule

I now turn to the characterization of optimal policy in the (realistic) case that not all of the stabilization objectives discussed in the previous chapter can be achieved simultaneously, so that it is not possible to fully eliminate all of the distortions that can be affected by monetary policy. It is in this case that the problem of optimal monetary policy becomes nontrivial, in that the character of the optimal equilibrium cannot be read directly from the nature of the loss function derived earlier. In this chapter I discuss how the constrained-optimal equilibrium pattern of responses to disturbances can be characterized in such a case and consider in general terms the problem of the choice of a policy rule intended to bring about the desired equilibrium.

The idea that it should be necessary to compromise among several stabilization goals, each desirable in itself but not mutually attainable in an absolute sense, is likely to be intuitive to most practical policymakers. It may be less obvious that it is desirable to attempt to characterize the optimal compromise among these objectives in terms of a *rule* for the systematic conduct of policy. One might think that it should suffice to clarify the proper *goals* of policy, on the one hand, and to develop a reliable quantitative model of the *effects* of alternative policy actions, on the other, and then simply to charge the central bank with the pursuit of the appropriate goals using an appropriate model to inform its decisions. Economists are often willing to suppose that households and firms do a fairly good job of pursuing their objectives without external guidance, even when the optimization problems that they face are quite complex. Why not similarly trust that central bankers can be relied upon to behave in something close to an optimal fashion once their objectives and constraints have been made clear?

But the reason that rules are important in monetary policy is not that central bankers cannot be relied upon to pursue the public interest or that their highly trained staffs cannot be expected to bring the latest knowledge to bear upon the analysis of the likely effects of alternative policies. It is rather that the central bank's stabilization goals can be most effectively achieved only to the extent that the central bank not only acts appropriately, but is also *understood* by the private sector to predictably act in a certain way. The ability to successfully steer private-sector expectations is favored by a decision procedure that is based on a rule, since in this case the systematic character of the central bank's actions can be most easily made apparent to the public.

Of course, one might imagine that market participants could become accurate predictors of central-bank behavior without any articulation by the central bank of the principles of its behavior, just as they predict the behavior of firms that do not commit themselves to rules of conduct. Yet while expertise of this kind certainly exists, the degree to which central-bank behavior can be confidently predicted simply through extrapolation from past actions is limited. The membership of monetary policy committees changes fairly often (and invites speculation about the consequences for future decisions), and new circumstances constantly arise that are not too closely analogous to others confronted by the central bank in the recent past. Articulation by the central bank of a rule that guides its decision process (and commitment by the bank to actually follow it!) can greatly improve the predictability of policy by the private sector, even when the rule is less explicit than a mechanical formula that yields an unambiguous prescription on the basis of publicly available data.

Moreover, an optimal pattern of conduct by the central bank does *not* generally correspond to what would result from *discretionary optimization,* as first stressed by Prescott (1977) and Kydland and Prescott (1977, 1980). By discretionary optimization I mean a procedure under which at each time that an action is to be taken, the central bank evaluates the economy's current state and hence its possible future paths from now on, and chooses the optimal current action in the light of this analysis, with no advance commitment about future actions, except that they will similarly be the ones that seem best in whatever state may be reached in the future. This might seem an eminently sensible procedure. It allows the bank to make use of all of its detailed knowledge about current conditions, rather than having to classify the current state as one of the coarsely described possible future states considered at some earlier time. It also avoids the necessity of making an explicit decision about anything other than the action that must currently be taken (although a view about likely future policy is implicit in the evaluation of alternative possible current actions). Moreover, it might seem to involve no loss of efficiency relative to a once-and-for-all optimal plan, insofar as a large literature on dynamic programming and optimal control has stressed the usefulness of recursive methods for the solution of dynamic-optimization problems. Under these methods, a dynamic problem is broken into a sequence of individual decision problems, in which the optimal action at each stage is chosen given the state at that time, taking as given the nature of optimizing behavior at stages yet to be reached.

But as Kydland and Prescott showed, these methods are appropriate only for the optimal control of a system that evolves mechanically as a function of its past state, exogenous disturbances, and the current action of the controller. They are not appropriate for the optimal control of a *forward-looking* system, in which people's expectations about future policy are one of the determinants of current outcomes. This is because a dynamic-programming approach considers the optimal action at a given point in time considering only the discounted current and future losses associated with alternative feasible continuation paths, given the system's current state. It thus neglects any effects of the *anticipation* at earlier dates of a different current action than the one that would be judged best by a discretionary optimizer. By credibly committing itself in advance to behave differently, a central bank can steer expectations in a way that furthers its stabilization goals.

It follows, once again, that successful management of expectations is unlikely to be possible except through commitment of the central bank to a fairly explicit rule for the determination of its appropriate action at any point in time. For conscious guidance by a rule is not only an aid to the private sector's understanding of policy; it also makes it more likely that the central bank itself will act correctly. Further, the temptation to behave in a discretionary fashion must be resisted; optimal policy requires that most of the time the central bank does *not* set interest rates at the level that would be optimal from the point of view of its stabilization objectives, taking as given past and future policy, as well as past, present, and future private-sector policy *expectations*.[1] This means that good will and a sound understanding of the effects of alternative policy actions and of the economic welfare associated with alternative possible paths for the economy are not enough. There must be a conscious commitment to a criterion for action that is counterintuitive for a discretionary policymaker, but that actually serves (and can be understood to serve) the bank's goals if pursued in a predictable way.

The importance of creating the right sort of expectations regarding future policy has another important lesson, of a somewhat subtler character, for the way that policy should be conducted: An optimal decision procedure is generally not *purely forward looking*, in the sense of allowing the proper current action to be determined solely from an analysis of the set of possible future paths for the economy given its current state. The point seems to be contrary to the intuition even of many who recognize the importance of commitment to a rule in order to avoid the dangers of discretionary

---

1. In the thought experiment proposed here, it is assumed that the private sector's current and future expectations about future policy are and will be correct, but that the current action need not be chosen in a way consistent with past expectations regarding this decision.

policy. Indeed, many popular current proposals for policy rules are purely forward looking in character. For example, inflation-forecast targeting as currently practiced at the Bank of England (see, e.g., the description in Vickers, 1998), or as described in the early analytical literature (e.g., Svensson 1997a, 1999a; Leitemo, 2000), selects a current interest-rate target on the basis of the conformity of projections of the economy's future evolution under that policy choice with a criterion that is purely forward looking (e.g., that RPIX inflation be predicted to equal 2.5 percent per year at a horizon 2 years in the future). Similarly, Taylor's classic formulation (Taylor, 1993) of his policy rule prescribes a reaction to current inflation and output-gap estimates that is independent of both past aggregate conditions and past monetary policy.[2] Moreover, in discussions elsewhere (e.g., Taylor, 1999b), Taylor stresses the desirability of immediately adjusting the federal funds rate target to changing aggregate conditions, without any of the partial-adjustment dynamics typically indicated by estimated Fed reaction functions, such as those described in Section 4.1 of Chapter 1.

The intuition of the proponents of purely forward-looking approaches, presumably, is that it is not desirable for policy to depend on "irrelevant" state variables, that is, on something that affects neither the set of possible future paths for the central bank's target variables nor the proper ranking of alternative paths. Yet such an argument would be incorrect, for the same reason that dynamic programming does not yield a truly optimal policy, as just discussed. Optimal policy must take account of the advantages of anticipating the policy at earlier dates; and for this reason it must generally be *history dependent* rather than purely forward looking. Past conditions should be taken into account in choosing the current policy setting, because it is desirable that people be able, at the earlier time, to count on the fact that the central bank will subsequently do so.

I begin this discussion of the advantages of policy commitment with a review in Section 1 of the most well-known disadvantage of discretionary policy, namely, the "inflation bias" stressed by Kydland and Prescott (1977) and Barro and Gordon (1983). This issue is one that can be treated in a purely deterministic analysis, and I consider the question first in such a setting. Once I allow in Section 2 for random disturbances, the bias in the long-run average inflation rate continues to exist, but there is a further problem

2. In the empirical implementation of the rule (Taylor 1993, 1999c), Taylor uses the cumulative increase in the log of the GDP deflator over the previous four quarters as his proposed measure of current inflation. This might appear to imply that Taylor's rule is somewhat history dependent, unlike the purely contemporaneous Taylor rules analyzed in much of the subsequent theoretical literature. However, it appears from Taylor's discussion of the logic of his proposal that the use of a measure of inflation over a year-long period should be understood as a simple attempt to estimate the current value of a target variable that is only imperfectly measured by higher-frequency data, rather than genuine advocacy of history-dependent policy.

with discretionary policy as well: suboptimal equilibrium responses to un-expected shocks. Unlike the inflation bias, the distortion of the response to shocks cannot generally be cured by any purely forward-looking policy. It is the emphasis on the inflation bias in many discussions of the disadvantages of discretionary policy that probably accounts for the widespread assumption that the advantages of commitment can be obtained within a decision framework that remains purely forward looking.

I then consider the problem of implementation of the desired equilibrium responses to disturbances through commitment of the central bank to an appropriate policy rule. A mere characterization of the desired state-contingent evolution of the economy does not suffice as a policy prescription, for a number of reasons outlined in Section 3. One of the simplest of these is that a specification of the future evolution of policy (say, a specification of the future path of overnight interest rates, to be concrete) that allows for enough contingencies to represent a desirable policy is too complex to actually write out in advance.

Instead, there are a variety of ways in which one may specify a *decision procedure* for the central bank that suffices (in the context of an evaluation of current conditions and possible future paths for the economy) to determine a policy action at each date, and such that an understanding that the central bank will follow the procedure determines a rational-expectations equilibrium in which the economy's state-contingent evolution is of the desired sort. I compare several alternatives in Sections 4 and 5, and argue in Section 5 for the particular desirability of a conception of rule-based policymaking under which the central bank seeks in each decision cycle to determine the current interest-rate operating target that is consistent with a projection of the economy's subsequent path that satisfies a "target criterion." Decision procedures of this kind are similar in form to the inflation-forecast targeting currently practiced at the Bank of England and a number of other central banks. But the content of the target criterion is likely to be somewhat different under an optimal rule than under current U.K. practice; in particular, an optimal criterion will be history dependent, as I illustrate here through a simple example.

1 The Optimal Long-Run Inflation Target

I begin this discussion of methods that can be used to characterize the economy's optimal evolution by considering the optimal rate of inflation in a purely deterministic setting. This problem is nontrivial when, for one of the reasons discussed in Section 3.3 of Chapter 6, it is not possible to simultaneously eliminate all of the distortions that are affected by monetary policy; and the problem provides a simple first setting in which to analyze the distortions resulting from discretionary policy. As it turns out, in the context of the linear-quadratic policy problems that are mainly studied in what follows, the optimal long-run average rate of inflation in the presence of random disturbances continues to be the same one as in the deterministic analysis presented here; this is a consequence of the familiar *certainty-equivalence* principle for such problems. Hence the characterization here of the optimal rate of inflation also applies to the stochastic settings considered in Section 2.

1.1 The Inflationary Bias of Discretionary Policy

Consider once again the basic neo-Wicksellian model of Chapter 4—a purely cashless economy with exogenous capital, flexible wages (and/or efficient labor contracting), and Calvo-style staggered pricing in goods markets—and suppose that there are no real disturbances ($\tilde{\xi}_t = 0$ for all t). Alternative possible perfect-foresight equilibrium paths for inflation and output must satisfy the "New Keynesian" aggregate-supply relation

$$\pi_t = \kappa x_t + \beta \pi_{t+1} \tag{1.1}$$

for all dates $t \geq 0$, where π_t is the rate of inflation, x_t is the output gap (here equivalent simply to detrended output), and the coefficients satisfy $\kappa > 0$, $0 < \beta < 1$. This is of course only a log-linear approximation to the exact relation derived in Section 2 of Chapter 3, valid for the characterization of possible equilibrium paths in which inflation is always near zero. But as we shall see, it is optimal in the present case for inflation to equal exactly zero, so that a comparison of paths in the neighborhood of this particular steady state suffices for a valid characterization of the optimal rate of inflation.

Equilibrium paths must also satisfy another restriction, the intertemporal Euler equation (or IS relation) that relates interest rates to the timing of expenditure. However, in the present case, the optimal paths of inflation and output can be determined without reference to that constraint, which simply determines the path of interest rates associated with any given equilibrium path for inflation and output. One does need to verify that the implied path for nominal interest rates is always nonnegative; but we shall see that in the present case, this is true for both the optimal commitment and the equilibrium resulting from discretionary optimization.

I have shown in Chapter 6 that a quadratic approximation to the utility of the representative household in this model is a decreasing function of

$$\sum_{t=0}^{\infty} \beta^t \left[\pi_t^2 + \lambda \left(x_t - x^* \right)^2 \right], \tag{1.2}$$

where $\lambda > 0$, $x^* \geq 0$ are functions of model parameters discussed in that chapter.[3] As discussed in Section 1 of Chapter 6, a log-linear approximation to the model structural equations suffices for a correct linear approximation to optimal policy only in the case that x^* is small enough. Specifically, since in the present case there are no random disturbances, the solution for the optimal paths for inflation and output obtained by minimizing (1.2) subject to the constraint that (1.1) hold each period is accurate up to a residual of order $\mathcal{O}(\|x^*\|^2)$. This suffices, however, for a characterization of the first-order effects of allowing for $x^* > 0$ (i.e., for inefficiency of the natural rate of output). And this, in turn, is enough to allow one to understand the basic character of the inflation bias resulting from discretionary policy, even if one cannot expect the analysis to yield an accurate estimate of the *size* of this bias except when x^* is small.[4]

I therefore consider the choice of monetary policy to minimize (1.2) subject to the sequence of constraints (1.1). Consider first the equilibrium outcome under discretionary optimization by the central bank. This is fairly simple to characterize, without any need to fully specify the strategic interaction between the central bank and the private sector. In the model just recalled, the set of possible equilibrium paths for inflation and output from any period T onward are independent of what inflation, output, or interest rates have been in any periods prior to T; nor does the central bank's evaluation of continuation paths from period T onward depend on prior history. Hence in a Markov equilibrium,[5] neither the equilibrium behavior of the private sector nor that of the central bank from period T onward should depend on what has happened earlier. This means that in such an equilibrium, the central bank can (correctly) assume in period t that the action it chooses has no effect on outcomes in any periods $T \geq t + 1$; nor (since the private sector has rational expectations) does it have any effect on the private sector's expectations in period t regarding π_{t+1}.

3. It does not matter for this characterization of optimal policy whether one assumes that the loss-function parameters are the ones that correctly reflect economic welfare as characterized in Chapter 6 or not. The results are equally applicable if (1.2) is taken to represent an ad hoc policy objective of some other kind.

4. As discussed in Section 5 of Chapter 6, expression (1.2) is correct to second order as an approximation to household utility only in the case that Φ_y is small. In the case of larger distortions, (1.2) must also include certain "transitory" quadratic terms. These do not affect the characterization in this chapter of optimal policy (under commitment) from a timeless perspective, but they would affect the characterization of optimizing policy under discretion. This extension of the theory is not taken up here.

5. There may, of course, be additional "reputational" equilibria in a policy game of this kind, as analyzed, e.g., by Chari et al. (1998) in the context of a sticky-price model with some prices fixed a period in advance. But for present purposes, the demonstration that *one* possible equilibrium under discretion is bad suffices to show that there is a potential gain from commitment to a suitable rule.

Let these equilibrium expectations be denoted π^e. (In a Markov equilibrium, inflation expectations are the same at all dates, owing to the time-invariant form of the continuation game.) Then the central bank perceives itself as being able to choose in period t among inflation-output pairs that satisfy the constraint

$$\pi_t = \kappa x_t + \beta \pi^e. \tag{1.3}$$

As it can no longer affect the contributions to (1.2) from periods prior to t and expects its current decision to have no effect on the contributions from later periods, a discretionary optimizer chooses an action in period t intended to bring about the inflation-output pair that minimizes $\pi_t^2 + \lambda(x_t - x^*)^2$ subject to this constraint. The first-order condition for this static optimization problem is given by

$$\pi_t + \frac{\lambda}{\kappa}\left(x_t - x^*\right) = 0. \tag{1.4}$$

Substitution of this into (1.3) implies that the bank generates inflation satisfying

$$\pi_t = \left(1 + \frac{\kappa^2}{\lambda}\right)^{-1} \left[\kappa x^* + \beta \pi^e\right] \tag{1.5}$$

in the case of any given expectations π^e.

Rational expectations on the part of the private sector, of course, require that π^e be such that exactly that same inflation rate is generated. Thus the expected rate of inflation under discretionary policy is

$$\pi^e = \frac{\kappa \lambda}{(1 - \beta)\lambda + \kappa^2}\, x^* > 0, \tag{1.6}$$

and this is also the rate of inflation that the central bank chooses to generate each period, given the (correctly) perceived inflation-output trade-off (1.3). Hence I have obtained the following result.

PROPOSITION 7.1. Consider a cashless economy with flexible wages, Calvo pricing, and no real disturbances. Assume that the initial dispersion of prices $\Delta_{-1} \equiv \mathrm{var}\{\log p_{-1}(i)\}$ is small,[6] and suppose furthermore that real

---

6. One should recall that this assumption was used in Chapter 6 in establishing that welfare is decreasing in (1.2), neglecting terms independent of policy and a residual of only third order. In the equilibrium described in this proposition, the condition continues to hold forever if it holds for the initial price distribution.

distortions (measured by Φ_y) are small as well, so that an approximation to the welfare of the representative household of the form (1.2) is possible, with $x^* > 0$ a small parameter ($x^* = \mathcal{O}(\Phi_y)$). Then, at least among inflation paths in which inflation remains forever near enough to zero, there is a unique Markov equilibrium with discretionary optimization by the central bank. In this equilibrium, inflation is constant at the value given by the right-hand side of (1.6), up to an error that is only of order $\mathcal{O}(\|\Delta_{-1}^{1/2}, \Phi_y, \tilde{\xi}\|^2)$.

But this outcome is not in fact the best possible rational-expectations equilibrium. Consider instead the problem of choosing bounded deterministic paths for inflation and output to minimize (1.2), subject to the constraint that the sequences must satisfy (1.1) each period. One can write a Lagrangian for this problem of the form

$$\mathcal{L} = \sum_{t=0}^{\infty} \beta^t \left\{ \frac{1}{2} \left[\pi_t^2 + \lambda \left(x_t - x^* \right)^2 \right] + \varphi_t \left[\pi_t - \kappa x_t - \beta \pi_{t+1} \right] \right\},$$

where φ_t is a Lagrange multiplier associated with the period t aggregate-supply relation. Differentiation of the Lagrangian with respect to each of its arguments yields a pair of first-order conditions

$$\pi_t + \varphi_t - \varphi_{t-1} = 0, \tag{1.7}$$

$$\lambda \left(x_t - x^* \right) - \kappa \varphi_t = 0, \tag{1.8}$$

for each $t \geq 0$, where in (1.7) for $t = 0$ one substitutes the value

$$\varphi_{-1} = 0, \tag{1.9}$$

as there is in fact no constraint associated with fulfillment of a period-minus-one aggregate-supply relation.

Using (1.7) and (1.8) to substitute for π_t and x_t respectively in (1.1) yields a difference equation for the evolution of the multipliers,

$$\beta \varphi_{t+1} - \left(1 + \beta + \frac{\kappa^2}{\lambda} \right) \varphi_t + \varphi_{t-1} = \kappa x^*, \tag{1.10}$$

that must hold for all $t \geq 0$, along with the initial condition (1.9). The characteristic equation

$$\beta \mu^2 - \left(1 + \beta + \frac{\kappa^2}{\lambda} \right) \mu + 1 = 0 \tag{1.11}$$

has two real roots

$$0 < \mu_1 < 1 < \mu_2,$$

as a result of which (1.10) has a unique nonexplosive solution consistent with the initial condition (1.9), given by

$$\varphi_t = -\frac{\lambda}{\kappa} x^* \left(1 - \mu_1^{t+1}\right) \tag{1.12}$$

for all $t \geq 0$. This solution, which is the only one satisfying the relevant transversality condition, represents the optimal perfect-foresight path from the standpoint of period zero. Substituting this solution for the multipliers into (1.7), one finds that the path of inflation under the optimal commitment is given by

$$\pi_t = (1 - \mu_1)\frac{\lambda}{\kappa} x^* \mu_1^t \tag{1.13}$$

for all $t \geq 0$.

This result indicates that discretionary optimization leads to excessive inflation. Indeed, under the optimal commitment, inflation should asymptotically approach zero, despite the assumption that $x^* > 0$. As was noted in Chapter 6, this results because the aggregate-supply relation (1.1) implies that in any perfect-foresight equilibrium, the objective (1.2) must equal

$$- 2\frac{x^*}{\theta}\pi_0 + \sum_{t=0}^{\infty} \beta^t \left[\pi_t^2 + \lambda x_t^2\right]$$

plus a positive constant. All the terms in the foregoing expression except the initial one are minimized by choosing $\pi_t = 0$ each period, regardless of the value of π^*; the presence of the initial term implies an advantage from an initial positive rate of inflation, but because the additional term applies only to inflation in the initial period, it remains optimal to commit to an inflation rate that is eventually zero.

Indeed, it is not obviously desirable to choose a positive inflation rate even initially. It is true that (1.2) is minimized by choosing the inflation path (1.13) rather than zero inflation from the initial date onward. This welfare gain, however, is obtained as a result of the fact that the inflation rate that is chosen initially has no consequences for expectations prior to date zero (that are taken as given at the time of the policy deliberations). This exploitation of the fact that initially existing expectations need not be fulfilled, however, is unattractive. It implies that the optimal policy determined on the foregoing grounds (optimality from the standpoint of date zero) is not *time consistent*: If the same reasoning is used at any later date $t > 0$ to determine the optimal policy commitment from *that* date onward, the policy chosen is not a continuation of the policy selected at date zero. (This can be seen from the fact that the inflation rate π_t varies with the date t in (1.13), even though the constraints defining the possible inflation paths from any date onward, and the social valuation of alternative inflation paths looking forward from any date, are the same at all times.) This failure of time consistency means that adherence to the policy must be due solely to a willingness to conform to a commitment entered into at an earlier date. In practice, it is difficult to imagine that a central bank would ever regard itself as being committed to a specific sequence of actions chosen at an earlier date simply because they seemed desirable at the earlier time,[7] whereas it is easier to imagine a bank being committed to a systematic *decision procedure* in the light of which its current actions are always to be justified. Furthermore, this analysis assumes that it is possible to commmit to an arbitrary time path for inflation and have this be expected by the private sector; it is assumed to be possible to choose inflation "just this time" while committing never to create inflation in the future. But there is reason to fear that the public should observe the central bank's method of reasoning, rather than its announced future actions, and conclude instead that in the present it should always wish to create inflation "just this time."

A similar problem of time consistency is familiar in the context of fiscal policy, and in that context it is common to conclude that if, say, one wishes the public to be able to confidently expect that capital will not be expropriated in the future, then one should adopt the rule of refusing to expropriate already existing capital, even though the latter action should not have the same kind of effects on investment incentives (since the investment decisions in question have already occurred). Similarly, if one wishes for the public to believe that a noninflationary policy will eventually be pursued and there is no difference between the current situation and the one that is anticipated in the future (except that one currently has an opportunity to create inflation without its having been expected), then it makes sense that the central bank should be willing to choose a noninflationary policy as well. Rather than doing one thing now but promising to behave differently in the future, one should follow a time-invariant policy that is of the kind that one would always wish *to have been expected* to follow. Woodford (1999b) calls such a policy "optimal from a timeless perspective."[8]

More specifically, I say that a time-invariant policy is optimal from a timeless perspective if the equilibrium evolution from any date t_0 onward (at which date one may consider the justification of the policy) is optimal

7. Such an understanding of the meaning of policy commitment raises the question posed by Svensson (1999b): "What is special about date zero?"

8. For additional discussions of the selection of policy rules from a timeless perspective, see McCallum and Nelson (2000), Giannoni and Woodford (2002a), Svensson and Woodford (2003), Section 3 in this chapter, and Section 1.1 of Chapter 8.

subject to the constraint that the economy's *initial* evolution be the one associated with the policy in question. (The presence of such a constraint on the initial outcomes that may be contemplated is a way of committing oneself to forswear the temptation to exploit the already given past expectations regarding those initial outcomes.) In the present context, a time-invariant policy implies a constant inflation rate $\bar{\pi}$. A constant inflation target $\bar{\pi}$ is optimal from a timeless perspective if the problem of maximizing (1.2) subject to the constraint that the bounded sequences $\{\pi_t, x_t\}$ satisfy (1.1) for each $t \geq 0$, and the additional constraint that $\pi_0 = \bar{\pi}$, has a solution in which $\pi_t = \bar{\pi}$ for all t.[9] The first-order conditions for this latter problem are again given by (1.7) and (1.8) for each $t \geq 0$, but now the initial condition (1.9) is replaced by the requirement that $\pi_0 = \bar{\pi}$. One easily sees that this system of equations has a solution in which $\pi_t = \bar{\pi}$ for all t if and only if $\bar{\pi} = 0$. Hence this is the uniquely optimal inflation target from a timeless perspective.

PROPOSITION 7.2. Consider a cashless economy with flexible wages, Calvo pricing, and no real disturbances, and again suppose that the initial dispersion of prices is small. Then a monetary policy under which inflation is zero for all t (up to an error of order $\mathcal{O}(\|\Delta_{-1}^{1/2}\|^2)$) is optimal from a timeless perspective and is the unique policy with this property among all policies under which inflation always remains in a certain interval around zero.

Note that for this proposition, unlike Proposition 7.1, it is not necessary for x^* to be small, since the optimal path is found to be near the zero-inflation steady state regardless of the value of x^*.

Under this analysis of the character of an optimal policy, there is a *constant* inflation bias associated with discretionary policy, which is clearly positive when $x^* = 0$. This is illustrated in Figure 7.1, which plots the time paths of inflation under discretionary policy, under the date-zero-optimal commitment, and under the policy that is optimal from a timeless perspective.[10] Inflation is lowest under the last of these policies, since only in this last case does the central bank refrain from the temptation to create inflation that cannot affect prior expectations, in both the short run and the long run.

9. See Section 2.1 in this chapter, and Section 1.1 of Chapter 8 for definitions of optimal policy from a timeless perspective in more general contexts.

10. In this numerical example, the values of β, κ are again those given in Table 6.1, λ is assigned the value given there for λ_x, and $x^* = 0.2$. This last value follows from equation (2.17) in Chapter 6 for the optimal output gap, under the assumptions that the elasticity of substitution among alternative differentiated goods (and hence the elasticity of demand faced by each firm) is equal to 7.88, the value obtained by Rotemberg and Woodford (1997) (see Table 4.1), and that there are no distorting taxes.

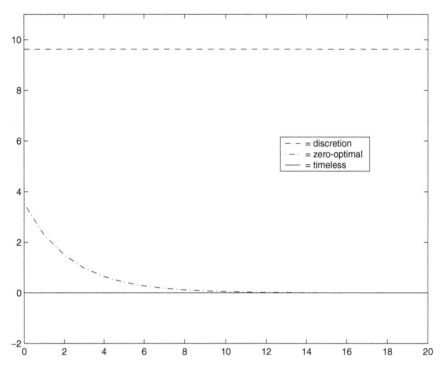

Figure 7.1 *Optimal policy from a timeless perspective compared to the result of discretionary optimization and to the policy commitment that is optimal from the standpoint of period zero.*

1.2 Extensions of the Basic Analysis

A striking conclusion of the previous section is that the optimal inflation rate is exactly zero in the baseline model with Calvo pricing, regardless of parameter values, including those that determine the size of the gap x^* between the optimal level of output and that consistent with zero inflation. However, this analysis neglects various other factors that may bear on the choice of a long-run average inflation target. Among the neglected factors are monetary frictions of the sort that led Friedman (1969) to argue for the optimality of deflation at the rate of time preference.

As shown in the previous chapter, in the presence of nonnegligible transactions frictions, the welfare-theoretic loss function takes the form

$$\sum_{t=0}^{\infty} \beta^t \left[\pi_t^2 + \lambda_x (x_t - x^*)^2 + \lambda_i (i_t - i_t^m)^2 \right], \quad (1.14)$$

where $\lambda_x > 0$ is the coefficient called λ in (1.2), $\lambda_i > 0$ as well, i_t is the short-term nominal interest yield on nonmonetary assets, and i_t^m is the interest rate paid on the monetary base.[11] In the event that monetary policy is implemented by varying i_t^m so as to maintain a constant interest differential regardless of the desired level of nominal interest rates—and that this differential is taken to be an institutional datum rather than an aspect of monetary policy—then the additional term in (1.14) relative to (1.2) makes no difference, as it is simply a constant independent of the chosen target path for inflation. In this case, the conclusions of the previous section continue to apply: The optimal policy from a timeless perspective involves a zero inflation rate at all times. But if, instead, the interest paid on the monetary base is an institutional datum, and $\bar{\imath}^m$ is lower than the rate consistent with zero inflation (e.g., if there is zero interest paid on money, as assumed by Friedman), then the rate of inflation that would otherwise be optimal may not be because of its consequences for nominal interest rates and hence the size of the last term in (1.14).

In the case that real balances enter the utility function in an additively separable way, transactions frictions do not affect the structural equations that determine equilibrium inflation and output, as discussed in Chapter 4. (While additively separability is not realistic, as discussed earlier, the quantitative magnitude of the real-balance effects that are neglected by such an assumption is likely to be small.) Feasible perfect-foresight equilibrium paths for inflation, output, and nominal interest rates must then satisfy (1.1), together with the corresponding deterministic IS equation

$$x_t = x_{t+1} - \sigma(i_t - \pi_{t+1} - \bar{r}), \tag{1.15}$$

for periods $t \geq 0$, where $\bar{r} > 0$ represents the constant natural rate of interest. A stationary policy commitment resulting in a constant inflation rate $\bar{\pi}$, output gap $\bar{x}$, and nominal interest rate $\bar{\imath}$ is optimal from a timeless perspective if the bounded sequences $\{\pi_t, x_t, \iota_t\}$ that minimize (1.14) subject to the constraints that (1.1) and (1.15) hold for each $t \geq 0$, and

$$\pi_0 = \bar{\pi}, \qquad x_0 = \bar{x},$$

are given by $\pi_t = \bar{\pi}$, $x_t = \bar{x}$, $i_t = \bar{\imath}$ for all t.

---

11. In the present chapter and the next one, i_t refers to the *continuously compounded* rate of interest on nonmonetary assets, $\log(1 + i_t)$ in the notation of the previous chapters, and similarly for the interest rate i_t^m paid on the monetary base and the natural rate of interest r_t^n, appearing in equation (2.23). Hence the interest differential $i_t - i_t^m$ is equal to $\hat{\imath}_t - \hat{\imath}_t^m + \bar{\Delta}$ in the notation of Chapter 6, up to a term of order $\mathcal{O}(\|\bar{\Delta}\|^2)$, which can be neglected in the quadratic approximation to the welfare-theoretic loss function. The change in notation should not create confusion, now that there is no longer any need to discuss the exact nonlinear equations that are log-linearized in deriving the linear structural relations assumed in this chapter and the next.

The Lagrangian for this generalization of the previous problem is of the form

$$\mathcal{L} = \sum_{t=0}^{\infty} \beta^t \left\{ \frac{1}{2} \left[\pi_t^2 + \lambda_x \left(x_t - x^* \right)^2 + \lambda_i \left(i_t - i^m \right)^2 \right] \right.$$

$$+ \varphi_{1t} \left[x_t - x_{t+1} + \sigma \left(i_t - \pi_{t+1} - \bar{r} \right) \right]$$

$$\left. + \varphi_{2t} \left[\pi_t - \kappa x_t - \beta \pi_{t+1} \right] \right\} - \beta^{-1} \varphi_{1,-1} \left[x_0 + \sigma \pi_0 \right] - \varphi_{2,-1} \pi_0,$$

where there are now Lagrange multipliers φ_{1t}, φ_{2t} corresponding to constraints (1.15) and (1.1), respectively, and multipliers $\beta^{-1} \varphi_{1,-1}$, $\varphi_{2,-1}$ corresponding to the constraints on the values of x_0 and π_0, respectively. (The notation chosen for these last multipliers is selected in order to give the following first-order conditions a time-invariant form.)

The first-order conditions are then

$$\pi_t - \beta^{-1} \sigma \varphi_{1,t-1} + \varphi_{2t} - \varphi_{2,t-1} = 0, \tag{1.16}$$

$$\lambda_x \left(x_t - x^* \right) + \varphi_{1t} - \beta^{-1} \varphi_{1,t-1} - \kappa \varphi_{2t} = 0, \tag{1.17}$$

$$\lambda_i \left(i_t - i^m \right) + \sigma \varphi_{1t} = 0 \tag{1.18}$$

for each period $t \geq 0$. Conditions (1.17) and (1.18) have a solution with the output gap and interest rate constant over time only if both Lagrange multipliers are also constant over time; but substituting constant values for the Lagrange multipliers in (1.16) and (1.18), one finds that these relations can be simultaneously satisfied only if

$$\lambda_i (\bar{i} - i^m) = -\beta \bar{\pi}.$$

At the same time, equation (1.15) is satisfied by constant values if and only if $\bar{i} = \bar{r} + \bar{\pi}$. These two relations are jointly satisfied if and only if the inflation target is equal to

$$\bar{\pi} = -\frac{\lambda_i}{\lambda_i + \beta} \left(\bar{r} - i^m \right). \tag{1.19}$$

I thus obtain the following result.

PROPOSITION 7.3. Consider an economy with flexible wages, Calvo pricing, and no real disturbances, with transactions frictions such that the quadratic approximation to welfare are given by (1.14), while the log-linear approximate structural relations are of the form (1.1) and (1.15). Suppose that the only feasible monetary policies are ones involving a constant interest rate i^m on the monetary base, where i^m is not too much below $\bar{r}$. Then the policy that is optimal from a timeless perspective involves a constant inflation rate equal to the right-hand side of (1.19), up to an error of order $\mathcal{O}(\|\Delta_{-1}^{1/2}, \bar{r} - i^m\|^2)$.

Note that in the case that $\lambda_i > 0$ and $i^m < \bar{r}$, the optimal inflation target is negative. In the limiting case of flexible prices, κ, and hence λ_i, becomes unboundedly large, and the optimal rate of deflation is $-(\bar{r} - i^m)$, the rate required to make the real return on money as high as $\bar{r}$, as argued by Friedman (1969). When prices are sticky, and κ is finite, the optimal rate of deflation is more moderate, and the optimal policy is one under which $\bar{\imath} > i^m$; but some deflation is still optimal, in order to reduce the distortions resulting from transactions frictions. In the cashless limit, in which $\bar{m}$ is negligible, λ_i is much smaller than β, and the optimal rate of inflation is essentially zero, as found in the previous section.

In the case that real-balance effects are nonnegligible in the aggregate-supply and IS equations, the same method can be employed as before, but (1.19) takes the more general form[12]

$$\bar{\pi} = -\frac{\lambda_i(\bar{r} - i^m) + \varphi \lambda_x x^*}{\lambda_i + \varphi^2 \lambda_x + \beta - (1 - \beta)\varphi\left(\theta^{-1} + \omega\right)}, \tag{1.20}$$

where the coefficient φ indexes the size of the real-balance effects, as in Chapter 4. If I use the calibrated parameter values from Table 6.1, but compute x^* from equation (4.6) of Chapter 6 under the assumption that $\Phi/\epsilon_{mc} = 0.2$ as assumed in the previous section, and assume that $i^m = 0$, this equation implies an optimal inflation rate of -0.4 percent per year.[13] This involves mild deflation, but much less deflation than would be suggested by the arguments of Friedman (1969) or Lucas (2000), according to which the optimal rate of inflation (under my parameter values and those of

---

12. Equation (1.20) applies in the case that this inflation rate implies a nominal interest rate no lower than i^m. In the case that this bound is not satisfied, the analysis must be modified to take account of the constraint on policy resulting from the zero lower bound on nominal interest rates, assumed not to bind in this derivation.

13. In this calculation, the values of λ_x, λ_i, $\bar{r}$, and β are taken directly from Table 6.1. The value used for φ is 0.22 years, the value implicit in the Table 6.1 parameter values, as discussed there; similarly, I assume the value $\theta = 7.88$ as in the derivation of the values given in the table. The values for ϵ_{mc}, σ^{-1}, χ, and η_y given in the table imply a value $\omega = 0.48$. In using equation (4.6) of Chapter 6 to evaluate x^*, recall that in the notation of that chapter, $i^* = -(\bar{r} - i^m)$. Finally, note that in the denominator of (1.20), if one uses an annual measure for φ, it is necessary to multiply $(1 - \beta)$ by 4 to obtain an annual discount rate as well.

Lucas) would be -3 percent per year. Moreover, one should recall that these parameter values have been chosen to exaggerate the size of real-balance effects; under the more plausible assumption that $\chi = 0.01$, one would obtain an optimal rate of deflation of only 0.2 percent per year.

It is perhaps surprising to observe that if $\varphi > 0$ (the empirically realistic case, as argued in Chapter 2), and if the denominator of (1.20) is positive (as must be true if real-balance effects are not too strong), a higher value of x^* actually *lowers* the optimal inflation target. It is commonly supposed that a higher value of x^* should justify higher inflation in a model (like the present one) that incorporates an upward-sloping long-run Phillips-curve relation between inflation and output. Yet this is not so. As shown in Chapter 6, in this model, commitment to a higher inflation rate in any period $t > t_0$ (i.e., any period for which the anticipation effects must be considered) does not change the discounted sum of output-gap terms implied by the aggregate-supply relation; for the increase in output in period t is exactly offset by a reduction in output in period $t - 1$. The only effects of policy that do *not* cancel in this way are the real-balance effects on aggregate supply, when these exist. If $\varphi > 0$, a lower nominal interest rate causes a favorable shift in the aggregate-supply relation each period, allowing a higher value for the discounted sum of output gaps. When $x^* > 0$, this channel creates a reason to prefer a lower nominal interest rate than the one consistent with zero inflation and hence to prefer deflation for reasons independent of Friedman's.

Thus far I have discussed only reasons why the optimal inflation target might be even *lower* than zero. Other considerations may instead justify a positive long-run average inflation rate. These include a desire to prevent the zero lower bound on nominal interest rates from being so tight a constraint on cyclical variation in real rates for stabilization purposes (Summers, 1991) or a desire to make a social norm that prohibits nominal-wage declines less of a constraint upon the degree to which real wages can decline when necessary for an efficient allocation of resources (Akerlof et al., 1996). These latter considerations matter only in the case of random disturbances and cannot be addressed without considering the optimal responses to such disturbances. It is worth noting, however, that they cast some doubt on the desirability of deliberately aiming for deflation, as opposed to zero inflation or even a very modest positive rate of inflation, of the sort typically aimed at by current inflation targeting central banks.

My analyses thus far have also argued for the optimality of a policy that would bring about a constant inflation rate in the absence of stochastic disturbances. Yet a number of countries that have actually adopted inflation targets in the past decade have thought it desirable to lower the target inflation rate from an (undesirably high) initial rate of inflation only gradually, over several years, rather than announcing an intention to immediately jump to the inflation rate that is regarded as optimal over the long run. The argument made for the desirability of gradualism of this sort generally involves a belief that there is substantial inertia in the inflationary process, though the models used previously do not allow for this. One can consider the effect of inflation inertia on the optimal time path for inflation, still within a purely deterministic context, by allowing for indexation of individual prices to a lagged price index, as considered in Section 3.2 of Chapter 3. In this case, the aggregate-supply relation (1.1) generalizes to

$$\pi_t - \gamma \pi_{t-1} = \kappa x_t + \beta(\pi_{t+1} - \gamma \pi_t), \tag{1.21}$$

where $0 \leq \gamma \leq 1$ indicates the degree of indexation, if I once again abstract from real-balance effects. Hence the possible perfect-foresight paths for inflation and output from any date t_0 onward depend upon the preexisting rate of inflation $t_0 - 1$.

As shown in Chapter 6, the welfare-theoretic loss function (1.2) for a cashless economy generalizes to

$$\sum_{t=0}^{\infty} \beta^t \left[(\pi_t - \gamma \pi_{t-1})^2 + \lambda(x_t - x^*)^2 \right] \tag{1.22}$$

in the presence of inflation inertia. Because both the constraints (1.21) and the loss function (1.22) are of the same form as before, but with $\pi_t - \gamma \pi_{t-1}$ replacing π_t in the previous equations, the same calculations as before may be used directly to characterize optimal policy (as well as the consequences of discretionary optimization), except that the previous solutions for the path of π_t now apply instead to the path of $\pi_t - \gamma \pi_{t-1}$.

Figure 7.2 shows the implied equilibrium paths for inflation under discretion, under an unconstrained optimal commitment from the standpoint of period zero, and under a policy that is optimal from a timeless perspective, when all parameters are the same as those assumed in Figure 7.1, except that $\gamma = 0.5$, and (since the initial inflation rate now matters) an inflation rate of 10 percent per year prior to period zero is assumed. In all three cases, the fact that the economy starts from a condition of fairly high inflation makes the inflation rate in the early periods higher than it would otherwise be; in fact, one can show that in each of the three cases, the equilibrium value of π_t is given by $\pi_{-1} \gamma^{t+1}$ plus a term that is independent of the initial condition. However, despite this effect of inertial inflation, the comparisons among the three paths remain of the kind discussed earlier: Discretion leads to an inflation rate that is permanently higher than the inflation that would occur under an optimal policy, and unconstrained (time-inconsistent) optimization at date zero leads to the choice of a higher inflation rate in the early periods, reflecting an attempt to exploit the initially given expectations of

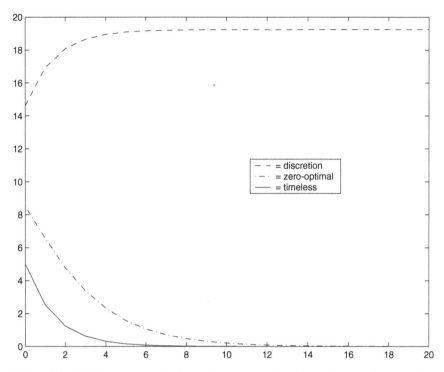

Figure 7.2 *Timelessly optimal policy, date-zero-optimal policy, and discretionary policy in the case of inflation inertia [$\gamma = 0.5$].*

inflation, though it leads to the same inflation rate as under a timelessly optimal policy in the long run.

The proof of Proposition 7.2 can be directly adapted to provide the following characterization of optimal policy in this case.

PROPOSITION 7.4. Consider an economy of the kind assumed in Proposition 7.2, except that prices are (partially) indexed to a lagged aggregate price index, to a degree measured by $0 \leq \gamma \leq 1$, and suppose that the initial inflation rate π_{-1} is not far from zero. Then the policy that is optimal from a timeless perspective involves a path of inflation along which

$$\pi_t = \gamma \pi_{t-1} \qquad\qquad (1.23)$$

at each date $t \geq 0$, up to an error of order $\mathcal{O}(\|\Delta_{-1}^{1/2}, \pi_{-1}\|^2)$.

This path has the property that the policy that minimizes discounted losses from any date t_0 onward, given the inflation history up through period t_0-1 and subject to the constraint that (1.23) hold in period t_0, is one in which

(1.23) holds for all $t \geq t_0$. Note that (1.23) can easily be solved to show that $\pi_t = \pi_{-1}\gamma^{t+1}$ for any $t \geq 0$. Once again one finds (in the case that $\gamma < 1$) that the optimal long-run inflation rate is zero; but it is now optimal to approach this inflation rate only over a period of time if the economy starts (for whatever reason) from an initial situation in which inflation has been higher.

In the case of full indexation ($\gamma = 1$), this result implies that it is not optimal *ever* to reduce inflation below whatever its initial level happens to be. Such a result should not be acceptable as having too much practical relevance. It comes about because, in the present simple model, all prices are adjusted to reflect past inflation in a perfectly synchronized way, except when they are reoptimized. When $\gamma = 1$, a policy that keeps inflation steady results in all prices being increased by exactly the same amount each period, so that no price dispersion is created, regardless of the rate of inflation. But in practice, even in an economy with substantial indexation (as one generally observes in economies with chronic high inflation), inflation results in price dispersion, and higher inflation is generally associated with greater dispersion. If the present model were extended to allow for this—for example, by supposing that prices are not continuously adjusted in response to variations in the aggregate price index between the occasions on which they are reoptimized, but that these mechanical price adjustments also occur only at certain intervals—then price dispersion would be minimized only with zero inflation, though one would again find that *changes* in the rate of inflation would increase price dispersion and hence lower welfare. I do not attempt to develop an extended indexation model of this kind here. But it is fairly obvious that one can in this or in various other ways justify the assumption that there are at least some distortions associated with a high rate of inflation, regardless of how steady it may be; and once even a small amount of such a distortion is introduced, it will again be optimal to eventually disinflate, regardless of the degree of inflation inertia.

For example, suppose that I again allow for transactions frictions and assume that the interest paid on the monetary base is constant. For simplicity, consider only the case in which $\chi = 0$ though $\lambda_i > 0$. Here, the structural equation (1.15) must be combined with (1.21) as constraints on possible perfect-foresight paths, and the welfare-theoretic loss function is of the form

$$\sum_{t=0}^{\infty} \beta^t \left[(\pi_t - \gamma\pi_{t-1})^2 + \lambda(x_t - x^*)^2 + \lambda_i(i_t - i^m)^2 \right].$$

The first-order condition (1.16) generalizes to

$$(\pi_t - \gamma\pi_{t-1}) - \beta\gamma\,(\pi_{t+1} - \gamma\pi_t) - \beta^{-1}\sigma\varphi_{1,t-1} + \varphi_{2t} - \varphi_{2,t-1} = 0,$$

while (1.17) and (1.18) continue to apply as previously indicated. The same analysis as before can again be used to derive a unique long-run steady-state rate of inflation that is consistent with these first-order conditions, given by

$$\bar{\pi} = -\frac{\lambda_i}{\lambda_i + \beta(1-\gamma)(1-\beta\gamma)}(\bar{r} - i^m) < 0,$$

generalizing (1.19).

While in the case that $\lambda_i = 0$ (the cashless case just considered), this equation yields a determinate outcome only when $\gamma \neq 1$, in the case that $\lambda_i > 0$, there is a uniquely optimal long-run inflation rate even when $\gamma = 1$, namely,

$$\bar{\pi} = -(\bar{r} - i^m),$$

the rate of deflation called for by Friedman (1969). It is worth noting that the degree to which it is eventually desirable to disinflate is independent of how large λ_i may be—it is simply necessary to allow for *some* frictions of this kind, which increase with the rate of expected inflation. In fact, if one assumes full indexation of prices to a lagged price index, this indexation actually *increases* the degree to which it is optimal to eventually lower the rate of inflation; for it is no longer true that steady deflation creates relative-price distortions owing to the failure of prices to be reoptimized at perfectly synchronized times. This last result, however, is again an example of an extreme conclusion that results from too simple a model of indexation. In reality, even steady deflation is likely to create distortions, for reasons identical to those noted in the case of steady inflation; and as a result, the optimal long-run rate of inflation is likely not to be as low as the Friedman rate.

2 Optimal Responses to Disturbances

The inflationary bias resulting from discretionary policy has been much discussed. However, emphasis on the problem of inflation bias has often led to a supposition that the problems resulting from discretion can be cured through a simple adjustment of the targets and/or the relative weights on alternative stabilization objectives assigned to the central bank, while allowing the central bank's decisionmaking framework to be otherwise one of unfettered discretion. For example, the baseline analysis in Section 1.1 implied an inflation bias equal to

$$\frac{\kappa\lambda}{(1-\beta)\lambda + \kappa^2} x^*,$$

when the central bank seeks to minimize the true social loss function, in which I have argued that $\lambda > 0$, $x^* > 0$. But if the central bank instead seeks to minimize a loss function of the form (1.2) with some other coefficients, the preceding analysis still applies. In particular, the equilibrium inflation rate is zero each period, even under discretion, as long as either $\lambda = 0$, $x^* = 0$, or both. Thus one might suppose that the problem can be solved by appointing a central banker with appropriate preferences or by charging the central bank with the task of minimizing a particular loss function that differs from true social welfare. The choice of a loss function with $\lambda = 0$ corresponds to Rogoff's (1985) proposal that a "conservative central banker" be chosen, while King (1997) and Blinder (1998) propose that the central bank should have an objective under which $x^* = 0$, that is, an output target consistent with its inflation target.

But while it is fairly simple to eliminate the bias in the average rate of inflation resulting from discretionary policy through either of these means, this does not suffice to yield an optimal policy framework, for in general the equilibrium responses to shocks that result are suboptimal, even if the long-run average values of the various state variables are the optimal ones. It is perhaps obvious that the Rogoff proposal to alter the relative weight on the two stabilization objectives often results in incorrect responses to disturbances; indeed, Rogoff discusses this as an important qualification to his proposal (so that the optimal degree of "conservativeness" is argued to be less than absolute in the presence of certain kinds of disturbances). But in the context of a linear-quadratic framework of the kind that I use here to approximate the central bank's problem, an adjustment of the target values of one or more variables affects the average equilibrium values of the endogenous variables resulting from central-bank optimization without having any effect on the equilibrium responses to shocks; hence one might think that the proposal of King and Blinder should not result in any distortion of stabilization policy.[14] But, in general, the equilibrium resulting from discretionary optimization is suboptimal, not only in the long-run average values of variables such as inflation, but *also* in the equilibrium responses of these variables to random shocks, for reasons discussed in the introduction; and an adjustment of the target values assigned to the central bank does nothing to solve this problem.

In this section, I contrast the optimal responses to shocks to those resulting from discretionary optimization in two simple examples and then discuss the structure of the problem more generally. I show not only that the former are generally different from the latter, but that they usually require that equilibrium be history dependent in a way that cannot result from

---

14. Indeed, King (1997) shows, in the context of a simple model in which an aggregate-supply relation of the New Classical form discussed in Chapter 3 is combined with an assumed stabilization objective of the form (1.2), that under his proposed modification of the central bank's loss function, the equilibrium resulting from discretionary optimization is optimal. However, this result depends on extremely special features of the example that he considers.

any purely forward-looking decision procedure for monetary policy. This implies, among other things, that an approach to the implementation of optimal policy that charges the central bank with the minimization of a loss function under discretion that involves the same target variables as the true social loss function—only with different target values and a different matrix of weights in the quadratic form over deviations from those target values—will generally be inadequate, as such a decision procedure is purely forward looking.

2.1   Cost-Push Shocks

Probably the simplest example of this general problem arises in the case of cost-push shocks that shift the aggregate-supply relation when written in terms of the welfare-relevant inflation and output-gap measures.[15] In the case of such disturbances, complete stabilization of both inflation and the output gap is impossible; thus one need not assume any concern with interest-rate stabilization, or other stabilization objectives, in order to conclude that there is an essential tension among the stabilization objectives of monetary policy. In such a case, discretionary policy does not generally lead to optimal responses to shocks.[16]

This can be seen by considering the minimization of a social loss function given by the expected value of (1.2), if the aggregate-supply relation each period is given by

$$\pi_t = \kappa x_t + \beta E_t \pi_{t+1} + u_t, \tag{2.1}$$

where u_t is an exogenous cost-push shock. Consider first the case of discretionary optimization by the central bank. Let s_t be the exogenous state at date t that contains all information available at that time about current and future cost-push disturbance terms. One observes that the set of possible

15. Several interpretations of such disturbances are possible, as discussed in Sections 4.5 and 5 of Chapter 6.

16. If complete stabilization of each of the target variables is simultaneously possible, then there is no difference in the responses to shocks under discretion and under an optimal commitment. A discretionary optimizer finds it optimal to completely stabilize each of the target variables in any given period, given the assumption that they will be stabilized in the future. Hence complete stabilization is an equilibrium under discretionary policy and is also optimal. This is obvious in the case that the target values of the various state variables are mutually consistent with equilibrium in the absence of shocks, so that it is possible for the loss function to equal zero at all times. But even when this is not so—when, e.g., x^* is too high to be consistent with zero inflation on average—the same result is true, because the equilibrium responses to shocks, both under discretion and under an optimal commitment, are independent of the assumed target values, which matter only for the average values of the variables in equilibrium.

equilibrium evolutions of inflation and the output gap from period t onward depend only on s_t, and in particular are independent of the past values of all endogenous variables. It follows that in a Markov equilibrium, π_t and x_t should be functions only of s_t. Hence the central bank in period t believes that its policy action in that period can have no effect on terms in the loss function for periods $T \geq t+1$, and also that its action has no effect on the private sector's expectations $E_t \pi_{t+1}$.

Then the central bank perceives itself as being able to choose in period t among inflation-output pairs that satisfy the constraint (2.1) for a *given* value of $E_t \pi_{t+1}$ (that depends only on s_t), and it chooses an action in period t intended to bring about the inflation-output pair that minimizes $\pi_t^2 + \lambda(x_t - x^*)^2$ subject to this constraint. The first-order condition for this static optimization problem is again given by (1.4). Substitution of this into (2.1) implies that the bank generates inflation satisfying

$$\pi_t = \left(1 + \frac{\kappa^2}{\lambda}\right)^{-1} \left[\kappa x^* + u_t + \beta E_t \pi_{t+1}\right], \tag{2.2}$$

generalizing (1.5). The Markov solution to this equation is then an inflation process

$$\pi_t = \frac{\kappa \lambda}{(1-\beta)\lambda + \kappa^2} x^* + \sum_{j=0}^{\infty} \beta^j \left(\frac{\lambda}{\lambda + \kappa^2}\right)^{j+1} E_t u_{t+j}. \tag{2.3}$$

PROPOSITION 7.5. Consider an economy of the same kind as in Proposition 7.1, except that the aggregate-supply relation (2.1) is perturbed by an exogenous disturbance process $\{u_t\}$ satisfying a uniform bound $\|\tilde{\xi}\|$. Then there is a neighborhood of zero in which there is a unique Markov equilibrium inflation process under discretionary optimization by the central bank, for any small enough bound on the expansion parameters $\|(\Delta_{-1}^{1/2}, \Phi_y, \tilde{\xi})\|$. In this equilibrium, inflation evolves according to (2.3), up to an error of order $\mathcal{O}(\|(\Delta_{-1}^{1/2}, \Phi_y, \tilde{\xi})\|^2)$.

The corresponding Markov solution for output can be obtained by substituting this solution for inflation into (2.1). Note that the long-run average rate of inflation in this equilibrium, given by the constant term in (2.3), is the same as in the deterministic analysis. The equilibrium responses of inflation and output are purely forward looking. If u_t is a Markov process, with the value of u_t being revealed only in period t, then equilibrium π_t and x_t depend only on the current disturbance u_t, and the effects of a disturbance on the paths of inflation and output are only as persistent as the disturbance itself.

Now consider instead the nature of an optimal policy commitment.[17] I first consider the state-contingent evolution from some period t_0 onward that minimizes the expected discounted sum of losses from that point forward, conditioning upon the state of the world in period t_0 and subject to the constraint that this evolution represent a possible rational-expectations equilibrium, that is, that it satisfy (2.1) for all periods $t \geq t_0$. The Lagrangian associated with this problem is of the form[18]

$$\mathcal{L}_{t_0} = E_{t_0} \sum_{t=t_0}^{\infty} \beta^{t-t_0} \left\{ \tfrac{1}{2} \left[\pi_t^2 + \lambda_x \left(x_t - x^* \right)^2 \right] + \varphi_t [\pi_t - \kappa x_t - \beta \pi_{t+1}] \right\}. \quad (2.4)$$

Once again, if there is no welfare loss resulting from nominal interest-rate variation, one may omit the constraint terms corresponding to the IS relation, as these constraints never bind. Moreover, in writing the constraint term associated with the period t AS relation, it does not matter that π_{t+1} is substituted for $E_t \pi_{t+1}$; for it is only the conditional expectation of the term at date t_0 that is significant in (2.4), and the law of iterated expectations implies that

$$E_{t_0} [\varphi_t E_t \pi_{t+1}] = E_{t_0} [E_t (\varphi_t \pi_{t+1})] = E_{t_0} [\varphi_t \pi_{t+1}]$$

for any $t \geq t_0$.

Differentiating (2.4) with respect to the levels of inflation and output each period, one obtains a pair of first-order conditions of exactly the form (1.7) and (1.8) for each period $t \geq t_0$ (and for each possible state of the world at that date), together with the initial condition

$$\varphi_{t_0-1} = 0. \quad (2.5)$$

Using (1.7) and (1.8) to substitute for π_t and x_t, respectively, in (2.1), one again obtains a difference equation for the evolution of the multipliers,

$$\beta E_t \varphi_{t+1} - \left(1 + \beta + \frac{\kappa^2}{\lambda} \right) \varphi_t + \varphi_{t-1} = \kappa x^* + u_t, \quad (2.6)$$

which is a stochastic generalization of (1.10). Once again, the characteristic equation (1.11) has two real roots $0 < \mu_1 < 1 < \mu_2$, as a result of which (2.6) has a unique bounded solution for $\{\varphi_t\}$, given by

---

17. Early treatments of this problem in the context of the present model with cost-push shocks include Clarida et al. (1999), Woodford (1999b), and Vestin (2002). Svensson and Woodford (2003) discuss a similar problem, but with a one-period delay in the effects of policy on both inflation and output.

18. The basic method used here to characterize the optimal policy commitment in the case of a forward-looking model was introduced by Kydland and Prescott (1980), Hansen et al. (1985), and Backus and Driffill (1986).

$$\varphi_t = \mu_1 \varphi_{t-1} - (1 - \mu_1)\frac{\lambda}{\kappa}x^* - \beta^{-1}\sum_{j=0}^{\infty}\mu_2^{-j-1}E_t u_{t+j} \qquad (2.7)$$

in the case of any bounded disturbance process $\{u_t\}$. Note that this equation can be solved recursively for the evolution of $\{\varphi_t\}$ starting from any initial condition for φ_{-1}. Substituting this solution for the path of the Lagrange multipliers into (1.7) and (1.8), one obtains unique bounded solutions for the paths of inflation and the output gap.

These bounded solutions necessarily satisfy the relevant transversality condition. Hence the solution obtained starting from the initial condition (2.5) represents the state-contingent evolution of inflation and output under the t_0-optimal commitment. (Note that the inflation solution thus obtained is a stochastic generalization of (1.13).) However, this solution contains a deterministic component that depends on the time that has elapsed since the date t_0 at which the plan was chosen, and so is not time consistent. Once again, there is a preference for a time-invariant policy that is optimal from a timeless perspective, meaning that continuation of the policy from any date t_0 forward leads to an equilibrium from that date onward that minimizes the expected discounted sum of losses, subject to a constraint of the form

$$\pi_{t_0} = \bar{\pi}_{t_0}, \qquad (2.8)$$

where the value of $\bar{\pi}_{t_0}$ may depend on the state of the world at date t_0.

Minimization of expected discounted losses subject to the constraint (2.8) leads to a Lagrangian of the same form (2.4), except for the addition of a term representing the additional constraint. This in turn leads to exactly the same system of first-order conditions, except that initial condition (2.8) replaces (2.5). Hence there is a unique bounded solution for the state-contingent evolution of inflation and output from date t_0 onward for any given specification of the initial condition. This solution is again of the form (2.7) for some choice of the initial value ϕ_{t_0-1}; the proper choice of this initial multiplier depends on the constraint value $\bar{\pi}_{t_0}$.

In order for such a policy to be time consistent, one needs to select the constraint value $\bar{\pi}_{t_0}$ as a function of exogenous and predetermined variables at date t_0, according to some time-invariant rule that is satisfied by the constrained-optimal state-contingent inflation path (i.e., the solution to the optimization problem with constraint (2.8)) at all dates $t > t_0$. One example of such a specification would be

$$\bar{\pi}_{t_0} = \beta^{-1}\sum_{j=0}^{\infty}\mu_2^{-j-1}E_{t_0}u_{t_0+j} - \beta^{-1}(1-\mu_1)\sum_{k=1}^{\infty}\sum_{j=0}^{\infty}\mu_1^{k-1}\mu_2^{-j-1}E_{t_0-k}u_{t_0+j-k}, \qquad (2.9)$$

as a consequence of the following result.

PROPOSITION 7.6. The state-contingent evolution of inflation $\{\pi_t\}$ from some date t_0 onward that minimizes the expected value of (1.2), taking as given the economy's evolution prior to date t_0 and subject to the constraint (2.8), where $\bar{\pi}_{t_0}$ is given by (2.9), is given by

$$\pi_t = \beta^{-1} \sum_{j=0}^{\infty} \mu_2^{-j-1} E_t u_{t+j} - \beta^{-1}(1-\mu_1) \sum_{k=1}^{\infty} \sum_{j=0}^{\infty} \mu_1^{k-1} \mu_2^{-j-1} E_{t-k} u_{t+j-k} \quad (2.10)$$

for all $t \geq t_0$.

The proof is given in Appendix F. Note that in the constrained-optimal evolution, inflation in every period after t_0 is chosen to be the same time-invariant function of past disturbances as it has been constrained to be in period t_0. This makes the constraint self-consistent in the desired sense.

One can easily show that (2.9) represents the only specification of $\bar{\pi}_{t_0}$ as a function of the history of exogenous disturbances (only) that is self-consistent in this sense. For regardless of the specification of $\bar{\pi}_{t_0}$, the constrained-optimal evolution from t_0 onward must satisfy (2.7) for some choice of φ_{t_0-1}. Solving for π_t as a function of φ_{t_0-1} and the history of disturbances between dates t_0 and t and then taking the limit as $t_0 \to -\infty$ for some fixed date t, one obtains (2.10), regardless of the assumed value of ϕ_{t_0-1}.[19] Hence regardless of the specification of $\bar{\pi}_{t_0}$, the dependence of inflation upon the history of disturbances must eventually be of the form (2.10). The only self-consistent specification of $\bar{\pi}_{t_0}$ as a function of the history of disturbances must then be of that same form.

This does not mean, however, that in order for a policy to be optimal from a timeless perspective, it must result in the state-contingent evolution of inflation indicated by (2.10). For one can also find self-consistent specifications of the initial inflation constraint that involve predetermined endogenous variables. As a simple example, the specification

$$\bar{\pi}_{t_0} = (1-\mu_1)\frac{\lambda}{\kappa} x_{t_0-1} + \beta^{-1} \sum_{j=0}^{\infty} \mu_2^{-j-1} E_{t_0} u_{t_0+j} \quad (2.11)$$

also results in a self-consistent constraint.

---

19. The asymptotic independence of the initial condition φ_{t_0-1} results from the fact that $|\mu_1| < 1$.

PROPOSITION 7.7. Consider the same optimization problem as in Proposition 7.6, but with $\bar{\pi}_{t_0}$ given by (2.11). Then in the constrained-optimal state-contingent evolution of inflation and output, the inflation rate satisfies

$$\pi_t = (1 - \mu_1)\frac{\lambda}{\kappa} x_{t-1} + \beta^{-1} \sum_{j=0}^{\infty} \mu_2^{-j-1} E_t u_{t+j} \tag{2.12}$$

at each date $t \geq t_0$.

The proof follows exactly the same lines as that of Proposition 7.6. Hence a time-invariant policy rule that results in a determinate equilibrium in which the inflation rate always satisfies (2.12) is optimal from a timeless perspective.

Yet another self-consistent constraint would be

$$\bar{\pi}_{t_0} = -(1 - \mu_1)(p_{t_0-1} - \bar{p}) + \beta^{-1} \sum_{j=0}^{\infty} \mu_2^{-j-1} E_{t_0} u_{t_0+j}, \tag{2.13}$$

where $p_t \equiv \log P_t$, and $\bar{p}$ is an arbitrary constant that has the interpretation of a target price level. (It is the long-run average log price level in the equilibrium that is optimal subject to this constraint, as discussed later.) In this case the initial constraint is perhaps most intuitively expressed as a constraint on the initial log price level, $p_{t_0} = \bar{p}_{t_0}$, where

$$\bar{p}_{t_0} = (1 - \mu_1)\bar{p} + \mu_1 p_{t_0-1} + \beta^{-1} \sum_{j=0}^{\infty} \mu_2^{-j-1} E_{t_0} u_{t_0+j}. \tag{2.14}$$

For any choice of $\bar{p}$, this is a self-consistent constraint, owing to the following result.

PROPOSITION 7.8. Consider the same optimization problem as in Proposition 7.6, but with $\bar{\pi}_{t_0}$ given by (2.13), or equivalently with a constraint on the initial price level given by (2.14). Then in the constrained-optimal state-contingent evolution of inflation and output, the equilibrium price level each period satisfies

$$\bar{p}_t = (1 - \mu_1)\bar{p} + \mu_1 p_{t-1} + \beta^{-1} \sum_{j=0}^{\infty} \mu_2^{-j-1} E_t u_{t+j}. \tag{2.15}$$

Again, the proof follows the same lines as that of Proposition 7.6. Note that this defines an entire one-parameter family of self-consistent constraints. For one particular choice of $\bar{p}$, namely,

$$\bar{p} = p_{t_0-1} + \frac{\lambda}{\kappa}x_{t_0-1},$$

this constraint is identical to (2.11), and the implied state-contingent evolutions are the same. But any other value for $\bar{p}$ would lead to a self-consistent constraint as well.

We see that the state-contingent evolution of inflation under a policy that is optimal from a timeless perspective is not uniquely determined. However, these alternative processes for inflation and output differ only in transitory, deterministic components of the solutions for inflation and the output gap; they agree both as to the long-run average values of both inflation and the output gap and as to the response of both variables to unexpected shocks in any period from t_0 onward.

PROPOSITION 7.9. Consider again an economy of the kind assumed in Proposition 7.5. Then in the case of any small enough bound $\|\Delta_{-1}^{1/2}, \Phi_y, \bar{\xi}\|$, and any initial values of any predetermined endogenous variables (that may matter for equilibrium determination as a result of the policy rule) that are close enough to the values associated with the zero-inflation steady state, the long-run average values of inflation and the output gap satisfy

$$\lim_{T\to\infty} E_t\pi_T = 0,$$

$$\lim_{T\to\infty} E_t x_T = 0$$

under the t_0-optimal policy that would be chosen at any date t_0. Moreover, the same is true of the equilibrium implemented by any policy that is optimal from a timeless perspective.

Furthermore, let the unexpected change in the forecast of any variable y_{t+m} at date t be denoted

$$I_t[y_{t+m}] \equiv E_t y_{t+m} - E_{t-1}y_{t+m}.$$

Then the effects of unanticipated shocks at any date t on the expected paths of inflation and output are given by

$$I_t[\pi_{t+m}] = \beta^{-1}\sum_{j=0}^{\infty}\mu_2^{-j-1}I_t[u_{t+j}]$$

$$-\beta^{-1}(1-\mu_1)\sum_{k=1}^{m}\sum_{j=0}^{\infty}\mu_1^{k-1}\mu_2^{-j-1}I_t[u_{t+m-k+j}], \qquad (2.16)$$

$$I_t[x_{t+m}] = -\beta^{-1} \sum_{k=0}^{m} \sum_{j=0}^{\infty} \mu_1^k \mu_2^{-j-1} I_t[u_{t+m-k+j}], \qquad (2.17)$$

for each $m \geq 0$ under a t_0-optimal policy chosen at any date $t_0 \leq t$. Again, the same is true of the equilibrium implemented by any policy that is optimal from a timeless perspective. (In each of these characterizations of the paths of inflation and the output gap, the results given are accurate up to an error term of order $\mathcal{O}(\|\Delta_{-1}^{1/2}, \Phi_y, \bar{\xi}\|^2)$.)

The proof is in Appendix F. Essentially, the result follows from the fact that in any of the cases allowed for, the economy's state-contingent evolution must satisfy (2.7).

Comparing Proposition 7.9 with Proposition 7.5, one again finds, as in the deterministic analysis in Section 1, that there is an inflationary bias to discretionary policy under the assumption that $x^* > 0$. (The size of the average-inflation bias is exactly the same as determined under the deterministic analysis, as a result of the well-known certainty-equivalence property of both the equilibrium outcome under discretionary optimization and the optimal plan under commitment in the case of linear-quadratic policy problems of the kind considered here.[20]) However, there is *also* a difference in the responses to shocks under an optimal policy commitment from those that result from discretionary optimization. Furthermore, this "stabilization bias" is present even when $x^* = 0$, so that there is no average-inflation bias associated with discretionary policy.[21]

The difference in the equilibrium responses to a cost-push shock under discretionary policy and under an optimal commitment are contrasted in Figure 7.3 in the simple case that the cost-push shock is purely transitory and unforecastable before the period in which it occurs (so that $E_t u_{t+j} = 0$ for all $j \geq 1$). Here the assumed values of β, κ, and λ are again as in Figure 7.1, and the shock in period zero is of size $u_0 = 1$, meaning that a 1 percent increase in the general level of prices would be required to prevent any decline in output relative to the natural rate (or more generally, its target

20. For discussions of certainty equivalence in the context of forward-looking models like the ones discussed in this chapter, see, e.g., Backus and Driffill (1986) and Currie and Levine (1993).

21. Thus the result of King (1997), according to which discretionary policy achieves an optimal state-contingent evolution for the economy as long as the output-gap target x^* in the central bank's loss function is modified so as to be consistent with its inflation target, is special to the specific simple model of aggregate supply that he assumes. Early discussions of stabilization bias in the context of other forward-looking models include Flodén (1996), Jonsson (1997), and Svensson (1997b).

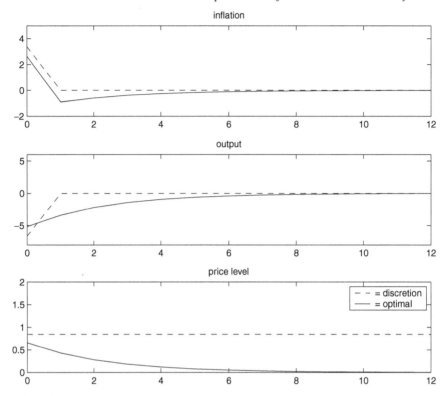

Figure 7.3 *Optimal responses to a transitory cost-push shock compared with equilibrium responses under discretionary policy.*

level) from occurring, on the assumption that prices are then stabilized at the new higher level. Once again, the periods represent quarters, and the inflation rate is plotted as an annualized rate, meaning that what is plotted is actually $4\pi_t$.

Under the discretionary policy characterized in Proposition 7.5, the effects of the disturbance on equilibrium inflation and the equilibrium output gap last only as long as the disturbance itself, so that both variables are expected to return to their normal levels by the following quarter. However, under an optimal commitment, monetary policy remains tight even after the disturbance has dissipated, so that the output gap returns to zero only much more gradually. As a result, while inflation overshoots its long-run target value at the time of the shock, it is held *below* its long-run target value for a time following the shock, so that the unexpected increase in prices is subsequently undone. In fact, as the bottom panel shows, under an optimal commitment, the price level eventually returns to exactly the same path that it would have been expected to follow if the shock had not occurred.

This simple example illustrates a very general feature of optimal policy once one takes account of forward-looking private-sector behavior: Optimal policy is almost always *history dependent* in a way that discretionary policy would not be. Discretionary policy (in a Markov equilibrium) is *purely forward looking*, in the sense that the action chosen at any date t depends solely upon the set of possible state-contingent paths for the target variables (here, inflation and the output gap) from period t onward, given the economy's state at that time (the values of predetermined or exogenous variables at date t). In the present example, the forward-looking aggregate-supply relation (2.1), which implies that the set of possible equilibrium paths for inflation and output from period t onward are independent of all lagged endogenous variables, and the assumption that the disturbance u_t is completely unforecastable together imply that the only aspect of the economy's state in period t that affects the set of possible paths for inflation and output from that period onward is the current disturbance u_t. Hence under any purely forward-looking decision procedure for monetary policy, π_t and x_t depend only on the current disturbance u_t, and the effects of a shock on the paths of these variables is as transitory as the effect on u_t itself. (The same is true of the associated path of nominal interest rates, if the intertemporal IS equation is of the form (2.23).) However, under an optimal policy, both π_t and x_t depend on disturbances in periods prior to t in the case of any period $t > t_0$.

Optimal policy is history dependent (and conventional optimal-control or dynamic-programming methods lead to suboptimal policy) because the *anticipation* by the private sector that future policy will be different as a result of conditions at date t—even if those conditions no longer matter for the set of possible paths for the target variables at the later date—can improve stabilization outcomes at date t. Suppose that there is a positive cost-push shock at date t, as illustrated in Figure 7.3. If the transitory disturbance is expected to have no effect on the conduct of policy in later periods (as under any purely forward-looking policy), then the short-run trade-off between inflation and the output gap in period t is shifted vertically by the amount of the disturbance, u_t, requiring that the central bank choose between an increase in inflation, a negative output gap, or some of each. If instead the central bank is expected to pursue a tighter policy in period $t + 1$ and later as a result of the shock in period t, as occurs under the optimal policy depicted in the figure, then the short-run trade-off between inflation and the output gap is shifted only by the amount of the total change in $u_t + \beta E_t \pi_{t+1}$, which is smaller than the increase in u_t. Hence greater stabilization (less of an increase in inflation, less of a reduction in output, or both) is possible in period t. (The anticipation of tighter policy later restrains price increases in period t, so that less contraction of output is needed in that period to achieve a given degree of moderation of inflationary pressure.)

Of course, to achieve this beneficial shift in expectations in period t, it is necessary that the central bank be committed to actually tightening policy later. This means less successful stabilization in later periods than would otherwise have been possible; but nonetheless, the discounted sum of expected stabilization losses can be reduced through some use of this tool.

It may not be obvious from Figure 7.3 that commitment to a history-dependent policy can simultaneously improve the stabilization of inflation and of the output gap, since in this numerical example, the overall variability of the output gap is higher under the optimal policy than under discretionary policy. (This need not have been true, but happens to be true for the calibrated parameter values used here, which involve quite a low relative weight λ on output-gap stabilization, for reasons discussed in Chapter 6.) The point can be illustrated numerically by computing the inflation-output variance frontier associated with history-dependent as opposed to purely forward-looking policies. These two variance frontiers are shown in Figure 6.6 in the case that β and κ are calibrated as in Figure 7.3, and u_t is assumed to be an AR(1) process,

$$u_t = \rho_u u_{t-1} + \epsilon_t^u, \tag{2.18}$$

with $\rho_u = .8$. (Here ϵ_t^u is an i.i.d. mean-zero random variable.)

The variance frontier in the case of general linear policies (allowing arbitrary history dependence) is obtained by computing the optimal responses to disturbances, characterized in Proposition 7.9, for values of $\lambda > 0$ that are allowed to vary over the entire positive real half-line. For each equilibrium in this one-parameter family, I compute the statistics $V[\pi]$ and $V[x]$, where I again use the discounted measure of variability

$$V[y] \equiv (1 - \beta) \sum_{t=0}^{\infty} \beta^t \mathrm{var}(y_t)$$

for any random variable $\{y_t\}$. Note that for each value of λ, the date-zero-optimal policy minimizes

$$E\left\{ \sum_{t=0}^{\infty} \beta^t [\pi_t^2 + \lambda(x_t - x^*)^2] \right\} = \sum_{t=0}^{\infty} \beta^t \left\{ (E[\pi_t])^2 + \lambda(E[x_t] - x^*)^2 \right\}$$

$$+ (1 - \beta)^{-1} V[\pi] + (1 - \beta)^{-1} \lambda V[x].$$

Furthermore, the first term on the right-hand side depends only on the deterministic component of policy, while the remaining two terms depend only on the prescribed responses to shocks. As these two aspects of policy can be independently specified, the optimal equilibrium responses to shocks minimize $V[\pi] + \lambda V[x]$. It follows that the responses to shocks characterized in Proposition 7.9 for alternative values of λ describe the policies on the $V[\pi]$-$V[x]$ efficient frontier.

The variance frontier for the more restricted class of purely forward-looking (linear) policies can similarly be obtained by computing the policy from within this class that minimizes $V[\pi] + \lambda V[x]$, for each possible value of $\lambda > 0$. In the present context, this means restricting consideration to state-contingent evolutions in which π_t and x_t are linear functions of the current value of u_t,

$$\pi_t = \bar{\pi} + f_\pi u_t, \qquad x_t = \bar{x} + f_x u_t. \tag{2.19}$$

State-contingent evolutions within this family represent possible rational-expectations equilibria if and only if the coefficients satisfy

$$(1 - \beta)\bar{\pi} = \kappa \bar{x}, \tag{2.20}$$

$$(1 - \beta\rho_u)f_\pi = \kappa f_x + 1, \tag{2.21}$$

as a consequence of (2.1). Finally, in the case of processes of the form (2.19),

$$V[\pi] + \lambda V[x] = \left[f_\pi^2 + \lambda f_x^2 \right] \mathrm{var}(u).$$

Thus I choose the response coefficients f_π, f_x so as to minimize $f_\pi^2 + \lambda f_x^2$ subject to constraint (2.21). The optimal response coefficients are easily seen to be

$$f_\pi = \frac{1 - \beta\rho_u}{\kappa^2\lambda^{-1} + (1 - \beta\rho_u)^2} > 0, \qquad f_x = -\frac{\kappa\lambda^{-1}}{\kappa^2\lambda^{-1} + (1 - \beta\rho_u)^2} < 0. \tag{2.22}$$

For each member of this one-parameter family of equilibria, the implied values of $V[\pi]$ and $V[x]$ yield a point on the dotted frontier shown in Figure 6.6. (Point B' on this frontier indicates the efficient plan in the case of the value $\lambda = 0.05$ corresponding to the welfare-theoretic loss function.) Observe that this frontier is entirely inside the one computed when policy is allowed to be history dependent; thus commitment to a history-dependent policy can simultaneously improve the stabilization of both inflation and the output gap.

A striking feature of the impulse responses under an optimal policy displayed in Figure 7.3 is the fact that following a cost-push shock, the unexpected inflation caused by the shock is entirely "undone," so that the price level returns completely to its previously anticipated path. This result is not special to the case of serially uncorrelated, completely unanticipated disturbances assumed in the figure.

PROPOSITION 7.10. Under the same assumptions as in Proposition 7.9, under the t_0-optimal plan, there exists a well-defined long-run expected price level,

$$\lim_{T \to \infty} E_t p_T = p_\infty,$$

that is the same in every period $t \geq t_0$, regardless of the history of disturbances between periods t_0 and t; and the same is true under any policy followed from period t_0 onward that is optimal from a timeless perspective. In the particular case of the latter sort that is optimal subject to the initial constraint (2.13) or (2.14), the long-run expected price level corresponds to the constant $\bar{p}$ in the constraint.

This is also shown in Appendix F. Note that the long-run price level p_∞ generally depends on initial conditions (including the preexisting price level p_{t_0-1}) at the time that the optimal policy is adopted; it is furthermore different (for given initial conditions) under different policies within the set to which the proposition applies. (In the case of initial constraints of the form (2.13) or (2.14), p_∞ is independent of initial conditions at the time that the policy is adopted, as it is in fact determined solely by the constant $\bar{p}$ in the initial constraint; but any long-run price level is possible under a suitable choice of $\bar{p}$.) Nonetheless, under any policy of the kind specified in the proposition, the initial conditions plus the form of optimal policy adopted determine a long-run price level, which is not subsequently affected by the realization of any random disturbances. Hence equilibrium fluctuations in the price level are stationary.

This feature of optimal policy may seem counterintuitive. Indeed, it is often argued that if one wishes to stabilize inflation and does not care about the absolute level of prices, then surprise deviations from the long-run average inflation rate should *not* have any effect on the inflation rate that policy aims for subsequently: One should "let bygones be bygones," even though this means allowing the price level to drift to a permanently different level. The claim is that "undoing" past deviations from the target rate of inflation simply creates additional, unnecessary variability in inflation. This would be correct if the commitment to subsequently undo target misses had no effect on the probability distribution of the unexpected deviations from the inflation target. However, if pricesetters are forward looking, the anticipation that a current increase in the general price level will predictably be undone soon gives suppliers a reason not to increase their own prices currently as much as they otherwise would, and so leads to smaller equilibrium deviations from the inflation target in the first place. Hence such a policy can reduce equilibrium inflation variability, and not simply the range over which the absolute price level varies.

Nonetheless, the result that optimal policy involves a stationary (or even trend-stationary) price level depends on fairly special assumptions. For example, in the event of partial indexation of prices to a lagged price index, it ceases to be optimal to completely restore the price level to the path that it would have been expected to follow in the absence of a shock, even though it continues to be optimal for positive-inflation surprises to be predictably followed by periods in which inflation is temporarily below its long-run average value. This is illustrated in Figures 7.4 and 7.5, which show the impulse responses to the same kind of shock as in Figure 7.3, but for economies with a range of values for the indexation parameter γ. (The case $\gamma = 0$ corresponds to the basic Calvo pricing model, the case already shown in Figure 7.3.) In Figure 7.4, the responses are shown in the case that the central bank optimizes under discretion, seeking to minimize the expected value of the loss function (1.22). In Figure 7.5, the corresponding responses are shown for an optimal policy commitment.

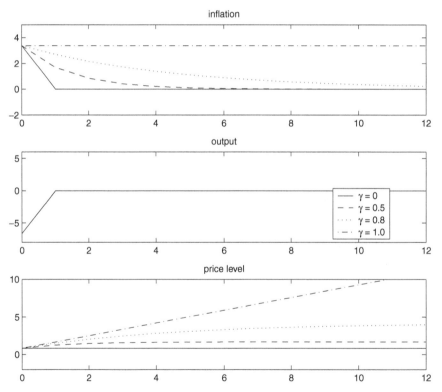

Figure 7.4 *Equilibrium responses to a transitory cost-push shock under discretionary policy for varying degrees of inflation inertia.*

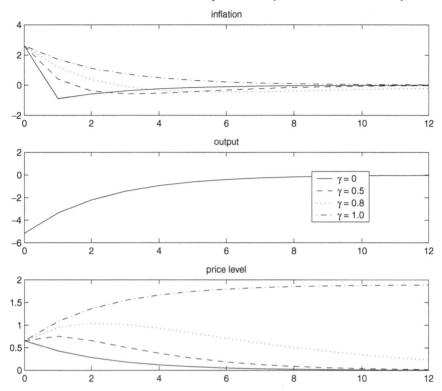

Figure 7.5 *Responses to a transitory cost-push shock under optimal policy, again for varying degrees of inflation inertia.*

In the case of discretionary policy, we see that a positive cost-push shock results not only in a burst of inflation during the period of the disturbance, but additional above-normal price increases in subsequent periods, as the rate of inflation only gradually returns to its normal level. As before, the perturbation of the target variable $\pi_t - \gamma\pi_{t-1}$ is as transitory as the disturbance u_t; but the inflation inertia resulting from the automatic indexation creates additional inflation for several more quarters. In the limiting case of full indexation ($\gamma = 1$), inflation remains permanently higher as a result of the transitory cost-push shock.

Under optimal policy, the initial unexpected increase in prices is eventually undone, as long as $\gamma < 1$; and this once again means that inflation eventually undershoots its long-run level for a time. However, for any large enough value of γ, inflation remains greater than its long-run level for a time even after the disturbance has ceased, and only later undershoots its long-run level; the larger the value of γ, the longer this period of above-average inflation persists. In the limiting case that $\gamma = 1$, the undershooting never occurs; inflation is simply gradually brought back to the long-run target level.[22] In this last case, a temporary disturbance causes a permanent change in the price level, even under optimal policy. (Under optimal policy, the price is an integrated process of order one, while under discretion it is an integrated process of order two, since there is a unit root in the *inflation rate*.)

Even if there is not full indexation to a lagged price index, the result that the price level is stationary under optimal policy is relatively fragile, given that welfare does not depend at all on the range of variation in the absolute level of prices. Under many small perturbations of the precise model considered here, optimal policy involves a price-level process with a unit root. This is true, for example, if there is even a small weight on interest-rate stabilization in the loss function, as discussed in the next section, or if the zero lower bound on nominal interest rates ever binds. The more robust conclusion about optimal policy is not that it is important for the price level to actually be stationary (or trend-stationary); it is rather that it is desirable for an inflationary disturbance to be followed by a period of tight monetary policy that keeps output below the natural rate for a time, the anticipation of which helps to restrain price increases as a result of the disturbance.

2.2 Fluctuations in the Natural Rate of Interest

I turn now to the optimal response to real disturbances that cause temporary fluctuations in the natural rate of interest r_t^n. In the case that inflation stabilization and output-gap stabilization are the only objectives of monetary policy (as in the case of loss function (1.2)), and the zero interest-rate bound never binds (as assumed thus far), fluctuations in the natural rate of interest do not prevent the central bank from completely stabilizing both inflation and the output gap; they only affect the kind of nominal interest-rate variations that are required in order to achieve this. In such a case, optimal policy continues to involve zero inflation and a zero output gap at all times, just as in the deterministic analysis in Section 1.1. In this special case, there is no difference between discretionary policy and an optimal policy commitment as regards the equilibrium responses to disturbances of this kind: In either case, inflation and the output gap do not respond at all to

22. The reason for this is easily seen. Optimal policy in the case that $\gamma > 0$ is the same as under the characterization in Proposition 7.9, except that π_t must be replaced by the quasi-differenced inflation rate $\pi_t - \gamma\pi_{t-1}$ in each expression. In the case that $\gamma = 1$, the optimal evolution of the inflation rate π_t is the same as the optimal evolution of p_t when $\gamma = 0$. Thus the impulse response of inflation (for $\gamma = 1$) in panel 1 of Figure 7.5 is the same as the impulse response of the price level (under optimal policy) in panel 3 of Figure 7.3. The scales are different because the inflation rate plotted is an annualized rate, $4\pi_t$ rather than π_t.

the disturbance, while the nominal interest-rate operating target perfectly tracks the current value of the natural rate of interest.[23]

However, the conclusion is different if the central bank is also concerned to minimize the degree of variability of nominal interest rates for either of the reasons discussed in Section 4 of Chapter 6, or perhaps for other reasons as well. In this case, as discussed in the previous chapter, it is possible to reduce interest-rate variation at the price of increased variability of inflation and the output gap, and optimal policy does this to some extent. Moreover, once simultaneous satisfaction of all of the stabilization objectives ceases to be possible, it is almost inevitably the case that optimal policy no longer coincides with discretionary policy, and indeed that optimal policy no longer is purely forward looking.

In particular, there are important advantages to a more *inertial* adjustment of interest rates than would occur under a purely forward-looking policy.[24] As discussed in Chapter 4, in an optimizing model, aggregate demand should depend on the expected path of (short-term) real interest rates far into the future, and not simply on their current level. Hence a commitment to maintain real rates at a moderately high level for a longer period of time can be as effective a way of preventing a surge in aggregate demand due to real disturbances as a sharper increase in real rates that is expected to be only temporary; but the former policy has the advantage of requiring less variable interest rates. Of course, as in the previous section, conditioning policy on past disturbances rather than on current conditions causes distortions; but the gains from anticipation of such behavior can make it nonetheless worthwhile to engage in such behavior to an extent. It can therefore be desirable for the central bank to raise interest rates only gradually in response to an increase in the natural rate of interest, and similarly to lower them again only gradually once the disturbance has passed— even though the type of loss function proposed in Chapter 6, Section 4, penalizes deviations of the *level* of nominal interest rates from the optimal level, rather than large *rates of change* in the interest rate. This is another example of the history dependence of optimal policy.

Woodford (1999a) shows that inertial interest-rate adjustment is optimal in the case of the basic neo-Wicksellian model presented in Chapter 4. If interest-rate variations matter for welfare, the aggregate-supply relation (2.1) must be augmented by an intertemporal IS relation,

$$x_t = E_t x_{t+1} - \sigma \left[i_t - E_t \pi_{t+1} - r_t^n \right], \tag{2.23}$$

---

23. These conclusions are easily obtained from the analysis of discretionary policy and optimal commitment in the previous section, since it did not matter in that analysis what was assumed about fluctuations in the natural rate of interest.

24. The basic intuition for this result is essentially that given by Goodfriend (1991).

generalizing (1.15), where now $\{r_t^n\}$ is an exogenous disturbance process. I wish to choose a policy to minimize a social loss function of the form

$$E_{t_0} \sum_{t=t_0}^{\infty} \beta^{t-t_0} \left[\pi_t^2 + \lambda_x \left(x_t - x^* \right)^2 + \lambda_i \left(i_t - i^* \right)^2 \right]. \tag{2.24}$$

Here $i^* = i^m$, as in (1.14), if the interest-rate stabilization objective appears solely as a result of transactions frictions; but one may wish to assign a higher value to i^* (and to λ_i) in order to reflect the need to avoid negative nominal interest rates.

Once again, the model is one in which the possible rational-expectations equilibrium paths of inflation, the output gap, and the nominal interest from any date t onward depend only on the real disturbances (r_t^n, u_t) at date t and upon information at date t about the subsequent evolution of those disturbances. Hence if these disturbances are Markovian, so that their current values contain all available information about their likely future evolution, then any purely forward-looking policy makes all three of the target variables vary solely in response to the current disturbances, and the effects of any disturbance on any of these variables is only as persistent as the disturbance itself.

The optimal responses to such disturbances can instead be characterized using the same Lagrangian method as in the previous section. I again obtain the first-order conditions (1.16)–(1.18) for each $t \geq t_0$.[25] In order to compute the t_0-optimal commitment, these conditions are solved under the initial conditions

$$\varphi_{1,t_0-1} = \varphi_{2,t_0-1} = 0. \tag{2.25}$$

A policy that is optimal from a timeless perspective is instead only required to minimize (2.24) subject to constraints of the form

$$\pi_{t_0} = \bar{\pi}_{t_0}, \qquad x_{t_0} = \bar{x}_{t_0}. \tag{2.26}$$

The equilibrium associated with such a policy solves the same system of first-order conditions, but with different initial values for the Lagrange multipliers $\varphi_{1,t_0-1}, \varphi_{2,t_0-1}$ than those given in (2.25). Hence the responses to disturbances under a timelessly optimal policy are of the same kind as under a t_0-optimal commitment.

The optimal responses to a disturbance to the natural rate of interest characterized by these equations are history dependent, as a result of the

---

25. In the general case, the coefficient i^m in (1.18) must be replaced by i^*.

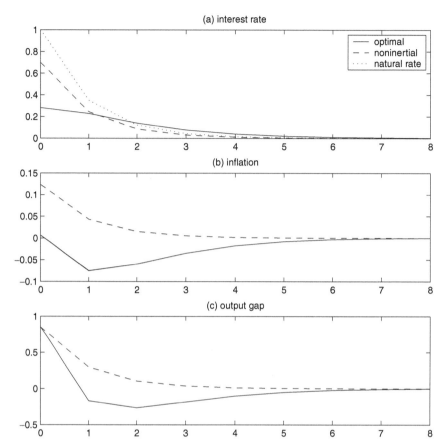

Figure 7.6   *Optimal responses to a disturbance to the natural rate of interest.*

presence of the lagged Lagrange multipliers in the first-order conditions. (For example, even in the case that $\{r_t^n\}$ is Markovian, the period t endogenous variables are not independent of the history of natural-rate disturbances prior to period t.) These optimal responses are illustrated by the solid lines in Figure 7.6 for the case of an AR(1) process for the natural rate of interest,

$$r_t^n = (1 - \rho_r)\bar{r} + \rho_r r_{t-1}^n + \epsilon_t^r, \tag{2.27}$$

with an autoregressive coefficient $\rho_r = 0.35$. (The numerical values for $\beta, \sigma, \kappa, \lambda_x$, and λ_i used in this example are taken from Table 6.1.) The impulse response of the natural rate of interest itself is shown by the dotted line in the first panel of the figure. The equilibrium responses of inflation, output, and the nominal interest rate under the best possible purely forward-looking policy (the "optimal noninertial plan," characterized in the next section) are also shown for purposes of comparison.

Under an optimal policy, the responses of these variables are not simple multiples of the current deviation of the natural rate of interest from its long-run average value. The nominal interest rate is raised much more gradually in response to an increase in the natural rate than under the optimal purely forward-looking policy, but the higher interest rates are maintained longer than the time for which the disturbance itself persists. This more persistent change in the level of interest rates restrains the initial increase in the output gap to the same extent as under the forward-looking policy, despite the more modest increase in interest rates; and it returns the gap to zero (and even undershoots) quickly, as people come to foresee real rates in the near future that will be even higher than the natural rate. Because the increase in the output gap is much more transitory (and is even soon reversed), the immediate increase in inflation is much smaller under the optimal policy. Yet this improved stabilization of inflation and output requires less volatility of nominal interest rates as well.

The way in which nominal interest rates evolve in an optimal equilibrium can be roughly described as partial adjustment toward a "desired" level that is a function of current and expected future levels of the natural rate; hence interest-rate inertia of the kind suggested by the estimated Fed reaction functions discussed in Chapter 1 is actually a feature of optimal policy, rather than an indication of failure to react quickly enough to changing conditions. The nature of the partial-adjustment dynamics can be seen especially clearly in a limiting case of this model, in which $\kappa = 0$, so that the inflation rate never varies (or at any rate evolves exogenously), regardless of the evolution of the output gap.

In this case, the problem reduces to one of choosing state-contingent paths for $\{x_t, i_t\}$ to minimize the discounted sum of losses resulting from output-gap and interest-rate variation, subject to the constraint that (2.23) be satisfied each period (given the exogenous path of inflation). The first-order conditions characterizing optimal policy are then simply (1.17) and (1.18), with the terms involving φ_{2t} omitted. Using the latter of these equations to eliminate the Lagrange multiplier φ_{1t} from the former yields[26]

---

26. In eliminating the lagged multiplier using the same relation, I am in effect choosing a particular time-invariant way of selecting the initial lagged multiplier φ_{1,t_0-1}, using a relation between this multiplier and i_{t_0-1} that *would* have been true in the case of any optimal commitment chosen at a date *earlier* than t_0. Hence the solution obtained here represents at least one of the possible equilibria from date t_0 onward that are optimal from a timeless perspective. Since the equilibrium responses to natural-rate disturbances from date t_0 onward are the same

$$\sigma \lambda_x \left(x_t - x^* \right) - \lambda_i \left[\left(i_t - i^* \right) - \beta^{-1} \left(i_{t-1} - i^* \right) \right] = 0.$$

When, in turn, this condition is used to eliminate x_t from (2.23), the latter relation becomes[27]

$$i_t - \beta^{-1} i_{t-1} = E_t \left[i_{t+1} - \beta^{-1} i_t \right] - \lambda_i^{-1} \lambda_x \sigma^2 \left(i_t - r_t^n \right). \qquad (2.28)$$

This equation has a unique bounded solution of the form

$$i_t = \mu_1 i_{t-1} + (1 - \mu_1) \bar{\imath}_t \qquad (2.29)$$

in the case of any bounded process for the disturbance $\{r_t^n\}$, where

$$\bar{\imath}_t = (1 - \mu_2) \sum_{j=0}^{\infty} \mu_2^{-j} E_t r_{t+j}^n, \qquad (2.30)$$

and $0 < \mu_1 < 1 < \mu_2$ are the two roots of the characteristic equation

$$\mu^2 - \left(1 + \beta^{-1} + \frac{\lambda_x \sigma^2}{\lambda_i} \right) \mu + \beta^{-1} = 0.$$

Equation (2.29) takes the form of partial-adjustment dynamics toward the time-varying desired level of short-term interest rates $\bar{\imath}_t$, with the root μ_1 determining the speed of adjustment. The desired level $\bar{\imath}_t$ is a weighted average of current and expected future natural rates of interest, with the root μ_2 determining how far in the future the expected values of the natural rate are averaged. In the case that the natural rate process is of the Markovian form (2.27), $\bar{\imath}_t$ is an increasing linear function of r_t^n (an average of r_t^n and the long-run average natural rate $\bar{r}$), with a slope less than one (though it gets closer to one as the fluctuations in the natural rate become more persistent). The optimal inertia coefficient μ_1 in these partial-adjustment dynamics is an increasing function of $\lambda_i / (\lambda_x \sigma^2)$. If interest-rate stabilization is sufficiently important relative to output-gap stabilization, the optimal rate of adjustment of the central bank's operating target in response to a shift in the current natural rate of interest may be quite slow.

While this simple characterization of optimal interest-rate dynamics is exactly true only in the limiting case in which $\kappa = 0$, the dynamics shown

---

in all such equilibria, the method used here gives the uniquely appropriate characterization of the optimal dynamic response to such a disturbance.

27. Here I assume that the limiting case with $\kappa = 0$ is one in which prices are so sticky that inflation is zero at all times. If instead inflation varies in response to exogenous cost-push shocks, then (2.28) again holds, but with the exogenous forcing process r_t^n replaced by the exogenous variation in $r_t^n + E_t \pi_{t+1}$.

in Figure 7.6 are fairly similar to those described by (2.29), as is discussed further in Woodford (1999a). For while $\kappa > 0$ in a realistic model, the slope of the aggregate-supply relation that is estimated econometrically is often fairly small; thus the limiting case just discussed provides considerable insight into the character of optimal interest-rate dynamics.

3 Optimal Simple Policy Rules

I have thus far discussed the character of the state-contingent evolution that one would ideally wish to arrange, and we have seen that this requires commitment to systematic behavior of a kind that would not be chosen by a discretionary optimizer. I turn now to the question of the type of *policy rule* to which a central bank should commit itself in order to reap the benefits of policy commitment that I have discussed.

Much of the recent literature has addressed this question by asking which rule would be best within some parametric family of relatively simple rules—for example, the family of contemporaneous Taylor rules,

$$ i_t = \bar{i} + \phi_\pi(\pi_t - \bar{\pi}) + \phi_x(x_t - \bar{x})/4. \tag{3.1} $$

Often it is supposed that commitment to a relatively simple rule of this sort represents the only feasible form of commitment, perhaps because of difficulties of explaining the nature of the central bank's commitment in some more complex case to the public. Here I consider the optimal choice of a policy rule from within such a restricted class from the point of view of the sort of forward-looking models of the effects of policy commitments presented earlier. I begin by discussing the optimality criterion that is appropriate in such an exercise.

It might seem that the obvious way in which to choose an optimal rule from within a family such as (3.1) is to compute the rational-expectations equilibrium associated with any given rule in the family, and evaluate a loss function such as (1.14) given the state-contingent evolution of the target variables in that equilibrium. The optimal rule within the family would then be the rule leading to the lowest expected loss. This is the definition of an "optimal simple rule" given, for example, in Levine (1991).

However, this criterion has undesirable features in the context of a forward-looking model of the effects of policy. As in the discussion of the t_0-optimal commitment in the previous two sections, one is evaluating alternative policies under a criterion that favors policies that exploit the fact that initial expectations are already given at the time that policy is chosen; and in general, this leads to a time-inconsistent policy choice, even when policies are restricted to a simple family. The criterion favors policies that create inflation in the initial periods following the policy choice, while committing to negligible average inflation farther in the future. If a rule from within family (3.1) is chosen at a time when negative output gaps are anticipated in the near term (while the long-run average output gap is expected to be zero), the preference is for a rule under which a negative output gap justifies a loosening of policy, exactly because this is expected to create the desired initial inflation without implying long-run inflation. But if the question of the optimal simple rule is reconsidered at a later date, at which a positive output gap is anticipated in the near term, a rule is preferred under which it is a *positive* output gap that justifies a loosening of policy. The choice of an optimal simple rule on these grounds is time inconsistent (as Currie and Levine (1993) note), for essentially the same reason as in the earlier discussion of the unconstrained policy problem. I wish to propose instead a criterion that results in a time-consistent selection.

Another disadvantage of this criterion is that even when applied to a class of policies flexible enough to include one that is optimal from a timeless perspective, that policy may well *not* be judged optimal within the restricted class of policies.[28] This can be seen from a reconsideration of the deterministic problem treated in Section 1.1. There the optimal policy from a timeless perspective was found to be one that resulted in zero inflation each period. One might also consider the optimal policy within the restricted class of policies that keep inflation constant at some rate $\bar{\pi}$ for all time. If one simply evaluates (1.2) for the paths of inflation and output associated with any such policy, one obtains a value

$$(1 - \beta)^{-1} \left[\bar{\pi}^2 + \lambda \left(\frac{1 - \beta}{\kappa} \bar{\pi} - x^* \right)^2 \right],$$

which is not minimized at $\bar{\pi} = 0$ in the case that $x^* > 0$. One instead would prefer a somewhat positive inflation rate under this criterion, in order to take advantage of the gains from unanticipated inflation in period t_0, even though the extent to which this is chosen is limited by the restriction that one must choose the same inflation rate for all later periods as well. In order to obtain a criterion that results in a choice of policy that is optimal from a timeless perspective when the class of simple policies is flexible enough to contain it, it is necessary to evaluate the outcomes associated with alternative rules from a perspective that penalizes a rule for taking advantage of preexisting expectations at the time of policy choice.

Thus, I propose to evaluate policy rules according to a criterion of the following sort. A quadratic loss criterion such as (1.2), evaluated conditional

---

28. For example, Jensen and McCallum (2002) find that the targeting rule (5.1), which brings about the equilibrium characterized by Proposition 7.7 and hence is optimal from a timeless perspective, is not optimal (in the sense that they consider) within a family of simple linear rules that includes rule (5.1). This is because they do not rank alternative policies according to the stabilization loss measure L^{stab} proposed below.

on the economy's state at date t_0, can be expressed as the sum of two components, $L^{det} + L^{stab}$, where L^{det} depends only on the deterministic component of the equilibrium paths of the target variables, and L^{stab} depends only on the equilibrium responses to unexpected shocks in periods after t_0. For example, in the case of (1.2), the deterministic component is given by

$$L^{det} = \sum_{t=t_0}^{\infty} \beta^{t-t_0} \left[\left(E_{t_0} \pi_t\right)^2 + \lambda\left(E_{t_0} x_t - x^*\right)^2 \right],$$

whereas the stabilization component is given by

$$L^{stab} = \sum_{t=t_0}^{\infty} \beta^{t-t_0} \left[\text{var}_{t_0}(\pi_t) + \lambda\text{var}_{t_0}(x_t) \right].$$

Under any policy rule that is optimal from a timeless perspective (or, for that matter, under a t-optimal commitment chosen at any date $t \leq t_0$), the equilibrium responses to shocks in periods after t_0 are exactly those that minimize L^{stab}, among the set of possible dynamic responses to shocks that are consistent with the (linear) structural equations. Hence I wish to evaluate rules within more restricted families of linear rules according to the same criterion: The coefficients that determine the equilibrium responses to shocks—for example, the coefficients ϕ_π, ϕ_x in the case of the family (3.1)—should be chosen so as to minimize L^{stab}, to the extent that this is possible within the class of simple rules considered. This is a criterion that allows a choice of these coefficients that is independent of the economy's state at date t_0. For that state may affect the predicted deterministic component of the paths of the target variables implied by given response coefficients, but it has no effect on the predicted variances that enter L^{stab}, given a linear model for the evolution of the disturbances. Thus the proposed criterion leads to a time-consistent choice. Furthermore, it is a criterion that implies that if the family of rules considered is flexible enough to include one that is optimal from a timeless perspective, the response coefficients in that rule are judged to be optimal.

Given this choice of the response coefficients, the coefficients that determine the long-run average values of the target variables with which the rule is consistent (the values $\bar{\imath}, \bar{\pi}, \bar{x}$ in (3.1)) are not then chosen to minimize L^{det}. Instead, in accordance with the discussion of deterministic policy problems in Section 1, a rule is chosen that is consistent with the long-run average values that occur under the t_0-optimal commitment. (These are the same values as would occur under an optimal commitment chosen at any other date or under a policy that is optimal from a timeless perspective.) Unlike the criterion of minimizing L^{det}, this criterion leads to a choice that is independent of the state at t_0, and hence that is time consistent. Moreover, it leads to a rule that is consistent with the same long-run average values of the target variables as any rule that is optimal from a timeless perspective; so if the family of rules under consideration includes such a rule, it is optimal within the restricted family. I turn now to some simple examples of policies that could be judged optimal within a restricted family of simple alternatives, though they are not fully optimal.

3.1   The Optimal Noninertial Plan

A restricted class of policies of particular interest is that of *purely forward-looking* policies, under which policy (and hence equilibrium outcomes) at each date depends only on the set of evolutions for the target variables that are possible from that date onward. Basing policy solely on projections of the economy's current and possible future states has a certain intuitive appeal, and the forecast-targeting procedures of central banks often seem to have this character; hence it may be of interest to know how different the best possible rules of this kind are from fully optimal policy.

In order to deal with this issue, I begin by considering which state-contingent evolution one should wish to bring about, among all those consistent with *any* purely forward-looking policy, and then subsequently ask which policy (or policies) can be used to implement the desired equilibrium. The set of possible state-contingent evolutions to which I restrict attention consists of those under which the current endogenous non-predetermined state variables z_t depend only on the (i) vector of exogenous states s_t that contains all the information available in period t about the disturbances to the structural equations in period t or later, and (ii) the vector Z_t of exogenous disturbances that matter for determination of the variables z_t. For the set of possible evolutions of the economy from date t onward depends only on the values of s_t and Z_t. It follows that if policy depends only on this set, it also depends only on those variables, and if the policy rule results in a determinate equilibrium, it must be one in which the equilibrium values z_t also depend only on (s_t, Z_t).

I call the optimal state-contingent evolution from within this restricted class the *optimal noninertial plan,* following Woodford (1999a). To be precise, this is the plan under which (i) the long-run average values of the variables z_t are those associated with a policy that is optimal from a timeless perspective, and (ii) the fluctuations in response to shocks are those that minimize the stabilization loss L^{stab}, subject to the constraint that z_t depend only on (s_t, Z_t).

As an example, consider again the model consisting of aggregate-supply relation (2.1), and suppose once more that social welfare is measured by the expected value of (1.2). For simplicity, suppose that the disturbance u_t evolves according to (2.18) for some $0 \leq \rho_u < 1$. As discussed earlier, in this case the set of variables (s_t, Z_t) reduces simply to the current value of u_t, and the only possible state-contingent paths that can be implemented by a purely forward-looking (linear) rule are ones in which π_t and x_t are linear functions of the current value of u_t, as in (2.19). Plans of this form are consistent with the equilibrium relation (2.1) if and only if

$$(1 - \beta)\bar{\pi} = \kappa\bar{x}, \tag{3.2}$$

$$(1 - \beta\rho_u)f_\pi = \kappa f_x + 1. \tag{3.3}$$

Furthermore, in the case of any plan of this form, the stabilization loss is given by

$$L^{stab} = \frac{\beta}{1 - \beta} \frac{1 - \rho_u^2}{1 - \beta\rho_u^2} \left[f_\pi^2 + \lambda f_x^2 \right] \sigma_u^2, \tag{3.4}$$

where σ_u^2 is the unconditional variance of the disturbance process $\{u_t\}$.

It follows from Proposition 7.2 that the long-run average values of inflation and the output gap associated with a timelessly optimal policy are $\bar{\pi} = \bar{x} = 0$. The optimal values of the coefficients (f_π, f_x) are those that minimize (3.4) or, equivalently, that minimize $f_\pi^2 + \lambda f_x^2$, subject to constraint (3.3). The solution to this latter problem is given by

$$f_\pi^{oni} = \frac{1 - \beta\rho_u}{\kappa^2\lambda^{-1} + (1 - \beta\rho_u)^2}, \qquad f_x^{oni} = -\frac{\kappa\lambda^{-1}}{\kappa^2\lambda^{-1} + (1 - \beta\rho_u)^2}. \tag{3.5}$$

Thus I obtain the following.

PROPOSITION 7.11. Consider the baseline (Calvo pricing) model, in which the aggregate-supply relation is of the form (2.1), and abstract from any grounds for a concern with interest-rate stabilization, so that the period loss function is of the form (1.2). Let the cost-push disturbance $\{u_t\}$ evolve according to (2.18) for some $0 \leq \rho_u < 1$. Then the optimal noninertial plan is a state-contingent evolution of the form (2.19) in which $\bar{\pi} = \bar{x} = 0$, and the coefficients f_π, f_x indicating the response to cost-push shocks are given by (3.5).

Applying (2.3) to the case of an AR(1) disturbance process (2.18), one finds that the equilibrium responses under discretion are also of the form (2.19), but with

$$\bar{\pi}^{disc} = \frac{\kappa\lambda}{(1 - \beta)\lambda + \kappa^2} x^* > 0$$

and

$$f_\pi^{disc} = \frac{\lambda}{\kappa^2 + (1 - \beta\rho_u)\lambda} \geq f_\pi^{oni},$$

where the last inequality is strict if $\rho_u > 0$. Thus discretionary policy is sub-optimal, even within the class of purely forward-looking policies, except in the special case that $x^* = 0$ and the cost-push shocks are serially uncorrelated. In general, discretionary policy leads both to too high an average rate of inflation (if $x^* > 0$), and too large an inflation response to cost-push shocks (if $\rho_u > 0$). It follows from (3.3) that too large a positive inflation response f_π also means too small a negative output-gap response f_x.

A similar analysis is possible in the case that welfare is reduced by variation in the level of nominal interest rates, for reasons such as those discussed in Chapter 6, Section 4. If the period loss function is of the form (2.24), then both (2.1) and (2.23) are constraints on possible equilibrium paths of the target variables $\{\pi_t, x_t, i_t\}$. If one assumes that the disturbances to both structural equations are Markovian—in particular, that $\{u_t\}$ evolves according to (2.18) for some $0 \leq \rho_u < 1$, and $\{r_t^n\}$ similarly evolves according to a law of motion (2.27) for some $0 \leq \rho_r < 1$—then under any purely forward-looking policy that results in a determinate equilibrium, each of the target variables must evolve according to equations of the form[29]

$$y_t = \bar{y} + f_y u_t + g_y r_t^n, \tag{3.6}$$

where $(\bar{y}, f_y, g_y)$ are constant coefficients for each of the variables $y = \pi, x, i$. The equilibrium relations (2.1) and (2.23) imply two linear restrictions on the coefficients f_y and another set of two linear restrictions on the coefficients g_y.

Under the assumption that the two disturbance processes are independent, the stabilization loss can be decomposed into two parts,

$$L^{stab} = L^{stab,r} + L^{stab,u},$$

corresponding to the losses resulting from responses to unexpected shocks of the two types. In the case of a plan of the form (3.6), these terms are equal to

---

29. It is not actually necessary to assume that the two disturbances evolve according to independent AR(1) processes, as posited here, in order for the form (3.6) to be correct; one might more generally assume that both r_t^n and u_t are linear functions of (r_{t-1}^n, u_{t-1}) plus an unforecastable innovation term, where the two innovation terms need not be uncorrelated with each other. Certainly there is no economic reason to assume that these disturbance processes must be independent. In the case that steady-state distortions are large, discussed in Chapter 6, Section 5, many types of disturbances, such as variations in government purchases, affect r_t^n and u_t simultaneously. However, the case of two independent disturbance processes is easier to treat, and allows one to conduct thought experiments such as the one considered in Figure 7.6.

3. Optimal Simple Policy Rules

$$L^{stab,r} = \frac{\beta}{1-\beta} \frac{1-\rho_r^2}{1-\beta\rho_r^2} \left[g_\pi^2 + \lambda_x g_x^2 + \lambda_i g_i^2 \right] \sigma_r^2, \tag{3.7}$$

$$L^{stab,u} = \frac{\beta}{1-\beta} \frac{1-\rho_u^2}{1-\beta\rho_u^2} \left[f_\pi^2 + \lambda_x f_x^2 + \lambda_i f_i^2 \right] \sigma_u^2, \tag{3.8}$$

where σ_r^2, σ_u^2 are the unconditional variances of the disturbance processes $\{r_t^n, u_t\}$, respectively. Note that $L^{stab,r}$ involves only the coefficients g_y, while $L^{stab,u}$ involves only the coefficients f_y.

The optimal noninertial plan is then the state-contingent evolution of the form (3.6) such that: (i) the coefficients $\bar{y}$ are the long-run average values under a timelessly optimal policy (characterized in Proposition 7.3), (ii) the coefficients f_y minimize $L^{stab,u}$ subject to the two constraints implied by (2.1) and (2.23), and (iii) the coefficients g_y minimize $L^{stab,r}$ subject to the corresponding two constraints on these coefficients. The solution to this problem, derived in Giannoni and Woodford (2002b), is presented in Section F.3 of Appendix F.[30] Here I note simply that the optimal response coefficients to either of the real disturbances (e.g., the coefficients g_y in the case of the natural-rate disturbance) are independent of the properties of the other disturbance; indeed, they are the same regardless of whether other (independent) disturbances are assumed to exist or not. The optimal response coefficients to a given disturbance are also independent of the degree of variability of that disturbance, though they do depend (as in Proposition 7.11) on the degree of its serial correlation.

3.2 The Optimal Taylor Rule

I now consider the optimal choice of a policy rule from within the simple family of Taylor rules (3.1). Suppose that inflation and output determination under such a rule are governed by equilibrium relations (2.1) and (2.23) of the basic neo-Wicksellian model introduced in Chapter 4. As shown in that chapter,[31] a rule of this kind (with $\phi_\pi, \phi_x \geq 0$) implies a determinate rational-expectations equilibrium if and only if it conforms to the Taylor principle, that is, its coefficients satisfy

---

30. Note that the dashed lines plotted in Figure 7.6 indicate the responses implied by the coefficients g_y in the case of the calibrated parameter values assumed in that figure.

31. In Chapter 4, I considered a version of the New Keynesian Phillips curve in which no disturbance term u_t appeared. But the analysis of determinacy of equilibrium there would be unaffected by the addition of such a term. The solutions given in Chapter 4 for the equilibrium evolution of inflation and the output gap must be modified to take account of the cost-push disturbances. However, the equations given in Chapter 4 remain applicable under the interpretation that the variable called x_t in Chapter 4 corresponds to $x_t + \kappa^{-1} u_t$ in the notation used in equation (2.1). In the notation of Chapter 4, then, the policy rule (3.1) would be one with a time-varying intercept (equal to $\bar{i} - (\phi_x/4\kappa)u_t$) in addition to the linear response to $x_t + \kappa^{-1} u_t$.

$$\phi_\pi + \frac{1-\beta}{4\kappa}\phi_x > 1. \tag{3.9}$$

In the case that the disturbance processes are of the form (2.18) and (2.27), this equilibrium is one in which the equilibrium values of π_t, x_t, and i_t all depend only on the current disturbances r_t^n and u_t. The state-contingent evolution of the target variables are then of the form (3.6) for certain coefficients $\bar{y}, f_y, g_y$ given in Appendix F.

I am thus interested in choosing the coefficients of the policy rule (3.1), from within the class of rules satisfying (3.9), so as to bring about a state-contingent evolution of the form (3.6) that achieves as low as possible a value for L^{stab}, together with the long-run average values $\bar{y}$ associated with a timelessly optimal policy. For at least a certain range of parameter values, it is possible to choose the coefficients of the Taylor rule so as to implement the best possible state-contingent evolution from within the restricted family (3.6), that is, so as to implement the optimal noninertial plan. (Note that the nine coefficients $\bar{y}, f_y, g_y$ must satisfy six equalities in order to be consistent with the equilibrium conditions (2.1) and (2.23). Hence a three-parameter family of policy rules suffices, in principle, to support any plan within this family; it is thus not fortuitous that, for a nontrivial range of parameter values, a Taylor rule can be found that implements the optimal noninertial plan.) An example of a case in which this is so is given by the following result of Giannoni and Woodford (2002b).

PROPOSITION 7.12. Suppose that the disturbance processes in the basic neo-Wicksellian model are of the form (2.18) and (2.27), with a common degree of serial correlation $\rho_r = \rho_u = \rho$. Then if ρ is in the range such that

$$0 < \left[\frac{(1-\beta\rho)(1-\rho)}{\kappa\sigma} - \rho\right]\lambda_i < \frac{(1-\beta)(1-\beta\rho)}{\kappa^2}\lambda_x + 1, \tag{3.10}$$

the optimal noninertial plan is consistent with a Taylor rule (3.1) with coefficients $\phi_\pi, \phi_x > 0$ that also satisfy (3.9). Hence commitment to this rule implies a determinate equilibrium, and implements the optimal noninertial plan. It follows that this is the optimal Taylor rule.

The coefficients of this optimal rule are given by

$$\bar{\pi} = \frac{\lambda_i}{\lambda_i + \beta}(i^* - \bar{r}), \qquad \bar{x} = \frac{1-\beta}{\kappa}\bar{\pi}, \qquad \bar{i} = \bar{r} + \bar{\pi}, \tag{3.11}$$

$$\phi_\pi = \left[\frac{(1-\beta\rho)(1-\rho)}{\kappa\sigma} - \rho\right]^{-1}\lambda_i^{-1}, \qquad \frac{\phi_x}{4} = (1-\beta\rho)\frac{\lambda_x}{\kappa}\phi_\pi. \tag{3.12}$$

The coefficients (3.11) and (3.12) are obtained by substituting the solution for the optimal noninertial plan, given in Section F.3 of Appendix F, into (3.1). Once the solution (3.12) has been obtained for the response co-efficients, it is easily seen that $\phi_x > 0$, and that $\phi_\pi > 1$ as long as λ_i satisfies the upper bound implied by (3.10). One can also show that the inequalities (3.10) are necessarily satisfied for ρ in some nonempty interval $\underline{\rho} < \rho < \bar{\rho}$, where $0 < \bar{\rho} < 1$, so that this interval also contains some positive values of ρ (but not values of ρ that are too close to one).[32] Hence in at least some cases, there exists a Taylor rule (with positive feedback coefficients satisfying the Taylor principle) that represents optimal policy, at least among the class of purely forward-looking policies.

Nor is this result dependent upon the assumption that $\rho_r = \rho_u$, made in Proposition 7.12 solely for the sake of algebraic simplification. One observes from the form of the equations that must be solved to ensure consistency of the optimal noninertial plan with a rule of the form (3.1) that there exists a pair of feedback coefficients (ϕ_π, ϕ_x) solving these equations for almost all possible parameter values, even when $\rho_r \neq \rho_u$. (Certain functions of the model parameters must be nonzero in order for a system of linear equations to have a solution; but this excludes only certain extremely special parameter values.) One must then check whether the required feedback coefficients satisfy the inequality (3.9), so that the rule implies a determinate equilibrium.[33] Proposition 7.12 shows that some parameter values exist for which the implied feedback coefficients (3.12) satisfy this inequality. Then, since the required feedback coefficients are continuous functions of the model parameters (except at the degenerate parameter values where no solution exists), the inequality is also satisfied for all model parameters (including values of ρ_r and ρ_u) that are sufficiently close to these. For any values of the other parameters, there is thus an open set of nonnegative values for (ρ_r, ρ_u) for which the results announced in Proposition 7.12 obtain, though the algebraic expressions for the optimal feedback coefficients are considerably more complex in the general case.[34]

Optimality of the Taylor rule within the class of purely forward-looking policies implies in particular that there is no gain from adopting a more

---

32. In the case of the calibrated parameter values given in Table 6.1 for β, κ, σ, λ_x, and λ_i, this interval corresponds to $0.17 < \rho < 0.68$.

33. This condition is necessary and sufficient for determinacy, as shown in Chapter 4, only under the restriction that $\phi_\pi, \phi_x \geq 0$. Thus one must also verify that these two additional inequalities are satisfied in order to ensure that the conclusions of Proposition 7.12 hold. Alternatively, one could allow for rules with negative feedback coefficients, as long as they imply a determinate equilibrium; but in that case, there are again additional inequalities that must be checked. The presence of these additional inequalities does not affect the validity of the argument made in the text; the statement "the inequality is also satisfied" should simply be modified to refer to "inequalities."

34. Proposition 4 of Giannoni and Woodford (2002b) gives an example of an open set of values for (ρ_r, ρ_u) for which this is true, though the conditions established in that result are again only sufficient conditions, and not necessary for existence of an optimal Taylor rule.

forward-looking interest-rate feedback rule, at least in the case of this simple model. For example, suppose that one considers rules of the form

$$i_t = \bar{\imath} + \phi_\pi \left(E_t \pi_{t+k} - \bar{\pi} \right) + \phi_x \left(E_t x_{t+k} - \bar{x} \right) /4, \qquad (3.13)$$

for some forecast horizon $k > 0$. Such a rule is again purely forward-looking, and so can at best implement the optimal noninertial plan. However, in a case such as that treated in Proposition 7.12, the Taylor rule already implements this plan, so that a consideration of rules with a forecast horizon $k > 0$ does not offer any possible improvement. In fact, forward-looking rules may be an inferior approach even to implementation of the optimal noninertial plan. It is true that it should be equally possible to find a rule of the form (3.13) that is consistent with that state-contingent evolution. For example, in the case treated in Proposition 7.12, there exists a rule of this form that is consistent with the optimal noninertial plan for any $k \geq 0$; it is the rule with coefficients $\bar{y}$ as in (3.11) and coefficients ϕ_y given by

$$\phi_y = \rho^{-k} \bar{\phi}_y, \qquad (3.14)$$

for $y = \pi, x$, where $\bar{\phi}_y$ refers to the coefficients given in (3.12). However, this alternative policy rule, while equally consistent with the optimal noninertial plan when $k > 0$, may not also imply determinacy of equilibrium.[35] Indeed, for large enough k, it necessarily does not, as established by Giannoni and Woodford (2002b).

PROPOSITION 7.13. Consider an economy satisfying the assumptions of Proposition 7.12. Then for all forecast horizons k longer than some critical value, the rule of the form (3.13) that is consistent with the optimal noninertial plan implies indeterminacy of rational-expectations equilibrium.

See Proposition 5 of Giannoni and Woodford.[36] Thus if the forecast horizon k is sufficiently long, it is not possible to implement the optimal noninertial plan using a rule of the form (3.13).[37] It follows that, at least when model parameters satisfy (or are close enough to satisfying) the conditions of Proposition 7.12, the best rule in this forward-looking family is not as desirable as the best purely contemporaneous Taylor rule.

---

35. Recall the discussion of this defect of forward-looking rules in Chapter 4, Section 2.2. Levin et al. (2001) also show that too long a forecast horizon can lead to indeterminacy.

36. Batini and Pearlman (2002) establish a related result for a general family of interest-rate feedback rules in which the current nominal interest rate operating target is a linear function of an inflation forecast and a lagged nominal interest rate.

37. For example, in the case of the calibrated parameter values given in Table 6.1, the rule (3.13) with coefficients (3.14) implies indeterminacy for all $k \geq 1$.

Yet even in this case, while the Taylor rule is optimal among the class of purely forward-looking policies, it does not follow that one cannot do better; for optimal policy is history dependent, as shown in Section 2.2. I demonstrate in Chapter 8 that a generalized Taylor rule that includes dependence of the right kind on lagged variables (in particular, lags of the nominal interest rate) can instead implement a fully optimal equilibrium (understood to mean one that is optimal from a timeless perspective). Moreover, even the optimality of the simple Taylor rule among purely forward-looking policies depends on fairly strong restrictions; for example, it is not true if the disturbances are not (at least jointly, if not individually) Markovian. Moreover, even when one is willing to assume Markovian disturbances, the coefficients of the optimal Taylor rule depend quite critically on the degree of serial correlation of the disturbances, as indicated by (3.12). As shown in Chapter 8, it is instead possible to choose a generalized Taylor rule with the property that the *same* feedback coefficients are optimal regardless of the serial correlation properties of the disturbances. Hence the more complex rule is better not only in terms of the expected losses in the case of a particular specification of the disturbance processes, but is also more robust.

4 The Optimal State-Contingent Instrument Path as a Policy Rule

I turn now to the problem of choosing a policy commitment that would be fully optimal—that would lead not only to the optimal long-run average values of the target variables characterized in Section 1, but also to the optimal responses to disturbances characterized in Section 2. It might be thought that the characterization of the economy's optimal state-contingent evolution in Section 2 has already given as complete a characterization of fully optimal policy as may be desired. For I have shown how to compute the optimal state-contingent paths of the various endogenous variables, including the optimal state-contingent path for the central bank's nominal interest-rate instrument. Moreover, it might be supposed that a solution for the optimal state-contingent instrument path—a formula that would tell what the nominal interest-rate operating target should be at each date, as a function of the history of disturbances up to that time—is itself a good example (perhaps even the canonical example) of a fully optimal policy rule. That is, one might propose that commitment to a fully optimal policy should mean a commitment by the central bank to choose its operating target in each decision cycle according to this formula.

I argue that this is not a desirable way of deriving an optimal policy rule; but it is first useful to illustrate what such an approach would mean. Consider again the model with cost-push shocks and no penalty for interest-rate variations treated in Section 2.1. Recall from Proposition 7.6 that equation (2.10) describes the state-contingent evolution of inflation under one kind of policy that would be optimal from a timeless perspective.[38] If I substitute a specific stochastic process for the disturbances $\{u_t\}$, such as (2.18), into this equation I obtain the solution

$$\pi_t = \frac{1}{\beta(\mu_2 - \rho_u)} \left\{ u_t - (1 - \mu_1) \sum_{k=1}^{\infty} \mu_1^{k-1} u_{t-k} \right\} \qquad (4.1)$$

for inflation as a function of the history of disturbances up through the current date. I may substitute this in turn into (2.1) to obtain a similar solution for x_t, and substitute both of these results into (2.23) to obtain the following solution for the path of the nominal interest rate.

PROPOSITION 7.14. Consider again the policy problem treated in Proposition 7.6, and suppose that the exogenous cost-push disturbances evolve according to (2.18). Then in the timelessly optimal equilibrium characterized in Proposition 7.6, the state-contingent evolution of the nominal interest rate is given by

$$i_t = r_t^n + \left(1 - \frac{\kappa}{\lambda \sigma}\right) \left\{ \frac{\mu_1 + \rho_u - 1}{\beta(\mu_2 - \rho_u)} u_t - \frac{1 - \mu_1}{\beta(\mu_2 - \rho_u)} \sum_{k=0}^{\infty} \mu_1^k u_{t-k} \right\}. \qquad (4.2)$$

One might then take equation (4.2) to specify an optimal rule for setting the central bank's interest-rate operating target; indeed, some may suppose that this kind of description of optimal policy, specifying the optimal instrument setting in each possible state of the world (identified by the history of exogenous disturbances), should represent the canonical specification of a policy rule. But this approach to the specification of optimal policy has serious disadvantages. One is that a commitment to the rule by the central bank, even if fully credible and correctly understood by the private sector, need not ensure that the desired (optimal) equilibrium evolution of inflation and output is realized.

A commitment to set interest rates according to (4.2), regardless of how inflation and output may evolve, is an example of a policy that would specify

---

38. While this is only one of several possible specifications of the initial inflation constraint $\bar{\pi}_{t_0}$ that is self-consistent in the sense discussed in Section 2.1, one can also show that it is the only specification of the initial constraint that leads to an expression (4.2) that is time invariant, i.e., independent of the date t_0 at which the policy rule is chosen. For example, the alternative specification (2.11) would lead instead to a state-contingent path for the nominal interest rate in periods $t \geq t_0$ that would depend on the value of x_{t_0-1} and on the number of periods $t - t_0$ that had elapsed since the date at which the commitment was chosen. Because I wish to choose a time-invariant policy rule in order to address the problem of time consistency discussed earlier, I accordingly assume that the specification of interest for present purposes is the one discussed in Proposition 7.6.

an exogenous nominal interest-rate path. It then follows from Proposition 4.1 that at least in the case of the basic model (considered here), rational-expectations equilibrium is indeterminate under such a policy. The optimal inflation path (4.2) is *one* possible equilibrium path for inflation under this policy, but there is also an uncountably infinite number of other nonexplosive equilibrium paths for inflation, including paths in which inflation (and hence output) responds to cost-push shocks in an entirely different way and paths in which inflation and output are affected by pure sunspot states. The fact that such a rule does not exclude these other, quite undesirable, equilibria makes this an unattractive approach to the implementation of optimal policy.

We have similarly seen in Chapter 4 that commitment to a rule of this kind, which specifies an exogenous path for the nominal interest rate, implies that the minimum-state-variable equilibrium (which in the present case corresponds to the optimal inflation evolution (4.1)) is not learnable through least-squares regression techniques. Hence from this point of view as well, a rule such as (4.2) represents an undesirable approach to the implementation of optimal policy.

Addressing both of these problems requires that the central bank's policy commitment be specified in a different way, so that the implied interest-rate path depends on the observed (or projected) paths of inflation and output, and not simply on the bank's evaluation of the history of exogenous disturbances. The Taylor rule is an example of a policy rule with this latter property, and we have seen in Chapter 4 that a rule of this kind results both in a determinate equilibrium and in one that is stable under least-squares learning dynamics. However, in the present context, we have seen that a simple (contemporaneous) Taylor rule does not result in an equilibrium that is optimal, as it fails to bring about the history dependence required for an optimal equilibrium. The question that remains to be addressed, then, is whether a rule can be found that introduces feedback from inflation and/or output to the central bank's interest-rate target of the kind needed to ensure determinacy and learnability, and that at the same time involves the sort of history dependence needed to implement an optimal equilibrium. I show in the next section how this is possible.

Equation (4.2) is also unappealing as a policy rule, but for a quite independent reason. The specific formula (4.2) has been shown to be consistent with an optimal state-contingent evolution of inflation and output only under a single very specific assumption about the statistical properties of the cost-push shocks—that they evolve according to a process of the form (2.18) with serial correlation coefficient ρ_u, with the innovation ϵ_t^u completely unforecastable before period t. Were I to assume any other stochastic process for the cost-push shock—something more complex than an AR(1) process or even an AR(1) process with a different degree of persistence or one with the same degree of persistence but with innovations revealed some number of periods in advance—then the solution for the optimal interest rate as a function of the history of the shocks would be given by a different formula.

Yet there is little practical interest in a characterization of optimal policy such as (4.2), which is valid only under the assumption that the real disturbances are of one specific type, no matter how that type is chosen. Suppose that I have estimated the coefficients of the aggregate-supply relation (2.1), have an accurate historical series for both inflation and the output gap, and thus can construct a historical series for the disturbance term u_t in this equation. I might then propose to estimate ρ_u using the historical disturbance series and could then compute the numerical coefficients of a rule of the form (4.2). But a central bank would be highly unlikely to be willing to commit itself to follow the rule even in that case.

For central bankers always have a great deal of highly specific information about the kind of disturbances that have just occurred, which are always somewhat different than those that have been faced at other times. Hence even if it is understood that "typically" cost-push disturbances have had a coefficient of serial correlation of .7, there are often grounds to suppose that the particular shock that has just occurred is likely to be either more persistent or less persistent than a typical disturbance. Moreover, it is unlikely that central bankers will be willing to commit themselves to stick rigidly to a rule that is believed to lead to outcomes that would be optimal in the case of typical disturbances, even in the case that they are aware of the economy's instead being subjected to atypical disturbances. In order for a proposed policy rule to be of practical interest, it must instead be believed that the rule is compatible with optimal (or at least fairly good) outcomes in the case of any of the extremely large number of possible types of disturbances that might be faced on different occasions.

Of course, the sort of analysis that I have used to derive (4.2) can be extended to deal with the case in which there are many different types of real disturbances that may shift the aggregate-supply relation. That is, I may suppose that the residual in equation (2.1) is actually of the form

$$u_t = \sum_j \psi_{jk} \epsilon^j_{t-k}, \tag{4.3}$$

where the $\{\epsilon^j_t\}$ are a large set of different types of shocks that may occur in period t that affect the aggregate-supply relation in that period or later to varying degrees, with varying degrees of persistence and in ways that are forecastable in advance to varying extents. Given a specification of the dynamic effects on the AS relation of a given type of shock ϵ^j_t, one can compute the response of the nominal interest rate to this particular type of shock in an optimal equilibrium. In principle this can be done for each of the types of shocks indexed by j to obtain an optimal state-contingent path for the nominal interest rate, where the state in period t is now specified by the histories of realizations of each of the different shocks. But in this case, the formula corresponding to (4.2) contains separate terms, with different numerical coefficients, for each of the possible types of shocks. Such a description of optimal policy thus becomes completely unwieldy in the case of any attempt to capture even in very coarse terms the sorts of differing situations that central banks actually confront at different times.

Giannoni and Woodford (2002a) show that if instead the central bank's policy commitment is described in terms of a relation among endogenous variables that the bank is committed to bring about—rather than in terms of a mapping from exogenous states to the instrument setting, as in (4.2)— it is possible, in a large class of policy problems, to find a rule that is *robustly optimal*, in the sense that the same rule (with given numerical coefficients) continues to be optimal regardless of the assumed statistical properties of the (additive) disturbance terms such as u_t. Indeed, the rule is optimal even if the disturbance terms in the model structural equations are actually composites of an extremely large (not necessarily finite) number of different types of real disturbances, as in (4.3). I illustrate how this is possible in the next section and discuss the kinds of policy rules to which this approach leads in greater detail in the next chapter. A rule of this kind represents a policy commitment that a central bank could reasonably make, despite its awareness that it is constantly receiving quite fine-grained information about current conditions. For a belief that the rule represents a good criterion for judging whether policy is on track does not require the central bank to believe that all shocks are alike, or even that all of the possible types of disturbances to which it may have to respond can all be listed in advance.

5 Commitment to an Optimal Targeting Rule

I now consider an alternative approach to the specification of a policy rule that can implement an optimal equilibrium, and show that this approach can avoid the problems just discussed with a specification of optimal policy in terms of a state-contingent instrument path. The alternative is what Svensson (1999a, 2003b) calls a *targeting rule*. Under such a rule, the central bank is committed to adjust its instrument as necessary in order to ensure that a certain *target criterion* is satisfied at all points in time, or more precisely (as this is all that is possible in practice), so that the criterion is *projected* to be satisfied, according to the central bank's forecast of the economy's evolution. The target criterion specifies a condition that the projected evolution of the bank's *target variables*—such as inflation, the output gap, and possibly interest rates as well—must be projected to satisfy if policy is to be regarded as "on track." A simple example would be the criterion that RPIX inflation 2 years in the future be expected to equal 2.5 percent per annum; this is the criterion used to explain the policy decisions of the Bank of England under current procedures (Vickers, 1998).

A rule of this kind represents a "higher-level" description of policy than an explicit specification of the instrument setting in each possible state of the world, such as (4.2). The instrument setting that is implied by such a rule at any point in time can only be determined through the use of a quantitative model of the effects of monetary policy on the economy. In each decision cycle, the central bank must use its model (and, of course, the judgment of policymakers) to determine what interest-rate operating target results in projections that satisfy the target criterion. But a targeting rule is not different, in this respect, from commitment to a rule like the Taylor rule discussed in Section 3.2. For in the present basic neo-Wicksellian model (the model for which the Taylor rule was shown to constitute an optimal purely forward-looking policy), both inflation and the output gap in period t depend on period t interest rates; hence the policy rule (3.1) does not indicate what the level of interest rates in period t should be without a calculation of what π_t and x_t are projected to equal in the case of one level of interest rates or another. The previous discussions about the consequences of commitment to such a rule assumed as in Chapter 4 that implementation of an "implicit instrument rule" of this kind is possible.[39]

While such incompleteness of the specification of prescribed central-bank behavior has some disadvantages—for example, it makes it more difficult for the private sector to be certain that the central bank is following the announced policy rule precisely—it has the important advantage of making possible a commitment to a rule that is optimal under a much broader range of circumstances, as discussed by Svensson and Woodford (2003c) and Giannoni and Woodford (2002a). This can be usefully illustrated through a further consideration of optimal policy in the case treated in Sections 2.1 and 4.

5.1   Robustly Optimal Target Criteria

Recall the characterization of timelessly optimal policy given in Section 2.1. For example, in the case to which Proposition 7.7 applies, the state-contingent evolution of inflation given by equation (2.12) is obtained by

---

39. McCallum (1999) has instead criticized the Taylor rule for not being an "operational" policy proposal, and proposed that one ought instead to consider only candidate rules that explicitly specify the interest-rate operating target as a function of data available to the central bank at the time that the numerical value of this target must be chosen. I do not accept this stricture here because of my interest in the design of robustly optimal rules.

solving a system of equations consisting of the first-order conditions (1.7) and (1.8) together with the structural equation (2.1), under the initial condition (2.11). Note further that conditions (1.7) and (1.8) must be satisfied in the equilibrium associated with a timelessly optimal policy for all periods $t \geq t_0$ (for some value of the initial Lagrange multiplier φ_{t_0-1}), regardless of the form of the initial constraint (2.8).

If one uses equation (1.8) to substitute for the Lagrange multiplier φ_t in (1.7), one obtains the relation

$$\pi_t + \frac{\lambda}{\kappa}(x_t - x_{t-1}) = 0 \tag{5.1}$$

which must hold for each $t \geq t_0 + 1$ under any timelessly optimal policy. One cannot show in the same way that the relation must hold at date $t = t_0$, for equation (1.8) need not hold for dates $t < t_0$, and so cannot be used to eliminate φ_{t_0-1}. Nonetheless, the fact that (5.1) must be satisfied for all dates $t \geq t_0+1$ under any timelessly optimal policy (and indeed, under a t_0-optimal commitment as well) makes a commitment to ensure that relation (5.1) holds at all times a reasonable candidate for a timelessly optimal policy rule. The following result shows that this guess is correct.

PROPOSITION 7.15. Consider again the problem of choosing monetary policy from date t_0 onward so as to minimize the expected value of (1.2), where the joint evolution of inflation and output must satisfy (2.1) for each date $t \geq t_0$. Let $\{u_t\}$ be a bounded exogenous disturbance process, the statistical character of which is otherwise unspecified. Then if the central bank commits itself to a policy that ensures that (5.1) is satisfied at each date $t \geq t_0$, there are unique bounded rational-expectations equilibrium processes $\{\pi_t, x_t\}$ for dates $t \geq t_0$ consistent with this policy rule. Furthermore, the equilibrium determined by this policy commitment is the same as the one characterized in Proposition 7.7. Thus the proposed policy rule is optimal from a timeless perspective.

This result is proved in Appendix F. Note that the result that the system of equations consisting of (2.1) and (5.1) for each $t \geq t_0$ has a determinate rational-expectations solution is important for two reasons. First, the *existence* of a solution is important in order for the proposed targeting rule to be *feasible*. Proposition 7.15 implies that there are in fact equilibrium paths for inflation and output that would satisfy the target criterion at all times. (I discuss the instrument settings required to implement such a rule in the next section.) Second, the *uniqueness* of the solution implies that this policy rule, unlike the proposed rule discussed in Section 4, is not only *consistent* with an optimal equilibrium, but is furthermore consistent with *no other* equilibria of a less desirable character. Hence a commitment to the targeting rule can be said to *implement* the desired equilibrium in a way that a commitment to the associated state-contingent interest-rate path does not.

The determinacy result announced in Proposition 7.15 is established directly in Appendix F, through a consideration of the equation system consisting of (2.1) and (5.1). However, the result has a simple intuition; it is a consequence of the existence of a unique bounded solution to the system of equations consisting of (1.7) and (1.8) together with (2.1), which characterize the t_0-optimal plan. For equation (5.1) is equivalent to conditions (1.7) and (1.8) plus the stipulation of an initial Lagrange multiplier[40]

$$\varphi_{t_0-1} = \frac{\lambda}{\kappa}\left(x_{t_0-1} - x^*\right). \tag{5.2}$$

However, the initial condition (5.2) is irrelevant for the question of whether a determinate solution exists; if such a solution exists in the case of the initial condition (2.5), then it also should exist in the case of the initial condition (5.2). Hence a commitment to achievement of the target criterion (5.1) implies a determinate rational-expectations equilibrium.

I thus have an example of a policy rule that results in a determinate equilibrium that is optimal from a timeless perspective. Moreover, the proposed rule is also *robustly* optimal in the sense of Giannoni and Woodford (2002a). For Proposition 7.15 relies on no assumptions about the nature of the exogenous disturbance process $\{u_t\}$, except that it is bounded (as is generally necessary in order for bounded equilibrium paths for inflation and the output gap to be possible under *any* monetary policy, and hence for my approximate characterizations of the equilibrium conditions and welfare to be valid) and that its effect on the aggregate-supply relation (2.1) is additive (in a log-linear approximation). The first-order conditions from which the target criterion (5.1) is derived are independent of any assumptions about the statistical properties of the disturbances, and so the optimal policy rule obtained in this way is optimal regardless of their character. Hence a commitment to bring about the optimality condition (5.1) is equally sensible regardless of the particular types of shocks that the central bank may believe to have most recently disturbed the economy.

The robustly optimal rule is an example of a flexible inflation targeting rule, in the sense discussed by Svensson (1999, 2003b).[41] The central bank commits itself to adjust the level of nominal interest rates so that the projected inflation rate is consistent at all times with the target criterion. How-

---

40. Note that (5.2) is just what the multiplier would have to have been equal to if the first-order condition (1.8) also held at date $t = t_0 - 1$, as it would in the case of an optimal commitment chosen at date $t_0 - 1$ or earlier.

41. To be more precise, the type of rule that I consider here corresponds to what Svensson calls a "specific" targeting rule.

ever, the acceptable inflation rate depends on the projected path of the output gap. An inflation rate higher than the long-run target rate (here, zero) is acceptable if the output gap is projected to decline, and a lower inflation rate could be achieved only by reducing the output gap even more sharply, making the left-hand side of (5.1) negative. Similarly, an inflation rate lower than the long-run target rate should be sought if even this rate of inflation requires a growing output gap, so that any higher current inflation rate would be possible only with a positive value for the left-hand side of (5.1).

However, the optimal target criterion (5.1) differs from a common conception of "flexible inflation targeting" in that it is the projected *rate of change* of the output gap, rather than the absolute level of the output gap, that should determine the acceptable deviation from the long-run inflation target. This might seem paradoxical, in that it is the absolute level of the output gap, rather than its rate of change, that one wishes to stabilize. But this is simply a reflection, once again, of the fact that optimal policy is not purely forward looking. The target criterion is history dependent in the sense that acceptable projections (π_t, x_t) depend on the value of the lagged output gap x_{t-1}, even though that gap is irrelevant both to the determination of current and future inflation and output gap and to the welfare evaluation of alternative possible paths for those variables from the present time onward. But this sort of history-dependence is exactly what is necessary in order for the targeting rule to bring about the kind of dynamic responses to a cost-push shock shown in Figure 7.3. Once an adverse cost-push shock has caused a negative output gap, the history-dependent target criterion requires that the output gap be restored only gradually to its long-run level and that inflation be kept below its long-run level during the period in which the output gap is catching up to its long-run level. This kind of dynamic response to a transitory cost-push shock implies that price-level increases due to the cost-push shock are subsequently undone, and as discussed earlier, the anticipation that this is the case restrains price increases at the time of the shock, reducing the extent to which either inflation or a negative output gap is necessary at that time.

The optimal target criterion (5.1) also differs from the kind of target criteria typically used by inflation-targeting central banks to justify their policy settings—such as the criterion used by the Bank of England, mentioned above—in that it specifies an acceptable near-term inflation rate (that is allowed to vary, under stated conditions) rather than a medium-term inflation objective (that should remain always the same, despite short-term inflation variability). It is important to note that this criterion does incorporate a long-run inflation target (namely, zero); because the change in the output gap from one quarter to the next must be zero on average, ensuring that (5.1) holds each quarter requires a zero inflation rate on average. Nonetheless, the rule requires the central bank to justify its instrument setting in each decision cycle by reference to whether it is projected to result in an acceptable near-term inflation rate, and not simply by reference to whether policy continues to be consistent with a projection that inflation should eventually approach the long-term target value.

A flexible (but specific!) target criterion of this kind provides a clearer guide to short-run policy decisions—that is, to the only kind of decisions that a central bank is actually called upon to make—than does a mere specification of the long-run inflation target. After all, the interest-rate decision made at any point in time is of little import for the expected long-run inflation rate, which should depend entirely on how policy is expected to be conducted in the future. A commitment to return inflation to its long-run target rate by a specified (not too distant) horizon may have less trivial implications for current policy, but a horizon that is short enough for such a commitment to determine current policy is likely to result in too rigid a criterion for such a commitment to be desirable. Hence the desirability of a target criterion that specifies the conditions under which near-term deviations from the long-run target are justifiable, rather than merely specifying the long-run target.

Actual inflation-targeting central banks have probably avoided the articulation of a flexible nearer-term target criterion of this kind out of skepticism about whether it is possible to specify in advance all of the conditions under which a given degree of temporary departure from the long-run inflation target should be justifiable. But we have seen that it is possible to derive a robustly optimal target criterion that correctly determines whether a given degree of departure of projected near-term inflation from the long-run target rate is consistent with the optimal state-contingent inflation path, *regardless* of the size and nature of the disturbances that have most recently affected the economy. If the soundness of such a criterion is accepted, then it ought to be possible for a central bank to commit itself to the conduct of policy in accordance with a nearer-term target criterion of this kind.

While (5.1) represents an example of a robustly optimal target criterion, it is not the only possible criterion with that property. Note that satisfaction of (5.1) each period implies that the quantity $p_t + (\lambda/\kappa)x_t$ never changes (since the left-hand side of (5.1) is just the first difference of this quantity). Hence in any equilibrium that is optimal from a timeless perspective, there exists some value of $\bar{p}$ such that

$$p_t + \frac{\lambda}{\kappa}x_t = \bar{p} \tag{5.3}$$

at all times. This suggests an alternative policy rule, namely, that the central bank commit to ensure that (5.3) holds each period. This too can be shown to be a robustly optimal targeting rule.

PROPOSITION 7.16. Under the same assumptions as in Proposition 7.15, suppose that the central bank commits itself to a policy that ensures that

(5.3) is satisfied at each date $t \geq t_0$. Then there are unique bounded rational-expectations equilibrium processes $\{\pi_t, x_t\}$ for dates $t \geq t_0$ consistent with this policy rule. Furthermore, the equilibrium determined by this policy commitment is the same as the one characterized in Proposition 7.8. Thus the proposed policy rule is optimal from a timeless perspective.

The proof is in Appendix F. This type of rule corresponds to the flexible price-level target advocated by Hall (1984).[42] Note that my analysis provides theoretical grounds for choosing a particular coefficient on the output gap in such a rule. As shown in Chapter 6, in the welfare-theoretic loss function, $\lambda = \kappa/\theta$, where $\theta > 1$ is the elasticity of substitution among alternative goods and also the elasticity of demand faced by each of the monopolistically competitive suppliers. It then follows that the optimal flexible price-level targeting rule stabilizes the value of $p_t + \theta^{-1}x_t$. Since a reasonable calibration of θ must be much larger than one (a value on the order of ten is most commonly assumed, in order for the model not to imply an implausible degree of market power), this implies that the weight on the output gap should be only a small fraction of the weight on the price level.

The targeting rule (5.3) is closely related to (5.1); indeed, committing to (5.1) from some date t_0 onward is equivalent to committing to a rule of the form (5.3) with a particular choice of the price-level target, namely,

$$\bar{p} = p_{t_0-1} + \frac{\lambda}{\kappa}x_{t_0-1}.$$

However, the choice of $\bar{p}$ is arbitrary, if one wishes only to ensure that the rule chosen is optimal from a timeless perspective. Different rules in the family lead to the same long-run average inflation rate (though different long-run average price levels), the same long-run average output gap, and the same equilibrium responses to shocks. The associated equilibria differ only in a transitory, deterministic component, as to which one can make no choice from a timeless perspective.

5.2 Implementation of a Targeting Rule

The results in the previous section (Propositions 7.15 and 7.16) describe the state-contingent evolution of inflation and output that should result,

---

42. The observation that timelessly optimal policies bring about equilibria consistent with a rule of this kind explains the comment, in Section 4.5 of Chapter 6, that the efficient frontier in Figure 6.6 corresponds to flexible price-level targets with alternative weights on the output gap. The efficient frontier is constructed by computing the optimal state-contingent evolution of inflation and of the output gap in the case of alternative values of λ ranging between 0 and $+\infty$. For each value of λ, the optimal policy is a member of the family (5.3), but with a different weight on the output gap in each case.

in a rational-expectations equilibrium, if the central bank succeeds in ensuring that the target criterion is satisfied at all times. But can a central bank actually ensure this, and hence bring about such an equilibrium? It is appropriate to discuss further what sort of adjustment of its interest-rate instrument this would involve. This means describing the conduct of policy in accordance with such a rule in terms of the associated *reaction function* for the nominal interest rate that is the policy instrument. One can then consider whether such a reaction function determines a unique (or at least a unique nonexplosive) rational-expectations equilibrium and whether this equilibrium should be learnable, along the lines of the analysis of the determinacy and learnability of equilibrium under simple interest-rate rules in Chapter 4.

First consider the implementation of the targeting rule (5.1). The policy rule specifies that i_t should be set in period t in such a way that the central bank projects values of π_t and x_t consistent with equation (5.1). The interest-rate decision that this implies depends on the way in which the central bank constructs the projections for current inflation and output conditional on alternative interest-rate decisions.

I suppose that the central bank's model of the effects of alternative policies is the correct one, that is, that it consists of equations (2.1) and (2.23), together with a correct understanding of the laws of motion of the exogenous disturbance processes. But this in itself does not answer the question of what the central bank's projection conditional on its interest-rate decision should be, for according to the equations of the structural model, current inflation and output, given the current nominal interest rate, depend on expectations regarding the economy's future evolution. One way of specifying these expectations would be for the central bank to assume that the private sector expects the economy to evolve in the future (i.e., in period $t+1$ and later) according to the rational-expectations equilibrium described in Proposition 7.15. That is, it assumes that the private sector expects it to succeed in enforcing the target criterion in all periods from $t+1$ onward, even though, for purposes of constructing the conditional projection, the central bank contemplates the consequences of deviation from the interest rate consistent with the policy rule in period t.

This means that the central bank believes that the private sector expects that in period $t+1$, inflation and the output gap will be given by

$$\pi_{t+1} = (1 - \mu_1)\frac{\lambda}{\kappa}x_t + \frac{1}{\beta}\sum_{j=0}^{\infty}\mu_2^{-j-1}E_{t+1}u_{t+j+1},$$

$$x_{t+1} = \mu_1 x_t + \frac{\kappa}{\beta\lambda}\sum_{j=0}^{\infty}\mu_2^{-j-1}E_{t+1}u_{t+j+1}.$$

Taking the expectations of these two expressions conditional upon period t information, one obtains solutions for $E_t \pi_{t+1}$ and $E_t x_{t+1}$ as linear functions of x_t and terms of the form $E_t u_{t+j}$. Substituting these solutions into the structural relations (2.1) and (2.23), one can then solve those two relations for π_t and x_t as linear functions of i_t, r_t^n, and terms of the form $E_t u_{t+j}$. The bank's projection of the current-period value of its target $\pi_t + (\lambda/\kappa) x_t$, conditional on its current instrument choice i_t and given its information about the exogenous disturbances, would then equal

$$\frac{-\sigma}{\lambda^{-1}\kappa - \sigma} \frac{1}{\mu_1(1 - \mu_1)} (i_t - r_t^n) + u_t - \frac{1}{\beta(1 - \mu_1)} \frac{\kappa^2 + \lambda}{\lambda} \sum_{j=1}^{\infty} \mu_2^{-j} E_t u_{t+j}.$$

If the central bank equates this expression to $(\lambda/\kappa) x_{t-1}$, as required in order for the projection to satisfy (5.1), it obtains a relation that can be solved for i_t, yielding

$$i_t = r_t^n + \mu_1 \left(1 - \frac{\lambda\sigma}{\kappa}\right) \left\{ \frac{(1 - \mu_1)\kappa}{\lambda\sigma} u_t - \frac{\kappa}{\beta\lambda\sigma} \left(1 + \frac{\kappa^2}{\lambda}\right) \right.$$

$$\left. \sum_{j=1}^{\infty} \mu_2^{-j} E_t u_{t+j} - \frac{1 - \mu_1}{\sigma} x_{t-1} \right\}. \qquad (5.4)$$

This is what Evans and Honkapohja (2002a) call the "fundamentals-based reaction function" for implementation of the target criterion (5.1),[43] which gives a formula for the central bank's operating target purely in terms of exogenous and predetermined variables.

However, while this relation is consistent with the desired state-contingent evolution of the interest rate and other variables, a commitment to set interest rates in this way does not necessarily imply a determinate equilibrium; Evans and Honkapohja show that for many parameter values, it does not.[44] For while the right-hand side of (5.4) does not depend solely on exogenous variables, all dependence on either current or expected future endogenous variables has been eliminated by substituting the values

43. They define this reaction function, like (5.5), only for the case of disturbance processes of the special forms (2.18) and (2.27); but the logic of their derivation is the one given here. Note that the determinacy of equilibrium when the central bank commits itself to a reaction function of this form does not depend on the statistical properties of the exogenous disturbance processes; only the coefficient with which the lagged endogenous variable x_{t-1} enters matters for that.

44. Svensson and Woodford (2003c) reach a similar conclusion in the case of a closely related reaction function in the case of a model in which the endogenous components of both inflation and output are predetermined a period in advance.

that these variables are expected to take in the desired equilibrium. But a
central bank that commits itself to act *as if* the desired equilibrium is being
realized regardless of whether or not this is observed to be the case does not
act sufficiently decisively to ensure that this equilibrium is realized, rather
than some other one which is less desirable.

An alternative approach, recommended by Evans and Honkapohja, is for
the central bank not to substitute out for what the expectations $E_t\pi_{t+1}$ and
$E_t x_{t+1}$ *ought* to be, given the economy's current state and the laws of motion
that obtain in the desired equilibrium, but rather to condition its policy decision on what it *actually observes* current private-sector expectations to be.
Under this approach, the central bank produces its projections for current-
period inflation and output by solving the structural equations (2.1) and
(2.23) for π_t and x_t as functions of i_t, period t expectations, and the exogenous disturbances. In this case, the bank's projection for $\pi_t + (\lambda/\kappa)x_t$
conditional on its current instrument choice is given by

$$-\sigma\frac{\kappa^2+\lambda}{\kappa}\left(i_t - r_t^n\right) + u_t + \left[\beta + \sigma\left(\frac{\kappa^2+\lambda}{\kappa}\right)\right]E_t\pi_{t+1} + \frac{\kappa^2+\lambda}{\kappa}E_t x_{t+1}.$$

Equating this to $(\lambda/\kappa)x_{t-1}$ and solving for i_t, one obtains the alternative
reaction function

$$i_t = r_t^n + \frac{\kappa}{\sigma(\kappa^2+\lambda)}u_t + \left[1 + \frac{\beta\kappa}{\sigma(\kappa^2+\lambda)}\right]E_t\pi_{t+1}$$

$$+ \frac{1}{\sigma}E_t x_{t+1} - \frac{\lambda}{\sigma(\kappa^2+\lambda)}x_{t-1}. \tag{5.5}$$

Evans and Honkapohja call this an "expectations-based reaction function,"
intended to implement (5.1).

If the central bank can commit itself to set interest rates in accordance
with this reaction function at all times, then rational-expectations equilibrium is necessarily determinate, due to the following result.

PROPOSITION 7.17. Consider an economy in which inflation and output
are determined by structural relations of the form (2.1) and (2.23), where
the exogenous disturbances $\{u_t, r_t^n\}$ are bounded processes but otherwise
unrestricted, and suppose that the central bank sets its nominal interest-rate
instrument in accordance with (5.5) in each period $t \geq t_0$. Then there is a
determinate rational-expectations equilibrium evolution for inflation, output, and the nominal interest rate in periods $t \geq t_0$, and the state-contingent
paths of inflation and output are the ones characterized in Proposition 7.7.
Hence such a policy is optimal from a timeless perspective.

The proof of this result is simple. Equation (5.5), together with (2.1) and (2.23), implies that (5.1) must hold in each period $t \geq t_0$. (This just reverses the steps in the derivation of (5.5) sketched above.) But, from Proposition 7.15, the system consisting of equations (2.1) and (5.1) has a unique bounded solution for inflation and output. Equation (2.23) can then be solved for the associated bounded solution for the path of the nominal interest rate. Furthermore, it is known from Proposition 7.15 that the equilibrium determined in this way is the one characterized in Proposition 7.7.

We thus see that a commitment to achieving the flexible inflation target (5.1) is actually an equivalent policy to one that results from a commitment to an interest-rate rule of the form (5.5). As in the case of the strict inflation target discussed in Chapter 4, the implied reaction function takes the form of a forward-looking Taylor rule, though in the present case, the rule is no longer *purely* forward looking, owing to the dependence of the period t interest rate on the previous period's output gap. Once again, we see that the optimal interest-rate rule satisfies the Taylor principle, since the long-run response coefficients are equal to

$$\Phi_\pi = 1 + \frac{\beta\kappa}{\sigma(\kappa^2 + \lambda)} > 1, \qquad \Phi_x/4 = \frac{\kappa^2}{\sigma(\kappa^2 + \lambda)} > 0.$$

Also note that the optimal interest-rate rule has an intercept that varies with fluctuations in the natural rate of interest, like the rules discussed in Chapter 4 that would completely stabilize inflation. However, the variation in the natural rate of interest is no longer the *only* relevant information about real disturbances; once the central bank's target criterion also involves the output gap, if the welfare-relevant output gap is not one that can be completely stabilized through stabilization of inflation, then cost-push disturbances (i.e., shifts in the equilibrium relation between the inflation rate and the welfare-relevant output gap) should enter into the central bank's reaction function as well.

It is perhaps interesting to note that a rule that not only leads to a determinate equilibrium, but that represents a robustly optimal policy, involves responses to variations in expected future inflation and output. As discussed in Chapter 4, a policy of strongly responding to variations in expected inflation as a way of preventing such fluctuations from occurring can be counterproductive, as it may actually enable instability of inflation due to self-fulfilling expectations. (See also Proposition 7.13.) The difference here is that in the case of the reaction function (5.5), the central bank is responding to private-sector expectations *solely in order to counteract them.* The target criterion (5.1), which describes the state of affairs that the central bank is trying to achieve through its policy, is not forward looking at all, and in particular is not affected by any change in perceived private-sector expectations. These expectations are relevant to the policy decision only insofar as they affect what the central bank expects to be able to achieve by setting interest rates at one level rather than another, in much the way that information about the current real disturbances r_t^n or u_t must also be taken into account. Responding to forecasts in this particular sense does not make the economy more vulnerable to self-fulfilling expectations; on the contrary, by counteracting the effects of such variations in expectations as may occur, it tends to protect the economy from this potential source of instability.

Thus far I have considered only the problem of indeterminacy of rational-expectations equilibrium under a given policy rule. As discussed in Chapter 4, it is also appropriate to consider whether one should expect private-sector beliefs to converge to those associated with a rational-expectations equilibrium through a process of learning from the statistical patterns in observed data. Evans and Honkapohja (2002a) consider the E-stability (in the sense discussed in Section 2.3 of Chapter 4) of the rational-expectations equilibrium determined by the target criterion (5.1) in the case that the target criterion is implemented through either of the reaction functions (5.4) or (5.5), with the conditional expectations $E_t[\cdot]$ replaced by subjective expectations $\hat{E}_t[\cdot]$ in each case. As with the E-stability analysis of Bullard and Mitra (2002) discussed in Chapter 4, they assume that inflation and output are determined by relations (2.16) and (2.17) of Chapter 4 in the case of arbitrary private-sector expectations and that private agents forecast using an OLS regression model. Evans and Honkapohja find that in the case of the fundamentals-based reaction function, the optimal rational-expectations equilibrium is often unstable under learning dynamics, whereas in the case of the expectations-based reaction function (5.5) it is necessarily E-stable. These findings again support the desirability of the latter approach to implementation of the target criterion.

The results of Evans and Honkapohja, however, depend on assuming a mapping from subjective expectations to the actual evolution of inflation and output that only makes sense (in terms of the underlying microfoundations of the basic neo-Wicksellian model) in the case that agents have rational expectations,[45] as discussed in Chapter 4. Preston (2002b) reconsiders the consequences of conducting monetary policy in accordance with these reaction functions under the assumption that inflation and output are determined by equations (2.29) and (2.30) of Chapter 4, so that longer-horizon private-sector forecasts also matter. In this case, he finds that not even the reaction function (5.5) always leads to stability of the rational-expectations equilibrium under learning dynamics. The reason is that when

---

45. Note that the central bank may reasonably wish to monitor private expectations even under that assumption, if it is concerned with the possibility of multiple rational-expectations equilibria.

the mapping from private-sector forecasts to actual outcomes is not the one assumed in the derivation of the expectations-based reaction function, then a central bank that acts in accordance with that formula does not actually succeed in causing the target criterion to be satisfied, unless the economy does happen to converge to a rational-expectations equilibrium.

However, Preston shows that similar reasoning can be used to compute the reaction function that the central bank would follow in order to implement the target criterion (5.1), in the case that private-sector forecasts are observable and the central bank correctly understands the way in which inflation and output are determined by these expectations. This results in an expectations-based reaction function that now requires the central bank to respond to long-horizon forecasts. This reaction function leads not only to determinacy of rational-expectations equilibrium (it is necessarily consistent with the same set of rational-expectations equilibria as the simpler reaction function (5.5)), but also to E-stability of these equilibria when agents forecast using OLS regression. Hence Preston also finds that commitment to a targeting rule, if implemented by a central bank that observes private-sector expectations and *correctly understands* how to project inflation and output conditional upon its policy decision in the light of those observed expectations, should result in convergence of learning dynamics to a rational-expectations equilibrium that is optimal from a timeless perspective.

CHAPTER 8

Optimal Monetary Policy Rules

I turn now to the question of the specific content of an optimal rule for the conduct of monetary policy. In the previous chapter, I characterized the optimal state-contingent responses to disturbances that monetary policy should seek to bring about and demonstrated the need for commitment to a policy rule in order for policy to be consistent with such an optimal equilibrium. I also argued for the desirability for a particular form of policy commitment, namely, a commitment to bring about paths for certain target variables (such as an inflation measure, a measure of the output gap, and the level of overnight interest rates) that satisfy (or at any rate, are projected to satisfy) a certain target criterion. The present chapter considers the choice of a suitable target criterion, or (in the case that the target criterion involves the current instrument setting) a suitable feedback rule that the central bank's interest-rate operating target should satisfy at all times.

My goal is not to derive a particular rule that can be presented as *the* optimal one for monetary policy. It is rather to expound a method that can be used to derive a desirable rule, given one's beliefs about the correct model of the monetary transmission, on the one hand, and one's conception of the appropriate aims of stabilization policy on the other. In principle, the aims of stabilization policy should *follow* from one's model of the economy, as discussed in Chapter 6. But the utility of the method proposed here does not depend on any such consistency between model and stabilization goals. This greatly increases the interest of the results, insofar as central banks are not always (indeed, are probably never entirely) able to decide by themselves on the goals of monetary policy.

I begin by presenting a general approach to the design of an optimal policy rule in the context of a fairly general class of linear-quadratic policy problems. (The quadratic stabilization objective and log-linear structural relations that define such a problem may be derived from local approximations of the kind explained in Chapter 6.) I then illustrate concretely how the form of the optimal policy rule depends on the model of the economy that one assumes by considering a series of fairly simple examples (though all more complex than the simple case described in Section 5 of Chapter 7). These examples are chosen not simply because they are easy to solve, but because they incorporate (albeit in a simpler context) various important features of the current generation of optimization-based quantitative models of the monetary transmission mechanism. Finally, I conclude with reflections on the extent to which currently popular proposals, of the kind discussed in Chapter 1, are similar to the kind of rules that could be justified on the criteria proposed here, in the light of my provisional conclusions about elements of a realistic model of the transmission mechanism.

1 A General Linear-Quadratic Framework

A common feature of many common prescriptions for monetary policy (as discussed in Chapter 1) is that a precise criterion is given that should be checked each time an interest-rate decision is made in order to determine whether the central bank's current interest-rate target is acceptable or not, given the observed or projected behavior of variables such as inflation and the output gap (i.e., the variables that define the bank's stabilization objectives, rather than any "intermediate" targets). Here I wish to consider the optimal choice of a criterion to be used in this way.[1] The question has been extensively discussed in recent years.[2] However, most of the recent literature assumes some low-dimensional parametric family of policy rules, and then optimizes over the coefficients of the rule, using an economic model to compute the equilibrium associated with each possible set of parameters. A characteristic weakness of such work,[3] in my view, is that the conclusions reached about the optimal values of certain parameters are likely to be strongly influenced by the parametric family of rules considered, that is, by which other kinds of feedback are assumed *not* to be possible. Hence I propose here to take a different approach: first to characterize the best possible pattern of equilibrium responses to disturbances—solving an optimization problem in which the structural equations of one's model of the economy appear as constraints, as in Chapter 7—and then to ask what kind of policy rule can bring about the desired equilibrium.

This alternative approach is standard in the theory of public finance, and is also used in optimal-control approaches to the analysis of monetary policy, such as that of Currie and Levine (1993). However, work of this latter kind typically assumes that optimal policy has been adequately characterized once one has solved for the optimal state-contingent paths of the various

1. This section is based on Giannoni and Woodford (2002a).
2. See, e.g., the papers in Taylor (1999a).
3. This includes my own previous studies, such as Rotemberg and Woodford (1999a).

endogenous variables, including a solution for the instrument setting as a function of the history of exogenous disturbances. Here my interest is rather in the further question of how best to choose a policy rule with which to *implement* the optimal pattern of responses to disturbances. A policy rule specified in terms of a mapping from the history of disturbances to the instrument setting is not the only possible type of policy rule that would be consistent with the optimal pattern of responses, and I have argued in Chapter 7 that it is generally not the best one. Hence I am led to consider rules that involve the projected paths of endogenous variables, such as inflation and output. Of course, once I do not insist on a particular canonical form for the criterion that policy is to satisfy, I find that *many* alternative policy rules would be equally consistent with the optimal equilibrium. I can then ask for a representation of optimal policy that has other desirable features as well.

For example, I demand that the policy rule be not merely consistent with the desired equilibrium, but also that commitment to the rule imply a *determinate* equilibrium, so that the rule is not equally consistent with other, less desirable equilibria. I am also looking for policy rules that are time invariant and that refer only to the evolution of certain state variables (those that I call *target* variables) that represent the central bank's stabilization goals. Finally, I seek to derive policy rules that continue to be optimal regardless of what the statistical properties of the exogenous disturbances hitting the economy are believed to be.

Giannoni and Woodford (2002a) present a method for deriving policy rules with these properties for a fairly general class of policy problems in which the monetary transmission mechanism is represented by a linear(ized) rational-expectations model and stabilization objectives are represented by a discounted quadratic loss function. I first give more precise statements of the general criteria that an optimal policy rule should satisfy and then present the solution to this problem given by Giannoni and Woodford. In this general discussion, the instrument of policy need not be an interest rate, and the stabilization goals need have nothing to do with nominal variables, though this is the application that motivates their formulation of the problem. Applications to the problem of interest-rate policy in the context of explicit optimizing models of the monetary transmission mechanism are then taken up in Sections 2 and 3.

1.1 Optimal State-Contingent Paths

I begin by describing the general linear-quadratic policy problem considered by Giannoni and Woodford (2002a). The linear(ized) structural equations, which represent the constraints on possible equilibrium outcomes under any policy, are assumed to be a system of the form

$$\hat{I} \begin{bmatrix} Z_{t+1} \\ E_t z_{t+1} \end{bmatrix} = A \begin{bmatrix} Z_t \\ z_t \end{bmatrix} + Bi_t + Cs_t, \tag{1.1}$$

where z_t is a vector of n_z nonpredetermined endogenous variables, Z_t is a vector of n_Z predetermined endogenous variables, i_t is the policy instrument (chosen by the policy authority in period t), and s_t is a vector of exogenous disturbances.[4] Each matrix in this equation has $n = n_z + n_Z$ rows, so that there are a sufficient number of independent structural relations each period to determine each of the endogenous variables. I futher suppose that the vector s_t includes all of the exogenous states that contain information about the possible future evolution of the variables Z_T and z_T for $T \geq t$.

I may further partition the matrices as

$$\hat{I} = \begin{bmatrix} I & 0 \\ 0 & \tilde{E} \end{bmatrix}, \quad A = \begin{bmatrix} A_{11} & A_{12} \\ A_{21} & A_{22} \end{bmatrix}, \quad B = \begin{bmatrix} 0 \\ B_2 \end{bmatrix}, \quad C = \begin{bmatrix} 0 \\ C_2 \end{bmatrix},$$

where in each case the upper blocks have n_Z rows, the lower blocks n_z rows, and the columns of $\hat{I}$ and A are partitioned in a manner conformable to the partition of the endogenous variables in (1.1). Here the assumed zero restrictions in the upper blocks reflect the fact that the first n_Z equations define the elements of Z_t as elements of z_{t-j} for some $j \geq 1$. (Because of this feature of the vector Z_{t+1}, the assumption that the lower left block of $\hat{I}$ is a zero matrix is also without loss of generality.) I assume that B_2 is not zero in all elements, so that the instrument has some effect, and that A_{22} is nonsingular, so that the last n_z equations can be solved for z_t as a function of Z_t, s_t, i_t, and expectations $E_t z_{t+1}$.

The objectives of stabilization policy are assumed to be represented by a discounted quadratic loss function of the form

$$E_{t_0} \sum_{t=t_0}^{\infty} \beta^{t-t_0} L_t, \tag{1.2}$$

where t_0 is the initial date at which a policy rule is adopted, $0 < \beta < 1$ is a discount factor, and the period loss L_t is of the form

$$L_t = \tfrac{1}{2}(\tau_t - \tau^*)' W (\tau_t - \tau^*), \tag{1.3}$$

---

4. I assume that both z_t and Z_t are vectors of finite length. The vector s_t, however, need not be; as I discuss in Section 1.3, I allow in principle for an infinite number of distinct types of random disturbances. In the case that s_t is not a finite vector, the references to "bounded disturbance processes" are to be understood to refer not simply to a bound upon each element of s_t, but also to a bound upon each element of Cs_t, so that the perturbations of the structural relations are bounded (and well-defined) each period.

where τ_t is a vector of *target variables*, τ^* specifies the vector of *target values* for these variables, and W is a symmetric, positive-definite matrix. The target variables are furthermore assumed to be linear functions of a subset of the endogenous variables mentioned earlier,

$$\tau_t = T y_t, \tag{1.4}$$

where

$$y_t \equiv \begin{bmatrix} Z_t \\ z_t \\ i_t \end{bmatrix},$$

and T is a matrix of coefficients.

As I have argued in Chapter 7, one should not generally wish to design a policy rule that, if adopted from some date t_0 onward, would bring about the rational-expectations equilibrium that minimizes (1.2), since this is a time-inconsistent criterion for the choice of policy: A reconsideration of policy at a later date on precisely the same criterion would not lead one to choose to continue the policy chosen at the earlier date, even if one's model of the economy and stabilization objectives had not changed at all in the interim. Instead, I am content with a rule that is optimal from a timeless perspective of the sort explained in the earlier chapter. In the present more general context, optimality of a policy rule from a timeless perspective can be defined as follows.

DEFINITION. A policy rule that determines a unique nonexplosive rational-expectations equilibrium is *optimal from a timeless perspective* if the equilibrium determined by the rule is such that:

1. The nonpredetermined endogenous variables z_t can be expressed as a *time-invariant* function of a vector of predetermined variables $\bar{Z}_t$ and a vector of exogenous variables $\bar{s}_t$.[5] That is, a relation of the form

$$z_t = f_0 + f_Z \bar{Z}_t + f_s \bar{s}_t, \tag{1.5}$$

    applies for all dates $t \geq t_0$;
2. The equilibrium evolution of the endogenous variables $\{y_t\}$ for all dates $t \geq t_0$ minimizes (1.2) among the set of all bounded

---

5. Here the vectors $\bar{Z}_t$ and $\bar{s}_t$ are allowed to differ from those that appear in (1.1), insofar as the policy rule may involve additional predetermined or exogenous state variables.

processes,[6] subject to the constraints implied by the economy's initial state Z_{t_0}, the requirements for rational-expectations equilibrium (i.e., the structural equations (1.1)), and a set of additional constraints of the form

$$\tilde{E}z_{t_0} = \bar{e} \equiv \tilde{E}\left[f_0 + f_Z\bar{Z}_{t_0} + f_s\bar{s}_{t_0}\right] \tag{1.6}$$

on the initial behavior of the nonpredetermined endogenous variables.

Here the additional constraints (1.6) restrict the possible values of the initial nonpredetermined variables z_{t_0} only insofar as expectations regarding the values of these variables should have affected equilibrium determination at earlier dates. Note also that these additional constraints refer *only* to period t_0 (the period in which the optimality of commitment to the rule is being considered). Thus the fact that it is judged desirable to commit to a rule that should imply evolution of the nonpredetermined variables according to (1.5) in periods $t > t_0$ does not depend on any assumed constraint on the evolution in those periods, other than that the expected evolution represent a rational-expectations equilibrium. Hence in submitting to the constraints (1.6) in period t_0, the central bank is choosing to conform to a rule to which it should have wished to be *expected* to conform had the question been considered earlier without any restriction of this kind upon conduct at date t_0.

Because the additional constraints (1.6) refer only to outcomes in period t_0, the equilibrium dynamics resulting from commitment to a policy that is optimal from a timeless perspective involve the *same* responses to unanticipated shocks in all periods $t > t_0$ as would occur under the t_0-optimal plan, that is, the evolution from date t_0 onward that would minimize (1.2) in the absence of the additional constraints. (Because of the assumed linearity of the equilibrium conditions (1.1), the planned linear response to an unanticipated shock at date t has no effect on the constraints on possible outcomes at earlier dates. This implies that the optimal response to a shock at date $t > t_0$ is independent of the constraint values $\bar{e}$ imposed on the choices for date t_0, and indeed is the same even if the constraints (1.6) are omitted

---

6. I consider only the optimal plan among possible plans satisfying some uniform bound, since the Taylor-series approximations involved in the derivation of the quadratic loss function and linear equilibrium conditions are generally valid only locally. Unbounded paths $\{y_t\}$ that yield a lower value of the objective (1.2) need not correspond to any feasible equilibrium of the exact model, and so are not considered here. Of course, my interest in policies that are optimal in this local sense depends on a belief that the optimal equilibrium of the exact model is in fact one that involves only small departures from the steady state around which I have linearized the equilibrium conditions; in that case, the locally optimal policy defined here should represent a linear approximation to the true optimal policy.

from the minimization problem.) Furthermore, if the solution to the optimization problem stated in the second part of the foregoing definition is
one under which the expected long-run average values of the endogenous
variables are independent of the initial conditions, then it follows that the
long-run average values under a rule that is optimal from a timeless perspective are the same as those under commitment to the t_0-optimal plan.

One can characterize the solution to this constrained minimization problem using the Lagrangian method illustrated in Chapter 7. In the present
general case, the Lagrangian can be written in the form

$$\mathcal{L}_{t_0} = E_{t_0} \left\{ \sum_{t=t_0}^{\infty} \beta^{t-t_0} \left[L(y_t) + \varphi'_{t+1} \tilde{A} y_t - \beta^{-1} \varphi'_t \tilde{I} y_t \right] \right\}, \tag{1.7}$$

where

$$\tilde{A} \equiv [A \quad B], \quad \tilde{I} \equiv [\hat{I} \quad 0].$$

Here $L(y_t)$ is the period loss L_t expressed as a quadratic function of y_t,
and φ_{t+1} is the vector of Lagrange multipliers associated with the constraints (1.1).

The conditional expectation has been eliminated from the term $E_t z_{t+1}$ in
these constraints, using the law of iterated expectations (since the entire expression is conditional upon information at date t_0 in any event). However,
because the last n_z constraints hold only in conditional expectation, the last
n_z elements of φ_{t+1} must be measurable with respect to period t information
(i.e., cannot depend upon shocks at date $t + 1$). I therefore introduce the
notation

$$\varphi_{t+1} \equiv \begin{bmatrix} \xi_{t+1} \\ \Xi_t \end{bmatrix},$$

where the partition is conformable to the partition of the rows of (1.1);
the different time subscript on Ξ_t (as in Svensson and Woodford, 2003a,b)
serves as a reminder that these elements of the vector are determined a
period earlier. I have suppressed the terms in the Lagrangian involving
the exogenous disturbances s_t, as these do not matter for the first-order
conditions derived below. Finally, the term

$$\varphi'_{t_0} \tilde{I} y_{t_0} = \xi'_{t_0} Z_{t_0} + \Xi'_{t_0-1} \tilde{E} z_{t_0}$$

has been added to the Lagrangian in (1.7). The first term on the right-
hand side represents the constraints imposed by the given initial values
Z_{t_0} for the predetermined variables, while the second term represents the
constraints (1.6).

The same Lagrangian can be used to characterize the t_0-optimal plan, that is, the time-inconsistent "optimal commitment" that is often considered in the literature on rules versus discretion. This is the path for the evolution of the endogenous variables from t_0 onward that minimizes the same criterion in the absence of any constraints of the form (1.6). The Lagrangian for such a minimization problem is of the same form as (1.7), except that the final term $\Xi'_{t_0-1}\tilde{E}z_{t_0}$ should be omitted. Alternatively, one may write the Lagrangian in the form (1.7) for the sake of symmetry, but impose the stipulation that

$$\Xi_{t_0-1} = 0. \tag{1.8}$$

Thus the t_0-optimal plan also minimizes a Lagrangian of the form (1.7), but with (1.8) imposed as an additional initial condition, rather than (1.6).

Differentiating the Lagrangian (1.7) with respect to the endogenous variables y_t yields the first-order conditions

$$\tilde{A}'E_t\varphi_{t+1} + T'W(\tau_t - \tau^*) - \beta^{-1}\tilde{I}'\varphi_t = 0 \tag{1.9}$$

for each $t \geq t_0$. An optimal plan must also satisfy a transversality condition, but this is necessarily satisfied in the case of any bounded solution to the structural equations, and I have already noted that I am restricting my attention to bounded solutions. Thus any bounded processes for the endogenous variables $\{y_t\}$ and the Lagrange multipliers $\{\varphi_t\}$ for dates $t \geq t_0$ that are consistent with the initial conditions for Z_{t_0} and with (1.8), satisfy the structural equations (1.1), and satisfy the first-order conditions (1.9) for each $t \geq t_0$ describe a t_0-optimal commitment. Alternatively, any bounded processes consistent with the initial conditions Z_{t_0} and (1.6) and satisfy (1.1) and (1.9) for each $t \geq t_0$ conform to the second part of the definition of optimality from a timeless perspective.

Giannoni and Woodford maintain the following assumption about their linear-quadratic policy problem.

ASSUMPTION 8.1. In the case of any bounded disturbance processes and any initial conditions Z_{t_0} and Ξ_{t_0-1}, there is a unique bounded solution to the system of equations consisting of (1.1) and (1.9). In particular, in the case of any such disturbance process and any initial conditions Z_{t_0}, there is a unique bounded solution to the system of equations consisting of (1.1), (1.8), and (1.9). Thus there exists a unique bounded t_0-optimal plan $\{y_t\}$, to which there is associated a bounded process $\{\varphi_t\}$ for the Lagrange multipliers as well.[7]

---

7. By a bounded optimal plan I mean a process $\{y_t\}$ that minimizes (1.2) among the class of bounded processes, subject to the other stated constraints.

In fact, under quite weak assumptions a linear-quadratic problem of this kind has a unique optimum (subject to bounds on the rate at which the endogenous variables may grow asymptotically), in which $\beta^{t/2} y_t$ and $\beta^{t/2} \varphi_t$ are bounded.[8] Assumption 8.1 thus represents only a small strengthening of the canonical assumptions, so that the optimal processes $\{y_t\}$ and $\{\varphi_t\}$ are bounded without the rescaling. It should also be noted that under the canonical assumptions, if there exists a bounded optimal plan—as one must assume in most applications of interest in order to justify working with a log-linear approximation to the exact equilibrium conditions in the characterization of optimal policy—then the first-order conditions must have a unique bounded solution, as assumed here, for other bounded solutions would have to correspond to alternative optimal plans.

Assumption 8.1 also states that there is a unique bounded solution regardless of the assumed value for Ξ_{t_0-1}, and not only in the case of the value Ξ_{t_0-1} associated with the t_0-optimal commitment. But in the generic case, the existence of a unique bounded solution to the system consisting of (1.1) and (1.9) depends only on the roots of a characteristic polynomial associated with the coefficients of these equations and is independent of the assumed vectors of initial conditions Z_{t_0} and Ξ_{t_0-1}. Hence a unique bounded solution almost always exists for arbitrary Z_{t_0} and Ξ_{t_0-1} if there is a unique bounded t_0-optimal plan for arbitrary Z_{t_0}.

It follows from the foregoing definition that in the equilibrium associated with a policy rule that is optimal from a timeless perspective, the evolution of the endogenous variables from date t_0 onward must satisfy (1.1) and (1.9) for each $t \geq t_0$, for some choice of the initial multipliers Ξ_{t_0-1}. Under Assumption 8.1, there is a unique bounded solution corresponding to any given specification of Ξ_{t_0-1} and in particular a unique implied value for

$$\tilde{E} z_{t_0} = e_0 + e_Z Z_{t_0} + e_s s_{t_0} + e_\Xi \Xi_{t_0-1}. \tag{1.10}$$

Hence corresponding to any specification of Ξ_{t_0-1} there is an associated value of $\bar{e}$, given by the right-hand side of (1.10), such that the unique bounded solution corresponding to this choice of Ξ_{t_0-1} represents the optimal evolution from date t_0 onward, subject to the additional constraints (1.6).

My definition of optimality from a timeless perspective can then be equivalently restated as follows. A policy rule that determines a unique bounded equilibrium is optimal from a timeless perspective if:

---

8. This is a general property of linear-quadratic optimization problems of this kind. One can show that the roots of the characteristic equation associated with the system consisting of (1.1) and (1.9) have the property that for every root μ_i, $\beta^{-1}\mu_i^{-1}$ is also a root. Hence exactly half of the roots have modulus less than $\beta^{-1/2}$. See Svensson and Woodford (2002b).

1. The equilibrium satisfies a time-invariant relation of the form (1.5).
2. In this equilibrium, the endogenous variables y_t for $t \geq t_0$ evolve according to the unique bounded solution to (1.1) and (1.9) for $t \geq t_0$, consistent with the given initial conditions Z_{t_0} and some initial Lagrange multipliers Ξ_{t_0-1}.
3. The initial multipliers are given by a linear rule of the form

$$\Xi_{t_0-1} = g_0 + g_Z \bar{Z}_{t_0} + g_s \bar{s}_{t_0}, \tag{1.11}$$

where the coefficients g_0, g_Z, g_s are such that in the equilibrium,

$$\tilde{E} z_t = e_0 + e_Z Z_t + e_s s_t + e_\Xi [g_0 + g_Z \bar{Z}_t + g_s \bar{s}_t] \tag{1.12}$$

at all dates $t \geq t_0$ and under all possible realizations of the exogenous disturbances; that is, the right-hand side of (1.5) premultiplied by $\tilde{E}$ coincides with the right-hand side of (1.12).

Here the second condition guarantees that the evolution of the endogenous variables from t_0 onward is optimal subject to some constraint of the form (1.6), while the third ensures that the constraint value $\bar{e}$ for which this is true is derivable from the initial conditions $\bar{Z}_{t_0}, \bar{s}_{t_0}$ using a time-invariant rule (1.12) that one wishes to commit to satisfying in all subsequent periods.

1.2 Alternative Forms of Policy Rules

I now discuss in general terms the properties that one would like a monetary policy rule to have in order for it to be considered a suitable approach to implementing the optimal responses to disturbances that one can characterize using the methods described in the previous section. A first issue is what one should consider to be a complete specification of a monetary policy rule. As noted earlier, I do *not* require that the rule explicitly specify an instrument setting for each possible state of the world (defined by a history of exogenous disturbances). Instead, I wish to consider rules that involve a commitment to bring about paths for the endogenous variables that satisfy a criterion of the form

$$\phi_i i_t + \phi_z' \bar{z}_t + \phi_Z' \bar{Z}_t + \phi_s' \bar{s}_t = \bar{\phi}, \tag{1.13}$$

where $\bar{z}_t$ is a vector of nonpredetermined endogenous variables, $\bar{Z}_t$ is a vector of predetermined endogenous variables (lags of variables that are included in $\bar{Z}_t$), $\bar{s}_t$ is a vector of exogenous state variables (disturbances), and the coefficients ϕ_i, ϕ_z, and so on are constants. Here each of the vectors $\bar{z}_t, \bar{Z}_t, \bar{s}_t$ may include additional elements not present in the corresponding vectors in (1.1). For there I sought to represent the structural equations in terms of the minimal set of state variables that were required to characterize the set of feasible equilibrium paths for the target variables, looking forward from any date t; but I do not wish to restrict consideration to policy rules that prescribe a purely contemporaneous relation among the variables in that minimal set.

Despite the apparently contemporaneous form of the criterion (1.13), this notation should be understood to allow dependence of current policy both on forecasts (e.g., the inflation forecast $E_t \pi_{t+k}$ may be an element of $\bar{z}_t$) and on past policy (as i_{t-j} may be an element of $\bar{Z}_t$). The assumption here that the intercept term $\bar{\phi}$ is not time-varying reflects a *time-invariance* property that is considered to be a desirable feature of a policy rule. This does not mean, however, that one may not consider rules with a time-varying inflation target; one simply requires that the target vary in a time-invariant way in response to variations in macroeconomic conditions.

I assume that either $\phi_i \neq 0, \phi_z \neq 0$, or both, so that (1.13) constrains possible endogenous outcomes at date t, rather than referring only to variables that cannot be affected by the policy decision at date t. In the case that $\phi_i \neq 0$, but $\phi_z = 0$, equation (1.13) can be solved for the instrument setting i_t as an explicit function of predetermined and exogenous state variables alone, which variables have determinate values independent of the policy decision. In this case the rule is what Svensson and Woodford (2003) call an *explicit instrument rule*. But not all proposals of practical interest are of this form, and indeed one finds that desirable policy rules can typically not be expressed in this form.

An implicit policy rule in which both ϕ_i and ϕ_z are nonzero is an *implicit instrument rule*. This is a formula for setting the policy instrument as a function of other variables, some of which must be *projected* by the central bank in order to implement the rule, with the projections themselves being *conditional upon* (and affected by) the instrument setting. The Taylor rules considered in Chapter 4 are of this kind, since the basic neo-Wicksellian model used there implies that current-quarter inflation and output should depend on current-quarter interest rates.[9] Other examples would include the rules, specifying the short-term nominal interest rate as a function of an inflation forecast, that are sometimes used to represent the policies of inflation-targeting central banks (e.g., Black et al., 1997b; Batini and Haldane, 1999).

Of course, given that such rules specify the instrument setting only implicitly, an obvious question arises as to whether they represent a well-defined policy specification at all. My view is that they do if and only if

---

9. On the other hand, if inflation and output are both predetermined variables, as in the models discussed in Section 2 of Chapter 5, then the classic Taylor (1993) rule would be an example of an explicit instrument rule.

the rule in question, when adjoined to the other equations of a structural model, is consistent with the existence of a rational-expectations equilibrium and implies a determinate solution for the state-contingent path of the policy instrument (in the sense described further in the next section). This means that the question whether a given implicit rule can be considered a well-defined policy specification is model dependent. However, it depends only on the coefficients by which the endogenous variables enter the (linear) structural equations of one's model, and not on the assumed properties of the exogenous disturbance processes. I subsequently argue that robustness to changes in beliefs about the nature of the exogenous disturbances is the primary sense in which it is important for a proposed policy rule to be robust.

Relation (1.13) can also describe a well-defined policy rule when $\phi_i = 0$, as long as $\phi_z \neq 0$. In this case, the equation must be understood to specify a *pure targeting rule* of the kind advocated by Svensson (1999a, 2003b).[10] The optimal targeting rule considered in Section 5 of Chapter 7 has already provided an illustration of the interest of policy specifications of this kind. Despite the fact that the target criterion makes no explicit reference to the policy instrument, such a rule may represent a feasible and complete specification of policy, just as with an implicit rule that provides a formula for the instrument setting. Once again, I consider that the rule represents a well-defined policy specification if, when adjoined to the other structural equations, it is consistent with the existence of a rational-expectations equilibrium and implies a determinate solution for the path of the instrument. Once I admit that implicit rules can represent well-defined policies, there is really no reason to restrict attention to rules that are expressed as formulas for the instrument setting, and indeed the distinction between instrument rules and targeting rules is probably not as important as that between explicit and implicit rules (of either type).

Insofar as the policy rule (1.13) involves nonzero coefficients on elements of $\bar{z}_t$ or $\bar{Z}_t$ not included in the subvectors z_t and Z_t, analysis of equilibrium determination under such a rule requires one to augment the equilibrium conditions (1.1) with the additional conditions that determine the equilibrium evolution of the additional endogenous variables. I suppose that the augmented system of equilibrium conditions can again be written in the form

$$\bar{I}\begin{bmatrix} \bar{Z}_{t+1} \\ E_t \bar{z}_{t+1} \end{bmatrix} = \bar{A}\begin{bmatrix} \bar{Z}_t \\ \bar{z}_t \end{bmatrix} + \bar{B}i_t + \bar{C}\bar{s}_t, \qquad (1.14)$$

---

10. Svensson further distinguishes between "general" and "specific" targeting rules; here I consider only the latter way of specifying a policy commitment. See also Svensson and Woodford (2003).

where the larger matrices $\bar{I}$ and $\bar{A}$ contain $\hat{I}$ and A, respectively, as diagonal blocks, the vector $\bar{B}$ contains B as a subvector, and so on.

I am concerned here solely with bounded solutions to these equations, that is, with solutions in which each element of $\bar{z}_t$ and $\bar{Z}_t$ satisfies some bound for all t, under the assumption that the disturbances are bounded (each element of $\bar{C}\bar{s}_t$ satisfies some bound for all t). In the case of an exact linear-quadratic model, one might want to consider unbounded solutions, subject perhaps to a transversality condition or some other particular bound with an economic interpretation. But in general (as in the cases treated in this study), the structural equations (1.14) are only linear approximations to a set of true, nonlinear equilibrium conditions, and there is reason to doubt whether unbounded solutions correspond to any solutions at all of the true equations. Accordingly I consider here only the set of bounded solutions consistent with a given policy rule and note that equilibrium is determinate when a unique solution of this kind exists.

DEFINITION. A policy rule (1.13) implies a *determinate* rational-expectations equilibrium if the system of equations obtained by conjoining this equation to the system (1.14) has a unique bounded solution for the endogenous variables in periods $t \geq t_0$, given the initial conditions $\bar{Z}_{t_0}$ and bounded disturbance processes for all periods $t \geq t_0$.

A special case of particular interest is that of a policy rule that specifies an instrument setting as a function of the history of exogenous disturbances. In this case, the complete system of equilibrium conditions is simply (1.1), with i_t replaced by a specified function of $\bar{s}_t$. Standard results then imply that the determinacy of equilibrium depends, in the generic case, on the roots of the characteristic equation associated with this system,

$$\det[A - \mu\hat{I}] = 0. \tag{1.15}$$

Rational-expectations equilibrium is (generically) determinate if the number of roots μ_i such that $|\mu_i| < 1$ is exactly equal to n_Z, the number of predetermined state variables.

In the applications considered in Chapter 7, and in Sections 2 and 3 of this chapter as well, the structural equations are such that this polynomial has more than n_Z roots inside the unit circle, and so a policy rule of this kind leads to indeterminacy.[11] This is the Sargent-Wallace (1975) problem with rules that specify an exogenous path for the nominal interest rate, discussed in Chapter 4. Hence I propose the following terminology.

---

11. Proposition 4.1 establishes this in the case of the basic neo-Wicksellian model.

DEFINITION. A system (1.1) has the *Sargent-Wallace property* if (1.15) has more than n_Z roots μ_i such that $|\mu_i| < 1$, where if A is singular, the zero root is counted $n - \text{rank}(A)$ times.

In such a case, it is important to consider as well the possibility of rules that prescribe feedback from the actual and/or projected paths of endogenous variables.

Finally, I give particular attention to policy rules that involve only a certain subset of the state variables. By a *direct* rule I mean one that involves only the observed and/or projected paths of the target variables, with no reference to any "intermediate target" variables. Many popular current proposals, including both the Taylor rule and standard formulations of inflation-forecast targeting, are direct rules in this sense. Direct rules evidently have a degree of practical appeal and probably facilitate communication with the public about the nature of policy as well. Reference to ambiguous state variables such as "the output gap" obviously presents some difficulties, both for the implementation of a policy rule and for the explanation of policy to the public; but if such terms of art must be used—and in general they must be, if the policy rule is to be *robustly* optimal—it is probably best to use terms that refer directly to the goals of policy, so that the meaning of the variable can be discussed in terms of what a desirable target (say, for output) is believed to be, rather than terms that have no meaning except in the context of a particular model of the economy.

I find that it is possible to formulate direct rules that are optimal, and indeed robustly optimal. I could formulate a large class of alternative rules that would also be robustly optimal (in the same sense) by substituting for one or another variable in terms of others using one or more of the structural equations of the present model of the economy. However, these alternative representations of optimal policy would all involve additional variables, such as the exogenous disturbances, that enter the structural equations of the model. Restricting attention to optimal *direct* rules allows me to reach much more definite conclusions about the nature of an optimal rule, and these are the results that I emphasize.

1.3 Robustness to Alternative Types of Disturbances

Finally, I reach much more specific conclusions as to the form of an optimal policy rule if I demand not simply that the rule bring about optimal state-contingent responses to shocks under the assumption that the kind of disturbances that matter are of a few very specific types, but rather that it imply optimal responses to *any* of an extremely large class of possible types of disturbances. This is important in order to overcome one of the most important practical objections to the idea of *commitment* to a policy rule simply because it can be shown to perform well in a stochastic-simulation exercise—that the fact that the rule is a good one when the economy is perturbed in the particular ways allowed for in the simulations may be no guarantee that it also performs well when one is faced by the (unforeseen) circumstances that happen to have actually occurred.

The actual conduct of monetary policy typically involves detailed discussion of current conditions (and projections for the next year or two), taking account of a wide range of sources of information, both qualitative and quantitative. Central bankers are likely neither to be willing to restrict themselves to the consideration of only a small number of statistics when surveying the economic outlook nor to identify the current situation with a particular realization from a probability distribution that could have been described in advance and used in conducting the stochastic simulations employed to analyze alternative policy rules. The fact is that there are *always* special circumstances of one sort or another, and it is difficult to imagine that central bankers will ever be willing to implement a rule that has been shown to be optimal only on the assumption that circumstances like those currently faced can never occur.

Yet much of the richness of actual central-bank discussions of the economic outlook can be allowed for within the context of a specific quantitative model of the economy, if one simply allows the additive *disturbance terms* in my equations to be extremely various in character. One should accept that the number of distinct types of disturbances that may occur in practice is too large to imagine listing them all once and for all, let alone estimating all of the parameters of a complete description of their statistical properties and their relative likelihoods. At the same time, one should recognize that central bankers have fairly specific ideas about the character of the particular disturbances that have most recently affected their national economies, and accordingly require that an analysis of optimal policy be able to address the specific question of how one should optimally respond to *those particular* disturbances.[12]

Interestingly, one can base policy on an analysis that allows for the possibility of the specific kinds of disturbances that happen to have occurred most recently, without policy reducing to discretionary optimization. This is

12. My point is related, but not identical, to Svensson's (2003b) advocacy of targeting rules on the grounds that they allow the use of "judgment." Svensson assumes that central bankers have information about certain state variables and could use this knowledge in implementing a targeting rule (by using the information in its forecasts of the target variables), but cannot adopt a rule that refers *explicitly* to those states. His analysis is thus based upon a distinction between disturbances to which policy may directly respond and others to which it must not. My own emphasis is instead upon the advantage, from the point of view of simplicity, of commitment to a rule that does not require explicit reference to particular types of disturbances at all, and not simply avoiding mention of certain particularly difficult-to-describe disturbances.

because it is possible to choose a policy rule to which commitment would be optimal (from the timeless perspective explained above) *regardless of the statistical properties of the additive disturbances* to the model equations, and indeed even if these can only be fully specified by a statistical model with millions of parameters. Specifically, Giannoni and Woodford show that it is possible to establish that a particular linear rule with constant coefficients is optimal under the hypothesis that the disturbance terms have unconditional means of zero, without any further assumptions about their statistical properties.

A given structural disturbance s_{jt} need only be assumed to be of the form

$$s_{jt} = \sum_{k=0}^{\infty} \sum_{m} \alpha_{m,k}^{j} \epsilon_{m,t-k}, \tag{1.16}$$

where the index m ranges over a possibly infinite list of possible types of disturbances, and where each of the random variables $\{\epsilon_{m,t}\}$ is an i.i.d. mean-zero variable, each with its own probability distribution. For each disturbance, the coefficients $\{\alpha_{m,k}^{j}\}$ indicate the degree to which it is forecastable in advance and the length of time for which its effects persist; this infinite list of parameters may be different for each disturbance. One may also suppose that for most if not all of the shocks, the distribution from which $\epsilon_{m,t}$ is drawn each period has a very large atom at the value zero, so that a shock of this type (of nonzero magnitude) is observed only infrequently. Thus it is logically possible both to assume that the central bank has a correct understanding of the nature of all of the disturbances that have hit the economy to date, and at the same time to suppose that it does not possess a complete list of all of the possible future disturbances or sufficient data to estimate their likelihood of occurrence within a certain time interval. Under the assumption that the (innumerable) shocks are all mean zero, such a bank would still be able to correctly evaluate both the history of the disturbance term, $s_{j,t-k}$ for all $k \geq 0$, and the conditional expectation of its future path, $E_t s_{j,T}$ for all $T \geq t+1$. In a log-linear (certainty-equivalent) model of the kind that I use to approximate my account of the monetary transmission mechanism, assumption of a (symmetric-information) rational-expectations equilibrium requires that I assume that everyone in the economy shares a common (correct) evaluation of these conditional expectations, though there need not be accurate knowledge of or even agreement upon other aspects of the probability distribution for future disturbances; it is for this reason that I assume correct knowledge of the *average* values of the disturbance terms, which I may then without loss of generality assume to be zero.

I seek a policy rule with the following property.

DEFINITION. A time-invariant policy rule (1.13) is *robustly optimal* if it is optimal from a timeless perspective, regardless of the specification of the coefficients $\{\alpha_{m,k}^{j}\}$ in (1.16) and regardless of the distributions from which the innovations $\epsilon_{m,t}$ are drawn (except that these must be bounded and have mean zero).

The key to the possibility of a robustly optimal policy rule in this sense is the *certainty equivalence* of optimal policy in the case of a linear-quadratic optimal policy problem of the kind that I consider here. This means that the central bank's optimal instrument setting may depend upon the conditional expectations of disturbances at various future horizons, as well as upon current and past disturbance terms, but that it is independent of other details of the probability distribution of future disturbances and thus can be expressed without any need to enumerate or assign probabilities to all of the possible types of future disturbances. In fact, as we shall see, it is possible to express optimal policy in terms of an instrument rule or targeting rule that makes no reference even to the disturbances that have already occurred, except insofar as these affect the bank's estimates of (and projections of the future paths of) its target variables (such as the output gap).

Even with the further stipulation of robust optimality, there are many possible policy rules with the desired property. Hence I further narrow the search to the category of *direct rules*—rules that involve only the target variables τ_t, though they may involve both leads and lags of these—for the reasons discussed earlier. Giannoni and Woodford show that it is quite generally possible to find a time-invariant direct policy rule that is robustly optimal. Indeed, even under these requirements, one cannot generally isolate a single uniquely optimal rule, though attention is narrowed to a small number of possibilities.

1.4   Existence of Robustly Optimal Policy Rules

My goal, then, is to find a time-invariant direct policy rule that results in a determinate equilibrium, and such that the equilibrium determined by this rule is robustly optimal (from a timeless perspective). I turn now to a sketch of the method proposed by Giannoni and Woodford (2002a) to construct such rules in the context of the general linear-quadratic policy problem defined above.

I now turn to the question of finding a policy rule that can be expected to bring about equilibrium dynamics of the kind characterized in the previous section. The key insight is that one can design a time-invariant target criterion (1.13) that implies that the endogenous variables must evolve in a way that is consistent with the system of first-order conditions (1.9) that characterize an optimal commitment,[13] under a particular rule (1.11) for

---

13. My approach generalizes the derivation of optimal specific targeting rules in Svensson (1997a, 2003b) and Svensson and Woodford (2003c).

the choice of the initial Lagrange multipliers. This kind of rule necessarily implies a determinate equilibrium because the system of first-order conditions has (under Assumption 8.1) a unique bounded solution. Furthermore, while the equilibrium does not in general coincide in its transition dynamics with the t_0-optimal commitment—for the initial Lagrange multipliers must generally not be set equal to zero, in order for the proposed rule to be time-consistent—the economy's equilibrium evolution is optimal from the timeless perspective defined above. Moreover, because the first-order conditions involve only the target variables (in addition to the Lagrange multipliers, which are eliminated in order to derive the policy rule), the optimal rule is a direct rule. Moreover, because the first-order conditions are independent of the assumed statistical properties of the disturbance processes, the optimal rule is robust to changes in that aspect of the model specification.

At the end of Section 1.1, I obtained the following characterization of optimality from a timeless perspective. The policy rule must determine an equilibrium in which the endogenous variables y_t evolve according to the unique bounded solution to (1.1) and (1.9) for $t \geq t_0$, consistent with the given initial conditions Z_{t_0} and some initial Lagrange multipliers Ξ_{t_0-1}. Furthermore, these initial multipliers must be given by a rule of the form (1.11), in which the coefficients are such that (1.12) holds at all dates $t \geq t_0$.

One case in which one may be sure that the rule (1.11) satisfies (1.12), of course, is if the corresponding relation

$$\Xi_{t-1} = g_0 + g_Z \bar{Z}_t + g_s \bar{s}_t \qquad (1.17)$$

holds for all $t > t_0$ in the unique bounded solution to the system consisting of (1.1) and (1.9) consistent with initial multipliers (1.11). This is the approach that Giannoni and Woodford take to the construction of a policy rule that is optimal from a timeless perspective. Note that in equilibrium, the multipliers Ξ_{t-1} for any $t > t_0$ depend only on the economy's state at date $t - 1$ (hence my choice of subscript). Thus (1.17) must have this property; that is, g_Z and g_s must put nonzero weight only on elements of $\bar{Z}_t$ and $\bar{s}_t$ that are known at date $t - 1$.

The approach of Giannoni and Woodford can now be sketched as follows. First, the structural equations (1.1) and stabilization objectives (1.2) allow me to define the optimal dynamics corresponding to any specification Ξ_{t_0-1} of the initial Lagrange multipliers. I then look for a rule (1.11) for choosing the initial multipliers with the property that the implied equilibrium satisfies the corresponding relation (1.17) at all later dates as well. This then determines the particular equilibrium evolution of the economy that I wish to implement. Finally, I seek to formulate a time-invariant target criterion referring only to the projected path of the target variables, with the property that commitment to fulfill this target criterion in all periods

$t \geq t_0$ implies a determinate rational-expectations equilibrium in which the endogenous variables evolve in the desired way.

In order for it to be applicable here, the Giannoni-Woodford method requires a further assumption about the matrices $\hat{I}$ and A in the structural equations (1.1).

ASSUMPTION 8.2. *The characteristic polynomial* (1.15) *has at least* n_Z *roots such that* $|\mu_i| < \beta^{-1}$, *that is, at least* rank(A) $- n_z$ *nonzero roots satisfying that bound, in addition to the zero root that is repeated* $n -$ rank(A) *times. Furthermore, it is possible to select a set of exactly* n_Z *roots, including the* $n -$ rank(A) *zeros, such that either:* (i) *the roots in this set consist entirely of real roots and of complex pairs, both elements of which belong to the set; or* (ii) *there is a single complex root* μ *in the set, the complex conjugate of which is not also in the set, and this root is such that* $|\mathrm{Re}\,\mu^{-1}| > \beta$.

In the generic case, the first part of Assumption 8.2 implies that in the case of a constant instrument setting, $i_t = \bar{\imath}$ for all t, there are one or more solutions to the structural equations (1.1) in which $\beta^t y_t$ remains bounded for all t, regardless of the initial conditions Z_{t_0} and regardless of the specification of the disturbance processes, as long as the disturbances are themselves bounded. This means that policy need not be adjusted in any special way in order to prevent explosive (at least, unduly explosive) dynamics; a nonexplosive equilibrium path for the endogenous variables exists as long as explosive dynamics are not required by the violent adjustment of the policy instrument. Note that this part of Assumption 8.2 is implied by the Sargent-Wallace property.

The further stipulation regarding the set of exactly n_Z roots is a relatively weak additional restriction. It is necessarily possible to choose a set of roots with property (i), *except* in the case that the nonzero roots satisfying $|\mu_i| < \beta^{-1}$ are all complex, *and* rank(A)$-n_z$ is odd. Even in this case, it is necessarily possible to choose a set of n_Z roots in which there is only one complex root such that the complex conjugate is not also in the set. Thus the only real restriction is the further stipulation that this root be such that $|\mathrm{Re}\,\mu^{-1}| > \beta$, which is stronger than the restriction already assumed on the modulus of the root.

Giannoni and Woodford also assume that these matrices satisfy two additional technical assumptions, Assumptions 8.3 and 8.4, given in Appendix G. Here I simply note that both of these assumptions hold for generic matrices A and $\tilde{E}$ of arbitrary ranks $0 \leq$ rank($\tilde{E}$) $\leq n_z$ and $n_z \leq$ rank(A) $\leq n$.

I now recall that conditions (1.9) may be separated into two sets of first-order conditions,

$$A' E_t \varphi_{t+1} + \tilde{T}' W \left(\tau_t - \tau^* \right) - \beta^{-1} \hat{I}' \varphi_t = 0, \qquad (1.18)$$

$$B'_2 \Xi_t + T^{i\prime} W \left(\tau_t - \tau^* \right) = 0, \qquad (1.19)$$

where the columns of

$$T \equiv \begin{bmatrix} \tilde{T} & T^i \end{bmatrix}$$

are partitioned conformably with those of $\tilde{A}$. Given any bounded process for the evolution of the target variables, it is possible to find a process for the multipliers that satisfies conditions (1.18).

PROPOSITION 8.1. Under Assumptions 8.2–8.4, there exist (real-valued) matrices Λ and Υ and linear operators $Q(L^{-1})$ and $R(L^{-1})$ such that bounded processes $\{\varphi_t\}$ and $\{\tau_t\}$ satisfy (1.18) for all $t \geq t_0$ if and only if they satisfy the conditions

$$\Xi_t = \Lambda \Xi_{t-1} + E_t \big[Q(L^{-1}) \tilde{T}' W (\tau_t - \tau^*) \big], \qquad (1.20)$$

$$\xi_t = \Upsilon \Xi_{t-1} + E_t \big[R(L^{-1}) \tilde{T}' W (\tau_t - \tau^*) \big] \qquad (1.21)$$

for all $t \geq t_0$. These linear operators are such that $Q(L^{-1})x_t$ and $R(L^{-1})x_t$ are well-defined and bounded processes in the case of any bounded process x_t.

The proof can be found in Giannoni and Woodford (2002a). In the case that there are exactly n_Z roots of (1.15) such that $|\mu_i| < \beta^{-1}$, the matrices Λ, Υ, Q, and R are uniquely defined, and there is a unique solution to (1.18) for the evolution of the multipliers $\{\varphi_t\}$ given a process for the evolution of the target variables $\{\tau_t\}$ and an initial condition Ξ_{t_0-1}. If instead there are more than n_Z such roots, there are many possible solutions for the evolution of the multipliers. Nonetheless, it is possible to select a solution in which Ξ_t and ξ_t are time-invariant functions of the lagged value Ξ_{t-1} and the expected path of the target variables from date t onward, as indicated in (1.20) and (1.21). In this case the values of Λ, Υ, Q and R are not uniquely determined, but there are only a small number of possibilities that work, corresponding to the different ways in which it is possible to select a set of n_Z roots of (1.15) with modulus $|\mu_i| < \beta^{-1}$.

I next observe that for any square matrix Λ of dimension n_z, there exist an $n_z \times n_z$ matrix polynomial $B(L)$ and a scalar polynomial $\alpha(L)$ such that

$$B(L)(I - \Lambda L) = \alpha(L)I. \qquad (1.22)$$

Here $\alpha(L) = \det(I - \Lambda L)$, and $B(L)$ is the adjoint of $(I - \Lambda L)$, that is, the transpose of the matrix of cofactors. Note that $\alpha(L)$ is of order rank$(\Lambda) = $ rank$(\tilde{E}) \equiv k$, whereas $B(L)$ is of order $d \equiv \min(k, n_z - 1)$. Premultiplying (1.20) by $B(L)$ yields

$$\alpha(L)\Xi_t = B(L)E_t \big[Q(L^{-1}) \tilde{T}' W (\tau_t - \tau^*) \big].$$

This equation holds for all $t \geq t_0 + k$ if (1.20) holds for all $t \geq t_0$, and conversely, if (1.20) holds for all $t_0 \leq t < t_0 + k$ and the above condition holds for all $t \geq t_0 + k$, it follows that (1.20) also holds for all $t \geq t_0 + k$.

Finally, premultiplying this last equation by B_2' and using (1.19) to eliminate the $B_2' \Xi_t$ terms, one obtains the condition

$$\alpha(L) T^{i'} W(\tau_t - \tau^*) + B_2' B(L) E_t \big[Q\left(L^{-1}\right) \tilde{T}' W\left(\tau_t - \tau^*\right) \big] = 0, \qquad (1.23)$$

which involves only the target variables. Under the optimal once-and-for-all commitment chosen at date t_0, the evolution of the target variables satisfies this criterion at all dates $t \geq t_0 + k$.[14] Thus a commitment by the policymaker to enforce condition (1.23) each period is an example of a policy that can be justified on the grounds that it *would have been* optimal to commit to such a policy in the case of any optimal commitment chosen at a date sufficiently far in the past.

Condition (1.23) is an example of a direct policy rule that takes the time-invariant form (1.13). Both are desirable properties of a policy rule, as discussed above. In order to express (1.23) in the form (1.13), it suffices that the vector $\bar{Z}_t$ be defined as

$$\bar{Z}_t \equiv \left(Z_t' \; q_{t-1}' \; \cdots \; q_{t-d}' \; v_{t-1} \; \cdots \; v_{t-k} \right)', \qquad (1.24)$$

where

$$q_t \equiv E_t \big[Q\left(L^{-1}\right) \tilde{T}' W(\tau_t - \tau^*) \big], \qquad (1.25)$$

$$v_t \equiv T^{i'} W(\tau_t - \tau^*), \qquad (1.26)$$

and that the vector $\bar{Z}_t$ include not only the nonpredetermined endogenous variables that matter for the current targets τ_t, but also the conditional expectations of future target variables that are involved in q_t. In general, (1.24) requires that the vector $\bar{Z}_t$ include elements beyond those needed in order to specify the possible evolution of the target variables from period t onward.[15] Thus the rule is in general not purely forward looking in the sense of Woodford (2000).

One can show quite generally that such a rule implies a determinate equilibrium. The following result relies upon an additional Assumption 8.5,

14. Under this optimal commitment, both (1.19) and (1.20) hold for all $t \geq t_0$. Once both (1.19) and (1.20) have held for the previous k periods, it is possible to use the derivation in the text to show that (1.23) must hold.

15. This is almost inevitably true if $\Lambda \neq 0$, which is the case as long as $\tilde{E} \neq 0$, i.e., as long as the structural equations are at all forward looking. See Section G.2 of Appendix G for the relation between the rank of Λ and the rank of $\tilde{E}$.

given in Appendix G; this condition is again one that holds for generic matrices of arbitrary rank.

PROPOSITION 8.2. Under Assumptions 8.1–8.5, a commitment to ensure that condition (1.23) holds at all dates $t \geq t_0$ results in a determinate rational-expectations equilibrium. In this equilibrium, z_t each period is given by a linear relation of the form (1.5), where $\bar{s}_t = s_t$ (the exogenous state vector required to define the possible evolution of the target variables from date t onward) and $\bar{Z}_t$ is given by (1.24).

Furthermore, the bounded process $\{y_t\}$ associated with this equilibrium minimizes (1.2) among all possible bounded evolutions of the endogenous variables from date t_0 onward that are consistent with conditions (1.1), the initial conditions Z_{t_0}, and the additional constraints

$$\tilde{E} z_{t_0} = \bar{e}, \qquad (1.27)$$

where $\bar{e}$ is the function of $\bar{Z}_{t_0}$ and s_{t_0} specified in (1.6).

The proof can again be found in Giannoni and Woodford (2002a). The essential idea is that one can uniquely determine a vector of initial Lagrange multipliers Ξ_{t_0-1} implied by the given initial conditions $\bar{Z}_{t_0}$, with the property that a bounded solution to the system consisting of (1.1) and (1.23) for all $t \geq t_0$ consistent with the initial conditions $\bar{Z}_{t_0}, s_{t_0}$ must correspond to a bounded solution to the system consisting of (1.1) and (1.9) consistent with the initial conditions $Z_{t_0}, \Xi_{t_0-1}, s_{t_0}$. The existence and uniqueness of the latter solution (under Assumption 8.1) then implies determinacy of rational-expectations equilibrium under the commitment to the target criterion (1.23). In addition, the fact that the determinate equilibrium satisfies the system of equations consisting of (1.1) and (1.9) for some choice of the initial multipliers Ξ_{t_0-1} implies that it is optimal subject to additional constraints of the form (1.27). The fact that the initial Lagrange multipliers are time-invariant functions of the initial conditions of the form (1.17) then guarantees that the additional constraints are the ones specified in (1.6).

This second part of Proposition 8.2 implies that policy rule (1.23) is optimal from a timeless perspective. I note further that the coefficients of this rule depend only upon the coefficients of the first-order conditions (1.9), which are independent of any assumptions about the statistical properties of the disturbances. Hence this policy rule is also robustly optimal.

1.5 Optimal Instrument Rules

The coefficient multiplying the current instrument setting i_t in (1.23) is[16]

16. Note that the foregoing definitions imply that $\alpha(0) = 1$, $B(0) = I$.

$$T^{i\prime}WT^{i} + B_{2}^{\prime}Q(0)\tilde{T}^{\prime}WT^{i}.$$

If this quantity is nonzero, the rule can be interpreted as an implicit instrument rule. The following is a case of particular interest.

ASSUMPTION 8.6. The target variables can be partitioned as

$$\tau_{t} = \begin{bmatrix} \hat{\tau}_{t} \\ i_{t} \end{bmatrix},$$

where $\hat{\tau}_{t} = \hat{T}\tilde{y}_{t}$ is a function only of $\tilde{y}_{t}$, the vector of endogenous variables other than the instrument, and the target values τ^{*} can similarly be partitioned into target values $\hat{\tau}^{*}$ and i^{*}. The matrix W in (1.3) is also block-diagonal, so that

$$L_{t} = \tfrac{1}{2}\left(\hat{\tau}_{t} - \hat{\tau}^{*}\right)^{\prime}\hat{W}\left(\hat{\tau}_{t} - \hat{\tau}^{*}\right) + \frac{\lambda_{i}}{2}\left(i_{t} - i^{*}\right)^{2},$$

where $\hat{W}$ is a symmetric, positive-definite matrix, and $\lambda_{i} \geq 0$.

This assumption is satisfied in all of the examples considered later in this chapter. Under this assumption, the coefficient multiplying i_{t} in (1.23) is simply λ_{i}. Then if $\lambda_{i} > 0$ (i.e., if the policymaker's objective includes a concern for stabilization of the instrument), the optimal rule is an implicit instrument rule, which may be expressed in the form

$$i_{t} = (1-\gamma(1))i^{*} + \gamma(L)i_{t-1} - \lambda_{i}^{-1}B_{2}^{\prime}B(L)\mathrm{E}_{t}\big[Q\big(L^{-1}\big)\,\hat{T}^{\prime}\hat{W}\big(\hat{\tau}_{t} - \hat{\tau}^{*}\big)\big]. \quad (1.28)$$

Here I have expressed the lag polynomial $\alpha(L)$ as $1 - \gamma(L)L$, where $\gamma(L)$ is a polynomial of order $k-1$.

I can say more about the form of the optimal instrument rule in the following case.

ASSUMPTION 8.7. The characteristic polynomial (1.15) has $n_{Z} + m$ roots such that $|\mu| < \beta^{-1}$, for some $m \geq 1$, where once again, if A is singular, the zero root is counted $n - \mathrm{rank}(A)$ times.

The models studied throughout this book have this property; note that Assumption 8.7 is implied by the Sargent-Wallace property (that holds in my examples). In such a case, I obtain the following stronger characterization of optimal policy.

PROPOSITION 8.3. In the case of a linear-quadratic policy problem satisfying Assumptions 8.1–8.7, with $\lambda_{i} > 0$, the optimal instrument rule (1.28) necessarily involves weights on lagged interest rates that are large enough for the lag polynomial $\alpha(L) = 1 - \gamma(L)L$ to have m zeros inside the unit circle.

Note that the result that $\alpha(L)$ has zeros inside the unit circle means that the instrument dynamics implied by (1.28) in the case of an arbitrary bounded path for the other target variables $\{\hat{\tau}_t\}$ is almost always *explosive*. Thus the finding of Rotemberg and Woodford (1999a) and Woodford (1999a) that an optimal interest-rate rule for certain forward-looking models involves superinertial interest-rate dynamics is no fluke; for an interesting general class of forward-looking models, every optimal instrument rule of the form (1.28) has this property. Of course, commitment to such a rule does not imply that interest-rate dynamics are explosive *in equilibrium;* on the contrary, I have shown that a rational-expectations equilibrium exists in which the interest rate (along with all of the other state variables) is bounded, and the fact that the dynamics are explosive in all *other* solutions to the system consisting of (1.1) and (1.28) is what makes this equilibrium determinate. In fact, under the assumption that private-sector expectations coordinate upon the determinate rational-expectations equilibrium consistent with a given policy rule, a commitment to set interest rates according to a superinertial rule represents a way of forcing the evolution of the other target variables to satisfy the condition that is required in order for the implied interest-rate dynamics *not* to be explosive.

Of course, there is not always a robustly optimal policy rule that can be represented as even an implicit instrument rule. If $\lambda_i = 0$, the optimal rule reduces to

$$B_2' B(L) E_t \left[Q \left(L^{-1} \right) \hat{T}' \hat{W} \left(\hat{\tau}_t - \hat{\tau}^* \right) \right] = 0. \tag{1.29}$$

The rule is in this case a *pure targeting rule*. Because Proposition 8.2 implies that there is a determinate rational-expectations equilibrium in which this criterion is fulfilled at all dates, the use of the instrument to ensure that this criterion holds is feasible and suffices to uniquely determine an implied instrument setting at each date.

Moreover, even when $\lambda_i > 0$, there may *also* exist robustly optimal policy rules that take the form of pure targeting rules. Note that a rule need not be of the form (1.23) at all to be a robustly optimal direct rule. Any rule of the form

$$a(L)' E_t \left[\Psi \left(L^{-1} \right) \left(\tau_t - \tau^* \right) \right] = 0 \tag{1.30}$$

is *equivalent* to the rule

$$E_t \left\{ \phi \left(L^{-1} \right) a(L)' E_t \left[\Psi \left(L^{-1} \right) \left(\tau_t - \tau^* \right) \right] \right\} = 0, \tag{1.31}$$

where $\phi(L^{-1})$ is any invertible (scalar) polynomial function of the inverse lag operator, that is, any polynomial such that all roots of $\phi(\mu) = 0$ are outside the unit circle. These rules are equivalent in the sense that a bounded process $\{\tau_t\}$ satisfies (1.30) if and only if it satisfies (1.31). One might suppose that the form (1.31) is necessarily a more complex specification, on the grounds that it involves projections of the target variables farther in the future, and therefore that (1.30) would unambiguously be preferred. But this need not be so. If one or more of the lag polynomials $a_i(L)$ can be factored as

$$a_i(L) = \gamma_1(L)\gamma_2(L),$$

where $\gamma_1(L)$ is a lag polynomial of order $m \geq 1$ such that all roots of $\gamma_1(\mu) = 0$ are inside the unit circle, one may choose $\phi(L^{-1}) = \tilde{\gamma}_1(L^{-1})^{-1}$, where $\tilde{\gamma}_1(L^{-1}) \equiv \gamma_1(L)L^{-m}$ is a polynomial of order m with all of its zeros *outside* the unit circle. In this case,

$$E_t\left\{\phi\left(L^{-1}\right) a_i(L)x_t\right\} = \gamma_2(L)x_{t-m},$$

for any bounded variable x_t, and this is a simpler function of x_t (involving fewer lags and no more leads) than is $a_i(L)x_t$.

In particular, this possibility arises when Assumption 8.7 is satisfied.

PROPOSITION 8.4. Consider again the case of a linear-quadratic policy problem satisfying Assumptions 8.1–8.7, with $\lambda_i > 0$. By Proposition 8.3, the lag polynomial $\alpha(L) = 1 - \gamma(L)L$ in (1.28) has m zeros inside the unit circle. Let this polynomial be factored as

$$\alpha(L) = \alpha_1(L)\,\alpha_2(L),$$

where $\alpha_1(L)$ is a polynomial of order m with all of its zeros inside the unit circle and $\alpha_2(L)$ is a polynomial of order $k - m$ with all of its zeros outside the unit circle.

Then another optimal policy rule is given by

$$E_t\left\{\tilde{\alpha}_1\left(L^{-1}\right)^{-1} B_2' B(L)E_t\left[Q\left(L^{-1}\right)\hat{T}'\hat{W}\left(\hat{\tau}_t - \hat{\tau}^*\right)\right]\right\} \\ + \lambda_i\alpha_2(L)\left(i_{t-m} - i^*\right) = 0, \tag{1.32}$$

where $\tilde{\alpha}_1(L^{-1}) \equiv \alpha_1(L)L^{-m}$. (Note that this is a pure targeting rule.) Rules (1.28) and (1.32) are equivalent in the sense that bounded processes $\{i_t\}$ and $\{\hat{\tau}_t\}$ satisfy (1.28) if and only if they satisfy (1.32). Thus (1.32) is an example of a robustly optimal direct targeting rule that cannot be interpreted as an instrument rule.

The existence of a representation of optimal policy in terms of a pure targeting rule (even though instrument smoothing is among the policy authority's stabilization objectives) is not unrelated to the fact that the optimal instrument rule is superinertial. I have noted that a commitment to set interest rates according to a superinertial rule represents a way of forcing the evolution of the other target variables to satisfy a particular condition, one that is required in order for the implied interest-rate dynamics *not* to be explosive. The expectation that the evolution of the target variables will satisfy this condition is exactly what is expressed by the target criterion (1.32). Thus a commitment to set interest rates according to (1.28) and a commitment to adjust interest rates as necessary to ensure that criterion (1.32) holds at all times are not really different policies; the representation of policy in terms of an implicit instrument rule simply specifies more directly the size of interest-rate adjustments that are involved.

The possibility of equivalent representations of optimal policy in terms of either an implicit instrument rule or a targeting rule is illustrated in the examples considered in Section 3. Note that the equivalence of the two representations holds not only in the case of a single specification of the disturbance processes, but for *all* possible disturbance processes. Thus neither representation is more robust than the other, or requires more information for its implementation than does the other, or allows more scope for the exercise of judgment than does the other. I accordingly see few grounds for drawing a sharp distinction between implicit instrument rules and targeting rules as general approaches to the conduct of monetary policy. If there are grounds for preferring one form of policy commitment to the other in a case of the sort described by Proposition 8.4, these presumably have to do with ease of communication with the public about commitments of the two types, rather than with any differences in the consequences associated with a credible commitment of either type.

2 Optimal Inflation Targeting Rules

I now offer some concrete examples of the way in which the optimal policy rule depends on the details of one's model of the monetary transmission mechanism.[17] I consider a series of simple examples, selected to illustrate the consequences of features that are often present in quantitative optimizing models of the monetary transmission mechanism. I then offer an example of the computation of an optimal policy rule in the case of a small quantitative model that is estimated using U.S. time series, the model of Giannoni and Woodford (2003b), discussed previously in Chapter 5.

In each of the examples considered in this section, I abstract both from transactions frictions and from any concern with the zero lower bound on

---

17. This section is largely based on Giannoni and Woodford (2003b).

interest rates; hence the welfare-theoretic stabilization objectives involve no concern for interest-rate stabilization. It then follows that robustly optimal policy rules derived in accordance with the principles discussed in Section 1 are necessarily pure targeting rules: that is, they involve a commitment to adjust interest rates as necessary to achieve a certain target criterion, where the target criterion itself is independent of the path of the interest-rate instrument.

In fact, in each of these examples, the optimal target criterion places particular weight on an inflation projection, though the projected change in a single price index is not the *only* variable that matters to the target criterion. Hence these policy rules may reasonably be described as "flexible inflation targeting rules." One of the primary goals of the analysis here is to clarify the way in which it is optimal for an inflation targeting rule to be "flexible"—that is, to explain which other variables should be taken into account in addition to the inflation projection, and to what extent. Of course, the answer is that it depends on the details of one's model of the monetary transmission mechanism; but I wish to illustrate how the answer is affected by various elements that are commonly found in quantitative optimizing models, including that of Giannoni and Woodford.

The analysis of Giannoni and Woodford (2002a) described in the previous section derives a robustly optimal target criterion for a general class of linear-quadratic policy problems, to which class the examples considered here belong. But here I illustrate the method by directly applying it to my simple examples, rather than invoking the general formula (1.29).

2.1 A Model with Inflation Inertia

I have already given one simple example of an optimal inflation targeting rule in Section 5 of Chapter 7. There I considered a model in which the relevant constraint upon stabilization policy comes from an aggregate-supply relation of the form

$$\pi_t = \kappa x_t + \beta E_t \pi_{t+1} + u_t, \tag{2.1}$$

derived from the Calvo model of staggered pricing (see Chapter 3), in which π_t is the change in the log of a general price index, x_t is the welfare-relevant output gap (discussed in Chapter 6), u_t is an exogenous cost-push disturbance (also discussed in Chapter 6) that precludes complete stabilization of both inflation and the output gap, and the coefficients satisfy $\kappa > 0, 0 < \beta < 1$. The objective of monetary policy was assumed to be to minimize the expected value of a loss function of the form

$$W = E_0 \left\{ \sum_{t=0}^{\infty} \beta^t L_t \right\}, \tag{2.2}$$

where the discount factor β is the same as in (2.1), and the loss each period is given by

$$L_t = \pi_t^2 + \lambda \left(x_t - x^* \right)^2 \tag{2.3}$$

for a certain relative weight $\lambda > 0$ and optimal level of the output gap $x^* > 0$. Under the same micro-foundations as justify the structural relation (2.1), I have shown in Chapter 6 that a quadratic approximation to the expected utility of the representative household is a decreasing function of (2.2), with

$$\lambda = \kappa/\theta \tag{2.4}$$

(where $\theta > 1$ is the elasticity of substitution between alternative differentiated goods) and x^* a function of both the degree of market power and the size of tax distortions. However, the analysis given in Chapter 7 applies in the case of any loss function of the form (2.3), regardless of whether the weights and target values are the ones that can be justified on welfare-theoretic grounds or not.

In Chapter 7, it is shown that in this case a robustly optimal target criterion is of the form

$$\pi_t + \phi(x_t - x_{t-1}) = 0, \tag{2.5}$$

with a coefficient $\phi = \lambda/\kappa > 0$. As noted previously, this is a form of flexible inflation target. It indicates that deviations of the projected inflation rate π_t from the long-run inflation target (here equal to zero) that are proportional to the degree to which the output gap is projected to decline over the same period that prices are projected to rise should be accepted. Note that the optimal criterion is *history dependent*, since the acceptability of a given projection (π_t, x_t) depends on the recent past level of the output gap; it is this feature of the criterion that results in the output gap's returning only gradually to its normal level following a transitory cost-push shock, as shown in Figure 7.3.

I now wish to consider the way in which the optimal targeting rule must be modified in the case that the aggregate-supply relation incorporates instead inflation inertia of the kind that is present in many empirical models of inflation dynamics. As in Chapters 6 and 7, I take account of inflation inertia in an optimizing model of pricing behavior by assuming, as Christiano et al. (2001) propose, that individual prices are indexed to an aggregate price index during the intervals between reoptimizations of the individual prices and that the aggregate price index becomes available for this purpose only with a one-period lag. When the Calvo model of staggered pricesetting is modified in this way, the aggregate-supply relation (2.1) takes the more general form

$$\pi_t - \gamma \pi_{t-1} = \kappa x_t + \beta E_t[\pi_{t+1} - \pi_t] + u_t, \qquad (2.6)$$

as shown in Chapter 3, where the coefficient $0 \leq \gamma \leq 1$ indicates the degree of automatic indexation to the aggregate-price index. In the limiting case of complete indexation ($\gamma = 1$), the case assumed by Christiano et al. and the case found to best fit U.S. data in the model estimated by Giannoni and Woodford (2003b), this relation is essentially identical to the aggregate-supply relation proposed by Fuhrer and Moore (1995a), which has been widely used in empirical work.

As shown in Chapter 6, the welfare-theoretic stabilization objective corresponding to this alternative structural model is of the form (2.2) with the period loss function (2.3) replaced by

$$L_t = (\pi_t - \gamma \pi_{t-1})^2 + \lambda \left(x_t - x^*\right)^2, \qquad (2.7)$$

where $\lambda > 0$ is again given by (2.4), and $x^* > 0$ is similarly the same function of underlying microeconomic distortions as before. If one considers the problem of minimizing (2.2) with loss function (2.7) subject to the sequence of constraints (2.6), the problem has the same form as in the case of no indexation (i.e., the standard Calvo model), except with π_t everywhere replaced by the quasi-differenced inflation rate

$$\pi_t^{qd} \equiv \pi_t - \gamma \pi_{t-1}. \qquad (2.8)$$

The solution is therefore also the same, with this substitution. (See Chapter 7, Section 2.1, for further details.)

The impulse responses of inflation, the output gap, and the price level to a transitory cost-push shock under optimal policy were shown in Figure 7.5 for economies with alternative values of the indexation parameter γ. Under an optimal commitment, the initial unexpected increase in prices is eventually undone, as long as $\gamma < 1$; and this once again means that inflation eventually undershoots its long-run level for a time. However, for any large enough value of γ, inflation remains greater than its long-run level for a time even after the disturbance has ceased, and only later undershoots its long-run level; and the larger the value of γ, the longer this period of above-average inflation persists. In the limiting case that $\gamma = 1$, the undershooting never occurs; inflation is simply gradually brought back to the long-run target level.[18] In this last case, a temporary disturbance causes

---

18. Note that the impulse response of inflation (for $\gamma = 1$) in panel 1 of Figure 7.5 is the same as the impulse response of the price level (under optimal policy) in panel 3 of Figure 7.3. The scales are different because the inflation rate plotted is an annualized rate, $4\pi_t$ rather than π_t.

a permanent change in the price level, even under optimal policy. However, the *inflation rate* is eventually restored to its previously anticipated long-run level under an optimal commitment, even though the rate of inflation (as opposed to the rate of *acceleration* of inflation) is not welfare-relevant in this model. Note that the optimal responses shown in Figure 7.5 for the case $\gamma = 1$ correspond fairly well to the conventional wisdom of inflation-targeting central banks; but my theoretical analysis allows me to compute an optimal rate at which inflation should be projected to return to its long-run target value following a disturbance.

As in the previous section, I can derive a target criterion that implements the optimal responses to disturbances regardless of the assumed statistical properties of the disturbances. This optimal target criterion is obtained by replacing π_t in (2.5) by π_t^{qd}, yielding

$$\pi_t - \gamma \pi_{t-1} + \phi(x_t - x_{t-1}) = 0, \tag{2.9}$$

where $\phi > 0$ is the same function of model parameters as before. This indicates that the acceptable inflation projection for the current period should depend not only on the projected change in the output gap, but also (insofar as $\gamma > 0$) on the recent past rate of inflation: A higher existing inflation rate justifies a higher projected near-term inflation rate in the case of any given output-gap projection.

In the special case that $\gamma = 1$, the optimal target criterion adjusts the current inflation target one-for-one with increases in the existing rate of inflation—the target criterion actually involves only the rate of acceleration of inflation. But this does not mean that disturbances are allowed to permanently shift the inflation rate to a new level, as shown in Figure 7.5. In fact, in the case of full indexation, an alternative target criterion that also leads to the optimal equilibrium responses to cost-push shocks is the simpler criterion

$$\pi_t + \phi x_t = \bar{\pi}, \tag{2.10}$$

where again $\phi > 0$ is the same coefficient as in (2.9), and the value of the long-run inflation target $\bar{\pi}$ is arbitrary (but not changing over time). Note that (2.5) is just a first-differenced form of (2.10), and a commitment to ensure that (2.9) holds in each period $t \geq t_0$ is equivalent to a commitment to ensure that (2.10) holds for a particular choice of $\bar{\pi}$, namely, $\bar{\pi} = \pi_{t_0-1} + \phi x_{t_0-1}$. But the choice of $\bar{\pi}$ has no effect on either the determinacy of equilibrium or the equilibrium responses of inflation and output to real disturbances (only on the long-run average inflation rate), and so any target criterion of the form (2.10) implements the optimal responses to disturbances. Note that this optimal target criterion is similar in form to the kind that Svensson (1999) suggests as a description of the behavior of actual inflation-targeting central banks, except that the inflation and output-gap projections in (2.10) are not so far in the future (they refer only to the coming quarter) as in the procedures of actual inflation targeters.

Any rule of the form (2.10) is also optimal from a timeless perspective, under the definition proposed in Section 1, in the case of complete in-dexation to the past price index. Note that alternative rules that result in equilibria that differ only in a transitory, deterministic component of the path of each of the target variables can each be considered optimal in this sense. This ambiguity as to the initial behavior of the target variables can-not be resolved if the concept of optimal policy is to be time consistent. In the present case, ambiguity about the required initial behavior of the target variable, inflation acceleration, implies ambiguity about the required long-run average level of the inflation rate, though there is no ambiguity about how inflation should respond to shocks.

The result that the long-run inflation target associated with an optimal target criterion is indeterminate depends, of course, on the fact that I have assumed a model in which no distortions depend on the inflation rate, as opposed to its rate of change. This is logically possible, but unlikely to be true in reality. (Distortions that depend on the level of nominal interest rates, considered in the next section, would be one example of a realistic complication that would break this result, even in the case of full indexa-tion.) Because the model considered here with $\gamma = 1$ does not determine any particular optimal long-run inflation target (e.g., it need *not* vary with the initially existing inflation rate), even a small perturbation of these as-sumptions is likely to determine an optimal long-run inflation target, and this is generally independent of the initially existing rate of inflation. The monetary frictions considered in Section 1.2 of Chapter 7 provide an exam-ple of this. One should recall the discussion there of the optimal long-run inflation target in the presence of indexation, which was found to be well-defined in the presence of any monetary frictions at all, even in the case that $\gamma = 1$. (The appropriate optimal target criterion for that case is considered in Section 3.2.)

It is worth noting that even though the optimal dynamic responses shown in Figure 7.5 for the case of large γ confirm the conventional wisdom of inflation-targeting central bankers with regard to the desirability of a grad-ual return of the inflation rate to its long-run target level following a cost-push shock, the optimal target criterion for this model does *not* involve a medium-term inflation forecast rather than a shorter-run projection. Even in the case that one supposes that the central bank often has advance in-formation about disturbances that will shift the aggregate-supply relation only a year or more in the future, the robust description of optimal policy is one that indicates how short-run output-gap projections should modify the acceptable short-run inflation projection, rather than one that checks only that some more distant inflation forecast is still on track. Of course, a commitment to the achievement of the target criterion (2.9) each period does imply that the projection of inflation several quarters in the future should never depart much from the long-run inflation target; but the latter stipulation is not an equally useful guide to what should actually be done with interest rates at a given point in time.

2.2 A Model with Wages and Prices Both Sticky

As discussed in Chapter 5, a number of studies have found that the joint dynamics of real and nominal variables are best explained by a model in which wages as well as prices are sticky (e.g., Amato and Laubach, 2003a; Christiano et al., 2001; Smets and Wouters, 2002; Altig et al., 2002; Giannoni and Woodford, 2003b). This is often modeled in the way suggested by Erceg et al. (2000), with monopolistic competition among the suppliers of different types of labor and staggered wagesetting analogous to the Calvo (1983) model of pricesetting. As shown in Section 4 of Chapter 3, the structural equations of the supply side of this model can be written in the form

$$\pi_t = \kappa_p \left(x_t + u_t \right) + \xi_p \left(w_t - w_t^n \right) + \beta E_t \pi_{t+1}, \tag{2.11}$$

$$\pi_t^w = \kappa_W (x_t + u_t) + \xi_W \left(w_t^n - w_t \right) + \beta E_t \pi_{t+1}^w, \tag{2.12}$$

together with the identity

$$w_t = w_{t-1} + \pi_t^w - \pi_t, \tag{2.13}$$

generalizing the single equation (2.1) for the flexible-wage model. Here π_t^w represents nominal wage inflation, $\hat{w}_t$ is the log real wage, $\hat{w}_t^n$ represents exogenous variation in the natural real wage, and the coefficients $\xi_p, \xi_w, \kappa_p, \kappa_w$ are all positive. The coefficient ξ_p indicates the sensitivity of goods-price inflation to changes in the average gap between marginal cost and current prices; it is smaller as prices are stickier. Similarly, ξ_w indicates the sensitivity of wage inflation to changes in the average gap between households' "supply wage" (the marginal rate of substitution between labor supply and consumption) and current wages, and it measures the degree to which wages are sticky.

Note furthermore that $\kappa_p \equiv \xi_p \omega_p$ and $\kappa_w \equiv \xi_w (\omega_w + \sigma^{-1})$, where $\omega_p > 0$ measures the elasticity of marginal cost with respect to the quantity supplied at a given wage; $\omega_w > 0$ measures the elasticity of the supply wage with respect to quantity produced, holding fixed households' marginal utility of income; and $\sigma > 0$ is the same intertemporal elasticity of substitution as appears in the intertemporal IS relation. In the limit of perfectly flexible wages, ξ_w is unboundedly large, and (2.12) reduces to the contemporaneous relation $w_t - w_t^n = (\omega_w + \sigma^{-1})(x_t + u_t)$. With this to substitute for w_t in (2.11), the latter relation then reduces to (2.1), where

$$\kappa \equiv \xi_p \left(\omega_p + \omega_w + \sigma^{-1} \right) \qquad (2.14)$$

and the cost-push shock u_t has been rescaled.

I have shown in Chapter 6 (following Erceg et al., 2000) that the appropriate welfare-theoretic stabilization objective is a discounted criterion of the form (2.2), with a period loss function of the form

$$L_t = \lambda_p \pi_t^2 + \lambda_w \pi_{wt}^2 + \lambda_x \left(x_t - x^* \right)^2, \qquad (2.15)$$

with $\lambda_p, \lambda_w, \lambda_x > 0$. (The optimal weights are given as functions of underlying model parameters in Chapter 6.) I wish to consider policies that minimize the criterion defined by (2.2) and (2.15), subject to the constraints (2.11)–(2.13).

The Lagrangian method used in Chapter 7 and in Section 1 of this chapter now yields a system of first-order conditions

$$\lambda_p \pi_t + \varphi_{pt} - \varphi_{p,t-1} + \upsilon_t = 0, \qquad (2.16)$$

$$\lambda_w \pi_t^w + \varphi_{wt} - \varphi_{w,t-1} - \upsilon_t = 0, \qquad (2.17)$$

$$\lambda_x \left(x_t - x^* \right) - \kappa_p \varphi_{pt} - \kappa_w \varphi_{wt} = 0, \qquad (2.18)$$

$$\upsilon_t = \xi_p \varphi_{pt} - \xi_w \varphi_{wt} + \beta E_t \upsilon_{t+1}, \qquad (2.19)$$

where $\varphi_{pt}, \varphi_{wt}, \upsilon_t$ are the Lagrange multipliers associated with constraints (2.11), (2.12), and (2.13), respectively. I can again use three of the equations to eliminate the three Lagrange multipliers, obtaining a target criterion of the form

$$(\kappa_w - \kappa_p)\pi_t^{asym} + (\xi_p + \xi_w)q_t$$
$$+(\kappa_w - \kappa_p)\left\{ E_t[\beta q_{t+1} - q_t] - E_{t-1}[\beta q_t - q_{t-1}] \right\} = 0, \qquad (2.20)$$

where

$$\pi_t^{asym} \equiv \lambda_p \xi_p \pi_t - \lambda_w \xi_w \pi_t^w$$

is a measure of the asymmetry between price and wage inflation,

$$\pi_t^{sym} \equiv \frac{\lambda_p \kappa_p \pi_t + \lambda_w \kappa_w \pi_t^w}{\lambda_p \kappa_p + \lambda_w \kappa_w}$$

is a (weighted) average of the rates of price and wage inflation, and

$$q_t \equiv (\lambda_p \kappa_p + \lambda_w \kappa_w) \left[\pi_t^{sym} + \frac{\lambda_x}{\lambda_p \kappa_p + \lambda_w \kappa_w} (x_t - x_{t-1}) \right]. \qquad (2.21)$$

In the special case that $\kappa_w = \kappa_p = \kappa > 0$, which empirical studies such as that of Amato and Laubach (2002) find to be not far from the truth,[19] the optimal target criterion (2.20) reduces simply to $q_t = 0$, or

$$\pi_t^{sym} + \phi(x_t - x_{t-1}) = 0, \qquad (2.22)$$

with $\phi = \lambda_x / \kappa$, as in the case with only sticky prices.[20] More generally, the optimal target criterion is more complex and slightly more forward looking (as a result of the inertia in the real-wage dynamics when both wages and prices are sticky[21]). But it still takes the form of an output-adjusted inflation target, involving the projected paths of both price and wage inflation; and since all terms except the first one in (2.20) are equal to zero under a commitment to ensure that $q_t = 0$ at all times, the target criterion (2.22) continues to provide a fairly good approximation to optimal policy even when κ_w is not exactly equal to κ_p.

This is of the same form as the optimal target criterion (2.5) for the case in which only prices are sticky, with the exception that the index of goods-price inflation π_t is now replaced by an index π_t^{sym} that takes account of both price and wage inflation. Of course, the weight that should be placed on wages in the inflation target depends on the relative weight on wage stabilization in the loss function (2.15). If one assumes a "traditional" stabilization objective of the form (2.3), so that $\lambda_w = 0$, then (2.22) is again identical to (2.5). However, one can show that expected utility maximization corresponds to minimization of a discounted loss criterion in which the relative weight on wage-inflation stabilization depends on the relative stickiness of wages and prices, as discussed by Erceg et al. (2000) and in Chapter 6.

---

19. In this case, the structural equations (2.11) and (2.12) imply that the real wage is unaffected by monetary policy, instead evolving as a function of the real disturbances alone, as discussed in Chapter 3. Empirical studies often find that the estimated response of the real wage to an identified monetary policy shock is quite weak, and not significantly different from zero. It is also not significantly different from zero in the results of Giannoni and Woodford (2003b), though the point estimates for their impulse response functions suggest that wages are not as sticky as prices, as discussed in Chapter 5.

20. Here I assume a normalization of the loss function weights in (2.15) in which $\lambda_p + \lambda_w = 1$, corresponding to the normalization in (2.3).

21. This only affects the optimal target criterion, of course, to the extent that the evolution of the real wage is endogenous, which requires that $\kappa_w \neq \kappa_p$.

2.3   A Model with Habit Persistence

In the simple models thus far, the intertemporal IS relation implies that aggregate demand is determined as a purely forward-looking function of the expected path of real interest rates and exogenous disturbances, as discussed in Chapter 4. Many empirical models of the monetary transmission mechanism instead imply that the current level of aggregate real expenditure should depend positively on the recent past level of expenditure, so that aggregate demand should change only gradually, even in the case of an abrupt change in the path of interest rates. A simple way of introducing this is to assume that private expenditure exhibits habit persistence of the sort assumed in the case of consumption expenditure by authors such as Fuhrer (2000), Edge (2000), Christiano et al. (2001), Smets and Wouters (2002), and Altig et al. (2002). As in Section 1.2 of Chapter 5, I consider here a model in which I continue to express all interest-sensitive private expenditure as if it were nondurable consumption, and so assume habit persistence in the level of aggregate private expenditure, as in the models of Amato and Laubach (2001) and Boivin and Giannoni (2003).

Specifically, I assume that the utility flow from interest-sensitive private expenditure C_t is an increasing, concave function of $C_t - \eta C_{t-1}$, where $0 < \eta < 1$ measures the degree of habit persistence. As discussed in Chapter 5, this modification of preferences changes the form of the aggregate-supply relation (2.1), in addition to its implications for the relation between private expenditure and real interest rates. For simplicity, I again consider the case of a model with flexible wages and Calvo pricing. In the presence of habit persistence, the aggregate-supply relation takes the form

$$\pi_t = \kappa \left[(x_t - \delta x_{t-1}) - \beta \delta E_t (x_{t+1} - \delta x_t) \right] + \beta E_t \pi_{t+1} + u_t, \qquad (2.23)$$

where $0 < \delta \leq \eta$ depends both on η (it is an increasing function of η, holding fixed the other parameters of preferences and technology) and on the relative importance of increasing marginal disutility of supplying output as opposed to decreasing marginal utility of income as factors that account for the increase in real marginal cost when economic activity increases. (The greater the relative importance of the increasing marginal disutility of supplying output, measured by the parameter ω, the smaller the value of δ for any given value of η.)

I have shown in Chapter 6 that the discounted loss criterion that corresponds to expected utility maximization in this case is again of the form (2.2), but now with a period loss function

$$L_t = \pi_t^2 + \lambda \left(x_t - \delta x_{t-1} - \hat{x}^* \right)^2, \qquad (2.24)$$

generalizing (2.3). Here λ is again defined as in (2.4), the parameters κ, δ are the same as in the aggregate-supply relation (2.23), and the size of $\hat{x}^* > 0$

depends once more on both the degree of market power and the size of tax distortions. Because both the aggregate-supply relation (2.23) and the loss function (2.24) are functions of the same quasi-differenced output gap $(x_t - \delta x_{t-1})$, there is no conflict between the goals of inflation stabilization and stabilization of the welfare-relevant quasi-differenced output gap, in the absence of the cost-push disturbance u_t, as discussed in Chapter 6. Here, however, I wish to derive a policy rule that is optimal even when such disturbances exist, and indeed, regardless of their statistical properties.

An optimal policy seeks to minimize the discounted sum of losses (2.24) subject to the sequence of constraints (2.23). The same Lagrangian method as above yields first-order conditions

$$\pi_t + \varphi_t - \varphi_{t-1} = 0, \tag{2.25}$$

$$\lambda\left(x_t - \delta x_{t-1} - \hat{x}^*\right) - \kappa\varphi_t + \delta\kappa\varphi_{t-1} = 0, \tag{2.26}$$

generalizing the corresponding pair of conditions obtained in Chapter 7 for the case without habit persistence. An optimal target criterion is again obtained by eliminating the Lagrange multiplier. In the case that $\delta < 1$, as is necessarily true (even in the extreme case where $\eta = 1$) given $\omega > 0$, (2.26) implies that a time-invariant way of identifying the Lagrange multiplier is

$$\varphi_t = (\lambda/\kappa)\left(x_t - x^*\right),$$

where $x^* \equiv \hat{x}^*/(1 - \delta)$. Substituting this into (2.25) yields

$$\pi_t + (\lambda_x/\kappa)(x_t - x_{t-1}) = 0. \tag{2.27}$$

Thus the optimal target criterion is *exactly the same* as in the baseline model and is unaffected by the estimated value of η. The estimated degree of habit persistence does matter for the central bank's judgment about which inflation/output paths are feasible and about the interest-rate path that is necessary in order to achieve them. But it has no consequences for the target criterion that should be used to judge whether a given inflation/output projection is acceptable.

2.4 Predetermined Spending and Pricing Decisions

As discussed in Chapter 5, many empirical models of the monetary transmission mechanism assume that both spending and pricing decisions are *predetermined* for some amount of time, so that there is inevitably a time lag in which neither output nor inflation can be affected by an unexpected change in monetary policy. (Examples include the models estimated by Rotemberg and Woodford, 1997, Amato and Laubach, 2003a, Christiano et al., 2001,

Altig et al., 2002, Boivin and Giannoni, 2003, and Giannoni and Woodford, 2003b.) Here I consider the consequences for optimal policy of allowing for such delays in the effect of policy, modeled in the way described in Section 1.1 of Chapter 5.

Consider a model with flexible wages, but sticky prices indexed to a lagged price index, as in Section 2.1, and assume that both price changes and aggregate private demand are predetermined d periods in advance for some $d \geq 0$. For simplicity, suppose that the efficient level of output is known d periods in advance as well, so that the output gap is also a predetermined variable.[22] In this case, the aggregate-supply relation takes the form

$$\pi_t - \gamma \pi_{t-1} = \kappa E_{t-d} x_t + \beta E_{t-d}(\pi_{t+1} - \gamma \pi_t) + E_{t-d} u_t. \qquad (2.28)$$

The welfare-theoretic loss function continues to be given by (2.2) and (2.7). The Lagrangian associated with the present policy problem is then of the form

$$\mathcal{L} = E_0 \sum_{t=0}^{\infty} \beta^t \left\{ \tfrac{1}{2} \left(\pi_t^{qd} \right)^2 + \frac{\lambda_x}{2} \left(x_t - x^* \right)^2 \right.$$
$$\left. + \varphi_{t-d} \left[\pi_t^{qd} - \kappa x_t - \beta E_{t-d} \pi_{t+1}^{qd} - E_{t-d} u_t \right] \right\},$$

where π_t^{qd} is again defined by (2.8). Here I write φ_{t-d}, the multiplier associated with the constraint (2.28), to indicate that the multiplier is determined at date $t - d$, given that there is one such constraint for each possible state of the world at date $t - d$.

Using the law of iterated expectations, the Lagrangian can equivalently be written as

$$\mathcal{L} = E_0 \sum_{t=d}^{\infty} \beta^t \left\{ \tfrac{1}{2} \left(\pi_t^{qd} \right)^2 + \frac{\lambda_x}{2} \left(x_t - x^* \right)^2 + \varphi_{t-d} \left[\pi_t^{qd} - \kappa x_t - \beta \pi_{t+1}^{qd} \right] \right\} \qquad (2.29)$$

dropping terms that are independent of policy. The first-order conditions that characterize an optimal policy under commitment are given by

$$\pi_t^{qd} + \varphi_{t-d} - \varphi_{t-d-1} = 0, \qquad (2.30)$$

---

22. Alternatively, in (2.28) one may interpret x_t to mean $\hat{Y}_t - E_{t-d} \hat{Y}_t^e$. In this case, the loss function (2.2)–(2.7) is still correct, up to terms (involving the component of $\hat{Y}_t^e$ that is not forecastable d periods in advance) that are independent of policy.

$$\lambda_x \left(x_t - x^* \right) - \kappa \varphi_{t-d} = 0, \tag{2.31}$$

for each $t \geq t_0 + d$. Note that these first-order conditions are of exactly the same form as those derived in Chapter 7 for the model with $d = 0$, except for the fact that the multiplier φ_t determined previously is now called φ_{t-d}. (Now this multiplier is a function only of the state of the world at date $t - d$, but the same is true of π_t^{qd} and x_t.)

Elimination of the Lagrange multipliers then yields exactly the same target criterion as before, namely (2.9), where ϕ is again equal to $\lambda/\kappa >$ 0. The only difference is that now all of the terms of this criterion are determined as of date $t - d$. Obviously, one cannot use a policy decision at date t to ensure that the criterion is satisfied. Moreover, in the event that private-sector decisions at date $t - d$ do happen to have satisfied the criterion, a commitment to have the criterion hold would not serve to determine the appropriate policy decision at date t, for the criterion would hold regardless of the decision made at that date.

The criterion (2.9) can nonetheless be used to define a coherent policy rule, if one understands (2.9) to be the criterion that determines the appropriate policy decision at date $t - d$. That is, at any given date t, the central bank acts so as to ensure that its projection for the economy's evolution from date $t + d$ onward satisfies[23]

$$\pi_{t+d} - \gamma_{t+d-1} + \phi(x_{t+d} - x_{t+d-1}) = 0. \tag{2.32}$$

This is a condition that involves target variables that can still be affected by the bank's decision in period t. Furthermore, the condition that (2.32) be projected to hold for each $t \geq t_0$, together with initial predetermined values for π_t and x_t in all periods $t < t_0 + d$, can be shown to determine unique nonexplosive equilibrium paths $\{\pi_t, x_t\}$.

Yet while the criterion (2.32) involves variables that are not completely determined prior to period t, it does *not* involve variables that can be affected by the choice of i_t. This is because, when spending decisions are predetermined, the IS relation of the model takes the form

$$x_t = E_{t-d} x_{t+1} - \sigma E_{t-d} \left(i_t - \pi_{t+1} - r_t^n \right), \tag{2.33}$$

---

23. Since both inflation and the output gap are assumed to be predetermined d periods in advance, one might equivalently write this criterion in terms of forecasts conditional upon period t information. In the case that inflation and output are assumed to be made up of endogenous predetermined components, determined in accordance with relations (2.28) and (2.33), plus exogenous nonpredetermined components, as in the model considered by Svensson and Woodford (2003), then the optimal target criterion is again given by (2.32), except that in this case it is essential to replace each of the terms by its conditional expectation at date t.

which implies that only the *forecastable component* of short-term interest rates, $E_{t-d}i_t$, has any effect on spending decisions, and hence on inflation dynamics as well. It follows that what the central bank must decide upon in its period t decision cycle, with a view to ensuring that (2.32) is projected to be satisfied, is the value of $E_t i_{t+d}$.

In fact, since unanticipated interest-rate movements cannot play any role in the stabilization of either inflation or output in this kind of model, it is desirable for the central bank to ensure that interest rates are completely forecastable (d periods in advance). As discussed in Chapter 6, there are various reasons why reduction of the volatility of nominal interest-rate fluctuations may also be an appropriate goal of stabilization policy. In this section, I have assumed that such concerns are of sufficiently minimal importance that it is never desirable to sacrifice inflation or output-gap stability for the sake of interest-rate stabilization. But if one admits even the tiniest preference for less volatile interest rates, it follows that optimal policy should reduce interest-rate variability to the extent that this is possible *without* sacrificing any other stabilization objectives. In the present case, this would mean complete elimination of unforecastable interest-rate variation, for any such component of the interest-rate process adds to the variability of interest rates while achieving no possible gains in terms of other stabilization goals. Hence

$$i_t = E_{t-d}i_t \tag{2.34}$$

is an additional requirement for optimal policy. The requirement that (2.34) hold each period in addition to (2.32) can be shown to uniquely determine a nonexplosive equilibrium path for $\{i_t\}$ as well as the other two target variables. (Condition (2.32) uniquely determines the path of $E_{t-d}i_t$, since this can be read off from (2.33) once one has determined the paths for inflation and the output gap. Condition (2.34) is then a complementary relation to determine the unanticipated component of the nominal interest rate.)

One may then imagine implementing optimal policy through a targeting procedure of the following sort (as proposed in Svensson and Woodford, 2003). In each period t, the central bank acts so as to achieve overnight interest rates i_t equal to the operating target $i_{t,t-d}$ decided upon during its period $t-d$ decision cycle. In addition, its policy committee deliberates about the appropriate target $i_{t+d,t}$ to set for interest rates in period $t+d$. This latter decision is made so as to result in a projected future evolution of the economy (given the bank's information in period t) that satisfies the target criterion (2.32). The target that is decided upon at that time might reasonably be announced at the time that it is decided upon, given that it is only private-sector anticipations of interest-rate changes that allow the central bank to achieve its stabilization goals.

2.5 Optimal Policy for a Small Quantitative Model

I now illustrate the consequences of applying this approach to a somewhat more complex model, the one estimated by Giannoni and Woodford (2003b), discussed previously in Section 2.2 of Chapter 5. This allows me to describe the quantitative character of the optimal inflation-targeting rule in the context of a model whose parameters have been chosen to match certain key features of the U.S. monetary transmission mechanism. The model incorporates each of the features that I have already discussed in isolation in this section: sticky wages as well as prices (with Calvo-style staggering); both wages and prices indexed to a lagged price index; habit persistence in aggregate private expenditure; and wages, prices, and real expenditure all determined a quarter in advance. (The interest-sensitive component of real expenditure is actually predetermined for two quarters, as in the model of Rotemberg and Woodford, 1997.)

The method expounded in Chapter 6 can be used to show that in the context of this model, the appropriate welfare-theoretic loss function, again abstracting from any grounds for concern with interest-rate stabilization, is given by

$$E_0 \sum_{t=0}^{\infty} \beta^t \left[\lambda_p \left(\pi_t - \gamma_p \pi_{t-1} \right)^2 + \lambda_w \left(\pi_t^w - \gamma_w \pi_{t-1} \right)^2 \right.$$

$$\left. + \lambda_x \left(x_t - \delta x_{t-1} - \hat{x}^* \right)^2 \right]. \tag{2.35}$$

In this expression, the weights $\lambda_p, \lambda_w, \lambda_x > 0$ are again

$$\lambda_p = \frac{\theta_p \xi_p^{-1}}{\theta_p \xi_p^{-1} + \theta_w \phi^{-1} \xi_w^{-1}} > 0, \qquad \lambda_w = \frac{\theta_w \phi^{-1} \xi_w^{-1}}{\theta_p \xi_p^{-1} + \theta_w \phi^{-1} \xi_w^{-1}} > 0, \tag{2.36}$$

$$\lambda_x = \lambda_p \frac{\kappa}{\theta_p} > 0, \tag{2.37}$$

as in the simpler loss function (2.15), where κ in the last expression is defined as

$$\kappa \equiv \xi_p \eta \varphi / \delta > 0, \tag{2.38}$$

as in (2.23). The coefficient $0 \le \delta \le \eta$ is the smaller root of the quadratic equation

$$\eta \varphi \left(1 + \beta \delta^2 \right) = \left[\omega + \varphi \left(1 + \beta \eta^2 \right) \right] \delta, \tag{2.39}$$

just as in (2.24); and $\hat{x}^* > 0$ is the same function of the microeconomic distortions affecting the efficiency of the steady-state output level as in (2.24).

The numerical coefficients of the welfare-theoretic loss function implied by the estimated parameter values reported in Table 5.3 are given by

$$\lambda_p = .9960, \qquad \lambda_w = .0040, \qquad \lambda_x = 0.0026, \qquad \delta = .035.$$

Interestingly, the estimated Giannoni-Woodford model implies that it is optimal for the central bank to put a much larger weight on the stabilization of goods-price inflation than on the stabilization of wage inflation or of the output gap. Moreover, despite the fact that they estimate a very high degree of habit formation, which implies that household utility depends on the rate of change of real expenditure rather than its level, the central bank's loss function does not involve the variability of the change in the output gap. Rather, it involves the variability of the level of the output gap relative to a small fraction of the lagged output gap.

These conclusions depend, of course, on their parameter estimates. It may seem surprising that the weight on wage inflation stabilization is so small, given that the estimates do not imply that wages are substantially more flexible than prices (e.g., ξ_w is larger than ξ_p, but not by a large factor). The conclusion that λ_w is nonetheless very much smaller than λ_p reflects mainly the fact that the estimates reported in Table 5.3 imply a value for θ_p that is much larger than $\phi^{-1}\theta_w$. This in turn results from the fact that the estimated value of ω_w is much larger than the calibrated value of ω_p.[24] Because it is not plausible to assume a technology for which ω_p could be nearly as large as the estimated value of ω_w, they are led to assume a value of θ_p substantially larger than $\phi^{-1}\theta_w$. The result that λ_p greatly exceeds λ_w then follows, using (2.36).

The conclusion that λ_x is small follows, using (2.37), from the small value of κ_p and the large value of θ_p implied by their parameter estimates. Since $\kappa_p \equiv \xi_p\omega_p$ and the value of θ_p is inferred from the value of ξ_p using the definition from Section 4.1 of Chapter 3, both of these conclusions depend crucially on the small estimated value for ξ_p. Essentially, the observed insensitivity of inflation to variations in output requires them to infer underlying microeconomic parameters that imply that variations in the output gap cause relatively modest distortions—this is the only way, in the context of the other assumptions of their model, to explain the fact that inflation is not more strongly affected (i.e., that the Phillips curve is not steeper).

Finally, the conclusion that δ is small (despite the fact that $\eta = 1$) follows, using (2.39), from the fact that the value of ω implied by their estimates is

---

24. If ξ_p and ξ_w were assigned equal values, then under the assumption of equal values for α_p and α_w, one would have to have equal values for $\omega_p\theta_p$ and $\omega_w\phi^{-1}\theta_w$. (See the definitions of ξ_w and ξ_p in Section 4.1 of Chapter 3, and recall that $\omega_w \equiv \nu\phi$.) The implied value of θ_p is then larger than $\phi^{-1}\omega_w$ by exactly the same factor as ω_w is larger than ω_p. In fact, their estimated value for ξ_p is smaller than their estimate of ξ_w, and this further increases the relative size of the implied value of θ_p.

large relative to the estimated value of φ. Essentially, the observed sensitivity of wages to variations in real activity on the one hand (implying a large value for ω_w) and the sensitivity of aggregate expenditure to interest-rate changes on the other (implying that φ cannot be too large) indicate preferences under which variations in the level of real activity create greater distortions than variations in the rate of growth of real activity. Even with an estimated coefficient of $\eta = 1$, the level of output matters to the representative household because of its consequences for the amount that the household must work; if the marginal disutility of output supply increases sharply with the level of real activity (as implied by a large value of ω), it is still relatively more important to stabilize the level of real activity than its rate of change.

The problem of minimizing (2.35) subject to the constraints implied by the structural equations of the estimated model (described in Chapter 5) results again in a system of first-order conditions that can be used to derive an optimal target criterion for monetary policy. I omit details of this derivation here, referring the reader instead to the technical appendix to Giannoni and Woodford (2003b). Here I simply summarize the content of the numerical characterization of optimal policy that they obtain.

A first observation about optimal policy in the Giannoni-Woodford model follows from the fact that wages, prices, and output are all predetermined for one quarter or longer in the model. As explained in the previous section, it follows that

$$i_t = E_{t-1} i_t \tag{2.40}$$

is a requirement for optimal policy. The instrument that the central bank must adjust in period t in order to ensure that its period t target criterion is projected to be satisfied is then not the period t interest rate i_t, but rather the bank's precommitted value $i_{t+1,t}$ for the level of short-term nominal interest rates in the following quarter.

The target criterion that the bank seeks to satisfy using this instrument can be stated purely in terms of the projected paths of the target variables π_t, π_t^w, and $x_t - \delta x_{t-1}$, or alternatively, in terms of projections for the paths of the inflation rate π_t, the real wage w_t, and the output gap x_t. In the present case, unlike the simpler ones discussed thus far, the most convenient representation of the requirements for optimal policy is not in terms of a single target criterion, but two distinct criteria. First of all, optimality requires that projections in any period t satisfy a condition of the form[25]

---

25. The target criterion could equivalently be expressed in the form $\phi_p F_t(\pi) + \phi_w F_t(\pi^w) = \bar{\pi}_t$, in which case the target criterion would refer solely to projected inflation of different sorts (both price and wage inflation). This would be a representation analogous to the one given in Section 2.2, and would make clear that only the projected future paths of variables that enter

$$F_t(\pi) + \phi_w[F_t(w) - w_t] = \bar{\pi}_t. \tag{2.41}$$

Here for each of the variables $z = \pi, w$, the expression $F_t(z)$ refers to a weighted average of forecasts of the variable z at various future horizons, conditional on information at date t,

$$F_t(z) \equiv \sum_{k=1}^{\infty} \alpha_k^z E_t z_{t+k}, \tag{2.42}$$

where the weights α_k^z sum to one. Thus the coefficient ϕ_w is actually the sum of the weights on real-wage forecasts at different horizons k.

Observe that this target criterion can be thought of as a wage-adjusted inflation target. In addition to the correction for the projected growth of real wages in the future, the acceptable rate of projected future inflation also varies due to time variation in the target $\bar{\pi}_t$. Optimality further requires that $\bar{\pi}_t$ be a function only of information available at date $t-1$, and hence that

$$\bar{\pi}_t = E_{t-1}\left[F_t(\pi) + \phi_W(F_t(w) - w_t)\right]. \tag{2.43}$$

In general, this optimal target is not constant over time.

In addition to the above requirement (which amounts to the condition that the left-hand side of (2.41) be forecastable a quarter in advance), optimality also requires that projections at date t also satisfy another condition of the form

$$F_t^*(\pi) + \phi_w^*\left[F_t^*(w) - w_t\right] + \phi_x^*\left[F_t^*(x) - x_t\right] = \pi_t^*, \tag{2.44}$$

where the expressions $F_t^*(z)$ are again weighted averages of forecasts at different horizons (but with relative weights α_k^{z*} that may be different in this case), and π_t^* is another time-varying target value, once again a predetermined variable. In this case the criterion specifies a target for a wage- and output-adjusted inflation projection.[26]

Optimality requires that the target value be given by an expression of the form

---

the loss function matter. However, the representation given here provides what is arguably a more convenient numerical summary of the content of the target criterion by collecting the central bank's projections regarding the future level of nominal quantities in a single variable, the projected future price level.

26. As with (2.41), one could equivalently express this criterion in terms of a linear function of projections for price inflation, wage inflation, and the output gap.

$$\pi_t^* = F_{t-1}^1(\pi) + \phi_w^* \left[F_{t-1}^1(w) - w_t \right] + \phi_x^* \left[F_{t-1}^1(x) - x_t \right]$$

$$+ \theta_\pi^* \left[F_{t-1}^1(\pi) - F_{t-2}^2(\pi) \right] + \theta_w^* \left[F_{t-1}^1(w) - F_{t-2}^2(w) \right] \qquad (2.45)$$

$$+ \theta_x^* \left[F_{t-1}^1(x) - F_{t-2}^2(x) \right],$$

where the expressions $F_t^j(z)$, for $j = 1, 2$, are still other weighted averages of forecasts at different horizons, with relative weights α_k^{zj} that again sum to one. Here, as with (2.43), the optimal target value depends on previous quarters' forecasts of the economy's subsequent evolution; this is a further example of the history dependence of optimal target criteria, already observed in the simpler cases treated earlier.

It is worth noting that for each of the three variables—the inflation rate, the real wage, and the output gap—it is only the *differences* between the projections for the variables and their current values or between current projections and projections for the same variables at an earlier date that matter for the optimal target criterion.[27] What this means is that one could alternatively express the target criterion entirely in terms of projections of the *first differences* of these three variables, with no dependence on the *absolute levels* of any of the variables.[28] The reasons are somewhat different, however, in each case. The inflation projections involve only the projected first difference of the inflation rate because in the loss function (2.35), it is only the values of $\pi_t - \pi_{t-1}$ and $\pi_t^w - \pi_{t-1}$ that matter,[29] rather than the absolute rate of either price or wage inflation. Projections for these two target variables can alternatively be expressed in terms of projections for $\pi_t - \pi_{t-1}$ and $w_t - w_{t-1}$. Because real-wage projections enter the target criterion only for this reason (i.e., as a substitute for wage-inflation projections), it is only projections for the first difference of the real wage that matter as well.

The observation that the optimal target criterion involves only the projected rate of change of the output gap, rather than its level, is not a consequence of the form of the loss function—for δ may be much less than one, as it is for the estimated parameter values. Nor is this a consequence

27. Note that the same is true of the short-run target criterion (2.41)–(2.43).

28. One could also simplify the algebraic statement of the target criterion by eliminating the $-\phi_w^* w_t - \phi_x^* x_t$ terms that appear both on the left-hand side of (2.44) and the right-hand side of (2.45). Giannoni and Woodford do not do so in order to make it clear that the target criterion does not actually require an estimate of either the absolute level of the output or of the deviation of the real wage from its trend path, but only of output-gap and real-wage *growth*. This is an important practical consideration, given that real-time estimates of the absolute levels of both variables are much more controversial.

29. The result thus depends on the fact that the parameter estimates of Giannoni and Woodford imply that $\gamma_p = \gamma_w = 1$.

of the estimated value $\eta = 1$. The optimality conditions just stated apply regardless of the value of η, and I note once again that, in any event, $\eta = 1$ does not imply $\delta = 1$. The result is rather an illustration of the generality of the conclusion, first obtained for the baseline model considered in Chapter 7, that the optimal target criterion involves the rate of change of the output gap rather than its absolute level, regardless of the degree of habit persistence.

It may be wondered how one can specify optimal policy in terms of two distinct target criteria involving different linear combinations of projections when the central bank has only one instrument at its disposal. The key to this is to observe that the target criterion specified by (2.41)–(2.43) restricts only the *surprise* components of the quarter t projections, that is, the way in which they may differ from the projections that were made in quarter $t - 1$ for the same variables. Hence it is only the *surprise* component of the central bank's interest-rate decision—the difference between the $E_t i_{t+1}$ announced in quarter t and $E_{t-1} i_{t+1}$—that can be determined by this criterion for optimal policy. The evolution of the (two-period-ahead) predetermined component of policy, $E_{t-2} i_t$, can instead be chosen so as to ensure that the second target criterion, specified by (2.44)–(2.45), is satisfied each period.

One may thus imagine the implementation of the optimal targeting rule to occur in the following way.[30] First, in each quarter t, the central bank intervenes in the money markets (through open-market operations, repurchases, standing facilities in the interbank market for central-bank balances, and so on) so as to implement the interest-rate target $i_{t,t-1}$ announced in quarter $t - 1$. Second, as part of the quarter t decision cycle, the bank must choose an operating target $i_{t+1,t}$ to announce for the following quarter. This is chosen in order to imply a projected evolution of (wage and price) inflation from quarter $t + 1$ onward that satisfies the target criterion (2.41), where $\bar{\pi}_t$ is a target value that had been determined in quarter $t - 1$. Third, it is also necessary, as part of the quarter t decision cycle, for the central bank to choose the target $\bar{\pi}_{t+1}$ for the following quarter. This is chosen so as to ensure that future policy is conducted in a way that allows the bank to project (conditional on its current information) that the target criterion (2.44) and (2.45) should be satisfied. In practice, this means that the central bank should use its model of the transmission mechanism to determine the future evolution of the economy under the assumption that (2.44) and

---

30. Because the Giannoni-Woodford empirical model is quarterly, it is simplest to discuss the policy process as if a policy decision is also made once per quarter, even though in reality most central banks reconsider their operating targets for overnight interest rates somewhat more frequently. The present discussion should not be taken to imply that it is optimal for the policy committee to meet only once per quarter; this would follow from the analysis only if (as in their model) all other markets were also open only once per quarter.

(2.45) hold in all future periods; this forecast then determines the target value $\bar{\pi}_{t+1}$ using (2.43).

Algebraic expressions for each of the coefficients in the optimal target criteria, as functions of the underlying model parameters, are given in the technical appendix to Giannoni and Woodford (2003b). Here I discuss only the numerical coefficients implied by their estimated parameter values. In the case of the short-term criterion (2.41), the coefficient ϕ_w is equal to 0.565.[31] Thus if unexpected developments in quarter t are projected to imply a higher future level of real wages than had previously been anticipated, policy must ensure that projected future price inflation is correspondingly reduced. This is because of a desire to stabilize (nominal) wage inflation as well as price inflation, and under circumstances of expected real-wage growth, inflation must be curbed in order that nominal-wage growth not be even higher.

The relative weights that this criterion places on projections at different future horizons are shown in Figure 8.1. The two panels plot the coefficients α_k^{π}, α_k^{w}, respectively, as functions of the horizon k. Note that the quarter for which the projections receive greatest weight is one quarter in the future in each case. However, while the real-wage projection that matters is primarily the projected growth in real wages between the present quarter and the next one, substantial weight is also placed on projected inflation farther in the future; in fact, the mean lead $\sum_k \alpha_k^{\pi} k$ is between ten and eleven quarters in the future in the case of the inflation projection $F_t(\pi)$. Thus the short-run target criterion is a (time-varying) target for the average rate of inflation that is projected over the next several years, adjusted to take account of expected wage growth, mainly over the coming quarter. Roughly speaking, optimal policy requires that the central bank choose $i_{t+1,t}$ in quarter t so as to head off any change in the projected average inflation rate over the next several years, due to developments not anticipated in quarter $t - 1$ (and hence reflected in the current target $\bar{\pi}_{t-1}$). This is a criterion in the spirit of inflation-forecast targeting as currently practiced at central banks such as the Bank of England, except that projected wage growth matters as well as price inflation and the target shifts over time.

However, in the case of the long-term criterion (2.44), the numerical coefficients of the target criterion are given by

$$\phi_w^* = 0.258, \qquad \phi_x^* = 0.135.$$

---

31. Here and below, I present the coefficients for a target criterion where the inflation rate is measured in annualized percentage points, rather than as a quarterly rate of change as in the equations of the Giannoni-Woodford model given in Chapter 5. When the variables are defined as in the model, the coefficients multiplying the real-wage and output-gap terms are only one-quarter as large as those given here and subsequently.

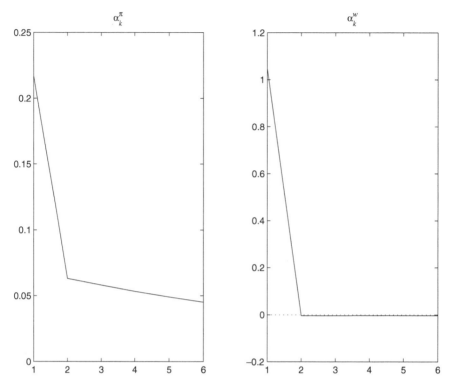

Figure 8.1 *Relative weights on projections at different horizons in the short-run target criterion (2.41). The horizontal axis indicates the horizon k in quarters. Source: Giannoni and Woodford (2003b).*

Output-gap projections matter here as well; a higher projected future output gap requires a reduction in the projected future rate of inflation, just as a higher projected future real wage does. The numerical size of the weight placed on the output-gap projection may appear modest; but Giannoni and Woodford (2003b) find that this is nonetheless a significant correction to the path of the target criterion, owing to the degree of variability of the output-gap projections implied by their model.

The relative weights on forecasts at different horizons in this criterion are plotted in the panels in the first row of Figure 8.2. Observe that in the case of this criterion, the projections that mainly matter are those for two quarters in the future; the criterion is nearly independent of projections regarding the quarter after the current one. Hence it makes sense to think of this criterion as the one that should determine the policy that the central bank plans on in periods two or more quarters in the future (and hence its

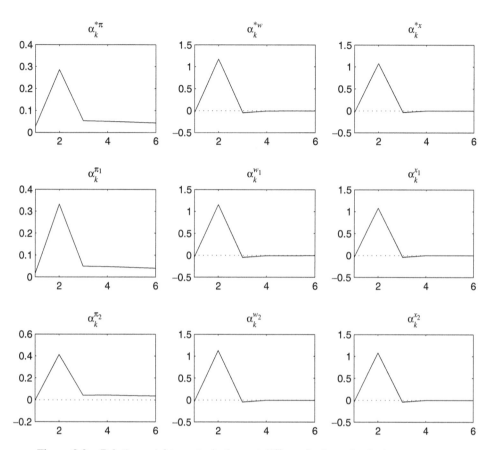

Figure 8.2 *Relative weights on projections at different horizons in the long-run target criterion. Panels in the first row indicate the projections in (2.44), while the other two rows indicate the projections from previous quarters that define the target value π_t^*. Source: Giannoni and Woodford (2003b).*

choice in quarter t of the target $\bar{\pi}_{t+1}$ to constrain its choice in the following period of $i_{t+2,t+1}$), but not as a primary determinant of whether the bank's intended policy in period $t+1$ is on track.

Finally, the coefficients of the rule (2.45) determining the target value for the long-term criterion are given by

$$\theta_\pi^* = 0.580, \qquad \theta_w^* = 0.252, \qquad \theta_x^* = 0.125.$$

The weights in the projections (conditional on information in the previous two quarters) at various horizons are plotted in the second and third rows of

Figure 8.2. Here too, it is primarily projections for two quarters in the future that matter in each case. Roughly speaking, then, the target value for the wage- and output-adjusted inflation projection two quarters in the future is high when a similar adjusted inflation projection (again for a time two quarters in the future) was high in the previous quarter or when the adjusted inflation projection in the previous quarter was high, not in absolute terms, but *relative* to a similar adjusted inflation projection two quarters previously.

Thus one finds that forecasting exercises, in which the central bank projects the evolution of both inflation and real variables many years into the future under alternative hypothetical policies on its own part, play a central role in a natural approach to the implementation of optimal policy. A forecast of inflation several years into the future is required in each (quarterly) decision cycle in order to check whether the intended interest-rate operating target for the following quarter is consistent with the criterion (2.41). In addition, the time-varying medium-term inflation target $\bar{\pi}_t$ must be chosen each period on the basis of yet another forecasting exercise. While the long-run target criterion (2.44) primarily involves projections for a time only two quarters in the future, the choice of $\bar{\pi}_{t+1}$ requires that the central bank solve for a projected path of the economy in which (2.44) is satisfied not only in the current period, but in all future periods as well. Hence this exercise also requires the construction of projected paths for inflation and real variables extending many years into the future. However, the relevant paths will not be constant-interest-rate projections (of the kind currently published by the Bank of England), but rather projections of the economy's future evolution given how policy is expected to evolve. Indeed, the projections are used to select constraints on the bank's own actions in future decision cycles (by choosing both the interest-rate operating target $i_{t+1,t}$ and the adjusted inflation target $\bar{\pi}_{t+1}$ in period t).

3   Optimal Interest-Rate Rules

In all of the examples considered in the previous section, interest-rate stabilization is not assumed to be among the goals of monetary policy, and, as a consequence, the optimal target criteria derived in accordance with the principles of Section 1 do not involve any explicit reference to the path of interest rates. However, central banks generally appear to care about reducing the volatility of nominal interest rates (Goodfriend, 1991), in addition to their concern with price stability and the stabilization of real activity. Such a concern can also be justified in terms of expected utility maximization, as discussed in Sections 4.1 and 4.2 of Chapter 6. Either of the grounds described there—the existence of nonnegligible transactions frictions or a concern to reduce the frequency with which a linear policy rule would require violation of the zero lower bound on nominal interest rates—can justify the choice of policy rules that minimize a loss function that includes a term of the form $\lambda_i(i_t - i^*)^2$, in addition to the terms discussed in the previous examples, for suitable choices of the coefficients $\lambda_i > 0$ and i^*.

If one assumes a loss function of this kind, the principles discussed in Section 1 lead to the choice of a target criterion for monetary policy that involves the path of the short-term nominal interest rate i_t, along with the other target variables. A commitment to achieve a target criterion of this form may be interpreted as an interest-rate feedback rule, which implicitly defines the desired instrument choice at each point in time, as discussed in Section 1.5. As we shall see, an optimal rule of this kind may well take the form of a generalized Taylor rule and may be similar in form to the estimated interest-rate rules discussed in Chapter 1.[32]

3.1 An Optimal Rule for the Basic Neo-Wicksellian Model

I first illustrate the possibility of a robustly optimal interest-rate rule in the context of the basic optimizing model of the monetary transmission mechanism developed in Chapter 4 and used as the basis for my analysis of the optimal equilibrium responses to real disturbances in Chapter 7. The structural equations of this model consist of the aggregate-supply relation (2.1) together with the intertemporal IS relation

$$x_t = E_t x_{t+1} - \sigma E_t \left(i_t - \pi_{t+1} - r_t^n \right). \tag{3.1}$$

This is a system of two equations each period for the determination of inflation and the output gap, given the central bank's control of the short-term nominal interest rate i_t and the exogenous disturbances u_t and r_t^n. (The IS relation must now be included among the constraints on the policy problem, owing to the inclusion of a concern with the variability of interest rates among the stabilization objectives.) The assumed objective of monetary policy is to minimize the expected value of a loss criterion of the form (2.2), where the period loss function is now of the form

$$L_t = \pi_t^2 + \lambda_x \left(x_t - x^* \right)^2 + \lambda_i \left(i_t - i^* \right)^2, \tag{3.2}$$

generalizing (2.3) as in Section 2.2 of Chapter 7.

I have already discussed the optimal dynamic responses of inflation, output, and interest rates to real disturbances in this case in Chapter 7. I now wish to consider the choice of a policy rule that can implement these desired responses as a determinate rational-expectations equilibrium, and that can

---

32. The results in this section are based directly on Giannoni and Woodford (2002b, 2003a).

do so regardless of the statistical properties of the exogenous disturbance processes $\{u_t, r_t^n\}$ appearing in the structural equations. As shown in Chapter 7, the optimal responses satisfy a system of first-order conditions

$$\pi_t - \beta^{-1}\sigma\varphi_{1,t-1} + \varphi_{2t} - \varphi_{2,t-1} = 0, \tag{3.3}$$

$$\lambda_x\left(x_t - x^*\right) + \varphi_{1t} - \beta^{-1}\varphi_{1,t-1} - \kappa\varphi_{2t} = 0, \tag{3.4}$$

$$\lambda_i\left(i_t - i^*\right) + \sigma\varphi_{1t} = 0 \tag{3.5}$$

for each period $t \geq t_0$. These equations are solved for unique nonexplosive paths for the variables $\{\pi_t, x_t, i_t\}$ for $t \geq t_0$ and the Lagrange multipliers $\{\varphi_{1t}, \varphi_{2t}\}$ for $t \geq t_0 - 1$ that are also consistent with specified initial values

$$\pi_{t_0} = \bar{\pi}_{t_0}, \ x_{t_0} = \bar{x}_{t_0}. \tag{3.6}$$

It is possible to eliminate the two Lagrange multipliers, employing (3.5) to solve for φ_{1t}, and then, after using this solution to eliminate φ_{1t} from (3.4), resorting to the latter relation to solve for φ_{2t}. Substituting these solutions for the two Lagrange multipliers into (3.3), one obtains a relation among the target variables $\pi_t, x_t, x_{t-1}, i_t, i_{t-1}$, and i_{t-2} that must hold in any period $t \geq t_0 + 2$ in an equilibrium that is optimal from a timeless perspective. Demanding that this relation hold for $t = t_0, t_0 + 1$ as well amounts to a way of choosing the initial constraints $\bar{\pi}_{t_0}, \bar{x}_{t_0}$ that is self-consistent, in the sense discussed in Chapter 7.

Because the relation in question involves a nonzero coefficient on i_t, it can be expressed as an implicit instrument rule of the form

$$i_t = (1 - \rho_1)i^* + \rho_1 i_{t-1} + \rho_2\Delta i_{t-1} + \phi_\pi\pi_t + \phi_x\Delta x_t/4, \tag{3.7}$$

where

$$\rho_1 = 1 + \kappa\sigma/\beta > 1, \qquad\qquad \rho_2 = \beta^{-1} > 1, \tag{3.8}$$

$$\phi_\pi = \kappa\sigma/\lambda_i > 0, \qquad\qquad \phi_x = 4\sigma\lambda_x/\lambda_i > 0. \tag{3.9}$$

Moreover, Giannoni and Woodford (2002b) show that commitment to this rule implies a determinate equilibrium.

PROPOSITION 8.5. Suppose that the problem of choosing a state-contingent plan $\{\pi_t, x_t, i_t\}$ for dates $t \geq t_0$ satisfying (2.1) and (3.1) and initial conditions (3.6) has a bounded solution in the case of any bounded disturbance processes. Then a commitment to the rule described by (3.7)–(3.9) implies a determinate rational-expectations equilibrium.

The proof is given in Appendix G. The equilibrium determined by commitment to this rule from date $t = t_0$ onward corresponds to the unique bounded solution to equations (3.3)–(3.5) when the initial Lagrange multipliers φ_{1,t_0-1}, φ_{2,t_0-1} are the ones that would be inferred from the historical values of x_{t_0-1}, i_{t_0-1}, and i_{t_0-2} in the case that an equilibrium of the kind determined by this policy had already existed in periods $t_0 - 2$ and $t_0 - 1$.

It follows that the equilibrium determined by commitment to the implicit instrument rule (3.7) is optimal from a timeless perspective, in the sense defined in Section 1.1. It is furthermore robustly optimal, in the sense defined in Section 1.3. Note that the present derivation of the optimal rule requires no hypotheses about the nature of the disturbance processes $\{r_t^n, u_t\}$, except that they are exogenously given and that they are bounded. In fact, the rule is optimal regardless of their nature. Commitment to this rule implies the optimal impulse responses displayed in Figure 7.6 in the case of the particular disturbance process assumed in the numerical illustration there, but it equally implies optimal responses in the case of any other types of disturbances to the natural rate of interest and/or cost-push shocks.[33] This robustness of the rule is a strong advantage from the point of view of its adoption as a practical guide to the conduct of monetary policy.

The optimal interest-rate rule (3.7) has a number of important similarities to the Taylor rule. It specifies the appropriate current level of the nominal interest rate as a function of inflation and the output gap and is similar to Taylor's recommendation in that the contemporaneous effect of an increase in either inflation or the output gap upon the federal funds rate operating target is positive ($\phi_\pi, \phi_x > 0$). The rule also satisfies the Taylor principle, given that $\phi_\pi > 0$ and $\rho_1 > 1$.[34] However, the optimal rule involves additional history dependence, owing to the nonzero weights on the lagged funds rate, the lagged rate of increase in the funds rate, and the lagged output gap. Moreover, the optimal degree of history dependence is nontrivial: The optimal values of ρ_1 and ρ_2 are both necessarily greater than

33. This is a substantial advantage of this instrument rule over the one proposed in Woodford (1999a), which expresses the federal funds rate as a function of the lagged funds rate, the lagged rate of increase in the funds rate, the current inflation rate, and the previous quarter's inflation rate. That rule would also be consistent with optimal responses to real disturbances, but only if (as assumed in the earlier calculation) all disturbances perturb the natural rate of interest in a way that can be described by an AR(1) process with a single specified coefficient of serial correlation, and have no effect on the natural rate of output that is different than the effect on the efficient rate of output (i.e., there are no cost-push shocks). In this special case, however, the rule discussed earlier has the advantage that its implementation requires no information on the part of the central bank other than an accurate measure of inflation (including an accurate projection of period t inflation at the time that the period t funds rate is set).

34. Recall the discussion in Section 2.2 of Chapter 4 of the generalization of this principle to the case of policy rules with interest-rate inertia.

one, while the optimal coefficient on x_{t-1} is as large (in absolute value) as the coefficient on x_t. It is particularly worth noting that the optimal rule implies not only intrinsic inertia in the dynamics of the funds rate—a transitory deviation of the inflation rate from its average value increases the funds rate not only in the current quarter, but in subsequent quarters as well—but is actually *superinertial:* The implied dynamics for the funds rate are explosive,[35] if the initial overshooting of the long-run average inflation rate is not offset by a subsequent undershooting (as actually always happens in equilibrium). In this respect this optimal rule is similar to those found to be optimal in the numerical analysis by Rotemberg and Woodford (1999a) of a more complicated empirical version of the model.[36]

In the case of the calibrated parameter values given in Table 6.1 and used in the numerical examples of Chapter 7, the coefficients of the optimal instrument rule are given by $\rho_1 = 1.15, \rho_2 = 1.01, \phi_\pi = 0.64$, and $\phi_x = 0.33$. These may be compared with the coefficients of the Fed reaction function of similar form estimated by Judd and Rudebusch (1998) for the Greenspan period, and reported in Table 1.1. These values were equal to $\rho_1 = 0.73, \rho_2 = 0.43, \phi_\pi = 0.42$, and $\phi_x = 0.30$, except that in the empirical reaction function ϕ_x represents the reaction to the current quarter's *level* of the output gap, rather than its first difference.[37] (Interestingly, Judd and Rudebusch find that an equation with feedback from the first difference of the output gap, rather than its level, fits best during an earlier period of Fed policy, under Paul Volcker's chairmanship.) The signs of the coefficients of the optimal rule agree with those characterizing actual policy; in particular, the estimated reaction function includes substantial positive coefficients ρ_1 and ρ_2, though these are still not as large as the optimal values. Thus the way in which actual Fed policy is more complex than adherence to a simple Taylor rule can largely be justified as movement in the direction of optimal policy, according to the simple model of the transmission mechanism assumed here.[38]

---

35. Technically, this corresponds to the observation that in the equivalent representation (3.10) of the policy rule given later, there exists a root $\lambda_2 > 1$. A sufficient condition for this is that $\rho_1 > 1$, in which case exactly one of the roots is greater than 1.

36. Levin et al. (1999) similarly find that a rule with $\rho_1 = 1$ (the largest value of the inertia coefficient that they consider) is optimal in the context of each of several forward-looking empirical models of the monetary transmission mechanism.

37. It should also be noted that the output-gap measure used in Judd and Rudebusch's empirical analysis, while a plausible measure of what the Fed is likely to have responded to, may not correspond to the welfare-relevant output gap indicated by the variable x_t in the optimal rule (3.7). In addition, ϕ_π indicates response to the most recent four-quarter growth in the GDP deflator, rather than an annualized inflation rate over the past quarter alone.

38. Kara (2003) proposes an interpretation of the difference between the Fed's estimated policy rule and the optimal rule. He shows that a central bank that is capable of only imperfect commitment—modeled as a constant hazard rate for arrival of an event in which policy is reoptimized without any constraint associated with prior commitment—should conduct policy

One finds that in the case of this simple model at least, it is not necessary for the central bank's operating target for the overnight interest rate to respond to forecasts of the future evolution of inflation or of the output gap in order for policy to be fully optimal—and not just optimal in the case of particular assumed stochastic processes for the disturbances, but robustly optimal. Thus the mere fact that the central bank may sometimes have information about future disturbances, which are not yet disturbing demand or supply conditions in any way, is not a reason for feedback from current and past values of the target variables to be insufficient as a basis for optimal policy. This does not mean that it may not be desirable for monetary policy to restrain spending and/or price increases even before the anticipated real disturbances actually take effect. But in the context of a forward-looking model of private-sector behavior, a commitment to respond to fluctuations in the target variables only contemporaneously and later does not preclude effective preemptive constraint of that kind. First of all, such a policy may well mean that the central bank *does* adjust its policy instrument immediately in response to the news, insofar as forward-looking private-sector behavior may result in an immediate effect of the news upon current inflation and output.[39] Moreover, and more importantly, in the presence of forward-looking private-sector behavior, the central bank mainly affects the economy through changes in expectations about the *future* path of its instrument; a predictable adjustment of interest rates *later,* once the disturbances substantially affect inflation and output, should be just as effective in restraining private-sector spending and pricing decisions as an immediate preemptive increase in overnight interest rates.

At the same time, it is important to note that the optimal rule (3.7), while not "forecast based" in the sense in which this term is usually understood, *does* depend upon projections of inflation and output in the same quarter as the one for which the operating target is being set. Thus the rule is not an explicit instrument rule in the sense of Svensson and Woodford (2003). Morever, this implicit character is crucial to the optimality of the rule, at least if one wishes to find an optimal rule that is also a direct rule (specifying feedback only from the target variables). For optimal policy requires an immediate adjustment of the short-term nominal interest rate in response to shocks, as shown in Chapter 7;[40] and so unless the rule is to be

---

according to a rule of the form (3.7), but with inertia coefficients ρ_1 and ρ_2 that are smaller than those specified in (3.8).

39. This is obviously not the case if, as more realistic models often assume, there are delays in the effect of any new information on prices and spending. But in this case, it is not desirable for overnight interest rates to respond immediately to news, either, as discussed in Sections 1.4 and 1.5.

40. This is not true if there are delays in the effects of shocks upon inflation and output, as discussed in Section 3.2. But in that case, even the *delayed* effect upon the central bank's

specified in terms of the central bank's response to particular shocks, it will have to specify a contemporaneous response to fluctuations in the target variables, and not simply a lagged response. Thus implementation of such a rule involves judgment of some sophistication about current conditions; it cannot be implemented mechanically on the basis of a small number of publicly available statistics.

Furthermore, the mere fact that I have exhibited a robustly optimal rule that involves no dependence on projections beyond the current quarter does not mean that a forecast-based rule cannot have equally desirable properties. In fact, the policy rule just discussed is *equivalent*, in a certain sense, to a forecast-based rule. This alternative representation of optimal policy also shows that even when $\lambda_i > 0$, it is possible for a robustly optimal policy rule to take the form of a pure targeting rule, rather than an expression that presents, even implicitly, a formula for the bank's interest-rate operating target.

One can write the implicit instrument rule (3.7) in the form

$$(1 - \lambda_1 L)(1 - \lambda_2 L)\hat{\imath}_t = \hat{q}_t, \tag{3.10}$$

where $\hat{\imath}_t \equiv i_t - \bar{\imath}$, and $\hat{q}_t$ similarly denotes the deviation of

$$q_t \equiv \phi_\pi \pi_t + (\phi_x/4)\Delta x_t, \tag{3.11}$$

the function of the target variables to which the central bank responds from its long-run average value $\phi_\pi \bar{\pi}$. Because the optimal coefficients (3.8) are such that $\rho_1 > 1, \rho_2 > 0$, the roots in the factorization (3.10) necessarily satisfy $0 < \lambda_1 < 1 < \lambda_2$. It then follows that relation (3.7) is equivalent to the relation

$$(1 - \lambda_1 L)\hat{\imath}_{t-1} = -\lambda_2^{-1} E_t \left[\left(1 - \lambda_2^{-1} L^{-1} \right)^{-1} \hat{q}_t \right], \tag{3.12}$$

in the following sense.

PROPOSITION 8.6. Two bounded stochastic processes $\{\hat{\imath}_t, \hat{q}_t\}$ satisfy (3.10) for all $t \geq 0$ if and only if they satisfy (3.12) for all $t \geq 0$.

The proof is given in Appendix G.

Thus there is no difference between the way in which a central bank must adjust its interest-rate instrument to ensure that (3.7) holds in all periods

---

instrument that is required by optimal policy cannot be implemented on the basis only of lagged observations of the target variables because of the delay with which shocks affect these variables.

and the way that it would adjust it to ensure that (3.12) holds in all periods, for the two conditions imply one another. (This does not mean that arranging for (3.12) to hold in a *single* period t is equivalent to arranging for (3.7) to hold in that single period, regardless of how policy is expected to be conducted thereafter; but a *permanent commitment* to either rule from some date t_0 onward has identical consequences.) This equivalence does not apply only in the case of processes that are possible equilibria of the model consisting of structural equations (2.1) and (3.1); thus the rules are equivalent regardless of whether that model is correctly specified, and regardless of whether the central bank expects the economy to actually evolve according to a rational-expectations equilibrium of that model or not (e.g., regardless of whether it is believed that the private sector correctly understands the bank's policy rule or not).

It follows from this equivalence that a commitment to ensure that (3.12) holds in all periods from some date onward represents a coherent complete specification of a monetary policy rule, at least in the context of the model described by equations (2.1) and (3.1). Hence this represents a well-defined targeting rule, even though the target criterion cannot be solved by itself to yield even an implicit expression for the period t instrument setting: the left-hand side involves only lagged interest rates, while the right-hand side refers only to the evolution of inflation and the output gap. A model of the monetary transmission mechanism must be used in order to determine the instrument setting that is consistent with a projection that satisfies the target criterion.[41]

The target criterion (3.12) can be expressed in the form

$$F_t(\pi) + \frac{\phi_x}{4}F_t(x) = \frac{\theta_x}{4}x_{t-1} - \theta_i\left(i_{t-1} - i^*\right) - \theta_\Delta\Delta i_{t-1}, \qquad (3.13)$$

where for each of the variables $z = \pi$, x I again use the notation $F_t(z)$ for a conditional forecast

$$F_t(z) \equiv \sum_{j=0}^{\infty} \alpha_{z,j} E_t z_{t+j},$$

involving weights $\{\alpha_{z,j}\}$ that sum to one. Thus the criterion specifies a time-varying target value for a weighted average of an inflation forecast and an output-gap forecast, where each of these forecasts is in fact a weighted average of forecasts at various horizons, rather than a projection for a specific

---

41. Note, however, that the situation is not really different in the case of a commitment to ensure that (3.7) is satisfied: A model is still needed to determine the instrument setting that should result in current period inflation and output that imply that the implicit instrument rule is satisfied.

future date. Once again, the optimal policy rule can be characterized as flexible inflation targeting.

In representation (3.13) of this policy rule, there is no constant term, indicating an inflation-forecast target of zero except insofar as this is corrected in response to deviations (past or projected) of the output gap and/or the nominal interest rate from their target values.[42] The optimal coefficients indicating the degree to which the inflation-forecast target is adjusted are given by

$$\phi_x = \theta_x = 4\left(1 - \lambda_2^{-1}\right)\frac{\lambda_x}{\kappa} > 0,$$

$$\theta_i = \lambda_2\left(1 - \lambda_1\right)(1 - \lambda_2^{-1})\frac{\lambda_i}{\kappa\sigma} > 0,$$

$$\theta_\Delta = \lambda_1\lambda_2\left(1 - \lambda_2^{-1}\right)\frac{\lambda_i}{\kappa\sigma} > 0,$$

while the optimal weights in the conditional forecasts are

$$\alpha_{\pi,j} = \alpha_{x,j} = \left(1 - \lambda_2^{-1}\right)\lambda_2^{-j}.$$

Thus the optimal conditional forecast is one that places positive weight on the projection for each future period, beginning with the current period, with weights that decline exponentially as the horizon increases. The mean distance in the future of the projections that are relevant to the target criterion is equal to

$$\sum_{j=0}^{\infty} \alpha_{z,j} j = (\lambda_2 - 1)^{-1}$$

for both the inflation and output-gap forecasts.

In the case of the calibrated parameter values reported in Table 6.1, the rate at which these weights decay per quarter is $\lambda_2^{-1} = .68$, so that the mean forecast horizon in the optimal target criterion is 2.1 quarters. Thus while my optimal example of a pure targeting rule can be expressed in terms of a target for inflation and output-gap forecasts, the forecast horizon involved is short compared to those typically considered in the recent literature, or those typical of the actual practice of inflation-forecast-targeting

---

42. Note, however, that this does not mean that the rule sets the inflation forecast equal to zero on average. This is because the target interest rate i^* is in general not consistent with an average inflation rate of zero.

central banks. For these same parameter values, the optimal relative weight on the output-gap forecast is $\phi_x = 0.15$, indicating that the target criterion is essentially an inflation-forecast target, albeit a modified one. Finally, the remaining optimal coefficients are $\theta_x = 0.15, \theta_i = 0.24$, and $\theta_\Delta = 0.51$, indicating a substantial degree of history dependence of the optimal modified inflation-forecast target. The fact that $\theta_x = \phi_x$ indicates that once again it is really the forecasted increase in the output gap relative to the previous quarter's level, rather than the absolute level of the gap, that should modify the inflation-forecast target, just as in the examples presented in Section 2. The signs of θ_i and θ_Δ imply that policy is tightened (in the sense of demanding a lower modified inflation forecast) when interest rates have been high and/or increasing in the recent past; this is another way of committing to interest-rate inertia of the kind discussed above.

The equivalence expressed in Proposition 8.6 implies that commitment to a history-dependent modified inflation-forecast target of this kind is a robustly optimal policy rule in exactly the same sense as the instrument rule (3.7). This alternative, forward-integrated representation of optimal policy has the possible advantage (from the point of view of successfully steering private-sector expectations) of emphasizing the way in which the outlook for inflation and the output gap are adjusted at each point in time (at least as far as the intentions of the central bank are concerned) in response to variations in the recent evolution of the target variables. While this is *implied* by a commitment to implement the instrument rule (3.7) from now on, it might not be clear to the private sector—for example, because the central bank's commitment to continue to implement the instrument rule in the future might not be clear. Hence communication with the public about current policy decisions in terms of their implications for inflation and output-gap forecasts might be a superior way of conveying the central bank's commitments with regard to subsequent developments.

The representation of optimal policy in terms of a pure targeting rule also has the advantage of continuing to be possible even in the limiting case that $\lambda_i = 0$, that is, even when reducing the variability of interest rates is not an independent concern. In that limit, the weights ϕ_π and ϕ_x in (3.7) become unboundedly large, so that a representation of optimal policy in terms of a direct instrument rule ceases to be possible. Instead, the coefficients of (3.13) remain well defined: θ_i and θ_Δ become equal to zero, while ϕ_x, θ_x and the weights $\{\alpha_{z,j}\}$ continue to take well-defined positive values. Thus in this limiting case, the optimal targeting rule is one in which the inflation-forecast target must be modified in proportion to the projected change in the output gap, but it is no longer also dependent on lagged interest rates. In fact, in the limit as λ_i approaches zero, the optimal target criterion (2.5) derived in Chapter 7 is recovered.

3.2 Consequences of Inflation Inertia

The basic neo-Wicksellian model is often criticized as being excessively forward looking, particularly in its neglect of any sources of intrinsic inertia in the dynamics of inflation. It might be suspected that this feature of the model is responsible for the strong result just obtained, according to which a robustly optimal policy rule need involve no dependence on forecasts of the target variables beyond the current period. In Svensson's (1997a) classic argument for the optimality of inflation-forecast targeting, it is the existence of lags in the effect of monetary policy on inflation that causes the optimal rule to involve a target criterion for a forecast, with the optimal forecast horizon coinciding with the length of the policy transmission lag. It might reasonably be suspected that forecasts are not necessary in the foregoing analysis because the simple model includes no lags in the effects of policy.

Here I consider this question by extending the analysis to the case of the model of inflation inertia developed in Section 3.2 of Chapter 3, and considered in Section 2.1 of the present chapter. The aggregate-supply relation is again assumed to be of the form (2.6), but I now adjoin the intertemporal IS relation (3.1) as an additional constraint, and assume a loss function for stabilization policy of the form

$$L_t = (\pi_t - \gamma \pi_{t-1})^2 + \lambda_x (x_t - x^*)^2 + \lambda_i (i_t - i^*)^2, \qquad (3.14)$$

for some $\lambda_i > 0$, generalizing (2.7).

I wish to consider policies that minimize the criterion defined by (2.2) and (3.14), subject to the constraints imposed by the structural equations (3.1) and (2.6), for arbitrary values of the indexation parameter $0 \leq \gamma \leq 1$.

In the case of this generalization of the policy problem, the first-order condition (3.3) becomes instead

$$\pi_t^{qd} - \beta \gamma E_t \pi_{t+1}^{qd} - \beta^{-1} \sigma \Xi_{1t-1} - \beta \gamma E_t \Xi_{2,t+1}$$
$$+ (1 + \beta \gamma) \Xi_{2t} - \Xi_{2t-1} = 0, \qquad (3.15)$$

where π_t^{qd} is again as defined in (2.8). Conditions (3.4) and (3.5) remain as before, and this system of three equations, together with an initial condition for π_{-1} and initial constraints (3.6) continues to define the optimal once-and-for-all commitment to apply from date $t = 0$ onward.

As before, one can use conditions (3.4) and (3.5) to eliminate the Lagrange multipliers in (3.15), obtaining an Euler equation of the form

$$E_t \left[A(L) \left(i_{t+1} - i^* \right) \right] = -f_t \qquad (3.16)$$

for the optimal evolution of the target variables. Here $A(L)$ is a cubic lag polynomial

$$A(L) \equiv \beta\gamma - (1+\gamma+\beta\gamma)L + \left(1+\gamma+\beta^{-1}(1+\kappa\sigma)\right)L^2 - \beta^{-1}L^3, \quad (3.17)$$

while the term f_t is a function of the observed and expected future paths of the target variables, defined by

$$f_t \equiv \tilde{q}_t - \beta\gamma E_t\tilde{q}_{t+1}, \quad (3.18)$$

$$\tilde{q}_t \equiv \frac{\kappa\sigma}{\lambda_i}\left[\pi_t^{qd} + \frac{\lambda_x}{\kappa}\Delta x_t\right]. \quad (3.19)$$

(Note that the above definition generalizes the earlier (3.11), and that in the limit where $\gamma = 0$, f_t is equal to $\tilde{q}_t$, which equals q_t.)

By an argument directly analogous to the proof of Proposition 8.5, one can show that if a bounded optimal state-contingent plan exists, the system obtained by adjoining (3.16) to the structural equations (2.6) and (3.1) implies a determinate rational-expectations equilibrium, in which the responses to exogenous disturbances are the same as under the optimal commitment. (The only difference between this equilibrium and the optimal once-and-for-all commitment just defined relates to the initial conditions, as in our earlier discussion, and once again this difference is irrelevant to the design of a policy rule that is optimal from a timeless perspective.) Hence one could regard (3.16) as implicitly defining a policy rule, and the rule would once again be robustly optimal. In the limiting case that $\gamma = 0$, (3.16) ceases to involve any dependence upon $E_t i_{t+1}$, and the proposed rule would coincide with the optimal instrument rule (3.7) discussed above.

However, (3.16) is an even less explicit expression for the central bank's interest-rate policy than the implicit instrument rules considered earlier, for (when $\gamma > 0$) it defines i_t only as a function of $E_t i_{t+1}$. This means that the central bank defines the way in which it is committed to set its instrument only as a function of the way that it expects to act further in the future. This failure to express the rule in "closed form" is especially undesirable from the point of view of the question about the optimal forecast horizon for a monetary policy rule. Expression (3.16) involves no conditional expectations for variables at dates more than one period in the future. However, this does not really mean that the central bank's forecasts for later dates are irrelevant when setting i_t. For this "rule" directs the bank to set i_t as a function of its forecast of i_{t+1}, and (if the same rule is expected to be used to set i_{t+1}) the bank's forecast at t of i_{t+1} should involve its forecast at t of $\tilde{q}_{t+2}$. It should also involve its forecast of i_{t+2} and thus (by similar reasoning) its forecast of

$\tilde{q}_{t+3}$, and so on. Hence it is more revealing to describe the proposed policy rule in a form that eliminates any reference to the future path of interest rates themselves and refers only to the bank's projections of the future paths of inflation and the output gap.[43]

To obtain an equivalent policy rule of the desired form, one needs to partially solve forward equation (3.16). This requires factorization of the lag polynomial as

$$A(L) \equiv \beta\gamma(1 - \lambda_1 L)(1 - \lambda_2 L)(1 - \lambda_3 L). \qquad (3.20)$$

I note the following properties of the roots of the associated characteristic equation.

PROPOSITION 8.7. Suppose that $\sigma, \kappa > 0, 0 < \beta < 1$, and $0 < \gamma \leq 1$. Then in the factorization (3.20) of the polynomial defined in (3.17), there is necessarily one real root $0 < \lambda_1 < 1$, and two roots outside the unit circle. The latter two roots are either two real roots $\lambda_3 \geq \lambda_2 > 1$, or a complex pair λ_2, λ_3 of roots with real part greater than 1. Three real roots necessarily exist for all small enough $\gamma > 0$, while a complex pair necessarily exists for all γ close enough to 1.

The proof is given in Appendix G. I use the conventions in the statement of this proposition in referring to the distinct roots in what follows. It is also useful to rewrite (3.16) as

$$E_t[A(L)\hat{\imath}_{t+1}] = -\hat{f}_t, \qquad (3.21)$$

where once again hats denote the deviations of the original variables from the long-run average values implied by the policy rule (3.16), or equivalently, by the optimal commitment.

---

43. A rule expressed in this way also conforms better to the evident preference of central banks to justify their monetary policy decisions to the public in terms of their projections for the future paths of inflation and output, rather than in terms of their assumptions about the future path of interest rates. Public communications such as the Bank of England's *Inflation Report* put projections for both inflation and output at center stage, while being careful not to express any opinion about the likely path of interest rates over the period under discussion. The forecast-based rules proposed later still refer to forecast paths conditional upon intended policy, rather than upon constant-interest-rate forecasts, and so it is not possible to implement these rules without taking a stand (at least for internal purposes) on the likely future path of interest rates. But the rules make it possible to discuss the way in which the current instrument setting is required by the bank's inflation and output projections, without also discussing the interest-rate path that is implicit in those projections, and to this extent they require a less radical modification of current procedures.

In the case that three real roots exist, the existence of two distinct roots greater than 1 allow for two distinct ways of solving forward, resulting in two alternative relations,

$$(1 - \lambda_1 L)(1 - \lambda_2 L)\hat{\imath}_t = (\beta\gamma\lambda_3)^{-1} E_t \left[\left(1 - \lambda_3^{-1} L^{-1}\right)^{-1} \hat{f}_t \right], \qquad (3.22)$$

or

$$(1 - \lambda_1 L)(1 - \lambda_3 L)\hat{\imath}_t = (\beta\gamma\lambda_2)^{-1} E_t \left[\left(1 - \lambda_2^{-1} L^{-1}\right)^{-1} \hat{f}_t \right]. \qquad (3.23)$$

I can also derive other relations of the same form by taking linear combinations of these. Of special interest is the relation

$$(1 - \lambda_1 L)\left(1 - \frac{\lambda_2 + \lambda_3}{2} L\right)\hat{\imath}_t = \tfrac{1}{2}(\beta\gamma\lambda_3)^{-1} E_t \left[\left(1 - \lambda_3^{-1} L^{-1}\right)^{-1} \hat{f}_t \right]$$
$$+ \tfrac{1}{2}(\beta\gamma\lambda_2)^{-1} E_t \left[\left(1 - \lambda_2^{-1} L^{-1}\right)^{-1} \hat{f}_t \right]. \qquad (3.24)$$

Here relations (3.22) and (3.23) are defined (with real-valued coefficients) only in the case that three real roots exist, while relation (3.24) can also be derived (and has real coefficients on all leads and lags) in the case that λ_2, λ_3 are a complex pair. Because $|\lambda_2|, |\lambda_3| > 1$, the right-hand side of each of these expressions is well defined and describes a bounded stochastic process in the case of any bounded process $\{\hat{f}_t\}$. (In what follows, I refer to the three possible expressions for an optimal instrument rule presented in (3.22)–(3.24) as rule I, rule II, and rule III, respectively.)

Each of the relations (3.22)–(3.24) can be solved for $\hat{\imath}_t$ as a function of two of its own lags and expectations at date t regarding current and future values of $\hat{f}_t$. These can thus be interpreted as implicit instrument rules, each of which now avoids any direct reference to the planned future path of the central bank's instrument (though assumptions about future monetary policy are implicit in the inflation and output-gap forecasts). Each of these policy rules is equivalent to (3.16), and they are accordingly equivalent to one another, in the following sense.

PROPOSITION 8.8. Under the assumptions of Proposition 8.7, and in the case that the factorization (3.20) involves three real roots, a pair of bounded processes $\{\hat{\imath}_t, \hat{f}_t\}$ satisfy any of the equations (3.22), (3.23), or (3.24) at all dates $t \geq t_0$ if and only if they satisfy (3.21) at all of those same dates. In the case that a complex pair exists, (3.24) is again equivalent to (3.21), in the same sense.

The proof is given in Appendix G. Each of the rules thus represents a feasible specification of monetary policy in the case that its coefficients are real valued, and when this is true it implies equilibrium responses to real disturbances that are those associated with an optimal commitment. Accordingly, each represents an optimal policy rule from a timeless perspective. (Note that although the coefficients differ, these are not really different policies. Proposition 8.8 implies that they involve identical actions, if the bank expects to follow one of them indefinitely, regardless of the model of the economy used to form the conditional forecasts.)

In the case that three real roots exist, one has a choice of representations of optimal policy in terms of an instrument rule and cannot choose among them on grounds of algebraic simplicity alone. Giannoni and Woodford (2002a) propose that in such cases the choice should be the "minimally inertial" representation of policy, the one that involves the smallest modulus for the largest autoregressive root of the lag polynomial multiplying the nominal interest rate in representation (1.28), so as to express the relation that the central bank is committed to maintain in as nearly contemporaneous a form as possible. In the present context, this would mean selecting rule I in the case that γ is small enough for all three rules to be defined (while selecting rule III for larger values of γ, as this is the only possibility). This choice is also uniquely desirable in the sense that rule I remains well defined in the limit as γ approaches zero. In this limit, rule I reduces to

$$(1 - \lambda_1 L)(1 - \lambda_2 L)\,\hat{\imath}_t = \hat{f}_t,$$

which is the optimal instrument rule (3.10) derived in the previous section.[44] Instead, in the case of any of the other rules, the coefficients on lagged interest rates become unboundedly large as γ approaches zero. Thus rule I is clearly the preferable specification of policy in the case of small γ. The desire for a rule that varies continuously with γ, so that uncertainty about the precise value of γ does not imply any great uncertainty about how to proceed, then makes rule I an appealing choice over the entire range of γ for which it is defined.

The instruction to follow rule I if three real roots exist but rule III if there is a complex pair also makes all coefficients of the policy rule continuous functions of γ at the critical value where one switches from rule I to rule III. The reason is that as γ passes through the critical value $\bar{\gamma}$ at which the real roots of the characteristic equation bifurcate, the two larger real roots, λ_2 and λ_3, come to exactly equal one another. When $\bar{\gamma}$ is approached from the other direction, the imaginary parts of the complex roots λ_2 and λ_3 approach zero; at the bifurcation point their common real value is the

---

44. Note that as $\gamma \to 0$, $\lambda_3 \to +\infty$, while $\gamma \lambda_3 \to \beta^{-1}$. Recall also that in this limiting case, $\hat{f}_t = \hat{q}_t$. One can show furthermore that the two smaller roots λ_1, λ_2 in the factorization (3.20) approach the two roots in the factorization (3.10) of the earlier quadratic lag polynomial.

repeated real root obtained as the common limit of the two real roots from the other direction. Hence when $\gamma = \bar{\gamma}$, rules I, II, and III are all identical. There is thus no ambiguity about whether rule I or rule III should be applied in this case and no discontinuity in the coefficients of the recommended rule as γ approaches $\bar{\gamma}$ from either direction. At the same time, this proposal results in a rule that remains well defined as γ approaches zero, and for small $\gamma > 0$ results in a rule that is very close to the one previously recommended for an economy with no inflation inertia.

Each of rules I, II, and III can be written in the form

$$i_t = (1 - \rho_1)i^* + \rho_1 i_{t-1} + \rho_2 \Delta i_{t-1} + \phi_\pi F_t(\pi)$$
$$+ \frac{\phi_x}{4} F_t(x) - \theta_\pi \pi_{t-1} - \frac{\theta_x}{4} x_{t-1}, \tag{3.25}$$

where here I have added the constant terms again to indicate the desired level of interest rates (and not just the interest rate relative to its long-run average level) and $F_t(z)$ again denotes a linear combination of forecasts of the variable z at various future horizons, with weights normalized to sum to one. This form of rule generalizes the specification (3.7) that suffices in the case $\gamma = 0$ in two respects: The interest-rate operating target i_t now depends upon lagged inflation in addition to the lagged variables that mattered before and upon forecasts of inflation and the output gap in future periods, and not simply upon the projections of those variables for the current period.

Except in these respects, the coefficients are qualitatively similar to those in (3.7), as indicated by the following proposition.

PROPOSITION 8.9. Under the assumptions of Proposition 8.7, and a loss function with $\lambda_x, \lambda_i > 0$, each of rules I, II, and III has a representation of the form (3.25) for all values of γ for which the rule is well defined, and in this representation,

$$\rho_1 > 1, \qquad \rho_2 > 0,$$
$$0 < \theta_\pi \le \phi_\pi,$$

and

$$0 < \theta_x = \phi_x.$$

Furthermore, for given values of the other parameters, as $\gamma \to 0$ (for rule I) the coefficient $\theta_\pi \to 0$, though ϕ_π approaches a positive limit; while as $\gamma \to 1$ (for rule III) the coefficients θ_π and ϕ_π approach the same positive limit.

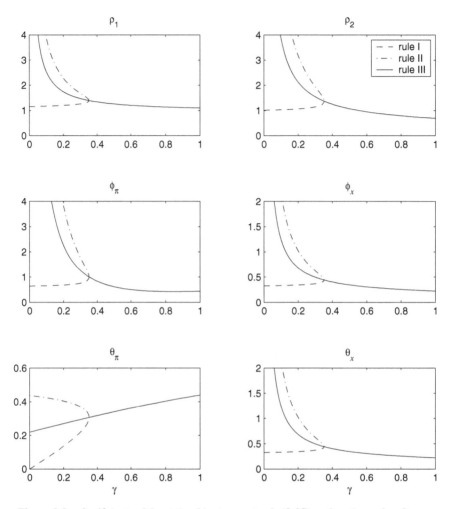

Figure 8.3   *Coefficients of the optimal instrument rule (3.25) as functions of γ. Source:
Giannoni and Woodford (2003a).*

The proof is in Appendix G. It is especially noteworthy that once again the
optimal instrument rule is superinertial. Also note that once again what
should matter is the projected output gap relative to the previous quarter's
output gap, rather than the absolute level of the projected gap; and once
again interest rates should be increased if the gap is projected to rise. Here,
too, a higher projected inflation rate implies that the interest rate should
be increased; but now the degree to which this is true is lower if recent
inflation has been high, and in the extreme case $\gamma = 1$, it is only the

projected inflation rate relative to the previous quarter's rate that should be significant.

The numerical values of these coefficients are plotted, for alternative values of γ ranging between zero and one, in the various panels of Figure 8.3, where the assumed values for the other parameters are again as in Table 6.1. For all values $\gamma < \bar{\gamma} = .35$, there are three real roots, and for each value of γ the three values corresponding to rules I, II, and III are each plotted; for $\gamma > \bar{\gamma}$, only rule III is defined. An interesting feature of these plots is that if one considers the coefficients associated with rule I for $\gamma \leq \bar{\gamma}$ and rule III for $\gamma \geq \bar{\gamma}$, one observes that the magnitude of each of the coefficients remains roughly the same, regardless of the assumed value of γ. (The exception is θ_π, which approaches zero for small γ, but becomes a substantial positive coefficient for large γ, as indicated by Proposition 8.9.)

The panels of Figure 8.4 similarly plot the relative weights $\alpha_{z,j}/\alpha_{z,0}$ for different horizons j of the inflation and output-gap forecasts to which the

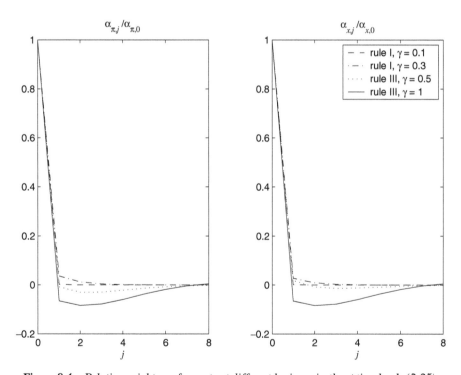

Figure 8.4 *Relative weights on forecasts at different horizons in the optimal rule (3.25). Source: Giannoni and Woodford (2003a).*

optimal instrument rule refers[45] for each of several different possible values of γ. (The weights associated with rule I are plotted in the case of values $\gamma < \bar{\gamma}$, and those associated with rule III in the case of values $\gamma > \bar{\gamma}$.) Observe that in this case the forecasts $F_t(z)$ are not actually weighted averages of forecasts at different horizons because the weights are not all nonnegative. Thus while in the presence of inflation inertia, the optimal instrument rule is to some extent forecast based, the optimal responses to forecasts of future inflation and output gaps are not of the sort generally assumed in forward-looking variants of the Taylor rule. In the case of high γ, a higher forecasted inflation rate (or output gap) in any of the next several quarters implies, for given past and projected current conditions, that a *lower* current interest rate is appropriate. According to the optimal rule, a higher current inflation rate should be tolerated in the case that high inflation is forecast for the next several quarters. This is because (in an economy with γ near one) it is sudden *changes* in the inflation rate that create the greatest distortions in the economy, as in this case automatic adjustment of prices in response to lagged inflation becomes a poor rule of thumb.

One notes that under the optimal rule it is only forecasts regarding the near future that matter much at all. Even if one considers only the weights put on forecasts for $j \geq 1$ quarters in the future, the mean future horizon of these forecasts, defined by

$$\sum_{j \geq 1} \alpha_{z,j}\, j \Big/ \sum_{j \geq 1} \alpha_{z,j},$$

is equal to only 2.2 quarters in the case of the calibrated example with $\gamma = 1$. Thus forecasts other than for the first year following the current quarter matter little under the optimal policy. Even more notably, none of the projections beyond the current quarter should receive too great a weight; in my example, the sum of the relative weights on *all* future quarters,

$$\sum_{j > 0} |\alpha_{z,j}| / \alpha_{z,0},$$

is equal to only 0.39 even in the extreme case $\gamma = 1$, while this fraction falls to zero for small γ. Thus while a robustly optimal direct instrument rule does have to be forecast based in the presence of inflation inertia, the degree to which forecasts matter under the optimal policy rule is still

---

45. Here I plot the relative weights, rather than the absolute weights, because it makes visual comparison between the degree of forecast dependence of optimal policy in the different cases easier. The absolute weights can be recovered by integrating the plots shown here, since the relative weights in each case must sum to $1/\alpha_{z,0}$.

relatively small. Instead, a strong response to projections of inflation and the output gap for the current period, as called for by the Taylor rule, continues to be the crucial element of optimal policy.

Of course, the fact that the optimal interest-rate rule is superinertial suggests that it should have an equivalent representation as a pure targeting rule, and this alternative representation of the policy rule is more forward looking. The presence of two roots outside the unit circle in the factorization (3.20) indicates that it would have been possible to solve *both* of them forward, rather than only one. This would eliminate the ambiguity about which one to solve forward, which required choosing between representations (3.22) and (3.23) of optimal policy. Solving both roots forward, one obtains instead a relation of the form

$$(1 - \lambda_1 L)\hat{\imath}_{t-1} = -(\beta\gamma\lambda_2\lambda_3)^{-1} E_t \left[\left(1 - \lambda_2^{-1}L^{-1}\right)^{-1} \left(1 - \lambda_3^{-1}L^{-1}\right)^{-1} \hat{f}_t \right]. \quad (3.26)$$

Once again, this relation can be shown to be equivalent to the Euler equation (3.16).

PROPOSITION 8.10. Under the assumptions of Proposition 8.7, a pair of bounded processes $\{\hat{\imath}_t, \hat{f}_t\}$ satisfy (3.26) at all dates $t \geq t_0$ if and only if they satisfy (3.21) at all of those same dates.

The proof is in Appendix G. Another advantage of solving both roots forward is that this relation, unlike either (3.22) or (3.23), has real coefficients for all leads and lags, whether or not there are complex roots.

This representation of optimal policy differs from any of the relations (3.22)–(3.24) in that it does not involve $\hat{\imath}_t$. Thus it represents a pure targeting rule, one that cannot be interpreted as an instrument rule. However, it follows from Proposition 8.7 that a commitment to adjust the short-term nominal interest rate so as to achieve a situation in which the bank's projections satisfy (3.26) represents a well-defined policy rule, and one that is equivalent to any of the three instrument rules discussed in the previous section (if these are defined). Hence one obtains an example of a robustly optimal pure targeting rule for the case of an economy with inflation inertia.

The optimal target criterion (3.26) can be written in the form

$$F_t(\pi) + \frac{\phi_x}{4} F_t(x) = \theta_\pi \pi_{t-1} + \frac{\theta_x}{4} x_{t-1} - \theta_i \left(i_{t-1} - i^*\right) - \theta_\Delta \Delta i_{t-1}, \quad (3.27)$$

generalizing (3.13). Note that the only difference as to the general form of this targeting rule is the presence of the term indicating dependence of the modified inflation-forecast target on lagged inflation π_{t-1}. One can also establish the following properties of the optimal coefficients, generalizing the previous results.

PROPOSITION 8.11. Under the assumptions of Proposition 8.9, the optimal target criterion has a representation (3.27) in which

$$\phi_x = \theta_x > 0,$$

$$0 < \theta_\pi \leq 1,$$

and

$$\theta_i, \theta_\Delta > 0.$$

Furthermore, for fixed values of the other parameters, as $\gamma \to 0$, $\theta_\pi \to 0$ and the other parameters approach the nonzero values associated with the target criterion (3.13). Instead, as $\gamma \to 1$, $\theta_\pi \to 1$.

Again, the proof is in Appendix G.

Once again, the optimal inflation-forecast target must be modified in response to variations in the output-gap projection; a higher inflation-forecast target is appropriate if the output gap is projected to fall relative to its recent past level. Once again the optimal inflation-forecast target must be history dependent, not only because the output-gap modification just mentioned depends upon the relation between the output-gap projections for current and future periods relative to a past level, but because the appropriate inflation-forecast target is lower if nominal interest rates have been high and/or increasing in the recent past.

The additional presence of a coefficient $\theta_\pi > 0$ when $\gamma > 0$ indicates that the modified inflation-forecast target should be higher when recent inflation has been higher. This makes sense given that the distortions associated with inflation variations are greater as the departure of the current inflation rate from the rate of automatic price adjustment in response to lagged inflation is greater. In the extreme case $\gamma = 1$, the inflation-forecast target is adjusted 100 percent in response to variations in the recent rate of inflation, since in this case it is actually the rate of *change* in inflation that one wants to stabilize.

Each of the coefficients in (3.27) is plotted as a function of γ in Figure 8.5, assuming the same calibrated values for the other parameters as before. (This time there are no separate plots for θ_x and ϕ_x, as these coefficients are necessarily identical.) An interesting feature of these results is that each of the coefficients indicating history dependence (θ_π, θ_x, θ_i, and θ_Δ) increases with γ. Thus if there is substantial inflation inertia, it is even more important for the inflation-forecast target to vary with changes in recent economic conditions. It is also worth noting that the degree to which the inflation-forecast target should be modified in response to changes in the output-gap projection (indicated by the coefficient ϕ_x) increases with γ. While the

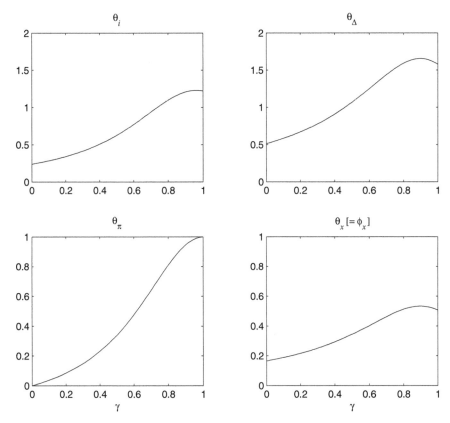

Figure 8.5 *Coefficients of the optimal targeting rule (3.27) as functions of γ. Source: Giannoni and Woodford (2002b).*

conclusion for the baseline model (an optimal targeting rule with $\phi_x = .15$) might have suggested that this sort of modification of the inflation-forecast target is not too important, it turns out that a substantially larger response is justified if γ is large (the optimal ϕ_x approaches the value 0.51 for $\gamma = 1$).

The panels of Figure 8.6 correspondingly show the relative weights $\alpha_{z,j}/\alpha_{z,0}$ on the forecasts at different horizons in the optimal target criterion (3.27) for each of several alternative values of γ. As before, this representation of optimal policy is more forward looking than the optimal instrument rule; one now finds, at least for high enough values of γ, that the optimal target criterion places nonnegligible weight on forecasts more than a year in the future. But it is not necessarily true that a greater degree of inflation inertia justifies a target criterion with a longer forecast horizon. Increases in γ increase the optimal weights on the current-quarter projections of both

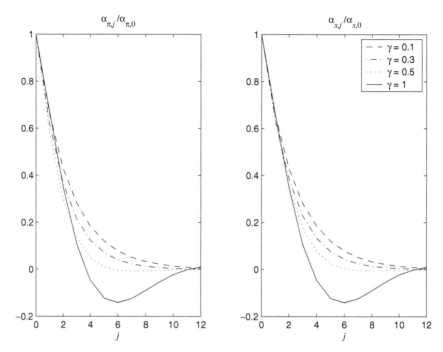

Figure 8.6   *Relative weights on forecasts at different horizons in the optimal rule (3.27).
Source: Giannoni and Woodford (2002b).*

inflation and the output gap (normalizing the weights to sum to one), and
instead make the weights on the projections for quarters more than two
quarters in the future less positive. At least for low values of γ (in which
case the weights are all nonnegative), this makes the optimal target criterion *less* forward looking. For high values of γ, increases in γ do increase
the absolute value of the weights on forecasts for dates 1 to 2 years in the
future (these become more negative). But even in this case, the existence of
inflation inertia does not justify the kind of response to longer-horizon forecasts that is typical of inflation-forecast-targeting central banks. An increase
in the forecast level of inflation and/or the output gap during the second
year of a bank's current projection should justify a *loosening* of current policy, in the sense of a policy intended to *raise* projected inflation and/or the
output gap in the next few quarters.

3.3   Predetermined Spending and Pricing Decisions

As discussed in Section 2.4, econometric models of the monetary transmission mechanism often assume that both spending and pricing decisions are

predetermined for some period of time, and this is again a reason for both inflation and output determination to be less purely forward looking than in the basic neo-Wicksellian model. Again it is important to consider to what extent the existence of lags of this kind in the effects of monetary policy should affect conclusions as to the form of an optimal policy rule.

Consider the same model as in Section 2.4, in which both spending and pricing decisions are predetermined for d periods, but now suppose that the objectives of stabilization policy are described by a loss function of the form (3.14) rather than (2.7). Because I now assume an interest-rate stabilization objective, the IS relation must be included among the constraints on feasible equilibrium paths for the target variables. Under the assumption of d-period delays, this takes the form (2.33).

The Lagrangian used in Section 3.1 to characterize optimal policy must be modified as a result of the predeterminedness of these decisions, along the lines already illustrated in Section 2.4. The first-order conditions that characterize optimal policy are then given by

$$\pi_t^{qd} - \beta\gamma E_{t-d}\pi_{t+1}^{qd} - \beta^{-1}\sigma\varphi_{1,t-d-1} - \beta\gamma E_{t-d}\varphi_{2,t-d+1}$$
$$+ (1+\beta\gamma)\varphi_{2,t-d} - \varphi_{2,t-d-1} = 0, \tag{3.28}$$

together with conditions (3.4) and (3.5), but with $\varphi_{i,t-d}$ substituted for φ_{it} (for $i = 1, 2$) in the latter equations. Each of the first-order conditions just listed holds for all $t \geq t_0 + d$. In addition, optimal policy must satisfy (2.34), just as in Section 2.4.

As in the previous section, one can substitute out the Lagrange multipliers, obtaining an Euler equation of the form

$$A_1(L)\left(i_t - i^*\right) + \beta\gamma E_{t-d}\left(i_{t+1} - i^*\right) = -E_{t-d}f_t, \tag{3.29}$$

where $A_1(L)$ is the quadratic lag polynomial such that

$$A(L) = \beta\gamma + LA_1(L)$$

is the polynomial defined in (3.17), and f_t is again defined in (3.18) and (3.19). It follows from this that under a policy that is optimal from a timeless perspective, i_t depends solely on public information at date $t - d$. Taking the expectation of (3.29) conditional upon information at date $t - d$, one obtains

$$E_{t-d}\left[A(L)\left(i_{t+1} - i^*\right)\right] = -E_{t-d}f_t,$$

which is identical to (3.16) except for the conditioning information set.

The same manipulations as in Section 3.2 can then be used to derive similar representations for optimal policy, simply changing the conditioning information set for expectations. There are once again the three possible forms for an optimal instrument rule discussed in Section 3.2, and each exists for the same values of γ as before. Each of the three rules is of the form

$$i_t = (1 - \rho_1)\, i^* + \rho_1 i_{t-1} + \rho_2 \Delta i_{t-1} + \phi_\pi E_{t-d} F_t(\pi)$$
$$+ \frac{\phi_x}{4} E_{t-d} F_t(x) - \theta_\pi \pi_{t-1} - \frac{\theta_x}{4} x_{t-1}, \tag{3.30}$$

where the coefficients are exactly the same functions of the model parameters as in (3.25). Similarly, optimal policy can again be represented by a pure targeting rule with a target criterion of the form

$$E_{t-d} F_t(\pi) + \frac{\phi_x}{4} E_{t-d} F_t(x) = \theta_\pi \pi_{t-1} + \frac{\theta_x}{4} x_{t-1} - \theta_i \left(i_{t-1} - i^* \right)$$
$$- \theta_\Delta \Delta i_{t-1}, \tag{3.31}$$

where the coefficients are exactly the same functions of the model parameters as in (3.27). Thus the optimal policy rules are of exactly the same form as before, except that now the period t interest rate should be chosen in period $t - d$ and on the basis of the inflation and output-gap projections that are available at that earlier date. The projections, however, should be for the same time periods as before.

In the case that $\gamma = 0$ (the basic model, with a standard New Keynesian Phillips curve, except for the d-period delays), the projections in (3.30) again are only for inflation and the output gap in period t. Since both of these variables are known at date $t - d$, according to the present model, the optimal instrument rule is once again of the form (3.7), with coefficients (3.8) and (3.9). Thus in this case there is *no change* at all in the optimal policy rule. It remains true that the delays imply that it is optimal for nominal interest rates to be perfectly forecastable d periods in advance. However, this principle does not imply that a rule that prescribes a response to contemporaneous inflation and output-gap variations, as under the Taylor rule, is therefore suboptimal. For under the present assumptions, inflation and the output gap are themselves completely forecastable d periods in advance. This example shows that an optimal policy rule need not be at all forward looking, even in the case that the effects of monetary policy are entirely delayed.

3.4 Optimal Policy under Imperfect Information

My analysis thus far has assumed that the central bank has complete information about the current state of the economy and thus can bring about an optimal state-contingent path for its instrument, regardless of how that may require its operating target to vary in response to disturbances. In reality, central-bank information about current conditions is imperfect. At the time that the operating target is chosen, the current quarter's inflation rate and level of real GDP—both required to implement a rule such as (3.7)—are not yet known, and must be forecasted based on a variety of indicators. The estimates available "in real time" differ substantially from the values that are eventually determined to have been correct (Orphanides, 2001). Still less does a central bank know the current quarter's efficient level of output in real time; estimates of "potential output" can be revised by several percentage points after some years if additional data become available. A proper analysis of optimal policy needs to take account of such constraints upon the central bank's information.

The Lagrangian method used earlier to characterize the optimal state-contingent plan can be adapted to a situation in which the central bank has imperfect information, as shown by Svensson and Woodford (2002b). One obtains similar first-order conditions, but with changes in the information sets with respect to which certain expectations are conditioned. As a simple example, consider again the basic neo-Wicksellian model, as in Section 3.1, but suppose now that the central bank has less information than the private sector each period. The first-order conditions (3.3) and (3.4) for the optimal state-contingent plan still apply, but (3.5) must now be replaced by

$$\lambda_i \left(i_t - i^* \right) + \sigma \varphi_{1t|t} = 0, \tag{3.32}$$

where I use the notation $z_{t|t}$ for the expectation of any variable z_t conditional upon the central bank's information set at the time that the period t instrument setting is chosen. This last condition is modified in the way indicated because the central bank must choose a single instrument setting for each of the possible states at date t that it is unable to distinguish on the basis of its information, though φ_{1t} (the shadow value to the bank of relaxing the constraint associated with the IS equation) may differ across those states.

In this case, one can no longer use (3.32) to eliminate φ_{1t} from the other two first-order conditions and so can no longer obtain an instrument rule that refers only to the evolution of the interest rate, the inflation rate, and the output gap. However, one can still define a variable

$$\bar{\imath}_t \equiv i^* - \frac{\sigma}{\lambda_i} \Xi_{1t}, \tag{3.33}$$

indicating an ideal instrument setting that *would* be optimal if the central bank had the information required to implement it. Then condition (3.33) can be used with (3.3) and (3.4) as before to show that this variable evolves according to a law of motion

$$\bar{\imath}_t = (1 - \rho_1)i^* + \rho_1 \bar{\imath}_{t-1} + \rho_2 \Delta \bar{\imath}_{t-1} + \phi_\pi \pi_t + \phi_x \Delta x_t / 4, \qquad (3.34)$$

where the coefficients are again defined in (3.8) and (3.9). (One can assign arbitrary initial conditions to begin this recursion and still obtain a policy rule that is optimal from a timeless perspective.) First-order condition (3.32) can then be written simply as

$$i_t = \bar{\imath}_{t|t}. \qquad (3.35)$$

This states that the central bank chooses an operating target for each period that equals the expected value of the ideal instrument setting conditional upon the bank's information set at the time that it must choose.

Under imperfect information, then, optimal policy can be described by the rule (3.35), where the ideal instrument setting referred to in this rule is defined by (3.34). In practice, estimation of the conditional expectation referred to in this rule requires the use of a Kalman filter, the coefficients of which depend on the law of motion of the ideal instrument setting (3.34). The coefficients of the Kalman filter also depend on the equilibrium comovement of the endogenous indicator variables with inflation and the output gap, which in turn depend on the coefficients of the Kalman filter (insofar as the central bank's policy is based on it). This fixed-point problem is discussed further in Svensson and Woodford (2002b).

Svensson and Woodford show that certain equations that describe the optimal instrument setting continue to hold in the case of imperfect information, except that variables not observed by the central bank are replaced by their expectations conditional upon the bank's information set. Thus this kind of linear-quadratic policy problem possesses a *certainty-equivalence* property.[46] Nonetheless, it is important to realize that one cannot naively apply this principle to *any* rule that describes optimal policy in the case of full information. For example, it would not be correct to set interest rates using (3.7), simply replacing each term on the right-hand side by the central bank's estimate of the term at the time that it sets i_t. This application of certainty equivalence would suggest a rule of the form

$$i_t = (1 - \rho_1)i^* + \rho_1 i_{t-1} + \rho_2 \Delta i_{t-1} + \phi_\pi \pi_{t|t} + \frac{\phi_x}{4}\left(x_{t|t} - x_{t-1|t}\right),$$

since i_{t-1} and i_{t-2} must be part of the central bank's information set. But this is *not* an optimal rule in the case of imperfect information; instead of i_{t-1} and i_{t-2}, the optimal rule responds to $\bar{\imath}_{t-1|t}$ and $\bar{\imath}_{t-2|t}$. These are not

---

46. Svensson and Woodford (2002a) provide a similar analysis in the case of symmetric but incomplete information on the part of both the central bank and the private sector.

the same, since in general, by the time that it sets i_t, the central bank has additional information about the correct values of $\bar{\imath}_{t-1}$ and $\bar{\imath}_{t-2}$, relative to its estimates at the time of its earlier interest-rate decisions. Hence the notion of certainty equivalence must be applied with care.[47]

Nonetheless, optimal policy under imperfect information is in many ways similar to optimal policy under full information. For example, it is often questioned whether an optimal policy rule should depend very strongly on central-bank estimates of the output gap, given that it is known from historical experience (as stressed by Orphanides, 2001, 2003) that real-time estimates of the gap have often proven to be highly inaccurate. The example discussed here shows that this is not a sufficient reason to regard it as unimportant to variations in the output gap, to the extent that these are judged to occur. In the optimal rule defined by (3.34) and (3.35), the coefficient ($\phi_x/4$) through which the current interest-rate operating target i_t should depend on the current estimate of the output gap $x_{t|t}$ is just as large as under full-information optimal policy, no matter how badly the output gap may be measured in real time.

Of course, it is important to remember that in this equation, $x_{t|t}$ represents an *optimal* (minimum mean-squared-error) estimate of the output gap, given the central bank's information set. If the available information is very uninformative, then the optimal estimate $x_{t|t}$ varies very little (as the central bank realizes that most of the time it has few grounds to suppose that the output gap is anything very different from its long-run average value), and in this sense the central bank's interest-rate policy has little to do with changes in the estimated output gap. But it remains true that when the bank *does* have reason to estimate a substantial change in the output gap, this should affect its policy. It is also important to recognize that the optimal (Kalman-filter-based) estimate of the output gap is generally based not solely on measures of real activity, but also on observations of other variables, such as inflation, which are known to be systematically related to variations in the gap. In the case that direct real-time information about changes in the natural rate of output is highly inaccurate, an optimal real-time estimate of the output gap may be largely based on observed variation

---

47. Aoki (2002) provides another example of this point. In the model considered by Aoki, there are no cost-push shocks, so that under full information optimal policy would completely stabilize inflation and the output gap, and so would involve a nominal interest rate equal at all times to the current natural rate of interest. But Aoki shows that when the central bank has incomplete information, it is not generally true that optimal policy involves setting the nominal interest rate equal to the central bank's optimal current *estimate* of the natural rate of interest. Indeed, he shows that optimal policy under incomplete information is generally history dependent: It is optimal for the central bank to commit itself to respond later to information that it obtains about its past errors in estimating the natural rate, and not simply to its estimate of the current natural rate.

in *inflation*. Hence the existence of a nontrivial coefficient on the output-gap estimate in the rule (3.34) and (3.35) may be consistent with an interest-rate policy that responds primarily to observed variations in inflation and relatively little to observed variations in real activity or employment.[48]

4   Reflections on Currently Popular Policy Proposals

As noted in the introduction to this chapter, my primary goal is to expound a method that can be used to design optimal policy rules in the light of current views as to the nature of the monetary transmission mechanism, rather than to advocate a specific rule. Not only are the details of the best sort of monetary policy rule likely to vary from country to country, but current understanding of the monetary transmission mechanism remains too provisional to expect to reach any final conclusion as to the form of the best policy rule at this time.[49] Nonetheless, one may seek to extract some provisional lessons from the range of examples of optimal policy rules discussed in this chapter. In particular, it may be useful to consider the extent to which the policy rules discussed in Chapter 1—which have been offered both as characterizations of the current behavior of some of the leading central banks and as normative proposals—are similar to those that are found to be optimal under the criteria proposed in this study.

4.1   The Taylor Rule

It should be clear from the results of this study that the formulation of the Taylor rule represented a step in the right direction, in several respects. One important accomplishment of Taylor's proposal has simply been to focus more attention, both in the United States and elsewhere, on the systematic character of sound monetary policy. As I have stressed throughout this study, there are important advantages both to rule-based policymaking and to

48. See Svensson and Woodford (2002a) for further development of this point in the context of a simple example.

49. Some may feel that the unlikelihood of *ever* reaching complete certainty as to the proper model of the economy is a reason why it should never be possible for a central bank to commit itself to a policy rule, and hence then my inquiry is pointless. But the conception of rule-based policymaking proposed here is not one in which it is necessary for a specific rule to be adopted at some date that can never be reconsidered at any later time. Instead, I have proposed a way of judging the optimality of a policy rule that allows the optimality of a given rule to be reconsidered as often as may be desired. In the absence of any change in one's beliefs about the correct model of the economy, there should be no grounds to depart from the rule previously adopted, if one wishes for policy to be optimal from a timeless perspective. At the same time, the adoption of such a rule at a given point in time does not prevent modification of the rule at such a time as the central bank's understanding of the transmission mechanism changes.

clearer public understanding of the systematic character of monetary policy, and the use of the Taylor rule, both within central banks and among market participants seeking to forecast central-bank behavior, has surely facilitated improvement on both fronts.

The specific rule proposed by Taylor also has several desirable features. The fact that it is formulated in terms of a direct relationship between the federal funds rate—the Fed's policy instrument—and measures of inflation and of the output gap—the target variables that matter most in judging the success of stabilization policy, without any reference to intermediate targets such as a monetary aggregate, has surely increased the appeal of the rule to policymakers while also increasing its intelligibility to the public. Some economists, though, have doubted that a rule of this kind represents a sound basis for a policy commitment, owing to the role assigned to monetary aggregates both in many theoretical accounts of the determinants of inflation and business fluctuations and in the best-known examples (at least prior to the 1990s) of proposed monetary policy rules. Indeed, the formulation of a policy commitment in terms of an interest-rate rule might seem to ignore the well-known criticisms of interest-rate rules by economists such as Friedman (1968) or Sargent and Wallace (1975) as inherent sources of instability, as systematic policies of this kind were argued to leave the economy vulnerable to self-fulfilling expectations.

The present analysis has shown that while some kinds of interest-rate rules are validly criticized on this score (such as the interest-rate peg, or exogenous nominal-interest-rate processes, with which the arguments both of Friedman and of Sargent and Wallace are really concerned), properly chosen interest-rate rules are not. Furthermore, at least in the context of certain simple models of the monetary transmission mechanism that I have considered, the classic Taylor rule is an example of the type of interest-rate rule that results both in a determinate rational-expectations equilibrium and in the convergence of plausible learning dynamics to that equilibrium.

Moreover, we have seen that a linear relation among target variables (quite possibly including the level of overnight interest rates) is a highly desirable form in which to express a policy commitment. It is possible to choose a relation of this kind in such a way that it represents a relation that one wishes to have hold at all times, regardless of the history of disturbances, essentially because the rule represents a first-order condition for the optimal evolution of the target variables. Such a first-order condition, which represents a particularly robust way of describing what it should mean for policy to be on track, is naturally formulated in terms of variables that are as directly related as possible to the distortions that one wishes to minimize. From this point of view, the level of nominal interest rates may well be a variable that should be taken into account (as a measure, e.g., of the distortions associated with an inefficiently low level of liquidity in the economy), whereas the money supply is not so directly a measure of any such distortion.[50]

One may, of course, view Taylor's proposal not as seeking to describe such a measure of whether the goals of policy are being achieved—a *target criterion*, in the terminology that I have used in Chapter 7 and in this one— but rather as a rough description of the *reaction function* that the central bank should use in order to ensure that such a target is achieved fairly well, like equation (5.5) in Chapter 7. If this is what one seeks to describe, then the fact that the rule is expressed as a rule for the federal funds rate simply reflects the fact that the funds rate is the instrument of policy under current Fed operating procedures. One might alternatively have derived a similar expression for the monetary base as a function of the various determinants of inflation and of the output gap, if one wished to implement a flexible-inflation-targeting rule using the base as the instrument of policy.

But again one can argue not merely that the choice of an overnight interest rate as the instrument of policy is an equally coherent choice, but that it has clear advantages. These are most obvious in the case that one supposes (as is true of the empirical models discussed in Chapter 5) that both spending and pricing decisions are predetermined for at least a short period of time. In this case, optimal policy requires that the overnight interest rate be completely forecastable over a similar time horizon, as discussed in Sections 2.4 and 3.3. This can easily be achieved through the choice of an operating target for the interest rate on the basis of information available at some earlier date. For example, in the case that both kinds of decisions are predetermined for d periods, the optimal target criterion (2.32)[51] can be implemented through a reaction function

$$
i_t = E_{t-d} r_t^n + \frac{\kappa}{\sigma(\kappa^2 + \lambda)} E_{t-d} u_t + \left[1 + \frac{\beta\kappa}{\sigma(\kappa^2 + \lambda)} \right] E_{t-d} \pi_{t+1}
$$

$$
+ \frac{1}{\sigma} E_{t-d} x_{t+1} - \frac{\lambda}{\sigma(\kappa^2 + \lambda)} E_{t-d} x_{t-1},
$$

(4.1)

---

50. While one might suppose that it is the quantity of money that should be most directly related to the severity of this distortion, the fact is that there is no time-invariant standard by which to judge how a given quantity of money compares to the level that would mitigate transactions frictions to any given degree, whereas the level of nominal interest rates that is associated with efficiency is invariant (namely, a zero opportunity cost of holding money). It is noteworthy that in Friedman's famous essay on "the optimum quantity of money"—the title of which indicates a desire to conceive the problem as one of choosing a monetary aggregate—the criterion for optimality actually obtained is defined in terms of the nominal interest rate: One should bring about money growth at the rate needed to reduce the nominal interest rate to zero.

51. Here I present the reaction function only for the special case in which $\gamma = 0$, i.e., the case of standard Calvo pricing, allowing a direct comparison with equation (5.5) of Chapter 7.

where the right-hand side is just the forecast in period $t-d$ of the right-hand side of equation (5.5) in Chapter 7. No equivalent reaction function could be written in terms of the monetary base in this case, except one that would involve responses to real disturbances that occur between periods $t-d$ and t; thus it would not be possible to determine the instrument as far in advance if the base were the instrument. The reaction function would also be more complex in that case, as it would necessarily respond to disturbances (money demand disturbances) that do not enter in (4.1).

The particular target variables selected by Taylor that the Fed should respond to, and so seek to stabilize—namely, measures of the general rate of inflation and the output gap—also receive considerable support from the present theoretical analysis. I have shown in Chapter 6 that there are good reasons to regard both of these variables (when properly defined) as measures of important distortions and hence as arguments of a loss function for stabilization policy that can be justified in terms of the welfare of individuals.

A particularly controversial feature of Taylor's proposal is the prescription that policy should respond to variations in the output gap, and not merely to inflation. The analysis in this study shows not only that one can make sense of the concept of an output gap, but that it is a useful one in modeling inflation dynamics. This has been true of each of the variety of types of models with nominal rigidities that I have examined in this book. We have also seen that welfare maximization can justify a goal of stabilizing an appropriately defined output gap, in addition to the pursuit of price stability, and that under some circumstances there can be a tension between these two goals, so that some degree of departure from complete price stability is desirable in order to allow greater stability of the output gap.

Furthermore, I have found that the robustly optimal policy rules derived in this chapter all prescribe interest-rate adjustments (or modification of the inflation target) in response to changes in the projected path of the (correctly defined) output gap. While it might also be possible to formulate policy rules consistent with an optimal equilibrium that would *not* involve explicit reference to this variable, such alternative representations of optimal policy would either not be *robustly* optimal like the rules derived here— the coefficients of the optimal rule would depend upon precise details of the assumed statistical character of the disturbances[52]—or they would not

52. For example, Woodford (1999a) derives an optimal policy rule for the model of Section 1 that involves only the short-term nominal interest rate and an inflation measure, and argues that this representation of optimal policy is desirable because it can be implemented without requiring the central bank to measure the output gap. However, the rule discussed there is optimal only under a very specific assumption about the disturbances: There are no cost-push shocks, and the natural rate of interest is an AR(1) process, with innovations that are

be *direct* rules—they would involve explicit reference to variables other than the target variables, such as specific exogenous disturbances. Hence, insofar as a robustly optimal direct rule is desirable, there is an important advantage to expressing the central bank's policy commitment in terms of a rule that involves the bank's estimate of (or projection of) the path of the output gap.

There are certainly substantial difficulties involved in accurate measurement of the output gap in practice. But many of these can be well represented by additive measurement error of the kind considered by Svensson and Woodford (2002a,b), so that certainty equivalence applies, as discussed in Section 3.4. In this case, it is still optimal to commit to a policy rule with the same coefficient on the central bank's estimate of the output gap as would be optimal under full information; the measurement error affects only the way in which it is optimal for the central bank to form its estimate of current and past output gaps. For example, an optimal estimate of the output gap generally makes use of information about wages and prices, and not simply available quantity measures. But this does not mean that it is not useful for the central bank to describe its policy commitment in terms of a relationship between the output gap and other variables. For *this* description of policy is much more robust than an explicit description of the way that the central bank should respond to specific indicator variables, which depends on the bank's current beliefs about the statistical properties of the various disturbances (including the ones responsible for the measurement problems).

It is also worth noting that the errors that have been observed historically in real-time estimates of the output gap (documented by Orphanides, 2003) have been much greater in the case of estimates of the absolute level of the output gap than in the case of estimates of the quarter-to-quarter changes in the gap. (Errors in the recognition of shifts in the trend rate of growth of potential output until years later have caused substantial, highly persistent misestimates of the absolute gap; but this particular source of measurement error has little effect on the higher-frequency components of the output-gap estimate.) However, the optimal rules obtained in this chapter involve only the projected path of quarter-to-quarter *changes* in the output gap, and are independent of the absolute *level* of the gap, even though it is the absolute size of the gap that one wishes to stabilize. Because of this, it is less obvious that output-gap mismeasurement is a more serious problem in the case of the optimal rules derived here than under common proposals that would

---

revealed in the same period that they affect the natural rate. Furthermore, the numerical coefficients of the optimal rule depend on the coefficient of serial correlation of the natural-rate disturbances. The rules discussed in Section 1 are equally optimal under this specification of the disturbances and a vast number of other possibilities.

make policy depend on the absolute level of the current or projected future output gap.

Finally, the particular kind of response to variations in inflation and in the output gap that Taylor calls for—a positive response of interest rates to increases in the output gap and a response coefficient greater than one in the case of inflation—is at least broadly similar to optimal policy in several of the analyses of simple models. We have seen that robustly optimal instrument rules, in the case of an interest-rate stabilization objective (Section 3), can be expressed as interest-rate rules that satisfy the Taylor principle and involve positive responses of interest rates to increases in either (current or expected future) inflation or output gaps. We have also seen that reaction functions associated with the implementation of an inflation target (equation (2.44) of Chapter 4 or equation (5.5) of Chapter 7), in the case that there is no such objective, can be expressed as interest-rate rules with these properties as well.

At the same time, the present analysis suggests several respects in which it would be possible to improve upon Taylor's original formulation. One concerns the appropriate definitions of the target variables to which the central bank should respond. In Taylor's (1993) comparison of his proposal with actual Fed behavior, he assumes that the appropriate inflation measure is change in the GDP deflator. But we have seen (in Chapter 6) that in general the best measure of the distortions associated with instability of prices is not an index of economy-wide prices that weights the prices of different goods in proportion to their share in domestic production; rather, it is appropriate to place a greater weight on stabilization of some kinds of prices than others, depending on sectoral characteristics such as the frequency with which different types of prices are adjusted. Hence a desirable policy rule would respond to variations in an (appropriately defined) measure of core inflation, rather than to any measure of the average rate of increase of all prices. We have also seen that instability of nominal-wage inflation may well produce economic distortions similar to those associated with goods-price inflation. It follows from this (as discussed in Chapter 6 and in Section 2.2 of this chapter) that an optimal policy rule may well require a response to wage as well as price inflation.[53]

Similarly, in Taylor's (1993) comparison of his proposal with historical policy, he identifies the output gap with linearly detrended real GDP. In most central-bank policy discussions as well, when output-gap measures are cited, they are usually measures of real GDP relative to some fairly

---

53. See Giannoni and Woodford (2002b, sec. 3.1) for analysis of a model with sticky wages and prices, for which there exists a robustly optimal instrument rule similar in form to (3.7), but with the inflation variable replaced by a weighted average of wage and price inflation.

smooth trend. But the welfare-relevant output gap according to the theoretical analysis—and so the variable that properly appears as an argument of an optimal policy rule of the kind characterized in this chapter—is the difference between real GDP and a target level that should vary in response to real disturbances of many sorts (including disturbances to preferences, technology, and fiscal policy), and it is not obvious that these real factors should all be expected to evolve as smooth trends.

Furthermore, we have seen that there is at least some evidence to suggest that conventional output-gap measures (essentially, detrended output) are not at all closely related to the output-gap variable in the theoretical analysis. As discussed in Section 2.1 of Chapter 3, under fairly general assumptions, the level of real marginal cost should be monotonically related to the theoretical output gap, and if one assumes a production technology with a constant elasticity of output with respect to the labor input, this quantity is in turn proportional to real unit labor cost (or the labor share). But, as noted by Gali and Gertler (1999) and Sbordone (2002), cyclical variations in real unit labor cost do not correspond at all closely to typical measures of detrended output—there is actually a substantial *negative* correlation between these series! Moreover, the fact that simple optimizing models of pricing dynamics fit aggregate U.S. inflation series fairly well when real unit labor cost is used as a proxy for the output gap, but not at all when detrended output is used, suggests that the real unit labor cost series is in fact the better measure of the output-gap concept that is relevant to inflation determination.[54] Neiss and Nelson (2002) reach a similar conclusion by constructing a theory-based output-gap measure, using estimates of the historical series of real disturbances to preferences and technology to infer the variation in the natural rate of output; again, their gap series is negatively correlated with detrended output measures, while better serving to explain historical variation in inflation. It follows that a central bank that raises interest rates when a conventional gap measure (detrended output) is high may be responding in quite a different way than my optimal rules would prescribe.

Moreover, while the responses to inflation and output-gap variations prescribed by Taylor agree in some significant ways with common properties of optimal rules, they are different in some important respects as well. Taylor prescribes a purely contemporaneous response, whereas optimal

---

54. Of course, the output gap that determines variations in inflation and the one that defines an appropriate stabilization objective need not move together at all times. Under certain assumptions, as discussed in Chapter 6, they should coincide; but there are a variety of plausible reasons for them to be somewhat different, as discussed in Section 5 of that chapter. Hence the mere fact that real unit labor costs seem to be a good measure of inflationary pressure does not require that they are also an accurate measure of the welfare-relevant output gap.

rules involve additional dynamics. Even in the case of a simple model of inflation and output determination, where lagged endogenous variables are of no causal significance, an optimal policy rule is *history dependent*, for reasons explained in Chapter 7. For example, all of the optimal rules derived in this chapter involve responses to observed and/or projected *changes* in the output gap, rather than to the absolute level of the gap, even though it is the level of the gap that measures a distortion that policy should aim to stabilize. Furthermore, in the case that interest-rate stabilization is a goal of policy, so that the target criterion that represents a first-order condition characterizing optimality can be expressed as an interest-rate feedback rule, the rule involves substantial dependence of the appropriate current level of nominal interest rates on lagged interest rates. We have seen in the examples given in Section 3 that optimal interest-rate rules are actually *superinertial,* and Proposition 8.3 shows that this is not an accidental feature of those examples; it must be true in the case of any model of the monetary transmission mechanism that possesses the Sargent-Wallace property.

Finally, it is sometimes questioned whether Taylor's classic formulation of the rule is not too backward looking, in that it prescribes a response only to inflation that has already occurred. We have seen in Section 3.1 that it is possible for a robustly optimal rule to specify feedback only from contemporaneous and lagged variables. On the other hand, it is important to note that even in this case, the optimal rule is only an *implicit* instrument rule: It specifies a relation between the current period's nominal-interest-rate target and that same period's values of variables that depends on the current level of interest rates. Hence implementation of the optimal rule requires that the central bank be able to *project* the effect on those variables of alternative possible decisions on its part, in order to decide what interest-rate decision would be consistent with the rule; a *structural model* of the transmission mechanism is therefore essential to the conduct of policy in accordance with such a rule. This is a fairly general characteristic of robustly optimal policy rules derived along the lines explained in this chapter.

It is not clear that Taylor's rule is intended to be of this kind. The assumption implicit in his proposal may well be that forecasts can be made of the inflation rate and output gap for the coming quarter that are independent of the policy decision (as monetary policy changes are generally regarded as having little effect on either prices or output so quickly), so that the rule can be applied without recourse to a structural model or conditional forecasts. If this is the intention, then an optimal rule of the kind described in this chapter almost never has this character. It is possible to suppose that both inflation and output are predetermined for some months; but in this case, optimal policy generally involves making an advance commitment regarding the interest-rate operating target for a time some months in the future, on the basis of projected conditions *at that time* that depend on the policy decision.

It is perhaps more accurate, then, to view the Taylor rule as intending to describe the central-bank *reaction function* that should be used to achieve a desirable path for the target variables, rather than as a *target criterion* that itself represents the measure of whether the paths of the target variables are of the sort desired. Under this view, it is appropriate to seek a formula that expresses the interest-rate operating target as a function of variables that can be observed (or at least estimated) by the central bank at the time that it must make its decision. Under this view, the Taylor rule does have certain basic features of the reaction functions associated with optimal policies. However, an optimal reaction function is unlikely to be quite so simple as the classic formulation of the Taylor rule (the one that John Taylor could print on his business card). An optimal reaction function surely involves responses to perceived real disturbances, and not merely to past and/or forecasted variations in inflation and the output gap. In particular, the optimal reaction functions that I have illustrated in my simple examples require that the central bank adjust its operating target for the nominal interest rate in response to variations in the Wicksellian natural rate of interest—variations that occur as a result of any of several kinds of real disturbances, as discussed in Chapter 4.[55]

Furthermore, if one interprets the Taylor rule in this light, then despite its usefulness as a simple rule of thumb, even a more sophisticated version of the rule is unlikely to prove an adequate substitute for the use of a full-fledged economic model to determine the policy setting that is most consistent with the achievement of desirable paths for the target variables. This is because the target criterion for optimal policy—the kind of first-order condition that can be derived on the principles explained in this chapter—is likely to be both simpler to express and more robust to possible changes in one's beliefs about the circumstances under which policy is conducted than an explicit formula for the reaction function that is required in order to implement the target criterion. It is therefore the target criterion to which it is more appropriate that the central bank commit itself, and it is also the target criterion that provides the more appropriate basis for communication with the public about the bank's policy commitments and the justification for policy actions that have been taken. While an understanding of the character of reaction function that is implied by a given target criterion can be useful both within the central bank and among market participants seeking to forecast future policy decisions, there is no need for a *commitment* to any such formula, given a commitment to a target criterion. The problem

55. For examples of efforts to construct empirical series for fluctuations in the natural rate of interest, see Laubach and Williams (2001) and Neiss and Nelson (2002).

that the reaction function solves can be solved on an ad hoc basis on each occasion when a policy action must be taken, without any need for a general formula.

4.2 Inflation-Forecast Targeting

The inflation-forecast targeting procedures now used by many central banks also represent an important advance in the practice of central banking. As I remarked about the Taylor rule, bringing focus and clarity to monetary policy deliberations and increasing the degree to which the public is able to understand and anticipate the systematic character of policy are in themselves important steps forward. Inflation-forecast targeting has been even more beneficial in this regard, as it has served to structure policy deliberations (in many countries) to an even greater extent than the Taylor rule, and it has been associated with particularly notable increases in the transparency of central-bank decisionmaking. It is quite possibly the fact that the inflation-targeting central banks *have* explicit targets and are committed to explaining their decisions to the public in the light of their policy commitments that are the most important features of inflation targeting.

But the specific form of policy commitment that exists at these central banks is also, in important respects, in accordance with my analysis of optimal policy rules. First of all, I have argued that optimal policy rules can quite generally be expressed as *targeting rules,* in which the central bank is committed to adjust interest rates in whatever way is judged necessary in order for the projected paths of various target variables to satisfy an explicit *target criterion.* Further, I have argued that the kind of target criterion that is robustly optimal is one that defines the appropriate instrument setting only *implicitly*; the use of an economic model to project the consequences of alternative interest-rate decisions is a crucial part of monetary policy decisions. Inflation-forecast targeting as practiced at the Bank of England, the Reserve Bank of New Zealand, the Swedish Riksbank, and the other banks that have followed their lead provides the best practical example of how policy can be conducted in accordance with a commitment of this kind.

The fact that the targeting procedures of these central banks emphasize their *inflation* targets is also a choice that receives substantial support from the analysis in this study. We have seen that under certain ideal circumstances, optimal policy would be characterized by complete stabilization of an appropriately chosen price index, as discussed in Chapter 6. Moreover, while the conditions under which complete price stability is optimal are somewhat special, my numerical investigations of the character of optimal policy in various calibrated examples have suggested that both the average rate of inflation and the degree of variation in inflation that are optimal under more realistic circumstances are still quite modest. Hence "price stability" is not a bad short description of the primary goal of sound policy.

Nonetheless, there remain important respects in which current inflation-forecast-targeting procedures (both those actually used by inflation-targeting central banks and those advocated in much of the scholarly literature) differ from the kind of optimal targeting rules discussed in this chapter. First of all, my comments about the appropriate target variables in connection with the Taylor rule apply here as well. Most inflation-targeting central banks target the rate of growth of some form of consumer price index, perhaps with a small number of adjustments, such as the RPIX inflation measure in the United Kingdom just mentioned. As I have discussed, an optimal target criterion places more weight on changes in some kinds of prices than others. Targeting a measure of core inflation would be closer to the theoretical ideal, though a fully optimal target criterion is likely to involve more than one inflation measure (since the optimal relative weights on different kinds of inflation need not be the same at all leads and lags). The optimal target criterion should also take account of wage as well as price inflation, as illustrated in Section 2.5.

Similarly, discussions in the literature of flexible inflation targeting advocate acceptance of temporary deviations from the long-run inflation target for the sake of a smaller output gap. But these discussions are often vague about the conception of the output gap that is intended. Here we have seen that optimal target criteria do often involve output-gap projections; but it is important to note that the output gap referred to in my theoretical analysis may behave quite differently from the output-gap measures most often used in policy discussions within central banks, as discussed in the previous section. Furthermore, the literature often proposes that the degree of acceptable departure from the long-run inflation target should be proportional to the projected absolute *level* of the output gap; but in the optimal target criteria derived here, it is only the projected *change* in the output gap from one quarter to the next that is relevant.

One fairly general respect in which inflation-forecast targeting in practice differs from the theoretical ideal expounded in this study is that current procedures are *purely forward looking*, at least as far as official rhetoric is concerned. At the beginning of each quarterly *Inflation Report* published by the Bank of England, one finds two "fan charts," indicating probability distributions for forecast paths for real GDP and RPIX inflation eight quarters into the future. The current level of overnight interest rates is presented as being justified by the character of these charts, on criteria that are evidently independent of what may have happened before, including the projections and the policy decisions that may have been made in prior quarters. One might think, using dynamic-programming reasoning, that it is entirely correct, and a sign of rationality, for the most recent policy decision to have been based solely on a consideration of the possible paths for the economy from that date onward. But as argued in Chapter 7, this is incorrect, insofar as it neglects the benefits that can be obtained from a history-dependent policy that can be relied upon in advance and that, as a result, shapes expectations at earlier dates in a desirable way. This does not mean that a forecast-targeting procedure cannot be a suitable form of policy commitment; but as a result of the forward-looking behavior of private agents, an optimal target criterion is almost always *history dependent.* Numerous examples in this chapter have illustrated the type of history dependence that may be appropriate.

Another problematic feature of the target criteria used in current forecast-targeting procedures is the sole emphasis on conditions to be achieved relatively far in the future. Thus the criterion emphasized in the Bank of England's discussion of its projections is the requirement that the projected rate of RPIX inflation eight quarters in the future equal 2.5 percent. The problem with this form of policy commitment is not that it involves a fixed inflation target for the medium term. In the examples that I have considered, optimal policy almost always involves a well-defined long-run inflation target, to which the inflation rate should return after a few quarters even if it is temporarily allowed to deviate from the long-run target as a result of real disturbances; and it is surely desirable for a central bank to be explicit about this aspect of its policy commitment, in order to anchor the public's medium-term inflation expectations.

Rather, the problem is that this sort of commitment is *insufficient* to determine what policy should actually be like in the near term—the time in which we are always actually living, as Keynes famously remarked. The mere fact that a central bank wishes to see inflation return to a rate of 2.5 percent at a horizon 2 years in the future is not sufficient to say which of the various possible transition paths that reach that endpoint should be preferred. There is always a range of possible scenarios consistent with the terminal condition: for example, looser policy this year to be compensated by tighter policy next year, or alternatively the reverse.

In practice, the Bank of England, like many other forecast-targeting banks, deals with this problem by demanding that a *constant-interest-rate* forecast satisfy the terminal condition. That is, the current level of overnight interest rates is held to be justified if a projection *under the assumption that that level of interest rates will be maintained* implies that RPIX inflation should equal 2.5 percent eight quarters in the future. However, this implies no commitment to actually maintain interest rates at the current level over that period, or even that interest rates are currently expected to remain at that level on average. (It is frequently the case that the published constant-interest-rate projection would itself imply that interest rates will have to be changed over the coming year, in order for the target criterion to be satisfied by a constant-interest-rate projection under the conditions that are forecasted to obtain by then.) It is thus hard to see how basing policy decisions on a forecast-targeting exercise of this particular kind can be expected to serve the goals of making monetary policy more transparent or improving the degree to which policy is correctly anticipated by the private sector.[56]

The conceptually superior approach, surely, is to base policy on a projection that is computed under the assumption that policy is made in accordance with the targeting rule in the future as well,[57] so that the projection that is used to justify current policy corresponds to the bank's own best forecast of how it should act in the future.[58] It is, of course, necessary to stress that the bank's only commitment is to the *rule* embodied in this projection, not to the particular time path of interest rates indicated as most likely. But given the use of fan charts to show that a variety of possible future scenarios can be envisioned, depending on how various types of uncertainty happen to be resolved, it is not clear why it should not be possible to talk about probability distributions for future interest rates along with those for inflation and real activity without giving rise to the appearance of a more specific commitment than is intended.

Once this is done, however, it becomes necessary to specify a target criterion that can determine the appropriate short-run dynamics for the economy, and not simply a terminal condition for a date some years in the future. Such a criterion accordingly places substantial weight on projections of the target variables over the coming year, as in the case of the optimal target criteria derived in this chapter. It also has to take a stand as to the kinds of projected departures of real variables from their long-run average values that justify short-run departures of the inflation projection from its long-run target value; it no longer suffices simply to specify the (unchanging) long-run inflation target. None of the inflation-targeting central banks actually believe that it is desirable to keep inflation as close as possible to the long-run target value at all times, which is why forecast-targeting procedures only seek to ensure that inflation is projected to return to the target

56. See Svensson (2003a) for related criticism of this aspect of current Bank of England procedures, and Goodhart (2001) for a defense. Another problem with basing policy on a constant-interest-rate forecast is the fact that many forward-looking models of the monetary transmission mechanism, including all of those discussed in this book, satisfy the Sargent-Wallace property, so that such models *yield no determinate answer* to the question of how inflation and other variables would evolve in the event that nominal interest rates are fixed indefinitely at a given level. Possible interpretations of constant-interest-rate forecast targeting as a policy rule are discussed by Leitemo (2000).

57. See Svensson and Woodford (2003) for further discussion of what this would mean in practice.

58. Currently, the Reserve Bank of New Zealand is the only inflation-targeting central bank to release projections based on its own forecast of future policy. These projections are made by solving a quantitative model, the Forecasting and Projection System, that includes an interest-rate rule intended to model the Reserve Bank's own future policy (Black et al., 1997a).

value after many quarters.[59] But by formulating no explicit doctrine as to the way in which one should choose among alternative transition paths to that medium-term goal, they avoid having to clarify the nature of acceptable trade-offs among competing stabilization goals.[60]

A coherent approach—and in particular, one that could be justified as seeking to implement the conditions for optimal policy discussed in this chapter—would instead have to make explicit the kind of projections for output and other real variables that should justify a modification of the short-run inflation target and the degree to which they should affect it. In all likelihood, the inflation-targeting banks have shied away from such explicitness out of a suspicion that the types of circumstances that might reasonably justify short-term departures from the inflation target are too various to be catalogued. But the theory developed here has sought to show that it is possible to state *short-run* target criteria (criteria that apply to the shortest horizon at which current policy decisions can still have an effect) that are *robustly* optimal, meaning that the same criterion continues to determine the correct degree of short-run departure from the long-run inflation target regardless of the nature of the disturbance that may have occurred.

One thus finds that there remains room for improvement in current inflation forecast-targeting procedures, though the approach advocated here would be a direct descendant of those pioneered by banks like the Bank of England. Agreement on the details of the optimal short-run target criterion, of course, depends upon agreement as to the details of the correct structural model of the monetary transmission mechanism; for while the optimal rules derived here are robust to alternative assumptions as to the character of the additive disturbance terms, the form of the structural equations and the response elasticities relating the endogenous variables to one another *do* matter. This requires further research, of a kind that is only likely to succeed as a result of cooperative effort between academic researchers and the staffs of the central banks. It is hoped that the present study will help to stimulate further work in this sphere and, in so doing, reveal as a practical possibility the sort of rational management of national standards of value that could only be dreamed of by the monetary reformers of a century ago.

---

59. On this point, see, e.g., Bernanke et al. (1999) or Svensson (1999).

60. The fact that a real GDP projection is always included along with the projection for RPIX inflation in the introduction to the Bank of England's *Inflation Report*—and, in fact, is always discussed *first*—suggests that some attention is paid to the projected path of output in deciding upon the appropriateness of the current level of interest rates. But the Bank's official target criterion, involving only the constant-interest-rate projection of RPIX inflation at the eight-quarter horizon, does not make explicit the way in which the output projection should be taken into account.

APPENDIXES

Addendum to Chapter 2

A.1 Proof of Proposition 2.1

PROPOSITION 2.1. Consider positive-valued stochastic processes $\{P_t, Q_{t,T}\}$ satisfying equations (1.10) and (1.11) of Chapter 2 at all dates, and let $\{C_t, M_t\}$ be non-negative-valued processes representing a possible consumption and money-accumulation plan for the household. Then there exists a specification of the household's portfolio plan at each date satisfying both the flow budget constraint (1.7) and the borrowing limit (1.9) at each date,[1] if and only if the plans $\{C_t, M_t\}$ satisfy the constraint

$$\sum_{t=0}^{\infty} E_0 Q_{0,t}\, [P_t C_t + \Delta_t M_t] \leq W_0 + \sum_{t=0}^{\infty} E_0 Q_{0,t}[P_t Y_t - T_t]. \qquad (A.1)$$

PROOF: Substituting s for the time index t in (1.7), taking the present value of both sides of the inequality at an earlier (or no later) date t, and summing over dates s from t through $T - 1$ yields

$$\sum_{s=t}^{T-1} E_t Q_{t,s}\, [P_s C_s + \Delta_s M_s] + E_t[Q_{t,T} W_T] \leq W_t + \sum_{s=t}^{T-1} E_t Q_{t,s}[P_s Y_s - T_s]$$

for any date $T \geq t + 1$. Combining this with the bounds (1.9) on the portfolios that may be chosen in the various possible states at date $T - 1$ (which are lower bounds upon the values of those portfolios in possible states at date T), one sees that a feasible plan must satisfy

$$\sum_{s=t}^{T-1} E_t Q_{t,s}\, [P_s C_s + \Delta_s M_s] \leq W_t + \sum_{s=t}^{\infty} E_t Q_{t,s}[P_s Y_s - T_s].$$

---

1. Within each appendix, equation numbers that are not otherwise qualified refer to the equations with those numbers in the chapter of the text to which the appendix relates.

Note that the right-hand side is now independent of the terminal date T. The left-hand side is a nondecreasing series in T, given positive goods prices at all dates (necessary for any finite level of consumption to be optimal), interest rates satisfying (1.11), and nonnegative levels of consumption and money balances at all times. The right-hand side, which is finite by (1.10), provides an upper bound for this series, which accordingly must converge as T grows. Furthermore, the limiting value of the series must itself satisfy the upper bound. Thus any feasible plan involves a sequence of state-dependent consumption levels and money balances satisfying the intertemporal budget constraint (1.13). In particular, under any feasible plan, the entire infinite stream $\{C_t, M_t\}$ from the initial date $t = 0$ onward must satisfy this constraint for date zero, given the household's initial financial wealth W_0. This establishes the necessity of (A.1).

It remains to show that this constraint is also *sufficient* for processes $\{C_t, M_t\}$ to be attainable. One easily shows that processes that satisfy (A.1) can be achieved by letting the household's choice of W_t at each date $t \geq 1$ (in each possible state) be given by the value that makes (1.13) hold at that date with equality. Given the hypothesized process for M_t, this then implies a value for A_{t+1} in each possible state, and thus completely specifies the household's portfolio plan at each date $t \geq 0$. The resulting plan obviously satisfies (1.9) at each date, and it is easily verified that it satisfies (1.7), and hence (1.2), at each date as well. Thus the entire sequence of flow budget constraints is equivalent to the single intertemporal constraint (A.1).

A.2 Proof of Proposition 2.2

PROPOSITION 2.2. Let assets be priced by a system of stochastic discount factors that satisfy equation (1.20) of Chapter 2, and consider processes $\{P_t, i_t, i_t^m, M_t^s, W_t^s\}$ that satisfy (1.15), (1.21), and (1.23) at all dates, given the exogenous processes $\{Y_t, \xi_t\}$. Then these processes satisfy (1.22) as well if and only if they satisfy

$$\lim_{T \to \infty} \beta^T E_t[u_c(Y_T; \xi_T)D_T/P_T] = 0. \tag{A.2}$$

In this proposition, note that the path of $\{D_t\}$ can be inferred from the processes that are specified using the identity

$$D_t = M_t^s + E_t[Q_{t,t+1}(W_{t+1}^s - (1 + i_t^m)M_t^s)].$$

PROOF: Note that (1.15) and (1.21) imply that

$$\beta E_t[u_c(Y_{T+1}; \xi_{T+1})(1 + i_T^m)M_T^s/p_{T+1}]$$

$$= \beta E_t \big[u_c(Y_{T+1}; \xi_{T+1})(1 + i_T) M_T^s / p_{t+1} \big]$$
$$= E_t \big[u_c(Y_T; \xi_T) M_T^s / P_T \big].$$

Adding this to the relation

$$\beta E_t \big[u_c(Y_{T+1}; \xi_{T+1}) A_{T+1}^s / p_{T+1} \big] = E_t \big[u_c(Y_T; \xi_T) B_T^s / P_T \big]$$

that follows from (1.4) and (1.20), one finds that

$$\beta E_t \big[u_c(Y_{T+1}; \xi_{T+1}) W_{T+1}^s / P_{t+1} \big] = E_t \big[u_c(Y_T; \xi_T) D_T / P_T \big].$$

It then follows that (1.22) holds if and only if (A.2) does.

In the case of the model with transactions frictions introduced in Section 3 of Chapter 2, a similar proposition continues to hold. A precise statement can be given as follows.

PROPOSITION 2.2′. Let assets be priced by a system of stochastic discount factors that satisfy (1.20), and consider processes $\{P_t, i_t, i_t^m, M_t^s, W_t^s\}$ that satisfy (1.21), (3.3), and (3.4) at all dates, given the exogenous processes $\{Y_t, \xi_t\}$. Then these processes satisfy (1.22) as well if and only if they satisfy

$$\lim_{T \to \infty} \beta^T E_t \big[u_c(Y_T, M_T^s / P_T; \xi_T) D_T / P_T \big] = 0. \qquad (A.3)$$

In this more general case, (1.21) and (3.3) can be used to show that

$$\beta E_t \big[u_c\big(Y_{T+1}, M_{T+1}^s / p_{T+1}; \xi_{T+1}\big)\big(1 + i_T^m\big) M_T^s / p_{T+1} \big]$$
$$= E_t \big[u_c\big(Y_T, M_T^s / P_T; \xi_T\big)(1 - \Delta_T) M_T^s / P_T \big]$$
$$= E_t \big[\big(u_c(Y_T, M_T^s / P_T; \xi_T) - u_m\big(Y_T, M_T^s / P_T; \xi_T\big)\big) M_T^s / P_T \big],$$

from which it follows as before that

$$\beta E_t \big[u_c\big(Y_{T+1}, M_{T+1}^s / p_{T+1}; \xi_{T+1}\big) W_{T+1}^s / p_{T+1} \big]$$
$$= E_t \big[u_c\big(Y_T, M_T^s / P_T; \xi_T\big) D_T / P_T \big] - E_t \big[u_m\big(Y_T, M_T^s / P_T; \xi_T\big) M_T^s / P_T \big].$$

Furthermore, (3.4) implies that

$$\lim_{T \to \infty} \beta^T E_t \big[u_m\big(Y_T, M_T^s / P_T; \xi_T\big) M_T^s / P_T \big] = 0.$$

Hence (1.22) holds if and only if (A.3) holds.

A.3   Log-Linearization and Determinacy of Equilibrium

A method that I use extensively in this study in order to yield an approximate characterization of equilibrium under alternative policy rules involves the solution of linear (typically, log-linear) approximations to the exact equilibrium conditions. The method is essentially an application of the implicit function theorem, analogous to the familiar method of "comparative statics" in the case of static economic models, that is, models in which only a finite number of variables are simultaneously determined.

In a typical comparative-statics problem, a finite number of variables (say n) are simultaneously determined by a system of n equilibrium conditions,

$$\Phi(p; u) = 0, \qquad\qquad (A.4)$$

where p is the vector of n endogenous variables, u is a vector of m parameters (possibly disturbances), and Φ is a vector of n differentiable functions. Suppose that one knows a solution $\bar{p}$ in the case that $u = 0$, that is, a vector $\bar{p}$ such that

$$\Phi(\bar{p}; 0) = 0.$$

Then the *inverse function theorem* of calculus allows one to show that this solution is locally unique in the case that the matrix of partial derivatives $D_p\Phi(\bar{p}; 0)$ is nonsingular. This means that there exists a neighborhood of $\bar{p}$ in which there are no solutions to (A.4) in the case that $u = 0$, other than $p = \bar{p}$. The *implicit function theorem* tells one that under the same hypothesis, there is also a locally unique solution $p(u)$ defined for all u close enough to 0. Moreover, the function $p(u)$ that is implicitly defined by (A.4) has a derivative

$$Dp(0) = -[D_p\Phi(\bar{p}; 0)]^{-1}D_u\Phi(\bar{p}; 0).$$

The last result implies that a first-order Taylor series approximation to the solution, for values of u near enough to 0, is given by

$$p(u) = \bar{p} - [D_p\Phi(\bar{p}; 0)]^{-1}D_u\Phi(\bar{p}; 0) \cdot u. \qquad\qquad (A.5)$$

This approximate solution is accurate up to an error term of order $\mathcal{O}(\|u\|^2)$, and the method used to obtain it can be described as follows. One first *linearizes* the equilibrium conditions (A.4), replacing each of the functions in the vector Φ by a first-order Taylor series approximation, expanding around the point $(\bar{p}; 0)$.[2] The approximate system of equilibrium conditions obtained is

---

2. This is a *log-linear* approximation to the equilibrium conditions in the case that the vector p actually represents the logs of various endogenous variables, as is the case of most of the applications in this book.

$$[D_p\Phi(\bar{p}; 0)](p - \bar{p}) + [D_u\Phi(\bar{p}; 0)]u = 0. \tag{A.6}$$

Next, one checks whether the linearized system of equations has a unique solution; this is true if and only if $D_p\Phi(\bar{p}; 0)$ is nonsingular, and therefore invertible. Third, one computes the unique solution to the linearized equations and uses this as the approximate solution to the exact equations. Note that the solution to the linearized system is just (A.5), so that the implicit function theorem (together with Taylor's theorem) implies that this is indeed a valid local approximation to the exact solution.

The same method can be applied, with a little care, to the equilibrium conditions of dynamic models as well. Suppose instead that I have a system of n equations *per period*, of the form

$$f(p_{t-1}, p_t, p_{t+1}; u_t) = 0, \tag{A.7}$$

for each $t \geq 0$, to determine the evolution of the sequence $\{p_t\}$ for $t \geq 0$, given an initial condition p_{-1} and a sequence of m disturbances per period $\{u_t\}$. Here I suppose that the entire sequence $\{u_t\}$ is known with certainty at date $t = 0$ and consider only equilibria in which the future evolution of the endogenous variables is known with certainty as well. Thus I wish to characterize *perfect-foresight equilibria* of the dynamic model. (The equilibrium condition indicates that p_t is affected at date t by the anticipated value of p_{t+1}; the actual value of p_{t+1} enters as an argument because of the assumption of perfect foresight.)

Suppose it is known that $\bar{p}$ is a *steady-state* equilibrium in the absence of disturbances; that is, that if the system starts off with initial condition $p_{-1} = \bar{p}$, and the disturbances are $u_t = 0$ for all t, then one possible perfect-foresight equilibrium is $p_t = \bar{p}$ for all t. This requires that the value $\bar{p}$ satisfy

$$f(\bar{p}, \bar{p}, \bar{p}; 0) = 0.$$

(Note that this is a system of n equations to determine the n elements of the steady-state values $\bar{p}$.) A first question to consider is whether this equilibrium is at least *locally* unique. (Global uniqueness would also be of interest, as discussed in Section 4 of Chapter 2, but cannot be determined using purely local methods.) The inverse function theorem (suitably generalized) can again be used to answer this question.

The complete sequence of equilibrium conditions (A.7) for all $t \geq 0$ can be thought of as a system of the form (A.4), where now p refers to the entire infinite sequence $\{p_t\}$ for $t \geq 0$; u is similarly the entire infinite sequence $\{u_t\}$ for $t \geq 0$, together with the specification of the initial condition p_{-1}; and Φ is a function that maps these infinite sequences to the infinite sequence $\{f_t\}$ for $t \geq 0$, where f_t is the vector of values of the n functions in (A.7) for period t. Near the particular solution $\bar{p}$ (the steady state) in the case that

$u = 0^3$ one may define the derivative mapping $D_p\Phi(\bar{p}; 0)$; this is the linear operator that maps a sequence of perturbations $\{\hat{p}_t\}$ for $t \geq 0$ (where one defines $\hat{p}_t \equiv p_t - \bar{p}$) into the sequence of perturbations $\{\hat{f}_t\}$ for $t \geq 0$, where

$$\hat{f}_t = f_1\hat{p}_{t-1} + f_2\hat{p}_t + f_3\hat{p}_{t+1} \tag{A.8}$$

for each $t \geq 0$.[4] Here for $j = 1, 2, 3, f_j \equiv D_j f(\bar{p}, \bar{p}, \bar{p}; 0)$ is the matrix of partial derivatives of the functions f with respect to their jth vector of arguments, evaluated at the steady-state values of those arguments.

Application of the inverse function theorem requires that this derivative mapping be a continuous linear operator *and* that it have a continuous inverse mapping.[5] In the finite-dimensional case, any matrix of partial derivatives represents a continuous linear operator, and the existence of a continuous inverse simply requires that the matrix be nonsingular. In the infinite-dimensional case, the requirement of continuity of the linear operator represented by the derivative mapping is not so trivial; it requires that the operator be bounded (which is no longer guaranteed by linearity alone). That is, the sequence $\{\hat{f}_t\}$ must be bounded in the case of any bounded sequence $\{\hat{p}_t\}$. Assuming the l_∞ (or sup norm) topology on the linear space of sequences, one then requires that $\hat{f}_t$ satisfy some uniform bound for all t in the case that each of the $\hat{p}_t$ satisfy some uniform bound. (This is necessarily true of the kind of linear operator represented by (A.8).) Similarly, invertibility of the derivative operator requires that the sequence of conditions has a unique bounded solution $\{\hat{p}_t\}$ in the case of any bounded sequence $\{\hat{f}_t\}$. This may or may not be true, even when all of the partial derivatives in the matrices f_j are well defined. In the case considered here, the condition obtains (generically) if and only if the characteristic equation

$$\det[f_3\lambda^2 + f_2\lambda + f_1] = 0 \tag{A.9}$$

has exactly n roots inside the unit circle (i.e., such that $|\lambda| < 1$) and n roots outside ($|\lambda| > 1$). If this condition obtains, the inverse function theorem implies that the steady state is a locally unique solution to the equilibrium conditions. That is, there is no other equilibrium in which p_t is within some neighborhood of $\bar{p}$ for all t, except the one in which $p_t = \bar{p}$ exactly for all t.

Note that (A.8) is again just a linearization of equations (A.7) for the case in which $p_{-1} = \bar{p}$ and $u_t = 0$ for all t, and the invertibility condition

3. Here I parameterize the element of u that specifies p_{-1} so that $u = 0$ implies that $p_{-1} = \bar{p}$,

4. The first term on the right-hand side is suppressed in the case that $t = 0$, since the definition of the sequence p does not include an element p_{-1}.

5. See, e.g., Lang (1983, chap. 6) for statements of the inverse and implicit function theorems for infinite-dimensional spaces.

simply requires that one check that the linearized equations can be uniquely solved. The only important detail is that in the infinite-dimensional case one must check for the existence of a unique *bounded* solution to the linearized equations. The inverse function theorem indicates that when the linearized equations have a unique bounded solution (the zero solution), the exact equations have a unique solution that remains forever near the steady state, namely, the steady state itself.

As in the finite-dimensional case, when this invertibility condition is satisfied, one can also use the implicit function theorem to show the existence of a locally unique solution in the case of any small enough perturbations of the equilibrium conditions. That is, it can be shown that for any initial condition p_{-1} close enough to $\bar{p}$ and for any disturbance sequence u_t that remains within a small enough neighborhood of zero for all t, there exists a locally unique associated equilibrium sequence $\{p_t\}$. That is, there exists a neighborhood of $\bar{p}$ such that this is the only perfect-foresight equilibrium for which p_t remains within this neighborhood for all t. Furthermore, this locally unique solution can be approximated (to first order) by the (unique bounded) solution $\{\hat{p}_t\}$ to the linearized equilibrium conditions

$$f_1\hat{p}_{t-1} + f_2\hat{p}_t + f_3\hat{p}_{t+1} = u_t \tag{A.10}$$

consistent with the initial condition $\hat{p}_{-1}$. The (locally unique) exact solution coincides with this solution to the linearized conditions up to an error term of order $\mathcal{O}(\|u\|^2)$, where now $\|u\|$ is both a uniform bound on the size of the disturbances u_t for all t and a bound on the distance $\hat{p}_{-1}$ of the initial condition from consistency with the steady state.[6]

Similar methods can be employed in the case of models with stochastic disturbances, or more generally when one is interested in possible equilibria in which the endogenous variables are stochastic (possibly responding to sunspot states). Suppose that the equilibrium conditions are of the form

$$E_t[f(p_{t-1}, p_t, p_{t+1}; u_t)] = 0 \tag{A.11}$$

for each period t. Here u_t is now a stochastic disturbance, and I allow the endogenous variables p_t to be functions of the exogenous state of the world s_t in period t, where s_t includes the complete history of the fundamental disturbances u_t, all information available at t about the probability distribution of future fundamentals, and possibly nonfundamental sunspot states as well. $E_t[\cdot]$ denotes the expectation conditional upon the state of the world s_t in period t.

6. See Woodford (1998) for further discussion of the method and an application.

This may again be viewed as a system of the form (A.4), where now p is a sequence of bounded measurable functions $\{p_t(s_t)\}$, u is a similar sequence of bounded measurable functions $\{u_t(s_t)\}$, together with a specification of the initial condition p_{-1}, and Φ maps these sequences of functions into a sequence of bounded measurable functions $\{f_t(s_t)\}$. Again the bounded measurable functions form a linear space, which is a Banach space (as required in order to use the generalized inverse and implicit function theorems) if I assume the L_∞ topology, under which the norm of a bounded measurable function $\hat{p}$ is the least bound, such that $\|p_t(s_t)\|$ satisfies the bound almost surely for all t.

The steady state $\bar{p}$ (now meaning that $p_t(s_t) = \bar{p}$ in every state of the world at each date t) is again a solution in the case that $p_{-1} = \bar{p}$ and $u_t = 0$ for all t (similarly, in every state of the world). I can again define a derivative mapping $D_p\Phi(\bar{p}; 0)$, evaluated at the steady state. This is the linear operator that maps a sequence of perturbations $\{\hat{p}_t\}$ for $t \geq 0$ (where for each t, $\hat{p}_t$ is now a bounded measurable function) into the sequence of perturbations $\{\hat{f}_t\}$ for $t \geq 0$, where

$$\hat{f}_t = f_1\hat{p}_{t-1} + f_2\hat{p}_t + f_3E_t\hat{p}_{t+1} \tag{A.12}$$

is also a bounded measurable function for each $t \geq 0$. The form of the linear operator (A.12) necessarily maps bounded processes $\{\hat{p}_t\}$ to bounded processes $\{\hat{f}_t\}$. The inverse and implicit function theorems can then be invoked if and only if the matrices of coefficients $\{f_j\}$ are such that the system (A.12) has a unique bounded solution $\{\hat{p}_t\}$ in the case of any bounded process $\{\hat{f}_t\}$. Again this is true, generically, if and only if (A.9) has exactly n roots inside the unit circle and n roots outside.[7]

When this invertibility condition is satisfied, the system of equations (A.11) has a locally unique solution (a solution that is always near the steady-state values $\bar{p}$) in the case of any initial condition p_{-1} near enough to $\bar{p}$ and any disturbance process $\{u_t\}$ that is small enough at all times. This locally unique solution can furthermore be approximated (to first order in a bound on the amplitude of the disturbances) by the unique bounded solution to the linearized equilibrium conditions

$$f_1\hat{p}_{t-1} + f_2\hat{p}_t + f_3E_t\hat{p}_{t+1} = u_t. \tag{A.13}$$

Accordingly, I proceed throughout this study by linearizing (or log-linearizing) the equilibrium conditions, proceeding from exact equilibrium relations of a form such as (A.11) to the corresponding linearized equations

---

7. See Woodford (1986) for further discussion of the application of the implicit function theorem to nonlinear rational-expectations models of this kind.

(A.13), and then address the question whether the latter system has a unique bounded solution in the case of bounded disturbances. The latter issue—what is called the (local) *determinacy* of rational-expectations equilibrium—is of interest not only because of the question of the local uniqueness of equilibrium, but also because this is the condition under which one can employ the implicit function theorem to justify approximation of the equilibrium of the present model by the unique bounded solution to the system of linearized equilibrium relations.

The question whether a particular linear model such as (A.12) has a unique bounded solution is thus one that recurs throughout this study. General methods for addressing it are discussed in references such as Blanchard and Kahn (1980), Klein (1997), and Soderlind (1998). Results for certain simple classes of linear models that occur repeatedly in this study are presented in Section A.4 and in Section C.1 of Appendix C.

A.4 Proof of Proposition 2.3

PROPOSITION 2.3. *Under a Wicksellian policy rule (1.30) with $\phi_p > 0$, the rational-expectations equilibrium paths of prices and interest rates are (locally) determinate; that is, there exist open sets $\mathcal{P}$ and $\mathcal{I}$ such that in the case of any tight enough bounds on the fluctuations in the exogenous processes $\{\hat{r}_t, \pi_t^*, v_t\}$, there exists a unique rational-expectations equilibrium in which $P_t/P_t^* \in \mathcal{P}$ and $i_t \in \mathcal{I}$ at all times. Furthermore, equations (1.37) and (1.38) of Chapter 2 give a log-linear (first-order Taylor series) approximation to that solution, accurate up to a residual of order $\mathcal{O}(\|\xi\|^2)$, where $\|\xi\|$ indexes the bounds on the disturbance processes.*

PROOF: This is a direct application of the implicit function theorem, as discussed in the previous section. As discussed in the text, (1.32) and (1.34) represent log-linear (first-order Taylor-series) approximations to the equilibrium relations (1.21) and (1.30). The existence of a unique bounded solution to the log-linearized relations implies the existence of a locally unique solution to the exact relations as well, in the case of any tight enough bound on the exogenous disturbances, using the inverse function theorem, and that solution to the log-linearized relations provides a first-order Taylor-series approximation to the solution to the exact relations, using the implicit function theorem. If the neighborhoods $\mathcal{P}$ and $\mathcal{I}$ are small enough, any solution to the exact relations restricted to these sets must also satisfy the transversality condition (1.24), and so represents a rational-expectations equilibrium.

It thus remains only to demonstrate that the system consisting of (1.32) and (1.34), together with the identity (1.35), has a unique bounded solution when $\phi_p > 0$. As shown in the text, these equations imply (1.36). This is a form of expectational difference equation that occurs repeatedly in Chapter 2, which may be written in the form

$$z_t = aE_t z_{t+1} + u_t, \tag{A.14}$$

where z_t is an endogenous variable and u_t is an exogenous disturbance process. In the present application, $z_t = \hat{P}_t$, $a = (1 + \phi_p)^{-1}$, and

$$u_t = (1 + \phi_p)^{-1} \left(\hat{r}_t + E_t \pi_{t+1}^* - v_t \right).$$

Any expectational difference equation of the form (A.14) has a unique bounded solution $\{z_t\}$ in the case of an arbitrary bounded disturbance process $\{u_t\}$ in the case that $|a| < 1$. Note that (A.14) implies that

$$E_t z_{t+j} = aE_t z_{t+j+1} + E_t u_{t+j}$$

for arbitrary $j \geq 0$. Multiplying this equation by a^j and summing from $j = 0$ through $k - 1$ yields

$$z_t = a^k E_t z_{t+k} + \sum_{j=0}^{k-1} a^j E_t u_{t+j}. \tag{A.15}$$

Note that this equation must hold for arbitrary k. If $\{z_t\}$ is a bounded process and $|a| < 1$, it follows that

$$\lim_{k \to \infty} a^k E_t z_{t+k} = 0.$$

Then, since the left-hand side of (A.15) is independent of k, it follows that the final term on the right must converge in value as k is made unboundedly large, and specifically to the value of the left-hand side. Thus one must have

$$z_t = \sum_{j=0}^{\infty} a^j E_t u_{t+j}. \tag{A.16}$$

(This solution is sometimes said to be obtained by solving (A.14) forward.)

Equation (A.15) represents not just one possible solution to (A.14), but the unique bounded solution. In the present application, (A.16) yields equation (1.37). Substitution of this into (1.34) then yields (1.38) as well.

For future reference, it is also useful to consider the case in which $|a| \geq 1$. In this case, the process $\{z_t\}$ recursively defined by

$$z_t = a^{-1}(z_{t-1} - u_{t-1}) + v_t \tag{A.17}$$

for all $t \geq 1$, starting from an arbitrary initial condition z_0, represents a solution to (A.14) in the case of any process $\{v_t\}$ such that $E_t v_{t+1} = 0$ for all t. If $|a| > 1$, (A.17) represents a bounded solution for $\{z_t\}$ in the case of any bounded process $\{v_t\}$, assuming that $\{u_t\}$ is bounded as well. Hence there is an extremely large set of bounded solutions $\{z_t\}$ to equation (A.14).

In the case that $|a| = 1$ exactly, not all solutions of the form (A.17) are bounded, even if both $\{u_t\}$ and $\{v_t\}$ are bounded processes. Nonetheless, if (A.14) has any bounded solution, it must have an uncountably infinite number of them. Let $\{\bar{z}_t\}$ be one bounded solution. (For example, in the case that

$$v_t \equiv \sum_{j=0}^{\infty} E_t u_{t+j}$$

is well-defined and bounded, as is true for any stationary ARMA process $\{u_t\}$ with bounded innovations, then one bounded solution to (A.14) is given by $\bar{z}_t = v_t$, the solution obtained by solving forward.) Then another bounded solution is recursively defined by

$$z_t = \bar{z}_t + (z_{t-1} - \bar{z}_{t-1}) + v_t$$

for all $t \geq 1$, starting from an arbitrary initial condition z_0, where $\{v_t\}$ is any stochastic process such that $E_t v_{t+1} = 0$ for all t, *and* such that $\sum_{t=1}^{T} v_t$ remains bounded for arbitrarily large T. This last stipulation can obviously be satisfied by a large number of mean-zero, unforecastable processes; for example, it suffices that v_t be bounded for each t, and equal to zero with probability one for all t greater than some date T. Hence in this case as well, there are clearly an uncountably infinite number of bounded solutions. Thus the condition that $|a| < 1$ is both necessary and sufficient for the existence of a unique bounded solution to (A.14).

A.5 Proof of Proposition 2.4

PROPOSITION 2.4. Consider a monetary policy under which the monetary base is bounded below by a positive quantity: $M_t^s \geq \underline{M} > 0$ at all times. (For example, perhaps the monetary base is nondecreasing over time, starting from an initial level $M_0^s > 0$.) Suppose furthermore that government debt is nonnegative at all times, so that $D_t \geq M_t^s$. Finally, suppose that $i_t^m = 0$ at all times. Then in the cashless economy described in Section 1.2 of Chapter 2, there exists no rational-expectations equilibrium path for the price level $\{P_t\}$.

PROOF: If $i_t^m = 0$ at all times, equation (1.15) of Chapter 2 requires that in any equilibrium, $i_t = 0$ at all times. Then (1.21) requires that

$$\beta E_t [u_c(Y_{t+1}; \xi_{t+1})/p_{t+1}] = u_c(Y_t; \xi_t)/P_t$$

at all times, and hence, by iteration, that

$$\beta^T E_t [u_c(Y_T; \xi_T)/P_T] = \beta^t u_c(Y_t; \xi_t)/P_t$$

for all $T \geq t$. But this, together with the lower bound $D_t \geq \underline{M} > 0$, implies that

$$\beta^T E_t [u_c(Y_T; \xi_T) D_T/P_T] \geq \underline{M}\beta^T E_t [u_c(Y_T; \xi_T)/P_T]$$
$$= \underline{M}\beta^t E_t [u_c(Y_t; \xi_t)/P_t] > 0,$$

which contradicts (A.2). Hence no equilibrium is possible.

In fact, equilibrium values could be defined under such a regime for *real* rates of return and asset prices. If one writes prices in terms of some real numeraire rather than monetary units, a well-defined equilibrium would exist, but would involve zero exchange value for money. In essence, under the regime described, money is a pure "bubble"—an asset the exchange value of which would have to be sustained purely by the expectation of a future exchange value, and not any dividends ever yielded by the asset—and cannot have an exchange value in a rational-expectations equilibrium, at least not in a representative-household model of the kind assumed here. (In fact, a similar result can be obtained in much more general environments, as shown by Santos and Woodford, 1997.) Instead, under the regime to which Proposition 2.3 applies, interest is paid on money, and—the crucial point—this interest is not simply additional money that remains forever in circulation. Because private-sector nominal claims on the government D_t are assumed to grow at a rate *less* than the rate at which interest is paid on money—recall that $\gamma_D < \bar{\pi}/\beta = 1 + \phi(1; 0) = 1 + \bar{\imath}^m$—at least some of the money received as interest payments is eventually redeemed by the government (accepted as payment for taxes), so that money ceases to be a pure bubble.

A.6   Proof of Proposition 2.5

PROPOSITION 2.5. *Let monetary policy be specified by an exogenous sequence of interest-rate targets, assumed to remain forever within a neighborhood of the interest rate $\bar{\imath} > 0$ associated with the zero-inflation steady state; and let these be implemented by setting i_t^m equal to the interest-rate* target each period. Let $\{M_t^s, D_t\}$ be exogenous sequences of the kind assumed in Proposition 2.3. Finally, let $\mathcal{P}$ be any neighborhood of the real number zero. Then for any tight enough bounds on the exogenous processes $\{Y_t, \xi_t D_t/D_{t-1}\}$ and on the interest-rate target process, there exists an uncountably infinite set of rational-expectations equilibrium paths for the price level, in each of which the inflation rate satisfies $\pi_t \in \mathcal{P}$ for all t. These include equilibria in which the inflation rate is affected to an arbitrary extent by fundamental disturbances (unexpected changes in Y_t or ξ_t), by pure sunspot states (exogenous randomness unrelated to the "fundamental" variables), or both.

As discussed in the text of Chapter 2, this can be established using the local methods discussed in Section A.3; see Woodford (1986). However, in the present case, the equilibrium relations are simple enough to analyze without any need to resort to linear approximation.

Proof: Let $\{v_t\}$ be any unforecastable mean-zero random variable (or martingale difference) such that $v_t < 1$ at all times. Then the inflation process given by

$$\frac{P_t}{p_{t-1}} = \beta \frac{1 + i_{t-1}^m}{u_c(Y_{t-1}; \xi_{t-1})} E_{t-1}[u_c(Y_t; \xi_t)(1 - v_t)] \frac{1}{1 - v_t}$$

satisfies equation (1.21) in Chapter 2 at all times. (Note that the solutions (2.3) presented in Chapter 2 are log-linear approximations to these processes.) In the case of tight enough bounds on both the exogenous variables and the fluctuations in $\{v_t\}$, this yields an inflation process such that $\pi_t \in \mathcal{P}$ at all times, and satisfies (A.2) as well. Hence any such solution represents a rational-expectations equilibrium. The solutions corresponding to different choices of $\{v_t\}$ represent distinct equilibria, since in each case the surprise component of inflation is given by

$$\pi_t - E_{t-1}\pi_t = -\log(1 - v_t).$$

Finally, the variable $\{v_t\}$ may be correlated in an arbitrary way with any of the fundamental variables, or it may be completely independent of them.

A.7 Proof of Proposition 2.7

PROPOSITION 2.7. Let monetary policy be described by a feedback rule of the form (2.9), at least near the zero-inflation steady state, with $\Phi_\pi \geq 0$. Then equilibrium is determinate if and only if $\Phi_\pi > 1$. When this condition is satisfied, a log-linear approximation to the equilibrium evolution of the smoothed inflation process is given by

$$\bar{\pi}_t = (1 - \delta) \sum_{j=0}^{\infty} (\delta + (1 - \delta)\Phi_\pi)^{-(j+1)} E_t\big[\hat{r}_{t+j} - \bar{\imath}_{t+j}\big]. \qquad \text{(A.18)}$$

A corresponding approximation to the equilibrium evolution of the single-period inflation rate π_t is then obtained by substituting (A.18) into

$$\pi_t = \frac{\bar{\pi}_t - \delta \bar{\pi}_{t-1}}{1 - \delta}. \qquad \text{(A.19)}$$

PROOF: The solution (2.12) for π_t given the evolution of $\bar{\pi}_t$ is obtained by inverting equation (2.8) of Chapter 2. Then substituting (2.9) into (1.32) to eliminate i_t gives

$$\Phi_\pi \bar{\pi}_t = E_t \pi_{t+1} + (\hat{r}_t - \bar{\imath}_t).$$

Substituting (2.12) for π_t in this equation, one obtains an expectational difference equation for the smoothed inflation measure,

$$[\delta + (1 - \delta)\Phi_\pi]\bar{\pi}_t = E_t \bar{\pi}_{t+1} + (1 - \delta)(\hat{r}_t - \bar{\imath}_t). \qquad \text{(A.20)}$$

This is again an equation of the form (A.14), allowing one to apply the same method as in the proof of Proposition 2.3. The equation can be solved forward to obtain a unique bounded solution if and only if

$$\delta + (1 - \delta)\Phi_\pi > 1,$$

which is to say, if and only if $\Phi_\pi > 1$, as required by the Taylor principle. When this condition holds, the solution (A.15) is given by (A.18).

A.8   Proof of Proposition 2.8

PROPOSITION 2.8. Let monetary policy be described by a feedback rule of the form of equation (2.12) of Chapter 2, at least near the zero-inflation steady state, with $\phi_\pi, \rho \geq 0$. Then equilibrium is determinate if and only if $\phi_\pi > 0$ and

$$\phi_\pi + \rho > 1. \qquad \text{(A.21)}$$

When these conditions are satisfied, a log-linear approximation to the equilibrium evolution of inflation is given by (2.14).

PROOF: The proof follows the same lines as in the case of Proposition 2.7. Using (2.12) to eliminate π_{t+1} in (1.32), one obtains an expectational difference equation

$$(\phi_\pi + \rho)\hat{\imath}_t = E_t\hat{\imath}_{t+1} + \phi_\pi\hat{r}_t + \rho\bar{\imath}_t - E_t\bar{\imath}_{t+1},$$

corresponding to (A.20) above, and once again this is of the form (A.14). Applying the same method as in the proof of Proposition 2.3, one finds that there is a unique bounded solution for $\{\hat{\imath}_t\}$ if and only if

$$|\phi_\pi + \rho| > 1 \tag{A.22}$$

is satisfied. Under the sign assumptions made in the statement of the proposition, condition (A.22) reduces to (A.21). By solving forward, that is, applying (A.15), one obtains (2.15) as the solution for the interest-rate process.

Corresponding to this solution for the path of the interest rate is a unique solution for $\{\pi_t\}$, obtained by inverting (2.12), if and only if $\phi_\pi \neq 0$. Hence there is a unique bounded solution for $\{\pi_t\}$ if $\phi_\pi > 0$ and (A.21) applies. Using the solution obtained for $\{\hat{\imath}_t\}$, one obtains the solution (2.14) for the inflation process.

If instead $\phi_\pi = 0$, there is a multiplicity of possible solutions for $\{\pi_t\}$, even when the equilibrium path $\{\hat{\imath}_t\}$ is uniquely determined. In fact, Proposition 2.5 again applies in this case. If $\phi_\pi > 0$ but $0 < \phi_\pi + \rho < 1$, there is an uncountably infinite number of solutions for $\{\hat{\imath}_t\}$, as one can show using the method discussed following the proof of Proposition 2.3. To each of these there corresponds a unique associated inflation process, but the set of equilibrium inflation processes is uncountably infinite.

As remarked in the text, determinacy of equilibrium does not require that $\phi_\pi > 0$, though that is the case of primary practical interest. The earlier analysis shows that in fact all that is required is that $\phi_\pi \neq 0$ and that (A.22) be satisfied. When $\rho > 1$, the latter condition is satisfied by all nonzero inflation-response coefficients $\phi_\pi > -(\rho-1)$, which would include moderately negative values. In such a case, (2.14) continues to provide a log-linear approximation to the equilibrium inflation process. The conditions for determinacy would also be satisfied by all $\phi_\pi < -(1+\rho)$. (Note that this means that determinacy results from sufficiently large negative values of ϕ_π even in the case that $\rho < 1$.) However, the equilibrium obtained in this case depends too crucially upon the assumption of a discrete sequence of dates on which markets are open to be of practical interest. (In the continuous-time limit of the model, no such equilibria are possible. See the discussion at the end of Section 3.4 of Chapter 2.)

A.9 Proof of Proposition 2.9

PROPOSITION 2.9. Suppose that the equilibrium real rate $\{\hat{r}_t\}$ follows an exogenously given stationary AR(1) process, and let the monetary policy rule be of the form of equation (2.12) of Chapter 2, with $\rho \geq 0, \phi_\pi > 0$ and a constant intercept consistent with the zero-inflation steady state (i.e.,

$\bar{\imath}_t = 0$). Consider the choice of a policy rule (ρ, ϕ_π) within this class so as to bring about a certain desired unconditional variance of inflation $\text{var}(\pi) > 0$ around the mean inflation rate of zero. For any large enough value of ρ, there exists a ϕ_π satisfying (A.21) such that the unconditional variance of inflation in the stationary rational-expectations equilibrium associated with this rule is of the desired magnitude. Furthermore, the larger is ρ, the *smaller* is the unconditional variance of interest-rate fluctuations $\text{var}(\hat{\imath})$ in this equilibrium.

PROOF: In the case of an AR(1) process

$$\hat{r}_t = \rho_r \hat{r}_{t-1} + \epsilon_t$$

for the equilibrium real rate, $E_t \hat{r}_{t+j} = \rho_r^j \hat{r}_t$ for all $j \geq 0$. Then for any policy rule (ρ, ϕ_π) that satisfies (A.21), (2.15) implies that

$$\hat{\imath}_t = \frac{\phi_\pi}{\phi_\pi + \rho - \rho_r} \hat{r}_t.$$

Hence $\{\hat{\imath}_t\}$ is also an AR(1) process, with variance and first-order autocovariance

$$\text{var}(\hat{\imath}) = \left(\frac{\phi_\pi}{\phi_\pi + \rho - \rho_r} \right)^2 \text{var}(\hat{r}), \qquad (A.23)$$

$$\text{cov}(\hat{\imath}_t, \hat{\imath}_{t-1}) = \rho_r \text{var}(\hat{\imath}).$$

Inverting (2.12) implies that $\pi_t = \phi_\pi^{-1}(\hat{\imath}_t - \hat{\imath}_{t-1})$, from which it follows that

$$\text{var}(\pi) = \phi_\pi^{-2} \text{var}(\hat{\imath}_t - \rho \hat{\imath}_{t-1})$$

$$= \phi_\pi^{-2} \left[(1 + \rho^2) \text{var}(\hat{\imath}) - 2\rho \text{cov}(\hat{\imath}_t, \hat{\imath}_{t-1}) \right]$$

$$= \frac{1 - 2\rho_r \rho + \rho^2}{(\phi_\pi + \rho - \rho_r)^2} \text{var}(\hat{r}). \qquad (A.24)$$

Condition (A.24) can be solved for the required inflation-response coefficient in order to obtain a given degree of variability of inflation, yielding

$$\phi_\pi = \left[(1 - 2\rho_r \rho + \rho^2) \frac{\text{var}(\hat{r})}{\text{var}(\pi)} \right]^{1/2} + \rho_r - \rho.$$

(Here I select the positive square root because I know that if a solution exists that satisfies (A.21), it must be such that $\phi_\pi > \rho_r - \rho$.) Note that for all large enough $\rho > 0$, the right-hand-side expression must exceed $1 - \rho$, in which case there is indeed a solution satisfying (A.21), as asserted in the proposition.

This solution can then be substituted for ϕ_π in (A.23), yielding

$$\sigma(\hat{\imath}) = \sigma(\hat{r}) - \frac{\rho - \rho_r}{(1 - 2\rho_r\rho + \rho^2)^{1/2}}\sigma(\pi), \qquad (A.25)$$

where $\sigma(x) \equiv (\mathrm{var}(x))^{1/2}$ in the case of any stationary random variable x. The expression

$$\frac{\rho - \rho_r}{(1 - 2\rho_r\rho + \rho^2)^{1/2}} = \frac{\rho - \rho_r}{[(1 - \rho_r^2) + (\rho - \rho_r)^2]^{1/2}}$$

is easily seen to be monotonically increasing in ρ, so that the right-hand side of (A.23) is monotonically decreasing in ρ, for any given value of ϕ_π.

A.10   Proof of Proposition 2.10

PROPOSITION 2.10. Consider a policy rule of the form (2.12), where $\rho > 1$ and $\{\bar{\imath}_t\}$ is a bounded process, to be adopted beginning at some date t_0. Then any bounded processes $\{\pi_t, \hat{\imath}_t\}$ that satisfy (2.12) for all $t \geq t_0$ must be such that the predicted path of inflation, looking forward from any date $t \geq t_0$, satisfies (2.17). Conversely, any bounded processes satisfying (2.17) for all $t \geq t_0$ also satisfy (2.12) for all $t \geq t_0$.

PROOF: Note that (2.12) can equivalently be written

$$\hat{\imath}_{t-1} - \bar{\imath}_{t-1} = -\rho^{-1}\phi_\pi\pi_t + \rho^{-1}E_t[\hat{\imath}_t - \bar{\imath}_t].$$

This is yet another stochastic difference equation of the form (A.14), where now $z_t \equiv \hat{\imath}_{t-1} - \bar{\imath}_{t-1}$ happens to be a variable that is predetermined at date t. It follows from the discussion in the proof of Proposition 2.3 that if $|a| < 1$, any bounded solution to (A.14) must satisfy (A.16). In the present case, this result applies if $\rho > 1$, since in this case $0 < \rho^{-1} < 1$, and equation (2.17) of Chapter 2 is just the condition corresponding to (A.16).

The converse is established by noting that (A.16) implies that z_t satisfies (A.14). This was implicit in the previous characterization of (A.16) as a "solution" of equation (A.14). In the present application, it does not make sense to call condition (2.17) a "solution" for the variable $\hat{\imath}_{t-1} - \bar{\imath}_{t-1}$, for this variable is determined at date $t - 1$, whereas the right-hand side of (2.17) depends on information at date t. Instead, (2.17) indicates the way in which the central bank's inflation target at date t varies depending on past conditions.

A.11   Proof of Proposition 2.11

PROPOSITION 2.11.   In the context of a Sidrauski-Brock model with additively separable preferences, consider the consequences of a monetary policy specified in terms of exogenous paths $\{M^s_t, i^m_t\}$, together with a fiscal
policy specified by an exogenous path $\{D_t\}$. Under such a regime, the
rational-expectations equilibrium paths of prices and interest rates are (lo-
cally) determinate; that is, there exist open sets $\mathcal{P}$ and $\mathcal{I}$ such that in the case
of any tight enough bounds on the fluctuations in the exogenous processes
$\{Y_t, \xi_t, M^s_t/M^s_{t-1}, i^m_t, D_t/D_{t-1}\}$, there exists a unique rational-expectations
equilibrium in which $P_t/M^s_t \in \mathcal{P}$ and $i_t \in \mathcal{I}$ at all times. Furthermore, a log-
linear approximation to the equilibrium path of the price level, accurate up
to a residual of order $\mathcal{O}(\|\xi\|^2)$, takes the form

$$\log P_t = \sum_{j=0}^{\infty} \varphi_j E_t \left[\log M^s_{t+j} - \eta_i \log \left(1 + i^m_t\right) - u_{t+j} \right] - \log \bar{m}, \quad \text{(A.26)}$$

where the weights

$$\varphi_j \equiv \frac{\eta_i^j}{(1 + \eta_i)^{j+1}} > 0$$

sum to one, and u_t is a composite exogenous disturbance

$$u_t \equiv \eta_y \hat{Y}_t - \eta_i \hat{r}_t + \epsilon^m_t - \eta_i \log(1 + \bar{i}^m).$$

PROOF: Once again, one may ignore conditions (1.24) and (3.4) of Chap-
ter 2, as these are satisfied by any processes $\{P_t/M^s_t, i_t, i^m_t, M^s_t/M^s_{t-1}, D_t/D_{t-1}, Y_t, \xi_t\}$ that satisfy tight enough bounds. It then suffices that one consider the
existence of bounded solutions to the system of log-linear relations consist-
ing of (1.32) and (3.6), augmented by the identity

$$\hat{m}_t = \hat{m}_{t-1} + \mu_t - \pi_t, \quad \text{(A.27)}$$

where $\mu_t \equiv \log(M^s_t/M^s_{t-1})$ is the exogenous rate of growth in the monetary
base. This comprises a system of three expectational difference equations
per period to determine the three endogenous variables $\hat{m}_t$, π_t, and $\hat{i}_t$.

Using (1.32) to eliminate $\hat{i}_t$ in (3.6), I obtain a discrete-time rational-
expectations version of the Cagan model of inflation determination,

$$\hat{m}_t = -\eta_i E_t \pi_{t+1} + \left[u_t + \eta_i \log \left(1 + i^m_t\right) \right], \quad \text{(A.28)}$$

where u_t is the composite exogenous disturbance defined in the statement
of the proposition. Then, when (A.27) is used to substitute for π_{t+1}, (A.28)
implies that

$$\hat{m}_t = \alpha E_t \hat{m}_{t+1} + (1-\alpha)\big[u_t + \eta_i \log\left(1+i_t^m\right) - \eta_i E_t \mu_{t+1}\big], \quad \text{(A.29)}$$

where $\alpha \equiv \eta_i/(1+\eta_i)$.

This is once again an expectational difference equation of the form (A.14). Because $\eta_i > 0$ implies that $0 < \alpha < 1$, (A.29) can be solved forward to obtain a unique bounded solution for $\{\hat{m}_t\}$, given by

$$\hat{m}_t = (1-\alpha)\sum_{j=0}^{\infty}\alpha^j E_t\big[u_{t+j} + \eta_i \log\left(1+i_t^m\right) - \eta_i \mu_{t+j+1}\big]. \quad \text{(A.30)}$$

Such a unique solution for $\{\hat{m}_t\}$ then implies a unique solution for $\{\hat{\imath}_t\}$, using equation (3.6) of Chapter 2, and for $\{\pi_t\}$, using (A.27). It then follows from the discussion in Section A.3 that there is also a locally unique solution to the exact equilibrium relations (1.21) and (3.5) in the case of tight enough bounds on the exogenous processes. Furthermore, this solution satisfies any desired bounds on $\hat{m}_t$ and $\hat{\imath}_t$. (Since $P_t/M_t^s = 1/m_t$, this allows me to ensure that $P_t/M_t^s \in \mathcal{P}$ at all times.) Finally, I observe that (A.29) can be rewritten as (A.26).

A.12 Proof of Proposition 2.12

PROPOSITION 2.12. In a Sidrauski-Brock model where utility is not necessarily separable, let monetary policy be specified by a Wicksellian rule, equation (1.30) of Chapter 2, for the central bank's interest-rate operating target. Suppose that $i_t^m = \bar{\imath}$ at all times, for some $0 \le \bar{\imath} < \beta^{-1} - 1$; and let fiscal policy again be specified by an exogenous process $\{D_t\}$. Finally, suppose that

$$\chi > -1/2\eta_i. \quad \text{(A.31)}$$

Then equilibrium is determinate in the case of any policy rule with $\phi_p > 0$. A log-linear approximation to the locally unique equilibrium price process is given by (3.17), where the weights are given by (3.18) and (3.19).

PROOF: Substituting (1.34) for $\hat{\imath}_t$ in (3.12), and setting $\hat{\imath}_t^m = 0$, one obtains the equilibrium relation

$$(1+(1+\eta_i\chi)\phi_p)\hat{P}_t = (1+\eta_i\chi\phi_p)E_t\hat{p}_{t+1}$$
$$+ \big[E_t\pi_{t+1}^* + (\tilde{r}_t - v_t) + \eta_i\chi(E_t v_{t+1} - v_t)\big] \quad \text{(A.32)}$$

as a generalization of (1.36). This is once again a stochastic difference equation of the form (A.14). It then follows from the discussion in Section A.4 that (A.32) can be solved forward to yield a unique bounded solution for $\{\hat{P}_t\}$, if and only if

$$|1 + \eta_i \chi \phi_p| < |1 + \phi_p(1 + \eta_i \chi)|.$$

Observe that as long as (A.31) holds, this determinacy condition is satisfied for all $\phi_p > 0$, just as was concluded in Section 1.2 of Chapter 2 for the case $\chi = 0$. Furthermore, in this case, the unique bounded solution is given by (A.16). Applying this result and rearranging terms, one obtains (3.17).

A.13   Proof of Proposition 2.13

PROPOSITION 2.13. Let monetary policy be specified instead by an interest-rate rule of the form of equation (2.12) of Chapter 2, with coefficients $\phi_\pi, \rho \geq 0$, and again suppose that $i_t^m = \bar{\imath}_t^m$ at all times. Finally, suppose that χ satisfies (A.31).Then equilibrium is determinate if and only if $\phi_\pi > 0$ and (A.21) holds. When these conditions are satisfied, a log-linear approximation to the equilibrium evolution of inflation is given by (3.20), where the weights are given by (3.21) and (3.22).

PROOF: Using (2.12) to eliminate π_{t+1} in (3.12), and again setting $i_t^m = 0$, one obtains a stochastic difference equation for the interest rate of the form

$$[(1 + \eta_i \chi)\phi_\pi + \rho]\hat{\imath}_t = [1 + \eta_i \chi \phi_\pi] E_t \hat{\imath}_{t+1} + \phi_\pi \tilde{r}_t + \rho \bar{\imath}_t - E_t \bar{\imath}_{t+1}. \quad \text{(A.33)}$$

This is again an equation of the form (A.14). It follows that equilibrium is locally determinate if and only if the term in square brackets on the left-hand side (call it γ_0) is larger in absolute value than the term in square brackets on the right-hand side (call it γ_1). Condition (A.31) suffices to guarantee that $\gamma_0 + \gamma_1 > 0$. It then follows that $|\gamma_0| > |\gamma_1|$, so that determinacy obtains, if and only if $\gamma_0 > \gamma_1$. This last inequality is in turn seen to be equivalent to (A.21). In the case that equilibrium is determinate, (A.16) can be applied again, yielding (3.20).

A.14   Proof of Proposition 2.14

PROPOSITION 2.14. Consider a sequence of economies with progressively smaller period lengths Δ, calibrated so that $\bar{\chi} \neq 0$. Assume in each case that monetary policy is specified by a contemporaneous Taylor rule (2.4), with a positive inflation-response coefficient $\phi_\pi \neq 1$ that is independent of Δ. Assume also that zero interest is paid on money. Then equilibrium is determinate for all small enough values of Δ if $\phi_\pi > 1$ and $\bar{\chi} > 0$, or if $0 < \phi_\pi < 1$ and $\bar{\chi} < 0$, but not otherwise.

PROOF: As discussed in the proof of Proposition 2.13, determinacy obtains if and only if $|\gamma_0| > |\gamma_1|$. In the limit as $\Delta \to 0$, both γ_0 and γ_1 become unboundedly large, while

$$\Delta\gamma_0, \Delta\gamma_1 \to \tilde{\eta}_i \bar{\chi} \phi_\pi. \tag{A.34}$$

Thus both γ_0 and γ_1 have the same sign as $\bar{\chi}$ for all small enough values of Δ. Note furthermore that

$$\gamma_0 - \gamma_1 = \phi_\pi - 1,$$

so that $\gamma_0 > \gamma_1$ if and only if $\phi_\pi > 1$. It then follows that $|\gamma_0| > |\gamma_1|$, and determinacy obtains, for all small enough values of Δ, if and only if either $\phi_\pi > 1$ and $\bar{\chi} > 0$ (so that $\gamma_0 > \gamma_1 > 0$) or $0 < \phi_\pi < 1$ and $\bar{\chi} < 0$ (so that $\gamma_0 < \gamma_1 < 0$).

A.15 Proof of Proposition 2.15

PROPOSITION 2.15. Again consider a sequence of economies with progressively smaller period lengths Δ, and suppose that

$$\bar{\chi} > -1/\psi \Phi_\pi \tilde{\eta}_i. \tag{A.35}$$

Let monetary policy instead be specified by an inertial Taylor rule, equation (2.12) of Chapter 2, with a long-run inflation-response coefficient $\Phi_\pi \equiv \phi_\pi/(1-\rho)$ and a rate of adjustment $\psi \equiv -\log \rho/\Delta > 0$ that are independent of Δ. Assume again that zero interest is paid on money. Then rational-expectations equilibrium is determinate if and only if $\Phi_\pi > 1$, that is, if and only if the Taylor principle is satisfied.

The unique bounded solution for the path of nominal interest rates in the determinate case is of the form

$$\hat{\imath}_t = \Lambda \bar{\imath}_t + \Gamma(1-\gamma) \sum_{j=0}^{\infty} \gamma^j E_t \tilde{r}_{t+j} - \tilde{\Gamma}(1-\gamma) \sum_{j=0}^{\infty} \gamma^j E_t \bar{\imath}_{t+j}, \tag{A.36}$$

with the solution for $\{\pi_t\}$ then obtained by inverting (2.12). In this solution, the coefficients $\Lambda, \Gamma, \tilde{\Gamma}$ approach well-defined limiting values as Δ is made arbitrarily small, while the rate of decay of the weights on expected disturbances farther in the future,

$$\xi \equiv -\log \gamma/\Delta > 0,$$

also approaches a well-defined limiting value. Furthermore, these limiting values are all continuous functions of $\bar{\chi}$ for values of $\bar{\chi}$ in the range satisfying (A.35), including values near zero.

PROOF: In this case, because ϕ_π approaches zero at the same rate as Δ (though we again maintain a long-run inflation-response coefficient independent of Δ), γ_0 and γ_1 do not become unboundedly large for small Δ. Instead of (A.34), one obtains

$$\gamma_0, \gamma_1 \to 1 + \tilde{\eta}_i \bar{\chi} \Phi_\pi \psi,$$

and this limiting value is positive given (A.35). Hence $\gamma_0, \gamma_1 > 0$ in the case of any small enough value of Δ, even if $\bar{\chi}$ is (modestly) negative. Furthermore I observe that in this case,

$$\gamma_0 - \gamma_1 = (\Phi_\pi - 1)(1 - \rho).$$

Hence I find once again that $\gamma_0 > \gamma_1$ if and only if $\Phi_\pi > 1$. Thus $|\gamma_0| > |\gamma_1|$, and equilibrium is determinate, if and only if $\Phi_\pi > 1$.

In the case of determinacy, the equilibrium solution for the nominal interest rate, derived in the course of the proof of Proposition 2.13, is given by

$$\hat{\imath}_t = \bar{\imath}_t + \sum_{j=0}^{\infty} \phi_\pi \varphi_j E_t \tilde{r}_{t+j} - \sum_{j=0}^{\infty} \phi_\pi \tilde{\varphi}_j E_t \bar{\imath}_{t+j},$$

where the coefficients $\{\varphi_j, \tilde{\varphi}_j\}$ are defined in (3.21) and (3.22). This is observed to be of the form (A.36), and allows one to identify the coefficients $\Lambda, \Gamma, \tilde{\Gamma}$, and γ in that representation of the solution.

Then observe that as Δ is made arbitrarily small,

$$\Lambda + \Gamma(1 - \gamma) - 1 = \frac{(1 + \eta_i \chi)\phi_\pi}{(1 + \eta_i \chi)\phi_\pi + \rho} \to \frac{\tilde{\eta}_i \bar{\chi} \Phi_\pi \psi}{1 + \tilde{\eta}_i \bar{\chi} \Phi_\pi \psi},$$

$$\Gamma = \frac{\phi_\pi}{\phi_\pi + \rho - 1} = \frac{\Phi_\pi}{\Phi_\pi - 1} > 0,$$

$$\tilde{\Gamma} = \frac{1 + (1 - \rho)\eta_i \chi}{1 + \eta_i \chi \phi_\pi} \Gamma \to \frac{1 + \tilde{\eta}_i \bar{\chi} \psi}{1 + \tilde{\eta}_i \bar{\chi} \Phi_\pi \psi} \frac{\Phi_\pi}{\Phi_\pi - 1} > 0,$$

and that ξ has the same limiting value as

$$\frac{1 - \gamma}{\Delta} = \frac{1}{\Delta} \frac{\phi_\pi + \rho - 1}{(1 + \eta_i \chi)\phi_\pi + \rho} \to \frac{(\Phi_\pi - 1)\psi}{1 + \tilde{\eta}_i \bar{\chi} \Phi_\pi \psi} > 0.$$

Since $\gamma \to 1$, observe also that

$$\Lambda \to 1 + \frac{\tilde{\eta}_i \bar{\chi} \Phi_\pi \psi}{1 + \tilde{\eta}_i \bar{\chi} \Phi_\pi \psi} > 0.$$

Hence $\Lambda, \Gamma, \tilde{\Gamma}$, and ξ all have well-defined limiting values, and each is a continuous function of $\bar{\chi}$.

A.16 Monetary Frictions with an Alternative Timing Convention

Some discrete-time models of economies with monetary frictions use an alternative timing convention, and hence alternative budget constraint, from that used in Section 3 of Chapter 2 (which derives from the classic work of Brock). Because many analyses of the determinacy of equilibrium under alternative monetary policy rules use the alternative convention (especially popularized by work on cash-in-advance models such as Lucas and Stokey, 1987), it is useful to compare the two approaches and to consider the extent to which the difference affects my conclusions.

In the alternative formulation (which I call Lucas-Stokey timing), the following sequence of events occurs within each discrete "period." First, at the beginning of period t, the state-contingent interest (or dividends) on financial assets acquired in the period $t - 1$ financial markets are paid. The representative household then has nominal financial wealth W_t. Next, taxes T_t are collected from each household, and financial markets open. At this time, households choose a portfolio allocation of their after-tax wealth between money balances M_t and state-contingent bond holdings (with total nominal value B_t at the time of purchase), subject to a budget constraint

$$M_t + B_t \leq W_t - T_t, \tag{A.37}$$

instead of equation (1.2) of Chapter 2. Third, goods markets open, and households' money balances are reduced by the nominal cost of their expenditure in these markets. At the same time, households' money balances are increased by the revenues that they receive from the sale of goods, so that end-of-period money balances equal

$$M_t + P_t Y_t - P_t C_t.$$

It follows that nominal wealth at the beginning of the following period is given by

$$W_{t+1} = A_{t+1} + \left(1 + i_t^m\right) [M_t + P_t Y_t - P_t C_t], \tag{A.38}$$

instead of (1.3).

Once again, the state-contingent value of the household's nonmonetary assets at maturity A_{t+1} is related to the value of the portfolio at the time of purchase B_t through the pricing relation (1.4). This gives a flow budget constraint in terms of beginning-of-period wealth that the household plans to have in the next period of the form

$$E_t\left[Q_{t,t+1} W_{t+1}\right] \leq W_t - T_t - \Delta_t M_t + (1 - \Delta_t)(P_t Y_t - P_t C_t), \tag{A.39}$$

instead of (1.7). With a borrowing limit that once again implies an ability to borrow any amount that can be repaid with certainty (but no more), one obtains an intertemporal budget constraint of the form

$$\sum_{s=t}^{\infty} E_t Q_{t,s} \left[(1-\Delta_s) P_s C_s + \Delta_s M_s \right] \leq W_t + \sum_{s=t}^{\infty} E_t Q_{t,s} \left[(1-\Delta_s) P_s Y_s - T_s \right] \text{ (A.40)}$$

instead of (1.13), looking forward from the beginning of any period t.

Assuming again preferences of the form (3.1)—though the money balances that supply liquidity services in period t are now those held before the goods markets open, rather than those held at the end of the period as under the Brock timing—one now obtains first-order conditions for an optimal household plan of the form

$$\frac{u_m(C_t, M_t/P_t; \xi_t)}{u_c(C_t, M_t/P_t; \xi_t)} = \frac{\Delta_t}{1 - \Delta_t}, \tag{A.41}$$

rather than (3.2), and

$$\frac{u_c(C_t, M_t/P_t; \xi_t)}{u_c(C_{t+1}, M_{t+1}/P_{t+1}; \xi_{t+1})} = \frac{\beta}{Q_{t,t+1}} \frac{P_t}{P_{t+1}} \frac{1 - \Delta_t}{1 - \Delta_{t+1}}, \tag{A.42}$$

rather than (1.16). Note that (A.42) can again be written in the form

$$\frac{\lambda(C_t, M_t/P_t; \xi_t)}{\lambda(C_{t+1}, M_{t+1}; \xi_{t+1})} = \frac{\beta}{Q_{t,t+1}} \frac{P_t}{P_{t+1}}, \tag{A.43}$$

but that now the function $\lambda(C, m; \xi)$ indicates not the marginal utility of consumption (as in the case of the model with Brock timing), but rather

$$\lambda(C, m; \xi) = u_c(C, m; \xi) + u_m(C, m; \xi). \tag{A.44}$$

As before, $\lambda(C_t, M_t/P_t; \xi_t)$ measures the marginal utility of additional real income in period t, received at the time that financial asset returns are received. But whereas with the Brock timing, the value of additional real income is always equal to the current marginal utility of consumption (as long as there is no binding borrowing limit), under the Lucas-Stokey timing, additional income received at the beginning of the period also has the benefit of increasing that period's money balances (and hence liquidity services), even if the additional income is spent during the same period.

However, these alternative assumptions about the precise way in which money balances yield liquidity services do not fundamentally change the form of the equilibrium conditions obtained. Under the Lucas-Stokey timing, one again sets an LM equation of the form

$$M_t^s/P_t = L(Y_t, \Delta_t; \xi_t), \tag{A.45}$$

and once again the assumption that both consumption and real balances are normal goods in the preferences (3.1) implies that the liquidity preference function is such that $L_Y > 0$, $L_\Delta < 0$. Here the liquidity preference function is obtained by solving (A.41) for required real money balances when consumption equals Y_t; because $\Delta_t/(1 - \Delta_t)$ is a monotonically increasing function of Δ_t, my previous conclusions about the existence of this function and the sign of its partial derivatives continue to obtain. Similarly, I again obtain a Fisher relation of the form

$$1 + i_t = \beta^{-1}\left\{E_t\left[\frac{\lambda(Y_{t+1}, M_{t+1}^s/P_{t+1}; \xi_{t+1})}{\lambda(Y_t, M_t/P_t; \xi_t)}\frac{P_t}{P_{t+1}}\right]\right\}^{-1}, \tag{A.46}$$

where the function λ is now defined as in (A.44).

Log-linearization of these two relations (the only ones that matter for analysis of local equilibrium determination under interest-rate rules of the kind considered in Section 3 of Chapter 2) again yields approximate equilibrium relations of the form (3.6) and (3.11). The only difference is that the definitions of the coefficients η_y, η_i, and χ in terms of derivatives of the utility function are different; for example, as a result of (A.44) I now have

$$\chi \equiv \frac{\bar{m}(u_{cm} + u_{mm})}{u_c + u_m}, \tag{A.47}$$

instead of (3.10). But since the results in Section 3 have already been framed in terms of the values of the coefficients η_y, η_i, and χ, all of the results continue to apply to a model with the Lucas-Stokey timing.

Why, then, do Carlstrom and Fuerst (2001) argue that the two alternative choices of timing convention "result in dramatic differences" in the conditions under which a policy rule results in a determinate equilibrium? Because they consider the conditions for determinacy of equilibrium when the model is specified in terms of assumptions regarding the form of the indirect utility function $u(C, m; \xi)$. Under a given assumption about the form of this function, one gets different conclusions because the implied coefficients of the log-linearized structural relations (3.6) and (3.11) are different under the alternative timing conventions. For example, in the case of the Brock timing, additive separability implies that $\chi = 0$, as noted in the text of Chapter 2. In the case of the Lucas-Stokey timing, instead, additive separability ($u_{cm} = 0$) implies that $\chi < 0$, using (A.47).

This does not, however, mean that the discussion in Sections 3.2 and 3.3 of equilibrium determination in the case that $\chi = 0$ is of interest only under the Brock timing convention. Even under the Lucas-Stokey timing, I can

identify assumptions that would lead to the special, simpler form of equilibrium relations that I first consider in the text. Suppose that household
utility in a given period is equal to

$$v(C; \xi) - w(c_2; \xi), \qquad (A.48)$$

where $v(\cdot; \xi)$ indicates the utility obtained from consumption of one's purchases, c_2 represents the quantity of goods that are purchased using a less-
convenient payment technology rather than by paying cash, and $w(\cdot; \xi)$
indicates the additional disutility of carrying out transactions of the latter
sort (for example, time-consuming verification of one's creditworthiness).
I assume that v is increasing and concave in C, whereas w is increasing and
convex in c_2.

The inconvenient payment technology must be used to the extent that
one holds insufficient cash balances to pay for one's purchases prior to the
opening of the goods market, so that one must satisfy

$$c_2 \geq \max(C - m, 0). \qquad (A.49)$$

Under this assumption about the underlying payment technology, the indirect utility function $u(C, m; \xi)$ is defined as the maximum attainable value
of (A.48) when one chooses c_2 optimally subject to the constraint (A.49).
The optimal choice of c_2 is obviously given by the right-hand side of (A.49),
so that

$$u(C, m; \xi) = v(C; \xi) - w(\max(C - m, 0); \xi).$$

The function $\lambda(C, m; \xi)$ is then equal to $v_C(C; \xi)$, regardless of the value of
m. In this case, the Euler equation (A.46) does not involve the path of real
money balances, and so the conclusions reached in Sections 3.2 and 3.3 of
the text apply to this case. (Of course, as stressed in the text, the case $\chi = 0$
is also of interest as it corresponds to the case of an economy in which monetary frictions do not distort the pattern of goods exchange very much.)

This example also illustrates the fact that cash-in-advance models of transactions frictions fall within the class to which these results apply; they correspond to a particular form of indirect utility function $u(C, m; \xi)$, in the case
of Lucas-Stokey timing. A common specification in the literature is the case
of a "cash/credit goods" model, following Lucas and Stokey (1987). Here
household utility each period is assumed to be of the form

$$V(c_1, c_2; \xi), \qquad (A.50)$$

where c_1 denotes the quantity of purchases made with cash, and c_2 again
denotes the quantity of purchases made with a payment technology that

does not require the payment of cash in advance (credit). Here substitution between the two payment technologies requires substitution between purchases of two types of goods; but there is no other cost of the use of credit. Purchases of cash goods are constrained by the cash-in-advance constraint

$$c_1 \leq m, \tag{A.51}$$

where m is real balances in units of cash goods that can be purchased. Note that this is equivalent to (A.49) if one writes

$$C \equiv c_1 + c_2 \tag{A.52}$$

for the total quantity of goods purchased of either type.

Lucas and Stokey assume furthermore that both types of goods are supplied at the same price P in a given period (they are perfect substitutes from the point of view of producers, though not for consumers). The quantity m in (A.51) then corresponds to a conventional definition of real money balances, and an indirect utility function $u(C, m; \xi)$ can be defined as the maximum attainable value of (A.50), when c_1 and c_2 are chosen optimally subject to the constraints (A.51) and (A.52). Here the quantity C in the indirect utility function is the real value of total consumption expenditure. Note that the example discussed just above can be viewed as a special case of this model, in which

$$V(c_1, c_2; \xi) = v(c_1 + c_2; \xi) - w(c_2; \xi).$$

In the literature, however, it is often assumed that V is additively separable between the two kinds of goods,

$$V(c_1, c_2; \xi) = v(c_1; \xi) + w(c_2; \xi).$$

In this case, the marginal utility of additional financial income equals

$$\lambda(C, m; \xi) = v_c(m; \xi)$$

in the case of any level of real balances m lower than the satiation level $\bar{m}(C; \xi)$, that is, the level at which constraint (A.51) ceases to bind. Strict concavity of the function $v(\cdot; \xi)$ then implies that λ is decreasing in m, so that $\chi < 0$ in models of this kind.

A.17 The Example of Schmitt-Grohé and Uribe

The model of Schmitt-Grohé and Uribe (2000), mentioned in Section 4.3 of Chapter 2, is an example of a cash/credit goods model of the kind just discussed, in which the fact that λ is decreasing in m is important for excluding self-fulfilling hyperinflations. These authors assume preferences of the form

$$V(c_1, c_2) = \log c_1 + \theta \log c_2, \tag{A.53}$$

for some $\theta > 0$. In this case, the optimal level of cash goods purchases is equal to

$$c_1 = \min(m, \; C/(1+\theta)).$$

Substituting this into the direct utility function (A.53), one obtains an indirect utility function $u(C, m)$. From this it is easily shown that the marginal utility of real (financial, i.e., beginning-of-period) income is given by

$$\lambda(C, m) = \frac{1}{\min(m, \; C/(1+\theta))}, \tag{A.54}$$

and that the money-demand function is of the form

$$L(Y, i) = \frac{Y}{1+\theta(1+i)}. \tag{A.55}$$

(In the latter expression, one simplifies by assuming $i^m = 0$, as do Schmitt-Grohé and Uribe.)

Substituting (A.55) into (A.54), one sees that in this model, the function $\lambda(i)$ referred to in equation (4.5) is of the form

$$\lambda(i) = \frac{1+\theta(1+i)}{\bar{Y}}$$

for all $i \geq 0$. This is a function with the properties discussed at the end of Section 4.3 in Chapter 2. It can be made unboundedly large in the case of a high enough interest rate, in which case the distortions associated with the cash-in-advance constraint become severe; note that this is true even if θ is quite small (though positive), so that the dependence of the marginal utility of income on the current level of nominal interest rates might be negligible for purposes of analyzing inflation determination in a low-inflation regime. Furthermore, the elasticity of $\lambda(i)$ with respect to i remains bounded below 1 for all i.

Schmitt-Grohé and Uribe consider a family of linear Taylor rules of the form

$$\phi(\Pi_t) = \beta^{-1}\left[\Pi^* + \phi_\pi(\Pi_t - \Pi^*)\right] - 1, \tag{A.56}$$

which are consistent with a steady-state inflation rate Π^*.[8] Such a rule satisfies the Taylor principle if and only if $\phi_\pi > 1$. In this case, one observes that $A(\Pi) \equiv \lambda(\phi(\Pi))/(1 + \phi(\Pi))$ is a monotonically decreasing function of Π that approaches the asymptotic value of $\theta > 0$ for large Π. Instead, the function $B(\Pi) \equiv \beta\lambda(\phi(\Pi))/\Pi$ is a monotonic function that approaches the asymptotic value of $\phi_\pi\theta > \theta$ for large Π. It follows that there exists a finite $\bar{\Pi}$ such that $A(\bar{\Pi}) = \phi_\pi\theta$. One then observes that in the case of any $\Pi_t \geq \bar{\Pi}$, there is no value for Π_{t+1} that would satisfy (4.5).

This allows me to infer that any perfect-foresight equilibrium consistent with such a policy rule involves $\Pi_t < \bar{\Pi}$ for all t. I can also show that $\Pi_t \leq \Pi^*$ at all times, using the argument sketched in the text of Chapter 2. Consider the sequence of bounds $\bar{\Pi}^{(k)}$, defined recursively by the equation

$$A(\bar{\Pi}^{(k+1)}) = B(\bar{\Pi}^{(k)})$$

for $k \geq 0$, starting from the initial bound $\bar{\Pi}^{(0)} = \bar{\Pi}$ defined above. One observes from the properties of the functions $A(\cdot)$ and $B(\cdot)$ noted in the previous paragraph that for any $\bar{\Pi}^{(k)} > \Pi^*$, this equation has a unique solution such that $\Pi^* < \bar{\Pi}^{(k+1)} < \bar{\Pi}^{(k)}$. One thus constructs a monotonically decreasing sequence of bounds that furthermore satisfy

$$\lim_{k \to \infty} \bar{\Pi}^{(k)} = \Pi^*.$$

It furthermore follows from (4.5) that if $\Pi_{t+1} < \bar{\Pi}^{(k)}$, one must have $\Pi_t < \bar{\Pi}^{(k+1)}$.

Thus one can show that it is not possible to have a perfect-foresight equilibrium sequence $\{\Pi - t\}$ in which $\Pi_t > \Pi^*$ in any period. For if this were the case, it would follow that $\Pi_t > \bar{\Pi}^{(k)}$ for some k, which would then be consistent with (4.5) only if $\Pi_{t+k} > \bar{\Pi}$, which has been shown to be impossible. Accordingly, self-fulfilling hyperinflations are impossible in this model in the case of a policy rule (A.56) consistent with the Taylor principle. As discussed in Section 4.2, self-fulfilling deflations are also impossible in the case of a balanced-budget fiscal policy. Thus Schmitt-Grohé and Uribe establish that in the case of an interest-rate rule satisfying the Taylor principle and a balanced-budget fiscal rule, the unique perfect-foresight equilibrium is the one in which $\Pi_t = \Pi^*$ at all times.

---

8. This form holds, obviously, only for inflation rates for which it implies a nonnegative interest rate. Because I am interested here solely in the possibility of self-fulfilling hyperinflations, I omit more precise discussion of the form of the rule for low inflation rates.

APPENDIX B

Addendum to Chapter 3

B.1 Non-CES Demand and Variable Markups

In the model of Kimball (1995), the consumption aggregate C_t is implicitly defined by a relation of the form

$$\int_0^1 \psi(c_t(i)/C_t)\,di = 1, \tag{B.1}$$

where $\psi(x)$ is an increasing, strictly concave function satisfying $\psi(1) = 1$. The demand curve for good i is then implicitly defined by

$$\psi'\left(\frac{y_t(i)}{Y_t}\right) = \psi'(1)\frac{p_t(i)}{P_t}, \tag{B.2}$$

where the price index P_t for aggregate (B.1) is implicitly defined by

$$\int_0^1 \frac{p_t(i)}{P_t}\psi'^{-1}\left(\psi'(1)\frac{p_t(i)}{P_t}\right)di = 1. \tag{B.3}$$

The elasticity of the demand curve (B.2) faced by supplier i is then equal to $\theta(y_t(i)/Y_t)$, where

$$\theta(x) \equiv -\frac{\psi'(x)}{x\psi''(x)}. \tag{B.4}$$

It follows that the desired markup of price over marginal cost for a flexible-price supplier is equal to $\mu(y_t(i)/Y_t)$, where

$$\mu(x) \equiv \frac{\theta(x)}{\theta(x) - 1}. \tag{B.5}$$

Note that in general, neither θ nor μ is a constant as assumed before; but I continue to assume a function $\psi(x)$ such that $\theta(x) > 1$ for all x in a neighborhood of 1, so that $\mu(x) > 1$ is well defined, at least in that neighborhood. The desired relative price of a flexible-price supplier is then given by equation (1.39) of Chapter 3 in the text, where the function $\mu(x)$ is defined by (B.5).

B.2   Proof of Proposition 3.3

PROPOSITION 3.3. Suppose that preferences over differentiated goods are defined by (1.38), and that the production technology is defined by (1.42). Then one again obtains a log-linear approximation to the notional SRAS curve of the form (1.34), with elasticity

$$\zeta = \frac{(1 - \mu s_m)(s_y + s_Y)}{1 + \theta[\epsilon_\mu + (1 - \mu s_m)s_y]}, \tag{B.6}$$

generalizing (1.41).

Here the real marginal cost of supplying value added by firm i has elasticity $s_y \geq 0$ with respect to value added by firm i, and elasticity s_Y with respect to aggregate value added. In the case of specific factor markets (as in Section 1.1 of Chapter 3), this expression holds with $s_y = \omega$, $s_Y = \sigma^{-1}$; instead, in the case of homogeneous factor markets (discussed in Section 1.4 of Chapter 3), $s_y = 0$, $s_Y = \omega + \sigma^{-1}$.

PROOF: It follows from production function (1.42) that if firms allocate their intermediate input purchases across goods j in a cost-minimizing way, the quantity purchased of good j for use in producing good i equals $m_t(i)(p_t(j)/P_t)^{-\theta}$ (or the corresponding generalization in the case of a non-Dixit-Stiglitz aggregator), and the cost per unit of materials inputs will be the same price index P_t as for consumption purposes. Total demand for firm i's output, given by the sum of final demand and intermediate-input demand from other producers, is still given by (1.5)—or more generally by (B.2)—where now aggregate demand Y_t is equal to

$$Y_t = C_t + \int_0^1 m_t(i)\,di. \tag{B.7}$$

It further follows from the production function (1.42) that real marginal cost for firm i equals

$$s_t(i) = (1 - s_m)s_t^{VA}(i) + s_m, \tag{B.8}$$

where $s_t^{VA}(i)$ is the real marginal cost of an additional unit of theoretical value added (the function of primary input use given by $A_t f(h_t(i))$), and I have used the fact that the price of the materials aggregate is P_t. The marginal cost of supplying value added is given by the same real marginal cost function derived earlier; for example, in the case of specific factor markets, it is given by

$$s_t^{VA}(i) = s\left((1 - s_m)y_t(i),\ Y_t - s_m X_t;\ \tilde{\xi}_t\right),$$

where X_t is the same alternative production aggregate as in (1.36), and $s(y, Y; \tilde{\xi})$ is again defined as in (1.10). The existence of a symmetric steady state then requires that $s_m < \mu^{-1}$, where the latter quantity represents the steady-state level of real marginal cost, given firms' desired markup of $\mu > 1$.[1] Such a steady state involves a constant level of final-goods demand (or real value added) $\bar{Y}$ implicitly defined by[2]

$$s\left(\bar{Y}, \bar{Y}; 0\right) = \frac{1 - \mu s_m}{\mu(1 - s_m)}. \tag{B.9}$$

Regardless of the factor market structure, one can show that a log-linear approximation to the real marginal cost function for value added is given by

$$\hat{s}_t^{VA}(i) = s_y \hat{y}_t(i) + s_Y \hat{Y}_t,$$

where the elasticities s_y and s_Y are the same as earlier (and related to underlying parameters of preferences and technology in the statement of the proposition). Log-linearization of (B.8) then implies that

$$\hat{s}_t(i) = (1 - \mu s_m)\left(s_y \hat{y}_t(i) + s_Y \hat{Y}_t\right).$$

It is the appearance of the multiplicative factor $1 - \mu s_m < 1$ here that explains how the economy's input-output structure gives rise to "real rigidity" of the sort that increases the strategic complementarity among pricing decisions. Substitution of the demand curve for $\hat{y}_t(i)$ as before then allows one to solve once again for firm i's desired relative price. One again obtains a log-linear relation (1.34), but now with elasticity ζ given by (B.6).

---

1. In the case that the desired markup is variable, we continue to use the coefficient μ to refer to the steady-state value, $\mu(1)$.

2. Note that the right-hand side of (B.9) is the reciprocal of the steady-state "value-added markup" or inefficiency wedge resulting from market power that Rotemberg and Woodford (1995) contrast with the steady-state "gross-output markup" or firm-level markup of price over marginal cost μ. Distinguishing between the two is essential in calibrating an imperfectly competitive model that abstracts from the existence of intermediate inputs.

B.3 Proof of Proposition 3.4

PROPOSITION 3.4. Suppose that $\{\log S_t\}$ is a difference-stationary process. Then there is a unique solution to equations (2.5) and (2.8) for the price index process such that $\{\log P_t\}$ is also difference-stationary (i.e., inflation is a stationary process), given by

$$\log P_t = \lambda_1 \log P_{t-1} + (1 - \lambda_1)\left(1 - \lambda_2^{-1}\right) \sum_{j=0}^{\infty} \lambda_2^{-j} \left[\log \mu + E_t \log S_{t+j}\right], \quad \text{(B.10)}$$

where $0 < \lambda_1 < 1 < \beta^{-1} < \lambda_2$ are the two roots of the characteristic polynomial

$$\mathcal{P}(\lambda) \equiv \beta \lambda^2 - (1 + \beta + \xi)\lambda + 1 = 0, \quad \text{(B.11)}$$

in which

$$\xi \equiv \frac{1 - \alpha}{\alpha}\frac{1 - \alpha\beta}{1 + \tilde{\omega}\theta} > 0. \quad \text{(B.12)}$$

PROOF. If (2.8) is expected to hold in period $t + 1$ as well as period t, it follows that

$$\log p_t^* = \frac{1 - \alpha\beta}{1 + \tilde{\omega}\theta}[\log \mu + \log S_t - \tilde{\omega}\theta \log P_t] + \alpha\beta E_t \log p_{t+1}^*.$$

Then, substituting $(\log P_t - \alpha \log P_{t-1})/(1 - \alpha)$ for $\log p_t^*$ as a consequence of (2.5), and making a similar substitution for $\log p_{t+1}^*$, I obtain

$$E_t[A(L) \log P_{t+1}] = -\xi[\log \mu + \log S_t], \quad \text{(B.13)}$$

where ξ is defined by (B.12), and

$$A(L) \equiv L^2 - (1 + \beta + \xi)L + \beta.$$

This lag polynomial can be factored as

$$A(L) = \beta(1 - \lambda_1 L)(1 - \lambda_2 L),$$

where λ_1, λ_2 are the two roots of (B.11). Note furthermore that $\mathcal{P}(0) > 0$, $\mathcal{P}(1) < 0$, and $\mathcal{P}(\beta^{-1}) < 0$, while $\mathcal{P}(\lambda) > 0$ for all large enough positive values of λ. It follows that there must be two real roots, satisfying $0 < \lambda_1 < 1 < \beta^{-1} < \lambda_2$, as stated in the proposition. Finally, comparing the factorization with the original lag polynomial, I observe that $\lambda_1 \lambda_2 = \beta^{-1}$. Using this factorization, I can write (B.13) as

$$E_t[(1 - \lambda_1 L)(1 - \lambda_2 L) \log P_{t+1}] = -\beta^{-1} \xi [\log \mu + \log S_t],$$

or as

$$z_t = \lambda_2^{-1} E_t z_{t+1} + \beta^{-1} \lambda_2^{-1} \xi [\log \mu + \log S_t], \qquad (B.14)$$

where

$$z_t \equiv (1 - \lambda_1 L) \log P_t.$$

Because $|\lambda_2^{-1}| < 1$, one solution to (B.14) can be obtained by solving forward, yielding

$$z_t = \bar{z}_t \equiv \beta^{-1} \lambda_2^{-1} \xi \sum_{j=0}^{\infty} \lambda_2^{-j} [\log \mu + E_t \log S_{t+j}].$$

Here the assumption that $\{\log S_t\}$ is a difference-stationary process implies that there exists a well-defined limiting growth rate of nominal marginal cost

$$\lim_{T \to \infty} E_t \Delta \log S_T = \gamma,$$

and hence that there exists a finite bound K such that

$$|E_t \log S_{t+j+1} - E_t \log S_{t+j}| \leq K$$

for all $j \geq 0$. It follows from this last bound that the infinite sum in the definition of $\bar{z}_t$ is well defined and finite; and while $\{\bar{z}_t\}$ inherits any unit root in $\{\log S_t\}$, it is also a difference-stationary process, with a long-run average growth rate

$$\lim_{T \to \infty} E_t \Delta \bar{z}_T = \gamma. \qquad (B.15)$$

Finally, it follows from (B.11) that

$$(1 - \lambda_1)(1 - \lambda_2) = (1 - \lambda_1)(1 - \beta \lambda_1)$$
$$= \mathcal{P}(\lambda_1) + \xi \lambda_1$$
$$= \xi \lambda_1 = \beta^{-1} \lambda_2^{-1} \xi,$$

so that the solution $\bar{z}_t$ can alternatively be written in the form (B.10). Moreover, the fact that $\{\bar{z}_t\}$ is a difference-stationary process implies that $\{\log P_t\}$ is one as well.

It remains to show that this is the *only* possible difference-stationary solution for $\{\log P_t\}$. Observe that (B.14) implies that

$$z_t - \bar{z}_t = \lambda_2^{-1} E_t[z_{t+1} - \bar{z}_{t+1}],$$

or equivalently, that

$$E_t[z_{t+1} - \bar{z}_{t+1}] = \lambda_2[z_t - \bar{z}_t].$$

This in turn implies that

$$E_t[z_{t+j+1} - \bar{z}_{t+j+1}] = \lambda_2[z_{t+j} - \bar{z}_{t+j}]$$

for any $j \geq 0$. One can then show by an iterative argument that

$$E_t[z_{t+j} - \bar{z}_{t+j}] = \lambda_2^j[z_t - \bar{z}_t],$$

for any $j \geq 0$. It follows that if $z_t \neq \bar{z}_t$, $E_t z_{t+j} - E_t \bar{z}_{t+j}$ must grow as λ_2^j. Since (B.15) implies that $E_t \bar{z}_{t+j}$ grows asymptotically only at the rate γj, $E_t z_{t+j}$ must grow asymptotically at the rate λ_2^j. This implies that $E_t \log P_{t+j}$ also grows aymptotically at the rate λ_2^j (since $\log P_t$ is an exponential moving average of z_{t-j}), and hence that $E_t \Delta \log P_{t+j}$ grows asymptotically at the rate λ_2^j. But this implies that $\{\Delta \log P_t\}$ would not be a stationary process. Hence the unique solution in which $\{\log P_t\}$ is difference-stationary is the one given by (B.10).

B.4 Proof of Proposition 3.5

PROPOSITION 3.5. Let the profit function of the supplier of an individual good again be of the form of equation (1.17) of Chapter 3 and satisfy Assumption 3.1, but suppose now that a fraction $0 < \alpha < 1$ of goods prices remain fixed each period, with each price having an equal probability of being revised in any given period, as in the model of Calvo (1983). Suppose also that profits are discounted using a stochastic discount factor that is equal on average to β, where $0 < \beta < 1$. Then the aggregate inflation rate and aggregate output in any period t must satisfy an aggregate-supply relation of the form

$$\pi_t = \kappa\left(\hat{Y}_t - \hat{Y}_t^n\right) + \beta E_t \pi_{t+1}, \tag{B.16}$$

where

$$\kappa = \frac{(1 - \alpha)(1 - \alpha\beta)}{\alpha} \zeta > 0.$$

PROOF. I have shown in the text of Chapter 3 that Calvo pricing implies that the aggregate price index should evolve (up to a log-linear approximation) according to (2.5), where p_t^* is given (up to a log-linear approximation) by (2.6). Solving this equation for $\log p_t^*$, subtracting $\log P_t$ from both sides, and expressing the expected change in the price index over various future horizons in terms of the expected inflation rate at various future dates, one obtains

$$\hat{p}_t^* = (1 - \alpha\beta) \sum_{T=t}^{\infty} (\alpha\beta)^{T-t} E_t \left[\sum_{s=t+1}^{T} \pi_s + \zeta \left(\hat{Y}_T - \hat{Y}_T^n \right) \right]$$

$$= \sum_{T=t}^{\infty} (\alpha\beta)^{T-t} E_t \left[\alpha\beta\pi_{T+1} + (1 - \alpha\beta)\zeta \left(\hat{Y}_T - \hat{Y}_T^n \right) \right],$$

where $\hat{p}_t^* \equiv \log(p_t^*/P_t)$ is the log relative price chosen by suppliers that revise their prices in period t. As in the proof of Proposition 3.4, this implies that

$$\hat{p}_t^* = [\alpha\beta E_t \pi_{t+1} + (1 - \alpha\beta)\zeta x_t] + \alpha\beta E_t \hat{p}_{t+1}^*. \qquad \text{(B.17)}$$

Equation (2.5) for the evolution of the price index implies (subtracting $\log P_t$ from both sides) that the inflation rate is proportional (up to a log-linear approximation) to the log relative price chosen by suppliers that revise their prices,

$$\pi_t = \frac{1 - \alpha}{\alpha} \hat{p}_t^*.$$

Using this relation to substitute for both $\hat{p}_t^*$ and $\hat{p}_{t+1}^*$ in (B.17), one obtains relation (B.16).

B.5 Proof of Proposition 3.6

PROPOSITION 3.6. Suppose that aggregate nominal expenditure evolves according to equation (2.15) of Chapter 3, where ϵ_t is an unforecastable monetary policy shock at date t, and the process $\{q_t\}$ is independent of the process $\{\epsilon_t\}$. Then in an economy with an aggregate-supply relation of the New Keynesian form (B.16), the impulse-response functions of the log price index and log real GDP to a unit positive innovation in ϵ_t (i.e., an unexpected permanent increase of one unit in the log of aggregate nominal expenditure) are given by

$$\tilde{p}_k = 1 - \lambda^{k+1}, \tag{B.18}$$

$$\tilde{y}_k = \lambda^{k+1}, \tag{B.19}$$

for $k \geq 0$, where $0 < \lambda < 1$ is the smaller of the two real roots of the characteristic polynomial

$$\beta\lambda^2 - (1 + \beta + \kappa)\lambda + 1 = 0. \tag{B.20}$$

PROOF. I have shown in the text of Chapter 3 that the impulse-response function for the log price index must satisfy (2.16) for $k \geq 0$, plus the initial and terminal conditions

$$\tilde{p}_{-1} = 0,$$

$$\lim_{k \to \infty} \tilde{p}_k = 1.$$

The difference equation can be written as

$$A(L)\tilde{p}_{k+1} = -\kappa, \tag{B.21}$$

where

$$A(L) \equiv L^2 - (1 + \beta + \kappa)L + \beta,$$

and the lag operator is now defined so that $L\tilde{p}_k \equiv \tilde{p}_{k-1}$.

This difference equation can be solved using the same method as in the proof of Proposition 3.4. Once again, $A(L)$ can be factored as

$$A(L) = \beta(1 - \lambda_1 L)(1 - \lambda_2 L),$$

where λ_1, λ_2 are the roots of the characteristic polynomial (B.20), and once again, one can show that $0 < \lambda_1 < 1 < \beta^{-1} < \lambda_2$, and that $\lambda_1\lambda_2 = \beta^{-1}$. Using the same method as before, one can show that the unique solution satisfying the terminal condition must be given by

$$z_k = \beta^{-1}\lambda_2^{-1}\kappa \sum_{j=0}^{\infty} \lambda_2^{-j}$$

$$= \frac{\beta^{-1}\kappa}{\lambda_2 - 1}$$

$$= 1 - \lambda_1,$$

where $z_k \equiv (1 - \lambda_1 L)\tilde{p}_k$. Equating z_k to the constant value $1 - \lambda_1$, one then has a difference equation for $\tilde{p}_k$,

$$\tilde{p}_k = \lambda_1 \tilde{p}_{k-1} + (1 - \lambda_1),$$

to solve subject to the initial condition. The solution to this equation is easily seen to be (B.18), in which we have written λ for the smaller root, λ_1.

Finally, the identity $\log \mathcal{Y}_{t+k} = \log P_{t+k} + \log Y_{t+k}$ implies that the impulse-response functions for the log price level and log output must satisfy

$$\tilde{p}_k + \tilde{y}_k = 1$$

for each $k \geq 0$. Then solution (B.18) for the response of the price level implies (B.19) for the response of output.

B.6 Proof of Proposition 3.7

PROPOSITION 3.7. Suppose that aggregate nominal expenditure evolves according to equation (2.21) of Chapter 3, where $0 < \rho < 1$, with $\rho \neq \lambda$, where $0 < \lambda < 1$ is again defined as in Proposition 3.6; ϵ_t is an unforecastable monetary policy shock at date t; and the process $\{q_t\}$ is independent of the process $\{\epsilon_t\}$. Then in an economy with an aggregate-supply relation of the New Keynesian form (2.12), the impulse-response function of log real GDP to a positive innovation of size $1 - \rho$ in ϵ_t (implying an eventual permanent increase of one unit in the log of aggregate nominal expenditure) is given by

$$\tilde{y}_k = \frac{(1 - \rho)(1 - \beta\rho)}{(\lambda - \rho)(\lambda^{-1} - \beta\rho)}(\lambda^{k+1} - \rho^{k+1}) \tag{B.22}$$

for each $k \geq 0$. The corresponding impulse-response function for the log price level is given by

$$\tilde{p}_k = 1 - \rho^{k+1} - \tilde{y}_k.$$

PROOF. The proof follows the same lines as in Proposition 3.6, except that now (2.21) implies that

$$\tilde{Y}_k \equiv (1 - \rho)\frac{\partial}{\partial \epsilon_t} E_t \log \mathcal{Y}_{t+k} = 1 - \rho^k \tag{B.23}$$

for each $k \geq -1$. As a result, (B.21) must be generalized to

$$A(L)\tilde{p}_{k+1} = -\kappa\left(1 - \rho^{k+1}\right), \tag{B.24}$$

where the lag polynomial $A(L)$ is unchanged. Because the primary interest here is in a solution for the impulse-response function of output, it is useful to rewrite this as a difference equation for $\{\tilde{y}_k\}$. Equation (B.23) implies that

$$A(L)\tilde{Y}_{k+1} = \beta\left(1 - \rho^{k+2}\right) - (1 + \beta + \kappa)\left(1 - \rho^{k+1}\right) + \left(1 - \rho^k\right)$$

for $k \geq 0$. Subtracting (B.24) from this, one obtains

$$A(L)\tilde{y}_{k+1} = -(1 - \rho)(1 - \beta\rho)\rho^k \tag{B.25}$$

for all $k \geq 0$. In addition, the impulse-response function for output must satisfy initial and terminal conditions

$$\tilde{y}_{-1} = 0,$$

$$\lim_{k \to \infty} \tilde{y}_k = 0.$$

Again factoring $A(L)$ as in the proof of Proposition 3.6, one can show that the unique solution consistent with the terminal condition is given by

$$(1 - \lambda_1 L)\tilde{y}_k = \beta^{-1}\lambda_2^{-1}(1 - \rho)(1 - \beta\rho)\sum_{j=0}^{\infty}\lambda_2^{-j}\rho^{j+k}$$

$$= C\rho^k$$

for each $k \geq 0$, where

$$C \equiv \frac{(1 - \rho)(1 - \beta\rho)}{\lambda_1^{-1} - \beta\rho} > 0.$$

It follows that

$$(1 - \rho L)(1 - \lambda_1 L)\tilde{y}_{k+1} = 0 \tag{B.26}$$

for each $k \geq 0$, where there is now an additional initial condition

$$\tilde{y}_0 = C.$$

The general solution to an autonomous second-order difference equation of the form (B.26) with two initial conditions, when $\rho \neq \lambda_1$ (as assumed in the proposition), is of the form

$$\tilde{y}_k = A_1 \lambda_1^k + A_2 \rho^k,$$

where the coefficients A_1 and A_2 are uniquely determined by the requirement that this solution satisfy the two initial conditions for $k = -1$ and $k = 0$. In the present case, the initial conditions require that

$$A_1 = \frac{\lambda_1}{\lambda_1 - \rho} C, \qquad A_2 = \frac{\rho}{\rho - \lambda_1} C,$$

so that this solution corresponds to (B.22), in which λ_1 is written simply as λ, as in the statement of Proposition 3.6. Note that $A_1 > 0, A_2 < 0$ if $0 < \rho < \lambda_1$, while the signs are reversed if $\lambda_1 < \rho < 1$. Thus one finds that the sign is positive on the term that is larger and decays less rapidly, as noted in the text in the discussion of this proposition.

B.7 Proof of Proposition 3.8

PROPOSITION 3.8. Consider a two-sector model of the kind described above, with Calvo pricing in each sector (and the fraction of prices that remain unchanged each period in sector j equal to $0 < \alpha_j < 1$), and sector-specific disturbances to tastes and technology. Then for each sector $j = 1, 2$, the sectoral inflation rate is related to the aggregate output gap through a relation of the form

$$\pi_{jt} = \kappa_j \left(\hat{Y}_t - \hat{Y}_t^n \right) + \gamma_j \left(\hat{p}_{Rt} - \hat{p}_{Rt}^n \right) + \beta E_t \pi_{j,t+1}, \tag{B.27}$$

generalizing (B.16), where

$$\kappa_j \equiv \frac{(1 - \alpha_j)(1 - \alpha_j \beta)}{\alpha_j} \frac{\omega + \sigma^{-1}}{1 + \omega\theta} > 0$$

for $j = 1, 2$, and

$$\gamma_1 \equiv n_2 \frac{(1 - \alpha_1)(1 - \alpha_1 \beta)}{\alpha_1} \frac{1 + \omega\eta}{1 + \omega\theta} > 0,$$

$$\gamma_2 \equiv -n_1 \frac{(1 - \alpha_2)(1 - \alpha_2 \beta)}{\alpha_2} \frac{1 + \omega\eta}{1 + \omega\theta} < 0.$$

PROOF. Under the assumptions described in the text, the gradient of the profit function is of the form

$$\Pi_p^j(p_t(i), P_{jt}, P_t; Y_t, \tilde{\xi}_t) = (1 - \theta) Y_{jt} P_{jt}^\theta p_t(i)^{-\theta - 1}$$

$$\left[p_t(i) - \mu s^j (Y_{jt}(p_t(i)/P_{jt})^{-\theta}, Y_t; \tilde{\xi}_t) \right]. \tag{B.28}$$

Here the real marginal cost of supplying good i in sector j is given by

$$s^j (y_t(i), Y_t; \tilde{\xi}_t) \equiv v_h \left(\frac{f^{-1}(y_t(i)/A_{jt}); \tilde{\xi}_{jt})}{u_c(Y_t; \xi_t)} \right) A_{jt} \, \Psi \, (y_t(i)/A_{jt}),$$

as a function of the quantity supplied of the individual good, aggregate output, and sector-specific real disturbances, generalizing equation (1.10) of Chapter 3, and the index of sectoral demand Y_{jt} is given by

$$Y_{jt} = n_j \varphi_{jt} \, Y_t (P_{jt}/P_t)^{-\eta}. \tag{B.29}$$

Because each firm faces a demand curve with constant elasticity θ as before, the desired markup is again μ.

One can then define a natural rate of output Y_{jt}^n for each sector j as the common equilibrium output of each good i in that sector in the case of flexible prices. These sectoral natural rates are implicitly defined by

$$\mu \, s^j \left(Y_{jt}^n, Y_t^n; \tilde{\xi}_t \right) = \left(\frac{Y_{jt}^n}{n_j \varphi_{jt} Y_t^n} \right)^{-1/\eta},$$

for $j = 1, 2$, where the right-hand side indicates the relative price P_{jt}/P_t required to induce the relative demand Y_{jt}^n/Y_t^n. The natural rate of aggregate output, Y_t^n, aggregates Y_{1t}^n and Y_{2t}^n using (2.22). In the case that $\tilde{\xi}_t = 0$ for all t, and in addition $\varphi_{jt} = 1$ for all t and both sectors, the flexible-price equilibrium involves a common level of output $\bar{Y}$ for all goods, defined in the same way as before. Log-linearizing around this allocation, the real marginal cost function in sector j can be approximated by

$$\hat{s}_t^j (i) = \omega \left(\hat{y}_t(i) - \hat{Y}_{jt}^n \right) + \sigma^{-1} \left(\hat{Y}_t - \hat{Y}_t^n \right) + \eta \left(\hat{\varphi}_{jt} + \hat{Y}_t^n - \hat{Y}_{jt}^n \right), \tag{B.30}$$

generalizing (1.15). (Here $\hat{\varphi}_{jt} \equiv \log \varphi_{jt}$, and the hatted output variables all represent log deviations from $\bar{Y}$.)

The choice of $p_t(i)$ by firms in sector j that revise their prices in period t so as to maximize the objective (2.24) implies a first-order condition for optimality of the form

$$E_t \left\{ \sum_{T=t}^{\infty} \alpha_j^{T-t} Q_{t,T} \Pi_p^j (p_{jt}^*, P_{jT}, P_T; Y_T, \tilde{\xi}_T) \right\} = 0. \qquad (B.31)$$

Substituting (B.28) into this and log-linearizing, one obtains

$$E_t \sum_{T=t}^{\infty} (\alpha_j \beta)^{T-t} \left\{ \hat{p}_{jt}^* - \left[\hat{s}_{t,T}^j - \hat{p}_{jT} + \sum_{\tau=t+1}^{T} \pi_{j\tau} \right] \right\} = 0, \qquad (B.32)$$

where $\hat{p}_{jt}^* \equiv \log(p_{jt}^*/p_{jt})$ is the relative price at date t (relative to other firms in the same sector) of the firms in sector j that have newly revised their prices, $\hat{p}_{jt} \equiv \log(P_{jt}/P_t)$ is the relative price index for sector j (relative to goods prices in the entire economy), and $\hat{s}_{t,T}^j$ is the value of $\hat{s}_T^j(i)$ for firms in sector j that last revised their prices at date t.

It further follows from (B.30) that

$$\hat{s}_{t,T}^j = \hat{s}_T^j - \omega\theta \left[\hat{p}_{jt}^* - \sum_{\tau=t+1}^{T} \pi_{j\tau} \right],$$

where $\hat{s}_t^j$ denotes the deviation of the log of the *average* level of real marginal cost in sector j from its steady-state value. Substitution of this into (B.32) then yields a log-linear pricing equation that can be written in the form (B.32).

A series of manipulations analogous to those used in the proof of Proposition 3.5 then yields a sectoral inflation equation of the form

$$\pi_{jt} = \xi_j (\hat{s}_t^j - \hat{p}_{jt}) + \beta E_t \pi_{j,t+1} \qquad (B.33)$$

for each sector, where

$$\xi_j \equiv \frac{1 - \alpha_j}{\alpha_j} \frac{1 - \alpha_j \beta}{1 + \omega\theta} > 0.$$

This generalizes the inflation equation (2.14) for the one-sector model.

Finally, (B.30) implies that

$$\hat{s}_t^j = \omega(\hat{Y}_{jt} - \hat{Y}_{jt}^n) + \sigma^{-1}(\hat{Y}_t - \hat{Y}_t^n) + \eta(\hat{\varphi}_{jt} + \hat{Y}_t^n - \hat{Y}_{jt}^n).$$

Substituting

$$\hat{Y}_{jt} = \hat{\varphi}_{jt} + \hat{Y}_t - \eta \hat{p}_{jt}$$

obtained from log-linearization of (B.29), one can alternatively express this as

$$\hat{s}_t^j - \hat{p}_{jt} = \left(\omega + \sigma^{-1}\right)\left(\hat{Y}_t - \hat{Y}_t^n\right) - (1 + \omega\eta)\left(\hat{p}_{jt} - \hat{p}_{jt}^n\right),$$

where $\hat{p}_{jt}^n$ is the log relative price index for sector j in a flexible-price equilibrium (a function solely of the exogenous real disturbances). Substituting this into (B.33), one obtains (B.27). Here I have written each of the sectoral relative prices as multiples of the single relative price $\hat{p}_{Rt} \equiv \log(P_{2t}/P_{1t})$ using the identities $\hat{p}_{1t} \equiv -n_2 \, \hat{p}_{Rt}$ and $\hat{p}_{2t} \equiv n_1 \, \hat{p}_{Rt}$, where $\hat{p}_{Rt}^n = n_1^{-1} \, \hat{p}_{2t}^n$ is the natural level of this relative price and the coefficients κ_j, γ_j are those stated in the proposition.

Addendum to Chapter 4

C.1 Determinacy of Equilibrium in Small Linear Models: Useful Results

The results on determinacy of equilibrium in Section 2.2 of Chapter 4 make use of the following general results regarding the eigenvalues of matrices.

PROPOSITION C.1. Consider a linear rational-expectations model of the form

$$E_t z_{t+1} = A z_t + a e_t,$$

where z_t is a 2-vector of nonpredetermined endogenous state variables, e_t is a vector of exogenous disturbance terms, and A is a 2×2 matrix of coefficients. Rational-expectations equilibrium is *determinate* if and only if the matrix A has both eigenvalues outside the unit circle (i.e., with modulus $|\lambda| > 1$).[1]

This condition in turn is satisfied if and only if *either* (Case I)

$$\det A > 1, \tag{C.1}$$

$$\det A - \text{tr} A > -1, \tag{C.2}$$

and

$$\det A + \text{tr} A > -1; \tag{C.3}$$

---

1. To be precise, these conditions are sufficient for determinacy, but only *generically* necessary. I omit consideration of nongeneric boundary cases, in which one or another of the conditions holds as an exact equality. In such cases, a log-linear approximation to the exact equilibrium conditions does not suffice to settle the question of whether equilibrium is locally determinate.

or (Case II)

$$\det A - \mathrm{tr} A < -1, \tag{C.4}$$

and

$$\det A + \mathrm{tr} A < -1. \tag{C.5}$$

PROOF. The eigenvalues of A are the two roots of the characteristic equation

$$P(\lambda) \equiv \lambda^2 + A_1 \lambda + A_0 = 0,$$

where $A_1 \equiv -\mathrm{tr} A$, $A_0 \equiv \det A$. I first show that either of the sets of conditions listed in the proposition imply that both roots of this equation are outside the unit circle. I begin with the conditions that define Case I.

Since the characteristic polynomial must equal $(\lambda - \lambda_1)(\lambda - \lambda_2)$, where λ_1, λ_2 are the two roots, observe that $\mathrm{tr} A = \lambda_1 + \lambda_2$ and $\det A = \lambda_1 \lambda_2$. Hence conditions (C.1)–(C.3) imply that

$$\lambda_1 \lambda_2 > 1, \tag{C.6}$$

$$(\lambda_1 - 1)(\lambda_2 - 1) > 0, \tag{C.7}$$

and

$$(\lambda_1 + 1)(\lambda_2 + 1) > 0. \tag{C.8}$$

In the case that there are two real roots, (C.7) and (C.8), respectively, imply that the two roots are on the same side of 1 and on the same side of -1. Hence they must either both be less than -1, or both greater than 1; in either case, both are outside the unit circle. Alternatively, in the case that the two roots form a complex pair, they have a common modulus, and $\lambda_1 \lambda_2$ is the square of that common modulus. Condition (C.6) then implies that this common modulus must be greater than 1, so that again both roots are outside the unit circle. Hence conditions (C.1)–(C.3) are sufficient for determinacy.

I next show that the conditions defining Case II are also sufficient. Conditions (C.4) and (C.5) correspondingly imply that

$$(\lambda_1 - 1)(\lambda_2 - 1) < 0, \tag{C.9}$$

and

$$(\lambda_1 + 1)(\lambda_2 + 1) < 0. \tag{C.10}$$

Hence they imply that the roots cannot form a complex pair, and that they must lie on opposite sides of both -1 and 1. Thus one root must lie below

-1 while the other is above 1. It follows that both roots are outside the unit circle, and conditions (C.4) and (C.5) are again sufficient for determinacy.

I now show that the conditions listed in the proposition are also (generically) necessary for determinacy. In other words, I show that if both roots of the characteristic equation are outside the unit circle, one or the other of these two sets of conditions must be satisfied.

There are again two cases to consider: that of two real roots with $|\lambda_1|$, $|\lambda_2| > 1$, and that of a complex pair with $|\lambda_1| = |\lambda_2| > 1$. In the case of two real roots, if both are greater than 1, then both are on the same side of -1 and also on the same side of 1, so that (C.7) and (C.8) must be satisfied. Further, the product of the two roots must be greater than 1, so that (C.6) must be satisfied as well. The same arguments apply if both roots are less than -1. Hence all three conditions defining Case I must be satisfied in the event of two real roots such that either $\lambda_1, \lambda_2 < -1$ or $\lambda_1, \lambda_2 > 1$. If, instead, $\lambda_1 < -1$ while $\lambda_2 > 1$, both (C.9) and (C.10) are satisfied, so that both conditions defining Case II are satisfied.

Finally, in the case of a complex pair outside the unit circle, the fact that the two roots form a complex pair implies that both (C.7) and (C.8) must hold; and the fact that the modulus is greater than 1 implies that the product of the two roots must be greater than 1, so that (C.6) is satisfied as well. Thus in this case, all three conditions defining Case I are satisfied. Thus in any possible case with both roots outside the unit circle, either the conditions defining Case I or those defining Case II must be satisfied.

PROPOSITION C.2. Consider a linear rational-expectations model of the form

$$\begin{bmatrix} E_t z_{t+1} \\ x_{t+1} \end{bmatrix} = A \begin{bmatrix} z_t \\ x_t \end{bmatrix} + a e_t$$

where z_t is again a 2-vector of nonpredetermined endogenous state variables, x_t is a single predetermined endogenous state variable, e_t is again a vector of exogenous disturbance terms, and A is a 3×3 matrix. Rational-expectations equilibrium is *determinate* if and only if the matrix A has *exactly one* eigenvalue inside the unit circle (i.e., with modulus $|\lambda| < 1$), and the other two eigenvalues outside the unit circle.

Let the characteristic equation of the matrix A be written in the form

$$\mathcal{P}(\lambda) \equiv \lambda^3 + \mathcal{A}_2 \lambda^2 + \mathcal{A}_1 \lambda + \mathcal{A}_0 = 0.$$

Then this equation has one root inside the unit circle and two roots outside (and the natural-expectations equilibrium is determinate) if and only if[2]:

---

2. As with Proposition C.1, these conditions are sufficient for determinacy but actually only *generically* necessary. I again omit discussion of certain nongeneric boundary cases.

either (Case I)

$$1 + A_2 + A_1 + A_0 < 0, \tag{C.11}$$

and

$$-1 + A_2 - A_1 + A_0 > 0; \tag{C.12}$$

or (Case II)

$$1 + A_2 + A_1 + A_0 > 0, \tag{C.13}$$

$$-1 + A_2 - A_1 + A_0 < 0, \tag{C.14}$$

and

$$A_0^2 - A_0 A_2 + A_1 - 1 > 0; \tag{C.15}$$

or (Case III) conditions (C.13) and (C.14) hold, and in addition[3]

$$A_0^2 - A_0 A_2 + A_1 - 1 < 0 \tag{C.16}$$

and

$$|A_2| > 3. \tag{C.17}$$

PROOF. I begin by establishing that each of the four cases listed is *sufficient* for determinacy. I start with Case I. Conditions (C.11) and (C.12) imply that $\mathcal{P}(1) > 0$ and $\mathcal{P}(-1) < 0$, respectively. Note also that $\mathcal{P}(\lambda) > 0$ for all large enough positive λ, and that $\mathcal{P}(\lambda) < 0$ for all large enough negative λ, as in either case the λ^3 term dominates the others. Then by continuity there must be three real roots, satisfying

$$\lambda_1 < -1 < \lambda_2 < 1 < \lambda_3.$$

Thus there is determinacy in this case.

I next consider Case II. Conditions (C.13) and (C.14) imply that $\mathcal{P}(1) < 0$ and $\mathcal{P}(-1) > 0$, respectively. By continuity there is then an odd number of real roots between -1 and 1 (i.e., inside the unit circle), as well as an even number less than -1 and an even number greater than 1. (These even numbers may be zero.)

---

3. Condition (C.16) is not actually needed in Case III in order for the proposition to be true. This condition is added in order to make the three cases mutually disjoint.

Noting that $\mathcal{P}(\lambda) = (\lambda - \lambda_1)(\lambda - \lambda_2)(\lambda - \lambda_3)$, one observes that the coefficients of the characteristic equation have the interpretations

$$A_0 = -\lambda_1\lambda_2\lambda_3,$$

$$A_1 = \lambda_1\lambda_2 + \lambda_1\lambda_3 + \lambda_2\lambda_3,$$

$$A_2 = -\lambda_1 - \lambda_2 - \lambda_3.$$

Substituting these into (C.15), one sees that (C.15) is equivalent to the requirement that

$$(\lambda_1\lambda_2 - 1)(\lambda_1\lambda_3 - 1)(\lambda_2\lambda_3 - 1) > 0.$$

Thus it implies that an *odd number* of the three *products* of roots are real numbers greater than 1. (If all three roots are real, so are all three products, and each factor above is a positive or negative real quantity depending on whether the product of the roots exceeds 1 or not. If roots λ_1 and λ_2 are a complex pair, then only the pair $\lambda_1\lambda_2$ is real, while $\lambda_1\lambda_3$ and $\lambda_2\lambda_3$ are *complex conjugates*. It follows that $(\lambda_1\lambda_3 - 1)(\lambda_2\lambda_3 - 1) > 0$, so that the inequality holds if and only if $\lambda_1\lambda_2 > 1$.)

These conditions suffice for determinacy. In the case that there exists one real root and a complex pair, conditions (C.13) and (C.14) imply that the real root must lie in the interval $-1 < \lambda_3 < 1$, while condition (C.15) implies that the complex pair must satisfy $|\lambda_1| = |\lambda_2| > 1$. Thus one has determinacy. Alternatively, if there exist three real roots, (C.13) and (C.14) imply that either one or three of them lie in the interval between -1 and 1. If all three do, all three products of the roots also lie between -1 and 1, contradicting (C.15). So instead one must lie inside the unit circle, and the other two outside. Thus one again has determinacy.

I next consider Case III. As above, conditions (C.13) and (C.14) imply that there is an odd number of real roots between -1 and 1. Furthermore, condition (C.17) implies that the sum of the roots $\lambda_1 + \lambda_2 + \lambda_3$ is either greater than 3 or less than -3. If all three roots are real, they cannot all lie between -1 and 1, as in that case their sum would lie between -3 and 3. But then the odd number of roots between -1 and 1 must be one, and the other two real roots must have absolute value greater than 1, so that there is determinacy. Alternatively, if there is one real root and a complex pair, the real root must lie between -1 and 1. The sum of the roots is in this case equal to the real root plus twice the real part of either of the complex roots. As the real root lies between -1 and 1, the only way that the sum of the roots can fail to lie between -3 and 3 is if the real part of the complex roots has an absolute value greater than one. But as the modulus of each complex root must be greater than the absolute value of the real part, it follows that both complex roots are outside the unit circle, and again one has determinacy. Thus the conditions stated in the proposition are sufficient for determinacy. (Note that the conditions listed under Case III would be sufficient even if one were not to require (C.16).)

I now establish that the conditions listed are (generically) *necessary* for determinacy as well, that is, that any (generic) case where determinacy obtains must satisfy the conditions for one of the three cases listed. I consider first the possibility that there exist three real roots. Then determinacy requires that exactly one of these lie between -1 and 1, while the other two each have an absolute value greater than 1. This requires that the roots satisfy one of the following three conditions:

(a) $\lambda_1 < -1 < \lambda_2 < 1 < \lambda_3$,
(b) $\lambda_1, \lambda_2 < -1 < \lambda_3 < 1$, or
(c) $-1 < \lambda_1 < 1 < \lambda_2, \lambda_3$.

I consider these possibilities in turn.

Case (a) requires that $\mathcal{P}(-1) > 0$ and $\mathcal{P}(1) < 0$, so that conditions (C.11) and (C.12) are satisfied. Thus the conditions for Case I of the proposition are satisfied. Cases (b) and (c) imply instead that $\mathcal{P}(-1) < 0$ and $\mathcal{P}(1) > 0$. Thus conditions (C.13) and (C.14) are satisfied in either of these cases.

Case (b) may be further subdivided into four (generic) subcases, in which

(b1) $\lambda_3^{-1} < \lambda_1, \lambda_2 < -1 < \lambda_3 < 0$,
(b2) $\lambda_1 < \lambda_3^{-1} < \lambda_2 < -1 < \lambda_3 < 0$,
(b3) $\lambda_1, \lambda_2 < \lambda_3^{-1} < -1 < \lambda_3 < 0$, or
(b4) $\lambda_1, \lambda_2 < -1 < 0 < \lambda_3 < 1$.

In each of these cases, the three products of the roots satisfy

(b1) $0 < \lambda_1\lambda_3, \lambda_2\lambda_3 < 1 < \lambda_1\lambda_2$,
(b2) $0 < \lambda_2\lambda_3 < 1 < \lambda_1\lambda_2, \lambda_1\lambda_3$,
(b3) $1 < \lambda_1\lambda_2, \lambda_1\lambda_3, \lambda_2\lambda_3$, and
(b4) $\lambda_1\lambda_3, \lambda_2\lambda_3 < 0 < 1 < \lambda_1\lambda_2$, respectively.

Observe that in cases (b1), (b3), and (b4), there is an odd number of products that are greater than 1. Thus these cases satisfy (C.15), and so all of the conditions required for Case II of the proposition are satisfied. However, in Case (b2), there is an even number of products greater than one, which implies that (C.16) is satisfied. Further observe that in this case the sum of the roots must satisfy

$$\lambda_1 + \lambda_2 + \lambda_3 < \lambda_3 + \lambda_3^{-1} - 1 < 3$$

so that (C.17) holds. Thus this case satisfies all of the conditions required for Case III of the proposition.

Case (c) can be treated in exactly the same way as Case (b), changing signs as appropriate. Thus in the case corresponding to (b2), one has instead

$$0 < \lambda_3 < 1 < \lambda_2 < \lambda_3^{-1} < \lambda_1,$$

which implies that the products of the roots again satisfy

$$0 < \lambda_2\lambda_3 < 1 < \lambda_1\lambda_2, \lambda_1\lambda_3,$$

while the sum of the roots satisfy

$$\lambda_1 + \lambda_2 + \lambda_3 > \lambda_3 + \lambda_3^{-1} + 1 > 3.$$

Thus once again (C.16) and (C.17) are satisfied, and so are all of the conditions required for Case III of the proposition. I conclude that if there are three real roots, any (generic) determinate case must satisfy one of the sets of conditions stated in the proposition.

I finally consider the possibility that there exist one real root and a complex pair. In this case, determinacy requires that the real root lie in the interval between −1 and 1, while the complex pair has a modulus greater than 1. Because there are no real roots less than −1 or greater than 1, in such a case one must have $\mathcal{P}(-1) < 0$ and $\mathcal{P}(1) > 0$. Thus conditions (C.13) and (C.14) are satisfied. Furthermore, in such a case, only one product of the roots is a real number, the product of the two complex roots, and this product is equal to the square of the modulus. As the modulus is greater than 1, this product is a real number greater than 1. Thus exactly one product is a real number greater than 1, and condition (C.15) is satisfied. It follows that all of the conditions required for Case II of the proposition are satisfied. I have thus shown that every (generic) determinate case satisfies one of the sets of conditions stated in the proposition.

C.2 Proof of Proposition 4.3

PROPOSITION 4.3. Suppose that monetary policy is conducted so as to ensure that the nominal interest rate satisfies a rule of the form of equation (1.14) of Chapter 4, where $\phi_\pi, \phi_x \geq 0$. Then equilibrium is determinate if and only if the response coefficients satisfy

$$\phi_\pi + \frac{1-\beta}{4\kappa}\phi_x > 1. \tag{C.18}$$

PROOF. The analysis of determinacy of equilibrium in this case proceeds along similar lines as for Proposition 4.2, discussed in the text of Chapter 4. In the present case, substitution of (1.14) into (1.12) to eliminate $\hat{\imath}_t$ again yields a system of the form

$$E_t z_{t+1} = A z_t + a \left(\hat{r}_t^n - \bar{\imath}_t + \bar{\pi} \right), \tag{C.19}$$

where now

$$z_t \equiv \begin{bmatrix} \pi_t - \bar{\pi} \\ x_t - \bar{x} \end{bmatrix},$$

and

$$A \equiv \begin{bmatrix} \beta^{-1} & -\beta^{-1}\kappa \\ \sigma \left(\phi_\pi - \beta^{-1} \right) & 1 + \sigma \left(\phi_x/4 + \beta^{-1}\kappa \right) \end{bmatrix}, \qquad a \equiv \begin{bmatrix} 0 \\ -\sigma \end{bmatrix}.$$

Observe that

$$\operatorname{tr} A = 1 + \beta^{-1}(1 + \kappa\sigma) + \sigma\phi_x/4, \qquad \det A = \beta^{-1} \left[1 + \sigma \left(\phi_x/4 + \kappa\phi_\pi \right) \right].$$

From Proposition C.1 in Section C.1, it is known that a 2×2 matrix with a positive determinant has both eigenvalues outside the unit circle (the condition for determinacy) if and only if either the inequalities defining Case I or those defining Case II are satisfied. Under the sign restrictions, (C.5) is necessarily violated, so Case II is not possible. Hence I may restrict attention to Case I, and equilibrium is determinate if and only if (C.1)–(C.3) are all satisfied.

Under the sign restrictions, the first and third of these inequalities necessarily hold, so that both eigenvalues are outside the unit circle if and only if (C.2) also holds. Given the above expressions for $\operatorname{tr} A$ and $\det A$ in the present case, this inequality is equivalent to (C.18). Hence that condition alone is necessary and sufficient.

C.3 Proof of Proposition 4.4

PROPOSITION 4.4. Suppose that monetary policy is conducted so as to ensure that the nominal interest rate satisfies a rule of the form of equation (2.8) in Chapter 4, where $\rho, \phi_\pi, \phi_x \geq 0$. Then equilibrium is determinate if and only if the response coefficients satisfy

$$\phi_\pi + \frac{1 - \beta}{4\kappa} \phi_x > 1 - \rho. \tag{C.20}$$

Proof: Substituting (2.8) into (1.12), I again obtain a system of equations that may be written in the form (C.19), but where now the vector of endogenous variables is

$$z_t \equiv \begin{bmatrix} \pi_t - \bar{\pi} \\ x_t - \bar{x} \\ \hat{\imath}_{t-1} - \bar{\imath}_{t-1} \end{bmatrix}, \tag{C.21}$$

and

$$A \equiv \begin{bmatrix} \beta^{-1} & -\beta^{-1}\kappa & 0 \\ \sigma(\phi_\pi - \beta^{-1}) & 1 + \sigma(\phi_x/4 + \beta^{-1}\kappa) & \sigma\rho \\ \phi_\pi & \phi_x/4 & \rho \end{bmatrix}, \qquad a \equiv \begin{bmatrix} 0 \\ -\sigma \\ 0 \end{bmatrix}.$$

As there is now a predetermined state variable (namely, $\hat{\imath}_{t-1} - \bar{\imath}_{t-1}$), equilibrium is determinate in this case if and only if the 3×3 matrix A has exactly two eigenvalues outside the unit circle.

Necessary and sufficient conditions for determinacy in a system of this form are given by Proposition C.2 of Section C.1. Note that in the present case, the characteristic equation of matrix A is of the form

$$\mathcal{P}(\mu) = \mu^3 + A_2\mu^2 + A_1\mu + A_0 = 0,$$

where

$$A_0 = -\beta^{-1}\rho < 0,$$

$$A_1 = \rho + \beta^{-1}(1 + \rho(1 + \kappa\sigma)) + \beta^{-1}\sigma(\kappa\phi_\pi + \phi_x/4) > 0,$$

$$A_2 = -\beta^{-1}(1 + \kappa\sigma) - 1 - \rho - \sigma\phi_x/4 < 0.$$

The proposition lists three possible sets of conditions under which there is determinacy. Because of the signs of the coefficients A_i, one sees immediately that condition (C.12) is violated and that condition (C.14) must hold instead; thus one can exclude Case I of the proposition. In the present case, the remaining conditions (in addition to (C.14) that, as I have just noted, is necessarily satisfied) required for Case II of the proposition reduce to

$$\phi_\pi + \frac{1-\beta}{4\kappa}\phi_x > 1 - \rho, \tag{C.22}$$

$$\phi_\pi + \frac{1-\rho}{4\kappa}\phi_x + (\beta^{-1} - 1)\left[\kappa^{-1}\sigma^{-1}(1-\rho)(\beta-\rho) - \rho\right] > 0. \tag{C.23}$$

The remaining conditions required for Case III[4] are instead (C.22) and

$$\beta^{-1}(1 + \kappa\sigma) + \rho + \sigma\phi_x/4 > 2. \tag{C.24}$$

Equilibrium is determinate if and only if the coefficients of the policy rule (2.8) satisfy both (C.22) and at least one of (C.23) and (C.24).

In fact, one can show that under the sign assumptions, (C.22) is both necessary and sufficient for determinacy. One proves this by showing that any parameter values that satisfy (C.22) and *not* (C.24) must necessarily satisfy (C.23). First note that under the sign assumptions, (C.24) can fail to hold only if $\rho < \beta$. (Here I use the fact that $\beta^{-1} + \beta > 2$.) Next observe that the left-hand side of (C.23) is a decreasing function of ρ, for given values of all the other parameters, for all values $\rho < \beta$. Thus the values of ϕ_π required in order for (C.23) not to hold become smaller, the smaller the value of ρ. On the other hand, the values of ϕ_π consistent with (C.22) become larger, as ρ becomes smaller. Thus if (C.22) is to be satisfied while (C.23) is not, for any given values of β, κ, σ, and ϕ_x, this must occur for the *largest* value of ρ consistent with (C.24) being (weakly) violated. (Note that this last quantity is independent of ϕ_π.)

Furthermore, the left-hand side of (C.23) is an increasing function of ϕ_π. Thus if (C.22) is to be satisfied while (C.23) is not, for any given values of β, κ, σ, ϕ_x, and ρ, this must occur for the *smallest* value of ϕ_π that is (weakly) consistent with (C.22). (The geometry of these regions is illustrated in Figure C.1.) It therefore suffices that one consider values of ρ and ϕ_π for which (C.22) and (C.24) hold as equalities for given values of the other parameters. (This is the point shown by the intersection of the solid and dashed lines in Figure C.1.) If (C.23) is not violated in this case, it can never be.

The algebra required to check this is simplest if one solves (C.22) and (C.24) for ϕ_π and ϕ_x as functions of ρ, rather than for ρ and ϕ_π as functions of ϕ_x. One obtains

$$\phi_\pi = (1 - \rho) - \frac{1 - \beta}{\kappa\sigma}\left[2 - \rho - \frac{1 + \kappa\sigma}{\beta}\right],$$

$$\phi_x = \frac{4}{\sigma}\left[2 - \rho - \frac{1 + \kappa\sigma}{\beta}\right].$$

---

4. In the statement of Proposition C.2 in Section C.1, another condition listed is (C.16), which is the denial that (C.23) holds. But this is not necessary, for if (C.23) holds instead, determinacy also obtains, as Case II then applies. Also condition (C.17) as written in the statement of the proposition allows the coefficient A_2 to be either less than -3 or greater than 3. But as in the present case A_2 is necessarily negative, it is only the possibility that A_2 may be less than -3 that is relevant; this is condition (C.24).

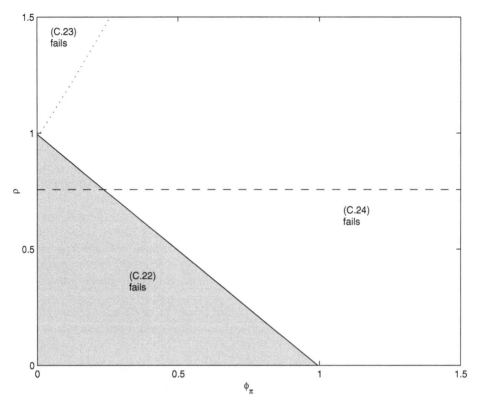

Figure C.1 *Regions in which each of three inequalities fail to hold. Gray region indicates policy rules for which equilibrium is indeterminate; white region indicates determinacy.*

Substituting these values into the left-hand side of (C.23) yields

$$\frac{1}{\beta \kappa \sigma}(\beta - \rho)^2 > 0,$$

which holds as a strict inequality because $\rho < \beta$. Thus (C.23) holds in this case, and so must hold in any case where (C.22) holds but (C.24) does not. (This is illustrated for particular numerical parameter values in Figure C.1.[5]) It follows that condition (C.22) is necessary and sufficient for determinacy.

---

5. The values assumed for β, κ, and σ are given in Table 5.1; the value assumed for ϕ_x is .05. This last value has no particular significance, except that the relative locations of the various regions are especially easily seen for a small positive value of this order.

C.4 Proof of Proposition 4.5

PROPOSITION 4.5. Suppose that monetary policy is conducted so as to ensure that the nominal interest rate satisfies a rule of the form (2.10), where $\phi_\pi, \phi_x \geq 0$. Then equilibrium is determinate if and only if the response coefficients satisfy both (C.18) and

$$\phi_\pi < 1 + \frac{1+\beta}{4\kappa}\left(\phi_x + 8\sigma^{-1}\right). \tag{C.25}$$

PROOF. Substituting (2.10) into (1.12) to eliminate $\hat{\imath}_t$, I again obtain an equation system of the form (C.19), but where now

$$z_t \equiv \begin{bmatrix} \pi_t - \bar{\pi} \\ x_t - \bar{x} \end{bmatrix},$$

and

$$A \equiv \begin{bmatrix} \beta^{-1} & -\beta^{-1}\kappa \\ \sigma\beta^{-1}(\phi_\pi - 1) & 1 + \sigma\left(\phi_x/4 - \beta^{-1}\kappa(\phi_\pi - 1)\right) \end{bmatrix}, \quad a \equiv \begin{bmatrix} 0 \\ -\sigma \end{bmatrix}.$$

Thus in this case one has

$$\operatorname{tr} A = 1 + \beta^{-1} + \sigma(\phi_x/4 - \beta^{-1}\kappa(\phi_\pi - 1)),$$

$$\det A = \beta^{-1}(1 + \sigma\phi_x/4).$$

As in the proof of Proposition 4.3, determinacy obtains if and only if either conditions (C.1)–(C.3) or conditions (C.4) and (C.5) are all satisfied. One may note (by summing the left-hand sides of the two inequalities) that (C.4) and (C.5) imply that $\det A < -1$. But under the sign assumptions, the expression just given for $\det A$ implies that $\det A > 1$. Hence Case II is not possible, as in the proof of Proposition 4.3, and once again equilibrium is determinate if and only if conditions (C.1)–(C.3) are jointly satisfied.

In the present case, the first condition takes a slightly different form than before, but it is again necessarily satisfied by all rules satisfying the sign assumptions (as just noted). The second condition again is equivalent to (2.7). However, the third condition now takes a slightly different form than in the case of conventional (backward-looking) Taylor rules, and is no longer necessarily satisfied by all rules satisfying our sign restrictions. This condition is now equivalent to (C.25). Hence both roots of the characteristic equation are outside the unit circle (the condition required for determinacy) if and only if the coefficients of the policy rule satisfy both (2.7) and (2.11).

C.5 Proof of Proposition 4.6

PROPOSITION 4.6. Suppose that monetary policy is conducted so as to ensure that the nominal interest rate satisfies a rule of the form of equation (2.12) of Chapter 4, where $\rho, \phi_\pi, \phi_x \geq 0$. Then it is necessary for determinacy of equilibrium that the response coefficients satisfy both (C.20), generalizing (C.18), and

$$\phi_\pi < 1 + \rho + \frac{1+\beta}{4\kappa}\left(\phi_x + 8\sigma^{-1}(1+\rho)\right), \tag{C.26}$$

generalizing (C.25).

PROOF: This rule again implies a system of equations that may be written in the form (C.19), but with a vector of endogenous variables given by (C.21) and coefficient matrices

$$A \equiv \begin{bmatrix} \beta^{-1} & -\beta^{-1}\kappa & 0 \\ \sigma\beta^{-1}(\phi_\pi - 1) & 1 + \sigma\left(\phi_x/4 - \beta^{-1}\kappa(\phi_\pi - 1)\right) & \sigma\rho \\ \beta^{-1}\phi_\pi & \phi_x/4 - \beta^{-1}\kappa\phi_\pi & \rho \end{bmatrix}, \quad a \equiv \begin{bmatrix} 0 \\ -\sigma \\ 0 \end{bmatrix}.$$

As in the proof of Proposition 4.4, there is a single predetermined state variable (namely, $\hat{\imath}_{t-1} - \bar{\imath}_{t-1}$), so that equilibrium is determinate if and only if A has exactly two eigenvalues outside the unit circle. Once again necessary and sufficient conditions for this are given by Proposition C.2 in Section C.1.

Observe that conditions (A.1) and (A.2) imply that $\phi_x < 0$, so that Case I is once again impossible under the sign assumptions. It then follows that conditions (A.3) and (A.4) are necessary for determinacy, as these are required by both Cases II and III of the proposition. In the present case, (A.3) corresponds once again to (C.20), while (A.4) corresponds to (C.26). Hence these conditions are both necessary for determinacy.

Additional restrictions may, however, be necessary in order to ensure that sufficient conditions for either Case II or Case III of Proposition C.2 are satisfied. For determinacy to obtain, either (A.5) must hold or one of the two cases allowed in (A.7) must hold, that is, either $A_2 > 3$ or $A_2 < -3$. I omit analysis of the sufficient conditions here, but note that they are satisfied in the numerical example shown in Figure 4.2. For the parameter values used in this figure, all policy-rule coefficients that satisfy (C.20) and (C.26) also satisfy at least one of the other three inequalities. Thus the two conditions listed in the proposition turn out to be both necessary and sufficient for determinacy, at least in this case.

C.6 Proof of Proposition 4.7

PROPOSITION 4.7. Suppose that monetary policy is conducted so as to ensure that the nominal interest rate satisfies a rule of the form (2.14), where $\phi_p > 0, \phi_x \geq 0$. Then equilibrium is necessarily determinate.

PROOF: In the case of a Wicksellian policy rule, it is useful to rewrite (1.10) in the form

$$\Delta(p_t - \bar{p}_t) = \kappa(x_t - \bar{x}) + \beta E_t \Delta(p_{t+1} - \bar{p}_{t+1}),$$

and to similarly replace the expression $E_t \pi_{t+1}$ in (1.12) by $E_t \Delta(p_{t+1} - \bar{p}_{t+1}) + \bar{\pi}$. The system of equations consisting of (1.10), (1.12), and (2.14) can then be expressed in the form (C.19), with a vector of endogenous variables given by

$$z_t \equiv \begin{bmatrix} p_t - \bar{p}_t \\ p_{t-1} - \bar{p}_{t-1} \\ x_t - \bar{x} \end{bmatrix}, \tag{C.27}$$

and coefficient matrices

$$A \equiv \begin{bmatrix} 1 + \beta^{-1} & -\beta^{-1} & -\beta^{-1}\kappa \\ 1 & 0 & 0 \\ \sigma\left(\phi_p - \beta^{-1}\right) & \sigma\beta^{-1} & 1 + \sigma\left(\phi_x + \beta^{-1}\kappa\right) \end{bmatrix}, \quad a \equiv \begin{bmatrix} 0 \\ 0 \\ -\sigma \end{bmatrix}.$$

This is again a case in which there is a single predetermined state variable (namely, $p_{t-1} - \bar{p}_{t-1}$), so that equilibrium is determinate if and only if A has exactly two eigenvalues outside the unit circle, and the relevant necessary and sufficient conditions are given by Proposition C.2.

As shown in Giannoni (2000, app. A.2), under the sign assumptions one can show that conditions (A.3) and (A.4) necessarily hold, and also that (A.7) holds (with $A_2 < -3$). As noted in the proof of Proposition C.2, these are sufficient conditions for determinacy. (In the definition of Case III in the proposition, condition (A.6) is included only to make Cases II and III disjoint.) Hence equilibrium is determinate in the case of any policy rule in this class.

C.7 Proof of Proposition 4.9

PROPOSITION 4.9. Again suppose that the mapping from beliefs to outcomes is the one proposed by Bullard and Mitra equations (2.16) and (2.17) in Chapter 4, and that policy is conducted according to an interest-rate rule in the class (1.14), with coefficients ϕ_π, $\phi_x \geq 0$. But suppose now that agents forecast inflation and the output gap through linear regression of z_τ on $\bar{s}_{\tau-1}$, with the coefficient estimates $\hat{\Gamma}_t$ used to forecast in period t based on inflation and output data from periods $\tau < t$. Then the rational-expectations equilibrium $\bar{\Gamma}$ is *E-stable* if and only if the response coefficients of the policy rule satisfy (C.18), that is, if and only if policy conforms to the Taylor principle.

PROOF: As with Proposition 4.8, the rational-expectations equilibrium (fixed point of T) is E-stable if and only if all eigenvalues of the Jacobian matrix $DT(\bar{\Gamma}) - I$ have a negative real part. Here one vectorizes Γ as

$$\begin{bmatrix} \Gamma_0 \\ \text{vec } \Gamma_s \end{bmatrix}$$

in order to write this array of derivatives as a matrix. In the present example, T is a linear mapping, given by

$$\Gamma_0 - \bar{z} = B[\hat{\Gamma}_0 - \bar{z}], \tag{C.28}$$

$$\Gamma_s - \bar{\Gamma}_s = B(\hat{\Gamma}_s - \bar{\Gamma}_s)C.$$

In terms of vec Γ_s, the latter mapping can be written

$$\text{vec } \Gamma_s - \text{vec } \bar{\Gamma}_s = \begin{bmatrix} C' \otimes B \end{bmatrix} \left(\text{vec } \hat{\Gamma}_s - \text{vec } \bar{\Gamma}_s \right). \tag{C.29}$$

It follows from (C.28) and (C.29) that DT is given by

$$DT = \begin{bmatrix} B & 0 \\ 0 & C' \otimes B \end{bmatrix}.$$

The eigenvalues of DT are therefore the eigenvalues of the two diagonal blocks. One set is thus the two eigenvalues of B. As shown in the proof of Proposition 4.8, these both have a real part less than one (as required for E-stability) if and only if the response coefficients of the policy rule satisfy (C.18). Hence (C.18) is again necessary for determinacy. It remains to show that this condition also implies that all of the other eigenvalues of DT have real part less than one.

The remaining eigenvalues of DT are the eigenvalues of $C' \otimes B$. The eigenvalues of the Kronecker product are the set of products of the form $\rho_i \lambda_j$, where ρ_i is an eigenvalue of C' and λ_j is an eigenvalue of B. If (C.18) is satisfied, $|\lambda_j| < 1$ for $j = 1, 2$. (This is shown in the proof of Proposition 4.3.) I have also assumed that each of the eigenvalues of C (and hence each of the eigenvalues of C') satisfies $|\rho_i| < 1$, as this is required for stationarity of the exogenous disturbances. It follows that $|\rho_i \lambda_j| < 1$ for all pairs (i, j), and hence that every eigenvalue of $C' \otimes B$ has a modulus less than one, and hence a real part less than one. Thus (C.18) is also a sufficient condition for E-stability.

C.8 Proof of Proposition 4.11

PROPOSITION 4.11. Consider again the basic neo-Wicksellian model of a cashless economy, and suppose that monetary policy is conducted in accordance with a rule of the form of equation (1.14) of Chapter 4, where ϕ_π, $\phi_x \geq 0$, while fiscal policy is determined by a rule of the form (4.3), with $\tau_b \leq 1$. Then if fiscal policy is *locally Ricardian* (i.e., if $\tau_b > 1 - \beta > 0$), the results reported in Proposition 4.3 apply: Equilibrium is determinate if and only if the monetary policy rule conforms to the Taylor principle, that is, the response coefficients satisfy (C.18). If the inequality in (C.18) is reversed, equilibrium is *indeterminate* as discussed in Section 2 of Chapter 4.

If, instead, fiscal policy is *locally non-Ricardian* (i.e., if $\tau_b < 1 - \beta$), equilibrium is determinate (generically) if and only if the monetary policy rule *violates* the Taylor principle, that is, the inequality in (C.18) is reversed. If instead monetary policy conforms to the Taylor principle, there is (for almost all possible initial conditions and realizations of the exogenous disturbances) no equilibrium in which the paths of the endogenous variables $\{b_t, \pi_t, Y_t, i_t\}$ remain forever within small intervals around their steady-state values, no matter how small the open sets of values from which the initial conditions and disturbances may be selected.

PROOF: When one adjoins the law of motion (4.5) for government debt to the equations considered in the proof of Proposition 4.3, one obtains a system of equations of the form

$$\begin{bmatrix} E_t z_{t+1} \\ \hat{b}_t \end{bmatrix} = \begin{bmatrix} A & 0 \\ c' & \beta^{-1}(1 - \tau_b) \end{bmatrix} \begin{bmatrix} z_t \\ \hat{b}_{t-1} \end{bmatrix} + \begin{bmatrix} a(\hat{r}_t^n - \bar{\imath}_t + \bar{\pi}) \\ f_t \end{bmatrix},$$

where A, a, and z_t are defined as in (C.19). Because the state vector contains one predetermined variable ($\hat{b}_{t-1}$) in addition to two nonpredetermined variables (the elements of z_t), equilibrium is determinate if and only if the large matrix has exactly two eigenvalues outside the unit circle. Because the matrix is block-diagonal, its eigenvalues are the two eigenvalues of A and the diagonal element $\beta^{-1}(1 - \tau_b)$.

In the case that the fiscal rule is locally Ricardian, the third eigenvalue is inside the unit circle, so that determinacy requires that both eigenvalues of A be outside the unit circle. This is the case already characterized in Proposition 4.3, and when A has the required property (i.e., when monetary policy conforms to the Taylor principle), the unique bounded solution for $\{z_t\}$ is the one given by (2.34).

If instead the fiscal rule is locally non-Ricardian, the third eigenvalue is outside the unit circle, so that determinacy requires that exactly one of the eigenvalues of A be outside the unit circle. This is the case that obtains if and only if the inequality is reversed in (C.18), and that results in indeterminacy when the fiscal rule is locally Ricardian. For further discussion of equilibrium determination in this case, see Woodford (1996).

Addendum to Chapter 5

D.1 Alternative Interpretation of the Habit Persistence Model

It might be thought inappropriate to specify habit persistence in the determination of private expenditure as a whole, given that the classic literature on habit persistence relates to theory of household consumption expenditure, while I pointed out (in Chapter 4) that when one models the determination of aggregate private expenditure by a single Euler equation, one does not really mean to assume that all private expenditure actually consists only of consumer spending. For purposes of understanding the monetary transmission mechanism, it is surely the effects of interest rates on investment spending with which one is principally concerned. (This is verified quantitatively in a model that explicitly models consumption and investment expenditure separately, in Section 3 of Chapter 5.) How, then, could it make sense to assume habit persistence in the kind of private expenditure that matters for the monetary transmission mechanism?

While the hypothesis of habit persistence is most familiar from the literature on consumption spending, one can also make sense of the specification proposed in Section 1.2 of Chaper 5 under the interpretation that C_t^h actually refers to investment expenditure (albeit modeled in a way that abstracts from the consequences of investment spending for the evolution of production costs). The parallel is clearest if we assume investment adjustment costs of the specific kind postulated by Basu and Kimball (2002).

Suppose that a household's utility flow from its investment expenditures each period are equal to a term νK_t^h, for some constant $\nu > 0$, indicating the direct utility flow obtained from possession of a capital stock of size K_t^h, minus a term $\psi(S_t^h; \xi_t)$, where for each possible value of the disturbance ξ_t, $\psi(\cdot; \xi_t)$ is an increasing, strictly convex function, indicating the effort that must be expended in order to start S_t^h new investment projects in a given period. (Here I model the household's demand for capital as if capital goods were simply durable consumer goods, and also assume no diminishing marginal utility from owning additional durables of this kind. For simplicity, I also assume that the household obtains no utility from any other kind of expenditures.)

The household's capital stock evolves according to a law of motion $K_{t+1}^h = I_t^h + (1 - \delta)K_t^h$, where I_t^h is the household's investment spending, and $0 < \delta < 1$ is the rate of depreciation of capital goods. Its rate of investment expenditure is given by $I_t^h = S_t^h + \eta I_{t-1}^h$, where $0 < \eta < 1$ indicates the degree to which investment projects involve "time to build." Starting a new project in period t implies a stream of investment expenditures of size η^j in each period $t + j$ for all $j \geq 0$.

In such a model, the relation between the marginal utility of additional real income and investment expenditure is of the form indicated by equation (1.23) of Chapter 5, with each term of the form $u_c(C_t - \eta C_{t-1}; \xi_t)$ replaced by $\gamma - \psi_s(I_t - \eta I_{t-1}; \xi_t)$, where $\gamma \equiv v\beta/[(1 - \beta\eta)(1 - \beta(1 - \delta))] > 0$. Note that this is a monotonically decreasing function of $I_t - \eta I_{t-1}$, for each possible value of ξ_t, just as with the function u_c in the case of (1.23).

Investment adjustment costs of a similar form are also argued to be empirically realistic by Christiano et al. (2001).

D.2   Proof of Proposition 5.1

PROPOSITION 5.1. In the model with endogenous capital accumulation the optimal relative price of a firm that revises its price in period t is given by

$$(a - b)\hat{p}_t^* = \sum_{k=0}^{\infty}(\alpha\beta)^k E_t \hat{s}_{t+k} + a\sum_{k=1}^{\infty}(\alpha\beta)^k E_t \pi_{t+k} - b\sum_{k=1}^{\infty}\mu_2^{-k} E_t \pi_{t+k}, \quad (D.1)$$

where

$$a \equiv \frac{1 + \omega\theta}{1 - \alpha\beta} + (\omega - v)\frac{\alpha}{1 - \alpha\beta}\frac{\Xi}{(1 - \alpha\beta\mu_1)(1 - \alpha\beta\mu_2)} > 0,$$

$$b \equiv (\omega - v)\frac{\alpha}{1 - \mu_2^{-1}}\frac{\Xi}{(1 - \alpha\beta\mu_1)(1 - \alpha\beta\mu_2)} > 0,$$

$$\Xi \equiv (1 - \beta(1 - \delta))\rho_y\theta\epsilon_\psi^{-1} > 0,$$

and μ_2 is the root greater than β^{-1} of the equation

$$\mathcal{P}(\mu) \equiv \beta\mu^2 - \left[1 + \beta + (1 - \beta(1 - \delta))\rho_k\epsilon_\psi^{-1}\right]\mu + 1 = 0. \quad (D.2)$$

PROOF: Equation (3.7) of Chapter 5 implies that

$$\epsilon_\psi \left[\tilde{k}_{t+1}(i) - \tilde{k}_t(i) \right] = \left[1 - \beta(1-\delta) \right] \left[\rho_y E_t \left(\hat{y}_{t+1}(i) - \hat{Y}_t \right) - \rho_k \tilde{k}_{t+1}(i) \right]$$
$$+ \beta \epsilon_\psi E_t \left[\tilde{k}_{t+2}(i) - \tilde{k}_{t+1}(i) \right].$$

Again using the demand curve to express relative output as a function of the firm's relative price, this can be written as

$$E_t \left[Q(L) \tilde{k}_{t+2}(i) \right] = \Xi E_t \hat{p}_{t+1}(i), \tag{D.3}$$

where the lag polynomial is

$$Q(L) \equiv \beta - \left[1 + \beta + (1 - \beta(1-\delta)) \rho_k \epsilon_\psi^{-1} \right] L + L^2,$$

and Ξ is defined as in the statement of the proposition.

The lag polynomial can be factored as

$$Q(L) = \beta(1 - \mu_1 L)(1 - \mu_2 L),$$

where μ_1 and μ_2 are the two roots of the characteristic polynomial (D.2). Given that $Q(0) = \beta > 0$, $Q(\beta) < 0$, $Q(1) < 0$, and that $Q(z) > 0$ for all large enough $z > 0$, one sees that $Q(z)$ has two real roots: one between 0 and β and another that is greater than 1. Hence the two roots of (D.2) satisfy $0 < \mu_1 < 1 < \beta^{-1} < \mu_2$.

One also notes that

$$\Xi = -\theta \frac{\rho_y}{\rho_k} Q(1) = \beta\theta \frac{\rho_y}{\rho_k} \mu_2 \left(1 - \mu_1 \right)(1 - \mu_2^{-1}).$$

It then follows that in the case of any bounded process $\{\hat{p}_t(i)\}$, (D.3) has a unique bounded solution for the evolution of $\{\tilde{k}_t(i)\}$, given an initial capital stock for the firm. This solution is given by

$$\tilde{k}_{t+1}(i) = \mu_1 \tilde{k}_t(i) - z_t(i), \tag{D.4}$$

which may be integrated forward starting from an initial condition $\tilde{k}_t(i)$; here I define

$$z_t(i) \equiv \beta^{-1} \Xi \sum_{j=1}^{\infty} \mu_2^{-j} E_t \hat{p}_{t+j}(i).$$

Equation (3.13) requires that one evaluate the infinite sum $\sum_{k=0}^{\infty}(\alpha\beta)^k E_t \tilde{k}_{t+k}(i)$. I note that (D.4) implies that

$$E_t \tilde{k}_{t+k+1}(i) = \mu_1 E_t \tilde{k}_{t+k}(i) - E_t z_{t+k}(i)$$

for all $k \geq 0$. Integrating this law of motion I then find that

$$E_t \tilde{k}_{t+k}(i) = \mu_1^k \tilde{k}_t(i) - \sum_{j=0}^{k-1} \mu_1^{k-1-j} E_t z_{t+j}(i),$$

from which it follows that

$$\sum_{k=0}^{\infty}(\alpha\beta)^k E_t \tilde{k}_{t+k}(i) = \frac{1}{1-\alpha\beta\mu_1}\tilde{k}_t(i) - \frac{\alpha\beta}{1-\alpha\beta\mu_1}\sum_{j=0}^{\infty}(\alpha\beta)^j E_t z_{t+j}(i). \tag{D.5}$$

Furthermore, the final term in this last relation can be expressed in terms of expected relative prices, yielding

$$\sum_{j=0}^{\infty}(\alpha\beta)^j E_t z_{t+j}(i) =$$

$$\frac{\Xi}{\beta(1-\alpha\beta\mu_2)}\left[\sum_{j=1}^{\infty}\mu_2^{-j} E_t \hat{p}_{t+j}(i) - \sum_{j=1}^{\infty}(\alpha\beta)^j E_t \hat{p}_{t+j}(i)\right]. \tag{D.6}$$

Now substituting (D.5) and (D.6) for the sum of expected relative capital stocks in (3.13), I obtain a relation that involves only the initial relative capital stock $\tilde{k}_t(i)$. This relation can be simplified if it is averaged over all of the firms i that choose new prices at date t. Because the Calvo model assumes that all firms are equally likely to choose new prices at date t, the average value of $\tilde{k}_t(i)$ is zero (even though the average value of $E_t \tilde{k}_{t+k}(i)$ need not be zero for horizons $k > 0$). The average value of $E_t \hat{p}_{t+k}(i)$ can also be expressed as

$$\hat{p}_t^* - \sum_{j=1}^{k} E_t \pi_{t+j},$$

where $\hat{p}_t^*$ denotes the average relative price (average value of $\log p_t(i)/P_t$) for the firms that choose new prices at date t. With these substitutions, (3.13) yields an equation for $\hat{p}_t^*$ of the form (D.1), where a and b are defined as in the statement of the proposition.

D.3 Proof of Proposition 5.2

PROPOSITION 5.2. Let $\check{Y}_t \equiv \hat{Y}_t - \hat{Y}_t^n$, where the natural rate of output $\hat{Y}_t^n$ represents the flexible-price equilibrium level of output given $\hat{K}_t$, and similarly let $\check{K}_{t+1} \equiv \hat{K}_{t+1} - \hat{K}_{t+1}^n$, where $\hat{K}_{t+1}^n$ represents the flexible-price equilibrium capital stock given $\hat{K}_t$ [the *actual* capital stock in period t, not what it *would* have been if prices had been flexible in earlier periods]. Then optimizing investment demand implies that the joint dynamics of the output and capital gaps $\{\check{Y}_t, \check{K}_{t+1}\}$ satisfy

$$[1 - \beta(1 - \delta)] \left[\rho_y \left(E_t \check{Y}_{t+1} + \eta_y \check{K}_{t+1} \right) - \rho_k \check{K}_{t+1} \right]$$

$$+ \beta \epsilon_\psi \left[\left(E_t \check{K}_{t+2} + \eta_k \check{K}_{t+1} \right) - \check{K}_{t+1} \right], \tag{D.7}$$

where the coefficients ρ_y, ρ_k, η_y, η_k are again defined as in equation (3.7) of Chapter 5.

PROOF: I first note that condition (3.7) of Chapter 5, which is independent of the assumptions about pricing, must hold in a flexible-price equation, just as in the sticky-price model. It follows that

$$\hat{\lambda}_t^n + \epsilon_\psi \left(\hat{K}_{t+1}^n - \hat{K}_t \right) = \beta(1 - \delta) \left[E_t \hat{\lambda}_{t+1} - \eta_\lambda \check{K}_{t+1} \right]$$

$$+ \left[1 - \beta(1 - \delta) \right] \left[\rho_y \left(E_t \hat{Y}_{t+1}^n - \eta_y \check{K}_{t+1} \right) - \rho_k \hat{K}_{t+1}^n - \omega q_t \right]$$

$$+ \beta \epsilon_\psi \left[\left(E_t \hat{K}_{t+2}^n - \eta_k \check{K}_{t+1} \right) - \hat{K}_{t+1}^n \right].$$

Here I use the fact that in a flexible-price equilibrium, the conditional expectation at t of period $t + 1$ output does not correspond to the value of $E_t Y_{t+1}^n$ at date t in the sticky-price equilibrium, for the latter depends upon the value of $\hat{K}_{t+1}$ in the *sticky-price equilibrium*, which is generally not the same as what the period $t + 1$ capital stock would be in a *flexible-price equilibrium*. Thus the conditional expectation at t of period $t+1$ output in a flexible-price equilibrium (beginning at t and conditional upon the actual period t capital stock) is actually equal to $E_t \hat{Y}_{t+1}^n - \eta_y \check{K}_{t+1}$; and similarly for the expectation at t of other variables determined at $t + 1$. Comparing this with (3.7), one sees that in the sticky-price equilibrium, the gap variables must satisfy (D.7).

Addendum to Chapter 6

E.1   Proof of Proposition 6.1

PROPOSITION 6.1. In the case of small enough fluctuations in the production of each good $\hat{y}_t(i)$ around the level $\bar{Y}$, small enough disturbances, and a small enough value of Φ_y, the utility flow to the representative household each period can be approximated by

$$U_t = -\frac{\bar{Y}u_c}{2}\left\{(\sigma^{-1}+\omega)\left(x_t-x^*\right)^2+(\theta^{-1}+\omega)\operatorname{var}_i\hat{y}_t(i)\right\}$$

$$+\,\text{t.i.p.}+\mathcal{O}\left(\|\Phi_y,\hat{y},\tilde{\xi}\|^3\right). \tag{E.1}$$

Here $\hat{y}_t(i) \equiv \log(y_t(i)/\bar{Y})$; $x_t \equiv \hat{Y}_t - \hat{Y}_t^n$, where $\hat{Y}_t \equiv \log(Y_t/\bar{Y})$ and $\hat{Y}_t^n$ denotes the (log of the) *natural rate* of output, the equilibrium level of output under complete price flexibility (as defined in Chapter 3), and $x^* \equiv \log(Y^*/\bar{Y})$ is the efficient level of the output gap, given by equation (2.9) of Chapter 6. The term t.i.p. collects terms that are independent of monetary policy, either constants or functions of purely exogenous disturbances, and so irrelevant to the welfare ranking of alternative equilibria.

PROOF: The first term in (2.3) can be approximated as

$$\tilde{u}\left(Y_t;\tilde{\xi}_t\right)=\bar{u}+u_c\tilde{Y}_t+u_\xi\tilde{\xi}_t+\tfrac{1}{2}u_{cc}\tilde{Y}_t^2+u_{c\xi}\tilde{\xi}_t\tilde{Y}_t+\tfrac{1}{2}\tilde{\xi}_t'u_{\xi\xi}\tilde{\xi}_t+\mathcal{O}\left(\|\hat{y},\tilde{\xi}\|^3\right)$$

$$=\bar{u}+\bar{Y}u_c\cdot\left(\hat{Y}_t+\tfrac{1}{2}\hat{Y}_t^2\right)+u_\xi\tilde{\xi}_t+\tfrac{1}{2}\bar{Y}^2u_{cc}\hat{Y}_t^2$$

$$+\,\bar{Y}u_{c\xi}\tilde{\xi}_t\hat{Y}_t+\tfrac{1}{2}\tilde{\xi}_t'u_{\xi\xi}\tilde{\xi}_t+\mathcal{O}\left(\|\hat{y},\tilde{\xi}\|^3\right)$$

$$=\bar{Y}u_c\hat{Y}_t+\tfrac{1}{2}\left[\bar{Y}u_c+\bar{Y}^2u_{cc}\right]\hat{Y}_t^2-\bar{Y}^2u_{cc}g_t\hat{Y}_t+\text{t.i.p.}+\mathcal{O}\left(\|\hat{y},\tilde{\xi}\|^3\right)$$

$$=\bar{Y}u_c\left\{\hat{Y}_t+\tfrac{1}{2}\left(1-\sigma^{-1}\right)\hat{Y}_t^2+\sigma^{-1}g_t\hat{Y}_t\right\}+\text{t.i.p.}+\mathcal{O}\left(\|\hat{y},\tilde{\xi}\|^3\right). \tag{E.2}$$

Here the first line represents the usual Taylor expansion,[1] in which $\bar{u} \equiv u(\bar{Y}; 0)$ and $\tilde{Y}_t \equiv Y_t - \bar{Y}$, and I assume fluctuations in $\tilde{Y}_t$ of order $\mathcal{O}(\|\hat{y}\|)$, where $\|\hat{y}\|$ indicates a bound on the size of fluctuations in the output (relative to $\bar{Y}$) of each of the differentiated goods, at each date and in each state of the world. The second line substitutes for $\tilde{Y}_t$ in terms of $\hat{Y}_t$, using the Taylor series expansion

$$Y_t/\bar{Y} = 1 + \hat{Y}_t + \tfrac{1}{2}\hat{Y}_t^2 + \mathcal{O}\left(\|\hat{y}\|^3\right).$$

The third line collects in the term t.i.p. all of the terms that are independent of policy, and uses the notation

$$g_t \equiv -\frac{u_{c\xi}\tilde{\xi}_t}{\bar{Y}u_{cc}}$$

introduced in Chapter 2 for the percentage variation in output required in order to keep the marginal utility of expenditure u_c at its steady-state level, given disturbances to preferences and/or government purchases. The final line collects terms in a useful way; note that the only part of this expression that differs across policies is the expression inside the curly braces.

I may similarly approximate $\tilde{v}(y_t(i); \xi_t)$ by

$$\tilde{v}(y_t(i); \xi_t) = \bar{Y}v_y\left\{\hat{y}_t(i) + \tfrac{1}{2}(1+\omega)\hat{y}_t(i)^2 - \omega q_t\hat{y}_t(i)\right\} + \text{t.i.p.} + \mathcal{O}\left(\|\hat{y}, \tilde{\xi}\|^3\right)$$

$$= \bar{Y}u_c\left\{(1 - \Phi)\hat{y}_t(i) + \tfrac{1}{2}(1+\omega)\hat{y}_t(i)^2 - \omega q_t\hat{y}_t(i)\right\}$$

$$+ \text{t.i.p.} + \mathcal{O}\left(\|\Phi_y, \hat{y}, \tilde{\xi}\|^3\right), \tag{E.3}$$

where $\hat{y}_t(i) \equiv \log(y_t(i)/\bar{Y})$, ω is the elasticity of real marginal cost with respect to own output discussed above, and

$$q_t \equiv -\frac{v_{y\xi}\tilde{\xi}_t}{\bar{Y}v_{yy}}$$

is the percentage variation in output required to keep the marginal disutility of supply v_y at its steady-state level, given the preference shock, already introduced in Chapter 3. The second line uses (2.7) and (2.8) to replace v_y by $(1 - \Phi_y)u_c$, and then drops terms that are of higher than second order

---

1. To simplify notation, I use ξ subscripts to denote partial derivatives with respect to the entire vector of exogenous disturbances $\tilde{\xi}_t$. Also, all u's with subscripts refer to partial derivatives of $\tilde{u}$, though I have used the subscript c rather than y for partial derivatives with respect to the level of production, as these derivatives are equal to the corresponding partial derivatives of the direct utility function u with respect to the consumption index.

given that Φ_y is an expansion parameter. Note that the term premultiplying the expression in curly braces is now the same as in (E.2).

Integrating this expression over the differentiated goods i yields

$$\int_0^1 \tilde{v}\big(y_t(i); \tilde{\xi}_t\big) = \bar{Y}u_c\Big\{(1 - \Phi_y)E_i\hat{y}_t(i) + \tfrac{1}{2}(1 + \omega)\big[\big(E_i\hat{y}_t(i)\big)^2 + \text{var}_i\hat{y}_t(i)\big]$$

$$- \omega q_t E_i\hat{y}_t(i)\Big\} + \text{t.i.p.} + \mathcal{O}\big(\|\Phi_y, \hat{y}, \tilde{\xi}\|^3\big)$$

$$= \bar{Y}u_c\Big\{(1 - \Phi_y)\hat{Y}_t + \tfrac{1}{2}(1 + \omega)\hat{Y}_t^2 - \omega q_t \hat{Y}_t$$

$$+ \tfrac{1}{2}(\theta^{-1} + \omega)\text{var}_i\hat{y}_t(i)\Big\} + \text{t.i.p.} + \mathcal{O}\big(\|\Phi_y, \hat{y}, \tilde{\xi}\|^3\big), \qquad \text{(E.4)}$$

using the notation $E_i\hat{y}_t(i)$ for the mean value of $\hat{y}_t(i)$ across all differentiated goods at date t, and $\text{var}_i\hat{y}_t(i)$ for the corresponding variance. In the second line, I use the Taylor series approximation to (2.6),

$$\hat{Y}_t = E_i\hat{y}_t(i) + \tfrac{1}{2}(1 - \theta^{-1})\text{var}_i\hat{y}_t(i) + \mathcal{O}\big(\|\hat{y}\|^3\big), \qquad \text{(E.5)}$$

to eliminate $E_i\hat{y}_t(i)$.

Combining (E.2) and (E.4), I finally obtain

$$U_t = \bar{Y}u_c\Big\{\Phi_y\hat{Y}_t - \tfrac{1}{2}\big(\sigma^{-1} + \omega\big)\hat{Y}_t^2 + \big(\sigma^{-1}g_t + \omega q_t\big)\hat{Y}_t - \tfrac{1}{2}(\theta^{-1} + \omega)\text{var}_i\hat{y}_t(i)\Big\}$$

$$+ \text{t.i.p.} + \mathcal{O}\big(\|\Phi_y, \hat{y}, \tilde{\xi}\|^3\big)$$

$$= -\frac{\bar{Y}u_c}{2}\Big\{\big(\sigma^{-1} + \omega\big)\big(x_t - x^*\big)^2 + \big(\theta^{-1} + \omega\big)\text{var}_i\hat{y}_t(i)\Big\}$$

$$+ \text{t.i.p.} + \mathcal{O}\big(\|\Phi_y, \hat{y}, \tilde{\xi}\|^3\big).$$

Here the second line rewrites the expression in terms of the output gap $x_t \equiv \hat{Y}_t - \hat{Y}_t^n$, using the result (from Chapter 3) that

$$\hat{Y}_t^n = \frac{\sigma^{-1}g_t + \omega q_t}{\sigma^{-1} + \omega} + \mathcal{O}\big(\|\tilde{\xi}\|^2\big), \qquad \text{(E.6)}$$

and the expression for x^* given by (2.9). I thus obtain (E.1).

E.2   Proof of Proposition 6.3

PROPOSITION 6.3. *Suppose that price changes are staggered as in the discrete-time Calvo model expounded in Chapter 3, with fraction α of prices remaining unchanged each period, and let price dispersion at any point in time be measured by*

$$\Delta_t \equiv \operatorname{var}_i \log p_t(i).$$

Then this dispersion measure evolves over time according to

$$\Delta_t = \alpha \Delta_{t-1} + \frac{\alpha}{1-\alpha}\pi_t^2 + \mathcal{O}\big(\|\Delta_{t-1}^{1/2}, \varphi, \xi\|^3\big) \tag{E.7}$$

in the case of a small enough initial price dispersion, small enough disturbances, and a policy rule that ensures a long-run average inflation rate near zero.

PROOF: The Calvo pricing model implies that each period, the distribution of prices $\{p_t(i)\}$ consists of α times the distribution of prices in the previous period, plus an atom of size $(1-\alpha)$ at the price p_t^* that is chosen at date t by all suppliers who choose a new price at that date. Letting

$$\bar{P}_t \equiv E_i \log p_t(i),$$

one observes from this recursive characterization of the distribution of prices at date t that

$$\bar{P}_t - \bar{P}_{t-1} = E_i\big[\log p_t(i) - \bar{P}_{t-1}\big]$$
$$= \alpha E_i\big[\log p_{t-1}(i) - \bar{P}_{t-1}\big] + (1-\alpha)\big(\log p_t^* - \bar{P}_{t-1}\big)$$
$$= (1-\alpha)\big(\log p_t^* - \bar{P}_{t-1}\big).$$

Similar reasoning about the dispersion measure Δ_t yields

$$\Delta_t = \operatorname{var}_i\big[\log p_t(i) - \bar{P}_{t-1}\big]$$
$$= E_i\left\{\big[\log p_t(i) - \bar{P}_{t-1}\big]^2\right\} - \big(E_i \log p_t(i) - \bar{P}_{t-1}\big)^2$$
$$= \alpha E_i\left\{\big[\log p_{t-1}(i) - \bar{P}_{t-1}\big]^2\right\} + (1-\alpha)\big(\log p_t^* - \bar{P}_{t-1}\big)^2 - \big(\bar{P}_t - \bar{P}_{t-1}\big)^2$$
$$= \alpha \Delta_{t-1} + \frac{\alpha}{1-\alpha}\big(\bar{P}_t - \bar{P}_{t-1}\big)^2. \tag{E.8}$$

Finally, $\bar{P}_t$ may be related to the Dixit-Stiglitz price index through the log-linear approximation

$$\bar{P}_t = \log P_t + \mathcal{O}\big(\|\Delta_{t-1}^{1/2}, \varphi, \tilde{\xi}\|^2\big).$$

Note that it follows from the aggregate-supply relation (2.18) of Chapter 6 that small-φ policies, in which the long-run average value of $\hat{Y}_t$ remains near zero, must also be policies in which the long-run average inflation rate is near zero. The bound on the residual given here follows from the fact that the equilibrium inflation process satisfies a bound of order $\mathcal{O}(\|\varphi, \tilde{\xi}\|)$, together with the bound on the degree of preexisting price dispersion. Substituting this into (E.8) yields (E.7).

E.3 Proof of Proposition 6.6

PROPOSITION 6.6. Suppose that the preferences of the representative household exhibit habit persistence of the form of equation (2.26) of Chapter 6, for some $0 \leq \eta \leq 1$. Then under the same assumptions (otherwise) as in Proposition 6.1, the utility flow to the representative household each period can be approximated by

$$U_t = -\frac{\bar{Y} u_c}{2} \left\{ \mu_x \left(x_t - \delta x_{t-1} - \hat{x}^* \right)^2 + \left(\theta^{-1} + \omega \right) \operatorname{var}_i \hat{y}_t(i) \right\}$$

$$+ \text{t.i.p.} + \mathcal{O}\!\left(\| \Phi_y, \hat{y}, \tilde{\xi} \|^3 \right), \tag{E.9}$$

where the coefficient $0 \leq \delta \leq \eta$ is again the smaller root of equation (1.28) in Chapter 5,

$$\mu_x \equiv \frac{1 - \beta \eta}{1 + \beta \delta^2} \left[\omega + \varphi \left(1 + \beta \eta^2 \right) \right] > 0,$$

and

$$\hat{x}^* \equiv \frac{1 + \beta \delta^2}{1 - \beta \delta} \frac{\Phi_y}{\omega + \varphi \left(1 + \beta \eta^2 \right)} \geq 0,$$

in which the expression $\varphi > 0$ is again defined as in equation (1.25) of Chapter 5.

PROOF: The derivation of this approximation follows the same lines as the proof of Proposition 6.1.[2] In the presence of habit persistence, (E.2) takes the more general form

$$u_t \equiv u \left((Y_t - G_t) - \eta (Y_{t-1} - G_{t-1}); \tilde{\xi}_t \right)$$

$$= \bar{Y} u_c \left\{ \left(\hat{Y}_t - \eta \hat{Y}_{t-1} \right) + \tfrac{1}{2} \left[\hat{Y}_t^2 - \eta \hat{Y}_{t-1}^2 - \sigma^{-1} \left(\hat{Y}_t - \eta \hat{Y}_{t-1} \right)^2 \right] \right.$$

$$\left. + \sigma^{-1} \left(g_t - \eta \hat{G}_{t-1} \right) \left(\hat{Y}_t - \eta \hat{Y}_{t-1} \right) \right\} + \text{t.i.p.} + \mathcal{O}\!\left(\| \hat{y}, \tilde{\xi} \|^3 \right). \tag{E.10}$$

---

2. For further details, see the technical appendix to Giannoni and Woodford (2003b), where a generalization of this result is obtained in the context of a more complex model.

This implies a discounted value

$$\sum_{t=0}^{\infty} \beta^t u_t = \bar{Y} u_c \sum_{t=0}^{\infty} \left\{ (1 - \beta\eta)\hat{Y}_t + \tfrac{1}{2}\left[(1 - \beta\eta) - \sigma^{-1}\left(1 + \beta\eta^2\right)\right]\hat{Y}_t^2 \right.$$

$$\left. + \eta\sigma^{-1}\hat{Y}_t\hat{Y}_{t-1} + \sigma^{-1}\tilde{g}_t\hat{Y}_t \right\} + \text{t.i.p.} + \mathcal{O}\left(\|\hat{y}, \tilde{\xi}\|^3\right), \qquad (\text{E}.11)$$

where

$$\tilde{g}_t \equiv \left(g_t - \eta\hat{G}_{t-1}\right) - \beta\eta E_t\left(g_{t+1} - \eta\hat{G}_t\right).$$

Equation (E.4) still holds as an approximation to the disutility of labor supply in period t, except that now the steady-state marginal disutility v_y must be equated to $(1 - \beta\eta)(1 - \Phi_y)u_c$, rather than simply to $(1 - \Phi_y)u_c$, so that the right-hand side of (E.4) must be multiplied by $(1 - \beta\eta)$. Forming a similar discounted sum of these terms and subtracting from (E.11) yields

$$\sum_{t=0}^{\infty} \beta^t U_t = (1 - \beta\eta)\bar{Y} u_c \sum_{t=0}^{\infty} \left\{ \Phi_y\hat{Y}_t - \tfrac{1}{2}\left[\omega + \varphi\left(1 + \beta\eta^2\right)\right]\hat{Y}_t^2 \right.$$

$$\left. + \eta\varphi\hat{Y}_t\hat{Y}_{t-1} + \left(\varphi\tilde{g}_t - \omega q_t\right)\hat{Y}_t - \tfrac{1}{2}\left(\theta^{-1} + \omega\right)\text{var}_i\hat{y}_t(i) \right\}$$

$$+ \text{t.i.p.} + \mathcal{O}\left(\|\hat{y}, \tilde{\xi}\|^3\right), \qquad (\text{E}.12)$$

where $\varphi \equiv (1 - \beta\eta)^{-1}\sigma^{-1} > 0$, as in Chapter 5. One can also show that the flexible-price equilibrium level of output in the model with habit persistence satisfies

$$E_t\left\{ \left[\omega + \varphi(1 - \eta L)\left(1 - \beta\eta L^{-1}\right)\right]\hat{Y}_t^n \right\} = \varphi\tilde{g}_t - \omega q_t$$

each period, generalizing (E.6). Using this to substitute for the second-order terms involving exogenous disturbances in (E.12), one obtains

$$\sum_{t=0}^{\infty} \beta^t U_t = (1 - \beta\eta)\bar{Y} u_c \sum_{t=0}^{\infty} \left\{ \Phi_y x_t - \tfrac{1}{2}\left[\omega + \varphi\left(1 + \beta\eta^2\right)\right]x_t^2 + \eta\varphi x_t x_{t-1} \right.$$

$$\left. - \tfrac{1}{2}\left(\theta^{-1} + \omega\right)\text{var}_i\hat{y}_t(i) \right\} + \text{t.i.p.} + \mathcal{O}\left(\|\hat{y}, \tilde{\xi}\|^3\right), \qquad (\text{E}.13)$$

where as usual $x_t \equiv \hat{Y}_t - \hat{Y}_t^n$.

Finally, note that by rearranging terms, I can express the quadratic terms in (E.13) involving the output gap as a sum of squared terms, using the relation

$$\sum_{t=0}^{\infty} \beta^t \left\{ -\tfrac{1}{2} \left[\omega + \varphi \left(1 + \beta \eta^2 \right) \right] x_t^2 + \eta \varphi x_t x_{t-1} \right\} = \tfrac{1}{2} \delta_0 \delta^2 x_{-1}^2$$

$$- \tfrac{1}{2} \delta_0 \sum_{t=0}^{\infty} \beta^t \left(x_t - \delta x_{t-1} \right)^2,$$

where $0 \le \delta \le \eta$ is the smaller root of the quadratic equation (1.28) of Chapter 5, and

$$\delta_0 \equiv \frac{\mu_x}{1 - \beta \eta} > 0,$$

with μ_x defined as in the statement of the proposition. The linear terms in the output gap can similarly be incorporated into the sum of squared terms by writing the latter terms as a discounted sum

$$\sum_{t=0}^{\infty} \beta^t \left(x_t - \delta x_{t-1} - \hat{x}^* \right)^2,$$

where the constant $\hat{x}^*$ is defined as in the statement of the proposition. Making this substitution (and noting that the x_{-1}^2 term is independent of policy), I obtain a quadratic approximation of the form (E.9).

E.4   Proof of Proposition 6.7

PROPOSITION 6.7. Assume a transactions technology satisfying Assumption 6.1. Then in the case of small enough fluctuations in the production of each good $\hat{y}_t(i)$ around the level $\bar{Y}$, small enough fluctuations in the interest-rate differential Δ_t around the level $\bar{\Delta}$, small enough disturbances, and small enough values of the steady-state distortions Φ, the utility flow to the representative household each period can be approximated by

$$U_t = -\frac{\bar{Y} u_c}{2} \left\{ \epsilon_{mc} \left(x_t - x^* \right)^2 + \bar{v}^{-1} \eta_i \left(\hat{\imath}_t - \hat{\imath}_t^m + \bar{\Delta} \right)^2 \right.$$

$$\left. + (\theta^{-1} + \omega) \mathrm{var}_i \hat{y}_t(i) \right\} + \text{t.i.p.} + \mathcal{O} \left(\| \Phi, \hat{y}, \hat{\Delta}, \xi \|^3 \right). \tag{E.14}$$

Here ϵ_{mc} is defined by equation (4.3) of Chapter 6, x_t is the output gap relative to the natural rate of output defined by (4.5), x^* is defined by (4.6), and $\bar{v} \equiv \bar{Y}/\bar{m} > 0$ is the steady-state "velocity of money," and $\eta_i > 0$ is the limiting value of the interest-rate semielasticity of money demand.

   PROOF. I again compute a second-order Taylor series expansion to the utility from private expenditure, obtaining

$$u\left(Y_t, m_t; \tilde{\xi}_t\right) = \bar{Y}u_c\left\{\hat{Y}_t + \tfrac{1}{2}\left(1 - \sigma^{-1}\right)\hat{Y}_t^2 + \sigma^{-1}g_t\hat{Y}_t + s_m\hat{m}_t\right.$$

$$+ \tfrac{1}{2}s_m\left(1 - \sigma_m^{-1}\right)\hat{m}_t^2 + \chi\,\hat{m}_t\,\hat{Y}_t + s_m\sigma^{-1}g_t\hat{m}_t$$

$$\left. + s_m\left(\chi + \sigma_m^{-1}\right)\epsilon_t^m\,\hat{m}_t\right\} + \text{t.i.p.} + \mathcal{O}\left(\|\hat{y}, \hat{m}, \tilde{\xi}\|^3\right) \tag{E.15}$$

as a generalization of (E.2), where (because of the discontinuity of u_{mm} at the satiation point) the expansion applies only to levels of real money balances at or below the satiation level. Here I define the elasticity $\sigma_m \equiv -u_m/\bar{m}u_{mm} > 0$ as in Chapter 2, the exogenous disturbance term g_t is defined as in the cashless model, and

$$\epsilon_t^m \equiv \left(\chi + \sigma_m^{-1}\right)^{-1}\left[\frac{u_{m\xi}}{u_m}\xi_t - \sigma^{-1}g_t\right]$$

is the exogenous disturbance term in the money-demand relation (4.1). These last quantities are well defined as a result of Assumption 6.1.

Once again, I can legitimately substitute into this the log-linear approximate solution to the structural equations only if the coefficients on the linear terms are at most of first order in the expansion parameters. This requires choosing $\bar{\Delta}$ as well as Φ_y as an expansion parameter, meaning that the welfare approximation is applicable only under the assumption that the economy is sufficiently close to being satiated in money balances. In order to contemplate a series of economies that come as close as I like to this limit, without having to change the specification of preferences or technology (including the transactions technology), it is important to allow for interest payments on the monetary base, which I suppose are always close to a steady-state rate of $\bar{i}^m$. The assumption that $\bar{\Delta}$ is small can then be taken to be an assumption that $\bar{i}^m$ is close to $\bar{i}$, which requires no assumption about the size of the latter quantity.

It follows from Assumption 6.1 that in the limit of small $\bar{\Delta}$, s_m is of order $\mathcal{O}(\bar{\Delta})$, as is σ_m, though the ratio $s_m\sigma_m^{-1}$ approaches a positive limit as $\bar{\Delta} \to 0$, since

$$\frac{s_m}{\sigma_m} = -\frac{\bar{m}^2 u_{mm}}{\bar{Y}u_c} + \mathcal{O}(\bar{\Delta}).$$

This allows me to drop some of the quadratic terms from (E.15), the coefficients of which are only of order $\mathcal{O}(\bar{\Delta})$.

Note also that in the limit of small $\bar{\Delta}$, the elasticities of the money-demand relation (4.1) reduce to

$$\eta_y = -\frac{\bar{Y}u_{cm}}{\bar{m}u_{mm}} + \mathcal{O}(\bar{\Delta}), \qquad \eta_i = -\frac{u_c}{\bar{m}u_{mm}} + \mathcal{O}(\bar{\Delta}). \tag{E.16}$$

I can then substitute $(\eta_i \bar{v})^{-1}$ for $s_m \sigma_m^{-1}$ and $\chi \eta_i \bar{v}$ for η_y in the coefficients of quadratic terms.[3] With these substitutions, (E.15) can be written as

$$u(Y_t, m_t; \xi_t) = \bar{Y} u_c \left\{ \hat{Y}_t + \tfrac{1}{2}\left(1 - \sigma^{-1}\right) \hat{Y}_t^2 + \sigma^{-1} g_t \hat{Y}_t + s_m \hat{m}_t \right.$$
$$\left. + \chi \hat{m}_t \hat{Y}_t - \tfrac{1}{2}(\eta_i \bar{v})^{-1} \left(\hat{m}_t - \epsilon_t^m\right)^2 \right\}$$
$$+ \text{t.i.p.} + \mathcal{O}\left(\|\hat{y}, \hat{m}, \tilde{\xi}\|^3\right). \tag{E.17}$$

Then (4.1) can be substituted for equilibrium real balances $\hat{m}_t$,[4] which gives

$$u(Y_t, m_t; \xi_t) = \bar{Y} u_c \left\{ \hat{Y}_t + \tfrac{1}{2}\left(1 - \sigma^{-1}\right) \hat{Y}_t^2 + \sigma^{-1} g_t \hat{Y}_t + s_m \eta_y \hat{Y}_t - s_m \eta_i \left(\hat{\imath}_t - \hat{\imath}_t^m\right) \right.$$
$$\left. + \tfrac{1}{2}\chi \eta_y \hat{Y}_t^2 + \chi \epsilon_t^m \hat{Y}_t - \tfrac{1}{2}\bar{v}^{-1} \eta_i \left(\hat{\imath}_t - \hat{\imath}_t^m\right)^2 \right\}$$
$$+ \text{t.i.p.} + \mathcal{O}\left(\|\hat{y}, \hat{\Delta}, \tilde{\xi}\|^3\right). \tag{E.18}$$

Subtracting (E.4) from (E.18), yields

$$U_t = \bar{Y} u_c \left\{ \left(\Phi_y + s_m \eta_y\right) \hat{Y}_t - s_m \eta_i \left(\hat{\imath}_t - \hat{\imath}_t^m\right) + \left[\sigma^{-1} g_t + \omega q_t + \chi \epsilon_t^m\right] \hat{Y}_t \right.$$
$$\left. - \tfrac{1}{2}\bar{v}^{-1} \eta_i \left(\hat{\imath}_t - \hat{\imath}_t^m\right)^2 - \tfrac{1}{2}\epsilon_{mc} \hat{Y}_t^2 - \tfrac{1}{2}\left(\theta^{-1} + \omega\right) \text{var}_i \hat{y}_t(i) \right\} + \text{t.i.p.}$$
$$+ \mathcal{O}\left(\|\Phi, \hat{y}, \hat{\Delta}, \tilde{\xi}\|^3\right)$$
$$= -\frac{\bar{Y} u_c}{2} \left\{ \epsilon_{mc}\left(x_t - x^*\right)^2 + \bar{v}^{-1} \eta_i \left(\hat{\imath}_t - \hat{\imath}_t^m + \bar{\Delta}\right)^2 \right.$$
$$\left. + \left(\theta^{-1} + \omega\right) \text{var}_i \hat{y}_t(i) \right\} + \text{t.i.p.} + \mathcal{O}\left(\|\Phi, \hat{y}, \hat{\Delta}, \tilde{\xi}\|^3\right)$$

as a generalization of (2.10).

E.5 Proof of Proposition 6.9

PROPOSITION 6.9. Consider the problem of minimizing an expected discounted sum of quadratic losses

---

3. The advantage of replacing η_y by $\chi \eta_i \bar{v}$ is that it is then clear what form the results take in the familiar special case in which it is assumed that $u_{cm} = 0$; I simply set χ equal to zero in the expressions derived later.

4. Note that in the log-linear approximate relation (4.1), the residual (which has been suppressed) is of order $\mathcal{O}(\|\hat{y}, \hat{\Delta}, \tilde{\xi}\|^2)$.

$$E_0 \left\{ (1 - \beta) \sum_{t=0}^{\infty} \beta^t L_t \right\} \tag{E.19}$$

subject to the constraints

$$E_0 \left\{ (1 - \beta) \sum_{t=0}^{\infty} \beta^t i_t \right\} \geq 0, \tag{E.20}$$

$$E_0 \left\{ (1 - \beta) \sum_{t=0}^{\infty} \beta^t i_t^2 \right\} \leq K \left[E_0 \left\{ (1 - \beta) \sum_{t=0}^{\infty} \beta^t i_t \right\} \right]^2 . \tag{E.21}$$

Then the optimal policy also minimizes a modified discounted-loss criterion of the form (E.19), but with L_t replaced by

$$\tilde{L}_t \equiv L_t + \tilde{\lambda}_i \left(\hat{i}_t - i^{**} \right)^2 , \tag{E.22}$$

under no constraints other than the structural equations. Here $\tilde{\lambda}_i \geq 0$, with a strictly positive value if and only if the constraint (E.21) binds. Moreover, in the event that the constraint binds, $i^{**} > 0$; that is, the target interest rate is higher than the nominal interest rate $\bar{i}$ associated with the zero-inflation steady state.

PROOF: Let m_1, m_2 be the discounted average values of i_t and i_t^2 associated with the policy that solves the constrained optimization problem stated in the proposition, and let $m_1^* \geq \bar{i} > 0$ and $m_2^* > 0$ be the values of these moments for the policy that minimizes (E.19) when the constraints are not imposed. (As shown above, the unconstrained optimal policy involves a deterministic path for inflation and the output gap, along which both are nonnegative at all times.) Note first that constraint (E.20) never binds. For (E.19) can be decomposed into components due to the deterministic component of policy, on the one hand, and the responses to shocks on the other, which two aspects of policy can be independently specified (given the linearity of the constraints implied by the structural equations). The stabilization component of policy (the specified responses to unexpected shocks) determines the value of $m_2 - (m_1)^2$, whereas the deterministic component determines the value of m_1. Since the unconstrained optimal specification of the deterministic component of policy involves $m_1 = m_1^* > 0$, and both constraints (E.20) and (E.21) place only a lower bound on the value of m_1 given any specification of the stabilization component of policy, there cannot be an advantage to choosing a deterministic component of policy such that $m_1 < m_1^*$, though one might choose $m_1 > m_1^*$ in order to relax constraint (E.21). Hence $m_1 \geq m_1^* > 0$, and (E.20) does not bind.

Furthermore, the constrained-optimal policy is also the policy that minimizes (E.19) subject to the two alternative constraints

$$E_0 \left\{ (1 - \beta) \sum_{t=0}^{\infty} \beta^t i_t \right\} \geq m_1,$$

$$E_0 \left\{ (1 - \beta) \sum_{t=0}^{\infty} \beta^t i_t^2 \right\} \leq m_2,$$

since any policy consistent with both of these also satisfies the weaker constraints (E.20) and (E.21).

Then by the Kuhn-Tucker theorem, the policy that minimizes the expected discounted value of (E.19) subject to (E.20) and (E.21) can be shown to also minimize an (unconstrained) loss criterion of the form

$$E_0 \left\{ (1 - \beta) \sum_{t=0}^{\infty} \beta^t L_t \right\} - \mu_1 E_0 \left\{ (1 - \beta) \sum_{t=0}^{\infty} \beta^t i_t \right\}$$

$$+ \mu_2 E_0 \left\{ (1 - \beta) \sum_{t=0}^{\infty} \beta^t i_t^2 \right\}, \tag{E.23}$$

where μ_1 and μ_2 are appropriately chosen Lagrange multipliers. Both multipliers are nonnegative, and if the constraint (E.21) binds,

$$\mu_1 = 2Km_1\mu_2 > 0, \tag{E.24}$$

since $2Km_1$ is the slope of the frontier of the constraint set (E.21), evaluated at the constrained optimum.

Finally, the terms in (E.23) can be rearranged to yield a discounted-loss criterion of the form (E.19), but with L_t replaced by

$$\tilde{L}_t \equiv L_t + \mu_2 \left(i_t - (\mu_1/2\mu_2) \right)^2. \tag{E.25}$$

(There is also a constant term involved in completing the square, but as usual this is dropped as it has no effect on the ranking of alternative policies. The final term appears only in the case that $\mu_2 > 0$, so that $\mu_1/2\mu_2$ is well defined in the case that this term appears.) Writing the final term in terms of a target value for $\hat{i}_t \equiv i_t - \bar{i}$ rather than i_t, for consistency with the previous results, I obtain a modified loss function of the form (E.22).

Observe that $\tilde{\lambda}_i = \mu_2 \geq 0$, with a strictly positive value if and only if (E.21) binds. In the event that $\lambda_i > 0$, observe further that

$$i^{**} = \mu_1/2\mu_2 - \bar{\imath} = Km_1 - \bar{\imath} > 0,$$

where the final inequality follows from the facts that $m_1 \geq \bar{\imath} > 0$ and $K > 1$.

E.6 Proof of Proposition 6.10

PROPOSITION 6.10. Consider the two-sector model with asymmetric disturbances described in Section 2.5 of Chapter 3. Then in the case of small enough fluctuations in aggregate output Y_t around the level $\bar{Y}$, small enough fluctuations in relative prices $\hat{p}_t(i) \equiv \log(p_t(i)/P_t)$ (and hence small variations in the relative quantities produced and consumed of different goods), small enough disturbances, and a small enough value of Φ_y, the utility flow to the representative household each period can be approximated by

$$U_t = -\frac{\bar{Y} u_c}{2} \left\{ \left(\sigma^{-1} + \omega \right) \left(x_t - x^* \right)^2 + n_1 n_2 \eta (1 + \omega \eta) \left(\hat{p}_{Rt} - \hat{p}_{Rt}^n \right)^2 \right.$$

$$\left. + \theta (1 + \omega \theta) \sum_{j=1}^{2} n_j \mathrm{var}_i^j \log p_t(i) \right\} + \text{t.i.p.} + \mathcal{O}\left(\|\Phi_y, \hat{Y}, \hat{p}, \tilde{\xi}\|^3 \right). \quad \text{(E.26)}$$

Here x_t once again denotes the output gap $\hat{Y}_t - \hat{Y}_t^n$, where $\hat{Y}_t^n$ is the (log of the) equilibrium level of aggregate output under complete price flexibility (defined in Chapter 3), and the efficient level of the output gap x^* is again given by equation (2.17) of Chapter 6. I also use the notation $\hat{p}_{Rt} \equiv \log(P_{2t}/P_{1t})$ for the (log) sectoral relative price and $\hat{p}_{Rt}^n$ for its natural value, that is, the equilibrium relative price under full price flexibility (a function solely of the asymmetric exogenous disturbances).

PROOF: A second-order expansion of the equation defining Y_t as a function of the sectoral-demand indices (see Chapter 3) is of the form

$$\hat{Y}_t = \sum_{j=1}^{2} n_j \left(1 + \eta^{-1} \hat{\varphi}_{jt} \right) \hat{Y}_{jt} + \tfrac{1}{2} n_1 n_2 \left(1 - \eta^{-1} \right) \left(\hat{Y}_{2t} - \hat{Y}_{1t} \right)^2$$

$$+ \text{t.i.p.} + \mathcal{O}\left(\|\hat{y}, \tilde{\xi}\|^3 \right), \quad \text{(E.27)}$$

where n_j is the fraction of the goods that belong to sector j, η is the elasticity of substitution between the composite products of the two sectors (assumed equal to one by Benigno, 2003), and $\hat{\varphi}_{jt}$ is the exogenous disturbance to the sectoral composition of demand. A similar second-order expansion of the index of sectoral demand is of the form

$$\hat{Y}_{jt} = E_i^j \hat{y}_t(i) + \tfrac{1}{2}\left(1 - \theta^{-1}\right) \text{var}_i^j \hat{y}_t(i) + \mathcal{O}(\|\hat{y}\|^3), \qquad (\text{E.28})$$

for each of the sectors $j = 1, 2$, generalizing (E.5). Here I introduce the notation $E_i^j(\cdot)$ and $\text{var}_i^j(\cdot)$ for the mean and variance of the distribution of values for the different goods i belonging to a given sector j.

Similarly, in the case of any good i in sector j, a second-order expansion of the disutility of output supply can be written in the form

$$\tilde{v}(y_t(i); \xi_t^j) = \bar{Y} u_c \left\{ (1 - \Phi_y)\hat{y}_t(i) + \tfrac{1}{2}(1 + \omega)\hat{y}_t(i)^2 - \omega q_{jt}\hat{y}_t(i) \right\}$$

$$+ \text{t.i.p.} + \mathcal{O}(\|\Phi_y, \hat{y}, \tilde{\xi}\|^3), \qquad (\text{E.29})$$

generalizing (E.3), where now

$$q_{jt} \equiv -\frac{\tilde{v}_{y\xi}\xi_t^j}{\bar{Y}\tilde{v}_{yy}}$$

represents the sector-specific variation in the level of output required to maintain a constant marginal disutility of supply. Integrating (E.29) over the goods i belonging to sector j, and using (E.28) to eliminate $E_i^j \hat{y}_t(i)$ yields

$$\int_{N_j} \tilde{v}(y_t(i); \xi_t^j) di = n_j \bar{Y} u_c \left\{ (1 - \Phi_y)\hat{Y}_{jt} + \tfrac{1}{2}(1 + \omega)\hat{Y}_{jt}^2 - \omega q_{jt}\hat{Y}_{jt} \right.$$

$$\left. + \tfrac{1}{2}\left(\theta^{-1} + \omega\right)\text{var}_i^j \hat{y}_t(i) \right\} + \text{t.i.p.} + \mathcal{O}(\|\Phi_y, \hat{y}, \tilde{\xi}\|^3).$$

Then summing over the two sectors and using (E.27) to eliminate $\sum_j n_j \hat{Y}_{jt}$ gives

$$\int_0^1 \tilde{v}(y_t(i); \xi_t) di = \bar{Y} u_c \left\{ (1 - \Phi_y)\hat{Y}_t + \tfrac{1}{2}(1 + \omega)\hat{Y}_t^2 \right.$$

$$- \sum_{j=1}^2 n_j \left(\omega q_{jt} + \eta^{-1}\hat{\varphi}_{jt}\right)\hat{Y}_{jt} + \tfrac{1}{2} n_1 n_2 \left(\eta^{-1} + \omega\right)\left(\hat{Y}_{2t} - \hat{Y}_{1t}\right)^2$$

$$\left. + \tfrac{1}{2}\left(\theta^{-1} + \omega\right) \sum_{j=1}^2 n_j \text{var}_i^j \hat{y}_t(i) \right\}$$

$$+ \text{t.i.p.} + \mathcal{O}(\|\Phi_y, \hat{y}, \tilde{\xi}\|^3), \qquad (\text{E.30})$$

generalizing (E.4).

Combining (E.2) and (E.30), I finally obtain

$$
U_t = \bar{Y} u_c \left\{ \Phi \hat{Y}_t - \tfrac{1}{2} \left(\sigma^{-1} + \omega \right) \hat{Y}_t^2 + \sum_{j=1}^{2} n_j \left(\sigma^{-1} g_t + \omega q_{jt} + \eta^{-1} \hat{\varphi}_{jt} \right) \hat{Y}_{jt} \right.
$$

$$
\left. - \tfrac{1}{2} n_1 n_2 \left(\eta^{-1} + \omega \right) \left(\hat{Y}_{2t} - \hat{Y}_{1t} \right)^2 - \tfrac{1}{2} \left(\theta^{-1} + \omega \right) \sum_{j=1}^{2} n_j \mathrm{var}_i^j \hat{y}_t(i) \right\}
$$

$$
+ \text{t.i.p.} + \mathcal{O} \left(\| \Phi_y, \hat{y}, \hat{\xi} \|^3 \right)
$$

$$
= -\frac{\bar{Y} u_c}{2} \left\{ \left(\sigma^{-1} + \omega \right) \left(x_t - x^* \right)^2 + n_1 n_2 \left(\eta^{-1} + \omega \right) x_{Rt}^2 \right.
$$

$$
\left. + \left(\theta^{-1} + \omega \right) \sum_{j=1}^{2} n_j \mathrm{var}_i^j \hat{y}_t(i) \right\} + \text{t.i.p.} + \mathcal{O} \left(\| \Phi_y, \hat{y}, \hat{\xi} \|^3 \right), \tag{E.31}
$$

generalizing (2.10). Here once again $x_t \equiv \hat{Y}_t - \hat{Y}_t^n$ is the aggregate output gap, and x^* is the optimal aggregate gap given by (2.17). I correspondingly define the relative output gap $x_{Rt} \equiv x_{2t} - x_{1t}$, where $x_{jt} \equiv \hat{Y}_{jt} - \hat{Y}_{jt}^n$ is the gap for sector j. Finally, in deriving (E.31) from the expression above, I use the fact that the definitions of the aggregate and sectoral natural rates of output in Chapter 3 imply that

$$
\left(\sigma^{-1} + \omega \right) \hat{Y}_t^n = \sigma^{-1} g_t + \sum_{j=1}^{2} n_j q_{jt},
$$

$$
\left(\eta^{-1} + \omega \right) \left(\hat{Y}_{2t}^n - \hat{Y}_{1t}^n \right) = \eta^{-1} (\hat{\varphi}_{2t} - \hat{\varphi}_{1t}) + \omega \left(q_{2t} - q_{1t} \right).
$$

If the sectoral-demand equation is used to write relative sectoral demand as a function of relative sectoral price, and the demand equation for an individual good is used to write sectoral-output dispersion as a function of sectoral price dispersion, (E.31) can then alternatively be written as (E.26). The bound on the residual is now written in a way that indicates that a bound on the range of variation in relative prices implies a corresponding bound on relative quantities.

E.7 Proof of Proposition 6.11

PROPOSITION 6.11. Consider a two-sector model with staggered (Calvo) pricing in each sector, but possibly with different frequencies of price adjustment in the two sectors. Then the discounted sum of utility of the representative household can again be approximated by an expression of the form of equation (2.21) of Chapter 6, where now the period loss function is of the form

$$L_t = \sum_{j=1}^{2} w_j \pi_{jt}^2 + \lambda_x \left(x_t - x^*\right)^2 + \lambda_R \left(\hat{p}_{Rt} - \hat{p}_{Rt}^n\right)^2, \tag{E.32}$$

generalizing (2.22). Here π_{jt} is the rate of price inflation in sector j, and the weights (normalized so that $w_1 + w_2 = 1$) are given by

$$w_j \equiv \frac{n_j \kappa}{\kappa_j} > 0, \qquad \lambda_x \equiv \frac{\kappa}{\theta} > 0, \qquad \lambda_R \equiv \frac{n_1 n_2 \eta (1 + \omega\eta)}{\sigma^{-1} + \omega} \lambda_x > 0,$$

where the coefficients κ_j are defined as in Proposition 3.8, and

$$\kappa \equiv \left(n_1 \kappa_1^{-1} + n_2 \kappa_2^{-1}\right)^{-1} > 0$$

is a geometric average of the two.

PROOF: This follows from Proposition 6.10 in the same way as I previously obtained Proposition 6.4 from Proposition 6.1. Using the same steps as in the proof of Proposition 6.3, one can show that the measure of sectoral price dispersion

$$\Delta_t^j \equiv \text{var}_i^j \log p_t(i)$$

evolves according to the approximate law of motion

$$\Delta_t^j = \alpha_j \Delta_{t-1}^j + \frac{\alpha_j}{1 - \alpha_j} \pi_{jt}^2 + \mathcal{O}\big(\|\Delta_{t-1}^{1/2}, \varphi, \tilde{\xi}\|^3\big),$$

where α_j is the fraction of prices that remain unchanged each period in sector j. (Here I again parameterize policy by coefficients φ, where a small norm for φ implies inflation near zero for all goods in the case of small disturbances.)

Summing over time then yields

$$\sum_{t=0}^{\infty} \beta^t \Delta_t^j = \frac{\alpha_j}{(1 - \alpha_j)(1 - \alpha_j \beta)} \sum_{t=0}^{\infty} \beta^t \pi_{jt}^2 + \text{t.i.p.} + \mathcal{O}\big(\|\Delta_{-1}^{1/2}, \varphi, \tilde{\xi}\|^3\big).$$

Using this substitution for the price-dispersion terms in (E.26), I again find that discounted lifetime utility can be approximated by an expression of the form (2.21), but with period loss function (E.32). Note that in the bound on the residual in (2.21), the norm of Δ_{-1} refers to a bound on the initial price dispersion in *each* of the two sectors.

E.8 Proof of Proposition 6.12

PROPOSITION 6.12. Consider a model with sticky wages as well as sticky prices, as described in Chapter 3, Section 4. Then in the case of small enough fluctuations in aggregate output Y_t around the level $\bar{Y}$, small enough fluctuations in relative prices $\hat{p}_t(i) \equiv \log(p_t(i)/P_t)$ and relative wages $\hat{w}_t(j) \equiv \log(w_t(j)/W_t)$, small enough disturbances, and a small enough value of Φ_y, the utility flow to the representative household each period can be approximated by

$$U_t = -\frac{\bar{Y}u_c}{2}\left\{ \left(\sigma^{-1} + \omega\right)\left(x_t - x^*\right)^2 + \theta_p\left(1 + \omega_p\theta_p\right)\mathrm{var}_i \log p_t(i)\right.$$

$$\left. + \theta_w\phi^{-1}\left(1 + \nu\theta_w\right)\mathrm{var}_j \log w_t(j)\right\} + \mathrm{t.i.p.} + \mathcal{O}\big(\|\Phi_y, \hat{Y}, \hat{p}, \hat{w}, \tilde{\xi}\|^3\big), \quad \text{(E.33)}$$

where the output gap x_t is defined as in the flexible-wage model, and the optimal output gap x^* is again given by (2.17).

PROOF: A quadratic expansion of $v(h_t(j); \xi_t)$, integrated over the continuum of different types of labor, yields

$$\int_0^1 v(h_t(j); \xi) \, dj = \bar{H}v_h\Big\{\hat{H}_t + \tfrac{1}{2}(1 + \nu)\hat{H}_t^2 - \nu\bar{h}_t\hat{H}_t$$

$$+ \tfrac{1}{2}\theta_w(1 + \nu\theta_w)\mathrm{var}_j \log w_t(j)\Big\} + \mathrm{t.i.p.} + \mathcal{O}\big(\|\hat{H}, \hat{w}, \tilde{\xi}\|^3\big), \quad \text{(E.34)}$$

where once again

$$\nu \equiv \frac{\bar{H}v_{hh}}{v_h} > 0.$$

Here I have used (4.27) to replace the dispersion of demand for different types of labor, $\mathrm{var}_j \log h_t(j)$, by $\theta_w^2\mathrm{var}_j \log w_t(j)$.

The aggregate demand for the composite labor input H_t is in turn given by

$$H_t = \int_0^1 f^{-1}(y_t(i)/A_t) \, di, \quad \text{(E.35)}$$

integrating over the demands of each of the firms i. Using a quadratic approximation to an individual firm's labor demand

$$f^{-1}(y_t(i)) = \bar{H}\left\{1 + \phi\hat{y}_t(i) + \tfrac{1}{2}(1 + \omega_p)\phi\hat{y}_t(i)^2\right\} + \mathcal{O}(\|\hat{y}\|^3),$$

where once again

$$\phi_h \equiv \frac{\bar{Y}}{\bar{H}f'} > 1, \qquad \omega_p \equiv -\frac{ff''}{(f')^2} > 0,$$

one can expand (E.35) as

$$
\begin{aligned}
\hat{H} &= \phi\left(E_i\hat{y}_t(i) - a_t\right) + \tfrac{1}{2}\left(1 + \omega_p - \phi_h\right)\phi_h\left(E_i\hat{y}_t(i) - a_t\right)^2 \\
&\quad + \tfrac{1}{2}(1 + \omega_p)\phi_h \, \mathrm{var}_i\hat{y}_t(i) + \mathcal{O}\left(\|\hat{y}, \tilde{\xi}\|^3\right) \\
&= \phi_h\left(\hat{Y}_t - a_t\right) + \tfrac{1}{2}\left(1 + \omega_p - \phi_h\right)\phi_h\left(\hat{Y}_t - a_t\right)^2 \\
&\quad + \tfrac{1}{2}\left(1 + \omega_p\theta_p\right)\theta_p\phi_h \, \mathrm{var}_i \log p_t(i) + \mathcal{O}\left(\|\hat{Y}, \hat{p}, \tilde{\xi}\|^3\right).
\end{aligned}
\tag{E.36}
$$

In the second line I have again used (E.5) to eliminate $E_i\hat{y}_t(i)$ and (2.12) to write $\mathrm{var}_i\hat{y}_t(i)$ as a function of the dispersion of individual goods prices, now using θ_p for the elasticity of substitution between differentiated goods.

Finally, substituting (E.36) for $\hat{H}_t$ in (E.34), and then combining this with (E.2), I obtain the expansion (E.33), where x_t and x^* are again defined as in the basic (flexible-wage) model. The bound on the residual in (E.33) is written in the way shown using the bound $\|\hat{H}\| = \mathcal{O}(\|\hat{Y}, \hat{p}, \tilde{\xi}\|)$, implied by (E.36).

Addendum to Chapter 7

F.1 Proof of Proposition 7.6

PROPOSITION 7.6. The state-contingent evolution of inflation $\{\pi_t\}$ from some date t_0 onward that minimizes the expected value of equation (1.2) of Chapter 7, taking as given the economy's evolution prior to date t_0 and subject to the constraint (2.8), where $\bar{\pi}_{t_0}$ is given by (2.9), is given by

$$\pi_t = \beta^{-1} \sum_{j=0}^{\infty} \mu_2^{-j-1} E_t u_{t+j}$$

$$- \beta^{-1}(1 - \mu_1) \sum_{k=1}^{\infty} \sum_{j=0}^{\infty} \mu_1^{k-1} \mu_2^{-j-1} E_{t-k} u_{t+j-k} \tag{F.1}$$

for all $t \geq t_0$.

PROOF: As discussed in the text, the solution to this optimization is described by bounded processes $\{\pi_t, x_t\}$ for $t \geq t_0$ and $\{\varphi_t\}$ for $t \geq t_0 - 1$ that satisfy (1.7) and (1.8) and (2.1) for each $t \geq t_0$, as well as the initial condition for π_{t_0}. Furthermore, it has been shown that the process $\{\varphi_t\}$ must be given by iterative solution of (2.7) for some initial value φ_{t_0-1}. The question is then to find the value for φ_{t_0-1} consistent with (2.8). Given this, the entire process $\{\varphi_t\}$ is determined, and the processes $\{\pi_t, x_t\}$ are then given by (1.7) and (1.8).

Substituting solution (2.7) into (1.7) yields

$$\pi_{t_0} = (1 - \mu_1)\left[\varphi_{t-1} + (\lambda/\kappa)x^*\right] + \beta^{-1} \sum_{j=0}^{\infty} \mu_2^{-j-1} E_t u_{t+j} \tag{F.2}$$

as the solution for π_{t_0} implied by any choice of φ_{t_0-1}. Equating this to the right-hand side of (2.9), one can solve for the initial Lagrange multiplier consistent with the initial constraint (2.8), obtaining

$$\varphi_{t_0-1} = -(\lambda/\kappa)x^* - \beta^{-1}\sum_{k=1}^{\infty}\sum_{j=0}^{\infty}\mu_1^{k-1}\mu_2^{-j-1}E_{t_0-k}u_{t_0+j-k}. \tag{F.3}$$

This allows one to completely characterize the solution to the constrained optimization problem described in the proposition.

Substituting (F.3) into (2.7) gives

$$\varphi_{t_0} = -(\lambda/\kappa)x^* - \beta^{-1}\sum_{k=1}^{\infty}\sum_{j=0}^{\infty}\mu_1^{k-1}\mu_2^{-j-1}E_{t_0+1-k}u_{t_0+1+j-k}$$

for φ_{t_0}. Proceeding recursively, one similarly obtains

$$\varphi_t = -(\lambda/\kappa)x^* - \beta^{-1}\sum_{k=1}^{\infty}\sum_{j=0}^{\infty}\mu_1^{k-1}\mu_2^{-j-1}E_{t+1-k}u_{t+1+j-k} \tag{F.4}$$

for arbitrary $t \geq t_0 - 1$. Substitution of this into (1.7) then yields (F.1).

F.2 Proof of Proposition 7.9

PROPOSITION 7.9. Consider again an economy of the kind assumed in Proposition 7.5. Then in the case of any small enough bound $||\Delta_{-1}^{1/2}, \Phi_y, \tilde{\xi}||$, and any initial values of any predetermined endogenous variables (that matter for equilibrium determination as a result of the policy rule) that are close enough to the values associated with the zero-inflation steady state, the long-run average values of inflation and the output gap satisfy

$$\lim_{T\to\infty} E_t\pi_T = 0,$$

$$\lim_{T\to\infty} E_t x_T = 0$$

under the t_0-optimal policy that would be chosen at any date t_0, and the same is true of the equilibrium implemented by any policy that is optimal from a timeless perspective.

Furthermore, let the unexpected change in the forecast of any variable y_{t+m} at date t be denoted

$$I_t[y_{t+m}] \equiv E_t y_{t+m} - E_{t-1}y_{t+m}.$$

Then the effects of unanticipated shocks at any date t on the expected paths of inflation and output are given by

$$I_t[\pi_{t+m}] = \beta^{-1} \sum_{j=0}^{\infty} \mu_2^{-j-1} I_t[u_{t+j}]$$

$$- \beta^{-1}(1-\mu_1) \sum_{k=1}^{m} \sum_{j=0}^{\infty} \mu_1^{k-1} \mu_2^{-j-1} I_t[u_{t+m-k+j}], \quad \text{(F.5)}$$

$$I_t[x_{t+m}] = -\beta^{-1} \sum_{k=0}^{m} \sum_{j=0}^{\infty} \mu_1^{k} \mu_2^{-j-1} I_t[u_{t+m-k+j}], \quad \text{(F.6)}$$

for each $m \geq 0$ under a t_0-optimal policy chosen at any date $t_0 \leq t$, and again the same is true of the equilibrium implemented by any policy that is optimal from a timeless perspective. (In each of these characterizations of the paths of inflation and the output gap, the results given are accurate up to an error term of order $\mathcal{O}(\|\Delta_{-1}^{1/2}, \Phi_y, \tilde{\xi}\|^2)$.)

PROOF: These results all follow from the fact that any of the kind of equilibria mentioned must involve processes $\{\pi_t, x_t, \varphi_t\}$ that satisfy equations (1.7) and (1.8) of Chapter 7 and (2.7) for all $t \geq t_0$, for some specification of the initial multiplier φ_{t_0-1}. (None of the results announced in the proposition depends on what the value of φ_{t_0-1} may be.) Because $|\mu_1| < 1$, equation (2.7) implies that

$$\lim_{T \to \infty} E_t \varphi_T = -(\lambda/\kappa)x^* < 0. \quad \text{(F.7)}$$

It then follows from this, using (1.7) and (1.8), that the long-run expected values of inflation and the output gap must be well defined and equal to zero.

Similarly, it follows from (2.7) that

$$I_t[\varphi_{t+m}] = \mu_1 I_t[\varphi_{t+m-1}] - \beta^{-1} \sum_{j=0}^{\infty} \mu_2^{-j-1} E_t[u_{t+m+j}]$$

for any horizon $m \geq 0$. Starting from the initial condition $I_t[\varphi_{t-1}] = 0$ and solving this difference equation recursively, one obtains

$$I_t[\varphi_{t+m}] = -\beta^{-1} \sum_{k=0}^{m} \sum_{j=0}^{\infty} \mu_1^{k} \mu_2^{-j-1} E_t[u_{t+m-k+j}].$$

Substitution of this equation for the forecast revisions of the Lagrange multipliers into (1.7) and (1.8) then yields the desired formulas (F.5) and (F.6) for the forecast revisions (or impulse responses) of inflation and the output gap.

F.3 Proof of Proposition 7.10

PROPOSITION 7.10. Under the same assumptions as in Proposition 7.9, under the t_0-optimal plan, there exists a well-defined long-run expected price level,

$$\lim_{T \to \infty} E_t p_T = p_\infty,$$

that is the same in every period $t \geq t_0$, regardless of the history of disturbances between periods t_0 and t; and the same is true under any policy followed from period t_0 onward that is optimal from a timeless perspective. In the particular case of the latter sort that is optimal subject to the initial constraint (2.13) or (2.14) of Chapter 7, the long-run expected price level corresponds to the constant $\bar{p}$ in the constraint.

PROOF: See the proof of Proposition 7.9 for the set of equilibrium conditions that must be satisfied by any of the equilibria of the kind considered in this proposition. One of these is (1.7), which may be rewritten

$$p_t + \varphi_t = p_{t-1} + \varphi_{t-1}. \tag{F.8}$$

Thus the sum $p_t + \varphi_t$ never changes in any of these equilibria, regardless of the disturbances that may occur. It follows that

$$\lim_{T \to \infty} E_t p_T = (p_t + \varphi_t) - \lim_{T \to \infty} E_t \varphi_T$$

$$= (p_t + \varphi_t) + (\lambda/\kappa) x^*, \tag{F.9}$$

using (F.7). Furthermore, since $p_t + \varphi_t$ never changes, regardless of the history of disturbances, it follows that the right-hand side of (F.9) never changes, so that the long-run expected price level p_∞ can never change (though it may differ across different equilibria of the kind covered by the proposition).

In the particular case of an equilibrium that is optimal subject to the initial constraint (2.13) or (2.14), observe that by equating (F.2) with (2.13), one can show that the initial Lagrange multiplier in this case is given by

$$\varphi_{t_0-1} = -(\lambda/\kappa) x^* - (p_{t_0-1} - \bar{p}).$$

Substituting this expression into (F.9), one sees that the long-run expected price level is equal to $\bar{p}$.

F.4 The Optimal Noninertial Plan

Suppose that the disturbances in the basic neo-Wicksellian model are of the form of equations (2.18) and (2.27) of Chapter 7, with respective coefficients of serial correlation ρ_u and ρ_r. Then the optimal noninertial plan is given by

$$z_t = \bar{z} + F e_t, \qquad i_t = \bar{i} + f_i e_t$$

where $z_t \equiv [\pi_t, x_t]'$, $e_t \equiv [\hat{r}_t^n, u_t]'$. The long-run average values $\bar{z}$, $\bar{i}$, and the response coefficients are given by

$$\bar{z} = \begin{bmatrix} \dfrac{(1-\beta)\kappa^{-1}\lambda_x x^* + \lambda_i\,(i^* - \bar{r})}{1 + (1-\beta)^2\kappa^{-2}\lambda_x + \lambda_i} \\[3ex] \dfrac{1-\beta}{\kappa}\,\dfrac{(1-\beta)\kappa^{-1}\lambda_x x^* + \lambda_i\,(i^* - \bar{r})}{1 + (1-\beta)^2\kappa^{-2}\lambda_x + \lambda_i} \end{bmatrix},$$

$$\bar{i} = \frac{(1-\beta)\kappa^{-1}\lambda_x x^* + \lambda_i\,(i^* - \bar{r})}{1 + (1-\beta)^2\kappa^{-2}\lambda_x + \lambda_i} + \bar{r},$$

and

$$F = \begin{bmatrix} \pi_r & \pi_u \\ x_r & x_u \end{bmatrix}, \qquad f_i = [\,i_r \quad i_u\,]$$

where the coefficients

$$\pi_r = \frac{\lambda_i\sigma^{-1}\,(\gamma_r - \rho_r\kappa\sigma)\,\kappa}{h_r}, \qquad\qquad \pi_u = \frac{\lambda_i\sigma^{-2}\,(\gamma_u - \rho_u\kappa\sigma)\,(1 - \rho_u) + \xi_u}{h_u},$$

$$x_r = \frac{\lambda_i\sigma^{-1}\,(\gamma_r - \rho_r\kappa\sigma)\,(1 - \beta\rho_r)}{h_r}, \qquad\qquad x_u = \frac{\rho_u\lambda_i\sigma^{-1}\,(\gamma_u - \rho_u\kappa\sigma) - \kappa}{h_u},$$

$$i_r = \frac{\xi_r\,(1 - \beta\rho_r) + \kappa^2}{h_r} > 0, \qquad\qquad i_u = \frac{\sigma^{-1}\kappa\,(1 - \rho_u) + \xi_u\rho_u}{h_u} > 0,$$

and

$$\gamma_j \equiv (1 - \rho_j)\,(1 - \beta\rho_j) > 0,$$

$$h_j \equiv \lambda_i \sigma^{-2} \left(\gamma_j - \rho_j \kappa \sigma \right)^2 + \lambda_x \left(1 - \beta \rho_j \right)^2 + \kappa^2 > 0,$$

$$\xi_j \equiv \lambda_x \left(1 - \beta \rho_j \right) > 0,$$

for $j \in \{r, u\}$.

F.5   Proof of Proposition 7.15

PROPOSITION 7.15. Consider again the problem of choosing monetary policy from date t_0 onward so as to minimize the expected value of (1.2), where the joint evolution of inflation and output must satisfy equation (2.1) of Chapter 7 for each date $t \geq t_0$. Let $\{u_t\}$ be a bounded exogenous disturbance process, the statistical character of which is otherwise unspecified. Then if the central bank commits itself to a policy that ensures that (5.1) is satisfied at each date $t \geq t_0$, there are unique bounded rational-expectations-equilibrium processes $\{\pi_t, x_t\}$ for dates $t \geq t_0$ consistent with this policy rule. Furthermore, the equilibrium determined by this policy commitment is the same as the one characterized in Proposition 7.7. Thus the proposed policy rule is optimal from a timeless perspective.

PROOF: The system of equilibrium conditions in the case of this kind of policy commitment consists of (2.1) and (5.1), each of which must hold for all $t \geq t_0$. Using (5.1) to eliminate π_t and π_{t+1} from (2.1), one obtains a stochastic difference equation

$$\beta E_t x_{t+1} - \left(1 + \beta + \kappa^2 / \lambda \right) x_t + x_{t-1} = (\kappa / \lambda) u_t$$

for the output gap. This equation is similar in form to (2.6). In particular, it has the same characteristic equation (1.11), which as noted before has two real roots $0 < \mu_1 < 1 < \mu_2$. This implies (just as in the derivation of (2.7)) that there is a unique bounded solution for the process $\{x_t\}$, given by

$$x_t = \mu_1 x_{t-1} - (\kappa / \lambda) \beta^{-1} \sum_{j=0}^{\infty} \mu_2^{-j-1} E_t u_{t+j}, \tag{F.10}$$

in the case of any bounded disturbance process $\{u_t\}$. This can be solved recursively for the process $\{x_t\}$ given the initial condition x_{t_0-1}. Substitution of this into (5.1) then yields a unique bounded solution for $\{\pi_t\}$ as well.

The evolution of inflation and the output gap in the solution to the constrained optimization problem stated in Proposition 7.7 are easily characterized using the method illustrated in the proof of Proposition 7.6. One finds that the process $\{x_t\}$ satisfies the difference equation (F.10) in that solution as well, again starting from the given initial value x_{t_0-1} (which matters to the solution of the constrained optimization problem because of its role in the constraint on π_{t_0}). Hence the $\{x_t\}$ associated with the timelessly optimal equilibrium is the same process as is determined by the policy rule (5.1). The same is true of the inflation process (which can be uniquely determined given the output-gap process, in either case, by solving forward (2.1)).

F.6 Proof of Proposition 7.16

PROPOSITION 7.16. Under the same assumptions as in Proposition 7.15, suppose that the central bank commits itself to a policy that ensures that equation (5.3) of Chapter 7 is satisfied at each date $t \geq t_0$. Then there are unique bounded rational-expectations-equilibrium processes $\{\pi_t, x_t\}$ for dates $t \geq t_0$ consistent with this policy rule. Furthermore, the equilibrium determined by this policy commitment is the same as the one characterized in Proposition 7.8. Thus the proposed policy rule is optimal from a timeless perspective.

PROOF: Note that a commitment to ensure that (5.3) holds at each date $t \geq t_0$ implies that (5.1) holds at each date $t \geq t_0 + 1$. Furthermore, (5.1) would hold for $t = t_0$ as well if it happens that

$$\bar{p} = p_{t_0-1} + (\lambda/\kappa)x_{t_0-1}. \tag{F.11}$$

One can think of this as saying that (5.1) would also hold for $t = t_0$ if x_{t_0} has a certain value (the one that would satisfy (F.11), given the value of p_{t_0-1}).

Since x_{t_0} plays no role in any of the other equilibrium conditions under this policy rule, it may be said that (5.1) holds for all $t \geq t_0$ if a *fictitious* initial value is supplied for x_{t_0-1} that depends on the values of p_{t_0-1} and $\bar{p}$. In this case, the proof of Proposition 7.15 can be used to show that there is a unique bounded solution for $\{x_t\}$, given by (F.10) starting from the fictitious initial condition for x_{t_0-1}. Thus the solution is given by

$$x_{t_0} = -\mu_1(\kappa/\lambda)(p_{t_0-1} - \bar{p}) - (\kappa/\lambda)\beta^{-1} \sum_{j=0}^{\infty} \mu_2^{-j-1} E_{t_0} u_{t_0+j}$$

together with (F.10) for all $t \geq t_0+1$. This unique bounded solution for $\{x_t\}$ implies a unique bounded solution for $\{p_t\}$ by substitution into (5.3), and hence a unique bounded solution for inflation as well. Furthermore, one easily verifies that these equilibrium paths, which depend on the initial condition $p_{t_0-1} - \bar{p}$, coincide with those that solve the constrained optimization problem in Proposition 7.8 (which depend on the same initial condition because of its role in the constraint on π_{t_0}).

Addendum to Chapter 8

G.1 Assumptions 8.3 and 8.4

A correct statement of Proposition 8.1 requires additional technical assumptions, beyond those given in the text.

ASSUMPTION 8.3. The characteristic polynomial (1.15) of Chapter 8 has rank $(\tilde{E})$ + rank $(A) - n_z$ distinct nonzero roots, in addition to the root zero if rank $(A) < n$ (i.e., if A is singular). In addition, if rank $(A) < n$, there are $n - $ rank (A) linearly independent vectors u_i such that $Au_i = 0$, and likewise $n - $ rank (A) linearly independent vectors f_i' such that $f_i'A = 0$. Similarly, if rank $(\tilde{E}) < n_z$, there are $n_z - $ rank $(\tilde{E})$ linearly independent vectors e_j' such that $e_j'\hat{I} = 0$, and likewise $n_z - $ rank $(\tilde{E})$ linearly independent vectors h_j such that $\hat{I}h_j = 0$.

Assumption 8.3 implies that there are rank $(\hat{I}) = n_z + $ rank $(\tilde{E})$ linearly independent vectors u_i with the property that

$$Au_i = \mu_i \, \hat{I}u_i \tag{G.1}$$

for some (scalar) *eigenvalue* μ_i. The eigenvalues correspond to the roots μ_i of (1.15), and there is one *eigenvector* for each of the nonzero roots, in addition to $n - $ rank (A) corresponding to the zero root. The eigenvectors associated with real eigenvalues are real-valued, while the eigenvectors associated with complex eigenvalues are complex-valued. Complex roots come in complex conjugate pairs, and if u_i is the eigenvector associated with a complex eigenvalue μ_i, then the eigenvector associated with $\mu_i^\dagger$ is $u_i^\dagger$, where the dagger denotes a complex conjugate. There is also an additional set of $n_z - $ rank $(\tilde{E})$ linearly independent vectors h_j such that $\hat{I}h_j = 0$, necessarily linearly independent of the set of eigenvectors. Taken together, these vectors comprise a set of n linearly independent vectors that can be used as a basis for C^n.

There are similarly at least rank (A) linearly independent vectors e_j' with the property that

$$\theta_j e_j' A = e_j' \hat{I} \tag{G.2}$$

for some θ_j.[1] Corresponding to each of the nonzero roots μ_i of (1.15) there is a *left eigenvector* e_i' satisfying this equation for $\theta_i = \mu_i^{-1}$. The remaining left eigenvectors are the $n_z - \text{rank}(\tilde{E})$ linearly independent vectors e_j' such that $e_j' \hat{I} = 0$; these satisfy (G.2) for $\theta_j = 0$. Again there is also an additional set of $n - \text{rank}(A)$ linearly independent vectors f_i' such that $f_i' A = 0$. Taken together, this set of n *generalized left eigenvectors* also forms a basis for C^n.

In the case of a left eigenvector e_j' and a right eigenvector u_i corresponding to eigenvalues such that $\theta_j \mu_i \neq 1$, one necessarily has

$$e_j' A u_i = e_j' \hat{I} u_i = 0. \tag{G.3}$$

The same condition can be shown to hold if either e_j' or u_i is one of the generalized eigenvectors, that is, if $e_j' A = 0$ or $\hat{I} u_i = 0$. One can also normalize the eigenvectors so that if e_j' and u_i are eigenvectors for which $\theta_j \mu_i = 1$, then

$$e_j' \hat{I} u_i = 1.$$

Assumptions 8.2 and 8.3 together imply that there exist at least n_z linearly independent vectors u_i satisfying (G.1) for which the associated eigenvalue satisfies $|\mu_i| < \beta^{-1}$. Thus one can form a $n \times n_z$ matrix J with the property that

$$AJ = \hat{I} J \Omega, \tag{G.4}$$

where Ω is a square matrix of dimension n_z, all of the eigenvalues of which satisfy $|\mu_i| < \beta^{-1}$. This last property implies that

$$\|\beta \Omega\| < 1. \tag{G.5}$$

The columns of J are linear combinations of n_z of the eigenvectors u_i, and the eigenvalues of Ω are the associated eigenvalues.[2] It is possible to include

---

1. Note that in the case of a complex-valued column vector or matrix e, I use the notation e' to denote the transpose of e, not the conjugate transpose.

2. In the case that one selects a complex conjugate pair of eigenvectors, it is convenient for the columns of J not to be the eigenvectors themselves, so that they can be real valued.

all of the vectors u_i such that $Au_i = 0$ among the eigenvectors used to form the columns of J, and I assume that J is constructed in this way.

Corresponding to this selection from among the right eigenvectors, one may similarly form two sets of (generalized) left eigenvectors, Φ and Ψ. Here the rows of Ψ' are n_z linearly independent combinations of the n_z left eigenvectors with eigenvalues equal to zero or to the reciprocals of roots of (1.15) that are not among the eigenvalues of Ω. It follows that there is a matrix Θ such that

$$\Theta'\Psi'A = \Psi'\hat{I}; \tag{G.6}$$

this matrix is of rank $k \equiv \text{rank}\,(\tilde{E})$ and has nonzero eigenvalues corresponding to the reciprocals of the roots of (1.15) just mentioned. It also follows from (G.3) that

$$\Psi'AJ = \Psi'\hat{I}J = 0. \tag{G.7}$$

Similarly, the rows of Φ' are n_z linear combinations of the $n - \text{rank}\,(A)$ vectors f_i' such that $f_i'A = 0$ and the rank $(A) - n_z$ left eigenvectors with eigenvalues that are the reciprocals of nonzero eigenvalues of Ω. One can select this matrix so that

$$\Phi'A = \Omega\Phi'\hat{I}, \tag{G.8}$$

$$\Phi'\hat{I}J = I. \tag{G.9}$$

Note that the columns of Ψ and Φ together form a basis for $\mathcal{C}^n$.

I can now state the remaining technical assumption used in Proposition 8.1.

ASSUMPTION 8.4. The matrix of left eigenvectors Ψ is such that: (i) the matrix $A'\Psi$ is of full rank (i.e., rank n_z); and (ii) if the rows of Ψ are partitioned

$$\Psi \equiv \begin{bmatrix} \Psi_1 \\ \Psi_2 \end{bmatrix},$$

conformably with the partition of the vector of endogenous variables in (1.1), then

$$\det[\text{Re}\,\Psi_2] \neq 0.$$

Both Assumptions 8.3 and 8.4 are satisfied by generic matrices A and $\tilde{E}$ of arbitrary ranks $0 \leq \text{rank}\,(\tilde{E}) \leq n_z \leq \text{rank}\,(A) \leq n$. I turn now to the proofs of the propositions in the text of Chapter 8.

G.2 Assumption 8.5

A precise statement of Proposition 8.2 relies upon the following additional assumption.

ASSUMPTION 8.5. The vector B_2' and the vectors $B_2' \Lambda^j$, for $j = 1, \ldots, k-1$, are linearly independent of one another. Similarly, the vectors $B_2' \Lambda^j$ for $j = 1, \ldots, k$ are linearly independent.

Note that this assumption is violated in particular in the special case in which B_2' is a left eigenvector of Λ, or indeed if B_2' is any linear combination of fewer than k of the left eigenvectors corresponding to nonzero eigenvalues, plus the left eigenvectors corresponding to zero eigenvalues. (Recall that rank $(\Lambda) = k$, so that there are exactly k nonzero eigenvalues.) It follows that Assumption 8.5 also requires that $B_2' g_i \neq 0$ for any right eigenvector g_i of Λ corresponding to a nonzero eigenvalue. Nonetheless, the assumption is clearly satisfied for generic matrices of arbitrary rank, since the elements of B_2 are not involved in the conditions that define the matrix Λ.

G.3 Technical Lemmas

The following technical lemmas are used in certain of the proofs that follow.

LEMMA G.1. For any real coefficients A_0, A_1, A_2, A_3, one has

$$A_3 z^3 + A_2 z^2 + A_1 z + A_0 = A_3 \left(B_0 + B_1 \zeta + \zeta^3 \right),$$

where

$$\zeta = z + \frac{A_2}{3A_3},$$

$$B_0 = \frac{27 A_0 A_3^2 + 2 A_2^3 - 9 A_3 A_2 A_1}{27 A_3^3},$$

$$B_1 = \frac{3 A_3 A_1 - A_2^2}{3 A_3^2}.$$

PROOF:

$$A_3 \left(B_0 + B_1 \zeta + \zeta^3 \right) = A_3 \left(\zeta^3 + \frac{1}{3} \frac{3 A_3 A_1 - A_2^2}{A_3^2} \zeta + \frac{1}{27} \frac{27 A_0 A_3^2 + 2 A_2^3 - 9 A_3 A_2 A_1}{A_3^3} \right)$$

$$= A_3 \left(\left(z + \frac{1}{3}\frac{A_2}{A_3} \right)^3 + \frac{1}{3}\frac{3A_3A_1 - A_2^2}{A_3^2}\left(z + \frac{1}{3}\frac{A_2}{A_3} \right) \right.$$

$$\left. + \frac{1}{27}\frac{27A_0A_3^2 + 2A_2^3 - 9A_3A_2A_1}{A_3^3} \right)$$

$$= A_3z^3 + A_2z^2 + \left(\frac{1}{3}\frac{A_2^2}{A_3} + \frac{1}{3}\frac{3A_3A_1 - A_2^2}{A_3} \right)z + \frac{1}{27}\frac{A_2^3}{A_3^2}$$

$$+ \frac{1}{27}\frac{27A_0A_3^2 + 2A_2^3 - 9A_3A_2A_1}{A_3^2} + \frac{1}{9}\frac{3A_3A_1 - A_2^2}{A_3^2}A_2$$

$$= A_3z^3 + A_2z^2 + A_1z + A_0.$$

LEMMA G.2. In the limit, as γ approaches 0, $\lambda_3 \to +\infty$, and $\gamma\lambda_3 \to \beta^{-1}$.

PROOF: In the limit, as γ tends to 0, the polynomial $A(L)$ reduces to

$$A(L) = \beta^{-1}\left(\beta - (1 + \beta + \kappa\sigma)L + L^2\right)(-L),$$

and can again be factorized as

$$A(L) = \beta^{-1}(z_1 - L)(z_2 - L)(z_3 - L),$$

where $z_3 = 0$, and z_1, z_2 are the two roots of the second-order polynomial

$$\tilde{A}(L) = \beta - (1 + \beta + \kappa\sigma)L + L^2.$$

Note that since $\tilde{A}(0) = \beta > 0$, and $\tilde{A}(1) = -\kappa\sigma < 0$, the two roots of $\tilde{A}(L)$ are real and satisfy $0 < z_2 < 1 < z_1$. It follows that

$$0 < \lambda_1 < 1 < \lambda_2 < \lambda_3 = +\infty,$$

where $\lambda_j \equiv z_j^{-1}$, for $j = 1, 2, 3$.

Furthermore, as (G.20) holds for all γ, one has

$$\lambda_3\gamma = \beta^{-1} + \gamma\left(1 + \beta^{-1} - \lambda_1 - \lambda_2\right).$$

Taking the limit as $\gamma \to 0$ on both sides and noting that λ_1 and λ_2 are bounded yields

$$\lim_{\gamma \to 0} \lambda_3\gamma = \beta^{-1}.$$

G.4 Proof of Proposition 8.5

PROPOSITION 8.5. Suppose that the problem of choosing a state-contingent plan $\{\pi_t, x_t, i_t\}$ for dates $t \geq t_0$ satisfying equations (2.1) and (3.1) of Chapter 8 and initial conditions (3.6) has a bounded solution in the case of any bounded disturbance processes. Then a commitment to the rule described by (3.7)–(3.9) implies a determinate rational-expectations equilibrium.

PROOF: The system of equations given by the structural equations (2.1) and (3.1), together with the policy rule (3.7)–(3.9), can be written in matrix form as

$$\bar{I} \begin{bmatrix} Z_{t+1} \\ E_t z_{t+1} \\ E_t i_{t+1} \end{bmatrix} = \begin{bmatrix} 0 \\ -\bar{\phi} \end{bmatrix} + \bar{A} \begin{bmatrix} Z_t \\ z_t \\ i_t \end{bmatrix} + \bar{C} s_t, \tag{G.10}$$

where $z_t \equiv [\pi_t, x_t]'$, $Z_t \equiv [x_{t-1}, i_{t-1}, i_{t-2}]'$, $s_t \equiv [r_t^n, u_t]'$, and

$$\bar{I} = \begin{bmatrix} 1 & 0 & 0 & 0 & 0 & 0 \\ 0 & 1 & 0 & 0 & 0 & 0 \\ 0 & 0 & 1 & 0 & 0 & 0 \\ 0 & 0 & 0 & \sigma & 1 & 0 \\ 0 & 0 & 0 & \beta & 0 & 0 \\ 0 & 0 & 0 & 0 & 0 & 0 \end{bmatrix},$$

$$\bar{A} = \begin{bmatrix} 0 & 0 & 0 & 0 & 1 & 0 \\ 0 & 0 & 0 & 0 & 0 & 1 \\ 0 & 1 & 0 & 0 & 0 & 0 \\ 0 & 0 & 0 & 0 & 1 & \sigma \\ 0 & 0 & 0 & 1 & -\kappa & 0 \\ -\dfrac{\sigma\lambda_x}{\lambda_i} & 1+\dfrac{\kappa\sigma}{\beta}+\beta^{-1} & -\beta^{-1} & \dfrac{\kappa\sigma}{\lambda_i} & \dfrac{\sigma\lambda_x}{\lambda_i} & -1 \end{bmatrix}.$$

As discussed in Section 1.2 of Chapter 8, the equilibrium is determinate if the characteristic polynomial $\det[\bar{A} - \mu\bar{I}]$ has exactly $n_Z = 3$ roots such that $|\mu| < 1$. Recall that if there are fewer such roots, there is no bounded solution at all. Since the rule (3.7)–(3.9) is derived from the first-order conditions (3.3)–(3.5), it must be consistent with the optimal state-contingent plan. Because I assume that a bounded optimal state-contingent plan exists, it must be the case that $\det\left[\bar{A} - \mu\bar{I}\right]$ admits at least three roots inside the unit circle.

I can rewrite the characteristic polynomial as

$$\det\left[\bar{A} - \mu\bar{I}\right] = -p\left(\mu\right)\beta\mu \tag{G.11}$$

where

$$p\left(\mu\right) \equiv \mu^4 - a\mu^3 + b\mu^2 - a\beta^{-1}\mu + \beta^{-2}, \tag{G.12}$$

and

$$a = 2\frac{1 + \beta + \sigma\kappa}{\beta} + \frac{\sigma^2\lambda_x}{\lambda_i},$$

$$b = \frac{1 + 2\kappa\beta\sigma + 2\sigma\kappa + \sigma^2\kappa^2 + 4\beta + \beta^2}{\beta^2} + \sigma^2\frac{(1 + \beta)\lambda_x + \kappa^2}{\beta\lambda_i}.$$

I can furthermore express $p\left(\mu\right)$ as

$$p\left(\mu\right) = (\mu - \mu_1)(\mu - \mu_2)(\mu - \mu_3)(\mu - \mu_4),$$

where, because of the symmetry in (G.12), the four roots μ_i satisfy

$$\mu_1 = (\beta\mu_2)^{-1} \quad \text{and} \quad \mu_3 = (\beta\mu_4)^{-1}. \tag{G.13}$$

Because $\det\left[\bar{A} - \mu\bar{I}\right]$ admits at least three roots inside the unit circle, (G.11) and (G.12) imply that $p\left(\mu\right)$ admits two, three, or four roots inside the unit circle. I consider each case in turn:

1. Suppose first, by way of contradiction, that all four roots of $p\left(\mu\right)$ are inside the unit circle. Then $|\mu_1| < 1$ by assumption. However (G.13) implies $|\beta\mu_2| > 1$, and thus $|\mu_2| > 1$, which contradicts the assumption that all four roots are inside the unit circle.
2. Suppose next that $p\left(\mu\right)$ has three roots inside the unit circle. If $|\mu_1| < 1$, then (G.13) implies again $|\mu_2| > 1$. It follows that the remaining two roots μ_3 and μ_4 must be inside the unit circle. But this is impossible, as $|\mu_3| < 1$ implies $|\mu_4| > 1$. Inversely, if $|\mu_1| > 1$, then the three remaining roots must be inside the unit circle. Again, this is impossible as $|\mu_3| < 1$ implies $|\mu_4| > 1$.

It follows that $p\left(\mu\right)$ must have exactly two roots inside the unit circle, and thus that the equilibrium is determinate.

G.5   Proof of Proposition 8.6

PROPOSITION 8.6. Assuming $0 < \lambda_1 < 1 < \lambda_2$, two bounded stochastic processes $\{\hat{\imath}_t, \hat{q}_t\}$ satisfy

$$(1 - \lambda_1 L)(1 - \lambda_2 L)\,\hat{\imath}_t = \hat{q}_t \qquad (G.14)$$

for all $t \geq 0$ if and only if they satisfy

$$(1 - \lambda_1 L)\,\hat{\imath}_{t-1} = -\lambda_2^{-1} E_t \left[\left(1 - \lambda_2^{-1} L^{-1}\right)^{-1} \hat{q}_t \right] \qquad (G.15)$$

for all $t \geq 0$.

PROOF: First, I show that (G.14) implies (G.15). Expanding the left-hand side of (G.14) gives

$$(1 - \lambda_1 L)\,\hat{\imath}_t - \lambda_2\,(1 - \lambda_1 L)\,\hat{\imath}_{t-1} = \hat{q}_t,$$

or equivalently

$$(1 - \lambda_1 L)\,\hat{\imath}_{t-1} = -\lambda_2^{-1} \left[\hat{q}_t - (1 - \lambda_1 L)\,\hat{\imath}_t \right]$$

$$= -\lambda_2^{-1} E_t \left[\hat{q}_t - (1 - \lambda_1 L)\,\hat{\imath}_t \right].$$

Substituting recursively for $(1 - \lambda_1 L)\,\hat{\imath}_{t+j}$ on the right-hand side yields

$$(1 - \lambda_1 L)\,\hat{\imath}_{t-1} = -\lambda_2^{-1} E_t \left[\sum_{j=0}^{\infty} \lambda_2^{-j} \hat{q}_{t+j} \right]$$

$$= -\lambda_2^{-1} E_t \left[\left(1 - \lambda_2^{-1} L^{-1}\right)^{-1} \hat{q}_t \right],$$

where the last equality holds since $0 < \lambda_2^{-1} < 1$. Thus (G.14) implies (G.15).
Second, I show that (G.15) implies (G.14). Since (G.15) holds for all $t \geq 0$, (G.15) implies

$$(1 - \lambda_1 L)\,\hat{\imath}_t = -\lambda_2^{-1} E_{t+1} \left[\left(1 - \lambda_2^{-1} L^{-1}\right)^{-1} \hat{q}_{t+1} \right].$$

Multiplying on both sides by $(1 - \lambda_2 L)$ and taking expectations at t yields

$$(1 - \lambda_1 L)(1 - \lambda_2 L)\,\hat{\imath}_t = E_t \left[\left(1 - \lambda_2^{-1} L^{-1}\right)^{-1} \left(L - \lambda_2^{-1}\right) \hat{q}_{t+1} \right]$$

$$= E_t \left[\left(1 - \lambda_2^{-1} L^{-1}\right)^{-1} \left(1 - \lambda_2^{-1} L^{-1}\right) L\hat{q}_{t+1} \right]$$

$$= E_t \left[L\hat{q}_{t+1} \right]$$

$$= \hat{q}_t.$$

Thus (G.15) also implies (G.14).

G.6   Proof of Proposition 8.7

PROPOSITION 8.7. Suppose that $\sigma, \kappa > 0, 0 < \beta < 1$, and $0 < \gamma \le 1$. Then in the factorization

$$A(L) = \beta\gamma \left(1 - \lambda_1 L\right) \left(1 - \lambda_2 L\right) \left(1 - \lambda_3 L\right) \tag{G.16}$$

of the polynomial

$$A(L) \equiv \beta\gamma - (1 + \gamma + \beta\gamma) L + \left(1 + \gamma + \beta^{-1} (1 + \kappa\sigma)\right) L^2 - \beta^{-1} L^3, \tag{G.17}$$

there is necessarily one real root $0 < \lambda_1 < 1$ and two roots outside the unit circle. The latter two roots are either two real roots $\lambda_3 \ge \lambda_2 > 1$, or a complex pair λ_2, λ_3 with a real part greater than 1. Three real roots necessarily exist for all small enough $\gamma > 0$, while a complex pair necessarily exists for all γ close enough to 1.

PROOF: Consider the following properties of the polynomial (G.17):

$$A(z) > 0, \forall z \le 0, \qquad A'(z) < 0, \forall z \le 0,$$
$$A(\beta) = \beta\kappa\sigma > 0, \qquad A'(\beta) = (1 - \beta) (1 - \gamma) + 2\kappa\sigma > 0,$$
$$A(1) = \beta^{-1}\kappa\sigma > 0,$$
$$A(+\infty) = -\infty.$$

From this, we know that for all $z \le 0$, $A(z)$ is positive and decreasing. As z is raised from 0 to β, $A(z)$ continues to decrease, reaches a minimum (where $A(z)$ may be positive or negative), and starts increasing as z approaches β. The polynomial $A(z)$ is positive for $z = 1$, but decreases again and tends to $-\infty$ as z becomes larger and larger. It follows that $A(z)$ admits one real root $z_1 > 1$ and either two real roots $0 < z_3 \le z_2 < 1$ or a pair of complex roots z_2, z_3.

Thus $A(L)$ can be written as

$$A(L) = \beta^{-1} (z_1 - L) (z_2 - L) (z_3 - L)$$

$$= \beta^{-1}\lambda_1^{-1}\lambda_2^{-1}\lambda_3^{-1}(1 - \lambda_1 L)(1 - \lambda_2 L)(1 - \lambda_3 L)$$

$$= \frac{1}{\beta\lambda_1\lambda_2\lambda_3} - \frac{\lambda_1 + \lambda_2 + \lambda_3}{\beta\lambda_1\lambda_2\lambda_3} L + \frac{\lambda_1\lambda_2 + (\lambda_1 + \lambda_2)\lambda_3}{\beta\lambda_1\lambda_2\lambda_3} L^2 - \beta^{-1}L^3 \quad \text{(G.18)}$$

where $\lambda_j \equiv z_j^{-1}$ for $j = 1, 2, 3$. Comparing the first terms of (G.18) and (G.17), one notes that

$$(\beta\lambda_1\lambda_2\lambda_3)^{-1} = \beta\gamma, \quad \text{(G.19)}$$

so that the polynomial $A(L)$ can be factorized as in (G.16), where $0 < \lambda_1 < 1$ and λ_2, λ_3 are either two real roots satisfying $1 < \lambda_2 \leq \lambda_3$, or a pair of complex roots.

I now show that in the case that λ_2, λ_3 form a pair of complex roots, their common real part is greater than 1. Comparing the second term of (G.18) with the corresponding term in (G.17), and using (G.19), note that

$$\beta\gamma(\lambda_1 + \lambda_2 + \lambda_3) = 1 + \gamma + \beta\gamma. \quad \text{(G.20)}$$

Furthermore, as $\beta\gamma\lambda_1 < 1$, one has

$$\beta\gamma\lambda_1 = 1 + \gamma - \beta\gamma(\lambda_2 + \lambda_3 - 1) < 1.$$

This implies

$$-\beta\gamma(\lambda_2 + \lambda_3 - 1) < -\gamma,$$

and thus

$$\lambda_2 + \lambda_3 > 1 + \beta^{-1} > 2.$$

Therefore

$$\text{Re } \lambda_2 = \text{Re } \lambda_3 = \frac{\lambda_2 + \lambda_3}{2} > 1.$$

It follows that the moduli $|\lambda_2| = |\lambda_3| > 1$.

I now show that three real roots $\lambda_1, \lambda_2, \lambda_3$ necessarily exist for all small enough $\gamma > 0$, while a complex pair λ_2, λ_3 necessarily exists for all γ close enough to 1. First note that each λ_j, for $j = 1, 2, 3$, is real if and only if the solution $z_j \equiv \lambda_j^{-1}$ of the equation

$$A(z) \equiv A_0 + A_1 z + A_2 z^2 + A_3 z^3 = 0$$

is real, where

$$A_0 = \beta\gamma,$$

$$A_1 = -(1 + \gamma + \beta\gamma),$$

$$A_2 = 1 + \gamma + \beta^{-1}(1 + \kappa\sigma),$$

$$A_3 = -\beta^{-1}.$$

Furthermore, since

$$A(z) = A_3 \left(B_0 + B_1 \zeta + \zeta^3 \right)$$

where

$$\zeta = z + \frac{A_2}{3A_3},$$

and

$$B_0 = \frac{27A_0 A_3^2 + 2A_2^3 - 9A_3 A_2 A_1}{27A_3^3},$$

$$B_1 = \frac{3A_3 A_1 - A_2^2}{3A_3^2}$$

are real coefficients, each λ_j is real if and only if the corresponding solution ζ_j of the equation

$$B_0 + B_1 \zeta + \zeta^3 = 0$$

is real, using Lemma G.1. From Cardano's formulas for the roots of a cubic equation, one knows that this equation admits:

(1) three different real roots if $\Delta \equiv 27B_0^2 + 4B_1^3 < 0$,
(2) three real roots, at least two of which are equal if $\Delta = 0$, and
(3) one real root and two complex roots if $\Delta > 0$.

Expressing Δ as a function of γ yields

$$\Delta(\gamma) = 27B_0^2 + 4B_1^3 = A_3^{-4}\left(27A_0^2 A_3^2 + 4A_0 A_2^3 - 18A_0 A_3 A_2 A_1 - A_2^2 A_1^2 + 4A_3 A_1^3\right)$$

$$= -\beta^4 (1 - \beta)^2 \gamma^4 - 2\beta^3 \left((1 + \beta^2 - 4\beta)\kappa\sigma - (1 + \beta)(1 - \beta)^2\right)\gamma^3$$

$$- \beta^2 \left(\kappa^2\sigma^2 (1 - 10\beta + \beta^2) + 2\kappa\sigma (1 + \beta)(1 + \beta + \beta^2)\right)$$

$$+ \left(1 + 4\beta + \beta^2\right)(1 - \beta)^2\right)\gamma^2$$

$$+ \beta^2 \left(4\kappa^3\sigma^3 + 10\left(1 + \beta\right)\kappa^2\sigma^2 + 4\left(2 + 2\beta^2 - \beta\right)\kappa\sigma\right.$$

$$+ 2\left(1 + \beta\right)\left(1 - \beta\right)^2\right)\gamma$$

$$- \beta^2 \left(2\beta\kappa\sigma + \kappa^2\sigma^2 + 2\kappa\sigma + \left(1 - \beta\right)^2\right),$$

which is a fourth-order polynomial in γ. Note that $\Delta\left(\gamma\right)$ is a continuous function of γ that admits at most four real roots, and has the following properties:

$$\Delta\left(-\infty\right) = -\infty,$$

$$\Delta\left(0\right) = -\beta^2 \left(2\beta\kappa\sigma + \kappa^2\sigma^2 + 2\kappa\sigma + \left(1 - \beta\right)^2\right) < 0,$$

$$\Delta\left(1\right) = \beta^2\kappa\sigma \left(4\kappa^2\sigma^2 + \left(8 + 20\beta - \beta^2\right)\kappa\sigma + 4\left(1 - \beta\right)^3\right) > 0,$$

$$\Delta\left(+\infty\right) = -\infty.$$

It follows that $\Delta\left(\gamma\right)$ admits either one or three roots between 0 and 1. Furthermore, $\Delta < 0$ for $\gamma > 0$ small enough, and $\Delta > 0$ for all γ close enough to 1. Thus three real roots necessarily exist for all small enough $\gamma > 0$, while a complex pair necessarily exists for all γ close enough to 1.

G.7 Proof of Proposition 8.8

PROPOSITION 8.8. *Under the assumptions of Proposition 8.7, and in the case that the factorization (3.20) of Chapter 8 involves three real roots, a pair of bounded processes $\{\hat{\imath}_t, \hat{f}_t\}$ satisfies any of the equations*

$$\left(1 - \lambda_1 L\right)\left(1 - \lambda_2 L\right)\hat{\imath}_t = \left(\beta\gamma\lambda_3\right)^{-1} E_t \left[\left(1 - \lambda_3^{-1}L^{-1}\right)^{-1}\hat{f}_t\right], \quad \text{(G.21)}$$

$$\left(1 - \lambda_1 L\right)\left(1 - \lambda_3 L\right)\hat{\imath}_t = \left(\beta\gamma\lambda_2\right)^{-1} E_t \left[\left(1 - \lambda_2^{-1}L^{-1}\right)^{-1}\hat{f}_t\right], \quad \text{(G.22)}$$

or

$$\left(1 - \lambda_1 L\right)\left(1 - \frac{\lambda_2 + \lambda_3}{2}L\right)\hat{\imath}_t = \frac{1}{2}\left(\beta\gamma\lambda_3\right)^{-1} E_t \left[\left(1 - \lambda_3^{-1}L^{-1}\right)^{-1}\hat{f}_t\right]$$

$$+ \frac{1}{2}\left(\beta\gamma\lambda_2\right)^{-1} E_t \left[\left(1 - \lambda_2^{-1}L^{-1}\right)^{-1}\hat{f}_t\right] \quad \text{(G.23)}$$

at all dates $t \geq t_0$ if and only if they satisfy

$$E_t \left[A(L)\,\hat{\imath}_{t+1}\right] = -\hat{f}_t \quad \text{(G.24)}$$

at all of those same dates. In the case that a complex pair exists, (G.23) is again equivalent to (G.24) in the same sense.

PROOF: Proposition 8.7 guarantees that the roots $\lambda_1, \lambda_2, \lambda_3$ in the factorization (3.20) are either real and satisfy $0 < \lambda_1 < 1 < \lambda_2 \leq \lambda_3$, or $0 < \lambda_1 < 1$, and λ_2, λ_3 are complex conjugates that lie outside the unit circle. Consider first the case in which $\lambda_1, \lambda_2, \lambda_3$ are real.

Rule I. I now show that (G.24) implies (G.21). Using (3.20) to substitute for $A(L)$, and expanding the left-hand side of (G.24), one obtains

$$\beta \gamma E_t \left[(1 - \lambda_1 L)(1 - \lambda_2 L)\, \hat{\imath}_{t+1} - (1 - \lambda_1 L)(1 - \lambda_2 L)\, \lambda_3 \hat{\imath}_t \right] = -\hat{f}_t,$$

or

$$(1 - \lambda_1 L)(1 - \lambda_2 L)\, \hat{\imath}_t = (\beta \gamma \lambda_3)^{-1} \hat{f}_t + \lambda_3^{-1} E_t \left[(1 - \lambda_1 L)(1 - \lambda_2 L)\, \hat{\imath}_{t+1} \right].$$

Substituting recursively for $(1 - \lambda_1 L)(1 - \lambda_2 L)\, \hat{\imath}_{t+j}$ on the right-hand side yields

$$(1 - \lambda_1 L)(1 - \lambda_2 L)\, \hat{\imath}_t = (\beta \gamma \lambda_3)^{-1} E_t \left[\sum_{j=0}^{\infty} \lambda_3^{-j} \hat{f}_{t+j} \right]$$

$$= (\beta \gamma \lambda_3)^{-1} E_t \left[\left(1 - \lambda_3^{-1} L^{-1} \right)^{-1} \hat{f}_t \right],$$

which corresponds to (G.21).

I now show that (G.21) implies (G.24). Since (G.21) holds for all $t \geq t_0$, (G.21) implies

$$(1 - \lambda_1 L)(1 - \lambda_2 L)\, \hat{\imath}_{t+1} = (\beta \gamma \lambda_3)^{-1} E_{t+1} \left[\left(1 - \lambda_3^{-1} L^{-1} \right)^{-1} \hat{f}_{t+1} \right].$$

Multiplying both sides by $\beta \gamma (1 - \lambda_3 L)$ and taking expectations at t, one obtains

$$E_t \left[A(L)\, \hat{\imath}_{t+1} \right] = \lambda_3^{-1} E_t \left[(1 - \lambda_3 L) \left(1 - \lambda_3^{-1} L^{-1} \right)^{-1} \hat{f}_{t+1} \right]$$

$$= E_t \left[\left(1 - \lambda_3^{-1} L^{-1} \right) \left(1 - \lambda_3^{-1} L^{-1} \right)^{-1} L \hat{f}_{t+1} \right]$$

$$= -E_t \left[L \hat{f}_{t+1} \right]$$

$$= -\hat{f}_t,$$

which corresponds to (G.24).

Rule II. To show that a pair of bounded processes $\{\hat{\imath}_t, \hat{f}_t\}$ satisfies (G.22) at all dates if and only if it satisfies (G.24) at all dates, one simply needs to repeat the above steps, replacing λ_2 with λ_3 and vice versa.

Rule III. Now allow λ_2, λ_3 to be either real values or complex conjugates lying outside the unit circle. Since (G.24) implies both (G.21) and (G.22), it is known that (G.24) implies

$$(1 - \lambda_1 L)\left[\frac{(1 - \lambda_2 L) + (1 - \lambda_3 L)}{2}\right]\hat{\imath}_t = \tfrac{1}{2}(\beta\gamma\lambda_3)^{-1} E_t\left[\left(1 - \lambda_3^{-1}L^{-1}\right)^{-1}\hat{f}_t\right]$$
$$+ \tfrac{1}{2}(\beta\gamma\lambda_2)^{-1} E_t\left[\left(1 - \lambda_2^{-1}L^{-1}\right)^{-1}\hat{f}_t\right],$$

which is obtained by summing (G.21) and (G.22) on both sides and dividing by 2. Thus (G.24) implies (G.23).

I now show that (G.23) implies (G.24). Since (G.23) holds for all $t \geq t_0$, (G.23) implies

$$(1 - \lambda_1 L)\left(1 - \frac{\lambda_2 + \lambda_3}{2}L\right)\hat{\imath}_{t+2} = (2\beta\gamma\lambda_3)^{-1} E_{t+2}\left[\left(1 - \lambda_3^{-1}L^{-1}\right)^{-1}\hat{f}_{t+2}\right]$$
$$+ (2\beta\gamma\lambda_2)^{-1} E_{t+2}\left[\left(1 - \lambda_2^{-1}L^{-1}\right)^{-1}\hat{f}_{t+2}\right].$$

Multiplying both sides by $\beta\gamma(1-\lambda_2 L)(1-\lambda_3 L)$ and taking expectations at t, one obtains

$$E_t\left[A(L)\left(1 - \frac{\lambda_2 + \lambda_3}{2}L\right)\hat{\imath}_{t+2}\right]$$
$$= \frac{1}{2\lambda_3}E_t\left[(1 - \lambda_2 L)(1 - \lambda_3 L)\left(1 - \lambda_3^{-1}L^{-1}\right)^{-1}\hat{f}_{t+2}\right]$$
$$+ \frac{1}{2\lambda_2}E_t\left[(1 - \lambda_2 L)(1 - \lambda_3 L)\left(1 - \lambda_2^{-1}L^{-1}\right)^{-1}\hat{f}_{t+2}\right]$$
$$= -\tfrac{1}{2}E_t\left[(1 - \lambda_2 L)\hat{f}_{t+1}\right] - \tfrac{1}{2}E_t\left[(1 - \lambda_3 L)\hat{f}_{t+1}\right]$$
$$= -E_t\left[\left(1 - \frac{\lambda_2 + \lambda_3}{2}L\right)\hat{f}_{t+1}\right].$$

It follows that

$$-E_t\left[A(L)\left(1 - \frac{2}{\lambda_2 + \lambda_3}L^{-1}\right)L\hat{\imath}_{t+2}\right] = E_t\left[\left(1 - \frac{2}{\lambda_2 + \lambda_3}L^{-1}\right)L\hat{f}_{t+1}\right],$$

and hence that

$$E_t \left[A(L) \left(1 - \alpha L^{-1} \right) \hat{\imath}_{t+1} \right] = v_t,$$

where $0 \le \alpha \equiv 2/(\lambda_2 + \lambda_3) < 1$, and $v_t \equiv -E_t[(1 - \alpha L^{-1})\hat{f}_t]$. This implies furthermore that

$$E_t \left[A(L) \, \hat{\imath}_{t+1} \right] = \alpha E_t \left[A(L) \, \hat{\imath}_{t+2} \right] + v_t$$

$$= E_t \left[\sum_{j=0}^{\infty} \alpha^j v_{t+j} \right]$$

$$= E_t \left[\left(1 - \alpha L^{-1} \right)^{-1} v_t \right]$$

$$= -\hat{f}_t,$$

which corresponds to (G.24).

G.8   Proof of Proposition 8.9

PROPOSITION 8.9. Under the assumptions of Proposition 8.7, and a loss function with $\lambda_x, \lambda_i > 0$, each of the Rules I, II, and III has a representation of the form

$$i_t = (1 - \rho_1) \, i^* + \rho_1 i_{t-1} + \rho_2 \Delta i_{t-1} + \phi_\pi F_t (\pi)$$

$$+ \frac{\phi_x}{4} F_t (x) - \theta_\pi \pi_{t-1} - \frac{\theta_x}{4} x_{t-1} \qquad \text{(G.25)}$$

for all values of γ for which the rule is well defined, and in this representation

$$\rho_1 > 1, \qquad \rho_2 > 0,$$

$$0 < \theta_\pi \le \phi_\pi,$$

$$0 < \theta_x = \phi_x.$$

Furthermore, for given values of the other parameters, as $\gamma \to 0$ (for Rule I) the coefficient θ_π approaches zero, though ϕ_π approaches a positive limit; while as $\gamma \to 1$ (for Rule III) the coefficients θ_π and ϕ_π approach the same limit.

PROOF: Proposition 8.7 guarantees that the roots $\lambda_1, \lambda_2, \lambda_3$ in the factorization (3.20) of Chapter 8 are either real and satisfy $0 < \lambda_1 < 1 < \lambda_2 \le \lambda_3$

or $0 < \lambda_1 < 1$, and λ_2, λ_3 are complex conjugates that lie outside the unit circle. Consider first the case in which λ_1, λ_2, λ_3 are real, so that both Rule I and Rule II are well defined.

Rule I. First note that Rule I, that is, (3.22) can be rewritten as

$$\hat{\imath}_t = \rho_1 \hat{\imath}_{t-1} + \rho_2 \Delta \hat{\imath}_{t-1} + (\beta\gamma\lambda_3)^{-1} v_t, \qquad \text{(G.26)}$$

where

$$\rho_1 = 1 + (\lambda_2 - 1)(1 - \lambda_1) > 1,$$
$$\rho_2 = \lambda_1 \lambda_2 > 0,$$

and

$$v_t \equiv E_t \left[\left(1 - \lambda_3^{-1} L^{-1} \right)^{-1} \hat{f}_t \right]$$

$$= E_t \left[\sum_{j=0}^{\infty} \lambda_3^{-j} \hat{f}_{t+j} \right].$$

Since $E_t \hat{f}_{t+j}$ is given by

$$E_t \hat{f}_{t+j} = \frac{\kappa\sigma}{\lambda_i} E_t \left(\hat{q}_{t+j} - \beta\gamma \hat{q}_{t+j+1} \right)$$

$$= \frac{\kappa\sigma}{\lambda_i} E_t \left[-\gamma \hat{\pi}_{t+j-1} + \left(1 + \beta\gamma^2 \right) \hat{\pi}_{t+j} - \beta\gamma \hat{\pi}_{t+j+1} \right]$$

$$+ \frac{\lambda_x \sigma}{\lambda_i} E_t \left[-\hat{x}_{t+j-1} + (1 + \beta\gamma) \hat{x}_{t+j} - \beta\gamma \hat{x}_{t+j+1} \right],$$

one has

$$v_t = \frac{\kappa\sigma}{\lambda_i} E_t \left[\sum_{j=0}^{\infty} \lambda_3^{-j} \left(-\gamma \hat{\pi}_{t+j-1} + \left(1 + \beta\gamma^2 \right) \hat{\pi}_{t+j} - \beta\gamma \hat{\pi}_{t+j+1} \right) \right]$$

$$+ \frac{\lambda_x \sigma}{\lambda_i} E_t \left[\sum_{j=0}^{\infty} \lambda_3^{-j} \left(-\hat{x}_{t+j-1} + (1 + \beta\gamma) \hat{x}_{t+j} - \beta\gamma \hat{x}_{t+j+1} \right) \right]$$

$$= \frac{\kappa\sigma}{\lambda_i} \sum_{j=-1}^{\infty} \tilde{\alpha}_{\pi,j} E_t \hat{\pi}_{t+j} + \frac{\lambda_x \sigma}{\lambda_i} \sum_{j=-1}^{\infty} \alpha_{x,j} E_t \hat{x}_{t+j},$$

where

$$\tilde{\alpha}_{\pi,-1} = -\gamma, \tag{G.27}$$

$$\tilde{\alpha}_{\pi,0} = 1 + \beta\gamma^2 - \lambda_3^{-1}\gamma, \tag{G.28}$$

$$\tilde{\alpha}_{\pi,j} = -\lambda_3^{-j+1}\beta\gamma + \lambda_3^{-j}\left(1 + \beta\gamma^2\right) - \lambda_3^{-j-1}\gamma, \qquad \forall j \geq 1 \tag{G.29}$$

and

$$\alpha_{x,-1} = -1, \tag{G.30}$$

$$\alpha_{x,0} = 1 + \beta\gamma - \lambda_3^{-1}, \tag{G.31}$$

$$\alpha_{x,j} = -\lambda_3^{-j+1}\beta\gamma + \lambda_3^{-j}\left(1 + \beta\gamma\right) - \lambda_3^{-j-1}, \qquad \forall j \geq 1. \tag{G.32}$$

The variable V_t can be written as

$$v_t = \frac{\kappa\sigma}{\lambda_i} S_\pi \sum_{j=0}^{\infty} \alpha_{\pi,j} E_t \hat{\pi}_{t+j} + \frac{\lambda_x\sigma}{\lambda_i} \sum_{j=0}^{\infty} \alpha_{x,j} E_t \hat{x}_{t+j} - \frac{\kappa\sigma\gamma}{\lambda_i} \hat{\pi}_{t-1}$$

$$- \frac{\lambda_x\sigma}{\lambda_i} \hat{x}_{t-1}, \tag{G.33}$$

where

$$S_\pi = \sum_{j=0}^{\infty} \tilde{\alpha}_{\pi,j}$$

$$= -\left(0 + \lambda_3^{-0} + \lambda_3^{-1} + \lambda_3^{-2} + \ldots\right)\beta\gamma + \left(\lambda_3^{-0} + \lambda_3^{-1} + \lambda_3^{-2} + \ldots\right)\left(1 + \beta\gamma^2\right)$$

$$- \left(\lambda_3^{-1} + \lambda_3^{-2} + \ldots\right)\gamma$$

$$= \left(1 - \lambda_3^{-1}\right)^{-1} \left(1 + \beta\gamma^2 - \beta\gamma - \lambda_3^{-1}\gamma\right),$$

and

$$\alpha_{\pi,j} = \frac{\tilde{\alpha}_{\pi,j}}{S_\pi}, \qquad \forall j \geq 0.$$

Note that the coefficients $\alpha_{\pi,j}$ satisfy

$$\sum_{j=0}^{\infty} \alpha_{\pi,j} = S_\pi^{-1} \sum_{j=0}^{\infty} \tilde{\alpha}_{\pi,j} = 1$$

and the coefficients $\alpha_{x,j}$ satisfy

$$\sum_{j=0}^{\infty} \alpha_{x,j} = -\left(0 + \lambda_3^{-0} + \lambda_3^{-1} + \lambda_3^{-2} + \ldots\right)\beta\gamma$$

$$+ \left(\lambda_3^{-0} + \lambda_3^{-1} + \lambda_3^{-2} + \ldots\right)(1 + \beta\gamma) - \left(\lambda_3^{-1} + \lambda_3^{-2} + \ldots\right)$$

$$= \left(1 - \lambda_3^{-1}\right)^{-1}\left(1 - \lambda_3^{-1}\right)$$

$$= 1.$$

Combining (G.26) and (G.33), one can rewrite Rule I as

$$\hat{\imath}_t = \rho_1 \hat{\imath}_{t-1} + \rho_2 \Delta \hat{\imath}_{t-1} + \phi_\pi F_t\left(\hat{\pi}\right) + \frac{\phi_x}{4} F_t\left(\hat{x}\right) - \theta_\pi \hat{\pi}_{t-1} - \frac{\theta_x}{4}\hat{x}_{t-1} \qquad \text{(G.34)}$$

where

$$\phi_\pi = (\beta\gamma\lambda_3)^{-1}\frac{\kappa\sigma}{\lambda_i}S_\pi = \frac{\kappa\sigma}{\lambda_i\beta}\frac{1 + \beta\gamma^2 - \beta\gamma - \lambda_3^{-1}\gamma}{\lambda_3\gamma\left(1 - \lambda_3^{-1}\right)},$$

$$\theta_\pi = (\beta\gamma\lambda_3)^{-1}\frac{\kappa\sigma\gamma}{\lambda_i} = \frac{\kappa\sigma}{\lambda_i\beta\lambda_3} > 0,$$

$$\phi_x = \theta_x = \frac{4\lambda_x\sigma}{\lambda_i\beta\gamma\lambda_3} > 0.$$

Note furthermore that

$$\phi_\pi = \theta_\pi\frac{\lambda_3 + \beta\gamma^2\lambda_3 - \beta\gamma\lambda_3 - \gamma}{\gamma\left(\lambda_3 - 1\right)} = \theta_\pi\left(1 + \frac{(1-\gamma)(1-\beta\gamma)}{\gamma\left(1 - \lambda_3^{-1}\right)}\right) \geq \theta_\pi. \quad \text{(G.35)}$$

Recalling that $\hat{z}_t \equiv z_t - \bar{z}$ for any variable z and that $\phi_x = \theta_x$, one can rewrite (G.34) as

$$i_t = (1 - \rho_1)\bar{\imath} - (\phi_\pi - \theta_\pi)\bar{\pi} + \rho_1 i_{t-1} + \rho_2\Delta i_{t-1} + \phi_\pi F_t\left(\pi\right)$$

$$+ \frac{\phi_x}{4}F_t\left(x\right) - \theta_\pi\pi_{t-1} - \frac{\theta_x}{4}x_{t-1}. \qquad \text{(G.36)}$$

It is known from Proposition 8.8 that (3.21) holds, and thus that (3.16) holds. In the steady state, equation (3.16) reduces to

$$A(L)\left(\bar{\imath} - \bar{\imath}^*\right) = -\bar{f}$$

where

$$\bar{f} = \frac{\kappa\sigma}{\lambda_i}\left(1 - \beta\gamma\right)\bar{q} = \frac{\kappa\sigma}{\lambda_i}\left(1 - \beta\gamma\right)\left(1 - \gamma\right)\bar{\pi}.$$

It follows from (3.20) that

$$\left(1 - \lambda_1\right)\left(1 - \lambda_2\right)i^* = \left(1 - \lambda_1\right)\left(1 - \lambda_2\right)\bar{i} + \frac{\kappa\sigma}{\lambda_i}\frac{\left(1 - \gamma\right)\left(1 - \beta\gamma\right)}{\beta\gamma\left(1 - \lambda_3\right)}\bar{\pi}. \qquad \text{(G.37)}$$

Given that

$$\left(1 - \lambda_1\right)\left(1 - \lambda_2\right) = 1 - \rho_1,$$

and that (G.35) implies

$$\frac{\kappa\sigma}{\lambda_i}\frac{\left(1 - \gamma\right)\left(1 - \beta\gamma\right)}{\beta\gamma\left(1 - \lambda_3\right)} = -\left(\phi_\pi - \theta_\pi\right),$$

one can rewrite (G.37) as

$$\left(1 - \rho_1\right)i^* = \left(1 - \rho_1\right)\bar{i} - \left(\phi_\pi - \theta_\pi\right)\bar{\pi}.$$

Combining this with (G.36) yields (G.25).

As γ approaches 0, one has $\lambda_3^{-1} \to 0$ and $\lambda_3\gamma \to \beta^{-1}$. It follows that

$$\lim_{\gamma\to 0}\phi_\pi = \lim_{\gamma\to 0}\frac{\kappa\sigma}{\lambda_i\beta}\frac{1 + \beta\gamma^2 - \beta\gamma - \lambda_3^{-1}\gamma}{\lambda_3\gamma\left(1 - \lambda_3^{-1}\right)} = \frac{\kappa\sigma}{\lambda_i} > 0,$$

$$\lim_{\gamma\to 0}\theta_\pi = \lim_{\gamma\to 0}\frac{\kappa\sigma}{\lambda_i\beta}\lambda_3^{-1} = 0,$$

$$\lim_{\gamma\to 0}\phi_x = \lim_{\gamma\to 0}\theta_x = \lim_{\gamma\to 0}\frac{4\lambda_x\sigma}{\lambda_i\beta\gamma\lambda_3} = \frac{4\lambda_x\sigma}{\lambda_i} > 0.$$

Rule II. Following the same development as for Rule I, but replacing λ_2 with λ_3 and vice versa, I can show that (3.23) can also be written as in (G.25), but where

$$\rho_1 = 1 + \left(\lambda_3 - 1\right)\left(1 - \lambda_1\right) > 1,$$

$$\rho_2 = \lambda_1\lambda_3 > 0,$$

$$\theta_\pi = \frac{\kappa\sigma}{\lambda_i\beta\lambda_2} > 0,$$

$$\phi_\pi = \theta_\pi \left(1 + \frac{(1-\gamma)(1-\beta\gamma)}{\gamma\left(1-\lambda_2^{-1}\right)} \right) \geq \theta_\pi,$$

$$\phi_x = \theta_x = \frac{4\lambda_x\sigma}{\lambda_i\beta\gamma\lambda_2} > 0.$$

Rule III. I now allow the roots λ_2 and λ_3 to be either real or complex. Recall from the proof of Proposition 8.7 that $(\lambda_2 + \lambda_3)/2$ is real and is greater than 1. Using this, Rule III (3.24) can be rewritten, for all values of $\gamma \in (0, 1]$, as

$$\hat{\imath}_t = \rho_1\hat{\imath}_{t-1} + \rho_2\Delta\hat{\imath}_{t-1} + \tfrac{1}{2}(\beta\gamma\lambda_3)^{-1}v_t^I + \tfrac{1}{2}(\beta\gamma\lambda_2)^{-1}v_t^{II} \qquad \text{(G.38)}$$

where ρ_1 and ρ_2 are now given by

$$\rho_1 = \lambda_1 + \frac{\lambda_2 + \lambda_3}{2} - \lambda_1\frac{\lambda_2 + \lambda_3}{2} = 1 + \left(\frac{\lambda_2 + \lambda_3}{2} - 1\right)(1 - \lambda_1) > 1, \quad \text{(G.39)}$$

$$\rho_2 = \lambda_1\frac{\lambda_2 + \lambda_3}{2} > 0, \qquad\qquad\qquad\qquad\qquad\qquad\qquad\qquad \text{(G.40)}$$

and

$$v_t^I \equiv E_t\left[\left(1 - \lambda_3^{-1}L^{-1}\right)^{-1}\hat{f}_t\right] = \frac{\kappa\sigma}{\lambda_i}\sum_{j=-1}^{\infty}\tilde{\alpha}_{\pi,j}^I E_t\hat{\pi}_{t+j}$$

$$+ \frac{\lambda_x\sigma}{\lambda_i}\sum_{j=-1}^{\infty}\alpha_{x,j}^I E_t\hat{x}_{t+j}, \qquad\qquad\qquad\qquad \text{(G.41)}$$

$$v_t^{II} \equiv E_t\left[\left(1 - \lambda_2^{-1}L^{-1}\right)^{-1}\hat{f}_t\right] = \frac{\kappa\sigma}{\lambda_i}\sum_{j=-1}^{\infty}\tilde{\alpha}_{\pi,j}^{II} E_t\hat{\pi}_{t+j}$$

$$+ \frac{\lambda_x\sigma}{\lambda_i}\sum_{j=-1}^{\infty}\alpha_{x,j}^{II} E_t\hat{x}_{t+j}, \qquad\qquad\qquad\qquad \text{(G.42)}$$

and where $\tilde{\alpha}_{\pi,j}^I, \alpha_{x,j}^I$ are defined in (G.27)–(G.32) for all $j \geq 1$ and $\tilde{\alpha}_{\pi,j}^{II}, \alpha_{x,j}^{II}$ are defined in the same way except that λ_3 is replaced with λ_2. Using (G.41) and (G.42), equation (G.38) can be written as

$$\hat{\imath}_t = \rho_1\hat{\imath}_{t-1} + \rho_2\Delta\hat{\imath}_{t-1} + \frac{\kappa\sigma}{\lambda_i\beta\gamma}\frac{S_\pi}{2}\sum_{j=0}^{\infty}\alpha_{\pi,j}E_t\hat{\pi}_{t+j} + \frac{\lambda_x\sigma}{\lambda_i\beta\gamma}\frac{S_x}{2}\sum_{j=0}^{\infty}\alpha_{x,j}E_t\hat{x}_{t+j}$$

$$-\frac{\kappa\sigma}{\lambda_i\beta}\frac{\lambda_2^{-1}+\lambda_3^{-1}}{2}\hat{\pi}_{t-1}-\frac{\lambda_x\sigma}{\lambda_i\beta\gamma}\frac{\lambda_2^{-1}+\lambda_3^{-1}}{2}\hat{x}_{t-1},\tag{G.43}$$

where

$$S_\pi = \sum_{j=0}^{\infty}\left(\lambda_3^{-1}\tilde{\alpha}_{\pi,j}^I + \lambda_2^{-1}\tilde{\alpha}_{\pi,j}^{II}\right),$$

$$S_x = \sum_{j=0}^{\infty}\left(\lambda_3^{-1}\alpha_{x,j}^I + \lambda_2^{-1}\alpha_{x,j}^{II}\right) = \lambda_2^{-1}+\lambda_3^{-1},$$

$$\alpha_{\pi,j} = S_\pi^{-1}\left(\lambda_3^{-1}\tilde{\alpha}_{\pi,j}^I + \lambda_2^{-1}\tilde{\alpha}_{\pi,j}^{II}\right),$$

$$\alpha_{x,j} = S_x^{-1}\left(\lambda_3^{-1}\alpha_{x,j}^I + \lambda_2^{-1}\alpha_{x,j}^{II}\right),$$

and

$$\sum_{j=0}^{\infty}\alpha_{\pi,j} = \sum_{j=0}^{\infty}\alpha_{x,j} = 1.$$

Equation (G.43) is of the form (G.34), where ρ_1 and ρ_2 are defined in (G.39) and (G.40), and

$$\phi_\pi = \frac{\kappa\sigma}{\lambda_i\beta\gamma}\frac{S_\pi}{2},\tag{G.44}$$

$$\theta_\pi = \frac{\kappa\sigma}{\lambda_i\beta}\frac{\lambda_2^{-1}+\lambda_3^{-1}}{2} > 0,\tag{G.45}$$

$$\phi_x = \theta_x = \frac{4\lambda_x\sigma}{\lambda_i\beta\gamma}\frac{\lambda_2^{-1}+\lambda_3^{-1}}{2} > 0.\tag{G.46}$$

(Note that if λ_2 and λ_3 are complex conjugates, then $\lambda_2^{-1}+\lambda_3^{-1} = (\lambda_2+\lambda_3)/\lambda_2\lambda_3$ is real.) Note furthermore that for all $\gamma \in (0,1]$, the coefficient ϕ_π satisfies

$$\phi_\pi = \frac{\kappa\sigma}{\lambda_i\beta}\left(\frac{\lambda_3^{-1}}{2}\frac{1+\beta\gamma^2-\beta\gamma-\lambda_3^{-1}\gamma}{\gamma\left(1-\lambda_3^{-1}\right)} + \frac{\lambda_2^{-1}}{2}\frac{1+\beta\gamma^2-\beta\gamma-\lambda_2^{-1}\gamma}{\gamma\left(1-\lambda_2^{-1}\right)}\right)$$

$$= \frac{\kappa\sigma}{\lambda_i\beta}\left(\frac{\lambda_3^{-1}}{2}\left(1+\frac{(1-\gamma)(1-\beta\gamma)}{\gamma\left(1-\lambda_3^{-1}\right)}\right) + \frac{\lambda_2^{-1}}{2}\left(1+\frac{(1-\gamma)(1-\beta\gamma)}{\gamma\left(1-\lambda_2^{-1}\right)}\right)\right)$$

$$= \theta_\pi - \frac{\kappa\sigma}{\lambda_i\beta\gamma} \frac{(1-\gamma)(1-\beta\gamma)}{(1-\lambda_2)(1-\lambda_3)} \left(1 - \frac{\lambda_2+\lambda_3}{2}\right) \qquad \text{(G.47)}$$

$$\geq \theta_\pi.$$

As for Rule I, I can rewrite (G.34) as in (G.36), but where the coefficients are given in (G.39), (G.40), and (G.44)–(G.46). Again, it is known from Proposition 8.8 that (3.16) holds, and thus that (G.37) holds. Multiplying both sides of (G.37) by $(1-\lambda_2)^{-1}(1-(\lambda_2+\lambda_3)/2)$ yields

$$(1-\lambda_1)\left(1 - \frac{\lambda_2+\lambda_3}{2}\right) i^* = (1-\lambda_1)\left(1 - \frac{\lambda_2+\lambda_3}{2}\right)\bar{i}$$

$$+ \frac{\kappa\sigma}{\lambda_i}\frac{(1-\gamma)(1-\beta\gamma)}{\beta\gamma(1-\lambda_2)(1-\lambda_3)}\left(1 - \frac{\lambda_2+\lambda_3}{2}\right)\bar{\pi}. \qquad \text{(G.48)}$$

Since (G.39) and (G.47) imply

$$(1-\lambda_1)\left(1 - \frac{\lambda_2+\lambda_3}{2}\right) = 1 - \rho_1,$$

$$\frac{\kappa\sigma}{\lambda_i\beta\gamma}\frac{(1-\gamma)(1-\beta\gamma)}{(1-\lambda_2)(1-\lambda_3)}\left(1 - \frac{\lambda_2+\lambda_3}{2}\right) = -(\phi_\pi - \theta_\pi),$$

one can rewrite (G.48) as

$$(1-\rho_1)i^* = (1-\rho_1)\bar{i} - (\phi_\pi - \theta_\pi)\bar{\pi}.$$

Combining this with (G.36) yields (G.25).

Finally, in the limit, as $\gamma = 1$, I have

$$\phi_\pi = \frac{\kappa\sigma}{\lambda_i\beta}\frac{\lambda_2^{-1}+\lambda_3^{-1}}{2} = \theta_\pi.$$

G.9 Proof of Proposition 8.10

PROPOSITION 8.10. Under the assumptions of Proposition 8.7, a pair of bounded processes $\{\hat{i}_t, \hat{f}_t\}$ satisfy

$$(1-\lambda_1 L)\hat{i}_{t-1} = -(\beta\gamma\lambda_2\lambda_3)^{-1} E_t\left[\left(1-\lambda_2^{-1}L^{-1}\right)^{-1}\left(1-\lambda_3^{-1}L^{-1}\right)^{-1}\hat{f}_t\right] \quad \text{(G.49)}$$

at all dates $t \geq t_0$ if and only if they satisfy

$$E_t[A(L)\hat{i}_{t+1}] = -\hat{f}_t \qquad \text{(G.50)}$$

at all of those same dates.

PROOF: Proposition 8.7 guarantees that $0 < \lambda_1 < 1$, and that λ_2, λ_3 are either real values or complex conjugates that lie outside the unit circle.

First I show that (G.50) implies (G.49). Using (3.20) to substitute for $A(L)$, and expanding the left-hand side of (G.50), I obtain

$$\beta \gamma \lambda_2 \lambda_3 E_t \left[(1 - \lambda_1 L) \left(\lambda_2^{-1} L^{-1} - 1 \right) \left(\lambda_3^{-1} L^{-1} - 1 \right) L^2 \hat{\imath}_{t+1} \right] = -\hat{f}_t,$$

or

$$E_t \left[D(L) \left(1 - \lambda_3^{-1} L^{-1} \right) \hat{\imath}_{t-1} \right] = v_t,$$

where

$$D(L) = (1 - \lambda_1 L) \left(1 - \lambda_2^{-1} L^{-1} \right),$$

$$v_t \equiv - (\beta \gamma \lambda_2 \lambda_3)^{-1} \hat{f}_t.$$

It follows that

$$E_t \left[D(L) \hat{\imath}_{t-1} \right] = \lambda_3^{-1} E_t \left[D(L) \hat{\imath}_t \right] + v_t$$

$$= E_t \left[\sum_{j=0}^{\infty} \lambda_3^{-j} v_{t+j} \right]$$

$$= E_t \left[\left(1 - \lambda_3^{-1} L^{-1} \right)^{-1} v_t \right].$$

This can be rewritten as

$$E_t \left[(1 - \lambda_1 L) \left(1 - \lambda_2^{-1} L^{-1} \right) \hat{\imath}_{t-1} \right] = \tilde{v}_t,$$

where

$$\tilde{v}_t \equiv - (\beta \gamma \lambda_2 \lambda_3)^{-1} E_t \left[\left(1 - \lambda_3^{-1} L^{-1} \right)^{-1} \hat{f}_t \right].$$

It follows that

$$E_t \left[(1 - \lambda_1 L) \hat{\imath}_{t-1} \right] = \lambda_2^{-1} E_t \left[(1 - \lambda_1 L) \hat{\imath}_t \right] + \tilde{v}_t$$

$$= E_t \left[\sum_{j=0}^{\infty} \lambda_2^{-j} \tilde{v}_{t+j} \right]$$

$$= E_t \left[\left(1 - \lambda_2^{-1} L^{-1}\right)^{-1} \tilde{v}_t \right]$$

$$= - (\beta \gamma \lambda_2 \lambda_3)^{-1} E_t \left[\left(1 - \lambda_2^{-1} L^{-1}\right)^{-1} \left(1 - \lambda_3^{-1} L^{-1}\right)^{-1} \hat{f}_t \right],$$

which corresponds to (G.49).

I now show that (G.49) implies (G.50). Since (G.49) holds for all $t \geq t_0$, (G.49) implies that

$$(1 - \lambda_1 L)\, \hat{i}_{t+1} = -(\beta \gamma \lambda_2 \lambda_3)^{-1} E_{t+2} \left[\left(1 - \lambda_2^{-1} L^{-1}\right)^{-1} \left(1 - \lambda_3^{-1} L^{-1}\right)^{-1} \hat{f}_{t+2} \right].$$

Multiplying on both sides by $\beta \gamma (1 - \lambda_2 L)(1 - \lambda_3 L)$ and taking expectations at date t, I obtain

$$E_t \left[A(L)\, \hat{i}_{t+1} \right] = -\lambda_2^{-1} \lambda_3^{-1} E_t \left[(1 - \lambda_2 L)(1 - \lambda_3 L) \left(1 - \lambda_2^{-1} L^{-1}\right)^{-1} \times \right.$$

$$\left. \left(1 - \lambda_3^{-1} L^{-1}\right)^{-1} \hat{f}_{t+2} \right]$$

$$= -E_t \left[L^2 \hat{f}_{t+2} \right]$$

$$= -\hat{f}_t,$$

which corresponds to (G.50).

G.10 Proof of Proposition 8.11

PROPOSITION 8.11. Under the assumptions of Proposition 8.9, the optimal target criterion

$$(1 - \lambda_1 L)\, \hat{i}_{t-1} = -(\beta \gamma \lambda_2 \lambda_3)^{-1} E_t \left[\left(1 - \lambda_2^{-1} L^{-1}\right)^{-1} \left(1 - \lambda_3^{-1} L^{-1}\right)^{-1} \hat{f}_t \right] \text{ (G.51)}$$

has a representation

$$F_t (\pi) + \frac{\phi_x}{4} F_t (x) = \theta_\pi \pi_{t-1} + \frac{\theta_x}{4} x_{t-1} - \theta_i \left(i_{t-1} - i^* \right) - \theta_\Delta \Delta i_{t-1} \quad \text{(G.52)}$$

in which

$$\phi_x = \theta_x > 0,$$

$$0 < \theta_\pi \leq 1,$$

and

$$\theta_i, \theta_\Delta > 0.$$

Furthermore, for fixed values of the other parameters, as $\gamma \to 0$, $\theta_\pi \to 0$ and the other parameters approach the nonzero values associated with the target criterion (3.13) of Chapter 8. Instead, as $\gamma \to 1$, $\theta_\pi \to 1$.

PROOF: The optimal target criterion (G.51) can be written as

$$\hat{\imath}_{t-1} - \lambda_1 \hat{\imath}_{t-2} = -\left(\beta\gamma\lambda_2\lambda_3\right)^{-1} v_t, \tag{G.53}$$

where

$$v_t \equiv E_t\left[\left(1 - \lambda_2^{-1}L^{-1}\right)^{-1}\left(1 - \lambda_3^{-1}L^{-1}\right)^{-1}\hat{f}_t\right]$$

and where $|\lambda_2|, |\lambda_3| > 1$. Note that in the case that $\lambda_2 \neq \lambda_3$,

$$\left(1 - \lambda_2^{-1}L^{-1}\right)^{-1}\left(1 - \lambda_3^{-1}L^{-1}\right)^{-1} = c_2\left(1 - \lambda_2^{-1}L^{-1}\right)^{-1} - c_3\left(1 - \lambda_3^{-1}L^{-1}\right)^{-1}$$

where $c_2 \equiv \lambda_3/\left(\lambda_3 - \lambda_2\right)$ and $c_3 \equiv \lambda_2/\left(\lambda_3 - \lambda_2\right)$. The variable V_t can therefore be rewritten as

$$v_t = E_t\left\{\left[c_2\left(1 - \lambda_2^{-1}L^{-1}\right)^{-1} - c_3\left(1 - \lambda_3^{-1}L^{-1}\right)^{-1}\right]\hat{f}_t\right\}$$

$$= E_t\left[\sum_{j=0}^{\infty}\left(c_2\lambda_2^{-j} - c_3\lambda_3^{-j}\right)\hat{f}_{t+j}\right].$$

Substituting for $\hat{f}_{t+j}$ as in the proof of Proposition 8.9, one obtains

$$v_t = \frac{\kappa\sigma}{\lambda_i}E_t\left[\sum_{j=0}^{\infty}\left(c_2\lambda_2^{-j} - c_3\lambda_3^{-j}\right)\left(-\gamma\hat{\pi}_{t+j-1} + \left(1 + \beta\gamma^2\right)\hat{\pi}_{t+j} - \beta\gamma\hat{\pi}_{t+j+1}\right)\right]$$

$$+ \frac{\lambda_x\sigma}{\lambda_i}E_t\left[\sum_{j=0}^{\infty}\left(c_2\lambda_2^{-j} - c_3\lambda_3^{-j}\right)\left(-\hat{x}_{t+j-1} + \left(1 + \beta\gamma\right)\hat{x}_{t+j} - \beta\gamma\hat{x}_{t+j+1}\right)\right]$$

$$= \frac{\kappa\sigma}{\lambda_i}\sum_{j=-1}^{\infty}\tilde{\alpha}_{\pi,j}E_t\hat{\pi}_{t+j} + \frac{\lambda_x\sigma}{\lambda_i}\sum_{j=-1}^{\infty}\alpha_{x,j}E_t\hat{x}_{t+j},$$

where

$$\tilde{\alpha}_{\pi,-1} = -\gamma,$$

$$\tilde{\alpha}_{\pi,0} = 1 + \beta\gamma^2 - \left(c_2\lambda_2^{-1} - c_3\lambda_3^{-1}\right)\gamma,$$

$$\tilde{\alpha}_{\pi,j} = -\left(c_2\lambda_2^{-j+1} - c_3\lambda_3^{-j+1}\right)\beta\gamma + \left(c_2\lambda_2^{-j} - c_3\lambda_3^{-j}\right)(1 + \beta\gamma^2)$$

$$- \left(c_2\lambda_2^{-j-1} - c_3\lambda_3^{-j-1}\right)\gamma, \forall j \geq 1,$$

and

$$\alpha_{x,-1} = -1,$$

$$\alpha_{x,0} = 1 + \beta\gamma - \left(c_2\lambda_2^{-1} - c_3\lambda_3^{-1}\right),$$

$$\alpha_{x,j} = -\left(c_2\lambda_2^{-j+1} - c_3\lambda_3^{-j+1}\right)\beta\gamma + \left(c_2\lambda_2^{-j} - c_3\lambda_3^{-j}\right)(1 + \beta\gamma)$$

$$- \left(c_2\lambda_2^{-j-1} - c_3\lambda_3^{-j-1}\right), \qquad \forall j \geq 1.$$

Furthermore one can write the variable V_t as

$$v_t = \frac{\kappa\sigma}{\lambda_i} S_\pi \sum_{j=0}^{\infty} \alpha_{\pi,j} E_t \hat{\pi}_{t+j} + \frac{\lambda_x\sigma}{\lambda_i} \sum_{j=0}^{\infty} \alpha_{x,j} E_t \hat{x}_{t+j} - \frac{\kappa\sigma\gamma}{\lambda_i} \hat{\pi}_{t-1} - \frac{\lambda_x\sigma}{\lambda_i} \hat{x}_{t-1}, \quad \text{(G.54)}$$

where

$$S_\pi = \sum_{j=0}^{\infty} \tilde{\alpha}_{\pi,j} = \frac{\lambda_3\left(1 + \beta\gamma^2 - \beta\gamma - \lambda_2^{-1}\gamma\right)}{(\lambda_3 - \lambda_2)\left(1 - \lambda_2^{-1}\right)} - \frac{\lambda_2\left(1 + \beta\gamma^2 - \beta\gamma - \lambda_3^{-1}\gamma\right)}{(\lambda_3 - \lambda_2)\left(1 - \lambda_3^{-1}\right)}$$

$$= \gamma + \frac{(1 - \gamma)(1 - \beta\gamma)}{\left(1 - \lambda_2^{-1}\right)\left(1 - \lambda_3^{-1}\right)} \quad \text{(G.55)}$$

$$\geq \gamma$$

and

$$\alpha_{\pi,j} = \frac{\tilde{\alpha}_{\pi,j}}{S_\pi}, \qquad \forall j \geq 0.$$

Note that the coefficients $\alpha_{\pi,j}$ and $\alpha_{x,j}$ satisfy

$$\sum_{j=0}^{\infty} \alpha_{\pi,j} = \sum_{j=0}^{\infty} \alpha_{x,j} = 1.$$

Combining (G.53) and (G.54), one can rewrite the optimal target criterion as

$$\frac{\kappa\sigma}{\lambda_i} S_\pi F_t\left(\hat{\pi}\right) + \frac{\lambda_x\sigma}{\lambda_i} F_t\left(\hat{x}\right) - \frac{\kappa\sigma\gamma}{\lambda_i}\hat{\pi}_{t-1} - \frac{\lambda_x\sigma}{\lambda_i}\hat{x}_{t-1} = -\beta\gamma\lambda_2\lambda_3\left(\hat{\imath}_{t-1} - \lambda_1\hat{\imath}_{t-2}\right).$$

Recalling that $\hat{z}_t \equiv z_t - \bar{z}$ for any variable z gives

$$\frac{\kappa\sigma}{\lambda_i} S_\pi\left(F_t\left(\pi\right) - \bar{\pi}\right) + \frac{\lambda_x\sigma}{\lambda_i} F_t\left(x\right) = \frac{\kappa\sigma\gamma}{\lambda_i}\left(\pi_{t-1} - \bar{\pi}\right) + \frac{\lambda_x\sigma}{\lambda_i} x_{t-1}$$

$$- \beta\gamma\lambda_2\lambda_3\left((1 - \lambda_1)(\imath_{t-1} - \bar{\imath}) - \lambda_1\Delta\imath_{t-2}\right),$$

or an equation of the form

$$F_t\left(\pi\right) + \frac{\phi_x}{4}F_t\left(x\right) = \theta_i\bar{\imath} + (1 - \theta_\pi)\,\bar{\pi} + \theta_\pi\pi_{t-1}$$

$$+ \frac{\theta_x}{4} x_{t-1} - \theta_i\imath_{t-1} - \theta_\Delta\Delta\imath_{t-1} \qquad (G.56)$$

where

$$\phi_x = \theta_x = \frac{4\lambda_x}{\kappa S_\pi} > 0,$$

$$\theta_\pi = \frac{\gamma}{S_\pi} > 0,$$

$$\theta_i = \frac{\lambda_i\beta\gamma\,(1 - \lambda_1)\,\lambda_2\lambda_3}{\kappa\sigma\,S_\pi} > 0,$$

$$\theta_\Delta = \frac{\lambda_i\beta\gamma\,\lambda_1\lambda_2\lambda_3}{\kappa\sigma\,S_\pi} > 0.$$

It is known from Proposition 8.8 that (3.21) holds, and thus that (3.16) holds. In the steady state, equation (3.16) reduces to

$$A(L)\left(\bar{\imath} - i^*\right) = -\bar{f}$$

where

$$\bar{f} = \frac{\kappa\sigma}{\lambda_i}\,(1 - \beta\gamma)\,\bar{q} = \frac{\kappa\sigma}{\lambda_i}\,(1 - \beta\gamma)\,(1 - \gamma)\,\bar{\pi}.$$

Furthermore, using (3.20) yields

$$\theta_i i^* = \theta_i \bar{\imath} + \frac{\theta_i}{A(1)} \frac{\kappa \sigma}{\lambda_i} (1 - \beta\gamma)(1 - \gamma)\bar{\pi}$$

$$= \theta_i \bar{\imath} + \frac{[\lambda_i \beta\gamma (1 - \lambda_1)\lambda_2\lambda_3] / \kappa\sigma S_\pi}{\beta\gamma (1 - \lambda_1)(1 - \lambda_2)(1 - \lambda_3)} \frac{\kappa\sigma}{\lambda_i} (1 - \beta\gamma)(1 - \gamma)\bar{\pi}$$

$$= \theta_i \bar{\imath} + \frac{(1 - \beta\gamma)(1 - \gamma)}{\left(1 - \lambda_2^{-1}\right)\left(1 - \lambda_3^{-1}\right)} \frac{1}{S_\pi} \bar{\pi}$$

$$= \theta_i \bar{\imath} + (S_\pi - \gamma) \frac{1}{S_\pi} \bar{\pi}$$

$$= \theta_i \bar{\imath} + (1 - \theta_\pi)\bar{\pi}.$$

Combining this with (G.56) yields (G.52).

As $\gamma \to 0$, it follows from Lemma G.2 that $\lambda_3^{-1} \to 0$, $\lambda_3\gamma \to \beta^{-1}$, $S_\pi \to \left(1 - \lambda_2^{-1}\right)^{-1} > 0$, and thus

$$\phi_x = \theta_x \to 4\left(1 - \lambda_2^{-1}\right)\frac{\lambda_x}{\kappa} > 0,$$

$$\theta_\pi \to 0,$$

$$\theta_i \to \lambda_2 (1 - \lambda_1)\left(1 - \lambda_2^{-1}\right)\frac{\lambda_i}{\kappa\sigma} > 0,$$

$$\theta_\Delta \to \lambda_1\lambda_2 \left(1 - \lambda_2^{-1}\right)\frac{\lambda_i}{\kappa\sigma} > 0.$$

Furthermore, $c_2 = \lambda_2^{-1}/\left(\lambda_2^{-1} - \lambda_3^{-1}\right) \to 1$, $c_3 = \lambda_3^{-1}/\left(\lambda_2^{-1} - \lambda_3^{-1}\right) \to 0$, and $\tilde{\alpha}_{\pi,j} \to \lambda_2^{-j}$, for all $j \geq 0$, so that

$$\alpha_{\pi,j} \to \left(1 - \lambda_2^{-1}\right)\lambda_2^{-j},$$

$$\alpha_{x,j} \to \left(1 - \lambda_2^{-1}\right)\lambda_2^{-j},$$

for all $j \geq 0$. Instead, as $\gamma = 1$, I have $S_\pi \to 1$, and

$$\theta_\pi \to 1.$$

So far, I have considered the case in which $\lambda_2 \neq \lambda_3$. Now suppose, alternatively, that $\lambda_2 = \lambda_3$. Then, since

$$\left(1 - \lambda_2^{-1}L^{-1}\right)^{-1}\left(1 - \lambda_3^{-1}L^{-1}\right)^{-1} = \left(1 - \lambda_2^{-1}L^{-1}\right)^{-2} = \sum_{j=0}^{\infty}(1 + j)\lambda_2^{-j}L^{-j}$$

one can write v_t as

$$v_t = E_t \left[\sum_{j=0}^{\infty} (1+j) \lambda_2^{-j} \hat{f}_{t+j} \right].$$

Substituting for $\hat{f}_{t+j}$ as in the proof of Proposition 8.9, I obtain

$$v_t = \frac{\kappa\sigma}{\lambda_i} E_t \left[\sum_{j=0}^{\infty} (1+j) \lambda_2^{-j} \left(-\gamma\hat{\pi}_{t+j-1} + \left(1 + \beta\gamma^2\right) \hat{\pi}_{t+j} - \beta\gamma\hat{\pi}_{t+j+1} \right) \right]$$

$$+ \frac{\lambda_x\sigma}{\lambda_i} E_t \left[\sum_{j=0}^{\infty} (1+j) \lambda_2^{-j} \left(-\hat{x}_{t+j-1} + (1 + \beta\gamma) \hat{x}_{t+j} - \beta\gamma\hat{x}_{t+j+1} \right) \right]$$

$$= \frac{\kappa\sigma}{\lambda_i} \sum_{j=-1}^{\infty} \tilde{\alpha}_{\pi,j} E_t \hat{\pi}_{t+j} + \frac{\lambda_x\sigma}{\lambda_i} \sum_{j=-1}^{\infty} \alpha_{x,j} E_t \hat{x}_{t+j},$$

where

$$\tilde{\alpha}_{\pi,-1} = -\gamma,$$

$$\tilde{\alpha}_{\pi,0} = 1 + \beta\gamma^2 - 2\lambda_2^{-1}\gamma,$$

$$\tilde{\alpha}_{\pi,j} = -j\lambda_2^{-j+1}\beta\gamma + (1+j) \lambda_2^{-j} \left(1 + \beta\gamma^2\right) - (2+j) \lambda_2^{-j-1}\gamma, \qquad \forall j \geq 1,$$

and

$$\alpha_{x,-1} = -1,$$

$$\alpha_{x,0} = 1 + \beta\gamma - 2\lambda_2^{-1},$$

$$\alpha_{x,j} = -j\lambda_2^{-j+1}\beta\gamma + (1+j) \lambda_2^{-j} (1 + \beta\gamma) - (2+j) \lambda_2^{-j-1}, \qquad \forall j \geq 1.$$

The variable v_t can again be written as in (G.54), where as before $\alpha_{\pi,j} = \tilde{\alpha}_{\pi,j}/S_\pi, \forall j \geq 0,$ and

$$S_\pi = \sum_{j=0}^{\infty} \tilde{\alpha}_{\pi,j} = - \left(1\lambda_2^{-0} + 2\lambda_2^{-1} + 3\lambda_2^{-2} + \ldots\right) \beta\gamma$$

$$+ \left(1\lambda_2^{-0} + 2\lambda_2^{-1} + 3\lambda_2^{-2} + \ldots\right) \left(1 + \beta\gamma^2\right)$$

$$- \left(2\lambda_2^{-1} + 3\lambda_2^{-2} + \ldots\right) \gamma$$

$$= \left(1 - \lambda_2^{-1}\right)^{-2} \left(-\beta\gamma + 1 + \beta\gamma^2 - \gamma\right) + \gamma$$

$$= \gamma + \frac{(1-\gamma)(1-\beta\gamma)}{\left(1 - \lambda_2^{-1}\right)^2}.$$

Note that S_π is equal to the value obtained in (G.55), when $\lambda_2 = \lambda_3$. In addition, the coefficients $\alpha_{\pi,j}$ and $\alpha_{x,j}$ satisfy again $\sum_{j=0}^{\infty} \alpha_{\pi,j} = \sum_{j=0}^{\infty} \alpha_{x,j} = 1$. It follows that the optimal target criterion can again be expressed as in (G.52), where the coefficients are defined as before.

REFERENCES

Aiyagari, S. Rao, and R. Anton Braun, "Some Models to Guide Monetary Policy-makers," *Carnegie-Rochester Conference Series on Public Policy* 48: 1–42, 1989.

Akerlof, George A., William T. Dickens, and George L. Perry, "The Macroeconomics of Low Inflation," *Brookings Papers on Economic Activity* 1996-1: 1–76, 1996.

Altig, David, Lawrence J. Christiano, Martin S. Eichenbaum, and Jesper Linde, "Technology Shocks and Aggregate Fluctuations," unpublished, Federal Reserve Bank of Cleveland, 2002.

Amato, Jeffery D., and Thomas Laubach, "Implications of Habit Formation for Optimal Monetary Policy," Finance and Economic Discussion Series no. 2001-58, Federal Reserve Board, 2001.

———, "Estimation and Control of an Optimization-Based Model with Sticky Prices and Wages," *Journal of Economic Dynamics and Control* 27: 1181–1215, 2003a.

———, "Rule-of-thumb behaviour and monetary policy," *European Economic Review,* forthcoming 2003b.

Andersen, Torben M., "Persistency in Sticky Price Models," *European Economic Review* 42: 593–603, 1998.

Anderson, Gary, and Andrew Levin, "A User-Friendly, Computationally-Efficient Algorithm for Obtaining Higher-Order Approximations of Non-Linear Rational Expectations Models," unpublished, Federal Reserve Board, 2002.

Aoki, Kosuke, "Optimal Monetary Policy Responses to Relative Price Changes," *Journal of Monetary Economics* 48: 55–80, 2001.

———, "Optimal Commitment Policy under Noisy Information," CEPR Discussion Paper No. 3370, May 2002.

Ascari, Guido, "Price/Wage Staggering and Persistence: A Unifying Framework," unpublished, University of Pavia, September 2001.

Backus, David, and John Driffill, "The Consistency of Optimal Policy in Stochastic Rational Expectations Models," CEPR Discussion Paper No. 124, August 1986.

747

Ball, Laurence, and David Romer, "Real Rigidities and the Non-Neutrality of Money," *The Review of Economic Studies* 57: 183–203, 1990.

Barro, Robert J., "Unanticipated Money Growth and Unemployment in the United States," *American Economic Review* 67: 101–115, 1977.

Barro, Robert J., and David B. Gordon, "A Positive Theory of Monetary Policy in a Natural Rate Model," *Journal of Political Economy* 91: 589–610, 1983.

Barth, Melvin J. III, and Valerie A. Ramey, "The Cost Channel of Monetary Transmission," NBER Working Paper No. 7675, April 2000.

Bassetto, Marco, "A Game-Theoretic View of the Fiscal Theory of the Price Level," *Econometrica* 70: 2167–2196, 2002.

Basu, Susanto, "Intermediate Goods and Business Cycles: Implications for Productivity and Welfare," *American Economic Review* 85: 512–531, 1995.

Basu, Susanto, and Miles Kimball, "Investment Planning Costs and the Effects of Fiscal and Monetary Policy," unpublished, University of Michigan, November 2002.

Batini, Nicoletta, and Joe Pearlman, "Too Much Too Soon: Instability and Indeterminacy with Forward-Looking Rules," unpublished, Bank of England, July 2002.

Batini, Nicoletta, and Andrew G. Haldane, "Forward-Looking Rules for Monetary Policy," in J. B. Taylor, ed., *Monetary Policy Rules,* Chicago: University of Chicago Press, 1999.

Batini, Nicoletta, Brian Jackson, and Stephen Nickell, "Inflation Dynamics and the Labour Share in the U.K.," External MPC Discussion Paper No. 2, Bank of England, November 2000.

Bean, Charles R., "Targeting Nominal Income: An Appraisal," *Economic Journal* 93: 806–819, 1983.

Bénassy, Jean-Pascal, *The Macroeconomics of Imperfect Competition and Nonclearing Markets,* Cambridge: MIT Press, 2002.

Benhabib, Jess, Stephanie Schmitt-Grohé, and Martín Uribe, "Monetary Policy and Multiple Equilibria," *American Economic Review* 91: 167–186, 2001a.

———, "The Perils of Taylor Rules," *Journal of Economic Theory* 96: 40–69, 2001b.

———, "Avoiding Liquidity Traps," *Journal of Political Economy* 110: 535–563, 2002.

Benigno, Pierpaolo, "Optimal Monetary Policy in a Currency Area," *Journal of International Economics,* forthcoming 2003.

Benigno, Pierpaolo, and Michael Woodford, "Inflation Stabilization and Welfare: The Case of Large Distortions," unpublished, Princeton University, April 2003.

Bergin, Paul R., and Robert C. Feenstra, "Staggered Price Setting, Translog Preferences, and Endogenous Persistence," *Journal of Monetary Economics* 45: 657–680, 2000.

Bernanke, Ben S., and Jean Boivin, "Monetary Policy in a Data-Rich Environment," unpublished, Princeton University, September 2000.

Bernanke, Ben S., and Michael Woodford, "Inflation Forecasts and Monetary Policy," *Journal of Money, Credit, and Banking* 24: 653–684, 1997.

Bernanke, Ben S., Thomas Laubach, Frederic S. Mishkin, and Adam S. Posen, *Inflation Targeting*, Princeton: Princeton University Press, 1999.

Beveridge, Stephen, and Charles R. Nelson, "A New Approach to the Decomposition of Economic Time Series into Permanent and Transitory Components with Particular Attention to Measurement of the 'Business Cycle'," *Journal of Monetary Economics* 7: 151–174, 1981.

Black, Fischer, "Banking in a World without Money: The Effects of Uncontrolled Banking," *Journal of Bank Research* 1: 9–20, 1970.

Black, Richard, Vincenzo Cassino, Aaron Drew, Eric Hansen, Benjamin Hunt, David Rose, and Alasdair Scott, "The Forecasting and Policy System: The Core Model," Research Paper No. 43, Reserve Bank of New Zealand, August 1997a.

Black, Richard, Tiff Macklem, and David Rose, "On Policy Rules for Price Stability," in T. Macklem, ed., *Price Stability, Inflation Targets and Monetary Policy*, Ottawa: Bank of Canada, 1997b.

Blanchard, Olivier J., "Price Asynchronization and Price-Level Inertia," in R. Dornbusch and M. H. Simonsen, eds., *Inflation, Debt and Indexation*, Cambridge: MIT Press, 1983.

Blanchard, Olivier J., and Stanley Fischer, *Lectures on Macroeconomics*, Cambridge: MIT Press, 1989.

Blanchard, Olivier J., and Charles Kahn, "The Solution of Linear Difference Equations under Rational Expectations," *Econometrica* 48: 1305–1311, 1980.

Blanchard, Olivier J., and Nobuhiro Kiyotaki, "Monopolistic Competition and the Effects of Aggregate Demand," *American Economic Review* 77: 647–666, 1987.

Blinder, Alan S., *Central Banking in Theory and Practice*, Cambridge: MIT Press, 1998.

Blinder, Alan S., Elie R. D. Canetti, David E. Lebow, and Jeremy B. Rudd, *Asking About Prices: A New Approach to Understanding Price Stickiness*, New York: Russell Sage Foundation, 1998.

Blinder, Alan S., Charles Goodhart, Philipp Hildebrand, David Lipton, and Charles Wyplosz, *How Do Central Banks Talk?*, Geneva Report on the World Economy No. 3, International Center for Monetary and Banking Studies, 2001.

Boivin, Jean, and Marc Giannoni, "Has Monetary Policy Become More Effective?" NBER Working Paper No. 9459, January 2003.

Brandt, R. E., *Ethical Theory*, Englewood Cliffs, N.J.: Prentice-Hall, Inc., 1959.

Brayton, Flint, Andrew Levin, Ralph Tryon, and John Williams, "The Evolution of Macro Models at the Federal Reserve Board," *Carnegie-Rochester Conference Series on Public Policy* 47: 43–81, 1997.

Brock, William A., "Money and Growth: The Case of Long-Run Perfect Foresight," *International Economic Review* 15: 750–777, 1974.

————, "A Simple Perfect Foresight Monetary Rule," *Journal of Monetary Economics* 1: 133–150, 1975.

Bryan, Michael F., Stephen G. Cecchetti, and Roisin O'Sullivan, "Asset Prices in the Measurement of Inflation," NBER Working Paper No. 8700, January 2002.

Buiter, Willem H., "The Fiscal Theory of the Price Level: A Critique," *Economic Journal* 112: 459–480, 2002.

Bullard, James, and Kaushik Mitra, "Learning about Monetary Policy Rules," *Journal of Monetary Economics* 49: 1105–1129, 2002.

Bulow, Jeremy, John Geanakoplos, and Paul Klemperer, "Multimarket Oligopoly: Strategic Substitutes and Complements," *Journal of Political Economy* 93: 488–511, 1985.

Cagan, Phillip, "The Monetary Dynamics of Hyperinflation," in M. Friedman, ed., *Studies in the Quantity Theory of Money,* Chicago: University of Chicago Press, 1956.

Calvo, Guillermo, "Staggered Prices in a Utility-Maximizing Framework," *Journal of Monetary Economics* 12: 383–398, 1983.

Caplin, Andrew, and John Leahy, "State-Dependent Pricing and the Dynamics of Money and Output," *Quarterly Journal of Economics* 106: 683–708, 1991.

Carlstrom, Charles T., and Timothy S. Fuerst, "Timing and Real Indeterminacy in Monetary Models," *Journal of Monetary Economics* 47: 285–298, 2001.

Chari, V. V., and Patrick J. Kehoe, "Optimal Fiscal and Monetary Policy," in J. B. Taylor and M. Woodford, eds., *Handbook of Macroeconomics,* Vol. 1C, Amsterdam: North-Holland, 1999.

Chari, V. V., Lawrence J. Christiano, and Martin S. Eichenbaum, "Expectation Traps and Discretion," *Journal of Economic Theory* 81: 462–492, 1998.

Chari, V. V., Patrick J. Kehoe, and Ellen R. McGrattan, "Sticky Price Models of the Business Cycle: Can the Contract Multiplier Solve the Persistence Problem?" *Econometrica* 68: 1151–1179, 2000.

Christiano, Lawrence J., Martin S. Eichenbaum, and Charles L. Evans, "Sticky Price and Limited Participation Models of Money: A Comparison," *European Economic Review* 41: 1201–1249, 1997.

————, "Monetary Policy Shocks: What Have We Learned and to What End?" in J. B. Taylor and M. Woodford, eds., *Handbook of Macroeconomics,* Vol. 1A, Amsterdam: North-Holland, 1999.

————, "Nominal Rigidities and the Dynamic Effects of a Shock to Monetary Policy," NBER Working Paper No. 8403, July 2001.

Clarida, Richard, Jordi Galí and Mark Gertler, "The Science of Monetary Policy: A New Keynesian Perspective," *Journal of Economic Literature* 37: 1661–1707, 1999.

————, "Monetary Policy Rules and Macroeconomic Stability: Evidence and Some Theory," *Quarterly Journal of Economics* 115: 147–180, 2000.

————, "Optimal Monetary Policy in Closed versus Open Economies: An Integrated Approach," NBER Working Paper No. 8604, November 2001.

Cochrane, John H., "What do the VARs Measure? Measuring the Output Effects of Monetary Policy," *Journal of Monetary Economics* 41: 277–300, 1998.

———, "Money as Stock: Price Level Determination with No Money Demand," NBER Working Paper No. 7498, January 2000.

Coletti, Donald, Benjamin Hunt, David Rose, and Robert Tetlow, "The Dynamic Model: QPM, The Bank of Canada's New Quarterly Projection Model, Part 3," Technical Report No. 75, Bank of Canada, May 1996.

Collard, Fabrice, and Michel Juillard, "Perturbation Methods for Rational Expectations Models," unpublished, CEPREMAP (Paris), February 2001.

Collard, Fabrice, Harris Dellas, and Guy Ertz, "Poole Revisited," unpublished, CEPREMAP (Paris), October 1998.

Cooley, Thomas F., and Gary D. Hansen, "The Inflation Tax in a Real Business Cycle Model," *American Economic Review* 79: 733–748, 1989.

Cooley, Thomas F., and Edward C. Prescott, "Economic Growth and Business Cycles," in T. F. Cooley, ed., *Frontiers of Business Cycle Research,* Princeton: Princeton University Press, 1995.

Costa, Claudia, and Paul DeGrauwe, "Monetary Policy in a Cashless Society," CEPR Discussion Paper No. 2696, February 2001.

Currie, David, and Paul Levine, *Rules, Reputation and Macroeconomic Policy Coordination,* Cambridge: Cambridge University Press, 1993.

Dixit, Avinash K., and Joseph E. Stiglitz, "Monopolistic Competition and Optimum Product Diversity," *American Economic Review* 67: 297–308, 1977.

Dotsey, Michael, Robert G. King, and Alexander L. Wolman, "State-Dependent Pricing and the General Equilibrium Dynamics of Money and Output," *Quarterly Journal of Economics* 114: 655–690, 1999.

Dunlop, John T., "The Movement of Real and Money Wage Rates," *Economic Journal* 48: 413–434, 1938.

Dupor, Bill, "Optimal Monetary Policy with Nominal Rigidities," unpublished, Wharton School, February 1999.

Edge, Rochelle M., "Time to Build, Time to Plan, Habit Persistence, and the Liquidity Effect," International Finance Discussion Paper No. 2000-673, Federal Reserve Board, July 2000.

———, "The Equivalence of Wage and Price Staggering in Monetary Business Cycle Models," *Review of Economic Dynamics* 5: 559–585, 2002.

Eggertsson, Gauti B., and Michael Woodford, "The Zero Interest-Rate Bound and Optimal Monetary Policy," unpublished, Princeton University, March 2003.

Erceg, Christopher J., and Andrew T. Levin, "Optimal Monetary Policy with Durable and Non-Durable Goods," ECB Working Paper No. 179, September 2002.

Erceg, Christopher J., Dale W. Henderson, and Andrew T. Levin, "Optimal Monetary Policy with Staggered Wage and Price Contracts," *Journal of Monetary Economics* 46: 281–313, 2000.

Evans, George W., and Seppo Honkapohja, *Learning and Expectations in Macroeconomics,* Princeton: Princeton University Press, 2001.

————, "Monetary Policy, Expectations and Commitment," CEPR Discussion Paper No. 3434, June 2002a.

————, "Policy Interaction, Learning, and the Fiscal Theory of Prices," unpublished, University of Oregon, July 2002b.

————, "Adaptive Learning and Monetary Policy Design," unpublished, University of Oregon, October 2002c.

Feenstra, Robert, "Functional Equivalence Between Liquidity Costs and the Utility of Money," *Journal of Monetary Economics* 17: 271–291, 1986.

Fisher, Irving, *Stable Money: A History of the Movement,* New York: Adelphi, 1934.

Fisher, Mark, and Christian Gilles, "Modeling the State-Price Deflator and the Term Structure of Interest Rates," unpublished, Research Department, Federal Reserve Bank of Atlanta, February 2000.

Flodén, Martin, "The Time Inconsistency Problem of Monetary Policy under Alternative Supply Side Modelling," unpublished, Stockholm University, 1996.

Freedman, Charles, "Monetary Policy Implementation: Past, Present and Future—Will Electronic Money Lead to the Eventual Demise of Central Banking?" *International Finance* 3: 211–227, 2000.

Friedman, Benjamin M., "The Future of Monetary Policy: The Central Bank as an Army with Only a Signal Corps?" *International Finance* 2: 321–338, 1999.

Friedman, Milton, "The Role of Monetary Policy," *American Economic Review* 58: 1–17, 1968.

————, "The Optimum Quantity of Money," in *The Optimum Quantity of Money and Other Essays,* Chicago: Aldine, 1969.

Friedman, Milton, and Anna J. Schwartz, *A Monetary History of the United States, 1867–1960,* Princeton: Princeton University Press, 1963.

Fuhrer, Jeffrey C., "Comment," *NBER Macroeconomics Annual* 12: 346–355, 1997.

————, "Habit Formation in Consumption and Its Implications for Monetary-Policy Models," *American Economic Review* 90: 367–390, 2000.

Fuhrer, Jeffrey C., and Geoffrey R. Moore, "Inflation Persistence," *Quarterly Journal of Economics* 110: 127–159, 1995a.

————, "Monetary Policy Trade-offs and the Correlation between Nominal Interest Rates and Real Output," *American Economic Review* 85: 219–239, 1995b.

————, "Forward-Looking Behavior and the Stability of a Conventional Monetary Policy Rule," *Journal of Money, Credit and Banking* 27: 1060–1070, 1995c.

Gabaix, Xavier, and David Laibson, "The 6D Bias and the Equity Premium Puzzle," HIER Discussion Paper No. 1947, Harvard University, March 2002.

Galí, Jordi, "New Perspectives on Monetary Policy, Inflation and the Business Cycle," unpublished, Universitat Pompeu Fabra, Barcelona, January 2001.

————, "The Conduct of Monetary Policy in the Face of Technological Change: Theory and Postwar U.S. Evidence," in *Stabilization and Monetary Policy: The International Experience,* Mexico City: Banco de Mexico, 2002.

Galí, Jordi, and Mark Gertler, "Inflation Dynamics: A Structural Econometric Analysis," *Journal of Monetary Economics* 44: 195–222, 1999.

Galí, Jordi, Mark Gertler, and J. David Lopez-Salido, "European Inflation Dynamics," *European Economic Review* 45: 1237–1270, 2001.

———, "Robustness of the Estimates of the Hybrid New Keynesian Phillips Curve," unpublished, Universitat Pompeu Fabra, January 2003.

Gesell, Silvio, *The Natural Economic Order* [1929]. English translation by Philip Pye, San Antonio: Free-Economy Publishing Co., 1934.

Giannoni, Marc P., "Optimal Interest-Rate Rules in a Forward-Looking Model, and Inflation Stabilization versus Price-Level Stabilization," unpublished, FRBNY, September 2000.

———, "Robust Optimal Monetary Policy in a Forward-Looking Model with Parameter and Shock Uncertainty," unpublished, Princeton University, 2001.

———, "Does Model Uncertainty Justify Caution? Robust Optimal Monetary Policy in a Forward-Looking Model," *Macroeconomic Dynamics* 6: 111–144, 2002.

Giannoni, Marc P., and Michael Woodford, "Optimal Interest-Rate Rules: I. General Theory," NBER Working Paper No. 9419, December 2002a.

———, "Optimal Interest-Rate Rules: II. Applications," NBER Working Paper No. 9420, December 2002b.

———, "How Forward-Looking is Optimal Monetary Policy?" *Journal of Money, Credit and Banking*, forthcoming 2003a.

———, "Optimal Inflation Targeting Rules," in B. S. Bernanke and M. Woodford, eds., *Inflation Targeting*, Chicago: University of Chicago Press, forthcoming 2003b.

Goodfriend, Marvin, "Interest-Rate Smoothing and Price-Level Trend-Stationarity," *Journal of Monetary Economics* 19:335–348, 1987.

———, "Interest Rate Smoothing in the Conduct of Monetary Policy," *Carnegie-Rochester Conference Series on Public Policy* 34: 7–30, 1991.

Goodfriend, Marvin, and Robert G. King, "The New Neoclassical Synthesis and the Role of Monetary Policy," *NBER Macroeconomics Annual* 12: 231–283, 1997.

Goodhart, Charles A. E., "The Conduct of Monetary Policy," *Economic Journal* 99: 293–346, 1989.

———, "The Objectives for, and Conduct of, Monetary Policy in the 1990s," in A. Blundell-Wignall, ed., *Inflation, Disinflation, and Monetary Policy*, Sydney: Ambassador Press, 1992.

———, "Time, Inflation and Asset Prices," unpublished, London School of Economics, August 1999.

———, "Can Central Banking Survive the IT Revolution?" *International Finance* 3: 189–209, 2000.

———, "Monetary Transmission Lags and the Formulation of the Policy Decision on Interest Rates," *Federal Reserve Bank of St. Louis Review*, July/August 2001, pp. 165–181.

Grandmont, Jean-Michel, "On Endogenous Competitive Business Cycles," *Econometrica* 53: 995–1046, 1985.

Grandmont, Jean-Michel, and Guy Laroque, "Stability of Cycles and Expectations," *Journal of Economic Theory* 40: 138–151, 1986.

Grimes, Arthur, "Discount Policy and Bank Liquidity: Implications for the Modigliani-Miller and Quantity Theories," Reserve Bank of New Zealand, Discussion Paper No. G92/12, October 1992.

Guerrieri, L., "Inflation Dynamics," International Finance Discussion Paper No. 715, Federal Reserve Board, December 2001.

Haavelmo, Trygve, "Wicksell on the Currency Theory vs. the Banking Principle," *Scandinavian Journal of Economics* 80: 209–215, 1978.

Hairault, Jean-Olivier, and Franck Portier, "Money, New Keynesian Macroeconomics, and the Business Cycle," *European Economic Review* 37: 1533–1568, 1993.

Hall, Robert E., "Employment Fluctuations and Wage Rigidity," *Brookings Papers on Economic Activity* 1980-1, pp. 91–123.

———, "Optimal Fiduciary Monetary Systems," *Journal of Monetary Economics* 12: 33–50, 1983.

———, "Controlling the Price Level," *Contributions to Macroeconomics* 2(1), Article 5, 2002. [http://www.bepress.com]

Hall, Robert E., and N. Gregory Mankiw, "Nominal Income Targeting," in N. G. Mankiw, ed., *Monetary Policy*, Chicago: University of Chicago Press, 1994.

Haltiwanger, John, and Michael Waldman, "Limited Rationality and Strategic Complements: The Implications for Macroeconomics," *Quarterly Journal of Economics* 104: 463–483, 1989.

Hansen, Gary D., "Indivisible Labor and the Business Cycle," *Journal of Monetary Economics* 16: 309–327, 1985.

Hansen, Lars P., Dennis Epple, and William Roberds, "Linear-Quadratic Duopoly Models of Resource Depletion," in T. J. Sargent, ed., *Energy, Foresight and Strategy*, Washington, D.C.: Resources for the Future, 1985.

Harsanyi, John C., "Morality and the Theory of Rational Behaviour," in A. Sen and B. Williams, eds., *Utilitarianism and Beyond*, Cambridge: Cambridge University Press, 1982.

Henderson, Dale, and Warwick J. McKibbin, "A Comparison of Some Basic Monetary Policy Regimes for Open Economies: Implications of Different Degrees of Instrument Adjustment and Wage Persistence," *Carnegie-Rochester Conference Series on Public Policy* 39(1): 221–318, 1993.

Howitt, Peter, "Interest-Rate Control and Nonconvergence to Rational Expectations," *Journal of Political Economy* 100: 776–800, 1992.

Huang, Kevin X. D., and Zheng Liu, "Staggered Contracts and Business Cycle Persistence," Discussion Paper No. 127, Federal Reserve Bank of Minneapolis, December 1998.

Humphrey, Thomas M., "Price-Level Stabilization Rules in a Wicksellian Model of the Cumulative Process," *Scandinavian Journal of Economics* 94: 509–518, 1992.

————, "Knut Wicksell and Gustav Cassel on the Cumulative Process and the Price-Stabilizing Policy Rule," *Economic Quarterly*, Federal Reserve Bank of Richmond, 88(3): 59–83, 2002.

Ireland, Peter N., "The Role of Countercyclical Monetary Policy," *Journal of Monetary Policy* 104: 704–723, 1996.

————, "A Small, Structural, Quarterly Model for Monetary Policy Evaluation," *Carnegie-Rochester Conference Series on Public Policy* 47: 83–108, 1997.

————, "Money's Role in the Monetary Business Cycle Model," NBER Working Paper No. 8115, February 2001.

Jadresic, Esteban, "Can Staggered Price-Setting Explain Short-Run Inflation Dynamics?" unpublished, IMF Research Department, October 2000.

Jensen, Christian, and Bennett T. McCallum, "The Non-Optimality of Proposed Monetary Policy Rules Under Timeless-Perspective Commitment," NBER Working Paper No. 8882, April 2002.

Jin, He-hui, and Kenneth L. Judd, "Perturbation Methods for General Dynamic Stochastic Models," unpublished, Stanford University, April 2002.

Jonas, Jiri, and Frederic Mishkin, "Inflation Targeting in Transition Economies: Experience and Prospects," in B. S. Bernanke and M. Woodford, eds., *Inflation Targeting*, Chicago: University of Chicago Press, forthcoming 2003.

Jondeau, E., and H. LeBihan, "Testing for a Forward-Looking Phillips Curve: Additional Evidence from European and U.S. Data," Notes d'Etudes et de Recherche No. 86, Bank of France, December 2001.

Jonsson, Gunnar, "Monetary Politics and Unemployment Persistence," *Journal of Monetary Economics* 39: 303–325, 1997.

Jonung, Lars, "Knut Wicksell's Norm of Price Stabilization and Swedish Monetary Policy in the 1930s," *Journal of Monetary Economics* 5: 459–496, 1979.

Judd, John F., and Glenn D. Rudebusch, "Taylor's Rule and the Fed: 1970–1997," *Federal Reserve Bank of San Francisco Economic Review* 1998(3), pp. 3–16.

Kara, Ali Hakan, "Optimal Monetary Policy Rules under Imperfect Commitment: Some Theory and Evidence," unpublished, Central Bank of Turkey, February 2003.

Kazemi, H. B., "An Intertemporal Model of Asset Prices in a Markov Economy with a Limiting Stationary Distribution," *Review of Financial Studies* 5: 85–104, 1992.

Kerr, William, and Robert G. King, "Limits on Interest Rate Rules in the IS Model," *Economic Quarterly*, Federal Reserve Bank of Richmond, 82: 47–76, 1996.

Keynes, John Maynard, *The General Theory of Employment, Interest, and Money*, New York: Macmillan, 1936.

Khan, Aubhik, Robert G. King, and Alexander L. Wolman, "Optimal Monetary Policy," NBER Working Paper No. 9402, December 2002.

Kiley, Michael T., "Partial Adjustment and Staggered Price Setting," *Journal of Money, Credit and Banking* 34(2): 283–298, 2002.

———, "Is Moderate-to-High Inflation Inherently Unstable with Forward-Looking Monetary Policy?" unpublished, OECD, January 2003.

Kim, Jinill, and Sunghyun Henry Kim, "Spurious Welfare Reversals in International Business Cycle Models," *Journal of International Economics,* forthcoming 2003.

Kim, Jinill, Sunghyun Kim, Ernst Schaumburg, and Christopher A. Sims, "Second Order Accurate Solution of Discrete Time Dynamic Equilibrium Models," unpublished, Princeton University, January 2003.

Kimball, Miles S., "The Quantitative Analytics of the Basic Neomonetarist Model," *Journal of Money, Credit and Banking* 27: 1241–1277, 1995.

King, Mervyn A., "Changes in UK Monetary Policy: Rules and Discretion in Practice," *Journal of Monetary Economics* 39: 81–97, 1997.

———, "Challenges for Monetary Policy: New and Old," in *New Challenges for Monetary Policy,* Kansas City: Federal Reserve Bank of Kansas City, 1999.

King, Robert G., and Sergio T. Rebelo, "Resuscitating Real Business Cycles," in J. B. Taylor and M. Woodford, eds., *Handbook of Macroeconomics,* Vol. 1B, Amsterdam: North-Holland, 1999.

King, Robert G., and Mark W. Watson, "Money, Prices, Interest Rates and the Business Cycle," *Review of Economics and Statistics* 78: 35–53, 1996.

King, Robert G., and Alexander L. Wolman, "Inflation Targeting in a St. Louis Model of the 21st Century," *Federal Reserve Bank of St. Louis Review* 78: 83–107, 1996.

———, "What Should the Monetary Authority Do when Prices are Sticky?" in J. B. Taylor, ed., *Monetary Policy Rules,* Chicago: University of Chicago Press, 1999.

King, Robert G., Charles I. Plosser, and Sergio T. Rebelo, "Production, Growth and Business Cycles: I. The Basic Neoclassical Model," *Journal of Monetary Economics* 21: 195–232, 1988.

Klein, Paul, "Using the Generalized Schur Form to Solve a System of Linear Expectational Difference Equations," in *Papers on the Macroeconomics of Fiscal Policy,* IIES Monograph Series No. 33, Stockholm University, 1997.

Koenig, Evan F., "A Dynamic Optimizing Alternative to Traditional IS-LM Analysis," Discussion Paper No. 87-07, Department of Economics, University of Washington, May 1987.

———, "Rethinking the IS in IS-LM: Adapting Keynesian Tools to Non-Keynesian Economies," *Economic Review,* Federal Reserve Bank of Dallas, Third Quarter 1993, pp. 33–50, and Fourth Quarter 1993, pp. 17–36.

Krugman, Paul, "It's Baaack! Japan's Slump and the Return of the Liquidity Trap," *Brookings Papers on Economic Activity* 1998-2, pp. 137–187.

Kurmann, André, "Quantifying the Uncertainty about the Fit of a New Keynesian Pricing Model," unpublished, Université de Québec à Montréal, December 2002.

Kydland, Finn E., and Edward C. Prescott, "Rules Rather than Discretion: The Inconsistency of Optimal Plans," *Journal of Political Economy* 85: 473–491, 1977.

———, "Dynamic Optimal Taxation, Rational Expectations and Optimal Control," *Journal of Economic Dynamics and Control* 2: 79–91, 1980.

———, "Time to Build and Aggregate Fluctuations," *Econometrica* 50: 1345–1370, 1982.

Lang, Serge, *Real Analysis*, 2nd ed., Reading, MA: Addison-Wesley, 1983.

Lange, Joe, Brian Sack, and William Whitesell, "Anticipations of Monetary Policy in Financial Markets," FEDS Paper No. 2001-24, Federal Reserve Board, April 2001.

Lau, Sau-Him Paul, "Aggregate Pattern of Time-Dependent Adjustment Rules, II: Strategic Complementarity and Endogenous Non-Synchronization," *Journal of Economic Theory* 98: 199–231, 2001.

Laubach, Thomas, and John C. Williams, "Measuring the Natural Rate of Interest," FEDS Discussion Paper No. 2001-56, Federal Reserve Board, November 2001.

Laxton, Douglas, and Paolo Pesenti, "Monetary Rules for Small, Open Emerging Economies," unpublished, International Monetary Fund, November 2002.

Leeper, Eric, "Equilibria under 'Active' and 'Passive' Monetary and Fiscal Policies," *Journal of Monetary Economics* 27: 129–147, 1991.

Leijonhufvud, Axel, "The Wicksell Connection—Variations on a Theme," in *Information and Coordination: Essays in Macroeconomic Theory*, Oxford: Oxford University Press, 1981.

Leitemo, Kai, "Targeting Inflation by Constant-Interest-Rate Forecasts," unpublished, University of Oslo, November 2000.

Lettau, Martin, and Timothy Van Zandt, "Robustness of Adaptive Expectations as an Equilibrium Selection Device," unpublished, Federal Reserve Bank of New York, March 2000.

Levin, Andrew, Volker Wieland, and John C. Williams, "Robustness of Simple Monetary Policy Rules under Model Uncertainty," in J. B. Taylor, ed., *Monetary Policy Rules*, Chicago: University of Chicago Press, 1999.

———, "The Performance of Forecast-Based Monetary Policy Rules under Model Uncertainty," FEDS Paper No. 2001-39, Federal Reserve Board, August 2001.

Levine, Paul, "Should Rules be Simple?" CEPR Discussion Paper No. 515, March 1991. [Reprinted as Chapter 6 of Currie and Levine, 1993.]

Lindahl, Erik, "The Dynamic Approach to Economic Theory," in *Studies in the Theory of Money and Capital*, London: Allan and Unwin, 1939.

Linde, Jesper, "Estimating New-Keynesian Phillips Curves: A Full Information Maximum Likelihood Approach," Working Paper No. 129, Bank of Sweden, April 2002.

Long, John B., and Charles I. Plosser, "Real Business Cycles," *Journal of Political Economy* 91: 39–69, 1983.

Loungani, Prakash, Assaf Razin, and Chi-Wa Yuen, "Capital Mobility and the Output-Inflation Tradeoff," *Journal of Development Economics* 64: 255–274, 2001.

Loyo, Eduardo H. M., "Tight Money Paradox on the Loose: A Fiscalist Hyperinflation," unpublished, Kennedy School of Government, June 1999.

Lubik, Thomas A., and Frank Schorfheide, "Testing for Indeterminacy: An Application to U.S. Monetary Policy," unpublished, Johns Hopkins University, July 2002.

Lucas, R. E., Jr., "Expectations and the Neutrality of Money," *Journal of Economic Theory* 4: 103–124, 1972.

———, "Econometric Policy Evaluation: A Critique," *Carnegie-Rochester Conference Series on Public Policy* 1: 19–46, 1976.

———, "Adaptive Behavior and Economic Theory," *Journal of Business* 59(supp.): 401–426, 1986.

———, "Inflation and Welfare," *Econometrica* 68: 247–274, 2000.

Lucas, R. E., Jr., and Nancy L. Stokey, "Money and Interest in a Cash-in-Advance Economy," *Econometrica* 55: 491–513, 1987.

Mankiw, N. Gregory, "Small Menu Costs and Large Business Cycles: A Macroeconomic Model of Monopoly," *Quarterly Journal of Economics* 100: 529–539, 1985.

Mankiw, N. Gregory, and Ricardo Reis, "Sticky Information versus Sticky Prices: A Proposal to Replace the New Keynesian Phillips Curve," NBER Working Paper No. 8290, May 2001a.

———, "Sticky Information: A Model of Monetary Non-Neutrality and Structural Slumps," NBER Working Paper No. 8614, December 2001b.

Marcet, Albert, and Thomas J. Sargent, "Convergence of Least-Squares Learning in Environments with Hidden State Variables and Private Information," *Journal of Political Economy* 97: 1306–1322, 1989.

Mash, Richard, "New Keynesian Microfoundations Revisited: A Generalized Calvo-Taylor Model and the Desirability of Inflation vs. Price-Level Targeting," Discussion Paper No. 109, Oxford University Department of Economics, June 2002.

McCallum, Bennett T., "Price Level Determinacy with an Interest Rate Policy Rule and Rational Expectations," *Journal of Monetary Economics* 8: 319–329, 1981.

———, *Monetary Economics: Theory and Policy*, New York: Macmillan, 1989.

———, "Issues in the Design of Monetary Policy Rules," in J. B. Taylor and M. Woodford, eds., *Handbook of Macroeconomics*, Vol. 1C, Amsterdam: North-Holland, 1999.

———, "Indeterminacy, Bubbles, and the Fiscal Theory of Price Level Determination," *Journal of Monetary Economics* 47: 19–30, 2001.

McCallum, Bennett T., and Edward Nelson, "An Optimizing IS-LM Specification for Monetary Policy and Business Cycle Analysis," *Journal of Money, Credit and Banking* 31: 296–316, 1999a.

————, "Performance of Operational Policy Rules in an Estimated Semi-Classical Structural Model," NBER Working Paper No. 6599, 1999b.

————, "Timeless Perspective vs. Discretionary Monetary Policy in Forward-Looking Models," NBER Working Paper No. 7915, November 2000.

McGrattan, Ellen R., "Predicting the Effects of Federal Reserve Policy in a Sticky-Price Model: An Analytical Approach," Federal Reserve Bank of Minneapolis Working Paper No. 598, December 1999.

Meade, James E., *The Theory of International Economic Policy, Vol. 1: The Balance of Payments,* London: Oxford University Press, 1951.

Monetary Policy Committee, "Minutes of the Monetary Policy Committee Meeting on 9–10 December 1998," *Inflation Report February 1999,* Bank of England, pp. 66–68.

Myrdal, Gunnar, *Monetary Equilibrium,* London: W. Hodge and Co., 1939 [orig. Swedish, 1931].

Neiss, Katherine S., and Edward Nelson, "Inflation Dynamics, Marginal Cost, and the Output Gap: Evidence from Three Countries," unpublished, Bank of England, July 2002.

————, "The Real Interest Rate Gap as an Inflation Indicator," *Macroeconomic Dynamics,* 7:239–262, 2003.

Nelson, Edward, "U.K. Monetary Policy 1972–1997: A Guide using Taylor Rules," in P. Mizen, ed., *Central Banking, Monetary Theory and Practice: Essays in Honour of Charles Goodhart,* Vol. 1, Cheltenham, UK: Edward Elgar, forthcoming 2003.

Nelson, Edward, and Kalin Nikolov, "Monetary Policy and Stagflation in the UK," CEPR Discussion Paper No. 3458, July 2002.

Niehans, Jurg, *A History of Economic Theory: Classic Contributions, 1720–1980,* Baltimore: Johns Hopkins University Press, 1990.

Obstfeld, Maurice, and Kenneth Rogoff, "Speculative Hyperinflations in Maximizing Models: Can We Rule Them Out?" *Journal of Political Economy* 91: 675–687, 1983.

————, "Ruling Out Divergent Speculative Bubbles," *Journal of Monetary Economics* 17: 349–362, 1986.

————, *Foundations of International Macroeconomics,* Cambridge: MIT Press, 1996.

Ohanian, Lee H., Alan Stockman, and Lutz Klian, "The Effects of Real and Monetary Shocks in a Business Cycle Model with Some Sticky Prices," *Journal of Money, Credit, and Banking* 27: 1209–1234, 1995.

Orphanides, Athanasios, "Monetary Policy Rules Based on Real-Time Data," *American Economic Review* 91: 964–985, 2001.

————, "Monetary Policy Rules, Macroeconomic Stability and Inflation: A View from the Trenches," *Journal of Money, Credit and Banking,* forthcoming 2003.

Phelps, Edmund S., "Phillips Curves, Expectations of Inflation and Optimal Unemployment over Time," *Economica* 34: 254–281, 1967.

————, "Disinflation without Recession: Adaptive Guideposts and Monetary Policy," *Weltwirtschaftliches Archiv* 114: 783–809, 1978.

Pigou, Arthur C., "The Classical Stationary State," *Economic Journal* 53: 343–351, 1943.

Poole, William, "Optimal Choice of Monetary Policy Instrument in a Simple Stochastic Macro Model," *Quarterly Journal of Economics* 84: 197–216, 1970.

Prescott, Edward C., "Should Control Theory Be Used for Economic Stabilization?" *Carnegie-Rochester Conference Series on Economic Policy* 7: 13–38, 1977.

Preston, Bruce, "Learning about Monetary Policy Rules when Long-Horizon Forecasts Matter," unpublished, Princeton University, August 2002a.

————, "Adaptive Learning and the Use of Forecasts in Monetary Policy," unpublished, Princeton University, December 2002b.

Razin, Assaf, and Chi-Wa Yuen, "The 'New Keynesian' Phillips Curve: Closed Economy versus Open Economy," *Economics Letters* 75: 1–9, 2002.

Roberts, John M., "New Keynesian Economics and the Phillips Curve," *Journal of Money, Credit and Banking* 27: 975–984, 1995.

Rogoff, Kenneth, "The Optimal Degree of Commitment to an Intermediate Monetary Target," *Quarterly Journal of Economics* 100: 1169–1190, 1985.

Rotemberg, Julio J., "Monopolistic Price Adjustment and Aggregate Output," *Review of Economic Studies* 49: 517–531, 1982.

————, "The New Keynesian Microfoundations," *NBER Macroeconomics Annual* 2: 69–104, 1987.

————, "Prices, Output and Hours: An Empirical Analysis Based on a Sticky Price Model," *Journal of Monetary Economics* 37: 505–533, 1996.

Rotemberg, Julio J., and Michael Woodford, "Oligopolistic Pricing and the Effects of Aggregate Demand on Economic Activity," *Journal of Political Economy* 100: 1153–1207, 1992.

————, "Dynamic General Equilibrium Models with Imperfectly Competitive Product Markets," in T. F. Cooley, ed., *Frontiers of Business Cycle Research*, Princeton: Princeton University Press, 1995.

————, "An Optimization-Based Econometric Framework for the Evaluation of Monetary Policy," *NBER Macroeconomics Annual* 12: 297–346, 1997.

————, "An Optimization-Based Econometric Framework for the Evaluation of Monetary Policy," NBER Technical Working Paper No. 233, May 1998.

————, "Interest-Rate Rules in an Estimated Sticky-Price Model," in J. B. Taylor, ed., *Monetary Policy Rules,* Chicago: University of Chicago Press, 1999a.

————, "The Cyclical Behavior of Prices and Costs," in J. B. Taylor and M. Woodford, eds., *Handbook of Macroeconomics,* Vol. 1B, Amsterdam: North-Holland, 1999b.

Rudebusch, Glenn D., and Lars E. O. Svensson, "Policy Rules for Inflation Targeting," in J. B. Taylor, ed., *Monetary Policy Rules,* Chicago: University of Chicago Press, 1999.

Santos, Manuel S., and Michael Woodford, "Rational Asset Pricing Bubbles," *Econometrica* 65: 19–58, 1997.

Sargent, Thomas J., and Neil Wallace, " 'Rational' Expectations, the Optimal Monetary Instrument, and the Optimal Money Supply Rule," *Journal of Political Economy* 83: 241–254, 1975.

Sbordone, Argia M., "Prices and Unit Labor Costs: A New Test of Price Stickiness," IIES Seminar Paper No. 653, Stockholm University, October 1998.

———, "Prices and Unit Labor Costs: A New Test of Price Stickiness," *Journal of Monetary Economics* 49: 265–292, 2002.

———, "Inflation Dynamics and Real Marginal Costs," unpublished, Rutgers University, February 2003.

Schmitt-Grohé, Stephanie, and Martín Uribe, "Price Level Determinacy and Monetary Policy under a Balanced-Budget Requirement," *Journal of Monetary Economics* 45: 211–246, 2000.

———, "Solving Dynamic General Equilibrium Models Using a Second-Order Approximation to the Policy Function," NBER Technical Working Paper No. 282, October 2002.

Sheffrin, Steven M., *Rational Expectations*, Cambridge: Cambridge University Press, 1996.

Sidrauski, Miguel, "Rational Choice and Patterns of Growth in a Monetary Economy," *American Economic Review* 57: 534–544, 1967.

Simons, H. C., *Economic Policy for a Free Society*, Chicago: University of Chicago Press, 1948.

Sims, Christopher A., "Fiat Debt as Equity: Domestic Currency Denominated Debt as Equity in the Primary Surplus," unpublished, Princeton University, August 1999.

———, "Limits to Inflation Targeting," in B. S. Bernanke and M. Woodford, eds., *Inflation Targeting*, Chicago: University of Chicago Press, forthcoming 2003.

Smets, Frank, and Raf Wouters, "Sources of Business Cycle Fluctuations in the U.S.: A Bayesian DSGE Approach," seminar presentation, Princeton University, November 1, 2002.

Soderlind, Paul, "Solution and Estimation of RE Macromodels with Optimal Policy," unpublished, Stockholm School of Economics, September 1998.

Steinsson, Jón, "Optimal Monetary Policy in an Economy with Inflation Persistence," unpublished, Harvard University, May 2002.

Summers, Lawrence, "How Should Long Term Monetary Policy Be Determined?" *Journal of Money, Credit and Banking* 23: 625–631, 1991.

Sutherland, Alan, "A Simple Second-Order Solution Method for Dynamic General-Equilibrium Models," unpublished, University of St. Andrews, July 2002.

Svensson, Lars E. O., "Sticky Goods Prices, Flexible Asset Prices, Monopolistic Competition and Monetary Policy," *Review of Economic Studies* 53: 385–405, 1986.

————, "Inflation Forecast Targeting: Implementing and Monitoring Inflation Targets," *European Economic Review* 41: 1111–1146, 1997a.

————, "Optimal Inflation Targets, 'Conservative' Central Banks, and Linear Inflation Contracts," *American Economic Review* 87: 98–114, 1997b.

————, "Inflation Targeting as a Monetary Policy Rule," *Journal of Monetary Economics* 43: 607–654, 1999.

————, "The Inflation Forecast and the Loss Function," unpublished, Princeton University, January 2003a.

————, "What is Wrong with Taylor Rules? Using Judgment in Monetary Policy through Targeting Rules," *Journal of Economic Literature*, forthcoming June 2003b.

Svensson, Lars E. O., and Michael Woodford, "Indicator Variables for Optimal Policy," *Journal of Monetary Economics*, forthcoming 2003a.

————, "Indicator Variables for Optimal Policy under Asymmetric Information," *Journal of Economic Dynamics and Control*, forthcoming 2003b.

————, "Implementing Optimal Policy through Inflation-Forecast Targeting," in B. S. Bernanke and M. Woodford, eds., *Inflation Targeting*, Chicago: University of Chicago Press, forthcoming 2003c.

Tarshis, Lorie, "Changes in Real and Money Wage Rates," *Economic Journal* 49: 150–154, 1939.

Taylor, John B., "Staggered Wage Setting in a Macro Model," *American Economic Review* 69(2): 108–113, 1979a.

————, "Estimation and Control of a Macroeconomic Model with Rational Expectations," *Econometrica* 47: 1267–1286, 1979b.

————, "Aggregate Dynamics and Staggered Contracts," *Journal of Political Economy* 88: 1–24, 1980.

————, "Discretion versus Policy Rules in Practice," *Carnegie-Rochester Conference Series on Public Policy* 39: 195–214, 1993.

————, "The Inflation/Output Variability Trade-off Revisited," in J. C. Fuhrer, ed., *Goals, Guidelines, and Constraints Facing Monetary Policymakers*, Boston: Federal Reserve Bank of Boston, 1995.

————, ed., *Monetary Policy Rules*, Chicago: University of Chicago Press, 1999a.

————, "Introduction," in J. B. Taylor, ed., *Monetary Policy Rules*, Chicago: University of Chicago Press, 1999b.

————, "A Historical Analysis of Monetary Policy Rules," in J. B. Taylor, ed., *Monetary Policy Rules*, Chicago: University of Chicago Press, 1999c.

————, "Expectations, Open Market Operations, and Changes in the Federal Funds Rate," *Federal Reserve Bank of St. Louis Review* 83(4): 33–47, 2001.

Van Hoose, D. "Monetary Targeting and Price Level Non-Trend Stationarity," *Journal of Money, Credit, and Banking* 21: 232–239, 1989.

Vestin, David, "Price Level Targeting versus Inflation Targeting in a Forward Looking Model," unpublished, European Central Bank, July 2002.

Vickers, John, "Inflation Targeting in Practice: The U.K. Experience," *Bank of England Quarterly Bulletin,* November 1998.

Walsh, Carl, *Monetary Theory and Policy,* Cambridge: MIT Press, 1998.

West, Kenneth D., "Targeting Nominal Income: A Note," *Economic Journal* 96: 1077–1083, 1986.

White, Bruce, "Central Banking: Back to the Future," Discussion Paper No. 2001/5, Reserve Bank of New Zealand, September 2001.

Wicksell, Knut, *Interest and Prices,* 1898. English translation by R. F. Kahn, London: Macmillan, for the Royal Economic Society, 1936. Reprinted New York: Augustus M. Kelley, 1962.

———, "The Influence of the Rate of Interest on Prices," *Economic Journal* 17: 213–220, 1907.

———, *Lectures in Political Economy, Vol. II: Money,* 1915. English translation of the second edition by E. Claasen, London: George Routledge and Sons, 1935. Reprinted Fairfield, N.J.: Augustus M. Kelley, 1978.

Williams, John C., "Simple Rules for Monetary Policy," Finance and Economics Discussion Series Paper No. 1999-12, Federal Reserve Board, February 1999.

Woodford, Michael, "Stationary Sunspot Equilibria: The Case of Small Fluctuations around a Deterministic Steady State," unpublished, University of Chicago, September 1986.

———, "The Optimum Quantity of Money," in B. M. Friedman and F. H. Hahn, eds., *Handbook of Monetary Economics,* Vol. II, Amsterdam: North-Holland, 1990.

———, "Discussion of Fuhrer and Madigan, 'Monetary Policy when Interest Rates are Bounded at Zero'," presented at Conference on Monetary Policy in a Low-Inflation Environment, Federal Reserve Bank of San Francisco, March 1994a.

———, "Monetary Policy and Price-Level Determinacy in a Cash-in-Advance Economy," *Economic Theory* 4: 345–380, 1994b.

———, "Price-level Determinacy Without Control of a Monetary Aggregate," *Carnegie-Rochester Conference Series on Public Policy* 43: 1–46, 1995.

———, "Control of the Public Debt: A Requirement for Price Stability?" NBER Working Paper No. 5684, July 1996. [Shorter version published in G. A. Calvo and M. King, eds., *The Debt Burden and its Consequences for Monetary Policy,* London: Macmillan, 1997.]

———, "Doing Without Money: Controlling Inflation in a Post-Monetary World," *Review of Economic Dynamics* 1: 173–219, 1998.

———, "Optimal Monetary Policy Inertia," NBER Working Paper No. 7261, August 1999a.

———, "Commentary: How Should Monetary Policy Be Conducted in an Era of Price Stability?" in *New Challenges for Monetary Policy,* Kansas City: Federal Reserve Bank of Kansas City, 1999b.

————, "Pitfalls of Forward-Looking Monetary Policy," *American Economic Review* 90(2): 100–104, 2000.

————, "Fiscal Requirements for Price Stability," *Journal of Money, Credit and Banking* 33: 669–728, 2001a.

————, "Monetary Policy in the Information Economy," in *Economic Policy for the Information Economy,* Kansas City: Federal Reserve Bank of Kansas City, 2001b.

Yun, Tack, "Nominal Price Rigidity, Money Supply Endogeneity, and Business Cycles," *Journal of Monetary Economics* 37: 345–370, 1996.

Zbaracki, Mark, Mark Ritson, Daniel Levy, Shantanu Dutta, and Mark Bergen, "The Managerial and Customer Dimensions of the Cost of Price Adjustment: Direct Evidence from Industrial Markets," unpublished, University of Pennsylvania, November 1999.

INDEX

Page numbers for entries occurring in figures are followed by an f; those for entries occurring in notes are followed by an n; and those for entries occurring in tables are followed by a t.

adaptive learning dynamics. *See* learning dynamics
Altig, David, 233, 332, 352, 568
Amato, Jeffery D., 233, 332, 345–47, 350, 567, 568
Amato-Laubach model, 345–47, 350; impulse response to shocks in, 345, 346f, 347; optimal policy rules for, 568; parameter values in, 346–47, 347t
Andersen, Torben M., 228–29
Anderson, Gary, 390
Aoki, Kosuke, 418, 436, 438
asset-price inflation, 13, 440–41
asset-pricing model in cashless economy, 64–74; conditions for rational-expectations equilibrium in, 71–72, 628–29; government liabilities in, 72–73; government purchases in, 73–74; household flow budget constraints in, 64–65, 66–67, 68–69, 70, 627–28; household optimization problem in, 69–70, 75; household portfolio decisions in, 65–66, 69, 627–28; indirect utility in, 74–75; intertemporal household budget

constraints in, 68–69, 75; nominal interest rates in, 65; utility functions in, 64, 74
asymmetric shocks: in Calvo staggered pricesetting model, 437; inflation and, 200–204, 666–69; optimal policy, 435–43, 442f; representative-household utility flow, 436, 703–5; in sticky price models, 417–18; welfare losses, 440, 441f
Australia, channel system, 26, 28

balanced-budget fiscal rule, 76
Ball, Laurence, 162
Bank of England: inflation-forecast targeting, 43, 291, 467, 468, 522, 579, 619, 621; *Inflation Reports*, 620; interest-rate forecasts, 621. *See also* United Kingdom
Barro, Robert J., 20, 143, 467
Barth, Melvin J., III, 330
basic neo-Wicksellian model, 238–39; aggregate demand in, 239–40, 242, 243, 321, 403–4; aggregate-supply relations, 284, 334–36, 415; comparison with variable-capital

indexation. *See* price indexation; wage indexation
indices. *See* price indices
inertial inflation models, 205
inflation: asset-price, 13, 440–41; bias in discretionary optimization policies, 19–21, 467, 469–75, 482, 484–85, 493; in Brazil, 317; cumulative process of, 46, 262; determinants in basic neo-Wicksellian model, 276–86; equilibrium evolution of, 95, 116–17, 118–19, 119f, 639–40; expectations of, 128, 159–60, 176–77, 188; hyper-, 136, 138; Keynesian view of, 4–5; measures of, 94, 121–22, 289; persistence of shock effects, 212–13, 281; predicted responses to shocks, 341, 347; prevention of panics, 135–38; as purely forward-looking process, 205; in reaction functions, 281; real-balance effects, 301–5; relative price distortions and, 396–405; sectoral asymmetries, 203–4, 437; self-fulfilling, 127, 129, 130–31, 130f, 135, 136–37; short-term, 120–21; spirals, 267, 272; during transition to optimal policy, 414; unexpected component of, 398, 413; in variable-capital model, 360, 361–62, 362f; wage, 14, 236, 418, 445–46, 620; Wicksellian explanation of, 49. *See also* impulse responses to shocks; prices; price stability
inflation inertia: aggregate-supply relations, 561–62; in basic neo-Wicksellian model, 284–86, 285f; determinate equilibria, 95, 96–97, 640–41; with discretionary optimization, 481, 482f, 499f, 499–501; effects on inflation path, 481–83; interest-rate rules and, 94–101, 592–604, 724–27; optimal policies with, 415–16, 499–501, 500f, 560–65, 592–604, 724–27; due to price indexation, 215, 402–3, 408–9, 415–16, 481–

83; timelessly optimal policy with, 481–83, 482f
inflation rates: core inflation, 14, 440, 615, 620; distortions caused by high, 483–84; distortions caused by variations in, 5; optimal, 401; persistence of changes, 98; relationship to price dispersion, 399–400, 483–84, 694–95; short-term, 622–23; in Taylor rule, 39; variability, 5, 98–99; zero as goal, 460, 462–63, 473, 475, 477. *See also* inflation-targeting rules; price indices
Inflation Reports, 17, 620
inflation-targeting central banks, 3, 381; interest-rate forecasts of, 621–22; policy rules of, 39, 43–44; procedures of, 564, 619; purely forward-looking, 21; reaction functions of, 293–94; reports to public, 17, 620; rules representing policies of, 544; strict inflation targeting, 290–95; Taylor principle and, 90–94. *See also* Bank of England
inflation-targeting rules, 90–94; arguments for, 5, 13; in basic neo-Wicksellian model, 286, 290–95; communication to public, 294; comparison to optimal policy, 619–23; comparison to Taylor rules, 294; constant rates as goal, 248; core inflation as target rate, 14, 440, 620; examples, 101, 559–60; flexible, 524–25, 526–27, 560, 561, 590, 714–15; goals, 382, 401, 402–3; gradually lower rates, 480–81; implementation of, 292–95; near-term inflation, 526–27; negative inflation targets, 479–80, 484; optimal, 559–60, 560–65, 592, 602–4; optimal long-run target, 468–69; positive long-run average rates, 480; in practice, 43–44, 291, 467, 468, 522, 525–26, 619, 621; purely forward-looking, 467, 620–21; robustly optimal, 591; target

Taylor rules (*continued*)
618; specification in terms of output gap, 245–46; statement of, 39; target variables, 613, 615; in variable-capital model, 375, 376

Taylor rules: determinacy of equilibrium and, 91–92, 116–17, 122, 128; in basic neo-Wicksellian model, 254, 676–77; in cashless economy, 314; with forward-looking variants, 256–57, 258f, 260f, 681; and interest rate inertia, 255–56, 677–80; proofs of, 646, 647–48

technology shocks, 461–62

time-invariant policy rules, 544, 549–55

timelessly optimal policy, 459–60, 474–75; definition- of, 538–39, 542–43; design of, 551–55; determinacy of equilibrium, 554–55; with inflation inertia, 481–83, 482f; inflation-targeting rules, 475, 476f, 477; long-run expected inflation rates, 490–93, 498, 712–13; responses to shocks, 490–93, 503, 509, 709–10; target criteria, 522–24; targeting rules, 524; Taylor rule, 517; time-invariance property, 549–50

time-varying distortions, 448–55

transactions frictions: alternative timing convention for, 649–53; basic neo-Wicksellian model with, 295–99; determinate equilibria, 106; equilibrium conditions, 104; equilibrium prices and interest rates, 114–16, 645–46; in general-equilibrium models, 12; implementation of monetary policy with, 105–6; importance in monetary theory, 82, 83; inflation targets with, 476–80; interest-rate rules with, 105–6; loss function justified by, 476–77, 483–84; model with, 102–5; natural rate of output with, 420–21; nominal interest rates and, 417; optimal policy with, 424–26, 429, 433, 434–35; optimizing

IS-LM model, 295–99; price-level determination with, 101–6; rational-expectations equilibrium with, 104–5; representative-household utility function, 420, 422–23, 698–700; welfare effects, 420–26; with Wicksellian interest-rate rule, 105–6. *See also* cashless economy; real-balance effects

transactions services, 102

transactions technology, 54–55. *See also* cashless economy

Treasury Department, U.S., 318

unit labor costs, 182–84, 183f, 184f, 186, 206

United Kingdom: inflation rates in, 40, 291; interest rates in, 40; proposed interest-rate rule, 40. *See also* Bank of England

United States: bond-price support regime in, 318; inflation in, 184–85, 185f, 206, 217; macroeconomic instability in, 40, 93; money-demand elasticities in, 306; money supply variations in, 118, 305–6; output fluctuation half-life, 195; output gap in, 42, 205–6; size of monetary base in, 118; unit labor costs in, 182–84, 183f, 206. *See also* federal funds rate; Federal Reserve; quantitative models of U.S. monetary transmission mechanism; Taylor principle, U.S. policy and; Taylor rules, relationship to U.S. policy

units of account, 37, 63

Uribe, Martin, 76, 123, 390, 653–55

value-added production functions, 170, 171, 657–58

variable-capital model, 352; adjustment costs in, 353–54; aggregate demand in, 367–68; aggregate supply in, 360, 361, 364; capital stock equilibrium in, 356; coefficients, 364, 366–67, 367f, 376–78, 377f; comparison with basic neo-Wicksellian model, 361–72;